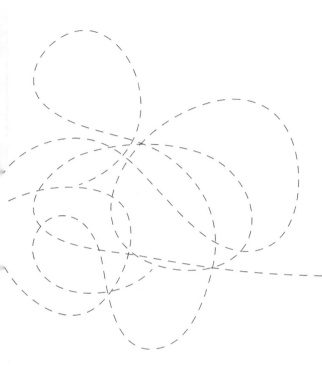

Contract Law
Commentaries, Cases and Perspectives

Philip Clarke | Julie Clarke

Second Edition

OXFORD
UNIVERSITY PRESS

Oxford University Press is a department of the University of Oxford.

It furthers the University's objective of excellence in research, scholarship, and education by publishing worldwide. Oxford is a registered trademark of Oxford University Press in the UK and in certain other countries.

Published in Australia by
Oxford University Press
253 Normanby Road, South Melbourne, Victoria 3205, Australia

© Philip Clarke and Julie Clarke 2012

The moral rights of the authors have been asserted.

First published 2008
Second edition published 2012

All rights reserved. No part of this publication may be reproduced, stored in a retrieval system, or transmitted, in any form or by any means, without the prior permission in writing of Oxford University Press, or as expressly permitted by law, by licence, or under terms agreed with the appropriate reprographics rights organisation. Enquiries concerning reproduction outside the scope of the above should be sent to the Rights Department, Oxford University Press, at the address above.

You must not circulate this work in any other form and you must impose this same condition on any acquirer.

National Library of Australia Cataloguing-in-Publication data

   Author: Clarke, Philip H.
   Title: Contract law: commentaries, cases and perspectives / Philip Clarke; Julie Clarke.
   Edition: 2nd ed.

   ISBN 9780195578454 (pbk.)

   Notes: Includes index.
   Subjects: Contracts.
             Contracts–Cases.
   Other Authors/Contributors: Clarke, Julie, 1976-
   Dewey Number: 346.02

Reproduction and communication for educational purposes
The Australian *Copyright Act 1968* (the Act) allows a maximum of one chapter or 10% of the pages of this work, whichever is the greater, to be reproduced and/or communicated by any educational institution for its educational purposes provided that the educational institution (or the body that administers it) has given a remuneration notice to Copyright Agency Limited (CAL) under the Act.

For details of the CAL licence for educational institutions contact:

Copyright Agency Limited
Level 15, 233 Castlereagh Street
Sydney NSW 2000
Telephone: (02) 9394 7600
Facsimile: (02) 9394 7601
Email: info@copyright.com.au

Edited by Carolyn Leslie
Cover design by Canvas
Text design by Eggplant Communications
Typeset by diacriTech
Proofread by Roz Edmond
Indexed by Trischa Baker
Printed by Sheck Wah Tong Printing Press Ltd

Links to third party websites are provided by Oxford in good faith and for information only. Oxford disclaims any responsibility for the materials contained in any third party website referenced in this work.

Table of Contents

Table of Cases   *v*
Table of Statutes   *xxiv*
List of Figures   *xxxiv*
Preface   *xxxvi*
Acknowledgments   *xxxvii*

PART 1   INTRODUCTION   1

Chapter 1   The Nature and Importance of Contract Law   3

PART 2   FORMATION   23

Chapter 2   Agreement   25
Chapter 3   Certainty and Conditional Contracts   86
Chapter 4   Consideration   114
Chapter 5   Intention to Create Contractual Relations   153
Chapter 6   Capacity   169
Chapter 7   Formalities   190

PART 3   SCOPE AND CONTENT   209

Chapter 8   Privity of Contract   211
Chapter 9   The Terms of a Contract   240
Chapter 10   Construction and Classification of Terms   276
Chapter 11   Exclusion Clauses   296

PART 4   AVOIDANCE   315

Chapter 12   Misleading or Deceptive Conduct   319

Chapter 13	Mistake	368
Chapter 14	Duress	403
Chapter 15	Undue Influence	423
Chapter 16	Unconscionable Conduct	440
Chapter 17	Unfair Terms	479
Chapter 18	Illegality and Public Policy	496

PART 5	PERFORMANCE AND TERMINATION	537
Chapter 19	Performance	539
Chapter 20	Discharge by Agreement	564
Chapter 21	Discharge for Breach	573
Chapter 22	Discharge by Frustration	616

PART 6	REMEDIES	651
Chapter 23	Damages and Liquidated Claims	653
Chapter 24	Equitable Remedies	702

Index   *737*

Table of Cases

400 George Street (Qld) Pty Ltd & Ors v BG International Ltd [2010] QSC 66   115
A v Hayden (1984) 156 CLR 532   508, **510–12**
A Roberts & Co Ltd v Leicestershire County Council [1961] Ch 555   392
AA Singh v Union of India AIR 1970 Mani 16   394
Abbott v Lance (1860) Legge 1283   81
ABC v XIVth Commonwealth Games Ltd (1988) 18 NSWLR 540   57
Abram v Bank of New Zealand (1996) ATPR 41-507   344
ACCC v 4WD Systems Pty Limited (2003) 59 IPR 435   460, 461
ACCC v Allphones Retail Pty Ltd (No 2) [2009] FCA 17   460
ACCC v CG Berbatis Holdings Pty Ltd (No 2) (2000) 96 FCR 491; (2003) 214 CLR 51
   26, 449, 456–7, 460
ACCC v Davis [2003] FCA 1227   418
ACCC v Keshow [2005] FCA 558   457
ACCC v McCaskey (2000) 104 FCR 8   418, 419
ACCC v Radio Rentals Ltd [2005] FCA 1133   **456–8**
ACCC v Samton Holdings Pty Ltd (2002) 117 FCR 301   457
ACCC v Simply No-Knead (Franchising) Pty Ltd (2000) 104 FCR 253   456, **458–9**, 460, 461
Accounting Systems 2000 (Developments) Pty Ltd v CCH Australia Ltd (1993) 42 FCR
   470   323, 339
Adaras Development Ltd v Marcona Corporation [1975] 1 NZLR 324   99
Administration of the Territory of Papua and New Guinea v Leahy (1961) 105 CLR 6   **165**
Afovos Shipping Co SA v Pagnan [1983] 1 All ER 449   **557–8**
AGC (Advances) Ltd v McWhirter (1977) 1 BPR 9454   **33–5**
Air Great Lakes Pty Ltd v KS Easter (Holdings) Pty Ltd [1985] 2 NSWLR 309   **154–7**
Air New Zealand Ltd & Enzedair Tours Ltd v Leibler, Leibant Investments Pty Ltd & Ninth
   Astjet Pty Ltd (VSC, 19 November 1996, Unreported), Hansen J   392
AKAS Jamal v Moolla Dawood Sons & Co [1916] 1 AC 175   660, 686
Alati v Kruger (1955) 94 CLR 216   357
Albazero, The [1977] AC 774   224, 659
Alfred McAlpine Construction Ltd v Panatown Ltd [2000] 3 WLR 946   **223–6**
Alliance Manufacturing Co Inc v Foti 146 So 2d 464 (1962)   63
Allied Steel & Conveyors Inc v Ford Motor Co 277 F 2d 907 (1960)   68
Allphones Retail Pty Ltd v Hoy Mobile Pty Ltd (2009) ATPR 42-294   580
Amadio Pty Ltd v Henderson (1998) 81 FCR 149   326

AMEV-UDC Finance Ltd v Austin (1986) 162 CLR 170   687
Andrews v Parker (1973) Qd R 93   **516–18,** 519, 527
Anotonovic v Volker (1986) 7 NSWLR 151   470
Ansett Transport Industries (Operations) Pty Ltd v The Commonwealth of Australia (1977) 139 CLR 54   177
Antaios Compania Neviera SA, The v Salen Rederierna AB [1985] 1 AC 191   283
Antonovic v Volker (1986) 7 NSWLR 151   467
ANZ Banking Group Ltd v Alirezai; Alirezai v ANZ Banking Group Ltd & Anor [2004] QCA 6   436
Aotearoa International Ltd v Scancarriers A/S [1985] 1 NZLR 513   87, 94
Argy v Blunts & Land Cove Real Estate Pty Ltd (1990) 26 FCR 112   324, 339, 343
Associated Japanese Bank (International) Ltd v Credit du Nord SA [1988] 3 All ER 902   370, 373, 379
Associated Newspapers Ltd v Bancks (1951) 83 CLR 322   **287–9,** 587
Atco Controls Pty Ltd (in liq) v Newtronics Pty Ltd (recs & mgrs apptd) (in liq) [2009] VSCA 238   75, 118, 154, 163
Attorney General v Blake (Jonathan Cape Ltd Third Party) [2001] 1 AC 268   654, 690, **691–4**
Attorney General of Belize v Belize Telecom Ltd [2009] UKPC 10   **262–5**
Attwells v Campbell [2000] NSWCA 132   163
Austin Instrument Inc v Loral Corp (1971) 29 NY 2d 124   413, 415
Australia and New Zealand Banking Group Ltd v Frost Holdings Pty Ltd [1989] VR 695   **92–6,** 99
Australia and New Zealand Banking Group Ltd v Karam [2005] NSWCA 344   404
Australia Estates Pty Ltd v Cairns City Council [2005] QCA 328   369, 379, 380, 381
Australian Woollen Mills Pty Ltd v The Commonwealth (1954) 92 CLR 424   **118–19,** 120, 153, 158, 165
Automatic Fire Sprinklers Proprietary Limited v Watson (1946) 72 CLR 435   545–6, 610
Avery v Bowden (1855) 5 E & B 714   584
Axelsen v O'Brien (1949) 80 CLR 219   90, 99

Bain v Fothergill (1874) LR 7 HL 158   681
Baird Textile Holdings Ltd v Marks & Spencer plc [2002] 1 All ER (Comm) 737   147
Baivijli v Nansa Nagar (1885) 10 Bom 152   523
Balfour v Balfour [1919] 2 KB 571   153, 154, 157, **160–1,** 164
Balfour & Clark v Hollandia Ravensthorpe NL (1978) 18 SASR 240   355
Ball v Hesketh (1697) 90 ER 541   127
Balla v Theophilos (No 2) (1957) 98 CLR 193   46
Baltic Shipping Co v Dillon (1993) 176 CLR 8   639, **667–9**
Bani Muncharan v Regina ILR 32 Bom 581   523
Bank Line, Limited v Arthur Capel and Company [1919] AC 435   **633–4**
Bank of New South Wales v The Commonwealth (1948) 76 CLR 1   325
Banque Brussels Lambert SA v Australian National Industries Ltd (1989) 21 NSWLR 502   164

Banwari Lal v Sukhdarshan Daya (1973) 1 SCC 294   166
Barber v Crickett [1958] NZLR 1057   109
Barry v Davies (trading as Heathcote Ball & Co) [2000] 1 WLR 1962   35
Barton v Armstrong [1976] AC 104   405, **406–8**
Batsakis v Demotsis 226 SW 2d 673 (1949)   124
Beaton v McDivitt (1987) 13 NSWLR 162   **119–21**
Beauchamp v Beauchamp (1972) 32 DLR (3d) 693; (1974) 40 DLR (3d) 160   109
Bell v Lever Bros Ltd [1988] 3 All ER 902; [1989] 1 WLR 255   **373–5,** 379, 380, 386, 387, 391
Bellgrove v Eldridge (1954) 90 CLR 613, High Court of Australia   676–8
Belna Pty Limited v Irwin [2009] NSWCA 46   **300–1**
Berry v Mahony [1933] VLR 314   610
Beswick v Beswick [1968] AC 58   **219–20,** 221, 222, **705–6**
Bettini v Gye (1876) 1 QBD 183   289, 587, 589
Bevanere Pty Ltd v Lubidineuse (1984) 7 FCR 325   **324–5**
Biotechnology Australia Pty Ltd v Pace (1988) 15 NSWLR 130   4, **88–91,** 99, **125–6**
Birch v Thomas [1972] 1 WLR 294   300
Blackpool and Fylde Aero Club Ltd v Blackpool Borough Council [1990] 3 All ER 25   **38–9**
Blomley v Ryan (1956) 99 CLR 362   **175–6,** 445, 446, 448, 450
Board of Control of Eastern Michigan University v Burgess 45 Mich App 183, 186; 206 NW2d 256 (1973)   41
Body Bronze International Pty Ltd v Fehcorp Pty Ltd [2011] VSCA 196   **459–62**
Bogigian v Bogigian 551 NE 2d 1149 (1990)   117, 124
Booker Industries Pty Ltd v Wilson Parking (Qld) Pty Ltd (1982) 149 CLR 600; 43 ALR 68   94, 96, 97
Borg v Howlett (1996) NSWSC 95001763   385
Borthwick v Carruthers (1787) 99 ER 1300   169
Bot v Ristevski [1981] VR 120   **610–11**
Boulton v Jones (1857) 2 H & N 564; 157 ER 232   52
Bowler v Hilda Pty Ltd (1998) 80 FCR 191   **334–5,** 342
BP Refinery (Westernport) Pty Ltd v Shire of Hastings (1977) 180 CLR 266   265, 267
Brackenbury v Hodgkin 102 A 106 (1917)   80
Bragg v Alam (1982) NSW Conv R 55-082   46
Brambles Holdings Ltd v Bathurst City Council (2001) 53 NSWLR 153   45, 75, **76–8**
Brehm v Wright [2007] NSWSC 1101   141
Brennan v Bolt Burdon [2005] QB 303; Champion Investments Ltd v Ahmed [2004] EWHC 1956   380
Bressan v Squires [1974] 2 NSWLR 460   **65–6**
Brian Constr & Dev Co Inc v Brighenti 405 A 2d 72 (1978)   131
Brikon Investments v Car [1979] 2 All ER 753   249
Brinkibon Ltd v Stahag Stahl und Stahl-Warenhandelsgesellschaft mbH [1983] 2 AC 34   **66–8**
Brisbane City Council v Group Projects Pty Ltd (1979) 145 CLR 143   622, **625–7**
British Road Services Ltd v Arthur v Crutchley & Co Ltd [1968] 1 Lloyd's Rep 271   56

British Russian Gazette and Trade Outlook Ltd v Associated Newspapers Ltd [1933] 2 KB 616   565
Broadnax v Ledbetter 99 SW 1111 (1907)   52, 231
Brodgen v Metropolitan Railway Co (1877) 2 App Cas 666   53, 55
Brooks v Burns Philp Trustee Co Ltd (1969) 121 CLR 433   530–1
Brooks Towers Corporation v Hunkin-Conkey Construction Co 454 F 2d 1203 (1972)   63
Buckwell v Commercial Banking Co of Sydney Ltd (1937) 58 CLR 155   127
Burger King Corp v Hungry Jack's Pty Ltd [2001] NSWCA 187   269
Burns v MAN Automotive (Aust) Pty Ltd (1986) 161 CLR 653, High Court of Australia   683–5
Butcher v Lachlan Elder Realty Pty Ltd (2004) 218 CLR 592   323, **340–2**
Butler v Fairclough (1917) 23 CLR 78   565
Butler Machine Tool Co Ltd v Ex-Cell-O Corp (England) Ltd [1979] 1 WLR 401   **54–6**
Butt v McDonald (1896) 7 QLJ 68   268
Byers v Dorotea Pty Ltd (1987) ATPR 40-760   327, 333, 342, 355
Byle v Byle (1990) 65 DLR (4th) 641   405
Byrne v Van Tienhoven (1880) LR 5 CPD 344   **42–3**, 65

Callisher v Bischoffsheim (1870), LR 2 QB 449   142
Cameron v Qantas Airways Ltd (1994) 55 FCR 147   457
Campbell v Backoffice Investments Pty Ltd (2009) 238 CLR 304   323, **338–9**, 342, **345**
Campbell v Metway Leasing Ltd (1998) ATPR 41-630   418
Car & Universal Finance Co Ltd v Caldwell [1963] 2 All ER 547   594
Carlill v Carbolic Smoke Ball Company [1893] 1 QB 256   **30–1**, 36, **43–4**, **60–1**, 63, 79, **122,** 166, 230, 231
Carter v Hyde (1923) 33 CLR 115   46
Casey's Patents, In Re; Stewart v Casey (1892) 1 Ch 104   127
CCP Australian Airships Ltd v Primus Telecommunications Pty Ltd [2004] VSCA 232   332
Cehave NH v Bremer Handelsgesellschaft mbH [1976] 1 QB 44   587
Cehave NV v Bremer Handelsgesellschaft mbH [1976] 1 QB 44l   287, **289–91**, 587
Central London Property Trust Ltd v High Trees House Ltd [1947] 1 KB 130   **146–7,** 148
Cermak v Ruth Consolidated Industries (2005) Aust Contract Reports 90–207; [2004] NSWSC 38   381, 391, 392
Chand Singh v Ram Kaur (1987) 2 Punj LR 70   430
Chandler v Webster[1904] 1 KB 493   640, 641
Chaplin v Hicks [1911] 2 KB 786   655, 663, **670–2**
Chappell & Co Ltd v Nestle Co Ltd [1960] AC 87   **123,** 124
Chinnaya v Ramayya (1882) 4 Mad 137   144
Chinnock v Marchioness of Ely (1865) 4 De GJ & S 638; 46 ER 1066   106
Chwee Kin Keong v Digilandmall.com Pte Ltd [2005] 1 SLR 502   391
Citibank NA v Brown Shipley & Co Ltd [1991] 2 All ER 690   387
City & Westminster Properties v Mudd [1959] 1 Ch 129   249
Clarke v Earl of Dunraven [1897] AC 59   75, 76

Close v Phipps (1844) 7 Man & G 586   414
CMI Clothesmakers Inc v ASK Knits Inc 380 NYS 2D 447 (1975)   63
Coal Cliff Collieries Pty Ltd v Sijehama Pty Ltd (1991) 24 NSWLR 1   **97–100,** 101
Coastal Estates v Melevende [1965] VR 433   358
Codelfa Construction Pty Ltd v State Rail Authority of New South Wales (1982) 149 CLR 337   **265–8,** 277, **280–1,** 284, 617, **622–5,** 631, 632
Cohen v Cohen (1929) 42 CLR 91   157
Cohen v Cowles Media Co 457 NW 2d 199 (1990)   153
Colonial Ammunition Co v Reid (1900) 21 LR (NSW) 338   39–40
Combe v Combe [1951] 1 All ER 767   147, 148
Commercial Bank of Australia v Amadio (1983) 151 CLR 447   441, **442–5,** 450
Commercial Banking Co of Sydney Ltd v Brown (1972) 126 CLR 337   359
Commission for the New Towns v Cooper (Great Britain) Ltd [1995] Ch 259   392
Commissioner of Stamp Duties (NSW) v Carlenka Pty Ltd (1995) 41 NSWLR 329   391
Commonwealth of Australia v Amann Aviation Pty Ltd (1991) 174 CLR 64, High Court of Australia   673–6
Commonwealth of Australia v Australian Commonwealth Shipping Board (1926) 39 CLR 1   177
Commonwealth of Australia v Crothal Hospital Services (Aust) Ltd (1981) 36 ALR 567   53
Commonwealth of Australia v Verwayen (1990) 170 CLR 394   4, 150
Concrete Constructions (NSW) Pty Ltd v Nelson (1990) 169 CLR 594   323
Con-Stan Industries of Australia Pty Ltd v Norwich Winterthur Insurance (Australia) Ltd (1985–1986) 160 CLR 226   **269–71**
Co-Operative Insurance Society Ltd v Argyll Stores (Holdings) Ltd [1998] AC 1   703, **716–18**
Couldery v Bartrum (1881) 19 ChD 394   145
Coulls v Bagot's Executor & Trustee Co Ltd (1967) 119 CLR 460   **129,** 141, 214, 215, 218, 220, **221–3,** 226
Council of the Upper Hunter County District v Australian Chilling and Freezing Co Ltd (1967) 118 CLR 429   **87–8**
Courtney & Fairbairn Ltd v Tolaini Brothers (Hotels) Ltd [1975] 1 WLR 297   98, 101
Cowan v Stanhill Estates Pty Ltd (No 2) [1967] VR 641   610
Coward v Motor Insurers Bureau [1963] 1 QB 259   153
Crawford Fitting Co v Sydney Valve and Fitting Pty Ltd (1988) 14 NSWLR 438   **568–9**
Creamoata Limited v The Rice Equalization Association Limited (1953) 89 CLR 286   564
Crescendo Management Pty Ltd v Westpac Banking Corporation (1988) 19 NSWLR 40   404, 405, **411–12**
Crown v Clarke (1927) 40 CLR 227   **50–1,** 52, 79
Cummings v Lewis (1993) 41 FCR 559   335
Curtis v Chemical Cleaning & Dyeing Co [1951] 1 KB 805   254
Curwen v Yan Yean Land Co Ltd (1891) 17 VLR 745   327
Cutter v Powell (1795) All ER Rep 159; 6 Term Rep 320   **544–5,** 548
CWT v Abdul Hussein (1988) 3 SCC 562   166

Darlington Borough Council v Wiltshier Northern Ltd [1995] 1 WLR 68   225
Darlington Futures Ltd v Delco Australia Pty Ltd (1986) 161 CLR 500   285, 297, 298, **301–3**
Daropti v Jaspat Rai (1905) PR 171   236
Daulia Ltd v Four Millbank Nominees Ltd [1978] 1 Ch 231   81
Davey v Challenger Managed Investments Ltd [2003] NSWCA 172   445
Davis Contractors Ltd v Fareham Urban District Council [1956] AC 696   267, **620–2**, 622, 627
Decro-Wall International SA v Practitioners in Marketing Ltd [1971] 1 WLR 361, 380   293, 581
Demagogue Pty Ltd v Ramensky (1993) ATPR 41-203; (1993) 110 ALR 608   329, 330
Depree v Bedhorough (1863), 4 Gift 479; 66 ER 795   610
Derry v Peek (1889) 14 App Cas 337   359, 361
Devaraja Urs v Ram Krishnaiah AIR 1952 Mys 109   236
Dharindhar v Kanhji Sahay, AIR 1949 Pat 250   532
Dick Bentley Productions Ltd v Harold Smith Motors [1965] 1 WLR 623   242, 244, 245
Dickinson v Dodds (1876) 2 Ch D 463   **41–2**, 46
Dickson Property Management Services Pty Ltd v Centro Property Management (Vic) Pty Ltd (2000) 180 ALR 485, Federal Court of Australia   726–7
Director of Consumer Affairs Victoria v AAPT Limited (Civil Claims) [2006] VCAT 1493   482, 485, **486–7**
Donkin v Official Trustee in Bankruptcy [2003] QSC 401   380
Donoghue v Stevenson [1932] AC 562   9, 218
Donwin [Crown Office List (UK), 2 March 1984, unreported]   98
Dougan v Ley (1946) 71 CLR 142   703, **711–12**
Dowsett v Reid (1912) 15 CLR 695, High Court of Australia   **707–8**
Drennan v Star Paving Co 333 P 2d 757 (1958)   47
Dularia Devi v Janardan Singh AIR 1990 SC 1173   399
Dunlop Pneumatic Tyre Co Ltd v Selfridge and Co Ltd [1915] AC 847   116, 119–20, 213, 214, 218, **687–9**
Dunton v Dunton (1892) 18 VLR 114   **123–4**

Eccles v Bryant [1948] 1 Ch 93   76
Edgington v Fitzmaurice (1885) 29 Ch D 459   108, 355
Effem Foods Pty Ltd v Lake Cumbeline Pty Ltd (1999) ATPR 41-686   326
Elder, Demster & Co v Paterson Zochinos & Co [1924] AC 522   227
Elder's Trustee & Executor Co Ltd v Commonwealth Homes & Investment Co Ltd (1941) 65 CLR 603   358
Elias v George Sahely & Co (Barbados) Ltd [1983] 1 AC 646   **196–7**
Elkofairi v Permanent Trustee Co Ltd [2002] NSWCA 413   442, 470
Ella v Wenham [1972] QdR 90   682
Ellul and Ellul v Oakes (1972) 3 SASR 377   **244–5**
Empirnall Holdings Pty Ltd v Machon Paull Partners Pty Ltd (1988) 14 NSWLR 523   52, 53, **62–4**
Entores Ltd v Miles Far East Corporation [1955] 2 All ER 493   64, 67

Equitable Life Assurance Society v Hyman [2002] 1 AC 408   263, 264
Ermogenous v Greek Orthodox Community of SA Inc (2002) 209 CLR 95   **158–60**
Errichetti Nominees Pty Ltd v Paterson Group Architects Pty Ltd [2007] WASC 77   381
Errington v Errington [1952] 1 All ER 149   **79–80**
Esso Petroleum Co Ltd v Mardon [1976] 1 QB 801   359
Ettridge v Vermin Board of the District of Mural Bay [1928] SASR 124   610

Fairline Shipping Corporation v Adamson [1975] QB 180   63
Far Horizons Pty Ltd v McDonald's Australia Ltd [2000] VSCA 310   269
Farley v Skinner [2002] 2 AC 732   667
Farmer v Honan (1919) 26 CLR 183   106
Farrani v Leburn [1970] WAR 179   611
Federal Commerce and Navigation Ltd v Molena Alpha Inc [1979] AC 757   **580–2**
Fells v Read [1896] All ER Rep 525   711
Felthouse v Bindley (1862) 11 CB (NS) 869; 142 ER 1037   **59–60**, 63
Fender v St John Mildmay [1938]   517
Fenwick v McDonald Frazer & Co (1904) 6 F (Ct of Sess) 850   34
Fibrosa Spolka Akcyjna v Fairbairn Lawson Combe Barbour Ltd [1943] AC 32   630, 632, **640–2**
Figjam Pty Ltd v Pedrini (2007) Aus Contract Reports 90-259   131
Filbay v Hounsell (1896) 2 Ch 737   106
Finelli v Dee (1968) 67 DLR 393   598, 600
First East Auction Holdings Pty ltd v Ange [2010] VSC 72   259
Fisher v Bell [1961] 3 All ER 731   32
Fitzgerald v FJ Leonhardt Pty Ltd (1997) 189 CLR 215   496, 497, **504–5**, 525, **529**
Fitzgerald v Masters (1956) 95 CLR 420, High Court of Australia   **565–7**
Fletcher v Kakemoto [2010] QSC 219   45
Foakes v Beer (1884) 9 App Cas 605, House of Lords   **140–1**, 146
Foley v Classique Coaches Ltd [1934] 2 KB 1   93
Foster v Wheeler (1888) 38 Ch D 130   90, 99
Fowler v Fowler (1859) 4 De G & J 250   381
Foxtel Management Pty Ltd v Seven Cable Television Pty Ltd (2000) 102 FCR 464   87
Franich v Swannell (1994) ATPR (Digest) 46-115   324
Freedom v AHR Constructions Pty Ltd [1987] 1 Qd R 59   199
Freeth v Burr (1874) LR 9 CP 208   577, 581, 583
Frost v Knight (1872) LR 7 Ex 111   682
Futuretronics International Pty Ltd v Gadzhis [1992] 2 VR 217   361

Garcia v National Australia Bank (1998) 194 CLR 395   **432–5**, 436
Garry Rogers Motors (Aust) Pty Ltd v Subaru (Aust) Pty Ltd (1999) ATPR 41-703   269, 457
Gates v City Mutual Life Assurance Society Ltd (1986) 160 CLR   249, 349
Gentry Bros Pty Ltd v Wilson Brown & Associates Pty Ltd (1992) ATPR 41-184   324
Gibbons v Wright (1954) 91 CLR 423   **171–4**
Gibson v Manchester City Council [1979] 1 WLR 294 at 297; [1979] 1 All ER 972   40, 77

Giliberto v Kenny (1983) 48 ALR 620   280
Glandore Pty Ltd v Elders Finance and Investment Co (1984) 57 ALR 186   355
Glasbrook Bros Ltd v Glamorgan County Council [1925] AC 270   **137–8**
Glynn v Margetson & Co [1893] AC 351   304
Godecke v Kirwan (1973) 129 CLR 629   90, **95–6,** 99
Gordon v Macgregor (1909) 8 CLR 316   **278–9**
Gore v Van Der Lann [1967] 1 All ER 360   221
Gould v Vaggelas (1985) 157 CLR 215   347, 356, 359
Governor & [Guardian] of the Poor of Kingston-upon-Hull v Petch (1854) 10 Exch 610; 156 ER 583   106
Grainger v Gough [1896] AC 325   36
Great Northern Railway Co v Witham LR 9 CF 16   230
Great Peace Shipping Ltd v Tsavliris Salvage (International) Ltd [2003] QB 679   369, 373, 380, 381
Greco v Bendigo Machinery Pty Ltd (1985) ATPR 40-521; Embo Holdings Pty Ltd v Camm (1998) ATPR (Digest) 46-184   326
Green v Sommerville (1979) 141 CLR 594, High Court of Australia   708–10
Grime v Bartholomew [1972] 2 NSWLR 827   108
GUS Property Management Ltd v Littlewoods Mail Order Stores Ltd, 1982 SLT 533   658
GW Sinclair & Co Pty Ltd v Cocks [2001] VSCA 47   268

H & E Van Der Sterren v Cibernetics (Holdings) Pty Ltd (1970) 44 ALJR 157   285
Hadley v Baxendale (1854) 9 Ex 341, Court of Exchequer   663–4, 665
Haji Abdul Rehman Allarakhia v Bombay and Persia Steam Navigation Co (1892) 16 Bom 561   394
Hall v Busst (1960) 104 CLR 206   92, 94, 96, 97
Hall v Wells (1962) Tas SR 122   184
Hamer v Sidway 124 NY 538 (1891)   124
Hamilton v Lethbridge (1912) 14 CLR 236   180
Harbutt's 'Plasticine' Ltd v Wayne Tank & Pump Co Ltd [1970] 1 QB 447   310
Harnett v Yielding (1805) 2 Sch & Lef 549   703
Harrington v Taylor 36 SE 2d 227 (1945)   **126–7,** 145
Harris v Digital Pulse Pty Ltd (2003) 56 NSWLR 298   380, 381
Harris v Nickerson (1873) LR 8 QB 286   35
Hart v O'Connor [1985] 1 AC 1000   **173–4**
Hartley v Ponsonby (1857) 119 ER 1471   131
Harvey v Edward Dunlop & Co Ltd (1927) 39 CLR 302   196
Harvey v Facey [1893] AC 552   40
Hawker Pacific Pty Ltd v Helicopter Charter Pty Ltd (1991) 22 NSWLR 298   **409–11,** 417
Haydon v Jackson (1988) ATPR 40-845   355
Helicopter Sales (Australia) Pty Ltd v Rotor-Work Pty Ltd (1974) 132 CLR 1   268
Hely v Stirling [1982] VR 246   96
Henjo Investments Pty Ltd v Collins Marrickville Pty Ltd (1988) ATPR 40-850; (1988) 79 ALR 83   329, 342, 343

Henry Kendall & Sons v William Lillico & Sons Ltd [1969] 2 AC 31   **259–61**
Henthorn v Fraser ([1892] 2 Ch 27   66
Henville v Walker (2001) 206 CLR 459   343, 344, **346–8,** 350
Heppingstone v Stewart (1911) 12 CLR 126   198
Hermann v Charlesworth [1905] 2 KB 123   **518–19**
Heyman v Darwins Ltd [1942] AC 356   573, 577, **602–3,** 605
Hill v C A Parsons & Co Ltd [1971] 3 All ER 1345; [1971] 3 WLR 995; [1972] 1 Ch 305   **727–8**
Hillas & Co Ltd v Arcos Ltd (1932) 147 LT 503; [1932] All ER Rep 494   88, 96, 98, 101
Hillingdon Estate co v Stonefield Estate Ltd [1952] Ch 627   712
Hochster v De La Tour (1853) 2 E & B 678   584
Hoenig v Isaacs [1952] 2 All ER 176   547–8
Hoffman v Cali [1985] Qd R 253   **681–2**
Holdcroft v Market Garden Produce Pty Ltd [2001] 2 Qd R 381   514
Holland v Wiltshire (1954) 90 CLR 409   **575–6, 594–5**
Holman v Johnson [1775–1802] All ER Rep 98; 1 Cowp 341; 98 ER 1120   497, **508–9**
Hongkong Fir Shipping Co Ltd v Kawasaki Kisen Kaisha Ltd   289, 290, 292, 577, 581, 588, **591–3**
Horlock v Beal [1916] 1 AC 486   631
Hornsby Building Information Centre Pty Ltd v Sydney Building Information Centre Ltd (1978) 140 CLR 216   326
Hospital Products Ltd v United States Surgical Corp (1984) 156 CLR 41   268
Household Fire and Carriage Accident Insurance Co Ltd v Grant, 4 Ex D 216   67
Howard Smith & Co v Varawa (1907) 5 CLR 68   65
Howe v Smith (1884), 27 ChD 89   610
Howe v Teefy (1927) 27 SR (NSW) 301, Supreme Court of New South Wales   672–3
Hoyt's Pty Ltd v Spencer (1919) 27 CLR 133   249
Hughes Aircraft Systems International v Airservices Australia (1997) 76 FCR 151   39, 269
Humphreys Estate [1987] 1 AC 114   149
Hungerfords v Walker (1989) 171 CLR 125   681
Huntoon Company v Kolynos (Incorporated) [1930] 1 Ch 528   549
Hurley v McDonald's Australia Pty Ltd (2000) ATPR 41-741   457
Hussey v Horne-Payne (1879) 4 App Cas 311   57
Hyde v Wrench (1840) 3 Beav 334   45, 55
Hyundai Heavy Industries Co Ltd v Papadopoulos [1980] 2 All ER 29   **608–10**

Ibberson v Neck (1886) 2 TLR 247   141
Igloo Homes Pty Ltd v Sammut Constructions Pty Ltd [2005] NSWCA 280   381, 382
Immer (No 145) Pty Ltd v Uniting Church in Australia Property Trust (NSW) (1992–1993) 182 CLR 26   358, **595–8**
Imperial Loan Co Ltd v Stone [1892] 1 QB 599   173
In Dies v British and International Mining Corporation [1939] 1 KB 724   608, 609
Ingram v Little [1961] 1 QB 31   387
Insight Vacations Pty Ltd v Young [2011] HCA 16   **303–4**

Integrated Computer Services Pty Ltd v Digital Equipment Corp (Aust) Pty Ltd (1988) 5 BPR 11,110 at 11,117–11,118   77
Interfoto Picture Library Ltd v Stiletto Visual Programmes Ltd [1989] 1 QB 433   **257–8,** 259
Investors Compensation Scheme Ltd v West Bromwich Building Society [1998] 1 WLR 896   262, 280, **282–3,** 284

J Lauritzen AS v Wijsmuller BV (the 'Super Servant Two') [1990] 1 Lloyds Rep 1   618, **636–7**
Jackson v Broatch (1900) 37 SLR 707   51
Jackson v Horizon Holidays [1975] 1 WLR 1468   215, 221
Jackson v Seymour 71 SE 2d 181 (1952)   124
Jackson v The Union Marine Insurance Company, Limited [1873] LR 10 CP 125   631
James Baird Co v Gimbel Bros Inc 64 F 2d 344 (1933)   44
Jamieson v Renwick 17 VLR 124   124
Jamna Das v Ram Autar (1911) 30 IA 7   236
JC Williamson Ltd v Lukey & Mulholland (1931) 45 CLR 282   **202–3,** 704, **714–16**
JJ Savage & Sons Pty Ltd v Blakney (1970) 118 CLR 435   **246–7**
John G Glass Real Estate Pty Ltd v Karawi Constructions Pty Ltd (1993) ATPR 41-249   339
Johnson v Agnew [1980] AC 367   577, 706, 730, **731–2**
Johnson v Buttress (1936) 56 CLR 113   425, 426, **427–9**
Jones v Dumbrell [1981] VR 199   327, 355
Jones v Padavatton [1969] 2 All ER 616   153, **161–2**
Jorden v Money (1854) 5 HLC 185   147

Kalibaksh Singh v Ram Gopal Singh (1913) 41 IA 23   430
Kandaswami v Narayanaswami 45 MLJ 551   523
Kapur Chand Godha v Mir Nawab Himayatalikhan Azamjah 1963 AIR 250   569
Karmot Auto Spares Pty Ltd v Dominelli Ford (Hurtsville) Pty Ltd (1992) ATPR 41-175   355
Karuppayee Ammal v Karuppish Pillai (1987) 1 Mad LJ 138   420
Kell v Harris (1915) 15 SR (NSW) 473; 32 WN (NSW) 133   89
Kelner v Baxter (1866) LR 2 CP 174   186, 196
Khoury v Government Insurance Office (NSW) (1984) 165 CLR 622   358, 596–7
Khwaja Muhammad Khan v Hussaini Begum (1910) 37 IA 152   236
Kimberley NZI Finance Ltd v Torero Pty Ltd (1989) ATPR 46-054   329, 330
Kingston v Preston (1773) 2 Doug 689   587
Kirkby v Turner [2009] NSWCA 131   100
Klans Mittelbachert v East India Hotels Ltd AIR 1997 Delhi 201   236
Kleinwort Benson Ltd v Malaysia Mining Corporation Berhad [1989] 1 WLR 379   164
Knight v Seattle First National Bank 589 P 2d 1279 (1979)   80
Kofi-Sunkersette Obu v A Strauss & Co Ltd [1951] AC 243   90, 125
Koompahtoo Local Aboriginal Land Council v Sanpine Pty Ltd [2007] HCA 61   **291–3,** 587

Koufos v C Czarnikow [1969] 1 AC 350, House of Lords   664–6
Krakowski v Eurolynx (1995) 183 CLR 563   355
Kranz v National Australia Bank Ltd (2003) 8 VR 310   436
Krell v Henry [1903] 2 KB 740   **628–30**
Kriketos v Livschitz [2009] NSWCA 96   75
Krishnaveni Constructions v Executive Engineer, Panchayat Raj, Darsi AIR 1995 AP 362   48
Kshirodebehari Datta v Mangobinda Panda AIR 1934 Cal 682   236

Lalman v Gauri Datt (1913) 11 All LJ 489   52
Lam v Ausintel Investments Australia Pty Ltd (1990) ATPR 40-990; (1990) 97 FLR 458   328, 344
Lang James Morrison & Co Ltd (1911) 13 CLR 1   52
Laurel Race Course Inc v Regal Construction Co Inc 333 A 2d 319 (1975)   63
Laurinda Pty Ltd v Capalaba Park Shopping Centre Pty Ltd (1988–1989) 166 CLR 623   **582–4**, 586
Laybutt v Amoco Australia Pty Ltd (1974) 132 CLR 57   41
Leda Holdings Pty Ltd v Oraka Pty Ltd (1998) ATPR 41-601   342
Lefkowitz v Great Minneapolis Surplus Store 86 NW 2d 689 (1957)   **36–7**, 47
Leigh Enterprises Pty Ltd v Transcrete Pty Ltd (1984) ATPR 40-452   344
Leroux v Brown (1852) 12 CB 801   198
L'Estrange v F Graucob Ltd [1934] 2 KB 294   250, 251, 253, 254
Lewandowski v Mead Carney-BCA Pty Ltd [1973] 2 NSWLR 640   91, 125
Lewis v Averay (1972) 1 QB 198   387, 391
Lewis v Brass (1877) LR 3 QBD 667   156
Life Insurance Co of Australia Ltd v Phillips (1925) 36 CLR 60   **103–4**
Life Savers (Australasia) Ltd v Frigmobile Pty Ltd (1983) 1 NSWLR 431   231
Linden Gardens Trust Ltd v Lenesta Sludge Disposals Ltd [1994] 1 AC 85   223, **658–9**
Liverpool City Council v Irwin [1977] AC 239   261, 266, 270
Lombok Pty Ltd v Supetina Pty Ltd (1987) 14 FCR 226   642
London Drugs Ltd v Kuchne & Napel International Ltd [1992] 3 SCR 299   227
Lord Strathcona SS Co v Dominion Coal Co [1925] All ER 87   231
Louinder v Leis (1982) 149 CLR 509   **555–6**
Louth v Diprose (1992) 175 CLR 621   **447–8**
Lovell and Christmas Ltd v Wall [1911] 104 LT 85   280
Lowe v Peers [1558–1774] All ER 364; (1768) 4 Burr 2225   **514–15**
Lucy v Commonwealth (1923) 33 CLR 229   714
Lucy v Zehmer 84 SE 2d 516 (1954)   26
Lumley v Wagner [1852] All ER Rep 368, Lord Chancellor's Court   722–3
Luna Park (NSW) Ltd v Tramways Advertising Pty Ltd (1938) 61 CLR 286   **540–2**, 587, 656–7
Lymquartz Pty Ltd v 2 Elizabeth Bay Road Pty Ltd [2007] NSWSC 457   327

McBride v Sandland (1918) 25 CLR 69   **203–4**, 205, 206
MacCormick v Nowland (1988) ATPR 40-852   324

McCutcheon v David MacBrayne Ltd [1964] 1 WLR 125   256, 260
Macdonald v Australian Wool Innovation Ltd [2005] FCA 105   461
McDonald v Dennys Lascelles Ltd (1933) 48 CLR 457   **606–8**, 610, 611
McKenzie v McDonald (1927) VLR 134   358
Mackman v Stengold Pty Ltd (1991) ATPR 41-105   353
McLaughlin v Daily Telegraph Newspaper Co Ltd (No 2) (1904) 1 CLR 243   173, 174
McPherson v Appanna AIR 1951 SC 184   47
McPhillips v Ampol Petroleum (Vic) Pty Ltd (1990) ATPR 41-014   333
McRae v Commonwealth Disposals Commission (1951) 84 CLR 377   **371–2**, 379
MacRobertson Miller Airline Services v Commissioner of State Taxation (Western Australia) (1975) 133 CLR 125   76
Mallozzi v Carapelli SpA [1976] 1 Lloyd's Rep 407   98, 99
Manchester Diocesan Council for Education v Commercial & General Investments Ltd [1970] 1 WLR 241   68
Mannai Investments Co Ltd v Eagle Star Life Assurance Co Ltd [1997] 2 WLR 945   283
Maritime National Fish Limited v Ocean Trawlers Limited [1935] AC 524   **635**
Marks v GIO Australia Holdings Ltd (1998) 196 CLR 494   344, 346, 350
Maskell v Horner [1915] 3 KB 106   414
Masters v Cameron (1954) 91 CLR 353   96, **104–6**
Maula Bux v Union of India (1969) 2 SCC 554   697
Maxitherm Boilers Pty Ltd v Pacific Dunlop Ltd [1998] 4 VR 559   **57–8**, **258–9**
May and Butcher Ltd v The King [1934] 2 KB 17(n)   90, 93
MC Chacko v State Bank of Travancore (1969) 2 SCC 343   236
Meates v Attorney-General [1983] NZLR 308   77
Medlin v State Government Insurance Commission   347
Meehan v Jones (1982) 149 CLR 571   91, 99, **107–11**, 125, 268
Merritt v Merritt [1970] 1 WLR 1211   162
Metal Fabrications (Vic) Pty Ltd v Kelcey [1986] VR 507   683
Midland Silicones Ltd v Scruttons Ltd [1962] AC 446   227, 228, 229
Miles v New Zealand Alford Estate Co (1885), 32 Ch D 266   142, 143
Miller v Miller 35 NW 464 (1887)   154
Miller v Miller [2011] HCA 9   498, 499
Miller & Associates Insurance Broking Pty Ltd v BMW Australia Finance Ltd (2010) 241 CLR 357   **330–2**
Misiaris v Saydels Pty Limited [1989] ANZ ConvR 403; (1989) NSW ConvR 55-474   392
Mobil Oil Australia Ltd v Wellcome International Pty Ltd (1998) 81 FCR 475   **80–3**
Mohori Bibee v Dhurmodas (1903) ILR 30 Cal 539   185
Money v Westpac Banking Corporation (1988) ATPR (Digest) 46-034   355
Mooljin Jaitha & Co v Seth Krodimal AIR 1961 Ker 21   58
Moorcock, The (1889) 14 PD 64   265
Morrison v Thoelke 155 So 2d 889 (1963)   65
Morton v Black (1988) ATPR (Digest) 46-037   355
Moschi v Lep Air Services [1972] 2 All ER 393   **604–5**
MS Madhusoodhanan v Kerala Kaumudi P Ltd (2004) 9 SCC 204   718

Murphy v Overton Investments Pty Ltd (2004) 216 CLR 388   **351–3**
Musumeci v Winadell Pty Ltd (1994) 34 NSWLR 723   **131–5**

Nash v Inman [1908] 2 KB 1   **179–80**
National Australia Bank v Nemur Varity Pty Ltd (2000) 4 VR 252   661
National Carriers v Panalpina (Northern) Ltd [1981] AC 675   617, 620, **637–9**
National Engineering Pty Ltd v Chilco Enterprises Pty Ltd [2001] NSWCA 291   **586–7**
National Westminster Bank v Morgan [1985] 1 AC 686   425
Nelson v Nelson (1995) 184 CLR 538   **500–1, 525–6**, 529
Nescor Industries Group Pty Ltd v Miba Pty Ltd (1998) ATPR 41-609   333
New Zealand Shipping Co v Societe des Ateliers et Chantiers France [1919] AC 1   111
New Zealand Shipping Co Ltd v AM Satterthwaite & Co Ltd [1975] AC 154   55, 136, **228–30**, 298, **299**
Newcombe v Newcombe (1934) 34 SR (NSW) 446   587
Niesmann v Collingridge (1921) 29 CLR 177   105
Nissho Iwai Australia Ltd v Malaysian International Shipping Corporation Berhad (1989) 167 CLR 219   305
Nordenfelt v The Maxim Nordenfelt Guns and Ammunition Company Ltd [1894] AC 535   **520–2**
Norman Baker Pty Ltd (in liq) v Baker (1978) 3 ACLR 856   180
North Ocean Shipping Co Ltd v Hyundai Construction Co Ltd [1979] 1 QB 705   **413–15**, 417
Norwich Union Fire Insurance Society Ltd v WmH Price, Ltd (1934) AC 455   378
NSW v Bardolph (1933–1934) 52 CLR 455   177
Nunin Holdings Pty Ltd v Tullamarine Estates Pty Ltd [1994] 1 VR 74   64

O'Brien v Dawson (1942) 66 CLR 18   105
O'Brien v Smolonogov (1983) 53 ALR 107   324, 325
Occidental Worldwide Investment Corp v Skibs A/S Avanti [1976] 1 Lloyd's Rep 293   404, 409
Ocean Tramp Tankers Corporation v V/O Sovfracht 'The Eugenia' [1964] 2 QB 226   617, 620, 632, 635
Oceanic Sun Line Special Shipping Company Inc v Fay (1988) 165 CLR 197   **255–7**
Odorizzi v Bloomfield School District 246 Cal App 2d 123 (1966)   424, 425
Office of Fair Trading v Abbey National plc [2009] UKSC 6   485
Ogle v Comboyuro Investments Pty Ltd (1976) 136 CLR 444   594
Oglebay Norton Co v Armco Inc 556 NE 2d 515 (1990)   97
Oil & Natural Gas Corpn Ltd v Saw Pipes Ltd [2003] INSC 236   689
Opat v National Mutual Life Assurance of Australia Ltd [1992] VR 283   218
Oscar Chess Ltd v Williams [1957] 1 WLR 370   242, 244, 245
O'Young v Walter Reid & Co Ltd (1932) 47 CLR 497   198

Pacific National (ACT) Limited v Queensland Rail (2006) 28 ATPR 46-268   460
Palmer v Temple (1839) 9 Ad & El 508; 112 ER 1304   607, 608, 609

Pao On v Lau Yiu Long [1980] AC 615   **127–8, 135–6**
Paradine v Jane [1558–1774] All ER Rep 172; 82 ER 897   **617–8**
Parkdale Custom Built Furniture Pty Ltd v Puxu Pty Ltd (1982) 149 CLR 191   325, 335, 360
Parker v South Eastern Railway Co (1877) 2 CPD 416   251, 258
Parker v The Queen (1963) 111 CLR 610   18
Partridge v Crittenden [1968] 1 WLR 1204   36
Paul George Pty Ltd v George as Executor for the late Hasbie George [2000] ANZ ConvR 4   399
Pavey & Mathews Pty Ltd v Paul (1986) 162 CLR 221   **199–201**
Payne v Cave (1789) 3 TR 148; 100 ER 502   34, 35
Payne v McDonald (1908) 6 CLR 201   528
Pearce v Brooks [1861–73] All ER Rep 102; [1866] LR 1 Ex 213   520
Petelin v Cullen (1975) 132 CLR 355   **397–9**
Peter Turnbull & Co Pty Ltd v Mundus Trading Co (Australasia) Pty Ltd (1953–1954) 90 CLR 235   584
Pettitt v Pettitt [1970] AC 777   153
Petty v Penfold Wines Pty Ltd (1994) 49 FCR 282   327
Phoenix Court Pty Ltd v Melbourne Central Pty Ltd (1997) ATPR (Digest) 46-179   **336–7**
Photo Production Ltd v Securicor Ltd [1980] AC 827   10, 298, **299**, 310
Pianta v National Finance & Trustees Ltd (1964) 180 CLR 146   712–13
Pinnel's Case (1602) 5 Co Rep 117a; 77 ER 237   139, 141
Pirie v Saunders (1960–1961) 104 CLR 149   196, 198
Placer Development Ltd v The Commonwealth (1969) 121 CLR 353   89, 125
Placer (Granny Smith) Pty Ltd v Thiess Contractors Pty Ltd [2003] HCA 10   **655–6**, 657
Poonoo Bibi v Fyaz Buksh (1874) 15 BLR App 5   532
Popiw v Popiw [1959] VR 197   **138–9**, 162, 196, 198
Port Jackson Stevedoring Pty Ltd v Salmon & Spraggon (Australia) Pty Ltd (1978) 139 CLR 231
Port Line Ltd v Ben Line Steamers Ltd [1958] 2 QB 146   231
Powell v Jones [1968] SASR 394   95, 99
Powell v Lee (1908) 99 LT 284   59
PR Subramania Iyer v Lakshmi Ammal (1973) 2 SCC 54   236
Pratt Contractors Ltd v Palmerston North City Council [1995] 1 NZLR 469   39
Prenn v Simmonds [1971] 1 WLR 1381   280, 282
Price v Strange [1978] Ch 337, [1977] 3 All ER 371   704, 706, 707
Progressive Mailing House Pty Ltd v Tabali Pty Ltd (1985) 157 CLR 17   639
Public Trustee v Taylor [1978] VR 289   355
Pukallus v Cameron (1982) 180 CLR 447   **382–3**

Raffles v Wichelhaus (1864) 2 H & C 906; 159 ER 375   89, 384, 385
Raghava Chariar v Srinivasa (1916) 40 Mad 308   185
Raguz v Sullivan [2000] 50 NSWLR 236   76
Rajendra v Abdul 39 IC 767   523

Ram Singh v Jethamal Wadhumal & Co AIR 1964 Raj 232   532
Re Ku-ring-gai Co-Operative Building Society (No 12) Ltd (1978) 36 FLR 134   324, 325
Re Moore & Co and Landauer & Co [1921] 2 KB 519   539
Real Estates Securities Ltd v Kew Golf Links Estate Pty Ltd [1935] VLR 114   610
Reardon v Morley Ford Pty Ltd (1980) 33 ALR 417   32
Reardon Smith Line Ltd v Yngvar Hansen-Tangen [1976] 1 WLR 989   282
Redgrave v Hurd (1881) 20 Ch D 1   343
Redken Laboratories (Aust) Pty Ltd v Docker (2000) Aust Contract R 90-113   268
Reg Glass Pty Ltd v Rivers Locking Systems Pty Ltd (1968) 120 CLR 516   **661–2**
Regency Media Pty Ltd v AAV Australia Pty Ltd [2009] NSWCA 199   277
Regent v Millett (1976) 133 CLR 679   **204–6**
Renard Constructions (ME) Pty Ltd v Minister For Public Works (1992) 26 NSWLR 234   261, 269
Ringrow Pty Ltd v BP Australia Pty Ltd (2005) 224 CLR 656   687
Roberts v Smith (1859) 4 H & N 315; 157 ER 861   125
Robertson v Robertson [1930] QWN 41   409
Robinson v Harman [1848] All ER Rep 383   654, 692
Roscorla v Thomas (1842) 3 QB 234   **126**
Rose & Frank Co v Crompton & Bros Ltd [1923] 2 KB 261   **163–4**
Ross T Smyth & Co Ltd v T D Bailey, Son & Co [1940] 3 All ER 60   577, 581
Rossiter v Miller (1878) 3 App Cas 1124   105
Royal Bank of Scotland v Etridge (No 2) [2002] AC 773   436
Royal Botanic Gardens and Domain Trust v South Sydney City Council (2002) 186 ALR 289   269, 280, **283–4**
Rust v Abbey Life Assurance Co Ltd [1979] 2 Lloyd's Rep 334   63
Rutter v Palmer [1922] 2 KB 92   305
Ruxley Electronics and Construction Ltd v Forsyth [1995] 1 AC 344   678–80

Sachs v Miklos [1948] 1 All ER 67   53
Saints Gallery Pty Ltd v Plummer (1988) 80 ALR 525   339
Santos Coffee Company Pty Ltd v Direct Freight Express Pty Ltd [2010] NSWCA 14   303
Sargent v ASL Developments Ltd (1974) 131 CLR 634   358, 597
Satyabrata v Mugneeram (1954) SCR 310   645
Saxon v Saxon [1976] 4 WWR 300   405
Scammell (G) & Nephew Ltd v Ouston [1941] AC 251   87, 88
Scanlan's New Neon Ltd v Tooheys Ltd (1943) 67 CLR 169   635
Schib Packaging Srl v Emrich Industries Pty Ltd [2005] 12 VR 268   65
Schuler AG v Wickman Machine Tool Sales Ltd [1974] AC 235   285, 591
Scott v Avery (1856) 5 HLC 811   513
Scriven Bros & Co v Hindley & Co [1913] 3 KB 564   386
Seddon v North Eastern Salt Co Ltd [1905] 1 Ch 326   358, 359
Segur v Franklin (1934) 34 SR (NSW) 67   612
Selectmove Ltd, In re [1995] 1 WLR 474   146
Sellars v Adelaide Petroleum NL (1994) 179 CLR 332   669

Semelhago v Paramedevan (1996) 136 DLR (4th) 1   713–14
Shanklin Pier Ltd v Detel Products Ltd [1951] 2 KB 854   249
Shepperd v The Council of the Municipality of Ryde (1952) 85 CLR 1   **246–7**
Shevill v The Builders Licensing Board (1982) 149 CLR 620   570, **576–9**, 694
Shirlaw v Southern Foundries (1926) Ltd [1939] 2 KB 206   264, 267
Shrimati v Sudhakar R Bhatkar AIR 1998 Bom 122   420
Shuey v United States 92 US 73 (1875)   44
Silver v Dome Resources NL (2007) Aust Contract Reports 90-258   214
Sinclair, Scott & Co Ltd v Naughton (1929) 43 CLR 310   105
Smith v Hughes [1871] LR 6 QB 597   **27**, 385, 386, **387–8**, 389
Smith v Kay (1859) 7 HLC 750   430
Smythe v Thomas [2007] NSWSC 844   36
Snelling v John G Snelling Ltd [1973] 1 QB 87   221
Software Integrators Pty Ltd v Roadrunner Couriers Pty Ltd (1997) ATPR (Digest) 46-177   **328–30**
Solle v Butcher [1949] 2 All ER   379, 380, 381, 389
Soper v Arnold (1889) 14 AC 429   610
South Australia v The Commonwealth (1962) 108 CLR 130   157, 159
South Australian Cold Stores Ltd v Electricity Trust of South Australia (1965) 115 CLR 247   **527–8**
Spedley Securities (in liq) v Bank of New Zealand (1991) ATPR ¶ 41-143   328
Spurling (J) Ltd v Bradshaw [1956] 1 WLR 461   310
St John Shipping Corp v Joseph Rank Ltd [1957] 1 QB 267   **498–9**, 527
St Martins Property Corpn Ltd v Sir Robert McAlpine Ltd [1994] 1 AC 85   223, 224, 225, 226
Startup v Macdonald (1843) 134 ER 1029   557
State Rail Authority of New South Wales v Health Outdoor Pty Ltd (1986) 7 NSWLR 191   279
Steadman v Steadman [1976] AC 536   202, 206
Steinberg v Scala (Leeds) Ltd [1923] 2 Ch 452   180
Stern v McArthur (1988) 165 CLR 489   457
Stevenson, Jaques and Co v McLean (1880) 5 QBD 346   45
Stewart v Kennedy (1890) 15 AC 75   703
Stilk v Myrick (1809) 2 Camp 317   130, 132, 134
Sudbrook Trading Estate Ltd v Eggleton [1982] 3 All ER 1   96, 97
Sudesh Prabhakar Volvoikar v Gopal Babu Savolkar (1996) 5 Bom CR 1   660
Suisse Atlantique Societe d'Armement Maritime SA v NV Rotterdamsche Kolen Centrale [1967] 1 AC 361   310, 577
Sullivan v Macquarie Pathology Services Pty Ltd (1995) ATPR (Digest) 46-143   344
Summergreene v Parker (1950) 80 CLR 304   106
Sumpter v Hedges [1898] 1 QB 673   612
Sunbird Plaza Pty Limited v Maloney (1988) 166 CLR 245   586
Sutton v AJ Thompson Pty Ltd (1987) 73 ALR 233   343, 353
Suttor v Gundowda Pty Ltd (1950) 81 CLR 418   111

Svanosio v McNamara (1956) 96 CLR 186   **376–8,** 379
Sweet & Maxwell Ltd v Universal News Services Ltd [1964] 2 QB 699   91, 99
Sydney City Council v West (1965) 114 CLR 481   298

TA Sundell & Sons Pty Ltd v Emm Yannoulatos (Overseas) Pty Ltd (1956) SR (NSW) 323   130
Tabcorp Holdings Ltd v Bowen Investments Pty Ltd (2009) 236 CLR 272   676, 678
Taft v Hyatt 180 Pac 213 (1919)   52
Tallerman & Co Pty Ltd v Nathan's Merchandise (Victoria) Pty Ltd (1957) 98 CLR 93   66
Tanwar Enterprises Pty Ltd v Cauchi (2003) 217 CLR 315   **552–5**
Tarsem Singh v Sukhminder Singh (1998) 3 SCC 471   385, 394
Taylor v Brewer (1813) 1 M & S 290; 105 ER 108   125
Taylor v Caldwell [1861–1873] All ER Rep 24; (1863) 3 B & S 826   **618–19**, 620, 630, 640
Taylor v Johnson (1983) 151 CLR 422   156, 379, 381, 385, 386, **388–90**, 594
Taylor v Johnston Sup 123 Cal Rptr 641 (1975)   **584–5**
TCN Channel 9 Pty Ltd v Hayden Enterprises Pty Ltd (1989) 16 NSWLR 130   683
The Council of the City of Sydney v West (1965) 114 CLR 481   **306–7**
The Moorcock (1889) 14 PD 64   264
Thomas Bates & Son Ltd v Wyndham's (Lingerie) Ltd [1981] 1 All ER 1077   392, **393–4**
Thomas Brown & Sons Ltd v Fazal Deen (1962) 108 CLR 391   **531–2**
Thomas National Transport (Melbourne) Pty Ltd v May & Baker (Australia) Pty Ltd (1966) 115 CLR 353   303, 305, **308–10**
Thompson v Ice Creameries of Australia Pty Ltd (1998) ATPR 41-611   327, 335
Thomson v McInnes (1911) 12 CLR 562   196, 198
Thorby v Goldberg (1964) 112 CLR 597   91, 93, 125, 135–6
Thornton v Shoe Lane Parking Ltd [1971] 2 QB 163   256, 257
Timmins v Moreland Street Property Co Ltd [1958] Ch 110   197
Tinn v Hoffmann & Co (1873) 29 LT 271   52
Toll (FGCT) Pty Ltd v Alphapharm Pty Ltd (2004) 219 CLR 165   **250–4**, 255, 277
Town & Country Property Management Services Pty Ltd v Kaltoum [2002] NSWSC 166   690
Toyota Motor Corporation Australia Ltd v Ken Morgan Motors Pty Ltd [1994] 2 VR 106   78
Tramways Advertising Pty Ltd v Luna Park (NSW) Ltd (1938) SR (NSW) 632   289, 594, 600
Trident General Insurance Co Ltd v McNiece Bros Pty Ltd (1987–1988) 165 CLR 107   212, 213, **214–17**, 218, 219, 221, 232, 235
Trollope & Colls Ltd v Atomic Power Constructions Ltd [1963] 1 WLR 333   55
Trollope & Colls Ltd v North West Metropolitan Regional Hospital Board [1973] 1 WLR 601   263
Tulk v Moxhay (1848) 41 ER 1143   231
Turner v Bladin (1951) 82 CLR 463   199, 200
Tweddle v Atkinson [1861–73] All ER Rep 369   116, 236
Twynam Pastoral Co Pty Ltd v Anburn Pty Ltd (1989) NSW Conv R 55-498   196

Ulbrick v Laidlaw [1924] VLR 247   35
United Group Rail Services Ltd v Rail Corporation New South Wales [2009] NSWCA 177   100, 101
United States v Bethlehem Steel Corporation et al 315 US 289 (1942)   404
United States v Stump Home Specialties Manufacturing, Incorporated 905F 2d 1117 (1990)   133
Universal Cargo Carriers Corporation v Citati [1957] 2 QB 401   586, 592
Universe Tankships Inc of Monrovia v ITWF [1982] 2 All ER 67   412
Upfull v Wright [1911] 1 KB 506   523
Upper Hunter District Council v Australian Chilling and Freezing Co Ltd (1968) 118 CLR 429   89

Vandepitte v Preferred Accident Insurance Corporation of New York [1932] All ER Rep 527   213, 214
Vantage Navigation Corporation v Suhail and Saud Bahwan Building Materials LLC [1989] 1 Lloyd's Rep 138   409
Veeramma v Appayya AIR 1957 AP 965   236
Veivers v Cordingley [1989] 2 Qd R 278   81
Vodafone Pacific Ltd v Mobile Innovations Ltd [2004] NSWCA 15   269
Von Hatzfeldt-Wildenburg v Alexander (1912) 1 Ch 284   106
Vroon BV v Foster's Brewing Group [1994] 2 VR 32   77

Wajid Khan v Raja Ewaz Ali Khan (1891) 18 IA 144   430
Walford v Miles [1992] 2 AC 128   **100–1**
Wallis, Son & Wells v Pratt & Haynes [1911] AC 394   303, 589
Waltons Stores (Interstate) Ltd v Maher (1988) 164 CLR 387   4, 115, 146, **148–50,** 198, 206
Ward v Byham [1956] 2 All ER 318   138
Ward v Premier Ice Skating Rink Pty Ltd (1986) ATPR 40-681   326
Wardley Australia Ltd v Western Australia   346, 351, 352
Warlow v Harrison (1859) 1 El & El 309; 120 ER 925   34
Warner v Elders Rural Finance Ltd (1992) 113 ALR 517   330
Warner Bros v Nelson [1937] 1 KB 209   724–6
Watt v State Bank of New South Wales [2003] ACTCA 7   436
Way v Latillar [1937] 3 All ER 759   125
Wells (Merstham) Ltd v Buckland Sand & Silica Ltd [1965] 2 QB 170   249
West v AGC (Advances) Ltd (1986) 5 NSWLR 610   **467–70**
Westpac Banking Corporation v Cockerill (1998) 152 ALR 267   416
Westpac Banking Corporation v Sugden [1988] NSW ConvR ¶55-377   467
Wheeler Grace & Pierucci Pty Ltd v Wright [1989] ATPR 50,239   334
White v John Warrick & Co Ltd [1953] 2 All ER 1021   305
White and Carter (Councils) Ltd v McGregor [1961] 3 All ER 1178   **598–600**
Whitlock v Brew (1968) 118 CLR 445   90, 99
Wigan v Edwards (1973) 47 ALJR 586   **141–3**

Wilkinson v Osborne (1915) 21 CLR 89   **513**
Williams v Carwardine (1833) 4 B & Ad 621   50
Williams v Roffey Bros & Nicholls (Contractors) Ltd [1991] 1 QB 1   131, 132, 134
Wilson v Darling Island Stevedoring & Lighterage Co Ltd (1956) 95 CLR 43   214, 227, 228
Wilson Parking Australia 1992 Pty Ltd v Leda Holdings Pty Ltd and National Mutual Trustee Ltd [1996] 982 FCA 1   639
Wisconsin Knife Works v National Metal Crafters 781 F 2d   133
Wong Lai Ying v Chinachem Investment Co Ltd (1979) 13 Build LR 81   **631–2**
Woolf v Associated Finance Pty Ltd (1956) VLR 51   184
Workers Trust and Merchant Bank Ltd v Dojap Investments Ltd [1993] AC 573   611, **695–6**
Wright v TNT Management Pty Ltd (1989) 15 NSWLR 679   334, 335

XCB Pty Ltd v Creative Brands Pty Ltd [2005] VSC 424   392

Yango Pastoral Co Pty Ltd v First Chicago Australia Ltd (1978) 139 CLR 410   497, 498, 502–4
Yerkey v Jones (1939) 63 CLR 649   426, 432, 433, 434, 435
Yorke v Lucas (1985) 158 CLR 661   340, 353

Zieme v Gregory [1963] VR 214   109

Table of Statutes

Australia

Commonwealth of Australia

Acts Interpretation Act 1901
   s 22(1)(aa)   482
Australian Consumer Law   7, 9, 26, 210, 218, 240, 243, 271, 325, 355, 376, 417, 449, 463, 480, 482, 490, 491, 506
   Part 2   480
   Part 2-2   449
   Part 2-3   480, 481, 483, 488–9
   Part 3-2   297, 311
   Part 5-2, Division 2   419
   Part 5-4, Division 2   235, 462
   ss 2–8   480
   s 2   219, 353
   s 4   333
   s 6   449
   s 18   241, 243, 245, 250, 320, 321, 322, 323, 348, 349, 360, 369, 386
   s 20   449
   s 20(1)   449
   s 20(2)   449
   s 21   452–3, 455
   ss 21–22   452, 455
   s 22   453–5
   s 22A   455
   ss 23–28   480
   s 23   311, 481, 489
   s 23(3)   482
   s 24   311, 481, 483, 488
   s 24(2)(b)   483
   s 24(4)   483
   s 25   487, 488–9
   s 26   487, 489
   s 26(1)   483
   s 26(2)   488
   s 27   483
   s 28   481–2
   s 25(1)(i)(k)   311
   s 27(1)   219
   s 35(1)   37
   s 39   53
   s 40   53
   s 41(1)   53
   s 41(4)   53
   s 42   53
   s 43   53
   s 50   417, 418, 419
   s 51   311, 376
   s 52   311
   s 53   311
   s 63   569
   s 64   8, 297, 311
   S 64(1)   505
   s 64A   311
   ss 51–64   26
   s 59   249
   ss   138–141
   s 139   218
   s 224(1)(a)(i)   462
   s 232   490
   s 232(1)   490
   s 232(2)   490
   s 232(6)   490
   s 236   344, 349, 419, 462
   s 236(1)   344, 345, 348, 349, 353
   s 236(2)   344, 462

s 237   462, 490
s 237(1)   354, 490
s 237(3)   462, 490
s 238(1)   354
s 239(1)   354
s 239(4)   490
s 243   354, 419
s 250(1)   490
Australian Securities and Investments Commission Act 2001   462
ss 12BF–12MB   491
s 12 CA   462
s 12CB   463
Banking Act 1959   502
Bankruptcy Act 1966 (Cth)
s 133(5A)   177
s 296   177
Bills of Exchange Act 1909 (Cth)   235
s 32   127
Carriage of Goods by Sea Act 1991   7, 227
Cheques Act 1986   7, 235
Competition and Consumer Act 2010   7, 26, 497
  Part XI   480
  s 4(2)   323
  s 5   231
  s 6   231
  s 45   497
  s 48   213
  s 131(1)   321
  s 131A   323
  s 131A(1)   462
  s 134A(2)(a)   462
  s 137B   343, 348
  s 137B(d)   349
  s 137C(1)   348
  s 137F   462
  s 139A(1)   311
  s 139A(4)   311
  s 139B(2)   343
  Schedule 2 (Australian Consumer Law)   7, 26, 417, 480

Competition and Consumer Legislation Amendment Act 2011   452
Corporations Act 2001   186
  s 9   482
  s 124(1)   186
  s 125(1) and (2)   186
  s 126(1)   186
  s 127(2)   186
  s 131   187
  s 1041K(2)   323
Defence Services Homes Act 1918   500
Electronic Transactions Act 1999 (Cth)   69
  s 5   69–70
  s 14   70
  s 14A   70–1
  s 14B   71
Electronic Transactions Amendment Act 2011   394
Insurance Contracts Act 1984   7
  s 13   272
  s 21   327
  s 48   214, 216, 234
Judiciary Act 1903
  Part IX   177
Marine Insurance Act 1909
  s 20(2)   234–5
  s 28   191
National Consumer Credit Protection Act 2009   471
  Schedule 1 (National Credit Code)   471
  National Credit Code   471–4
  s 76   471–3
  s 77   473
  s 78   474
  s 80   474
Trade Practices Act 1974   7, 245, 528
  Part IV   7, 350, 520
  Part V   336, 350, 352
  Part V, Division 2   219
  Part VI   352
  s 4(2)(a)   328
  s 4(k)   352

Trade Practices Act 1974(cont.)
　s 51A　333, 334, 335, 336, 337, 338
　s 51A(2)　336
　s 51AA　449, 450, 451, 452, 456, 458, 459, 460
　s 51AB　455, 456, 457, 458
　s 51AB(1)　456
　s 51AB(2)(a)　458
　s 51AB(2)(c)　458
　s 51AC　455, 458, 459, 460, 461, 463
　s 51AC(3)　459, 460, 462
　s 51AC(3)(d)　459
　s 51AC(3)(g)　459
　s 51AC(3)(j)　459
　s 51AC(3)(k)　459
　s 51AC(3)(l)　459
　s 52　80, 245, 320, 321, 322, 324, 326, 328, 329, 330, 331, 332, 334, 335, 336, 338, 340, 346, 349, 350, 353, 360, 460, 592
　s 52A(1)　452
　s 60　417
　s 74(1)　304
　s 74G　249
　s 75B　353
　s 82　346, 347, 348, 349, 350, 351, 352
　s 82(1)　344, 345
　s 82(1B)　348
　s 82(2)　245, 321
　s 87　352, 353, 355, 363
　Schedule 5, item 2　7
Trade Practices Amendment (Australian Consumer Law) Act (No 2) 2010　7
　Schedule 7, items 6(1) and 7(1)　245, 321

All States
Consumer Credit Code (not in WA)　195, 471
　Part 2, Division 1　191
　s 12　194
　s 16　194
　s 18　194–5
Credit Acts　7

Crown Proceedings Acts　177
Fair Trading Acts　7, 320, 417
Sale of Goods Acts　7, 18, 92, 178, 240, 271
Sale of Goods (Vienna Convention) Acts　44

Australian Capital Territory
Civil Law (Property) Act 2006
　Pt 2.6　548
Civil Law (Wrongs) Act 2002
　Ch 13　359
　s 102　685
　s 173　358
Consumer Credit Act 1995　7
Crown Proceedings Act 1992　177
Electronic Transactions Act 2001　69
Fair Trading (Australian Consumer Law) Act 1992　7
　s 6　321
　s 7　321
　s 11　333
　s 12　320
Law Reform (Miscellaneous Provisions) Act 1955
　s 54(1)　192
Leases (Commercial & Retail) Act 2001 463 s 22
Mercantile Law Act 1962
　s 15　181
Sale of Goods Act 1954　7
　s 7　174, 178
　s 11　372
　s 12　372
　s 13(2)　92
　ss 17–19　271, 287
　s 17(a)　376
Sea-Carriage Documents Act 1997　235
Supreme Court Act 1933
　ss 26–27　730

New South Wales
Builders Licensing Act 1971　199
　s 45　199

Consumer Credit (New South Wales)
    Act 1995   7
Contracts Review Act 1980   464–5, 467,
    469, 470, 471
    s 4   465, 468
    s 4(1)   470
    s 7   465
    s 7(1)   470, 468
    s 8   470
    s 9   465–6
    s 9(2)   468
    s 9(2)(a)   468
    s 9(2)(d)   468
    s 9(2)(e)   468
    s 9(2)(g)   468
    s 9(2)(i)   468
    s 9(2)(j)   468
    s 9(4)   468
Conveyancing Act 1919 (NSW)
    s 13   551
    s 38(1)   115
    s 54A(1)   192, 193, 195, 205
    s 54B   681
    s 55(2A)   611
    s 142   548
    s 144   548
Credit (Commonwealth Powers)
    Act 2010   471
Crown Proceedings Act 1988   177
Electronic Transactions
    Act 2000   69
Fair Trading Act 1987   7
    s 12   320
    s 27   321
    s 28   321
    s 41   333
    s 42   340
Frustrated Contracts Act 1978
    ss 11–13   642
Home Building Act 1989
    s 7   8
Industrial Relations Act 1996
    s 106   480

Law Reform (Miscellaneous Provisions)
    Act 1965
    Part 3   685
Minors (Property and Contracts) Act
    1970   181
    s 19   181
    s 30   181, 182
    s 31   181, 182
    0s 35   181, 182
    s 37   181, 182–3
Restraints of Trade Act 1976   520
Retail Leases Act 1994
    s 62A   463
    s 62B   463
Sale of Goods Act 1923   7
    s 7   174
    s 11   372
    s 12   372
    s 13(2)   92
    ss 17–19   271, 287
    s 17(1)   376
    s 38(2)   358
Sea-Carriage Documents Act 1997   235
    ss 8 and 10   235
Supreme Court Act 1970
    s 68   730
Workers Compensations
    Act 1987
    s 155   8

Northern Territory[1]

Business Tenancies (Fair Dealings)
    Act 2003
    Part 10   463
Consumer Affairs and Fair Trading
    Act 1990   7
    s 26   321
    s 27   321
    s 41   333
    s 42   320
Consumer Credit (National Uniform
    Legislation) Implementation
    Act 2010   471

---

[1]   Note: Northern Territory legislation bears a date when first enacted but once an Act has been amended the date is omitted.

Consumer Credit (Northern Territory)
    Act 1995   7
Crown Proceedings Act 1993   177
Electronic Transactions Act (Northern
    Territory) 2000   69
Law of Property Act 2000
    s 56   232
    s 58   193
    s 62   192
    ss 211–213   548
Law Reform (Miscellaneous Provisions) Act
    Part V   685
Sale of Goods Act   7
    s 7   174, 178
    s 11   372
    s 12   372
    s 13(2)   92
    ss 17–19   271, 287
Sea-Carriage Documents Act 1998   235
    ss 8 and 10   235
Supreme Court Act
    ss 62–63   730
Water Act 1992   504

Queensland

Consumer Credit (Queensland)
    Act 1994   7, 191
Credit (Commonwealth Powers)
    Act 2010   471
Crown Proceedings Act 1980   177
Electronic Transactions (Queensland)
    Act   69
Fair Trading Act 1989   7
    s 15   321
    s 16   321
    s 37   333
    s 38   320
Industrial Relations Act 1999
    s 276(1)   480
Law Reform Act 1995   685
Property Law Act 1974 (Qld)   232
    Part 17   548
    s 12   234
    s 55   232, 233–4
    s 55(1)(6)(c)   232
    s 56   193

s 59   192
s 62   551
s 68   681
s 72   601–2
Retail Shop Leases Act 1994
    s 46A   463
Sale of Goods Act 1896   7
    s 5   174, 178
    s 9   372
    s 10   372
    s 11(2)   92
    ss 15–17   271, 287
    s 15(a)   376
Sea-Carriage Documents Act 1996   235
    ss 6 and 8   235

South Australia

Building Work Contractors Act 1995
    s 28   195
    s 28(1)   195, 198
Consumer Credit (South Australia)
    Act 1995   7
Credit (Commonwealth Powers)
    Act 2010   471
Crown Proceedings Act 1992   177
Electronic Transactions Act 2000   69
Fair Trading Act 1987   7
    s 13   321
    s 14   321
    s 54   333
    s 56   320
Frustrated Contracts Act 1988   642
Law of Property Act 1936
    Part 7   548
    s 16   551
    s 26(1)   192
Law Reform (Contributory Negligence
    and Apportionment of Liability)
    Act 2001   685
Minors' Contracts (Miscellaneous
    Provisions) Act 1979
    ss 4–8   183
    s 4   181
Misrepresentation Act 1972   359
    s 6   358
Prices Act, 1948–1951   528

Sale of Goods Act 1895   7
   s 2   174, 178
   s 6   372
   s 7   372
   s 8(2)   92
   ss 12–14   271, 287
   s 121   376
Sea-Carriage Documents
   Act 1998   235
   ss 7 and 9   235
Supreme Court Act 1935
   s 30   730

Tasmania

Apportionment Act 1871
   ss 2–3   548
Australian Consumer Law (Tasmania)
   Act 2010
   s 5   321
   s 6   321
Consumer Credit (Tasmania)
   Act 1996   7
Conveyancing and Law of Property
   Act 1884
   s 36(1)   192
Credit (Commonwealth Powers)
   Act 2009   471
Crown Proceedings Act 1993   177
Electronic Transactions Act 2000   69
Fair Trading Act 1990   7
   s 11   333
   s 14   320
Fair Trading (Code of Practice for Retail
   Tenancies) Regulations 1998   463
Mercantile Law Act 1935
   s 6   193
Sale of Goods Act 1896   7
   s 7   174, 178
   s 9   193
   s 11   372
   s 12   372
   s 13(2)   92
   ss 17–19   271, 287
   s 17(a)   376

Sea-Carriage Documents Act 1997   235
   ss 7 and 9   235
Supreme Court Civil Procedure Act 1932
   s 11(7)   551
   s 11(13)   730
Wrongs Act 1954
   s 4   685

Victoria

Consumer Credit (Victoria) Act 1995   7
Credit (Commonwealth Powers)
   Act 2010   471
Crimes Act 1958
   s 321   508
Crown Proceedings Act 1958   177
Electronic Transactions (Victoria)
   Act 2000   69, 194
Fair Trading Act 1985
   s 10A   338
   s 11   337, 338
Fair Trading Act 1999   7, 487
   Part 2B   480, 486
   Part 2C   642, 643
   s 4   333, 338
   s 8   321
   s 9   320, 321, 337
   s 32   594
   s 32OA   358
   s 32OA(1)   600
   s 32P   600–1
   s 32PA   601
   s 32W   485, 486
   s 32Y   480
   s 32Y(3)   480
   s 32ZG   643
   s 32ZH   643, 644
   s 32ZI   643–4
   s 32ZJ   644
   s 32ZK   644
   s 32ZL   644
   s 32ZM   645
   s 33ZF   643
   s 33ZG   643, 644
   s 33ZH   643

Fair Trading Amendment (Unfair Contract
    Terms) Act 2010   480
Goods Act 1958   7
    s 7   174, 178, 180
    s 11   372
    s 12   372
    s 13   92, 94
    s 13(2)   92
    s 14   551
    s 15   551
    ss 17–19   271, 287
    s 17(a)   376
    s 64(b)   36
    s 102(2)   249
Instruments Act 1958   199
    s 126   192, 193, 198, 704, 730
    s 128   202
    s 129   196
Property Law Act 1958
    s 41   551
    s 49(2)   611
Residential Tenancies Act 1997
    s 28   464
Retail Leases Act 2003
    s 78   463, 464
    s 79   464
    s 80   464
Sea-Carriage Documents
    Act 1998   235
    ss 8 and 10   235
Supreme Court Act 1986
    s 38   730
    s 49   184
    s 50   181, 184
    s 51   184, 185
    s 51(2)(3)   184
    ss 53–56   548
    s 54   549
Wrongs Act 1958
    s 25   685
    s 26   686

Western Australia

Credit (Commonwealth Powers) Act
    2010   471

Crown Suits Act 1947   177
Electronic Transactions Act 2003   69
Fair Trading Act 1987   7
    s 9   333
    s 10   320
    s 18   321
    s 19   321
Law Reform (Contributory Negligence
    and Tortfeasors' Contribution)
    Act 1947   685
Law Reform (Statute of Frauds)
    Act 1962   192
Motor Vehicle (Third Party Insurance)
    Act 1943
    s 4   8
Property Law Act 1969
    Part VX   548
    s 11   232–3
    s 11(2)   232
    s 11(2)(c)   232
    s 21   551
Sale of Goods Act 1895   7
    s 2   174, 178
    s 4   193
    s 6   372
    s 7   372
    s 8(2)   92
    ss 12–14   271, 287
    s 12(1)   376
Sea-Carriage Documents Act 1997   235
    ss 8 and 10   235

International Instruments

Hague Rules
    Art III, rule 6   229, 298
UNIDROIT Principles of International
    Commercial Contracts 2004
    Art 1.2   192
    Art 1.7   269, 272
    Art 3.2   114
United Nations Commission on
    International Trade Law's
    (UNCITRAL) 1996 Model Law on
    Electronic Commerce   69

United Nations Convention on Contracts
  for the International Sale of Goods,
  1980 (Vienna Convention)   44
 Art 16   44
 Art 16(2)   47
 Art 17   45
 Art 19   46
 Art 19(1)   58
 Art 19(2)   58
 Art 19(3)   58
 Art 20(1)   47
 Art 21(1)   47
United Nations Convention on the Use
  of Electronic Communications in
  International Contracts 2005   394
 Art 14   395

India

Indian Contract Act 1872   20–1, 154, 166,
  236, 272, 312, 360, 383, 394, 429–30,
  441, 491, 506, 522, 532, 542, 549,
  558, 560, 569, 612, 645, 655, 660,
  686, 697, 718, 728
 ss 1–75   21
 s 1   21
 s 2   27–8, 30, 102
 s 2(a)   166
 s 2(c)   166
 s 2(d)   121, 143, 144, 145, 218
 s 2(j)   363
 s 3   48, 72
 s 4   48, 52, 71, 72–3
 s 5   48, 72, 73
 s 6   48
 s 7   58, 59, 73
 s 7(2)   72
 s 8   73
 s 9   73
 s 9   29, 30
 s 10   28, 115, 166, 170, 191–2, 385,
    419, 430, 506
 s 11   170, 174, 185, 186
 s 12   174
 s 13   385–6, 395, 399

 s 14   395, 419, 430
 s 15   420
 s 16   430–1
 s 17   360–1, 362, 395–6
 s 17(1)   361
 s 18   361
 s 18(1)   361
 s 19   361–2, 363, 395
 s 19A   431
 s 20   383
 s 21   383
 s 22   395
 s 23   143–4, 506–7, 522–3
 s 24   532
 s 25   115–16, 143, 144
 s 25(i)   116
 s 26   523
 s 27   523
 s 28   523–4
 s 29   102
 s 30   524
 s 37   542
 s 38   542
 s 39   542–3, 549, 612
 s 46   558
 s 47   559
 s 48   559
 s 50   543
 s 51   550
 s 53   560
 s 54   561
 s 55   559
 s 56   383, 645–6
 s 62   569
 s 63   543, 569
 s 64   362, 363
 s 65   362, 363, 532, 646
 s 66   363
 s 67   561
 s 68   171
 s 73   655, 660, 666–7, 686
 s 74   689
 s 75   362, 363, 612
Indian Majority Act 1875
 s 3   186

Indian Partnership Act 1932 21
Sale of Goods Act 1930 21
Specific Relief Act
  s 10 718–19
  s 12 719
  s 14 719–20
  s 15 720
  s 16 720
  s 17 720
  s 20 720–1
  s 21 733
  s 26 383
  s 33(2) 185–6
  s 33(2)(b) 185
  s 36 728
  s 37 728
  s 38 728–9
  s 39 729
  s 40 733
  s 41 729
  s 41(e) 729
  s 42 729

New Zealand

Contracts (Privity) Act 1982 232

United Kingdom

Bills of Lading Act 1855 229
Contracts (Rights of Third Parties) Act 1999 213, 232
Financial Services Act 1986 282
Infants Relief Act 1874 (UK)
  s 1 184
Law of Property (Miscellaneous Provisions) Act 1989
  s 2 202
Lord Cairns' Act 1858 730, 732
Pharmacy and Poisons Act 1933 32
Police Pensions Act 1890 137
Sale of Goods Act 1893 18, 289, 303, 592
  s 61(2) 290
Sale of Goods Act 1979 271, 286
  s 57(2) 36
Statute of Frauds 1677 18, 138, 190, 191, 192, 193, 195, 197, 197, 199, 202, 205, 206, 278
  s 4 192, 193
  s 17 192, 193
Statute of Frauds (Amendment) Act 1828 (UK) (Lord Tenterden's Act) 181
Unfair Terms in Consumer Contracts Regulation 1999
  reg 6(2)

China

Civil Code 1929 21
Contract Law of the People's Republic of China 1999 20, 21, 166, 312, 360, 431–2, 441, 491, 507, 524, 532, 543, 550, 560, 561, 569, 612, 646, 655, 660, 667, 686, 690, 721, 730
Art 2 28, 114, 166, 733
Art 3 28
c
Art 5 28, 272, 492
Art 6 28, 272, 492
Art 7 507
Art 8 507
Art 9 170, 171
Art 10 192
Art 12 273
Art 13 29, 30
Art 14 29, 30, 166
Art 15 47, 49
Art 16 49
Art 17 49
Art 18 49
Art 19 49
Art 20 49
Art 21 30
Art 22 73
Art 23 72, 73–4
Art 24 72, 74
Art 25 74
Art 26 72, 74
Art 27 74
Art 28 72, 74
Art 29 72, 74

Art 30   58, 59
Art 31   58, 59
Art 32   72, 74
Art 33   72, 74
Art 35   72, 74
Art 42   363
Art 39   492
Art 40   492
Art 45   111
Art 46   112
Art 47   170, 171
Art 52   364, 420, 507, 524
Art 53   311, 312, 492
Art 54   364, 384, 385, 394, 395, 420, 432, 441, 493
Art 54(i)   399
Art 55   364
Art 56   364, 441
Art 57   364
Art 58   364
Art 60   273, 543, 561
Art 61   102, 272
Art 62   273, 560
Art 62(i)–(iii)   102
Art 62(iv)–(vi)   103
Art 63   103
Art 64   237
Art 65   237
Art 67   550
Art 72   544
Art 91   543, 570
Art 92   570
Art 93   570
Art 94   612, 613, 647
Art 97   612, 613, 660
Art 107   722
Art 108   612, 613

Art 109   722
Art 110   647, 721, 722, 730
Art 111   660–1
Art 112   660, 661
Art 113   667
Art 114   690
Art 115   613, 697
Art 116   613, 697
Art 117   647
Art 118   647
Art 119   687
Art 231   647
Draft Civil Code 1912   21
Economic Contract Law 1981   21
Foreign Economic Contract Law 1985   21
Technology Contract Law 1987   21

Japan

Japanese Civil Code   21

United States

Fair Trade Commission Act 1914
  s 5   360
Restatement of the Law, Contracts (2d) 1981   14, 78
  Chapter 3   136
  s 22(2)   77
  s 71   121
  s 75(1)   120
  s 84(d)   136
  s 87(2)   47
  s 90   47
  s 241   593
Uniform Commercial Code   78
  s 1–203   269
  s 45   360

List of Figures

Summary of Chapter 1: The Nature and Importance of Contract Law	22
Summary of Chapter 2: Agreement	84
Summary of Chapter 3: Certainty and Conditional Contracts	112
Sale of goods: Relationship between seller and buyer	117
Summary of Chapter 4: Consideration	151
Summary of Chapter 5: Intention to Create Contractual Relations	167
Summary of Chapter 6: Capacity	188
Summary of Chapter 7: Formalities	207
Contract to benefit third party C	212
Contract to obligate third party C	212
Summary of Chapter 8: Privity of Contract	238
Summary of Chapter 9: The Terms of a Contract	274
Summary of Chapter 10: Construction and Classification of Terms	294
Summary of Chapter 11: Exclusion Clauses	313
Summary of Chapter 12: Misleading or Deceptive Conduct	365
Summary of Chapter 13: Mistake	400
Summary of Chapter 14: Duress	421
Summary of Chapter 15: Undue Influence	437
Summary of Chapter 16: Unconscionable Conduct	475
Summary of Chapter 17: Unfair Terms	493
Summary of Chapter 18: Illegality and Public Policy	533
Summary of Chapter 19: Performance	562
Summary of Chapter 20: Discharge by Agreement	571
Summary of Chapter 21: Discharge for Breach	614
Summary of Chapter 22: Discharge by Frustration	648

Summary of Chapter 23: Damages and Liquidated Claims: Overview   698
Summary of Chapter 23: Damages and Liquidated Claims:
           Approach to Damages   699
Summary of Chapter 24: Equitable Remedies   734

Preface

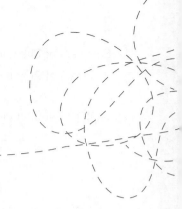

As in the first edition, we seek in this book to provide a current, succinct and comprehensive exposition of Australian contract law and at the same time introduce readers to international perspectives on that area of law, especially from India and China.

Since writing in June 2007, contract law has undergone considerable change, especially as it relates to the broad area of consumer protection and fair trading. This edition responds to those changes. In particular, it incorporates a treatment of the unfair contract terms provisions of the *Australian Consumer Law* (ACL), which came into operation on 1 January 2011, and adjusts the first edition's references to the *Trade Practices Act 1974* to the corresponding provisions of the *Competition and Consumer Act 2010* and the ACL. It also takes account of other statutory developments in areas such as frustration and consumer law. In order to be as current as possible, it anticipates (presciently, we hope!) the passage of the *Competition and Consumer Legislation Amendment Act 2011*, dealing with unconscionable conduct, which by November had passed the House of Representatives but was still before the Senate. As developments in contract law have occurred as a result of judicial decision, as well as statutory enactment, this edition also incorporates reference to, or extracts from, important cases decided since 2007. These include *Attorney General of Belize v Belize Telecom Ltd* [2009] UKPC 10 (implied terms), *Koompahtoo Local Aboriginal Land Council v Sanpine Pty Ltd* [2007] HCA 61 (classification of terms), *Miller & Associates Insurance Broking Pty Ltd v BMW Australia Finance Ltd* (2010) 241 CLR 357 and *Campbell v Backoffice Investments Pty Ltd* (2009) 238 CLR 304 (the scope of the prohibition of misleading conduct), and *Body Bronze International Pty Ltd v Fehcorp Pty Ltd* [2011] VSCA 196 (statutory prohibition of unconscionable conduct).

To assist the reader this edition includes, at the end of each chapter, a diagrammatic summary and a number of review questions designed to raise issues based on the material covered in the chapter.

As noted above, this edition retains its international perspectives. In this respect, it adopts an approach to legal education consistent with that advocated in the Australian Learning & Teaching Council's *Academic Standards Statement for the Bachelor of Laws* (December 2010), which we applaud.

In the preparation of this edition we have benefited from the unflagging support, cooperation and tolerance of the editorial staff at Oxford University Press, especially Estelle Tang and Michelle Head. We would also like to thank Carolyn Leslie for her comprehensive editorial work. We are very grateful to them all.

Philip H Clarke, Gherang
Julie N Clarke, Geelong

Acknowledgments

The author and the publisher wish to thank the following copyright holders for reproduction of their material:

Material from *A Guide to the Unfair Contract Terms Law* reproduced by permission of the ACCC © Commonwealth of Australia; Restatement, Second, Contracts, © 1981 by The American Law Institute. Reproduced with permission. All rights reserved—all legislative material herein is reproduced by permission but does not purport to be the official or authorised version. It is subject to Commonwealth of Australia copyright; Carswell, a Thomson Reuters company, for the DLR extract; CCH for extracts from ANZ ConvR and ATPR; Extracts from NSWLR © Council of Law Reporting for New South Wales [1974–1994]; HCA case extracts reproduced by permission of the High Court of Australia; Extracts from WLR reproduced by permission of the International Council of Law Reporting; Extracts from ALL ER reproduced by permission of Reed Elsevier (UK) Limited trading as LexisNexis; LexisNexis Australia for extracts from the Journal of Contract Law, ALR, QR, BPR and VR; Extracts from NZLR reproduced by permission of the New Zealand Council of Law Reporting; the Office of the Queensland Parliamentary Counsel for permission to reproduce Queensland State Government legislation; South Australian legislation reproduced by permission of the Attorney-General for the State of South Australia; Extracts from legislation of the Parliament of the State of Victoria, Australia, are reproduced with the permission of the Crown in right of the State of Victoria, Australia. The State of Victoria accepts no responsibility for the accuracy and completeness of any legislation contained in this publication; Judgements from the Judicial Committee of the Privy Council—www.jcpc.gov.uk—licensed under the Open Government Licence v1.0 (UK); Case extracts from the Supreme Court of Victoria reproduced by permission of His Honour Justice Beach, Chair of the Victorian Council of Law Reporting; Thomson Reuters for extracts from CLR and FCR; the United Nations for the extract from the 2005 United Nations Convention on the Use of Electronic Communications in International Contracts, article 14, and the United Nations Convention on Contracts for the International Sale of Goods, 1980, articles 16, 17 & 19; Extracts from the University of Cincinnati Law Review reproduced by permission; the Attorney-General for the State of Western Australia for the extract from the *Property Law Act 1969* (WA) section 11.

Every effort has been made to trace the original source of copyright material contained in this book. The publisher would be pleased to hear from copyright holders to rectify any errors or omissions.

PART 1

Introduction

This book describes Australian contract law and outlines the comparable provisions in two countries that are of great and growing importance to this country—China and India. It also seeks to introduce some of the theories that have been advanced to explain this area of law, thereby facilitating its evaluation. By way of introduction, in Part 1 we:

- define what a contract is and identify the essential features of a contractual relationship
- explain why contract law is so important in modern societies
- identify the defining characteristics of Australian contract law and why it should be seen as distinctive
- identify some of the theories that have been advanced to explain the nature of contract law
- provide a brief international perspective and an introduction to Chinese and Indian contract law.

CHAPTER 1

The Nature and Importance of Contract Law

1	What is a contract?	03
2	The importance of contract law	04
3	The nature of contract law	07
	a Contract law is largely judge-made law	07
	b Contractual obligations are largely self-imposed	08
	c The law of contract not contracts	09
	d Relationship with other branches of law	09
4	Contract theory	09
	a The will theory	12
	b The bargain theory	14
	c The promise theory	14
	d The reasonable expectations theory	15
	e The reliance theory	16
	f Miscellaneous	17
5	Australian contract law	18
6	Summary	22
7	Questions	22

1   What is a contract?

A contract is a promise (or a set of promises) that is legally binding; by legally binding we mean that the law will compel the person making the promise ('the promisor') to perform, or to pay damages to compensate the person to whom it was made ('the promisee') for non-performance. Promises are a common feature of our lives; individuals make promises to family members and their friends, promises are made within the workplace, suppliers and their customers make promises about the supply and acquisition of goods and services, and political parties make election promises. However, only some of these promises are legally binding and only some of those that are binding are contracts. For a promise to give rise to a contract it must in substance amount to an undertaking by the promisor that is proffered in exchange for something sought in return from the promisee; for example, a promise by A to let B have her car if B pays A $10,000. The concept of 'bargain'—I will do something if you do something in return—inherent in promises of this nature is the defining characteristic of a contract.

As we have noted, some promises are binding even though they are not contractual in nature. Thus, a promise that does not contain the element of a bargain may still give rise to legal rights and obligations if the promisee has relied upon that promise in circumstances in which it would be unjust to allow the promisor to resile with impunity. This was established for Australia by *Waltons Stores (Interstate) Ltd v Maher*[1] the effect of which is 'that an equitable estoppel yields a remedy in order to prevent unconscionable conduct on the part of the party who, having made a promise to another who acts to his detriment, seeks to resile from the promise'.[2]

2 The importance of contract law

Contract law is important because it underpins our society;[3] without it, life as we know it could not exist. This is because in countries such as Australia most goods and services are created and distributed through markets and markets have at their heart a contract. Consider for a moment this issue from the point of view of a business: almost every transaction it will make will involve a contract; for example it will purchase raw materials, lease premises, hire equipment, sell its products or services, and use banking and related systems to make or receive payments. Likewise, most transactions by consumers involve the purchase of goods or services facilitated by a contract. As with business, it is difficult to think of many transactions entered into by consumers that are not of this nature.[4] Finally, from the perspective of governments, although most of what they do derives from an act of the relevant parliament, increasingly the services they provide are being privatised and delivered pursuant to a contract. This is consistent with Maine's thesis that the movement of progressive societies is from 'status to contract'.[5]

The importance of contracts to our society helps to explain one of the principal reasons why the law enforces them. This reason and the moral justifications for contract law are discussed in the following extract from the work of Professor PS Atiyah, one of the leading contract scholars of the twentieth century.

---

1   (1988) 164 CLR 387. This case is extracted at p 148, below.
2   *The Commonwealth of Australia v Verwayen* (1990) 170 CLR 394 at 428–429, per Brennan J.
3   A similar view was expressed by Kirby P in *Biotechnology Australia Pty Ltd v Pace* (1988) 15 NSWLR 130 at 132 when his Honour said that 'the law of contract … underpins the economy…'.
4   As citizens, members of the public engage in activities, such as visiting a public park or using a footpath, that are not contractual. However, when doing so they are not consumers in the conventional sense.
5   In *Ancient Law*, 14th edn, John Murray, London, 1891, Chapter V, Sir Henry Maine argued that as societies develop they progress from relying on status for their organisation to relying on contract. Thus, while in 'ancient law' individuals were bound together by status, in modern societies they are free to make contacts and form associations with whoever they chose.

Stephen A Smith, Atiyah's Introduction to the Law of Contract,
Clarendon Press, Oxford, 2005

[at 3] The Justification for Contract Law

[W]hat, if anything, is the justification for contract law? Assuming that contracts are voluntary undertakings, why should the law enforce such undertakings? Stated differently, on what basis is it legitimate for the state, acting through the courts, to sanction individuals for breaking contracts? Why lend the state's support to what is an essentially private complaint?

Virtually all societies have evolved laws for the enforcement of contracts, so it is no surprise that most commentators believe that, while certain aspects of the law may pose difficulties, in broad terms the law of contract is justifiable. More specifically, two kinds of justifications are typically given for the law of contract. The first, which is associated with 'economic' and other broadly 'utilitarian' approaches to law, justifies contract law on the basis that it facilitates mutually beneficial exchanges, and so promotes overall social welfare or social 'wealth' (broadly defined). The underlying idea is that where two parties freely agree on a contract involving, say, a simple exchange of money for goods, the seller does so because he thinks he will be better off with the money than with the goods, and the buyer does so because she prefers the goods to the money. Both parties thus emerge from the exchange better off (in one sense) than they were before, and since society's wealth is made up of the total wealth of its members, even a simple exchange of this kind can improve social wealth. In short, contract law (and the officials needed to enforce the law) is a justified use of the state's resources because it helps everyone to become better off. ... <4> ...

From an economic perspective, the primary reason a law of contract is needed is that most exchanges of any complexity cannot be performed simultaneously. One or both parties will have to perform in the future, which means that the other party has to have confidence that she will perform. Suppose that I want a special machine made to order for my factory. A manufacturer could make the machine, and then sell the finished product to me in a simultaneous exchange of machine for cash. But the manufacturer is likely to be worried that I might change my mind at the last minute, leaving him with a machine that is difficult to sell. I might also worry that the manufacturer will change his mind, and decide not to make the machine. Admittedly, there are many reasons aside from the law that each of us might keep to our agreement, such as our interests in our reputation or simply our sense of morality. Nonetheless, it is clear that the risk of non-performance will sometimes dissuade people from entering otherwise beneficial deferred exchanges. It is because of this risk that a law of contract is needed. The fundamental role of contract law, in the economic theory now being considered, is to facilitate the making and performing of deferred exchanges. The law fulfils this role in many ways, but the most fundamental is by providing remedies for breaches of contract, either in the form of orders that breaching parties perform or orders that they pay damages.

Thus interpreted, contract law's essential purpose is to secure cooperation in human behaviour, and particularly in exchange. In sophisticated modern societies this cooperation has led to a massive and elaborate system of credit—and 'credit' is simply another word for 'trust' or 'reliance'. In the simplest sort of case, where businesses provide goods or services on credit to consumers, they trust or rely on the consumer to pay and in the meantime they allow the consumers to have the goods. Generally, the consumers will ultimately pay, but if they fail to do so some sanction is needed: the law of contract provides that sanction. So contract law ultimately provides the backing needed to support the whole institution of credit. A moment's reflection is enough to show to what extent this is true not only in commercial matters, but in all walks of life. The value of consumers' bank accounts, their right to occupy their houses if rented or mortgaged, their employment, their insurance, their shareholdings, and many other matters of vital importance to them, all depend on the fact that the law of contract will enable them to <5> realise their rights. In the striking phrase of Roscoe Pound, 'Wealth, in a commercial age, is made up largely of promises.'

The second general justification that is commonly given for the law of contract can be described more quickly. The individualist or 'moral' justification focuses not on the social benefits of contracting, but on the rights and duties of individual contracting parties. According to this view, when courts order that contracts be performed, the reason is that the defendants have duties, *owed to the claimants* (not society), to do what they contracted to do. And when courts order that damages be paid, the reason is not merely to encourage future contracting or to bring about any other social benefit, but to remedy the injustice caused by the defendant having infringed the claimant's rights. In this view, the payment of damages reflects the idea that the defendant has *wronged* the claimant, and so must repair the harmful consequences of that wrong. Damages correct the injustice *to the individual claimant* caused by the breach. Of course, the defenders of this view do not deny that contracts are socially beneficial, and that contract law facilitates the making of contracts. But they regard these advantages merely as side-effects of an institution whose primary purpose is to ensure that justice is done between individuals.

The economic and moral justifications each provide a plausible justification for the general institution of contract law and, as we shall see in later chapters, for many specific contract law rules. It seems plausible to suppose, therefore, that the best overall justification for the law of contract combines each of these accounts. The idea that contract law is justified on two grounds—an economic ground and a moral ground—is indeed a common conclusion. And as a matter of history, it is clear that lawmakers have been influenced by both grounds (and many others as well). But it is worth noting that many contract scholars are uncomfortable defending a 'mixed' justification of this kind. The reason is straightforward: the two justifications have opposite starting points. The economic view supposes that society's interests take precedence over those of the individual, while the moral view supposes the opposite. A justification for contract law that simultaneously adopts both justifications thus might be thought to raise as many questions as it answers.

3 The nature of contract law

a Contract law is largely judge-made law

Contract law is composed almost entirely of judge-made law and as such is primarily to be found in judicial decisions accumulated over the years. As a result, most books on the subject consist largely of the author's interpretation and rationalisation of those decisions. However, scholarly books have also played an important role in ordering judicial decisions and presenting them in a coherent manner. This was especially the case with early writers such as Chitty, Pollock, and Anson,[6] who played a crucial role in developing a coherent law of contract in the nineteenth century. Indeed, the doctrines they developed in that period remain central to modern contract law.

Increasingly, however, statutes are being passed which regulate, or have an impact upon, substantial areas of contract law. Examples include (at the Commonwealth level) the *Insurance Contracts Act 1984*, the *Cheques Act 1986* and the *Carriage of Goods by Sea Act 1991*; and (at the state and territory level) the Sale of Goods Acts,[7] Fair Trading Acts[8] and Credit Acts.[9] Perhaps the most significant, at least from the perspectives of the volume of litigation and the regulation of consumer contracts, has been what is now the *Competition and Consumer Act 2010* (Cth)[10] which has revolutionised contract law in the areas such as misrepresentation, implied terms, manufacturers' liability and unconscionable conduct. All of these statutes affect areas that were once the sole preserve of judge-made law. As a result, although judge-made law remains the more important ingredient, especially in commercial transactions, Australian contract law is now a complex mix of judge-made and statute law.

---

6   J Chitty, *The Law of Contracts*, S Sweet, London, 1826; F Pollock, *Principles of Contract at Law and in Equity*, Stevens, London, 1878; WR Anson, *Principles of the Law of Contract*, Callaghan & Co, Chicago, 1880.
7   *Sale of Goods Act 1954* (ACT); *Sale of Goods Act 1923* (NSW); *Goods Act 1958* (Vic); *Sale of Goods Act 1896* (Qld); *Sale of Goods Act 1895* (SA); *Sale of Goods Act 1896* (Tas); *Sale of Goods Act 1895* (WA); *Sale of Goods Act* (NT).
8   *Fair Trading (Australian Consumer Law) Act 1992* (ACT); *Fair Trading Act 1987* (NSW); *Fair Trading Act 1999* (Vic); *Fair Trading Act 1989* (Qld); *Consumer Affairs and Fair Trading Act 1990* (NT); *Fair Trading Act 1987* (WA); *Fair Trading Act 1987* (SA); *Fair Trading Act 1990* (Tas).
9   *Consumer Credit Act 1995* (ACT); *Consumer Credit (New South Wales) Act 1995* (NSW); *Consumer Credit (Queensland) Act 1994* (Qld); *Consumer Credit (South Australia) Act 1995* (SA); *Consumer Credit (Tasmania) Act 1996* (Tas); *Consumer Credit (Victoria) Act 1995* (Vic); *Consumer Credit (Western Australia) Act 1996* (WA); *Consumer Credit (Northern Territory) Act 1995* (NT).
10 This act was originally known as the *Trade Practices Act 1974* (Cth); it was renamed the *Competition and Consumer Act 2010* (Cth), as part of a major revision of Australian consumer law in 2010, by the *Trade Practices Amendment (Australian Consumer Law) Act (No 2) 2010*, Schedule 5, item 2. The provisions of this act of most relevance to contract law are: (i) those in Part IV (and associated provisions) dealing with restrictive trade practices which prohibit certain agreements because they are anti-competitive; and (ii) those in the *Australian Consumer Law*, located in Schedule 2, which prohibit certain forms of conduct and create certain rights that have either an impact on contractual dealings generally, or only on those involving consumers, or consumer goods or services.

An important challenge presented by this mix of case and statute law is that the statutory modifications of case law are not conveniently collated in a single source and are constantly being added to. This means that English texts (upon which great reliance was placed until comparatively recently) may no longer accurately represent important areas of Australian contract law and Australian texts, which do integrate local statutory modifications, may soon become dated in certain areas. As a result, it is important for anyone practising or studying contract law to be alert for statutory modifications to the common law, modifications which can sometimes appear in unlikely places.

b Contractual obligations are largely self-imposed

In contrast to most other areas of law, contractual obligations are largely self-imposed. Unlike, for example, the criminal law or the law of torts which impose obligations upon individuals whether or not they consent to them, contract law merely provides a framework within which individuals can create their own rights and obligations if, but only if, they wish to do so. In *Baltic Shipping Co v Dillon*[11] Brennan J expressed this defining characteristic of a contract succinctly when he said that it was an institution 'by which parties are empowered to create a charter of their rights and obligations *inter se*'. As a result of contract being of this nature, generally speaking, individuals are free to decide whether or not to enter into a contract at all; and if they do decide to do so:

- what the nature and content their respective rights and obligations will be; and
- what the consequences will be of those obligations not being honoured, or rights infringed.

There are, of course, limits to this freedom. Thus, in some cases it is mandatory to enter into contracts; third party personal injury insurance in relation to the use of motor vehicles[12] and workers' compensation insurance[13] are prime examples. In other cases, terms are prescribed,[14] or prohibited[15] for certain contracts. More common still, inequality in bargaining position and the associated use of standard form contracts often means that, in practice, if a person wishes to enter into a contract they must do so on the terms laid down by the other party. In such cases, by entering into the contract, the former is taken to have agreed to the latter's terms notwithstanding that they felt that they had no choice about the matter. Only if the dominant party's conduct constitutes duress or undue influence, or

---

11 (1993) 176 CLR 344 at 369.
12 See *Motor Vehicle (Third Party Insurance) Act 1943* (WA) s 4.
13 See *Workers Compensation Act 1987* (NSW) s 155.
14 See the *Home Building Act 1989* (NSW) s 7.
15 For example, it is now common for consumer protection legislation to prohibit (in the sense of making void) contractual provisions that would take away the protection given to consumers by the legislation: see the *Australian Consumer Law*, s 64.

is unconscionable in some way, or the terms in question form part of a standard form consumer contract and are judged to be 'unfair', will such a contract be unenforceable.[16]

c   The law of contract not contracts

Unlike the position in some jurisdictions, Anglo-Australian common law recognises a general law of contract that applies equally to all types of agreements; in other words, that there is a law of *contract*, rather than a law of *contracts*. However, principally as a result of legislation, special rules have been introduced to govern particular types of contracts; examples include those statutes dealing with contracts for the sale of goods, insurance, consumer credit, the carriage of goods, and building and construction. Typically, the focus of these statutes is the content of the contract and they leave the general law to govern its formation and the remedies for breach. However, in other cases aspects of these matters are also covered and in some instances the operation of the general law is eliminated almost entirely.[17]

d   Relationship with other branches of law

Contract and other branches of the law are not mutually exclusive. Thus, a particular event may give the rise to rights or obligations under more than one regime. For example, consumers who purchase goods or services which prove to be faulty will have a remedy for breach of contract against the supplier for any loss that this causes them and a statutory right to claim compensation from that person.[18] In addition, if the goods cause personal injury or damage to other property, as well as a contractual claim against the seller they will have a claim for the tort of negligence[19] and a statutory claim against the manufacturer.[20]

4   Contract theory

The description of contract law in the previous section is a traditional one and reflects what is often referred to as 'classical' and 'neoclassical' contract theory. Classical contract theory enjoyed its zenith during the heyday of laissez-faire in the nineteenth century and had at its centre the doctrines of freedom of contract and sanctity of contract. According to the former, individuals are the best judges of what is in their own interests and they should be 'free', within the broad limits

---

16   For a discussion of these topics see chapters 14–17, below.
17   For example, employment law is now almost entirely governed by subject matter specific statutory provisions.
18   Under the *Australian Consumer Law*, a consumer has certain statutory rights against the supplier of goods or services in relation to the quality of and title to the goods or services supplied: see ss 51–63 and associated remedy provisions.
19   See *Donoghue v Stevenson* [1932] AC 562.
20   Under ss 138–141 of the *Australian Consumer Law*, a consumer has certain statutory rights against the manufacturer of goods if those goods have a safety defect that causes injury or property damage.

of the criminal law and public policy, to contract upon whatever terms they wish. In the words of Lord Diplock in *Photo Production Ltd v Securicor Ltd*,[21] it is 'A basic principle of the common law of contract ... that the parties to a contract are free to determine for themselves what primary obligations they will accept.' The doctrine of sanctity of contract takes this concept one step further by saying that a contract, once made, is 'sacred' and should, therefore, be enforced according to its terms and not rewritten by the courts because they may think that the parties have made a bargain that is unsatisfactory in some way.

Developments in the twentieth century, however, revealed the practical limitations of the classical theory. In its pure form, it could not accommodate the sympathy that developed for the position of those who lacked the bargaining power to protect their own interests, or the growing desire of the courts to intervene in order to ensure just outcomes. This saw it metamorphose into neoclassical theory. This process and the relationship between the two are explained further in the following extract.

Jay M Feinman, 'The Significance of Contract Theory'

(1990) 58 *University of Cincinnati Law Review* 1283

[at 1285] 1. Neoclassical Contract Law

Modern contract law is often usefully referred to as neoclassical contract law. This term aptly situates today's contract law in its historical context. The essential quality of neoclassical contract is that it is the product of the attempt to accommodate classical contract law and subsequent critiques of it. The word 'neoclassical' suggests the partial nature of the accommodation, indicating that neoclassical contract has not so far departed from classical law that a wholly new name is appropriate.

... <1286> Classical law in general was structured by a series of dichotomies which defined the relationships among legal actors. For example, the Federal government and state governments had separate spheres of authority, as did legislatures and courts. The most fundamental dichotomy was between the individual and the community. Therefore, relations among individuals were governed by private law, which was distinct from public law, which regulated relations between individuals and the state. Within private law, contract law embodied the dichotomy between individual and community by imagining a realm of private agreement in which individual freedom was protected from state coercion. The image that motivated this realm was the isolated bargain between independent, self-interested individuals. Steely-eyed bargainers carefully calculated their interests in a particular exchange, gave a promise or performance only in return for something else, and embodied their transaction in an agreement that carefully defined the terms of performance and therefore could provide the basis for a determinate remedy in case of breach.

---

21 [1980] AC 827 at 848.

Accordingly, as conceived by classical contract law, liability was always voluntarily assumed by the individual through his making of a promise or an agreement, unlike in tort law, in which liability was imposed by the legal system without regard for the individual's consent. Contract doctrines such as narrow formation rules and bargain consideration followed logically from these principles and assured that the individual actually had consented to a bargained-for exchange. When courts mechanically applied these abstract, formal doctrines, they protected the individual's right to assume contractual <1287> obligation or to avoid it at the same time as they provided a predictable basis for commercial transactions.

The problems of classical contract law quickly became apparent to judicial and scholarly commentators. Contractual liability, like all other legal liability, did not arise solely from the individual's choice but came from the court's imposition of legal obligation as a matter of public policy; a contract was binding because the court determined that imposing liability served social interests, not because the individual had voluntarily assumed liability through his manifestation of assent. Nor could the parties' words in creating the contract exclusively define the scope of liability; courts had to interpret, fill gaps, and even impose pre-contractual and quasi-contractual liability, either to make the parties' contract meaningful in its commercial context or to serve social interests other than individual choice, such as fairness. Because of the inherent limits of language and the infinite variability of facts, courts could not state doctrinal rules in such a way that they could be mechanically applied to all fact situations that might arise; moreover, the changing needs of commerce made it undesirable to attempt to do so. ...

As with classical law, neoclassical law can be evoked by presenting the image of its prototypical case as well as by describing its substance, method, and social role. The prototype of neoclassical contract posits parties in an economic relationship that is neither entirely isolated nor wholly encompassing. The parties seek individual advantage through the transaction, but their individual advantage is tied to the success of their mutual venture. The relationship arises through voluntary bargaining which defines the basic terms of the agreement, but the terms can only be understood by examining the context within which the agreement is reached, so that context sometimes supplies interpretations and additional terms.

Proceeding from this image, as a matter of substantive principle neoclassical contract law attempts to balance the individualist ideals <1288> of classical contract with communal standards of responsibility to others. The core remains the principle of freedom of contract, distinguishing contract from tort and other areas, but this principle is 'tempered both within and without [contract's] formal structure by principles, such as reliance and unjust enrichment, that focus on fairness and the interdependence of parties rather than on parties' actual agreements.' In deciding the scope of contractual liability, courts weigh the classical values of liberty, privacy, and efficiency against the values of trust, fairness, and cooperation, which have been identified as important by post-classical scholars.

Neoclassical contract accommodates these conflicting values through a method that is flexible and pragmatic. Logic and analytic rigor remain important in contract law because they are a source of legal authority and an important element of professional culture. In contrast to classical law, though, neoclassical law tempers rigid logic by the use of policy analysis, empirical inquiry, and practical reason. Contract doctrine, more often formulated as general standards rather than mechanical rules, guides judges, sometimes quite strongly, but it allows them enough discretion in hard cases to reach just, socially desirable results.

Through this flexible body of principles and methods for their application, neoclassical contract serves the important social goal of supporting and regulating economic transactions. It does this in two general ways. First, it provides a framework for parties who engage in business planning. The framework helps them to create legal relations, to determine their content, to avoid them altogether, and to sort out difficulties when planning goes awry. Second, it provides a background set of norms for fair market relations. Even without the direct threat of enforcement, these norms are used by business people to set standards and limits for their conduct.

This description of neoclassical contract law and how it has arisen should be largely unobjectionable. Mainstream scholars believe that the neoclassical adaptation has successfully responded to the defects of earlier contract law and that it can continue to evolve as the need for further development arises.

[footnotes omitted]

A valuable summary of some of the other theories that have been advanced to explain the nature of a contract and the existence of contractual liability are contained in the following extract.

Brian Coote, 'The Essence of Contract'

(1988) 1 *Journal of Contract Law* 91

[at 99] The theories stated
a The will theory

Under the will theory, contracts are seen as expressions of the human will and, for that reason, as being inherently worthy of respect. In that premise are found both the justification of contract law and the basis of many of its incidents. The theory asserts the liberal principle of individual self-determination and the value of individual judgment and volition. Both are thought to be enhanced when two or more wills meet in agreement.

The idea of contract as an expression of will or intention can be traced back at least to classical Greece and Rome. Later it was developed particularly by the Pandectists, the scholars who reintroduced the study of Roman law to Europe from the Renaissance onwards. Through them the theory influenced provisions of the French and German Civil Codes as well as of Scottish law. In turn, it influenced the development of the common law in the nineteenth century, through the writings of such European theorists as Pothier and Savigny.

Associated with the will theory, or derived from it, have been the concepts of contract as agreement, of consensus *ad idem*, offer and acceptance, intention to contract, privity and the *vinculum juris*, and construction and interpretation by reference to the intention of the parties. The theory has also lent support to defences such as mistake, misrepresentation, duress and undue influence and hence to the idea that consent to a contract should be full, free and true. In the common <100> law of the classical period, perhaps its best-known manifestation was freedom of contract, a doctrine which both reinforced, and was itself reinforced by the then-prevailing philosophy of laissez-faire. So pervading did that doctrine become that it found its way into the constitutions of both the United States and Germany.

Subject to a limited number of restrictions, the law of contract could be seen to have delegated to individual citizens a form of legislative authority. While this could mean that one party could place him or herself to some degree under the control of another, the power to do so was itself an expression of individual autonomy and an incident of freedom. The most often-quoted judicial statement of the freedom of contract doctrine was that of Sir George Jesse in the 1875 case of *Printing and Numerical Registering Co v Sampson* where he said:

> if there is one thing which more than another public policy requires it is that men of full age and competent understanding shall have the utmost liberty of contracting, and that their contracts when entered into freely and voluntarily shall be held sacred and shall be enforced by Courts of Justice.

In the common law context, however, the will theory has its weaknesses, both as a justification for the enforcement of contracts and as a basis for prediction. Under the postal rule, for example, it is clear that an offerer could be bound to an offer he had already attempted to withdraw. The theory is also prima facie incompatible with the existence of implied-by-law terms. The most obvious weakness is the impossibility in practice of determining what the will of the parties might be, even supposing an exact concurrence of wills could ever exist about all aspects of any particular contract. The common law response has, of course, been to apply objective tests of will and intention. The parties are bound, not by what they actually intended, but by the inferences to be drawn from what they said and did. This objective approach has meant that a search for the apparent intention of the parties has been a practical possibility. But it also means that the existence of contract law can hardly be justified by reference to some mystical need to give effect to the human will, since it is not necessarily the actual will which is the determinant.

The use of standard forms which gained momentum in the nineteenth century and which has accelerated since, has also undermined the idea of consensus *ad idem*. There has, too, been a retreat from the notion of freedom of contract, coinciding with a retreat from laissez-faire <101> economics which has only recently been reversed. These matters will be adverted to again in due course.

b   The bargain theory

The bargain theory is a common law development from the notion of contract as agreement. It incorporates what has been called the bargain theory of consideration, attributed in the United States to O W Holmes, which sees consideration in terms of reciprocal conventional inducement. The distinguishing feature of a contract at common law is said to be a bargain or exchange between the parties. As a theory it is necessarily confined to the common law system, which is the only one to contain, through the doctrine of consideration, any requirement of reciprocity between the parties.

… *Cheshire & Fifoot* subscribe to this theory. They are seemingly not alone. Professor C J Hanson, for example, has suggested that 'consideration, offer and acceptance are an indissoluble trinity, facets of one identical notion which is that of bargain'. The requirement of reciprocal consideration ensures that the parties make their undertakings to each other and that, since each makes a 'payment', each desires those undertakings to be made. The bargain theory, therefore, reinforces the ideas of privity, request and mutuality.

An obvious drawback to the theory is its exclusiveness. Not only has it to be confined to contracts at common law. Within the common law it fails to include contracts by deed made without consideration. On the other hand, it can also be argued in its favour that it does not exclude the possibility of gratuitous contracts. Even if simple contracts must be bargains, the common law does not require any equivalence of exchange. If the promise of a peppercorn can be a sufficient consideration, the bargain theory could be said to include the possibility of a contract being made by way of gift, otherwise than by use of a deed.

c   The promise theory

The promise theory says in effect that contracts are promises, that promises should be kept, and that it is therefore appropriate that the law should enforce them.

The idea of a promise as something to be kept is an ancient one and has drawn support from the Jewish, Christian and Muslim religions. The nearest Roman law came to a general type of contract took the form of a ritual promise. In Roman times and since, the bindingness of <102> promises has been seen to be required by natural law. In England, promises were important to the Anglo-Saxons. For centuries they were also enforced by the ecclesiastical courts. In the King's courts, the writ of *assumpsit* was, in form, an action on the case for damage caused by breach of promise. In more recent times, as we have already seen, textbook definitions of contract have frequently been cast in terms of promise, as was the definition in the Restatement of Contracts.

The promise theory, then, has the advantages of reflecting a practice of some antiquity and of giving legal expression to widely held intuitions of what is fair and right. It is not confined to agreements. But as a theory of contract it, too, has its drawbacks. It assumes that contracts are enforced because they are promises but, in practice, no legal system has ever enforced every promise and life would be intolerable under any system which did so, human nature being what it is.

On the other hand, as has already been pointed out, some promises are nowadays enforceable which would not have been recognised as contracts under classical common law. There are problems too about what comprises a promise, why promises should be kept and why the law should intervene to enforce them.

It seems generally to be agreed that promisors place themselves under obligation to their promisees and in that sense surrender a measure of autonomy to them. Promises are seen as voluntary acts and the resultant obligation as being in some sense or another voluntarily incurred by the promisor. There is less agreement as to what constitutes a promise. Some regard it as merely an emphatic expression of intent, a statement of resolve or commitment, or a prediction. For others, it depends on an intention by the promisor to accept obligation in respect of whatever he or she has undertaken. The problem of futurity has already been mentioned. <103>

As to why promises should be kept and, in particular, why the law should intervene to enforce them, there is again an absence of agreement. In the past, morality and religion have been accepted reasons. Professor Roscoe Pound argued that the extensive modern use of common forms had, in itself, 'relaxed' the claims of morality for the enforcement of contracts. Even so, Professor Fried has recently argued the moral basis of contracts. More widely acceptable nowadays might be claims of utility and convenience. Promising can be regarded as a socially useful practice which it is in the interests of society to foster and protect. It could be said to provide facilities for its members in the form of systems of rules which give them the power, at their choice, to place themselves under obligation.

This latter view of promises, too, has its detractors, principally on the ground that it presupposes an intention to be bound on the part of the promisor. If promises depend on intention, argued Adam Smith, a promise made without an intention to perform it would never be binding. Other commentators would claim that the search for intention is an unnecessary fiction. In practice, of course, the common law derives intention objectively, on the basis of the appearance of what the promisor has said and done.

For himself, Adam Smith preferred to found obligation on the reasonable expectations induced in the promisee. Some later commentators have taken the argument a step further by basing obligation on reliance by the promisee in pursuance of his or her reasonable expectations. These approaches have both been sufficiently important in contract theory to justify separate treatment here.

d   The reasonable expectations theory

Adam Smith's theory of the foundation of contract law has come down to us in transcripts made by his students of his lectures in Jurisprudence. He based the obligation to perform a contract on the reasonable expectations induced by a <104> promise and the disappointment of those obligations occasioned by breach.

In the classical period and since, views similar to those seem to have been shared very widely. In England, for example, they have appeared in such textbooks as *Pollock, Holland, Salmond, Anson* and *Cheshire and Fifoot* and to have had the endorsement of Austin and Goodhart. In the United States, they were supported by *Corbin* and were incorporated by Roscoe Pound into one of his jural postulates. In Canada they have the support of contributors to *Studies in Contract Law* and are endorsed, for example, in Professor Waddams' *Contract* text. So widespread has been their acceptance that they have been described by Professor Atiyah as being now traditional.

It is not immediately obvious why the reasonable expectations theory should have held so much appeal, for so long. No doubt, promises and contracts do usually raise expectations and in most cases are intended to do so. But in practice, the raising of reasonable expectations is neither sufficient nor necessary for the existence of a promise or contract. A statement that I am likely to call at your home on Saturday afternoon may well raise expectations of a visit but it would not be a promise. On the other hand a statement would not be any less a promise merely because the promisee did not believe it could or would be performed. And a promise made by deed can be a binding contract even though the beneficiary is unaware of its existence. Then, too, there is a certain circularity in the theory. What marks it as especially reasonable to base expectations on a promise or contract if not that it is regarded as binding?

There is a further problem in the nature of expectation itself. Life is full of disappointments but we do not ordinarily expect the law to make <105> provision for them to be compensated, even when the expectations themselves are reasonable. And if contract law exists to protect reasonable expectations, how are we to explain the decision of the House of Lords in *Addis v Gramophone Co Ltd*, the effect of which in most cases is to deny compensation for the 'disappointment of mind' caused by breach of contract?

It was doubtless reasons of this kind, at least in part, which led to the development of the reliance theory.

e The reliance theory

This theory, in its strongest form, is that a contract arises (or should arise) whenever a promisee has relied upon a promise in a way which would cause detriment if it were not kept. Writing in 1933 about justifications for contract liability, Professor M R Cohen described it as 'the favourite theory today'. Since then, it has attracted strong support from Fuller and Perdue in their famous 1937 article on 'The Reliance Interest in Damages' and, in more recent times, from Professors Horwitz and Atiyah in particular.

Since it is based on loss or injury to the promisee, the theory has the advantage of appearing both objective (in not depending upon the intentions of the promisor) and fair (in visiting liability on the one who by inviting reliance has caused the loss or injury). It appears, too, to draw some historical justification from the earliest actions in *assumpsit*, which could be said to have been based on loss or damage suffered as the result of reliance on the defendant's promise. Professor Cohen recognised that in basing liability on loss or damage the theory would appeal to those who wished to see contract integrated with other forms of obligation and particularly with tort.

Nevertheless, as a theory of contract it has serious limitations. For example, damages in contract characteristically are measured not by the loss suffered by the promisee in reliance on the promise but by the loss <106> resulting from the promisor's failure to perform. The promisee is entitled in general to be put in the position he or she would have occupied had the contract been performed, the so-called 'expectation' measure. Fuller and Perdue's answer to this objection was to extend their concept of 'reliance' to include failure by the promisee to make alternative contractual arrangements in reliance on the promise (lost opportunity costs). On that basis, they suggested, the expectation measure was essentially a rule-of-thumb means of assessing reliance loss, followed by the courts for the sake of efficiency and convenience.

The reliance theory also seemingly fails to explain why, as is the case, executory contracts are binding from the moment of their formation and are enforceable independently of whether either party has acted to his or her detriment. Professor Atiyah would answer that the law has been wrong in this respect. A less drastic answer might be to say that, in enforcing wholly executory contracts, the object of the law is to protect not only particular acts of reliance but also the practice of relying on contracts generally.

A third difficulty is that neither reliance nor a tendency to induce reliance is either sufficient or necessary for the existence of a contract. Promises made in a social context, such as an invitation to dinner, may induce reliance but are not contracts. The same can be true of invitations to treat, such as advertisements for the holding of an auction, or offers such as tenders, which may induce reliance before being withdrawn. On the other hand, a contract by deed can bind even though it has not been communicated to, let alone been relied upon by, the promisee. Like the reasonable expectations theory the reliance theory also contains an element of circularity.

Finally, the reliance theory bases contractual obligation, not on what a promisor said or did, but on the reactions of another to those things. As such it would be a potential instrument for the imposition of obligations for which the promisor had not contracted.

f   Miscellaneous

In his 1933 article on the basis of contract, Professor Cohen identified three theories in justification of contract liability apart from those already mentioned. <107>

One was a theory of O W Holmes that the parties to a contract had in effect an option to perform it or pay damages. In respect of matters outside the control of a promisor, the theory contains an element of truth. The same could be true of cases where the law does not allow for specific enforcement. But as a theory of contract generally, it is inconsistent with the availability of specific performance and of actions in debt for the recovery of contract sums.

A second theory was that the formalities associated with contracts in different cultures and at different times were not only designed to make evidence secure but were also, in large part, expressions of a fundamental human need for formality and ceremony. This theory draws attention to what may well be an important feature of formation but it does not, for example, supply any very obvious explanation of or justification for contract liability, let alone indicate what constitutes a contract.

The third theory, which Cohen put forward as his own, was that the role played by the State in contract enforcement made the law of contract part of public law. The law was justified in placing limitations on the extent of the parties' freedom to invoke the power of the State. Again, the emphasis of the theory is on just one feature of the law of contract, albeit an important one.

[footnotes omitted]

5   Australian contract law

As will be apparent from the material that follows, Australian contract law is largely derived from England. When the various colonies were established in the eighteenth and nineteenth centuries the colonists brought with them the English common law including those statutes, such as the *Statute of Frauds 1677*, that could be applied locally. Even after the colonies gained independence, English court decisions continued to be influential; indeed, it was not until 1963 in *Parker v The Queen*[22] that the High Court finally decided that it was free not to follow decisions of the House of Lords. English statutes have also been influential and many local provisions are merely adaptations of them.[23] Therefore, it is not surprising that extracts from English cases appear frequently in this work. However, Australian contract law is increasingly diverging from its English counterpart. Our courts are developing the common law differently from courts in England and our statutes are creating a distinct Australian law. The significance of this for contract scholarship and practice is considered in the following extract.

MP Ellinghaus, 'An Australian Contract Law'

(1989) 2 *Journal of Contract Law* 13

[at 28] Diminution of English influence

What is at stake is not, of course, the development of a law of contract branded with specifically Australian virtues and loaded with local colour, or isolated from outside influence, but simply one that cleaves to our own social condition. Although some similarities between English and Australian society continue to exist, rooted as they are in language <29> and modern history, and reinforced by the continuing import of English immigrants, entertainments and ideas, it is nevertheless true that there are fundamental differences between the two countries. For example, Australians inhabit a continent of 7,682,000 square kilometres with a population density of

---

22   (1963) 111 CLR 610.
23   The state and territory Sale of Goods Acts are a prime example, each being modelled on the *Sale of Goods Act 1893* (UK).

2.1 per square kilometre; the English inhabit an island of 244,000 square kilometres at a density of 231.3 per square kilometre. In 1986 3.4 million of a total population of 16 million, or one in five, Australians were foreign born; of these, 2.2 million, or one in seven Australians, were from other than the United Kingdom, Ireland and North America, in other words, from legal systems presumably not derived from the English model. In the United Kingdom 3.3 million of a total population of 56 million, or one in 17, was foreign born.

Moreover, Australia is situated in proximity to Asia and Oceania, where its trading partners are increasingly to be found, and which supply an increasing percentage of its immigrants. The United Kingdom is an island adjunct of Europe, on the opposite side of the globe, and is now a member of the European Economic Community. Increasing divergencies in the law of contract are a certain result of their respective situations.

Such points of comparison may vary in the degree to which they manifestly bear on issues of legal order, and specifically on the issue whether the contract law of the one place should be hitched to that of the other. Nevertheless they are structurally significant for the functioning of their respective societies. Given 'the profoundly indigenous sources of social being', the differences which they reflect must have enough impact on transactions to make it unwise to apply to the contracts of one the law devised in the other. Despite this, the combined efforts of Australian judges, practitioners, and scholars have created a situation in which, notwithstanding its formal independence, much of Australian contract law continues to be made in London. We have continued to <30> accept 'ready-made solutions from the United Kingdom instead of evolving answers for ourselves'.

Affirmative action is needed to accelerate the rate of change in this situation. All ex-colonial cultures must endure this irritating phase of 'self-conscious attempt to turn one's back on the parent tradition and to create a new one rooted in the native soil', before reaching a stage 'where self-consciousness has largely disappeared'.

The routine citation of English cases should therefore be dropped. This is so particularly of the 'classic decisions'. 'The classic decisions—usually English—should not be omitted merely because of their age or origin', say the authors of the most recent of our casebooks on contract. The revealing phrase in this otherwise unexceptionable proposition is that between hyphens: 'usually English'. Whose classics are we talking about? Would it not seem odd now in, say, literature, painting or history, to number Wordsworth, Constable, or Gibbon among ours?

It is not enough, moreover, merely to stipulate that 'if there is relevant Australian authority it should be cited in preference to English authority'. Contingencies which have not yet been considered by Australian courts are contingencies for which there is as yet no specific Australian rule, and for which the leeways of choice are open. The argument in such a case should be about what principle is best applied in Australia, not about the degree of persuasiveness of an English decision in point.

Above all, Australian contract lawyers need a much more vigorous and comprehensive exposure to their own case law. The space taken up in Australian reports, casebooks and texts by the discussion of English precedent is not vacant space, but could be filled many times over with Australian material. Only the full exposure of that material, and its scrutiny without the constant bifurcation of attention to English doctrine, will enable such questions to be answered as: What elements of contract law have been found to be most important for transactions in and with Australia, situated in its particular global, continental and social geography? What are the most articulate opinions, the best passages, the classic dicta, of Australian judges and commentators? Precisely to what doctrine are we committed by Australian decision, and what remains in the realm, at best, of the persuasive? In law above all, with its constant tendency to ossify, it is important that Australian lawyers realise fully the extent of their leeways of choice; without this <31> realisation the will and capacity to devise their own solutions must remain stunted.

[footnotes omitted]

INTERNATIONAL PERSPECTIVES

Because of its English origins, some international perspective is inherently part of Australian contract law. In addition, as English influences on our law have waned, those of other countries, especially those sharing our common law heritage such as the United States, New Zealand and Canada, have increased. As a result, Australian contract law has not developed in splendid isolation and this is reflected in the materials we have selected in the following chapters. In addition, we have included specific international perspectives from China and India. There are two reasons for choosing these jurisdictions. In the first place, they are countries that are becoming increasingly important to Australia. China is now Australia's largest trading partner and our commercial links with India are destined to expand rapidly. Consequently, it will be advantageous for Australian lawyers to have some familiarity with the commercial law of those countries. Second, India and China present valuable perspectives from which to evaluate Australian law. The *Indian Contract Act, 1872* put into statutory form much of the common law of contract that India had adopted from England. Consequently, comparing and contrasting its provisions with current Australian law will deepen and enrich our understanding of the latter. This is also the case with the *Contract Law of the People's Republic of China* adopted and promulgated in 1999. This was formulated after an extensive review of contract law regimes around the world, including Australia's, and although many of its provisions are directed towards uniquely Chinese situations it nevertheless represents one important view of what an ideal contract law would look like.

a. Background to the *Indian Contract Act, 1872*

Ancient Indian law did not recognise a separate law of contract.[24] As a result, during the period of English colonial rule, especially in the eighteenth and early

---

24   See generally, HK Saharay, *Dutt on Contract*, 10th edn, Eastern Law House, Kolkata, 2006.

nineteenth centuries, the common law was introduced into India. However, its relationship with local law, which did regulate particular forms of commercial activity, was ambiguous, so much so that the Second and Third Law Commissions in India suggested codification of contract law. This resulted in the passage of the *Indian Contract Act, 1872*. Sections 1–75 of this Act contain general provisions that apply to all agreements. Subsequent parts then deal with indemnities and guarantees, bailment and agency. Originally, the Act also dealt with the sale of goods and partnership; these matters have since been made the subject of separate statutes.[25] The *Indian Contract Act* is not a code. That is, it does not purport to deal with all aspects of contract law and s 1 specifically preserves 'any usage or custom of trade, [or] any incident of a contract, not inconsistent with the provisions of this Act'.[26] As a result, the common law as interpreted by Indian courts continues to apply where the Act is silent.

b. Background to the Chinese *Contract Law 1999*

The first meaningful attempt to develop contract law in China was in 1911 during the Qing Dynasty. This Draft Civil Code was largely modelled on the Japanese Civil Code and disappeared together with the last Chinese emperor when the Republic of China was established in 1912.

In 1929 the Republic of China promulgated a new Civil Code, the development of which was influenced by European and Japanese codifications of contract law. However, after the establishment of the People's Republic of China (PRC) in 1949, this code was abolished and contract law remained undeveloped during the formative years of the new regime. This situation became untenable with the rapid expansion of the Chinese economy following the reform programs and open-door policies introduced after 1978. These saw business activity grow in scale and complexity, both domestically and internationally, and necessitated significant reform. Three statutes were enacted in response— the *Economic Contract Law* (the ECL) in 1981, the *Foreign Economic Contract Law* (the FECL) in 1985 and the *Technology Contract Law* (the TCL) in 1987. Unfortunately, each of these statutes was drafted to deal with a particular type of economic activity and none was applicable to all commercial transactions with the result that gaps remained in some areas and overlap and inconsistency occurred in others. This led to calls for the development of a unified contract law to accommodate China's business and social needs. After Chinese legislators had spent six years examining the contract laws of civil and common law countries and various international models, the result was the promulgation on 1 October 1999 of the *Contract Law of the People's Republic of China* and the repeal of the ECL, FECL and TCL.[27]

---

25   See *Sale of Goods Act 1930* and the *Indian Partnership Act 1932*.
26   See also the comments to s 1 of the Act.
27   For the detailed account of the development of Chinese contract law, see B Ling, *Contract Law in China*, Sweet & Maxwell, Hong Kong, 2002.

6 Summary

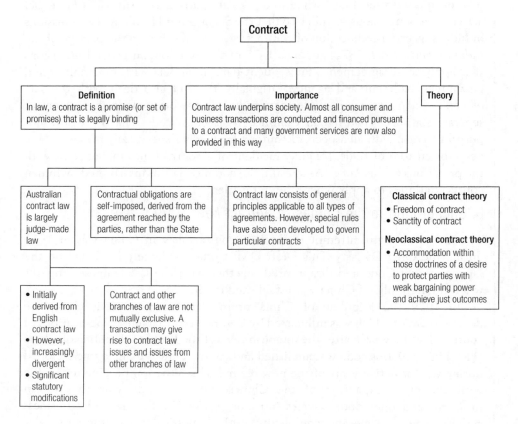

7 Questions

1. Why is contract law so important in countries with market economies? Could they operate without a law of contract? When considering this question, reflect on what contracts you have made in the last few days and whether you could have avoided making them.

2. What are the doctrines of 'freedom of contract' and 'sanctity of contract'? How relevant are they today in influencing the content and nature of contractual relations?

3. What are the principal sources of Australian contract law? How are the sources of contract law different in India and China? Do these jurisdictions present any lessons for Australia; in particular, should Australian contract law be codified in some way?

PART 2

Formation

In Part 1, we defined a contract as a promise (or set of promises) that is legally binding and noted that only some promises are binding and contractual in nature. In Part 2 we examine in more detail the preconditions that must be satisfied for a promise to be contractual; these are as follows:

- the promise must arise through an agreement reached between two or more parties about its subject matter
- this agreement must be sufficiently certain and complete to be enforceable, should there be a dispute between the parties; in other words, its language must be sufficiently clear to reveal the intention of the parties and deal with all the matters that the law regards as essential for this purpose
- the party to whom the promise is made—the 'promisee'—must pay for the promise by providing what is known as 'consideration'; alternatively, the promise must be recorded as a deed; that is, recorded in a document that is signed, sealed and delivered by the person making the promise—the 'promisor'—and intended by that person to be a deed

- the parties must intend that their agreement is to be a contract and be enforceable as such
- the parties must have the legal capacity to enter into the contract in the terms of their agreement
- any formalities prescribed for the enforcement of the agreement in question must be complied with.

Each of these six preconditions is the subject of a separate chapter in this Part.

CHAPTER 2

Agreement

1	Introduction	25
2	The nature of an agreement	26
3	Offer and acceptance	28
4	The nature and duration of offers	30
	a To whom can an offer be made?	30
	b Offers distinguished from invitations to deal	31
	c Offers distinguished from requests for information or statements of possible terms	40
	d Termination of offers	40
5	Acceptance	50
	a The relationship between offer and acceptance	50
	b Who may accept an offer?	52
	c Acceptance by conduct	52
	d Correspondence between offer and acceptance	53
	e Communication of acceptance	59
6	Agreements reached without offer and acceptance	75
7	Bilateral and unilateral contracts	78
8	Summary	84
9	Questions	84

1 Introduction

The central requirement of a contract is the existence of an agreement between two parties concerning the promise in question. What is to be understood by this requirement and how the law determines whether it is satisfied (and if it is, when and where this happened) is considered below; in particular we will examine:

- the nature of an agreement
- the offer and acceptance process used in connection with this requirement
- the situations in which agreements can be reached without a discernable process of offer and acceptance
- the need for the agreement to concern a promise, and the distinction between bilateral and unilateral agreements.

2 The nature of an agreement

For the purposes of contract law, an agreement is an understanding between two parties that one of them will do something, or will promise to do so, in return for the other doing something, or promising to do so. Thus, there are two elements: a meeting of the minds of the parties (which is why agreement is often referred to as a *consensus ad idem*) and at least one promise. It is the need for this second element that distinguishes a contractual agreement from other types of agreement. For example, while, colloquially, we may say that A and B have reached an agreement if, after discussion, they reach a common understanding that a particular car has a new engine, this would not be a contractual agreement as there is no promise involved. On the other hand, it would be a contractual agreement if A promised B that the engine was new in return for B making a promise, or actually doing something nominated by A.

It is also essential that the agreement is entered into voluntarily; that is, it must not be the result of illegitimate pressure being exerted by one party on the other. However, although the concepts of 'consensus' and 'free association' lie at the heart of 'agreement' in contract law, they are interpreted narrowly. In particular:

- whether the parties have reached an agreement is determined objectively, not subjectively[1]
- agreement is required only about entering into the contract and its terms; it is not concerned with the desirability of doing so, or what motivates the parties
- an agreement can exist even though one, or both, of the parties believes that they were obliged to enter into it because of their economic or personal circumstances
- an agreement can exist even though one of the parties is not happy about its terms and has entered into it only reluctantly.

As a result, where one party is in a superior bargaining position to the other, as a general proposition, the law does not prevent that power being used to drive a bargain that is overwhelmingly in that party's favour.[2] However, there are two important qualifications to this proposition. First, the general or 'unwritten law' will render a contract voidable at the instigation of the weaker party if the agreement was induced by the use of 'illegitimate' pressure (discussed in chapter 14), or was attributable to some other form of reprehensible conduct on the part of the dominant party (discussed in chapters 15 and 16). Second, the *Australian Consumer Law* (*ACL*) creates a number of 'consumer guarantees' in favour of consumers that cannot be excluded by an agreement between the parties.[3]

---

1   As a result, if one party was only joking when they entered into an agreement they will, nevertheless, be bound where a reasonable person would have concluded that they had intended to enter into a contract: see *Lucy v Zehmer* 84 SE 2d 516 (1954).
2   See, for example, the observation of Gleeson CJ in *ACCC v CG Berbatis Holdings Pty Ltd* (2003) 214 CLR 51 at 64 that 'good conscience does not require parties to contractual negotiations to forfeit their advantages, or neglect their own interests'.
3   The *ACL* is set out in Schedule 2 of the *Competition and Consumer Act 2010* (Cth); the provisions referred to are ss 51–64.

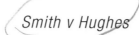

Smith v Hughes

[1871] LR 6 QB 597, Court of Queen's Bench

[Smith offered to sell oats to Hughes and showed him a sample of what was for sale. Believing that what he had been shown were old oats, Hughes agreed to purchase them at the price stated by Smith. When he later discovered that they were new oats, Hughes sought to return them and avoid paying. Smith, who had known that the oats were new, refused to take them back and sued for the contract price. At first instance the jury found for the defendant (Hughes) after having been directed by the judge that they should do so if they concluded that the plaintiff was aware of the defendant's mistake. On appeal]

Cockburn CJ [at 606]: It only remains to deal with an argument which was pressed upon us, that the defendant in the present case intended to buy old oats, and the plaintiff to sell new, so the two minds were not ad idem; and that consequently there was no contract. This argument proceeds on the fallacy of confounding what was merely a motive operating on the buyer to induce him to buy with one of the essential conditions of the contract. Both parties were agreed as to the sale and purchase of this particular parcel of oats. The defendant believed the oats to be old, and was thus induced to agree to buy them, but he omitted to make their age a condition of the contract. All that can be said is, that the two minds were not ad idem as to the age of the oats; they certainly were ad idem as to the sale and purchase of them.

Blackburn J [at 607]: If, whatever a man's real intention may be, he so conducts himself that a reasonable man would believe that he was assenting to the terms proposed by the other party, and that other party upon that belief enters into a contract with him, the man thus conducting himself would be equally bound as if he had intended to agree to the other party's terms.

New trial ordered

INTERNATIONAL PERSPECTIVES

The concept of a contract being a voluntary agreement between two parties is explicitly reproduced in the Indian and Chinese law. However, China appears to go further than the common law in relation to requiring fairness and good faith in the formation and performance of contracts.

Indian Contract Act, 1872

Section 2 …

(e) Every promise and set of promises, forming consideration for each other, is an agreement.

…

(h) An agreement enforceable by law is a contract

Section 10

All agreements are contracts if they are made with the free consent of the parties, competent to contract, for lawful consideration and with lawful object, and are not expressly declared to be void.

This definition raises the question, considered in chapter 5, of whether intention to create contractual relations is a separate requirement for the existence of a contract under Indian law.

Contract Law of the People's Republic of China, 1999

Article 2. Definition of Contract

For purposes of this law, a contract is an agreement between natural persons, legal persons or organisations with equal standing, for the purpose of establishing, altering, or discharging a relationship of civil rights and obligations.

Article 3. Equal Standing of Parties

Contract parties enjoy equal rights and neither party may impose its will on the other party.

Article 4. Right to Enter into Contract Voluntarily

A party is entitled to enter into a contract voluntarily under the law, and no entity or individual may unlawfully interfere with such right.

Article 5. Fairness

The parties shall abide by the principle of fairness in prescribing their respective rights and obligations.

Article 6. Good Faith

The parties shall abide by the principles of good faith in exercising their rights and performing their obligations

3 Offer and acceptance

In most cases, the issue of whether an agreement has been reached is determined by analysing the dealings between the parties in terms of 'offer' and 'acceptance'. Such an analysis seeks to determine whether one party has communicated to the other an offer which the latter has accepted; if this is found to have occurred, the parties are said to have reached an agreement. Although the parties may not have used the language of offer and acceptance in their communications, it is usually possible to discern from their words, or conduct, what the law regards as one or the other. In substance, an offer is a promise by one person (the 'offeror') to do something, or not to do something, if the person to whom it is addressed (the 'offeree') responds in a stipulated manner. Any form of words or conduct intentionally communicating such a promise can amount to an offer. Examples include:

- stating a willingness to sell goods, or supply services, in exchange for a stipulated price
- advertising that a reward, or a prize, will be paid to anyone providing certain information, or acting in a certain way
- making a bid at an auction
- displaying an automatic vending machine, or a sign, proffering goods or services in exchange for payment
- submitting a tender for the supply of goods or services for a stipulated price.

An acceptance is an affirmative response to an offer by the offeree; in effect, the offeree saying 'yes'. The clearest way for the offeree to do this is to literally state, orally or in writing, that the offer is accepted. However, in some cases this is impractical. Thus, unless there is a stipulation to the contrary, any form of words or conduct can amount to an acceptance, so long as an intention can be discerned on the part of the offeree to accept the offer on the terms stipulated.

The process of analysing the communications and conduct of the parties in terms of offer and acceptance is used to determine not only *whether* an agreement has been reached, but also *when* this occurred and *where*. These issues can be important because of the bearing they have on such matters as the terms of the contract and the jurisdiction in which disputes should be adjudicated. Subject to the qualifications to be considered later, the general rule is that an agreement is reached *when* and *where* the offeree's acceptance is communicated to the offeror.

INTERNATIONAL PERSPECTIVES

The common law approach to determining whether an agreement has been reached (analysing transactions in terms of offer and acceptance) has been adopted in India and China. Both also adopt the concept of an offer being, in essence, a promise to act in a certain way if the person to whom it is directed responds positively. In India, this is done by defining an offer (called a 'proposal') and then providing that when this is accepted it becomes a promise which is then defined as an agreement. The common law position that offers and acceptances can be conveyed by conduct as well as by words is specifically acknowledged (s 9). The Chinese provisions (Articles 13 and 14) are more direct.

Indian Contract Act, 1872

Section 2 ...

(a) When one person signifies to another his willingness to do or to abstain from doing anything, with a view to obtaining the assent of that other to such an act of abstinence, he is said to make a proposal.

(b) When the person to whom the proposal is made signifies his assent thereto, the proposal is said to be accepted. A proposal when accepted becomes a promise.

(c) The person making the proposal is called the 'promisor', and the person accepting the proposal is called the 'promisee'.

Section 9 Promises, express and implied

In so far as the proposal or acceptance of any promise is made in words, the promise is said to be express. In so far as such proposal or acceptance is made otherwise than in words, the promise is said to be implied.

Contract Law of the People's Republic of China, 1999

Article 13. Offer-Acceptance

A contract is concluded by the exchange of an offer and an acceptance.

Article 14. Definition of Offer

An offer is a party's manifestation of intention to enter into a contract with the other party, which shall comply with the following:

(i) its terms are specific and definite;

(ii) it indicates that upon acceptance by the offeree, the offeror will be bound thereby.

Article 21. Definition of Acceptance

An acceptance is the offeree's manifestation of intention to assent to an offer.

4 The nature and duration of offers

a To whom can an offer be made?

An offer can be made to a particular person, to a group, or to the whole world.

Carlill v Carbolic Smoke Ball Company

[1893] 1 QB 256, English Court of Appeal

[The Carbolic Smoke Ball Company manufactured and sold a medical preparation called 'The Carbolic Smoke Ball' which was designed to prevent users contracting a cold or influenza. To promote this product, the company published an advertisement in the *Pall Mall Gazette*, part of which read:

> £100 reward will be paid by the Carbolic Smoke Ball Company to any person who contracts the increasing epidemic influenza, colds, or any disease caused by taking cold, after having used the ball three times daily for two weeks according to the printed directions supplied with each ball. £1,000 is deposited with the Alliance Bank, Regent Street, showing our sincerity in the matter.

In response to this advertisement, Mrs Carlill bought one of the balls and used it as directed. Nevertheless, she contracted influenza, whereupon she claimed the reward advertised. Her claim succeeded at first instance and the company then appealed.]

Bowen LJ [at 268]: It was also said that the contract is made with all the world—that is, with everybody; and that you cannot contract with everybody. It is not a contract made with all the world. There is the fallacy of the argument. It is an offer made to all the world; and why should not an offer be made to all the world which is to ripen into a contract with anybody who comes forward and performs the condition? It is an offer to become liable to anyone who, before it is retracted, performs the condition, and, although the offer is made to the world, the contract is made with the limited portion of the public who come forward and perform the condition on the faith of the advertisement. It is not like cases in which you offer to negotiate, or you issue advertisements that you have got a stock of books to sell, or houses to let, in which case there is no offer to be bound by any contract. Such advertisements are offers to negotiate—offers to receive offers—offers to chaffer, as, I think, some learned judge in one of the cases has said. If this is an offer to be bound, then it is a contract the moment the person fulfils the condition.

[In separate judgments, AL Smith and Lindley LJJ agreed on this point with the reasoning of Bowen LJ.]

Appeal dismissed

b Offers distinguished from invitations to deal

Most legal systems draw a distinction, based upon the intention of the party making the communication, between an offer and an invitation to deal (sometimes referred to as an 'invitation to treat'). A communication will be characterised as an offer if the party making it intended that an affirmative response would immediately give rise to an agreement. If, on the other hand, the communication was intended to merely initiate negotiation, it will be characterised as an 'invitation to deal'. The distinction between the two is important; if a communication is characterised as an offer, an affirmative response will create an agreement, whereas if it is characterised as an invitation to deal, such a response can only be an offer which the party issuing the invitation may accept or reject. The types of communication that have raised this issue include displaying goods in shops or shop windows, conducting or advertising auctions, advertising goods or services for sale, circulars promoting sales, calls for tender, operating a public transport system, displaying an automatic vending machine, and issuing tickets.

Displaying goods

The display of goods in a self-service store, or in a shop window, is usually regarded as merely an invitation to deal, rather than an offer to sell, even though the display is accompanied by the price tag of some kind.[4] This issue is important because, as the following case shows, it determines the point in time when a contract of sale is made, and whether a customer can insist upon purchasing goods they have selected.

Pharmaceutical Society of Great Britain v Boots Cash Chemists (Southern) Ltd

[1953] 1 QB 401, English Court of Appeal

[Boots operated a self-service store which contained a pharmacy department. Customers wishing to purchase items from the store selected them from the shelves and took them to a cashier's desk at one of the exits where they were paid for. When a drug was involved, the transaction at the cashier's desk was supervised by the pharmacist in control of the pharmacy department. The Pharmaceutical Society alleged that by operating in this manner, Boots infringed the *Pharmacy and Poisons Act 1933* which required the sale of certain drugs to be supervised by a registered pharmacist. In a case stated, the Chief Justice found that Boots had not infringed the Act. The Society appealed.]

Somervell LJ [at 405]: The point taken by the plaintiffs [the Society] is this: it is said that the purchase is complete if and when a customer going round the shelves takes an article and puts it in the receptacle which he or she is carrying, and that therefore, if that is right, when the customer comes to the pay desk, having completed the tour of the premises, the registered pharmacist, if so minded, has no power to say: 'This drug ought not to be sold to this customer.' Whether and in what circumstances he would have that power we need not inquire, but one can, of course, see that there is a difference if supervision can only be exercised at a time when the contract is completed.

I agree with the Lord Chief Justice in everything that he said, but I will put the matter shortly in my own words. Whether the view contended for by the plaintiffs is a right view depends on what are the legal implications of this layout—the invitation to the customer. Is a contract to be regarded as being completed when the article is put into the receptacle, or is this to be regarded as a more organized way of doing what is done already in many types of shops—and a bookseller is perhaps the best example—namely, enabling customers to have free access to what is in the shop, to look at the different articles, and then, ultimately, having got the

---

4   See *Fisher v Bell* [1961] 3 All ER 731 at 733 and *Reardon v Morley Ford Pty Ltd* (1980) 33 ALR 417.

ones which they wish to buy, to come up to the assistant saying 'I want this'? The assistant in 999 times out of 1,000 says 'That is all right,' and the money passes and <406> the transaction is completed. I agree with what the Lord Chief Justice has said, and with the reasons which he has given for his conclusion, that in the case of an ordinary shop, although goods are displayed and it is intended that customers should go and choose what they want, the contract is not completed until, the customer having indicated the articles which he needs, the shopkeeper, or someone on his behalf, accepts that offer. Then the contract is completed. I can see no reason at all, that being clearly the normal position, for drawing any different implication as a result of this layout.

The Lord Chief Justice, I think, expressed one of the most formidable difficulties in the way of the plaintiffs' contention when he pointed out that, if the plaintiffs are right, once an article has been placed in the receptacle the customer himself is bound and would have no right, without paying for the first article, to substitute an article which he saw later or a similar kind and which he perhaps preferred. I can see no reason for implying from this self-service arrangement any implication other than that which the Lord Chief Justice found in it, namely, that it is a convenient method of enabling customers to see what there is and choose, and possibly put back and substitute, articles which they wish to have, and then to go up to the cashier and offer to buy what they have so far chosen. On that conclusion the case fails, because it is admitted that there was supervision in the sense required by the Act and at the appropriate moment of time.

[Birkett and Romer LJJ delivered separate judgments to the same effect.]

Appeal dismissed

Auctions

If a sale of property by auction is advertised and bids called, is that communication an offer to sell to the highest bidder, or merely an invitation asking bids to be made? The answer to this question is complicated by the fact that an auction involves three parties—the seller, the auctioneer and the bidder. In addition, the auction may be advertised as being subject to a 'reserve price' (a price below which the property will not be sold) or 'without reserve' (that is, without a minimum or 'reserve' price being set by the seller). The law's response to these issues is discussed in the following case.

AGC (Advances) Ltd v McWhirter

(1977) 1 BPR 9454, Supreme Court of New South Wales

[AGC held a mortgage over land owned by a company of which the McWhirters were the directors. Because the company was in default, AGC exercised its power under the mortgage to sell the property by auction. During this auction the auctioneer announced that an initial reserve had been withdrawn, whereupon

Mr McWhirter bid the highest price. He was informed that this bid was not acceptable and eventually the property was knocked down to an earlier bidder for a lower price. The McWhirters then placed a caveat on the title to the land, arguing that they were entitled to the land under a contract made at the auction. In this action, AGC sought to have the caveat removed.]

Holland J [at 9456]: The basis of the defendants' assertion that a contract had come into existence was that, once the reserve price was withdrawn and it was announced at the auction that the property was 'on the market', the plaintiff became an offerer for sale to the highest bidder and Mr McWhirter's bid, being the highest, constituted acceptance of the offer, thereby making a contract irrespective of whether the auctioneer actually knocked the property down to him. The theory of this submission was that a vendor who puts a property up for sale by auction without reserve to the highest bidder undertakes to sell to the highest bidder and that each bidder is a conditional purchaser, the condition being that no-one bids a higher price. This theory of such an auction was rejected by the King's Bench Division of the Courts in England nearly 200 years ago in *Payne v Cave* (1789) 3 TR 148; 100 ER 502. ... The trial judge, Lord Kenyon, non-suited the plaintiff and the King's Bench Division upheld the non-suit. The court said (at TR 149; ER 503);

> The auctioneer is the agent of the vendor, and the assent of both parties is necessary to make the contract binding; that is signified on the part of the seller by knocking down the hammer, which was not done here till the defendant had retracted. An auction is not unaptly called *locus poenitentiae*. Every bidding is no <9457> more than an offer on one side, which is not binding on the other side till it is assented to. But according to what is now contended for, one party would be bound by the offer, and the other not, which can never be allowed.

It is clear that the *ratio decidendi* of *Payne v Cave*, was that the bidder is not a conditional purchaser but is no more than an offeror and that consequently no contract can come into existence unless and until his bid is accepted, usually, by the fall of the hammer. In my opinion, this is still the law of auctions and was not affected in the present case by the announcement at the auction that the highest bidder should be the purchaser and that no bidding should be retracted or by the announcement to the effect that the sale was no longer subject to a reserve price. This means that it is open to the vendor to withdraw the property from sale at any time before a bid has been accepted or, as in this case, to decline to accept a bid from a party with whom the vendor does not wish to contract.

The question whether an express statement by or on behalf of the vendor that the auction sale will be 'without reserve' constitutes a definite offer to sell to the highest bidder has been the subject of debate. The proposition that it does was rejected by a Scottish court in *Fenwick v McDonald Frazer & Co* (1904) 6 F (Ct of Sess) 850 which held that no agreement was made unless and until the auctioneer acknowledged acceptance of the bid by the fall of his hammer; however, some obiter dicta in *Warlow v Harrison* ... has kept the question open.

[On appeal in that case (1859) 1 El & El 309; 120 ER 925] <9458> None of the judges suggested that, by being the highest bidder, the plaintiff had made a contract for sale with the vendor. The only issue in the case was whether the bidder had a right of action against the auctioneer. The majority of the Court of Exchequer Chamber appear to have been of the opinion that a collateral contract arose between the highest bona fide bidder and the auctioneer arising out of a holding out by the auctioneer that the sale would be without reserve. It is difficult to see what consideration there could be for such a contract particularly when it appears to be settled law that the advertisement of an auction is an invitation to treat and not an offer to sell: *Harris v Nickerson* (1873) LR 8 QB 286. In my opinion, *Warlow v Harrison* leaves the general law on auctions where it was decided in *Payne v Cave, supra*.

I should mention that *Warlow v Harrison* was followed in *Ulbrick v Laidlaw* [1924] VLR 247 in an action by a bidder against an auctioneer for breach of contract in failing to put the property up again when there was a dispute between the bidder and another bidder as to whose bid the auctioneer had accepted. However, the authority of *Payne v Cave* was not questioned in that case and its decision has never been overruled.

The possibility of an action against an auctioneer as canvassed in *Warlow v Harrison* is not something I have to decide in this case but I think that if such an action is open it would be an anomaly in the law of auctions.

... An auction remains, in my opinion, an invitation to treat. If the fact that there is a reserve price is notified, it indicates to the bidders that an offer below the reserve price will or may not be considered. If the sale is advertised as being without reserve or to the highest bidder, it means that the highest bid is an offer that is liable to be accepted and, if accepted, will make a contract but the vendor remains free to withdraw the property from sale or decline to accept any bid ....

[His Honour ordered that the caveat be removed.]

The decision in *Warlow v Harrison*,[5] although doubted by Holland J in the instant case, was followed by the English Court of Appeal in *Barry v Davies (trading as Heathcote Ball & Co)*.[6] As a result, it is likely that advertising an auction without reserve will be characterised as the auctioneer making an offer to sell to the highest bidder. This offer can then be accepted by anyone who makes a bid. In this event, a collateral contract is created between the auctioneer and the bidder, the terms of which are that the property will be sold to the highest bidder. If this does not happen then, as occurred in *Barry v Davies*, the bidder will have an action in damages for breach of contract against the auctioneer. However, this does alter the characterisation of the bid as merely an offer as far as the seller is concerned, with the result that there is still no contract of sale between the seller and the bidder if it has not been accepted by the auctioneer.

As far as the auction of goods is concerned, the position adopted in *AGC (Advances) Ltd v McWhirter* is adopted in sale of goods legislation which provides that until the auctioneer announces the completion of the sale, any bidders

---

5 (1859) 1 El & El 309; 120 ER 925.
6 [2000] 1 WLR 1962.

may retract their bids: see *Goods Act 1958* (Vic), s 64(b); *Sale of Goods Act 1979* (UK), s 57(2).

In the case of online auctions, it has been held that a seller who lists goods for sale with a disclosed reserve price is making an offer to sell to anyone who makes the highest bid within the specified time, provided this bid is at or above the reserve price and made without a qualification not previously agreed to by the seller. As a result, such a person's bid amounts to an acceptance and a contract is created thereby.[7]

Advertisements

Advertisements are the quintessential example of invitations to deal because this accords with what advertisers usually intend.[8] Were it otherwise, each person who responded to an advertisement would thereby make a contract with the advertiser, with the result that, should the advertisement generate more response than anticipated, the advertiser could be faced with contracts they have no capacity to honour. This problem is avoided by making the advertisement only an invitation to deal: responses can then only be offers made to the advertiser and can be rejected when supply is exhausted.[9] However, this is not always the advertiser's intention, as *Carlill v Carbolic Smoke Ball Company* (pp 30–1, above)[10] reminds us. It is always crucial to examine the facts of individual cases and be wary of generalisation. The following case is a more recent illustration.

Lefkowitz v Great Minneapolis Surplus Store

86 NW 2d 689 (1957), Supreme Court of Minnesota

[The defendant store published an advertisement in a newspaper which read

'Saturday, 9 AM Sharp. 3 brand new fur coats worth to $100.00. First served $1 each'

The plaintiff was the first customer to ask for one of these coats but was refused.]

Murphy J [at 691]: There are numerous authorities which hold that a particular advertisement in a newspaper or circular letter relating to a sale of articles may be construed by the court as constituting an offer, acceptance of which would complete a contract. ...

The test of whether a binding obligation may originate in advertisements addressed to the general public is 'whether the facts show that some performance was promised in positive terms in return for something requested.' I Williston, *Contracts* (Rev.ed.) §27.

---

7   See *Smythe v Thomas* [2007] NSWSC 844.
8   See *Partridge v Crittenden* [1968] 1 WLR 1204.
9   This was the explanation given in *Grainger v Gough* [1896] AC 325 for characterising the advertisement as an invitation to deal.
10   [1893] 1 QB 256.

The authorities ... emphasize that, where the offer is clear, definite and explicit, and leaves nothing open to negotiation, it constitutes an offer, acceptance of which will complete the contract. ...

Whether in any individual instance a newspaper advertisement is an offer rather than an invitation to make an offer depends on the legal intention of the parties and the surrounding circumstance. We are of the view on the facts before us that the offer by the defendant of the Lapin fur was clear, definite, and explicit, and left nothing open for negotiation. The plaintiff having successfully managed to be the first one to appear at the seller's place of business to be served, as requested by the advertisement, and having offered the stated purchase price of the article, was entitled to performance on the part of the defendant. We think the trial court was correct in holding that there was the conduct of the parties a sufficient mutuality of obligation to constitute a contract sale.

Bait advertising

The distinction between an offer and an invitation to deal facilitates 'bait advertising' by retail stores. This is the practice of advertising certain goods at extremely low prices to attract customers to the store with the intention of selling them other goods, at normal prices, rather than, or in addition to, those advertised. By ensuring that such advertisements are invitations to deal, rather than offers, retailers are able to avoid exposing themselves to the risk of having to supply any (or many) items at the advertised price. This practice is now prohibited by the Australian Consumer Law.

The Australian Consumer Law

Section 35(1): A person must not, in trade or commerce, advertise goods or services for supply at a specified price if:

(a) there are reasonable grounds for believing that the person will not be able to offer for supply those goods or services at that price for the period that is, and in the quantities that are, reasonable having regard to:
   (i) the nature of the market in which the person carries on business and
   (ii) the nature of the advertisement; and
(b) the person is aware or ought to be aware of those grounds.

Calls for tender

A call for tenders will usually be regarded as merely an invitation to make an offer which, if made, can be accepted or rejected by the person making the call. However, as the following case shows, a call for tenders may contain an undertaking to treat the tender in a specified manner which the law will characterise as an offer. In such cases, by submitting a tender, the invitee accepts this offer and thereby creates a contract in the terms of the undertaking, regardless of whether the tender itself is ultimately accepted, or not.

Blackpool and Fylde Aero Club Ltd v Blackpool Borough Council
[1990] 3 All ER 25, English Court of Appeal

[The Blackpool Council invited the Aero Club and six other parties to tender for the operation of pleasure flights from its airport. These invitations stated that tenders were to be submitted in an envelope provided and that tenders received after a specified date would not be considered. The club submitted a tender by the due date. However, due to an error within the Council's office, this tender was recorded as being received late and not considered. The club took proceedings against the Council, arguing that it had promised to consider all tenders received before the specified date and that it had not done so. The club succeeded at first instance and the Council appealed.]

Bingham LJ [at 29]: Firstly, it was submitted that an invitation to tender in this form was well established to be no more than a proclamation of willingness to receive offers. ... [It] was an invitation to treat, and no contract of any kind would come into existence unless or until, if ever, the council chose to accept any tender or other offer.

Secondly, counsel submitted that on a reasonable reading of this invitation to tender the council could not be understood to be undertaking to consider all timely tenders submitted. The statement that late tenders would not be considered did not mean that timely tenders would. If the council had meant that it could have said it. ... <30>

I found great force in the submissions made on behalf of the council and agree with much of what was said. ... But I am in the end persuaded that the argument proves too much. During the hearing the following questions were raised: what if, in a situation such as the present, the council had opened and thereupon accepted the first tender received, even though the deadline had not expired and other invitees had not yet responded? Or if the council had considered and accepted a tender admittedly received well after the deadline? Counsel answered that although by so acting the council might breach its own standing orders, and might fairly be accused of discreditable conduct, it would not be in breach of any legal obligation because at that stage there would be none to breach. This is a conclusion I cannot accept, and if it were accepted there would in my view be an unacceptable discrepancy between the law of contract and the confident assumptions of commercial parties ....

A tendering procedure of this kind is, in many respects, heavily weighted in favour of the invitor. He can invite tenders from as many or as few parties as he chooses. He need not tell any of them who else, or how many others, he has invited. The invitee may often, although not here, be put to considerable labour and expense in preparing a tender, ordinarily without recompense if he is unsuccessful. The invitation to tender may itself, in a complex case, although again not here, involve time and expense to prepare, but the invitor does not commit himself to proceed with the project, whatever it is; he need not accept the highest tender; he need not accept any tender; he need not give reasons to justify his acceptance or rejection of any tender received. The risk to which the tenderer is exposed does not end with the risk that his tender may not be the highest (or, as the case may be, lowest). But where, as here, tenders are solicited from selected parties all of them known to the invitor, and where a local authority's invitation prescribes a clear, orderly and familiar procedure (draft contract conditions available for inspection and plainly not open to negotiation, a prescribed common form of tender, the supply of envelopes designed to preserve the absolute anonymity of tenderers and clearly to identify the tender in question and an absolute deadline) the invitee is in my judgment protected at least to this extent: if he submits a conforming tender before the deadline he is entitled, not as a matter of mere expectation but of contractual right, to be sure that his tender will after the deadline be opened and considered in conjunction with all other conforming tenders or at least that his tender will be considered if others are. ... <31> ...

In all the circumstances of this case ... I have no doubt that the parties did intend to create contractual relations to the limited extent contended for. ... I think it plain that the council's invitation to tender was, to this limited extent, an offer, and the club's submission of a timely and conforming tender an acceptance.

[Stocker and Farquharson LJJ agreed.]

Appeal dismissed

Contracts of this kind are often referred to as 'pre-award contracts'. The approach to deciding whether a tender gives rise to such a contract, adopted in *Blackpool*, was followed in *Hughes Aircraft Systems International v Airservices Australia*[11] where Finn J approved the following summary of the law from *Pratt Contractors Ltd v Palmerston North City Council*:

> Authority makes it clear that the starting point is that a simple uncomplicated request for bids will generally be no more than an invitation to treat, not giving rise to contractual obligations, although it may give rise to obligations to act fairly. On the other hand, it is obviously open to persons to enter into a preliminary contract with the expectation that it will lead in defined circumstances to a second or principal contract ... Whether or not the particular case falls into one category or the other will depend upon a consideration of the circumstances and the obligations expressly or impliedly accepted.[12]

The effect of accepting a tender depends upon its terms: it may obligate both parties or only the person submitting the tender. *Colonial Ammunition Co v Reid* is an example of the latter. Here, Colonial Ammunition entered into an agreement with the New South Wales Government to supply it with ammunition for a period of seven years at specified prices. The ammunition was to be delivered in such quantities as the government might, from time to time, order. Ammunition was ordered and supplied under this agreement. However, the government subsequently

---

11 (1997) 76 FCR 151
12 [1995] 1 NZLR 469 at 478–479.

purchased ammunition from other firms, whereupon Colonial sued for breach of contract. Its claim failed as the court found that there was

> no contract on the part of the government to take any ammunition, except such ammunition as the government chose to order. Once they order the ammunition there is a contract to take the ammunition, but until they give the order, this agreement is nothing more than a tender on the part of the plaintiffs to supply the government at the prices therein named with the ammunition ordered.[13]

c Offers distinguished from requests for information or statements of possible terms

For the same reasons as those discussed in relation to invitations to deal and with the same consequences, offers are also distinguished from statements of the terms upon which a person may be willing to contract and responses to requests for information about the subject matter of a possible contract. As a result, the response to such a statement cannot be an acceptance; at most it will be an offer which the maker of the initial statement can accept or reject. For example, in *Harvey v Facey*[14] the plaintiffs asked the defendants at what price they would be prepared to sell certain land. The defendants replied with a certain figure which the plaintiffs, treating it as an offer, accepted. The Privy Council, however, held that the defendants' reply, rather than being an offer, was merely a statement of the minimum price at which they may be willing to sell. Therefore, the plaintiffs' communication could not amount to an acceptance; it could only be an offer which, on the facts, the defendants had not accepted. Similarly, in *Gibson v Manchester City Council*,[15] a letter from a municipal council, whose policy at the time was to sell council houses to tenants, and which read in part 'The corporation may be prepared to sell the house to you at the purchase price of £2,725 less 20 per cent = £2,180 (freehold)' was held not to be an offer to sell but merely a statement of the terms upon which it might be willing to sell in due course.

d Termination of offers

An offer may be terminated in several ways. Once this has happened, it can no longer be accepted and thereby give rise to an agreement.

Revocation

Revocation occurs when an offer is withdrawn and the offeror communicates this decision to the offeree. An offer can be revoked at any time before it is accepted. Once acceptance has occurred this is no longer possible. This means that, in a given case, which occurs first (revocation or acceptance) will determine whether or not a contract is formed. Also, an offer cannot be revoked if the offeror has granted the

---

13 (1900) 21 LR (NSW) 338, per Darley CJ at 345.
14 [1893] AC 552
15 [1979] 1 WLR 294.

offeree an option covering it; for present purposes, an option involves a promise by the offeror not to revoke the offer, made in exchange for consideration[16] provided by the offeree.[17]

What is required to revoke an offer and other aspects of revocation are discussed in the following case.

Dickinson v Dodds

(1876) 2 Ch D 463, English Court of Appeal

[On 10 June Dodds offered in writing to sell a house to Dickinson and said that the offer was 'to be left over until Friday, 9 o'clock am 12th June 1874'. Dickinson decided to accept this offer but did nothing to communicate his decision to Dodds. Then, on 11 June, he was informed by a third party that Dodds had sold the property to another buyer. Hearing this, Dickinson left a formal acceptance of the offer at Dodds' residence and an agent of his gave a copy to Dodds personally before 9:00 on 12 June. Dodds declined to transfer the house to Dickinson who commenced proceedings for specific performance. He succeeded at first instance and Dodds appealed.]

James LJ [at 471]: The document, [by which Dodds offered to sell his house to Dickinson] though beginning 'I hereby agree to sell,' was nothing but an offer, and was only intended to be an offer, for the Plaintiff himself tells us that he required time to consider whether he would enter into an agreement or not. Unless both parties had then agreed there was no concluded agreement then made; it was <472> in effect and substance only an offer to sell. ... There was no consideration given for the undertaking or promise, ... to keep the property unsold until 9 o'clock on Friday morning. ... [I]t is clear settled law, on one of the clearest principles of law, that this promise, being a mere *nudum pactum*, was not binding, and that at any moment before a complete acceptance by *Dickinson* of the offer, *Dodds* was as free as *Dickinson* himself. Well, that being the state of things, it is said that the only mode in which *Dodds* could assert that freedom was by actually and distinctly saying to *Dickinson*, 'Now I withdraw my offer.' It appears to me that there is neither principle nor authority for the proposition that there must be an express and actual withdrawal of the offer, or what is called a retraction. It

---

16   As the following case shows, a promise not to revoke that is made without consideration being given in return is not enforceable. See also *Board of Control of Eastern Michigan University v Burgess* 45 Mich App 183, 186; 206 NW2d 256 (1973).

17   The precise nature of an option is the subject of debate; one view is that it is an irrevocable offer, another is that it is a conditional contract. These views are discussed in *Laybutt v Amoco Australia Pty Ltd* (1974) 132 CLR 57 at 71–76. In most cases it will be irrelevant which view is adopted and the outcome may depend upon the wording of the option. However, where an interest in land is involved, whether an option is one or the other may be important. On the conditional contract theory, if the owner of land grants an option to purchase, the person to whom the option is granted gains an immediate interest in the land, rather than merely an opportunity to enter into a contract to purchase it in the future. If so, this would enhance that party's chances of obtaining an order for specific performance in the event of the option being exercised but the vendor seeking to renege on their agreement.

must, to constitute a contract, appear that the two minds were at one, at the same moment of time, that is, that there was an offer continuing up to the time of the acceptance. If there was not such a continuing offer, then the acceptance comes to nothing. Of course it may well be that the one man is bound in some way or other to let the other man know that his mind with regard to the offer has been changed; but in this case, beyond all question, the Plaintiff knew that *Dodds* was no longer minded to sell the property to him as plainly and clearly as if *Dodds* had told him in so many words, 'I withdraw the offer.' This is evident from the Plaintiff's own statements in the bill. <473>

It is impossible, therefore, to say there was ever that existence of the same mind between the two parties which is essential in point of law to the making of an agreement. I am of opinion, therefore, that the Plaintiff has failed to prove that there was any binding contract between *Dodds* and himself.

Mellish LJ: I am of the same opinion. <474> ...

The question which arises is this—If an offer has been made for the sale of property, and before that offer is accepted, the person who has made the offer enters into a binding agreement to sell the property to somebody else, and the person to whom the offer was first made receives notice in some way that the property has been sold to another person, can he after that make a binding contract by the acceptance of the offer? I am of opinion that he cannot.

Appeal allowed

Revocation will not be effective unless, and until, it is communicated to the offeree. In this connection the postal rule does not apply.[18] The leading case establishing these propositions is *Byrne v Van Tienhoven*.

Byrne v Van Tienhoven

(1880) LR 5 CPD 344, Court of Common Pleas

[In a letter dated 1 October, Van Tienhoven offered to sell goods to Byrne. However, on 8 October he posted a second letter revoking his offer; this letter was received on 20 October. In the meantime, on 11 October, Byrne had telegraphed Van Tienhoven accepting the offer and had resold the goods for a profit. Van Tienhoven refused to supply the goods, whereupon Byrne sued to recover damages for their non-delivery.]

Lindley J [at 347]: There is no doubt that an offer can be withdrawn before it is accepted, and it is immaterial whether the offer is expressed to be open for acceptance for a given time or not. ... For the decision of the present case, however, it is necessary to consider two other questions, viz: 1. Whether a withdrawal of an offer has any effect until it is communicated to the person to whom the offer has been sent? 2. Whether posting a letter of withdrawal is a communication to the person to whom the letter is sent?

---

18   This rule applies only to the communication of an acceptance: see below at p 64.

It is curious that neither of these questions appears to have been actually decided in this country. As regards the first question, I am aware that Pothier and some other writers of celebrity are of opinion that there can be no contract if an offer is withdrawn before it is accepted, although the withdrawal is not communicated to the person to whom the offer has been made. The reason for this opinion is that there is not in fact any such consent by both parties as is essential to constitute a contract between them. Against this view, however, it has been urged that a state of mind not notified cannot be regarded in dealings between man and man; and that an uncommunicated revocation is for all practical purposes and in point of law no revocation at all. This is the view taken in the United States [and] appears to me much more in accordance with the general principles of English law than the view maintained by Pothier. I pass, to the next question, <348> viz, whether posting the letter of revocation was a sufficient communication of it to the plaintiff. The offer was posted on the 1st of October, the withdrawal was posted on the 8th, and did not reach the plaintiff until after he had posted his letter of the 11th, accepting the offer. It may be taken as now settled that where an offer is made and accepted by letters sent through the post, the contract is completed the moment the letter accepting the offer is posted ... even although it never reaches its destination. When, however, these authorities are looked at, it will be seen that they are based upon the principle that the writer of the offer has expressly or impliedly assented to treat an answer to him by a letter duly posted as a sufficient acceptance and notification to himself, or, in other words, he has made the post office his agent to receive the acceptance and notification of it. But this principle appears to me to be inapplicable to the case of the withdrawal of an offer.

In my opinion the withdrawal by the defendants on the 8th of October of their offer of the 1st was inoperative; and a complete contract binding on both parties was entered into on the 11th of October, when the plaintiffs accepted the offer of the 1st, which they had no reason to suppose had been withdrawn. Before leaving this part of the case it may be as well to point out the extreme injustice and inconveniences which any other conclusion would produce. If the defendants' contention were to prevail no person who had received an offer by post and had accepted it would know his position until he had waited such a time as to be quite sure that a letter withdrawing the offer had not been posted before his acceptance of its. It appears to me that both legal <349> principles, and practical convenience require that a person who has accepted an offer not known to him to have been revoked, shall be in a position safely to act upon the footing that the offer and acceptance constitute a contract binding on both parties.

Judgment for the plaintiffs

[citations omitted]

Where an offer has been directed to a particular individual or identifiable group, revocation must be communicated to that person or group. However, in the case of an offer made to the world at large, as in *Carlill v Carbolic Smoke*

Ball Company,[19] requiring this level of communication would be impractical. Therefore, in such cases, it is sufficient to publish a notice of revocation that is at least as prominent as the notice making the original offer. This was the conclusion reached by the United States Supreme Court in *Shuey v United States*,[20] concerning a proclamation published in newspapers offering a reward to anyone providing information leading to the arrest of a named individual who was believed to have been involved in the assassination of President Lincoln. This offer was revoked by proclamation that was publicised in a similar manner. However, unaware of this revocation, Shuey provided the information sought. His claim was rejected on the ground that the offer had been revoked effectively by the publication of the second proclamation.

The common law rule allowing an offeror, in the absence of an option, to revoke an offer at any time before acceptance has the potential to cause harm to an unwary offeree. *James Baird Co v Gimbel Bros Inc*[21] provides an example. To prepare a tender for a building project, Baird used a quotation obtained from Gimbel for the supply of a component needed in the project. Subsequently, Gimbel discovered that the quotation was incorrect and it was withdrawn. Baird's tender was successful and it then sought to accept Gimbel's quotation. The court held that no contract existed as Gimbel had withdrawn its offer before Baird's acceptance had occurred. As a result, Baird had a contract with its employer but without the benefit of a subcontract with Gimbel, even though Gimbel's quotation had been relied upon to secure that contract.

In relation to international sales of goods, a more flexible approach is taken. Such sales are governed by what is commonly referred to as 'the *Vienna Convention*',[22] Article 16 of which provides as follows:

United Nations Convention on Contracts for the International Sale of Goods, 1980

Article 16

(1) Until a contract is concluded an offer may be revoked if the revocation reaches the offeree before he has despatched an acceptance.
(2) However, an offer cannot be revoked:
    (i) if it indicates, whether by stating a fixed time for acceptance or otherwise, that it is irrevocable; or
    (ii) if it was reasonable for the offeree to rely on the offer as being irrevocable and the offeree has acted in reliance on the offer.

---

19   [1893] 1 QB 256.
20   92 US 73 (1875).
21   64 F 2d 344 (1933).
22   This convention came into force in Australia on 1 April 1989 and applies to international contracts for the sale of goods. It has force in Australia by virtue of Sale of Goods (Vienna Convention) Acts in each state and territory.

Rejection, or counter-offer, by the offeree

Rejection is a communication saying, in effect, 'no' to an offer. A counter-offer, on the other hand, is a communication by the offeree indicating that the offer is acceptable in substance, but seeking to vary the terms of the proposed contract. Although different in intent, at common law both have the effect of terminating the offer so that it can no longer be accepted.[23] The leading authority is *Hyde v Wrench*.[24] The defendant offered to sell land to the plaintiff for £1,000; the plaintiff replied offering to buy the land for £950. The defendant refused to sell at this price whereupon the plaintiff said that he would pay £1,000 as the defendant had originally offered. The defendant refused and the plaintiff commenced proceedings seeking specific performance. The claim failed; the court held that the plaintiff's offer to buy for £950 amounted to a rejection of the defendant's offer and that this had the effect of terminating it—a state from which it could not be revived by a subsequent expression of acceptance.

Because it has the effect of terminating the offer, a counter-offer must be distinguished from a mere request by the offeree for information, or clarification. Such requests leave the offer open. The importance of this distinction is illustrated by *Stevenson, Jaques and Co v McLean*.[25] Stevenson, in response to a written offer from McLean, telegrammed the latter asking whether the time of delivery and payment were negotiable. McLean treated this communication as a rejection and sold the items in question to a third party. However, the court held that it was merely a request for information, with the result that Stevenson's subsequent acceptance of McLean's offer created a contract. A counter-offer should also be distinguished from a request to alter the terms of the offer. If the offeror agrees to do this and the revised offer is then put to the offeree who accepts, a contract will be created.[26]

If the terms of a purported acceptance differ in any meaningful way from those of the offer, it would appear that at common law this communication will amount to a counter-offer and, as such, will terminate the offer. This contrasts with the position under the *Vienna Convention*, the relevant provisions of which are set out in Article 19(2), below.

United Nations Convention on Contracts for the International Sale of Goods, 1980

Article 17

An offer, even if it is irrevocable, is terminated when a rejection reaches the offeror.

---

23 One qualification to this proposition was recognised in *Brambles Holdings Ltd v Bathurst City Council* (2001) 53 NSWLR 153 where a contract was found to exist, despite the offer having been rejected by the offeree, on the ground that the offeree had subsequently acted in a manner that would have caused a reasonable person in the position of the offeror to believe that the offer had been accepted.
24 (1840) 3 Beav 334.
25 (1880) 5 QBD 346.
26 See *Fletcher v Kakemoto* [2010] QSC 219 esp at para 28.

Article 19

(1) A reply to an offer which purports to be an acceptance but contains additions, limitations or other modifications is a rejection of the offer and constitutes a counter-offer.
(2) However, a reply to an offer which purports to be an acceptance but contains additional or different terms which do not materially alter the terms of the offer constitutes an acceptance, unless the offeror, without undue delay, objects orally to the discrepancy or despatches a notice to that effect. If he does not so object, the terms of the contract are the terms of the offer with the modifications contained in the acceptance.
(3) Additional or different terms relating, among other things, to the price, payment, quality and quantity of the goods, place and time of delivery, extent of one party's liability to the other or the settlement of disputes are considered to alter the terms of the offer materially.

Lapse of time

If an offer specifies a time within which it must be accepted, acceptance after that time will be ineffective unless the offeror agrees to waive the stipulation. However, if the offeror intentionally avoids receiving an acceptance within the stipulated time, acceptance communicated after that will still be effective.[27] If the duration of an offer is not stipulated, the offer will come to an end after a reasonable time; what is reasonable depends upon the circumstances of the case.[28]

Death

As a general rule, an offer will lapse with the death of the offeror and cannot be accepted thereafter.[29] However, there are at least two qualifications to this rule. First, if the offeree does not know of the offeror's death, acceptance may still be possible unless this is precluded by the terms or nature of the offer, that is, the proposed transaction contemplated personal performance by the offeror. Second, even where the offeree does know of the offeror's death, acceptance may be possible if the terms of the offer contemplate that the contract could be performed by the offeror's estate, or if the offer was accompanied by an option not to revoke for a period of time that had not yet elapsed.

Whether the death of the offeree terminates the offer, so that it cannot be accepted by that person's estate, similarly appears to depend upon whether the offer was personal to the deceased or not. Thus, if it is clear that performance was to be by the offeree alone, or that only they were to benefit from the proposed contract, the offer will lapse.[30]

---

27 See *Bragg v Alam* (1982) NSW Conv R 55–082.
28 See *Balla v Theophilos (No 2)* (1957) 98 CLR 193.
29 See *Dickinson v Dodds* (1876) 2 Ch D 463 at 475, per Mellish LJ.
30 See *Carter v Hyde* (1923) 33 CLR 115 at 121.

Failure of a condition

If an offer is made conditional upon the occurrence or non-occurrence of an event, or state of affairs, then the offer will lapse if the event does, or does not, occur respectively.

United Nations Convention on Contracts for the International Sale of Goods, 1980

Article 20(1)

A period of time for acceptance fixed by the offeror in a telegram or letter begins to run from the moment the telegram is handed in for despatch or from the date shown on the letter, or if no such date is shown, from the date shown on the envelope. A period of time fixed for acceptance by the offeror by telephone, telex or other means of instantaneous communication, begins to run from the moment that the offer reaches the offeree.

Article 21(1)

A late acceptance is nevertheless effective as an acceptance if without delay the offeror orally so informs the offeree or despatches a notice to that effect.

INTERNATIONAL PERSPECTIVES

The distinction between offers and invitations to deal is accepted in other common law countries and in India[31] and China. The latter makes this explicit in Article 15 (extracted below) using examples familiar to the common law, while at the same time also recognising that advertisements such as that in *Lefkowitz v Great Minneapolis Surplus Store* may be offers.

The Indian and Chinese provisions relating to the termination of offers resemble the common law. However, there are some important differences including the following:

- China has adopted, in Article 19, provisions very similar to Article 16(2) of the *Vienna Convention*. As a result an offer will be irrevocable if it is expressed to be so, or if the offeree has reasonably relied on the offer.[32]

---

31   See *McPherson v Appanna* AIR 1951 SC 184.
32   In the United States the common law position has similarly been ameliorated by s 87(2) of the *Restatement of Contracts (2d)* which provides:
an offer which the offeror should reasonably expect to induce action or forbearance of substantial character on the part of the offeree before acceptance and which does induce such action or forbearance is binding as an option contract to the extent necessary to avoid injustice.
As a result of this provision, a case like *James Baird Co v Gimbel* is now likely to be decided in favour of the party in Baird's position: see for example, *Drennan v Star Paving Co* 333 P 2d 757 (1958), which also invokes s 90 dealing with reasonable reliance on promises.

- India, on the other hand, has adopted the common law position of requiring consideration to be present before a promise not to revoke an offer will be binding.[33]
- The *Indian Contract Act* prescribes specific rules to govern the communication of offers and their revocation which may produce different outcomes from the common law.

Indian Contract Act, 1872

Section 3. Communication, acceptance and revocation of proposals

The communication of proposals, the acceptance of proposals, and the revocation of proposals and acceptances, respectively, are deemed to be made by any act or omission of the party proposing, accepting or revoking, by which he intends to communicate such proposal, acceptance or revocation, or which has the effect of communicating it.

Section 4. Communication when complete

The communication of a proposal is complete when it comes to the knowledge of the person to whom it is made. …
 The communication of a revocation is complete,—

- as against the person who makes it, when it is put into the course of transmission to the person to whom it is made, so as to be out of the power of the person who makes it;
- as against the person to whom it is made, when it comes to his knowledge.

Section 5. Revocation of Proposals and Acceptances

A proposal may be revoked at any time before the communication of its acceptance is complete as against the proposer, but not afterwards. …

Section 6. Revocation how made

A proposal is revoked—

(i) by the communication of notice of revocation by the proposer to the other party;
(ii) by lapse of the time prescribed in such proposal for its acceptance, or, if no time is so prescribed, by the lapse of a reasonable time, without communication of acceptance;
(iii) by the failure of the acceptor to fulfil a condition precedent to acceptance; or
(iv) by the death or insanity of the proposer, if the fact of the death or insanity comes to the knowledge of the acceptor before acceptance.

---

33 See *Krishnaveni Constructions v Executive Engineer, Panchayat Raj, Darsi* AIR 1995 AP 362.

Contract Law of the People's Republic of China, 1999

Article 15. Invitation to Offer

An invitation to offer is a party's manifestation of intention to invite the other party to make an offer thereto. A delivered price list, announcement of an auction, call for tender, prospectus, or commercial advertisement, etc is an invitation to offer.

A commercial advertisement is deemed an offer if its contents meet the requirement of an offer.

Article 16. Effectiveness of Offer. Offer through Electronic Message

An offer becomes effective when it reaches the offeree.

When a contract is concluded by the exchange of electronic messages, if the recipient of an electronic message has designated a specific system to receive it, the time when the electronic message enters into such specific system is deemed its time of arrival; if no specific system has been designated, the time when the electronic message first enters into any of the recipient's systems is deemed its time of arrival.

Article 17. Withdrawal of Offer

An offer may be withdrawn. The notice of withdrawal shall reach the offeree before or at the same time as the offer.

Article 18. Revocation of Offer

An offer may be revoked. The notice of revocation shall reach the offeree before it has despatched a notice of acceptance.

Article 19. Irrevocable Offer

An offer may not be revoked:

(i) if it expressly indicates, whether by stating a fixed time for acceptance or otherwise, that it is irrevocable;
(ii) if the offeree has reason to regard the offer as irrevocable, and has undertaken preparation for performance.

Article 20. Extinguishment of Offer

An offer is extinguished in any of the following circumstances:

(i) The notice of rejection reaches the offeror;
(ii) The offeror lawfully revokes the offer;
(iii) The offeree fails to despatch its acceptance at the end of the period for acceptance;
(iv) The offeree makes a material change to the terms of the offer.

5 Acceptance

a The relationship between offer and acceptance

We have defined 'acceptance' as an affirmative response to an offer. A key element of this definition is that the offeree's conduct occurs in *response* to the offer; merely doing what the offeror asks is not sufficient. The leading illustration is *Crown v Clarke*.

Crown v Clarke
(1927) 40 CLR 227, High Court of Australia

[The Crown offered a reward for information leading to the arrest and conviction of the murderers of two police officers. Clarke was arrested in connection with these murders and while in custody gave the police information which led to the conviction of two other men. Clarke was released and he claimed the reward. When this was refused he brought proceedings to recover the sum promised. His claim failed at first instance; he successfully appealed to the Western Australian Full Court; the Crown then appealed to the High Court.]

Isaacs ACJ [at 231]: The facts of this case, ... are not ... in dispute. They amount to this: the information for which Clarke claims the reward was given by him when he was under arrest ... and was given by him in circumstances which show that in giving the information he was not acting on or in pursuance of or in reliance upon or in return for the consideration contained in the proclamation, but exclusively in order to clear himself of the false charge of murder. ... The learned Chief Justice held that <232> Clarke never accepted or intended to accept the offer in the proclamation, and, unless the mere giving of the information without such intention amounted in law to an acceptance of the offer ... there was [no] 'acceptance' ... and therefore there was no contract. I do not understand either of the learned Judges who formed the majority to controvert this. But they held that *Williams v Carwardine* (1833) 4 B & Ad 621 has stood for so long that it should be regarded as accurate, and that, so regarded, it entitled the respondent to judgment. As reported in the four places where it is found, it is a difficult case to follow. I cannot help thinking that it is somewhat curtly reported. ... But two circumstances are important. One is the pregnant question of *Denman* CJ as to the plaintiff's knowledge of the handbill. ... The other circumstance is the stress placed on motive. The Lord Chief Justice clearly attached importance to the answer given to his question. He, doubtless, finally drew the inference that, having knowledge of the request in the handbill, the plaintiff at last determined to accede, and did accede, to that request, and so acted in response to it, although moved thereto by the incentive supplied by her stings of conscience. <233>

If the decision in *Williams v Carwardine* went no further than I have said, it is in line with the acknowledged and settled theories of contract. ...

It is unquestionable—putting aside what are called formal contracts or quasi-contracts—that to create a contractual obligation there must be both offer and acceptance. It is the union of these which constitutes the binding tie, the *obligatio*. The present type of case is no exception. It is not true to say that since such an offer calls for information of a certain description, then, provided only information of that description is in fact given, the informant is entitled to the reward. That is not true unless the word 'given' is interpreted as 'given in exchange for the offer'—in other words, given in performance of the bargain which is contemplated by the offer and of which the offer is intended to form part. Performance in that case is the implied method of acceptance, and it simultaneously effects the double purpose of acceptance and performance. But acceptance is essential to contractual obligation, because without it there is no agreement, and in the absence of agreement, actual or imputed, there can be no contract. Lord Kinnear in *Jackson v Broatch* (1900) 37 SLR 707, at p 714 said: 'It is an excellent definition of a contract that it is an agreement which produces an obligation.' ... <234> ...

The controlling principle, then, is that to establish the *consensus* without which no true contract can exist, acceptance is as essential as offer, even in a case of the present class where the same act is at once sufficient for both acceptance and performance. But acceptance and performance of condition, as shown by the judicial <235> reasoning quoted, involve that the person accepting and performing must act on the offer. ...

Instances easily suggest themselves where precisely the same act done with reference to an offer would be performance of the condition, but done with reference to a totally distinct object would not be such a performance. An offer of £100 to any person who should swim a hundred yards in the harbour on the first day of the year, would be met by voluntarily performing the feat with reference to the offer, but would not in my opinion be satisfied by a person who was accidentally or maliciously thrown overboard on that date and swam the distance simply to save his life, without any thought of the offer. The offeror might or might not feel morally impelled to give the sum in such a case, but would be under no contractual obligation to do so. <236> ...

On the question of fact whether Clarke in making his statement of 10th June acted upon the offer in the proclamation, the learned Chief Justice, who saw and heard him give his testimony, answered that question in the negative.

The appeal, should, in my opinion, for the reasons stated, be allowed, and the judgment of *McMillan* CJ restored.

[Higgins and Starke JJ delivered separate judgments to the same effect.]

Appeal allowed

If responding to the offer was at least one of the reasons for the offeree's action, it seems clear that acceptance will be found to have occurred even though it was not the offeree's principal motivation. Also, dicta in the instant case by Higgins J (at 241) and Starke J (at 244) suggest that where the offeree knew of the offer it will be presumed that their action was in response to it.[34] The same position has been adopted in the United States[35] and in India applying s 4 of the *Indian Contract Act, 1872* which provides that the communication of a proposal is complete when it comes to the knowledge of the person to whom it is made. This has been interpreted to mean that a proposal (offer) cannot be regarded as having been accepted unless the offeree was aware of it when they performed the action sought.[36]

The requirement that the offeree's conduct occurs in response to the offeror's offer is a natural corollary of the need for the parties to have reached an agreement. The parties in *Crown v Clarke* clearly had not agreed that Clarke would be paid a reward for providing information because he acted without any reference to a communication of that nature from the Crown. At no stage were they *ad idem*. For the same reason, if A writes to B offering to sell on certain terms and B writes to A offering to purchase on the same terms, their simultaneous communications, each in ignorance of the other, (often referred to as 'cross offers') do not create an agreement.[37]

b Who may accept an offer?

An offer can be accepted only by the person to whom it is addressed. This is illustrated by *Boulton v Jones* in which the defendant's order for goods, directed to a named trader, was, without the defendant's knowledge, accepted and executed by the plaintiff to whom the trader had transferred his business.[38] The defendant refused to pay for the goods and the plaintiff's claim for the price failed on the ground that there was no contract between them. The defendant's offer was not directed to the plaintiff and, therefore, the plaintiff could not accept it. According to Griffith CJ in *Lang v James Morrison & Co Ltd*,[39] a purported acceptance in such a case would amount to a counter-offer, on the terms of the original offer, which the offeror could accept or refuse. However, in cases of this nature, the courts look at the substance of the offer, rather than merely its form: was it to the named person and that person alone (in which case no one else can accept it) or was it to whoever was in that person's position? Thus, in *Boulton v Jones*, it appears to have been crucial that the defendant was owed money by the named person and it was his intention to set that debt off against the price of the goods he ordered; for that reason, the identity of the offeree was central to the transaction.

c Acceptance by conduct

In certain circumstances, an offer may be accepted by conduct, rather than words. *Empirnall Holdings Pty Ltd v Machon Paull Partners Pty Ltd*,[40] is an example.

---

34 See also *Port Jackson Stevedoring Pty Ltd v Salmon & Spraggon (Australia) Pty Ltd* (1978) 139 CLR 231 at 244.
35 See *Broadnax v Ledbetter* 99 SW 1111 (1907) and *Taft v Hyatt* 180 Pac 213 (1919).
36 See *Lalman v Gauri Datt* (1913) 11 All LJ 489.
37 See *Tinn v Hoffmann & Co* (1873) 29 LT 271.
38 (1857) 2 H & N 564; 157 ER 232.
39 (1911) 13 CLR 1.
40 (1988) 14 NSWLR 523.

Machon Paull, a firm of architects, was engaged to carry out certain work for Empirnall. After doing some of the work they submitted a written contract to Empirnall for signature and return. This document was never signed. However, Machon Paull continued to work for Empirnall and the latter made payments in accordance with the terms of the document. On these facts the New South Wales Court of Appeal concluded:

> Empirnall's acceptance of the work, when considered objectively, should be taken as an acceptance of the work on the terms and conditions offered by Machon. The case is not so much one of acceptance by silence as one of taking the benefit of an offer with knowledge of its terms and knowledge of the offeror's reliance on payment being made in return for his work.[41]

One situation that has the potential to be characterised as acceptance by conduct is the non-return of unsolicited goods: the despatch of goods being regarded as an offer to sell and their retention by the consumer as acceptance of that offer. To protect consumers against being lulled into a contract by their inactivity, or the liability that may arise in torts as a gratuitous bailee,[42] the following provision is contained in the *Australian Consumer Law*:

> Section 41(1): If a person, in trade or commerce, supplies unsolicited goods to another person, the other person:
> (a) is not liable to make any payment for the goods; and
> (b) is not liable for loss of or damage to the goods, other than loss or damage resulting from the other person doing a wilful and unlawful act in relation to the goods during the recovery period.[43]

d Correspondence between offer and acceptance

To amount to an acceptance, the words or conduct of the offeree must, expressly or by implication, indicate assent to all the terms of the offer. Should the offeree's response, even though couched in terms of 'acceptance', introduce new terms or seek to derogate from those proposed by the offeror, that response will amount to a counter-offer and terminate the original offer. In lengthy negotiations between businesses, each concerned to contract on their own standard terms, this can give rise to what is known as a 'battle of the forms'. Who wins this 'battle' will determine when and where a contract is concluded and on whose terms.

---

41   (1988) 14 NSWLR 523 at 535–6, per McHugh JA. See also *Brogden v Metropolitan Railway Co* (1877) 2 App Cas 666 and *Commonwealth of Australia v Crothal Hospital Services (Aust) Ltd* (1981) 36 ALR 567.
42   See *Sachs v Miklos* [1948] 1 All ER 67.
43   The recovery period is prescribed by s 41(4) of the *ACL*. Sections 39, 40, 42 and 43 of the *ACL* deal with other aspects of supplying, unsolicited, credit or debit cards, goods, or services.

Butler Machine Tool Co Ltd v Ex-Cell-O Corp (England) Ltd

[1979] 1 WLR 401, English Court of Appeal

Lord Denning MR [at 403]: On May 23, 1969, the sellers offered to deliver one 'Butler' double column plane-miller for the total price of £75,535. Delivery 10 months (subject to confirmation at time of ordering) other terms and conditions are on the reverse of this quotation. On the back there were 16 conditions in small print starting with this general condition:

> 'All orders are accepted only upon and subject to the terms set out in our quotation and the following conditions. These terms and conditions shall prevail over any terms and conditions in the buyer's order.'

Clause 3 was the price variation clause. It said:

> 'Prices are based on present day costs of manufacture and design and having regard to the delivery quoted and uncertainty as to the cost of labour, materials etc. during the period of manufacture, we regret that we have no alternative but to make it a condition of acceptance of order that goods will be charged at prices ruling upon date of delivery.'

The buyers replied on May 27, 1969, giving an order in these words: 'Please supply on terms and conditions as below and overleaf.' Below there was a list of the goods ordered, but there were differences from the quotation of the sellers in these respects: (i) there was an additional item for the cost of installation, £3,100 and (ii) there was a different delivery date: instead of 10 months, it was 10–11 months.

Overleaf there were different terms as to the cost of carriage: in that it was to be paid to the delivery address of the buyers: whereas the sellers' terms were ex warehouse. There were different terms as to the right to cancel for late delivery. The buyers in their conditions reserved the right to cancel if delivery was not made by the agreed date: whereas the sellers in their conditions said that cancellation of order due to late delivery would not be accepted.

On the foot of the buyers' order there was a tear-off slip headed:

> 'Acknowledgment: Please sign and return to Ex-Cell-O. We accept your order on the terms and conditions stated thereon-and undertake to deliver by-Date-signed.'

In that slip the delivery date and signature were left blank ready to be filled in by the sellers.

On June 5, 1969, the sellers wrote this letter to the buyers:

> 'We have pleasure in acknowledging receipt of your official order dated May 27 covering the supply of one Butler Double Column Plane-Miller. This being delivered in accordance with our revised quotation of May 23 for delivery in 10/11 months, ie, March/April 1970. We return herewith duly completed your acknowledgment of order form.'

They enclosed the acknowledgment form duly filled in with the delivery date March/April 1970 and signed by the Butler Machine Tool Co.

No doubt a contract was then concluded. But on what terms? The sellers rely on their general conditions and on their last letter which said <404> 'in accordance with our revised quotation of May 23' (which had on the back the price variation clause). The buyers rely on the acknowledgment signed by the sellers which accepted the buyer's order 'on the terms and conditions stated thereon' (which did not include a price variation clause).

If those documents are analysed in our traditional method, the result would seem to me to be this: the quotation of May 23, 1969, was an offer by the sellers to the buyers containing the terms and conditions on the back. The order of May 27, 1969, purported to be an acceptance of that offer in that it was for the same machine at the same price, but it contained such additions as to cost of installation, date of delivery and so forth that it was in law a rejection of the offer and constituted a counter-offer. That is clear from *Hyde v Wrench* (1840) 3 Beav 334. As Megaw J. said in *Trollope & Colls Ltd v Atomic Power Constructions Ltd* [1963] 1 WLR 333, 337: 'the counter-offer kills the original offer.' The letter of the sellers of June 5, 1969, was an acceptance of that counter-offer, as is shown by the acknowledgment which the sellers signed and returned to the buyers. The reference to the quotation of May 23 referred only to the price and identity of the machine.

To go on with the facts of the case. The important thing is that the sellers did not keep the contractual date of delivery which was March/April 1970. The machine was ready about September 1970 but by that time the buyers' production schedule had to be re-arranged as they could not accept delivery until November 1970. Meanwhile the sellers had invoked the price increase clause. They sought to charge the buyers an increase due to the rise in costs between May 27, 1969 (when the order was given), and April 1, 1970 (when the machine ought to have been delivered). It came to £2,892. The buyers rejected the claim. The judge held that the sellers were entitled to the sum of £2,892 under the price variation clause. He did not apply the traditional method of analysis by way of offer and counter-offer. He said that in the quotation of May 23, 1969, 'one finds the price variation clause appearing under a most emphatic heading stating that it is a term or condition that is to prevail.' So he held that it did prevail.

I have much sympathy with the judge's approach to this case. In many of these cases our traditional analysis of offer, counter-offer, rejection, acceptance and so forth is out of date. This was observed by Lord Wilberforce in *New Zealand Shipping Co Ltd v AM Satterthwaite & Co Ltd* [1975] AC 154, 167. The better way is to look at all the documents passing between the parties and glean from them, or from the conduct of the parties, whether they have reached agreement on all material points—even though there may be differences between the forms and conditions printed on the back of them. As Lord Cairns said in *Brodgen v Metropolitan Railway Co* (1877) 2 App Cas 666, 672:

> '... there may be a consensus between the parties far short of a complete mode of expressing it, and that consensus may be discovered from letters or from other documents of an imperfect and incomplete description; ... '

Applying this guide, it will be found that in most cases when there is a 'battle of forms,' there is a contract as soon as the last of the forms is sent and received without objection being taken to it. That is well observed in *Benjamin's Sale of Goods*, 9th ed (1974), p 84. The difficulty is to decide which form, or which part of which form, is a term or condition of the contract. In some cases the battle is won by the man who fires the last shot. <405> He is the man who puts forward the latest terms and conditions: and, if they are not objected to by the other party, he may be taken to have agreed to them. Such was *British Road Services Ltd v Arthur V Crutchley & Co Ltd* [1968] 1 Lloyd's Rep 271, 281–282, per Lord Pearson; and the illustration given by Professor Guest in *Anson's Law of Contract*, 24th ed, pp 37, 38 when he says that 'the terms of the contract consist of the terms of the offer subject to the modifications contained in the acceptance'. In some cases the battle is won by the man who gets the blow in first. If he offers to sell at a named price on the terms and conditions stated on the back: and the buyer orders the goods purporting to accept the offer—on an order form with his own different terms and conditions on the back—then if the difference is so material that it would affect the price, the buyer ought not to be allowed to take advantage of the difference unless he draws it specifically to the attention of the seller. There are yet other cases where the battle depends on the shots fired on both sides. There is a concluded contract but the forms vary. The terms and conditions of both parties are to be construed together. If they can be reconciled so as to give a harmonious result, all well and good. If differences are irreconcilable—so that they are mutually contradictory—then the conflicting terms may have to be scrapped and replaced by a reasonable implication.

In the present case the judge thought that the sellers in their original quotation got their blow in first: especially by the provision that 'these terms and conditions shall prevail over any terms and conditions in the buyer's order.' It was so emphatic that the price variation clause continued through all the subsequent dealings and that the buyers must be taken to have agreed to it. I can understand that point of view. But I think that the documents have to be considered as a whole. And, as a matter of construction, I think the acknowledgment of June 5, 1969, is the decisive document. It makes it clear that the contract was on the buyers' terms and not on the sellers' terms: and the buyers' terms did not include a price variation clause.

I would therefore allow the appeal and enter judgment for the defendants.

[In separate judgments Lawton and Bridge LJJ agreed that the appeal should be allowed.]

Appeal allowed

The evocative description 'battle of the forms' does not mean, however, that where the parties have engaged in lengthy negotiations, the formation of a contract and the terms on which the contract is made are determined simply by whether there exists a penultimate communication from one party, containing all the terms of an offer, followed by an unqualified acceptance by the other party. Commercial negotiations are rarely so pristine. Rather, where negotiations are drawn out and multiple documents exchanged, it is necessary to consider the communications between the parties as a whole to determine when a contract is made and on whose terms. This is illustrated by the following extract.

Maxitherm Boilers Pty Ltd v Pacific Dunlop Ltd
[1998] 4 VR 559, Victorian Court of Appeal

[Maxitherm submitted a quotation to Pacific Dunlop for the installation of an autoclave. This quotation was expressed to be subject to terms and conditions attached; however, none were attached. Subsequently, on 22 March 1989 a fax was sent to Pacific Dunlop saying that supply would be on Maxitherm's standard terms 'as per previous quotation'. Immediately upon its receipt, this fax was accepted orally by Pacific Dunlop. Further discussions took place between the parties concerning specifications and on 3 April a document setting out Maxitherm's standard terms was sent to Pacific Dunlop. Pacific Dunlop then prepared an amended purchase order form and sent it, together with a cheque for 25% of the price to Maxitherm. This form contained no terms other than a reproduction of one of Maxitherm's standard terms dealing with the method of payment. The autoclave was manufactured and installed at Pacific Dunlop's premises. Unfortunately, it exploded causing extensive damage to those premises. As a result, Pacific Dunlop sued Maxitherm for breach of contract and by way of defence Maxitherm relied on an exclusion clause contained in its standard terms and conditions. At first instance, it was held that these terms were not part of the contract; Maxitherm appealed.]

Buchanan JA [at 567]: In my opinion Pacific Dunlop and Maxitherm did not reach a concluded agreement on 22 March 1989. On that day the parties were in the course of working out the terms upon which the autoclave would be supplied, and neither regarded the process as complete. In determining whether and when a contract is made in the course of an ongoing series of communications, it is necessary to consider the communications as a whole. As Earl Cairns LC said in *Hussey v Horne-Payne* (1879) 4 App Cas 311 at 316:

> ... it is one of the first principles applicable to a case of the kind that where you have to find your contract, or your note or memorandum of the terms of the contract in letters, you must take into consideration the whole of the correspondence which has passed. You must not at one particular time draw a line and say, 'We will look at the letters up to this point and find in them a contract or not, but we will look at nothing beyond.' In order fairly to estimate what was arranged and agreed, if anything was agreed between the parties, you must look at the whole of that which took place and passed between them.

See also *ABC v XIVth Commonwealth Games Ltd* (1988) 18 NSWLR 540 at 547–8 per Gleeson CJ.

I think that the ready acceptance by Pacific Dunlop of Maxitherm's request for payment of a deposit supports the conclusion that no concluded agreement was made earlier. If the parties had then regarded themselves as bound to a concluded agreement, Pacific Dunlop could have rejected the request for a benefit by Maxitherm for which Pacific Dunlop received no countervailing advantage. In my opinion the contract comprised an offer made by Maxitherm constituted by the original quotation, the confirming fax and the upper case specifications, and acceptance by Pacific Dunlop of that offer. While there is room for debate as to the precise form which Pacific Dunlop's acceptance took, the correspondence and conversations viewed as a whole in my view describe a contract coming into existence in that manner.

The original quotation incorporated Maxitherm's standard terms. A reasonable reader of the quotation would have concluded that Maxitherm intended to contract in accordance with certain conditions, and that those conditions, which were not contained in the body of the quotation, could be identified. I do not think that the failure to attach the terms would be reasonably taken to countermand the words 'subject to conditions of tender'. However, even if the absence of attached terms might have been taken to mean that Maxitherm did not intend to contract according to any 'conditions of tender', that impression could not have survived the confirming fax, for that document stated in type, not print, that the offer was '… based on our standard terms and conditions as per previous quotation …'. Accordingly, in my opinion Maxitherm's standard terms were made terms of the contract because they formed part of the offer which Pacific Dunlop accepted.

[Ormiston and Callaway JJA gave separate judgments to the same effect. As a result, the appeal was allowed in part.]

As we have seen (at p 46, above), the position in relation to international sales of goods is less rigid. Article 19(2) of the *Vienna Convention* allows an affirmative response to an offer to constitute acceptance, even though it differs from the terms of the offer, as long as it does 'not materially alter' those terms and the offeror does not object 'without undue delay'. If these conditions are satisfied, the terms of the contract become those of the original offer as modified by the offeree's response. If the offeror does object, or the differences are material,[44] according to Article 19(1) the response will amount to a rejection and constitute a counter-offer.

INTERNATIONAL PERSPECTIVES

Section 7 of the *Indian Contract Act* follows the common law in requiring the terms of acceptance to correspond exactly with those of the offer. Consequently, the introduction of even a small variation will prevent an agreement being concluded.[45]

Articles 30 and 31 of the Chinese *Contract Law*, on the other hand, adopt the same position as the *Vienna Convention*. As a result, an acceptance containing

---

44 Article 19(3) provides that additional or altered terms relating to such matters as price, payment, quality, quantity, time and place of delivery, the extent of liability, or the settlement of disputes will be considered to be material.
45 See *Mooljin Jaitha & Co v Seth Krodimal* AIR 1961 Ker 21.

immaterial differences will still constitute a valid acceptance, so long as the offeror does not object to the differences within a reasonable time and the terms of the offer did not indicate that acceptance must be exact.

Indian Contract Act, 1872

Section 7. Acceptance must be absolute

In order to convert a proposal into a promise, the acceptance must—
(i) be absolute and unqualified.
(ii) ...

Contract Law of the People's Republic of China, 1999

Article 30. Acceptance Containing Material Change

The terms of the acceptance shall be identical to those of the offer. A purported acceptance dispatched by the offeree which materially alters the terms of the offer constitutes a new offer. A change in the subject matter, quantity, quality, price or remuneration, time, place and method of performance, liabilities for breach of contract or method of dispute resolution is a material change to the terms of the offer.

Article 31. Acceptance Containing Non-material Changes

An acceptance containing non-material changes to the terms of the offer is nevertheless valid and the terms thereof prevail as the terms of the contract, unless the offeror timely objects to such changes or the offer indicated that acceptance may not contain any change to the terms thereof.

e Communication of acceptance

As a general rule, an acceptance will not be effective unless and until it is communicated. It is not sufficient for an offeree merely to decide to accept an offer, even where there are outward manifestations of this decision; to be operative, it must be communicated to the offeror. Furthermore, communication must be by the offeree, or by a person they have authorised to communicate the acceptance. Communication by an unauthorised third party will not be effective.[46] The leading authority dealing with the need for communication is *Felthouse v Bindley*.

Felthouse v Bindley

(1862) 11 CB (NS) 869; 142 ER 1037, Court of Common Pleas

[After discussing the matter with him, Felthouse wrote to his nephew offering to buy a horse and saying 'If I hear no more about him, I consider the horse mine.'

---

46   See *Powell v Lee* (1908) 99 LT 284.

The nephew did not reply but decided to accept this offer and told the defendant, Bindley, an auctioneer engaged to sell certain property, not to sell the horse. However, by mistake, Bindley sold the horse to a third party. Felthouse sued Bindley for the tort of conversion. This required him to establish that, at the time of sale, the horse was his property.]

Willes J [1040]: The nephew might, no doubt, have bound his uncle to the bargain by writing to him: the uncle might also have retracted his offer at any time before acceptance. It stood an open offer: and so things remained until 25 February, when the nephew was about to sell his farming stock by auction. The horse in question being catalogued with the rest of the stock, the auctioneer (the defendant) was told that it was already sold. It is clear, therefore, that the nephew in his own mind intended his uncle to have the horse at the price which he (the uncle) had named, — £30 15s: but he had not communicated such his intention to his uncle, or done anything to bind himself. Nothing, therefore, had been done to vest the property in the horse in the plaintiff down to 25 February, when the horse was sold by the defendant. It appears to me that, independently of the subsequent letters, there had been no bargain to pass the property in the horse to the plaintiff, and therefore that he had no right to complain of the sale. [His Honour went on to conclude that those letters did not alter this outcome.]

[Keating and Byles JJ agreed with Willes J.]

There are several exceptions to the rule that acceptance must be communicated; these include where:

- the offeror waives the need to communicate
- the silence of the offeree, in the special circumstances of the case, constitutes acceptance
- the offeror is estopped from denying communication
- the 'postal acceptance rule' operates
- the offeror has specified a special mode for indicating acceptance that does not involve communication.

Waiver

It is possible for the offeror to waive the need for communication, to indicate to the offeree that, should the offeree decide to accept the offer, it is not necessary to communicate that decision. The nature and operation of this exception is discussed in the following extract.

Carlill v Carbolic Smoke Ball Company

[1893] 1 QB 256, English Court of Appeal

[The facts of this case are set out at page 30, above.]

Bowen LJ [at 269]: One cannot doubt that, as an ordinary rule of law, an acceptance of an offer made ought to be notified to the person who makes the offer, in order that the two minds may come together. Unless this is done the two minds may be apart, and there is not that consensus which is necessary according to the English law—I say nothing about the law of other countries—to make a contract. But there is this clear gloss to be made upon the doctrine, that as notification of acceptance is required for the benefit of the person who makes the offer, the person who makes the offer may dispense with notice to himself if he thinks it desirable to do so, and I suppose there can be no doubt that where a person in an offer made by him to another person, expressly or impliedly intimates a particular mode of acceptance as sufficient to make the bargain binding, it is only necessary for the other person to whom such offer is made to follow the indicated method of acceptance; and if the person making the offer, expressly or impliedly intimates in his offer that it will be sufficient to act on the proposal without communicating <270> acceptance of it to himself, performance of the condition is a sufficient acceptance without notification. ...

Now, if that is the law, how are we to find out whether the person who makes the offer does intimate that notification of acceptance will not be necessary in order to constitute a binding bargain? In many cases you look to the offer itself. In many cases you extract from the character of the transaction that notification is not required, and in the advertisement cases it seems to me to follow as an inference to be drawn from the transaction itself that a person is not to notify his acceptance of the offer before he performs the condition, but that if he performs the condition notification is dispensed with. It seems to me that from the point of view of common sense no other idea could be entertained. If I advertise to the world that my dog is lost, and that anybody who brings the dog to a particular place will be paid some money, are all the police or other persons whose business it is to find lost dogs to be expected to sit down and write me a note saying that they have accepted my proposal? Why, of course, they at once look after the dog, and as soon as they find the dog they have performed the condition. The essence of the transaction is that the dog should be found, and it is not necessary under such circumstances, as it seems to me, that in order to make the contract binding there should be any notification of acceptance. It follows from the nature of the thing that the performance of the condition is sufficient acceptance without the notification of it, and a person who makes an offer in an advertisement of that kind makes an offer which must be read by the light of that common sense reflection. He does, therefore, in his offer impliedly indicate that he does not require notification of the acceptance of the offer.

[In separate judgments, AL Smith and Lindley LJJ summarised the law in similar terms.]

In cases of waiver, unless the offeror (in the words of Bowen LJ, above) 'intimates a particular mode of acceptance', acceptance is effective once the offeree has decided to accept. As the other rules about offer and acceptance continue to apply, the only difficulty this poses for the offeree is being able to prove, should this be challenged, that a decision to accept has been made and when and where this occurred.

Silence

The waiver exception is permitted because it disadvantages only the party who initiates it—the offeror—while relieving the offeree of the burden of communicating a decision that has, in fact, been made. As a result, it does not allow the offeror to impose upon the offeree the burden of rejecting an offer as the alternative to entering into a contract; in other words, the offeror cannot say: 'Here is my offer, if I do not hear from you to the contrary, we will have a contract.' In short, silence alone cannot be treated as assent. However, where silence is combined with other factors the outcome may be different, especially where the offeree's conduct can be characterised as acceptance by conduct. These rules and the reasons for them are discussed in the following case.

Empirnall Holdings Pty Ltd v Machon Paull Partners Pty Ltd

(1988) 14 NSWLR 523, New South Wales Court of Appeal

[Empirnall, engaged Machon Paull, a firm of architects, to redevelop a site it owned. After carrying out certain work, Machon Paull submitted a written contract to Empirnall for signature and return. This document was never signed. However, Machon Paull continued to carry out work on the site and Empirnall made payments in accordance with its terms. Eventually, Empirnall became insolvent owing Machon Paull a considerable sum of money. At issue between the parties was whether there was a contract between them in the terms of the written document. This was important because if there was such a contract, a clause in it granted Machon Paull a charge over the land; if not it was relegated to being one of a number of unsecured creditors. Machon Paull succeeded at first instance and Empirnall appealed.]

Kirby P [at 527]: The starting point for the legal classification of the facts which I have set out is that an offeror may not impose a contractual obligation upon an offeree by stating, that if the latter does not expressly reject the offer as made, it will be taken to have accepted it. This general principle is accepted throughout the common law world. ...

Various explanations may be offered for this principle. One is that it derives from the disinclination of the common law to impose legal liability <528> upon individuals for omissions. Another is that it is a consequence of the common law's protective attitude towards liberty of conduct and its resistance to the unilateral imposition of obligations. Still another is that it derives from the contractual theory of the common law that a binding and legally enforceable agreement must be *mutually* achieved by offer and acceptance. Whatever the history of and reasons for the general rule, its existence is not in doubt. ...

McHugh J A (with whom Samuels J A agreed) [at 534]: Under the common law theory of contract, the silent acceptance of an offer is generally insufficient to create any contract. ... The objective theory of contract requires an external manifestation of assent to an offer. Convenience, and especially commercial convenience, has given rise to the rule that the acceptance of the offer should be communicated to the offeror. After a reasonable period has elapsed, silence is seen as a rejection and not an acceptance of the offer. Nevertheless, communication of acceptance is not always necessary. The offeror will be bound if he dispenses with the need to communicate the acceptance of his offer: *Carlill v Carbolic Smoke Ball Co* [1893] 1 QB 256 at 269. However, an offeror cannot erect a contract between himself and the offeree by the device of stating that unless he hears from the offeree he will consider the offeree bound. He cannot assert that he will regard silence as acceptance: *Felthouse v Bindley* (1862) 11 CB (NS) 869 at 875; 142 ER 1037 at 1040 and *Fairline Shipping Corporation v Adamson* [1975] QB 180 at 189. The common law's concern with the protection of freedom is opposed to the notion that a person must take action to reject an uninvited offer or be bound by contractual obligations.

Nevertheless, the silence of an offeree in conjunction with the other circumstances of the case may indicate that he has accepted the offer: *Rust v Abbey Life Assurance Co Ltd* [1979] 2 Lloyd's Rep 334 at 340. The offeree may be under a duty to communicate his rejection of an offer. If he fails to do so, his silence will generally be regarded as an acceptance of the offer sufficient to form a contract. Many cases decided in United States jurisdictions have held that the custom of the trade, the course of dealing, or the previous relationship between the parties imposed a duty on the offeree to reject the offer or be bound: *CMI Clothesmakers Inc v ASK Knits Inc 380* NYS 2D 447 (1975); *Brooks Towers Corporation v Hunkin-Conkey* <535> *Construction Co* 454 F 2d 1203 (1972); *Alliance Manufacturing Co Inc v Foti* 146 So 2d 464 (1962). But more often than not the offeree will be bound because, knowing of the terms of the offer and the offeror's intention to enter into a contract, he has exercised a choice and taken the benefit of the offer. In *Laurel Race Course Inc v Regal Construction Co Inc* 333 A 2d 319 (1975) a contractor proposed that it would do additional work upon the basis that, if the work was the result of its defective workmanship under the original contract, there would be no charge. Otherwise the work would be charged on a 'cost-plus' basis. The building owner made no reply to this offer. The contractor commenced work on the job to the knowledge of the building owner who was held bound by the terms of the offer. Speaking for the Court of Appeals for Maryland, Judge Levine said (at 329):

> 'Where the offeree with reasonable opportunity to reject offered services takes the benefit of them under circumstances which would indicate to a reasonable person that they were offered with the expectation of compensation, he assents to the terms proposed and thus accepts the offer.'

This formulation states acceptance in terms of a rule of law. However, the question is one of fact. A more accurate statement is that where an offeree with a reasonable opportunity to reject the offer of goods or services takes the benefit of them under circumstances which indicate that they were to be paid for in accordance with the offer, it is open to the tribunal of fact to hold that the offer was accepted according to its terms. ...

[His Honour then examined the facts in detail and concluded that] Empirnall's acceptance of the work, when <536> considered objectively, should be taken as an acceptance of the work on the terms and conditions offered by Machon. The case is not so much one of acceptance by silence as one of taking the benefit of an offer with knowledge of its terms and knowledge of the offeror's reliance on payment being made in return for his work.

Appeal dismissed

Estoppel

In the present context, estoppel arises when conduct of the offeror prevents that party from asserting that communication of acceptance has not occurred. In such cases, the law treats the offeree's acceptance as having been communicated to the offeror even though, in fact, it has not been. In *Entores Ltd v Miles Far East Corporation* Denning LJ gave the following examples:

> But suppose that [the offeree] does not know that his message [of acceptance using the telephone] did not get home. He thinks it has. This may happen if the listener on the telephone does not catch the words of acceptance, but nevertheless does not trouble to ask for them to be repeated: or if the ink on the teleprinter fails at the receiving end, but the clerk does not ask for the message to be repeated: so that the man who sends an acceptance reasonably believes that his message has been received. The offeror in such circumstances is clearly bound, because he will be estopped from saying that he did not receive the message of acceptance. It is his own fault he did not get it.[47]

Postal acceptance rule

According to what has become known as 'the postal acceptance rule', acceptance is deemed to be effective at the time and place a letter of acceptance is posted, or a telegram is handed in for transmission, rather than when and where it is received. Furthermore, where the rule operates, an acceptance will still be deemed to have been communicated even though the letter, or telegram, becomes lost in the postal system and is never delivered, so long as this is not the offeree's fault.[48]

The postal rule exists primarily for the benefit of the offeree[49] and being an exception to the general rule it is kept within strict limits. In particular, the postal rule:

- will only apply if the terms and circumstances of the offer indicate that the offeror contemplated that acceptance could be by post—it will not apply if there is a contrary stipulation in the offer,[50] or if it was unreasonable to use the

---

47   [1955] 2 All ER 493 at 495.
48   An example of fault of this kind would be the offeree wrongly addressing the letter.
49   The rule is regarded as being beneficial to the offeree because, once the letter is posted, the offeree will know that a contract has been concluded but the offeror does not know this (and will not do so) until the letter is delivered.
50   See *Nunin Holdings Pty Ltd v Tullamarine Estates Pty Ltd* [1994] 1 VR 74.

post (for example members of the postal service were on strike) or (possibly) if the offer was made using a quicker means of communication[51]
- does not apply to instantaneous forms of communication such as the telephone, telex or email[52]
- does not apply to the *revocation* of an offer—a contract will be formed even though a letter of acceptance is posted after a letter of revocation has been despatched to the offeree but before it arrives[53]
- may not prevent the offeree countermanding a posted acceptance before it reaches the offeror. Applied strictly, the rule would prevent this happening because its operation makes the formation of a contract complete when the letter, or equivalent, is posted.[54] However, this is an unsatisfactory outcome where the offeror knows of the offeree's latest decision before the letter of acceptance is received. For this reason, and because such an outcome would conflict with the rule's rationale, it is suggested that such an outcome would not now be adopted.

The nature of the rule and its parameters are discussed in the following cases.

Bressan v Squires

[1974] 2 NSWLR 460, Equity Division of the New South Wales Supreme Court

[Squires gave Bressan an option to purchase land, clause 1 of which provided that it may be exercised 'by notice in writing addressed to me at any time on or before 20 December, 1972'. On 18 December 1972, Bressan posted a notice, addressed to Squires, exercising this option. It was received on 21 December. Squires denied that the option had been exercised properly and refused to sell the land. Bressan claimed that the option had been exercised and sued for specific performance.]

Bowen CJ in Eq [at 461]: The general rule is, of course, that a contract is not concluded until acceptance of an offer is actually communicated to the offeror. To this rule there is an exception in the case of acceptance by post.

There have been various formulations of the exception and various reasons assigned for its existence. Many of these reasons have later been said to be unsound. The exception, it seems, is really based upon notions of expediency and convenience, as these are envisaged by the courts from time to time. It is an important exception, since it may determine not only whether or when a contract has been made but also where it has been made.

---

51 See dicta to this effect in *Howard Smith & Co v Varawa* (1907) 5 CLR 68 at 79, per Griffith CJ.
52 See *Schib Packaging Srl v Emrich Industries Pty Ltd* [2005] 12 VR 268.
53 See *Byrne v Van Tienhoven* (1880) LR 5 CPD 344 (above at p 42).
54 See *Morrison v Thoelke* 155 So 2d 889 (1963). In this case, the Florida District Court of Appeal held that the plaintiff could not, by calling the offeror, revoke an acceptance after it had been posted but before it had been received. See also the discussion by AH Hudson 'Retraction of Letters of Acceptance' (1966) 82 *LQR* 168 and A Samek 'Reassessment of the present rule relating to postal acceptance' (1961) 35 *ALJ* 38.

A formulation of the exception, which is often quoted, is that of Lord Herschell in *Henthorn v Fraser* ([1892] 2 Ch 27, at p 33). His Lordship said: 'Where the circumstances are such that it must have been within the contemplation of the parties that, according to the ordinary usages of mankind, the post might be used as a means of communicating the acceptance of an offer, the acceptance is complete as soon as it is posted.'

According to this formulation, all that needs to be in contemplation of the parties is the post as a mode, indeed as a possible or permitted mode, <462> for the law to impose the consequence that the contract is concluded by the action of posting. It is not required that it should be within the contemplation of the parties that the action of posting should have the consequence of concluding the contract; this, of course, would apply in relatively fewer cases, and would narrow the application of the exception.

At first reading, it might be thought that the formulation by Dixon CJ and Fullagar J in *Tallerman & Co Pty Ltd v Nathan's Merchandise (Victoria) Pty Ltd* ((1957) 98 CLR 93, at p 111) constituted an adoption of this narrower basis. Their Honours said: 'The general rule is that a contract is not completed until acceptance of an offer is actually communicated to the offeror, and a finding that a contract is completed by the posting of a letter of acceptance cannot be justified unless it is to be inferred that the offeror contemplated and intended that his offer might be accepted by the doing of the act: see *Henthorn v Fraser* ([1892] 2 Ch 27, at pp 35, 36), per Kay, LJ.'

The reference made by their Honours to the judgment of Kay LJ in *Henthorn v Fraser*, however, suggests to my mind they were not intending to narrow the exception.

In the present case the parties must, in my view, have contemplated that the option might be exercised by means of a notice sent through the post. Accordingly the exception applies and there is here a concluded contract, unless there is some other ground for holding this result does not follow.

[His Honour went on to conclude that the proper interpretation of the option was that actual notice of acceptance was required and that as such notice had not been received by the stipulated date it had not been exercised properly and the plaintiff's case failed.]

Brinkibon Ltd v Stahag Stahl und Stahl-Warendhandelsgesellschaft mbH

[1983] 2 AC 34, House of Lords

[In this case, Brinkibon (an English company) wished to sue Stahag (an Austrian company) for breach of contract. To be able to do so it was necessary to determine where the contract was made—in England or Austria. This raised the issue of whether a telexed acceptance of a counter-offer, sent from England to Austria, was effective when sent (in which case the contract was made in England) or when it was received (in which case the contract was made in Austria). Brinkibon succeeded at first instance but lost on appeal to the Court of Appeal; it then appealed to the House of Lords.]

Lord Wilberforce [at 41]: [The question is] ... whether an acceptance by telex sent from London but received in Vienna causes a contract to be made in London, or in Vienna. If the acceptance had been sent by post, or by telegram, then, on existing authorities, it would have been complete when put into the hands of the post office—in London. If on the other hand it had been telephoned, it would have been complete when heard by the offeror—in Vienna. So in which category is a telex communication to be placed? Existing authority of the Court of Appeal decides in favour of the latter category, i.e. a telex is to be assimilated to other methods of instantaneous communication: see *Entores Ltd v Miles Far East Corporation* [1955] 2 QB 327. The appellants ask that this case, which has stood for 30 years, should now be reviewed. ... <42> ...

In *Entores Ltd v Miles Far East Corporation* [1955] 2 QB 327 the Court of Appeal classified [a telex communication] with instantaneous communications. Their ruling, which has passed into the textbooks, including *Williston on Contracts*, 3rd ed (1957), appears not to have caused either adverse comment, or any difficulty to business men. I would accept it as a general rule. Where the condition of simultaneity is met, and where it appears to be within the mutual intention of the parties that contractual exchanges should take place in this way, I think it a sound rule, but not necessarily a universal rule. Since 1955 the use of telex communication has been greatly expanded, and there are many variants on it. The senders and recipients may not be the principals to the contemplated contract. They may be servants or agents with limited authority. The message may not reach, or be intended to reach, the designated recipient immediately: messages may be sent out of office hours, or at night, with the intention, or upon the assumption, that they will be read at a later time. There may be some error or default at the recipient's end which prevents receipt at the time contemplated and believed in by the sender. The message may have been sent and/or received through machines operated by third persons. And many other variations may occur. No universal rule can cover all such cases: they must be resolved by reference to the intentions of the parties, by sound business practice and in some cases by a judgment where the risks should lie: see *Household Fire and Carriage Accident Insurance Co Ltd v Grant*, 4 Ex D 216, 227 per Baggallay LJ and *Henthorn v Fraser* [1892] 2 Ch 27 per Lord Herschell.

The present case is, as *Entores Ltd v Miles Far East Corporation* [1955] 2 QB 327 itself, the simple case of instantaneous communication between principals, and, in accordance with the general rule, involves that the contract (if any) was made when and where the acceptance was received. This was on May 4, 1979, in Vienna.

[The other members of the House of Lords agreed with the conclusion reached by Lord Wilberforce that generally, though not invariably, the postal rule will not apply to a telex. Their reasons included the following:

- Once a telex message has been received on the offeror's telex machine, it should be regarded as delivered because it is the offeror's responsibility to arrange for prompt handling of messages within its office.
- An offeree who sends a message by telex can generally tell if the message has not been received on the offeror's machine, whereas the offeror will not know if an unsuccessful attempt has been made to send an acceptance. Therefore, being in the better position, the offeree should have the responsibility of ensuring that the message is received.
- Commercial expediency, used to justify the postal rule, has no application when the means of communication employed between the offeror and the offeree is instantaneous.]

Mode specified by the offeror

The offeror can specify the mode in which acceptance is to occur and this may include dispensing with the need for actual communication. The law in this area was conveniently summarised by Buckley J in *Manchester Diocesan Council for Education v Commercial & General Investments Ltd* in these terms:

> If an offeror stipulates by the terms of his offer that it may, or that it shall, be accepted in a particular manner a contract results as soon as the offeree does the stipulated act, whether it has come to the notice of the offeror or not. In such as case the offeror conditionally waives either expressly or by implication the normal requirement that acceptance must be communicated to the offeror to conclude a contract. ... It may be that an offeror who by the terms of his offer insists upon acceptance in a particular manner, is entitled to insist that he is not bound unless acceptance is effected or communicated in that precise way, although it seems probable that, even so, if the other party communicates his acceptance in some other way, the offeror may by conduct or otherwise waive his right to insist upon the prescribed method of acceptance. Where, however, the offeror has prescribed a particular method of acceptance, but not in terms insisting that only acceptance in that mode shall be binding, I am of the opinion that acceptance communicated to the offeror by any other mode which is no less advantageous to him will conclude the contract.[55]

Allied Steel & Conveyors Inc v Ford Motor Co illustrates the latter situation.[56] Here, Ford ordered machinery from Allied on an order form that provided that 'acceptance should be executed on acknowledgment copy which should be returned to the buyer'. Allied began installing the machinery without doing this and when a dispute arose it argued that it had not effectively accepted Ford's offer. However, the court held the method of acceptance prescribed by Ford was

---

55 [1970] 1 WLR 241 at 245–6.
56 277 F 2d 907 (1960).

merely a suggestion and that by beginning performance with Ford's knowledge and consent Allied had validly accepted its offer.

Electronic communications

The formation of contracts by means of electronic communications is now governed by legislation in all Australian jurisdictions.[57] This legislation is designed to implement in Australia the United Nations Commission on International Trade Law's (UNCITRAL) 1996 Model Law on Electronic Commerce. In 2005, this Model Law was updated by a United Nations Convention on Electronic Communications and in May 2011 the Commonwealth *Electronic Transactions Act* was amended to align it with that Convention. However, the Australian Act, unlike the Convention, is not restricted to business transactions but also applies to personal, family and household contracts. The key provisions of the Act, relevant to the formation of contracts, are reproduced below. In due course, the corresponding state and territory provisions will be amended to bring them into line with the Commonwealth Act.

Electronic Transactions Act 1999 (Cth)

Section 5. Definitions

(1) In this Act, unless the contrary intention appears:
addressee of an electronic communication means a person who is intended by the originator to receive the electronic communication, but does not include a person acting as an intermediary with respect to the electronic communication.
automated message system means a computer program or an electronic or other automated means used to initiate an action or respond to data messages in whole or in part, without review or intervention by a natural person each time an action is initiated or a response is generated by the system. ...
consent includes consent that can reasonably be inferred from the conduct of the person concerned. ...
electronic communication means:

(a) a communication of information in the form of data, text or images by means of guided and/or unguided electromagnetic energy; or
(b) a communication of information in the form of speech by means of guided and/or unguided electromagnetic energy, where the speech is processed at its destination by an automated voice recognition system. ...

originator of an electronic communication means a person by whom, or on whose behalf, the electronic communication has been sent or generated before

---

57 See *Electronic Transactions Act 1999* (Cth); *Electronic Transactions Act 2000* (NSW); *Electronic Transactions (Victoria) Act 2000* (Vic); *Electronic Transactions (Queensland) Act 2001* (Qld); *Electronic Transactions Act 2000* (SA); *Electronic Transactions Act 2003* (WA); *Electronic Transactions Act 2000* (Tas); *Electronic Transactions Act 2001* (ACT); *Electronic Transactions Act (Northern Territory) 2000* (NT).

storage, if any, but does not include a person acting as an intermediary with respect to the electronic communication. ...

place of business means:

(a) in relation to a person, other than an entity referred to in paragraph (b)—a place where the person maintains a non-transitory establishment to pursue an economic activity other than the temporary provision of goods or services out of a specific location; or

(b) in relation to a government, an authority of a government or a non-profit body—a place where any operations or activities are carried out by that government, authority or body.

transaction includes:

(a) any transaction in the nature of a contract, agreement or other arrangement; and

(b) any statement, declaration, demand, notice or request, including an offer and the acceptance of an offer, that the parties are required to make or choose to make in connection with the formation or performance of a contract, agreement or other arrangement; and

(c) any transaction of a non-commercial nature.

Section 14. Time of dispatch

(1) For the purposes of a law of the Commonwealth, unless otherwise agreed between the originator and the addressee of an electronic communication, the time of dispatch of the electronic communication is:

(a) the time when the electronic communication leaves an information system under the control of the originator or of the party who sent it on behalf of the originator; or

(b) if the electronic communication has not left an information system under the control of the originator or of the party who sent it on behalf of the originator—the time when the electronic communication is received by the addressee.

Note: Paragraph (b) would apply to a case where the parties exchange electronic communications through the same information system.
...

Section 14A. Time of receipt

(1) For the purposes of a law of the Commonwealth, unless otherwise agreed between the originator and the addressee of an electronic communication:

(a) the time of receipt of the electronic communication is the time when the electronic communication becomes capable of being retrieved by the addressee at an electronic address designated by the addressee; or

(b) the time of receipt of the electronic communication at another electronic address of the addressee is the time when both:

(i) the electronic communication has become capable of being retrieved by the addressee at that address; and
(ii) the addressee has become aware that the electronic communication has been sent to that address.

...

Section 14B. Place of dispatch and place of receipt

(1) For the purposes of a law of the Commonwealth, unless otherwise agreed between the originator and the addressee of an electronic communication:
   (a) the electronic communication is taken to have been dispatched at the place where the originator has its place of business; and
   (b) the electronic communication is taken to have been received at the place where the addressee has its place of business.

(2) For the purposes of the application of subsection (1) to an electronic communication:
   (a) a party's place of business is assumed to be the location indicated by that party, unless another party demonstrates that the party making the indication does not have a place of business at that location; and
   (b) if a party has not indicated a place of business and has only one place of business, it is to be assumed that that place is the party's place of business; and
   (c) if a party has not indicated a place of business and has more than one place of business, the place of business is that which has the closest relationship to the underlying transaction, having regard to the circumstances known to or contemplated by the parties at any time before or at the conclusion of the transaction; and
   (d) if a party has not indicated a place of business and has more than one place of business, but paragraph (c) does not apply—it is to be assumed that the party's principal place of business is the party's only place of business; and
   (e) if a party is a natural person and does not have a place of business—it is to be assumed that the party's place of business is the place of the party's habitual residence.

INTERNATIONAL PERSPECTIVES

Both the Indian and Chinese Acts contain detailed provisions dealing with acceptance and its communication. Broadly, the Indian provisions (extracted below) follow the same approach as the common law; however, there are some important differences including the following:

- The postal rule is entrenched as the norm for communications using the post or similar services. This is the effect of s 4 which provides that in all such cases the offeror (proposer) is bound by an acceptance once it is 'put in the course of transmission to him'.

- Section 5 makes it clear that an offeree (acceptor) can revoke a posted acceptance so long as the revocation reaches the offeror before the posted acceptance does. It was suggested earlier, this is what the common law position should be. However, there is considerable authority to the contrary. The Indian Act clarifies the situation by clearly making the offeree's revocation effective in this situation.
- Section 7(2), dealing with the effect of the offeree not complying with a prescribed manner for acceptance, adopts rules that are more indulgent to the offeree (making effective an acceptance that does not comply with a mandatory prescription, where the offeror does not object within a reasonable time) and rules that may be more strict (allowing the offeror to object to an effective acceptance where it does not comply with a direction about the manner of acceptance).

The common law remains, however, a powerful influence. Thus, for example, despite the apparent breadth of the terms 'communication' and 'a course of transmission' used in s 4, the section has been held not to apply to instantaneous means of communication.[58]

The Chinese provisions follow the common law in requiring an acceptance to be communicated to the offeror before it is effective (Article 26) and in making that the time and place at which the contract is formed (see also Articles 32 and 35). Article 27, allowing the withdrawal of an acceptance, also accords with what has been suggested the common law should be, as do the detailed provisions in Articles 23, 24 and 28, dealing with the time for acceptance. However, there is no equivalent to the postal rule (although Article 29 does make provision for delays in the transmission of an acceptance) and the reference in Article 33 to a 'confirmation letter' is also unknown to the common law.

Indian Contract Act, 1872

Section 3. Communication, acceptance and revocation of proposals

The communication of proposals, the acceptance of proposals, and the revocation of proposals and acceptances, respectively, are deemed to be made by any act or omission of the party proposing, accepting or revoking, by which he intends to communicate such proposal, acceptance or revocation, or which has the effect of communicating it.

Section 4. Communication when complete

The communication of a proposal is complete when it comes to the knowledge of the person to whom it is made. The communication of an acceptance is complete,—

- as against the proposer, when it is put in a course of transmission to him so as to be out of the power of the acceptor;

---

58   See *Bhagwandas Goverdhandas Kedia v Girdharilal Parshottamdas & Co* (1966) 1 SCR 656.

- as against the acceptor, when it comes to the knowledge of the proposer.

The communication of a revocation is complete,—

- as against the person who makes it, when it is put into a course of transmission to the person to whom it is made, so as to be out of the power of the person who makes it;
- as against the person to whom it is made, when it comes to his knowledge.

Section 5. Revocation of proposals and acceptance

A proposal may be revoked at any time before the communication of its acceptance is complete as against the proposer, but not afterwards.

An acceptance may be revoked at any time before the communication of the acceptance is complete against the acceptor, but not afterwards.

Section 7. Acceptance must be absolute

In order to convert a proposal into a promise the acceptance must—

(1) be absolute and unqualified;
(2) be expressed in some usual and reasonable manner, unless the proposal prescribes the manner in which it is to be accepted. If the proposal prescribes a manner in which it is to be accepted, and the acceptance is not made in such manner, the proposer may, within a reasonable time after the acceptance is communicated to him, insist that his proposal shall be accepted in the prescribed manner, and not otherwise; but, if he fails to do so, he accepts the acceptance.

Section 8. Acceptance by performing conditions, or receiving consideration

Performance of the conditions of a proposal, or the acceptance of any consideration for a reciprocal promise which may be offered with a proposal, is an acceptance of the proposal.

Section 9. Promises, express and implied

In so far as the proposal or acceptance of any promise is made in words, the promise is said to be express. In so far as such proposal or acceptance is made otherwise than in words, the promise is said to be implied.

Contract Law of the People's Republic of China, 1999

Article 22. Mode of Acceptance; Acceptance by Conduct

An acceptance shall be manifested by notification, except where it may be manifested by conduct in accordance with the relevant usage or as indicated in the offer.

Article 23. Timely Dispatch of Acceptance

An acceptance shall reach the offeror within the period prescribed in the offer.

Where the offer does not prescribe a period for acceptance, the acceptance shall reach the offeror as follows:

(i) Where the offer is made orally, the acceptance shall be dispatched immediately, unless otherwise agreed by the parties;

(ii) Where the offer is made in a non-oral manner, the acceptance shall reach the offeror within a reasonable time.

Article 24. Commencement of the Period for Acceptance

Where an offer is made by a letter or a telegram, the period for acceptance commences on the date shown on the letter or the date on which the telegram is handed in for dispatch. If the letter does not specify a date, the period commences on the posting date stamped on the envelope. Where the offer is made through an instantaneous communication device such as telephone or facsimile, etc, the period for acceptance commences once the offer reaches the offeree.

Article 25. Contract Formed upon Effectiveness of Acceptance

A contract is formed once the acceptance becomes effective.

Article 26. Effectiveness of Acceptance

A notice of acceptance becomes effective once it reaches the offeror. Where the acceptance does not require notification, it becomes effective once an act of acceptance is performed in accordance with the relevant usage or as required by the offer.

Where a contract is concluded by the exchange of electronic messages, the time of arrival of the acceptance shall be governed by Paragraph 2 of Article 16 hereof.

Article 27. Withdrawal of Acceptance

An acceptance may be withdrawn. The notice of withdrawal shall reach the offeror before or at the same time as the acceptance.

Article 28. Late Acceptance

An acceptance dispatched by the offeree after expiration of the period for acceptance constitutes a new offer, unless the offeror timely advises the offeree that the acceptance is valid.

Article 29. Delayed Transmission of Acceptance

If the offeree dispatched its acceptance within the period for acceptance, and the acceptance, which would otherwise have reached the offeror in due time under normal circumstances, reaches the offeror after expiration of the period for acceptance due to any other reason, the acceptance is valid, unless the offeror timely advises the offeree that the acceptance has been rejected on grounds of the delay.

> Article 32. Time of Formation in Case of Memorandum of Contract
>
> Where the parties enter into a contract by a memorandum of contract, the contract is formed when it is signed or sealed by the parties.
>
> Article 33. Time of Formation in Case of Letters or Electronic Messages: Confirmation Letter
>
> Where the parties enter into a contract by the exchange of letters or electronic messages, one party may require execution of a confirmation letter before the contract is formed. The contract is formed upon execution of the confirmation letter.
>
> Article 34. Place of Formation; Electronic Messages
>
> The place where the acceptance becomes effective is the place of formation of a contract.
> Where a contract is concluded by the exchange of electronic messages, the recipient's main place of business is the place of formation of the contract, if the recipient does not have a main place of business, its habitual residence is the place of formation of the contract. If the parties have agreed otherwise, such agreement prevails.
>
> Article 35. Place of Formation in Case of Memorandum of Contract
>
> Where a contract is concluded by a memorandum of contract, its place of formation is the place where the parties sign or seal the contract.

6 Agreements reached without offer and acceptance

There are many instances in which the common law will conclude that an agreement has been reached between two parties even though it is not possible to realistically analyse their dealings in terms of offer and acceptance. A leading example is provided by *Clarke v Dunraven* which concerned whether there was a contract between the participants in a yacht race.[59] When applying to enter the race, applicants dealt only with the organisers and not with each other. However, when doing so they agreed with the organisers that they would be bound by the race rules and knew that other applicants would do likewise. In these circumstances, even though there was no communication between applicants, the House of Lords concluded that there was a contract between them in the terms of the race rules. A useful discussion of other instances of this nature is found in *Brambles Holdings Ltd v Bathurst City Council*.[60]

---

59 [1897] AC 59.
60 See also *Atco Controls Pty Ltd (in liq) v Newtronics Pty Ltd (recs & mgrs apptd) (in liq)* [2009] VSCA 238 and *Kriketos v Livschitz* [2009] NSWCA 96.

Brambles Holdings Ltd v Bathurst City Council
(2001) 53 NSWLR 153, New South Wales Court of Appeal

[In the period 1982–1989, pursuant to a formal contract, Brambles managed the Council's solid waste disposal depot. A second contract was concluded in July 1990 that referred to general waste and provided that part of the fees received by Brambles was to be remitted to the Council. In September 1991, the Council wrote to Brambles saying that it could increase the fees charged for receiving liquid waste but stipulating that part of these fees should be remitted to the Council to fund the construction of a liquid treatment plant. Brambles began charging the higher fees but refused to remit any part thereof to the Council, arguing that liquid waste was not covered by the new contract and that it had rejected any offer contained in the September letter. In these proceedings, the Council claimed a portion of these fees; it succeeded at first instance and Brambles appealed.]

Heydon JA [at 176]: The defendant's contention that the rejection of the Council's offer meant that it was no longer capable of acceptance by conduct, and its related contention that its conduct did not constitute acceptance, depend heavily on the view that offer and acceptance analysis must invariably be employed in reaching decisions about the formation of contracts. While the process by which many contracts are arrived at is reducible to an analysis turning on the making of an offer, the rejection of the offer by a counter-offer and so on until the last counter-offer is accepted, that analysis is neither sufficient to explain all cases nor necessary to explain all cases. Offer and acceptance analysis does not work well in various circumstances. One example is a contract for the transportation of passengers on mass public transport (*MacRobertson Miller Airline Services v Commissioner of State Taxation (Western Australia)* (1975) 133 CLR 125 at 136–140). Another is the contract between competitors in a regatta: though they did not communicate with each other but only with the organiser of the regatta, they are bound by their conduct in 'entering for the race, and undertaking to be bound by [the] rules to the knowledge of each other' (*Clarke v Earl of Dunraven* [1897] AC 59 at 63). That case was applied in *Raguz v Sullivan* [2000] 50 NSWLR 236 at 250 at [65]–[67]. Another example concerns the exchanges of contracts to sell land, which are hard to analyse in offer and acceptance terms; despite that Lord Greene MR observed of the practice:

> 'Parties become bound by contract when, and in the manner in which, they intend and contemplate becoming bound. It is a question of the facts of each case …'
> (*Eccles v Bryant* [1948] 1 Ch 93 at 104).

Another example concerns simultaneous manifestations of consent (Horst K Lucke 'Striking A Bargain' (1962) 1 *Adel LR* 293 at 295–299). Another example concerns contracts between numerous parties, or even two parties, negotiated at meetings but not assented to until each party executes counterparts. Another is where the contract is made through a single broker acting for both parties. Another is where the parties are deadlocked and they agree to submit to a solution reached by a third party. … <177> …

Thus offer and acceptance analysis is a useful tool in most circumstances, and indeed is 'normal' and 'conventional' (*Gibson v Manchester City Council* [1979] 1 WLR 294 at 297; [1979] 1 All ER 972 at 974 per Lord Diplock). But limited recognition has been given to the possibility of finding that contracts exist even though it is not easy to locate an offer or acceptance. In *Integrated Computer Services Pty Ltd v Digital Equipment Corp (Aust) Pty Ltd* (1988) 5 BPR 11, 110 at 11, 117–11, 118 McHugh JA (Hope and Mahoney JJA concurring) said:

> 'It is often difficult to fit a commercial arrangement into the common lawyers' analysis of a contractual arrangement. Commercial discussions are often too unrefined to fit easily into the slots of 'offer', 'acceptance', 'consideration' and 'intention to create a legal relationship' which are the benchmarks of the contract of classical theory. In classical theory, the typical contract is a bilateral one and consists of an exchange of promises by means of an offer and its acceptance together with an intention to create a binding legal relationship ...
>
> Moreover, in an ongoing relationship, it is not always easy to point to the precise moment when the legal criteria of a contract have been fulfilled. Agreements concerning terms and conditions which might be too uncertain or too illusory to enforce at a particular time in the relationship may by reason of the parties' subsequent conduct become sufficiently specific to give rise to legal rights and duties. In a dynamic commercial relationship new terms will be added or will supersede older terms. It is necessary therefore to look at the whole relationship and not only at what was said and done when the relationship was first formed.'

Those passages were cited with approval by Ormiston J in *Vroon BV v Foster's Brewing Group* [1994] 2 VR 32 at 82–3. He also approved the following statement of Cooke J in *Meates v Attorney-General* [1983] NZLR 308 at 377:

> 'I would not treat difficulties in analysing the dealings into a strict classification of offer and acceptance as necessarily decisive in this field, although any difficulty on that head is a factor telling against a contract. The acid test in the case like the present is whether, viewed as a whole and objectively from the point of view of reasonable persons on both sides, the dealings show a concluded bargain.'

Ormiston J said at 81:

> '... I am prepared to accept ... that agreement and thus a contract can be extracted from circumstances where no acceptance of an offer can be established or inferred and where the most that can be said is that a manifestation of mutual assent must be implied from the circumstances. <178> In the language of para 22(2) of the *Second Restatement on Contracts:* 'A manifestation of mutual assent may be made even though neither offer or acceptance could be identified and even though the moment of formation cannot be determined'.'

He concluded at 83:

> 'there is now sufficient authority to justify the court inquiring as to the existence of an agreement evidenced otherwise than by offer and acceptance' ....

While in *Toyota Motor Corporation Australia Ltd v Ken Morgan Motors Pty Ltd* [1994] 2 VR 106 at 178 Tadgell J exhibited some caution about the finding of a contract merely on the basis of a manifestation of mutual assent, he did quote *Williston on Contracts*, Vol I, para 4:3, p 258, to the following effect:

> 'It is not necessary to insist that assent must always be manifested by means of offer and acceptance, but cases where offer and acceptance are lacking are so rare that for purposes of general discussion they may be <179> disregarded. When they arise, they can be easily reduced to fundamental principles, particularly in the light of the modern view, adopted by both the Uniform Commercial Code and Restatement (Second), that so long as a manifestation of mutual assent is present, a contract can be found to exist though no offer or acceptance can be identified and though the precise moment that the contract thereby comes into being cannot be determined.'

He continued:

> 'If a contract is to be discerned in the absence of offer and acceptance I venture the suggestion that ... it is to be discovered by inferring from the relevant facts the conclusion that the parties have agreed to incur reciprocal promissory obligations ... As *Williston* suggests, the necessity or opportunity so to infer in the absence of offer and acceptance is likely to be rare ... .'

If offer and acceptance analysis is not always necessary or sufficient, principles such as the general principle that a rejection of an offer brings it to an end cannot be universal. A rejected offer could remain operative if it were repeated, or otherwise revived, or if in the circumstances it should for some other reason be treated, despite its rejection, as remaining on foot, available for acceptance, or for adoption as the basis of mutual assent manifested by conduct.

In the light of the above cases, it is relevant to ask: in all the circumstances can an agreement be inferred? Has mutual assent been manifested? What would a reasonable person in the position of the Council and a reasonable person in the position of the defendant think as to whether there was a concluded bargain?

[His Honour concluded that Brambles, by charging higher fees, had accepted the offer contained in the Council's September letter. As a result, the appeal was dismissed. Mason P and Ipp A-JA reached the same conclusion on different grounds.]

7 Bilateral and unilateral contracts

A bilateral contract is one in which each party makes a promise to the other. Most consumer and business contracts are of this nature. For example, in a contract of sale the seller promises to supply goods and the purchaser promises to pay for them. As a result, if one or the other does not perform their promise, then (assuming the other elements of a contract are satisfied) the other can sue for breach of contract.

A unilateral contract, on the other hand, is one in which only one party makes a promise. There are still two parties, but while one has made a promise the other has not made one in return. *Carlill v Carbolic Smoke Ball Company* is a leading example.[61] A promise was made by the Carbolic Smoke Ball Company (to pay £100 to persons catching a cold after having used the smoke ball as directed) but Mrs Carlill, when she responded, did not make a promise in return. Nevertheless, a contract was created between them once she had done all that the company had asked for in return for its promise.

Whether a contract is bilateral or unilateral depends upon the intention of the parties; in particular, upon whether they understood the response elicited by the offeror's promise to be a reciprocal promise or not. For example, were O to say to A 'I will pay you $1,000 to paint my fence', A's response 'yes' is likely be understood as a promise to paint the fence and will, therefore, give rise to a bilateral contract. As a result, A could sue O if the latter did not pay the money once the fence had been painted and O could sue A if A did not paint it. On the other hand, were O to say to A 'I will pay you $1,000 to find my lost dog', A's response 'yes' is unlikely to be understood as a promise that A will find the dog. Whereas O *has* promised to pay the reward to A if A finds the dog, A has not made a reciprocal promise to do so. As a result, if A found the dog, A could sue O if O did not pay the reward; on the other hand, if A did not find the dog, or did not even try to do so, O could not sue A as A has not made a promise to this effect.

Although most contracts are bilateral, unilateral contracts are still not uncommon. They tend to be used when the offeror wishes to induce the offeree to behave in a certain way, but knows that the vagaries of the situation are such that the offeree is unlikely to respond by promising to do what the offeror seeks; offers of rewards (as in *Crown v Clarke*) and advertisements (as in *Carlill*) are examples.

Some of the key issues arising out of unilateral contracts include:

- What constitutes acceptance of the offer of a unilateral contract, when does this occur and does it have to be communicated?
- Is it possible for the offeror to revoke an offer after the offeree has commenced performing the acts requested in that offer?
- If an offer is revokable after the offeree commences performing the requested acts in an offer but before they are completed, does the offeree have any redress?

These issues were central to the following cases in which contrasting responses are given.

Errington v Errington

[1952] 1 All ER 149, English Court of Appeal

[A father bought a house for his son and daughter-in-law, financed through a mortgage taken out on the property. He promised them that if they made the payments due under this mortgage the house would be theirs upon his death. They

---

61 [1983] 1 QB 256 (extracted at p 30, above). See also *Crown v Clarke* (1927) 40 CLR 227.

did this and occupied the house. Nine years later, the father died leaving the house to his widow. After the couple separated, although the wife continued to occupy the house and pay the instalments, the widow sued for possession. Her claim failed at first instance and she appealed.]

Denning LJ [at 153]: It is to be noted that the couple never bound themselves to pay the instalments to the building society; and I see no reason why any such obligation should be implied. It is clear law that the court is not to imply a term unless it is necessary; and I do not see that it is necessary here. Ample content is given to the whole arrangement by holding that the father promised that the house should belong to the couple as soon as they paid off the mortgage. The parties did not discuss what was to happen if the couple failed to pay the instalments to the building society, but I should have thought it clear that, if they did fail to pay the instalments, the father would not be bound to transfer the house to them. The father's promise was a unilateral contract—a promise of the house in return for their act of paying the instalments. It could not be revoked by him once the couple entered on performance of the act, but it would cease to bind him if they left it incomplete and unperformed, which they have not done. If that was the position during the father's lifetime, so it must be after his death. If the daughter-in-law continues to pay all the building society instalments, the couple will be entitled to have the property transferred to them as soon as the mortgage is paid off; but if she does not do so, then the building society will claim the instalments from the father's estate and the estate will have to pay them. I cannot think that in those circumstances the estate would be bound to transfer the house to them, any more than the father himself would have been. …

Appeal dismissed

[Somervell and Hodson LJJ in separate judgments also dismissed the appeal but on other grounds.][62]

Mobil Oil Australia Ltd v Wellcome International Pty Ltd

(1998) 81 FCR 475, Federal Court of Australia (Full Court)

[At a convention held for its dealers Mobile represented that a dealer who performed at a prescribed level for six years would be given a franchise for a further nine years at no cost to the dealer (referred to as the 'nine-for-six offer'). Mobil later discontinued this scheme. In these proceedings a number of dealers claimed that Mobil's conduct amounted to a breach of contract, misleading conduct contrary to s 52 of the *Trade Practices Act 1974*, or constituted an estoppel. Some dealers

---

62 On very similar facts, in *Brackenbury v Hodgkin* 102 A 106 (1917) the same result was reached by the Supreme Court of Maine, relying on the same grounds as those advanced by Denning LJ. See also the cases relied upon by the trial judge in *Mobil Oil Australia v Wellcome International Pty Ltd* (extracted below) and *Knight v Seattle First National Bank* 589 P 2d 1279 (1979).

succeeded at first instance and Mobil appealed. The following extract covers only the contract claim.]

The Court [at 500]: A unilateral contract is one in which the act of acceptance of the offer is also an executed consideration for the promise offered. The act of acceptance called for by the offer, once completed by the offeree, leaves the contract executory only on the part of the offeror. A familiar illustration is the offer of a reward for the return of lost goods or for the provision of information. The supposed nine-for-six promise was the offer of a reward (nine years' free tenure) in return for an act (the attaining of 90 per cent or better in Circle of Excellence judgings over the six years 1992–1997).

A distinction must be recognised. In the case of some unilateral contracts, it may remain within the offeree's power unilaterally to complete the act of acceptance, and thereby to furnish the executed consideration sought, that is to say, without the necessity of cooperation by the offeror and even notwithstanding a purported revocation of the offer. An example is the furnishing of sought information by posting it in an envelope addressed in a particular way. There may also be a case (it is, perhaps, difficult to imagine one) in which the offeror may prevent the offeree from completing the act of acceptance, and thereby furnishing the executed consideration sought, yet the offer will be held not to have been revoked. In the present case, Mobil made it clear to its dealers that its supposed nine-for-six-offer was revoked. But, in addition, by terminating the system of Circle of Excellence judgings, it made it impossible for its dealers to complete the act of acceptance called for by that supposed offer. In the present section of these reasons, we address only the question whether Mobil effectively revoked its supposed offer. <501> ...

His Honour referred to discussions of the question whether an offeror of a promise for an act can effectively revoke the offer where performance of the act of acceptance has been embarked upon but not completed. He referred to *Cheshire & Fifoot The Law of Contract* (2nd Australian edition) at 137–139; Carter & Harland, *Contract Law in Australia* (3rd ed) at 67–69; *Abbott v Lance* (1860) Legge 1283; *Daulia Ltd v Four Millbank Nominees Ltd* [1978] 1 Ch 231; and *Veivers v Cordingley* [1989] 2 Qd R 278. He considered that the weight of authority was in favour of the proposition that,

> ' ... a person who makes an offer susceptible of acceptance by performance of an act, may not revoke that offer after the offeree has embarked upon performance of the act'.

While his Honour thought that there was some difference in the authorities as to the proper juristic basis of this proposition and that 'in a technical sense' he was not bound to follow the decisions to which he referred, he considered that he should follow them unless positively satisfied that they were wrong. He recorded that he was not so satisfied.

We would make several observations at the outset. It has been suggested to be unjust that an offeror should be at liberty to revoke the offer once performance of the act, which is at once the act of acceptance and the executed consideration, has commenced. This proposition is usually stated as if its truth were self-evident and universal. We do not think that it is either.

(a) The respective positions of offeror and offeree vary greatly from the case of one unilateral contract to another. The following factors illustrate:
  (i) The offeror may or may not know that the offeree has commenced performance;
  (ii) The offeree may or may not have an understanding that the offeror is at liberty to revoke and that any incomplete performance of the act of acceptance by the offeree will be at his or her risk;
  (iii) The notion of 'commencement of performance of the act of acceptance' or 'embarking upon the act of acceptance' is problematical and can lead to a result which is unjust to the offeror. <502> By reference to the facts of the present case, could it be suggested that attainment of ninety per cent in the first year or even perfect operation of a service station for a day, a week or a month, albeit by reference to the offer, represents a commencement of attainment of ninety per cent in all six years so as immediately to bind Mobil not to revoke?
  (iv) The act called for by the offer may be detrimental to the offeree, or of some benefit to the offeree as well as to the offeror, as in the present case;
  (v) Although the offeree is not obliged to perform, or to continue performing, the act of acceptance and is at liberty to cease performing at any time, *ex hypothesi*, the offeror remains bound, perhaps over a lengthy period as in the present case, to keep its offer open for completion of the act of acceptance, without knowing whether the offeree will choose to complete or not to complete that act;
  (vi) The circumstances of the particular case may or may not, by reference to conventional criteria, suggest that the parties intended that the offeror should not be at liberty to revoke once the offeree had performed the act of acceptance to some extent.
  (vii) We do not accept that it is universally unjust that an offeror be at liberty to revoke once the offeree has 'commenced' or 'embarked upon' performance of an act which is both the sought act of acceptance of the offer and the sought executed consideration for the promise.

(b) A juristic basis which has been suggested to support the general proposition is that of an implied ancillary unilateral contract by which the offeror promises not to revoke once the offeree commences the act of acceptance of the principal offer. But even if such an ancillary contract should be implied in all cases, it is one thing to say that there is a contractually binding promise not to revoke and another thing to say that a purported revocation will be ineffective. The normal remedy for a revocation in breach of the ancillary contract would be an award of damages, the amount of which would be assessed, no doubt, by reference to the prospect that the act of acceptance would have been completed, and, by the same act, the offered promise duly 'paid for'. No doubt it might be possible for the offeree to seek specific relief in the form of an injunction restraining the offeror from revoking the offer and from preventing the offeree from providing the executed consideration. In the present case, the franchisees did not seek orders that Mobil maintain its Circle of Excellence judgings and that it not act upon or implement its purported revocation. Perhaps no-one thought of doing so. Perhaps the view was taken that an application for such relief would probably fail. We make no comment as to the prospects of success which any such application would have enjoyed.

(c) It seems that the general undifferentiated proposition could produce unintended and unjust results. Assume that X made a public offer of payment for the collection and supply of information of a kind described in the offer; that A, B and C embark upon collecting the information; and that A supplies it to X. According to the general proposition, X is bound not to revoke the offer made to B and C, notwithstanding the inutility of their subsequently supplying to X the information that A has already provided. It may be replied that the terms of the offer would include an <503> implied qualification. But this very response bespeaks the inadequacy of a universal rule.

[The Court then considered the authorities relied upon by the trial judge and concluded at 506:]

For the reasons indicated earlier, we do not accept that there is a universal proposition that an offeror is not at liberty to revoke the offer once the offeree 'commences' or 'embarks upon' performance of the sought act of acceptance (being also the sought executed consideration for the offered promise). If and to the extent that any of the authorities to which we have referred say otherwise, we would respectfully disagree. In any event, even if it be assumed that an offeror has impliedly promised not to revoke in consideration of a commencement of performance of the act of acceptance, it would not follow that a purported revocation would be ineffective. On the contrary, in the absence of specific relief in respect of that promise, the offeror's revocation would be effective, although leaving the offeror liable in damages.

It should not be thought that the absence of a universal rule is unjust. In the circumstances of a particular case, it may be appropriate to find that the offeror has entered into an implied ancillary contract not to revoke, or that the offeror is estopped from falsifying an assumption, engendered by it, that the offeree will not be deprived of the chance of completing the act of acceptance.

We see no basis in the particular facts of the present case for concluding that Mobil should be taken to have offered to all those franchisees who would but commence or embark upon performing the prescribed act of acceptance of its principal offer (of a promise of nine-for-six), an ancillary promise not to revoke that offer.

[After considering other issues the Court allowed the appeal.]

8 Summary

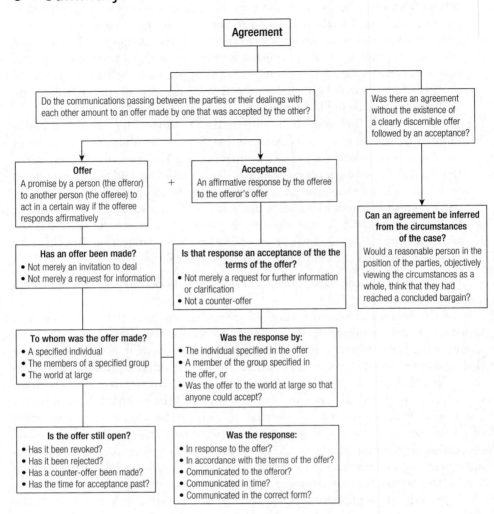

9 Questions

1. On 15 September, Olivia advertised her car for sale in the local newspaper for $15,000. In response to this advertisement, David inspected the car and having done so said to Olivia 'I want to buy the car and I am prepared pay for it in three instalments over the next three months.' Olivia replied that she 'would think about it'. However, later in the day, David posted a letter to Olivia saying that he wanted the car and could now pay for it immediately.

    While at work on the following day, David learnt from a friend that that Olivia had sold the car to Imogen for $16,000 early that morning. On 17 September Olivia received David's letter. Olivia still has possession of the car but both Imogen and David are now claiming ownership.

Please advise Olivia, Imogen and David about their contractual position in relation to the car.

2. Rhonda's distinctive fibreglass racing bike was stolen. In the hope of recovering the bike, she placed an advertisement in the local paper advertising a reward of $1,000 to anyone who found it and returned it to her. Bill, who had not seen the advertisement, discovered the bike abandoned on a piece of waste land and took it home. His wife, Libby, on seeing the bike, recognised it as the one for which the reward had been offered and showed Bill the advertisement. Bill immediately returned the bike to Rhonda. However, she refused to pay him the $1,000, saying that she no longer wanted the bike as her boyfriend, Chris, had purchased a new one for her as an engagement present.

Please advise Bill whether he or Libby has a contractual claim to the reward.

3. By email dated 10 June, Moriac Ltd offered to supply certain pine timber to Belmont Ltd for $10,000 and red gum for $50,000. Belmont Ltd decided to accept these offers late in June and an internal memorandum recorded this decision. However, due to an administrative error, its letter of acceptance relating to the pine timber was posted to the wrong address and it did not reach Moriac until 18 October. Similarly, an email it sent accepting the red gum was lost in transmission and was never received by Moriac. Not having heard from Belmont Ltd, Moriac sold the timber to another company.

Please advise Belmont whether it has a contract of sale with Moriac in relation to the pine, or in relation to the red gum.

CHAPTER 3

Certainty and Conditional Contracts

1	Introduction	86
2	Types of uncertainty	87
	a Vague or ambiguous terms	87
	b Illusory agreements	88
	c Incompleteness	91
	d Agreements to agree and agreements to negotiate	97
	e Agreements to negotiate in good faith to resolve a contractual dispute	101
3	Severance	103
4	Conditional contracts	104
	a Subject to contract	104
	b Subject to finance	106
5	Summary	112
6	Questions	112

1 Introduction

An agreement will not give rise to contractual rights and obligations unless it is sufficiently 'certain'—unless it is expressed with sufficient clarity to enable a court to determine the intention of the parties and give effect to that intention. As a result, an apparent agreement will fail on the ground that it is uncertain where:

- the terms of the agreement are too vague, or ambiguous, to show what the parties intended
- the agreement is illusory
- the agreement fails to deal with matters that are essential for agreements of its kind
- the agreement amounts to no more than an agreement to enter into an agreement in the future.

2 Types of uncertainty

a Vague or ambiguous terms

If the terms of an agreement are so vague, or ambiguous, that meaning cannot be given to them, the agreement will not be enforced. For example, in *Scammell v Ouston*,[1] the House of Lords held that in the particular circumstances, an agreement for the acquisition of a new lorry on 'hire purchase terms' was too vague to constitute a contract. Five possible meanings were attributed to these words and this ambiguity led their Lordships to conclude that 'no contract between the parties existed at all, notwithstanding that they may have thought otherwise'.[2]

However, the courts will seek to uphold agreements wherever possible, seeing it as their duty to resolve uncertainty and correct defects in the words used by the parties if, by doing so, they can give effect to a discernable common intention. This is especially so in the case of commercial agreements[3] and agreements that have been partly performed.[4] The devices used to do this include admitting extrinsic evidence, referring to custom, correcting clerical errors and importing standards of reasonableness. On the other hand, a court will not make a contract for the parties by constructing for them what they should have agreed to for themselves.[5] Some the key principles are discussed and applied in the following case.

The Council of the Upper Hunter County District v Australian Chilling and Freezing Co Ltd

(1967) 118 CLR 429, High Court of Australia

[The Council entered into a contract to supply the company with electricity. Clause 5 of this agreement provided that 'if the Supplier's costs shall vary in other respects than has been hereinbefore provided the Supplier shall have the right to vary the maximum demand charge and energy charge ...'. The council sought to increase its charges under clause 5; the company challenged its right to do so arguing that the clause, in particular a reference to 'supplier's costs' was void for uncertainty. The New South Wales Supreme Court agreed; the Council appealed to the High Court.]

Barwick CJ [at 436]: [A] contract of which there can be more than one possible meaning or which when construed can produce in its application more

---

1   [1941] 1 All ER 14.
2   See Lord Russell at [1941] 1 All ER 14 at 20.
3   See, for example, the observation of Viscount Maugham in *Scammell v Ouston* [1941] 1 All ER 14 at 16 that 'In commercial documents connected with dealings in a trade with which the parties are perfectly familiar, the court is very willing, if satisfied that the parties thought that they had made a binding contract, to imply terms, and, in particular, terms as to the method of carrying out the contract, which it would be impossible to supply in other kinds of contract.'
4   See *Foxtel Management Pty Ltd v Seven Cable Television Pty Ltd* (2000) 102 FCR 464 at 504.
5   See *Aotearoa International Ltd v Scancarriers A/S* [1985] 1 NZLR 513, esp at 556 (PC).

than one result is not therefore void for uncertainty. As long as it is capable of a meaning, it will ultimately bear that meaning which the courts, or in an appropriate case, an arbitrator, decides is its proper construction: and the court or arbitrator <437> will decide its application. The question becomes one of construction, of ascertaining the intention of the parties, and of applying it. Lord Tomlin's words in this connexion in *Hillas & Co Ltd v Arcos Ltd* (1932) 147 LT 503, at p 512 ought to be kept in mind. So long as the language employed by the parties, to use Lord Wright's words in *Scammell (G) & Nephew Ltd v Ouston* [1941] AC 251 is not 'so obscure and so incapable of any definite or precise meaning that the Court is unable to attribute to the parties any particular contractual intention', the contract cannot be held to be void or uncertain or meaningless. In search for that intention, no narrow or pedantic approach is warranted, particularly in the case of commercial arrangements. Thus will uncertainty of meaning, as distinct from absence of meaning or of intention, be resolved.

I do not think there is any uncertainty or for that matter ambiguity in the expression 'supplier's costs' in cl 5, however wide may be the area of possible disagreement as to its denotation in a particular case. A contract to build a bridge at cost could not, in my opinion, be held void for uncertainty: it could not properly, in my opinion, be said to be meaningless: nor is it, in my opinion, ambiguous. Endless might be the arguments pro and con as to whether or not in marginal cases some item of expenditure is as claimed a cost, or as to how much of an expenditure is a cost, of the particular activity. But to my mind, generally speaking, the concept of a cost of doing something is certain in the sense that it provides a criterion by reference to which the rights of the parties may ultimately and logically be worked out, if not by the parties then by the courts. There are no elements in the circumstances of this contract to deprive the concept of that certainty.

[McTiernan, Kitto and Windeyer JJ agreed with Barwick CJ; in a separate judgment Menzies J also agreed that clause 5 was not void.]

Appeal allowed

b Illusory agreements

An illusory agreement is one that makes the performance of a party's promises entirely a matter for that party's discretion. A stark example is provided by *Davis v General Foods Corp* 21 F Supp 445 (1937) in which General Foods agreed to buy services from Davis at a price 'solely within [its] discretion'. Such agreements are said to be void for uncertainty.

Biotechnology Australia Pty Ltd v Pace

(1988) 15 NSWLR 130, New South Wales Court of Appeal

[Pace entered into a contract of employment with Biotechnology which, *inter alia*, provided that he would have 'the option to participate in the company's senior staff equity sharing scheme'. No such scheme existed at the time and none had been finalised when Pace resigned several years later. Pace sued for breach of contract, alleging that Biotechnology had promised to establish a scheme that would give him the opportunity to acquire shares in the company. He succeeded at first instance and Biotechnology appealed.]

Kirby P [at 134]: *The legal principles applicable:* The case law on ambiguous, uncertain and illusory contracts is enormous. Some of it is difficult to reconcile because of the different ways in which judges have classified disputed terms, for example, as so illusory as to deny a contract at all or so ambiguous or uncertain as to deny enforcement of the contract, although clearly one was intended. Some commentators urge that it is essential to maintain a 'sharp distinction' between terms which are vague, uncertain or ambiguous and those which are illusory: see, eg, H K Lucke, 'Illusory, Vague and Uncertain Contractual Terms' (1977) 6 *Adel LR* 1 at 2. Others suggest that the concepts are interchangeable or at least merge into each other along a spectrum which begins with the vague, passes through the ambiguous, reaches the uncertain and finally disappears into the illusory. <135> In the High Court of Australia, Taylor and Owen JJ sought to explain the distinction between terms which are illusory and those which are real but uncertain. They do so in their joint judgment in *Placer Development Ltd v The Commonwealth* (1969) 121 CLR 353 at 359–360:

> '… a promise to pay an unspecified amount of money is not enforceable where it expressly appears that the amount to be paid is to rest in the discretion of the promisor and the deficiency is not remedied by a subsequent provision that the promisor will, in this discretion, fix the amount of the payment. Promises of this character are treated by Pollock (*Principles of Contract*, 12th ed (1946) pp 38, 39) not as vague and uncertain promises—for their meaning is only too clear—but as illusory promises […].'

Accepting, therefore, the distinction (but acknowledging that, at the margins, there will be legitimate differences of view about the legal classification to be applied in the particular case), the following general observations may be made about the task of classification required in cases of this sort:

(1) The determination of every case depends upon its own facts. The meaning of the agreement between the parties must be discovered objectively. Where there is suggested ambiguity or vagueness or where it is urged that a term is illusory, it may sometimes be both necessary and appropriate to have regard to extrinsic evidence in order to give meaning to that to which the parties have agreed: see, eg, *Kell v Harris* (1915) 15 SR (NSW) 473 at 479; 32 WN (NSW) 133 at 136 and *Raffles v Wichelhaus* (1864) 2 H & C 906; 159 ER 375.

(2) The court will endeavour to uphold the validity of the agreement between the parties: see *Hillas & Co Ltd v Arcos Ltd*. The court will attempt to avoid frustrating the wishes of the contracting parties so far as those wishes may be ascertained from the agreement between them: see *Meehan* (at 589); see also Barwick CJ in *Upper Hunter District Council v Australian Chilling and Freezing Co Ltd* (1968) 118 CLR 429 at 437 where his Honour said that:

'… In the search for that intention, no narrow or pedantic approach is warranted, particularly in the case of commercial arrangements.'

(3) But the court will not do so, where, in effect, it is asked to spell out, to an unacceptable extent, that to which the parties have themselves failed to agree. Nor will the court clarify that which is irremediably obscure. Most particularly, the court will not accept for itself a discretion which the parties have, by their agreement, reserved to one or other of them. To do so would not be to effect the contract but to change it: *Kofi-Sunkersette Obu v A Strauss & Co Ltd* [1951] AC 243 at 250 (PC).

(4) Views will differ about the classification of the challenged provision and whether the court can or cannot give effect to it. Usually, there is no objectively right decision in these cases. That fact is illustrated by the frequency with which there are strongly expressed differences of judicial opinion concerning whether the case falls on one side of the line or the other. … <136> …

(5) Nevertheless, the differences of result are not simply the result of differing judicial opinion based on nothing more than personal predilection. True, it is possible that being the willingness of courts to fashion with precision a term which the parties have failed or neglected to clarify could be analysed in terms of differing fundamental attitudes concerning the role of courts in disturbing the economic relations of contracting parties. I say no more of that. Alternatively, it has been suggested that the willingness of courts to give content to the expression 'subject to finance' in land title conveyancing transactions derives from the special nature of such transactions. In them, judges, familiar with the incidents of such contracts, feel confident that they can fill the gaps which the parties have left. In other cases, less familiar, they do not: see, eg, the comment by Professor KCT Sutton, 'Certainty of Contract' (1977) 7 *Qld Law Soc J* 5 at 11. However that may be, the court will pay regard to features of the agreement, of the relationship between the parties and of relevant external reference points in order to determine whether the term which is challenged can or cannot be sustained.

(6) Matters which have been considered relevant in the determination of these cases include the following:

    (a) The provision in question, although an essential terms, may be left in adequately clear terms to be settled by an identified third party who is given power to settle ambiguities and uncertainties: see, eg, *Foster v Wheeler* (1888) 38 Ch D 130 and *Axelsen v O'Brien* (1949) 80 CLR 219.

    (b) But even then, if the term is so vital that leaving it to one only of the parties unacceptably removes certainty in the arrangement, the court may or may not refuse to enforce it as illusory or unacceptably uncertain: contrast, eg, *May and Butcher Ltd v The King* [1934] 2 KB 17(n) and the comment of Gibbs J in *Godecke v Kirwan* (1973) 129 CLR 629 at 646–647.

    (c) Where there is a readily ascertainable external standard which is proved, the court will have regard to it in order to add flesh to the provision which, on its own, is unacceptably vague and uncertain or apparently illusory.

This is what happened in *Sweet & Maxwell Ltd v Universal News Services Ltd* [1964] 2 QB 699: see also *Meehan v Jones* (at 589).

(d) Where a contract provides a term containing a specified range of possibilities, a court, rather than avoiding the contract will hold the party to providing at least the minimum provision in the range, that is to say the one which is the most favourable to it. This is what occurred in *Lewandowski v Mead Carney-BCA Pty Ltd* [1973] 2 NSWLR 640 at 643. The contract had provided for the payment of a salary in the range of $7,000 to $9,000 per annum. This Court (Jacobs P; Hardie and Bowen JJA concurring) held that the effect of the agreement between the parties was to prescribe the minimum of $7,000 so that the contract was not void for uncertainty. ... <137> ...

The contract is illusory or its terms unenforceable: The problem for the Court is that the term is just too uncertain of content. It depends for fulfilment upon the decision of one party to the agreement only, namely the appellant. There is no external standard which can be appealed to in order to fix an 'appropriate' or 'reasonable' equity participation scheme, even assuming that to be what was intended or what the law would impute to the appellant. ...

If, however, contrary to my view, the promise was not illusory for these reasons, it was nonetheless void for uncertainty because the challenged term contained within it too many elements which are uncertain. How many shares in Biotech were to be devoted to the participation scheme? What class of shares were to be held by the senior scientists such as the respondent? What were to be the terms of the options upon the shares would issue? In any differentiation between employees, where would the respondent stand? What rights would attach to the shares? Upon what terms were they to be acquired and subject to what terms disposed of by employees? ... <138> ...

I am of the opinion that the promise of the appellant did not, in the words of Kitto J in *Placer* (at 357), create any contractual obligation to the respondent which he may enforce in a court of law. It was rather, in his Honour's words in *Thorby v Goldberg* (1964) 112 CLR 597 at 603, a provision for 'future arrangements' not a contract concluded before the parties. Alternatively, if it was a term of the contract, it was irredeemably vague and uncertain and so unenforceable.

[In a separate judgment McHugh JA reached the same conclusion as Kirby P; Hope JA dissented.]

Appeal allowed

c Incompleteness

An agreement will not be enforceable as a contract if it does not deal with all essential matters. What is essential for this purpose depends upon the nature of the agreement. For example, a lease agreement must specify the term of the lease[6]

---

6 See *Whitlock v Brew* (1968) 118 CLR 445.

and a contract for the sale of land must fix, in some way, the price to be paid.[7] On the other hand, fixing a price is not essential in contracts for the sale of goods as the various state and territory Sale of Goods Acts provide that, if the parties do not set the price, 'a reasonable price is to be paid'.[8] This requirement does not, however, mean that the agreement must finalise the matter immediately, or in great detail. Thus, according to Ipp J in *Anaconda Nickel Lt v Tarmoola Australia Pty Ltd* [2000] WASCA 27, 'It is well recognised that parties may enter into a valid contract containing a limited number of terms comprising those terms essential to the bargain that they wish to conclude, in the expectation that at a later date a further contract will be arrived at containing additional terms that would facilitate and clarify the initial contract. That is to say, a binding contract may be arrived at even though it leaves unresolved many matters which might arise in future.' It is also possible for the agreement to leave an essential matter for final determination in the future so long as this does not require any further agreement to be reached between the parties.

Goods Act 1958 (Vic)

Section 13

(1) The price in a contract of sale may be fixed by the contract or may be left to be fixed in manner thereby agreed or may be determined by the course of dealing between the parties.

(2) Where the price is not determined in accordance with the foregoing provisions the buyer must pay a reasonable price. What is a reasonable price is a question of fact dependent on the circumstances of each particular case.

Australia and New Zealand Banking Group Ltd v Frost Holdings Pty Ltd

[1989] VR 695, Victorian Full Court

[Frost submitted a proposal to the ANZ Bank for the production of calendars. This was accepted in principle, subject to certain changes. Subsequently, however, the bank advised Frost that it did not wish to proceed with the project. Frost claimed damages for breach of contract and succeeded at first instance. The bank appealed.]

Kaye J (with whom Marks and Teague JJ agreed) [at 700]: [On] 16 April there was no agreement between the parties upon essential terms of the plaintiff's proposals.

---

7   See *Hall v Busst* (1960) 104 CLR 206. According to Fullagar J at 222, there cannot be a binding contract for the sale of land unless three essential elements are agreed upon. They are 'the parties, the subject matter and the price'.

8   See *Sale of Goods Act 1923* s 13(2) (NSW); *Goods Act 1958* s 13(2) (Vic); *Sale of Goods Act 1896* s 11(2) (Qld); *Sale of Goods Act 1895* s 8(2) (SA); *Sale of Goods Act 1895* s 8(2) (WA); *Sale of Goods Act 1896* s 13(2) (Tas); *Sale of Goods Act 1954* s 13(2) (ACT); *Sale of Goods Act 1972* s 13(2) (NT).

'It is a first principle of the law of contracts that there can be no binding and enforceable obligation unless the terms of the bargain, or at least it's essential or critical terms, have been agreed upon. So, there is no concluded contract where an essential or critical term is expressly left to be settled by future agreement of the parties': per Sugarman J in the Full Court of the Supreme Court of New South Wales, quoted on appeal with approval by Menzies J in *Thorby v Goldberg* (1964) 112 CLR 597, at p 607. See also *May and Butcher Ltd v R* (HL) [1934] 2 KB 17, at p 20, per Lord Buckmaster and, at p 22, per Lord Warrington.

An agreement by a term of which a relevant or critical term will be the subject of future agreement between the parties is not enforceable. This general principle of the law of contract was stated by Viscount Dunedin in *May and Butcher Ltd v R*, at p 21 in the following passage: 'To be a good contract there must be a concluded bargain, and a concluded contract is one which settles everything that is necessary to be settled and leaves nothing <701> to be settled by agreement between the parties. Of course it may leave something which still has to be determined, but then that determination must be a determination which does not depend upon the agreement between the parties. In the system of law in which I was brought up, that was expressed by one of those brocards of which perhaps we have been too fond, but which often express very neatly what is wanted: '*Certum est quod certum reddi potest.*' Therefore, you may very well agree that a certain part of the contract of sale, such as price, may be settled by someone else. As a matter of the general law of contract all the essentials have to be settled. What are the essentials may vary according to the particular contract under consideration. We are here dealing with sale, and undoubtedly price is one of the essentials of sale, and if it is left still to be agreed between the parties, then there is no contract.' ...

No doubt the principle is founded on recognition that the parties might subsequently fail to agree upon the undecided term, and that in such event the agreement would fail for want of agreement concerning a relevant term. The situation is distinguished from a contract made by parties leaving an essential term to be agreed upon by them, and if they fail to agree the disputed term is to be determined by a third party or by arbitration. Such was the situation in *Foley v Classique Coaches Ltd* [1934] 2 KB 1, where a term of a supplemental agreement to an agreement for the sale of land provided that the purchasers would buy from the vendor, who was the proprietor of a petrol station situated on the land, all of his supplies of petrol from the vendor of the land at a price to be agreed upon by the parties from time to time. The supplemental agreement further provided that any dispute or difference about the subject matter or construction of the agreement should be submitted to arbitration. The judgments of both Scrutton LJ and Greer LJ, holding the supplemental agreement to be valid and binding on the purchasers, proceeded largely upon the existence of the arbitration clause in the supplemental agreement. Scrutton LJ, at p 10, stated that the arbitration clause applied to any failure of the parties to agree upon the price of petrol available for supply.

Greer LJ, at pp 11–12, distinguished the case before the court and *May & Butcher Ltd v R*. His Lordship expressed his view that to give effect to what the parties intended the court was justified in implying that, in the absence of agreement as to price, a reasonable price must be paid, and that if they failed to agree upon a reasonable price then arbitration must take place: see also *Booker Industries Pty Ltd v Wilson Parking (Qld) Pty Ltd* (1982) 149 CLR 600, at p 604; 43 ALR 68.

The amendment to para 5 of the statement of claim allowed by the trial judge was directed to overcome the absence of agreement on 16 April concerning the style, size, quality and price of the proposed calendar. The parties not having agreed to a term of their bargain in such effect, his <702> Honour implied into the agreement a term of an alternative price of 'a higher price as would be reasonable in the event that the defendant stipulated a larger or better quality calendar than was originally specified by the plaintiff'. However, the law does not permit a court to imply a term into a bargain between parties for the purposes of making their bargain an enforceable contract. Lord Roskill, delivering the judgment of the Privy Council in *Aotearoa International Ltd v Scancarriers A/S* [1985] 1 NZLR 513, at p 556, said: 'But the first question must always be whether any legally binding contract has been made, for until that issue is decided a Court cannot properly decide what extra terms, if any, must be implied into what is ex hypothesis a legally binding bargain, as being both necessary and reasonable to make that legally binding bargain work. It is not correct in principle, in order to determine whether there is a legally binding bargain, to add to those terms which alone the parties have expressed, further implied terms upon which they have not expressly agreed and then by adding the express terms and the implied terms together thereby create what would not otherwise be a legally binding bargain.'

It would seem that the learned trial judge, implying a term for payment of a reasonable price, relied upon the following statement of Fullagar J in *Hall v Busst* (1960) 104 CLR 206, at p 222: 'So far as contracts for the sale of goods are concerned, there may or may not be a general rule, applicable in respect of executory, as distinct from executed, contracts, that, where the price is not otherwise determined, a promise to pay a reasonable price is to be implied: ... But such a rule, if it exists, is anomalous.'

It is apparent from his statement that Fullagar J entertained doubt whether a term as to a reasonable price might be implied into an executory contract for the sale of goods. ...

Section 13 of the *Goods Act* 1958 contains provisions relating to ascertainment of a price under a contract of sale of goods where the parties had either reserved the fixing of the price or have made no provisions for it. ... <703> ...

The section is seen to be concerned with an existing contract of sale of goods, that is to say, the contract by which the parties have agreed upon all the essential contractual terms and obligations except for the price. The provisions of subs (2) for payment of a reasonable price are confined to an existing contract. It follows that if a term as to a reasonable price may be implied to an executory agreement, in my opinion, it may be implied only where the parties have reached agreement on all other essential contractual terms: see Sutton, *Sales and Consumer Law in Australia and New Zealand* (1983), pp 110–13.

In the present case the plaintiff and the defendant neither on 16 April nor at any material time thereafter reached agreement upon all the essential contractual terms of their bargain. In addition to the means of fixing the price per unit, they had not agreed upon matters of design, style, quality and size of paper, and content of the calendar, and the number of calendars to be supplied to the defendant. These were not merely specifications of the calendar. Apart from the quantity to be supplied, those were matters which constituted the subject matter of the negotiations. Differences about those matters were not capable of resolution by implication. ... <704> ...

In my opinion, therefore, the project of a calendar proposed by the plaintiff and the defendant's confirmed involvement in the project did not constitute a binding and enforceable agreement for the sale of calendars produced by the plaintiff.

Appeal allowed

Godecke v Kirwan

(1973) 129 CLR 629, High Court of Australia

[Godecke and Kirwan entered into a written agreement for the sale of land. Clause 6 of this agreement provided that if required to do so by Kirwan, Godecke would execute a further agreement 'containing the foregoing and such other covenants and conditions as [Kirwan's solicitors] may reasonably require'. Kirwan refused to proceed with the sale whereupon Godecke lodged a caveat over the land. Kirwan applied to have this removed and it was agreed that this application should determine the rights and obligations of the parties under the agreement. At first instance it was held that the agreement was not binding. Godecke appealed to the High Court.]

Walsh J [at 642]: It is clearly established that a binding agreement may be made which leaves some important matter, eg the price, to be settled by the decision of a third party. I agree with respect with the view of Bray CJ [in *Powell v Jones* [1968] SASR 394] that, subject to the qualifications to which he refers [1968] SASR at p 398, there is no reason in principle for holding that there cannot be any binding contract if some matter is left to be determined by one of the contracting parties.

In the present case the parties set out all the principal terms which were to govern the sale and purchase of the land and these included provisions which imposed by implication an obligation to execute a formal contract. There was also a promise by the purchaser to execute, if required to do so, a further agreement in accordance with cl 6. In my opinion, that clause should be construed as limited to permitting the insertion of covenants and conditions not inconsistent with those contained in the offer. It was limited also by the reference to the reasonableness of requiring the inclusion of the covenants and conditions. In my opinion this does not mean that anything may be required which in the opinion of the solicitors is reasonable. It means that what is required must be reasonable in an objective sense, and in case of <643> dispute this is a matter which the court can decide. Clause 6 does not mean that the purchaser is making an agreement to agree later upon additional provisions to govern the bargain. It means that he is agreeing presently to accept as part of the bargain such additional provisions, if any, as are required, provided that they satisfy the requirements of consistency with the other terms and of reasonableness to which I have referred. ...

For the foregoing reasons I am unable to agree with the view of the learned primary judge that this was a case in which all the terms of the contract had not been settled and which for that reason fell within the third class of the cases discussed in *Masters v Cameron* (1954) 91 CLR 353. I am of opinion that a binding agreement was made.

[Mason J agreed with Walsh J; in a separate judgment Gibbs also agreed that there was a binding contract.]

Appeal allowed

As noted above, the parties can leave essential matters to be determined in the future, so long as this does not require them to reach a further agreement between themselves. This can be done by including in their agreement 'formula' or 'mechanism' provisions that, when operated, will finalise the matter. Provisions of this nature can be structured so that they operate together (as when the agreement provides that prescribed machinery is to use a certain formula) or separately.

Formula

A formula provision is a provision designed to settle the content of an essential term without the need for further negotiation between the parties. For example, it has been held possible to leave the price to be determined by reference to a nominated price list[9] or the consumer price index.[10]

Machinery

A machinery provision is a mechanism agreed upon by the parties to resolve the precise content of a term sometime in the future. Such a device may be used, for example, when the parties do not know what would be appropriate at that time. Examples include nominating a particular person, or a designated officer holder, to fix the sale price of land,[11] or the rent to be paid upon the renewal of a lease.[12]

Where the parties have included a machinery provision in their agreement, problems may arise should it require their cooperation in the future and this is not forthcoming, or should it not work because, for example, the person nominated to fix the price refuses to do so. To deal with the first situation, courts in England[13] and

---

9   *Hillas & Co Ltd v Arcos Ltd* [1932] All ER Rep 494.
10 *Hely v Stirling* [1982] VR 246.
11 See *Hall v Busst* (1960) 104 CLR 206 at 222.
12 See *Booker Industries Pty Ltd v Wilson Parking (Qld) Pty Ltd* (1982) 149 CLR 600.
13 See *Sudbrook Trading Estate Ltd v Eggleton* [1982] 3 All ER 1 at 5.

Australia[14] have found that the parties are under an implied contractual obligation to cooperate with each other in order to enable a formula, or machinery provision, to operate. However, in relation to the second situation differing positions have been taken. In England, should a machinery provision not work, the courts are now willing to substitute their own machinery so that effect can be given to the agreement. Thus, for example, should an agreement for sale provide that the price is to be a reasonable price determined by a named person and that person declines to fix the price, the court will do so itself.[15] Australian courts, on the other hand have so far declined to intervene in this manner. According to Fullagar J in *Hall v Busst*,[16] 'if the named or described person dies or cannot or will not fix the price or value, the contract cannot, as a general rule, be enforced'. There are grounds for thinking, however, that a more interventionist approach may now be taken where the clear intention of the parties would otherwise be thwarted.

d Agreements to agree and agreements to negotiate

When the parties wish to extract a commitment from each other, but do not feel able to finalise the terms of a complete contract immediately, they may seek to enter into an 'agreement to agree' (an agreement to enter into an agreement in the future) or an 'agreement to negotiate' (an agreement to negotiate the terms of a contract in the future). The attitude of the courts to such agreements and to 'lock-out agreements' (not to deal with a third person for a specified time) is discussed in the following cases.

Coal Cliff Collieries Pty Ltd v Sijehama Pty Ltd

(1991) 24 NSWLR 1, New South Wales Court of Appeal

[In 1981, Coal Cliff and Bulli Main Colliery (of which Sijehama was the major shareholder) entered into a 'heads of agreement' for the joint development of coal mining rights owned by Bulli. This agreement envisaged the execution of a joint venture agreement between the parties. The parties failed to reach a final agreement and negotiations were terminated in October 1985. Sijehama alleged that this amounted to a breach of the heads of agreement for which damages could be recovered. It succeeded at first instance and Coal Cliff appealed.]

Kirby P [at 22]: I have already noted the basic law that courts will not enforce an agreement to agree. This is accepted by the High Court of Australia as part of the law of this country: see [*Booker Industries Pty Ltd v Wilson Parking (Qld) Pty Ltd* (1982) 149 CLR 600 at 604]. But that principle falls far short of resolving the

---

14 See *Booker Industries Pty Ltd v Wilson Parking (Qld) Pty Ltd* (1982) 149 CLR 600 at 605.
15 See *Sudbrook Trading Estate Ltd v Eggleton* [1982] 3 All ER 1. A similar position has been adopted in the United States: *Oglebay Norton Co v Armco Inc* 556 NE 2d 515 (1990).
16 (1960) 104 CLR 206, at 222. See also *Booker Industries Pty Ltd v Wilson Parking (Qld) Pty Ltd* (1982) 149 CLR 600 at 605.

issue presented by the present case upon which there is no clear binding authority of the High Court or of this Court.

The issue has arisen in England in a number of cases; but there have has [sic] been a conflict of dicta. In *Hillas & Co Ltd v Arcos Ltd* [1932] All ER Rep 494; 147 LT 503; 38 Com Cas 23, Lord Wright, in the House of Lords, observed (at 505–507; 515–517; 39–43):

> '... There is ... no bargain except to negotiate, and negotiations may be fruitless and end without any contract ensuing; yet even then, in strict theory, there is a contract (if there is good consideration) to negotiate, though in the event of repudiation by one party the damages may be nominal, unless a jury thinks that the opportunity to negotiate was of some appreciable value to the injured party ... <23> ...'

This 'flirtation' with the idea that, by construction, a negotiation contract could be treated as final and enforced according to its terms, was condemned by Lord Denning MR in [*Courtney & Fairbairn Ltd v Tolaini Brothers (Hotels) Ltd* [1975] 1 WLR 297]. Of Lord Wright's dictum, Lord Denning said (at 301; 720):

> 'That tentative opinion by Lord Wright does not seem to me to be well-founded. If the law does not recognise a contract to enter into a contract (when there is a fundamental term yet to be agreed) it seems to me it cannot recognise a contract to negotiate. The reason is because it is too uncertain to have any binding force. No court could estimate the damages because no-one could tell whether the negotiations would be successful or would fall through: or if successful what the result would be. It seems to me that a contract to negotiate, like a contract to enter into a contract, is not a contract known to the law.'

Lord Diplock, sitting in the Court of Appeal, agreed with Lord Denning and added (at 302; 720):

> 'I ... would only add my agreement that the dictum, for it is no more, of Lord Wright in *Hillas & Co Ltd v Arcos Ltd* ... to which Lord Denning MR has referred, though an attractive theory, should in my view be regarded as bad law.'

Courtney was applied in the English Court of Appeal in *Mallozzi v Carapelli SpA* [1976] 1 Lloyd's Rep 407. ...

[at 26]: From the foregoing it will, I hope, be clear that I do not share the opinion of the English Court of Appeal that no promise to negotiate in good faith would ever be enforced by a court. I reject the notion that such a contract is unknown to the law, whatever its term. I agree with Lord Wright's speech in *Hillas* that, provided there was consideration for the promise, in some circumstance a promise to negotiate in good faith will be enforceable, depending upon its precise terms. Likewise I agree with Pain J in *Donwin* [Crown Office List, 2 March 1984, unreported] that, so long as the promise is clear and part of an undoubted agreement between the parties, the courts will not adopt a general principle that relief for the breach of such promise must be withheld. It follows that in this regard I agree with the conclusion of Clarke J on the principle presented by the first issue before him—and now before this Court.

Nevertheless, alike with Goff LJ in *Mallozzi* and the substantial body of United States authority which has been cited in this case, I believe that the proper approach to be taken in each case depends upon the construction of the particular contract: see *Australia and New Zealand Banking Group Ltd v Frost Holdings Pty Ltd* [1989] VR 695; see note (1991) 65 ALJ 59. In many contracts it will be plain that the promise to negotiate is intended to be a binding legal obligation to which the parties should then be held. The clearest illustration of this class will be cases where an identified third party has given the power to settle ambiguities and uncertainties: see *Foster v Wheeler* (1888) LR 38 Ch D 130; *Axelsen v O'Brien* (1949) 80 CLR 219 and *Biotechnology* (at 136). But even in such cases, the court may regard the failure to reach agreement on a particular term as such that the agreement should be classed as illusory or unacceptably uncertain: *Godecke v Kirwan* <27> (at 646f) and *Whitlock v Brew* (1968) 118 CLR 445 at 456. In that event, the court will not enforce the arrangement.

In a small number of cases, by reference to a readily ascertainable external standard, the court may be able to add flesh to a provision which is otherwise unacceptably vague or uncertain or apparently illusory: see, eg, *Powell v Jones* [1968] SASR 394; *Sweet and Maxwell Ltd v Universal News Services Ltd* [1964] 2 QB 699; cf *Meehan v Jones* (1982) 149 CLR 571 at 589; *Jillcy Film Enterprises* (at 521); *Ridgeway Coal Co* (at 408).

Finally, in many cases, the promise to negotiate in good faith will occur in the context of an 'arrangement' (to use a neutral term) which by its nature, purpose, context, other provisions or otherwise makes it clear that 'the promise is too illusory or too vague and uncertain to be enforceable': see McHugh JA in *Biotechnology* (at 156) and *Adaras Development Ltd v Marcona Corporation* [1975] 1 NZLR 324 at 331.

In the present case, with every respect to Clarke J, I am of the opinion that this contract should be so classified. ... This was not a case where an external arbitrator was nominated to resolve outstanding differences. There were many such differences at the time of the heads of agreement and a number remain even three years later when negotiations were finally broken off. A court would be extremely ill-equipped to fill the remaining blank spaces and to resolve questions which three years of painful negotiation between the solicitors for the parties had failed to remove. A court could not, in this case, appeal to objective standards or to its own experience as it might in filling a blank space in a lease of domestic premises or a contract less complex and more familiar than one for a major mining development. At stake are commercial decisions involving adjustments which would contemplate binding the parties for years and deciding issues that lie well beyond the expertise of a court. How mining executives, attending to the interests of their corporation and its shareholders might act in negotiating such a complex transaction is quite unknowable. Therefore, although I agree with Clarke J that some contracts to negotiate in good faith may be enforced by our law, this was not such a contract.

[Waddell A-JA expressed general agreement with Kirby P; Handley JA agreed that the appeal should be allowed but in the course of doing so expressed the opinion that agreements to negotiate were not enforceable.][17]

Appeal allowed

Walford v Miles

[1992] 2 AC 128, House of Lords

[Mr and Mrs Miles agreed to negotiate with Walford for the sale of a photographic processing business and to terminate negotiations for the sale of the business to any other purchaser, provided they were furnished with a 'comfort letter' confirming that the financial resources needed to finalise the sale to Walford were available. This letter was provided and they ended negotiations with a third party. However, they subsequently decided not to proceed with negotiations with Walford and eventually sold the business to the third party. Walford sued for breach of contract and misrepresentation. He succeeded at first instance but this decision was reversed by the Court of Appeal. Walford then appealed to the House of Lords.]

Lord Ackner [at 139 on the issue of the validity of lock-out agreements]: I believe it helpful to make these observations about a so-called 'lock-out' agreement. There is clearly no reason in the English contract law why A, for good consideration, should not achieve an enforceable agreement whereby B, agrees for a specified period of time, not to negotiate with anyone except A in relation to the sale of his property. There are often good commercial reasons why A should desire to obtain such an agreement from B. B's property, which A contemplates purchasing, may be such as to require the expenditure of not inconsiderable time and money before A is in a position to assess what he is prepared to offer for its purchase or whether he wishes to make any offer at all. A may well consider that he is not prepared to run the risk of expending such time and money unless there is a worthwhile prospect, should he desire to make an offer to purchase, of B, not only then still owning the property, but of being prepared to consider his offer. A may wish to guard against the risk that, while he is investigating the wisdom of offering to buy B's property, B may have already disposed of it or, alternatively, may be so advanced in negotiations with a third party as to be unwilling or for all practical purposes unable, to negotiate with A. But I stress that this is a negative

---

17 In *United Group Rail Services Ltd v Rail Corporation New South Wales* [2009] NSWCA 177, this decision and the authorities preceding and following it, dealing with whether an agreement to negotiate in good faith is enforceable, were reviewed at length by Allsop P (with whom Ipp JA and Macfarlan JA agreed). His Honour concluded that (at 63) 'Kirby P's reasons are more persuasive than the competing authority' and that he agreed 'with the statements of principle by Kirby P' (at 67). However, as the case concerned an agreement to resolve a dispute in good faith (discussed below), it was not necessary to decide the matter. In *Kirkby v Turner* [2009] NSWCA 131, the parties and on that basis the Court of Appeal, assumed (at 31) that there 'is nothing inherently unenforceable' about an agreement to negotiate.

agreement—B by agreeing not to negotiate for this fixed period with a third party, locks himself out of such negotiations. He has in no legal sense locked himself into negotiations with A. What A has achieved is an exclusive opportunity for a fixed period, to try and come to terms with B, an opportunity for which he has, unless he makes his agreement under seal, to give good consideration.

[Lord Ackner concluded that the agreement in this case was an agreement to negotiate in good faith and that as such agreements were unenforceable the present appeal should be dismissed. In the course of his speech he approved of the decision in *Courtney & Fairbairn Lt v Tolaini Brothers (Hotels) Ltd* and disapproved of Lord Wright's dictum in *Hill & Co Ltd v Arcos Ltd*. The other members of the House of Lords concurred.]

Appeal dismissed

e   Agreements to negotiate in good faith to resolve a contractual dispute

A distinction has been drawn between an agreement to negotiate in good faith so as to finalise an agreement (the matter discussed in *Coal Cliff*, above) and an agreement in a concluded contract to negotiate in good faith should a dispute arise between the parties about its performance. In relation to the latter, Allsop P, speaking for the New South Wales Court of Appeal in *United Group Rail Services Ltd v Rail Corporation New South Wales* [2009] NSWCA 177 at 74 said:

> 'With respect to those who assert to the contrary, a promise to negotiate (that is to treat and discuss) genuinely and in good faith with a view to resolving claims to entitlement by reference to a known body of rights and obligations, in a manner that respects the respective contractual rights of the parties, giving due allowance for honest and genuinely held views about those pre-existing rights is not vague, illusory or uncertain. It may be comprised of wide notions difficult to falsify. However, a business person, an arbitrator or a judge may well be able to identify some conduct (if it exists) which departs from the contractual norm that the parties have agreed, even if doubt may attend other conduct. If business people are prepared in the exercise of their commercial judgment to constrain themselves by reference to express words that are broad and general, but which have sensible and ascribable meaning, the task of the Court is to give effect to, and not to impede, such solemn express contractual provisions. It may well be that it will be difficult, in any given case, to conclude that a party has not undertaken an honest and genuine attempt to settle a dispute exhibiting a fidelity to the existing bargain. In other cases, however, such a conclusion might be blindingly obvious. Uncertainty of proof, however, does not mean that this is not a real obligation with real content.'

INTERNATIONAL PERSPECTIVES

Indian Contract Act, 1872

Section 2. Interpretation …

(i) An agreement which is enforceable by law at the option of one or more of the parties thereto, but not at the option of the other or others, is a voidable contract.

Section 29. Agreements void for uncertainty

Agreements, the meaning of which is not certain, or capable of being made certain, are void.

Contract Law of the People's Republic of China, 1999

Article 61. Indeterminate Terms; Supplementary Agreement

If a term such as quality, price or remuneration, or place of performance etc was not prescribed or clearly prescribed, after the contract has taken effect, the parties may supplement it through agreement; if the parties fail to reach a supplementary agreement, such term shall be determined in accordance with the relevant provisions of the contract or in accordance with the relevant usage.

Article 62. Gap Filling

Where a relevant term of the contract was not clearly prescribed, and cannot be determined in accordance with Article 61 hereof, one of the following provisions applies:

(i) If quality requirement was not clearly prescribed, performance shall be in accordance with the state standard or industry standard; absent any state or industry standard, performance shall be in accordance with the customary standard or any particular standard consistent with the purpose of the contract;

(ii) If price or remuneration was not clearly prescribed, performance shall be in accordance with the prevailing market price at the place of performance at the time the contract was concluded, and if adoption of a price mandated by the government or based on government issued pricing guidelines is required by law, such requirement applies;

(iii) Where the place of performance was not clearly prescribed, if the obligation is payment of money, performance shall be at the place where the payee is located; if the obligation is delivery of immovable property, performance shall be at the place where the immovable property is located; for any other subject matter, performance shall be at the place where the obligor is located;

(iv) If the time of performance was not clearly prescribed, the obligor may perform, and the obligee may require performance, at any time, provided that the other party shall be given the time required for preparation;

(v) If the method of performance was not clearly prescribed, performance shall be rendered in a manner which is conducive to realizing the purpose of the contract;

(vi) If the party responsible for the expenses of performance was not clearly prescribed, the obligor shall bear the expense.

Article 63. Performance at Government Mandated Price

Where a contract is to be implemented at a price mandated by the government or based on government issued pricing guidelines, if the government adjusts the price during the prescribed period of delivery, the contract price shall be the price at the time of delivery. Where a party delays in delivering the subject matter, the original price applies if the price has increased, and the new price applies if the price has decreased. Where a party delays in taking delivery or making payment, the new price applies, if the price has increased, and the original price applies if the price has decreased.

3 Severance

If uncertainty afflicts only part of an agreement it may be possible to sever that part from the rest and leave the remainder enforceable. The circumstances in which this can occur are discussed in *Life Insurance Co of Australia Ltd v Phillips*.

Life Insurance Co of Australia Ltd v Phillips

(1925) 36 CLR 60, High Court of Australia

[Phillips purchased two life assurance polices from the company. These provided for payments to be made by the company on his death, or on a specified date, and gave him the right to a housing loan after his policy had been in operation for three years. After four years, Phillips sought to rescind the policies, or have them declared void, and recover the premiums he had paid. He failed at first instance but on appeal the Victorian Full Court held that the agreements were too vague to be enforced. The Company then appealed to the High Court.]

Knox CJ [at 71]: The next question is whether the policies are void for uncertainty. The argument for the respondent on this point was founded on the clause in each policy which provides for a loan of £500 after three <72> annual premiums shall have been paid. It was said that the words of that clause were so vague that the obligation which it was intended to impose on the Company could not be enforced. But, assuming this to be established, it does not necessarily follow that the whole agreement embodied in the policy is void. When a contract contains a number of stipulations one of which is void for uncertainty, the question whether the whole contract is void depends on the intention of the parties to be gathered from the instrument as a whole. If the contract be divisible, the part which is void may be separated from the rest and does not affect its validity. In this case I think it is clear that the stipulations contained in the contract are divisible. There is no uncertainty or ambiguity in the promise on the part of the Company that in consideration of the payment of the annual premiums it will on 5th February 1939, or on the death of the respondent if occurring before that date, pay to the respondent or his representatives, as the case may be, the sum of £500.

[In separate judgments Isaacs and Starke JJ agreed with the Chief Justice.]

Appeal allowed

4 Conditional contracts

An agreement may be entered into in terms that make it conditional in some manner upon the occurrence or non-occurrence of an event or other circumstance. In such cases, whether the parties are bound by the agreement before the event occurs (or does not occur) and if they are, the content of their obligations, depends upon the nature of the condition. This is determined by reference to the intention of the parties as disclosed by the language they have used. Common examples of conditional contracts are those that are made 'subject to contract' or 'subject to finance'. The following cases discuss the effects of such clauses; in particular, the extent to which the parties are bound before the condition is fulfilled and the nature of the obligations they impose, if any, to facilitate that event occurring.

a Subject to contract

Masters v Cameron

(1954) 91 CLR 353, High Court of Australia

[Cameron agreed to sell a farm to Masters. This agreement provided that the sale was 'subject to the preparation of a formal contract of sale which shall be acceptable to my solicitors on the above terms and conditions'. Subsequently, Masters refused to proceed with the sale and a dispute arose concerning his entitlement to a deposit he had paid. The outcome of this dispute depended upon whether there had been a binding agreement between the parties. At first instance it was decided that there was such an agreement and Masters' claim failed. He appealed to the High Court.]

Dixon CJ, McTiernan and Kitto JJ [at 360]: The first question in the appeal is whether, as *Wolff* J considered, this document on its true construction constitutes a binding contract between the respondent and the appellants, or only a record of terms upon which the signatories were agreed as a basis for the negotiation of a contract. Plainly enough they were agreed that there should be a sale and purchase, and the parties, the property, the price, and the date of possession were clearly settled between them. All the essentials of a contract are there; but whether there is a contract depends entirely upon the meaning and effect of the final sentence in that portion of the document which the appellant signed.

Where parties who have been in negotiation reach agreement upon terms of a contractual nature and also agree that the matter of their negotiation shall be dealt with by a formal contract, the case may belong to any of three classes. It may be one in which the parties have reached finality in arranging all the terms of their bargain and intend to be immediately bound to the performance of those terms, but at the same time propose to have the terms restated in a form which will be full or more precise but not different in effect. Or, secondly, it may be a case in which the parties have completely agreed upon all the terms of their bargain and intend no departure from or addition to that which their agreed terms express or imply, but nevertheless have made performance of one or more of the terms conditional upon the execution of a formal document. Or, thirdly, the case may be one in which the intention of the parties is not to make a concluded bargain at all, unless and until they execute a formal contract.

In each of the first two cases there is a binding contract: in the first case a contract binding the parties at once to perform the agreed terms whether the contemplated formal document comes into existence or not, and to join (if they have so agreed) in settling and executing the formal document; and in the second case a contract binding the parties to join in bringing the formal contract into existence and then to carry it into execution. Of these two cases the first is the more common. Throughout the decisions on this branch of the law the proposition is insisted upon which Lord <361> *Blackburn* expressed in *Rossiter v Miller* (1878) 3 App Cas 1124 when he said that the mere fact that the parties have expressly stipulated that there shall afterwards be a formal agreement prepared, embodying the terms, which shall be signed by the parties does not, by itself, show that they continue merely in negotiation. His Lordship proceeded: '... as soon as the fact is established of the final mutual assent of the parties so that those who draw up the formal agreement have not the power to vary the terms already settled, I think the contract is completed' (1878) 3 App Cas, at p 1151: see also *Sinclair, Scott & Co Ltd v Naughton* (1929) 43 CLR 310, at p 317. A case of the second class came before this Court in *Niesmann v Collingridge* (1921) 29 CLR 177 where all the essential terms of a contract had been agreed upon, and the only reference to the execution of a further document was in the term as to price, which stipulated that payment should be made 'on the signing of the contract'. *Rich and Starke JJ* observed (1921) 29 CLR, at pp 184, 185 that this did not make the signing of a contract a condition of agreement, but made it a condition of the obligation to pay, and carried a necessary implication that each party would sign a contract in accordance with the terms of agreement. Their Honours, agreeing with *Knox CJ*, held that there was no difficulty in decreeing specific performance of the agreement, 'and so compelling the performance of a stipulation of the agreement necessary to its carrying out and due completion' ((1921) 29 CLR, at p 185): see also *O'Brien v Dawson* ((1942) 66 CLR 18, at p 31).

Cases of the third class are fundamentally different. They are cases in which the terms of agreement are not intended to have, and therefore do not have, any binding effect of their own: *Governor & [Guardian] of the Poor of Kingston-upon-Hull v Petch* (1854) 10 Exch 610 [156 ER 583]. The parties may have so provided either because they have dealt only with major matters and contemplate that others will or may be regulated by provisions to be introduced into the formal document, as in *Summergreene v Parker* (1950) 80 CLR 304 or simply because they wish to reserve to themselves a right to withdraw at any time until the formal document is signed. ... <362> ...

So, as *Parker J* said in *Von Hatzfeldt-Wildenburg v Alexander* (1912) 1 Ch 284, at p 289 in such a case there is no enforceable contract, either because the condition is unfulfilled or because the law does not recognize a contract to enter into a contract.

The question depends upon the intention disclosed by the language the parties have employed, and no special form of words is essential to be used in order that there shall be no contract binding upon the parties before the execution of their agreement in its ultimate shape: *Farmer v Honan* (1919) 26 CLR 183. Nor is any formula, such as 'subject to contract', so intractable as always and necessarily to produce that result: cf *Filbay v Hounsell* (1896) 2 Ch 737. But the natural sense of such words was shown by the language of Lord *Westbury* when he said in *Chinnock v Marchioness of Ely* (1865) 4 De GJ & S 638 [46 ER 1066]: 'if to a proposal or offer an assent be given subject to a provision as to a contract, then the stipulation as to the contract is a term of the assent, and there is no agreement independent of that stipulation' (1865) 4 De GJ & S 638, at p 646 [46 ER, at p 1069]. ...

This being the natural meaning of 'subject to contract', 'subject to the preparation of a formal contract', and expressions <363> of similar import, it has been recognized throughout the cases on the topic that such words prima facie create an overriding condition, so that what has been agreed upon must be regarded as the intended basis for a future contract and not as constituting a contract.

[Their Honours concluded that there was nothing in the present transaction to displace this meaning being adopted here.]

Appeal allowed

b Subject to finance

It is very common for contracts for the purchase of residential property to provide that the transaction is 'subject to finance'. Generally speaking, such provisions are designed to enable a purchaser to withdraw from the transaction should they be unable to obtain the finance needed to pay the purchase price. Important issues arising from subject to finance clauses include:

- To what extent are the parties bound before finance is obtained? In particular, is the purchaser bound to seek finance, or can they allow the transaction to fail merely by not seeking a loan?

- What level of detail must be included about such matters as the amount to be borrowed, the source of the finance, the interest rate to be paid and the length of the loan, to prevent the provision being void for uncertainty?
- Can the provision be waived by either party without the consent of the other?

These issues are considered in the case below.

Meehan v Jones

(1982) 149 CLR 571, High Court of Australia

[Jones agreed to sell land to Meehan. This agreement contained a provision (condition 1(b)) which made the agreement subject to 'The Purchaser or his nominee receiving approval for finance on satisfactory terms and conditions in an amount sufficient to complete the purchase hereunder.' Before the date specified for this condition to be fulfilled, Jones purported to rescind the agreement on the ground that it was void for uncertainty. Jones then entered into a contract to sell the land to a third party. However, within the time allowed, Meehan informed Jones that the condition had been fulfilled. Meehan sued for specific performance. He failed at first instance and on appeal. He then appealed to the High Court.]

Gibbs CJ [at 578]: Of course it is obvious enough that every [subject to finance clause] must depend on the particular words of the contract in question, and that it is not profitable to compare with each other cases decided on different contractual provisions. However, it may be possible to state principles which will provide some guidance through the thicket of decisions.

When the words of a condition state that a contract is subject to finance, or to suitable finance, or to satisfactory finance, the question immediately arises whether the test which is required to be applied is a subjective or an objective one. On the one hand, the contract may be conditional upon the purchaser obtaining finance which he finds sufficient or satisfactory—such finance as he honestly thinks he needs to complete the purchase. On the other hand, the condition may be fulfilled if finance is available which the purchaser ought to find sufficient, or which ought reasonably to satisfy him, even though he honestly, but unreasonably, regards it as insufficient or unsatisfactory. The fact that opinions may differ as to which of these two meanings is given to the words of the clause does not mean that the clause is uncertain. If the Court, in construing the contract, can decide which of the two possible meanings is that which the parties intended, there will be no uncertainty. ...

If the words of the condition are understood to import a subjective test—if the condition is fulfilled if the purchaser honestly thinks that the finance is satisfactory—it is impossible in my opinion to regard the condition as uncertain. The question whether the purchaser does think the finance satisfactory is a simple question of fact. In most cases it will be a question easily answered; if the purchaser thinks the finance satisfactory, he will normally seek to complete the contract, whereas if he does not think it satisfactory, usually he will not attempt to complete. In any case, whether the purchaser is satisfied is simply a question of fact, because, to use the well known words of Bowen LJ, 'the state of a man's mind is as <579> much a fact as the state of his digestion' (*Edgington v Fitzmaurice* (1885) 29 ChD 459, at p 483). However if the test is purely subjective, the question will arise whether any binding agreement has been made at all. That is a question which I shall later discuss.

On the other hand, if the test is an objective one, and the question is whether the finance ought reasonably to be regarded as satisfactory, I should not have thought that the clause is too indefinite for the courts to be able to attribute any particular contractual intention to the parties. It is true that the condition may, as Holland J said in *Grime v Bartholomew* [1972] 2 NSWLR 827, at p 838, be 'silent as to amount, term of the loan, rate of interest, conditions of repayment, class of lender, secured or unsecured or form of security'. Nevertheless, a court which had evidence of the financial position of the purchaser, the amount required the complete the contract and the prevailing rates and conditions on which loans are made by various classes of lenders should not find it unduly difficult to decide what finance a reasonable man, in the position of the purchaser, would regard as satisfactory. … <580> …

It seems to me that unless a clause of this kind makes a clear indication to the contrary, its natural effect is to leave it to the purchaser to determine whether or not the available finance is suitable to his needs. A clause such as special condition 1 (b), which speaks of 'satisfactory terms and conditions', in its natural meaning requires that the purchaser be satisfied. A cautious purchaser might be satisfied only with finance which was repayable over a long term and at comparatively low rates of interest, whereas a more adventurous purchaser might wish to proceed with the sale even though the term of the loan was short and the rate of interest high. It would be strange if an adventurous purchaser, having obtained finance on terms which were satisfactory to him, but at which a reasonable man might cavil, could be told by the vendor that the sale would not proceed, although the vendor was to be paid out in full and would have no interest in the purchaser's financial situation thereafter. Equally it would hardly seem likely that the parties would intend that a purchaser should be bound to complete if he honestly regarded the terms and conditions on which finance was available as unsatisfactory, notwithstanding that a court might take a different view. The intention of such a clause in my opinion is to leave it to the purchaser himself to decide whether the terms and conditions on which finance is available are satisfactory. The <581> condition prevents a purchaser from being obliged to go through with a sale when he does not believe that he can raise the necessary funds. Such a condition is generally entirely for the protection of the purchaser, and it is the satisfaction of the purchaser, not that of some hypothetical reasonable man, that will satisfy the condition. No doubt it may be implied that the purchaser will act honestly in deciding whether or not he is satisfied. However, it does not seem to me necessary, in order to give business efficacy to a contract, that a condition should be implied that the purchaser will make reasonable efforts to obtain finance. The parties may expect that he will, but he does not contract to so do.

Although there is nothing uncertain about a clause which speaks of terms and conditions which satisfy the purchaser, the question nevertheless arises, when a contract is made conditional on such a clause, whether the contract is illusory. ... The submission on behalf of the respondents in the present case was that the condition left a discretion or option to the purchaser to decide whether he would carry out the contract and that the purported contract was therefore illusory. In my opinion that principle does not apply where the discretion or option of the contracting party relates, not to the performance of the contractual obligations themselves, but only to the fulfilment of a condition upon which the contract depends. ... <582> ... [In the case of a conditional agreement] There is a concluded agreement as to the terms of the contract which, if the condition is satisfied, leaves no discretion in either party as to whether he shall carry them out. Once the condition is fulfilled, within the time allowed by the contract for its fulfilment, the contract becomes completely binding.

It is clear that the condition in special condition 1 (b) is not a condition precedent to contract. Certain obligations under the contract attached immediately the contract was signed although the condition had not been fulfilled. For example, the provisions with regard to deposit, and with regard to the giving and answering of requisitions on title, became immediately effective. Whether the contract is described as a condition precedent to completion, or as a condition subsequent, seems largely a matter of words. ...

For these reasons, special condition 1 (b) effectively and certainly described a condition on whose fulfilment the obligation to complete the contract depended. Once approval was given by any lender for the making of a loan on terms and conditions regarded as satisfactory by the purchaser or his nominee the condition was fulfilled. Thereafter both the vendors and the purchaser were bound to complete.

Mason J [His honour agreed with Gibbs CJ that subject to finance clauses, such as the one in question, were not too uncertain to be enforced. In relation to other issues raised by such clauses, he made the following observations starting at 588]: Primarily the object of such a clause is to benefit or protect the purchaser (*Zieme v Gregory* [1963] VR 214 at pp 216, 222; *Barber v Crickett* [1958] NZLR 1057, at p 1058; *Beauchamp v Beauchamp* (1972) 32 DLR (3d) 693; affd (1974) 40 DLR (3d) 160), by ensuring that he is not under a binding obligation to complete if he is unable to obtain finance. Here there is nothing in the contract or other materials to suggest that the object of the clause was not to protect the purchaser, though there is the question whether the condition is exclusively for his benefit, a matter to be discussed later. The primary object of the condition being the protection of the purchaser, it is sensible to treat it as stipulating for finance that is satisfactory to the purchaser or his nominee, subject to an implied obligation that he will act honestly, or honestly and reasonably, in endeavouring to obtain finance and in deciding whether to accept or reject proposals for finance.

In general this is the view which has been taken in New Zealand. ... In New South Wales a contrary view has been taken. ... <589> ...

To say that a 'subject to finance' or 'subject to finance on satisfactory terms and conditions' clause denotes finance which is satisfactory to the purchaser is not to say that he has an absolute or unfettered right to decide what is satisfactory. To concede such a right would certainly serve the object of the clause in protecting him. But it would do so at the expense of the legitimate expectations of the vendor by enabling the purchaser to escape from the contract on a mere declaration that he could not obtain suitable finance. With some justification the vendor can claim that the agreement made by the parties is not an option but a binding contract which relieves the purchaser from performance only in the event that, acting honestly, or honestly and reasonably, he is unable to obtain suitable finance.

There is in this formulation no element of uncertainty—the courts are quite capable of deciding whether the purchaser is acting honestly and reasonably. The limitation that the purchaser must act honestly, or honestly and reasonably, takes the case out of the principle that: '… where words which by themselves constitute a promise are accompanied by words which show that the promisor is <590> to have a discretion or option as to whether he will carry out that which purports to be the promise, the result is that there is no contract on which an action can be brought.' … The judgment of the purchaser as to what constitutes finance on satisfactory terms is not an unfettered discretion—it must be reached honestly, or honestly and reasonably. …

In this case it is not necessary to decide whether the purchaser, in <591> deciding whether finance is on satisfactory terms, is bound to act honestly or whether he is also bound to act reasonably. The cases already mentioned appear to support the first rather than the second alternative. And there is some ground for thinking that the parties contemplated that the question was to be left to the honest judgment of the purchaser rather than to the judgment of a court as to whether the purchaser acted reasonably in the circumstances.

On the other hand, it has been said that a condition of this type imports an obligation or promise on the part of the purchaser to act honestly and reasonably. … The reasoning which underlies the decisions of this Court upholding the implication of an obligation on the part of a party to a contract to do all that was reasonable on his part to obtain a statutory consent applies with equal force here. …

Here the expressed intention of the parties was that the purchaser would obtain finance; his obtaining of finance on satisfactory terms was necessary to give the transaction its intended efficacy. The consequence would be that he had an obligation to do all that was reasonable on his part to obtain that finance. It would make for greater consistency to say that, if the purchaser is bound to act reasonably in seeking to obtain finance, he is bound to act reasonably as well as honestly in deciding whether the finance was satisfactory. So understood the special condition would preserve an even balance between the vendors and the purchaser. However, I have no need to decide the question. Here it makes no difference whether the purchaser was under an obligation to act honestly or honestly and reasonably in deciding whether the terms of an offer of finance were satisfactory.

Although the binding words of the special condition suggest that <592> its effect is to make the existence of the contract conditional, it is more sensible to regard the provision as one which provides for the determination of a valid and binding contract in the event that the purchaser or his nominee is unable to obtain approval for satisfactory finance on or before the appointed date. In accordance with the principle established in *New Zealand Shipping Co v Societe des Ateliers et Chantiers France* [1919] AC 1 and extended in *Suttor v Gundowda Pty Ltd* (1950) 81 CLR 418, at pp 440–442, each party has the right to avoid the contract on the non-performance of the condition, notwithstanding that non-performance may occur without default on the part of the purchaser, i.e. he may fail to procure finance despite every endeavour on his part. I say 'each party' because it seems to me that, although the primary object of the condition is to protect the purchaser, it is perhaps difficult to assert that the clause is for his benefit exclusively when it states that the result of non-performance is that the contract shall be null and void, rather than null and void at the option of the purchaser. I see no justification for implying a right of avoidance on the part of the purchaser alone. In other circumstances to make this implication would be to reach a one-sided interpretation, allowing the purchaser to keep the contract on foot, despite non-performance of the condition, but denying the vendor the right to avoid. Here the vendors were protected by the fixing of the date for completion and the making of time of the essence. Even so, there is no adequate basis for concluding that the special condition authorized the purchaser alone to terminate.

Whether the condition is to be described as precedent or subsequent is an artificial and theoretical question. In one sense performance of the condition or non-avoidance for breach of it is precedent to the right of a party to call for the performance of a contract. In another sense there is a valid and binding contract which may be determined for non-performance of the condition, and in this sense the condition is subsequent, not precedent.

For the reasons I have given special condition 1(b) is valid.

[In separate judgments: Murphy J agreed with the conclusions reached by Gibbs CJ and Wilson J agreed with Mason J. The fifth member of the Court, Aickin J died before judgment was delivered.]

INTERNATIONAL PERSPECTIVES

Contract Law of the People's Republic of China, 1999

Article 45. Conditions Precedent; Conditions Subsequent; Improper Impairment or Facilitation

The parties may prescribe that effectiveness of a contract be subject to certain conditions. A contract subject to a condition precedent becomes effective once such condition is satisfied. A contract subject to a condition subsequent is extinguished once such a condition is satisfied.

Where in order to further its own interests, a party improperly impaired the satisfaction of a condition, the condition is deemed to have been satisfied; where a party improperly facilitated the satisfaction of a condition, the condition is deemed not to have been satisfied.

Article 46. Contract Term

The parties may prescribe a term for a contract. A contract subject to a time of commencement becomes effective at such time. A contract subject to a time of expiration is extinguished at such a time.

5 Summary

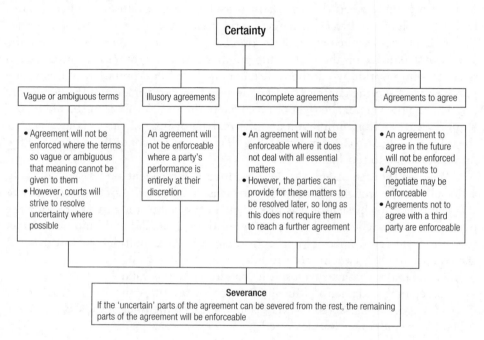

6 Questions

1. On November 2, Toby advertised his house for sale for $500,000. Later that day, an estate agent called at the house and gave him a document headed 'Offer to Purchase' under the terms of which Sophie stated that she offered to buy it $500,000 payable as follows: by a deposit of $50,000 to be paid on Toby's acceptance of the offer and by payment of the balance ($450,000) on or before 30 November, on which date possession of the house was to be given to Sophie. The offer was made subject to finance being arranged by the purchaser as follows: first mortgage for $250,000 at not more than 10% interest per annum and a second mortgage for the balance at not more than 12% interest per annum. The offer also stated that the price included all floor coverings and curtains in the house. At the foot of the document were printed the following words:

Acceptance of offer.
I hereby accept the above offer.
(Signature) ....

Toby signed in the space thus provided, but first wrote in, above his signature, 'provided that the purchase price is increased to $510,000 and that the floor coverings and curtains are not included in the sale'. Toby also added 'This acceptance is subject to my solicitor approving the purchaser's method of arranging finance for this sale.' The document was then sent to Sophie who wrote at the bottom 'I agree', signed her name and added the date. She then, via the agent, gave Toby a cheque for $50,000.

On November 14, Sophie telephoned Toby and told him that she had decided not to buy the house as she had received an overseas posting in Foreign Affairs, and requested the return of her $50,000. Toby replied that she could not act in this way and that he no longer required her method of financing the sale to be approved by his solicitor. However, Sophie insisted that she would not go on with the sale and demanded that Toby give back the $50,000 deposit. Toby has refused to do so.

Advise Sophie of her position in relation to this transaction.

2. On 1 March, Sheldon Ltd and Hardwick Ltd entered into a written agreement pursuant to which Sheldon leased commercial premises from Hardwick. The lease was for a term of three years, commencing on 25 March, at an annual rental of $100,000. Clause 48 of this agreement provides that at the end of the three-year term, Sheldon will have the option to purchase the property for its market value. Clause 50 provides that should any dispute arise between the parties they will meet and undertake genuine and good faith negotiations to resolve their differences.

On 15 March Hardwick informed Sheldon that it no longer wished to lease the premises as it had received from Frederick Ltd a very favourable offer to purchase the premises with vacant possession which it intends to accept.

Having made arrangements to move into the premises, Sheldon remains keen to enforce the lease. Please advise Sheldon whether it will be able to do so.

3. Brown is a breeder of stud rams and currently has a flock of 100 rams on her property just outside Hamilton. On 1 June, in urgent need of funds to repay a bank loan that would fall due on 30 June, she entered into an agreement with Black, negotiated over the telephone, to sell him her 'five best rams for their fair market value, delivery and payment on 25 June'. Black was keen to acquire these rams in order to expand his flocks of sheep and take advantage of improving wool prices. Unfortunately, however, Black suffered a farming accident on 15 June. As a result, he was no longer able to expand his flocks as planned. Therefore, he contacted Brown on 20 June and advised her that he no longer wished to purchase the rams.

Brown wishes to proceed with the sale as her need for the funds it will generate is now critical. Please advise her.

CHAPTER 4

Consideration

1	Introduction	114
2	The meaning of consideration	116
3	The nature of consideration	122
	a Consideration can be anything stipulated by the promisor	122
	b Consideration must be real but need not be as valuable as the promise	124
	c Consideration must be contemporaneous with the promise	126
	d Consideration must move from the promisee but it need not pass to the promisor	128
	e Performing an existing duty may be consideration	130
	f Part payment of a debt is not consideration for a promise to forego the balance	139
	g Settling a legal dispute or giving up a claim can be consideration	141
4	Criticism of the doctrine of consideration	145
5	Promissory estoppel	146
6	Summary	151
7	Questions	151

1   Introduction

A distinctive and controversial feature of the common law is the requirement that an agreement will amount to a contract only if the promises it contains were made in exchange for 'consideration'. To be enforceable, promises must be bargained for, rather than given gratuitously. As a result, a contractual relationship will not exist between two parties merely because they have reached an agreement, even though they intend that agreement to be legally binding and even though they may have acted upon it. There must also be consideration; without consideration their agreement is a *nudum pactum* and unenforceable as a contract. This contrasts with the position in most civil law jurisdictions[1] and in certain international regimes.[2]

There are two minor qualifications to this position; first, a promise contained in a deed is enforceable even though given without consideration. Such contracts are

---

1   For a recent example, see the *Contract Law of the People's Republic of China, 1999*, Article 2 of which defines a contract merely in terms of an agreement entered into for the purpose of establishing or altering the civil rights and obligations of the parties.

2   See, for example, Article 3.2 of the *Unidroit Principles of International Commercial Contracts 2004* which provides that 'a contract is concluded … by the mere agreement of the parties, without any further requirement'.

referred to as being 'formal'. A deed is a formal written document that is signed, sealed (or deemed to have been sealed) and delivered, and which is intended to operate as a deed.[3] Typically, the requirements for making a deed are now specified by statute[4] and merely recording an agreement in a signed document is not of itself sufficient to make that document a deed. Somewhat misleadingly, contracts not recorded in a deed and which, therefore, require consideration, are often referred to as being 'simple' or 'informal' even though they may be exceedingly complex and accompanied by considerable formality.

The second qualification arises from the operation of the doctrine of promissory estoppel which in Australia, since the decision of the High Court in *Waltons Stores (Interstate) Ltd v Maher*,[5] allows certain promises to be enforced where they have been relied upon and the circumstances are such that it would be unconscionable for the promisor to be able to renege on the promise. This doctrine is discussed in more detail below.

In this chapter we will examine:

- the meaning of consideration
- the nature of consideration
- criticisms of the doctrine of consideration
- the doctrine of promissory estoppel.

INTERNATIONAL PERSPECTIVES

The doctrine of consideration is given statutory force in Indian law and the provisions involved largely reflect the common law. However, as we shall see, there are some very important differences. Chinese law, on the other hand does not require consideration to be present for an agreement to have contractual force, though the requirements of fairness and good faith (dealt with in chapter 2) may, on occasion, fulfil a similar role by making gratuitous promises unenforceable.

Indian Contract Act, 1872

Section 10

All agreements are contracts if they are made ... for a lawful consideration ...

Section 25

An agreement made without consideration is void ...

A number of exceptions to the requirement of consideration are set out in s 25(1)–(3). However, these do not include agreements recorded as deeds and

---

3   For a discussion of this and the other requirements of a deed see *400 George Street (Qld) Pty Ltd & Ors v BG International Ltd* [2010] QSC 66 at 44–69.
4   See, for example, *Conveyancing Act 1919* (NSW), s 38(1) which provides that 'Every deed, whether or not affecting property, shall be signed as well as sealed, and shall be attested by at least one witness not being a party to the deed; but no particular form of words shall be requisite for the attestation.'
5   (1988) 164 CLR 387.

it has never been held that such agreements are enforceable in the absence of consideration.⁶ On the other hand there is a limited exception for agreements recorded in writing where it is 'registered under the law for the time being in force for the registration of documents and is made on account of natural love and affection between the parties in a near relation to each other': s 25(1).

There is no equivalent at common law which does not recognise natural love and affection as being valuable consideration.⁷

2 The meaning of consideration

What then is 'consideration'? The most satisfactory definition is that it is the price stipulated for the promise by the promisor;⁸ in other words, it is what the promisor asks the promisee to 'pay' in exchange for receiving the promise. 'Payment' can take any one of three forms: (i) performing an act; (ii) forbearing from performing an act; or more commonly (iii) promising to do something in return.

Examples

i A promises a reward of $100 to anyone who finds a lost dog. The act of finding the dog is the consideration stipulated for A's promise to pay the reward.

ii A promises to pay $100 if B stops smoking. Should B stop smoking, this act of forbearance is the consideration for A's promise to pay $100.

iii S offers to sell goods to B for $100 and B agrees to buy them. This is a typical sales transaction, the most common contract of all. Unlike examples (i) and (ii), it is bilateral as both parties have made a promise: S has promised to sell goods and B has promised to pay for them. Consequently, there must be two sets of consideration as follows:
- the consideration for S's promise to sell the goods is B's reciprocal promise to pay S $100;
- the consideration for B's promise to pay S $100 is S's reciprocal promise to deliver the goods.

There are two important points to note about the third transaction. First, as it is bilateral, when being analysed in terms of consideration, it is important to identify whose promise is in issue. That party will then become the relevant promisor and it will be the other (the promisee) who must have provided consideration. Second, in this transaction the consideration is the *promise* to pay $100, or deliver the goods, not the actual payment or delivery itself. Consequently, a contract is made as soon as B agrees to pay and S agrees to deliver, regardless of whether B or S eventually

---

6 See HK Saharay, *Dutt on Contract*, 10th edn, Eastern Law House, Kolkata, 2006.
7 See *Tweddle v Atkinson* [1861–73] All ER Rep 369, per Crompton J.
8 See *Dunlop Pneumatic Tyre Co Ltd v Selfridge and Co Ltd* [1915] AC 847 at 885, per Lord Dunedin. This definition has been criticised as being too vague and preference expressed for an analysis in terms of benefit and detriment: see AG Guest, *Chitty on Contracts*, 26th edn, Sweet & Maxwell, London, 1989, para 157.

perform their promises. The consideration involved is referred to as 'executory' because what the promisor asks for is yet to be performed. In contrast, in examples (i) and (ii) consideration is not provided until the act is actually performed, or the forbearance occurs. Such consideration is referred to as 'executed'.

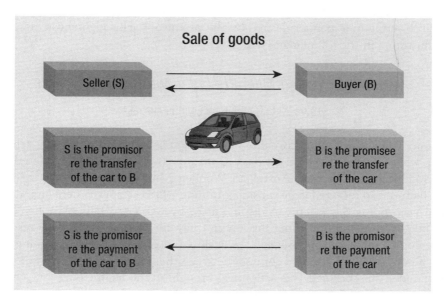

Consideration is also often referred to in terms of benefit and detriment—as something that is of benefit to the promisor, or a detriment to the promisee. In the above example: when S is the relevant promisor (promising to sell)—receiving the price is a benefit to S and paying it is a detriment to B. Conversely, when B is the relevant promisor (promising to buy)—receiving the goods is a benefit to B and parting with them is a detriment to S. Usually, as these examples show, consideration is simultaneously a benefit to the promisor and a detriment to the promisee. However, as we shall see later, this is not essential as the law allows the promisor to nominate that the consideration is to pass to a third party—in which case, while the promisee suffers a detriment the promisor receives no corresponding benefit.

Defining consideration as the 'price for a promise' has the advantage of drawing attention to three essential elements of consideration, namely:

- it must be something of value in the eye of the law
- it must be nominated by the promisor
- it must be given in exchange (often referred to as the *quid pro quo*) for the promise.

The last element is most important; consideration must be 'bargained for'; it cannot be thrust upon the promisor.[9] This significantly qualifies the analysis of

---

9 *Bogigian v Bogigian* 551 NE 2d 1149 (1990) is an illustration of an attempt to make a contract by thrusting consideration upon the promisor. Here, to secure his wife's agreement to release him from a court judgment worth $10,000, the defendant gave her $5. When, in an action brought on the judgment, the defendant sought to rely upon the agreement as a defence, the court held that it was not binding as the wife had not bargained for the $5.

consideration in terms of benefit and detriment: a detriment suffered by the promisee, or a benefit conferred on the promisor, will only amount to consideration if, expressly or by implication, it was requested by the promisor. Merely because the promisee suffered a detriment, or conferred a benefit, will not usually suffice, even though this happened because of the agreement and even though it involved the promisee acting in a manner desired by the promisor.[10] This element is discussed and illustrated in the following extracts.

Australian Woollen Mills Pty Ltd v The Commonwealth

(1954) 92 CLR 424, High Court of Australia

[In June 1946 the Commonwealth Government announced a subsidy scheme under which a subsidy would be paid to manufacturers for wool purchased and used for local manufacture. Australian Woollen Mills purchased wool for local manufacture and received large subsidies. In June 1948 the government announced that it was ending the scheme. A dispute arose between Australian Woollen Mills and the government concerning the amount payable to the former. This resulted in the company instituting proceedings against the Commonwealth, arguing that the scheme had given rise to a contract between them and that certain sums were owing under this contract. This action was brought in the High Court.]

The Court [at 456]: The contract put forward by the plaintiff is ... of that type which is commonly said to be constituted by an offer of a promise for an act, the offer being accepted by the doing of the act. ...

In cases of this class it is necessary, in order that a contract may be established, that it should be made to appear that the statement or announcement which is relied on as a promise was really offered as consideration for the doing of the act, and that the act was really done in consideration of a potential promise inherent in the statement or announcement. Between the statement or announcement, which is put forward as an offer capable of acceptance by the doing of an act, and the act which is put forward as the executed consideration for the alleged promise, there must subsist, so to speak, <457> the relation of a *quid pro quo*. One simple example will suffice to illustrate this. A, in Sydney, says to B in Melbourne: 'I will pay you £1,000 on your arrival in Sydney.' The next day B goes to Sydney. If these facts alone are proved, it is perfectly clear that no contract binding A to pay £1,000 to B is established. For all that appears there may be no relation whatever between A's statement and B's act. It is quite consistent with the facts proved that B intended to go to Sydney anyhow, and that A is merely announcing that, if and when B arrives in Sydney, he will make a gift to him. The necessary relation is not shown to exist between the announcement and the act. Proof of further facts, however, might suffice to establish a contract. For example, it might

---

10   See, for example, the discussion in *ATCO Controls Pty Ltd v Newtronics Pty Ltd* [2009] VSCA 238 at 62–69.

be proved that A, on the day before the £1,000 was mentioned, had told B that it was a matter of vital importance to him (A) that B should come to Sydney forthwith, and that B objected that to go to Sydney at the moment might involve him in financial loss. These further facts throw a different light on the statement on which B relies as an offer accepted by his going to Sydney. They are not necessarily conclusive but it is now possible to infer (a) that the statement that £1,000 would be paid to B on arrival in Sydney was intended as an offer of a promise, (b) that the promise was offered as the consideration for the doing of an act by B, and (c) that the doing of the act was at once the acceptance of an offer and the providing of an executed consideration for a promise. The necessary connection or relation between the announcement and the act is provided if the inference is drawn that A has requested B to go to Sydney.

[at 460] Coming to the present case, it is impossible, in our opinion, to hold that any contract was constituted at any stage binding the Commonwealth to pay a subsidy to the plaintiff, or to any manufacturer, in consideration of a purchase of wool for local manufacture. ... <461> ... No relation of *quid pro quo* between a promise and an act can be inferred. If we ask whether there was an implied request or invitation to purchase wool, we cannot say that there is. If we ask whether the announcement that a subsidy would be paid was made in order to induce the purchase of wool, no such intention can be inferred.

Judgment for the defendant

Beaton v McDivitt

(1987) 13 NSWLR 162, New South Wales Court of Appeal

[McDivitt (the respondent) owned a large block of land which he feared he would not be able to afford to keep when, as was likely, it was rezoned by the local council. With this in mind he promised to transfer part of the land to Beaton if he would move onto the land and cultivate it in a certain way. Beaton did this, building a house on the land and cultivating it as McDivitt had prescribed. After seven years a dispute arose between the parties and McDivitt ordered Beaton off the land. At first instance, Young J found that there was a contract between the parties but that it had been frustrated and Beaton was not entitled to stay on the land. Beaton appealed.]

Kirby P [at 168]: By our law, consideration is an essential requirement for an enforceable contract. Without consideration, a promise is unenforceable at law. The modern theory of consideration has arisen from the notion that a contract is a bargain struck between the parties by an exchange. By that modern theory, consideration must be satisfied in the form of a price in return for the promisor's promise or a quid pro quo. The price can be in the form of an act, forbearance or promise. In *Pollock on Contracts* (13th ed; 1950) p 133 Sir Frederick Pollock, in words adopted by Lord Dunedin in *Dunlop Pneumatic Tyre Co Ltd v Selfridge and*

Co Ltd [1915] AC 847, 855 expressed the idea of consideration as the 'price in return' in the following way:

> 'An act or forbearance of one party, or the promise thereof, is the price for which the promise of the other is bought, and the promise thus given for value is enforceable.'

The triumph of the bargain theory of consideration necessary for a contract amounts to a rejection of the theory of contractual obligation based upon reliance. …. Whatever the origins and explanations for this shift … it was necessary, thereafter, to have resort to Courts of Equity for the enforcement of claims based on relationships. For in the courts of law, duties arising from bargains entered between free parties were to be enforced, not duties deriving from suggested moral obligations.

The High Court of Australia [in *Australian Woollen Mills Pty Ltd v Commonwealth* (1954) 92 CLR 424, 456–457] has accepted this 'modern' or bargain doctrine of consideration. … <169> …

Young J (rightly in my opinion) was unable to find consideration in this sense in the facts of the present case. It is just not possible, however indulgently one approaches those facts with sympathy to the appellant, to classify the promises he made as a quid pro quo for the suggested promise of the respondent, in certain circumstances, to transfer title in the land to him.

McHugh JA [at 181]: In the United States the bargain theory has been extended to the point where nothing is regarded as consideration 'which is not regarded as such by both parties' (*Restatement, Contracts*, 2d, s 75(1)). English law has not gone so far (see Treitel, 'Consideration: A Critical Analysis of Professor Atiyah's Fundamental Restatement' (1976) 50 *ALJ* 439, 440). However, the essential elements of the bargain theory were adopted in *R v Clarke* and in *Australian Woollen Mills Pty Ltd v Commonwealth*.

The ratio decidendi of *Australian Woollen Mills Pty Ltd v Commonwealth* is that the expenditure of money in reliance on an announcement by the government that it would pay a subsidy to a manufacturer on wool purchased and used for local manufacture is not itself sufficient to create a contract to pay the subsidy. …

The reasoning of the High Court may not amount to an adoption of the extremes of the bargain theory of contract as understood in the United States. But the reasoning of the High Court in insisting on the necessity for a quid pro quo accepts the basic element of the bargain theory of consideration and amounts to a rejection of a reliance based theory of consideration.

[at 183]: In the present case, I think that the promise made by Mr McDivitt was an offer which was intended to give rise to an obligation on the part of himself and his wife upon the plaintiff coming and working on the land. …

The consideration for the transfer of the block was the act of the plaintiff in coming and working the block by means of organic farming at the request of the McDivitts. … <184> …

By entering onto lot B and performing work, the plaintiff had suffered sufficient detriment to constitute consideration even though he was obliged to work the land until the time of subdivision before he was entitled to the transfer of lot B (cf Treitel, *Law of Contract*, pp 115–116).

[Mahoney JA agreed with McHugh JA that a contract had been formed. However, he concluded that it had been frustrated and on this ground agreed with Kirby P that the appeal should be dismissed.]

Appeal dismissed

INTERNATIONAL PERSPECTIVES

The following definitions of consideration emphasise the requirement that to constitute consideration, the promisee's conduct must have been sought by the promisor. They also indicate that consideration can be any act or omission, or a reciprocal promise.

Restatement (2d) Contracts, American Law Institute, 1981

Section 71

(1) To constitute consideration, a performance or return promise must be bargained for.
(2) A performance or return promise is bargained for if it is sought by the promisor in exchange for his promise and is given by the promisee in exchange for that promise.
(3) The performance may consist of
    (a) an act other than a promise, or
    (b) a forbearance, or
    (c) the creation, modification, or destruction of a legal relation.

Indian Contract Act, 1872

Section 2(d)

When, at the desire of the promisor, the promisee or any other person has done or abstained from doing, or does or abstains from doing, or promises to do or abstains from doing, something, such an act or abstinence or promise is called consideration for the promise.

The *Restatement* expressly provides that the promisee's conduct must be 'bargained for' and it is this which explains some of the technical rules that make up the doctrine of consideration. The *Indian Contract Act*, on the other hand requires only that the promisee's conduct occur at 'the desire of the promisor'. It need not be bargained for. Thus, for example, if P asks A to perform a service and A does so, and later P promises to pay for it, the service would come within the definition of consideration and P's promise would be binding. This is quite different from the common law.

3 The nature of consideration

a Consideration can be anything stipulated by the promisor

It follows from the nature of consideration as something the promisor has bargained for that it may be anything stipulated by the promisor, expressly or by implication, that it is not illegal or illusory. This means that consideration can be things of real value to the promisor, or promisee, and things that are not. The nature of consideration as what the promisor has asked for in exchange for the promise is illustrated by the following cases.

Carlill v Carbolic Smoke Ball Company
[1893] 1 QB 256, English Court of Appeal

[The facts of this case are set out at page 30, above.]

Bowen LJ [at 270]: A further argument for the defendants was that this was a <271> *nudum pactum*—that there was no consideration for the promise—that taking the influenza was only a condition, and that the using the smoke ball was only a condition, and that there was no consideration at all; in fact, that there was no request, express or implied, to use the smoke ball. ... The short answer, ... is, it seems to me, that there is here a request to use involved in the offer. Then as to the alleged want of consideration. The definition of 'consideration' given in Selwyn's *Nisi Prius*, 8th ed p 47, which is cited and adopted by Tindal, CJ, in the case of *Laythoarp v Bryant* is this: 'Any act of the plaintiff from which the defendant derives a benefit or advantage, or any labour, detriment, or inconvenience sustained by the plaintiff, provided such act is performed or such inconvenience suffered by the plaintiff, with the consent, either express or implied, of the defendant.' Can it be said here that if the person who reads this advertisement applies thrice daily, for such time as may seem to him tolerable, the carbolic smoke ball to his nostrils for a whole fortnight, he is doing nothing at all—that it is a mere act which is not to count towards consideration to support a promise (for the law does not require us to measure the adequacy of the consideration). Inconvenience sustained by one party at the request of the other is enough to create a consideration. I think, therefore, that it is consideration enough that the plaintiff took the trouble of using the smoke ball. But I think also that the defendants received a benefit from this user, for the use of the smoke ball was contemplated by the defendants as being indirectly a benefit to them, because the use of the smoke balls would promote their sale.

[AL Smith and Lindley LLJ delivered separate judgments to the same effect.]
[footnotes omitted]

Chappell & Co Ltd v Nestle Co Ltd

[1960] AC 87, House of Lords

[To promote the sale of its chocolate, Nestle advertised that it would supply a gramophone record to anyone who sent it a sum of money and three chocolate wrappers. In connection with a copyright dispute over the record, the question arose as to whether the wrappers formed part of the consideration for its sale.]

Lord Somervell [at 114]: The question, then, is whether the three wrappers were part of the consideration or, as Jenkins LJ held, a condition of making the purchase, like a ticket entitling a member to buy at a co-operative store.

I think they are part of the consideration. They are so described in the offer. 'They,' the wrappers, 'will help you to get smash hit recordings.' They are so described in the record itself: 'all you have to do to get such a new record is to send three wrappers from Nestle's 6d milk chocolate bars, together with postal order for 1s 6d'. This is not conclusive but, however described, they are in my view, in law part of the consideration. It is said that when received the wrappers are of no value to Nestle's. This I would have thought irrelevant. A contracting party can stipulate for what consideration he chooses. A peppercorn does not cease to be good consideration if it is established that the promisee does not like pepper and will throw away the corn. As the whole object of selling the <115> record, if it was a sale, was to increase the sales of chocolate, it seems to me wrong not to treat the stipulated evidence of such sales as part of the consideration.

Dunton v Dunton

(1892) 18 VLR 114, Victorian Full Court

[Mr Dunton agreed to pay maintenance to his former wife, Mrs Dunton, so long as she shall 'conduct herself with sobriety, and in a respectable, orderly, and virtuous manner'. When Mr Dunton did not pay the maintenance, Mrs Dunton sought to enforce the agreement. This raised the issue of whether there was consideration for his promise.]

Higinbotham CJ [at 118]: I am of opinion that this agreement is binding, and that it is not *nudum pactum*, or void for want of consideration. It has been contended for the defendant that the written agreement discloses no consideration for the defendant's promise to pay the plaintiff 6*l*. per month, that his promise therefore was a purely voluntary one, and performance of it cannot be enforced by action. The agreement was signed by the plaintiff. The terms of it clearly imply, in my opinion, a promise on her part that she will conduct herself with sobriety, and in a respectable, orderly, and virtuous manner. But <119> it was said that this was only a promise to do that which the plaintiff was already bound to do, and that such a promise does not constitute a good consideration. It is true that if a person promises not to do something which he cannot lawfully do, and which, if done, would be either a legal wrong to the promisee, or an act forbidden by law, such promise is no consideration for the promise of the other party to the alleged contract founded on mutual promises. The case of *Jamieson v Renwick* [17 VLR 124] and the authorities there cited, support that rule. But they also show that a promise not to do, or to do something which the promisor may lawfully and without wrong to the promisee do or abstain from doing, is a good consideration. In the present case the plaintiff was released by the decree for the dissolution of marriage from her conjugal obligation to the defendant to conduct herself with sobriety, and in a respectable, orderly, and virtuous manner; and conduct of an opposite character would not necessarily involve a breach on her part of any human law other than the law of marriage, which had ceased to bind her. She was legally at liberty, so far as the defendant was concerned, to conduct herself in these respects as she might think fit, and her promise to surrender her liberty and to conduct herself in the manner desired by the defendant constituted, in my opinion, a good consideration for his promise to pay her the stipulated amount.

[In a separate judgment, Williams J agreed; Hood J dissented on the ground that there was no implied promise by Mrs Dunton and that even if there was, it was too uncertain.][11]

b   Consideration must be real but need not be as valuable as the promise

Consideration must be real in the sense of not being illusory. However, as the peppercorn example given by Lord Sommervell in *Chappell & Co Ltd v Nestle Co Ltd* illustrates, it need not be of substantial commercial value. In particular, it need not be comparable to the promise. Thus, something that is insignificant can still be good consideration for a very valuable promise. However, where there is a disparity between the two, it may indicate that the contract is voidable because of some form of misconduct on the part of the promisee,[12] or that there was no contract at all because what is relied upon as consideration was not really intended as the price for the promise.[13]

---

11   In a similar vein, see *Hamer v Sidway* 124 NY 538 (1891) in which an uncle's promise to pay his nephew $5,000 if he gave up drinking, smoking, swearing and gambling until he was 21 was held to be enforceable. The nephew's forbearance from lawful activity was held to amount to consideration; it was what the uncle had bargained for in exchange for his promise.

12   For example, duress, undue influence, unconscionable or misleading conduct. *Jackson v Seymour* 71 SE 2d 181 (1952) illustrates the vigilance of the courts where such conduct may explain the inadequacy of consideration. Here, the defendant purchased land from his sister and shortly thereafter cut and marketed timber from the land valued at ten times what he had paid her. In setting this agreement aside, the court noted that (at 185) 'where inadequacy of price is such as to shock conscience equity is alert to seize upon the slightest circumstances indicative of fraud, either actual or constructive'. Compare *Batsakis v Demotsis* 226 SW 2d 673 (1949) in which payment of approximately $25 was held to be good consideration for a promise to pay $2,000 as the promisor got exactly what she bargained for.

13   *Bogigian v Bogigian* 551 NE 2d 1149 (1990), outlined above at p 117, fn 9, is an example.

Biotechnology Australia Pty Ltd v Pace

(1988) 15 NSWLR 130, New South Wales Court of Appeal

[The facts of this case are set out above at page 88. The following extract deals only with the issue of consideration.]

McHugh JA [at 150]: *Was the consideration illusory?* A contract made for a consideration which is illusory is unenforceable: *Placer Development Ltd v The Commonwealth* (1969) 121 CLR 353 at 356, <151> 360–361 and *Meehan v Jones* (1982) 149 CLR 571 at 581. A consideration is illusory if its payment or fulfilment depends upon an unfettered discretion vested in the promisor. Thus a promise by the Commonwealth that it will pay a subsidy 'of an amount or at a rate determined by the Commonwealth from time to time' is an illusory consideration: *Placer Development Ltd v The Commonwealth*. So is a promise that any services rendered by a person would 'be taken into consideration, and such remuneration be made as should be deemed right': *Taylor v Brewer* (1813) 1 M & S 290; 105 ER 108. Likewise the consideration is illusory where an employer promises to pay 'such sum of money as I may deem right as compensation for labour done': *Roberts v Smith* (1859) 4 H & N 315; 157 ER 861. The decision of the Privy Council in *Kofi-Sunkersette Obu v A Strauss & Co Ltd* [1951] AC 243 is also an illustration of an illusory consideration. The agreement between the parties provided that a 'commission is also to be paid to me by the company which I have agreed to leave to the discretion of the company'. The Judicial Committee said (at 250) that the court could not determine the basis and rate of the commission. 'To do so would involve not only making a new agreement for the parties but varying the existing agreement by transferring to the court the exercise of the discretion vested' in the company.

In all these cases, there was an express or implied statement that the consideration was payable only if the promisor elected to do so. However, in the case of a commercial or employment agreement under which the promisee provides services, the proper conclusion ordinarily to be drawn is that the services or consideration were not intended to be performed gratuitously: cf *Way v Latillar* [1937] 3 All ER 759 at 763. In the absence of express words or necessary implication, it will be proper to conclude that the services were to be paid for by reference to some standard of measurement. The usual standard is that of reasonable remuneration based on market or industry criteria. Where there is a firm promise to pay or remunerate the promisee in return for his services, a conclusion that the consideration was illusory will only be drawn where no standard exists by which the promise can be valued. But even when no objective criterion of measurements is available, it may still be possible to infer a promise to act honestly and/or reasonably. Moreover, notwithstanding that the promisor retains a discretion, the consideration will not be illusory if the discretion must be exercised within specified parameters. In *Lewandowski v Mead Carney-BCA Pty Ltd* [1973] 2 NSWLR 640, this Court held that a promise to pay 'a salary within a range of $7,000–$9,000 per annum' was not illusory. The promise imported an obligation to pay a minimum salary of $7,000 per annum. In *Thorby v Goldberg*

(1964) 112 CLR 597, the High Court held that a contract was made although one party was given 'considerable discretion' as to how it carried out its obligations. Kitto J said (at 605) that 'an agreement is not void for uncertainty because it leaves one party or group of parties a latitude of choice as to the manner in which agreed stipulations shall be carried into effect, nor does it for that reason fall short of being a concluded contract'. ...

[His Honour concluded on the facts that the consideration was illusory as its content was solely at the discretion of Biotech and there were no objective standards available to limit that discretion to some minimum.]

c Consideration must be contemporaneous with the promise

It follows from the requirement that consideration must be bargained for that, to be effective, what is asserted to be consideration must be given in return for the promise. Therefore, an act, promise or forbearance cannot amount to consideration if it occurred before the promise was given—often expressed as the proposition that 'past consideration cannot be good consideration'. Similarly, something done, or promised, independently of the promise in question cannot be consideration for it.

Roscorla v Thomas

(1842) 3 QB 234, Court of Queen's Bench

[The parties entered into a contract for the sale of a horse. After it was concluded, the seller promised the purchaser that the horse was 'sound and free from vice'. Subsequently, the purchaser alleged that this was not correct and sued for breach of contract. The purchaser succeeded at first instance. However, the seller appealed on the ground that no consideration was provided for the promise.]

Lord Denman CJ for the Court [at 236]: It may be taken as a general rule, subject to excep-<237>-tions not applicable to this case, that the promise must be coextensive with the consideration. In the present case, the only promise that would result from the consideration, as stated, and be coextensive with it, would be to deliver the horse upon request. The precedent sale, without warranty, though at the request of the defendant, imposes no other duty or obligation upon him. It is clear, therefore, that the consideration stated would not raise an implied promise by the defendant that the horse was sound or free from vice.

[The Court went on to conclude that for the same reason, the alleged consideration would not support an express promise.]

Harrington v Taylor

36 SE 2d 227 (1945), Supreme Court of North Carolina

The Court [at 227]: The defendant had assaulted his wife, who took refuge in plaintiff's house. The next day the defendant gained access to the house and began another assault upon his wife. The defendant's wife knocked him down with an axe, and was on the point of cutting his head open or decapitating him while he was laying on the floor, and the plaintiff intervened, caught the axe as it was descending, and the blow intended for defendant fell upon her hand, mutilating it badly, but saving the defendant's life.

Subsequently, the defendant orally promised to pay the plaintiff her damages; but, after paying a small sum, failed to pay anything more.

The question presented is whether there was consideration recognised by our law as sufficient to support the promise. The Court is of the opinion that, however much the defendant should be impelled by common gratitude to alleviate the plaintiff's misfortune, a humanitarian act of this kind, voluntarily performed, is not such consideration as would entitle her to recover by law.

[The decision at first instance dismissing the claim was affirmed.]

There are a number of exceptions to the general rule that past consideration cannot be good consideration. These are:

- A service performed in the past may be good consideration for a subsequent promise to pay for that service if it was performed at the promisor's request and it was understood that it would be paid for.[14]
- A debt incurred by an infant may be good consideration for a promise to pay made after the person has become an adult.[15]
- A statute barred debt may be good consideration for a subsequent promise to pay the amount owed.[16] The revival of liability for such debts more generally is governed by the Limitation Acts in each state and territory.
- A technical exception is created by s 32 of the *Bills of Exchange Act 1909* (Cth) which provides that an antecedent debt or liability can be good consideration for a bill of exchange.

Pao On v Lau Yiu Long

[1980] AC 615, Privy Council on appeal from Hong Kong

[In February 1973 Pao On agreed to sell shares to Fu Chip, a public company controlled by Long as the majority shareholder, in consideration for shares issued in that company. To protect the value of the shares in Fu Chip, Pao On and Fu Chip agreed that the former would retain 60% of the shares so acquired until April 1974. In April 1973, Pao On refused to proceed with the sale unless Long agreed to indemnify him against the value of the shares he retained falling below a certain sum. Long agreed to this demand because of fear that delay caused by litigation would threaten public confidence in the company. The sale proceeded and some

---

14 See *In Re Casey's Patents; Stewart v Casey* (1892) 1 Ch 104 and *Pao On v Lau Yiu Long* [1980] AC 615.
15 See *Ball v Hesketh* (1697) 90 ER 541.
16 See *Buckwell v Commercial Banking Co of Sydney Ltd* (1937) 58 CLR 155, esp 163–165.

time later Pao On sought to enforce the indemnity. Having failed in the Hong Kong Court of Appeal, he appealed to the Privy Council.]

Lord Scarman for the Board [at 629]: The Board agrees ... that the consideration expressly stated in the written guarantee is sufficient in law to support the defendants' promise of indemnity. An act done before the giving of a promise to make a payment or to confer some other benefit can sometimes be consideration for the promise. The act must have been done at the promisors' request: the parties must have understood that the act was to be remunerated either by a payment or the conferment of some other benefit: and payment, or the conferment of a benefit, must have been legally enforceable had it been promised in advance. All three features are present in this case. The promise given to Fu Chip under the main agreement not to sell the shares for a year was at the first defendant's request. The parties understood at the time of the main agreement that the restriction on selling must be compensated for by the benefit of a guarantee against a drop in price: and such a guarantee would be legally enforceable.

[The Board advised that the appeal be allowed. Other aspects of its opinion concerning consideration are extracted below.]

d Consideration must move from the promisee but it need not pass to the promisor

The promisee must provide the consideration stipulated by the promisor. It is not sufficient for this to pass to the promisor from some other source. On the other hand, the terms of the promise may stipulate that the consideration pass to a third party, rather than to the promisor. Expressed in terms of benefit and detriment, the promisee must suffer a detriment; it is not essential for the promisor to receive a benefit.

Examples

i   S promises B to deliver goods to B if B pays S $100. This is the most common situation and involves the $100 passing from the promisee to the promisor. That sum is good consideration as it passes from the promisee.

ii S promises B to deliver goods to B if A pays S $100. The sum of $100, even if paid to S, is not good consideration as it has passed from A and not from the promisee (B).

iii S promises B to deliver goods to B if B pays A $100. The sum of $100 is good consideration as it passes from the promisee (B) even though it does not go to the promisor (S).

iv S promises B and A to deliver goods to them if B pays S $100. In this case as B and A are joint promisees, A can enforce the promise.

The fourth situation is an important gloss on the principal rule. It was established for Australia in the following case.

Coulls v Bagot's Executor & Trustee Co Ltd
(1967) 119 CLR 460, High Court of Australia

[Mr Coulls (the deceased) entered into an agreement with O'Neil Construction giving the latter the right to quarry part of his land. The company was authorised to pay royalties to Mr Coulls and his wife as joint tenants. O'Neil and Mr and Mrs Coulls signed the document evidencing this agreement. After Mr Coulls' death, his executor (Bagot's) sought a determination of whether O'Neil was bound to pay the royalties under the agreement to his estate or to Mrs Coulls. In the High Court, a majority (McTiernan, Taylor and Owen JJ) decided that, as a matter of construction, the agreement constituted a contract between O'Neil and Mr Coulls alone so that the royalties were payable to his estate and not Mrs Coulls. Barwick CJ and Windeyer J dissented, concluding that Mrs Coulls was a party to the contract. On the issues of privity and consideration, however, Windeyer, Taylor and Owen JJ gave separate judgments to the same effect as Barwick CJ.]

Barwick CJ [at 478]: [A]s I construe this writing, we have here not a promise by A with B for consideration supplied by B to pay C. It was, in my opinion, a promise by A made to B and C for consideration to pay B and C. In such a case it cannot lie in the mouth of A, in my <479> opinion, to question whether the consideration which he received for his promise moved from both B and C or, as between themselves, only from one of them. His promise is not a gratuitous promise as between himself and the promisees as on the view I take of the agreement it was a promise in respect of which there was privity between A on the one hand and B and C on the other. Such a promise, in my opinion, is clearly enforceable in the joint lifetime of B and C: But it is only enforceable if both B and C are parties to the action to enforce it. B, though he only supplied the consideration, could not sue alone. If C were unwilling to join in the action as plaintiff, B no doubt, after suitable tender of costs, could join C as a defendant. And A's promise could be enforced. But the judgment would be for payment to B and C. If B would not join in an action to enforce A's promise, I see no reason why C should not sue joining B as a defendant. Again, in my opinion, A's promise would be enforced and a judgment in favour of B and C would result. In neither of these cases could A successfully deny either privity or consideration. ...

Upon the death of one of the joint promisees the promise remains on foot and remains enforceable but it is still the same promise given to B and C though, because of the death of one and the right of survivorship, the promise is now to pay the survivor. C, it seems to me, being the survivor, may enforce the promise by an action to which both B's estate and C are parties. However, C could not, in any event, in my opinion, be the sole plaintiff against A because A's promise was not made with C alone. Consequently, B's personal representative would need to be either a co-plaintiff or joined as a defendant, though in this case the judgment would be for C alone, the promise with B and C being to pay the survivor of them.

e Performing an existing duty may be consideration

Performing, or promising to perform, a duty that the promisee is already obliged to perform, may be good consideration for a promise. At first blush, this may seem self-evident as it accords with the notion that consideration can be anything the promisor chooses, so long as it is not illegal or illusory. However, out of concern that recognising the performance of an existing duty as consideration could lead to forms of corruption, or the exploitation of the promisor, and thus be inimical to the public interest, the law's response has been more qualified.

Three forms of existing duty have been identified, according to the source of the duty. Whether performance can amount to consideration in a particular case may depend upon which form is involved. Therefore, when this issue arises, the first response should always be to categorise the duty. The possibilities are:

i   the duty may be a contractual one that the promisee already owes to the promisor
ii the duty may be a contractual one that the promisee already owes to a third party
iii the duty may be a public duty.

A contractual duty owed to the promisor

The duty that the promisee performed, or promised to perform, as consideration for the promise may be one that the promisee is already contractually bound to the promisor to perform.

Example

B had a contract with O to carry out building work on O's land for $1m with a completion date of 30 June. Although much of the work was carried out by late May, nevertheless it was clear that it would not be finished on time and O was concerned about this. O discussed the matter with B and they agreed that B would be able to complete the work on time if O agreed to pay B an additional $10,000. After the work was completed on 30 June, B sought payment of the extra $10,000. Is O obliged to pay, bearing in mind that in completing the original contract on time B was doing no more than performing a contractual duty already owed to O?

The dilemma the law faces in this situation is this: if O's promise was extracted by B taking advantage of O's vulnerability it would be against public policy for B's performance to be good consideration. On the other hand, if O initiated the second transaction to advance O's own interests, then, possibly, the position should be different.

The decided cases reflect this dilemma. They establish that if the promisee does nothing more than perform an existing duty, conferring no additional benefit on the promisor of any kind, performance will not be good consideration.[17] On the

---

17 See *Stilk v Myrick* (1809) 2 Camp 317 and *TA Sundell & Sons Pty Ltd v Emm Yannoulatos (Overseas) Pty Ltd* (1956) SR (NSW) 323 at 327.

other hand, if the promisor does something extra, or performs when circumstances have terminated the original duty,[18] or if performance is pursuant to a compromise about the existence of the duty,[19] performance can be good consideration. The difficulty here has been determining what can be regarded as 'something extra'. The following extract deals with leading cases and arguments on this topic.

Musumeci v Winadell Pty Ltd

(1994) 34 NSWLR 723, New South Wales Supreme Court

[Mr and Mrs Musumeci leased a shop in a shopping centre operated by Winadell. During the term of this lease, Winadell decided to lease another shop in the centre to a business that would compete with theirs. Believing that this would damage their business, the Musumecis asked for a reduction in their rent. This was agreed to. Subsequently, however, a dispute arose between the parties and Winadell attempted to terminate the lease. This led the Musumecis to bring these proceedings seeking damages for breach of a covenant for quiet enjoyment and relief against forfeiture of the lease. This raised the question of whether there was consideration for Winadell's promise to reduce the rent.]

Santow J [at 738]: Practical benefit or detriment as consideration?

[T]he second basis for putting the plaintiffs' contention that consideration was in fact provided for the rent concession ... relies upon the decision of the Court of Appeal in *Williams v Roffey Bros & Nicholls (Contractors) Ltd* [1991] 1 QB 1. That case held that A's promise to B to perform an existing duty owed to B may be consideration, notwithstanding the rule that a promise to perform an existing duty is not consideration. This rule is avoided only where the promisor in fact obtains in practice a benefit or obviates a 'disbenefit', from the promise or its performance, so enabling the promisee's reciprocal promise to be enforced. This is despite such benefit (or avoidance of disbenefit) not being expressly promised.

In that case, the principal contractor B agreed to pay a subcontractor A an additional sum over and above what was payable under the subcontract in order to secure the benefit of more assured performance from A. Thus the benefits which the defendant B was said to have obtained by so securing the plaintiff A's performance were twofold. First, there was a measure of protection against the risk that, as a result of the main contract to refurbish, B would be liable to pay liquidated damages if A failed to perform when that was a real risk and, secondly, avoidance of trouble and expense in finding a replacement for A.

---

18 See *Hartley v Ponsonby* (1857) 119 ER 1471 and *Figjam Pty Ltd v Pedrini* (2007) Aus Contract Reports 90-259. In the United States, courts have developed what is sometimes called the 'unforseen circumstances' exception under which continuing to perform a contractual obligation in such circumstances is good consideration for a new promise by the party to whom the obligation was owed: see *Brian Constr & Dev Co Inc v Brighenti* 405 A 2d 72 (1978).

19 This exception is discussed above at p 117, fn 9.

Essentially the plaintiffs in the present case have to overcome the difficulty that ... [they] might be said to be merely promising, as consideration, to perform a contractual duty already owed to the lessor and nothing more. If so, this could not be good consideration: *Stilk v Myrick* (1809) 2 Camp 317; 170 ER 1168. This decision has not been overruled, though is possibly explicable today as denying enforcement to a promise exacted by duress. The duress was by threatening desertion and thus a breach of contract, so as to secure more advantageous terms to perform an existing contractual duty. There was, after all, a similar practical benefit to the shipowner (or the Captain) from performance by the sailors of their duty to complete the voyage (despite desertion by two of them) of the sort that would have satisfied the *Williams v Roffey* test.

[at 740]: Glidewell LJ in *Williams v Roffey* (at 15–16) departed from [the] traditional approach, when allowing consequential practical benefits to suffice that were never explicitly the subject of the parties' promised bargain. He did so in reasoning encapsulated in the following five elements leading to the conclusion in (vi):

> 'The present state of the law on this subject can be expressed in the following proposition:
>
> (i) if A has entered into a contract with B to do work for, or to supply goods or services to, B in return for payment by B; and <741>
> (ii) at some stage before A has completely performed his obligations under the contract B has reason to doubt whether A will, or be able to, complete his side of the bargain; and
> (iii) B thereupon promises A an additional payment in return for A's promise to perform his contractual obligations on time; and
> (iv) as a result of giving his promise, B obtains in practice a benefit, or obviates a disbenefit; and
> (v) B's promise is not given as a result of economic duress or fraud on the part of A; then,
> (vi) the benefit to B is capable of being consideration for B's promise, so that the promise will be legally binding.'

So far as element (iii) is concerned, conceptually it can make no difference whether B promises A an additional payment for A's promise of performance or grants A the equivalent concession of promising a reduction in A's payment obligations, where these pre-exist. To reflect this, it is suggested element (iii) should have added the words 'or other concession (such as reducing A's original obligation)' immediately after 'payment'.

In either case the question is whether such a payment is nonetheless made for an illusory consideration in that it buys merely a promise by the same party to perform its existing contractual obligation.

Williams v Roffey—should it be followed in Australia?

There are three reasons which might be put as to why a contract to perform an existing obligation should not be enforced.

First, to protect the promisor from extortion, such as may result from threatening to breach a contract in order to exact a concession. ... <742> ...

Posner J sets out incisively the policy issues as he saw them in *United States v Stump Home Specialties Manufacturing, Incorporated* 905F 2d 1117 (1990) at 1121–1122:

> 'The requirement of consideration has, however, a distinct function in the modification setting—although one it does not perform well—and that is to prevent coercive modifications. Since one of the main purposes of contracts and of contract law is to facilitate long-term commitments, there is often an interval in the life of a contract during which one party is at the mercy of the other. A may have ordered a machine from B that A wants to place in operation on a given date, specified in their contract; and in expectation of B's complying with the contract, A may have made commitments to his customers that it would be costly to renege on. As the date of scheduled delivery approaches, B may be tempted to demand that A agree to renegotiate the contract price, knowing that A will incur heavy expenses if B fails to deliver on time. A can always refuse to renegotiate, relying instead on his right to sue B for breach of contract if B fails to make delivery by the agreed date. But legal remedies are costly and uncertain, thereby opening the way to duress. Considerations of commercial reputation will deter taking advantage of an opportunity to exert duress on a contract partner in many cases, but not in all. ... <743>
>
> [7] The rule that modifications are unenforceable unless supported by consideration strengthens A's position by reducing B's incentive to seek a modification. But it strengthens it feebly, as we pointed out in *Wisconsin Knife Works v National Metal Crafters, supra*, 781 F 2d at 1285. The law does not require that consideration be adequate—that it be commensurate with what the party accepting it is giving up. Slight consideration, therefore, will suffice to make a contract or a contract modification enforceable. ... And slight consideration is consistent with coercion. To surrender one's contractual rights in exchange for a peppercorn is not functionally different from surrendering them for nothing.
>
> The sensible course would be to enforce contract modifications (at least if written) regardless of consideration and rely on the defence of duress to prevent abuse. ... All coercive modifications would then be unenforceable, and there would be no need to worry about consideration, and inadequate safeguard against duress.'

I conclude that even if duress is not a fully developed doctrine, it is nonetheless a useful weapon. It, with fraud, is already introduced by element (v) of Glidewell LJ's formulation, precluding enforcement of a promise so induced. Logically though, one should expand that element also to exclude promises induced by undue influence or unconscionable conduct, at the least. ... <744> ... Thus such a reformulation of element (v) might read as follows:

> '(v) B's promise is not given as a result of economic duress or fraud, or undue influence or unconscionable conduct on the part of A nor is it induced otherwise by unfair pressure on the part of A, having regard to the circumstances'

The second reason … why the new promise should not be enforced, is that the promisee suffered no *legal* detriment in performing what was already due from him. Nor did the promisor receive any *legal* benefit in receiving what was already due to him. [after considering this argument His Honour concluded that] the very fact that a concession is extended by B, without extortion, supports an inference, though by no means conclusively, that consideration from A, in a real and practical sense, has moved that concession. …<745>

[T]he third possible reason for why such a promise should not be enforced … is expressed in the proposition that a benefit which is merely the hoped-for end result of performance cannot constitute consideration. …. But that assumes that existing rule has not even residual utility and I do not accept that proposition.

Thus, *William v Roffey* and subsequent cases … have been at pains to treat *Stilk's* case as still good law, though only 'where there is a wholly gratuitous promise' (at 545). But it should be apparent that *Stilk's* case involved no less a practical benefit than was upheld as sufficient for consideration in *Williams v Roffey*.

What then is a sufficient practical benefit to B, so as to take the situation beyond a wholly gratuitous promise by B? The answer … [is] … inherent in the situation posed by *Williams v Roffey* itself (and indeed in *Stilk's* case itself, despite the decision). There the subcontractor A's performance was worth more to B (the principal contractor) than likely damages, even taking into account the cost of any concession to obtain greater assurance of that performance. This suggests there should be an addition to element (iv) of Glidewell LJ's formulation … [A]s I have expanded it, should be divided into two parts, the second as follows:

(iv) (a) …, or
(b) As a result of giving this promise, A suffers in practice a detriment (or obviates a benefit), provided that A is thereby foregoing the opportunity of not performing the original contract in circumstances where such non performance, taking into account B's likely remedy against A (and allowing for any defences or cross-claims) is being capable of being viewed by A as worth more to A than performing that contract, in the absence of B's promised payment or concession to A. … <746> …

Accordingly, I am satisfied to conclude that subject to the earlier recasting of the five elements of Glidewell LJ, *Williams v Roffey* should be <747> followed in allowing a practical benefit or detriment to suffice as consideration…. One particular issue [to be refined with experience] is the extent to which a benefit or detriment, said to be 'practical', as distinct from explicitly bargained for, must nonetheless be consistent with, and not extraneous to, the bargaining process, as at least its intended result if not necessarily its moving force. …

Application of William v Roffey to present circumstances:

Applying that reasoning to the present circumstances, the practical benefit that the lessor gained from the concession of lower future rental, was argued to be the enhanced capacity of the plaintiffs to stay in occupation, able to carry out their future reduced lease obligations, notwithstanding substantial newly introduced competition from the other tenant. What this practical benefit consists of therefore is enhanced capacity for the lessor to maintain a <748> full shopping centre with another competing tenant, when the original tenant is no longer at so great a risk of defaulting and more likely to stay. That is a practical benefit, even though legally there be no inhibition on the lessor to introduce new competition.

[His Honour concluded that there was consideration for varying the lease.]

A contractual duty owed to a third party

The duty that the promisee performed, or promised to perform, as consideration for the promise may be one that the promisee is already contractually bound to a third party to perform.

Example

B had a contract with O to carry out building work on O's land for $1m with a completion date of 30 June. Concerned to ensure that this work was completed by that date X promised to pay B $10,000 if B finished the work on time. B did so. Is X obliged to pay B, bearing in mind that in completing the original contract on time B was doing no more than performing a contractual duty already owed to O?

In situations such as this, common law has had less difficulty in concluding that performing an existing contractual duty can be consideration. The following case considers the principal authorities and arguments relevant to this issue and the considerations that may influence the outcome in individual cases.

Pao On v Lau Yiu Long
[1980] AC 615, Privy Council on appeal from Hong Kong

[The facts of this case are set out on page 130]

Lord Scarman for the Board [at 632]: Their Lordships do not doubt that a promise to perform, or the performance of, a pre-existing contractual obligation to a third party can be valid consideration. ...

Unless, therefore, the guarantee was void as having been made for an illegal consideration or voidable on the ground of economic duress, the extrinsic evidence establishes that it was supported by valid consideration.

Mr Leggatt for the defendants submits that the consideration is illegal as being against public policy. He submits that to secure a party's promise by a threat of repudiation of a pre-existing contractual obligation owed to another can be, and in the circumstances of this case was, an abuse of a dominant bargaining position and so contrary to public policy. This, he submits, is so even though economic duress cannot be proved. This submission found favour with the majority in the Court of Appeal. Their Lordships, however, consider it misconceived. ... <633>

[W]here the pre-existing obligation is a contractual duty owed to a third party, some other ground of public policy must be relied on to invalidate the consideration (if otherwise legal); the defendants submit that the ground can be extortion by the abuse of a dominant bargaining position to threaten the repudiation of a contractual obligation. It is this application of public policy which Mr Leggatt submits has been developed in the American cases. Beginning with the general rule that 'neither the performance of duty nor the promise to render a performance already required by duty is a sufficient consideration' the courts have (according to *Corbin on Contracts*, vol 1, s 171) advanced to the view

> 'that the moral and economic elements in any case that involves the rule should be weighed by the court, and that the fact of pre-existing legal duty should not be in itself decisive.' <634>

The American Law Institute in its *Restatement of the Law, Contracts*, chapter 3, section 84(d), has declared that performance (or promise of performance) of a contractual duty owed to a third person is sufficient consideration. This view (which accords with the statement of our law in *New Zealand Shipping Co Ltd v AM Satterthwaite & Co Ltd* [1975] AC 154) appears to be generally accepted but only in cases where there is no suggestion of unfair economic pressure exerted to induce the making of what *Corbin on Contracts* calls 'the return promise'. ...

[The question under consideration] is whether, in a case where duress is not established, public policy may nevertheless invalidate the consideration if there has been a threat to repudiate a pre-existing contractual obligation or an unfair use of a dominating bargaining position. Their Lordships' conclusion is that where businessmen are negotiating at arm's length it is unnecessary for the achievement of justice, and unhelpful in the development of the law, to invoke such a rule of public policy. It would also create unacceptable anomaly. It is unnecessary because justice requires that men, who have negotiated at arm's length, be held to their bargains unless it can be shown that their consent was vitiated by fraud, mistake or duress. If a promise is induced by coercion of a man's will, the doctrine of duress suffices to do justice. The party coerced, if he chooses and acts in time, can avoid the contract. If there is no coercion, there can be no reason for avoiding the contract where there is shown to be a real consideration which is otherwise legal.

Such a rule of public policy as is now being considered would be unhelpful because it would render the law uncertain. It would become a question of fact and degree to determine in each case whether there had been, short of duress, an unfair use of a strong bargaining position. It would create anomaly because, if public policy invalidates the consideration, the effect is to make the contract void. But unless the facts are such as to support a plea of *'non est factum'*, which is not suggested in this case, duress does no more than confer upon the victim the opportunity, if taken in time, to avoid the contract. It would be strange if conduct less than duress could render a contract void, whereas duress does no more than render a contract voidable.

[His Lordship concluded that performing the existing duty in this case, owed to a third party, was consideration.]

A public duty

The duty that the promisee performed, or promised to perform, as consideration for the promise may be one that the promisee is already required to perform by virtue of some public office or statutory obligation.

> **Example**
>
> Concerned to protect valuable property, O promised to pay a retainer of $100 per week to P, a local police officer, to patrol the neighbourhood. Is O obliged to pay P, bearing in mind the duties that police officers owe in relation to the prevention of criminal activity?

Glasbrook Bros Ltd v Glamorgan County Council
[1925] AC 270, House of Lords

[Glasbrook sought police protection for its premises during a miners' strike. The Council formed the view that a mobile force of police officers, available when required, would be sufficient for this purpose. Glasbrook, on the other hand, wanted officers billeted on the premises. Believing that this was unnecessary, the Council refused unless Glasbrook agreed to pay for the costs involved. Glasbrook agreed and officers were billeted on its premises until the strike ended without incident. However, Glasbrook refused to pay, whereupon the Council took proceeding to enforce the agreement. The Council succeeded at first instance and in the Court of Appeal. Glasbrook then appealed to the House of Lords.]

Viscount Cave LC [at 277]: There is an absolute and unconditional obligation binding the police authorities to take all steps which appear to them to be necessary for keeping the peace, for preventing crime, or for protecting property from criminal injury; and the public, who pay for this protection through the rates and taxes, cannot lawfully be called upon to make a further payment for that which is their right. ... <278> ...

[A]ny attempt by a police authority to extract payment for services which fall within the plain obligations of the police force, should be firmly discountenanced by the Courts. But it has always been recognized that, where individuals desire that services of a special kind which, though not within the obligations of a police authority, can most effectively be rendered by them, should be performed by members of the police force, the police authorities may (to use an expression which is found in the *Police Pensions Act 1890*) 'lend' the services of constables for that purpose in consideration of payment. Instances are the lending of constables on the occasions of large gatherings in and outside private premises, as on the occasions of weddings, athletic or boxing contests or race meetings, and the provision of constables at large railway stations.

[at 281] [Applied here] If in the judgment of the police authorities, formed reasonably and in good faith, the garrison was necessary for the protection of life

and property, then they were not entitled to make a charge for it, for that would be to exact a payment for the performance of a duty which they clearly owed to the appellants and their servants; but if they thought the garrison a superfluity and only acceded to Mr James' request with a view to meeting his wishes, then in my opinion they were entitled to treat the garrison duty as special duty and to charge for it.

[Viscount Finlay and Lord Shaw delivered speeches to the same effect; Lords Carson and Blanesburgh dissented on the ground that the police had not acted beyond their obligations to Glasbrook.]

Appeal dismissed

Popiw v Popiw

[1959] VR 197, Supreme Court of Victoria

[Mr and Mrs Popiw separated. Mr Popiw then promised Mrs Popiw to put the title of the matrimonial home in their joint names if she returned to live with him. In response she did this until they again separated three or four weeks later. Mrs Popiw then commenced proceedings seeking a determination of her interest in the home and an order for its sale and a division of the proceeds. One of the grounds upon which her claim was based was that there was a contract between the parties relating to their home. Mr Popiw argued that there was no enforceable contract because (i) there was no intention to create legal relations; (ii) there was no consideration for his promise; and (iii) the agreement was not recorded in writing as required by the *Statute of Frauds*. The following extract deals with consideration.]

Hudson J [at 198]: The objection that the act of the applicant in returning to cohabitation did not amount to a valid consideration for the respondent's promise was founded on the view that the applicant was already under a duty as the wife of the respondent to return to cohabitation and this being so it could not be said that by the act of the applicant she suffered any detriment or that the respondent gained any advantage in <199> exchange for his promise. It is stated in *Pollock on Contracts* (13th ed), at p 146 that 'neither the promise to do a thing nor the actual doing of it will be a good consideration if it is a thing which the party is already bound to do either by the general law or by a subsisting contract with the other party'.

The learned editor is not alone among text book writers in expressing this view of the law and authority is not lacking for his proposition. But this view of the law was clearly rejected by the Court of Appeal in the case of *Ward v Byham*, [1956] 2 All ER 318 .... There it was held that the mother of an illegitimate child, already under a statutory duty to support that child, could enforce a promise by the father to pay her a weekly sum given in consideration for her promise to look after the child. No question of compromise of affiliation proceedings was involved and Lord Denning, at p 319, said: 'I approach the case, therefore, on the footing that the mother, in looking after the child, is only doing what she is legally bound to do. Even so, I think there is sufficient consideration to support the promise. I have always thought that a promise to perform an existing duty, or the performance of it, should be regarded as good consideration, because it is a benefit to the person to whom it is given. Take this very case. It is as much a benefit for the father to have the child looked after by the mother as by a neighbour. If he gets the benefit for which he stipulated, he ought to honour his promise; and he ought not to avoid it by saying that the mother was herself under a duty to maintain the child.' In the face of this decision the respondent's contention in the present case appears to be untenable. I might say, however, that even if the rule were as stated in *Pollock on Contracts*, I should think it would have no application to the facts of the present case. Although it may be true to state that the applicant was under a duty to cohabit with the respondent there was no remedy open to the respondent to compel the performance of that duty. Furthermore there was evidence which I am prepared to accept that the respondent had assaulted and beaten the applicant, and though these assaults on the evidence before me fell far short of what would be necessary to constitute constructive desertion they might well have given the applicant just cause for leaving and remaining away from the matrimonial home.

From a practical point of view therefore what the respondent was to get in exchange for his promise was something which must be regarded as far more advantageous to him than the right of cohabiting with his wife which he had no means of enforcing and the applicant in returning was submitting to a detriment in placing herself in a position which she could not have been compelled to occupy. On any view therefore I think there was good consideration for the respondent's promise.

f   Part payment of a debt is not consideration for a promise to forgo the balance

Where the promisee owes money to the promisor, paying part of the sum owed will not, as a general rule, be consideration for a promise not to claim the balance. This is often called the rule in *Pinnel's Case*.[20]

> *Examples*
>
> i   D owed C $1,000. Concerned that because of D's financial position none of this amount would be recovered, C agreed with D that C would regard the debt as having been repaid in full if D paid C $700. After the sum of $700 has been paid can C claim the balance?

---

20   (1602) 5 Co Rep 117a; 77 ER 237.

> ii D leased business premises from C for $1,000 per week. Due to a general downturn in business D could no longer afford to pay this sum and considered vacating the premises, even though this would breach the lease. Concerned that this not happen, C promised to reduce the rent to $700 per week for the remainder of the lease. In response, D remained in occupancy, paying the lower rent. Can C claim the balance of the rent due under the lease?

In these examples all that D has done in response to C's promise is to perform, partially, a contractual duty already owed to C. As such they fall squarely within the rule that, generally speaking, performance of this nature cannot be consideration. However, although frequently discussed in that light, this situation is considered separately as special rules have developed in relation to the part payment of a debt.

Foakes v Beer

(1884) 9 App Cas 605, House of Lords

[Foakes was indebted to Beer under a judgment. Beer agreed not to enforce this debt if Foakes paid the amount of the judgment by certain instalments. Foakes did this. However, Beer then claimed interest and the issue between the parties became whether she was precluded from recovering this amount by virtue of their agreement. At first instance it was held that the agreement precluded recovery. The Court of Appeal reversed this decision and Foakes appealed to the House of Lords.]

Earl of Selborne LC [at 612]: The doctrine, as stated in *Pinnel's Case* [5 Co Rep 117a] is 'that payment of a lesser sum on the day' (it would of course be the same after the day), 'in satisfaction of a greater, cannot be any satisfaction for the whole, because it appears to the Judges, that by no possibility a lesser sum can be a satisfaction to the plaintiff for a greater sum. ... <613> ...

If the question be (as, in the actual state of the law, I think it is), whether consideration is, or is not, given in a case of this kind, by the debtor who pays down part of the debt presently due from him, for a promise by the creditor to relinquish, after certain further payments on account, the residue of the debt, I cannot say that I think consideration is given, in the sense in which I have always understood that word as used in our law. ... What is called 'any benefit, or even any legal possibility of benefit', in Mr Smith's notes to *Cumber v Wane* [1 Sm LC 8th ed 366], is not <614> (as I conceive) that sort of benefit which a creditor may derive from getting payment of part of the money due to him from a debtor who might otherwise keep him at arm's length, or possibly become insolvent, but is some independent benefit, actual or contingent, of a kind which might in law be a good and valuable consideration for any other sort of agreement not under seal.

[His Lordship concluded that there was no additional benefit present on the facts in this case with the result that no consideration was given for Beer's promise.

In separate speeches, the other members of the House of Lords reached the same conclusion.]

Appeal dismissed

As Lord Selborne indicates, the rule in *Pinnel's Case* does not apply where the debtor, at the creditor's request, provides something additional to the lesser sum as consideration for the creditor's promise. For example, paying that sum earlier than it is due, or paying it together with an object of nominal value will suffice. As a result, if the creditor is willing to make such a stipulation, it is easy for the parties to avoid placing the debtor in the situation in which Foakes found himself. There are also a number of other exceptions or qualifications to this rule including:

- where the payment relates to an unliquidated debt[21]
- where payment is part of a composition agreement made between a debtor and their creditors or where the payment is made by a third party—the usual explanation for these exceptions is that if the creditor's claim were allowed it would amount to a fraud on the other creditors, or the third party[22]
- where the doctrine of promissory estoppel applies—this exception is discussed in more detail below.

g   Settling a legal dispute or giving up a claim can be consideration

Agreeing to settle or give up a claim, or performing an obligation that the promisee disputes having to perform, will constitute consideration for the promisor's promise where this was sought by the promisor[23] and the promisee acted honestly. This is so even if it should transpire that, in fact, the promisee's claim was not well founded (at least where it was not vexatious or frivolous), or that the promisee was bound by the obligation. This situation is illustrated and discussed in the following case.

Wigan v Edwards

(1973) 47 ALJR 586, High Court of Australia

[Wigan sold land to Mr and Mrs Edwards on which he had recently erected a house. The contract of sale did not contain any warranty that the house had been constructed in a proper manner. However, the Edwards gave Wigan a list of matters that they said required attention before they would finalise the sale. In response, Wigan promised to fix minor defects within one week of finance being approved

---

21 See *Ibberson v Neck* (1886) 2 TLR 247.
22 In some instances, another justification could be that the debtor and the other creditors or third party were joint promisees for the purposes of the joint promisee rule described in *Coulls v Bagot's Executor and Trustee Company Ltd* (1967) 119 CLR 460.
23 Merely acting in the ways described will not constitute consideration; it must be preceded by an actual or implied request from the promisor to so act as the price for the promisor's promise: see the discussion in *Brehm v Wright* [2007] NSWSC 1101 at 25–33.

and any 'major faults in construction five years from purchase date.' Settlement then took place. Wigan did not remedy defects or faults as promised. Therefore, the Edwards took proceedings to recover the cost of this work, arguing that Wigan's failure to do so was a breach of contract. They succeeded at first instance and on appeal; Wigan then appealed to the High Court.]

Mason J [at 594]: An important qualification to the general principle [that performing an existing contractual duty is not good consideration] is that a promise to do precisely what the promisor <595> is already bound to do is a sufficient consideration, when it is given by way of a bona fide compromise of a disputed claim, the promisor[24] having asserted that he is not bound to perform the obligation under the pre-existing contract or that he has a cause of action under that contract. The qualification recognizes that for the court itself to examine and determine the correctness of the promisor's claim would be a pointless exercise when the new bargain indicates that the promisee regarded the fresh promise as a benefit, presumably viewing the promise of performance as more advantageous than the remedies available to him for breach of contract. But the law, by insisting that the claim in dispute is one which was honestly or bona fide made, prevents the qualification from assisting the party who would seek to gain an unfair advantage by threatening unscrupulously to withhold performance under a contract.

It is no objection to the existence of a bona fide compromise of a dispute that the court considers that the claim made by the promisor that he was not bound under the former contract would not have succeeded had the issue been litigated (*Callisher v Bischoffsheim* (1870), LR 2 QB 449; *Miles v New Zealand Alford Estate Co* (1885), 32 Ch D 266). But it is perhaps open to question whether a bona fide compromise of a dispute is sufficiently established by showing that the promisor honestly believed that his claim was well founded. It has been said that it must also be shown that the claim was not vexatious or frivolous. In *Miles v New Zealand Alford Estate Co* (supra, at pp 291–292) Bowen LJ expressed himself in favour of the second formulation, whereas in the same case Cotton LJ (at pp 283–284) and Fry LJ (at pp 297–298) expressed themselves more obliquely. However, as I understand their observations, they are not inconsistent with what Bowen LJ had to say. In many courts in the United States a similar test to that adopted by Bowen LJ has been adopted. *Williston on Contracts* 3rd ed, s135B, states: 'In many jurisdictions the tendency is to make the test the honesty of the claimant, provided the invalidity of the claim in law or in fact is not entirely obvious.' Even so, according to the author, the forbearance is insufficient consideration 'if the claim

---

24　His Honour's allocation of the descriptions 'promisor' and 'promisee' here is apt to be confusing unless it is realised that he has called the party to whom the relevant promise is made and who, therefore, must provide consideration (and who we would normally refer to as 'the promisee') 'the promisor' because what that party is providing as consideration is a promise. It is suggested that this nomenclature is undesirable as it is likely to confuse the analysis of an individual transaction. A better approach is to identify the promise in respect of which consideration needs to be found and thereafter refer to the party who gave that promise as 'the promisor' and the party that must provide consideration as 'the promisee', even though the consideration they allege is, as in the instant case, a reciprocal promise.

forborne is so lacking in any foundation as to make its assertion incompatible with both honesty and a reasonable degree of intelligence'.

The different expressions of the principle do not reflect an important conceptual difference. There will be few cases involving an honest or bona fide belief in a claim which is vexatious or frivolous. In this case it is unnecessary to choose between the competing formulations, for in my view the more stringent test, that favoured by Bowen LJ in *Miles'* case (supra), is satisfied.

The judge found that the respondents honestly believed that, having regard to the defective condition of the house, they were not bound to complete. In my opinion his Honour was correct in so finding. Although it is my view that the majority of the defects on which the respondents relied would not have justified a refusal to complete the contract, there were many defects. In addition, the water had not been connected and the fence had not been erected. In these circumstances the respondents' claim that they would not complete cannot be described as a frivolous or vexatious claim.

[Although finding that there was a contract between the parties requiring Wigan to carry out repairs, Mason J (with whom Walsh and Gibbs JJ agreed) concluded that he was not in breach of this contract when proceedings had been commenced. Therefore, the Edwards had no cause of action at that time. For this reason the appeal was allowed. McTiernan ACJ and Menzies J dissented on this issue.]

Appeal allowed

INTERNATIONAL PERSPECTIVES

The nature of consideration in Indian law is essentially the same as it is in Anglo-Australian common law. It can be anything that is not illegal or illusory and the important rule that so long as it is real it need not be adequate is expressly provided in *Explanation 2* to s 25. Like the common law, this provision also recognises that inadequate consideration may, however, signal lack of real consent—in which case no contract will exist. In addition to s 2(d), already extracted, the key provisions are ss 23 and 25.

Indian Contract Act, 1872

Section 23. What considerations and objects are lawful, and what not

The consideration or object of an agreement is lawful, unless—

- it is forbidden by law; or
- is of such a nature that, if permitted, it would defeat the provisions of any law; or
- is fraudulent; or
- involves or implies injury to the person or property of another; or
- the Court regards it as immoral, or opposed to public policy.

In each of these cases, the consideration or object of an agreement is said to be unlawful. Every agreement of which the object or consideration is unlawful is void.

Section 25

An agreement made without consideration is void, unless—

(1) it is expressed in writing and registered under the law for the time being in force for the registration of documents, and is made on account of natural love and affection between parties standing in a near relation to each other; or unless
(2) it is a promise to compensate, wholly or in part; a person who has already voluntarily done something for the promisor, or something which the promisor was legally compellable to do; or unless
(3) it is a promise, made in writing and signed by the person to be charged therewith, or by his agent generally or specially authorized in that behalf, to pay wholly or in part a debt of which the creditor might have enforced payment but for the law for the limitation of suits.

In any of these cases, such an agreement is a contract.
Explanation 1. —Nothing in this section shall affect the validity, as between the donor and donee, of any gift actually made.
Explanation 2. —An Agreement to which the consent of the promisor is freely given is not void merely because the consideration is inadequate; but the inadequacy of the consideration may be taken into account by the Court in determining the question whether the consent of the promisor was freely given.

Indian law differs from the common law in the following respects:

- *Consideration need not move from the promisee*: the definition of consideration in s 2(d) expressly allows it to move from 'the promisee or any other person'.[25] Thus, if S promises B to deliver goods to B if A pays S $100, payment by A will amount to consideration.
- *Consideration need not be contemporaneous with the promise*: the definition of consideration in s 2(d) is wide enough to cover conduct by the promisee that occurs before the promise was made, so long as it was desired by the promisor. This reflects the common law exception that past conduct can be consideration if it was requested by the promisor, but is broader in so far as it contains no requirement that the parties understood, when the conduct occurred, that it would be paid for by the promisor.
- *A promise to compensate past voluntary conduct is enforceable without consideration:* s 25(2) makes enforceable a promise to compensate a person

---

25 For an example, see *Chinnaya v Ramayya* (1882) 4 Mad 137.

who has voluntarily done something for the promisor, or something that the promisor was legally compelled to do, even though no consideration was given for the promise. Thus, for example, a promise such as that in *Harrington v Taylor* (extracted above at p 126) would be enforceable in India.

The difference between this provision and s 2(d) which also applies to past conduct appears to be this: if the promisee's conduct was requested by the promisor, that conduct will amount to consideration, within the definition in s 2(d), for any subsequent promise made. On the other hand, if it was not requested, but was performed 'voluntarily', that conduct will not amount to consideration. However, in that case, a promise to compensate the promisee for what they have done will be enforceable even though made without consideration.

4 Criticism of the doctrine of consideration

As is apparent from our treatment, the doctrine of consideration is highly technical and includes rules that, if applied strictly, can allow agreements to be enforced, or avoided, without regard to their substantive merits. A prime illustration is the rule that consideration can be nominal and need bear no resemblance to the value of the promise. As a result, for example, an agreement to transfer property in exchange for only nominal value, such as a peppercorn, is enforceable whereas a bare agreement to do so is not—even though in substance the two agreements are the same. It was this kind of situation that led Jessel MR to say in *Couldery v Bartrum*:

> According to English common law a creditor might accept anything in satisfaction of his debt except a less amount of money. He might take a horse, or a canary, or a tomtit if he chose, and that was accord and satisfaction; but, by a most extraordinary peculiarity ... he could not take 19s 6d in the pound; that was a *nudum pactum*.[26]

Arguably, the doctrine also serves no purpose that is not already covered by the requirements that the parties must have reached an agreement, and must have intended that agreement to be binding. For reasons such as these it has been the subject of much criticism.[27] Perhaps more importantly, it has experienced significant judicial manipulation as courts have sought to prevent it producing unjust outcomes in individual cases. As a result, the doctrine is now sufficiently flexible to allow, in many instances at least, the court to decide a case according

---

26 (1881) 19 ChD 394 at 399.
27 See, for example, PS Atiyah, 'Consideration: a Restatement' in PS Atiyah, *Essays on Contract*, Clarendon Press (1986), p 179. This essay is a revised version of Atiyah's inaugural lecture at the Australian National University in 1971. GH Treitel's seminal response to that lecture appears as 'Consideration: a Critical Analysis of Professor Atiyah's Fundamental Restatement' (1976) 50 *ALJ* 439.

to the judge's view of its inherent merits, rather than strictly in accordance with legal rules. The modification, in *Williams v Roffey Bros & Nicholls (Contractors) Ltd*,[28] of the rule that performance of an existing contractual obligation cannot be good consideration is one example.[29] Another is the development of the doctrine of promissory estoppel (considered below) which, in Australia, at least since the decision of the High Court in *Waltons Stores (Interstate) Ltd v Maher*,[30] allows gratuitous promises to be enforced where they have been relied upon and the circumstances are such that it would be unconscionable for the promisor not to be bound by them.

5   Promissory estoppel

Under the doctrine of promissory estoppel a promisee can enforce a promise, even though no consideration has been provided, where it has been relied upon and it would be inequitable to allow the promisor to renege. This is a developing area of law. As a result, the precise circumstances in which the promise will be enforced and the full extent of the rights the promisee can acquire remain in a state of flux. It is also an area in which Australian law may have moved beyond the position in England.

The modern origins of the doctrine are found in the following case.

Central London Property Trust Ltd v High Trees House Ltd

[1947] 1 KB 130, King's Bench Division

[Central London leased a block of flats to High Trees for 99 years. During World War II it became apparent that High Trees would not be able to lease all the flats in the block so, in 1940, Central London agreed to reduce the ground rent by 50%. This rent was paid until 1945 by which time all the flats were fully let. In the meantime, Central London had gone into receivership and in September 1945 the receiver, having ascertained the rent prescribed by the lease, demanded the full rent and arrears. However, in these proceedings, Central London claimed only the increased rent from 1 July 1945; in its defence, High Trees relied upon the undertaking to reduce the rent.]

Denning J [at 133]: [T]he variation here <134> might be said to have been made without consideration. With regard to estoppel, the representation made in relation to reducing the rent, was not a representation of an existing fact. It was a

---

28   [1991] 1 QB 1.
29   But contrast see *In re Selectmove Ltd* [1995] 1 WLR 474 at 481 in which the Court of Appeal declined to apply *Williams v Roffey* to a case in which the existing obligation was to pay a debt on the ground that this would 'in effect leave the principle in *Foakes v Beer* 9 App Cas 605 without any application'.
30   (1987) 164 CLR 387.

representation, in effect, as to the future, namely, that payment of the rent would not be enforced at the full rate but only at the reduced rate. Such a representation would not give rise to an estoppel, because, as was said in *Jorden v Money* ((1854) 5 HLC 185), a representation as to the future must be embodied as a contract or be nothing.

But what is the position in view of developments in the law in recent years? The law has not been standing still since *Jorden v Money* ((1854) 5 HLC 185). There has been a series of decisions over the last fifty years which, although they are said to be cases of estoppel are not really such. They are cases in which a promise was made which was intended to create legal relations and which, to the knowledge of the person making the promise, was going to be acted on by the person to whom it was made, and which was in fact so acted on. In such cases the courts have said that the promise must be honoured. ... *Jorden v Money* ((1854) 5 HLC 185) can be distinguished, because there the promisor made it clear that she did not intend to be legally bound, whereas in the cases to which I refer the proper inference was that the promisor did intend to be bound. In each case the court held the promise to be binding on the party making it, even though under the old common law it might be difficult to find any consideration for it. The courts have not gone so far as to give a cause of action in damages for the breach of such a promise, but they have refused to allow the party making it to act inconsistently with it. It is in that sense, and that sense only, that such a promise gives rise to an estoppel.

[His Honour concluded that the parties intended the rent reduction to be temporary only so that the full rent could be claimed once the flats were all let. Therefore, Central London's claim succeeded.]

This case has been described as one of the most important of the twentieth century.[31] The development it gave rise to was, however, initially rather limited. It applied only to a variation of an existing contract and was restricted to providing the promisee with a defence to a claim made by the promisor, a restriction commonly referred to as being 'a shield and not a sword'.[32] Both these limitations are illustrated by *High Trees* itself: the promise there was one to reduce the rent due under an existing lease and had the doctrine applied (it was not on the facts of the case) it would have been only so as to provide a defence to a claim by the landlord for back rent.

These limitations appear still to apply in England, although they have been interpreted narrowly.[33] However, they do not apply in Australia as the following decision shows.

---

31   See GH Treitel, *Some Landmarks of Twentieth Century Contract Law*, Oxford University Press, Oxford, 2002 at 29.
32   See *Combe v Combe* [1951] 1 All ER 767 at 772, per Birkett LJ.
33   For example, in *Combe v Combe* [1951] 1 All ER 767 it was accepted that estoppel could be part of a cause of action, by providing a plaintiff with a means of resting a defence that might otherwise have been available to the defendant. See also *Baird Textile Holdings Ltd v Marks & Spencer plc* [2002] 1 All ER (Comm) 737 at para 98.

Waltons Stores (Interstate) Ltd v Maher

(1988) 164 CLR 387, High Court of Australia

[In September 1983, Waltons entered into negotiations with Mr and Mrs Maher for the lease of a new building which was to be constructed to meet the Waltons' needs. As Waltons knew, this would involve the demolition of an old building on the site. Late in October, Waltons' solicitors sent a draft lease to the solicitors acting for the Mahers and later informed them that amendments they had suggested were acceptable. A revised lease incorporating these amendments was executed by the Mahers and sent to Waltons' solicitors. In November, the Mahers' solicitors informed Waltons that demolition work had commenced on the old building and that it was important to conclude the lease quickly so that the Mahers could organise labour and building supplies before the Christmas shut down. Late in November, Waltons started to have reservations about proceeding with the lease and having learned from their solicitors that they were not bound by the lease, because they had not exchanged copies, instructed them to 'go slow'. Early in January 1984, the Mahers commenced building in accordance with plans Waltons had approved. However, later in the month, Waltons' solicitors informed the Mahers' solicitors that it did not want to proceed with the lease. By then the building was 40% complete. The Mahers commenced proceedings seeking a declaration that there was an enforceable agreement for lease and an order for specific performance or damages in lieu. At first instance the Mahers succeeded and recovered damages. An appeal by Waltons failed; it then appealed to the High Court.]

Mason CJ and Wilson J [at 399]: Promissory estoppel certainly extends to representations (or promises) as to future conduct. ... So far the doctrine has been mainly confined to precluding departure from a representation by a person in a pre-existing contractual relationship that he will not enforce his contractual rights, whether they be pre-existing or rights to be acquired as a result of the representation .... But Denning J in *Central London Property Trust Ltd v High Trees House Ltd* [[1947] KB 130, at pp 134–135], treated it as a wide-ranging doctrine operating outside the pre-existing contractual relationship. In principle there is certainly no reason why the doctrine should not apply so as to preclude departure by a person from a representation that he will not enforce a non-contractual right . ... <400>

There has been for many years a reluctance to allow promissory estoppel to become the vehicle for the positive enforcement of a representation by a party that he would do something in the future. Promissory estoppel, it has been said, is a defensive equity and the traditional notion has been that estoppel could only be relied upon defensively as a shield and not as a sword. ... *High Trees* [[1947] KB 130] itself was an instance of the defensive use of promissory estoppel. But this does not mean that a plaintiff cannot rely on an estoppel. Even according to traditional orthodoxy, a plaintiff may rely on an estoppel if he has an independent cause of action, where in the words of Denning LJ in *Combe v Combe* [[1951]

2 KB at p 220], the estoppel 'may be part of a cause of action, but not a cause of action in itself'.

But the respondents ask us to drive promissory estoppel one step further by enforcing directly in the absence of a pre-existing relationship of any kind a non-contractual promise on which the representee has relied to his detriment. ... The principal objection to the enforcement of such a promise is that it would outflank the principles of the law of contract.

[Their Honours then discussed several cases on estoppel and continued at p 406] The foregoing review of the doctrine of promissory estoppel indicates that the doctrine extends to the enforcement of voluntary promises on the footing that a departure from the basic assumptions underlying the transaction between the parties must be unconscionable. As failure to fulfil a promise does not of itself amount to unconscionable conduct, mere reliance on an executory promise to do something, resulting in the promisee changing his position or suffering detriment, does not bring promissory estoppel into play. Something more would be required. *Humphreys Estate* [[1987] 1 AC 114] suggests that this may be found, if at all, in the creation or encouragement by the party estopped in the other party of an assumption that a contract will come into existence or a promise will be performed and that the other party relied on that assumption to his detriment to the knowledge of the first party. ...

The application of these principles to the facts of the present case is not without difficulty. ... But the crucial question remains: was <407> the appellant entitled to stand by in silence when it must have known that the respondents were proceeding on the assumption that they had an agreement and that completion of the exchange was a formality? The mere exercise of its legal right not to exchange contracts could not be said to amount to unconscionable conduct on the part of the appellant. But there were two other factors present in the situation which require to be taken into consideration. The first was the element of urgency that pervaded the negotiation of the terms of the proposed lease. ...

The second factor of importance is that the respondents executed the counterpart deed and it was forwarded to the appellant's solicitor on 11 November. The assumption on which the respondents acted thereafter was that completion of the necessary exchange was a formality. The next their solicitor heard from the appellant was a letter from its solicitors dated 19 January, informing him that the appellant did not intend to proceed with the matter. It had known, at least since 10 December, that costly work was proceeding on the site.

It seems to us, in the light of these considerations, that the appellant was under an obligation to communicate with the respondents within a reasonable time after receiving the executed counterpart deed and certainly when it learnt on 10 December that demolition was proceeding. It had to choose whether to complete the contract or to warn the respondents that it had not yet decided upon the course it would take. It was not entitled simply to retain the counterpart deed executed by the respondents and do nothing. ... The appellant's inaction, in all the circumstances, constituted clear encouragement or inducement to the respondents to continue to act on the basis of the assumption which they had made. It was unconscionable for it, knowing that the respondents were exposing themselves to detriment by acting on the basis of a false assumption, to adopt a course <408> of inaction which encouraged them in the course they had adopted. To express the point in the language of promissory estoppel the appellant is estopped in all the circumstances from retreating from its implied promise to complete the contract. ...

Brennan J [at 428]: In my opinion, to establish an equitable estoppel, it is necessary for a plaintiff to prove that (1) the plaintiff assumed that a particular legal relationship then existed between the plaintiff and the defendant or expected that a particular legal relationship would exist between them and, in the latter case, that the defendant would not be free to withdraw from the expected legal relationship; (2) the <429> defendant has induced the plaintiff to adopt that assumption or expectation; (3) the plaintiff acts or abstains from acting in reliance on the assumption or expectation; (4) the defendant knew or intended him to do so; (5) the plaintiff's action or inaction will occasion detriment if the assumption or expectation is not fulfilled; and (6) the defendant has failed to act to avoid that detriment whether by fulfilling the assumption or expectation or otherwise. For the purposes of the second element, a defendant who has not actively induced the plaintiff to adopt an assumption or expectation will nevertheless be held to have done so if the assumption or expectation can be fulfilled only by a transfer of the defendant's property, a diminution of his rights or an increase in his obligations and he, knowing that the plaintiff's reliance on the assumption or expectation may cause detriment to the plaintiff if it is not fulfilled, fails to deny to the plaintiff the correctness of the assumption or expectation on which the plaintiff is conducting his affairs. ...

[In a separate judgments, Deane and Gaudron JJ also dismissed the appeal.]

Appeal dismissed

It is clear that the doctrine of promissory estoppel, as expounded in this case, is an important qualification to the proposition that for a promise to be enforceable the promisee must provide consideration. However, it is not a universal substitute for this requirement. In the first place, an estoppel will only arise if there is unconscionable conduct on the part of the promisor and merely failing to honour a promise will not, in itself, amount to such conduct. Secondly, the relief available is limited to removing the disadvantage suffered by the promisee. In the words of Mason CJ in *The Commonwealth v Verwayen*,[34] it 'will permit a court to do what is required in order to avoid detriment to the party who has relied on the assumption induced by the party estopped, but no more'. As a result, it cannot be used to actually enforce the promise made unless 'the minimum equity will not be satisfied by anything short of enforcing the promise'.[35]

---

34 (1990) 170 CLR 394 at 412.
35 *The Commonwealth v Verwayen* (1990) 170 CLR 394 at 429, per Brennan J.

6 Summary

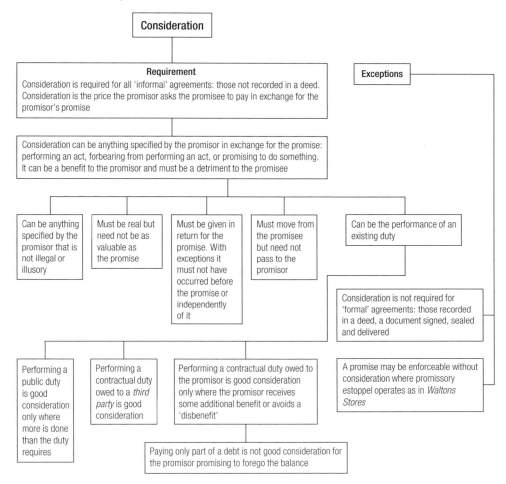

7 Questions

1. Sally is a university student. At the beginning of her first year she started smoking and drinking to excess and attending parties on most nights. As a result she failed all the mid-year tests and assignments in the subjects she was studying. In June, she also became pregnant. With a view to encouraging her to improve her results and with an eye to the future health of her baby, Sally's Aunt Prudence promised Sally that she would pay her $10,000 if she stopped smoking, drinking and attending parties until after her final exams and the birth of the baby. Sally did this and passed all her exams very well. The baby was born in February and is in excellent health. However, Prudence has refused to pay Sally as promised on the ground that Sally and the baby have benefited from Sally's changed lifestyle.

Please advise Sally whether she has a contractual claim for the sum promised by Prudence.

2   Bill and Rhonda are a very happy couple. From time to time they have discussed starting a family but have postponed doing so until Rhonda completed her PhD in international competition law. However, during a Federal election campaign they noted with interest a government announcement about the introduction of a new 'Baby Bonus' as part of its master plan to increase the Australian population. This was very detailed and formed a central plank of the government's election platform; indeed it was described by the Prime Minister as a 'core promise'. Printed information about the Baby Bonus was sent to all households in Australia; this provided that:

(i) The Baby Bonus would be paid in respect of all children born after 1 January.
(ii) The Baby Bonus would consist of a cash grant of $3,000 and free child care for the child for up to eight hours per day from the age of three months until he or she was five years of age.

The government was re-elected and introduced the Baby Bonus in the following Federal Budget. Relying on this initiative Bill and Rhonda decided that they would start a family immediately as the Baby Bonus would have the effect of enabling Rhonda to continue work on her PhD with only minimum disruption. Matters progressed well and Bill and Rhonda were delighted when Rhonda gave birth to Oliver. Unfortunately, however, at that time the government decided to discontinue the Baby Bonus. As the Minister for Human Services explained in a public announcement, cost blow-outs made it necessary for the government to trim expenditure and the Baby Bonus was a victim of this process.

Rhonda and Bill were very distressed by this announcement. They incurred $5,000 in maternity expenses when Oliver was born and that Rhonda has not been able to resume working on her PhD because they cannot afford child care. Please advise them of their contractual position in relation to the Baby Bonus.

3   In an agreement for the lease of a house to four university students, would the rent be good consideration for the landlord's promise to allow the students occupancy if the agreement stipulated that the rent be paid:

(a) by the students directly to the landlord's mortagee?
(b) to the landlord by the parents of the students?
(c) by one of the students?

4   Pursuant to a building contract, Davos Pty Ltd is due to pay Ceres Builders Ltd $100,000 on 20 May for work carried out on its behalf. However, Davos is experiencing financial difficulty and has only $90,000 available for this purpose. Fortunately for Davos, Ceres is also experiencing financial difficulty and in order to ensure that it receives most of what it is owed is prepared to accept $90,000 in settlement of its account.

(a) If, on 10 May, Ceres tells Davos that it would accept $90,000 in full settlement of its account, what would you advise Davos to do to protect its position?
(b) How, if at all, would your advice differ if Ceres made this offer on 20 May when asking Davos for payment?

CHAPTER 5

Intention to Create Contractual Relations

1	Introduction	153
2	Proving intention	158
3	Intention in practice	160
	a Domestic, family and social agreements	160
	b Commercial agreements	163
	c Agreements with a government	164
4	Summary	167
5	Questions	167

1   Introduction

In Anglo-Australian law an agreement will only have contractual effect if the parties intend it to do so. It is not sufficient that they are *ad idem* and that consideration for their promises is present; quite separately, they must also intend that should the agreement not be honoured, the aggrieved party can seek redress in the courts for breach of contract.[1] Examples of agreements that have been held not to be contracts on this ground include those between a husband and wife for an allowance,[2] a parent and adult child for the occupancy of a house,[3] friends to operate a car pool,[4] an investigative journalist and his source to keep the latter's identity confidential,[5] and between a government and a private firm to receive a subsidy.[6]

Although it is couched in terms of giving effect to the intention of the parties and although their intention will determine the matter if that is clearly expressed, the rule in question is also rooted in public policy considerations. This is most evident in relation to the reluctance of the courts to enforce family or domestic agreements.

---

1   The intention required is to create *contractual* relations. As Lord Diplock explains in *Pettitt v Pettitt* [1970] AC 777, the parties may well contemplate that *other* legal consequences will flow if their agreement is put into effect without intending that the agreement, while still executory, would constitute a contract.
2   *Balfour v Balfour* [1919] 2 KB 571.
3   *Jones v Padavatton* [1969] 2 All ER 616.
4   *Coward v Motor Insurers Bureau* [1963] 1 QB 259.
5   *Cohen v Cowles Media Co* 457 NW 2d 199 (1990).
6   *Australian Woollen Mills Pty Ltd v Commonwealth* (1955) 93 CLR 546.

Here two such considerations have been especially influential, both expressed in the seminal judgment of Atkin LJ in *Balfour v Balfour* (extracted below at p 160).[7] They are of the view that agreements between husband and wife (at least when they are in an amicable relationship) should be 'outside the realm of contract altogether'[8] and concern that if such agreements were enforceable this could result in an unacceptable amount of litigation requiring, according to his Lordship, 'the small Courts ... to be multiplied one hundredfold'. As a result, to a significant degree, whether a contract exists in a given case will be 'a consequence which the law imposes upon, or sees as a result of, what the parties have said or done', rather than merely the outcome of their subjective intention.[9]

The requirement that the parties must intend to create contractual relations, as an essential and distinct element of the formation of a contract, has been criticised on the ground that it is inconsistent with the objective approach adopted by the common law in relation to the formation of contracts.[10] It is argued that if a promise is made seriously and supported by consideration, nothing more should be required to create a contract.[11] As we shall see later, this view is reflected in the *Indian Contract Act, 1872* which contains no reference to this requirement. It is suggested, however, that the better view is expressed by the Victorian Court of Appeal in *ATCO Controls Pty Ltd v Newtronics Pty Ltd*,[12] namely, that while it 'may be that the rules as to consideration supply the answer as to whether the parties intend to enter into a legally binding bargain ... [even so] ... in some cases consideration and intention to create legal relations can be distinct; as where, for example, although application of the rules as to consideration as such suggest the formation of a legally binding agreement, the parties have otherwise expressly or impliedly signified that they do not intend their arrangement to be legally binding'. There has also been uncertainty about the meaning of 'intention' in this context; in particular, does it mean the parties must subjectively have the required intention, or is it sufficient if they do so objectively, or does the law consider both? These and related issues are discussed in the following extract.

Air Great Lakes Pty Ltd v KS Easter (Holdings) Pty Ltd

[1985] 2 NSWLR 309, New South Wales Court of Appeal

[The parties entered into an agreement for the sale of an airline business. Air Great Lakes alleged that this agreement had been repudiated by Easter and sought damages for breach of contract. In these proceedings it was argued by Easter that

---

7 [1919] 2 KB 571 at 579.
8 See also *Miller v Miller* 35 NW 464 (1887) Supreme Court of Iowa.
9 See *Air Great Lakes Pty Ltd v KS Easter (Holdings) Pty Ltd* [1985] 2 NSWLR 309 at 330, per Mahoney JA.
10 See S Williston, *Williston on Contracts* 3rd ed, Baker, Voorhis, Mount Kisco, 1957–1991, s 21. See also M Furmston (ed), *Butterworths Common Law Series: The Law of Contract*, Butterworths, London, 1999, para 2.165.
11 Ibid.
12 [2009] VSCA 238 per Warren CJ, Nettle and Mandie JJA at 60.

the parties did not intend the document they signed to be legally binding. This was accepted at first instance and Air Great Lakes appealed.]

Mahoney JA [at 330]: It is generally accepted that, in determining whether what the parties have done results in a binding contract, their intention is significant. And there is reference in the cases and the textbooks to the question whether, for there to be a binding contract, it is necessary that the parties have an actual or subjective intention to contract. ... But questions in that form are, I think, apt to mislead: it is, in my opinion, of more assistance to ask whether actual or subjective intention to contract plays a part in determining whether there is a binding contract, and (if it does) what part it plays.

The proper view is, in my opinion, that the existence of a contract is a consequence which the law imposes upon, or sees as a result of, what the parties have said and done. Actual subjective intention to contract is a factor which the law takes into account in determining whether a contract exists but it is not, or not always, the determining factor.

The matter may be tested by an example: A says, 'I promise to sell Black Acre to B for $100'; and B says, 'I promise to buy Black Acre from A for that price', the promises being made orally. In such a case, a binding contract will be held to exist. And this will be so even though neither A nor B subjectively adverted to (and therefore had no actual subjective intention as to) whether, by the exchange of those promises, a binding contract would be made. The law will hold a binding contract to have been made even though neither had any actual subjective intention that there be a contract, in the sense that neither party gave any thought to the matter.

The law looks, in this regard, to what the parties have done, viz, to their exchange of promises to buy and sell; and it treats the fact of that exchange prima facie sufficient for imposing on them the legal relationship of contract. It will determine whether, according to what they said and did, they exchanged congruent promises: if they did, a contract will prima facie result.

But this does not mean that actual subjective intention qua contract may not be relevant. Thus, if A, notwithstanding what he said, had the actual subjective intention that no contract should result, a binding contract may not be held to exist. If the terms of A's promise were such that B, as a reasonable man, would take it to involve a legal commitment and B did not know that A did not intend that there be a binding contract, then a binding <331> contract would result. A would not be permitted to set up, against such a meaning of what he had said, a contrary subjective intention.

But the result would not, I think, be the same if B knew of A's actual subjective intention. The law would not, I think, impose the relationship of contract where, eg, A though he was play-acting and B knew of that fact. A's actual subjective intention would be effective to prevent the contract arising. A fortiori, if both A and B had the intention that no contract should result, and each knew of it, then none would be imposed. And, I think, this notwithstanding that a reasonable bystander would take from what they said and did that there was an exchange of congruent promises and a mutual purpose to contract. I put aside for this purpose special cases, of estoppel, third party rights, and the like.

The result is therefore that intention to contract, in the subjective sense, is relevant to but not determinative of the existence of a binding contract. It acts, in a sense, as a limiting factor, that is, as a reason for not giving to what on the face of it is an exchange of congruent promises, the legal consequences which would otherwise be given to it. And on this basis, it is, in principle relevant to know what was the actual subjective intention of each party, in the example that I have given, in order to determine whether the legal relationship of contract is to be held to exist. More correctly, it is relevant to know the intention of the one party where it is the intention of or known to the other.

McHugh JA [at 335]: The publication by O W Holmes Jnr of *The Common Law* (1881) hastened the emergence of both a unified theory of contract and the supremacy of the objective theory of contract. The transition between the subjective and objective theories can be seen in a note in the 3rd edition of Anson's *Principles of the English Law of Contract*, at 9, where the author said:

> 'I hold that the law does require the wills of the parties to be at one, but that when men present all the phenomena of agreement they are not allowed to say that they were not agreed.'

Since then most courts and writers have championed the objective theory. ... In *Taylor v Johnson* (1983) 151 CLR 422 at 429 Mason ACJ, Murphy and Deane JJ said that, while 'the sounds of conflict have not been completely stilled, the clear trend in decided cases and academic writings has been to leave the objective theory in command of the field'. Nevertheless, some of the most influential writers have refused to accept either the subjective or objective theory as explaining the law of contract. ... Moreover, a nice question remains as to the manner of applying the objective theory: is it objectivity from the point of view of the promisor, the promisee or the detached bystander? Support for each view can be found in the cases. ...

Lewis v Brass (1877) LR 3 QBD 667 ... is an express decision, never overruled, that a subjective intention to contract is necessary to the formation of a binding contract. ... Although [this case] seems to have escaped both criticism and overruling, I do not think that it can now be accepted as authority for the proposition that a subjective intention to contract is a necessary element in the formation of a contract. The weight of authority in favour of the objective theory is too great. But the decision is consistent with what I think is clearly the Anglo-Australian law, namely, that an intention to create a legally enforceable contract is a necessary element in the formation of a contract. ... Nor does the rejection of the subjective element in *Lewis v Brass* mean that the intention to create an enforceable contract can only be deduced from the terms of the document when a document has 'integrated' the parties' negotiations and discussions. Thus a party may show that a document, which to all outward appearances constitutes a contract, is subject to a condition precedent. He may prove, for example, by oral evidence that the agreement was subject to another person's approval. ... A party may prove that words which manifest a contract were made in jest or as a joke or a dramatic performance, although he will be bound even in that class of case if a reasonable person would have understood his words in a promissory sense. ... Again a party may prove that a 'contract' was a sham. ... Moreover, the court is entitled to look beyond the promissory words to the relationship of the parties for the purpose of determining whether they intended to create a legally enforceable contract. In *Balfour v Balfour* [1919] 2 KB 571 and *Cohen v Cohen* (1929) 42 CLR 91 it was held that agreements made between husband and wife were not legally enforceable. In *South Australia v The Commonwealth* (1962) 108 <337> CLR 130 McTiernan, Taylor and Windeyer JJ were of the opinion that the agreement in question gave rise to political obligations only and not to legal obligations enforceable by a court. Windeyer J said (at 154):

'... An agreement deliberately entered into and by which both parties intend themselves to be bound may yet not be an agreement that the courts will enforce. The circumstances may show that they did not intend, or cannot be regarded as having intended, to subject their agreement to the adjudication of the courts. The status of the parties, their relationship to one another, the topics with which the agreement deals, the extent to which it is expressed to be finally definitive of their deals, the extent to which it is expressed to be finally definitive of their concurrence, the way in which it came into existence, these, or any one or more of them taken in the circumstance, may put the matter outside the realm of contract law.'

In my opinion it follows from *Pym v Campbell*, and the other cases to which I have referred, that a party is able to prove that, before signing a document, the signatories agreed that it did not constitute a binding contract. Accordingly, it would be an odd result if one of the signatories could not prove that, before signing, they agreed that the document was to be a binding contract. Of course, the agreement of the parties may turn out to be incorrect because a necessary formality, such as consideration, capacity or a statutory requirement, was not fulfilled. In principle, I see no reason why the intention to create a legal relationship cannot be proved by material outside the document, including the statements of the parties. ...

The intention to create a legally binding contract although a matter to be proved objectively, may, nevertheless, in my opinion, be proved by what the parties said and did as well as by what they wrote. The intention may be proved in that way even in a case where the document is intended to compromise all the terms of their bargain. This is because the intention to be bound is a jural act separate and distinct from the *terms* of their bargain.

[All members of the Court agreed that there was a binding agreement between the parties. However, Hope JA did not agree that, in the case of a written agreement, regard could be paid to extrinsic material to help to determine whether there was an intention to create legal relations.]

Appeal allowed

2 Proving intention

Until the decision of the High Court in *Ermogenous v Greek Orthodox Community of SA Inc*[13] it was generally understood that the issue of intention was to be resolved by reference to two rebuttable presumptions: in the case of agreements that were regarded as social or domestic in nature, it was presumed that the parties did not intend to create contractual relations so that no contract would be held to exist unless the party asserting that there was a contract proved that there was such an intention in the particular case. On the other hand, in the cases of commercial agreements, it was presumed that the parties did intend to create contractual relations so that it was not necessary for the party asserting that a contract existed to prove that this element was actually present; it would be in issue only if the other party asserted that it was not present—in which case that party bore the burden of proving that this was the case. As a result, where intention was contested, a preliminary matter would almost invariably be the categorisation of the agreement as one, or the other, as this determined who bore the burden of proof on the issue. While this appears to remain the position in England, the use of these presumptions was rejected by the Australian High Court in *Ermogenous* for the reasons set out in the following extract.

Ermogenous v Greek Orthodox Community of SA Inc

(2002) 209 CLR 95, High Court of Australia

[Ermogenous was employed by the Greek Orthodox community as its Archbishop for 23 years. During this period he received a stipend but nothing for annual or long service leave. Following the termination of his employment he brought an action in the Industrial Relations Court of South Australia seeking payment in respect of this leave. He succeeded at first instance before an industrial magistrate. However, on appeal this decision was reversed by the Full Court of the Supreme Court of South Australia on the ground that there was no intention to create legal relations between the parties. Ermogenous then appealed to the High Court.]

Gaudron, McHugh, Hayne and Callinan JJ [at 105]:
Intention to create contractual relations
[24] 'It is of the essence of contract, regarded as a class of obligations, that there is a voluntary assumption of a legally enforceable duty.' (*Australian Woollen Mills Pty Ltd v The Commonwealth* (1954) 92 CLR 424 at 457 per Dixon CJ, Williams, Webb, Fullagar and Kitto JJ) To be a legally enforceable duty there must, of course, be identifiable parties to the arrangement, the terms of the arrangement must be certain, and, unless recorded as a deed, there must generally be real consideration for the agreement. Yet '[t]he circumstances may show that [the parties] did not intend, or cannot be regarded as having intended, to subject their agreement to the

---

13 (2002) 209 CLR 95.

adjudication of the courts' (*South Australia v The Commonwealth* (1962) 108 CLR 130 at 154 per Windeyer J).

[25] Because the inquiry about this last aspect may take account of the subject matter of the agreement, the status of the parties to it, their relationship to one another, and other surrounding circumstances, not only is there obvious difficulty in formulating rules intended to prescribe the kinds of cases in which an intention to create contractual relations should, or should not, be found to exist, it would be wrong to do so. Because the search for the 'intention to create contractual relations' requires an objective assessment of the state of affairs between the parties (as distinct from the identification of any uncommunicated subjective reservation or intention that either may harbour) the circumstances which might properly be taken into account in deciding whether there was the relevant intention are so varied as to preclude the formation of any prescriptive rules. Although the word 'intention' is used in this context, it is used in the same sense as it is used in other contractual contexts. It describes what it is that would objectively be conveyed by what was said or done, having regard to <106> the circumstances in which those statements and actions happened. It is not a search for the uncommunicated subjective motives or intentions of the parties.

[26] In this context of intention to create legal relations there is frequent reference to 'presumptions'. It is said that it may be presumed that there are some 'family arrangements' which are not intended to give rise to legal obligations and it was said in this case that it should not be presumed that there was an intention to create legal relations because it was a matter concerning the engagement of a minister of religion. For our part, we doubt the utility of using the language of presumptions in this context. At best, the use of that language does no more than invite attention to identifying the party who bears the onus of proof. In this case, where issue was joined about the existence of a legally binding contract between the parties, there could be no doubt that it was for the appellant to demonstrate that there was such a contract. Reference to presumptions may serve only to distract attention from that more basic and important proposition.

[27] More importantly, the use of the language of presumptions may lead, as it did in this case, to treating one proposition (that an intention to create legal relations is not to be presumed) as equivalent to another, different proposition (that generally, or usually, or it is to be presumed that, an arrangement about remuneration of a minister of religion will not give rise to legally enforceable obligations). References to 'the usual non-contractual status of a priest or minister' and factors which 'generally militate against' a finding of intention to create legal relations illustrate the point. The latter proposition may then be understood as suggesting, in some way, that proof to the contrary is to be seen as particularly difficult and yet offer no guidance at all about how it may be done. Especially is that so when the chief factor said to justify the proposition that an intention to create legal relations must be proved (the essentially spiritual role of a minister of religion) is then put forward as the principal reason not to find that intention in a particular case, and any other matters suggesting that there may be an intention

to create legal relations are treated as dealing only with 'collateral' or 'peripheral' aspects of the relationship between the parties. In practice, the latter proposition may rapidly ossify into a rule of law, that there cannot be a contract of employment of a minister of religion, distorting the proper application of basic principles of the law of contract.

[Their Honours concluded that the magistrate at first instance had not failed to consider whether the parties had intended to create legal relations and that even if he had done so, there was no ground for the Full Court inferring that there was no such intention. In a separate judgment Kirby J reached the same conclusion.]

Appeal allowed

3 Intention in practice

Following the decision in *Ermogenous*, the position in Australia is that the party asserting the existence of a contract will always bear the burden of proving, along with the other elements required, that the parties intended to enter into contractual relations. When considering this issue regard can be paid to all surrounding circumstances including what the parties said or wrote, their relationship and the nature and terms of the agreement. These are assessed objectively by asking whether a reasonable person, with knowledge of them, would conclude that both parties intended the agreement to be an enforceable contract. Some examples of the situations that may arise in practice are set out below.

a Domestic, family and social agreements

Examples of agreements within this category include those between husband and wife and those relating to friendly activities such as purchasing lottery tickets jointly and car-pooling arrangements. Because agreements of this nature are generally not intended to be legally binding, a party asserting that in the particular instance the parties did have this intention will need to show that there were unusual circumstances present which would make this intention clear to a reasonable person.

Balfour v Balfour

[1919] 2 KB 571, English Court of Appeal

[When illness prevented her from returning to Ceylon with him, Mr Balfour promised to pay Mrs Balfour an allowance until she was able to travel. The parties remained apart and their relationship deteriorated. Mr Balfour ceased paying the allowance and Mrs Balfour commenced proceedings to recover the amount outstanding. By this time she had already obtained an order for alimony. At first instance Mrs Balfour succeeded; Mr Balfour appealed.]

Atkin LJ [at 578]: It is quite common, and it is the natural and inevitable result of the relationship of husband and wife, that the two spouses should make arrangements between themselves. ... To my mind those agreements, or many of them, do not result in contracts at all, and they do not result in contracts even though there may be what as between other parties would constitute consideration for the agreement. ... <579> ... Nevertheless they are not contracts, and they are not contracts because the parties did not intend that they should be attended by legal consequences. To my mind it would be of the worst possible example to hold that agreements such as this resulted in legal obligations which could be enforced in the courts. ... [T]he small courts of this country would have to be multiplied one hundredfold if these arrangements were to result in legal obligations. They are not sued upon, not because the parties are reluctant to enforce their legal rights when the agreement is broken, but because the parties, in the inception of the arrangement, never intended that they should be sued upon. Agreements such as these are outside the realm of contracts altogether. The common law does not regulate the form of agreements between spouses. ... [I]t appears to me to be plainly established that the promise here was <580> not intended by either party to be attended by legal consequences. I think the onus was upon the plaintiff, and the plaintiff has not established any contract.

[Warrington and Duke LJJ gave separate judgments to the same effect.]

Appeal allowed

Jones v Padavatton

[1969] 2 All ER 616, English Court of Appeal

[Jones desired her daughter, Padavatton, to leave Washington, where she worked, become a barrister in England and then return to Trinidad. To induce her to do this, Jones promised to pay Padavatton an allowance. After she had moved to England and studied for some time, Jones agreed to acquire a large house for Padavatton and to allow her to reside there and derive an income by letting spare rooms to tenants. After a number of years, Jones commenced proceedings to gain possession of the house. At first instance, it was decided that there was a contract between the parties which entitled Padavatton to possession of the house. Jones appealed.]

Danckwerts LJ [at 620]: There is no doubt that this case is a most difficult one, but I have reached a conclusion that the present case is one of those family arrangements which depend on the good faith of the promises which are made and are not intended to be rigid, binding agreement. *Balfour v Balfour* was a case of husband and wife, but there is no doubt that the same principles apply to dealings between other relations, such as father and son and daughter and mother. This, indeed, seems to me a compelling case. The mother and the daughter seem to have been on very good terms before 1967. The mother was arranging for a career for the daughter which she hoped would lead to success. This involved a visit to

England in conditions which could not be wholly foreseen. What was required was an arrangement which was to be financed by the mother and was such as would be adaptable to circumstances, as it in fact was. The operation about the house was, in my view, not a completely fresh arrangement, but an adaptation of the mother's financial assistance to the daughter due to the situation which was found to exist in England. It was not a stiff contractual operation any more than the original arrangement.

Salmon, LJ [at 621]: Did the parties intend the arrangement to be legally binding? This question has to be solved by applying what is sometimes (although perhaps unfortunately) called an objective test. The court has to consider what the parties said and wrote in the light of all the surrounding circumstances, and then decide whether the true interference is that the ordinary man and woman, speaking or writing thus in such circumstances, would have intended to create a legally binding agreement.

Counsel for the mother has said, quite rightly, that as a rule when arrangements are made between close relations, for example, between husband and wife, parent and child or uncle and nephew in relation to an allowance, there is a presumption against an intention of creating any legal relationship. This is not a presumption of law, but of fact. It derives from experience of life and human nature which shows that in such circumstances men and women usually do not intend to create legal rights and obligations, but intend to rely solely on family ties of mutual trust and affection. ... There may, however, be circumstances in which this presumption, like all other presumptions of fact, can be rebutted.

[His Lordship concluded that the parties did intend their agreement to have contractual force because it required Padavatton to give up a secure and well paid job in Washington to move to London, involving considerable dislocation for her and her son and because it had been confirmed by lawyers acting for her mother. However, he also concluded that the contract had been properly terminated and for this reason agreed that the appeal should be dismissed. In a separate judgment, Fenton Atkinson LJ agreed with Danckwerts LJ that the parties had not intended to create contractual relations.]

Appeal allowed

An important factor in these cases appears to have been that the parties were on amicable terms when the agreement was entered into. When this is not the case, for example, when a husband and wife are in the process of separating and the agreement relates to a division of matrimonial property or spousal maintenance, the parties are more likely to intend to create contractual relations and a different outcome will result as was the case in *Popiw v Popiw*[14] and *Merritt v Merritt*.[15]

---

14   [1957] VR 197. In this case Hudson J observed at 198: 'The promise made in the present case was given after the relationship had broken down and was made in an effort to restore it and related to a matter that had been one of the causes of dissension. Any doubt I might otherwise have had that the parties intended to affect their legal relationship is removed by the fact of their visit to the respondent's solicitor to give him instructions to take the steps necessary to carry out the respondent's promise.'

15   [1970] 1 WLR 1211.

As a result, regard must always be paid to the particular circumstances of the case including, for example, the extent to which the parties changed their positions as a result of the agreement; whether the agreement was negotiated or recorded using lawyers; the certainty of the terms used; whether the parties were on good terms when the agreement was made; and whether there was consideration for the promises involved. Circumstances such as these may show that the parties did intend their agreement to be contractually binding. *Attwells v Campbell*[16] is an example. Here, an agreement between Mr Attwells and Miss Campbell, concerning the latter's financial support, was held to be binding notwithstanding the intimacy of their relationship. This conclusion was reached having regard to the terms in which the agreement was expressed, the fact that it was recorded in writing and the acrimonious circumstances in which it was reached.

b Commercial agreements

In the present context, commercial agreements are those made in the course of business, or between parties whose only dealing with each other is in relation to the agreement in question. Generally speaking, the parties to such agreements do intend that they have contractual effect and in practice little evidence will be required to establish this element; indeed, the courts may well 'strive to give legal effect to such arrangements'.[17]

The parties to a commercial agreement may, however, not wish it to be a contract, but rather, to be binding only 'in honour'. One way of doing this is to include a provision in the agreement, often called an 'honour clause', to this effect. Since the decision in *Ermogenous* such a clause will make it more difficult, or even impossible if properly drafted, for the party asserting that there was a contract to establish the presence of an intention to create contractual relations. This is because that party will now bear the burden of doing so unassisted by a formal presumption that such an intention existed.

Rose & Frank Co v Crompton & Bros Ltd

[1923] 2 KB 261, English Court of Appeal

[The parties entered into a commercial agreement which included the words 'This arrangement is not entered into ... as a formal or legal agreement, and shall not be subject to legal jurisdiction in the law courts ... '. Crompton repudiated the agreement and Rose & Frank brought an action for breach of contract. At first instance, it was decided that the clause quoted was against public policy as an attempt to oust the jurisdiction of the courts and Rose & Frank succeeded in its claim. Crompton appealed.]

---

16 [2000] NSWCA 132.
17 *ATCO Controls Pty Ltd v Newtronics Pty Ltd* [2009] VSCA 238 per Warren CJ, Nettle and Mandie JJA at 68.

Atkin LJ [at 293]: To create a contract there must be a common intention of the parties to enter into legal obligations, mutually communicated expressly or impliedly. Such an intention ordinarily will be inferred when parties enter into an agreement which in other respects conforms to the rules of law as to the formation of contracts. It may be negatived impliedly by the nature of the agreed promise or promises, as in the case of offer and acceptance of hospitality, or of some agreements made in the course of family life between members of a family as in *Balfour v Balfour*. If the intention may be negatived impliedly it may be negatived expressly. In this document, construed as a whole, I find myself driven to the conclusion that the clause in question expresses in clear terms the mutual intention of the parties not to enter into legal obligations in respect to the matters upon which they are recording their agreement. I have never seen such a clause before, but I see nothing necessarily absurd in business men seeking to regulate their business relations by mutual promises which fall short of legal obligations, and rest on obligations of either honour or self-interest, or perhaps both.

[Bankes and Scrutton LJJ in separate judgments reached the same conclusion about the effect of the clause.]

Appeal allowed

The ability of parties to enter into non-binding commercial agreements explains the use of what are sometimes called 'letters of comfort'—documents in which the author makes a representation to the recipient about the commercial viability of a third party, but without the formality (and clear intention of making a binding commitment) associated with giving a gurantee. *Kleinwort Benson Ltd v Malaysia Mining Corporation Berhad*[18] is an example. Here, to support a loan application being made by its subsidiary, a company gave a letter to the finance company considering making the loan which included a statement that it is 'our policy to ensure that the business of [our subsidiary] is at all times in a position to meet its liabilities to you …'. Because of this statement, it was held that the letter did not to give rise to any enforceable legal obligation; it was not promissory, but merely a representation of the company's intentions. However, there is no general rule that letters of comfort are not binding; ultimately, this depends upon the intention of the parties as revealed by the circumstances of the particular case. Thus, for example, in *Banque Brussels Lambert SA v Australian National Industries Ltd*[19] a comfort letter was held to be binding because it was promisory in character and had been given after negotiation and the exchange of drafts.

c Agreements with a government

While in practice the normal commercial agreements of government—buying and selling of goods and services—will be intended to be contractual, this may not be so where an agreement relates to a policy initiative. In such a case, although all the

---

18   [1989] 1 WLR 379.
19   (1989) 21 NSWLR 502.

other elements of a contract are present, intention to contract may be absent. This is especially likely where the government is able to achieve its objective without needing to incur liability to the other party. An example is the wool subsidy scheme at issue in *Australian Woollen Mills Pty Ltd v Commonwealth* and it is suggested that lack of contractual intention is the best explanation of the decision in that case.[20] Another example is the arrangement discussed in the following extract.

Administration of the Territory of Papua and New Guinea v Leahy

(1961) 105 CLR 6, High Court of Australia

[At Leahy's request, the parties entered into an agreement whereby a government department would conduct a program to eradicate the ticks infesting his cattle. The program was unsuccessful and Leahy sued the department for breach of contract. His claim succeeded at first instance and the department appealed.]

Dixon CJ [at 10]: In my opinion this appeal must be allowed on the simple ground that the facts in no way support the conclusion that the defendant, the Administration of the Territory, entered into any such contractual relation with the plaintiff as his pleading alleges or as has been found in his favour. I am clearly of opinion that the Administration of the Territory, by its officers, did not contract with the plaintiff; there was no intention on their part to enter into any contract, to undertake contractual obligations or to do or undertake more than was considered naturally and properly incident to carrying out their governmental or departmental function in the conditions prevailing. They were merely pursuing the policy adopted for the eradication of tick. ...

McTiernan J [at 11]: The arrangement consisted of agreed promises but that is not enough to make a contract, unless it was the common intention of the parties to enter into legal obligations, mutually communicated, expressly or impliedly. It was not an express or implied term of the arrangement that the respondent should make any payment for the treatment of the cattle. I cannot agree that the Administration through its officers intended to enter into legal relations when, at the request of the respondent, it undertook the organization of the tick eradication campaign with respect to his cattle. The conduct of the parties constituted an administrative arrangement by which the Administration in pursuance of its agricultural policy, gave assistance to an owner of stock to prevent that stock contracting a disease which was prevalent in the Territory. The work done by the Administration was analogous to a social service which generally does not have as its basis a legal relationship of a contractual nature and from which no right of action would arise in favour of the citizen who is receiving the services if the government acts inefficiently in performing them.

[In a separate judgment, Kitto J reached the same conclusion.]

Appeal allowed

---

20 (1955) 93 CLR 546 (PC).

INTERNATIONAL PERSPECTIVES

India

Intention to create contractual relations did not exist as a distinct prerequisite to a contract in English law until the late nineteenth century,[21] appreciably after the passage of the *Indian Contract Act* in 1872. Although, no doubt, this explains why the Act is silent about the matter, this silence when coupled with s 10 which provides that: 'All agreements are contracts if they are made with the free consent of the parties, competent to contract, for lawful consideration and with lawful object' suggests that Indian law does not recognise intention to contract as a separate requirement. This appears to have been the Supreme Court's view in *CWT v Abdul Hussein* (1988) 3 SCC 562. However, a similar concept may be introduced into Indian law by saying that a communication cannot be a proposal within s 2(a), or an acceptance within s 2(c), unless the party involved intended to enter into a contract. Thus, for example, it has been suggested that it is the absence of this intention that explains why a sales puff is not regarded as a proposal.[22]

China

The *Contract Law of the People's Republic of China* also does not explicitly require the parties to have an intention to create contractual relations. However, as 'an offer' is defined (Article 14) as 'a party's manifestation of intention to enter into a contract' and as a contract is defined (Article 2) as an agreement 'for the *purpose* (emphasis added) of establishing, altering or discharging a relationship of civil rights and obligations', intention to create contractual relations is required implicitly. Thus, unlike the position in Anglo-Australian law, a communication cannot amount to an 'offer' (and hence an agreement cannot be reached) in Chinese contract law unless the offeror intends to create contractual relations should it be accepted. This is reinforced by the exclusion in Article 2 which provides that 'an agreement concerning personal relationships such as marriage, adoption, guardianship etc shall be governed by other applicable laws'.

---

21 Although Professor Simpson attributes its introduction to *Carlill v Carbolic Smoke Ball* [1893] 1 QB 256 (see AWB Simpson, *Leading Cases in the Common Law*, Oxford University Press, Oxford, 1995 at 281) arguably it was not clearly identified as a distinct element until *Balfour v Balfour* [1919] 2 KB 571.

22 See *Banwari Lal v Sukhdarshan Daya* (1973) 1 SCC 294.

4 Summary

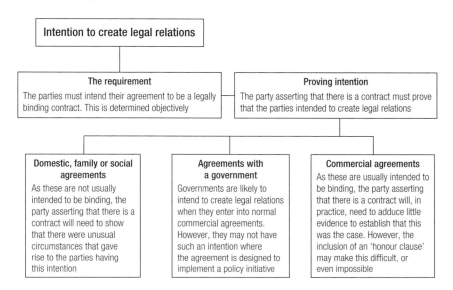

5 Questions

1. For many years, during the football season Anne has conducted a 'footy tipping' competition for staff members at her place of work. Members wishing to participate pay Anne a joining fee of $10 at the beginning of the season. According to the terms of the competition, drafted by Anne, a prize will be awarded each week to the person tipping the most winners that week and a major prize will be awarded at the end of the season to the person who has picked the most winners over the entire season. The competition has proved to be very popular and now over 150 staff members are participating. As a result, running the competition is placing a heavy burden on Anne, especially since her employer introduced a new workloads model, and halfway through the season she announced that she would no longer conduct the competition. This has caused uproar. Please advise Anne of her contractual position in relation to the competition.

2. Nelson Ltd operated two plants in New South Wales, one in Sydney and the other in Newcastle. It decided to close the Sydney plant. However, in an announcement to its workforce about the closure, the company said that it would pay a relocation allowance of $2,000 to any member of its Sydney workforce who chose to relocate to and work in the Newcastle plant. The announcement described the allowance as an 'ex gratia' payment and said that while Nelson was not obliged to make such a payment, it would to do so as a 'show of good faith'. Bill moved to Newcastle in response to this announcement and commenced work in Nelson's Newcastle plant. However, Nelson has refused to pay him the relocation allowance. Please advise Bill whether he has a contractual right to the allowance.

3. Libby wished to study drama at a long established Australian university. She applied to this university for a place in its highly regarded drama course and in due course received an offer of a place. She accepted this offer by the due date and paid the necessary fees. However, shortly before the course was due to commence, Libby was notified that due to declining interest in drama, the course would no longer be offered. Instead, she was offered a place in the university's Arts course, as part of which drama subjects could be studied. Libby does not wish to do this and seeks your advice concerning her contractual position in relation to the university; please advise her.

CHAPTER 6

Capacity

1	Introduction	169
2	Mental incapacity	171
3	Intoxication	175
4	Bankruptcy	177
5	The Crown	177
6	Minors	178
	a Common law	178
	b The effect of minority at common law	180
	c Statutory intervention	181
7	Companies	186
	a Common law	186
	b Contractual capacity under the *Corporations Act*	186
	c Pre-incorporation contracts	186
8	Summary	188
9	Questions	188

1 Introduction

Contractual capacity refers to a person's ability to make an agreement that can be enforced by the other party. At common law, it was presumed that all persons had such capacity. However, a number of exceptions were recognised that allowed a person to avoid contractual liability by rebutting this presumption.[1] The categories of those in this position, and the reasons why they receive special treatment, vary considerably. In the case of some categories, such as minors, drunks and the insane, it arose out of concern that a person's age or disability made them vulnerable to exploitation and so was designed to protect them from this occurring. In other cases, it arose because for technical reasons certain people were not able to make contracts; the now largely defunct exceptions relating to married women and corporations are examples. In the case of the Crown, the exception was because at common law the Crown could not be sued. This variety has caused some writers to

---

[1] See *Borthwick v Carruthers* (1787) 99 ER 1300.

warn that it is misleading 'to speak of certain classes of persons lacking capacity to contract'.[2] It also explains why some writers locate this topic, as we have done, in their treatment of formation of contract, while others locate it in their treatment of those factors that limit the enforcement of contracts.

This area of law is a complicated mix of common law and statute. In the case of minors this is especially so as there has been considerable statutory intervention. Unfortunately, this has not been uniform across Australia. At one end of the spectrum, New South Wales has codified the area, while at the other, Western Australia, Tasmania, Queensland and the territories have left it largely to the common law. Victoria and South Australia occupy a middle position. It is no wonder, therefore, that there have been calls for national law reform.[3]

In this chapter, we will examine the principal circumstances in which an agreement will not be enforceable on the grounds of contractual incapacity and the consequences.

INTERNATIONAL PERSPECTIVES

Both the Indian and Chinese Acts contain provisions dealing with capacity and both treat capacity as an issue of formation. In the case of India, this is made clear in s 10 of the *Indian Contract Act* which provides that an agreement will be a contract only if the 'parties are competent to contract'. Who is competent is defined in s 11. Agreements entered into by persons made incompetent to contract by this provision (principally minors and those of unsound mind) are of no effect and therefore impose no obligations upon them. However, some relief from the consequences of this outcome is provided by s 68 which allows a supplier to obtain reimbursement for necessaries supplied to an incompetent person.

In the case of China, Article 9 of the *Contract Law* requires the parties to have 'appropriate capacities' for civil rights and acts and special provision is made in Article 47 for contracts made by persons with limited capacity. This is an especially notable provision because, unlike the position at common law and in India, gradation is envisaged so that persons with limited capacity can make contracts appropriate to their 'age, intelligence or mental health'.

Indian Contract Act, 1872

Section 11. Who are competent to contract

Every person is competent to contract who is of the age of majority according to the law to which he is subject, and who is of sound mind and is not disqualified from contracting by any law to which he is subject.

---

2   See L Willmott, S Christensen and D Butler, *Contract Law*, 2nd edn, Oxford University Press, Melbourne, 2005, 351.
3   Ibid at 360.

Section 68. Claim for necessaries supplied to a person incapable of contracting, or on his account

If a person, incapable of entering into a contract, or any one whom he is legally bound to support, is supplied by another person with necessaries suited to his condition in life, the person who has furnished such supplies is entitled to be reimbursed from the property of such incapable person.

Contract Law of the People's Republic of China, 1999

Article 9. Capacity

In entering into a contract, the parties shall have the appropriate capacities for civil rights and civil acts.

Article 47. Contract by Person with Limited Capacity

A contract concluded by a person with limited capacity for civil act is valid upon ratification by the legal agent thereof, provided that a contract from which such person accrues benefits only or the conclusion of which is appropriate for his age, intelligence or mental health does not require ratification by his legal agent.

The other party may demand that the legal agent ratify the contract within one month. If the legal agent fails to manifest his intention, he is deemed to have declined to ratify the contract. Prior to ratification of the contract, the other party in good faith is entitled to cancel the contract. Cancellation shall be effected by notification.

2 Mental incapacity

A person is able to avoid a contract if, at the time it was entered into, they lacked the mental capacity to understand its nature and this was known, or should have been known, to the other party. However, it is not essential that the contract is unfair to that person, although if it is, this may indicate lack of a proper understanding on their part. Precisely what the law requires for a contract to be voidable on this ground, and who can rely upon it, is discussed in the following extracts.

Gibbons v Wright

(1954) 91 CLR 423, High Court of Australia

[Gibbons and her two sisters-in-law became owners of land as joint tenants. Subsequently, however, the sisters executed documents which converted the joint tenancy into a tenancy in common. After they had both died, Gibbons claimed that these documents were ineffectual because the sisters lacked the mental capacity to make them and that therefore she was the sole owner of the land as the surviving joint tenant. She commenced proceedings against Wright, as the executor of the sisters' estates, seeking a declaration to this effect. She failed in the Tasmanian Full Court and appealed to the High Court.]

Dixon CJ, Kitto and Taylor JJ [at 437]: The law does not prescribe any fixed standard of sanity as requisite for the validity of all transactions. It requires, in relation to each particular matter or piece of business transacted, that each party shall have such soundness of mind as to be capable of understanding the general nature of what he is doing by his participation. ... <437> ...

The principle ... appears to us to be that the mental capacity required by the law in respect of any instrument is relative to the particular transaction which is being effected by means of the instrument, and may be described as the capacity to understand the nature of that transaction when it is explained. ...

Ordinarily the nature of the transaction means in this connection the broad operation, the 'general purport' of the instrument; but in some cases it may mean the effect of a wider transaction which the instrument is a means of carrying out. In the present case, it was necessary, we think that the two sisters should have been capable of understanding, if the matter had been explained to them, that by the executing the mortgages and the memorandum of transfer they would be altering the character of their interest in the properties concerned, so that instead of the last survivor of the three joint tenants becoming entitled to the whole, each of them would be entitled to a one-third <439> share which would pass to her estate if she still owned it at her death. [Having regard to the finding of the jury, their Honours proceeded to consider the case on the footing that the sisters lacked this capacity; they continued.]

But proof of this was not enough to entitle the appellant to succeed in the action if the result was that the instruments were merely voidable; for an instrument voidable by reason of the incapacity of a party, or by reason of any form of imposition upon a party, is valid unless and until it is avoided by that party or his representative. It is clearly not open to other persons, such as one claiming adversely to the party, to elect against the validity of the instrument; ... Neither Ethel Rose Gibbons nor Olinda Gibbons purported in her lifetime to avoid the instruments severing the joint tenancy, and the respondent as their executor has always affirmed their validity. Consequently the appellant must fail unless the law is that a deed disposing of property is absolutely void if at the time of its execution the disponor was incapable of understanding what he was doing, in the sense we have mentioned.

[After reviewing numerous authorities, their Honours concluded that lack of understanding did not have this effect; it made the transaction voidable only. For that reason, the appellant's claim failed.]

Appeal dismissed

[footnotes omitted]

Hart v O'Connor

[1985] 1 AC 1000, Privy Council on appeal from New Zealand

[As trustee of an estate, the vendor sold trust property (a farm) to Hart. At the time of the sale the vendor was 83 and of unsound mind. However, Hart did not know this and negotiated the sale fairly with the vendor's solicitors. Hart went into occupation and made improvements to the land. Subsequently, O'Connor (one of the vendor's brothers) as the new trustee of the estate took proceedings to set the contract aside on the grounds, *inter alia*, that the vendor was of unsound mind and that the transaction was unconscionable. O'Connor failed at first instance but succeeded in the New Zealand Court of Appeal. Hart then appealed to the Privy Council.]

Lord Brightman for the Board [at 1015]: The Court of Appeal found that there was ample evidence to support the finding of fact that the vendor lacked the requisite contractual capacity. They upheld the judge's finding that the bargain was 'unfair'. They also said that the decision in *Archer v Cutler* correctly represented the law, and rejected the submission that there must be overreaching behaviour before a bargain can be set aside by an incompetent (whose incapacity is not known) on the ground of unfairness. ...

[Their Lordships continued at 1021]: *Imperial Loan Co Ltd v Stone* [1892] 1 QB 599 was considered and accepted as correct by the High Court of Australia in *McLaughlin v Daily Telegraph Newspaper Co Ltd* (No 2) (1904) 1 CLR 243, where Griffith CJ delivering the judgment of the court said of the *Imperial Loan* case and its predecessor *Molton v Camroux*, at p 272:

> 'The principal of the decision seems, however, to be the same in both cases, which, in our judgment, establish that a contract made <1022> by a person actually unsound, but apparently of sound, mind with another who deals with him directly, and who has no knowledge of the unsoundness of mind, is as valid as if the unsoundness of mind had not existed. If the man dealing with the person of unsound mind is aware of his insanity, the contract is voidable at the option of the latter, but the party who takes advantage of the other cannot himself set up the incapacity. In this respect the matter is treated on the same footing as cases of fraud inducing a contract. There is, indeed, authority for saying that the equitable doctrines governing the validity or invalidity of a contract made with an insane person are only a particular instance of the general doctrines relating to fraudulent contracts. In the cases last mentioned no unfairness of dealing could be imputed to the persons who sought to take advantage of the contract, which was, in fact, made, in each case, with an apparently sane person. The principle appears to be that the validity of a contract made with an apparently sane person is to be determined by the application of the same rules as are applied in ordinary cases.'

[Their Lordships continued at 1027]: [T]o accept the proposition enunciated in *Archer v Cutler* that a contract with a person ostensibly sane but actually of unsound mind can be set aside because it is 'unfair' to the person of unsound mind in the sense of contractual imbalance, is unsupported by authority, is illogical and would distinguish the law of New Zealand from the law of Australia, as exemplified in *McLaughlin's* case (1904) 1 CLR 243 and *Tremills'* case, 18 VLR 607, for no good reason, as well as from the law of England from which the law of Australia and New Zealand and other 'common law' countries has stemmed. In so saying, their Lordships differ with profound respect from the contrary view so strongly expressed by the New Zealand courts.

To sum the matter up, in the opinion of their Lordships, the validity of a contract entered into by a lunatic who is ostensibly sane is to be judged by the same standards as a contract by a person of sound mind, and is not voidable by the lunatic or his representatives by reason of 'unfairness' unless such unfairness amounts to equitable fraud which would have enabled the complaining party to avoid the contract even if he had been sane.

[Their Lordships also found that the sale was not unconscionable. Therefore, they advised that the appeal should be allowed.]

A contract made while a person lacked mental capacity may be ratified by that person if they recover the necessary capacity, or during a lucid period. In addition, an exception is created in the case of contracts for necessities by state and territory Sale of Goods Acts. These provide that a person who by reason of 'mental incapacity or drunkenness is incompetent to contract' must nevertheless pay a reasonable price for necessities sold to them.[4]

INTERNATIONAL PERSPECTIVES

Section 11 of the *Indian Contract Act, 1872* makes persons of unsound mind incompetent to contract. This provision has been held to also apply to persons who 'owing to drink and debauchery' are incapable of understanding a contract and forming a rational view of its effect on their interests.[5] What is meant by being of 'unsound mind' is indicated by s 12 of the Act.

Indian Contract Act, 1872

Section 12. Who is of sound mind for purposes of contracting

A person is said to be of sound mind for the purpose of making a contract, if, at the time when he makes it, he is capable of understanding it and of forming a rational judgment as to its effect upon his interests.

A person who is usually of unsound mind, but occasionally of sound mind, may make a contract when he is of sound mind.

A person who is usually of sound mind, but occasionally of unsound mind, may not make a contract when he is of unsound mind.

---

4 See *Sale of Goods Act 1954* (ACT) s 7; *Sale of Goods Act 1923* (NSW) s 7; *Goods Act 1958* (Vic) s 7; *Sale of Goods Act 1972* (NT) s 7; *Sale of Goods Act 1896* (QLD) s 5; *Sale of Goods Act 1895* (SA) s 2; *Sale of Goods Act 1896* (TAS) s 7; *Sale of Goods Act 1895* (WA) s 2.

5 HK Saharay, *Dutt on Contract*, 10th edn, Eastern Law House, Kolkata, 2006, 181.

3 Intoxication

Intoxication, or the influence of drugs, will make a contract voidable at the election of the affected person only where it impaired their judgment to such a degree that they did not properly understand what they were doing, and this was known to the other party. In this respect the position is essentially the same as it is with mental incapacity. However, perhaps reflecting the opprobrium associated with intoxication, it appears to be also necessary to show that the other party took advantage of the situation and concluded an agreement unfair to the person intoxicated. These matters and the different responses of equity and the common law are discussed in the following extract.

Blomley v Ryan

(1956) 99 CLR 362, High Court of Australia

[Blomley entered into a contract to purchase a grazing property from Ryan. At the time of the sale, Ryan was 78 and his faculties were gravely impaired by the prolonged and excessive consumption of alcohol. Ryan did not proceed with the sale and Blomley commenced proceedings seeking specific performance or damages. By way of defence, Ryan sought to avoid the contract. The action was brought in the original jurisdiction of the High Court as the parties lived in different states; the claim failed at first instance and Blomley appealed.]

Fullagar J [at 404]: The authorities which I have cited ... <405> ... show also that cases in which an allegation of intoxication is a main feature are approached with great caution by Courts of Equity. This is, I think, not so much because intoxication is a self-induced state and a reprehensible thing, but rather because it would be dangerous to lend any countenance to the view that a man could escape the obligation of a contract by simply proving that he was 'in liquor' when it was made. So we find it said again and again that *mere* drunkenness affords no ground for resisting a suit to enforce a contract. Where, however, there is real ground for thinking that the judgment of one party was, to the knowledge of the other, seriously affected by drink, equity will generally refuse specific performance at the suit of that other, leaving him to pursue a remedy at law if he so desires. And, where the court is satisfied that a contract disadvantageous to the party affected has been obtained by 'drawing him in to drink', or that there has been real unfairness in taking advantage of his condition, the contract may be set aside.

One other general observation may be made before proceeding to the facts of the present case. The circumstances adversely affecting a party, which may induce a court of equity either to refuse its aid or to set a transaction aside, are of great variety and can hardly be satisfactorily classified. Among them are poverty or need of any kind, sickness, age, sex, infirmity of body or mind, drunkenness, illiteracy or lack of education, lack of assistance or explanation where assistance or explanation is necessary. The common characteristic seems to be that they have the effect of placing one party at a serious disadvantage *vis-à-vis* the other. It does not appear to be essential in all cases that the party at a disadvantage should suffer loss or detriment by the bargain. In *Cooke v Clayworth*, in which specific performance was refused, it does not appear that there was anything actually unfair in the terms of the transaction itself. But inadequacy of consideration, while never of itself a ground for resisting enforcement, will often be a specially important element in cases of this type. It may be important in either or both of two ways—firstly as supporting the inference that a position of disadvantage existed, and secondly as tending to show that an unfair use was made of the occasion. Where, as here, intoxication is the main element relied upon as creating the position of disadvantage, the question of adequacy or inadequacy of consideration is, I think, likely to be a matter of major, and perhaps decisive, importance. It will almost always, <406> I think, be '… an important ingredient in considering whether a person did exercise any degree of judgment in making a contract, or whether there is a degree of unfairness in accepting the contract. … '(per *Page Wood* VC in *Wiltshire v Marshall*).

[His Honour examined the terms of the contract and noted that the sale price was significantly below market price, the deposit paid was only £5 (when the sale price was £25,000) and that the price was payable over four years with interest below market rates. He continued at 407]: The learned trial judge found the explanation of this remarkable transaction in the facts that the defendant was an old man, whose health and faculties had been impaired by habitual drinking to excess over a long period, who was at the material time in the middle of a prolonged bout of heavy drinking of rum, and who was utterly incapable of forming a rational judgment about the terms of any business transaction. Having carefully read and considered the evidence, I agree with this view. His Honour also held that the defendant's condition must have been patent to the plaintiff's father, who acted as the plaintiff's agent, and to Stemm, who acted (ostensibly) as the defendant's agent, and that these persons took such an unfair advantage of that condition that a court of equity could not allow the contract to stand. I agree with this view also.

[After rejecting an argument that Ryan had affirmed the contract when not intoxicated, his Honour concluded at 412]: I am satisfied that we have here an example of a thoroughly unconscionable transaction, which no court of equity could possibly enforce itself, or allow to be enforced at law. I would regard specific performance as out of the question, and to let the contract be enforced at law would, in this particular case, be, in effect, to allow the overreaching party to reap the full reward of his inequitable conduct. The appeal should, in my opinion, be dismissed.

[In a separate judgment, McTiernan also dismissed the appeal; Kitto J dissented.]

Appeal dismissed

[footnotes omitted]

4 Bankruptcy

Bankruptcy does not invalidate any contracts that were made by the bankrupt person before that event occurred. However, under s 133(5A) of the *Bankruptcy Act 1966* (Cth), the trustee in bankruptcy may avoid such contracts if they are unprofitable, or with the consent of the court. These provisions are designed to assist the trustee to protect the assets of the bankrupt's estate for the benefit of creditors. A bankrupt person may enter into a contract. However, they have limited ability to bind the trustee or the assets of their estate. Furthermore, because a person contracting with a bankrupt will have fewer effective remedies in the event of a breach of contract, s 269 of the *Bankruptcy Act* makes it an offence for a bankrupt to enter into certain types of contract without disclosing their bankruptcy. Non-compliance with this requirement is an offence and makes the contract voidable by the other party.

5 The Crown

At common law the Crown had largely unlimited contractual capacity. However, it also enjoyed immunity from suit which meant, in effect, that should it breach the contract the other party was without an enforceable remedy. This immunity has now been abolished by statute, at the Commonwealth level by Part IX of the *Judiciary Act 1903* and in the states and territories by Crown Proceedings Acts.[6] There are, however, a number of respects in which the Crown remains in a special position. These are as follows:

- The Crown's power to contract, although not needing to be created by legislation,[7] may be limited by statute and a similar restriction may be placed on government authorities and agencies.[8] Similarly, it has been suggested that the Commonwealth Crown can enter into a contract only if the subject matter is one about which the Commonwealth Parliament has legislative powers.[9]
- The Crown cannot contract in a manner that disables itself from performing a statutory duty, or from exercising a discretionary power. For example, it cannot contract in a manner that has the effect of binding a public official to exercise a statutory discretion in the future in a particular way. The consequences of the Crown doing so, however, are unclear. One suggestion is that whilst the official is able to exercise the discretion without being constrained by the contract, the Crown may be liable to pay damages for breach of contract.[10]

---

6   *Crown Proceedings Act 1992* (ACT); *Crown Proceedings Act 1988* (NSW); *Crown Proceedings Act 1980* (Qld); *Crown Proceedings Act 1992* (SA); *Crown Proceedings Act 1993* (Tas); *Crown Proceedings Act 1958* (Vic); *Crown Suits Act 1947* (WA); *Crown Proceedings Act 1993* (NT).
7   See *NSW v Bardolph* (1933–1934) 52 CLR 455 esp at 509.
8   See *Commonwealth of Australia v Australian Commonwealth Shipping Board* (1926) 39 CLR 1.
9   For a discussion of this complex topic see: N Seddon, *Government Contracts, Federal, State and Local*, 2nd edn, The Federation Press, Sydney, 1999, ch 5.
10   See the discussion by Mason J in *Ansett Transport Industries (Operations) Pty Ltd v The Commonwealth of Australia* (1977) 139 CLR 54, at 74–78.

- The ability of a plaintiff to recover damages from the Crown may be limited. This is because the expenditure of public monies requires parliamentary appropriation and if no such appropriation is available to meet a monetary judgment awarded against the Crown for breach of contract the claim will remain unsatisfied.

6 Minors

As noted earlier, the most complex category in this area concerns the capacity of minors[11] to make contracts. It comprises statute and common law, the exact mix of which varies between Australian jurisdictions. For this reason, our treatment starts with the common law and then looks at the principal statutory provisions.

a Common law

At common law, the general rule is that a contract made by a minor is voidable. However, this is only a general rule and there are a number of important exceptions which, in some cases, have been given statutory effect.

Contracts for necessities

A contract made by a minor to obtain necessities is binding on both parties. Necessities are goods and services needed by the minor to maintain their existing lifestyle and which are actually needed by them to do so. Thus, what is a necessity will vary depending upon the minor's circumstances, a position given statutory effect by Sale of Goods legislation in each state and territory other than New South Wales.[12] An example of this legislation is extracted below. Further, benefiting the minor is not sufficient; the minor must actually need the goods or services in question. The basis upon which a supplier can claim against the minor (whether it is in contract or restitution) and the issue of what can constitute necessities are discussed in the following case.

Nash v Inman

[1908] 2 KB 1, English Court of Appeal

[Nash entered into a contract to supply Inman, a Cambridge undergraduate student, with 11 fancy waistcoats and other clothes. At the time, Inman was an infant and was amply supplied with proper clothes by his father. Nash claimed the cost of

---

11   As result of Age of Majority legislation in each state and territory, the age of majority in Australia is now 18 years.
12   *Sale of Goods Act 1954* (ACT) s 7; *Sale of Goods Act 1972* (NT) s 7; *Sale of Goods Act 1896* (Qld) s 5; *Sale of Goods Act 1895* (SA) s 2; *Sale of Goods Act 1896* (Tas) s 7; *Goods Act 1958* (Vic) s 7; *Sale of Goods Act 1895* (WA) s 2.

these clothes and was met with a defence based on infancy. Inman succeeded on this ground at first instance and Nash appealed.]

Fletcher-Moulton LJ [at 8]: An infant, like a lunatic, is incapable of making a contract of purchase in the strict sense of the words; but if a man satisfies the needs of the infant or lunatic by supplying to him necessaries, the law will imply an obligation to repay him for the services so rendered, and will enforce that obligation against the estate of the infant or lunatic. The consequence is that the basis of the action is hardly contract. Its real foundation is an obligation which the law imposes on the infant to make a fair payment in respect of needs satisfied. ... <9> ...

Buckley LJ [at 11]: At common law ... the contracts of an infant were voidable except such as were necessarily <12> to his prejudice; these last were void. Speaking generally, the consequence of the infant's contract was that inasmuch as he was an infant the contract (with the exception of certain contracts) could not during infancy be enforced against him, but when he came to majority he might, if he pleased, ratify and confirm it, and if he did so both parties were bound. The obligation was in contract, but contract of such a kind that as against the infant at any rate it could not be enforced. It was a voidable contract. ... The plaintiff, when he sues the defendant for goods supplied during infancy, is suing him in contract on the footing that the contract was such as the infant, notwithstanding infancy, could make. The defendant, although he was an infant, had a limited capacity to contract. In order to maintain his action the plaintiff must prove that the contract sued on is within that limited capacity. The rule as regards liability for necessaries may, I think, be thus stated: an infant may contract for the supply at a reasonable price of articles reasonably necessary for his support in his station in life if he has not already a sufficient supply. To render an infant's contract for necessaries an enforceable contract two conditions must be satisfied, namely, (1) the contract must be for goods reasonably necessary for his support in his station in life, and (2) he must not have already a sufficient supply of these necessaries. The defence that the goods were not necessaries will be made out by shewing either that in what I may call their innate quality, having regard to the position in life of the defendant, they were such that he could not want them, or that, <13> supposing the goods were capable of being necessaries, he had already enough, so that he did not want them. If in the action it is put in issue that the goods supplied were not necessaries on those two grounds, or on either of them, the onus is on the plaintiff to shew that they are necessaries. He is suing upon a contract which the defendant cannot make except under defined circumstances, and it is for him to shew that the defined circumstances enabling the infant to contract existed.

[In their separate judgments, Cozens-Hardy MR and Fletcher-Moulton LJ reached the same conclusion as Buckley LJ concerning what a plaintiff must prove in a case such as this one and agreed that the trial judge was correct in finding that the plaintiff had failed to prove the elements his Lordship identified.]

Appeal dismissed

Goods Act 1958 (Vic)

Section 7

(1) Capacity to buy and sell is regulated by the general law concerning capacity to contract and to transfer and acquire property: Provided that where necessities are sold and delivered to an infant or minor or to a person who, by reason of mental incapacity or drunkenness, is incompetent to contract, he must pay a reasonable price therefor.

(2) 'Necessities' in this section means goods suitable to the condition in life of such infant or minor or other person and to his actual requirements at the time of such sale and delivery.

Beneficial contracts of employment

Contracts of employment are binding on a minor provided they are for the minor's benefit; that is, they are not unfair or oppressive. However, unlike contracts for necessities, the minor can repudiate the contract upon achieving adulthood.[13]

b   The effect of minority at common law

Contracts that do not fall within one or other of the two exceptions outlined are voidable. However, the effect of being 'voidable' in this area differs from the norm in contract law and depends upon the nature of the contract. Contracts in which the minor acquires permanent property, or which involve ongoing obligations, are binding *unless* avoided by the minor. Examples include contracts for the purchase of land or shares and a partnership agreement. In the case of such contracts, the parties remain bound until the minor elects to avoid the contract. Should this happen, avoidance terminates the contract *in futuro*: that is, for the future. As a result, the minor is relieved only from those obligations that would have arisen under the contract at some time in the future; the minor remains bound by those that have arisen prior to the date of termination.[14] In this regard, avoidance is more akin to discharge for breach of contract, than avoidance for a vitiating element such as misrepresentation or unconscionable conduct.

All other voidable contracts are not binding *unless* they are ratified by the minor upon becoming an adult. This requires the minor to take some positive steps to affirm the contract. If this does not occur within a reasonable time of adulthood being achieved the contract is not binding. In this connection, to protect a person from being unfairly pressured into ratifying a contract made while a

---

13   See *Hamilton v Lethbridge* (1912) 14 CLR 236 in which articles of clerkship, containing a restrictive covenant, were held binding as they had been ratified after the minor had become an adult.

14   See *Norman Baker Pty Ltd (in liq) v Baker* (1978) 3 ACLR 856 applying *Steinberg v Scala (Leeds) Ltd* [1923] 2 Ch 452.

minor, legislation in most jurisdictions requires ratification to be in writing[15] and in Victoria the effect of s 50 of the *Supreme Court Act 1986* is to make ratification ineffective entirely.

c Statutory intervention

As we have seen already, all jurisdictions have some legislation affecting aspects of the contractual capacity of minors, usually as part of a broader provision dealing with other persons as well. However, in New South Wales, South Australia and Victoria this subject has received specific legislative attention, although only in New South Wales does this amount to a code that replaces the operation of the common law.

New South Wales

The *Minors (Property and Contracts) Act 1970* deals with all aspects of a minor's capacity to make a contract and the power of the courts to afford protection. Key provisions of this Act are extracted below to indicate its approach and scope. In summary:

- Beneficial contracts made by a minor are presumptively binding. This is the effect of s 19 when read with the definition of 'civil act' in s 6(1) which includes 'a contract'. Section 35 provides that such contracts cannot be repudiated by the minor.
- Non-beneficial contracts can be repudiated by a minor under s 31, so long as this is done before the person reaches 18 years of age.
- When repudiation occurs the courts have very wide powers under s 37 to make adjustments between the parties to ensure that they make just compensation for the benefits they have derived under the contract.
- A non-beneficial contract can be affirmed by a minor once the age of majority is reached, or in the other instances listed in s 30. When affirmed, the contract is presumptively binding.

Minors (Property and Contracts) Act 1970 (NSW)
Section 19. Beneficial civil act

Where a minor participates in a civil act and his or her participation is for his or her benefit at the time of his or her participation, the civil act is presumptively binding on the minor.

---

15 See *Minors' Contracts (Miscellaneous Provisions) Act 1979* (SA) s 4; *Mercantile Law Act 1962* (ACT) s 15; in WA and the NT the UK *Statute of Frauds (Amendment) Act 1828* (Lord Tenterden's Act) applies as part of the law inherited through British settlement. This Act requires ratification to be written and signed by the party before they can be bound.

Section 30. Affirmation

(1) Where a person participates in a civil act while the person is a minor, the civil act may be affirmed:
   (a) while the person remains a minor, on the person's behalf by order of a court having jurisdiction under this section,
   (b) after the person attains the age of eighteen years, by the person, or
   (c) after the person's death, by the person's personal representative.
(2) The court may affirm a civil act on behalf of a minor participant in the civil act under paragraph (a) of subsection (1) on application by the minor participant or by any other person interested in the civil act.
(3) Subject to section 36, the court shall not affirm a civil act on behalf of a minor participant in the civil act under paragraph (a) of subsection (1) unless it appears to the court that the affirmation is for the benefit of the minor participant.
(4) Where a civil act is affirmed pursuant to this section by or on behalf of a minor participant in the civil act, or by the personal representative of a deceased minor participant in the civil act, the civil act is presumptively binding on the minor participant.
(5) An affirmation of a civil act under this section by a minor participant in the civil act or by the personal representative of a deceased minor participant in the civil act:
   (a) may be by words, written or spoken, or by conduct, and
   (b) need not be communicated to any person.

Section 31. Repudiation by minor

(1) Where a minor has participated in a civil act, then, subject to sections 33 and 35 and subject to subsection (2), the minor participant may repudiate the civil act at any time during his or her minority or afterwards but before the minor attains the age of nineteen years.
(2) A repudiation of a civil act by a minor participant in the civil act does not have effect if it appears that, at the time of the repudiation, the civil act is for the benefit of the minor participant.

Section 35. Restriction on effect of repudiation

(1) Where a civil act is presumptively binding on a minor participant in the civil act in favour of another party to the civil act or in favour of any other person, a repudiation of the civil act under any of sections 31, 32 and 34 by or on behalf of the minor participant, or, if the minor participant has died, by his or her personal representative, does not have effect as against that other party or person.

Section 37. Adjustment on repudiation

(1) Where a civil act is repudiated under any of sections 31, 32 and 34, a court having jurisdiction under this section may, on the application of any person interested in the civil act, make orders:

(a) for the confirmation, wholly or in part, of the civil act or of anything done under the civil act, or
(b) for the adjustment of rights arising out of the civil act or out of the repudiation or out of anything done under the civil act.
...
(4) Subject to subsection (3), and except so far as the court confirms the civil act or anything done under the civil act, the court shall make such orders as are authorised by this section and as the court thinks fit for the purpose of securing so far as practicable that:
(c) each minor participant in the civil act makes just compensation for all property, services and other things derived by him or her by or under the civil act to the extent that the derivation of that property or of those services or things is for his or her benefit,
(d) each other participant in the civil act makes just compensation for all property, services and other things derived by him or her by or under the civil act, and
(e) subject to paragraphs (a) and (b), the parties to the civil act and those claiming under them are restored to their positions before the time of the civil act.

South Australia

The key provisions of the *Minors Contracts (Miscellaneous Provisions) Act 1979*, ss 4–8, can be summarised as follows:

- The common law continues to determine what contracts made by a minor are binding or not. However, the Act provides that those that are not binding remain unenforceable unless ratified in writing when the minor becomes an adult.
- Application can be made to a court by a minor, their parent or guardian, or the other party for approval to enter into a contract. If given, the contract is as binding as if the minor had been an adult.
- Where, under an unenforceable contract, property has passed from a minor to the other party before the contract was avoided, the minor may apply to a court for an order recovering that property. This may be granted on such terms as the court considers just. This is a significant alteration of the common law position.
- The guarantor of a minor cannot avoid their liability under the guarantee on the ground that the minor is not liable under the principal contract because of their age. This reverses the common law position which is that a guarantee is not enforceable if the minor repudiates the principal contract as in such a case there is no longer a primary obligation to which the guarantee can attach.
- A court may, upon application by a minor, or their parent or guardian, appoint a person to transact any specific business or execute documents on the minor's behalf. If this is done, the minor is bound by any liabilities so incurred.

Victoria

Section 49 of the *Supreme Court Act 1986* (extracted below) makes three classes of contract void. Although these classes cover the most common contracts minors are likely to make, there are some important contracts not caught including those for the purchase of land, the provision of services, or employment. In relation to these, the common law continues to apply.

Section 49 is derived from s 1 of the *Infants Relief Act 1874* (UK) and like that provision it makes certain contracts 'void'. However, it appears that in this context, 'void' is given a meaning more akin to 'unenforceable'. Thus, it has been held that property can still pass under a contract for the sale of goods[16] and that money paid by a minor can be recovered only if there is a total failure of consideration,[17] even though the contracts involved fall within the section or its UK equivalent. Also, because paragraphs (a) and (b) refer only to the 'repayment' of money and the 'payment for goods', respectively, loan contracts and contracts for the sale of goods can be enforced by (although not against) a minor.

Sections 50 and 51 give further protection to minors by reducing the degree to which they are bound by confirmatory conduct, after adulthood is achieved, regarding promises or contracts made, or debts incurred, while a minor. However, in the case of agreements to repay a loan, this protection is reduced, in the case of certain third parties, by s 51(2)(3).

Supreme Court Act 1986 (Vic)

Section 49. Certain contracts by minors to be void

The following contracts entered into by a minor are void–
(a) contracts for the repayment of money lent or to be lent;
(b) contracts for payment for goods supplied or to be supplied, other than necessaries;
(c) accounts stated.

Section 50. No proceeding to be brought on ratification of minor's contract

(1) No proceeding can be brought to charge a person—
   (a) on a promise made after full age to pay a debt contracted during minority; or
   (b) on a ratification made after full age of a promise or contract made during minority.
(2) This section applies whether or not there was any new consideration for the promise or ratification.

---

16 See *Hall v Wells* (1962) Tas SR 122.
17 See *Woolf v Associated Finance Pty Ltd* (1956) VLR 51.

Section 51. Avoiding contract for payment of loan advanced during minority

(1) If a minor who has contracted a loan (a contract for the repayment of which is void under this Division) agrees after full age to repay all or part of that loan, that agreement and any instrument relating to it is, subject to sub-sections (2) and (3), void against everyone.

INTERNATIONAL PERSPECTIVES

The age of majority in India is generally 18 years.[18] The effect of s 11 of the *Indian Contract Act* is that a person under this age cannot make a contract. Unlike the common law, which provides that certain contracts made by a minor are merely voidable or unenforceable, it has been held that in India there is no contract at all.[19] As a result, an agreement cannot be enforced against a minor, nor can a minor ratify an agreement upon becoming an adult and thereby make it contractual. It has also been held that minors who fraudulently misrepresent their age cannot be estopped from proving that they were a minor when a contract was made and cannot be sued in tort on the ground of their deceit. However, there are some important qualifications to this extreme position which ameliorate its effect:

- Because it is not a contract, an agreement pursuant to which property physically passes to a minor will not transfer title in that property to the minor. As a result, the transferor will be able to recover the property in restitution by relying upon their continuing title.
- Section 33(2)(b) of the *Specific Relief Act* empowers a court to order a minor to restore a benefit received under an agreement where, in an action to enforce the agreement, s 11 of the *Indian Contract Act* has been relied upon by the minor as a defence.
- The courts have crafted a limited beneficial contracts exception to allow minors to enforce agreements that are beneficial to them, at least where the minor's obligations have been performed. Thus, for example, a minor has been held able to enforce a mortgage executed in his favour by a person to whom he had advanced the whole of the mortgage money.[20]
- As noted earlier, s 68 of the Act allows reimbursement in the case of necessaries supplied to persons incompetent to contract, including minors.

Indian Specific Relief Act 1963

Section 33(2)

Where a defendant successfully resists any suit on the grounds—
(b) that the agreement sought to be enforced against him in the suit is void by reason of his not having been competent to contract under Section

---

18 See *The Indian Majority Act 1875*, s 3.
19 *Mohori Bibee v Dhurmodas* (1903) ILR 30 Cal 539 (PC).
20 *Raghava Chariar v Srinivasa* (1916) 40 Mad 308.

> 11 of the *Indian Contract Act, 1872*, the court may, if the defendant has received any benefit under the agreement from the other party, require him to restore, so far as may be, such benefit to that party, to the extent to which he or his estate has benefited thereby.

7 Companies

a Common law

At common law, the contractual capacity of a company was limited by its constitution. As a result, if a company entered into a contract that was not authorised by its constitution, the contract was considered to be *ultra vires* and of no effect. Parties dealing with a company were taken to have notice of the limits of a company's power to make contracts.

b Contractual capacity under the *Corporations Act*

The contractual capacity of corporations is now largely governed by provisions in the *Corporations Act 2001* (Cth). Section 124(1) reverses the common law position by giving corporations the same legal capacity and powers as 'an individual'; this includes the power to make contracts. Further, s 125(1) and (2) abolish the doctrine of *ultra vires*, so far as contractual capacity is concerned, by providing that the actions of a company shall not be invalid merely because they are contrary to a restriction in its constitution.

Companies may make contracts in two ways: under s 126(1) by acting through an individual who has the company's express or implied authority to contract on their behalf and under s 127(2) by formally affixing the company's common seal.

c Pre-incorporation contracts

A pre-incorporation contract is a contract entered into by a person on behalf of a company before it has been created ('incorporated'). Such contracts are made when, for commercial reasons, it is not possible or desirable to wait until that time. They are made with the intention that the company will assume the rights and obligations created by the contract when the formalities of incorporation have been completed.

At common law, pre-incorporation contracts were not enforceable against the company, following its incorporation, nor could it ratify them.[21] Consequently, the company would avoid liability under such a contract, unless the contract was remade, leaving the individuals who had acted for it, or in some cases the other

---

21 See *Kelner v Baxter* (1866) LR 2 CP 174.

contracting party, to bear any resulting loss. However, under the *Corporations Act*, the relevant provisions of which are extracted below, the position is now significantly different. In particular, pre-incorporation contracts can be ratified under s 131(1) and provision is made for cases in which the company is either not formed, or it choses not to ratify.

Corporations Act 2001 (Cth)
Section 131. Contracts before registration

(1) If a person enters into, or purports to enter into, a contract on behalf of, or for the benefit of, a company before it is registered, the company becomes bound by the contract and entitled to its benefit if the company, or a company that is reasonably identifiable with it, is registered and ratifies the contract:
   (a) within the time agreed to by the parties to the contract; or
   (b) if there is no agreed time—within a reasonable time after the contract is entered into.
(2) The person is liable to pay damages to each other party to the pre-registration contract if the company is not registered, or the company is registered but does not ratify the contract or enter into a substitute for it:
   (a) within the time agreed to by the parties to the contract; or
   (b) if there is no agreed time—within a reasonable time after the contract is entered into.
   The amount that the person is liable to pay to a party is the amount the company would be liable to pay to the party if the company had ratified the contract and then did not perform it at all.
(3) If proceedings are brought to recover damages under subsection (2) because the company is registered but does not ratify the pre-registration contract or enter into a substitute for it, the court may do anything that it considers appropriate in the circumstances, including ordering the company to do 1 or more of the following:
   (a) pay all or part of the damages that the person is liable to pay;
   (b) transfer property that the company received because of the contract to a party to the contract;
   (c) pay an amount to a party to the contract.
(4) If the company ratifies the pre-registration contract but fails to perform all or part of it, the court may order the person to pay all or part of the damages that the company is ordered to pay.

8 Summary

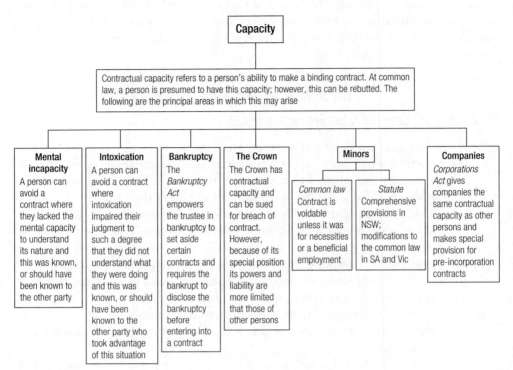

9 Questions

1. Jenny was a precocious student who entered university to study medicine shortly after her 17th birthday. Anxious to arrange accommodation near the university before teaching commenced, she entered into a lease agreement with Land Holdings Ltd for a two-bedroom apartment. This agreement was for three years (the duration of her initial medical studies) at a fortnightly rental of $650. Unfortunately, contrary to her expectations, Jenny was unable to secure a part-time job and soon experienced great difficulty in paying this rent. Therefore, she entered into a loan agreement with the University Credit Union, the essence of which was that in return for an immediate loan of $10,000 she would pay the Credit Union $12,000, 18 months later. However, after six months, Jenny decided to defer her studies and to travel around the world. As a result, she now wishes to know whether these agreements are enforceable. Please advise her, indicating the jurisdiction within which you have assumed these facts occurred. Would your advice differ if Jenny signed a document confirming these agreements after her 18th birthday?

2. Tom attended a party to celebrate Ivan's 20th birthday and drank various alcoholic beverages during the event. As he was about to leave the party, Tom thanked Ivan for his hospitality and said to him 'Ivan, you are a great mate. If there is anything you want, just let me know.' Ivan

replied that he would like to purchase Tom's new car, to which Tom replied: 'It's yours for $1000.' Ivan immediately gave Tom a cheque for $1000 and said that he would collect the car on the following day. The car is in fact worth at least $20,000 and when Ivan arrived to collect it, Tom refused to hand over the keys, instead returning Ivan's cheque. Please advise parties whether they have a contract for the sale of the car.

3. On 1 March, Bob entered into a contract to lease premises from Land Holdings Ltd. He did so to secure the premises for Barwon Pty Ltd, a company that he and his brother Bert were in the process of establishing. Barwon Pty Ltd was incorporated on 1 April. However, the business venture Bob and Bert had planned for Barwon Pty Ltd did not materialise and the premises are no longer required by the company. Please advise the parties of their rights and obligations in relation to the lease.

CHAPTER 7

Formalities

1	Introduction	190
2	Contracts for which formalities are prescribed	192
	a Contracts for the sale of land, or an interest in land	192
	b Contracts for the sale of goods	193
	c Contracts of guarantee	193
	d Consumer contracts	194
3	Satisfying the formalities	195
	a A note or memorandum is sufficient	195
	b The document must have been created before proceedings are commenced	198
	c Signature	198
4	The consequences of non-compliance	198
	a Common law rights independent of the contract	199
	b The equitable doctrine of part performance	202
	c Estoppel	206
5	Summary	207
6	Questions	207

1 Introduction

Contrary to popular perception, the general rule in most jurisdictions is that contracts can be made without the parties reducing their agreement to writing, or complying with any other formalities. As far as Anglo-Australian law is concerned, so long as the elements of agreement, consideration and intention are present, parties with contractual capacity can chose to make contracts orally, by conduct, in writing, or by a combination of these methods. They are all equally enforceable. However, there are a number of exceptions and the principal ones form the subject of this chapter. They have been created by statute and typically take one of the following forms:

- *The essential terms of a contract are required to be recorded in writing and the document signed*. Here, all that is required is that the essential terms of the agreement are recorded in a written document that is signed. This is the least formal approach and the one taken in the *Statute of Frauds* (1677)—

historically the most significant provision in this area—and the Australian state and territory provisions derived from this statute.
- *The contract is required to take a particular written form.* Here, the statute prescribes the particular form that the contract must take and gives the parties little or no flexibility in this regard. An example is s 28 of the *Marine Insurance Act 1909* (Cth) which provides that a contract of marine insurance, to be admissible, must be 'embodied in a marine policy in accordance with this Act'.
- *The contract is required to be in writing and other formalities are prescribed.* Here, the statute may require other formalities, such as pre-contractual disclosure and the delivery of a copy to a consumer. An example is Part 2, Division 1 of the *Consumer Credit Code*.[1]

Formalities such as these are adopted for a variety of reasons. These include:

- to reduce fraud by making it more difficult for a person to falsely claim that a contract existed—this was the rationale for the *Statute of Frauds*
- to protect consumers by ensuring that the contract contains terms for their benefit and that they receive a copy
- to make proof of a contract and its terms easier and thereby assist any court that may have to adjudicate upon a dispute between the parties
- to increase the formality of the transaction with the objective of enhancing the awareness of the parties of the obligations they are undertaking.

In this chapter we will:

- identify the principal types of contract in respect of which formalities are prescribed and the nature of those formalities
- examine the ways in which those formalities can be satisfied
- examine the consequences of non-compliance.

INTERNATIONAL PERSPECTIVES

> The following extracts illustrate law's inclination not to prescribe formalities for the making or enforcement of contracts. Formalities are the exception, not the rule.
>
> ### *Indian Contract Act, 1872*
>
> Section 10. What agreements are contracts
>
> All agreements are contracts if they are made by the free consent of the parties, competent to contract, for a lawful consideration and with a lawful object, and are not hereby expressly declared to be void.
>
> Nothing herein contained shall affect any law in force in India and not hereby expressly repealed by which any contract is required to be made in

---

1 This code is an appendix to the *Consumer Credit (Queensland) Act 1994*. It has been incorporated by reference into the law of all other states and territories except WA which has adopted its own legislation.

writing or in the presence of witnesses, or any law relating to the registration of documents.

Contract Law of the People's Republic of China, 1999

Article 10. Forms of Contract; Writing Requirement

A contract may be made in writing, in an oral conversation, as well as in any other form. A contract shall be in writing if a relevant law or administrative regulation so requires. A contract shall be in writing if the parties have so agreed.

UNIDROIT Principles of International Commercial Contracts, 2004

Article 1.2. Nothing in these Principles requires a contract, statement or any other act to be made in or evidenced by a particular form. It may be proved by any means, including witnesses.

2 Contracts for which formalities are prescribed

As part of the statute law of England at the time, the *Statute of Frauds* was automatically incorporated into Australian law when the various states were colonised in the eighteenth and nineteenth centuries. Its key provisions, ss 4 and 17, provided that certain agreements were not enforceable unless the agreement, or 'some memorandum or note thereof shall be in writing, and signed by ...' the party against whom it was being enforced. These provisions covered a miscellaneous group of agreements including those for the sale of goods over £10, for the sale of an interest in land, guaranteeing the liability of another person, and agreements that would not be performed within one year, or were made in consideration of marriage. Subsequently, in all Australian jurisdictions except Western Australia,[2] the statute was repealed or replaced by local legislation. Examples of some of the more important of these local derivatives are set out in the following extracts. Also reproduced are examples of the kinds of formalities that have been prescribed in consumer protection legislation to assist consumers.

a Contracts for the sale of land, or an interest in land

In all jurisdictions, to be enforceable, contracts for the sale of land, or of an interest in land, must be in writing.[3] Although there is a slight variation between them, these provisions all extend beyond sale contracts to include other dispositions of an

---

2   In WA the *Statute of Frauds* is retained in an amended form by the *Law Reform (Statute of Frauds) Act 1962*.
3   *Law Reform (Miscellaneous Provisions) Act 1955* (ACT) s 54(1); *Conveyancing Act 1919* (NSW) s 54A(1); *Law of Property Act 2000* (NT) s 62; *Property Law Act 1974* (Qld) s 59; *Law of Property Act 1936* (SA) s 26(1); *Conveyancing and Law of Property Act 1884* (Tas) s 36(1); *Instruments Act 1958* (Vic) s 126.

interest in land; for example, contracts of lease, mortgages and options concerning land. They are by far the most important provisions derived from the *Statute of Frauds*.

Example

Conveyancing Act 1919 (NSW)

Section 54A(1)

No action or proceedings may be brought upon any contract for the sale or other disposition of land or any interest in land, unless the agreement upon which such action or proceedings is brought, or some memorandum or note thereof, is in writing, and signed by the party to be charged or by some other person thereunto lawfully authorised by the party to be charged.

b Contracts for the sale of goods

Tasmania[4] and Western Australia[5] retain a requirement that contracts for the sale of goods, valued at or above a specified amount ($20), will be enforceable only if the buyer accepts and receives them, or gives something in earnest, or if there is a written note or memorandum of the contract, signed by the party to be bound. In other jurisdictions, these formalities, derived from s 17 of the *Statute of Frauds*, have been repealed.

c Contracts of guarantee

Local legislation[6] in Queensland, Tasmania, Victoria, Western Australia and the Northern Territory, derived from s 4 of the *Statute of Frauds*, makes contracts of guarantee enforceable only if the contract is evidenced by a note or memorandum, signed by the party to be bound.

Example

Instruments Act 1958 (Vic)

Section 126

(1) An action must not be brought to charge a person upon a special promise to answer for the debt, default or miscarriage of another person or upon a contract for the sale or other disposition of an interest in land unless the agreement on which the action is brought, or a memorandum or note of the agreement, is in writing signed by the person to be charged or by a person lawfully authorised in writing by that person to sign such an agreement, memorandum or note.

---

4   *Sale of Goods Act 1896* (Tas) s 9.
5   *Sale of Goods Act 1895* (WA) s 4.
6   *Property Law Act 1974* (Qld) s 56; *Mercantile Law Act 1935* (Tas) s 6; *Instruments Act 1958* (Vic) s 126; *Statute of Frauds 1677* (WA); *Law of Property Act 2000* (NT) s 58.

(2) It is declared that the requirements of subsection (1) may be met in accordance with the *Electronic Transactions (Victoria) Act 2000*.

d   Consumer contracts

To protect consumers, legislation sometimes prescribes that a particular contract must be in writing and that it must contain certain terms designed to safeguard the consumer's interests. Typically, the signature of both parties is required (although sometimes nominated exceptions are allowed) and a copy of the contract must be given to the consumer. In some cases it is also made an offence not to comply with these formalities.

Examples

National Credit Code

Section 14

(1) A credit contract must be in the form of
   (a) A written contract document signed by the debtor and the credit provider; or
   (b) A written contract document signed by the credit provider and constituting an offer by the debtor that is accepted by the debtor in accordance with the terms of the offer.
(4) In the case of a contract document consisting of more than one document, it is sufficient compliance with this section if one of the documents is duly signed and the other documents are referred to in the signed document.

[Section 17 sets out in detail the matters that must be in the contract document; these include: the credit provider's name, the amount of credit provided, the annual percentage rates under the contract, the method of calculating interest, the total amount of interest payable, the credit fees and charges payable, the default rate and the enforcement expenses payable in the event of default.]

Section 18

The contract document must conform to the requirements of the regulations as to its form and the way it is expressed and, subject to any such requirements, may consist of one or more separate documents.

Section 20

(1) If a contract document is to be signed by the debtor and returned to the credit provider, the credit provider must give the debtor a copy to keep.
(2) A credit provider must, not later than 14 days after a credit contract is made, give a copy of the contract in the form in which it was made to the debtor.
(3) Subsection (2) does not apply if the credit provider has previously given the debtor a copy of the contract document to keep.

Building Work Contractors Act 1995 (SA)

Section 28

(1) The following requirements must be complied with in relation to a domestic building work contract:
 (a) the contract must be in writing;
 (b) the contract must set out in full all the contractual terms;
 (c) the contract must set out the name in which the building work contractor carries on business under the contractor's licence, the contractor's licence number and the names and licence numbers of any other persons with whom the contractor carries on business as a building work contractor in partnership;
 (d) the contract must comply with any requirements of the regulations as to the contents of domestic building work contracts;
 (e) the contract must be signed by the building work contractor and the building owner personally or through an agent authorised to act on behalf of the contractor building owner;
 (f) the building owner must be given a copy of the signed contract as soon as reasonably practicable after it has been signed by both parties together with a notice in the prescribed form containing the prescribed information;
 (g) the copy of the contract and the notice given to the building owner must (apart from signatures or initials) be readily legible.
(2) If any of the requirements of subsection (1) is not complied with, the building work contractor is guilty of an offence.

3 Satisfying the formalities

What is required to satisfy a particular provision is determined by reference to the provision itself and as will be apparent from the examples given above this can vary considerably. Thus for example, the requirements of s 28(1) of the *Building Work Contractors Act 1995* (SA) and the *National Credit Code* are significantly more onerous than those of s 54A(1) of the *Conveyancing Act 1919* (NSW). For this reason, the following general observations are made only in relation to the provisions derived from the *Statute of Frauds*.

a A note or memorandum is sufficient

As the *Statute of Frauds* makes clear, it is not necessary for the contract itself to be in writing; a written note or memorandum is sufficient. Thus, although it will usually be desirable for them to do so, it is not necessary for the parties to prepare a formal contractual document. Further, it is not necessary for there to be a single document, or for the document relied upon to have been created for the purpose of satisfying the statute.[7] However, the courts have decided that it must contain the following:

- all the essential terms of the contract, including the identity of the parties[8]
- a clear description of the property[9]
- the consideration,[10] except in the case of a contract of guarantee[11]
- an acknowledgement that there was an agreement.[12]

What is required to allow documents to be joined together has been contentious. The narrow view is that this is possible only if the document signed actually refers to the other document.[13] The broader view is that reference can also be to a transaction through which another document is identified. This issue is discussed in the following extract.

Elias v George Sahely & Co (Barbados) Ltd

[1983] 1 AC 646, Privy Council

[Elias entered into an oral contract to purchase a property from the respondent. His lawyer then wrote to the respondent's lawyer describing the land, naming the parties and the price, and asking for a contract of sale to be forwarded for signature. Subsequently, the respondent's lawyer sent a receipt for the deposit paid that acknowledged that the land had been sold by the respondent. When the respondent refused to proceed, Elias sought specific performance. He succeeded at first instance but lost on appeal to the Court of Appeal of Barbados. He then appealed to the Privy Council.]

Lord Scarman for the Board [at 653]: The critical question is, therefore, whether it is admissible to read the letter and the receipt together. If they are so read, they constitute a sufficient memorandum provided, of course, that the defendant's points on agency and construction are rejected. The defendant's counsel submits that it is not permissible to place the two documents side by side and so to construct a memorandum of the terms of the contract. He makes two

---

7   See for example, *Popiw v Popiw* [1959] VR 197 at 200–201.
8   See *Harvey v Edward Dunlop & Co Ltd* (1927) 39 CLR 302 at 307 and *Pirie v Saunders* (1960–1961) 104 CLR 149 at 155–156.
9   In *Pirie v Saunders* (1960–1961) 104 CLR 149, for example, the description 'part of Lot B, Princess Highway, Sylvania Heights' was held to be insufficient.
10 See *Twynam Pastoral Co Pty Ltd v Anburn Pty Ltd* (1989) NSW Conv R 55–498 at 58,633.
11 See, for example, *Instruments Act 1958* (Vic), s 129.
12 *Pirie v Saunders* (1960–1961) 104 CLR 149. The High Court said that the document being relied upon was insufficient because 'Neither the existence of the document nor its content are indicative of the existence of a binding contract.'
13 See *Thomson v McInnes* (1911) 12 CLR 562 at 569.

points: first that the receipt neither expressly nor by necessary implication refers to the letter, and secondly that to constitute a sufficient memorandum the receipt must refer either to a written transaction or to a document which by acceptance becomes an integral part of the transaction. ...

In *Timmins v Moreland Street Property Co Ltd* [1958] Ch 110 ... Jenkins LJ, with whose judgment Romer and Sellers LJJ agreed, said, at p 130:

> 'it is still indispensably necessary, in order to justify the reading of documents together for this purpose, that there should be a document signed by the party to be charged, which, while not containing in itself all the necessary ingredients of the required memorandum, does contain some reference, express or implied, to some other document or transaction. Where any such reference can be spelt out of a document so signed, then parol evidence may be given to identify the other document referred to, or, as the case may be, to explain the other transaction, and to identify any document relating to it. If by this process a document is brought to light which contains in writing all the terms of the bargain so far as not contained in the document signed by the party to be charged, then the two documents can be read together ...'

Their Lordships accept this passage as a correct statement of the modern law. The first inquiry must, therefore, be whether the document signed by or on behalf of the person to be charged on the contract contains some reference to some other document or transaction. The receipt in this case clearly did refer to some other transaction, namely an agreement to sell the property in Swan Street. Parol evidence can, therefore, be given to explain the transaction, and to identify any document relating to it. Such evidence was led in the present case: it brought to light a document, namely Mr Forde's letter of February 10, 1975, which does contain in writing all the terms of the bargain. It is a writing which evidences the transaction, though not itself the transaction. This distinction is, however, not material ... Moreover, it would be contrary to the intendment of the *Statute of Frauds* to limit the rule to cases in which the reference in the signed document must be to a writing intended to have contractual force. The *Statute of Frauds* is concerned to suppress not evidence but fraud. In seeking a sufficient memorandum it is not necessary to shoulder the further burden of searching for a written contract. Evidence in writing is what the statute requires. ... If, therefore, a document signed by the party to be charged refers to a transaction of sale, parol evidence is admissible both to explain the reference and to identify any document relating to it. Once identified, the document may be placed alongside the signed document. If the two contain all the terms of a concluded contract, the statute is satisfied. Accordingly, their Lordships are of the opinion that Douglas CJ was right to admit the oral evidence of Mr Forde to explain the transaction to which the receipt referred and to identify as a document relating to it his letter of February 10, 1975. Their Lordships also agree with the Chief Justice that the letter contained all the terms of a concluded contract of sale of land.

The Board advised that the appeal be allowed

b The document must have been created before proceedings are commenced

Usually, the document will be created after the oral agreement is concluded. However, this is not essential; it has been held, for example, that a written offer, accepted orally can be sufficient.[14] On the other hand, the document must be created before proceedings are commenced to enforce the agreement. Thus, in *Popiw v Popiw*,[15] it was held that an affidavit sworn in connection with the proceedings could not be relied upon in those proceedings to satisfy what is now s 126 of the *Instruments Act 1958* (Vic). However, the Court noted that it could be used in new proceedings should the applicant choose to bring them.

c Signature

An important feature of the *Statute of Frauds* and its derivatives is that the required document needs to be signed only by the party against whom it is being used. Thus for example, if A has signed a document but B has not done so, B can successfully sue A on the contract it records, but A cannot similarly sue B.[16] One situation in which this could arise is where a written offer is signed by the offeror and accepted verbally by the offeree.[17]

The requirement of a signature has been interpreted liberally. It covers signing a document in person, signing a document using an amanuensis, acknowledging one's name on a document in a manner that expresses assent to its contents and binding nature, and signing via an authorised agent.[18]

4 The consequences of non-compliance

The consequences of non-compliance vary significantly. In the case of the *Statute of Frauds* and its derivatives, the contract is not made void, merely unenforceable.[19] As a result, it remains valid so that if the parties choose to abide by its terms and enforceability is not made an issue between them, the contract can still operate to affect their rights and liabilities. On the other hand, some statutes make a non-compliant contract void, so that it cannot operate at all. Other statutes go further still and make non-compliance an offence as well: see s 28(1) the *Building Work Contractors Act 1995* (SA).

---

14   See *O'Young v Walter Reid & Co Ltd* (1932) 47 CLR 497.
15   [1959] VR 197.
16   In such a case, it is possible that A may have some other, non-contractual, remedy as was the case in *Waltons Stores (Interstate) Ltd v Maher* (1988) 164 CLR 387.
17   See *Heppingstone v Stewart* (1911) 12 CLR 126.
18   See *Thomson v McInnes* (1911) 12 CLR 562 at 573 and *Pirie v Saunders* (1960–1961) 104 CLR 149 at 154. In the case of an agent, in Victoria, the appointment of the agent must be in writing signed by the defendant: *Instruments Act 1958* s 126.
19   *Leroux v Brown* (1852) 12 CB 801 at 824.

a   Common law rights independent of the contract

Because non-compliance with the *Statute of Frauds* and its derivatives does not make a contract void, should the parties perform part or all of its terms, their actions may create rights that can be relied upon at common law where this does not involve enforcing the contract as such. For example, a vendor of land can retain a deposit paid by a purchaser who has wrongfully repudiated the contract and, conversely, a purchaser can recover the deposit in the event of the vendor's repudiation.[20]

The precise ground upon which the common law will allow a claim to be brought, arising out of the performance of an unenforceable contract, has been the subject of considerable debate. In *Turner v Bladin*, Williams, Fullagar and Kitto JJ expressed the view that in a contract for the sale of land, where the land had been transferred but not paid for:

> [T]he *Instruments Act* was [not a] defence to the plaintiff recovering at law in an action of *indebitatus assumpsit* the amount of the instalments which had become payable at the date of the writ and overdue interest to the date of judgment in the action. The consideration moving from the plaintiffs to the defendant was fully executed with the result that the defendant became indebted to the plaintiffs for the balance of purchase money and interest. An action to recover these sums would not be an action brought on the agreement but an action of *indebitatus assumpsit*.[21]

However, this approach has since been doubted by members of the High Court. Instead, it is argued, a party who has performed part or all of an unenforceable contract may have a remedy under the law of restitution. This possibility is discussed in the following extract.

Pavey & Mathews Pty Ltd v Paul

(1986) 162 CLR 221, High Court of Australia

[Pavey & Mathews was a builder licensed under the *Builders Licensing Act 1971* (NSW). Pursuant to an oral contract it carried out building work for Paul and was paid part of the amount due. However, although the work was satisfactory, Paul declined to pay the balance and when this was claimed raised non-compliance with the formalities prescribed by s 45 of the Act. Pavey & Mathews succeeded at first instance but Paul's s 45 defence was upheld by the New South Wales Court of Appeal. Pavey & Mathews then appealed to the High Court.]

Mason CJ and Wilson J [at 224]: The important issue in this appeal is whether a builder may bring an action in *indebitatus assumpsit* for the value of work done and materials supplied under an oral building contract, notwithstanding the provisions of s 45 of the *Builders Licensing Act 1971* (NSW) ('the Act'). That section provides:

---

20   See *Freedom v AHR Constructions Pty Ltd* [1987] 1 Qd R 59.
21   (1951) 82 CLR 463 at 474.

'A contract (in this section referred to as a 'building contract') under which the holder of a licence undertakes to carry out, by himself or by others, any building work or to vary any building work or the manner of carrying out any building work, specified in a building contract is not enforceable against the other party to the contract unless the contract is in writing signed by each of the parties or his agent in that behalf and sufficiently describes the building work the subject of the contract.' ... <225> ...

The Court of Appeal in this case, and in *Schwarstein v Watson*, in which judgment was delivered on the same day, considered that an action in *indebitatus assumpsit* to recover the agreed remuneration for building work done pursuant to an oral contract that was wholly executed was an action to enforce that <226> contract. Their Honours arrived at this conclusion after a very lengthy review of the history of *indebitatus assumpsit* as a result of which they found that in order to succeed in the action the plaintiff must plead and prove the special contract for building work under which he claims remuneration. Their Honours reinforced the conclusion reached in this way by invoking considerations of legislative policy which, they thought, supported a legislative intention to prevent a builder from recovering any remuneration in respect of building work unless the contract is in writing and complies with the statutory requirements. ... <227> ...

Deane J, whose reasons for judgment we have had the advantage of reading, has concluded that an action on a *quantum meruit*, such as that brought by the appellant, rests, not on implied contract, but on a claim to restitution or one based on unjust enrichment, arising from the respondent's acceptance of the benefits accruing to the respondent from the appellant's performance of the unenforceable oral contract. This conclusion does not accord with the acceptance by Williams, Fullagar and Kitto JJ in *Turner v Bladin* of the views expressed by Lord Denning in his articles in the *Law Quarterly Review*, vol 41 (1925), p 79, and vol 55 (1939), p 54, basing such a claim in implied contract. These views were a natural reflection of prevailing legal thinking as it had developed to that time. ... Since then the shortcomings of the implied contract theory have been rigorously exposed ... and the virtues of an approach based on restitution and unjust enrichment ... widely appreciated. ... We are therefore now justified in recognizing, as Deane J has done, that the true foundation of the right to recover on a *quantum meruit* does not depend on the existence of an implied contract.

Once the true basis of the action on a *quantum meruit* is established, namely execution of work for which the unenforceable contract provided, and its acceptance by the defendant, it is difficult to regard the action as one by which the plaintiff seeks to enforce the oral contract. True it is that proof of the oral contract may be an indispensable element in the plaintiff's success but that is in order to show that (a) the benefits were not intended as a gift, and (b) that the <228> defendant has not rendered the promised exchange value. ... The purpose of proving the contract is not to enforce it but to make out another cause of action having a different foundation in law.

If the effect of bringing an action on a *quantum meruit* was simply to enforce the oral contract in some circumstances only, though not in all the circumstances in which an action on the contract would succeed, it might be persuasively contended that the action on a *quantum meruit* was an indirect means of enforcing the oral contract. So, if all the plaintiff had to prove was that he had fully executed the contract on his part and that he had not been paid the contract price, there would be some force in the suggestion that the proceeding amounted to an indirect enforcement of the contractual cause of action. However, when success in a *quantum meruit* depends, not only on the plaintiff proving that he did the work, but also on the defendant's acceptance of the work without paying the agreed remuneration, it is evident that the court is enforcing against the defendant an obligation that differs in character from the contractual obligation had it been enforceable. …

[Their Honours then considered whether s 45 should be interpreted so as to prevent a claim of any kind being made by the plaintiff and continued at 228]:

On one view the purpose of s 45 is to protect the building owner against spurious claims by a builder by preventing the enforcement by him of nonconforming contracts. This in substance was the view taken by the Court of Appeal in this case and in *Schwarstein v Watson*. <229> That purpose includes the protection of the building owner against a claim by a builder on a written contract that fails to describe the building work sufficiently, even in a case where the builder has fully executed the contract on his part. But it would be going a very long way indeed to assert that the statutory protection extends to a case where the building owner requests and accepts the building work and declines to pay for it on the ground that the contract fails to comply with the statutory requirements. True it is that the informal contract, though not enforceable by the builder, is enforceable against him. But it is not to be supposed that it is enforceable against him on the footing that the building owner is under no liability to pay for building work upon which he insists and the performance of which he accepts. The consequences of the respondent's interpretation are so draconian that it is difficult to suppose that they were intended. An interpretation that serves the statutory purpose yet avoids a harsh and unjust operation is to be preferred.

[In a separate judgment, Deane J also allowed the appeal on substantially the same grounds as Mason CJ and Wilson J. Brennan J dissented. Dawson J also allowed the appeal, agreeing that s 45 did not prevent the plaintiff's claim. However his Honour also observed at 269:

> 'I cannot, with respect, agree that an action upon a *quantum meruit* is an action upon an implied contract or, at all events, an implied contract which covers the same ground as an existing contract. Whether or not restitution, released from its abode in *indebitatus assumpsit*, would also support a claim in those circumstances is something which it was unnecessary to consider in order to decide that case as it is unnecessary in this case. In my view, the observations of this Court in *Turner v Bladin* and those apparently made originally by Denning LJ in *James v Thomas H Kent & Co Ltd* are correct.']

Appeal allowed

[footnotes omitted]

b   The equitable doctrine of part performance

The *Statute of Frauds* had not been in operation for very long before it became apparent that it could produce unjust results. Such an outcome would be likely, for example, in a case in which an oral contract of sale was repudiated by the vendor after the purchaser had entered the property, pursuant to the contract, and carried out substantial improvements. Not allowing the purchaser to enforce the contract in such a case, because it did not comply with the statute, could see the vendor being unfairly enriched by those improvements at the purchaser's expense. The response to situations of this kind was not an amendment to the statute but the development, by courts, of the equitable doctrine of part performance. As its name suggest, this doctrine allows a contract to be enforced where it has been 'partly performed' and this is necessary to produce an equitable outcome between the parties.

The precise requirements of the doctrine are not beyond dispute and on some points Australian courts have been more restrictive than they were in England when the doctrine still operated in that country.[22] The rationale for the doctrine and the requirements for its operation in Australia are summarised in the following extracts.

JC Williamson Ltd v Lukey & Mulholland

(1931) 45 CLR 282, High Court of Australia

[Williamson, the lessee of a theatre, agreed to grant Lukey and Mulholland an exclusive right to sell confectionary in the theatre for a period exceeding one year. However, no note or memorandum was made of this agreement as required by s 128 of the *Instruments Act 1928* (Vic). Lukey and Mulholland acted pursuant to the agreement for some time before it was repudiated by Williamson. Following this occurrence, they sought various equitable remedies designed to enforce the agreement. By way of defence, Williamson relied on s 128. At first instance, Lukey and Mulholland succeeded on the ground that there had been part performance of the agreement; Williamson appealed to the High Court.]

Evatt J [at 308]: The equitable doctrine of part performance has had many champions. … The *Statute of Frauds* must not, it was claimed, be used as an instrument of fraud. The consequence was a substantial alteration of the *Statute of Frauds* itself which, as Lord *Blackburn* pointed out in *Maddison v Alderson* was interpreted by Courts of Equity as if it contained a positive exception—'or unless possession of the land shall be given and accepted.' The judicial gloss on the statute

---

22   The doctrine was, in effect, eliminated by s 2 of the *Law of Property (Miscellaneous Provisions) Act 1989* (UK). However, previously, in *Steadman v Steadman* [1976] AC 536 the House of Lords had said that it was sufficient for the doctrine if the acts of part performance relied upon pointed to 'some contract' between the parties and that the payment of money could be a sufficient act of part performance. Neither point has been accepted in Australia as the extracts in the text indicate.

was regarded by him as an unjustified interpolation. Its justification was historical, not logical. Indeed, the speech of the Earl of *Selborne* in the same case, which puts forward the doctrine from the point of view of Courts of Equity in the most effective and plausible way, has running through it, I fancy, an undercurrent which admits the force of Lord *Blackburn's* criticism. 'In a suit founded on such part performance,' said the Lord Chancellor <309> 'the defendant is really 'charged' upon the equities resulting from the acts done in execution of the contract, and not (within the meaning of the statute) upon the contract itself. If such equities were excluded, injustice of a kind which the statute cannot be thought to have had in contemplation would follow.' His Lordship went on to give an illustration from a case of possession of land, showing a very harsh result from the literal application of the statute.

[On the facts in this case, his Honour concluded that the doctrine of part performance was not applicable as it could be used only in conjunction with the remedy of specific performance which, he said, could not be invoked here.[23] In separate judgments, Starke, Dixon (with whom Gavan Duffy CJ agreed) and McTiernan JJ arrived at the same conclusion.]

Appeal allowed

[footnotes omitted]

McBride v Sandland

(1918) 25 CLR 69, High Court of Australia

[In 1895, McBride promised to allow his daughter, Mrs Sandland, and her husband to occupy a certain farming property during his lifetime and to transfer it to them upon his death. This promise was made in exchange for certain undertakings on their part. The Sandlands occupied the land for a number of years and after Mr Sandland's death Mrs Sandland continued to do so under a lease from McBride. In 1916, at the expiration of this lease, McBride claimed possession of the land; Mrs Sandland refused to give up possession on the ground that she had an interest in the land pursuant to the 1895 promise. At first instance the court decided that Mrs Sandland had an equitable interest in the land pursuant to an agreement with McBride; McBride appealed to the High Court.]

Isaacs and Rich JJ [at 77]: It will conduce to precision in dealing with the voluminous and complicated circumstances detailed in the evidence to state, so far as material to the present case, certain elements of part performance essential to raise the equity:

(1) The act relied on must be unequivocally and in its own nature referable to 'some such agreement as that alleged.' That is, it must be such as could be done with no other view than to perform such an agreement.

---

23 Extracts from this case dealing with the availability of the remedies of injunction and specific performance are set out at p 714.

(2) By 'some such agreement as that alleged' is meant some contract of the general nature of that alleged.

(3) The proved circumstances in which the 'act' was done must be considered in order to judge whether it refers unequivocally to such an agreement as is alleged. Expressions are found in some cases which, if literally read, are to the effect that mere possession by a stranger is sufficient to let in parol evidence of any contract alleged. Those cases were prior to *Maddison v Alderson*, and the expressions literally read appear to be too wide, because, so read, they would conflict with the requirement that the act must unequivocally refer to some such contract as is alleged, and because bare possession does not necessarily connote trespass or, alternatively, a contract at all; indeed, some contracts would not justify the act done. Possession may be the result of mere permission. But if the circumstances under which the possession was given are proved, then the Court may judge whether the act indicates permission or contract, and, if <79> contract, its general character. …

(4) It must have been in fact done by the party relying on it on the faith of the agreement, and further the other party must have permitted it to be done on that footing. Otherwise there would not be 'fraud' in refusing to carry out the agreement, and fraud, that is moral turpitude, is the ground of jurisdiction.

(5) It must be done by a party to the agreement.

These requirements must be satisfied before the actual terms of the alleged agreement are allowed to be deposed to.

Further, when those terms are established, it still remains to be shown:

(6) That there was a completed agreement.

(7) That the act was done under the terms of that agreement by force of that agreement.

[Their Honours concluded that the 1895 promise did not give rise to a contract as alleged by Mrs Sandland and that her actions and those of her husband did not constitute part performance. In separate judgments Higgins J (with whom Gavan Duffy J agreed) and Powers J reached the same conclusion.]

Appeal allowed

[footnotes omitted]

Regent v Millett

(1976) 133 CLR 679, High Court of Australia

[Mr and Mrs Regent agreed to transfer a house to their daughter and her husband, Mr and Mrs Millett, in consideration of them paying off a mortgage over the house. This agreement was oral. The Milletts went into occupation, commenced paying off a mortgage and effected substantial renovations and repairs. However, the Regents refused to transfer the house and the Milletts sought specific performance. The Milletts succeeded at first instance and on appeal; the Regents then appealed to the High Court.]

Gibbs J [with whom Stephen, Mason, Jacobs and Murphy JJ agreed, at 682]: In the action the appellants pleaded the *Statute of Frauds* (whose equivalent in New South Wales is s 54A of the *Conveyancing Act 1919*, as amended). There is no suggestion that the agreement is evidenced by any note or memorandum in writing and the sole question now raised in the case is whether there was part performance. The acts of part performance on which the respondents relied were (1) the taking of possession; (2) the effecting of repairs before December 1972; (3) the doing of the work on the renovations and additions in January 1973; (4) the making of the mortgage repayments.

The learned trial judge held that these acts amounted to sufficient part performance and ordered specific performance of the agreement. His decision was affirmed by the Court of Appeal.

The principle upon which the doctrine of part performance rests was stated by Lord Cranworth, Lord Chancellor in *Caton v Caton* in words which appear to have a direct application to the present case. He said:

> '… when one of two contracting parties has been induced, or allowed by the other, to alter his position on the faith of the contract, as for instance by taking possession of land, and expending money in building or other like acts, there it would be a fraud in the other party to set up the legal invalidity of the contract on the faith of which he induced, or allowed, the person contracting with him to act, and expend his money.'

The books are full of cases in which it has been held that the entry into possession alone, or the taking of possession coupled with the expenditure of money by one party on the improvement of property, with the cognizance of the other party to the contract, may amount to part performance (see the cases cited in *Halsbury's Laws of England*, 3rd ed, vol 36, par 416).

The argument advanced on behalf of the appellants, when reduced to its essentials, depends upon two propositions. First, it was said that the acts relied on were not unequivocally referable to some such contract as that alleged by the respondents. Indeed, it was submitted that a narrower test should be adopted and that <683> it was necessary to establish 'such a performance as must necessarily imply the existence of the contract'—to use the words of Lord O'Hagan in *Maddison v Alderson*. However, the test suggested by the Earl of Selborne LC in that case, that the acts relied upon as part performance 'must be unequivocally, and in their own nature, referable to some such agreement as that alleged', has been consistently accepted as a correct statement of the law. It is enough that the acts are unequivocally and in their own nature referable to some contract of the general nature of that alleged (see *McBride v Sandland*).

The second proposition submitted for the appellants was that the acts relied upon must have been done in part performance of the agreement alleged; in other words, the acts must have been done under the terms of that agreement and by force of that agreement. In support of this proposition particular reliance was placed on *Cooney v Burns* and *McBride v Sandland*.

It may be said immediately that if the reasoning of their Lordships in the recent case of *Steadman v Steadman* is accepted, the appellants' arguments must fail. However, it is unnecessary for the present decision to consider the questions that are raised by that case.

In the present case the giving and taking of possession by itself was sufficient part performance of the contract and it is therefore unnecessary to consider whether the other acts relied upon would also, either alone or together, amount to part performance. The change of possession of land has been described as 'the act of part performance par excellence'—Williams: *The Statute of Frauds, Section IV*, p 256. Of course, it may be proved that the taking of possession was referable to some other authority than the contract alleged. That was the situation in *McBride v Sandland*. However, in the present case the circumstances under which possession was given indicate contract, to echo the words in *McBride v Sandland* and the possession was unequivocally referable to some such contract as that alleged. The taking of possession was pursuant to the contract. It is true that the contract did not require the respondents to take possession, but if it were necessary that the acts of part performance should have been done in compliance with a requirement of the contract, the utility of the equitable doctrine would be reduced to vanishing point, and many cases which have proceeded on the <684> opposite view would have been wrongly decided. The Judicial Committee in *White v Neaylon* indeed appears to have held that the effecting of improvements on property which were neither required nor permitted by the contract may be acts of part performance; but however that may be, it is clear that if a vendor permits a purchaser to take possession to which a contract of sale entitles him, the giving and taking of that possession will amount to part performance notwithstanding that under the contract the purchaser was entitled rather than bound to take possession.

For these reasons the Court below was, in my opinion, right in holding that there were sufficient acts of part performance and the appeal should be dismissed.

Appeal dismissed

[footnotes omitted]

c Estoppel

The doctrine of estoppel, considered in chapter 4, may also enable a contract to be enforced even though prescribed formalities were not complied with. This possibility is illustrated by Australia's leading case on estoppel, *Waltons Stores (Interstate) Ltd v Maher* (extracted at p 148).[24] In this case, the Mahers were unable to directly enforce the contract made with Waltons because, although they had signed the lease document, Waltons had not done so. However, the High Court held that because of its conduct Waltons was estopped from denying that it was bound, thereby enabling the Mahers to recover damages in lieu of specific performance.

---

24 (1988) 164 CLR 387.

5 Summary

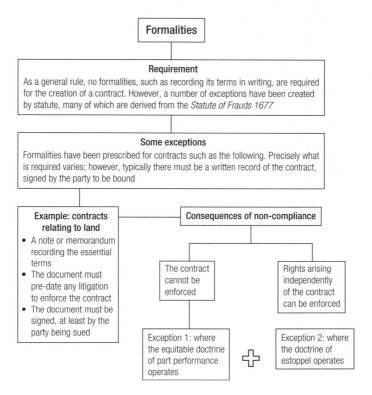

6 Questions

1. On 16 March, Peter wrote to Sally, the solicitor acting for Barwon Ltd, offering to purchase Barwon's old factory on certain specified terms. However, no price was mentioned beyond a reference to a fair market price. After taking instructions, Sally advised Peter that Barwon was willing to sell the factory, on the terms suggested, for $800,000. By letter dated 19 April, Peter replied that he agreed to pay this sum. With his letter he enclosed a cheque for $80,000, being a 10% deposit as provided for in the terms of sale specified in his letter of 16 March. On 23 April, Sally acknowledged Peter's letter and enclosed a receipt for the deposit he had paid.

    Peter no longer wishes to proceed with this transaction. Please advise him whether he is contractually bound to do so.

2. On 10 January, Able and Penny agreed that Penny would purchase Able's house for $450,000. This agreement provided for settlement on 14 March. The precise terms of their agreement were recorded in a letter which Penny wrote to Able on 12 January. Penny signed this letter and enclosed a cheque for $45,000, being the amount of the deposit they had agreed upon. Able received this letter on 14 January and banked the deposit. As Able's house was unoccupied, with his permission, Penny attended to the garden by mowing the lawns and watering various plants and young trees.

On 10 March, Able received another offer for the house of $500,000 which he accepted. He then refused to transfer the house to Penny on 14 March, even though she was ready and willing to pay the balance of the purchase price. He justified his action on the ground that he was not bound by the agreement made with her as he had not signed anything.

Please advise Penny of her rights under the agreement with Able.

PART 3

Scope and Content

Part 3 deals with the scope and content of a contract.

'Scope' refers to the ability of a contract to confer rights, or impose obligations, upon non-parties. In particular, we will examine the extent to which the two parties to a contract, A and B, can by agreement create a contractual right in favour of a third party, C, or impose a contractual obligation or restriction upon that person. This topic is dealt with in Chapter 8, Privity of Contract.

'Content' refers to the terms of the contract; that is, its prescription of the rights and obligations that the parties have created by their agreement. This involves considering three issues. First, the determination of precisely what terms the parties have agreed to. As in many cases, contractual terms may be (i) recorded in writing, (ii) entirely oral, or (iii) a combination of both, it is not surprising that most of the controversy surrounding this issue will arise when the contract is oral or partly oral, or is asserted by one of the parties to be so. This is dealt with in Chapter 9, The Terms of a Contract.

The second issue is the determination of the meaning to be given to the terms of the contract and their relative importance to the parties. This is dealt with in Chapter 10, Construction and Classification. As well as illuminating the rights and obligations of the parties, the construction and classification of terms is important because of its relationship to the remedy of discharge for breach of contract—the right an innocent party has to terminate a contract because of the other party's failure to perform the contract as agreed. Briefly, this remedy is only available where that failure amounts to a major breach of contract and this will usually occur only when the term or terms not complied are 'fundamental' to the contract as opposed to being of relatively minor importance.

The third issue concerns exclusion clause—clauses included in a contract to reduce, or qualify in some way, one party's obligations to the other, or to limit the remedies available to the latter in the event of the former's breach of a contractual or other duty. This is a controversial issue and may involve the determination, in the first place, of whether such clauses form part of the contract and then, if they do, whether they actually cover the particular situation in question. Therefore, to obtain a complete understanding of the *contractual* rights and obligations of the parties (as distinct from those that may be created by statute, such as the consumer guarantees established by the *Australian Consumer Law*) it is necessary to look at the substantive provisions of the contract *and* any exclusion clauses it contains. This is the subject of Chapter 11, Exclusion Clauses.

CHAPTER 8

Privity of Contract

1	Introduction	211
2	The origins and scope of the doctrine	213
	a Origins and development	213
	b Privity and consideration	218
	c Non-contractual rights and liabilities	218
3	Contracts for the benefit of third parties	219
	a Enforcement by the promisee	219
	b Enforcement by a joint promisee	226
	c Enforcement by the third party	226
4	Contracts obligating third parties	231
5	Exceptions to the privity doctrine	232
	a Introduction	232
	b Abolition: Western Australia, Queensland and Northern Territory	232
	c Specific exceptions	234
	d Common law and equitable circumventions	235
6	Summary	238
7	Questions	238

1 Introduction

The object of most contracts is to benefit, or obligate, the parties to the contract and those persons alone. In the case of a typical sales contract, for example, on one side of the transaction the seller gains the benefit of receiving price and incurs the obligation of delivering the property, while on the other, the purchaser gains the property and incurs the obligation of paying the price. However, the object of some contracts is to benefit or obligate a third party. Examples of contracts designed to benefit a third party include those between parents and a service provider to have services provided to children, or between employers and their customers to extend the benefit of exclusion clauses to their sub-contractors or employees. Examples of contracts designed to obligate a third party are vertical transactions in relation to property or services in which the contracting parties agree to impose restrictions on a third party in relation to the property or services sold. In such cases, although the promise and the consideration for the promise pass between the parties, the benefit or obligation created by the contract relates to the third party as illustrated by the following diagrams.

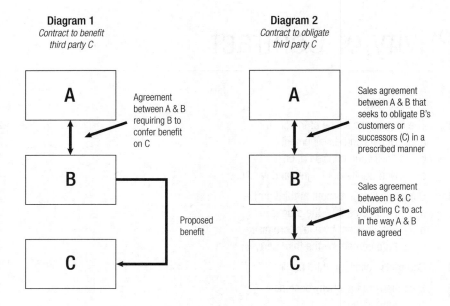

The doctrine of privity of contract deals with these situations. In its simplest form it provides that the third parties (C in these diagrams) cannot enforce the contract, or have the contract enforced against them; in other words

- In Diagram 1: C cannot compel B to perform the promise B has made to A, even though B has received from A the consideration B sought in exchange for that promise.
- In Diagram 2: A cannot compel C to act in the manner prescribed in the contract between A and B, or to adhere to the promise C made to B, even though C has received from B the consideration C sought in exchange for that promise.

Justification for the doctrine centres on the notion that contracts are essentially private bargains, exclusive to the parties. While they can be used to confer benefits on third parties, their exclusivity means that it is for the parties alone to choose whether to enforce them or not. This freedom would be eroded if third parties were able to enforce promises made in their favour, because such a right would necessarily involve fettering the otherwise unfettered power contracting parties have to vary their original agreement.[1] However, while there is force in this argument and while in many cases the doctrine will not actually thwart the intention of the parties because the promise involved can be enforced by the other party (A in Diagram 1 and B in Diagram 2), in many other cases it will do just that.

---

1   See generally the discussion in *Trident General Insurance Co Ltd v McNiece Bros Pty Ltd* (1987–1988) 165 CLR 107 at 122 and the authorities cited.

This is because the remedies available to the other contracting party (A or B, above) may not provide an adequate remedy, or may be limited, or in the circumstances it may be impossible, or impractical, for that party to enforce them.[2] For this reason, the doctrine of Privity of Contract has been the subject of sustained criticism and considerable judicial and statutory modification, including its abolition in England[3] and parts of Australia. Nevertheless, it remains part of the law in most Australian jurisdictions and applies to most contracts.

In this chapter we will:

- note the origins and scope of the doctrine
- examine the enforceability of contracts made for the benefit of third parties
- examine the enforceability of contracts seeking to impose obligations on third parties
- outline the common law and statutory exceptions to the doctrine

2 The origins and scope of the doctrine

a Origins and development

The doctrine of privity of contract does not have a long history, emerging only in Anglo-Australian law in the mid-nineteenth century in conjunction with the bargain theory of contract. However, it was sufficiently entrenched by the time of the decision in *Dunlop Pneumatic Tyre Co Ltd v Selfridge & Co Ltd* for Viscount Haldane LC to describe as 'fundamental' in the law of England the principle that 'only a person who is a party to a contract can sue on it'.[4] This case concerned a retail price maintenance scheme,[5] pursuant to which Selfridge contractually promised its supplier, Dew, to observe the price list of a third party, Dunlop, when it sold to its customers Dunlop tyres purchased from Dew. Selfridge did not honour this promise and Dunlop sued for breach of contract. This claim failed because, although the promise in question had been made for Dunlop's benefit and although Selfridge had received consideration for that promise from Dew, Dunlop was a third party to the contract between Selfridge and Dew and, as such, prevented by the principle quoted above from enforcing it.

Dunlop v Selfridge was applied by the Privy Council to contracts of car insurance in *Vandepitte v Preferred Accident Insurance Corporation of New York*.[6] As a result, coverage was denied to a third party in that case even though she came within the

---

2   See the discussion in *Trident General Insurance Co Ltd v McNiece Bros Pty Ltd* (1987–1988) 165 CLR 107 at 118–121, extracted below.
3   *Contracts (Rights of Third Parties) Act 1999* (UK).
4   [1915] AC 847.
5   Such schemes are prohibited in Australia by s 48 of the *Competition and Consumer Act 2010*; as a result, a contract such as the one in this case would be unenforceable as an illegal contract and the parties liable to prosecution under the Act.
6   [1932] All ER Rep 527.

terms of the insurance policy in question which provided cover for the insured and 'anyone operating the car with his permission', as she had been doing at the time of the accident. In Australia it was applied by the High Court to deny third parties the protection of exclusion clauses expressed in their favour[7] and to prevent a surviving spouse from enforcing a promise, made to her deceased husband, to make royalty payments to her after his death.[8] As these cases indicate, the doctrine not only prevents effect being given to the express intention of the parties but can also create great injustice where the third party and the promisee have assumed that the promise would be enforceable and have arranged their affairs accordingly; for example, by not taking out their own insurance cover, or not making their own contract with the promisor. Not surprisingly, therefore, it has been subjected to considerable criticism and calls for reform. These were discussed by members of the High Court in *Trident General Insurance Co Ltd v McNiece Bros Pty Ltd*, extracted below. A majority in this case decided that a third party, McNiece, could enforce an insurance contract expressed in its favour and did so in terms that foreshadowed the possibility of the Court one day dismantling the privity doctrine entirely. However, the actual decision in the case was limited to insurance contracts, a type of contract in respect of which the privity rule had recently been abolished by statute in any case,[9] and subsequent courts have not progressed in this direction.[10] Therefore, in all probability, abolition will require legislation.

Trident General Insurance Co Ltd v McNiece Bros Pty Ltd

(1987–1988) 165 CLR 107, High Court of Australia

[Trident Insurance contracted with Blue Circle to provide insurance cover against liability to the public. This contract covered Blue Circle and 'all its subsidiary, associated and related Companies, all Contractors and Sub-Contractors and/or Suppliers'. During the currency of the contract, McNiece, a contractor working for Blue Circle, sought indemnity from Trident in relation to a claim brought against it. Trident denied liability on the ground that McNiece was not a party to the insurance contract and could not sue on it, relying on *Dunlop v Selfridge* and *Vandepitte v Preferred Accident Insurance*. McNiece succeeded at first instance; Trident appealed unsuccessfully to the New South Wales Court of Appeal; it then appealed to the High Court.]

Mason CJ and Wilson J [at 116]: These 'fundamental' traditional rules, where they survive, have been under siege throughout the common law world. In the United Kingdom the Law Revision Committee, which included many distinguished lawyers under the chairmanship of Lord Wright, recommended the abolition of the consideration rule and the privity rule in its Sixth Interim Report. ... The

---

7   See *Wilson v Darling Island Stevedoring & Lighterage Co Ltd* (1956) 95 CLR 43.
8   See *Coulls v Bagot's Executor & Trustee Co Ltd* (1967) 119 CLR 460.
9   *Insurance Contracts Act 1984* (Cth) s 48. This provision did not apply to the facts in the case as they arose before this provision came into effect.
10 See, for example, *Silver v Dome Resources NL* (2007) Aust Contract Reports 90-258 at 89,968.

Committee stated that the English common law (an expression which, in the context of the Report in 1937, may be taken to include the Australian common law) was alone among modern systems of law in its insistence on the privity rule and observed that the United States had taken steps to mitigate the rigour of the rule. Even in England, the Committee noted, Parliament had found it necessary to create legislative exceptions. ...

The Committee recommended that the statutory recognition of third party rights should be carefully limited. The proposed limitations were: (1) no third party right should be acquired unless given by the express terms of the contract; (2) the promisor should be able to raise against the third party any defence available against the promisee; and (3) the right of the promisor and of the promisee to cancel the contract at any time should be preserved unless the third party has received notice of the agreement and has adopted it. It might be noted that this regime is much like that which has <117> developed in the United States. ... <118> ...

There is much substance in the criticisms directed at the traditional common law rules as questions debated in the cases reveal. First, there is the vexed question whether the promisee can recover substantial damages for breach by the promisor of his promise to confer a benefit on the third party. The orthodox view is that ordinarily the promisee is entitled to nominal damages only because non-performance by the promisor, though resulting in a loss of the third party benefit, causes no damage to the promisee. <119> ...

It is clear enough that the availability of an action for damages at the suit of the promisee for breach of the promise to benefit the third party is not a sufficient sanction to secure performance of the promise. What is more, the uncertain status of the decision in *Jackson v Horizon Holidays Ltd* is a telling indictment against the law as it presently stands. There, the plaintiff recovered substantial damages for the travel company's breach of contract to provide a satisfactory family holiday, but the basis on which the decision can be supported is by no means clear, even after the comments by the House of Lords in *Woodar*. Rules which generate uncertainty in their application to ordinary contracts commonly entered into by the citizen call for reconsideration.

Next, there is the question whether the contract to confer a benefit on the third party is capable of specific performance. In *Coulls* Barwick CJ considered that where a promisor promises to make a payment to a third party the promisee may obtain specific performance of the promises at least where the nature of the consideration would have allowed the remedy. Windeyer J went even further, asserting that contracts to pay money or transfer property to a third party are always or very often contracts for breach of which damages are an inadequate remedy and that on this ground such contracts are susceptible of specific performance. We agree with his Honour's comment and with his additional observations which point the way to a more general recognition of the availability of specific performance as a remedy. ... <120> ... But, even if we assume the availability of specific performance at the suit of the promisee in a wide variety of situations, there are nonetheless situations, such as that in *Jackson v Horizon Holidays Ltd*, where specific performance is not a suitable remedy and damages are inadequate. In these situations the incapacity of the third party to sue means that the law gives less protection to the promisee and the third party than the promisor: ... And, assuming the availability of specific performance, the third party is nonetheless dependent on the willingness of the promisee to exercise his rights, in the absence of a trust, an agency relationship or an enforceable agreement between the promisee and the third party.

Then there is the trust of the contractual promise on which the appellant places particular reliance as a palliative of the difficulties generated by the common law principles. ... [C]ritics of the common law rules have pointed to the uncertainty surrounding the <121> circumstances in which the courts will recognize a trust in contracts for the benefit of third parties as a reason for rejecting the trust concept as a sufficient answer to the difficulties caused by those rules. ...

And in the ultimate analysis it seems incongruous that we should be compelled to import the mechanism of a trust to ensure that a third party can enforce the contract if the intention of the contracting parties is that he should benefit from performance of the contract. *A fortiori* is that so if the intention common to the parties is that the third party should be able to sue the promisor.

[Their Honours then considered the justifications advanced for the privity doctrine and the legislative changes to it made by s 48 of the *Insurance Contracts Act 1984* (Cth) and in Queensland, Western Australia and New Zealand. They continued at 123]: The variety of these responses to the problems arising from contracts to benefit a third party indicate the range of the policy choices to be made and that there is room for debate about them. A simple departure from the traditional rules would lead to third party enforceability of such a contract, subject to the preservation of a contracting party's right to rescind or vary, in the absence of reliance by the third party to his detriment, and to the availability in an action by the third party of defences against a contracting party. The adoption of this course would represent less of a departure from the traditional exposition of the law than other legislative choices which have been made. Moreover, as we have seen, the traditional rules, which were adopted here as a consequence of their development in the United Kingdom, have been the subject of much criticism and of legislative erosion in the field of insurance contracts. Regardless of the layers of sediment which may have accumulated, we consider that it is the responsibility of this Court to reconsider in appropriate cases common law rules which operate unsatisfactorily and unjustly. The fact that there have been recent legislative developments in the relevant field is not a reason for continuing to insist on the application of an unjust rule as it stood before its alteration by the *Insurance Contracts Act 1984* (Cth).

In the ultimate analysis the limited question we have to decide is whether the old rules apply to a policy of insurance. The injustice which would flow from such a result arises not only from its failure to give effect to the expressed intention of the person who takes out the insurance but also from the common intention of the parties and the circumstance that others, aware of the existence of the policy, will order their affairs accordingly. ... <124> ...

In the circumstances, notwithstanding the caution with which the Court ordinarily will review earlier authorities and the operation of long-established principle, we conclude that the principled development of the law requires that it be recognized that McNiece was entitled to succeed in the action.

For the foregoing reasons, we would dismiss the appeal.

Toohey J [at 168]: I do not accept that a non-party assured is, as the common law presently stands, able to sue. But equally I accept that the law which precludes him from doing so is based on shaky foundations and, in its widest form, lacks support both in logic or in jurisprudence. My concern is whether the law is so well entrenched that nothing short of legislative interference can fairly budge it.

My conclusion is that the law is not so well entrenched as to be incapable of change.

[After discussing criticisms of the privity doctrine and considering the implications of 'declaring the law to be otherwise than hitherto accepted' his Honour concluded at 172]: The proposition which I consider this Court should now indorse may be formulated along these lines. When an insurer issues a liability insurance policy, identifying the assured in terms that evidence an intention on the part of both insurer and assured that the policy will indemnify as well those with whom the assured contracts for the purpose of the venture covered by the policy, and it is reasonable to expect that such a contractor may order its affairs by reference to the existence of the policy, the contractor may sue the insurer on the policy, notwithstanding that consideration may not have moved from the contractor to the insurer and notwithstanding that the contractor is not a party to the contract between the insurer and assured.

No doubt, a decision upholding the Court of Appeal will itself give rise to a number of questions. Are there other situations in which a third party may sue on a contract when consideration has not moved from the third party to the promisor? What defences are available to the promisor in such cases? These are questions which do not now require an answer. Other situations must await another day; the terms on which special leave to appeal was granted preclude a decision in wider terms than have been expressed in these reasons. The defences available to an insurer against whom action may lie at the suit of a third party do not have to be explored for none was advanced on behalf of the appellant before this Court.

The appeal should be dismissed.

[Gaudron J agreed that the appeal should be dismissed and that McNiece could enforce the insurance contract. However, her Honour based her conclusion on the grounds of unjust enrichment, rather than contract, and opined that this did not abrogate the privity doctrine. Deane J concluded that McNiece should be given the opportunity to establish that the contract created a trust in its favour. Brennan and Dawson JJ dissented on the ground that McNiece was not a party to the insurance contract and therefore could not enforce it.]

Appeal dismissed

[footnotes omitted]

b   Privity and consideration

Although in *Dunlop v Selfridge* Viscount Haldane identified them as separate,[11] it has been argued that the principle that a person must be privy to a contract before they can enforce it, is merely a different way of expressing the principle that a contract not under seal will be enforceable only if the promisee has provided consideration. However, while in most contracts the two principles do merge— because most promisees (who are by definition party to the contract) will provide consideration for the promise made to them—it is possible for this not to be the case. The example often given to illustrate this possibility is as follows: assume A, B and C enter into an agreement whereby A promises B and C to confer a benefit on C in exchange for consideration moving from B alone; in such a case, although a party to the contract, C will not be able to enforce A's promise as C did not provide consideration.[12] Indian contract law also recognises this separation by retaining a privity of contract doctrine even though s 2(d) of the *Indian Contract Act, 1872* allows consideration to be provided by a third party.

c   Non-contractual rights and liabilities

The principle that only a person who is a party to a contract can enforce, or be bound by it, does not mean that a contract cannot affect the legal position of third parties at all. The principle only restricts *contractual* rights and liabilities; it does not apply to rights and liabilities arising from other sources. Perhaps the best example of this point is *Donoghue v Stevenson*.[13] Here, the House of Lords established that a consumer could maintain an action for the tort of negligence against the manufacturer of a dangerous product, even though they were not a party to the contracts used by the manufacturer to distribute the product to consumers. Similarly, in *Opat v National Mutual Life Assurance of Australia Ltd*,[14] a builder was held liable in negligence to a third party who suffered loss as a result of the builder having performed a building contract negligently. The fact that the builder's contract was with the original owner of the property on which the work was carried out, did not preclude the builder owing a duty of care to a third party who subsequently purchased the property from the owner. Qualifications to the doctrine of this nature have also been created by statute, some of the most important of which are now contained in the *Australian Consumer Law (ACL)*. Thus, to replace reliance upon *Donoghue v Stevenson*, ss 138 and 139 of the *ACL* create statutory rights of action against the manufacturer of goods in favour of individuals who are injured, or who suffer loss or damage because others are injured, as a result of the goods having a safety defect. An even more significant qualification is created by s 271, which enables a person who has acquired goods

---

11   [1915] AC 847 at 853.
12   See *Trident General Insurance Co Ltd v McNiece Bros Pty Ltd* (1987–1988) 165 CLR 107 at 115– 116. Of course, if B provided consideration on behalf of both B and C, *Coulls v Bagot's Executor & Trustee Co Ltd* (1967) 119 CLR 460 suggests that C could enforce A's promise.
13   [1932] AC 562.
14   [1992] VR 283.

from a consumer to recover damages from the manufacturer of those goods where the statutory guarantee as to quality is not complied with.[15]

3 Contracts for the benefit of third parties

In this section we examine situations illustrated by Diagram 1. In particular, we identify the circumstances in which a contract made for the benefit of a third party (C) can be enforced directly by the promisee (A), or can create other contractual rights which C can enforce directly. Exceptions or qualifications to the privity doctrine are considered in section 5 below.

a Enforcement by the promisee

The party (A) who has made a contract designed to confer a benefit on a third party (C) can enforce that contract against the other contracting party (B) by either obtaining an order for specific performance or an injunction, or by recovering an award of damages for breach of contract. However, for the reasons outlined in *Trident General Insurance*, extracted above, these remedies are limited.

Specific performance or injunction

Assume B in Diagram 1, does not honour the promise made to A; for example, B does not transfer property to C as promised, or commences proceedings against C contrary to a promise not to do so. In such a case, A may be able to obtain an order for specific performance compelling B to transfer the property to C, or an injunction, restraining B from taking proceedings against C. The outcome of such proceedings is that C will receive the benefit that A and B agreed would be conferred by the latter.

The circumstances in which specific performance is available are discussed in the following extract.

Beswick v Beswick

[1968] AC 58, House of Lords

[In 1962 Peter Beswick sold his business to John Beswick (the appellant). Under this agreement, John promised to pay Peter £6 10s per week for the remainder of Peter's life and after his death to pay his wife £5 per week until her death. John made these payments until Peter's death in 1963. Thereafter, he made only one payment to Peter's widow (Mrs Beswick, the respondent). Mrs Beswick in

---

15   Section 271 (1) of the *ACL* confers this right on 'an affected person in relation to the goods'; such persons are defined in s 2. The statutory guarantee in relation to quality is created by s 54 and replaces the implied terms as to quality previously contained in Division 2 of Part V the *Trade Practices Act 1974* (Cth).

her personal capacity and as the administratrix of Peter's estate commenced proceedings to recover arrears in payments and an order for specific performance of the agreement. She failed at first instance but succeeded in the Court of Appeal; John then appealed to the House of Lords.]

Lord Pearce [at 88]: The administratrix is entitled, if she so prefers, to enforce the agreement rather than accept its repudiation, and specific performance is more convenient than an action for arrears of payment followed by separate actions as each sum falls due. Moreover, damages for breach would be a less appropriate remedy since the parties to the agreement were intending an annuity for a widow; and a lump sum of damages does not accord with this. And if <89> (contrary to my view) the argument that a derisory sum of damages is all that can be obtained be right, the remedy of damages in this case is manifestly useless. The present case presents all the features which led the equity courts to apply their remedy of specific performance. The contract was for the sale of a business. The defendant could on his part clearly have obtained specific performance of it if Beswick senior or his administratrix had defaulted. Mutuality is a ground in favour of specific performance. Moreover, the defendant on his side has received the whole benefit of the contract and it is a matter of conscience for the court to see that he now performs his part of it. ... It is argued that since the widow personally had no rights which she personally could enforce the court will not make an order which will have the effect of enforcing those rights. I can find no principle to this effect. The condition as to payment of an annuity to the widow personally was valid. The estate (though not the widow personally) can enforce it. Why should the estate be barred from exercising its full contractual rights merely because in doing so it secures justice for the widow who, by a mechanical defect of our law, is unable to assert her own rights? Such a principle would be repugnant to justice and fulfil no other object than that of aiding the wrongdoer. I can find no ground on which such a principle should exist. ... <90> ...

Recently in *Coulls v Bagot's Executor and Trustee Co Ltd* the learned Chief Justice of Australia, Sir Garfield Barwick, in commenting on the report of the Court of Appeal's decision in the present case, said:

> 'I would myself, with great respect, agree with the conclusion that where A promises B for a consideration supplied by B to pay C that B may obtain specific performance of A's promise, at least where the nature of the consideration given would have allowed the debtor to have obtained specific performance. I can see no reason whatever why A in those circumstances should not be bound to perform his promise. That C provided no part of the consideration seems to me irrelevant.'

I respectfully agree with these observations.

[In separate speeches, Lords Reid, Hodson, Guest and Upjohn agreed that Mrs Beswick could obtain specific performance in her capacity as administratrix of Peter's estate.]

Appeal dismissed

[footnotes omitted]

As far as the remedy of injunction is concerned, it has been established that if B has made a clear promise to A not to take proceedings against C, then (always assuming that there is no statutory provision to the contrary) A can restrain any action B may commence against C where this action would be detrimental to A's interests; for example, where A would have to indemnify C should B succeed.[16]

Damages

In a situation such as that in Diagram 1 it is clear that if A suffers loss as a result of B not conferring on C the promised benefit, A can recover that loss. Assume, for example, that A owed C $100 to be paid by a certain date and B owed A $100; in this situation, A and B might agree that B's debt to A will be discharged by B paying C $100 on A's behalf by the due date. Here, if B does not pay C as promised, A will remain indebted to C and perhaps incur additional liability, thus causing A loss. A could recover that loss from B as damages for breach of contract.

However, where A does not suffer loss but C does, or where C suffers loss in addition to loss suffered by A, the position is less clear. The first of these situations is illustrated by *Beswick v Beswick*, extracted above, as Peter Beswick's estate suffered no loss as a result of John Beswick not paying the promised benefit to Mrs Beswick. The members of the House of Lords were divided on the issue of whether, as administratrix of the estate, Mrs Beswick could recover substantial, as distinct from nominal, damages from John Beswick.[17] This matter was left unresolved as their Lordships decided, instead, to order specific performance of John's promise. An illustration of the second is *Jackson v Horizon Holidays Ltd* in which both the contracting party (Mr Jackson) and his family suffered loss as a result of the defendant's breach of contract.[18] Although the plaintiff recovered substantial damages in respect of both his own loss and that of his family, the status of this decision has been described as 'uncertain'.[19] Then, assuming that substantial damages *can* be recovered by A in relation to C's loss, the further issue arises of whether A must pay the amount recovered to C. These issues are discussed in the following extracts.

Coulls v Bagot's Executor & Trustee Co Ltd

(1967) 119 CLR 460, High Court of Australia

[The facts of this case are set out above at p129. The central issue before the Court was whether Mrs Coulls was a party to the agreement her husband had made with O'Neil. As a matter of construction, the majority concluded that she was not

---

16 *Gore v Van Der Lann* [1967] 1 All ER 360; *Snelling v John G Snelling Ltd* [1973] 1 QB 87.
17 *Beswick v Beswick* [1968] AC 58; Lords Reid (at 73) and Upjohn (at 102) assumed that only nominal damages could be recovered and Lord Hodson held that this was the case. On the other hand, Lord Pearce said that substantial damages could be recovered (at 88).
18 [1975] 1 WLR 1468.
19 *Trident General Insurance Co Ltd v McNiece Bros Pty Ltd* (1987–1988) 165 CLR 107 at 119, per Mason CJ and Wilson J.

and, therefore, that Mr Coulls' estate was entitled to the royalty payments made by O'Neil, rather than her. In the course of his dissenting judgment, Windeyer J made the following observations about whether damages could be recovered by one contracting party from the other when the latter does not confer a benefit on a third party as promised. He was the only member of the Court to address this issue.]

Windeyer J [at 501]: The question which presents itself at this point is what is the measure of damages for breach of a promise to confer a benefit upon a third party? Take the case supposed above—a contract by A with B under which B is to pay $500 to C. A sues B for breach of contract. There are authorities which say that he could recover only nominal damages, because it is C who has suffered not he: see *West v Houghton; Viles v Viles*; but cf *Drimmie v Davies*. As Else-Mitchell J remarked in *Cathels v Commissioner of Stamp Duties*, the cases on this point are 'conflicting and unsatisfactory'. No difficulty would arise if a statement of Lush LJ in *Lloyd's v Harper*, could be accepted without qualification and regardless of its context. He said:

> 'I consider it to be an established rule of law that where a contract is made with A for the benefit of B, A can sue on the contract for the benefit of B and recover all that B could have recovered if the contract had been made with B himself.'

But I think we must take it that when the learned Lord Justice spoke of a contract for the benefit of B he was thinking of a contract of which A was a trustee for B—that is to say of a case in which A held his legal rights under a contract as a trustee for B. In such a case of course the question disappears: but the case I have supposed, a contract by A with B that B will pay C $500, is a transaction at law devoid of any equity in C. Yet I do not see why, if A sued B for a breach of it, he must get no more than nominal damages. If C were A's creditor, and the $500 was to be paid to discharge A's debt, then B's failure to pay it would cause A more than nominal damage. Or, suppose C was a person whom A felt he had a duty to reward or recompense, or was someone who, with the aid of $500 was to engage in some activity which A wished to promote or from which he might benefit—I can see no reason why in such cases the damages which A would suffer upon B's breach of his contract to pay C $500 would be merely nominal: I think that, in accordance with the ordinary rules for the assessment of damages <502> for breach of contract, they could be substantial. They would not necessarily be $500; they could I think be less, or more. ...

Suppose that A does recover substantial damages for B's failure to perform his promise to A to pay C $500—the next question is does he recover these damages for himself or for C. Notwithstanding the statements in *Beswick v Beswick* suggesting that he would recover them for C, I do not see why this should be. On the hypothesis of a purely contractual right with no trust attached, why should A hold for C the proceeds of his action? He sued at law for damages he himself suffered, not as the representative of C. C had no right of action. A, not being a trustee of his contractual rights, might, had he wished, have released B from his contract, or declined to sue him for breach of it; or by agreement between A and B the contract could have been varied. C could not have complained. Why then is it said that proceedings brought by A to enforce his legal right give C a right against A when previously he had none? (I leave out of consideration the possibility of a bargain between A and C supported by consideration moving from C.) Of course A, whose purpose had miscarried because of B's breach of contract, might make over any damages he recovered to C: but that would not be because C had a right to them, but because A still wished to give effect to his plan to confer a benefit on him. In a case in which specific performance was an available remedy, A might choose to seek that form of redress against B, and thus obtain a judgment that B pay C $500. But that would not be because A was enforcing a right of C, but because he was enforcing his own right against B by obtaining an order that B perform his contract with him, A. For this reason—and always on the assumptions that there was no trust and that the transaction was as between A and C wholly gratuitous—I am not persuaded that C could force A to seek redress from B, or dictate to him what form of redress, specific performance or damages, he should seek.

Alfred McAlpine Construction Ltd v Panatown Ltd

[2000] 3 WLR 946, House of Lords

[Panatown contracted with McAlpine to have a building constructed on land owned by UIPL. This work was carried out in breach of contract with the result that UIPL suffered considerable loss. However, not being the owner of the land, Panatown suffered no loss itself. Nevertheless, it sued to recover the loss suffered by UIPL, notwithstanding the existence of a duty of care deed ('the DCD') between UIPL and McAlpine which gave the former direct contractual rights against the latter should it fail to exercise reasonable skill and care. In proceedings brought by Panatown, McAlpine argued that Panatown was debarred from recovering damages as it was not the owner of the land. Panatown's claim failed at first instance but it succeeded on appeal to the Court of Appeal; McAlpine then appealed to the House of Lords.]

Lord Browne-Wilkinson [at 999]: My Lords, this appeal raises again the question which was considered by the House in *St Martins Property Corpn Ltd v Sir Robert McAlpine Ltd* (heard with *Linden Gardens Trust Ltd v Lenesta Sludge Disposals Ltd*) [1994] 1 AC 85, viz, where A enters into a contract with B for the erection by B of a building on land belonging to C and the building so erected is defective, have either A or C a remedy against B? The general rule is that A can only recover compensation for damage that A has suffered; it is argued that, since neither the building nor the land belonged to A, no compensatable damage has been suffered by A. C as owner of the land and building has suffered damage but, not being a party to the contract, it is said that C has no claim against B. ...

In the *St Martins* case, one company in the group (A) contracted with McAlpine (B) for the erection of a building on land which at the date of contract belonged to A but which, before the date of breach, had been transferred to another company in the group (C). The building was defective. The contract contained no provision enabling C to sue B for the defect in the building. B argued that no damages were recoverable by A: the wrong done had fallen into a black hole where no one had a claim. Your Lordships rejected that submission on what was called in argument 'the narrower ground'.

The narrower ground starts by accepting the basic proposition that A, not owning the land at the date of breach, can show no compensatable loss and therefore no substantial damage suffered by A. However, the majority of the members of the Committee extended the reasoning in <1000> *The Albazero* [1977] AC 774, to cover the case so as to hold that where A enters into a contract with B relating to property and it is envisaged by the parties that ownership of that property may be transferred to a third party, C, so that the consequences of any breach of contract will be suffered by C, A has a cause of action to recover from B the loss suffered by C. However, two points are clearly established by the decision in both *The Albazero* and the *St Martins* case. First, A is accountable to C for any damages recovered by A from B as compensation for C's loss: *The Albazero*, at p 888d. Second, the exceptional principle does not apply (because it is not needed) where C has a direct remedy against B: see the *The Albazero*, at p 848, and the decision itself which, whilst recognising the exception, held that it did not apply to that case since the consignee of the goods had a direct claim; *St Martins* case [1994] 1 AC 85, 115e–f.

Lord Griffiths decided the *St Martins* case on what has been called 'the broader ground'. In the present case it is argued that the broader ground represents the right approach in law and that it applies even in cases where the third party has a cause of action directly against the defaulting promisor. ... <1001> ...

In my judgment the direct cause of action which UIPL has under the DCD is fatal to any claim to substantial damages made by Panatown against McAlpine based on the narrower ground. First, the principle in *The Albazero* as applied to building contracts by the *St Martins* case is based on the fact that it provides a remedy to the third party 'where no other would be available to a person sustaining loss which under a rational legal system ought to be compensated by the person who has caused it': see *The Albazero* at p 847b and the *St Martins* case at p 114g. If the contractual arrangements between the parties in fact provide the third party with a direct remedy against the wrongdoer the whole rationale of the rule disappears. Moreover, as I have said, both the decision in *The Albazero* case itself and dicta in the *St Martins* case, at p 115f, state that where the third party (C) has a direct claim against the builder (B) the promisee under the building contract (A) cannot claim for the third party's damage.

I turn now to the broader ground on which Lord Griffiths decided the *St Martins* case. He held that the building contractor (B) was liable to the promisee

(A) for more than nominal damages even though A did not own the land at the date of breach. He held in effect that by reason of the breach A had himself suffered damage, being the loss of the value to him of the performance of the contract. On this view even though A might not be legally liable to C to provide him with the benefit which the performance of the contract by B would have provided, A has lost his 'performance interest' and will therefore be entitled to substantial damages being, in Lord Griffiths's view, the cost to A of providing C with the benefit. In the *St Martins* case Lord Keith of Kinkel, Lord Bridge of Harwich and I all expressed sympathy with Lord Griffiths's broader view. However, I declined to adopt the broader ground until the possible consequences of so doing had been examined by academic writers. That has now happened and no serious difficulties have been disclosed. However, there is a division of opinion as to whether the contracting party, A, is accountable to the third party, C, for the damages recovered or is bound to expend the damages on providing for C the benefit which B was supposed to provide. Lord Griffiths in the *St Martins* case, at p 97g, took that view. But as I understand them Lord Goff of Chieveley and Lord Millett in the present case (in agreement with Steyn LJ in *Darlington Borough Council v Wiltshier Northern Ltd* [1995] 1 WLR 68, 80h) would hold that, in the absence of the specific circumstances of the <1002> present case A, is not accountable to C for any damages recovered by A from B.

I will assume that the broader ground is sound in law and that in the ordinary case where the third party (C) has no direct cause of action against the building contractor (B) A can recover damages from B on the broader ground. Even on that assumption, in my judgment Panatown has no right to substantial damages in this case because UIPL (the owner of the land) has a direct cause of action under the DCD.

The essential feature of the broader ground is that the contracting party A, although not himself suffering the physical or pecuniary damage sustained by the third party C, has suffered his own damage being the loss of his performance interest, ie the failure to provide C with the benefit that B had contracted for C to receive. In my judgment it follows that the critical factor is to determine what interest A had in the provision of the service for the third party C. If, as in the present case, the whole contractual scheme was designed, *inter alia*, to give UIPL and its successors a legal remedy against McAlpine for failure to perform the building contract with due care, I cannot see that Panatown has suffered any damage to its performance interests: subject to any defence based on limitation of actions, the physical and pecuniary damage suffered by UIPL can be redressed by UIPL exercising its own cause of action against McAlpine. It is not clear to me why this has not occurred in the present case: but, subject to questions of limitation which were not explored, there is no reason even now why UIPL should not be bringing the proceedings against McAlpine. The fact that the DCD may have been primarily directed to ensuring that UIPL's successors in title should enjoy a remedy in tort against McAlpine is nothing to the point: the contractual provisions were directed to ensuring that UIPL and its successors in title did have the legal right to sue McAlpine direct. So long as UIPL enjoys this right Panatown has suffered no failure to satisfy its performance interest.

The theoretical objection to giving the contracting party A substantial damages for breach of the contract by B for failing to provide C with a benefit which C itself can enforce against B is further demonstrated by great practical difficulties which such a view would entail. Let me illustrate this by postulating a case where, before the breach occurred, UIPL had with consent assigned the benefit of the DCD to a purchaser of the site, X. What if Panatown itself was entitled to, and did, sue for and recover damages from McAlpine? Presumably McAlpine could not in addition be liable to X for breach of the DCD: yet Panatown would not be liable to account to X for the damages it had recovered from McAlpine. The result would therefore be another piece of legal nonsense: the party who had suffered real, tangible damage, X, could recover nothing but Panatown which had suffered no real loss could recover damages. Again, suppose that X agrees with McAlpine certain variations of McAlpine's liability under the building contract. What rights would Panatown then have against McAlpine? ... <1003> ...

For these reasons I would allow the appeal.

[In separate speeches, Lords Clyde and Jauncey agreed that the appeal should be allowed; Lords Goff and Millett would have dismissed the appeal. Although their Lordships were divided as to the outcome of the case, they all agreed that third party beneficiary cases give rise to an exception to the general rule that 'A can only recover compensation for damage that A has suffered.' The extract from Lord Browne-Wilkinson's speech was selected because it most clearly raised the issues that Australian courts will need to consider when similar cases arise here and because he gave the leading speech in the *St Martins* case.]

Appeal allowed

b Enforcement by a joint promisee

Coulls v Bagot's Executor & Trustee Co Ltd[20] establishes for Australia that if A makes a promise to B and C jointly, C can take action to enforce the promise against A, although it will be necessary for C to join B as a party to such an action.

c Enforcement by the third party

As we have noted already, one type of contract made for the benefit of a third party is a contract between A and B pursuant to which B promises not to take proceedings against C. Such contracts are quite common in commercial transactions and often arise when an employer, or contractor, seeks to obtain protection for their employees or sub-contractors.

---

20   (1967) 119 CLR 460.

> ### Example
>
> A is a carrier who uses employees, or independent contractors, to carry goods for its customers. Its standard contract of carriage includes an exclusion clause reducing A's liability to its customers (B) should A damage, or not deliver, the goods carried. Such an arrangement allocates the risk of loss, or damage, to B who can take out appropriate insurance if it wishes to; conversely, A does not need to insure that risk and may use the savings made to offer a lower contract price. However, this allocation of risk and associated costs would be circumvented if B were able to sue A's employees or sub-contractors (C) where they were responsible for losing, or damaging, the goods. This is because, were B to succeed, A could expect some form of negative reaction from its employees or sub-contractors. To prevent this happening, A would include a provision in its exclusion clause whereby B exempts C as well as A from liability.

As we have seen, in such a case A may be able to obtain an injunction restraining B from suing C. However, this remedy is limited in scope and for this reason, other, more direct means of enforcement have been sought.

Vicarious immunity

In *Elder, Demster & Co v Paterson Zochinos & Co* the House of Lords decided that an exclusion clause of the kind described in the above example, conferred protection on C directly.[21] This decision gave rise to what became known as the 'doctrine of vicarious immunity' according to which employees, agents or sub-contractors enjoyed the same immunity from liability as their employer. However, this doctrine subsequently encountered difficulty with privity of contract when the High Court in *Wilson v Darling Island Stevedoring & Lighterage Company*[22] and then the House of Lords in *Midland Silicones Ltd v Scruttons Ltd*[23] decided that as C was not privy to the contract between A and B it could not rely on an exclusion clause contained in their contract, even though the clause was expressed in its favour. In Canada, on the other hand, the Supreme Court in *London Drugs Ltd v Kuchne & Napel International Ltd* decided that employees, at least, do enjoy vicarious immunity where the exclusion clause extends to them and they were acting in the course of their employment to confer the services sought by the plaintiff.[24] Vicarious immunity has now also been created by statute in the case of the servants and agents (but not independent contractors) of sea carriers by the *Carriage of Goods by Sea Act 1991*.

---

21 [1924] AC 522.
22 (1956–7) 95 CLR 43.
23 [1962] AC 446.
24 [1992] 3 SCR 299.

Finding a contract between B and C

The commercial inconvenience of C not being able to rely for protection on an exclusion clause contained in a contract between A and B was acknowledged in *Midland Silicones Ltd v Scruttons Ltd*.[25] This led Lord Reid to envisage that if four conditions were fulfilled a contract could be created between B and C that conferred protection upon the latter.[26] At the heart of these conditions is the requirement that A, when contracting with B to confer protection on C (usually A's employees, agents or sub-contractors), must have been acting as C's agent so as to create a contract between B and C. Where this is the case, C is transformed from being a third party to a contract between A and B into a party contracting directly with B through the agency of A. This approach was adopted and explained in *The Eurymedon*, extracted below.

New Zealand Shipping Co Ltd v AM Satterthwaite & Co Ltd

[1975] AC 154, Privy Council

[The shipper of goods engaged a carrier to transport them from Liverpool to Wellington on board *The Eurymedon*. The Bill of Lading setting out the terms of their contract contained exclusion clauses in favour of the carrier and any independent contractors it engaged to carry out the contract. The carrier engaged New Zealand Shipping as a stevedore to unload the goods in Wellington; it did so negligently and the goods were damaged. Satterthwaite, as consignee of the goods, sued New Zealand Shipping in negligence claiming the cost of repairing the goods. As the consignee of the goods, Satterthwaite was bound by the terms of the Bill of Lading. The issue, therefore, was whether New Zealand Shipping could rely upon the terms of the Bill of Lading to which it was not a party. At first instance Beattie held that it could; this decision was reversed by the New Zealand Court of Appeal, whereupon New Zealand Shipping appealed to the Privy Council.]

Lord Wilberforce delivering the advice of the majority of the Board [at 166]: The question in the appeal is whether the stevedore can take the benefit of the time limitation provision. The starting point, in discussion of this question, is provided by the House of Lords decision in *Midland Silicones Ltd v Scruttons Ltd* [1962] AC 446. There is no need to question or even to qualify that case in so far as it affirms the general proposition that a contract between two parties cannot be sued on by a third person even though the contract is expressed to be for his benefit. Nor is it necessary to disagree with anything which was said to the same effect in the Australian case of *Wilson v Darling Island Stevedoring & Lighterage Company* (1956–7) 95 CLR 43. Each of these cases was dealing with a simple case of a contract the benefit of which was sought to be taken by a third person not a party to it, and the emphatic pronouncements in the speeches and

---

25 [1962] AC 446.
26 [1962] AC 446 at 474.

judgments were directed to this situation. But *Midland Silicones* left open the case where one of the parties contracts as agent for the third person: in particular Lord Reid's speech spelt out, in four propositions, the prerequisites for the validity of such an agency contract. There is of course nothing unique to this case in the conception of agency contracts: well known and common instances exist in the field of hire purchase, of bankers' commercial credits and other transactions. Lord Reid said this:

> 'I can see a possibility of success of the agency argument if (first) the bill of lading makes it clear that the stevedore is intended to be protected by the provisions in it which limit liability, (secondly) the bill of lading makes it clear that the carrier, in addition to contracting for these provisions on his own behalf, is also contracting as agent for the stevedore that these provisions should apply to the stevedore, (thirdly) the carrier has authority from the stevedore to do that, or perhaps later ratification by the stevedore would suffice, and (fourthly) that any difficulties about consideration moving from the stevedore were overcome. And then to affect the consignee it would be necessary to show that the provisions of the *Bills of Lading Act, 1855*, apply.' (l.c. p.474)

The question in this appeal is whether the contract satisfies these propositions. Clause 1 of the Bill of Lading, whatever the defects in its drafting, is clear in its relevant terms. The carrier, on his own account, stipulates for certain exemptions and immunities: among these is that conferred by Article III, rule 6 of the *Hague Rules* which discharges the carrier from all liability for loss or damage unless suit is brought within one year after delivery. In addition to these stipulations on his own account, the carrier as agent for, *inter alios*, independent contractors stipulates for the same exemptions. Much was made of the fact that the carrier also contracts as agent for numerous other persons; the relevance of this argument is not apparent. It cannot be disputed that among such independent contractors, for whom, as agent, the carrier contracted, is the appellant company which habitually <167> acts as stevedore in New Zealand by arrangement with the carrier and which is, moreover, the parent company of the carrier. The carrier was, indisputably, authorised by the appellant to contract as its agent for the purposes of Clause 1. All of this is quite straightforward and was accepted by all of the learned judges in New Zealand. The only question was, and is, the fourth question presented by Lord Reid, namely that of consideration.

It was on this point that the Court of Appeal differed from Beattie J, holding that it had not been shown that any consideration for the shipper's promise as to exemption moved from the promisee, ie the appellant company. If the choice, and the antithesis, is between a gratuitous promise, and a promise for consideration, as it must be in the absence of a *tertium quid*, there can be little doubt which, in commercial reality, this is. The whole contract is of a commercial character, involving service on one side, rates of payment on the other, and qualifying stipulations as to both. The relations of all parties to each other are commercial relations entered into for business reasons of ultimate profit. To describe one set of promises, in this context, as gratuitous, or *nudum pactum*, seems paradoxical and is *prima facie* implausible. It is only the precise analysis of this complex of relations into the classical offer and acceptance, with identifiable consideration, that seems to present difficulty, but this same difficulty exists in many situations of daily life eg sales at auction; supermarket purchases; boarding an omnibus; purchasing a train ticket; tenders for the supply of goods; offers of rewards; acceptance by post; warranties of authority by agents; manufacturers' guarantees; gratuitous bailments; bankers' commercial credits. These are all examples which show that English law, having committed itself to a rather technical and schematic doctrine of contract, in application takes a practical approach, often at the cost of forcing the facts to fit uneasily into the marked slots of offer, acceptance and consideration.

In their Lordships' opinion the present contract presents much less difficulty than many of those above referred to. It is one of carriage from Liverpool to Wellington. The carrier assumes an obligation to transport the goods and to discharge at the port of arrival. The goods are to be carried and discharged, so the transaction is inherently contractual. It is contemplated that a part of this contract, *viz* discharge, may be performed by independent contractors—*viz* the appellant. By clause 1 of the Bill of Lading the shipper agrees to exempt from liability the carrier, his servants and independent contractors in respect of the performance of this contract of carriage. Thus, if the carriage, including the discharge, is wholly carried out by the carrier, he is exempt. If part is carried out by him, and part by his servants, he and they are exempt. If part is carried out by him and part by an independent contractor, he and the independent contractor are exempt. The exemption is designed to cover the whole carriage from loading to discharge, by whomsoever it is performed: the performance attracts the exemption or immunity in favour of whoever the performer turns out to be. There is possibly more than one way of analysing this business transaction into the necessary components; that which their Lordships would accept is to say that the Bill of Lading brought into existence a bargain initially unilateral but capable of becoming mutual, <168> between the shippers and the appellants, made through the carrier as agent. This became a full contract when the appellant performed services by discharging the goods. The performance of these services for the benefit of the shipper was the consideration for the agreement by the shipper that the appellant should have the benefit of the exemptions and limitations contained in the Bill of Lading. The conception of a 'unilateral' contract of this kind was recognised in *Great Northern Railway Co v Witham* LR 9 CF 16 and is well established. This way of regarding the matter is very close to if not identical to that accepted by Beattie J in the Supreme Court: he analysed the transaction as one of an offer open to acceptance by action such as was found in *Carlill v Carbolic Smoke Ball Company* [1893] I QB 256. But whether one describes the shipper's promise to exempt as an offer to be accepted by performance or as a promise in exchange for an act seems in the present context to be a matter of semantics. The words of Bowen LJ in *Carlill v*

Carbolic Smoke Ball Co, 'Why should not an offer be made to all the world which is to ripen into a contract with anybody who comes forward and performs the condition?' (ie p 268) seem to bridge both conceptions: he certainly seems to draw no distinction between an offer which matures into a contract when accepted and a promise which matures into a contract after performance, and, though in some special contexts (such as in connection with the right to withdraw) some further refinement may be needed, either analysis may be equally valid.

[Their Lordships went on to hold that New Zealand Shipping provided consideration by unloading the goods, notwithstanding that it was contractually bound to the carrier to perform this task.]

Their Lordships advised that the appeal be allowed

Initially, *The Eurymedon* was not well received in Australia and a majority of the High Court in *Port Jackson Stevedoring Pty Ltd v Salmon and Spraggon (Australia) Pty Ltd*[27] declined to apply it to the almost identical facts of that case. However, on appeal, this decision was reversed by the Privy Council which enjoined courts not to 'search for fine distinctions which would diminish the general applicability, in the light of established commercial practice, of the principle' it established.[28] Since then it has been followed in this country and applied to road transport as well.[29]

4 Contracts obligating third parties

Diagram 2 (p 212) illustrates those situations in which the two contracting parties, A and B, seek to impose an obligation on a third party, C. As a general rule, the privity doctrine prevents A in this situation from enforcing the obligation A and B have prescribed for C, or from enforcing the promise C has made to B. In the former situation C is a third party to the agreement between A and B and, therefore, not bound by it; in the latter situation, A is not privy to the contract between B and C and, therefore, cannot enforce it. However, property law has qualified this position in certain respects. Thus, for example, a restrictive covenant included in a contract for the sale of land may bind the purchaser's successors in title[30] and covenants in a lease may bind the assignees of the lessor or lessee. A similar rule has been applied to ships,[31] but the extent of this qualification is unclear and has not been extended to other goods.[32]

---

27 (1978) 139 CLR 231.
28 [1981] 1 WLR 138 at 144.
29 *Life Savers (Australasia) Ltd v Frigmobile Pty Ltd* (1983) 1 NSWLR 431.
30 See *Tulk v Moxhay* (1848) 41 ER 1143.
31 See *Lord Strathcona SS Co v Dominion Coal Co* [1925] All ER 87.
32 See *Port Line Ltd v Ben Line Steamers Ltd* [1958] 2 QB 146.

5   Exceptions to the privity doctrine

a   Introduction

Whatever its merits,[33] the privity doctrine is inconvenient in many situations. As a result, it has been abolished in the United Kingdom,[34] New Zealand[35] and three Australian jurisdictions[36] and modified in relation to specific types of contracts. Equity and the common law have also provided other devices which have enabled the doctrine to be circumvented.

b   Abolition: Western Australia, Queensland and Northern Territory

The *Property Law Act* in each of these jurisdictions has, in effect, abolished the privity doctrine in relation to all contracts. These Acts are substantially the same, although there are some noteworthy differences between the shorter Western Australian provisions and the more elaborate ones in Queensland and the Northern Territory. When reading the extracts below the following points should be noted:

- the Northern Territory Act is identical in all material respects to that in Queensland
- section 11(2) of Western Australian Act requires only that A and B intend to confer a benefit on C whereas the effect of s 55(1)(6)(c) of the Queensland Act is that A and B must also intend that C be able to sue on the promise[37]
- there is no equivalent in the Queensland Act to s 11(2)(c) of the Western Australian Act which requires each party named in the contract to be joined as a party to any proceedings taken to enforce it
- the Acts allow a defendant to raise in an action brought by C any defence that they would have been able to raise had C been named as a party to the contract
- the Acts allow A and B to agree to discharge or modify the contract at any time before it has been 'adopted', or there has been 'acceptance' of it, by C.

Property Law Act 1969 (WA)

Section 11. Persons taking who are not parties

(1) A person may take an immediate or other interest in land or other property, or the benefit of any condition, right of entry, covenant or agreement over or respecting land or other property, although he is not named as a party to the conveyance or other instrument that relates to the land or property.

---

33   For a defence of the privity doctrine see SA Smith, 'Contracts for the Benefit of Third Parties: In Defence of the Third-Party Rule' (1997) *17 Oxford Journal of Legal Studies* 643 and P Kincaid, 'Privity and Private Justice in Contract' (1997) *12 Journal of Contract Law* 47.
34   *Contracts (Right of Third Parties) Act 1999.*
35   *Contracts (Privity) Act 1982.*
36   *Property Law Act 1969* (WA) s 11; *Property Law Act 1974* (Qld) s 55; *Law of Property Act 2000* (NT) s 56. The Queensland and Western Australian provisions are extracted below.
37   See the comment on this difference in *Trident General Insurance Co Ltd v McNiece Bros Pty Ltd* (1987–1988) 165 CLR 107 at 123.

(2) Except in the case of a conveyance or other instrument to which subsection (1) applies, where a contract expressly in its terms purports to confer a benefit directly on a person who is not named as a party to the contract, the contract is, subject to subsection (3), enforceable by that person in his own name but
  (a) all defences that would have been available to the defendant in an action or proceeding in a court of competent jurisdiction to enforce the contract had the plaintiff in the action or proceeding been named as a party to the contract, shall be so available;
  (b) each person named as a party to the contract shall be joined as a party to the action or proceeding; and
  (c) such defendant in the action or proceeding shall be entitled to enforce as against such plaintiff, all the obligations that in the terms of the contract are imposed on the plaintiff for the benefit of the defendant.
(3) Unless the contract referred to in subsection (2) otherwise provides, the contract may be cancelled or modified by the mutual consent of the persons named as parties thereto at any time before the person referred to in that subsection has adopted it either expressly or by conduct.

Property Law Act 1974 (Qld)

Section 55. Contracts for the benefit of third parties

(1) A promisor who, for a valuable consideration moving from the promisee, promises to do or to refrain from doing an act or acts for the benefit of a beneficiary shall, upon acceptance by the beneficiary, be subject to a duty enforceable by the beneficiary to perform that promise.
(2) Prior to acceptance the promisor and promisee may, without the consent of the beneficiary, vary or discharge the terms of the promise and any duty arising from it.
(3) Upon acceptance—
  (a) the beneficiary shall be entitled in the beneficiary's own name to such remedies and relief as may be just and convenient for the enforcement of the duty of the promisor, and relief by way of specific performance, injunction or otherwise shall not be refused solely on the ground that, as against the promisor, the beneficiary may be a volunteer; and
  (b) the beneficiary shall be bound by the promise and subject to a duty enforceable against the beneficiary in the beneficiary's own name to do or refrain from doing such act or acts (if any) as may by the terms of the promise be required of the beneficiary; and
  (c) the promisor shall be entitled to such remedies and relief as may be just and convenient for the enforcement of the duty of the beneficiary; and
  (d) the terms of the promise and the duty of the promisor or the beneficiary may be varied or discharged with the consent of the promisor and the beneficiary.

(4) Subject to subsection (1), any matter which would in proceedings not brought in reliance on this section render a promise void, voidable or unenforceable, whether wholly or in part, or which in proceedings (not brought in reliance on this section) to enforce a promissory duty arising from a promise is available by way of defence shall, in like manner and to the like extent, render void, voidable or unenforceable or be available by way of defence in proceedings for the enforcement of a duty to which this section gives effect.

(5) In so far as a duty to which this section gives effect may be capable of creating and creates an interest in land, such interest shall, subject to section 12, be capable of being created and of subsisting in land under any Act but subject to that Act.

(6) In this section—
— *acceptance* means an assent by words or conduct communicated by or on behalf of the beneficiary to the promisor, or to some person authorised on the promisor's behalf, in the manner (if any), and within the time, specified in the promise or, if no time is specified, within a reasonable time of the promise coming to the notice of the beneficiary.
— *beneficiary* means a person other than the promisor or promisee, and includes a person who, at the time of acceptance is identified and in existence, although that person may not have been identified or in existence at the time when the promise was given.
— *promise* means a promise—
   (a) which is or appears to be intended to be legally binding; and
   (b) which creates or appears to be intended to create a duty enforceable by a beneficiary; and includes a promise whether made by deed, or in writing, or, subject to this Act, orally, or partly in writing and partly orally.
— *promisee* means a person to whom a promise is made or given.
— *promisor* means a person by whom a promise is made or given.

(7) Nothing in this section affects any right or remedy which exists or is available apart from this section.

(8) This section applies only to promises made after the commencement of this Act.

c Specific exceptions

Insurance contracts

Section 48 of the *Insurance Contracts Act 1984* (Cth) enables a person who, in a contract of general insurance, is specified as someone to whom the insurance cover extends, to recover their loss from the insurer even though they were not a party to a contract. A similar outcome is created in respect of marine insurance by s 20(2) of the *Marine Insurance Act 1909* (Cth) which enables a person having an interest in the subject matter of a marine insurance contract to insure the interests of other persons as well as their own.

Conferral of rights on third parties

A variety of statutes confer on third parties a right of action against a person with whom they have no contract, but who has indirectly supplied them with goods or services. Strictly, these provisions do not create an exception to the privity doctrine: the right being enforced is a statutory one, not one created by a contract to which they are not a party. In most cases, however, the outcome is substantially the same. A prime example is Division 2 of Part 5-4 of the *ACL* which gives 'an affected person' a direct cause of action against the manufacturer of goods that do not comply with the guarantee as to quality created by s 54, even though those goods were acquired from a retailer who in turn acquired them from the manufacturer. Other examples are provided by the *Bills of Exchange Act 1909* (Cth) and the *Cheques Act 1986* (Cth) and by the state and territory Sea-Carriage Documents Acts.[38]

d   Common law and equitable circumventions

The common law and equity have adapted a number of established devices to enable the privity doctrine to be circumvented. As Brennan J observed in *Trident General Insurance*,[39] although these devices are sometimes referred to as exceptions to the doctrine, they are really applications of other legal principles to the relationship created by the contracting parties.

Agency

In Diagram 1 (on p 212), if A, when contracting with B, did so as an agent for C, then a contract will be created between B and C which C can enforce. The same situation would arise in Diagram 2 (also on p 212) if B, when contracting with C, was doing so as an agent for A; in such a case a contract would be created between A and C which A could enforce.

Trust

If a contracting party (A in Diagram 1 and B in Diagram 2—see p 212) enters into a contract as a trustee for a third party (C in Diagram 1 and A in Diagram 2) then the third party can enforce the contract in equity, provided the trustee is joined as a party to the action.

---

38   *Sea-Carriage Documents Act 1997* (ACT); *Sea-Carriage Documents Act 1997* (NSW) ss 8 and 10; *Sea-Carriage Documents Act 1998* (NT) ss 8 and 10; *Sea-Carriage Documents Act 1996* (Qld) ss 6 and 8; *Sea-Carriage Documents Act 1998* (SA) ss 7 and 9; *Sea-Carriage Documents Act 1997* (Tas) ss 7 and 9; *Sea-Carriage Documents Act 1998* (Vic) ss 8 and 10; *Sea-Carriage Documents Act 1997* (WA) ss 8 and 10.

39   (1987–1988) 165 CLR 107 at 135.

INTERNATIONAL PERSPECTIVES

India

Although the *Indian Contract Act, 1872* does not require privity of consideration (s 2(d) allows the promisor to stipulate that consideration is to be provided by a third party) and although the doctrine of privity of contract is not referred to in the Act, it has been incorporated into Indian law by decisions of the Privy Council[40] and Supreme Court.[41] However, the following exceptions are recognised:

- *Trust*: as is the case in Australian law, if a contracting party enters into a contract as trustee for a third party, the latter, as the beneficiary of the trust, can enforce the agreement. This exception has been especially important in India in connection with contracts made between parents for the benefit of their children who are about to marry. For example, in *Khwaja Muhammad Khan v Hussaini Begum*[42] the Privy Council held that a woman could enforce a contract made between her father and the father of her husband to be, according to which the latter promised to pay her an allowance after marriage. Importantly, the promisor had charged certain property with the payment of this allowance and this showed that the parties intended to create a trust in her favour.[43] However, the identification of property in this manner is not essential. Thus, for example, where an airline entered into a contract with a hotel to accommodate its employees, an employee injured as a result of the hotel's negligence was able to sue it for breach of contract, as well as in tort.[44]
- *Family arrangements*: where, under a family arrangement, a contract is made for the benefit of a third party, the third party can enforce the contract. Examples include those between a husband and his wife's father providing for her maintenance[45] and between children for the maintenance of their parents.[46]
- *Estoppel*: If a contract made for the benefit of a third party is partially performed by the promisor, the promisor will incur liability to the third party. The express or implied acknowledgement of liability to the third party constituted by part-performance creates a relationship between them which the courts will enforce.[47]

---

40   *Jamna Das v Ram Autar* (1911) 30 1A 7.
41   *MC Chacko v State Bank of Travancore* (1969) 2 SCC 343; *PR Subramania Iyer v Lakshmi Ammal* (1973) 2 SCC 54.
42   (1910) 37 IA 152.
43   It is this aspect of the case that distinguishes it from *Tweddle v Atkinson* [1861–73] All ER Rep 369 in which, on very similar facts, the third party was not able to enforce the father's promise. Had the father in that case charged specific property with the payment of the allowance, the outcome of the case may have been different.
44   *Klans Mittelbachert v East India Hotels Ltd* AIR 1997 Delhi 201.
45   See *Daropti v Jaspat Rai* (1905) PR 171.
46   See *Veeramma v Appayya* AIR 1957 AP 965.
47   See *Devaraja Urs v Ram Krishnaiah* AIR 1952 Mys 109; *Kshirodebehari Datta v Mangobinda Panda* AIR 1934 Cal 682.

China

Although it does not deal with privity specifically, the implication to be drawn from Articles 64 and 65 of the *Contract Law* is that it adopts a position very similar to the common law. This is because those articles, which deal with performance for the benefit of a third person and performance by a third person, only allow a contract to be enforced by, or against, a party to the contract. Article 64, for example, rather than making the obligor liable to the third person, makes them liable to the obligee only.

Contract Law of the People's Republic of China, 1999

Article 64. Performance towards a Third Person

Where the parties prescribed that the obligator render performance to a third person, if the obligator fails to render its performance to the third person, or rendered non-conforming performance, it shall be liable to the obligee for breach of contract.

Article 65. Performance by a Third Person

Where the parties prescribed that a third person render performance to the obligee, if the third person fails to perform, or rendered non-conforming performance, the obligator shall be liable to the obligee for breach of contract.

6 Summary

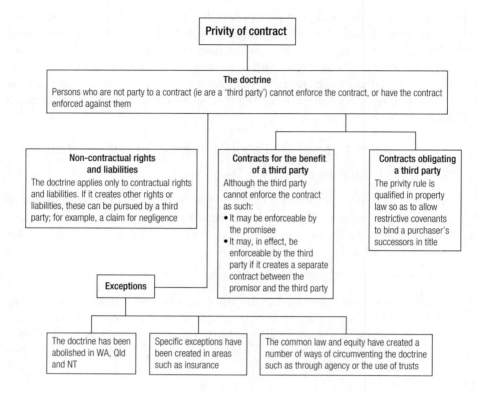

7 Questions

1. For a number of years, Karl worked for a consulting company, Ajax Ltd, and was due to retire. However, Veronica, a client of Ajax's, wished Karl to remain with the company for three more years so that he could carry out an important project for her. As a result, Ajax and Karl entered into a contract the terms of which were that, as an employee of Ajax, Karl would continue to work on Veronica's project for three years in return for Ajax making an annual payment of $100,000 into Karl's superannuation fund. However, after only 12 months, Karl become disenchanted with his work and resigned.

    Please advise Karl, Ajax and Veronica of their rights and obligations under this contract arising from Karl's resignation.

2. Quick Carriers Ltd entered into a contract with Magnetic Ltd to transport mining equipment from Sydney to Exmouth in Western Australia. This contract contained an exclusion clause protecting Quick and its employees and sub-contractors from liability in the event of the machinery being damaged during transit.

    To transport the machinery on the Western Australian leg of the journey, Quick engaged Dalkeith Ltd, a local trucking company. Unfortunately, while driving a truck containing the machinery on the North West Coastal Highway, Dalkeith's driver, Ben Belmont, fell asleep. A crash resulted and the machinery was very badly damaged. Magnetic has commenced proceedings seeking damages from both Dalkeith and Belmont.

Please advise Dalkeith and Belmont whether or not they can rely on the exclusion clause in Magnetic's contract with Quick. Should you need additional information to provide your advice, please indicated what this is and why it is needed.

CHAPTER 9

The Terms of a Contract

1	Introduction		240
2	Express terms		241
	a	Pre-contractual statements	241
	b	The test	243
	c	Collateral contracts	246
	d	Tripartite collateral contracts	249
	e	Signed documents	250
	f	Terms displayed or delivered	255
	g	Course of dealing	259
3	Implied terms		261
	a	Common law	261
	b	Statute	271
4	Summary		274
5	Questions		275

1 Introduction

This chapter deals with the determination of the terms of a contract; that is, deciding precisely what are the contractual rights and obligations the parties have agreed to, or (in exceptional cases) are imposed on them by statute because of the nature of the contract they have entered into. In our treatment of this issue we distinguish between express and implied terms. Express terms are those that, in one way or another, are actually articulated by the parties during the formation process. Implied terms, on the other hand, are those that are not referred to by the parties but nevertheless form part of the contract through the operation of law. Often, a party's contractual rights and obligations will be determined by a mix of both. However, since 1 January 2011, this will be less common in practice now that the *Australian Consumer Law* (*ACL*) has, in the case of consumer contracts, replaced non-excludable statutory implied terms with statutory guarantees. Nevertheless, such a mix will still exist in the case of consumer contracts made before that date and, for example, in the case of commercial contracts for the sale of goods where the parties have not excluded the terms implied by state and territory *Sale of Goods* legislation.[1]

---

1   See p. 271, below.

It is also important to note that the terms of their contract are not the only determinants of the rights and obligations of the parties arising out of their contractual relationship. In particular, their pre-contractual negotiations and their post-contractual conduct may give rise to *non-contractual* rights and obligations that operate in addition to, and independently of, those created by the terms of the contract. For example, a pre-contractual statement that is false or misleading may (and if uttered by a business or in a commercial context almost certainly will) give rise to liability for contravention of s 18 of the *ACL*. Thus, important though they are, it should not be thought that the rights and obligations of the parties to a contract are solely determined by its terms.

As a result of the foregoing, when seeking to determine the rights and obligations of the parties to a contract it is necessary to consider at least the following issues:

- What are the express terms of the contract?
- Are any terms implied into the contract?
- What do these terms mean and how relatively important are they?
- Are there any exclusion clauses that curtail what would otherwise be a party's obligations?
- Has the conduct of the parties given rise to non-contractual rights and obligations?

2 Express terms

As noted above, express terms are those terms that the parties articulate in some way as they negotiate their contract. This may be done orally (when the parties verbally spell out the terms they want), or by one party proffering to the other a printed document containing contractual terms, or making reference to a sign, or a ticket or a similar statement that contains such terms. A contract can consist entirely of written express terms, or entirely of oral express terms, or a combination of both.

The first issue to arise when considering the express terms of a contract is to determine what those terms are. This is contentious where the parties do not clearly indicate what items from their pre-contractual discussions, or what documents or other printed material, form part of the contract they made.

a Pre-contractual statements

During pre-contractual negotiations, statements relating to the subject matter of the proposed contract will often be made that influence the decision making of one of the parties. Such statements may be made by the other party, or by a third party.

> **Example**
>
> S advertised her car for private sale. During discussions with B, a prospective purchaser, she told B that the car had a new automatic transmission, had travelled only 50,000 km and was regarded as the best model ever manufactured. While B accepted these statements, he arranged for the car to be examined by a mechanic (M) who informed him that the car was in excellent working order. Relying upon these statements, B purchased the car. Unfortunately, he discovered that (i) the car had recently had a reconditioned automatic transmission installed; (ii) the car's odometer had malfunctioned and although it read 50,000 km, the car had actually travelled 80,000 km; (iii) it was universally accepted that many models of the car were superior to this model; and (iv) the car had defective brakes and suspension.

In such a case, the categorisation of each individual statement is important as this will determine the remedies available to the party (B in the example) to whom they were made. Statements may be categorised as:

- sales puff
- terms of the contract of sale
- collateral contracts or
- representation.

Sales puff

A 'sales puff' is a hyperbolical statement that the speaker does not intend to be taken literally and that a reasonable person would recognise as merely exaggerated sales talk. As a result, no remedy is available should the statement prove to be false. In the above example, S's statement that the car was the 'best model ever manufactured' is likely to be categorised in this way.

Term of the contract

A term is the contractual expression of a promise that has been made by one party to the other. In other words, it articulates the former's contractual obligations to the latter. As a result, if a statement is categorised as a term of the contract, should it prove to be false, the party that made it will be guilty of breach of contract and the other party will have a remedy on that ground. The statements made by S about the car's automatic transmission and the distance it had travelled could well be categorised as a term of the contract just as similar statements were in the case of *Dick Bentley Productions Ltd v Harold Smith Motors*.[2] On the other hand, the statements by M could not form part of the contract between S and B as M was not privy to that contract.

---

2   [1965] 1 WLR 623. But compare it with *Oscar Chess Ltd v Williams* [1957] 1 WLR 370.

Collateral contract

A collateral contract is a secondary contract that exists collaterally to the main contract between the parties. Typically it will consist of only one term. If a statement is categorised as a collateral contract, should it prove to be false, the party that made it will be guilty of breaching that contract and the other party will have access to the usual remedies available for breach of contract. However, they will not be guilty of breaching the main contract as the statement did not form part thereof. In the above example, if the statements made by S about the car's automatic transmission and the distance it had travelled were found not to be terms of her contract of sale with B, they could still constitute a collateral contract between them. It is also possible that the statement made by M, if found to be promissory, could constitute a tripartite collateral contract[3] between M and B. In such a case, M would be liable to B for breach of contract.

Representation

A representation is a statement made by one person to another (the representee) that was not intended or understood by the parties to be a promise. As it is not promissory, it will not form part of any contract made between them. If a statement is categorised as a representation, the position can be summarised as follows:

- At common law, the only remedy available to the representee is to rescind the contract on the ground of misrepresentation; damages cannot be recovered except in the unlikely event that representor was also guilty of the tort of negligence. Furthermore, the remedy of rescission will be lost if restitution is not possible.[4]
- On the other hand, if the statement comes within the scope of s 18 of the *ACL*, the representee will have remedies under the *ACL* which include being able to recover damages.[5]

Thus, in the above example, if the statements made by S and M were found not to be terms of the contract of sale and not to constitute a collateral contract, the remedies available to B would depend very significantly upon whether the transaction came within the scope of the *ACL*, or was governed only by the common law.

b The test

Because at common law the remedies available for breach of contract are usually far superior to those available for a mere misrepresentation, whether a particular pre-contractual statement is one or the other is most important. The test used by the courts to resolve this issue is discussed in the following case.

---

3   This form of contract is discussed on p 249, below.
4   See p 357, below.
5   See p 343, below.

Ellul and Ellul v Oakes

(1972) 3 SASR 377, Supreme Court of South Australia

[The Elluls purchased a house from Oakes relying on a statement made in a real estate agent's listing form to the effect that the property was sewered. This form was signed by Oakes. In fact, the property was not sewered and the Elluls claimed damages for breach of contract. At first instance their claim failed on the ground that the statement in the form did not form part of the contract of sale. They appealed to the Full Court.]

Zelling J [at 387]: The position, as is set out by the decisions of the Court of Appeal in *Oscar Chess Ltd* v *Williams* and *Dick Bentley Products Ltd* v *Harold Smith (Motors) Ltd* is this, namely, that as Lord *Denning* said at page 627:

> 'If a representation is made in the course of dealings from a contract for the very purpose of inducing the other party to act upon it, and actually inducing him to act upon it, by entering into the contract, that is *prima facie* ground for inferring that it was intended as a warranty. It is not necessary to speak of it as being collateral. Suffice it that it was intended to be acted upon and was in fact acted upon.'

That in my opinion is the position here. The respondent made the representation through the Multiple Listing Bureau to induce a purchaser, and in this case the appellants, to buy his property and succeeded thereby in doing so, and this provided a *prima facie* case which the respondent had to meet. The only real answer could be if the inspection which took place afterwards displaced the effect of that warranty. The various questions which have to be considered are well set out in *Anson's Law of Contract*, 23rd ed (1969), pp 117–118 as follows:

> 'In endeavouring to reach a conclusion on this point, the Courts can be said to take into account a number of factors. First, they may have regard to the time which elapsed between the time of making the statement and the final manifestation of agreement; if the interval is a long one, this points to a representation. Secondly, they may consider the importance of the statement in the minds of the parties; a statement which is important is likely to be classed as a term of the contract. Thirdly, if the statement was followed by the execution of a formal contract in writing, it will probably be regarded as a representation should it not be incorporated in the written document. Finally, where the maker of the statement is, *vis-à-vis* the other party, in a better position to ascertain the accuracy of the statement, the Courts will tend to regard it as a contractual term.
>
> But all of these factors are at best only secondary guides, and they are subsidiary to the main test of *contractual intention*, that is, whether there is evidence of an intention by one or both parties that there should be contractual liability in respect of the accuracy of the statement. The question therefore is: On the totality of evidence, must the person making the statement be taken to have *warranted* its accuracy, ie promised to make it good? This overriding principle was laid down in *Heilbut, Symons & Co* v *Buckleto*'<388> ...

... The question here, therefore, should have been: whether on the totality of the evidence should the respondent, the person making the statement, be taken to have warranted its accuracy, in other words did he promise to make it good. In my opinion he did and it is not a question of what he intended or of any consensus of minds but of what effect that statement would have on the mind of a reasonable person so as to make him think that such a representation was contractual in its nature, in other words that this would form part of the basis of the contract hereafter to be entered into. In *Erskine v Adeane* Mellish LJ said:

> 'No doubt, as a rule of law, if parties enter into negotiations affecting the terms of a bargain, and afterwards reduce it into writing, verbal evidence will not be admitted to introduce additional terms into the agreement; but, nevertheless, what is called a collateral agreement, where the parties have entered into an agreement for a lease or for any other deed under seal, may be made in consideration of one of the parties executing that deed, unless, of course, the stipulation contradicts the terms of the deed itself.'

In following the *Oscar Chess* and *Dick Bentley* Cases I do not want to be taken as assenting to the remainder of the observations of the Master of the Rolls in the *Dick Bentley* Case that the maker of the representation can rebut the *prima facie* inference by showing that the misrepresentation was innocent, that he was innocent of fault in making it and it would not be reasonable in the circumstances for him to be bound by it. I find myself in <389> respectful agreement with the comment on this case contained in (1965) *Cambridge Law Journal*, at page 181, as follows:

> 'It is not the function of the law of contract to absolve a defendant if he has behaved as a reasonable man would have done, but to hold him to his promises and make him answerable in damages if he has not. The issue whether an assertion is to be construed as a legally binding promise cannot depend upon whether the man who made it was well-meaning or irresponsible, saint or sinner.'

[In separate judgments Bray CJ and Wells J agreed.]

Appeal allowed

[footnotes omitted]

Before leaving this issue, please note that it is much less important now than it was before the passage of the *Trade Practices Act* (TPA) in 1974, the most relevant provision of which (s 52) now appears in the *ACL* as s 18. This is because where that Act[6] or the *ACL* apply, damages for a mere representation can be obtained on the grounds of misleading or deceptive conduct by invoking s 52, or s 18, respectively. Consequently, the recovery of damages is not restricted as it once was

---

6   Section 52 of the *TPA* continues to apply to conduct that occurred before 1 January 2011 and for the purpose of proceedings, based on it having been contravened, that were commenced before that date: see *Trade Practices Amendment (Australian Consumer Law) Act (No.2) 201*, Schedule 7 items 6(1) and 7(1). As a result, because the limitation period for seeking damages under the *TPA* is six years (see *TPA* s 82(2)) that Act will continue to be relevant to claims arising out of contractual transactions for quite some time.

(and still is where the Act or the *ACL* do not apply) to cases in which the pre-contractual statement became a term of the contract or the statement was tortious.

c Collateral contracts

A pre-contractual statement not forming part of the main contract between the parties may still have contractual effect if it constitutes a collateral contract. In such a case there will be two contracts between the parties—the main contract containing the principal terms relating to the bargain the parties have made and the collateral contract containing the statement. The most common situation in which a collateral contract is found to exist is where the parties have recorded their agreement in writing but have omitted a promissory statement made by one party to the other which induced the latter to enter into the contract. In such a case, to avoid the strictures of the parol evidence rule,[7] which prevents the statement being added to the document, the courts have been willing to regard it as a collateral contract so that it can still have contractual effect, rather than being relegated to the status of a mere representation. However, to be capable of being so characterised the statement must:

- be promissory in nature
- not contradict the main contract and
- be made in exchange for consideration.

The statement must be promissory. The parties must have intended it to be a promise, rather than a mere representation. This is usually the central issue where one party claims that a pre-contractual statement amounted to a collateral contract. The following extracts illustrate the approach taken by the courts to this issue.

Shepperd v The Council of the Municipality of Ryde
(1952) 85 CLR 1, High Court of Australia

[During pre-contractual discussions concerning the purchase of a house from the defendant, the plaintiff was told, by reference to a council plan and promotional brochure, that land opposite the house would become a park. The importance to the plaintiff of this being the case was made clear to the defendant. However, a year after the contract was completed, the defendant decided to subdivide the land. The plaintiff sought an injunction to restrain the defendant from doing this and from using the land other than as a park as shown in its housing scheme. His claim having failed at first instance the plaintiff appealed to the High Court.]

Dixon, McTiernan, Fullagar and Kitto JJ [at 12]: It is convenient to state first why we think that he has made out a *prima facie* case of a collateral promise or warranty that the areas in question shall be used as a park or parks and not otherwise. The question is very much one of fact. But it appears to us that in formulating Housing

---

7 The parol evidence rule is discussed on p 277, below.

Project No 4 as part of the Ryde Housing Scheme the Council was putting forward something conceived as an entirety. ... The plan records in diagrammatic form the features of the project of which the subdivision into lots is only a part. When a prospective purchaser was invited to buy a lot with a home erected upon it, it was upon the footing of the project, the existence and effectiveness of which was, as it appears <13> to us, an assumption from which the transaction was intended to proceed. ... The reluctance of courts to hold that collateral warranties or promises are given or made in consideration of the making of a contract is traditional. But a chief reason for this is that too often the collateral warranty put forward is one that you would expect to find its place naturally in the principal contract. In a case like the present it is, we think, otherwise. Doubtless the main contract might have included a clause by which the Council undertook not to depart from the housing scheme. But it seems to be not unnatural that the parties should treat the contract as devoted to the purchase of the lot which the individual purchaser acquired, the existence and stability of the project of which the transaction was an outcome being presupposed as something antecedent upon which the purchaser might implicitly rely. It is the common intention that he would so rely upon it and on that basis proceed to contract to buy the particular lot allocated to him. It is because of this that the assurance which is embodied in the plan, when it is read in the light of the pamphlet, obtains its effect as a collateral promise.

[Webb J agreed that the appeal should be allowed.]

Appeal allowed

JJ Savage & Sons Pty Ltd v Blakney

(1970) 118 CLR 435, High Court of Australia

[Blakney engaged Savage to build him a motor boat. During their negotiations Savage said that the boat, when fitted with a particular engine, would have an estimated speed of 15 miles per hour. However, no reference was made to this matter in the written contract subsequently executed by the parties. When built, the boat was not capable of travelling more than 12 miles per hour and Blakney sued the defendant for breach of contract. The trial judge held that the statement about the boat's speed did not form part of the main contract, nor did it constitute a collateral contract. On appeal by Blakney, the Full Court of the Supreme Court of Victoria held that the representation did amount to a collateral contract. Savage then appealed to the High Court.]

Barwick CJ, Kitto, Menzies, Owen and Walsh JJ [at 441]: The trial judge was of opinion that the statement in the appellant's letter was an estimate only, expressed as an expectancy, and not an unequivocal promise of a future speed. The Full Court, after referring to a dictionary meaning of the word 'estimate', thought the expression 'estimated speed 15 mph' in the appellant's <442> letter should be construed as 'approximate speed 15 mph'. In our opinion, this was an unwarranted substitution which stripped the words of the letter of their most significant meaning. The actual words used by the appellant in the letter should be considered. So far from being a promissory expression, 'estimated speed 15 mph' indicates, in our opinion, an expression of opinion as the result 'of approximate calculation based on probability' to use the dictionary equivalent of 'estimate' referred to by the Full Court. ... The words in themselves tend, in our opinion, against the inference of a promise that the boat would in fact achieve the nominated speed.

The Full Court seems to have thought it sufficient in order to establish a collateral warranty that without the statement as to the estimated speed the contract of purchase would never have been made. But that circumstance is, in our opinion, in itself insufficient to support the conclusion that a warranty was given. So much can be said of an innocent representation inducing a contract. The question is whether there was a promise by the appellant that the boat would in fact attain the stated speed if powered by the stipulated engine, the entry into the contract to purchase the boat providing the consideration to make the promise effective. The expression in *De Lassalle v Guildford* that without the statement the contract in that case would not have been made does not, in our opinion, provide an alternative and independent ground on which a collateral warranty can be established. Such a fact is but a step in some circumstances towards the only conclusion which will support a collateral warranty, namely, that the statement so relied on was promissory and not merely representational.

When the letter which we have quoted was written, the negotiations for the construction and delivery of the boat were incomplete. On receipt of the letter there were three courses open to the respondent. He could have required the attainment of the speed to be inserted in the specification as a condition of the contract; or he could have sought from the appellant a promise—however expressed, whether as an assurance, guarantee, promise or otherwise—that the boat would attain the speed as a prerequisite to his ordering the boat; or he could be content to form his own judgment as to the suitable power unit for the boat relying upon the opinion of the appellant of whose reputation and experience in the <443> relevant field he had, as the trial judge found, a high regard. Only the second course would give rise to a collateral warranty.

In our opinion, there is nothing in the evidence before the trial judge to support the view that the respondent took either the first or second of these courses: the only conclusion open upon that evidence was that the respondent took the third course; ... That the statement actually made by the appellant was intended to have some commercial significance upon a matter of importance to the respondent can be conceded; that the respondent was intended to act upon it, and that he did act upon it, is clearly made out. But those facts do not warrant the conclusion that the statement was itself promissory.

In our opinion, so far from it being shown that the trial judge was wrong in refusing to draw the conclusion that the appellant made a promissory statement as to the attainable speed of the cruiser (which he did by deciding that there was no condition of the contract in the stated terms) we are satisfied that he took the only course permitted by the material before him.

Appeal allowed

[footnotes omitted]

The statement must not contradict the main contract. While the statement can add to the totality of the parties' contractual relationship, it must not, for example, say that a term of the main contract is to be ignored. This was established in Australia by the decision of the High Court in *Hoyt's Pty Ltd v Spencer*,[8] which argued that as the consideration for the promise contained in the collateral contract was the promisee agreeing to enter into the main contract, the two must be consistent.[9] Although this requirement has been criticised[10] and is not the law in England,[11] it has been affirmed by the High Court.[12]

Consideration. Like all promises not under seal, the promise contained in the collateral statement must be given in exchange for consideration if it is to have contractual effect. As just noted, according the High Court in *Hoyt's Pty Ltd v Spencer*[13] in such cases the consideration is usually the person to whom the statement is made (the promisee) agreeing to enter into the contract.

d Tripartite collateral contracts

Most collateral contracts are made between the parties to the main contract; in other words, the parties to both contracts are the same. However, the law also recognises that a collateral contract may be made between one of the parties to the main contract and a third party. Such contracts are sometimes referred to as 'tripartite collateral contracts' and have typically been found to exist when a third party has made a statement about a product that has induced the representee to enter into a contract to acquire it from a supplier.[14] In such a case, the main contract is made between the supplier and the representee and a tripartite collateral contract is made between the representee and the third party. Before they were made enforceable by statute[15] this was the means by which a consumer could enforce the guarantees given by a manufacturer about its products which induced the consumer to purchase the product from a retailer. Similarly, in our earlier example (see p 242 above) it could provide a means by which B could recover damages from M based on M's misleading advice about the car's condition. However, in situations such as this, the importance of tripartite collateral contracts

---

8   (1919) 27 CLR 133.
9   See (1919) 27 CLR 133 at 139–140 and 147–148.
10 N Seddon, 'A Plea for the Reform of the Rule in *Hoyt's Pty Ltd v Spencer*' (1978) 52 *ALJ* 372.
11 See *City & Westminster Properties v Mudd* [1959] 1 Ch 129 and *Brikon Investments v Car* [1979] 2 All ER 753.
12 *Gates v City Mutual Life Assurance Society Ltd* (1986) 160 CLR 1 at 11.
13 (1919) 27 CLR 133.
14 See *Shanklin Pier Ltd v Detel Products Ltd* [1951] 2 KB 854; *Wells (Merstham) Ltd v Buckland Sand & Silica Ltd* [1965] 2 QB 170. In the first of these cases, it appears to have been important that the maker of the statement was the ultimate supplier of the product (for example, a manufacturer who supplies to a retailer who then supplies to the representee). However, in the latter case, it was suggested that this connection was not necessary. The latter view is given statutory effect for certain transactions by s 102(2) of the *Goods Act 1958* (Vic).
15 See *ACL* s 59 which substantially replaces s 74G of the *TPA*.

has been greatly reduced by the ability of B to take action against M on the ground of misleading or deceptive conduct, relying on s 18 of the *ACL*.[16]

e Signed documents

The most effective way for the parties to ensure that a particular provision becomes a term of their contract is to record it in a contractual document that they then sign. Such a document may, at one extreme, be the product of protracted negotiations and the exchange between the parties of multiple drafts. At the other extreme, it may take the form of one party proffering to the other for signature its standard terms on a 'take it or leave it' basis. However, in all cases, the position at common law is that, as a general rule, the signatory of a contractual document is bound by its terms whether or not they have read or understood the document in question. The reasons for this rule, sometimes referred to as the rule in *L'Estrange v Graucob*,[17] after the case to which it is ascribed, and some of the exceptions to it, are discussed in the following extract.

Toll (FGCT) Pty Ltd v Alphapharm Pty Ltd

(2004) 219 CLR 165, High Court of Australia

[Toll, (referred to in the judgment by its previous name, 'Finemores') entered into a signed contract with Richard Thomson Pty Ltd ('Richard Thomson'), acting on behalf of Alphapharm, to store and transport goods being imported into Australia for Alphapharm. It was alleged that Finemores performed this contract negligently, causing Alphapharm substantial loss. In its defence, Finemores relied upon an exclusion clause in the contract it entered into with Richard Thomson. At first instance and on appeal to the New South Wales Court of Appeal, this defence failed on two grounds; first that the exclusion clause did not form part of the contract and second, that when it entered into the contract, Richard Thomson was not acting for Alphapharm so that the latter was not bound by the contract (and hence the exclusion clause) in any case. Finemores appealed to the High Court against both of these conclusions.]

Gleeson CJ, Gummow, Hayne, Callinan and Heydon JJ [at 176]: [29] Each of the four parties to the case is a substantial commercial organisation, capable of looking after its own interests. This hardly seems an auspicious setting for an argument that a party who signs a contractual document is not bound by its terms because its representative did not read the document. ... <177–178> ...

[37] It is not in dispute that Finemores stored and transported the goods pursuant to a contract made between Finemores and Richard Thomson. The role of Alphapharm in that contract is a matter of dispute, and is the subject of the

---

16 See chapter 12.
17 [1934] 2 KB 294.

agency issue. It may be put to one side for the moment. The issue presently under consideration concerns the identification of the terms on which Finemores and Richard Thomson contracted. ... <179–180> ...

[42] Consistent with this objective approach to the determination of the rights and liabilities of contracting parties is the significance which the law attaches to the signature (or execution) of a contractual document. In *Parker v South Eastern Railway Co*, Mellish LJ drew a significant distinction as follows:

> 'In an ordinary case, where an action is brought on a written agreement which is signed by the defendant, the agreement is proved by proving his signature, and, in the absence of fraud, it is wholly immaterial that he has not read the agreement and does not know its contents. The parties may, however, reduce their agreement into writing, so that the writing constitutes the sole evidence of the agreement, without signing it; but in that case there must be evidence independently of the agreement itself to prove that the defendant has assented to it.'

[43] More recently, in words that are apposite to the present case, in *Wilton v Farnworth* Latham CJ said:

> 'In the absence of fraud or some other of the special circumstances of the character mentioned, a man cannot escape the consequences of signing a document by saying, and proving, that he did not understand it. Unless he was prepared to take the chance of being bound by the terms of the document, whatever they might be, it was for him to protect himself by abstaining from signing the document until he understood it and was satisfied with it. Any weakening of these principles would make chaos of every-day business transactions.'

[45] It should not be overlooked that to sign a document known and intended to affect legal relations is an act which itself ordinarily conveys a representation to a reasonable reader of the document. The <181> representation is that the person who signs either has read and approved the contents of the document or is willing to take the chance of being bound by those contents, as Latham CJ put it, whatever they might be. That representation is even stronger where the signature appears below a perfectly legible written request to read the document before signing it.

[46] The statements in the above authorities accord with the well-known principle stated by Scrutton LJ in *L'Estrange v F Graucob Ltd* that '[w]hen a document containing contractual terms is signed, then, in the absence of fraud, or, I will add, misrepresentation, the party signing it is bound, and it is wholly immaterial whether he has read the document or not'. Scrutton LJ, in turn, was repeating the substance of what had been said by Mellish LJ in *Parker v South Eastern Railway Co*. ... In his lecture published as 'Form and Substance in Legal Reasoning: The Case of Contract', Professor Atiyah posed, with reference to *L'Estrange v Graucob*, the question why signatures are, within established limits, regarded as conclusive. He answered:

> 'A signature is, and is widely recognized even by the general public as being a formal device, and its value would be greatly reduced if it could not be treated as a conclusive ground of contractual liability at least in all ordinary circumstances.'

Professor Atiyah added:

'However, what is, I think, less clear is what is the underlying reason of substance in this kind of situation. The usual explanation for holding a signature to be conclusively binding is that it must be taken to show that the party signing has agreed to the contents of the document; but another possible explanation is that the other party can be treated as having relied upon the signature.' ... < 182> ...

[47] The importance which, for a very long time, the common law has assigned to the act of signing is not limited to contractual documents. *Wilton v Farnworth* was not a contract case. The passage from the judgment of Latham CJ quoted above is preceded by a general statement that, where a man signs a document knowing that it is a legal document relating to an interest in property, he is in general bound by the act of signature. Legal instruments of various kinds take their efficacy from signature or execution. Such instruments are often signed by people who have not read and understood all their terms, but who are nevertheless committed to those terms by the act of signature or execution. It is that commitment which enables third parties to assume the legal efficacy of the instrument. To undermine that assumption would cause serious mischief.

[48] In most common law jurisdictions, and throughout Australia, <183> legislation has been enacted in recent years to confer on courts a capacity to ameliorate in individual cases hardship caused by the strict application of legal principle to contractual relations. As a result, there is no reason to depart from principle, and every reason to adhere to it, in cases where such legislation does not apply, or is not invoked. ...

[50] An application of settled principle in the present case leads to the conclusion that the terms and conditions on the reverse of the Application for Credit formed part of the contract governing the storage and transportation of the goods.

[51] The reasoning of the primary judge, accepted by the Court of Appeal, was based upon the proposition that, in order for those terms and conditions to be made part of the contract, it was necessary for Finemores to establish that it had done what was reasonably sufficient to give Richard Thomson notice of the terms and conditions (the major premise), and the further proposition that Finemores had not done what was reasonably sufficient to give Richard Thomson such notice (the minor premise).

[52] It would be possible to dispose of the appeal by disagreeing with the minor premise. What more Finemores could have done to give Richard Thomson notice of the terms and conditions than requiring their representative to sign a document, and to place his signature immediately below a request that he read the conditions on the reverse side of the document before signing, is difficult to imagine.

[53] Of wider importance, however, is the major premise. If correct, it involves a serious qualification to the general principle concerning the <184> effect of signing a contract without reading it. The proposition appears to be that a person who signs a contractual document without reading it is bound by its terms only if

the other party has done what is reasonably sufficient to give notice of those terms. If the proposition is limited to some terms and not others, it is not easy to see what the discrimen might be.

[54] It appears from the reasoning of the primary judge and the Court of Appeal that the proposition was given a narrower focus, and was limited to exclusion clauses, or, perhaps, exclusion clauses which are regarded by a court as unusual and onerous. The present happens to be a case about exclusion clauses, but there is no apparent reason why the principle, if it exists, should apply only to them. Nor is the criterion by which a court might declare a contractual provision to be unusual or onerous always easy to identify. The origin of the proposition, clearly enough, is in the principles that apply to cases, such as ticket cases, in which one party has endeavoured to incorporate in a contract terms and conditions appearing in a notice or an unsigned document. When an attempt is made to introduce the concept of sufficient notice into the field of signed contracts, there is a danger of subverting fundamental principle based on sound legal policy. There are circumstances in which it is material to ask whether a person who has signed a document was given reasonable notice of what was in it. Cases where misrepresentation is alleged, or where mistake is claimed, provide examples. No one suggests that the fact that a document has been signed is for all purposes conclusive as to its legal effect. At the same time, where a person has signed a document, which is intended to affect legal relations, and there is no question of misrepresentation, duress, mistake, or any other vitiating element, the fact that the person has signed the document without reading it does not put the other party in the position of having to show that due notice was given of its terms. Furthermore, it may be asked, where would this leave a third party into whose hands the document might come?

[55] In *L'Estrange v Graucob*, Scrutton LJ said that the problem in that case was different from what he described as 'the railway passenger and cloak-room ticket cases, such as *Richardson, Spence & Co v Rowntree*', where 'there is no signature to the contractual document, the document being simply handed by the one party to the other'. His Lordship said:

> 'In cases in which the contract is contained in a railway ticket or other unsigned document, it is necessary to prove that an alleged party was aware, or ought to have been aware, of its terms and conditions. These cases have no application when the document has been signed.' <185>

[56] In the same case Maugham LJ, who agreed with Scrutton LJ, referred to three possible circumstances in which the party who signed the document might not have been bound by its terms. The first was if the document signed was not a contract but merely a memorandum of a previous contract which did not include the relevant term. The second was a case of *non est factum*. The third was a case of misrepresentation.

[57] If there is a claim of misrepresentation, or *non est factum*, or if there is an issue as to whether a document was intended to affect legal relations or whether, on the other hand, it was tendered as a mere memorandum of a pre-existing contract,

or a receipt, or if there is a claim for equitable or statutory relief, then even in the case of a signed document it may be material to know whether a person who has signed it was given sufficient notice of its contents. The general rule, which applies in the present case, is that where there is no suggested vitiating element, and no claim for equitable or statutory relief, a person who signs a document which is known by that person to contain contractual terms, and to affect legal relations, is bound by those terms, and it is immaterial that the person has not read the document. *L'Estrange v Graucob* explicitly rejected an attempt to import the principles relating to ticket cases into the area of signed contracts. It was not argued, either in this Court or in the Court of Appeal, that *L'Estrange v Graucob* should not be followed. ... <186–187> ...

[63] There may be cases where the circumstances in which a document is presented for signature, or the presence in it of unusual terms, could involve a misrepresentation. No such problem exists in the present case. There could also be circumstances in which one party would not reasonably understand another party's signature to a document as a manifestation of intent to enter into legal relations, or of assent to its terms. Again, that is not this case. It was reasonable of Finemores to treat Mr Gardiner-Garden's [Richard Thomson's Operations Manager (ed)] signature as a manifestation of assent to the conditions he had been invited to read before signing.

[The Court concluded that as none of these exceptions was established by the facts of the case, the general rule should apply with the result that Richard Thomson was bound by its signature. The Court then considered the agency issue and found that Richard Thomson had acted as Alphapharm's agent so that the latter was also bound by the exclusion clause in the contract made with Finemores.]

Appeal allowed

[footnotes omitted]

As the Court in *Toll* noted, there are a number of important qualifications to the rule in *L'Estrange v F Graucob*:

- it applies only when the document in question was understood by the signatory to be a contract, as distinct from merely a receipt or other document not having contractual effect[18]
- it does not apply where the party proffering the document misrepresents its terms[19]
- it does not apply where the signatory was mistaken about the very nature of the document and so can invoke the plea of *non est factum*[20] and

---

18 See *L'Estrange v F Graucob Ltd* [1934] 2 KB 294 esp at 402–403.
19 See *Curtis v Chemical Cleaning & Dyeing Co* [1951] 1 KB 805 in which the plaintiff was held not to be bound by an exclusion clause that excluded liability for loss generally, and which was contained in a document she signed, because, before she signed, the defendant misrepresented that the exclusion clause covered only very specific losses.
20 This topic is dealt with in chapter 13.

- statutory exceptions have been created in connection with provisions dealing generally with unconscionable conduct, duress or unfair terms,[21] that may enable a signatory to avoid the effect of having signed certain types of contract.

f Terms displayed or delivered

Terms can also be incorporated into a contract without being mentioned during pre-contractual negotiations, or included in a signed document. This may occur as a result of the terms being set out in a sign at a party's place of business, or contained in a ticket or receipt that is delivered by one party to the other. Examples of the former are terms displayed at the entrance to premises that seek to reduce the liability of the owner. Examples of the latter are tickets issued to passengers travelling on commercial or public transport and receipts issued to acknowledge the delivery or collection of goods or services. The cases dealing with these situations, frequently referred to as the 'ticket cases',[22] establish that the terms will be incorporated into the contract only if the party seeking to do so did all that was reasonable in the circumstances of the case to bring them to the attention of the other party and this occurred before the contract was concluded. The following cases illustrate these two requirements.

Oceanic Sun Line Special Shipping Company Inc v Fay

(1988) 165 CLR 197, High Court of Australia

[Through a New South Wales travel agent, Fay, a resident of Queensland, booked a cruise of the Greek Islands on a Greek-registered ship owned by Oceanic. Before paying for the cruise, Fay was shown a brochure which said that the transportation of passengers was governed by the terms and conditions printed on the passenger ticket which could be inspected at any Sun Line office. However, Fay did not read that part of the brochure and the travel agent did not have tickets available for inspection. The travel agent issued Fay with an 'exchange order' to be exchanged for a ticket in Athens where he boarded the ship. Clause 13 of this ticket provided that any action against Oceanic must be brought in Athens and excluded the jurisdiction of all other courts. Fay was injured while on the voyage and brought an action for negligence against Oceanic in the Supreme Court of New South Wales. Oceanic applied to stay the proceedings. This application was refused at first instance and on appeal by the Court of Appeal. Oceanic then appealed to the High Court. The following extract deals with the issue of whether the ticket formed part of the contract between the parties.]

Brennan J [at 228]: It was too late after the original contract was made to add conditions which were not incorporated in it. The inclusion of cl 13 on the ticket

---

21   See chapters 14, 16 and 17.
22   The leading ticket cases are discussed by the High Court in the extracts from *Toll v Alphapharm*, reproduced on p 250, above.

could not alter the terms of a contract already made: *Olley v Marlborough Court*. A condition printed on a ticket is ineffective to alter a contract of carriage if the ticket is issued after the contract is made: *Daly v General Steam Navigation Co Ltd* (*The 'Dragon'*). Perhaps the defendant expected that the contract made when the exchange order was issued would contain all the terms and conditions which, according to the brochure given to Dr Fay, were printed on 'the Passenger Ticket Contract which may be inspected at any Sun Line office'. But, as we shall see, that expectation was not fulfilled, and not simply because no copy of the Passenger Ticket Contract was available at JMA Tours in Sydney.

If a passenger signs and thereby binds himself to the terms of a contract of carriage containing a clause exempting the carrier from liability for loss arising out of the carriage, it is immaterial that the passenger did not trouble to discover the contents of the contract. But where an exemption clause is contained in a ticket or other <229> document intended by the carrier to contain the terms of carriage, yet the other party is not in fact aware when the contract is made that an exemption clause is intended to be a term of the contract, the carrier cannot rely on that clause unless, at the time of the contract, the carrier had done all that was reasonably necessary to bring the exemption clause to the passenger's notice: *Hood v Anchor Line (Henderson Brothers) Ltd*; *McCutcheon v David Macbrayne Ltd*; *Thornton v Shoe Lane Parking Ltd* per Lord Denning MR, and per Megaw LJ. In differing circumstances, different steps may be needed to bring an exemption clause to a passenger's notice, especially if the clause is an unusual one. In the present case, the only step which the defendant took to bring the exclusive foreign jurisdiction clause to the plaintiff's notice before the fare was paid was the note in the brochure that the conditions of carriage were printed in the (unavailable) Passenger Ticket Contract. In *Hollingworth v Southern Ferries Ltd* (*The 'Eagle'*), it was held that a mere statement in a carrier's brochure that the carrier contracted on its conditions of carriage was not enough to make those conditions terms of a contract of carriage subsequently made with an intending passenger who had read the brochure.

The exchange order mentions 'the Sun Line passage contract' but gives particulars only of Art 2 of that document. It does not bring to the notice of the passenger any exclusive foreign jurisdiction clause. As Dr Fay was unaware of that clause, it did not become incorporated into the contract made when the exchange order was issued. In *'The Dragon'* Brandon J (as he then was) pointed out that, if the carrier's conditions are not incorporated into the contract of carriage when it is made, the carrier cannot subsequently, 'by issuing a ticket containing the conditions concerned, however clearly referred to in it, introduce such conditions into the contract when it was not subject to them originally'.

As the contract of carriage was made when the exchange order was issued and as the exclusive jurisdiction clause contained in cl 13 of the ticket was not then known to Dr Fay and as insufficient was done to bring such a clause to his attention, that clause was not incorporated into the contract of carriage and could not subsequently be incorporated by insertion in the ticket issued pursuant to the original contract.

[The other members of the court agreed that the contract had been concluded in New South Wales and that the ticket did not form part of that contract. However, only Deane and Gaudron JJ agreed with Brennan J that the action should be stayed; Wilson and Toohey JJ dissented on that issue.]

Appeal dismissed

[footnotes omitted]

Interfoto Picture Library Ltd v Stiletto Visual Programmes Ltd
[1989] 1 QB 433, English Court of Appeal

[By telephone, Stiletto ordered photographic transparencies from Interfoto's lending library. These were delivered by the latter, together with a delivery note containing nine printed conditions one of which (Condition 2) provided that the transparencies were to be returned within 14 days, otherwise a holding fee of £5 per day would be charged for each transparency. Stiletto did not read the conditions and returned the transparencies four weeks later, whereupon Interfoto, relying on Clause 2, claimed £3,783. Stiletto refused to pay and Interfoto brought an action to recover this sum. This claim succeeded at first instance and Stiletto appealed to the Court of Appeal.]

Dillon LJ [at 438]: Condition 2 of these plaintiffs' conditions is in my judgment a very onerous clause. The defendants could not conceivably have known, if their attention was not drawn to the clause, that the plaintiffs were proposing to charge a 'holding fee' for the retention of the transparencies at such a very high and exorbitant rate.

At the time of the ticket cases in the last century it was notorious that people hardly ever troubled to read printed conditions on a ticket or delivery note or similar document. That remains the case now. In the intervening years the printed conditions have tended to become more and more complicated and more and more one-sided in favour of the party who is imposing them, but the other parties, if they notice that there are printed conditions at all, generally still tend to assume that such conditions are only concerned with ancillary matters of form and are not of importance. In the ticket cases the courts held that the common law required that reasonable steps be taken to draw the other parties' attention to the printed conditions or they would not be part of the contract. It is in my judgment a logical development of the common law into modern conditions that it should be held, as it was in <439> *Thornton v Shoe Lane Parking Ltd* [1971] 2 QB 163 that, if one condition in a set of printed conditions is particularly onerous or unusual, the party seeking to enforce it must show that that particular condition was fairly brought to the attention of the other party.

In the present case, nothing whatever was done by the plaintiffs to draw the defendants' attention particularly to condition 2; it was merely one of four columns' width of conditions printed across the foot of the delivery note. Consequently condition 2 never, in my judgment, became part of the contract between the parties.

I would therefore allow this appeal and reduce the amount of the judgment which the judge awarded against the defendants to the amount which he would have awarded on a *quantum meruit* on his alternative findings, ie the reasonable charge of £3.50 per transparency per week for the retention of the transparencies beyond a reasonable period, which he fixed at 14 days from the date of their receipt by the defendants.

[In a separate judgment Bingham LJ reached the same conclusion.]

Appeal allowed

Maxitherm Boilers Pty Ltd v Pacific Dunlop Ltd

[1998] 4 VR 559, Victorian Court of Appeal

[The facts of this case appear at p 57, above. In the course of considering whether Maxitherm's standard terms and conditions, which contained the exclusion clauses it relied upon, formed part of the contract the Court made the following observations about the relevance to this issue of the nature of those clauses.]

Buchanan JA [at 568]: When a party is issued with a ticket or document containing terms, and the ticket or document performs a function other than being the embodiment of the terms of the contract, proof of consent will usually depend upon the efforts taken to bring the terms to the attention of the recipient of the ticket or other document. In *Parker v South Eastern Railway Co* (1877) 2 CPD 416, Mellish LJ said at 423:

> The railway company, as it seems to me, must be entitled to make some assumptions respecting the person who deposits luggage with them: I think they are entitled to assume that he can read, and that he understands the English language, and that he pays such attention to what he is about as may reasonably be expected from a person in such a transaction as that of depositing luggage in a cloak-room. The railway company must, however, take mankind as they find them, and if what they do is sufficient to inform people in general that the ticket contains conditions, I think that a particular plaintiff ought not to be in a better position than other persons on account of his exceptional ignorance or stupidity or carelessness. But if what the railway company do is not sufficient to convey to the minds of people in general that the ticket contains conditions, then they have received the goods on deposit without obtaining the consent of the persons depositing them to the conditions limiting their liability.

On the other hand, a party relying upon a document containing conditions may be relieved of the need to take steps to inform the other party that the document contains conditions where the other party expressly accepts an offer of which the document forms part.

I do not intend to convey that express acceptance of an offer which incorporates other terms by reference necessarily connotes acceptance of all those terms. In a case where the person expressing consent has not read the terms, his consent may be taken to be a consent to those terms which are appropriate to a contract of the type in question. If the terms include provisions which no one would anticipate in a contract of the type in question, it would not be appropriate to assume consent to those provisions. The basic enquiry remains whether it is reasonable to assume that a contracting party has assented to the terms put forward by the other party. ...

[After considering several cases including *Interfoto* his Honour continued at 569]: As I have said, in my opinion the inclusion of an unusual term, at least in an unsigned document, may require its proponent to take special steps to bring it to the attention of the other party, for otherwise it may not be reasonable to assume consent to the term. Whether special steps are required, and what those steps must be, will depend upon the circumstances of each case. Further, I think that a term may be unusual because it is more than ordinarily onerous. However, I do not consider that the mere fact that a provision is onerous entitles a court applying the common law to reject it as a term unless special steps have been taken to draw attention to it. The relevant question is whether a contracting party can be reasonably taken to have assented to a particular term, not whether a contracting party should be subject to an unreasonable term.

In the present case I doubt that any of Maxitherm's standard terms was so exceptional that it was unreasonable to suppose that Pacific Dunlop was not assenting to it by expressly accepting the offer that incorporated the terms.

g Course of dealing

Terms may be incorporated into a contract without being discussed, referred to, or displayed at the time the contract was concluded where the previous dealings of the parties are such as to give reasonable notice to the party against whom they are being invoked that the other intended to contract on those terms. Furthermore, even where the number of previous dealings is insufficient to do this, the fact that certain terms were present in previous dealings between the parties may be relevant to the issue of whether the party seeking to invoke them took all reasonable steps to bring them to the other party's attention.[23]

Henry Kendall & Sons v William Lillico & Sons Ltd

[1969] 2 AC 31, House of Lords

[The initial proceedings in this case arose out of a claim by the Hardwick Game farm against SAPPA for breach of contract in supplying it with defective animal feed. SAPPA joined, as third parties to those proceedings, Lillico and Grimsdale, two

---

23   See *First East Auction Holdings Pty ltd v Ange* [2010] VSC 72 at 144.

firms that had supplied it with the ingredients used to make the feed. They in turn joined as fourth parties their suppliers Kendall and Holland Colombo. Hardwick succeeded against SAPPA. The current proceedings concerned SAPPA's claim against Lillico and Grimsdale and their claim against the fourth parties. At first instance and on appeal to the Court of Appeal, SAPPA succeeded in its claim against Lillico and Grimsdale as did they against Kendall and Holland Colombo. In connection with SAPPA's claim it was argued by Grimsdale that it could rely upon an exclusion clause contained in a document called a 'contract note' that it sent to SAPPA shortly after each contract of sale was entered into. The following extract from Kendall's appeal to the House of Lords deals only with this issue.]

Lord Morris [at 90]: A separate issue arises, however, as between Grimsdale and SAPPA. There were three contracts between Grimsdale and SAPPA. They were oral. The learned judge found that there had been frequent prior transactions between them. There had been three to four deals a month during the previous three years. The practice had been that Grimsdale would send a contract note to SAPPA either later on the day of an oral contract or on the day following. SAPPA would expect to receive such a contract note. It was routine practice. The same practice was indeed followed when SAPPA bought this type of material (cakes and meals) from London wholesalers. On the back of the contract notes there were certain terms or conditions. Mr Golden who acted for SAPPA knew that there were such conditions though he had not read them. One term on the contract notes was as follows: 'The buyer under this contract takes the responsibility of any latent defects.' It was the contention of Grimsdale (a) that the terms or conditions on the contract notes were terms of or were incorporated into the relevant contracts of sale and (b) that the above-quoted term operated, on the facts of the present case, to relieve Grimsdale from any liability to SAPPA. As to (a), the learned judge, after considering the case of *McCutcheon v David MacBrayne Ltd* [1964] 1 WLR 125, HL, held that the conditions in the contract note were not incorporated into the contracts of sale. In agreement with all the members of the Court of Appeal I consider that they were. Over the course of a long period prior to the three oral contracts which are now in question SAPPA knew that when Grimsdale sold they did so on the terms that they had continuously made known to SAPPA. In these circumstances it is reasonable to hold that when SAPPA placed an order to buy they did so on the basis and with the knowledge that an acceptance of the order by Grimsdale and their agreement to sell would be on the terms and conditions set out on their contract notes to the extent to which they were applicable.

Lord Pearce [at 113]: SAPPA had regularly received more than a hundred similar contract notes from Grimsdale in the course of dealing over three years. They knew of the existence of the conditions on the back of the contract note. They never raised any query or objection. ... The court's task is to decide what each party to an alleged contract would reasonably conclude from the utterances, writings or conduct of the other. The question, therefore, is not what SAPPA themselves thought or knew about the matter but what they should be taken as representing to Grimsdale about it or leading Grimsdale to believe. The only reasonable inference from the regular course of dealing over so long a period is that SAPPA were evincing an acceptance of, and a readiness to be bound by, the printed conditions of whose existence they were well aware although they had not troubled to read them. Thus the general conditions became part of the oral contract.

[Lords Guest and Wilberforce agreed that the exclusion clause formed part of the contract between SAPPA and Grimsdale. However, all of their Lordships went on to conclude that it did not protect Grimsdale. The other member of the panel, Lord Reid did not discuss the matter.]

Appeal dismissed

3 Implied terms

As noted in our introduction, implied terms are terms that form part of a contract even though they were not mentioned, or referred to, by one or other of the parties during the formation process. Terms of this nature may implied by the common law and by statute.

a Common law

The common law will imply terms in a variety of situations. To assist analysis of these situations, attempts have been made to identify distinct categories of cases in which terms will be implied; the principal ones are used below. There is considerable overlap between these categories—rather than being sharply distinct, they are really shades 'on a continuous spectrum'.[24]

There are two grounds upon which terms are implied at common law. The first of these is to give effect to the intention of the parties. Here, the term is implied because it is determined that the parties would have expressly agreed to it had they thought about the matter when the contract was being negotiated. Terms of this nature are sometimes referred to as 'ad hoc'[25] as they will be designed specifically for the contract in question. However, although in connection with such terms reference is made to 'the intention of the parties', this is not determined subjectively, but rather, objectively by reference to what a reasonable person would have concluded having regard to the relevant circumstances surrounding the case. The second ground involves implying, in effect, standard implied terms because they are regarded as 'a legal incident of a particular class of contract'.[26] Here, the courts are not concerned about the actual intention of the parties but rather what it is appropriate to imply into a contract of the kind in question. The basis upon

---

24 *Liverpool City Council v Irwin* [1977] AC 239, per Lord Wilberforce at 254.
25 See HK Lucke, 'Ad hoc Implications in Written Contracts' (1973–1976) 5 *Adelaide Law Review* 32.
26 See *Renard Constructions (ME) Pty Ltd v Minister for Public Works* (1992) 26 NSWLR 234 at 256, per Priestley JA.

which terms are to be implied into contracts was recently discussed at length by the Privy Council in the following case. Although no longer binding in Australia, the Board's pronouncements are likely to be very influential to the approach taken by courts in this country.

Attorney General of Belize v Belize Telecom Ltd
[2009] UKPC 10, Privy Council

[This case concerned the construction of the articles of association of Belize Telecommunications Ltd; in particular, whether a provision should be implied into those articles providing for the removal of certain directors when the shareholders who appointed them no longer had the shareholding required to appoint or remove directors. Although not concerning the construction of a contract, the Board approached the case on the basis that the principles being expounded applied also to contractual instruments.]

Lord Hoffman [for the Board at 16]: Before discussing in greater detail the reasoning of the Court of Appeal, the Board will make some general observations about the process of implication. The court has no power to improve upon the instrument which it is called upon to construe, whether it be a contract, a statute or articles of association. It cannot introduce terms to make it fairer or more reasonable. It is concerned only to discover what the instrument means. However, that meaning is not necessarily or always what the authors or parties to the document would have intended. It is the meaning which the instrument would convey to a reasonable person having all the background knowledge which would reasonably be available to the audience to whom the instrument is addressed: see *Investors Compensation Scheme Ltd v West Bromwich Building Society* [1998] 1 WLR 896, 912–913. It is this objective meaning which is conventionally called the intention of the parties, or the intention of Parliament, or the intention of whatever person or body was or is deemed to have been the author of the instrument.

[17] The question of implication arises when the instrument does not expressly provide for what is to happen when some event occurs. The most usual inference in such a case is that nothing is to happen. If the parties had intended something to happen, the instrument would have said so. Otherwise, the express provisions of the instrument are to continue to operate undisturbed. If the event has caused loss to one or other of the parties, the loss lies where it falls.

[18] In some cases, however, the reasonable addressee would understand the instrument to mean something else. He would consider that the only meaning consistent with the other provisions of the instrument, read against the relevant background, is that something is to happen. The event in question is to affect the rights of the parties. The instrument may not have expressly said so, but this is what it must mean. In such a case, it is said that the court implies a term as to what will happen if the event in question occurs. But the implication of the term is not an addition to the instrument. It only spells out what the instrument means.

[19] The proposition that the implication of a term is an exercise in the construction of the instrument as a whole is not only a matter of logic (since a court has no power to alter what the instrument means) but also well supported by authority. In *Trollope & Colls Ltd v North West Metropolitan Regional Hospital Board* [1973] 1 WLR 601, 609 Lord Pearson, with whom Lord Guest and Lord Diplock agreed, said:

> [T]he court does not make a contract for the parties. The court will not even improve the contract which the parties have made for themselves, however desirable the improvement might be. The court's function is to interpret and apply the contract which the parties have made for themselves. If the express terms are perfectly clear and free from ambiguity, there is no choice to be made between different possible meanings: the clear terms must be applied even if the court thinks some other terms would have been more suitable. An unexpressed term can be implied if and only if the court finds that the parties must have intended that term to form part of their contract: it is not enough for the court to find that such a term would have been adopted by the parties as reasonable men if it had been suggested to them: it must have been a term that went without saying, a term necessary to give business efficacy to the contract, a term which, though tacit, formed part of the contract which the parties made for themselves.

[20] More recently, in *Equitable Life Assurance Society v Hyman* [2002] 1 AC 408, 459, Lord Steyn said:

> If a term is to be implied, it could only be a term implied from the language of [the instrument] read in its commercial setting.

[21] It follows that in every case in which it is said that some provision ought to be implied in an instrument, the question for the court is whether such a provision would spell out in express words what the instrument, read against the relevant background, would reasonably be understood to mean. It will be noticed from Lord Pearson's speech that this question can be reformulated in various ways which a court may find helpful in providing an answer—the implied term must 'go without saying', it must be 'necessary to give business efficacy to the contract' and so on—but these are not in the Board's opinion to be treated as different or additional tests. There is only one question: is that what the instrument, read as a whole against the relevant background, would reasonably be understood to mean?

[22] There are dangers in treating these alternative formulations of the question as if they had a life of their own. Take, for example, the question of whether the implied term is 'necessary to give business efficacy' to the contract. That formulation serves to underline two important points. The first, conveyed by the use of the word 'business', is that in considering what the instrument would have meant to a reasonable person who had knowledge of the relevant background, one assumes the notional reader will take into account the practical consequences of deciding that it means one thing or the other. In the case of an instrument such as a commercial contract, he will consider whether a different construction would

frustrate the apparent business purpose of the parties. That was the basis upon which *Equitable Life Assurance Society v Hyman* [2002] 1 AC 408 was decided. The second, conveyed by the use of the word 'necessary', is that it is not enough for a court to consider that the implied term expresses what it would have been reasonable for the parties to agree to. It must be satisfied that it is what the contract actually means.

[23] The danger lies, however, in detaching the phrase 'necessary to give business efficacy' from the basic process of construction of the instrument. It is frequently the case that a contract may work perfectly well in the sense that both parties can perform their express obligations, but the consequences would contradict what a reasonable person would understand the contract to mean. Lord Steyn made this point in the *Equitable Life* case (at p. 459) when he said that in that case an implication was necessary 'to give effect to the reasonable expectations of the parties.'

[24] The same point had been made many years earlier by Bowen LJ in his well known formulation in *The Moorcock* (1889) 14 PD 64, 68:

> In business transactions such as this, what the law desires to effect by the implication is to give such business efficacy to the transaction as must have been intended at all events by both parties who are business men

[25] Likewise, the requirement that the implied term must 'go without saying' is no more than another way of saying that, although the instrument does not expressly say so, that is what a reasonable person would understand it to mean. Any attempt to make more of this requirement runs the risk of diverting attention from the objectivity which informs the whole process of construction into speculation about what the actual parties to the contract or authors (or supposed authors) of the instrument would have thought about the proposed implication. The imaginary conversation with an officious bystander in *Shirlaw v Southern Foundries (1926) Ltd* [1939] 2 KB 206, 227 is celebrated throughout the common law world. Like the phrase 'necessary to give business efficacy', it vividly emphasises the need for the court to be satisfied that the proposed implication spells out what the contact would reasonably be understood to mean. But it carries the danger of barren argument over how the actual parties would have reacted to the proposed amendment. That, in the Board's opinion, is irrelevant. Likewise, it is not necessary that the need for the implied term should be obvious in the sense of being immediately apparent, even upon a superficial consideration of the terms of the contract and the relevant background. The need for an implied term not infrequently arises when the draftsman of a complicated instrument has omitted to make express provision for some event because he has not fully thought through the contingencies which might arise, even though it is obvious after a careful consideration of the express terms and the background that only one answer would be consistent with the rest of the instrument. In such circumstances, the fact that the actual parties might have said to the officious bystander 'Could you please explain that again?' does not matter.

[26] In *BP Refinery (Westernport) Pty Ltd v Shire of Hastings* (1977) 180 CLR 266, 282–283 Lord Simon of Glaisdale, giving the advice of the majority of the Board, said that it was 'not ... necessary to review exhaustively the authorities on the implication of a term in a contract' but that the following conditions ('which may overlap') must be satisfied:

> (1) it must be reasonable and equitable; (2) it must be necessary to give business efficacy to the contract, so that no term will be implied if the contract is effective without it; (3) it must be so obvious that 'it goes without saying' (4) it must be capable of clear expression; (5) it must not contradict any express term of the contract.

[27] The Board considers that this list is best regarded, not as series of independent tests which must each be surmounted, but rather as a collection of different ways in which judges have tried to express the central idea that the proposed implied term must spell out what the contract actually means, or in which they have explained why they did not think that it did so. The Board has already discussed the significance of 'necessary to give business efficacy' and 'goes without saying'. As for the other formulations, the fact that the proposed implied term would be inequitable or unreasonable, or contradict what the parties have expressly said, or is incapable of clear expression, are all good reasons for saying that a reasonable man would not have understood that to be what the instrument meant.

Terms needed to give a contract 'efficacy'

It was established in *The Moorcock*[27] that where it is necessary to do so the courts will imply a term, based on the presumed intention of the parties, to give a transaction 'such efficacy as both parties must have intended that at all events it should have.'[28] On that basis, it was held in the case that in a contract between the owner of a ship and the owner of a wharf allowing the ship to berth at the wharf, there was to be implied a term that the latter would take reasonable care to see that the berth was safe. What must be established before a term will be implied and the approach to be taken by the courts is discussed in the following extract.

Codelfa Construction Pty Ltd v State Rail Authority of New South Wales

(1982) 149 CLR 337, High Court of Australia

[Codelfa contracted with the NSW Rail Authority to excavate railway tunnels within a specified period of time. When the contract was entered into, both parties assumed that Codelfa would be able to work three shifts per day, seven days a

---

27 (1889) 14 PD 64.
28 (1889) 14 PD 64 at 68, per Bowen LJ.

week and at first it did so. However, local residents disturbed by the noise of the works obtained an injunction that restricted Codelfa to working only two shifts per day and to not excavating on Sunday. This increased Codelfa's cost and it claimed that increase from the Authority on the ground that there was an implied term to the effect that if it was prevented from working as planned, the Authority would indemnify it against the additional costs incurred. Alternatively, it argued that the contract was frustrated. The arbitrator, the judge at first instance and the Court of Appeal all concluded that terms were to be implied into the contract in Codelfa's favour. However, when it appealed against other aspects of those decisions, the Authority cross appealed against this conclusion. The following extract deals only with the implied terms issue.]

Mason J [at 345]: The appellant's case is that a term has to be implied in the contract to give it business efficacy, to make it workable. Consequently, there is no contest as to what constitutes the contract; rather the contest is as to its meaning and effect. ...

Of course, I am speaking of an implied term necessary to give business efficacy to a particular contract, not of the implied term which is a legal incident of a particular class of contract, of which *Liverpool City Council v Irwin* is an example. The difference between the two categories of implied term was mentioned by Viscount Simonds in *Lister v Romford Ice and Cold Storage Co Ltd*, at p 576, where he referred to the search for the second category of <346> implied term as being based 'upon more general considerations', a comment endorsed by Lord Wilberforce in *Irwin*.

The implication of a term is to be compared, and at the same time contrasted, with rectification of the contract. In each case the problem is caused by a deficiency in the expression of the consensual agreement. A term which should have been included has been omitted. The difference is that with rectification the term which has been omitted and should have been included was actually agreed upon; with implication the term is one which it is presumed that the parties would have agreed upon had they turned their minds to it—it is not a term that they have actually agreed upon. Thus, in the case of the implied term the deficiency in the expression of the consensual agreement is caused by the failure of the parties to direct their minds to a particular eventuality and to make explicit provision for it. Rectification ensures that the contract gives effect to the parties' actual intention; the implication of a term is designed to give effect to the parties' presumed intention.

For obvious reasons the courts are slow to imply a term. In many cases, what the parties have actually agreed upon represents the totality of their willingness to agree; each may be prepared to take his chance in relation to an eventuality for which no provision is made. The more detailed and comprehensive the contract the less ground there is for supposing that the parties have failed to address their minds to the question at issue. And then there is the difficulty of identifying with any degree of certainty the term which the parties would have settled upon had they considered the question.

Accordingly, the courts have been at pains to emphasize that it is not enough that it is reasonable to imply a term; it must be necessary to do so to give business efficacy to the contract. ...

The basis on which the courts act in implying a term was expressed by MacKinnon LJ in *Shirlaw v Southern Foundries <347> (1926) Ltd*, at p 227 in terms that have been universally accepted: '*Prima facie* that which in any contract is left to be implied and need not be expressed is something so obvious that it goes without saying ...'

The conditions necessary to ground the implication of a term were summarized by the majority in *BP Refinery (Westernport) Pty Ltd v Hastings Shire Council* at p 26: '(1) it must be reasonable and equitable; (2) it must be necessary to give business efficacy to the contract, so that no term will be implied if the contract is effective without it; (3) it must be so obvious that 'it goes without saying'; (4) it must be capable of clear expression; (5) it must not contradict any express term of the contract.'

[354] To say that the maintenance of three eight hour shifts a day for six days a week was a matter of common contemplation between the parties is not enough in itself to justify the implication of a term. ... It must appear that the matter of common contemplation was necessary to give the contract business efficacy and that the term sought to be implied is so obvious that it goes without saying. <355> In this case the problem, as I see it, lies not so much in saying that the implication of a term is necessary to give business efficacy to the contract, as in concluding that the particular term to be implied is so obvious that 'it goes without saying'.

[T]here remains an insurmountable problem in saying that 'it goes without saying' that had the parties contemplated the possibility that their legal advice was incorrect and that an injunction might be granted to restrain noise or other nuisance, they would have settled upon the term implied by the Court of Appeal or that implied by the Arbitrator and by Ash J at first instance. I doubt whether the fiction of treating the parties as reasonable and fair makes the problem any the less difficult. This is not a case in which <356> an obvious provision was overlooked by the parties and omitted from the contract. Rather it was a case in which the parties made a common assumption which masked the need to explore what provision should be made to cover the event which occurred. In ordinary circumstances negotiation about that matter might have yielded any one of a number of alternative provisions, each being regarded as a reasonable solution.

The difficulty which I have with the implication of a term here is much the same as the difficulty that Lord Reid had in *Davis Contractors Ltd v Fareham Urban District Council* in accepting that the doctrine of frustration rests on an implied term. It is greater because in many situations it is easier to say that the parties never agreed to be bound in a fundamentally different situation which has unexpectedly emerged than it is to assert that in a like situation the parties have impliedly agreed that the contract is to remain on foot with a new provision, not adverted to by them, governing their rights and liabilities.

My reluctance to imply a term is the stronger because the contract in this case was not a negotiated contract. The terms were determined by the Authority in advance and there is some force in the argument that the Authority looked to Codelfa to shoulder the responsibility for all risks not expressly provided for in the contract. It is a factor which in my view makes it very difficult to conclude that either of the terms sought to be implied is so obvious that it goes without saying.

Accordingly, my conclusion is that, if Codelfa is entitled to any relief in respect of the changed circumstances, that relief is more appropriately founded on the doctrine of frustration than on the implication of a term.

[Stephen and Wilson JJ agreed with Mason J; Aickin and Brennan JJ gave separate judgments to the same effect on the implied terms issue. However, a majority (Brennan J dissenting) concluded that the contract was frustrated.]

Cross appeal allowed

[footnotes omitted]

Standard implied terms

At common law certain standard terms will be implied into particular categories of contract unless the parties have made it clear that this is not to happen. They are implied on the basis that the parties would have agreed to them had they thought about the matter. They are regarded as 'standard' because the courts have determined that they are a normal incident of the kind of contract in question. Examples include:

- in a contract for work and materials, an implied term that the materials are of good quality and fit for their intended purpose[29]
- in a contract for the provision of professional services, an implied term that the services will be provided with reasonable care[30]
- in a distribution agreement for goods, an implied term that the supplier and distributor would use their best efforts to, respectively, supply or sell the goods.[31]

Terms to make the contract work as intended

Where a contract cannot operate unless one or both of the parties act in a certain way, or cooperate with each other, a term will be implied that they take reasonable steps to act as required.[32] For example, in the case of a contract that is subject to finance, a term may be implied that the purchaser take reasonable steps to obtain finance.[33]

---

29 See *Helicopter Sales (Australia) Pty Ltd v Rotor-Work Pty Ltd* (1974) 132 CLR 1.
30 See *GW Sinclair & Co Pty Ltd v Cocks* [2001] VSCA 47 and *Redken Laboratories (Aust) Pty Ltd v Docker* (2000) Aust Contract R 90-113.
31 See *Hospital Products Ltd v United States Surgical Corp* (1984) 156 CLR 41.
32 See *Butt v McDonald* (1896) 7 QLJ 68, esp at 70–71.
33 See *Meehan v Jones* (1982) 149 CLR 571, esp Mason J at 591.

Terms requiring good faith and fair dealing

In recent years, Anglo-Australian courts have grappled with the issue of whether our law recognises, or should recognise, a general implied obligation of 'good faith and fair dealing'.[34] In doing so they have, in part at least, been responding to the presence of such a requirement in other legal systems[35] and in international restatements of the law.[36] In Australia, the lead on this issue has been taken by the New South Wales Court of Appeal which, in a series of decisions, has recognised the existence of such a duty.[37] Support for this position has also come from the Federal Court[38] and the Victorian Court of Appeal.[39] However, the High Court has yet to pronounce on this matter and recently declined the opportunity to do so.[40] Until it does, issues such as the content of the implied term, its impact on other rules, whether it can be excluded by the parties and whether it applies to pre-contractual conduct as well as conduct during performance will remain unsettled.

Terms implied by custom

A term may be implied because it is customary in the particular trade, profession or locality. In the following extract, the High Court sets out the requirements for a term being implied on this basis.

Con-Stan Industries of Australia Pty Ltd v Norwich Winterthur Insurance (Australia) Ltd

(1985–1986) 160 CLR 226

[Con-Stan obtained insurance cover from Norwich. It paid the required premium to the broker who arranged this cover. However, the broker failed to pay Norwich and later a winding up order was made against it. Having failed to recover the premium from the broker, Norwich sought to recover it from Con-Stan. Its claim failed at first instance on the ground that as a result of custom there was an implied term in non-marine insurance contracts to the effect that an insurer had no

---

34   For a compilation of the leading authorities and commentaries see L Willmott, S Christensen and D Butler, *Contract Law*, 2nd edn, Oxford University Press, Melbourne, 2005 and J Carter and E Peden, 'Good Faith in Australian Contract Law' (2003) 19 *Journal of Contract Law* 155.

35   See section 1–203 of the United States *Uniform Commercial Code* which provides that 'every contract or duty within the Act imposes an obligation of good faith in its performance or enforcement.'

36   See *UNIDROIT Principles of International Commercial Contracts 2004*, Art 1.7, reproduced on p 272, below.

37   Discussion of this topic usually commences with the obiter remarks of Priestley JA in *Renard Constructions (ME) Pty Ltd v Minister For Public Works* (1992) 26 NSWLR 234 esp at 263–268. Decisions in which a term of good faith was implied include *Burger King Corp v Hungry Jack's Pty Ltd* [2001] NSWCA 187 and *Vodafone Pacific Ltd v Mobile Innovations Ltd* [2004] NSWCA 15.

38   See *Hughes Aircraft Systems International v Airservices Australia* (1997) 76 FCR 151 at 191–193 and *Garry Rogers Motors (Aust) Pty Ltd v Subaru (Aust) Pty Ltd* (1999) ATPR 41-704, esp 43,014.

39   See *Far Horizons Pty Ltd v McDonald's Australia Ltd* [2000] VSCA 310.

40   See *Royal Botanic Gardens and Domain Trust v South Sydney City Council* (2002) 186 ALR 289 at 301.

recourse against an assured if the assured had paid the premiums to the broker who arranged the insurance. Norwich successfully appealed to the New South Wales Court of Appeal; Con-Stan then appealed to the High Court.]

Gibbs CJ, Mason, Wilson, Brennan and Dawson JJ [at 236]: The circumstances in which trade custom or usage may form the basis for the implication of terms into a contract have been considered in many cases. The cases have established the following propositions:

(1) The existence of a custom or usage that will justify the implication of a term into a contract is a question of fact: *Nelson v Dahl*. The critical dependence of a finding of custom on the facts of the particular case means there is little to be gained by referring (as counsel for the appellant urged us to do) to the practices of the London marine market in the last century, notwithstanding that those practices formed the basis for the implication, in contracts of marine insurance, of a term similar to the first of the terms alternatively contended for in this case: see *Power v Butcher*; *Xenos v Wickham*; *Universo Insurance Co of Milan v Merchants Marine Insurance Co Ltd*.

(2) There must be evidence that the custom relied on is so well known and acquiesced in that everyone making a contract in that situation can reasonably be presumed to have imported that term into the contract: *Young v Tockassie*; *Summers v The Commonwealth*; *Majeau Carrying Co Pty Ltd v Coastal Rutile Ltd*. In the words of Jessel MR in *Nelson v Dahl*, approved by Knox CJ in *Thornley v Tilley*:

> '[The custom] must be so notorious that everybody in the trade enters into a contract with that usage as an implied term. It must be uniform as well as reasonable, and it must have quite as much certainty as the written contract itself.'

However, it is not necessary that the custom be universally accepted, for such a requirement would always be defeated by the denial by one litigant of the very matter that the other party seeks to prove in the proceedings.

(3) A term will not be implied into a contract on the basis of <237> custom where it is contrary to the express terms of the agreement: *Summers v The Commonwealth*; *Rosenhain v Commonwealth Bank of Australia*. ...

It has sometimes been said that the implication of a term into a contract does not depend on the parties' intention, actual or presumed, but on broader considerations: *Shell UK Ltd v Lostock Garage Ltd*; *Lister v Romford Ice and Cold Storage Co Ltd*; *Liverpool City Council v Irwin*. But these statements are directed to situations in which the courts have been asked to imply terms amounting to rules of law applicable to all contracts of a particular class. The present case is of a different kind in which it may be necessary to speak of presumed intention. In matters of this kind, that phrase means no more than that the general notoriety of the custom makes it reasonable to assume that the parties contracted on the basis of the custom, and that it is therefore reasonable to import such a term into the contract.

(4) A person may be bound by a custom notwithstanding the fact that he had no knowledge of it. ... The result is that in modern times nothing turns on the presence or absence of actual knowledge of the custom; that matter will stand or fall with the resolution of the issue of the degree of notoriety which the custom has achieved. ...

In order to establish a custom to the effect that a broker is alone liable to an insurer for payment of a premium on a policy of insurance, it is not sufficient to show that in the ordinary course of events the premium is paid to the insurer by the broker, nor is it sufficient to show that where a broker has failed to pay a premium the insurer makes its first demand for payment from the broker. Both circumstances are consistent with the continued liability of the assured. It is necessary to establish a clear course of conduct under which insurers do not look to the assured for payment of the premium. This may be established by proving either an absence of claims by insurers against assured, or the existence of claims directed exclusively to brokers as a practice rarely if ever departed from. Having examined the evidence of custom that was led in the present case, we do not think this requirement is satisfied.

[Their Honours concluded that there was no implied term such as that alleged by Con-Stan.]

Appeal dismissed

[footnotes omitted]

b Statute

A number of statutes imply terms into contracts. In the case of early examples, such as the United Kingdom *Sale of Goods Act 1893*, these terms usually reflected the position at common law and the parties were allowed to exclude the terms if they wished.[41] More recently, statutory implied terms have been used to make certain types of contracts more equitable where the legislature has been of the opinion that, because of the unequal bargaining power of the parties, this could not be achieved by negotiation between them. The most notable examples were the terms implied into consumer contracts by the *TPA* and its state and territory equivalents. However, this approach to consumer protection was eschewed by the *ACL*, which instead created a number of consumer guarantees, non-compliance with which give rise to statutory remedies, rather than to an action for breach of contract. Nevertheless, the approach of incorporating non-excludable implied

---

41   Sale of goods legislation in each state and territory implies into contracts for the sale of goods terms relating to the title to the goods, about the goods corresponding with their description and about their quality. However, these terms can be excluded by the contract. See, *Sale of Goods Act 1954* (ACT) ss 17–19; *Sale of Goods Act 1923* (NSW) ss 17–19; *Sale of Goods Act 1972* (NT) ss 17–19; *Sale of Goods Act 1896* (Qld) ss 15–17; *Sale of Goods Act 1895* (SA) ss 12–14; *Sale of Goods Act 1896* (Tas) ss 17–19; *Goods Act 1958* (Vic) ss 17–19; *Sale of Goods Act 1895* (WA) ss 12–14.

terms into certain contracts in order to protect parties with little bargaining power is still used in some areas such as insurance.[42]

INTERNATIONAL PERSPECTIVES

UNIDROIT Principles of International Commercial Contracts 2004

Article 1.7

(1) Each party must act in accordance with good faith and fair dealing in international trade.
(2) The parties may not exclude or limit this duty.

India

The *Indian Contract Act, 1872* contains no provisions dealing with the terms of a contract. Rather, this matter is left to the unwritten law which is essentially the same as it is in Anglo-Australian law.

China

On the other hand, the *Contract Law of the People's Republic of China, 1999* deals extensively with contractual terms. Its provisions fall into three broad categories. The first (Articles 5, 6 and 61) deals with fairness and good faith and requires the parties to exhibit fairness when prescribing their rights and obligations and good faith when performing the contract. The second (Article 12) prescribes what terms the parties should normally include in their contract. Provision is also made for the use of standard contracts. The third (Articles 61 and 62) deals with adding terms to a contract where important matters were not dealt with in the initial agreement. In such a case, the parties are encouraged to supplement the agreement as required; if they are unable to reach an agreement about the terms needed, this is to be determined by reference to the rest of the contract, usage or a number of prescribed gap filling terms.

Article 5. Fairness

The parties shall abide by the principle of fairness in prescribing their respective rights and obligations.

Article 6. Good Faith

The parties shall abide by the principle of good faith in exercising their rights and performing their obligations.

---

[42] For example, a term that the parties act with the 'utmost good faith' towards each other is implied into insurance contracts by s 13 of the *Insurance Contracts Act 1984*.

Article 12. Terms of Contract

The terms of a contract shall be prescribed by the parties, and generally include the following:

(i)   names of the parties and domicile thereof;
(ii) subject matter;
(iii) quantity;
(iv) quality;
(v)   price or remuneration;
(vi) time, place and method of performance;
(vii) liabilities for breach of contract;
(viii) method of dispute resolution.

The parties may enter into a contract by referencing a model contract for the relevant contract category.

Article 60. Full Performance; Performance in Good Faith

The parties shall fully perform their respective obligations in accordance with the contract. The parties shall abide by the principle of good faith, and perform obligations such as notification, assistance, and confidentiality, etc in light of the nature and purpose of the contract and in accordance with relevant usage.

Article 61. Indeterminate Terms; Supplementary Agreement

If a term such as quality, price or remuneration, or place of performance etc was not prescribed or clearly prescribed, after the contract has taken effect, the parties may supplement it through agreement; if the parties fail to reach a supplementary agreement, such term shall be determined in accordance with the relevant provisions of the contract or in accordance with the relevant usage.

Article 62. Gap Filling

Where a relevant term of the contract was not clearly prescribed, and cannot be determined in accordance with Article 61 hereof, one of the following provisions applies:

(i) If quality requirement was not clearly prescribed, performance shall be in accordance with the state standard or industry standard; absent any state or industry standard, performance shall be in accordance with the customary standard or any particular standard consistent with the purpose of the contract;
(ii) If price or remuneration was not clearly prescribed, performance shall be in accordance with the prevailing market price at the place of

performance at the time the contract was concluded, and if adoption of a price mandated by the government or based on government issued pricing guidelines is required by law, such requirement applies;

(iii) Where the place of performance was not clearly prescribed, if the obligation is payment of money, performance shall be at the place where the payee is located; if the obligation is delivery of immovable property, performance shall be at the place where the immovable property is located; for any other subject matter, performance shall be at the place where the obligor is located;

(iv) If the time of performance was not clearly prescribed, the obligor may perform, and the obligee may require performance, at any time, provided that the other party shall be given the time required for preparation;

(v) If the method of performance was not clearly prescribed, performance shall be rendered in a manner which is conducive to realizing the purpose of the contract;

(vi) If the party responsible for the expenses of performance was not clearly prescribed, the obligor shall bear the expenses.

4 Summary

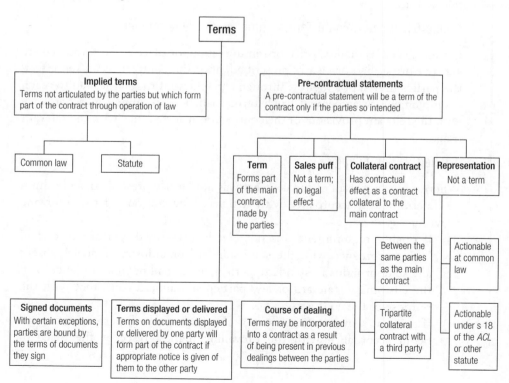

5 Questions

1. In January, David, a postgraduate business student, purchased a car-parking permit that allowed him to park his new BMW car in certain university car parks for the rest of the year. Although these permits were costly, providing car-parking spaces was a non-commercial activity for the university, one that it undertook only to provide an amenity for its students. In April, the university erected signs at the entrance to its car parks stating that cars were parked 'at the owner's risk' and that the university 'accepted no responsibility' in relation to them. David noticed that these signs had been erected but did not read them as, always in a rush to secure a front seat in the lectures he attended, he drove past them too quickly to do so. In June, while parked in a university car park, David's car was badly damaged by university employees carelessly carrying out maintenance work.

    David wishes to recover from the university the cost of repairing his car but is concerned that he may be precluded from doing so by the new signs. Please advise him about this matter.

    Were the university to seek your advice about the steps it should take to ensure that the signs were effective to protect its interests, what would your advice be?

2. Bob Pty Ltd (Bob) is a building company that has contracted to erect the frames for a large shopping centre. While carrying out some of the work required, one of its large cranes malfunctioned and it became necessary for the company to lease a replacement. Therefore, Bob's managing director, Michelle, contacted Easy Hire Ltd (Easy) to enquire whether it had a suitable replacement crane available. Michelle was assured by the manager of Easy that its 'High Lift' crane would meet Bob's load requirements and on this basis Michelle signed Easy's standard contract, leasing the crane for six months. Although she was given the opportunity to do so, Michelle did not read this document as she was in a rush to get the crane onto the building site and working.

    Unfortunately, while lifting certain material, the crane collapsed due to a faulty component that had recently been fitted to the crane by Crane Supplies Ltd (Supplies) during a regular service. This caused considerable damage to the building site for which Bob has been held responsible. Bob now wishes to know whether it can recover from Easy the amount it has been required to pay in damages to the owner of the building site. As part of your instructions, Bob has given you a copy of its contract with Easy, signed by Michelle, and your attention has been drawn to a well-drafted exclusion clause in that contract purporting to exempt Easy from any liability whatsoever should the crane malfunction. You are informed that a similar clause is also displayed on a number of signs in the office where Easy's leasing contracts are executed and inside the cabin of the crane.

    Please advise Bob.

    Would your advice differ if (i) Bob had regularly leased machinery from Easy during the previous 12 months; or (ii) due to an oversight, Michelle had not signed Easy's standard contract; or (iii) Michelle had not received assurances about the crane's load capacity?

CHAPTER 10

Construction and Classification of Terms

1	Introduction	276
2	Rules of construction	276
	a The basic rule	276
	b The parol evidence rule	277
	c Exceptions to the parol evidence rule	279
	d Some aids to construction	284
3	Classification of terms	285
	a Nature of the term	285
	b Nature of the operation	286
	c Importance	286
4	Summary	294
5	Questions	294

1   Introduction

Once the terms of a contract have been ascertained, the next step in determining the contractual rights and obligations of the parties is to construe those terms in order to discover their meaning and their relative importance. This chapter deals with both of these issues. We begin by considering the rules of construction used by the courts to give meaning to the terms of a contract including what is known as 'the parol evidence rule'. This governs the degree to which material external to a written contractual document can be used to add to, vary or contradict the language used in that document. We then address the ways in which contractual terms are classified, the basis upon which this is done and why this is important.

2   Rules of construction

a   The basic rule

The basic rule of construction is that a contract is to be given the meaning intended by the parties. The role of the courts is to ascertain that intention and give effect to it. However, with few exceptions, intention is determined objectively; that is, by reference to the conclusions that would be drawn by a reasonable person from the words used by the parties having regard to the whole document and where appropriate, its commercial purpose.[1] As a result, evidence cannot be given of what the parties *actually* intended; instead, the focus is on their presumed intention. In the words of the High Court in *Toll (FGCT) Pty Ltd v Alphapharm Pty Ltd* (2004) 219 CLR 165 at 179:

> It is not the subjective beliefs or understandings of the parties about their rights and liabilities that govern their contractual relations. What matters is what each party by words and conduct would have led a reasonable person in the position of the other party to believe. References to the common intention of the parties to a contract are to be understood as referring to what a reasonable person would understand by the language in which the parties have expressed their agreement. The meaning of the terms of a contractual document is to be determined by what a reasonable person would have understood them to mean. That, normally, requires consideration not only of the text, but also of the surrounding circumstances known to the parties, and the purpose and object of the transaction.

b   The parol evidence rule

This rule operates where the parties have recorded their contract in writing and deals with the admissibility of extrinsic evidence (evidence of matters external to the document) to determine what the terms of the contract are and the meaning of those terms. In *Codelfa Construction Pty Ltd v State Rail Authority of New South Wales* Mason J summarised the purpose and operation of the rule as follows:

> The broad purpose of the parol evidence rule is to exclude extrinsic evidence (except as to surrounding circumstances), including direct statements of intention (except in cases of latent ambiguity) and antecedent negotiations, to subtract from, add to, vary or contradict the language of a written instrument .... Although the traditional expositions of the rule did not in terms deny resort to extrinsic evidence for the purpose of interpreting the written instrument, it has often been regarded as prohibiting the use of extrinsic evidence for this purpose. No doubt this was due to the theory which came to prevail in English legal thinking in the first half of this century that the words of a contract are ordinarily to be given their plain and ordinary meaning. Recourse to extrinsic evidence is then superfluous. At best it confirms what has been definitely established by other means; at worst it tends ineffectively to modify what has been so established.[2]

The following extract illustrates the operation of the rule and explains its rationale.

---

1   See *Regency Media Pty Ltd v AAV Australia Pty Ltd* [2009] NSWCA 199 at 47.
2   (1982) 149 CLR 337 at 347–348.

Gordon v Macgregor

(1909) 8 CLR 316, High Court of Australia

[The parties entered into a written agreement pursuant to which Gordon was to supply Macgregor with a quantity of logs. The document specified that the logs were to have an average girth of not less than 10 ft 6 and delivered at a rate of not less than a certain quantity every three months. Gordon did not deliver the logs and Macgregor claimed damages for breach of contract. In response, Gordon argued that the contract did not comply with the *Statute of Frauds* because it did not record two essential terms agreed upon by the parties, namely, that delivery was to commence three months after the date of the contract and that the minimum girth was to be of six feet. This argument was accepted at first instance and judgment given for Gordon. Macgregor successfully appealed to the Queensland Full Court; Gordon then appealed to the High Court.]

Isaacs J [at 323]: Now, as I say, we start here with the legal presumption—the *prima facie* presumption—that this is a binding record of the contract, and there is nothing to displace it. Once you arrive at that position, the rule that you cannot introduce parol evidence to vary it is distinct, and perhaps the most authoritative place where you find the principle enumerated is in *Inglis v John Buttery & Co* at p 577. Lord *Blackburn* in his speech there quotes with approval the observations of Lord *Giffard*. He says:

> 'Now, I think it is quite fixed—and no more wholesome or salutary rule relative to written contracts can be devised—that where parties agree to embody, and do actually embody, their contract in a formal written deed, then in determining what the contract really was and really meant, a Court must look to the formal deed and to that deed alone. That is only carrying out the will of the parties. The only meaning of adjusting a formal contract is, that the formal contract shall supersede all loose and preliminary negotiations—that there shall be no room for misunderstandings which may often arise, and which do constantly arise, in the course of long, and it may be desultory conversations, or in the course of correspondence or negotiations during which the parties are often widely at issue as to what they will insist on and what they will concede. The very purpose of a formal contract is to put an end to the disputes which would inevitably <324> arise if the matter were left upon verbal negotiations or upon mixed communings partly consisting of letters and partly of conversations. The written contract is that which is to be appealed to by both parties, however different it may be from their previous demands or stipulations, whether contained in letters or in verbal conversation. There can be no doubt that this is the general rule, and I think the general rule, strictly and with peculiar appropriateness, applies to the present case.'

Once that position is established the defendant, in order to escape from the effect of the document, would have to show that it was not intended to be the record of the contract—he would have to show some reason for defeating the plaintiff, either by showing fraud, or by showing that by mistake the contract was not properly recorded, but neither of those things has been attempted to be shown here. Therefore, looking at the matter as part of the preliminary negotiations, no case whatever has been made, in my opinion, even if there were evidence as to what the negotiations were, to vary the effect of the written document.

[Griffith CJ, with whom O'Connor J agreed, gave a separate judgment to the same effect.]

Appeal dismissed

c Exceptions to the parol evidence rule

As the above extract makes clear, the rule operates only when the parties intended the document to embody entirely the agreement they have made. Thus, according to McHugh JA in *State Rail Authority of New South Wales v Health Outdoor Pty Ltd*:

> It has no operation until it is first determined that the terms of the agreement are wholly contained in writing. The tendering of oral evidence to prove a contractual term, therefore, cannot be excluded until it is determined that any terms in writing record the whole of the parties' agreement ... .[3]

As a result it has been described as no more than a circular statement to the effect that

> when it is proved or admitted that the parties to a contract intend that all the express terms of the agreements should be recorded in a particular document or documents, evidence will be inadmissible (because it is irrelevant) if it is tendered for the purpose of adding to, varying, subtracting from or contradicting the express terms of that contract'.[4]

For this reason, it has been doubted that it should be accorded the status of being a 'rule' at all.[5]

In addition to being inapplicable where the parties did not intend the document to be a complete record of their agreement, the parol evidence rule will not operate in the following situations:

- **Where the evidence goes to the validity of the contract**—extrinsic evidence can be given to establish that, despite appearances, there is no binding contract between the parties. For example, the parties contracted under the influence of mistake or misleading conduct, or had no intention to be contractually bound, or that the contract was to be conditional upon an event that has not materialised.
- **Where the evidence shows the true nature of the agreement**—extrinsic evidence may be given to show that a named party was really contracting as an

---

3   (1986) 7 NSWLR 170 at 191.
4   The Law Commission: The Parol Evidence Rule Cmnd 9700, Law Com No 154, 1986, para 2.7.
5   Ibid.

agent for another person,[6] or what the real consideration was, or to justify the rectification of the document so that it accords with what the parties actually agreed.
- **Where the evidence establishes a collateral contract**—the existence of a written document embodying a contract between the parties does not preclude extrinsic evidence being given to establish that there was also a collateral contract between them. Technically, the written contract is not altered in any way; rather, the collateral contract merely adds to the totality of the contractual relationship between the parties.
- **Where the evidence is of surrounding circumstances**—when determining, objectively, the intention of the parties, the courts can look beyond the actual words used in the contract. At one time, the approach taken by the courts was to 'construe the document according to the ordinary grammatical meaning of the words used therein, and without reference to anything which has previously passed between the parties to it'.[7] More recently, however, the courts have been willing to also look at the 'matrix of facts'[8] surrounding the contract, rather than just focusing on its grammatical construction. Unfortunately, the circumstances in which they will do this remains a matter of debate as the following extracts indicate. In *Codelfa*, the High Court took a relatively conservative position, suggesting that evidence of surrounding circumstances should only be given when there is ambiguity in the words used by the parties. On the other hand, the House of Lords in the more recent *West Bromwich* case argued that reference can be made to such circumstances in all instances. More recently still, the High Court in *Royal Botanic Gardens* declined to resolve the issue for Australia, saying that until it did so Australian courts should follow *Codelfa*. While it is thought likely that the more liberal *West Bromwich* view will eventually prevail, as it should, until the High Court so decides uncertainty about the matter will remain.[9]

Codelfa Construction Pty Ltd v State Rail Authority of New South Wales

(1982) 149 CLR 337, High Court of Australia

[The facts of this case are set out at p 265, above.]

Mason J [at 352]: The true rule is that evidence of surrounding circumstances is admissible to assist in the interpretation of the contract if the language is ambiguous or susceptible of more than one meaning. But it is not admissible to

---

6   See *Giliberto v Kenny* (1983) 48 ALR 620.
7   *Lovell and Christmas Ltd v Wall* [1911] 104 LT 85, per Cozens-Hardy MR at 88.
8   See *Prenn v Simmonds* [1971] 1 WLR 1381 at 1383, per Lord Wilberforce.
9   For a critique of *Codelfa* and the other cases mentioned, see J Carter and A Stewart, 'Interpretation, Good Faith and the "True Meaning" of Contracts: The Royal Botanic Decision' (2002) 18 *Journal of Contract Law* 182.

contradict the language of the contract when it has a plain meaning. Generally speaking facts existing when the contract was made will not be receivable as part of the surrounding circumstances as an aid to construction, unless they were known to both parties, although, ... if the facts are notorious knowledge of them will be presumed.

It is here that a difficulty arises with respect to the evidence of prior negotiations. Obviously the prior negotiations will tend to establish objective background facts which were known to both parties and the subject matter of the contract. To the extent to which they have this tendency they are admissible. But in so far as they consist of statements and actions of the parties which are reflective of their actual intentions and expectations they are not receivable. The point is that such statements and actions reveal the terms of the contract which the parties intended or hoped to make. They are superseded by, and merged in, the contract itself. The object of the parol evidence rule is to exclude them, the prior oral agreement of the parties being inadmissible in aid of construction, though admissible in an action for rectification.

Consequently when the issue is which of two or more possible meanings is to be given to a contractual provision we look, not to the actual intentions, aspirations or expectations of the parties before or at the time of the contract, except in so far as they are expressed in the contract, but to the objective framework of facts within which the contract came into existence, and to the parties' presumed intention in this setting. We do not take into account the actual intentions of the parties and for the very good reason that an investigation of those matters would not only be time consuming but it would also be unrewarding as it would tend to give too much weight to these factors at the expense of the actual language of the written contract.

There may perhaps be one situation in which evidence of the actual intention of the parties should be allowed to prevail over their presumed intention. If it transpires that the parties have refused to include in the contract a provision which would give effect to the presumed intention of persons in their position it may be proper to receive evidence of that refusal. After all, the court is interpreting <353> the contract which the parties have made and in that exercise the court takes into account what reasonable men in that situation would have intended to convey by the words chosen. But is it right to carry that exercise to the point of placing on the words of the contract a meaning which the parties have united in rejecting? It is possible that evidence of mutual intention, if amounting to concurrence, is receivable so as to negative an inference sought to be drawn from surrounding circumstances. ...

The importance of this evolution of the law as it affects the construction of contracts is that it centres upon the presumed, rather than the actual, intention of the parties.

[Stephen and Wilson JJ agreed with Mason J on this issue as did Brennan J, (although dissenting on the outcome of the case). Aickin J did not discuss the matter.]

[footnotes omitted]

Investors Compensation Scheme Ltd v West Bromwich Building Society

[1998] 1 WLR 896, House of Lords

[These proceedings concerned a compensation scheme established under the *Financial Services Act 1986* (UK). At issue was the meaning to be given to provisions in a claims form used as part of the scheme. In the course of his speech, Lord Hoffmann summarised the principles to be applied.]

Lord Hoffmann [at 912]: I do not think that the fundamental change which has overtaken this branch of the law, particularly as a result of the speeches of Lord Wilberforce in *Prenn v Simmonds* [1971] 1 WLR 1381, 1384–1386 and *Reardon Smith Line Ltd v Yngvar Hansen-Tangen* [1976] 1 WLR 989, is always sufficiently appreciated. The result has been, subject to one important exception, to assimilate the way in which such documents are interpreted by judges to the common sense principles by which any serious utterance would be interpreted in ordinary life. Almost all the old intellectual baggage of 'legal' interpretation has been discarded. The principles may be summarised as follows:

(1) Interpretation is the ascertainment of the meaning which the document would convey to a reasonable person having all the background knowledge which would reasonably have been available to the parties in the situation in which they were at the time of the contract.

(2) The background was famously referred to by Lord Wilberforce as the 'matrix of fact,' but this phrase is, if anything, an understated description of what the background may include. Subject to the requirement that it should have been reasonably available to the parties and to the exception to be mentioned next, it includes absolutely anything which would have affected the way in which the language of the document would have been understood by a reasonable man.

(3) The law excludes from the admissible background the previous negotiations of the parties and their declarations of subjective intent. They are admissible only in an action for rectification. The law makes this distinction for reasons of practical policy and, in this respect only, legal interpretation differs from the way we would interpret utterances in ordinary life. The boundaries of this exception are in some respects unclear. But this is not the occasion on which to explore them.

(4) The meaning which a document (or any other utterance) would convey to a reasonable man is not the same thing as the meaning of its words. The meaning of words is a matter of dictionaries and grammars; the meaning of the document is what the parties using those words against the relevant background would reasonably have been understood to mean. The background may not merely enable the reasonable man to choose between the possible meanings of words which are ambiguous but even (as occasionally happens in ordinary life) to conclude that the parties must, for whatever reason, have used the wrong

words or syntax. (see *Mannai Investments Co Ltd v Eagle Star Life Assurance Co Ltd* [1997] 2 WLR 945.

(5) The 'rule' that words should be given their 'natural and ordinary meaning' reflects the common sense proposition that we do not easily accept that people have made linguistic mistakes, particularly in formal documents. On the other hand, if one would nevertheless conclude from the background that something must have gone wrong with the language, the law does not require judges to attribute to the parties an intention which they plainly could not have had. Lord Diplock made this point more vigorously when he said in *The Antaios Compania Neviera SA v Salen Rederierna AB* [1985] 1 AC 191, 201:

> ' ... if detailed semantic and syntactical analysis of words in a commercial contract is going to lead to a conclusion that flouts business commonsense, it must be made to yield to business commonsense.'

Royal Botanic Gardens and Domain Trust v South Sydney City Council

(2002) 186 ALR 289, High Court of Australia

[The trustees of land known as 'the Domain' leased it to the Council for 50 years. This lease included a provision (clause 4(b)(iv)) for the lessor to periodically increase the rent having regard 'to additional costs and expenses which [it] may incur' relating to the surface of the Domain in the vicinity of a parking station maintained by the lessee. At issue in these proceedings was whether this provision allowed the lessor to have regard to matters other than those additional costs and expenses. The lessee sought a declaration that it did not, but failed at first instance. However, it succeeded on appeal to the New South Wales Court of Appeal which concluded that clause 4(b)(iv) exhaustively listed the material to which the lessor could have regard; the lessor then appealed to the High Court.]

Gleeson CJ, Gaudron, McHugh, Gummow and Hayne JJ [292]: [10] In *Codelfa*, Mason J (with whose judgment Stephen J and Wilson J agreed) referred to authorities which indicated that, even in respect of agreements under <293> seal, it is appropriate to have regard to more than internal linguistic considerations and to consider the circumstances with reference to which the words in question were used and, from those circumstances, to discern the objective which the parties had in view. In particular, an appreciation of the commercial purpose of a contract:

> ... presupposes knowledge of the genesis of the transaction, the background, the context, the market in which the parties are operating.

Such statements exemplify the point made by Brennan J in his judgment in *Codelfa*:

> The meaning of a written contract may be illuminated by evidence of facts to which the writing refers, for the symbols of language convey meaning according to the circumstances in which they are used.

[11] In the Court of Appeal, Fitzgerald JA said that, when, consistently with *Codelfa*, the lease was read against the background of what he identified as the principal, potentially material, surrounding circumstances, para (iv) specified exhaustively the considerations material to the determination of rent by the lessor. The surrounding circumstances identified by his Honour were:

(a) the parties to the transaction were two public authorities;
(b) the primary purpose of the transaction was to provide a public facility, not a profit;
(c) the lessee was responsible for the substantial cost of construction of the facility;
(d) the facility was to be constructed under the lessor's land and would not interfere with the continued public enjoyment of that land for its primary object, recreation;
(e) the parties' concern was to protect the lessor from financial disadvantage from the transaction; and
(f) the only financial disadvantage to the lessor which the parties identified related to additional expense which it would or might incur immediately or in the future.

[12] That summary should be accepted. In order to show why this is so, it is convenient to return both to the legislative antecedents of the parties and to the dedication of the relevant portion of the Domain to public recreational purposes. … <294–299> …

[After considering various authorities, antecedent materials and circumstances relating to the dealings between parties before entering into the lease and other provisions in that document their Honours concluded that the clause did specify exhaustively the matters that the lessor could take into account when setting the rent. They then continued at 301]:

[39] [R]eference was made in argument to several decisions of the House of Lords, delivered since *Codelfa* but without reference to it. Particular reference was made to passages in the speeches of Lord Hoffmann in *Investors Compensation Scheme Ltd v West Bromwich Building Society* and of Lord Bingham of Cornhill and Lord Hoffmann in *Bank of Credit and Commerce International SA v Ali*, in which the principles of contractual construction are discussed. It is unnecessary to determine whether their Lordships there took a broader view of the admissible 'background' than was taken in *Codelfa* or, if so, whether those views should be preferred to those of this court. Until that determination is made by this court, other Australian courts, if they discern any inconsistency with *Codelfa*, should continue to follow *Codelfa*.

Appeal dismissed

[footnotes omitted]

d Some aids to construction

The following is a non-exhaustive list of some of the aids the courts use when called upon to interpret a contract:

- **Words are given their ordinary meaning.** As the parties are assumed to have meant the words they have used to bear their ordinary meaning, that meaning will be adopted unless the circumstances show that their intention was otherwise. Dictionaries, therefore, are useful aids. Examples of circumstances in which a court may deviate from normal meaning include where the word has a special meaning when used in connection with the subject matter of the contract, where the word is a technical legal word or is defined in a special way in a definition section in the contract, and where the word has a customary meaning in the locality where the contract was made.
- **Words are interpreted to promote validity.** Where a word is ambiguous and one meaning would invalidate the contract, but not the other, then the latter will be preferred.[10]
- **Words are not read in isolation.** Individual words should always be read in the context of, not in isolation from, the rest of the document in which they appear. This may show that the ordinary meaning is not to be adopted.[11]
- **Words are construed** *contra proferentem*. According to this rule, in cases of ambiguity, a document should be construed against the person responsible for its drafting. Although of general application, this rule is especially relevant to the construction of exclusion clauses.[12]

3 Classification of terms

Terms may be classified in a number of ways and for different purposes. One important classification, between express and implied terms, was considered in the previous chapter. Some others, including the most important classifications—conditions, warranties and intermediate terms—are considered in this section.

a Nature of the term

Terms may be classified according to their inherent nature: whether they are promissory or merely adjectival. This classification is important because only the former can lead to a breach of contract and a claim for damages. Promissory terms are those that express the promises made by the parties. They are the main terms of the contract, reflecting the reasons why it was made. In some cases, a contract will consist entirely of promissory terms. Adjectival terms, on the other hand, merely regulate aspects of the contract; they do not constitute promises made by either party. A choice of law clause, indicating the law of which jurisdiction is to govern the contract, is an example. Typically, adjectival terms appear when a professionally prepared document is used to record the agreement and an attempt is made to cover all contingencies.

---

10 See *H & E Van Der Sterren v Cibernetics (Holdings) Pty Ltd* (1970) 44 ALJR 157, esp at 158.
11 See, for example, *L Schuler AG v Wickman Machine Tool Sales Ltd* [1974] AC 235.
12 See *Darlington Futures Ltd v Delco Australia Pty Ltd* (1986) 161 CLR 500, esp at 510.

b Nature of the operation

Terms may be classified according to the nature of their operation: whether they operate as conditions precedent or conditions subsequent. This classification is important because it can determine whether the parties are contractually bound to each other at all, or if they are, on what terms and at what times. In the present context, a condition precedent is a term that regulates the commencement of the contract or its obligations. For example, it may provide that unless and until certain events occur, the contract is not to be binding at all, or that certain obligations are to be suspended. A subject to contract clause, discussed above in our treatment of agreement, is of this nature. A condition subsequent, on the other hand, is a term providing for the contract, or parts thereof, to be brought to an end in specified circumstances. Unless and until those circumstances operate, the parties are bound. Subject to finance clauses in contracts for the sale of land are sometimes of this nature. As a result, the parties are bound by the contract as soon as it is entered into but their obligations will cease should finance not be obtained within the time nominated; if finance is obtained, on the other hand, the contract will continue to be binding.

c Importance

Terms may be classified according to their importance: whether they are conditions, warranties or intermediate terms. This is the most important classification because with most contracts it will determine what remedies are available to the innocent party in the event of the other party breaching a particular term. Briefly, if the term is a condition the innocent party will have the option of rescinding the contract and claiming damages, or affirming the contract and merely claiming damages. If the term is a warranty, the innocent party is not able to rescind the contract and can only claim damages for breach. If the term is an intermediate one, whether or not the innocent party has the option of rescinding the contract will depend upon the seriousness of the consequences of the breach.

Conditions

The word 'condition' is used in a variety of ways in contract law including as a generic alternative to the word 'term'. In the present context, however, it refers only to those terms that are fundamentally important to the contract. It is because a condition is of this nature that any breach will present the innocent party with the opportunity to rescind the contract, rather than merely claiming damages. Whether a term is a condition, or not depends upon:

- **Whether the term is made a condition by statute.** The United Kingdom *Sale of Goods Act 1893* used the word 'condition', in relation to certain terms it implied into contracts for the sale of goods, to signify that any breach of the terms would allow the innocent party to rescind the contract. This use has been adopted in each Australian state and territory in their corresponding sale of goods legislation.[13]

- **Whether the courts have characterised the term as a condition.** Where the courts have decided that certain terms are by their nature so important that they are to be considered conditions they will be so regarded, unless the parties clearly provide otherwise.
- **Whether the parties have made the term a condition.** It is common for the parties to describe certain terms as conditions where they wish to indicate that they are particularly important. However, the use of this word will not be conclusive if other aspects of the contract indicate that this was not the parties' intention.
- **Whether it is fundamental to the contract.** A term will be a condition if, as a matter of construction, it is apparent that the term is fundamental to the contract.

The approaches taken by the courts to determine whether a term is a condition or not is discussed in *Associated Newspaper v Bancks* and *Cehave v Bremer* extracted below.

Associated Newspapers Ltd v Bancks

(1951) 83 CLR 322, High Court of Australia

[The parties had a contract which provided that Bancks, an artist, would prepare weekly comic drawings for one of Associated's newspapers and that these drawings would appear on the front page of the paper's comic section. These terms were complied with for almost two years; then, owing to a shortage of newsprint, the drawings were published on the third page. Following protests by Bancks, he gave notice that he was rescinding the contract. In response, Associated sought an injunction restraining this threatened breach of contract. At issue in these proceedings was whether the term relating to where the drawings would be published was a condition of the contract, or not. At first instance it was held that Bancks was entitled to rescind the contract; Associated then appealed to the High Court.]

Dixon CJ, Williams, Webb, Fullagar and Kitto JJ [at 336]: The first question is whether the company's undertaking to present the defendant's drawings on the front page of the comic is a condition or essential term of the contract going to its very root, the breach of which would immediately entitle the defendant at his option to rescind the contract and sue for damages for the loss of the contract, or a mere warranty or non-essential and subsidiary term the breach of which would entitle the defendant to damages. Various tests have been advanced by the courts

---

13 See, *Sale of Goods Act 1954* (ACT) ss 17–19; *Sale of Goods Act 1923* (NSW) ss 17–19; *Sale of Goods Act 1972* (NT) ss 17–19; *Sale of Goods Act 1896* (Qld) ss 15–17; *Sale of Goods Act 1895* (SA) ss 12–14; *Sale of Goods Act 1896* (Tas) ss 17–19; *Goods Act 1958* (Vic) ss 17–19; *Sale of Goods Act 1895* (WA) ss 12–14.

from time to time to determine what is a condition as opposed to a warranty. In *Bettini v Gye*, at p 186 *Blackburn* J (as he then was) said that to determine this question the court must ascertain the intention of the parties to be collected from the instrument and the circumstances legally admissible with reference to which it is to be construed. Later in the same case his Lordship said that in the absence of any express declaration by the parties, as in the present case, 'we think that we are to look at the whole contract and applying the rule stated by *Parke* B to be acknowledged in *Graves v Legg*, see whether the particular stipulation goes to the root of the matter, so that a failure to perform it would render the performance of the rest of the contract by the plaintiff a thing different in substance from what the defendant has stipulated for; or whether it merely partially affects it and may be compensated for in damages'. In *Bentsen v Taylor, Sons & Co (No 2)*, at pp 280, 281 *Bowen* LJ, discussing the distinction between a condition and a warranty, points out that in order to decide this question one of the first things you would look to is, to what extent the truth of what is promised would be likely to affect the substance and foundation of the adventure which the contract is intended to carry out. Perhaps the test is better formulated by *CB Morison* in his *Principles of Rescission of Contracts* (1916), at p 86. 'You look at the stipulation broken from the point of view of its probable effect or importance as an inducement to enter into the contract.' ... <337> .... The test was succinctly stated by *Jordan* CJ in *Tramways Advertising Pty Ltd v Luna Park (NSW) Ltd*. The decision was reversed on appeal, but his Honour's statement of the law is not affected. He said: 'The test of essentiality is whether it appears from the general nature of the contract considered as a whole, or from some particular term or terms, that the promise is of such importance to the promisee that he would not have entered into the contract unless he had been assured of a strict or a substantial performance of the promise, as the case may be, and that this ought to have been apparent to the promisor: ... If the innocent party would not have entered into the contract unless assured of a strict and literal performance of the promise, he may in general treat himself as discharged upon any breach of the promise, however slight.'

At least it is clear that the obligation of the defendant to supply a weekly full-page drawing of 'Us Fellers' and the plaintiff's undertaking to present the drawing each week on the front page of the comic section are concurrent and correlative promises. And it would not seem open to doubt that the obligation of the defendant is a condition. He was not an ordinary employee of the plaintiff. He was employed as a comic artist and his true work was to produce this weekly drawing. It was for this production that his substantial weekly salary was principally payable. It was what he was really engaged to do. It would be strange if his obligation was a condition of the contract while the undertaking of the plaintiff was a subsidiary term the breach of which would only sound in damages. The undertaking is really a composite undertaking comprising three ingredients: (1) to present a full-page drawing; (2) to present it weekly; and (3) to present it on the front page of the comic section. It is impossible to attach different values to the defendant's obligation and the plaintiff's undertaking. The plaintiff would not have employed the defendant unless it had been assured that the defendant would perform his promise, and the <338> defendant would not have made the promise unless he was assured that his work would be published in a particular manner. Obviously it was of prime importance to the defendant that there should be continuity of publication so that his work should be kept continuously before the public, that his work should be published as a whole and not mutilated, and that it should be published on the most conspicuous page of the comic section.

[Their Honours concluded that Associated's undertaking to publish Banck's drawings on the front page of its comic section was a condition of their contract, breach of which entitled him to treat that contract as at an end.]

Appeal dismissed

[footnotes omitted]

Warranties

The word 'warranty' has a number of different meanings including, as we saw in the last chapter, a pre-contractual statement that has become a term of the contract as distinct from a mere representation. In the present context, however, it is used to refer to a term that is of secondary importance so that, unlike a condition, its breach will not entitle the innocent party to rescind the contract. This use was adopted in the United Kingdom *Sale of Goods Act 1893* in relation to the less important implied terms, a classification that has been adopted in Australia in similar legislation ever since.

Intermediate terms

An intermediate term is one that has not been, or could not be, classified as a condition or warranty when the contract was made. As a result, whether or not its breach will enable the innocent party to rescind the contract will depend upon the significance of the breach. Thus, unlike conditions and warranties, it is not possible to know in advance what remedies will be open to the innocent party should a breach occur. The modern origins of the concept of intermediate terms, the considerations that justify their existence and their reception in Australia are discussed in the following extracts. The leading authority discussed in them, *Hongkong Fir Shipping Co Ltd v Kawasaki Kisen Kaisha Ltd*, is extracted on p 591.

Cehave NV v Bremer Handelsgesellschaft mbH

[1976] 1 QB 44, English Court of Appeal

[Bremer sold goods to Cehave which were to be shipped 'in good condition'. A small part of the goods shipped were damaged and on this ground Cehave purported to rescind the contract and reject the goods. At first instance, it was held that the term 'in good condition' was a condition of the contract, breach of which entitled Cehave to act as it did. Bremer appealed to the Court of Appeal.]

Lord Denning MR [at 59]: [U]ntil the year 1893 there was much confusion in the use of the words 'condition' and 'warranty.' But that confusion was removed by the Act itself and by the judgment of Bowen LJ in *Bentsen v Taylor Sons & Co* [1893] 2 QB 274, 280. Thenceforward those words were used by lawyers as terms of art. The difference between them was this: if the promisor broke a *condition* in any respect, however slight, it gave the other party a right to be quit of his obligations and to sue for damages: unless he by his conduct waived the condition, in which case he was bound to perform his future obligations but could sue for the damage he had suffered. If the promisor broke a *warranty* in any respect, <60> however serious, the other party was not quit of his future obligations. He had to perform them. His only remedy was to sue for damages. ...

Now that division was not exhaustive. It left out of account the vast majority of stipulations which were neither 'conditions' nor 'warranties', strictly so called, but were intermediate stipulations, the effect of which depended on the breach. The cases about these stipulations were legion. ... I cannot believe that Parliament in 1893 intended to give the go-by to all these cases, or to say that they did not apply to the sale of goods. Those cases expressed the rules of the common law. They were preserved by s 61(2) of the 1893 Act, which said:

> 'The rules of the common law, including the law merchant, save in so far as they are inconsistent with the express provisions of this Act ... shall continue to apply to contracts for the sale of goods.'

There was nothing in the Act inconsistent with those cases. So they continued to apply.

In 1962 in *HongKong Fir Shipping Co Ltd v Kawasaki Kisen Kaisha Ltd* [1962] 2 QB 26, the Court of Appeal drew attention to this vast body of case law. They showed that, besides conditions and warranties, strictly so called, there are many stipulations of which the effect depends on this: if the breach goes to the root of the contract, the other party is entitled to treat himself as discharged; but if it does not go to the root, he is not. In my opinion, the principle embodies in these cases applies to contracts for the sale of goods just as to all other contracts.

The task of the court can be stated simply in the way in which Upjohn LJ stated it. First, see whether the stipulation, on its true construction, is a condition strictly so called, that is a stipulation such that, for any breach of it, the other party is entitled to treat himself as discharged. Second, if it is not such a condition, then look to the extent of the actual breach which has taken place. If it is such as to go to the root of the contract, the other party is entitled to treat himself as discharged; but, otherwise, not. ...

This brings me back to the particular stipulation in this case: 'shipped in good condition'. Was this a condition strictly so called, so that any breach of it entitled the buyer to reject the goods? Or was it an intermediate stipulation, so that the buyer cannot reject unless the breach is so serious as to go to the root of the contract?

<61> If there was any previous authority holding it to be a condition strictly so called, we should abide by it, just as we did with the clause 'expected ready to load'. ... But there is no such authority with the clause 'shipped in good condition'. I regard this clause as comparable to a clause as to quality, such as 'fair average quality'. If a small portion of the goods sold was a little below that standard, it would be met by commercial men by an allowance off the price. The buyer would have no right to reject the whole lot unless the divergence was serious and substantial. ... Likewise with the clause 'shipped in good condition', if a small portion of the whole cargo was not in good condition and arrived a little unsound, it should be met by a price allowance. The buyers should not have a right to reject the whole cargo unless it was serious and substantial.

In my opinion, therefore, the term 'shipped in good condition' was not a condition strictly so called; nor was it a warranty strictly so called. It was one of those intermediate stipulations which gives no right to reject unless the breach goes to the root of the contract.

[Lord Denning went on to conclude that Cehave was not entitled to reject the goods but could claim damages for breach of contract. In separate judgments, Roskill and Ormrod LJJ reached the same conclusion.]

Appeal allowed

[footnotes omitted]

Koompahtoo Local Aboriginal Land Council v Sanpine Pty Ltd

[2007] HCA 61, High Court of Australia

[Koompahtoo and Sanpine entered into a joint venture agreement to develop land vested in the former. This did not proceed satisfactorily and, on the ground that Sanpine was in breach of contract, the administrator appointed to manage Koompahtoo's affairs, on its behalf, terminated the agreement. In response, Sanpine commenced proceedings in the New South Wales Supreme Court, seeking a declaration that this termination was invalid. At first instance, this action was dismissed. However, Sanpine successfully appealed to the Court of Appeal, whereupon Koompahtoo appealed to the High Court. At issue was whether Sanpine's breaches of contract gave Koompahtoo the right to terminate the contract.]

Gleeson CJ, Gummow, Heydon and Crennan JJ [at 47]: For present purposes, there are two relevant circumstances in which a breach of contract by one party may entitle the other to terminate. The first is where the obligation with which there has been failure to comply has been agreed by the contracting parties to be essential. Such an obligation is sometimes described as a condition. ...

[49] The second relevant circumstance is where there has been a sufficiently serious breach of a non-essential term. In *Hongkong Fir Shipping Co Ltd v Kawasaki Kisen Kaisha Ltd*, the English Court of Appeal was concerned with a stipulation as to seaworthiness in a charterparty. Breaches of such a stipulation could vary widely in importance. They could be trivial or serious. The Court of Appeal held that to the accepted distinction between 'conditions' and 'warranties', that is, between stipulations that were in their nature essential and others, there must be added a distinction, operative within the class of non-essential obligations, between breaches that are significantly serious to justify termination and other breaches. This was a recognition that, although as a matter of construction of a contract it may not be the case that *any* breach of a given term will entitle the other party to terminate, some breaches of such a term may do so. Diplock LJ said that the question whether a breach by one party relieves the other of further performance of his obligations cannot always be answered by treating a contractual undertaking as either a 'condition' or a 'warranty'. Of some stipulations 'all that can be predicated is that some breaches will and others will not give rise to an event which will deprive the party not in default of substantially the whole benefit which it was intended that he should obtain from the contract; and the legal consequences of a breach of such an undertaking, unless provided for expressly in the contract, depend upon the nature of the event to which the breach gives rise'.

[50] In this way Diplock LJ set the policy of the law favouring certainty of outcome through the classification of terms as conditions against that which encourages contractual performance and favours restriction of the right to terminate to cases where breach occasions serious prejudice. As it is put in the eleventh edition of Treitel:

> [T]he policy of leaning in favour of classifying stipulations as intermediate terms can be said to promote the interests of justice by preventing the injured party from rescinding on grounds that are technical or unmeritorious.

Perhaps the adoption of other taxonomies for contractual stipulations might achieve similar outcomes. However, *Hongkong Fir* was decided in 1961 and has long since passed into the mainstream law of contract as understood and practised in Australia.

[51] It may be true that this Court has yet to accept *Hongkong Fir* as an essential element in the grounds for decision in any particular case. However, in *Ankar Pty Ltd v National Westminster Finance (Australia) Ltd*, Mason ACJ, Wilson, Brennan and Dawson JJ referred to *Hongkong Fir* with evident approval and said that the concept of the intermediate and innominate term brings a greater flexibility to the law of contract. With that in mind, it was entirely appropriate for Campbell J to proceed with an analysis of the facts in which *Hongkong Fir* was applied.

[52] The practical utility of a classification which includes intermediate terms, and the consequent greater flexibility of which the Court spoke in *Ankar*, appears

from several consequences. First, the interests of justice are promoted by limiting rights to rescind to instances of serious and substantial breaches of contract. Secondly, a just outcome is facilitated in cases where the breach is of a term which is inessential.

[53] As will appear later in these reasons, we rest our decision in the appeal not upon the ground of breach of an essential obligation, but upon application of the doctrine respecting intermediate terms.

[54] We add that recognition that, at the time a contract is entered into, it may not be possible to say that any breach of a particular term will entitle the other party to terminate, but that some breaches of the term may be serious enough to have that consequence, was taken up in *Ankar*. Breaches of this kind are sometimes described as 'going to the root of the contract', a conclusory description that takes account of the nature of the contract and the relationship it creates, the nature of the term, the kind and degree of the breach, and the consequences of the breach for the other party. Since the corollary of a conclusion that there is no right of termination is likely to be that the party not in default is left to rely upon a right to damages, the adequacy of damages as a remedy may be a material factor in deciding whether the breach goes to the root of the contract.

[55] A judgment that a breach of a term goes to the root of a contract, being, to use the language of Buckley LJ in *Decro-Wall International SA v Practitioners in Marketing Ltd*, 'such as to deprive the injured party of a substantial part of the benefit to which he is entitled under the contract', rests primarily upon a construction of the contract. Buckley LJ attached importance to the consequences of the breach and the fairness of holding an injured party to the contract and leaving him to his remedy in damages. These, however, are matters to be considered after construing the agreement the parties have made. A judgment as to the seriousness of the breach, and the adequacy of damages as a remedy, is made after considering the benefit to which the injured party is entitled under the contract.

[56] A question as to contractual intention, considered in the light of the language of the contract, the circumstances in which the parties have contracted and their common contemplation as to future performance, is different from a question as to the intention evinced by one of the parties at the time of breach, such as arises in cases of alleged renunciation. That difference is exemplified by the way in which the majority in the Court of Appeal dealt with the decision of the primary judge in this case.

[Their Honours concluded that Sanpine's breaches of contract deprived Koompahtoo 'of a substantial part of the benefit for which it contracted' and justified its termination of the contract. Kirby J reached the same conclusion but disagreed with the approach of the majority to the classification of terms.]

Appeal allowed

[footnotes omitted]

4 Summary

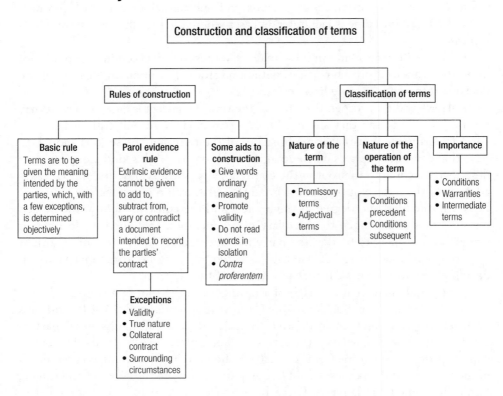

5 Questions

Brisbane Development Pty Ltd (Brisbane) a building and land development company, entered into a contract with Rhonda to sell her a house-and-land package for a total price of $250,000. This contract provided that the house was to be built in accordance with detailed plans that Rhonda had seen and approved. The contract also specified that the purchase price was to be paid by instalments, including a final payment of $150,000 to be made on the completion of the house. It was a condition of the contract that the house be constructed using bricks manufactured by the Besser Brick Company. The contract also provided that the walls of the kitchen would be painted white; it also specified a colour for each of the house's other ten rooms.

After the contract document recording this agreement was signed by Brisbane and Rhonda, Rhonda told Brisbane's representative that she wished to have the roof of the house constructed using colour-bond sheeting, rather than tiles. Brisbane's representative replied that, as this was no more expensive, he would ensure that colour-bond sheeting was used.

The house has now been completed and Brisbane is ready to transfer the house and the land to Rhonda in exchange for her final payment of $150,000. However, Rhonda does not wish to proceed with the transaction and wishes to recover from Brisbane the instalments (totalling $100,000) she has already paid to the company.

Please advise Rhonda of her position in the following scenarios:

1. The house was not constructed using bricks manufactured by the Besser Brick Company. Instead, Brisbane used better-quality bricks manufactured by another company.

2. The kitchen was painted light grey, rather than white.

3. Each of the other ten rooms in the house was painted in the wrong colour and it would cost $5,000 to repaint them in the correct colour.

4. The roof was constructed using tiles, rather than colour-bond sheeting.

Should you require further information before advising Rhonda, please say what this is and why it is required.

CHAPTER 11

Exclusion Clauses

1	Introduction	296
2	The nature and operation of exclusion clauses	297
	a Types of exclusion clauses	297
	b The importance of exclusion clauses	298
	c The use of exclusion clauses	298
	d Preconditions to effectiveness	299
3	The construction of exclusion clauses	300
	a The general approach to construction	301
	b Aids to construction	303
4	Legislative control	310
5	Summary	313
6	Questions	313

1 Introduction

Exclusion clauses[1] are clauses that are used to protect, in one way or another, a person from what otherwise would be their liability. In this chapter we identify the different types of exclusion clauses that are in common use and consider their importance, why they are used and what is required for them to be effective. We then examine approaches adopted by the courts to the construction of exclusion clauses and note some of the legislative restrictions that have been imposed on their use.

Although in this chapter we focus on contractual exclusion clauses and clauses that provide protection against liability for breach of contract, we also address the use of exclusion clauses in non-contractual situations and to protect against other forms of liability.

---

1   Exclusion clauses are sometimes called 'exemption clauses', 'exception clauses' or 'limitation clauses'.

2 The nature and operation of exclusion clauses

a Types of exclusion clauses

Over the years, lawyers have devised a number of different types of exclusion clauses to protect their clients and it is not uncommon for several types to be employed at once. Adopting this practice maximises the protection afforded to the client because, should one clause not succeed, another might still do so.[2] The principle types of clauses are as follows:

- **Clauses that seek to reduce, or eliminate altogether, the duty that would otherwise be owed to another person.** For example, a clause seeking to exclude from a contract of sale the implied terms relating to the quality of the goods sold that would otherwise form part of the contract. In his seminal work *Exception Clauses* (1964),[3] Coote refers to these as 'substantive' exclusion clauses because, by reducing a party's obligations, they prevent a breach of contract, or some other form of liability, from arising.
  Examples—clauses designed to preclude statutory implied terms[4]

  I acknowledge that [Deakin Computer Shop] DCS is not in a position to fully assess my needs and motivations and covenant that the computer system or any part thereof is not being acquired for any particular purpose made known to DCS.

  Except as expressly stated in any warranty by the manufacturer and as provided for in legislation referred to above, all other warranties, conditions and liability implied by statute and by rule of law are hereby expressly excluded and negated.[5]

- **Clauses that provide a guilty party with a defence.** In effect, such clauses seek to shield that party from liability for the wrong they have committed. Coote[6] refers to these as 'procedural' exclusion clauses.
  Example—clauses designed to exclude liability for breach of contract or in tort

  DCS shall not be liable in any event and whether caused by the negligence of DCS or otherwise for any damages resulting from loss of data, programs, profits, use of products or for any incidental or consequential damage, even if advised of the possibility of such damage. This limitation applies regardless of the form of action, whether in contract or tort.[7]

---

2 For an example of this approach succeeding, see *Darlington Futures Ltd v Delco Australia Pty Ltd* (1986) 161 CLR 500.
3 B Coote, *Exception Clauses*, Sweet and Maxwell, London, 1964.
4 This is only possible in the case of non-consumer transactions; in the case of consumer transactions covered by Part 3-2 of the *Australian Consumer Law*, s 64 of the *ACL* makes void any contractual term designed to 'exclude, restrict or modify' a guarantee created by that Part; see also, p 310 below.
5 This example is taken from the Deakin Computer Shop, 'Conditions: Computer purchases for staff and students', Deakin University, Geelong, Vic.
6 Coote, *Exception Clauses*, above n 3.
7 This example is taken from the Deakin Computer Shop, 'Conditions: Computer purchases for staff and students', Deakin University, Geelong, Vic.

- **Clauses that seek to protect the guilty party by imposing restrictions on a claimant's ability to bring an action against them.** Such a restriction may take the form of a time limit within which a claim must be brought,[8] or a limit on the amount of damages that can be recovered in the event that a claim is successful.

  Example—clauses designed to limit the amount of damages recoverable

  > Any liability on the agent's part ... shall not in any event (whether or not such liability results from or involves negligence) exceed one hundred dollars.[9]

- **Clauses that require a successful claimant to indemnify the guilty party.** In effect, this requires the successful claimant to repay any damages they may recover from the guilty party. As such, these clauses are designed to discourage the claimant from taking proceedings in the first place.

b The importance of exclusion clauses

Exclusion clauses are used widely and are incorporated, to the extent the law allows, in most standard form contracts. This is especially true of those contracts involving consumers who, typically, lack the bargaining power to exclude them. For this reason, when seeking to assess the rights and obligations of the parties, it is always important to look not only at the substantive terms of the contract but also for any exclusion clauses it may contain. Only by reading the two sets of terms together can an accurate assessment be made of the relative position of the parties.

c The use of exclusion clauses

In consumer transactions, exclusion clauses are typically used to reduce the supplier's liability to the consumer and are proffered on a take it or leave it basis. For this reason, the courts have traditionally construed such clauses strictly against the supplier. As a result, although the development of special doctrines designed to limit the effectiveness of exclusion clauses has been rejected,[10] a rigorous application of the ordinary rules of construction has generally enabled the courts to prevent them from being used unconscionably. This has been reinforced by statutory provisions, considered below, preventing exclusion clauses from being used to defeat the interests of consumers.

On the other hand, where an exclusion clause has been incorporated into a commercial contract between firms of comparable bargaining power, the courts have adopted a more sympathetic attitude. It has been recognised that in such

---

8   An example of a time limitation clause is Article III (6) of the *Hague Rules*, which discharges a carrier from all liability for loss or damage unless suit is brought within one year after delivery, relied upon in *New Zealand Shipping Co Ltd v AM Satterthwaite & Co Ltd* [1975] AC 154.

9   See *Darlington Futures Ltd v Delco Australia Pty Ltd* (1986) 161 CLR 500 at 505–506.

10 See *Photo Production Ltd v Securicor Ltd* [1980] AC 827 in which the House of Lords rejected the 'doctrine of fundamental breach'. According to this doctrine, an exclusion clause could not provide protection against liability for a 'fundamental breach', regardless of how widely it was drafted. This doctrine was never accepted by the High Court: see *Sydney City Council v West* (1965) 114 CLR 481.

cases, the clause may represent a deliberate attempt by the parties to allocate between themselves the risks and costs associated with the transaction and for this reason, should be given full effect. The following quotations are two of the more significant expressions of this approach.

New Zealand Shipping Co Ltd v AM Satterthwaite & Co Ltd [1975] AC 154

Lord Wilberforce at 169: 'In the opinion of their Lordships, to give the stevedore the benefit of the exemptions and limitations contained in the bill of lading is to give effect to the clear intentions of a commercial document, and can be given within existing principles. They see no reason to strain the law or the facts in order to defeat these intentions. It should not be overlooked that the effect of denying validity to the clause would be to encourage actions against servants, agents and independent contractors in order to get round exemptions (which are almost invariable and often compulsory) accepted by shippers against carriers, the existence, and presumed efficacy, of which is reflected in the rates of freight. They see no attraction in this consequence.'

Photo Production Ltd v Securicor Ltd [1980] AC 827

Lord Diplock at 851: 'In commercial contracts negotiated between business-men capable of looking after their own interests and of deciding how risks inherent in the performance of various kinds of contract can be most economically borne (generally by insurance), it is, in my view, wrong to place a strained construction upon words in an exclusion clause which are clear and fairly susceptible of one meaning only even after due allowance has been made for the presumption in favour of the implied primary and secondary obligations.'

d   Preconditions to effectiveness

As a general rule, an exclusion clause will protect a party only if:

- the clause was incorporated into a contract between that party and the claimant—what is required to achieve this was considered in chapter 9[11]
- the exclusion clause is, as a matter of construction, wide enough to cover the breach of contract, or other wrong, relied upon by the complainant—this issue is discussed below.

An important qualification to the first of these requirements is that a person can avoid non-contractual liability, such as liability in tort for negligence, where they are able to rely upon an exclusion clause to set up a defence of *volenti non fit injuria*—a defence that the claimant consented to the risk of injury. In such a case,

---

11   The circumstances in which a person can rely upon an exclusion clause that is contained in a contract to which they were not a party is considered in chapter 8.

it is not necessary for there to be a contract between the parties containing the exclusion clause because the clause is not operating contractually, but via the law of torts. *Birch v Thomas* is an example of an exclusion clause being effective in this manner.[12] Here, the driver of a motor car was held to be protected from liability to a passenger by a sticker he had placed on the passenger car window excluding liability in the event of an accident. In a similar fashion, the occupiers of land can reduce their liability to entrants by erecting appropriately prominent and worded signs at the entrance to the land, warning of dangers that may be present and advising entrants that entry is at their own risk.

3   The construction of exclusion clauses

In contract cases, once it has been established that an exclusion clause forms part of the contract between the parties the only remaining issue concerning the clause is whether, as a matter of construction, it is wide enough to cover the event complained of: the breach of contract or other wrong complained of by the claimant. This is 'simply' a matter of construction and means that (leaving aside for the moment restrictions imposed by statute) protection can always be conferred by an exclusion clause if it is drafted skilfully and covers all the possible forms of liability that may be incurred by the party on whose behalf it is prepared. On the other hand, if it is not—if it employs imprecise concepts or language— it is likely to be treated unsympathetically by the courts, as the following extract illustrates.

Belna Pty Limited v Irwin

[2009] NSWCA 46, New South Wales Court of Appeal

[Irwin suffered personal injury while in a gym operated by the appellant under the name 'Fernwood'. At first instance, she recovered damages for breach of contract on the ground that Fernwood had breached an implied term of its contract with Irwin that it 'would exercise reasonable skill and care in its performance'. Fernwood appealed to the Court of Appeal, inter alia, on the ground that it was protected by the following clause:

> It is my expressed interest in signing this agreement, to release Fernwood Fitness Centre, its Directors, Franchises, Officers, Owners, Heirs and assigns from any and all claims for professional or general liability, which may arise as a result of my participation, whether fault may be attributed to myself or its employees. I understand that I am totally responsible for my own personal belongings whilst at the Centre. I also understand that each member or guest shall be liable for any property damage and/or personal injury while at the Centre.

---

12   [1972] 1 WLR 294.

Ipp JA (with whom McColl JA and Handley AJA agreed) [at 39]: There are several problems with the clause. It records an 'expressed interest', which is a concept of indeterminate meaning. At best for Fernwood, the clause provides for a release, which ordinarily has effect only after liability has been incurred. A release, ordinarily, is not an exclusion of liability for breaches of duty that may occur in the future. The phrase 'professional or general liability' may or may not encompass negligence or breach of contract. The phrase 'fault ... attributed to myself or its employees' is difficult to understand. The purpose and meaning of the last sentence of the clause casts further obscurity on its meaning as a whole.

Toner DCJ rightly said, 'The clause is not merely ambiguous, it is likely unintelligible'. His Honour held that cl 7 was so vague as to be meaningless and could not reasonably be construed as exempting Fernwood from liability as it contended. I agree.

Application for leave to appeal dismissed

a   The general approach to construction

The courts now approach the construction of exclusion clauses as they do other contractual terms; that is, by interpreting them as the parties intended, giving the words used their ordinary, grammatical meaning assisted, where appropriate, by reference to the context in which the contract was formed. The leading exposition of this approach is contained in the following extract.

Darlington Futures Ltd v Delco Australia Pty Ltd

(1986) 161 CLR 500, High Court of Australia

[Delco engaged Darlington to deal in commodity futures on its behalf as a means of minimising its tax liability using a device known as a 'tax straddle'. Darlington's authority to do this, however, was limited by the terms of their contract. Deliberately ignoring this limitation, Darlington dealt in commodities on Delco's behalf and incurred heavy losses. Delco commenced proceedings to recover those losses; it failed at first instance as the trial judge found that, although the transactions causing them were not authorised, Darlington was protected by an exclusion clause, clause 6 below. Delco appealed successfully to the South Australian Full Court; Darlington then appealed to the High Court. The relevant parts of the exclusion clauses Darlington relied upon are as follows:

> Clause 6: ... The Client [Delco] finally acknowledges that the Agent [Darlington] will not be responsible for any loss arising in any way out of any trading activity undertaken on behalf of the Client whether pursuant to this Agreement or not, ...
>
> Clause 7(c): Any liability on the Agent's part or on the part of its servants or agents for damages for or in respect of any claim arising out of or in connection with the

relationship established by this agreement or any conduct under it or any orders or instructions given to the Agent by the Client, other than any liability which is totally excluded by paragraphs (a) and (b) hereof, shall not in any event (and whether or not such liability results from or involves negligence) exceed one hundred dollars.]

Mason, Wilson, Brennan, Deane and Dawson JJ [at 510]: [T]he interpretation of an exclusion clause is to be determined by construing the clause according to its natural and ordinary meaning, read in the light of the contract as a whole, thereby giving due weight to the context in which the clause appears including the nature and object of the contract, and, where appropriate, construing the clause *contra proferentem* in case of ambiguity. Notwithstanding the comments of Lord Fraser in *Ailsa Craig*, the same principle applies to the construction of limitation clauses. As King CJ noted in his judgment in the Supreme Court, a limitation clause may be so severe in its operation as to make its effect virtually indistinguishable from that of an exclusion clause. And the principle, in the form in which we have expressed it, does no more than express the general approach to the interpretation of contracts and it is of sufficient generality to accommodate the different considerations that may arise in the interpretation of a wide variety of exclusion and <511> limitation clauses in formal commercial contracts between business people where no question of the reasonableness or fairness of the clause arises.

Turning now to cl 6 of the contract between the appellant and the respondent, the question is whether the relevant losses arose 'in any way out of any trading activity undertaken on behalf of the Client whether pursuant to this agreement or not'. Read in context these words plainly refer to trading activity undertaken by the appellant for the respondent with the respondent's authority, whether pursuant to the agreement or not. It can scarcely be supposed that the parties intended to exclude liability on the part of the appellant for losses arising from trading activity in which it presumed to engage on behalf of the respondent when the appellant had no authority so to do.

The final question is whether the appellant is protected by cl 7(c) of the contract. This provision limits the liability of the appellant to $100 in relation to claims of three kinds: (1) claims arising out of or in connexion with the relationship established by the agreement; (2) claims arising out of or in connexion with any conduct under the agreement; and (3) claims arising out of or in connexion with any orders or instructions given by the client to the broker. The Full Court of the Supreme Court considered that cl 7(c) by its terms had no application to claims arising out of conduct which is outside the scope of the agreement and the relationship between the parties established by it. This, in our opinion, is to place a more restrictive interpretation on the clause than its language will naturally bear. In particular, it is expressed to comprehend claims arising out of or *in connexion with* the relationship established by the agreement. A claim in respect of an unauthorized transaction may nonetheless have a connexion, indeed a substantial connexion, with the relationship of broker and client established by the agreement. We are unable to discern any basis on which cl 7(c) can be construed so as not to apply to such a claim. The present case is one in which the respondent's claim arises in connexion with the relationship of broker and client established by the contract between the parties, notwithstanding the finding that the relevant transactions were not authorized.

In the result cl 7(c) operates to limit the appellant's liability to $100 in respect of each of the unauthorized coffee and silver contracts.

Appeal allowed

b   Aids to construction

The aids to construction discussed in the previous chapter apply to exclusion clauses with the *contra proferentem* rule being especially relevant. However, the construction of exclusion clauses has also given rise to the framing of a number of distinct rules that are uniquely relevant to them. Although expressed in different ways, essentially, each of these rules amounts to no more than determining whether an exclusion clause confers protection 'by construing the language that the parties used, read in its context and with any necessary implications based upon their presumed intention'.[13] However, they can be important guides to the objective determination of what the parties intended.

Contra proferentem

As we have seen, in cases of ambiguity this rule requires the ambiguity to be resolved against the author of the document, or the party seeking to rely upon it.[14] *Wallis, Son & Wells v Pratt & Haynes*[15] illustrates this rule very well. Here the defendants sold goods to the plaintiff in circumstances amounting to a breach of a condition implied by the *Sale of Goods Act 1893* (UK). In an action for breach of contract, the defendants sought to rely upon an exclusion clause which provided that the seller gave no 'warranty' as to the description of the goods. The House of Lords held that as the *Sale of Goods Act* drew a clear distinction between 'condition' and 'warranty' it could not be contended that when the clause said that the seller gave no 'warranty' it meant also that the seller would not be responsible for breach of a 'condition'. Consequently, the seller was not protected by the exclusion clause.

Insight Vacations Pty Ltd v Young

[2011] HCA 16, High Court of Australia

[Mrs Young purchased a European tour package from Insight Vacations. While travelling by coach from Prague to Budapest as part of this tour, she got out of her seat to get something from a bag in the overhead luggage shelf. As she did

---

13   *Thomas National Transport (Melbourne) Pty Ltd v May & Baker (Australia) Pty Ltd* (1966) 115 CLR 353 at 376, per Windeyer J.
14   For a recent example of the rule being used in relation to a party seeking to rely upon an exclusion clause, other than its author, see *Santos Coffee Company Pty Ltd v Direct Freight Express Pty Ltd* [2010] NSWCA 14 at paragraph 11.
15   [1911] AC 394.

so, the coach braked suddenly. As a result, she fell and suffered personal injuries. Upon returning to Australia, Mrs Young took proceedings against Insight Vacations alleging that it had breached the implied term, created by s 74(1) of the *TPA*, that its services would be provided with due care and skill. As a defence, the company sought to rely upon an exclusion clause that provided:

> 'Where the passenger occupies a motorcoach seat fitted with a safety belt, neither the Operators nor their agents or cooperating organisations will be liable for any injury, illness or death or for any damages or claims whatsoever from any accident, if the safety belt is not being worn at the time of such accident or incident.'

Mrs Young succeeded at first instance. An appeal by the company to the New South Wales Court of Appeal was dismissed, whereupon it appealed to the High Court.

French CJ, Gummow, Hayne, Kiefel and Bell JJ [at 38]: The text of the clause was set out earlier. It will be recalled that the first part of the clause read: 'Where the passenger *occupies* a motorcoach *seat* fitted with a safety belt' (emphasis added). That element of the clause should be given its ordinary meaning. It limits the times to which the clause applies to the times when the passenger occupies a seat. That is, it should be read as referring only to times when the passenger is seated, not to times when the passenger stands up to move around the coach or to retrieve some item from an overhead shelf or for some other reason. The contract of carriage did not require passengers to remain seated at all times while the coach was in motion. The provision of a lavatory at the rear of the coach shows that the operator accepted that a passenger could, and sometimes would, get out of his or her seat.

[39] If the introductory words of the exemption clause had omitted the word 'seat', it might have been possible to say that the exemption clause applied to any occasion when the passenger was aboard (or 'occupie[d]') a motorcoach fitted with seat belts, regardless of whether and why the passenger got out of the seat. But that is not how the clause was cast. The words 'occupies a motorcoach seat' should be understood as meaning sitting in the seat and able to wear the safety belt. Mrs Young was not sitting in her seat when she fell. The exemption clause did not apply.

Appeal dismissed

[footnotes omitted]

Main purpose rule

According to this rule, in cases of ambiguity, an exclusion clause will not be construed so as to conflict with the main purpose of the contract. The rule derives from the assumption that the parties would not have intended the clause to be construed so as to cover events the occurrence of which would defeat the purpose they sought to achieve by making the contract. *Glynn v Margetson & Co*[16] provides

---

16   [1893] AC 351.

an example. Here, Glynn, a ship-owner, agreed to carry a cargo of oranges from the port of Malaga to Liverpool pursuant to a contract containing a clause purporting to allow the vessel to proceed to any port or ports in the Mediterranean or other specified areas (a 'liberty clause'). After leaving Malaga, the vessel sailed in the opposite direction to Liverpool to a port 350 miles away and loaded another cargo. After it had done so it then proceeded to Liverpool. As a result of the length of this voyage the oranges were delivered in a damaged condition and the plaintiffs sued to recover their loss; in response, Glynn relied upon the liberty clause. The House of Lords rejected this defence on the grounds that the main purpose of the contract was to carry the oranges from Malaga to Liverpool and that this purpose would have been defeated were the clause interpreted so as to allow the ship-owner 'to proceed anywhere that he pleased'.[17] According to Lord Herschell LC, where general words are used it may be justifiable to read them down by reference to the main purpose of the contract.[18] However, this is a rule of construction only, and it may be clear that the parties intended an exclusion clause to be interpreted broadly and so cover events that defeat the main purpose of the contract.[19]

Negligence only rule

An exclusion clause can exclude liability for negligence. However, to do so it must use words that make clear that this was the intention of the parties and in the absence of an express reference to negligence, the courts will not readily draw this conclusion. *White v John Warrick & Co Ltd*[20] reflects this approach. Here, a clause in a contract hiring a tradesman's tricycle provided that 'Nothing in this agreement shall render the owners liable for any personal injuries to riders of the machines hired.' Despite the apparent breadth of this clause, in an action by the plaintiff seeking damages for personal injury suffered as a result of the defective condition of the tricycle it was held that the clause would not protect the defendant from liability for negligence. This was because the defendant could be liable in both contract and tort and in the absence of clear words covering negligence, the clause was to be construed as exempting the owners only from liability in contract, and not both. However, this does not mean that negligence must always be mentioned expressly; according to what is sometimes referred to as the 'negligence only rule', if the only ground upon which the defendant could be liable is negligence, it is (at least) more likely to be construed as covering such conduct.[21] According to Windeyer J in *Thomas National Transport (Melbourne) Pty Ltd v May & Baker (Australia) Pty Ltd* an exclusion clause 'is not to be construed as relieving [a defendant] against liability for negligence ... unless it expressly or by

---

17 Ibid at 354, per Lord Herschell LC.
18 Ibid.
19 *Nissho Iwai Australia Ltd v Malaysian International Shipping Corporation Berhad* (1989) 167 CLR 219.
20 [1953] 2 All ER 1021.
21 See *Rutter v Palmer* [1922] 2 KB 92.

implication covers such liability. It will by implication do so if there be no ground of liability other than negligence to which it could refer ... .'[22]

Four corners rule

According to this rule, an exclusion clause will confer protection only in respect of conduct that occurred in the performance of the contract. In other words, it will not protect a defendant while acting in a manner that is outside its 'four corners'. This rule is illustrated by the following extract.

The Council of the City of Sydney v West

(1965) 114 CLR 481, High Court of Australia

[West left his car at the Council's car park pursuant to a contract containing an exclusion clause which sought to protect the Council from the loss of, or damage to, parked vehicles. A thief tricked a parking attendant into issuing a duplicate ticket for the car and allowing him to remove it from the car park. The plaintiff sued the Council for damages and it responded by invoking the exclusion clause. This defence succeeded at first instance. However, West successfully appealed to the New South Wales Full Court; the Council then appealed to the High Court.]

Barwick CJ and Taylor J [at 488]: There is no doubt, of course, that in the case where a contract of bailment contains an exempting clause much as we have to consider the protection afforded by the clause will be lost if the goods the subject of the bailment are stored in a place or in a manner other than that authorized by the contract or if the bailee consumes or destroys them instead of storing them or if he sells them. But we would deny the application of such a clause in those circumstances simply upon the interpretation of the clause itself. Such a clause contemplates that loss or damage may occur by reason of negligence on the part of the warehouseman or his servants in carrying out the obligations created by the contract. But in our view it has no application to negligence in relation to acts done with respect to a bailor's goods which are neither authorized nor permitted by the contract. For instance, if, in the present case, one of the attendants at the parking station had been allowed by the management to use the respondent's car for his own purposes and, in the course of driving it, had caused damage to it by his negligent driving, the clause would afford no protection. Negligence in these circumstances would be right outside the purview of the clause. The same result would follow if an attendant had proceeded, without authority, to make adjustments or repairs to the respondent's vehicle while it was in the parking station and had carried out such work negligently and thereby caused damage. To our minds the clause clearly appears as one which contemplates that, in the performance of the Council's obligations under the contract of bailment, some loss or damage may be caused by reason of its servants' negligence but it does not contemplate or

---

22   (1966) 115 CLR 353 at 376.

provide an excuse for negligence on the part of <489> the Council's servants in doing something which it is neither authorized nor permitted to do by the terms of the contract. ...

It is, therefore, necessary to consider the question whether the loss, ... was a loss resulting merely from the failure on the part of the appellant to use reasonable care to keep the car safely whilst it was in its possession as a bailee or whether by some positive act the appellant can be said to have delivered possession of the car to 'Robinson'. If it did then, in our view, this constituted an unauthorized act performed by the appellant in relation to the respondent's car and he is entitled to recover. ... In order to drive out of the parking station 'Robinson' had to pass through a designated exit where an attendant was stationed and it was this official's function to permit vehicles to proceed only upon the surrender by the driver of an appropriate parking ticket. It was such a ticket which, as was said by the superintendent of the parking station, entitled 'a person to go into the parking station and drive a car out of the parking station after handing that ticket in to the attendant at the exit'. The parking ticket was his 'entrance card into and out of the parking station'. Possession of any car leaving the station, it seems to us, was, therefore, retained by the appellant until presentation and surrender of such a ticket by the driver of the car. To our minds, therefore, the act of the attendant in permitting 'Robinson' to proceed after handing over the duplicate ticket which he had obtained constituted an unauthorized delivery of possession by him to 'Robinson' and not a mere act of negligence in relation to some act authorized by the contract of bailment. ...

The fact that the attendant at the exit through which the car was driven was negligent is of no consequence in the case; the act of delivery was one which was neither authorized nor permitted <490> by the contract and in our view the appellant was not entitled to be exonerated by the exempting clause.

[In a separate judgment Windeyer J arrived at the same conclusion as Barwick CJ and Taylor J on the narrower ground that the Council had agreed to deliver the car only upon presentation of a valid ticket and not otherwise. However, his Honour acknowledged that in another case he might have been 'ready to follow their path' (at 503). Kitto and Menzies JJ dissented.]

Appeal dismissed

Deviation

In a number of shipping cases it has been held that an exclusion clause designed to protect a ship-owner will do so only while the vessel was sailing on the agreed route. If the ship deviated from that route, protection would be lost during the deviation and even once the agreed route had been resumed unless, in the latter instance only, the loss or damage complained of would have been suffered even if there had been no deviation. This rule, which is regarded as a rule of construction, has been applied to land transport as the following extract illustrates.

Thomas National Transport (Melbourne) Pty Ltd v May & Baker (Australia) Pty Ltd

(1966) 115 CLR 353, High Court of Australia

[TNT contracted to carry goods for May & Baker. To perform this contract, a sub-contractor (Pay) was engaged to collect the goods and deliver them to TNT's depot. However, by the time the sub-contractor had collected the goods the depot was closed so he stored them overnight in a shed at his home. The shed was destroyed by fire and the goods were damaged. In an action brought by May & Baker in respect of the damage done to its goods, TNT relied on exclusion clauses which provided that May & Baker accepted responsibility for any such loss or damage while the goods were in TNT's custody and that TNT accepted no responsibility for them while they were 'in transit or in storage'. At first instance, May & Baker succeeded against TNT and the sub-contractor; they both appealed to the High Court.]

McTiernan, Taylor and Owen JJ [at 365]: It seems to us that it must have been taken to have been implicit in the contract which TNT made with the respondent that its goods would be taken to TNT's depot and that the depot would be available for their reception at the conclusion of the pick-up round. It is, to our minds, unthinkable that it was within the contemplation of the parties that an extremely valuable consignment of goods was to be kept overnight by TNT's servant or sub-contractor in the yard of a suburban cottage. On the contrary, the only conclusion consistent with its primary obligation was that they would be taken to and received in the depot at the conclusion of the 'pick-up' round. This conclusion is <366> unaffected by consideration of the clause—incorporated in a number of the contracts—that the carrier 'is hereby expressly authorized by the Consignor to carry all goods or to have them carried by any *method* as he in his absolute discretion deems fit and notwithstanding any instruction verbal or otherwise of the Consignor that the goods are to be carried by another method'. The italics are ours and it seems to us that the expression 'method', which must mean method of carriage, is quite inappropriate to cover the circumstances of this case. What the respondent complains of is not the method which was employed to carry the goods but, rather, that the goods were carried, not to TNT's depot but to Pay's home and kept there overnight.

A variety of cases may be cited to illustrate how and in what circumstances a carrier so far departs from his contract of carriage as to preclude him from relying upon exempting provisions designed to relieve him from liability for loss or damage occurring during the performance of his contract. But it is sufficient to refer to *Bontex Knitting Works, Ltd v St Johns Garage* the decision in which case was approved by the Court of Appeal and referred to with evident approval by the Judicial Committee in *Sze Hai Tong Bank Ltd v Rambler Cycle Co Ltd*. The facts of that case are dissimilar but the present case is, if anything, stronger from the point of view of the respondent.

The effect of this conclusion is, of course, that TNT cannot protect itself by seeking to rely upon the exemption clauses and there is the clearest authority for the proposition that, in such circumstances as the present, it must be held liable for the damage which occurred whether or not it can be said to have resulted from lack of care or to have been directly caused by TNT's unauthorized departure from the terms of the contract.

Windeyer J [at 379]: The first question in all such cases is therefore what did the party who relies upon the exception clause contract to do. That being ascertained, the next question is was there such a radical breach by him of his obligations under the contract that, upon the true construction of the contract as a whole including the exception clause, he cannot rely upon the exception clause.

Cases concerning the effect of deviations in a voyage upon contracts of affreightment by sea are merely an example of these general principles of the law of contract. Their peculiar character is only in the strictness of the established rule that any deviation from the contract voyage—that is the one expressly stipulated for in the contract, or stipulated by implication as the usual and customary route of the vessel—is a breach that goes to the root of the contract of affreightment, a breach that entitles the cargo owner to treat the whole contract as at an end, unless with knowledge of the breach he has affirmed the contract. As Fletcher Moulton LJ put it:

> 'The cases show that, for a long series of years, the courts have held that a deviation is such a serious matter, and changes the character of the contemplated voyage so essentially, that a ship-owner who has been guilty of a deviation cannot be considered as having performed his part of the bill of lading contract, but something fundamentally different, and therefore he cannot claim the benefit of stipulations in his favour contained in the bill of lading: *Joseph Thorley Ltd Orchis Steamship Company Ltd*.' ... <380> ...

The strictness of the rule as to deviation in sea voyages appears to be based upon the assumption that deviation alters the risks of the voyage, and to be related to, perhaps a by-product of, the law of marine insurance. A deviation alters the risks of the contemplated voyage by adding or substituting the hazards of further time and a different place. In some cases, especially in war-time, a deviation may actually reduce the perils of a voyage. Nevertheless the general principle is that a deviation, except for a purpose recognized and permitted by the contract, discharges the underwriter simply because it substitutes a risk that is different, whether it be in fact greater or less than before: ... <381> ...

A common carrier by land is deemed to contract to carry by his customary route if no route be expressly stipulated. And the strictness of the rule about deviations in contracts of carriage by sea has been imported by analogy into the contracts of carriage by land. And now the term 'deviation' has come to be used sometimes to describe not only departures from a carrier's geographical route, but also other radical branches of his contract. But, except in the case of deviations from the contract route, it inverts the question to ask of a departure in method, Is it a deviation?—and say that if it is, it is a breach of a term that lies at the root of the contract. The correct question is, Is this departure a radical breach of the contract? If it is, it may sometimes be conveniently called a deviation simply because it has the consequences which by law geographical deviations have long had in contracts of carriage. ... <384> ...

A further aspect of deviations is of some importance. It is that a deviation does not mean only that an exception clause will not avail a carrier against liability for loss occurring during the deviation. It also prevents him relying upon the exception clause in the event of a loss occurring afterwards, unless it be shown that the same loss would have occurred if there had not been a deviation: ... This tends to be lost sight of when, as in the present case, the loss occurs during the alleged deviation. But if, as the respondent May & Baker contends, TNT cannot rely upon the conditions endorsed on the freight note because the goods were in Pay's garage for the night—that being, it is claimed, a deviation—then it could not rely upon them if they had been delivered safely to the depot next morning but had thereafter been lost or damaged by the negligence of some servant of TNT at the depot or had been later lost or damaged at some stage on their inter-State journey to their destination. This merely brings into sharp relief that a deviation means a departure from a fundamental obligation of the contract.

[McTiernan, Taylor and Owen JJ were joined by Barwick CJ in concluding that TNT had departed from the terms of the contract and that this prevented it from relying on its exclusion clauses. As a result, its appeal was dismissed. Windeyer J dissented on the ground that, in his opinion, TNT was under no contractual obligation to take the goods to its depot and that therefore, as it had not deviated from the contract, the exclusion clauses gave it protection. The whole court agreed that the sub-contractor was not negligent and allowed his appeal.]

4 Legislative control

Attempts by some judges, most notably Lord Denning MR through the 'doctrine of fundamental breach', to impose limits on the extent to which one party can exclude its liability to the other by the use of an exclusion clause have been unsuccessful.[23] As a result, at common law it is possible, using an appropriately drafted exclusion clause properly included into their contract, for one party to exclude its liability to the other for even the most serious breaches of contract. While this situation may be acceptable in commercial contracts made between parties of comparable bargaining power, it has been seen as not being so in the case of consumer contracts, or contracts made by small firms with their major suppliers or customers. For this reason, some legislative

---

23   According to the first version of this doctrine, as a matter of law, an exclusion clause could not protect a party from liability for a 'fundamental breach' no matter how widely it was drafted: see *Spurling (J) Ltd v Bradshaw* [1956] 1 WLR 461. This was rejected by the House of Lords in *Suisse Atlantique Societe d'Armement Maritime SA v NV Rotterdamsche Kolen Centrale* [1967] 1 AC 361. In a later version, Lord Denning argued that if a contract was discharged by breach (a fundamental breach) an exclusion clause could not then operate to protect the guilty party because it would have been discharged with the contract containing it: see *Harbutt's 'Plasticine' Ltd v Wayne Tank & Pump Co Ltd* [1970] 1 QB 447. This version was rejected by the House of Lords in *Photo Production Ltd v Securicor Ltd* [1980] AC 827.

control has been exerted over exclusion clauses. The most notable examples are the provisions in the *ACL*, set out below, that prevent suppliers protecting themselves from liability for breach of the statutory guarantees created by Part 3-2 of the *ACL* and which made void unfair terms in standard form consumer contracts.[24] However, these provisions recognise the especially vulnerable position of the suppliers of recreational services by allowing them to exclude, restrict or modify their liability to consumers for death or personal injury,[25] except where such liability is caused by the supplier's reckless conduct.[26] They also permit suppliers who supply non-consumer goods or services, to limit in certain ways their liability (but not to entirely exclude that liability) even though the contract of supply is covered by the *ACL*.

Australian Consumer Law

64 Guarantees not to be excluded etc. by contract

(1) A term of a contract (including a term that is not set out in the contract but is incorporated in the contract by another term of the contract) is void to the extent that the term purports to exclude, restrict or modify, or has the effect of excluding, restricting or modifying:

 (a) the application of all or any of the provisions of this Division; or
 (b) the exercise of a right conferred by such a provision; or
 (c) any liability of a person for a failure to comply with a guarantee that applies under this Division to a supply of goods or services.

(2) A term of a contract is not taken, for the purposes of this section, to exclude, restrict or modify the application of a provision of this Division unless the term does so expressly or is inconsistent with the provision.

64A Limitation of liability for failures to comply with guarantees

(1) A term of a contract for the supply by a person of goods other than goods of a kind ordinarily acquired for personal, domestic or household use or consumption is not void under section 64 merely because the term limits the person's liability for failure to comply with a guarantee (other than a guarantee under section 51, 52 or 53) to one or more of the following:

 (a) the replacement of the goods or the supply of equivalent goods;
 (b) the repair of the goods;
 (c) the payment of the cost of replacing the goods or of acquiring equivalent goods;
 (d) the payment of the cost of having the goods repaired.

---

24 See *ACL* ss 23, 24 and 25(1)(i)(k).
25 See *Competition and Consumer Act 2010* (Cth) s 139A(1).
26 Ibid, s 139A(4).

(2) A term of a contract for the supply by a person of services other than services of a kind ordinarily acquired for personal, domestic or household use or consumption is not void under section 64 merely because the term limits the person's liability for failure to comply with a guarantee to:

(a) the supplying of the services again; or
(b) the payment of the cost of having the services supplied again.

(3) This section does not apply in relation to a term of a contract if the person to whom the goods or services were supplied establishes that it is not fair or reasonable for the person who supplied the goods or services to rely on that term of the contract.

(4) In determining for the purposes of subsection (3) whether or not reliance on a term of a contract is fair or reasonable, a court is to have regard to all the circumstances of the case, and in particular to the following matters:

(a) the strength of the bargaining positions of the person who supplied the goods or services and the person to whom the goods or services were supplied (the *buyer*) relative to each other, taking into account, among other things, the availability of equivalent goods or services and suitable alternative sources of supply;
(b) whether the buyer received an inducement to agree to the term or, in agreeing to the term, had an opportunity of acquiring the goods or services or equivalent goods or services from any source of supply under a contract that did not include that term;
(c) whether the buyer knew or ought reasonably to have known of the existence and extent of the term (having regard, among other things, to any custom of the trade and any previous course of dealing between the parties);
(d) in the case of the supply of goods, whether the goods were manufactured, processed or adapted to the special order of the buyer.

INTERNATIONAL PERSPECTIVES

India

The *Indian Contract Act, 1872* contains no provision dealing with exclusion clauses. As a result, Indian law on this subject is governed by India's unwritten law which is essentially the same as Anglo-Australian common law, outlined above.

China

The *Contract Law of the People's Republic of China, 1999* has no special provisions dealing with the incorporation or interpretation of exclusion clauses. However, Article 53 does impose some restriction on the exclusion of liability for certain kinds of loss and wrongs.

> Article 53. Invalidity of Certain Exculpatory Provisions
>
> The following exculpatory provisions in a contract are invalid:
> (i) excluding one party's liability for personal injury caused to the other party;
> (ii) excluding one party's liability for property loss caused to the other party by its intentional misconduct or gross negligence.

5 Summary

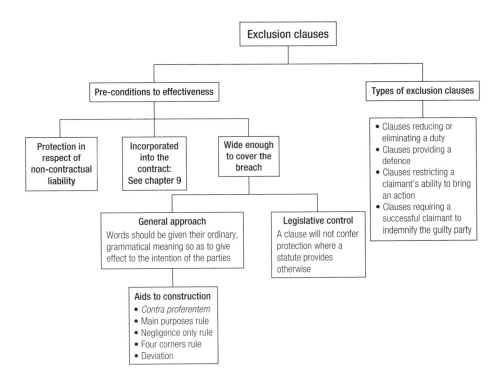

6 Questions

1. Steel Fabricators Ltd (Steel) entered into a contract to purchase 50 tons of steel piping from ABC Ltd (ABC). Clause 15 of the contract provided that:

    'ABC gives no guarantee regarding the goods that are the subject of this contract and accepts no responsibility for any loss or damage howsoever caused that they may occasion due to inherent defects therein or otherwise.'

    The piping was duly delivered to Steel, which commenced using it to make components for industrial air-conditioning equipment. Unfortunately, due to problems with the ore used to manufacture the piping, it proved to be unsuitable for this purpose. However, this was not discovered until after one of the air-conditioners exploded because of the defect, causing considerable damage to Steel's premises.

Please advise Steel. They wish to know whether they can successfully take proceedings against ABC, having regard to Clause 15.

2   Julie travelled by car to the football. She parked her car in a large car park, operated by Yarra Parking Ltd (Yarra), adjacent to the ground. Upon paying the parking fee, she received a ticket from Yarra's attendant which contained a clause that read 'Vehicles are parked and driven at customer's risk.' During the game, one of Yarra's attendants, who was listening to it on her radio, became so excited that she negligently drove her patrol vehicle into Julie's car, causing it significant damage.

Advise Julie whether she can take proceedings against Yarra, or the attendant, to recover the cost of repairing her car.

PART 4

Avoidance

An agreement that appears to meet all of the preconditions to the formation of a contract will, nevertheless, not be binding where it was concluded in circumstances that prevented one, or both, of the parties giving real or properly formed consent, or where one party did not fulfil important obligations owed to the other, or where it would be against public policy to enforce the agreement. The principal circumstances that can give rise to this situation are: misleading or deceptive conduct, the abuse by one party of a dominant position they occupy in relation to the other (unconscionable conduct, duress and undue influence), mistake and illegality. Where an agreement is concluded in one or more of these situations the apparent contract will be rendered void, voidable or unenforceable and this will usually mean that one party will be able to 'avoid' the contract by electing to bring it to an end or have it declared void. However, in some situations a court may choose not to enforce a contract on its own initiative (this is the case with certain types of illegality) while in others, both parties may have this option open to them.

A 'void 'contract is one that is completely ineffective and is so without the parties needing to elect to set it aside. As a result, it cannot create contractual rights, or impose contractual obligations, with the result that neither party can take action against the other for breach of contract. Most importantly, a void contract is incapable of transferring title to property from one party to the other, or to a third party. However, action taken by the parties pursuant to a void contract may give rise to other rights, or obligations, that can be enforced independently of contract; for example, money paid under a void contract will normally be recoverable in restitution and property transferred (or its value) may be recoverable in tort.

A 'voidable' contract, on the other hand, is one that is operative unless and until it is set aside. There are two important and inter-related consequences to a contract being of this nature. First, although the circumstances in which it was made render it vulnerable, unless the party who is entitled to complain about that matter chooses to avoid the contract, it will remain effective to confer contractual rights and impose contractual obligations on the parties. In effect, that party has the option to 'affirm' the contract (to keep it operative notwithstanding the circumstances that made it voidable) or to rescind it (to bring it to an end). Should the latter choice be made, the effect of rescission is to restore the parties to their original position—the contract is rescinded *ab initio* (from the beginning). However, because rescission has this effect, it can occur only where the parties can be restored to their original position without adversely affecting third parties. Second, because the contract remains operative until it is rescinded, unlike a void contract, it can to transfer property between the parties, or to a third party. As a result, where, before rescission occurs, a person acquires an interest in property of which the law will not deprive them, that person is able to retain the property notwithstanding rescission.

The difference between a contract being void and a contract being voidable is illustrated by the following example.

Examples

Assume S sold her car to B on 1 June; and B then sold the car to C on 25 June.

Where the contract between S and B is void

B will never obtain title to the car from S and therefore, cannot transfer title to C. As a result, although possession of the vehicle may pass from S to B and then from B to C, title will remain throughout in A, who will be able to recover possession of the car from C based on her ownership. In such a scenario, C is left only with a claim against B.

Where the contract between S and B is voidable at the option of S

1. B will obtain title to the car on 1 June. Should S not seek to rescind the contract until *after* 25 June (for example, because the grounds for avoidance were not discovered until after that date), B will still have title to the car on 25 June and will be able to give a good title to C on that date. In this scenario, provided C was a *bona fide* purchaser, S will not be able to rescind the contract because the law will not allow rescission to

> defeat the property interests acquired by *bona fide* purchasers for value. Therefore, C will be able to retain the car and S will be left to enforce any personal claim she may have against B; for example, for misleading or deceptive conduct.
>
> 2 However, should S rescind the contract *before* 25 June, the contract will be rescinded *ab initio* and title will revert to A, assuming that restitution is still possible. In this scenario, B will have no title to the car on 25 June when the contract between B and C was made, with the consequence that C will not obtain title to it as B had none to transfer. Therefore, S will be able to recover the car from C, relying on her title. In this situation, rescission does defeat any property interest C has in the car as, in fact, none had been obtained because of A's decision to rescind her contract with B before 25 June.

An 'unenforceable' contract is one that is operative but incapable of being enforced by one or both of the parties. For example, as we saw in Chapter 7, a contract for the sale of land can be enforced against a person only if they have signed a note or memorandum evidencing that contract. However, where there is no such document, although it will be unenforceable, the contract can still operate to transfer the title to the land from the vendor to the purchaser and once that has occurred, the purchaser can enforce all the rights that flow from having title. A similar situation may arise in the case of certain contracts that are unenforceable on the grounds of illegality.

In Part 4 we examine the circumstances that may render a contract, void, voidable or unenforceable. These have been grouped by the courts and writers into a number of well-recognised categories, based on the nature of the conduct involved. Each is the subject of one the following chapters. This approach should not, however, convey the impression that these categories are mutually exclusive; on the contrary, very often the facts of a particular case will make it possible to challenge a contract under more than one of them. This is especially the case with misleading or deceptive conduct which is very often present with one or more of the other grounds of avoidance.

CHAPTER 12

Misleading or Deceptive Conduct

1	Introduction		320
2	The prohibitions of misleading or deceptive conduct		321
3	The nature and scope of the prohibitions		322
4	Preconditions to liability		323
	a	Corporation or person	323
	b	Engaging in conduct	323
	c	Trade or commerce	324
	d	Misleading or deceptive	325
5	Application to contracts		326
	a	Representations of fact	326
	b	Expressions of opinion or law	326
	c	Sales puffs	327
	d	Silence or non-disclosure	327
	e	Statements about the future	333
	f	Contractual promises	337
	g	Relaying information	339
	h	Exclusion clauses	342
	i	Failure to exercise care	343
	j	Vicarious liability	343
6	Remedies		343
	a	Damages	344
	b	Other remedies	354
7	Misrepresentation at common law		355
	a	Pre-contractual misrepresentation: definition and preconditions	355
	b	Remedies	356
	c	Exclusion clauses	359
	d	Legislative modifications	359
8	Summary		365
9	Questions		365

1 Introduction

A person's decision to enter into a contract will often be influenced, at least to some degree, by communication from the other party, or a third party. The form and content of such communications vary enormously. Common examples (and in practice the most important) are the oral or written statements made by suppliers, to prospective customers, about the goods or services they are seeking to sell or lease to them. Other examples include:

- advertising or other promotional material about products
- advice from external experts about the suitability or quality of goods or services
- representations about the terms of the contract being proposed
- statements by consumers about their capacity to purchase, or their familiarity with the terms of the contract.

Communications such as these give rise to legal disputes when the party they influence (referred to below as 'the representee') claims that the communication was misleading and that this caused them loss.

At common law, the consequence of misleading conduct in relation to contracts is governed by the law of misrepresentation. If the conduct complained of was that of the other contracting party and it induced the contract, the law of pre-contractual misrepresentation applies, making the contract voidable in certain circumstances. Damages, however, are not recoverable unless the conduct also amounts to a tort, or has become a term of the contract, or this is allowed under a statutory modification of the common law. On the other hand, if the conduct involved was that of a third party, or if occurred after the contract was made, the law of negligent misrepresentation applies and a remedy will be available only if negligence can be established. This is a complicated legal regime and one that is far from satisfactory, both in terms of *when* remedies can be obtained and *what* those remedies are. Fortunately, in Australia, it now has very little application in practice as it has been largely usurped by the enactment of a broad statutory prohibition of misleading or deceptive conduct. This prohibition was introduced into Australian law in 1974 by s 52 of the *Trade Practices Act 1974* (Cth) (*TPA*) which was directed primarily at 'corporations'. A decade or so later, its reach was extended to all 'persons' by equivalent provisions in the Fair Trading Acts of each state and territory.[1] Since 1 January 2011 it has existed in the form of s 18 of the *Australian Consumer Law* (*ACL*).[2] However, since s 18 applies only to conduct occurring on or after that

---

1 *Trade Practices Act 1974* (Cth) s 52; *Fair Trading (Australian Consumer Law) Act 1992* (ACT) s 12; *Fair Trading Act 1987* (NSW) s 42; *Fair Trading Act 1999* (Vic) s 9; *Fair Trading Act 1989* (Qld) s 38; *Consumer Affairs and Fair Trading Act 1990* (NT) s 42; *Fair Trading Act 1987* (WA) s 10; *Fair Trading Act 1987* (SA) s 56; *Fair Trading Act 1990* (Tas) s 14.
2 The *ACL* is contained in Schedule 2 of the *Competition and Consumer Act 2010*.

date, s 52 of the *TPA* will continue to apply to earlier conduct[3] until the applicable limitation period bars action based upon its contravention.[4]

There are a number of reasons why the statutory prohibitions of misleading or deceptive conduct dominate this area of law and are the preferred means for seeking redress in cases of contract-related misleading conduct. These include that they are broader in scope, have fewer preconditions, cannot easily be avoided by the use of exclusion clauses and provide a much broader range of remedies. As a result, the common law has effectively been relegated to those rare cases in which the prohibitions cannot be used. Consequently, they are the focus of our treatment of this subject and only brief additional references are made to the position at common law.

In this chapter we will examine:

- the nature of the prohibitions and their scope
- the preconditions to liability
- the application of the prohibitions to contracts
- the remedies available
- the common law and its role.

2 The prohibitions of misleading or deceptive conduct

As noted above, the statutory prohibition of misleading or deceptive conduct is now contained in s 18 of the *ACL*. For constitutional reasons, the prohibitions contained in the *ACL*, including s 18, operate as a law of Commonwealth and as a law of each state and territory. As a law of the Commonwealth, although expressed in terms of prohibiting 'a person' from engaging in certain forms of conduct, they apply only to corporations.[5] As a law of each state and territory, on the other hand, they apply to all persons through the operation of state and territory application laws that apply the *ACL* in each jurisdiction.[6] For present purposes, the practical importance of this bifurcation is that it determines whether s 18 can be relied upon as Commonwealth law, or whether it must be relied upon as the law of the state or territory in which the conduct occurred. Where the person whose conduct is impugned is incorporated, the former is the case; where they are a natural person, generally speaking it will be the latter.

---

3   See *Trade Practices Amendment (Australian Consumer Law) Act (No 2) 2010*, Sch 7, items 6(1) and 7(1).
4   This is six years: see *TPA* s 82(2). As a result, it is to be expected that actions will still be brought alleging contravention of under s 52 of the *TPA* for at least that period.
5   See *Competition and Consumer Act 2010* s 131(1). Although ss 5 and 6 of the Act extend the operation of the *ACL* to individuals in certain situations, these are now of limited importance.
6   See New South Wales: *Fair Trading Act 1987* ss 27 and 28; Victoria: *Fair Trading Act 1999* ss 8 and 9; Queensland: *Fair Trading Act 1989* ss 15 and 16; Western Australia: *Fair Trading Act 2010* ss 18 and 19; South Australia: *Fair Trading Act 1987* ss 13 and 14; Tasmania: *Australian Consumer Law (Tasmania) Act 2010* ss 5 and 6; Northern Territory: *Consumer Affairs and Fair Trading Act* ss 26 and 27; Australian Capital Territory: *Fair Trading (Australian Consumer Law) Act 1992* ss 6 and 7.

The prohibition of misleading or deceptive conduct in s 18 of the *ACL* is expressed in terms that are identical in all material respects to those used in the former s 52 of the *TPA*. For this reason, the very considerable case law and literature that developed concerning s 52 will be directly relevant to s 18. For this reason, that material will be referred to in connection with s 18 as if that section had been its subject matter at the time it was written.

Australian Consumer Law

Section 18. Misleading or Deceptive Conduct

(1) A person must not, in trade or commerce, engage in conduct that is misleading or deceptive or is likely to mislead or deceive.

(2) Nothing in Part 3-1 (which is about unfair practices) limits by implication subsection (1).

3 The nature and scope of the prohibition

An important aspect of s 18 of the *ACL* is that it is a prohibition. Unlike the common law which merely provides the victims of misrepresentation with a remedy, s 18 *prohibits* misleading or deceptive conduct as well. This has influenced the courts to interpret the provision broadly as remedial legislation[7] and to reject all attempts to exclude liability for its contravention by the use of exclusion clauses.

Also, the prohibition is not restricted to pre-contractual conduct between the parties but is of general application and can apply in all contract-related situations:

Examples

1. A misleads B in order to induce B to enter into a contract with A.
2. A misleads B with the result that B enters into a contract with C.
3. A misleads B about some aspect of a contract that A and B have already made.

Of these situations, only the first (albeit the most common) is also within the ambit of the common law relating to contractual misrepresentation.

Because of its broad scope, s 18 has the potential to overlap considerably with other branches of contract law. For example, conduct that amounts at common law, or in equity, to duress, undue influence, unconscionable conduct, operative mistake or even in some cases breach of contract, can also constitute misleading or deceptive conduct. In such cases, choosing to rely upon s 18, rather than the common law or equity, may provide the aggrieved party with the more effective remedy.

The potential for s 18 to apply to all forms of misleading conduct that in some way are connected with commercial activity has caused concern. It has been

---

[7] See *Accounting Systems 2000 (Developments) Pty Ltd v CCH Australia Ltd* (1993) 42 FCR 470, esp at 503.

argued, for example, that it should be restricted to consumer transactions and not be available as a general remedy in all types of transactions.[8] While this view has not been accepted, some legislative restrictions have been imposed. In particular, s 18 no longer applies to 'the supply, or possible supply, of services that are financial services'.[9] Instead, misleading or deceptive conduct in relation to financial services is now prohibited by s 12DA of the *Australian Securities and Investments Commission Act 2001* (Cth) and s 1041H of the *Corporations Act 2001* (Cth). In addition, s 18 no longer applies to publications, other than advertisements, by 'information providers',[10] although this limitation has only very marginal relevance to contract-related conduct.

4 Preconditions to liability

The preconditions to liability arising for misleading or deceptive conduct under s 18 of the *ACL* are as follows:

- the defendant must be a 'corporation' or a 'person'
- the defendant must engage in conduct
- the conduct must occur in trade or commerce
- the conduct must be misleading or deceptive, or likely to be so.

a Corporation or person

As we have seen, as a law of the Commonwealth, s 18 is directed only towards the conduct of corporations, whereas as state or territory law is directed towards that of 'a person'. As a result, the section has the potential to apply to everyone—regardless of whether they are incorporated or not—their legal status as a corporation or natural person merely determining the level at which it can be invoked.

b Engaging in conduct

'Engaging in conduct' is defined broadly in s 4(2) of the *Competition and Consumer Act 2010* (Cth) so as to cover positive conduct, refusing to act and failing to act (other than inadvertently). As a result, the prohibition cover all of the forms of conduct that are likely to arise in connection with a contract including, for example, oral or written representations of fact, expressions of opinion or law, non-verbal communications, and withholding information. Importantly, 'the expression "conduct" in s 18 extends beyond "representations"'[11] so that, even though in most cases a representation will be involved, conduct can still contravene the section despite not being of this nature.

---

8   See *Concrete Constructions (NSW) Pty Ltd v Nelson* (1990) 169 CLR 594 at 617.
9   See *Competition and Consumer Act 2010* (Cth) s 131A. In relation to the Fair Trading Acts, see s 1041K(2) of the *Corporations Act 2001* (Cth).
10 See *ACL* s 19.
11 *Butcher v Lachlan Elder Realty Pty Ltd* (2004) 218 CLR 592 per Gleeson CJ, Hayne and Heydon JJ at 603. See also *Campbell v Backoffice Investments Pty Ltd* (2009) 238 CLR 304 at 341.

c Trade or commerce

Section 18 prohibits misleading or deceptive conduct only if it occurs in 'trade or commerce'. Although this concept has been interpreted widely to cover any activity that is trading or commercial in nature, it remains the principal limitation on the use of s 18 as it cannot be invoked in relation to contractual conduct unless that conduct can be characterised in this way. For example, it will not apply to the private sale of property where neither the buyer, nor seller, acted as part of a business.[12] However, while it should not be overlooked, this limitation has little effect in practice as almost all significant contracts have at least one commercial party, or are made using the services of a business agent and as a result satisfy the requirement. Thus, all consumer contracts are covered (as the supplier acts as a business) as are all commercial contracts (as both parties act as businesses) and all contracts where the conduct in question was that of an agent (as the conduct occurs as part of the agent's business).[13]

Bevanere Pty Ltd v Lubidineuse

(1984) 7 FCR 325, Federal Court of Australia (Full Court)

[Bevanere sold a cosmetic clinic to Lubidineuse. In the course of discussions between the parties prior to the sale, Bevanere engaged in conduct that was found to have been misleading in relation to staff at the clinic. On this basis, Lubidineuse recovered damages for contravention of s 52 of the *TPA*. Bevanere appealed, arguing, *inter alia*, that the conduct in question had not occurred in trade or commerce as it was a one-off sale of a business asset.]

The Court [at 328]: In our opinion the activities of the appellant in and about conducting and selling the clinic fall well within the confines of 'trade' or 'commerce'. As Deane J said in *Re Ku-ring-gai Co-Operative Building Society (No 12) Ltd* (1978) 36 FLR 134 at 167, the terms 'trade' and 'commerce' are not terms of art and are of the widest import. ...

The appellant's general proposition that the sale by a corporation of its only capital asset, where the corporation is not engaged in the business of buying or selling such capital assets, does not constitute conduct in trade or commerce was based upon the decision in *O'Brien v Smolonogov* (1983) 53 ALR 107. In that case it was held that the sale of a parcel of vacant land did not amount to conduct in

---

12 See *O'Brien v Smolonogov* (1983) 53 ALR 107, and *Franich v Swannell* (1994) ATPR (Digest) 46-115. However, if the sale was part of a series of transactions entered into for profit, then it may be characterised as trade or commerce: see *Gentry Bros Pty Ltd v Wilson Brown & Associates Pty Ltd* (1992) ATPR 41-184.

13 *MacCormick v Nowland* (1988) ATPR 40-852 and *Argy v Blunts & Lane Cove Real Estate Pty Ltd* (1990) 26 FCR 112 show that in the case of a private sale of land, although the seller may not have acted in trade or commerce, a real estate agent acting on their behalf will have done so. As a result, misleading conduct on the agent's part will contravene s 52 of the *Trade Practices Act*, even though such conduct on the part of its principal will not. However, it should be noted that the agent will escape liability if its conduct involves no more than relaying information from its principal to the plaintiff as in such a case its conduct will not be misleading: see 5(g) below.

trade or commerce. The case is distinguishable from the present. The land was not used for any business activity. The Court derived assistance in reaching its decision from a series of United States decisions under consumer protection legislation. It observed that in the American cases the view had been consistently taken that a private sale of property by an individual is not conduct in trade or commerce except if done in the course of a business activity or otherwise arising in a 'business context'. ... <331> ...

We do not think the decision in *O'Brien's* case assists the appellant. The Court was careful to point out that the land which was sold in that case was not used for any business activity. Nothing was said in *O'Brien's* case that lends support to the proposition that the sale of a capital item used for business purposes will not constitute conduct in trade or commerce unless it forms part of a business of buying or selling such capital assets.

The appellant submitted that the expression 'in trade or commerce' necessarily connoted a course of conduct as opposed to isolated and unusual or extraordinary conduct. The *Ku-ring-gai* case (supra) at 625 and *Bank of New South Wales v The Commonwealth* (1948) 76 CLR 1 at 284 and 381 were relied upon for this proposition. It was said in those cases that historically the use of the word 'trade' was founded upon the elements of use, regularity and course of conduct. But that is not to say that a corporation must engage in multiple transactions of a similar kind for it to be engaged in trade or commerce. It was submitted that, whilst the appellant engaged in trade or commerce when conducting the beauty clinic, the sale of the clinic was not something done in trade or commerce because the sale terminated the appellant's ability to engage in trade or commerce. In our opinion, the making of the arrangements necessary to dispose of the clinic were part and parcel of the totality of the appellant's activities in trade or commerce.

Appeal dismissed

d   Misleading or deceptive

The key precondition, of course, is that the conduct involved was 'misleading or deceptive or [was] likely to mislead or deceive'. The concept of 'misleading or deceptive' is not defined in the *ACL* but a widely accepted definition is that it means 'to lead into error' without any connotation of 'craft or overreaching' being required.[14] This gives it a broad meaning that extends beyond merely being false. On the other hand, the extension of the prohibition to conduct that is 'likely to mislead or deceive', while potentially important in cases of false advertising where it may be difficult to identify a particular person who was misled, is of little relevance in contract cases. This is because, in order to establish that their loss was caused by the defendant's misleading or deceptive conduct, the plaintiff in such cases will invariably need to show that they were actually misled.

Although the conduct referred to in s 18 is not confined to representations, in practice, for it to apply in contractual situations will usually require there to have

---

14   See *Parkdale Custom Built Furniture Pty Ltd v Puxu Pty Ltd* (1982) 149 CLR 191 at 198, per Gibbs CJ.

been a representation of some kind. In particular, it is not sufficient for a plaintiff to show that there was conduct on the defendant's part and that they were misled by that conduct; rather, they must show that the conduct itself was misleading (or likely to be so) and this will usually require a representation of some kind on the defendant's part. Thus, for example, in *Effem Foods Pty Ltd v Lake Cumbeline Pty Ltd*[15] the High Court held that Effem did not contravene s 52 by entering into a genuine contract with a supplier, even though this misled Lake Cumbeline into thinking that the supplier was a good investment. Although Effem was aware that the contract would be shown to people thinking of investing in the firm, according to the Court, this did not constitute making representation to them to this effect.

5 Application to contracts

a Representations of fact

A false representation of fact, made by one party to the other during pre-contractual negotiations, will amount to misleading or deceptive conduct if the latter was in fact misled. This is so regardless of whether it was made innocently or fraudulently and even though the representor had taken all possible care to ensure that it was correct.[16] A statement that is literally correct can also amount to misleading conduct where, despite being true, it misled the person to whom it was directed.[17] In that connection, whether the representation is misleading or not is determined by reference to how it could reasonably have been understood by the person to whom it was directed. Thus, for example, in *Ward v Premier Ice Skating Rink Pty Ltd*,[18] a statement that a business advertised for sale had an 'overhead of $1,600 pw' was found to be misleading because it was reasonable for the plaintiff to interpret this as referring to total expenses when in fact it referred only to the business' fixed costs.

b Expressions of opinion or law

Expressions of opinion, including those about the law, cannot be characterised as misleading or deceptive merely because subsequent events show that they were inaccurate. This is because the only information communicated in such cases is that the speaker actually holds the opinion expressed or, perhaps, that it is based upon reasonable grounds or research. If this is correct, the person to whom the opinion was directed was not misled about those matters. On the other hand, if the speaker did not hold the opinion,[19] or if their expression contained a representation that it

---

15 (1999) ATPR 41-686.
16 See *Greco v Bendigo Machinery Pty Ltd* (1985) ATPR 40-521; *Embo Holdings Pty Ltd v Camm* (1998) ATPR (Digest) 46-184.
17 *Hornsby Building Information Centre Pty Ltd v Sydney Building Information Centre Ltd* (1978) 140 CLR 216 at 227.
18 (1986) ATPR 40-681.
19 See *Amadio Pty Ltd v Henderson* (1998) 81 FCR 149.

was based upon research, or the existence of reasonable grounds,[20] and this was not the case, then liability can arise.

c   Sales puffs

Exaggerated statements of fact or opinion that a reasonable person would not understand as intended to be taken literally will not amount to misleading conduct. When determining if a statement is of this nature, relevant considerations include whether the statement was made in a publication designed to attract attention, rather than convey reliable information; whether the statement was subjective in nature, rather than factual; whether it was clear that the person to whom it was made was expected to form their own judgment about the subject matter, rather than rely upon the statement; and whether detailed information was subsequently provided to that person.[21] However, the courts have not been easily persuaded to characterise statements made in a commercial context in this way. Thus, for example, statements that a building would be 'bigger and better' than an existing building,[22] and that a customer was 'getting the best deal'[23] have been held to be actionable and not merely puffs.

d   Silence or non-disclosure

Not infrequently, contracts are negotiated in circumstances in which one party has information which, if available to the other party, would influence the latter's decision about whether to enter into the contract or not, or the terms upon which it was willing to do so. At common law, there is no general duty to disclose information of this kind so that failure to do so does not make the contract voidable, or give that party any other remedy. Only if the contract falls within one of the limited categories of contracts that are regarded *uberrimae fidei* (of utmost good faith) can the non-disclosure of information have this effect.[24]

Two related situations should also be noted. The first arises when a representation is made which was correct when made, but which subsequently becomes false due to changed circumstances. These may be known, or unknown to the representor. The second is where the representor discloses some information about a subject but not other relevant information that is available. At common law, non-disclosure in these circumstances will make the contract voidable.[25]

All of these situations now come within the scope of the prohibition of misleading or deceptive conduct. Considerable attention has been given to the issue of whether this, in effect, imposes upon the parties to a contract a greater

---

20   See *Thompson v Ice Creameries of Australia Pty Ltd* (1998) ATPR 41-611.
21   See, for example, *Lymquartz Pty Ltd v 2 Elizabeth Bay Road Pty Ltd* [2007] NSWSC 457 at 183–195
22   *Byers v Dorotea Pty Ltd* (1987) ATPR 40-760.
23   *Petty v Penfold Wines Pty Ltd* (1994) 49 FCR 282.
24   The principal examples are insurance contracts where the duty is now significantly regulated by statute: *Insurance Contracts Act 1984* (Cth), s 21.
25   See *Curwen v Yan Yean Land Co Ltd* (1891) 17 VLR 745 (partial disclosure); *Jones v Dumbrell* [1981] VR 199 (changed circumstances).

duty to disclose information to each other than existed at common law. This issue is considered in the following extracts.

Software Integrators Pty Ltd v Roadrunner Couriers Pty Ltd

(1997) ATPR (Digest) 46-177, Supreme Court of South Australia

[The parties entered into a contract whereby Software Integrators was to supply a computer software system and related services to Roadrunner. During negotiations, Software failed to inform Roadrunner that it would be difficult and time consuming to transfer client information to the new system. Had Roadrunner known this it would not have entered into the contract. At first instance, the magistrate found that the contract had been validly rescinded on this ground and ordered the repayment of money Roadrunner had paid to Software. Software appealed to the Supreme Court.]

Doyle CJ [at 54,421]: There can no longer be any doubt that silence can constitute misleading and deceptive conduct within the meaning of s 52 of the *Trade Practices Act 1974*. However, silence or non- disclosure, without more, will not amount to misleading and deceptive conduct. Silence and non-disclosure, by themselves, are not misleading and deceptive conduct for at least two reasons. For one thing, mere silence or non-disclosure cannot cause a person to be misled or deceived. For an applicant to establish that a contravention of s 52 has occurred, it is not sufficient to show that it was laboring under an erroneous belief. The applicant must prove its belief was caused by the defendant's conduct. That requisite causal nexus is necessarily absent in cases of mere silence or non-disclosure.

The second reason is closely allied to the first. In cases of silence the defendant's conduct must fall within the purview of 'engaging in conduct' which is the essential threshold hurdle to be cleared for any s 52 action. As that expression is defined to include refusing to do an act 'otherwise than inadvertently' (s 4(2)(a)) it has been interpreted as including an omission to disclose information only where that omission is deliberate, see: *Spedley Securities (in liq) v Bank of New Zealand* (1991) ATPR ¶ 41-143 at 35,065 per Cole J. It is also pertinent to bear in mind the comments of Gleeson CJ in *Lam v Ausintel Investments Australia Pty Ltd* (1990) ATPR 40-990; (1990) 97 FLR 458 (at ATPR 50,880; FLR 475):

> 'Where parties are dealing at arm's length in a commercial situation in which they have conflicting interests it will often be the case that one party will be aware of information which, if known to the other, would or might cause that other party to take a different negotiating stance. This does not in itself impose any obligation on the first party to bring the information to the attention of the other party, and failure to do so would not, without more, ordinarily be regarded as dishonesty or even sharp practice.'

Despite the foregoing comments, it is now beyond question that silence or non-disclosure can be misleading when combined with other factors such as the provision of incomplete information, or half-truths, or the failure to correct a representation which has become false. Section 52 plainly contemplates that misleading and deceptive conduct may be constituted by a factual matrix consisting of silence as well as the paradigm situations concerned with overt activity.

At common law, a failure to correct a representation which has become false may constitute an actionable misrepresentation. Such a failure could also be misleading and deceptive conduct. A duty of disclosure may also exist where there is the provision of incomplete information or half-truths. An example of the latter situation is *Henjo Investments Pty Ltd v Collins Marrickville Pty Ltd* (1988) ATPR 40-850; (1988) 79 ALR 83. In that case Lockhart J stated the position as follows (at ATPR 40,850; ALR 95):

> 'At common law, silence can give rise to an actionable misrepresentation where there is a duty upon the representor to reveal if a matter exists, and where the other party is therefore entitled to infer that matter does not exist from the silence of the representor.'

However, the law has moved on from this statement. Contemporary authority approaches the question from the perspective of whether the circumstances are such that they give rise to a reasonable expectation that if a relevant fact exists, it will be disclosed. The notion of a reasonable expectation, which is becoming common in modern jurisprudence, was employed in this context by French J in *Kimberley NZI Finance Ltd v Torero Pty Ltd* (1989) ATPR 46-054 (at 53,195):

> 'unless the circumstances are such as to give rise to the reasonable expectation that if some relevant fact exists it would be disclosed, it is difficult to see how mere <54,422> silence could support the inference that the fact does not exist.'

This test has subsequently been endorsed by a decision of the Full Court of the Federal Court. In *Demagogue Pty Ltd v Ramensky* (1993) ATPR 41-203; (1993) 110 ALR 608 the circumstances in which silence may amount to conduct in contravention of s 52 were the subject of exhaustive analysis by Gummow J, with whose reasoning Black CJ and Cooper J agreed. His Honour identified the proper approach to be taken in determining the issue of liability, when silence on the part of the respondent's conduct is central to the applicant's case, in the following way (at ATPR 40,851; ALR 618):

> 'But, consistently with regard to the natural meaning of the terms of s 52, the question is whether in the light of all the relevant circumstances constituted by acts, omissions, statements or silence, there has been conduct which is or is likely to be misleading or deceptive. Conduct answering that description may not always involve misrepresentation.'

In addition to expressing his agreement with Gummow J, the Chief Justice observed (at ATPR 40,844–5; ALR 609–610):

> 'Silence is to be assessed as a circumstance like any other. To say this is certainly not to impose any general duty of disclosure; the question is simply whether, having regard to all the relevant circumstances, there has been conduct that is misleading or deceptive or that is likely to mislead or deceive. To speak of 'mere silence' or a duty of disclosure can divert attention from the primary question. Although "mere

silence" is a convenient way of describing some fact situations, there is in truth no such thing as "mere silence" because the significance of silence falls to be considered in the context in which it occurs. That context may or may not include facts giving rise to a reasonable expectation, in the circumstances of the case, that if particular matters exist they will be disclosed.'

The decision in *Demagogue* was followed in *Warner v Elders Rural Finance Ltd* (1992) 113 ALR 517 where Hill J made it clear that whilst analogies can be drawn to duties to speak at common law, silence for the purposes of s 52 is dealt with as a question of statutory construction. In determining whether silence falls within the four corners of s 52, the term 'misleading and deceptive conduct' may be enlivened by, but not constrained by, consideration of those circumstances where there is a duty of disclosure in the general law, see: *Kimberley NZI Finance Ltd v Torero Pty Ltd* (1989) ATPR (Digest) 46-054 at 53,195 per French J. Thus, assistance may be gained from consideration of cases at common law and in equity dealing with related types of situations, but the reach of s 52 is not confined by such cases because s 52 is concerned with the interpretation and application of the words of a particular statute. Hence, s 52 is, in some cases, wider than the common law. As Hill J explained (at 522–523):

'Of course, where a duty to speak is imposed by the general law, the circumstances will obviously be such that the person to whom the duty is owed will be entitled to infer from the silence that no danger or detriment exists. Failure to speak will thus easily be seen to constitute misleading and deceptive conduct. The converse is clearly not true. The fact that no duty to speak is imposed by the general law will not conclude the inquiry whether that failure to speak is to be characterised as conduct which is misleading or deceptive.'

[His Honour concluded that Roadrunner was entitled to assume that any difficulties about the transfer of information would be brought to its attention so that Software's failure to do this amounted to misleading or deceptive conduct.]

Appeal dismissed

Miller & Associates Insurance Broking Pty Ltd v BMW Australia Finance Ltd

(2010) 241 CLR 357, High Court of Australia

[Miller negotiated a loan to a client from BMW. This loan was not fully repaid and BMW suffered loss. In these proceedings, BMW sought to recover this loss, arguing that when negotiating the loan, Miller engaged in misleading or deceptive conduct by not disclosing certain relevant information to BMW. At first instance, this non-disclosure was found not to be misleading. BMW successfully appealed to the Victorian Court of Appeal; Miller then appealed to the High Court.]

French CJ and Kiefel J [at 369]: Gummow J [Author's note: in *Demagogue*] referred to the limitation that 'unless the circumstances are such as to give rise to the reasonable expectation that if some relevant fact exists it would be disclosed, it is difficult to see how mere silence could support the inference that the fact does not exist'.

The language of reasonable expectation is not statutory. It indicates an approach which can be taken to the characterisation, for the purposes of s 52, of conduct consisting of, or including, non-disclosure of information. That approach may differ in its application according to whether the conduct is said to be misleading or deceptive to members of the public, or whether it arises between entities in commercial negotiations. An example in the former category is non-disclosure of material facts in a prospectus.

In commercial dealings between individuals or individual entities, characterisation of conduct will be undertaken by reference to its circumstances and context. Silence may be a circumstance to be considered. The knowledge of the person to whom the conduct is [370] directed may be relevant. Also relevant, as in the present case, may be the existence of common assumptions and practices established between the parties or prevailing in the particular profession, trade or industry in which they carry on business. The judgment which looks to a reasonable expectation of disclosure as an aid to characterising non-disclosure as misleading or deceptive is objective. It is a practical approach to the application of the prohibition in s 52.

To invoke the existence of a reasonable expectation that if a fact exists it will be disclosed is to do no more than direct attention to the effect or likely effect of non-disclosure unmediated by antecedent erroneous assumptions or beliefs or high moral expectations held by one person of another which exceed the requirements of the general law and the prohibition imposed by the statute. In that connection, Robson A-JA in the Court of Appeal spoke of s 52 as making parties 'strictly responsible to ensure they did not mislead or deceive their customer or trading partners'. Such language, while no doubt intended to distinguish the necessary elements of misleading or deceptive conduct from those of torts such as deceit, negligence and passing off, may take on a life of its own. It may lead to the imposition of a requirement to volunteer information which travels beyond the statutory duty 'to act in a way which does not mislead or deceive'. Cicero, in his famous essay *On Duties*, seems to have contemplated such a standard when he wrote:

> 'Holding things back does not always amount to concealment; but it does when you want people, for your own profit, to be kept in the dark about something which *you* know and would be useful for *them* to know.'

It would no doubt be regarded as an unrealistic expectation, inconsistent with the protection of that 'superior smartness in dealing' of which Barton J wrote in *W Scott, Fell & Co Ltd v Lloyd*, that people who hold things back for their own profit are to be regarded as engaging in misleading or deceptive conduct. As Burchett J observed in *Poseidon Ltd v Adelaide Petroleum NL*, s 52 does not strike at the traditional secretiveness and obliquity of the bargaining process. But his Honour went on to remark that the bargaining process is not to be seen as a licence to deceive, and gave the example of a bargainer who had no intention of contracting on the terms discussed and whose silence was to achieve some undisclosed and ulterior purpose harmful to a competitor. [371]

However, as a general proposition, s 52 does not require a party to commercial negotiations to volunteer information which will be of assistance to the decision-making of the other party. A fortiori it does not impose on a party an obligation to volunteer information in order to avoid the consequences of the careless disregard, for its own interests, of another party of equal bargaining power and competence. Yet that appears to have been, in practical effect, the character of the obligation said to have rested upon Miller in this case. Reasonable expectation analysis is unnecessary in the case of a false representation where the undisclosed fact is the falsity of the representation. A party to pre-contractual negotiations who provides to another party a document containing a false representation which is not disclaimed will, in all probability, have engaged in misleading or deceptive conduct. When a document contains a statement that is true, non-disclosure of an important qualifying fact will be misleading or deceptive if the recipient would be misled, absent such disclosure, into believing that the statement was complete. In some cases it might not be necessary to invoke non-disclosure at all where a statement which is literally true, but incomplete in some material respect, conveys a false representation that it is complete.

[Their Honours concluded that Miller's non-disclosure was not misleading or deceptive. In a separate judgment, Heydon, Crennan and Bell JJ reached the same conclusion.]

Appeal allowed

[footnotes omitted]

As noted in these extracts, the courts have been concerned not to allow the prohibitions of misleading or deceptive conduct to restrict the freedom that parties have traditionally enjoyed to bargain in their own interests during pre-contractual negotiations. However, a party must be careful not to advance its own interests in a manner that misleads or deceives the other party; if they do, liability can arise. Thus, as Nettle JA observed in *CCP Australian Airships Ltd v Primus Telecommunications Pty Ltd*:

> [A]lthough s.52 may not strike at the traditional secretiveness and obliquity of the bargaining process, one purpose of the section ... is to ensure that the bargaining process is not seen as a licence to deceive. Hence, ... if the bargainer has no intention of contracting on the terms discussed, his conduct in seeming to bargain may accurately be stigmatised as misleading. I add, that just as certainly, if a bargainer having no more capacity than a hope and a prayer of providing goods or services conducts negotiations in a fashion calculated to create the impression that he has the capacity to do so, and extracts payment on the faith of that assumption, his conduct is liable to be stigmatised as misleading and deceptive.[26]

---

26   [2004] VSCA 232 at paragraph 33.

e Statements about the future

To help persuade the other party to conclude a contract, a person may make statements about the subject matter that pertain to the future: for example, that a shop being sold could achieve a certain level of sales if properly managed,[27] that a building under construction would have superior facilities to its neighbours,[28] or that the purchaser of a business being sold would have no difficulty in obtaining an extension of a franchise.[29] Problems will arise when such a statement does not come true: when the shop does not achieve the level of sales stated, or the completed building is not superior.

This has proved to be such an important aspect of liability that in 1986 a special provision was introduced to deal with it, located in s 51A of the *TPA*.[30] This provision now appears as s 4 of the *ACL*.

Australian Consumer Law

Section 4. Misleading representations with respect to future matters

(1) If:
   (a) a person makes a representation with respect to any future matter (including the doing of, or the refusing to do, any act); and
   (b) the person does not have reasonable grounds for making the representation; the representation is taken, for the purposes of this Schedule, to be misleading.

(2) For the purposes of applying subsection (1) in relation to a proceeding concerning a representation made with respect to a future matter by:
   (a) a party to the proceeding; or
   (b) any other person;
      the party or other person is taken not to have had reasonable grounds for making the representation, unless evidence is adduced to the contrary.

(3) To avoid doubt, subsection (2) does not:
   (a) have the effect that, merely because such evidence to the contrary is adduced, the person who made the representation is taken to have had reasonable grounds for making the representation; or
   (b) have the effect of placing on any person an onus of proving that the person who made the representation had reasonable grounds for making the representation.

The circumstances in which statements about the future will give rise to liability under the rubric of misleading or deceptive conduct and the operation of what is now s 4 of the *ACL*, are discussed in the following extracts.

---

27 See *Nescor Industries Group Pty Ltd v Miba Pty Ltd* (1998) ATPR 41-609.
28 See *Byers v Dorotea Pty Ltd* (1987) ATPR 40-760.
29 See *McPhillips v Ampol Petroleum (Vic) Pty Ltd* (1990) ATPR 41-014.
30 The state and territory equivalents are: *Fair Trading Act 1992* (ACT) s 11; *Fair Trading Act 1987* (NSW) s 41; *Fair Trading Act 1999* (Vic) s 4; *Fair Trading Act 1989* (Qld) s 37; *Consumer Affairs and Fair Trading Act 1990* (NT) s 41; *Fair Trading Act 1987* (WA) s 9; *Fair Trading Act 1987* (SA) s 54; *Fair Trading Act 1990* (Tas) s 11.

Bowler v Hilda Pty Ltd

(1998) 80 FCR 191, Federal Court of Australia (Full Court)

[Hilda sold a unit in a strata title development to Bowler. Prior to this sale, its agent (Leader) represented that when the development was completed it would be possible for Bowler to use the unit as a residence. At the time this was not possible, although Hilda had sought permission for the unit to be used in this manner. When the sale was completed, permission had still not been obtained by Hilda. Bowler sought to set the sale aside on the ground that the representation contravened, *inter alia*, s 52 of the *TPA*. The application failed at first instance and Bowler appealed.]

Heerey J [at 203]: *Representations involving the future.* There has been for some time a divergence of views as to the applicability of s 52 to such representations.

The first view is that conduct can only be misleading and deceptive if it involves a false representation as to the existence or non-existence of some fact at the time the representation is made. This proposition has usually been stated in terms of the mental state of the representor. Thus it is said that a promise is only misleading or deceptive if it falsely represents that the representor has a present intention to perform the promise in the future, and a prediction is only misleading and deceptive if the representor does not presently hold an opinion that the predicted event will occur. Expressed in this way, this view has given rise to a corollary: representations involving the future can only be misleading and deceptive if they involve a statement as to the representor's state of mind. ...

[at 205]: A second view is that expounded in, DW Greig and JLR Davis, *The Law of Contract* (1987), pp 811–815 and summarised (p 815) where the learned authors say:

> 'If the respondent makes a contractual promise, the applicant may reasonably believe that it will be performed; when the promise is not performed, the applicant's belief is found to be erroneous and it may fairly be said that the respondent's original promise, together with his subsequent repudiation thereof, is conduct which has led the applicant into error.' ...

In *Wright v TNT Management Pty Ltd* (1989) 15 NSWLR 679 at 690, McHugh JA reached a similar conclusion, although with reasoning which relied essentially on s 51A. His Honour said:

> 'At common law a representation outside a contract would only give rise to legal consequences if it was in respect of an existing or past face; a contractual promise as to the future did not have legal consequences. But for the purposes of Pt V, s 51A must be taken to have abolished the distinction between a promise and a representation with respect to a future event. A promise to do something in the future is to be regarded as a representation that it will be performed. It will be deemed misleading, therefore, unless the corporation proves that it had reasonable grounds for making the promise.'

A third view is to be found in the judgment of Lee J (when a member of the Full Court) in *Wheeler Grace & Pierucci Pty Ltd v Wright* [1989] ATPR 50,239 at 50,251. His Honour said:

'A positive unqualified prediction by a corporation may be misleading conduct in trade or commerce if relevant circumstances show the need for some qualification to be attached to that statement or the possibility of its non-fulfilment to be disclosed as a requirement of fair trading. The fact that the corporation believed or had reasonable grounds for belief that the prediction would be fulfilled, would not answer the question as to whether the conduct was misleading or deceptive conduct in trade or commerce. The misleading or deceptive conduct may be found in the failure to qualify the statement or disclose the risk of non-fulfilment and the event of non-fulfilment of a prediction or promise may be evidence that raises an inference that such a risk of non-performance existed or that qualification of the positive statement, prediction or promise was required. Each case will depend upon its own circumstances, but the assessment of misleading or deceptive conduct is an objective test not dependent upon the proof of an intent to mislead or deceive on the part of the corporation (see *Parkdale Custom Built Furniture Pty Ltd v Puxu Pty Ltd* (1982) 149 CLR 191) and <206> restriction of the application of s 52 in respect of promissory or predictive statements by a corporation to conduct of the corporation which involves a lack of belief on the part of the corporation or absence of grounds upon which the corporation performs such a belief would be inconsistent with the thrust of the section.'

This statement is consistent with the first view (*Thompson, Stack, Bill Acceptance* and *Global Sportsman*) and contrary to the second view (Greig and Davis and *Wright*) in that it looks for conduct that is misleading or deceptive in some way at the time the conduct is engaged in—albeit in a way that can only be revealed by reference to subsequent circumstances. However it differs from the first view in declining to make the representor's state of mind an essential element.

I respectfully agree with Lee J's statement of the law, which is consistent with two basic principles that have emerged in the jurisprudence of s 52: first, it is the objective nature of the alleged contravener's conduct that is ultimately determinative of liability and not his or her state of mind; secondly, the words of the statute are to be given their natural meaning and not moulded to fit the pre-existing common law. It might also be noted that this view does not depend on s 51A. It would be equally applicable to the Act in the form it took before s 51A was introduced. That this should be so is consistent with s 51A being an evidentiary rather than substantive provision: *Cummings v Lewis* (1993) 41 FCR 559 at 567.

Lee J's statement is particularly apposite to the application of s 52 to the present case. Leader's statement as to the use which the appellants' unit might be put was quite unqualified. It gave no hint that in truth there was at best a hopeful expectation. Still worse, Leader must be credited with knowledge of Mr Ryman's letter of 7 July 1993 which amounts to an acceptance that most of the units, including unit 23, could not be used for residential purposes.

[Black CJ agreed with Heerey J that the appeal should be allowed. Cooper J would have dismissed the appeal; nevertheless, he agreed with Heerey J concerning the evidentiary nature of s 51A.]

Appeal allowed

Phoenix Court Pty Ltd v Melbourne Central Pty Ltd

(1997) ATPR (Digest) 46-179, Federal Court of Australia

[Phoenix entered into a lease for two shops in a shopping complex operated by Melbourne Central. The shops were not successful and the lease was terminated. Phoenix alleged that the leases and the guarantees that supported them were induced by misleading conduct on the part of Melbourne Central, contrary to s 52. The representations alleged concerned future matters. These proceedings concerned whether its reliance on s 51A was pleaded correctly.]

Goldberg J [at 54,431]: Prior to the enactment of s 51A it was well settled that an applicant could not adequately plead misleading and deceptive conduct invoking s 52 simply by asserting a representation as to future conduct or as to a future event and then asserting that the subject-matter had not come to pass. …

Although the mere fact that a representation as to future conduct or the happening of a future event does not occur does not make the representation misleading or deceptive, such a representation can ripen into misleading or <54,432> deceptive conduct for the purposes of s 52 in a number of circumstances; namely, if there is an implied statement in the representation as to a present or past fact; if the representation represents impliedly that the representor has a present intention to make good the promise or has the means or ability to do so; if the representation involves a representation that the representor has a present state of mind; or if a representation is made, which having regard to relevant circumstances at the time, requires a qualification because of the possibility of its non-fulfilment. … In any of these circumstances it is necessary to plead more than simply the fact of the representation as to the future matter and the fact that it does not occur. One has to plead material facts in relation to the implication in the statement of the present or past fact, the present intention and the means to carry it out, the relevant state of mind and the fact that there was no basis for it, and the relevant circumstance giving rise to the qualification. Without pleading such matters all the material facts necessary to complete the cause of action have not been stated and the respondent does not know what case it has to meet.

However, as a result of the enactment of s 51A the situation has altered because that section makes it clear that a representation with respect to a future matter is misleading unless the representor had reasonable grounds for making it. Section 51A(2) makes it clear that an applicant does not have to establish as an ingredient of its cause of action that the representor did not have reasonable grounds for making the representation. That sub-section rather throws the evidentiary burden on a respondent to establish that reasonable grounds for making the representation existed and in the absence of such evidence the deeming provision has the consequence that the representation is taken to be misleading. Section 51A does not create an independent cause of action separate from s 52 and other sections in Pt V of the Act but rather casts the burden of proof on the respondent and if that burden is not discharged then a breach of s 52 is established by the applicant proving the representation as to the future matter and the fact that it did not come to pass. …

[His Honour concluded that the pleadings invoking s 51A should be allowed to stand and that leave granted to allow Phoenix to raise it.]

f Contractual promises

The issue here is whether, and if so in what circumstances, a party's failure to perform a contractual promise amounts to, or is evidence of, misleading or deceptive conduct. This may be important where the innocent party's contractual remedies are inadequate, or excluded altogether by an exclusion clause. In such a case, relying on s 18 may provide the only means of redress available. The circumstances in which this may be possible are discussed in the following extracts.

Futuretronics International Pty Ltd v Gadzhis

[1992] 2 VR 217, Supreme Court of Victoria

[Futuretronics auctioned a commercial building. Gadzhis made the highest bid at this auction and it was knocked down to him. However, he refused to sign the written contract of sale. As a result, the contract could not be enforced because it did not comply with the formalities prescribed for land contracts. Unable to enforce the contract, Futuretronics commenced proceedings under s 11 of the *Fair Trading Act 1985* (Vic) (now s 9 of the *Fair Trading Act 1999*), arguing that Gadzhis's conduct was misleading or deceptive.]

Ormiston J [at 238]: It is wrong to view every contractual obligation as an unqualified promise to perform the stipulated act. Indeed it is rare that a contractual promise is not in some way qualified by some reciprocal obligation to be performed by the promisee or by some other circumstance. If the promise induced the other party to enter into the agreement, as one can readily accept it would, then it is that promise and the circumstances then surrounding it which must be examined. The promise can only be said to be misleading or deceptive if it was in some way inaccurate; otherwise every unfulfilled mutual contractual promise will constitute misleading or deceptive conduct, a consequence which I cannot believe those who drafted the Act intended. If intention be relevant, the promise may be misleading if the promisor had no intention to fulfil it at the time it was made and accepted. If intention be irrelevant, then the promise may be misleading if the promisor had no ability to perform it at that time. If one were to go to the breach to determine whether there has been misleading or deceptive conduct, the breach may, but only *may*, provide some evidence from which one could infer that the promisor never intended or never had the ability to fulfil his obligation.

[After considering the nature of contractual promises and various authorities, His Honour continued at 239]: It would seem on the authorities that, at the least, a contractual promise would amount to an implied representation that the promisor then had an intention to carry out that promise. If it can be shown that he had no such intention, he would be guilty of misleading or deceptive conduct. Likewise it would seem that such a representation connotes a present ability to fulfil that promise which, if shown to be untrue at the time of making, would likewise characterise the implied representation as misleading or deceptive.

[His Honour then considered the effect of s 51A of the *Trade Practices Act* and s 10A of the *Fair Trading Act 1985* (Vic)—now s 4 of the *Fair Trading Act 1999*—and continued at 240]: In my opinion, ... accepting that s 51A and s 10A each assumes that a promise may give rise to an implied representation that the promisor will perform an act in the future, namely the promised act, then the promisee is not, in proceedings under s 52 or s 11, bound to show that the promisor had no intention or no ability to perform the promise at the time of its making. The promisor will be deemed *not* to have reasonable grounds for making the representation or promise, unless he satisfies the court by evidence to the contrary that he had reasonable grounds for making that representation. He may achieve this, in part, by showing that he had a genuine intention to perform his promise and that he had the ability at the time to perform it, but in the end he must show objectively that he had reasonable grounds for making the representation. For present purposes I am not prepared to accept that the plaintiff can make out its case by showing merely promise and breach. In my opinion, that evidence, on its own, is insufficient to show that the promisee was 'led into error' unless the plaintiff can rely on s 10A or s 51A. ...

It follows from what has been said that I am not persuaded that one should treat every contractual promise as giving rise to an implied <241> representation of the kind referred to in s 10A (and s 51A). However, I am persuaded that if there be an unconditional promise which forms part of the contractual obligations, then it is proper to treat the giving of that promise, at least in the ordinary case, as the making of a representation as to a future matter, being either the doing of an act or the 'refusing' (*sic*) to do an act, being in each case the subject of the promise. Perhaps conditional promises may also be treated as the making of a representation as to future conduct, but in each case the qualified terms of the promise would usually lead to the conclusion that the maker had reasonable grounds therefor, unless it could be shown that under no circumstances would the promisor have fulfilled his promise. It is, however, not necessary to determine this latter point.

[His Honour went on to find that Gadzhis had made a representation that he intended to sign the contract and did not have reasonable grounds for making this representation. As a result, his conduct was misleading. However, the plaintiff's case failed because it was unable to show that Gadzhis' conduct had caused it any loss. This was because there was no other bidder interested in the property who may have bought it but for his conduct.]

Campbell v Backoffice Investments Pty Ltd

(2009) 238 CLR 304, High Court of Australia

French CJ [at 322]: The term 'conduct which is misleading or deceptive or likely to mislead or deceive' is apt to cover a large variety of possible circumstances in which the conduct of one has a tendency to lead another into error. There is no reason in principle why the fact that a false statement is contained in a contractual document thereby takes the use of that statement in the document out of the scope of 'misleading or deceptive conduct'. Whether the proffering of a contractual document containing a false statement amounts to a misrepresentation or to misleading or deceptive conduct, is a matter of fact to be determined by reference to all the circumstances. The circumstance that such a representation is the subject of a contractual warranty does not, as a matter of law, exclude the making of it from the purview of the statutory prohibition. This is consistent with the observation by Lockhart and Gummow JJ in *Accounting Systems 2000 (Developments) Pty Ltd v CCH Australia Ltd*: 'the making of a statement as to a presently existing state of affairs, if false, may be the engaging in misleading or deceptive conduct, where the statement is embodied as a provision of a contract.'

The question whether the giving of a warranty about the accuracy of a statement of present fact or a forecast of performance is misleading or deceptive raises slightly different considerations. The giving of a warranty embodying a false statement of present fact may be characterised as misleading or deceptive conduct simply because it involves the making of that false statement. A warranty as to a forecast of performance may fall within the category of, or involve the making of, a statement as to a future matter. Such a statement can be characterised as misleading or deceptive or likely to mislead or deceive according to whether there were reasonable grounds for making it or whether any other implied representations which it conveyed were true.

g Relaying information

The information one contracting party provides to the other will often have originated from a third party. In such a situation, where it is made clear that the information is merely being relayed from that source, liability for misleading or deceptive conduct cannot arise even though the information itself is false in some way.[31] This is because the only relevant conduct is the act of relaying the information and it is not this that has misled the recipient. On the other hand, if the party relaying the information adopts it as their own, that is, does not make clear that it is merely being relayed, liability can arise because it will be their conduct that has misled the recipient.[32]

The latter situation can give rise to rather poignant cases where a private contract has been made with the assistance of an agent. In such cases, false information provided by one of the parties to the other will not attract liability because it will not have been communicated in trade or commerce. However, if the same information is communicated by an agent, without the agent making clear that it is merely relaying information, the agent will be liable as *its* conduct will have the required commercial character.[33] On the other hand, as the following case shows, if the agent does make this clear liability will not arise.

---

31 See *Saints Gallery Pty Ltd v Plummer* (1988) 80 ALR 525.
32 See *John G Glass Real Estate Pty Ltd v Karawi Constructions Pty Ltd* (1993) ATPR 41-249.
33 See *Argy v Blunts & Lane Cove Real Estate Pty Ltd* (1990) 26 FCR 112.

Butcher v Lachlan Elder Realty Pty Ltd

(2004) 218 CLR 592, High Court of Australia

[The purchasers (Mr Butcher and Ms Radford) purchased at auction a residential property (the Rednal land) from a Mr Hawkins (the vendor). Before bidding at the auction, the purchasers had been given a brochure prepared by a real estate agent (the respondent, Lachlan Elder Realty Pty Ltd) containing a survey diagram showing a swimming pool entirely within the boundary of the land. In fact, only part of the pool was within the land. The brochure indicated that the information it provided had been obtained from other sources and that its accuracy could not be guaranteed. When the true position of the swimming pool was discovered a dispute arose between the purchasers and the vendor which led to the latter forfeiting the purchasers' deposit. Arising out of this dispute, the purchasers commenced proceedings against the vendor and against the agent. At first instance, it was held that the vendor was guilty of misrepresentation by authorising the preparation of the brochure and the inclusion of the inaccurate survey diagram. On this ground, the vendor was ordered to repay the deposit. However, the vendor's conduct, although misleading, was held not to contravene s 42 of the *Fair Trading Act 1987* (NSW) as it had not occurred in trade or commerce. In relation to the agent, the trial judge concluded that because it had merely passed on information prepared by others and because of disclaimers in the brochure, its conduct had not been misleading. The vendor appealed against the purchasers to the Court of Appeal; this was dismissed. The purchasers appealed against the agent; this was also dismissed. The purchasers then appealed to the High Court.]

Gleeson CJ Hayne and Heydon JJ [at 605] [38] *The relevant principles*. In *Yorke v Lucas*, Mason A-CJ, Wilson, Deane and Dawson JJ said that a corporation could contravene s 52 even though it acted honestly and reasonably:

> That does not, however, mean that a corporation which purports to do no more than pass on information supplied by another must nevertheless be engaging in misleading or deceptive conduct if the information turns out to be false. If the circumstances are such as to make it apparent that the corporation is not the source of the information and that it expressly or impliedly disclaims any belief in its truth or falsity, merely passing it on for what it is worth, we very much doubt that the corporation can properly be said to be itself engaging in conduct that is misleading or deceptive.

[39] In applying those principles, it is important that the agent's conduct be viewed as a whole. It is not right to characterise the problem as one of analysing the effect of its 'conduct' divorced from 'disclaimers' about that 'conduct' and divorced from other circumstances which might qualify its character. Everything relevant the agent did up to the time when the purchasers contracted to buy the Rednal land must be taken into account. It is also important to remember that the relevant question must not be reduced to a crude inquiry: 'Did the agent realise the purchasers were relying on the diagram?' To do that would be impermissibly to dilute the strict liability which s 52 imposes.

[40] For the following reasons, the agent did not engage in conduct towards the purchasers which was misleading. Whatever representation the vendor made to the purchasers by authorising the agent to issue the brochure, it was not made by the agent to the purchasers. The agent did no more than communicate what the vendor was representing, without adopting it or endorsing it. That conclusion flows from the nature of the parties, the character of the transaction contemplated, and the contents of the brochure itself.

[As far as the nature of parties was concerned, at paragraphs 41–44, their Honours noted that the purchasers had considerable business and investment experience involving complex property and financial dealings and that they were 'intelligent, shrewd and self-reliant ... [who would have] appeared that way to the officers of the agent.' On the other hand, the agent did not possess and did not hold itself out as possessing research skills, or the means of independently verifying title details about the property. Furthermore, the legal relationship between the purchasers and the vendor was created not through the agent, but by the purchasers bidding at the auction and signing a contract. As far as the character of the transaction was concerned, at paragraphs 45 and 46 their Honours noted that it involved the purchase of a very expensive property as an investment and that the purchasers had engaged professional advisers to assist them—an accountant, an architect, a builder and solicitors. As far as the contents of the brochure were concerned, at paragraph 47 it was noted that it was plain that the diagram shown had not been made by the agent and that the circumstances 'negated any suggestion that the agent had adopted the surveyor's diagram as its own, or that it verified its accuracy.' Their Honours also considered the effect of two disclaimers on the brochure and made the following observations about them commencing at page 608.]

[49] It is now necessary to consider the two disclaimers, one on the front and one on the back. ... If the disclaimers are examined from the point of view of what the agent was trying to do, the first at least establishes that it was trying not to make any representations about the accuracy of the information conveyed, save that it believed the sources of it to be reliable. If the disclaimers are examined from the point of view of a careful reader, they communicate the same message. ... [T]hough the disclaimers were in small type, the brochure was a short document, there was very little written on it, and the disclaimers were there to be read. Only persons of very poor eyesight would find them illegible, and there is no evidence that the eyesight of Mr Butcher or Ms Radford was in any way defective.

[50] The Court of Appeal declined to 'accord [the disclaimers] decisive significance', but they do have some significance. If the 'conduct' of the agent is what a reasonable person in the position of the purchasers, taking into account what they knew, would make of the agent's behaviour, reasonable purchasers would have read the whole document, given its importance, its brevity, and their use of it as the source of instructions to professional advisers. There are circumstances in which the 'conduct' of an agent would depend on different tests. For example, those tests might turn on what purchasers actually made of the agent's behaviour, whether they were acting reasonably or not, and they might also call for consideration of how the agent perceived the purchasers. Tests of that latter kind might be appropriate

for plaintiffs of limited experience acting without professional advice in rushed circumstances. They are not appropriate in the present <609> circumstances. Hence, in the circumstances, the brochure, read as a whole, simply meant:

'The diagram records what a particular surveyor found on a survey in 1980. We are not surveyors. We did not do the survey. We did not engage any surveyor to do the survey. We believe the vendor and the surveyor are reliable, but we cannot guarantee the accuracy of the information they have provided. Whatever you rely on, you must rely on your own enquiries.'

[51] Hence it would have been plain to a reasonable purchaser that the agent was not the source of the information which was said to be misleading. The agent did not purport to do anything more than pass on information supplied by another or others. It both expressly and implicitly disclaimed any belief in the truth or falsity of that information. It did no more than state a belief in the reliability of the sources.

[McHugh and Kirby JJ dissented]

Appeal dismissed

[footnotes omitted]

h   Exclusion clauses

At common law, a contractual exclusion clause can protect a party from liability for innocent misrepresentation.[34] This is not possible in the case of misleading or deceptive conduct.[35] However, it has been envisaged that an appropriately drafted clause delivered at the appropriate time may be able to prevent misleading conduct occurring in the first place, or, by breaking the required nexus between the defendant's conduct and the plaintiff's loss, prevent damages being recovered.[36] The position is conveniently summarised by French CJ in *Campbell v Backoffice Investments Pty Ltd* (2009) 238 CLR 304 at 321 in the following terms:

> Where the impugned conduct comprises allegedly misleading pre-contractual representations, a contractual disclaimer of reliance will ordinarily be considered in relation to the question of causation. For if a person expressly declares in a contractual document that he or she did not rely upon pre-contractual representations, that declaration may, according to the circumstances, be evidence of non-reliance and of the want of a causal link between the impugned conduct and the loss or damage flowing from entry into the contract. In many cases, such a provision will not be taken to evidence a break in the causal link between misleading or deceptive conduct and loss. The person making the declaration may nevertheless be found to have been actuated by the misrepresentations into entering the contract. The question is not one of law, but of fact.

---

34   See *Byers v Dorotea Pty Ltd* (1987) ATPR 40-760 at 48,230.
35   See *Henjo Investments Pty Ltd v Collins Marrickville Pty Ltd* (1988) 39 FCR 546; *Bowler V Hilda Pty Ltd* (1998) 80 FCR 191.
36   See *Leda Holdings Pty Ltd v Oraka Pty Ltd* (1998) ATPR 41-601.

i Failure to exercise care

Where misleading or deceptive conduct is established, it is no defence for the guilty party to show that the plaintiff would have discovered the error and avoided loss by exercising reasonable care and properly looking after their own interests.[37] Thus, for example, failing to verify the accuracy of a representation, even though this could have been done easily,[38] or failing to notice that documents were incomplete,[39] or failing to instruct a solicitor when executing a major financial investment[40] will not prevent liability arising where the plaintiff was misled. The position is the same at common law in relation to pre-contractual misrepresentation.[41] However, it has been envisaged that a plaintiff's failure to exercise care may show that they were not influenced by the defendant's misleading conduct and so prevent them showing that it caused them loss.[42] It may also reduce the damages recoverable when causation is still present.[43]

j Vicarious liability

A person or corporation engaged in trade or commerce will be liable for the misleading or deceptive conduct of their employees or agents where the employee or agent was acting on their behalf. This is the result of the application of the common law relating to a principal's vicarious liability as extended by statutory provisions dealing with this situation.[44]

6 Remedies

In cases of contract-related misleading conduct, one of the advantages to a plaintiff of being able to rely upon s 18 of the *ACL* is that the remedies available are significantly more extensive than those provided by the common law. In particular, damages can be obtained without the need to establish that the conduct was fraudulent, or had been incorporated as a term of the contract. In addition, where the conduct induced a contract, the courts are not restricted to only being able to choose between rescinding the contract or not, but also have very broad powers to vary or adjust the contract in order to ensure that the plaintiff is adequately compensated.

---

37 See *Henville v Walker* (2001) 206 CLR 459.
38 See *Sutton v AJ Thompson Pty Ltd* (1987) 73 ALR 233, esp at 240–241; *Henjo Investments Pty Ltd v Collins Marrickville Pty Ltd* (1988) 39 FCR 546, esp at 558.
39 See *Argy v Blunts & Land Cove Real Estate Pty Ltd* (1990) 26 FCR 112, esp at 136–138.
40 *Idem.*
41 See *Redgrave v Hurd* (1881) 20 Ch D 1.
42 See *Argy v Blunts & Land Cove Real Estate Pty Ltd* (1990) 26 FCR 112 at 138; *Henville v Walker* (2001) 206 CLR 459 at 468 [13].
43 See *Competition and Consumer Act 2010* (Cth) s 137B discussed below.
44 See *Competition and Consumer Act 2010* (Cth) s 139B(2).

a Damages

Anyone who suffers loss or damage as a result of a contravention of s 18 has a statutory right to recover compensatory damages under s 236(1) of the *ACL* from the person whose conduct caused that loss or damage and any other person involved in the contravention.[45] Section 236(2) requires actions to be commenced within six years of the date upon which the cause of action accrued.

Scope of the remedy

Damages are recoverable by anyone who suffers loss as a result of misleading conduct. Recovery is not restricted to persons who enter into a contract with the guilty party, nor is it restricted to those who are the immediate target of the misleading conduct. The variety of situations within the scope of the remedy is illustrated below.

Examples

1. D communicated with P and this induced P to enter into a contract with D (in practice, the most common situation).
2. D communicated with P and this induced P to enter into a contract with a third party C.
3. D communicated with C who to D's knowledge relayed the communication to P who entered into a contract with T.

Causation

Damages are recoverable only in respect of loss or damage that was caused by the defendant's misleading conduct and the plaintiff bears the burden of proof on this issue. This follows from the requirement in s 236 that it be suffered 'because of the conduct' of the defendant, a phrase which 'clearly requires causation'. Consequently, damages cannot be recovered by a person who was not influenced by the defendant's conduct,[46] or whose loss was attributable to other causes and not that conduct.[47] A further consequence is that where a person does not take reasonable steps to mitigate their loss, they may be unable to recover damages in respect of that part of the loss that could have been avoided, as the required causation will not the present.[48] On the other hand, it has been held in relation to the precursor to s 236(1), s 82(1) of the *TPA*, that it is not necessary to show that the defendant's conduct was the immediate, only or even major cause of the plaintiff's loss.[49] A useful summary of the approach to be taken to causation is contained in

---

45   Punitive damages cannot be awarded under s 236(1): *Marks v GIO Australia Holdings Ltd* (1998) 196 CLR 494.
46   See *Abram v Bank of New Zealand* (1996) ATPR 41-507.
47   See *Lam v Ausintel Investments Australia Pty Ltd* (1990) ATPR 40-990 and *Sullivan v Macquarie Pathology Services Pty Ltd* (1995) ATPR (Digest) 46-143.
48   See *Leigh Enterprises Pty Ltd v Transcrete Pty Ltd* (1984) ATPR 40-452.
49   See *Henville v Walker* (2001) 206 CLR 459, esp Hayne J at 507–510.

the following extract; it also serves to emphasise the importance, in contract cases, of considering the effect of the defendant's conduct on the particular plaintiff and of considering that conduct in the context of the entire transaction.

Campbell v Backoffice Investments Pty Ltd
(2009) 238 CLR 304, High Court of Australia

French CJ [at 319]: In *Butcher v Lachlan Elder Realty Pty Ltd* (73) the approach to characterisation of conduct directed to identified individuals was set out in the joint judgment of the majority as follows:

> The plaintiff must establish a causal link between the impugned conduct and the loss that is claimed. That depends on analysing the conduct of the defendant in relation to that plaintiff alone. So here, [320] it is necessary to consider the character of the particular conduct of the particular agent in relation to the particular purchasers, bearing in mind what matters of fact each knew about the other as a result of the nature of their dealings and the conversations between them, or which each may be taken to have known.

Although this passage begins by referring to the need to establish a causal link between the impugned conduct and the claimed loss, it is clear that thereafter their Honours were addressing the task of characterisation.

Determination of the causation of loss or damage may require account to be taken of subjective factors relating to a particular person's reaction to conduct found to be misleading or deceptive or likely to mislead or deceive. A misstatement of fact may be misleading or deceptive in the sense that it would have a tendency to lead anyone into error. However, it may be disbelieved by its addressee. In that event the misstatement would not ordinarily be causative of any loss or damage flowing from the subsequent conduct of the addressee.

A person accused of engaging in misleading or deceptive conduct may claim that its effects were negated by a contemporaneous disclaimer by that person, or a subsequent disclaimer of reliance by the person allegedly affected by the conduct. The contemporaneous disclaimer by the person engaging in the impugned conduct is likely to go to the characterisation of the conduct. A subsequent declaration of non-reliance by a person said to have been affected by the conduct is more likely to be relevant to the question of causation.

[footnotes omitted]

Remoteness

Section 236(1) of the *ACL* makes no mention of whether, when causation has been established, nevertheless the remoteness of the plaintiff's loss from the defendant's conduct will preclude damages being awarded. However, the common law concept of remoteness has been used in relation to s 82(1) of the *TPA* and it is always the case that the more remote the connection between contravening conduct and loss, the more likely it will be that the required causation between the two will be found not to exist. The requirement of causation and the issue of remotenesss are analysed in the following extract.

Henville v Walker

(2001) 206 CLR 459, High Court of Australia

[Henville, an architect and developer asked Walker to locate land suitable for development. Walker did this. Walker also represented that there was a demand for luxury home units in the locality and that if units were built on the land, Henville was likely to be able to sell them for between $250,000 and $280,000 each. After these statements were made but before he purchased the land, Henville prepared a feasibility study for the construction of three units which incorporated the lower end of Walker's estimate. This study was erroneous. Henville purchased the land and built the units, but was only able to sell them for a total of $545,000. In proceedings against Walker, alleging a contravention of s 52, he claimed damages under s 82. At first instance, he was awarded the difference between the sale price represented by Walker ($750,000) and the actual sale price. Walker succeeded on appeal to the Full Court of the Western Australian Supreme Court. According to the court, the errors Henville made in the feasibility study broke the causal connection between his loss and Walker's misleading conduct. Henville appealed to the High Court.]

McHugh J [at 489] [95]: This Court's decision in *Wardley Australia Ltd v Western Australia* established that the term 'by' in s 82 invokes the common law concept of causation. ...

[96] But this does not mean that common law conceptions of causation should be rigidly applied without regard to the terms or objects of the Act. .... In *Marks v GIO Australia Holdings Ltd*, Hayne and Callinan JJ and I pointed out that the section can apply to many different kinds of cases, not just those where a breach of s 52 is alleged. Moreover, the objects of the Act indicate that a court should strive to apply s 82 in a way that promotes competition and fair trading and protects consumers. The width of the potential application of s 82 and the objects of the Act tell against a narrow, inflexible construction of the section. No doubt in most cases, applying common law conceptions of causation will be sufficient to answer the issues posed by s 82 in its application to <490> contraventions of the Act. But care must be taken to avoid a mechanical application of those conceptions to issues arising under the section. ...

[97] The common law concept of causation recognises that conduct that infringes a legal norm may be causally connected with the sustaining of loss or damage even though other factors may have contributed to the loss or damage. Every event is the product of a number of conditions that have combined to produce the event. Some philosophers draw a distinction between a *condition* that is necessary only and a *cause* that is both necessary and sufficient to produce the event. The common law has avoided the technical controversies inherent in the logic of causation. Unlike science and philosophy, the common law is not concerned

to discover universal connections between phenomena so as to enable predictions to be made. The common law concept of causation looks backward because its function is to determine whether a person should be held responsible for some past act or omission. ... <493> ...

[105] ... [T]he course of judicial reasoning in this area has produced certain principles that assist tribunals of fact in deciding causation issues.

[106] If the defendant's breach has 'materially contributed' to the loss or damage suffered, it will be regarded as a cause of the loss or damage, despite other factors or conditions having played an even more significant role in producing the loss or damage. As long as the breach materially contributed to the damage, a causal connection will ordinarily exist even though the breach without more would not have brought about the damage. In exceptional cases, where an abnormal event intervenes between the breach and damage, it may be right as a matter of common sense to hold that the breach was not a cause of damage. But such cases are exceptional.

[107] Of particular importance to the present case is the long-standing recognition of the possibility that two or more causes may jointly influence a person to undertake a course of conduct. In separate judgments in *Gould v Vaggelas* Wilson and Brennan JJ emphasised that a representation need not be the sole inducement in sustaining the loss. If 'it plays some part even if only a minor part', in contributing to the course of action taken—in that case the formation of a contract—a causal connection will exist.

[108] This principle has been applied in cases where a complicating factor <494> is the intervention of some act or decision of the plaintiff or a third party that allegedly constitutes a more immediate cause of the loss or damage. Thus, in *Medlin v State Government Insurance Commission* Deane, Dawson, Toohey and Gaudron JJ said:

> 'The ultimate question must, however, always be whether, *notwithstanding the intervention of the subsequent decision*, the defendant's wrongful act or omission is, as between the plaintiff and the defendant and as a matter of commonsense and experience, properly to be seen as having caused the relevant loss or damage. Indeed, in some cases, it may be potentially misleading to pose the question of causation in terms of whether an intervening act or decision has interrupted or broken a chain of causation which would otherwise have existed. An example of such a case is where the negligent act or omission was itself a direct or indirect contributing cause of the intervening act or decision.' (Emphasis added.)

[109] Similarly, in respect of claims under s 82, courts have accepted that loss or damage is causally connected to a contravention of the Act if a misrepresentation was one of the causes of the loss or damage sustained by the claimant. ... <504> ...

[136] Given the long history of the common law's recognition of the concept of remoteness in assessing damages in contract and tort and its relationship with the issue of causation, it seems proper to read the term 'by' in s 82 as including the concept of remoteness. By remoteness, I mean that the loss or damage was not reasonably foreseeable even in a general way by the contravener. ...

[His Honour concluded that Walker's misrepresentations were causally connected to the loss sustained by Henville and that the appeal should be allowed. Gleeson CJ, Gaudron and Hayne JJ delivered separate judgments to the same effect; Gummow J expressly agreed with McHugh J.]

Appeal allowed

[footnotes omitted]

Types of loss or damage compensable

Damages can be recovered under s 236(1) of the *ACL* in respect of all types of loss or damage with the exception of that resulting from death or personal injury which are excluded by s 137C(1) of the *Competition and Consumer Act* 2010 (Cth) unless resulting from smoking or the use of tobacco. This includes pecuniary loss, loss of goodwill or an opportunity, injury to reputation, inconvenience and mental distress.

Failure to take care

In *Henville v Walker*, the High Court decided that s 82 of the *TPA* did not allow the courts to reduce an award of damages on account of the plaintiff's failure to exercise reasonable care, even though this contributed to their loss or damage. According to McHugh J:

> Nothing in the common law, in ss 52 or 82 or in the policy of the Act supports the conclusion that a claimant's damages under s 82 should be reduced because the loss or damage could have been avoided by the exercise of reasonable care on the claimant's part. There is no ground for reading into s 82 doctrines of contributory negligence and apportionment of damages. No doubt, if part of the loss or damage would not have occurred but for the unreasonable conduct of the claimant, it will be appropriate in assessing damages under s 82 to apply notions of reasonableness in assessing how much of the loss was caused by the contravention of the Act. But that proposition is concerned with the items that go to the computation of the loss.[50]

Parliament, however, was not persuaded and in 2004, s 82(1B) was inserted into the *TPA* to, in effect, reverse this decision. This was carried forward into the *Competition and Consumer Act 2010* (Cth) in the form of s 137B, which provides that where a 'claimant' suffers economic loss or property damage partly as a result of their own 'failure to take reasonable care' and partly as a result of the defendant's breach of s 18 of the *ACL*, the damages they can recover from the defendant under s 236(1) of the *ACL* are to be reduced to the 'extent to which the court thinks just and equitable having regard to the claimant's share in the responsibility for the loss or damage'. Consequently, where a person has failed to take reasonable care to look after their own interests and this has contributed to the loss they have suffered as a result of the defendant's contravention of s 18, their damages are likely to be

---

50 (2001) 206 CLR 459 at 505 [140].

reduced in proportion to that contribution. However, as a result of s 137(B)(d) this will not apply where the defendant intended to cause the loss or damage, or caused it fraudulently.[51]

Measure of damages

No particular measure of damages is prescribed in relation to s 236(1). The one most commonly employed in cases of representations contravening s 52 of the *TPA* has been that used in tort, rather than that used for breach of contract, and it is likely that this will continue in relation to s 18. In *Gates v City Mutual Life Assurance Society Ltd* Mason, Wilson and Dawson JJ described the difference as follows:

> In contract, damages are awarded with the object of placing the plaintiff in the position in which he would have been had the contract been performed—he is entitled to damages for loss of bargain (expectation loss) and damage suffered, including expenditure incurred, in reliance on the contract (reliance loss). In tort, on the other hand, damages are awarded with the object of placing the plaintiff in the position in which he would have been had the tort not been committed (similar to reliance loss).[52]

According to their Honours, the tort measure is appropriate for most cases involving misleading or deceptive conduct as the guilty party's conduct 'is similar both in character and effect to tortious conduct, particularly fraudulent misrepresentation and negligent misstatement'.[53] Applied to the facts of the case, this measure meant that Gates could recover nothing because, although City Mutual had misrepresented the benefits he was entitled to under the insurance policy sold to him, that policy was still worth what he had paid for it. In other words, he was not worse off as a result of entering into the transaction than he would have been had he not done so. The result would have been different, however, had Gates been able to show that if the representation had not been made he would have entered into a contract that *did* give him the benefits City Mutual had represented. In such a case, his reliance on City Mutual's misrepresentation would have caused him loss.

Although in *Gates* the court applied the 'difference between real value and price paid' test, it acknowledged that this was only the *prima facie* measure used in tort cases and that, for example, a plaintiff could also recover consequential loss directly flowing from their reliance on misleading conduct. Furthermore, it envisaged that there might be cases in which the tort measure was not appropriate at all. This possibility has been emphasised in subsequent cases. The High Court, in particular, has stressed that when considering claims under s 82 of the *TPA* (and now presumably s 236 of the *ACL*), the courts are not bound by the approaches taken at common law. Guidance is provided in the following extracts.

---

51 For a full analysis of this provision, see S Christensen and A Stickley, 'Will apportionment of responsibility for misleading conduct erode the consumer protection potency of the *Trade Practices Act 1974* (Cth)?' (2006) 34 *ABLR* 119.
52 (1986) 160 CLR 1 at 11–12.
53 *Gates v City Mutual Life Assurance Society Ltd* (1986) 160 CLR 1 at 14.

Henville v Walker

(2001) 206 CLR 459, High Court of Australia

McHugh J [at 501]: *Damages*

[130] This Court has addressed the question of assessment of damages under s 82 on several occasions. The Court has concluded that in most cases the measure of damages in tort is the appropriate guide in determining an award of damages under s 82. However, in assessing damages under s 82, courts are not bound to choose between the measure of damages in deceit or other torts or contract. In *Marks v GIO Australia Holdings Ltd*, the Court said that the central issue under s 82 is to establish a causal connection between the loss claimed and the contravening conduct. Once such a connection is found to exist, nothing in s 82 suggests that the recoverable amount should be limited by drawing an analogy with contract, tort or equitable remedies although they will usually be of <502> great assistance. As Gummow J said in *Marks*, '[a]nalogy, like the rules of procedure, is a servant not a master'.

[131] Indeed, general principles for assessing damages may have to give way altogether in particular cases to solutions best adapted to give the injured claimant an amount which will most fairly compensate for the wrong suffered.

[132] In this case, the most appropriate approach is to identify what Mr Henville has suffered by way of prejudice or disadvantage in consequence of altering his position by reason of the breach of the Act. The measure of that loss is not determined by reference to what he would have received if Mr Walker's representations had been true. ... [T]he wrong which s 52 of the Act prohibits is the making of, not the failure to honour, the false representation. By entering upon the project, Mr Henville has lost $319,846.51. If Mr Walker had not made representations in breach of the Act, none of this loss would have occurred. The loss suffered is therefore directly attributable to a contravention of the Act even though other factors played their part in bringing about the loss. ... <503> ...

[135] ... The purposes of the Act include promoting fair trading and protecting consumers from contraventions of the Act. Those purposes are more readily achieved by ensuring that consumers recover the actual losses they have suffered as the result of contraventions of the Act. Where a person contravenes the Act and induces a person to enter upon a course of conduct that results in loss or damage, an award of damages that compensates for the actual losses incurred in embarking on that course of conduct best serves the purposes of the Act and should ordinarily be awarded. In *Elna Australia Pty Ltd v International Computers (Aust) Pty Ltd (No 2)*, Gummow J said, correctly in my opinion:

> 'Wrapped up within s 82 are ... concepts the common law would describe by the terms "causation" and "remoteness" and "measure of damages". ... [I]t would be an error to translate automatically to the particular statute what appeared the closest analogue from the common law "rules" as to causation. It is rather a question of statutory construction. ... Thus, in construing s 82 it is appropriate to bear in mind such matters as the scope and purpose of Pts IV and V ... the wide range of

subject-matters dealt with in Pts IV and V but all linked to s 82 ... the absence of any direct provision to apportion responsibility for loss or damage ... and the apparent telescoping of what to the common law would be issues of causation, remoteness and measure of damages.'

[footnotes omitted]

Murphy v Overton Investments Pty Ltd
(2004) 216 CLR 388, High Court of Australia

[Mr and Mrs Murphy contracted with Overton to lease a unit in a retirement village it operated. Prior to it being executed, Overton made representations about the outgoings the Murphys would have to pay under the lease. These were found to be misleading. The Murphys would not have entered into the lease had they known the true position. They commenced proceedings seeking various remedies; the following extract deals only with their claim for damages. This failed at first instance and on appeal to the Full Federal Court. The Murphys then appealed to the High Court.]

Gleeson CJ, Gummow, Kirby, Hayne, Callinan and Heydon JJ [at 402]:
Conclusions at trial

[29] The trial judge concluded that the appellants had not proved that they had suffered any loss or damage. There were two steps taken to reach that conclusion. First, his Honour said that:

> 'When a claimant is induced by a misrepresentation to enter into an agreement that proves to be to his or her disadvantage, the claimant sustains a detriment, in a general sense, on entry into the agreement. That is because the agreement subjects the claimant to <403> obligations and liabilities that exceed the value or worth of the rights and benefits that it confers upon the claimant. However, detriment in that general sense is not universally equated with the legal concept of *"loss or damage"*— *Wardley Australia Ltd v Western Australia* ... Where a misrepresentation induces a claimant to enter into an agreement to purchase property, the claimant's loss, apart from any question of consequential damage, is measured by the difference between the price paid or payable under the agreement and the value of the property at the date of the agreement—*Potts v Miller*.'

As has been said above, there was no evidence of any difference between price paid under the agreement and the value of the property at the date of the agreement.

[30] Secondly, it was said that, because the lease obliged the appellants to pay the sums claimed as outgoings, and there was no evidence that the appellants were 'not receiving value for the maintenance fees that they [were] paying', they suffered no loss 'by reason of the level of maintenance fees that they [were] liable to pay'. It was said that the appellants had done nothing to their detriment after the respondent indicated that it intended to charge all that it was entitled to charge under the lease for outgoings. Their obligation to make those payments was undertaken when they took their lease and that obligation was not 'contingent in the sense that was referred to in *Wardley*'.

[31] Two comments about this reasoning may be made at once. First, the difference between price and value will often be an important element in assessing the damage suffered by a person who, by a misrepresentation, has been induced to buy an item of property. As the trial judge said, there may also be questions of consequential damage. It would be wrong, however, to assume that in every case of misrepresentation (leave aside other forms of misleading or deceptive conduct) the only kind of damage which may be suffered, and compensated or redressed by orders under Pt VI of the Act, is any difference between price and value or any consequential losses. In particular, care must be exercised before seeking to apply what it described as the 'rule in *Potts v Miller*' to claims made for relief under Pt VI of the Act. This is especially so when it is recalled that while the only monetary remedy for the tort of deceit is damages, a far wider range of remedies is available where contravention of the Act has caused or is likely to cause loss or damage to a party to the proceeding. <404>

[32] Secondly, while the trial judge rightly pointed out that there was no evidence that the appellants did not receive value for the maintenance fees they paid, it does not necessarily follow that there was no loss incurred by the appellants if the outgoings for which they were liable included sums of a kind which had not been taken into account in forming the estimate they were given. ... <407> ...

Some general principles affecting remedies under Pt VI.
[44] This Court has now said more than once that it is wrong to approach the operation of those provisions of Pt VI of the Act which deal with remedies for contravention of the Act by beginning the inquiry with an attempt to draw some analogy with any particular form of claim under the general law. No doubt analogies may be helpful, but it would be wrong to argue from the content of the general law that has developed in connection, for example, with the tort of deceit, to a conclusion about the construction or application of provisions of Pt VI of the Act. To do so distracts attention from the primary task of construing the relevant provisions of the Act. In the present case, analogies with the tort of deceit appear to have led to an assumption, at least at trial, that a person can suffer only one form of loss or damage as a result of a contravention of Pt V of the Act.

[45] The Act's references to 'loss or damage' can be given no narrow meaning. Section 4k of the Act provides that loss or damage includes a reference to injury. It follows that the loss or damage spoken of in ss 82 and 87 is not confined to economic loss. What kinds of detriment constitute loss or damage, when a detriment is to be identified as occurring or likely to occur, and what remedies are to be awarded, may all raise further difficult questions. Especially is that so when it is recalled that remedies may be awarded to compensate, prevent or reduce loss or damage that has been or is likely to be suffered by conduct in contravention of the Act.

[46] In *Wardley Australia Ltd v Western Australia*, a case about the application of s 82 of the Act, not s 87, a majority of the Court held that risk of loss is not itself a category of loss, and that, if a <408> plaintiff enters a contract which exposes the plaintiff to a *contingent* loss or liability, that plaintiff 'sustains no actual damage until the contingency is fulfilled and the loss becomes actual'. *Wardley* illustrates

that it is necessary to identify the detriment which is said to be the loss or damage which has occurred (or, when considering the application of s 87, has occurred or is likely to occur). In that case, the mere entry into obligations which might, but need not, have had detrimental consequences in the future was held not to have occasioned loss or damage to the party making the contract. ... <415> ...

Conclusion
[74] The reasoning employed by the Full Court in reaching the conclusion that the appellants proved no loss or damage was erroneous. The appellants did establish that they had undertaken an <416> obligation which, in the events that happened, proved to be larger than the respondent's misleading conduct led them to believe. Though at the end of the day the appellants may fail to prove any loss or damage, it is possible that they will demonstrate that they have suffered loss or damage. The matter should be remitted to the trial judge to assess the damages, if any, to be allowed to the appellants. The trial judge, while hearing the remitted issues, may think it proper to draw inferences in favour of the appellants, if it is concluded that the respondent's wrong itself made quantification difficult. ...

Appeal allowed

[footnotes omitted]

The liability of persons 'involved'

Damages can be recovered under s 236(1) not only from the party whose conduct contravened s 18 but also from 'any person involved in the contravention'. *Sutton v AJ Thompson Pty Ltd* provides an example.[54] Here, the respondent was induced to purchase a business by misrepresentations made by the vendor in contravention of s 52 of the *TPA*. In proceedings against the vendor and its accountant, the court found both liable; in the case of the accountant, this was because he had played a significant part in the contravention by keeping important information from the purchaser and accepting joint responsibility for some of the false statements made by the vendor.[55] Being able to proceed in this way is particularly valuable to a plaintiff when a corporate defendant is insolvent, as it provides a means of obtaining redress from the individuals who acted on its behalf.

Although the 'person involved' limb of s 236(1) is advantageous to plaintiffs it should be noted that it is more difficult to proceed against such a person than it is against the person who actually contravened the Act. This is because, as a result of the definition of 'involved' in s 2 of the *ACL*, such a person can only be liable if they knew that the conduct in question was misleading and participated in the deception.[56] As we have seen, this is not required in the case of the person whose conduct was itself misleading.

---

54 (1987) 73 ALR 233.
55 See also *Mackman v Stengold Pty Ltd* (1991) ATPR 41-105.
56 See *Yorke v Lucas* (1985) 158 CLR 661; this case concerned s 75B of the *TPA*, the precursor provision to the definition of 'involved' in s 2 of the *ACL*.

b Other remedies

Section 237(1) of the *ACL* gives the court a broad discretionary power to make such orders as it thinks appropriate against a person who has contravened, *inter alia*, s 18, where this will compensate, prevent or reduce the plaintiff's loss or damage. The kinds of orders that can be made under this provision include those set out in s 243 extracted below.

Australian Consumer Law
Section 243. Kind of orders that may be made

Without limiting section 237(1), 238(1) or 239(1), the orders that a court may make under any of those sections against a person (the *respondent*) include all or any of the following:

(a) an order declaring the whole or any part of a contract made between the respondent and a person (the *injured person*) who suffered, or is likely to suffer, the loss or damage referred to in that section, or of a collateral arrangement relating to such a contract:
 (i) to be void; and
 (ii) if the court thinks fit—to have been void ab initio or void at all times on and after such date as is specified in the order (which may be a date that is before the date on which the order is made);
(b) an order:
 (i) varying such a contract or arrangement in such manner as is specified in the order; and
 (ii) if the court thinks fit—declaring the contract or arrangement to have had effect as so varied on and after such date as is specified in the order (which may be a date that is before the date on which the order is made);
(c) an order refusing to enforce any or all of the provisions of such a contract or arrangement;
(d) an order directing the respondent to refund money or return property to the injured person;
(e) except if the order is to be made under section 239(1)—an order directing the respondent to pay the injured person the amount of the loss or damage;
(f) an order directing the respondent, at his or her own expense, to repair, or provide parts for, goods that had been supplied by the respondent to the injured person;
(g) an order directing the respondent, at his or her own expense, to supply specified services to the injured person;
(h) an order, in relation to an instrument creating or transferring an interest in land, directing the respondent to execute an instrument that:
 (i) varies, or has the effect of varying, the first mentioned instrument; or
 (ii) terminates or otherwise affects, or has the effect of terminating or otherwise affecting, the operation or effect of the first mentioned instrument

Using powers such as these under the equivalent provision in the *TPA* (s 87), courts have ordered the refund of money,[57] declared transactions void,[58] varied the terms of a contract,[59] restrained mortgagees,[60] and ordered the refund of the purchase price and the return of goods[61] and the repayment of deposits.[62]

7 Misrepresentation at common law

The common law relating to misrepresentation remains relevant where the *ACL* does not apply. That is, where the misrepresentation occurs in a non-commercial context; in other words, where neither the representor, nor the representee were acting in trade or commerce. In practice, such instances involving contracts of significant monetary value are uncommon, perhaps the most likely examples being the private, one-off sale of a motor vehicle, or family home. For this reason, it is rarely invoked and our treatment can, therefore, be brief.

a Pre-contractual misrepresentation: definition and preconditions

Pre-contractual misrepresentation is a false statement of fact that induces the representee to enter into a contract with the representor. It is to be distinguished from a statement that becomes a term of their contract, or a collateral contract between them (both of which can give rise to an action for breach of contract), or a mere puff (which does not give rise to legal consequences). For a statement to give rise to an actionable misrepresentation the following preconditions must be fulfilled:

- **There must be a false representation.** A representation can be made orally, in writing or by conduct. Whether it is false, or not, is determined by reference to the sense in which it would be understood by a reasonable person in the position of the representee.[63] As under the *ACL*, misrepresentation can be constituted by silence, one example being the failure to correct a statement which, although correct when made, became incorrect to the knowledge of the representor.[64]
- **The representation must be one of fact.** The statement must be one that a court can find to have been true or false at the time it was made. Thus a statement of opinion, or of law, or about the future will not suffice. However, if such a statement contained within it an implied statement of fact (for example, that the speaker believed the opinion being expressed, or that a statement about the future reflected existing policy) that statement, if false, will be actionable.[65]

---

57 See *Haydon v Jackson* (1988) ATPR 40-845.
58 See *Morton v Black* (1988) ATPR (Digest) 46-037.
59 See *Money v Westpac Banking Corporation* (1988) ATPR (Digest) 46-034.
60 See *Glandore Pty Ltd v Elders Finance and Investment Co* (1984) 57 ALR 186.
61 See *Karmot Auto Spares Pty Ltd v Dominelli Ford (Hurtsville) Pty Ltd* (1992) ATPR 41-175.
62 See *Byers v Dorotea Pty Ltd* (1987) ATPR 40-760.
63 See *Krakowski v Eurolynx* (1995) 183 CLR 563.
64 See *Jones v Dumbrell* [1981] VR 199.
65 See *Edgington v Fitzmaurice* (1885) 29 Ch D 459; *Public Trustee v Taylor* [1978] VR 289; *Balfour & Clark v Hollandia Ravensthorpe NL* (1978) 18 SASR 240.

- **The representation must be made to the other party.** A representation will only affect the validity of a contract if it was made by one party to the other. A representation that induces the representee to make a contract with a third party will not affect the validity of that contract unless, of course, the representor was acting on behalf of the third party. However, in such a case, if the representor acted fraudulently, or negligently, they may be liable to representee for the tort of deceit, or negligence, respectively.
- **The representation must induce the contract.** The representation must be made before the contract is made and must be at least one of the reasons why the representee entered into the contract. In a frequently quoted passage, Wilson J, in *Gould v Vaggelas*, summarised the law as follows:
  1. Notwithstanding that a representation is both false and fraudulent, if the representee does not rely upon it, he or she has no case.
  2. If a material representation is made which is calculated to induce the representee to enter into a contract and that person in fact enters into a contract there arises a fair inference of fact that he or she was induced to do so by the representation.
  3. The inference may be rebutted, for example by showing that the representee, before he or she entered into the contract, either was possessed of actual knowledge of the true facts and knew them to be true or alternatively made it plain that whether he or she knew the true facts or not he or she did not rely on the representation.
  4. The representation need not be the sole inducement. It is sufficient so long as it plays some part, even if only minor, in contributing to the formation of the contract.[66]

b Remedies

At common law, the principal remedy for pre-contractual misrepresentation is rescission of the contract. Damages are not recoverable unless the representation has become a term of the contract (in which case any action based upon it is for breach of contract) or it is tortious. South Australia and the Australian Capital Territory have special misrepresentation legislation that modifies the common law.

Rescission

Pre-contractual misrepresentation makes a contract voidable. This means that upon discovering the misrepresentation, the representee is presented with a choice: to rescind the contract, or affirm it notwithstanding the misrepresentation. Except South Australia and the Australian Capital Territory, adopting the latter option involves the representee overlooking the misrepresentation as no other remedy is available for the misrepresentation as such.[67] The contract continues according

---

66 (1985) 157 CLR 215 at 236.
67 The remedies that may be available in tort are outlined below.

to its terms, the parties remain bound to perform the obligations it imposes and enjoy the rights it creates as if the misrepresentation had not occurred. Electing to rescind the contract, on the other hand, brings it to an end *ab initio*: that is, as from the beginning. The rights and obligations it created are dissolved as of that moment and no longer bind the parties. Not only are the parties excused from further performance, but they are to be returned, at least substantially, to the position they were in immediately before the contract was entered into. For example, in the case of a contract for the sale of goods, this would involve the purchaser returning the goods to the seller and the seller refunding the price to the purchaser.

Rescission is the act of the representee. It is brought about by that party informing the representor that the contract is rescinded and seeking to return, or recover, as the case may be, any property or money that has passed between them pursuant to the contract. No particular form is required; it may be done orally, in writing or by conduct. However, as it may be contested, a method that allows the representee to easily prove that they made this election and communicated it to the representor is desirable. Because rescission is the act of the representee, a court will become involved only if the representee's action is disputed, or its aid is sought to achieve restitution.

Limits on the right to rescind

The representee will not be able to rescind, or will lose the right to do so, in the following circumstances:

- **If restitution is not possible.** Because rescission is designed to return the parties to the position they were in immediately before the contract was entered into, it is possible only if substantial restitution can be achieved. This is usually expressed by saying that rescission is possible only if *restitutio in tergum* is possible. Thus for example, if goods sold have been used up in a manufacturing process, or property has substantially deteriorated, rescission cannot occur. However, only *substantial* restitution is required and the courts have wide powers to make orders to achieve this, especially in cases of fraudulent misrepresentation. Thus, for example, in *Alati v Kruger*, a case involving the sale of a fruit business, the court effected a substantial restitution by ordering the purchaser to return those goods that remained to the vendor and the vendor to return the purchase price less an allowance for goods the purchaser was unable to return and an allowance for rental of the property used for the business.[68]
- **If the representee affirms.** Once the representee affirms the contract it can no longer be rescinded. In the present context, affirmation is the willingness to proceed with the contract notwithstanding the misrepresentation. It can occur expressly (the representee announcing a desire to continue with the contract) or by implication drawn from the representee continuing to perform its terms.

---

68   (1955) 94 CLR 216.

In both cases, however, the election must be communicated to the representor 'in clear and unequivocal terms'.[69]

- For affirmation to be found to have occurred, it is essential that the representee was aware, at the time, that there had been a misrepresentation. Anything said, or done, in ignorance of the misrepresentation cannot amount to affirmation. On the other hand, it is less clear whether the representee must also be aware that the misrepresentation gave them the choice to rescind or affirm the contract. The preponderance of opinion appears to be that this is not required.[70] However, at least where the representor has not been disadvantaged by the representee's conduct, it is less likely that the latter's conduct will be held to amount to an unequivocal election to affirm where they were unaware that they had the right to do otherwise.
- **If lapse of time constitutes affirmation.** Lapse of time alone, especially in cases of fraudulent misrepresentation, will not prevent rescission.[71] However, if the representee does not rescind within a reasonable time following discovery of the misrepresentation, this will amount to evidence that they have affirmed.
- **If a third party would suffer.** Rescission is not possible if this would prejudice the interests of the bona fide third party who has given value for those interests. For example, if S sold property to B as a result of B's misrepresentation, S will not be able to rescind the contract if, before this was discovered, B had sold the property to a bona fide third party, C.[72]
- **If the contract has been performed.** According to the rule in *Seddon v North Eastern Salt Co Ltd*,[73] if a contract has been executed (performed by the parties) it cannot thereafter be rescinded. However, this rule is now quite limited. In the first place, it applies only to innocent misrepresentation. Second, it does not apply where the parties have on-going obligations and so the contract is not fully executed. And third, it has been abolished or limited, by statute in South Australia, the Australian Capital Territory, Victoria and New South Wales.[74]

Damages

Damages are not recoverable at common law for pre-contractual misrepresentation as such. However, if the misrepresentation was negligent, or fraudulent, damages may be recovered in tort. In the case of negligence, this is difficult as it requires

---

69   *Immer (No 145) Pty Ltd v Uniting Church in Australia Property Trust (NSW)* (1992–1993) 182 CLR 26 at 39.
70   See *Khoury v Government Insurance Office (NSW)* (1984) 165 CLR 622 at 633–4 and *Immer (No 145) Pty Ltd v Uniting Church in Australia Property Trust (NSW)* (1992–1993) 182 CLR 26. Compare *Coastal Estates v Melevende* [1965] VR 433 where it was held that, at least in cases of fraudulent misrepresentation, the representee must be aware that they have a choice.
71   See *Elder's Trustee & Executor Co Ltd v Commonwealth Homes & Investment Co Ltd* (1941) 65 CLR 603; *Sargent v ASL Developments Ltd* (1974) 131 CLR 634.
72   See *McKenzie v McDonald* (1927) VLR 134.
73   [1905] 1 Ch 326.
74   *Misrepresentation Act 1972* (SA) s 6; *Civil Law (Wrongs) Act 2002* (ACT) s 173; *Fair Trading Act 1999* (Vic) s 32OA; *Sale of Goods Act 1923* (NSW) s 38(2).

showing that the representor owed the representee a duty to exercise reasonable care and failed to do so. Nevertheless, it is possible.[75] In the case of fraud, the challenge is much less formidable. If the representee can establish that the representor made the false representation knowing that it was untrue, or without believing it to be true or recklessly, not caring whether it was true or false, fraud will be established[76] and damages recoverable for the tort of deceit. The usual measure is the amount needed to put the representee in the position they were in had the representation not been made. As a claim for damages can be made whether or not the representee has rescinded the contract, the precise amount recoverable will depend upon which election is made. For example, if property is sold following a fraudulent misrepresentation by the seller and the contract is affirmed, the buyer will recover the difference (if any) between what was paid for the property and its true value. On the other hand, if the contract is rescinded and the buyer is repaid the purchase price, they will be able to recover only any consequential loss suffered such as wasted transactional expenses.[77]

c   Exclusion clauses

At common law it is possible to exclude liability for innocent or negligent misrepresentation but not for fraud.[78]

d   Legislative modifications

Legislation exists in South Australia and the Australian Capital Territory[79] which modifies the common law in the following ways:

- The remedy of rescission is expanded by the removal of certain bars, namely, the rule in *Seddon's* case and the doctrine of merger (the doctrine that if a representation becomes a term of the contract it 'merges' with and cannot be grounds for rescission.) There are strong grounds for saying the latter was not part of Australian law in any case; however these statutes put the matter beyond doubt.
- The courts are empowered to award damages in lieu of rescission where they consider it just and equitable to do so. In South Australia, this applies to all forms of misrepresentation. In the ACT, however, it does not apply in cases of fraud.
- A right to recover damages for innocent misrepresentation is created. However, this right is qualified by the creation of a defence which allows the representors to avoid liability if they can show that they 'had reasonable grounds to believe, and did believe, that the representation was true.'

---

75   See *Esso Petroleum Co Ltd v Mardon* [1976] 1 QB 801.
76   See *Derry v Peek* (1889) 14 App Cas 337.
77   See *Gould v Vaggelas* (1984) 157 CLR 215.
78   See *Commercial Banking Co of Sydney Ltd v Brown* (1972) 126 CLR 337.
79   *Misrepresentation Act 1972* (SA); *Civil Law (Wrongs) Act 2002* (ACT), chp 13.

- The effectiveness of exclusion clauses is restricted to instances in which the court considers them to be 'fair and reasonable in the circumstances of the case.'

INTERNATIONAL PERSPECTIVES

There is no provision comparable to s 18 of the *ACL* in any of the jurisdictions we are examining for international perspective. It is unique in scope and power. However, it does bear some resemblance to s 5 of the United States *Fair Trade Commission Act 1914* which prohibits 'unfair or deceptive acts or practices in or affecting commerce'.[80] In the early cases interpreting s 52 of the *TPA*, guidance was often sought from this provision and cases relying upon it, as United States statutes and the cases interpreting them had influenced the drafting of the *TPA*. However, in a number of seminal decisions involving s 52 the High Court emphasised the difference between the scope of the two provisions and reference to Fair Trade Commission is now much less frequent.[81]

The *Indian Contract Act, 1872*, on the other hand, having the same derivation, is similar to Australian common law. However, it contains some startling innovations that align it in important respects with the Misrepresentation Acts in South Australia and the Australian Capital Territory. This is especially so in relation to the remedies available to the representee.

The *Contract Law of the People's Republic of China* contains no provisions dealing with misleading conduct as such. However, in keeping with its emphasis on good faith and protecting the interests of the state it has provisions that cover many of the situations we would consider falling under that rubric. However, perhaps because of that emphasis, fewer remedies are available to the representee; in particular, rescission is not possible except in cases of fraud that harm the interests of the state.

Indian Contract Act, 1872

Section 17. 'Fraud' defined

'Fraud' means and includes any of the following acts committed by a party to a contract, or with his connivance, or by his agents, with intent to deceive another party thereto or his agent, or to induce him to enter into the contract:

(1) the suggestion as a fact, of that which is not true, by one who does not believe it to be true;
(2) the active concealment of a fact by one having knowledge or belief of the fact;
(3) a promise made without any intention of performing it;

---

80 *United States Code* s 45.
81 See *Parkdale Custom Built Furniture Pty Ltd v Puxu Pty Ltd* (1982) 149 CLR 191, esp at 202.

(4) any other act fitted to deceive;
(5) any such act or omission as the law specially declares to be fraudulent.

Explanation: Mere silence as to facts likely to affect the willingness of a person to enter into a contract is not fraud, unless the circumstances of the case are such that, regard being had to them, it is the duty of the person keeping silence to speak, or unless his silence is, in itself, equivalent to speech.

Section 18. 'Misrepresentation' defined.

'Misrepresentation' means and includes-
(1) the positive assertion, in a manner not warranted by the information of the person making it, of that which is not true, though he believes it to be true;
(2) any breach of duty which, without an intent to deceive, gains an advantage to the person committing it, or any one claiming under him; by misleading another to his prejudice, or to the prejudice of any one claiming under him;
(3) causing, however innocently, a party to an agreement, to make a mistake as to the substance of the thing which is the subject of the agreement.

These provisions define innocent and fraudulent misrepresentation for the purposes of the Act. Essentially they replicated the common law. For example, s 17(1) is understood to cover all three forms of fraud identified by Lord Herschell in *Derry v Peek*[82] and while active concealment is also covered, the *Explanation* makes clear mere silence on the part of a person will not amount to misrepresentation unless they are under a duty to speak. However, there are some interesting inclusions in the definitions (for example, the specific reference within the definition of fraud to making a promise 'without any intention of performing it')[83] and some uncertainty about the scope of others; in particular the three forms of innocent misrepresentation identified in s 18. Thus, while s 18(1) appears narrower than misrepresentation at common law (which does not require that an assertion not be warranted by the information available to the representee) the other two subsections appear much broader.

Section 19. Voidability of agreements without free consent

When consent to an agreement is caused by coercion, fraud or misrepresentation, the agreement is a contract voidable at the option of the party whose consent was so caused.

A party to a contract, whose consent was caused by fraud or misrepresentation, may, if he thinks fit, insist that the contract shall be

---

82 (1889) 14 App Cas 337 at 374.
83 Compare the discussion which arrived at the same outcome in *Futuretronics International Pty Ltd v Gadzhis* [1992] 2 VR 217.

performed, and that he shall be put in the position in which he would have been if the representations made had been true.

Exception: If such consent was caused by misrepresentation or by silence, fraudulent within the meaning of section 17, the contract, nevertheless, is not voidable, if the party whose consent was so caused had the means of discovering the truth with ordinary diligence.

Explanation: A fraud or misrepresentation which did not cause the consent to a contract of the party on whom such fraud was practised, or to whom such misrepresentation was made, does not render a contract voidable.

Section 64. Consequence of rescission of a voidable contract

When a person at whose option a contract is voidable rescinds it, the other party thereto need not perform any promise therein contained in which he is the promisor. The party rescinding a voidable contract shall, if he has received any benefit thereunder from another party to such contract restore such benefit, so far as may be, to the person from whom it was received.

Section 65. Obligation of person who has received advantage under void agreement, or contract that becomes void

When an agreement is discovered to be void, or when a contract becomes void, any person who has received any advantage under such agreement or contract is bound to restore it, or to make compensation for it, to the person from whom he received it.

Section 75. Party rightfully rescinding contract, entitled to compensation

A person who rightfully rescinds a contract is entitled to consideration for any damage which he has sustained through the non-fulfilment of the contract.

Section 19 deals with the consequences of misrepresentation and ss 64, 65 and 75 deal with the rights and liabilities of the parties when a contract has been avoided. Both fraudulent and innocent misrepresentation make a contract voidable. However, the *Explanation* makes it clear that, like the common law, this will be so only where the misrepresentation induced the contract. A further qualification is added by the *Exception* which provides that a contract will not be voidable if the representee 'had the means of discovering the truth with ordinary diligence'. It is suggested that this exception reverses the common law position, established in cases such as *Redgrave v Hurd*, that a representee's failure to take advantage of a readily available opportunity to check the accuracy of a representation, will not prevent the avoidance of a contract induced by that representation.[84] However, its precise limits are unclear.

---

84 (1881) 20 Ch D 1. See HK Saharay, *Dutt on Contract*, 10th ed, Eastern Law House, Kolkata, 2006, 240–1.

Section 19 allows the innocent party to affirm the contract. However, in a further departure from the common law, it provides that they can also insist on being placed in the position they would have been in if the representation had been true. In effect, this converts the representation into a promise and provides for the enforcement thereof. While this is possible under the broad powers given to a court by s 87 of the *Trade Practices Act*, it goes further than the South Australian and ACT Misrepresentation Acts which allow only the recovery of damages and even then, only on the basis they would be been awarded had the representation been fraudulent.

Section 66 of the Act provides that the communication of a decision to rescind, or of a decision to revoke a rescission, is to be governed by the same rules as those that apply to offers.

Where a voidable contract is avoided it becomes void under s 2(j). Upon this occurring, s 64 provides that the representor need no longer perform any of their obligations under the contract and that where the representee has received a benefit under it, that benefit must be returned as far as this is possible. This situation is amplified by s 65, which provides that 'any person' who has received a benefit under the contract must return it, or compensate the person from whom it was received. This covers a situation in which A and B contract with each other and property passes between them and also one in which A and B contract that B confer a benefit on C. In such a case, C must return the benefit to B. Importantly, the section applies equally to the representee and representor.

Section 75, however, gives a representee who has rescinded a contract, an additional right to claim damages for any loss suffered as a result of the contract not being performed. This section is located in the part of the Act dealing with the consequences of breach of contract and the right it gives is analogous to that given at common law to a party who discharges a contract on the grounds of breach of contract. Notwithstanding its location, the Act envisages that s 75 applies to rescission for misrepresentation and in giving the representee the same right to claim damages as the victim of a breach of contract, it marks another departure from the position at common law.

Contract Law of the People's Republic of China, 1999

Article 42. Pre-contract Liabilities

Where in the course of concluding a contract, a party engaged in any of the following conducts, thereby causing loss to the other party, it shall be liable for damages:

(i) negotiating in bad faith under the pretext of concluding a contract;
(ii) intentionally concealing a material fact relating to the conclusion of the contract or supplying false information;
(iii) any other conduct which violates the principle of good faith.

Article 52. Invalidating Circumstances

A contract is invalid in any of the following circumstances:

(i) One party induced conclusion of the contract through fraud or duress, thereby harming the interests of the state; …

Article 54. Contract Subject to Amendment or Cancellation

…

If a party induced the other party to enter into a contract against its true intention by fraud …. the aggrieved party is entitled to petition the People's Court or an arbitration institution for amendment or cancellation of the contract.

Where a party petitions for amendment of the contract, the People's Court or arbitration institution may not cancel the contract instead.

Article 55. Extinguishment of Cancellation Right

A party's cancellation right is extinguished in any of the following circumstances:

(i) It fails to exercise the cancellation right within one year, commencing on the date when the party knew or should have known the cause for the cancellation;
(ii) Upon becoming aware of the cause for cancellation, it waives the cancellation right by express statement or by conduct.

Article 56. Effect of Invalidation or Cancellation; Partial Invalidation or Cancellation

An invalid or cancelled contract is not legally binding *ab initio*. Where a contract is partially invalid, and the validity of the remaining provisions thereof is not affected as a result, the remaining provisions are nevertheless valid.

Article 57. Independence of Dispute Resolution Provision

The invalidation, cancellation or discharge of a contract does not impair the validity of the contract provision concerning the method of dispute resolution, which exists independently in the contract.

Article 58. Remedies in Case of Invalidation or Cancellation

After a contract was invalidated or cancelled, the parties shall make restitution of any property acquired thereunder; where restitution in kind is not possible or necessary, allowance shall be made in money based on the value of the property. The party at fault shall indemnify the other party for its loss sustained as a result. Where both parties were at fault, the parties shall bear their respective liabilities accordingly.

8 Summary

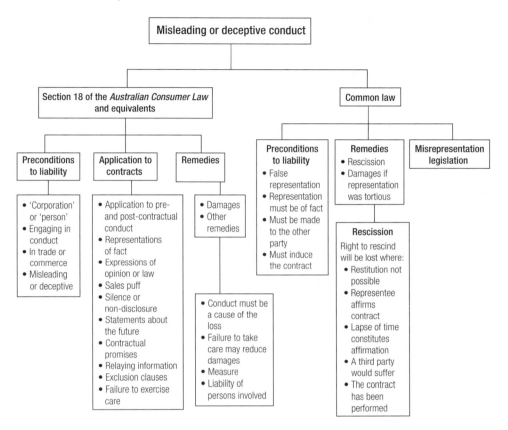

9 Questions

1. Betty retired recently and decided to sell her house and move into a home unit in Rocklands. To this end, she visited Burwood Estate Agency (BEA) and asked them to act on her behalf. During their negotiations, Betty informed BEA that her house had a steel frame as this was what she had been told when she purchased the house 10 years earlier. BEA also drew to her attention an attractive brochure describing new units that were being built in Rocklands by Rock Units Ltd (RU). Betty was very impressed with what she read, especially a description of the swimming pool that was attached to the units. Having read the brochure and having been told by BEA that the site upon which the units were being constructed could be accessed by boat (as BEA had been informed of this by RU) Betty entered into a contract to purchase one of the units for $400,000. Betty also sold the house on the same day, through BEA, to Peter for $350,000.

When the units were finished, Betty went into occupation only to discover that there was no swimming pool (it had been removed from the development as a cost-cutting measure) and that the site could not be accessed by boat. To make matters worse for her, Peter has discovered that Betty's house has a wooden frame and not a steel one as he had been told by BEA.

Please advise the parties of their legal position arising out of these transactions. Should you require further information to provide your advice, please say what you require and why.

2   Mr and Mrs Li have a daughter, Amy. She is their only child and they are devoted to advancing her education and ensuring that she has a successful career. To this end, in March they secured a place for her at the University of Eastern Melbourne (UEM) to study political science during the following academic year.

Mr and Mrs Li had been attracted to UEM by an information evening it conducted in June the previous year. The evening had featured various presentations about UEM's politics program and had, as its centrepiece, a lecture entitled 'The Politics of the Clinton Era' by a former member of the US Clinton administration. During the evening, the following statements were made about UEM and its politics program (these were also repeated in various brochures):

- Politics 101 would be taught by Adjunct Professor Bill Clinton, who would come from the USA
- all courses would be supported by EMOL (East Melbourne On-line) a computer-based teaching platform
- UEM enjoyed 'world-class' sporting facilities
- summer study opportunities were available that could enable students to accelerate their studies
- a study tour to China would be conducted in June.

During their discussions with representatives of UEM, Mr and Mrs Li indicated that they were very keen for Amy to be taught by leading figures, to finish her degree quickly and to be able to continue playing polo. They explained that Amy was a member of the Australian women's polo team and expected to play professionally upon graduation.

Unfortunately, Amy's experience at UEM was a great disappointment to both her and her parents.

Amy has come to you for advice. In particular, she has advised you of the following:

- Politics 101 was taught by a man whose name is 'Bill Clinton' and who is an Adjunct Professor from California. However, he is not the former president of the USA, as Amy had thought. Furthermore, he was a very poor teacher (he scored only 1 out of 5 on his teaching evaluations) and Amy gained very little, if anything, by attending his classes. Despite hard work on her part, she failed this subject.
- EMOL worked only in March and April. Late in April, a bushfire ravaged UEM's campus and destroyed its computer facilities. As a result, no computer-based teaching took place and students lost the opportunity to have access to notes, teaching materials and library resources. These seriously hampered Amy's study.
- UEM had very poor sporting facilities. In particular, they had no polo pitches with the result that Amy was unable to continue her training and lost her place in the Australian team. This

caused her great distress and the loss of a possible sponsorship contract with *Polo Girl* magazine.
- UEM did not offer a summer program that year. As a result, Amy was unable to study in that period and this has delayed the completion of her degree by at least six months.
- Amy arranged with the Politics Department of UEM to participate in the June study tour to Beijing and Tianjin. However, whist she was visiting the Tianjin Market as part of the tour, the tour bus left the market without her and she was stranded in that remote city for two days before her absence from the tour party was detected and she was located. This caused her parents and Amy herself great distress and substantial additional cost.

Amy and her parents consult you about their position arising out of this series of events. Please advise them, giving your reasons. Should you require further information to do this properly, please say what it is and why it is relevant.

CHAPTER 13

Mistake

1	Introduction	368
2	Common mistake	369
	a Common Law	369
	b Equity	379
3	Mutual mistake	384
4	Unilateral mistake	386
	a Common Law	386
	b Equity	387
5	*Non est factum*	396
6	Summary	400
7	Questions	400

1   Introduction

In circumstances where one or both parties are mistaken about some important aspect of their contract, the common law or equity may provide a remedy to the mistaken party, or parties, to deal with the consequences of the mistake. The availability of a remedy and the form that remedy will take depend upon the nature of the mistake. In particular, whether the mistake was common to both parties (a 'common mistake'), whether both parties were mistaken, but about different aspects of the contract (a 'mutual mistake'), or, more commonly, whether only one party was mistaken (a 'unilateral mistake').

The circumstances giving rise to the mistake may also provide an affected party with relief on other grounds. For example:

- where a party is mistaken because they have been misled by the other party, a remedy on the grounds of misleading or deceptive conduct,[1] or common law misrepresentation or fraud, may be available
- where there was an actionable non-disclosure which gave rise to the mistake
- where there was unconscionable conduct by one party, a remedy on this ground may be available to the other[2]

---

1   See further chapter 12.
2   See further chapter 16.

- where the mistake relates to a term of the contract, it may be possible to bring an action for breach of contract.

Consequently, in any instance where mistake is an issue, other possible causes of action should always be considered. Indeed, in cases of unilateral mistake attributable to one party's misleading or deceptive conduct, a cause of action based on s 18 of the *Australian Consumer Law (ACL)* will almost always be a preferable cause of action—which explains why there are now comparatively few new cases in which mistake is relied upon.

2 Common mistake

A common mistake[3] occurs when both parties are mistaken as to the same thing in relation to their contract. Both the common law and equity offer remedies in cases of common mistake provided certain criteria have been met.

a Common law

Adherence to the doctrine of sanctity of contracts means that validly formed contracts will be preserved by the common law courts in all but the most extreme circumstances. Consequently, the common law will rarely provide a remedy for common mistake. Where an operative mistake does exist, the common law will render that contract void *ab initio*; that is, it will be treated as if no contract ever came into existence. As this remedy has the potential to adversely affect third parties, it is important to define the precise scope of operative mistake at common law.

In *Australia Estates Pty Ltd v Cairns City Council*[4] Jerrard JA noted, with approval, the elements required for common mistake to avoid a contract at common law as articulated by the English Court of Appeal in *Great Peace Shipping Ltd v Tsavliris Salvage (International) Ltd*:

i there must be a common assumption as to the existence of a state of affairs;
ii there must be no warranty by either party that that state of affairs exists;
iii the non-existence of the state of affairs must not be attributable to the fault of either party;
iv the non-existence of the state of affairs must render performance of the contract impossible;
v the state of affairs may be the existence, or a vital attribute, of the consideration to be provided or circumstances which must subsist if performance of the contractual adventure is to be possible.[5]

---

3 In early cases, in particular, common mistakes were sometimes referred to as 'mutual mistakes' which we have classed in a separate category. Please keep this in mind when reading the cases relating to common mistake.
4 [2005] QCA 328.
5 [2003] QB 679 at para 48.

To assist in determining whether these elements have been met, the courts have identified various types of common mistake, including mistake as to the existence of subject matter, mistake as to the quality of subject matter and mistake as to the terms of the contract.

Mistake as to the existence of subject matter

The courts have been willing to find an operative mistake at common law where the mistake relates to the existence of the subject matter of the contract.

> ### Example
>
> John contracts to sell a car to Lily. Unbeknown to both parties, the car was destroyed in a fire prior to the conclusion of the contract. It is likely that this will constitute an operative common mistake at common law.

This issue arose in *Associated Japanese Bank (International) Ltd v Credit du Nord SA*.[6] Mr Bennet (B) sold goods to Associated Japanese Bank (A) and leased them back under a lease-back arrangement for the purpose of obtaining tax benefits and immediate cash incentives in excess of £1m. Credit du Nord (C) acted as a guarantor of the lease. B defaulted on the lease and A sued C on the guarantee. It was discovered that the goods in fact never existed; B had fraudulently claimed the goods to obtain cash from A. At all relevant times both A and C believed the goods existed. On the question of whether the guarantee could be avoided by C on the ground of common mistake, Steyn J held that the existence of the machines was the primary security for the guarantee provided and the non-existence of the machines therefore made the contract one that was essentially different from what the parties believed it to be; consequently mistake at common law was established.

If, however, one of the parties makes a promise, either expressly or by implication, that the subject matter of the contract exists, that party cannot rely on mistake to terminate the contract if they later discover that the subject matter does not in fact exist.

> ### Example
>
> John contracts to sell a car to Lily. Clause 3 of the contract states that the car is currently and will continue to be held in a garage at John's premises until the time of transfer.
>
> The statement that the car is currently garaged at John's premises contains a promise that the car in fact exists. Consequently, if it is later discovered that the car does not exist then, although John was mistaken about its existence, he cannot rely on this mistake to escape the contract. Instead, he would be guilty of a breach of contract.

---

6   [1988] 3 All ER 902: The Court's decision in favour of C was based on a finding that there was an implied condition precedent in the guarantee that the goods were in existence. As this condition was not met A could not recover under the guarantee.

Similarly, a party may not rely on mistake if they have caused the mistaken belief of the other.

McRae v Commonwealth Disposals Commission

(1951) 84 CLR 377, High Court of Australia

[The Commonwealth Disposals Commission invited tenders for the purchase of an oil tanker said to be lying on Jourmaund Reef, north of Samarai, and containing oil. The plaintiffs won the tender and sought, unsuccessfully, to locate the tanker. In fact there was no tanker at the locality indicated. The plaintiffs sought damages for breach of contract, deceit and negligence. The defendants claimed there had been a mutual mistake[7] regarding the identity of the subject matter and therefore no contract. On the issue of mistake, Webb J at first instance held that the contract was void. The plaintiff's appealed.]

Dixon and Fullagar JJ [at 408]: [Their Honours noted that the Commission's officers, in advertising the tanker, had acted with a 'reckless and irresponsible attitude' and continued]: ... a party cannot rely on mutual mistake where the mistake consists of a belief which is, on the one hand, entertained by him without any reasonable ground, and, on the other hand, deliberately induced by him in the mind of the other party. ... [In this case a] finding of actual knowledge [that the Commission] had nothing to sell does not seem justified by the evidence, though it is difficult to credit them at the time of the publication of the advertisements with any honest affirmative belief that a tanker existed. ... <409> ... even if they be credited with a real belief in the existence of a tanker, they were guilty of the grossest negligence. It is impossible to say that they had any reasonable ground for such belief. ... They took no steps to verify what they were asserting, and any 'mistake' that existed was induced by their own culpable conduct. In these circumstances it seems out of the question that they should be able to assert that no contract was concluded. It is not unfair or inaccurate to say that the only 'mistake' the plaintiffs made was that they believed what the Commission told them. ... <410> ... The only proper construction of the contract is that it included a promise by the Commission that there was a tanker in the position specified. The Commission contracted that there was a tanker there. 'The sale in this case of a ship implies a contract that the subject of the transfer did exist in the character of a ship.' ... If ... this case ought to be treated as [a case] raising a question of 'mistake', then the Commission cannot in this case rely on any mistake as avoiding the contract, because any mistake was induced by the serious fault of their own servants, who asserted the existence of a tanker recklessly and without any reasonable ground. There was a contract, and the Commission contracted that a tanker existed in

---

7   The Court uses the term 'mutual mistake'. The parties were in fact claiming a 'common mistake'. They were both mistaken about the same thing—the existence of a tanker in a specified location. See above n 3.

the position specified. Since there was no such tanker, there has been a breach of contract, and the plaintiffs are entitled to damages for that breach. ...

Appeal allowed

[footnotes omitted]

In cases where goods that form the subject of the contract cease to exist prior to the risk in those goods passing to the buyer, statute provides rules for determining the rights of the parties.

Goods Act 1958 (Vic)

Section 11

Where there is a contract for the sale of specific goods, and the goods without the knowledge of the seller have perished at the time when the contract is made the contract is void.[8]

Section 12

Where there is an agreement to sell specific goods, and subsequently the goods without any fault on the part of the seller or buyer perish before the risk passes to the buyer, the agreement is thereby avoided.[9]

In addition to those based specifically on mistake, other causes of action may exist where the subject matter of the contract is later discovered not to exist.[10] For example, an action may be available for total failure of consideration, for misrepresentation or for breach of an implied condition precedent that the property exists.

Mistake as to quality

A common mistake as to quality occurs when both parties are mistaken about some aspect of the subject matter of the contract. For example, the parties may be mistaken about the age of an antique piece of furniture or the authenticity of a piece of artwork. Common law courts have been reluctant to provide a remedy for such mistakes and have held that avoidance for mistake will only be granted where the mistake renders the subject matter essentially different from what the parties believed it to be. This is an extremely high threshold and, consequently, will be

---

8   See also *Sale of Goods Act 1954* (ACT) s 11; *Sale of Goods Act 1923* (NSW) s 11; *Sale of Goods Act 1972* (NT) s 11; *Sale of Goods Act 1896* (Qld) s 9; *Sale of Goods Act 1895* (SA) s 6, *Sale of Goods Act 1896* (Tas) s 11; *Sale of Goods Act 1895* (WA) s 6.

9   See also *Sale of Goods Act 1954* (ACT) s 12; *Sale of Goods Act 1923* (NSW) s 12; *Sale of Goods Act 1972* (NT) s 12; *Sale of Goods Act 1896* (Qld) s 10; *Sale of Goods Act 1895* (SA) s 7, *Sale of Goods Act 1896* (Tas) s 12; *Sale of Goods Act 1895* (WA) s 7.

10 *McRae v Commonwealth Disposals Commission* (1951) 84 CLR 377 provides an example of this situation.

rarely satisfied.[11] The test, and the reasons behind it, were summarised by Steyn J in *Associated Japanese Bank (International) Ltd v Credit du Nord SA*:

The first imperative must be that the law ought to uphold rather than destroy apparent contracts. Second, the common law rules as to a mistake regarding the quality of the subject matter, like the common law rules regarding commercial frustration, are designed to cope with the impact of unexpected and *wholly exceptional circumstances* on apparent contracts. Third, such a mistake in order to attract legal consequences must substantially be shared by both parties, and must relate to facts as they existed at the time the contract was made. Fourth, and this is the point established by *Bell v Lever Bros Ltd*, the mistake must render the subject matter of the contract *essentially and radically different from the subject matter which the parties believed to exist*. ... Fifth, there is a requirement which was not specifically discussed in *Bell v Lever Bros Ltd*. What happens if the party who is seeking to rely on the mistake had no reasonable grounds for his belief? An extreme example is that of the man who makes a contract with minimal knowledge of the facts to which the mistake relates but is content that it is a good speculative risk. In my judgment a party cannot be allowed to rely on a common mistake where the mistake consists of a belief which is entertained by him without any reasonable grounds for such belief: ... [emphasis added][12]

The leading case dealing with common mistake as to subject matter is *Bell v Lever Bros*.

Bell v Lever Bros Ltd

[1932] AC 161, House of Lords

[Bell and Snelling (the defendants/appellants) entered into separate agreements with Lever (the plaintiff/respondent) to provide services to Lever for a period of five years. Following the merger of a Lever subsidiary and its main competitor, the services of Bell and Snelling were no longer required. Lever terminated its contracts with Bell and Snelling in exchange for a substantial compensation payment. Lever later discovered that, as a result of a secretive 'pooling agreement' involving Bell and Snelling, they could have lawfully terminated their agreements without providing compensation. Lever sought repayment of the compensation moneys on the ground that they were paid under a mistake of fact. They succeeded at first instance. Bell and Snelling appealed.]

Lord Atkin [at 215]: [In the Court of Appeal it was accepted] that there was a duty upon the defendants to disclose to the plaintiffs their misconduct ... and that the contracts under which the money was paid were in consequence voidable. ...

---

11 In this respect, it has been observed that 'cases where contracts have been found to be void in consequence of common mistake are few and far between': *Great Peace Shipping Ltd v Tsavliris Salvage (International) Ltd* [2003] QB 679, para 85.
12 [1988] 3 All ER 902 at 912–913, [1989] 1 WLR 255 at 267.

... the rules of law dealing with the effect of mistake on contract appear to be established with reasonable clearness. If mistake operates at all it operates so as to negative or in some cases to nullify consent. The parties may be mistaken in the identity of the contracting parties, or in the existence of the subject matter of the contract at the date of the contract, or in the quality of the subject matter of the contract. These mistakes may be by one party, or by both, and the legal effect may depend upon the class of mistake above mentioned. Thus a mistaken belief by A that he is contracting with B, whereas in fact he is contracting with C, will negative consent where it is clear that the intention of A was to contract only with B. So the agreement of A and B for the purchase of a specific article is void if in fact the article had perished before the date of sale. ...

<218> ... *Mistake as to quality of the thing contracted for ... will not affect assent unless it is the mistake of both parties, and is as to the existence of some quality which makes the thing without the quality essentially different from the thing as it was believed to be* [emphasis added]. Of course it may appear that the parties contracted that the article should possess the quality which one or other or both mistakenly believed it to possess. But in such a case there is a contract and the inquiry is a different one, being whether the contract as to quality amounts to a condition or a warranty, a different branch of the law. ...

<223> [In this case the] agreement, which as part of the contract was terminated, had been broken so that it could be repudiated. Is an agreement to terminate a broken contract different in kind from an agreement to terminate an unbroken contract, assuming that the breach has given the one party the right to declare the contract at an end? I feel the weight of the plaintiffs' contention that a contract immediately determinable is a different thing from a contract for an unexpired term, and that the difference in kind can be illustrated by the immense price of release from the longer contract as compared with the shorter. And I agree that an agreement to take an assignment of a lease for five years is not the same thing as to take an assignment of a lease for three years, still less a term for a few months. But, on the whole, I have come to the conclusion that it would be wrong to decide that an agreement to terminate a definite specified contract is void if it turns out that the contract had already been broken and could have been terminated otherwise. The contract released is the identical contract in both cases, and the party paying for release gets exactly <224> what he bargains for. It seems immaterial that he could have got the same result in another way, or that, if he had known the true facts, he would not have entered into the bargain. [His Honour then considered a number of scenarios in which mistake would not provide a remedy, including the following classic example:] A buys a picture from B; both A and B believe it to be the work of an old master, and a high price is paid. It turns out to be a modern copy. A has no remedy in the absence of representation or warranty. ...

This brings the discussion to the alternative mode of expressing the result of a mutual mistake. It is said that in such a case as the present there is to be implied a stipulation in the contract that a condition of its efficacy is that the facts should be as understood by both parties—namely, that the contract would not be terminated till the end of the current term. The question of the existence of conditions, express

<225> or implied, is obviously one that affects not the formation of contract, but the investigation of the terms of the contract when made. A condition derives its efficacy from the consent of the parties, express or implied. They have agreed, but on what terms. ... [Counsel for the respondents] formulated for the assistance of your Lordships a proposition which should be recorded: 'Whenever it is to be inferred from the terms of a contract or its surrounding circumstances that the consensus has been reached upon the basis of a particular contractual assumption, and that assumption is not true, the contract is avoided: ie it is void *ab initio* if the assumption is of present fact and it ceases to bind if the assumption is of future fact.'

I think few would demur to this statement, ...

<226> Nothing is more dangerous than to allow oneself liberty to construct for the parties contracts which they have not in terms made by importing implications which would appear to make the contract more businesslike or more just. The implications to be made are to be no more than are 'necessary' for giving business efficacy to the transaction, and it appears to me that, both as to existing facts and future facts, a condition should not be implied unless the new state of facts makes the contract something different in kind from the contract in the original state of facts. ... We therefore get a common standard for mutual mistake, <227> and implied conditions whether as to existing or as to future facts. Does the state of the new facts destroy the identity of the subject matter as it was in the original state of facts? To apply the principle to the infinite combinations of facts that arise in actual experience will continue to be difficult, ...

... in the present case the identity of the subject-matter was not destroyed by the mutual mistake, if any, ...

[Lord Blanesburgh and Lord Thankerton also held that the mistake related to quality of services and not subject matter. Viscount Hailsham and Lord Warrington of Clyffe dissented.]

Appeal allowed

Mistake as to the terms of a contract

Where the mistake the parties complain of relates only to the terms of a contract, no remedy is available at common law. Thus, for example, if both parties believe the contract includes a term relating to the agreed damages for breach of contract, but no such term exists, the contract will not be void as a result. However, these facts may give rise to the remedy of rectification in equity.

Mistake as to title

Two situations may give rise to a mistake as to title. First, A may contract to buy property from B, both parties believing that B owns the property, only to later discover that it is already owned by A. Second, A may contract to buy property from B, both parties believing that B owns the property, only to later discover that it is actually owned by C. The first situation was discussed by Lord Atkin in *Bell v Lever Bros* as follows:

Corresponding to mistake as to the existence of the subject-matter is mistake as to title in cases where, unknown to the parties, the buyer is already the owner of that which the seller purports to sell him. The parties intended to effectuate a transfer of ownership: such a transfer is impossible: the stipulation is *naturali ratione inutilis*. This is the case of *Cooper v Phibbs* where A agreed to take a lease of a fishery from B, though contrary to the belief of both parties at the time A was tenant for life of the fishery and B appears to have had no title at all. To such a case Lord Westbury applied the principle that, if parties contract under a mutual mistake and misapprehension as to their relative and respective rights the result is that the agreement is liable to be set aside as having proceeded upon a common mistake. Applied to the context the statement is only subject to the criticism that the agreement would appear to be void rather than voidable. Applied to mistake as to rights generally it would appear to be too wide. Even where the vendor has no title, though both parties think he has, the correct view would appear to be that there is a contract: but that the vendor has either committed a breach of a stipulation as to title, or is not able to perform his contract. The contract is unenforceable by him but is not void. [footnotes omitted][13]

In the case of personal property supplied to a consumer, the *ACL* now provides a guarantee in relation to title, so that if the supplier does not have title they will generally be liable for contravention of that guarantee, even if both parties were mistaken about the supplier having such title.[14]

Australian Consumer Law

Section 51

(1) If a person (the ***supplier***) supplies goods to a consumer, there is a guarantee that the supplier will have a right to dispose of the property in the goods when that property is to pass to the consumer.

The second situation was discussed by the High Court in *Svanosio v McNamara*, extracted below.

Svanosio v McNamara

(1956) 96 CLR 186, High Court of Australia

[Svanosio purchased land from McNamara together with a licensed hotel that was said to be erected on the land. Both parties mistakenly believed that the hotel was

---

13   [1932] AC 161 at 218.
14   See also chapter 9 discussing consumer guarantees. Section 51 of the *ACL* applies only to consumer contracts. Some state laws may also imply terms into commercial contracts; see for example *Sale of Goods Act 1954* (ACT) s 17(a); *Sale of Goods Act 1896* (Qld) s 15(a); *Sale of Goods Act 1923* (NSW) s 17(1); *Sale of Goods Act 1895* (SA) s 12I; *Sale of Goods Act 1896* (Tas) s 17(a); *Goods Act 1958* (Vic) s 17(a); *Sale of Goods Act 1895* (WA) s 12(i).

situated wholly on the land also being sold; in fact approximately one-third of the hotel was situated on Crown lands. Svanosio claimed this was a fundamental mistake permitting avoidance of the contract.

The Supreme Court of Victoria held that the contract was not void as a result of this mistake. The contract itself provided for the possibility of such a mistake by providing that if no objections were made within a certain period of time the purchaser would be deemed to have accepted title. Svanosio did not make a survey of the land prior to the conveyance and only after entering possession sought to identify the exact boundaries of the land, thereupon discovering the mistake. Svanosio appealed to the High Court.]

Dixon CJ and Fullagar J [at 195]: ... So far as the contract is concerned, it may be assumed that all parties believed that the hotel stood wholly on the land sold. In that sense there was a 'common mistake'. It may also be assumed that the appellant, if he had known that a considerable part of the building stood on Crown land, would not have entered into the contract. But these facts do not make the contract void. ... <196> ...

'Mistake' might, of course, afford a ground on which equity would refuse specific performance of a contract, and there may be cases of 'mistake' in which it would be so inequitable that a party should be held to his contract that equity would set it aside. No rule can be laid down *a priori* as to such cases: ... But we would agree ... that it is difficult to conceive any circumstances in which equity could properly give relief by setting aside the contract unless there has been fraud or misrepresentation or a condition can be found expressed or implied in the contract. In the present case there was no fraud or misrepresentation, and the position must depend on the terms, express and implied, of the contract. The contract in express terms provides that the vendor sells 'All that piece of land being Crown allotment 15 of section O ... *together with the licensed premises known as the 'Bull's Head Hotel' erected thereon'*. The words 'erected thereon' have been discovered to be an inaccurate description. ... it is, in our opinion, clearly involved in the description of the property sold that the vendors are promising to convey the whole of the land on which the hotel is erected: ... <198> ...

In considering whether equitable relief can or should be granted to the appellant, we may confine our attention to contracts for the sale of land: ... <199>. Contracts for the sale of land present peculiar features of their own, ... It is the purchaser's business to investigate the title thoroughly before he pays his money, ... <200> ... The terms of the contract would not, as we have said, have precluded the appellant from rescinding the contract before conveyance, but, having failed to take the opportunity which those terms gave him, and having taken a conveyance, he falls within the general and reasonable rule that equity will not interfere unless there is fraud or what amounts practically to a total failure of consideration. There is no suggestion of fraud, and it cannot be said that there was a failure of consideration. ...

McTiernan, Williams and Webb JJ [at 204]: ... In one sense there is always a common mistake where a vendor sells land to the whole of which he honestly believes he has a good title and the purchaser honestly believes that if he contracts to purchase this land he will get a good title to the whole of it. But if the vendor contracts to sell the land to the purchaser and the purchaser contracts to purchase it, the fact that they would not have entered into a contract but for such a common misapprehension does not avoid the contract. The vendor contracts to sell the land on the basis that he has a good title to the whole of it and the purchaser contracts to purchase it on that basis. If the vendor <205> cannot make title he commits a breach of the contract and, apart from special conditions, the purchaser is entitled to repudiate it. If the contract states that certain premises are erected on the land sold, that is a representation that the vendor will make title to land on which those premises are erected. The representation becomes a promise contained in the contract and can no longer be relied on as an independent ground for rescission: .... If the premises are not erected wholly on the land sold the vendor will fail to fulfill the promise or in other words will fail to make a good title to the whole of the land described in the contract. A purchaser who purchases land which is represented to have a building erected thereon expects to obtain a complete building and not a building partly erected on land to which the vendor cannot make title. When the purchaser discovers that part of the building is not on the land he should object to the title. ... If the contract contemplates and makes provision for such a misdescription of the land sold how can it be said that it is void or voidable for common mistake. ... the mistaken belief of both parties that the hotel building stood wholly on the subject land ... could not possibly avoid a contract which contemplates and provides for it. ...

<207> It may be possible in exceptional cases to obtain relief on the ground of common mistake after a contract for the sale of land has been completed. But the cases must be very rare. They are unlikely to go beyond cases where there has been a total failure of consideration. One case is where it is found, after completion, that the purchaser and not the vendor is the owner of the land so that the purchaser is really paying for his own property. ...

Appeal dismissed

[footnotes omitted]

Mistake as to law

Traditionally, mistake as to law would not provide grounds for avoiding a contract. More recent authority, however, suggests that it may be possible to recover moneys paid under mistake of law in an action based on unjust enrichment where the mistake of law relates to private rights[15] rather than public rights.

---

15   *Norwich Union Fire Insurance Society Ltd v WmH Price, Ltd* (1934) AC 455. Here insurers made payment for goods on the mistaken belief that the cause of the destruction was one covered by the policy. It was not—the goods (lemons) had been sold in transit because they were ripening. The insurers were entitled to recover as a result of the common mistake.

b Equity

Where there is an actionable common mistake in equity the remedies of rescission and rectification may be available.

Rescission

In *Solle v Butcher*, Denning LJ in the Court of Appeal held that a court has equitable power to set a contract aside for common mistake in wider circumstances than those permitted at common law.[16] Equity, while requiring that the operative mistake be one which is 'fundamental', does not require the mistake to render the contract something 'radically different' from that which the parties intended. Lord Denning formulated the requirement as follows:

> A contract is ... liable in equity to be set aside if the parties were under a common misapprehension either as to facts or as to their relative and respective rights, provided the misapprehension was fundamental and that the party seeking to set it aside was not himself at fault.[17]

Similarly, Evans LJ, in *William Sindall p/c v Cambridgeshire* CC, observed:

> It must be assumed, I think, that there is a category of mistake which is 'fundamental' so as to permit the equitable remedy of rescission, which is wider than the kind of 'serious and radical' mistake which means that the agreement is void and of no effect in law ... The difference may be that the common law rule is limited to mistakes with regard to the subject matter of the contract, whilst equity can have regard to a wider and perhaps unlimited category of 'fundamental' mistake.[18]

The Australian High Court gave the principal in *Solle v Butcher* a cautious reception but has accepted that the equitable principle goes beyond that of the common law.[19]

The circumstances in which rescission will be available in equity for common mistake have, however, become less clear in recent years, following the decision

---

16   In *Associated Japanese Bank (International) Ltd v Credit du Nord SA* [1989] 1 WLR 255 at 270, Steyn J confirmed that equity would provide relief in a wider range of cases than the common law and would provide more flexible remedies.

17   *Solle v Butcher* [1949] 2 All ER 1107 at 1120; [1950] 1 KB 671 at 693. The case has been criticised. See C Slade, 'The Myth of Mistake in the Law of Contract' (1954) 70 *LQR* 385. On the other hand, it has also been suggested that this approach is entirely satisfactory: 'No one could fairly suggest that in this difficult area of the law there is only one correct approach or solution. But a narrow doctrine of common law mistake (as enunciated in *Bell v Lever Bros Ltd*), supplemented by the more flexible doctrine of mistake in equity (as developed in *Solle v Butcher* and later cases), seems to me to be an entirely sensible and satisfactory state of the law': Steyn J in *Associated Japanese Bank (International) Ltd v Credit du Nord SA* [1988] 3 All ER 902.

18   [1994] 3 All ER 932 at 959.

19   See *McRae v Commonwealth Disposals Commission* (1951) 84 CLR 377, *Svanosio v McNamara* (1956) 96 CLR 186 and *Taylor v Johnson* (1983) 151 CLR 422. For discussion of High Court consideration of this case see Jerrard JA in *Australia Estates Pty Ltd v Cairns City Council* [2005] QCA 328 from para 53.

of the English Court of Appeal in *Great Peace Shipping Ltd v Tsavliris Salvage (International) Ltd*[20] which overruled *Solle v Butcher*. The Court held that where the contract is valid and enforceable at common law[21] a court has no jurisdiction to grant rescission in equity.

Great Peace Shipping Ltd v Tsavliris Salvage (International) Ltd

[2003] QB 679, Court of Appeal, England

[The ship, *Cape Providence*, required urgent rescue and engaged Tsavliris Salvage to arrange for salvage. Tsavliris engaged the ship, *Great Peace*, to provide salvage services. This arrangement was made under the mistaken belief that the vessels were much closer—more than 350 miles closer—than they were. When the mistake was discovered by the *Cape Providence* they engaged a closer vessel to perform the rescue. Great Peace claimed a breach of contract and Tsavliris claimed the contract was terminated due to common mistake.

The Court concluded there was no mistake sufficient to justify avoidance at common law and then considered whether an equitable remedy was available.]

Lord Phillips of Worth Matravers MR, May and Laws LJJ [at 724]: [It has not, in over 50 years,] proved possible to define satisfactorily two different qualities of mistake, one operating in law and one in equity.

In *Solle v Butcher* Denning LJ identified the requirement of a common misapprehension that was 'fundamental', and that adjective has been used to describe the mistake in those cases which have followed *Solle v Butcher*. We do not find in possible to distinguish, by process of definition, a mistake which is 'fundamental' from Lord Atkin's mistake as to quality [in *Bell v Lever Bros*] which 'makes the thing contracted for essentially different from the thing that it was believed to be …'.

<725> Our conclusion is that it is impossible to reconcile *Solle v Butcher* with *Bell v Lever Bros Ltd*. The jurisdiction asserted in the former case has not developed. … in practice it has given rise to a handful of cases that have merely emphasised the confusion of this area of our jurisprudence. … If coherence is to be restored to this area of our law, it can only be by declaring that there is no jurisdiction to grant rescission of a contract on the ground of common mistake where the contract is valid and enforceable on ordinary principles of contract law. …

Appeal dismissed

---

20   [2003] QB 679: The case was applied in Australia in *Australia Estates Pty Ltd v Cairns City Council* [2005] QCA 328 and *Donkin v Official Trustee in Bankruptcy* [2003] QSC 401, and also cited in *Harris v Digital Pulse Pty Ltd* (2003) 56 NSWLR 298. The case has been followed in England in *Brennan v Bolt Burdon* [2005] QB 303; *Champion Investments Ltd v Ahmed* [2004] EWHC 1956. Indeed, in *Australia Estates Pty Ltd v Cairns City Council* [2005] QCA 328 [at para 45] Jerrard JA observed that '[t]he problem with reliance on [cases derived from *Solle v Butcher*] is that *Solle v Butcher* has itself been overruled by the Court of Appeal in England in *Great Peace Shipping Ltd v Tsavliris Salvage (International) Ltd*'.

21   This includes the situation where a contract is not able to be avoided at common law for common mistake.

This decision has attracted criticism[22] and is not binding in Australian jurisdictions. However, it has met with approval in the Queensland Court of Appeal where Jerrard JA stated that *Great Peace Shipping* should be followed in Australia in preference to *Solle v Butcher*.[23]

... the persuasiveness of the Court's reasoning in *Great Peace Shipping v Tsavliris Salvage*, together with the negative reference to *Solle v Butcher* by Heydon JA in *Harris v Digital Pulse* and the somewhat qualified approach taken to *Solle v Butcher* by the High Court, ... suggests that the law as stated in *Great Peace Shipping* should be applied by this Court in preference to the law as stated in *Solle v Butcher* and the cases which have followed it.

Rectification

Equity provides a remedy of rectification for common mistake in limited circumstances. Rectification permits the terms of a contract to be altered to give effect to the intent of the parties where the written contract has erred in recording that intent. In order for the remedy to be available 'it is necessary to find a contractual intention that a particular term should be included in the written document'.[24] The key elements of rectification for common mistake were summarised by Justice Ipp in *Igloo Homes Pty Ltd v Sammut Constructions Pty Ltd*[25]:

> [88] The essential basis of a claim for rectification is that, by mutual mistake, the parties' common intention has been incorrectly recorded in the written contract. It follows that the relevant time for assessing whether rectification should be ordered is the moment when the written contract was entered into, that is, when it was executed. ...
>
> [168] ... it has often been said that for a claim of rectification to succeed the requirements must be established by 'convincing proof' and that mere suspicion, although strong, is not enough. [The High Court] quoted with approval the following statement by Lord Chelmsford in *Fowler v Fowler* (1859) 4 De G & J 250 at 265:
>
>> It is clear that a person who seeks to rectify a deed upon the ground of mistake must be required to establish, in the clearest and most satisfactory manner, that the alleged intention to which he desires it to be made conformable continued concurrently in the minds of all parties down to the time of its execution ...

---

22 See Andrew Tettenborn, 'Agreements, Common Mistake and the Purpose of Contract' (2011) 27 *Journal of Contract Law* 91, Nick Seddon, 'Contract: Mistake Mistake' (2006) 80 *Australian Law Journal* 95, RMB Reynolds, 'Reconsider the Contract Textbooks' (2003) 119 (Apr) *LQR* 177–180 and SB Midwinter, 'The Great Peace and Precedent' (2003) 119 (Apr) *LQR* 180–182. The Court in *Great Peace* acknowledged that the decision may not always lead to desirable results and that 'there is scope for legislation to give greater flexibility to our law of mistake than the common law allows' [para 161]. More recently, in *Errichetti Nominees Pty Ltd v Paterson Group Architects Pty Ltd* [2007] WASC 77, the Court observed that recent developments have resulted in the law relating to common mistake becoming 'even more "arcane, uncertain in application, complex and controversial"'.
23 *Australia Estates Pty Ltd v Cairns City Council* [2005] QCA 328 at para 52. These comments were, however, obiter, with the court finding no mistake that would provide a remedy at common law or even under the *Taylor v Johnson* formulation.
24 Master Macready in *Cermak v Ruth Consolidated Industries* [2004] NSWSC 38 at para 4.
25 [2005] NSWCA 280.

Igloo Homes was one of a number of cases following the introduction of the GST in Australia in which one party argued that a price included in a contract was intended by the parties to be inclusive of GST, but contained a provision requiring payment of the GST. The case failed on the basis that the Court was not satisfied the purchase price was intended by *both* parties to be inclusive of GST.

Pukallus v Cameron

(1982) 180 CLR 447, High Court of Australia

[The parties contracted for the sale of a parcel of land, both believing that the land included a bore and 27 acres of cultivation. It was subsequently discovered through survey that the land contracted for did not include this area of land. The appellant purchasers sought rectification of the contract to include these areas on the ground of common mistake. They succeeded at first instance, but lost an appeal to the Full Court. They appealed to the High Court.]

Wilson J [at 450]: [The trial judge found that] Mr Cameron [for the respondents (vendors)] had honestly believed that the boundary was further to the south than it finally proved to be and in that belief he had represented to the appellants that the bore and cultivated area would fall within the land the subject of the sale. His Honour concluded that the case was one of mutual mistake contributed to by innocent misrepresentation and ... ordered rectification. He was mindful of the obligation resting upon the plaintiffs to show precisely the form to which the contract should conform. He noted [evidence at trial] which indicated some uncertainty about the precise representation. <451> ...

Nevertheless, his Honour stated:

> The parties had not determined exactly how far south of the cultivation the boundary would go. But it was clearly understood by them that it would at least skirt the southernmost part of the 27 acres of cultivation. This is a sufficient identification of the land to be included. The land lies between the true boundary and a line parallel to it passing through the southernmost point of the cultivation.

... <452> ... On appeal to the Full Court their Honours were unable to sustain the trial judge's finding as to the contractual intention of the parties. ...

The case raises no issue as to the principles which govern the rectification of a contract. Those principles are not in dispute. There need not be a concluded antecedent contract, but there must be an intention common to both parties at the time of contract to include in their bargain a term which by mutual mistake is omitted therefrom. So long as there is a continuing common intention of the parties, it may not be necessary to show that the accord found outward expression, ... It is unnecessary to pursue the distinction in the present case because the representation of the respondent and its acceptance by the appellants plainly established such an accord.

... <453> ... the application of each of the principles I have mentioned creates difficulty for the appellants. In the first place, the term which it is sought to include in the contract is clearly inconsistent with the expressed description of the land to be sold. ... From beginning to end the sale was of subdivision 1 of Portion 1154. ... There is no evidence to support a finding of an intention to contract for the sale of the bore and cultivated area. The intention was to effect a transfer of subdivision 1 of Portion 1154, a parcel of land which was thought erroneously, to include the bore and cultivated area. If the mistake had been discovered before the conveyance was effected, the appellants could no doubt have avoided the contract. ...

Secondly, even if a new boundary was in contemplation, the appellants face the difficulty of proving the precise term which it is said was agreed between the parties and which through mutual mistake was not incorporated in the written contract. It is not enough merely to prove that the bore and twenty-seven acres of cultivated land were intended to be included in the land the subject of the sale. ... <454> ... The ... established principles concerning rectification ... require convincing proof of the precise variation to the written agreement. Here there is no convincing proof. ...

[Gibbs CJ and Brennan J reached the same decision in separate judgments.]

Appeal dismissed

[footnotes omitted]

INTERNATIONAL PERSPECTIVES

The concept of common mistake is reproduced in the *Indian Contract Act*. The key requirements of avoidance for common mistake are a mistake of fact by both parties which relates to an essential element of the contract.[26] As is the case in Australia, mistake as to the value or quality of an object will not render a contract void. However, mistakes relating to the existence of goods (including where goods have been destroyed or have ceased to exist at the time of contract),[27] mistakes as to title and mistakes as to the identity of parties are mistakes of fact sufficient to render a contract void.

Rectification is also possible under s 26 of the *Specific Relief Act 1963* where the written agreement fails to reflect the intention of the parties.

Indian Contract Act, 1872

Section 20

Where both the parties to an agreement are under mistake as to a matter of fact essential to the agreement, the agreement is void. *Explanation:* An erroneous opinion as to the value of the thing which forms the subject-matter of the agreement, is not to be deemed a mistake as to a matter of fact.

---

26 Section 21 makes clear that mistake as to a law in force in India will not make a contract voidable. However, a mistake as to a law that is not enforce in India—for example, an Australian law—is treated as a mistake of fact.

27 Note that in this case the contract would also be void under s 56 of the Act because the agreement is to perform an impossible act and also under s 7 of the *Sale of Goods Act 1930* (India) due to the goods being non-existent at the time of contract.

> ### Contract Law of the People's Republic of China, 1999
>
> Chinese contract law gives parties the right to have a contract cancelled or amended where it was concluded due to a 'material' mistake.
>
> Article 54
>
> Either of the parties may petition the People's Court or an arbitration institution for amendment or cancellation of a contract if:
>
> (i) the contract was concluded due to a material mistake ...

3 Mutual mistake

A mutual mistake exists where both parties are mistaken, but their respective mistakes relate to different aspects of the contract.[28]

Example

A contracts with B to purchase B's boat. A mistakenly believes that the boat is registered; an unregistered boat is worth considerably less than a registered boat. B does not share this mistake. However, B mistakenly believes that the boat is not seaworthy and has reduced the price of the boat considerably as a result. A, who is more knowledgeable about boats, has inspected the boat and knows it to be seaworthy. Neither party is aware of the other's mistake. In this scenario, both parties are mistaken as to an important matter, but not as to the same matter; there is a mutual mistake.

Historically it was claimed that as, subjectively, in cases of mutual mistake the parties are at cross-purposes regarding an important aspect of the contract, there could be no '*consensus ad idem*' and therefore no contract could exist. This appears to have been the basis for the Court's decision in *Raffles v Wichelhaus*.[29] In that case the plaintiff entered into a contract to sell cotton to the defendant. The cotton was to be transported on the ship *Peerless* sailing from Bombay. There were, in fact, two ships sailing from Bombay carrying cotton; one in October and one in December. The plaintiff intended to sell the cotton from the ship sailing in

---

[28] Compare Law Book Company, *Laws of Australia*, vol 7 (at 31 August 2006) 2 Mistake, '7.2.510 Distinctions of practical significance are used to distinguish common, mutual and unilateral mistakes, leaving aside mistakes concerning the nature or extent of a written document' in which the author suggests mutual mistake occurs whenever one party is mistaken and the other party is unaware that that party is mistaken. The author would also restrict unilateral mistake to those circumstances in which the unmistaken party knew, or ought to have known of the other party's mistake. This view of mutual mistake will lead to the same result as that described in this chapter and perhaps highlights the confusion that has sometimes occurred in accurately classifying mistakes.

[29] (1854) 2 H & C 906; 159 ER 325.

December and the defendants intended to purchase the cotton sailing in October. The Court held that there was no contract as a result of the mutual mistake.[30]

As *Raffles* was decided when the subjective theory of contract still dominated, doubt has been expressed as to whether the same result would be reached today.[31] The objective test now prevails on issues of intent in contractual formation so that if, objectively, it would appear to a reasonable bystander that the parties had reached an agreement, then such consensus will be deemed, regardless of private subjective beliefs.[32] For example, in *Borg v Howlett* the parties were at cross-purposes regarding the sale of a horse, each believing the sale was for a different horse.[33] The Court held that, objectively, there was a contract and the Court simply had to determine to which horse the contract referred.

It is also unlikely that equity will intervene in cases of mutual mistake. Where both parties are mistaken and unaware of the other party's mistake there cannot be said to be any unconscionable conduct to justify equity's intervention.

The cases in which mutual mistake arise are likely, in any event, to be rare and, where such a mistake exists for which an objective intention cannot be determined, the contract is likely to be void for ambiguity or uncertainty without the need for reference to mistake as a vitiating factor.

INTERNATIONAL PERSPECTIVES

Under the *Indian Contract Act* mutual mistake will result in there being an absence of consent—*consensus ad idem*—necessary to form a binding contract,[34] as was the case in *Raffles*. Article 54 of the Chinese law, extracted above, encompasses mutual as well as common mistake, enabling a party to petition the court for amendment or cancellation of the contract.

Indian Contract Act, 1872

Section 13. 'Consent' defined

Two or more persons are said to consent when they agree upon the same thing in the same sense.

---

30 (1854) 2 H & C 906; 159 ER 325.
31 See *Borg v Howlett* (1996) NSWSC 95001763. For discussion of this case see also G Gilmore, *The Death of Contract*, Ohio State University Press, Columbus, 1974; AWB Simpson, *Leading Cases in the Common Law*, Clarendon Press, Oxford, 1995 and WF Young Jnr, 'Equivocation in the Making of Agreements' (1964) 64 *Columbia Law Review* 619. See also Hannen J in *Smith v Hughes* [1871] LR 6 QB 597.
32 See *Taylor v Johnson* (1983) 151 CLR 422.
33 (1996) NSWSC 95001763.
34 Free consent is required for a contract: s 10. See *Tarsem Singh v Sukhminder Singh* (1998) 3 SCC 471, where each party intended land to be sold in different units of measurement and the agreement was held to be void.

4 Unilateral Mistake

Unilateral mistake occurs when one party is mistaken as to an aspect of the contract but the other party is not. Normally this will not present the mistaken party with a remedy, but in certain circumstances, where the unmistaken party can be said to be at fault in some way, the mistaken party will have a remedy at common law or in equity. The reason no remedy is generally available is that, although subjectively there may be no *consensus ad idem*, objectively, if a reasonable bystander would believe the parties had reached agreement, the consensus requirement will be deemed to have been met. In these circumstances it would be considered unfair on the unmistaken party to avoid a contract for the other party's unilateral mistake. On the other hand, where the unmistaken party can be said to be at fault in some material respect, there is no need for the law to protect them and remedies for the mistaken party may be appropriate. However, given the requirement of fault, it will generally be the case that superior remedies, such as those available for breaches of s 18 of the *ACL* or unconscionable conduct, will also be available. It will rarely be the case that a party will rely solely on unilateral mistake for relief.

a Common law

It is very rare for the common law to render a contract void for unilateral mistake. The High Court has held that unilateral mistake as to terms of a contract will not render the contract void.[35] Similarly, unilateral mistake as to quality will not, by itself, render a contract void at common law,[36] although where the mistake as to quality was caused or contributed to by the unmistaken party, that party will not be able to enforce the contract at common law.[37] In such cases the mistaken party may also be protected by consumer protection regimes which imply terms as to quality or may have a claim for misleading and deceptive conduct.[38] Atkin LJ provided some examples of unilateral mistake which would not give rise to a common law remedy for mistake in *Bell v Lever Bros Ltd*:

> A buys B's horse; he thinks the horse is sound, and he pays the price of a sound horse: he would certainly not have bought the horse if he had known as the fact is that the horse is unsound. If B has made no representation as to soundness and has not contracted that the horse is sound A is bound, and cannot recover back the price. ... A agrees to take on lease or to buy from B an unfurnished dwelling-house. The house is in fact uninhabitable. A would never have entered into the bargain if he had known the fact. A has no remedy: and the position is the same whether B knew the fact or not, so long as he made no representation or gave no warranty. A buys a roadside garage business from B abutting on a public thoroughfare: unknown to A, but known to B, it has already been decided to construct a by-pass road which will divert substantially the whole of the traffic from passing A's garage. Again A has no remedy. All these cases involve hardship on A and benefit B, as most people

---

35 See *Taylor v Johnson* (1983) 151 CLR 422.
36 See *Smith v Hughes* [1871] LR 6 QB 597.
37 See *Scriven Bros & Co v Hindley & Co* [1913] 3 KB 564.
38 *ACL* s 18.

would say, unjustly. They can be supported on the ground that it is of paramount importance that contracts should be observed: and that if parties honestly comply with the essentials of the formation of contracts, ie, agree in the same terms on the same subject-matter they are bound: and must rely on the stipulations of the contract for protection from the effect of facts unknown to them.[39]

The only scenario in which unilateral mistake has rendered a contract void at common law is where the mistake relates to the identity of the other party and the identity of the other party is a matter of vital importance.[40] Whether this remains the case is, however, the subject of some uncertainty.[41] Furthermore, in most cases of mistaken identity the mistake will have arisen because the unmistaken party has purported to be somebody else, in which case the remedies available for misleading or deceptive conduct and for fraud may provide suitable alternatives for the mistaken party. The only exception to this being the case may be where a third party has obtained an interest in the property, the subject of the contract, before the mistake was discovered and acted upon by the innocent party.

b Equity

Equity provides remedies for unilateral mistake in a far greater range of circumstances than the common law. The remedy available will depend upon the type of mistake and the conduct of the unmistaken party.

Rescission

Where a unilateral mistake has been made the contract will be voidable at the option of the mistaken party if:

- the mistake was about an important matter
- the unmistaken party was aware, or ought to have been aware, of the mistake and
- the unmistaken party acted in a manner designed to ensure that the other party did not become aware of their mistake.

Mere silence as to a material fact, in the absence of a legal obligation to divulge, will, however, not provide the mistaken party with a remedy.[42]

Smith v Hughes

[1871] LR 6 QB 597, Court of Queen's Bench

[The plaintiff contracted to sell oats to the defendant. The defendant believed the sale was for 'old' oats. The plaintiff tendered 'new' oats and the defendant refused

---

39 [1932] AC 161.
40 See *Ingram v Little* [1961] 1 QB 31.
41 See *Lewis v Averay* (1972) 1 QB 198 and *Citibank NA v Brown Shipley & Co Ltd* [1991] 2 All ER 690.
42 Lord Atkin, in *Bell v Lever Bros* [1932] AC 161.

to complete the sale. The evidence conflicted as to whether reference was made to the oats being 'old' at the time of agreement.]

Cockburn CJ [at 603]: [His Honour assumed that the defendant believed the oats were old oats and that the plaintiff was aware of this belief, 'but did nothing directly or indirectly to bring it about …' and posed the question 'whether under such circumstances the passive acquiescence of the seller in the self-deception of the buyer will entitle the latter to avoid the contract'. He answered the question in the negative.]

I take the true rule to be that where a specific article is offered for sale without express warranty or without circumstances from which the law will imply a warranty … if [the buyer] chooses to act on his own judgment, the rule caveat coupler applies. … Here the defendant agreed to buy a specific parcel of oats. The oats were what they were sold as, namely, good oats according to the sample. The buyer persuaded himself they were old oats, when they were not so; but the seller neither said nor did anything to contribute to his deception. He has himself to blame.

[On the question of whether the parties' minds were *ad idem* his Honour continued at 606]: All that can be said is that the two minds were not *ad idem* as to the age of the oats; they certainly were *ad idem* as to the sale and purchase of them.

Blackburn J [at 606]: In this case I agree that on the sale of a specific article, unless there be a warranty making it part of the <607> bargain that it possesses some particular duality, the purchaser must take the article he has bought, though it does not possess that quality. And I agree that, even if the vendor was aware that the purchaser thought that the article possessed that quality, and would not have entered into the contract unless he had so thought, still the purchaser is bound, unless the vendor was guilty of some fraud or deceit upon him. A mere abstinence from disabusing the purchaser of that impression is not fraud or deceit, for, whatever may be the case in a court of morals, there is no legal obligation on the vendor to inform the purchaser that he is under a mistake which has not been induced by the act of the vendor.

Taylor v Johnson

(1983) 151 CLR 422, High Court of Australia

[Mrs Johnson granted an option to Mr Taylor (or his nominee) to purchase two five-acre lots of vacant land for a purchase price of $15,000. Mr Taylor subsequently exercised this option and a contract was entered into between Mrs Johnson and Mr Taylor's children for the sale of the land with the purchase price of $15,000.

Mrs Johnson later declined to perform the contract, claiming that she believed the contract she signed provided for a consideration of $15,000 per acre which would have amounted to approximately $150,000. The land was valued at around $50,000 which would have increased to around $195,000 if proposed rezoning occurred. The Taylor's sought specific performance of the contract and Mrs Johnson sought rectification of the contract or, alternatively, an order setting the contract aside.

The trial judge concluded that the contract was binding and ordered specific performance. He held that while Mrs Johnson did mistakenly believe the consideration specified was $15,000 per acre, Mr Taylor was unaware of this mistake. Mrs Johnson successfully appealed to the New South Wales Court of Appeal. The Taylors' appealed to the High Court.]

Mason ACJ, Murphy and Deane JJ [at 427]: In our view, a general inference which flows from the evidence is that Mr Taylor and Mrs Johnson each believed that the other was acting under a mistake or misapprehension, either as to price or value, in agreeing to a sale at the purchase price which he or she believed the other had accepted. ... We also consider that the evidence leads <428> to an inference that Mr Taylor, by refraining from again mentioning price and by the manner in which he procured the execution by Mrs Johnson of the option, deliberately set out to ensure that Mrs Johnson was not disabused of the mistake or misapprehension under which he believed her to be acting. ...

The judgments of Blackburn and Hannen JJ in *Smith v Hughes*, ... provide support for the proposition that a contract is void if one party to the contract enters into it under a serious mistake as to the content or existence of a fundamental term and the other party has knowledge of that mistake. That approach accorded with what has been called the 'subjective theory' of the nature of the assent necessary to constitute a valid contract .... The 'subjective theory' ... is that the true consent of the parties is essential to a valid contract. The contrary view, namely that described as the 'objective theory'... is that the law is concerned, not with the real intentions of the parties, but with the outward manifestations of those intentions. ...

<429> ... the clear trend in decided cases and academic writings has been to leave the objective theory in command of the field. ... <430> ...

For the present, but not without hesitation ... <431> ... we are prepared to accept [the general proposition that neither party to a contract can rely on his own mistake to avoid the contract *ab initio*, even if the mistake was fundamental and the other party was aware of the mistake] as applicable to a case, such as the present, where the mistake is as to the existence or content of an actual term in a formal written contract. It therefore becomes necessary to consider the scope of the basis upon which relief in equity is available from the contractual consequences of unilateral mistake. ...

In *Torrance v Bolton*, ... James LJ ... explained the basis upon which a contract for sale was set aside in a case of unilateral mistake as being the ordinary jurisdiction of equity 'to deal with' any instrument or other transaction 'in which the Court is of opinion that it is unconscientious for a person to avail himself of the legal advantage which he has obtained'. Special circumstances will ordinarily need to be shown before it would be unconscientious for one party to a written contract to enforce it against another party who was under a mistake as to its terms or its subject matter. In *Solle v Butcher* Denning LJ gave, as examples of such special circumstances, the case where the mistake of the one party has been induced by a material misrepresentation of the other and the case where 'one party, knowing that the other is mistaken about the terms of an offer, or the identity of the person by whom it is made, lets him remain under his delusion and concludes a contract on the mistaken terms instead of pointing out the mistake'. ... <432> ...

The particular proposition of law which we see as appropriate and adequate for disposing of the present appeal may be narrowly stated. It is that a party who has entered into a written contract under a serious mistake about its contents in relation to a fundamental term will be entitled in equity to an order rescinding the contract if the other party is aware that circumstances exist which indicate that the first party is entering the contract under some serious mistake or misapprehension about either the content or subject matter of that term and deliberately sets out to ensure that the first party does not become aware of the existence of his mistake or misapprehension. [This] is a principle which is best calculated to do justice between the parties to a contract in the situation which it contemplates. In such a <433> situation it is unfair that the mistaken party should be held to the written contract by the other party whose lack of precise knowledge of the first party's actual mistake proceeds from wilful ignorance because, knowing or having reason to know that there is some mistake or misapprehension, he engages deliberately in a course of conduct which is designed to inhibit discovery of it. Our comment can, for present purposes, be limited in its application to the case where the second party has not materially altered his position and the rights of strangers have not intervened.

Applying the above-mentioned principle to the present case, it is apparent that the appeal must fail. It is now common ground between the parties that, at the time she signed both option and contract, Mrs Johnson mistakenly believed that the relevant document stipulated that the purchase price was $15,000 per acre whereas the stipulated purchase price was $15,000 in total. The stipulation as to price was plainly a fundamental term of the contract ... both at the time when Mrs Johnson executed the option and at the time when she executed the contract, Mr Taylor believed that she was under some serious mistake or misapprehension about either the terms (the price) or the subject matter (its value) of the relevant transaction. The avoidance of mention of the purchase price after the 'idle curiosity' conversation and the circumstances in which Mr Taylor procured the execution of the option, including his wrong statement that he did not have a copy of the option which he could make available to Mrs Johnson, lead, in our view, plainly to the inference that he deliberately set out to ensure that Mrs Johnson did not become aware that she was being induced to grant the option and, subsequently, to enter into the contract by some material mistake or misapprehension as to its terms or subject matter.

...

[Justice Dawson dissented on the ground that the Court of Appeal should not have substituted its findings of fact regarding Mr Taylor's knowledge of Mrs Johnson's mistake for that of the trial judge.]

Appeal dismissed

[footnotes omitted]

The issue of unilateral mistake has arisen in the context of online sales. *Chwee Kin Keong v Digilandmall.com Pte Ltd*[43] involved an internet purchase of commercial laser printers. The six appellants, who were friends, purchased a total of 1,606 printers from the defendant's web site. Due to an employee error, the respondent had mistakenly advertised the printers for $66 each; in fact the real price for the printers was $3,854 each. Upon discovering the error (within a few hours of the appellants' purchase) the defendant corrected the web site and notified those who had placed orders that, due to the error, the order would not be met. The appellants brought an action seeking to enforce the contract and the respondents claimed that the contract was voidable on the ground of unilateral mistake. The appellants claimed they were unaware of the respondent's mistake at the time of contracting. There was, however, clear evidence that they were aware of the mistake and, in this respect, Rajah JC in the Singapore High Court at first instance concluded:

> The claims by the plaintiffs are audacious, opportunistic and contrived. ... This is not a case about bargain hunting—which is a time honoured and perfectly legitimate pursuit. This is a case about predatory pack hunting. ...[44]

The Singapore Court of Appeal agreed that the appellants knew of the mistake and further that in the event there was no actual knowledge their Honours indicated that constructive knowledge along with some form of unconscionable conduct—which might, as in this case, take the form of not bringing to the attention of the other party suspicions held about an error in price—was sufficient to justify equity intervening to set the contract aside.[45]

Where the mistake relates not to a term of the contract but to the identity of the other party the contract will be voidable in equity only where the identity of the other party is of vital importance.[46]

Rectification

Rectification, where available, will amend a contract to give effect to the true intention of the parties. Rectification will only be ordered where

> it is established by clear and convincing proof that at the time of the execution of the instrument the relevant party or parties as the case may be had an actual intention (if more than one party, a common intention) as to the effect which the instrument would have which was inconsistent with the effect which the instrument as executed did have in some clearly identified way.[47]

---

43 [2005] 1 SLR 502.
44 *Chwee Kin Keong v Digilandmall.com Pte Ltd* [2004] 2 SLR 594 at 637.
45 See further LP Woan, 'Unilateral Mistake in Law and Equity—*Solle v Butcher* Reinstated' (2006) 22 *Journal of Contract Law* 81 and A Phang, 'Contract Formation and Mistake in Cyberspace' (2005) 21 *Journal of Contract Law* 197.
46 *Lewis v Averay* (1972) 1 QB 198 at 209, per Megaw LJ. Lord Atkin has observed 'a mistaken belief by A that he is contracting with B, whereas in fact he is contracting with C, will negative consent where it is clear that the intention of A was to contract only with B': *Bell v Lever Bros* [1932] AC 161.
47 MH McLelland AJA in *Commissioner of Stamp Duties (NSW) v Carlenka Pty Ltd* (1995) 41 NSWLR 329, 345; cited and applied by Master Macready in the New South Wales Supreme Court in *Cermak v Ruth Consolidated Industries* (2005) Aust Contract Reports 90-207; [2004] NSWSC 38.

The following prerequisites must be established:

- one party must be mistaken about a particular term of the contract (or about the omission of a particular term)
- the unmistaken party must be aware of the other party's mistake[48] and
- the unmistaken party must not have drawn the mistake to the other party's attention.

Arguably, the following elements are also required before rectification will be granted:

- the unmistaken party must benefit from resisting rectification[49]
- the unmistaken party must be guilty of some 'sharp practice'—or fraud[50]—in not revealing the mistake (this would generally be achieved by *deliberately* concealing the mistake).[51]

Even in cases where fraud or 'sharp practice' has not been required, the courts have generally required some sort of unconscionable conduct on the part of the unmistaken party before rectification will be ordered. For example, in *XCB Pty Ltd v Creative Brands Pty Ltd*, Whelan J held that:

> Mere knowledge of a mistake and a failure to correct will be sufficient only 'in some circumstances', and those circumstances will be 'special.' The circumstances must be such as to render it unconscionable for the non-mistaken party to rely on the terms entered into by the mistaken party.[52]

---

48 '... As a matter of principle, and subject always to the particular facts, where a party does nothing to correct a mistake in a document of which he is aware and allows the other party to sign the document unaware of the mistake, rectification will ordinarily lie; ...': Hansen J, in *Air New Zealand Ltd & Enzedair Tours Ltd v Leibler, Leibant Investments Pty Ltd & Ninth Astjet Pty Ltd* (VSC, 19 November 1996, Unreported), at 94. Note also that it is likely to be sufficient if the unmistaken party suspects the other party is mistaken—in this respect, actual knowledge has been held to encompass 'wilfully shutting one's eyes to the obvious' and 'wilfully and recklessly failing to make such inquiries as an honest and reasonable man would make': Stuart-Smith, Evans and Farquarson LJJ in *Commission for the New Towns v Cooper (Great Britain) Ltd* [1995] Ch 259 at 280.

49 See *Thomas Bates & Son Ltd v Wyndham's (Lingerie) Ltd* [1981] 1 All ER 1077; Buckley LJ, but not Everleigh LJ, believed that this was a requirement.

50 Rectification for unilateral mistake is permitted 'where the party who is not mistaken is guilty of fraud, whether actual, constructive or equitable': Master Macready in the New South Wales Supreme Court in *Cermak v Ruth Consolidated Industries* (2005) Aust Contract Reports 90–207; [2004] NSWSC 38 at para [8]. In the same case Master Macready noted the suggestion that for purposes of rectification for unilateral mistake, even if no actual knowledge of mistake exists, it is enough that the defendant *strongly suspects* the other party is mistaken in a fundamental way. See further Young J in *Misiaris v Saydels Pty Limited* [1989] ANZ ConvR 403; (1989) NSW ConvR 55–474.

51 Buckley and Everleigh LLJ, in *Thomas Bates & Son Ltd v Wyndham's (Lingerie) Ltd* [1981] 1 All ER 1077, did not believe that 'sharp practice' was required. See further David Mossop, 'Rectification for Unilateral Mistake' (1996) 10 *Journal of Contract Law* 259 and *A Roberts & Co Ltd v Leicestershire County Council* [1961] Ch 555 at 570 by Pennycuick J.

52 [2005] VSC 424 at [10] (Supreme Court of Victoria).

Thomas Bates & Son Ltd v Wyndham's (Lingerie) Ltd

[1981] 1 All ER 1077, England and Wales Court of Appeal (Civil Division)

[The parties agreed to a fourteen-year lease of premises with rent set for five years to be reviewed every five years thereafter. It was intended that the lease would make a provision for determining rent by arbitration in default of agreement between the parties. By oversight the landlords omitted to include this arbitration clause and simply stated rent was to be 'such rents as shall have been agreed between the lessor and the lessee'. The tenants were aware of the omission when the lease was executed and did not bring it to the landlord's attention. Subsequently rent could not be agreed and the landlord sought to refer the matter to arbitration. The tenants rejected the referral to arbitration. The landlords sought rectification of the rent review clause to provide for determination of rent by arbitration in default of agreement. The trial judge ordered rectification. The tenants appealed.]

Buckley LJ [at 1086]: [After finding that the omission of reference to arbitration was due to a mistake on the part of the landlords his Honour held that for rectification for unilateral mistake] the conduct of the defendant must be such as to make it inequitable that he should be allowed to object to the rectification of the document. If this necessarily implies 'some measure' of sharp practice, so be it; but for my part I think that the doctrine is one which depends more on the equity of the provision. The graver the character of the conduct involved, no doubt the heavier the burden of proof may be; but, in my view, the conduct must be such as to affect the conscience of the party who has suppressed the fact that he has recognised the presence of a mistake.

[For rectification for unilateral mistake to apply] I think it must be shown: first, that one party, A, erroneously believed that the document sought to be rectified contained a particular terms or provision, or possibly did not contain a particular term or provision which, mistakenly, it did contain; second, that the other party, B, was aware of the omission or the inclusion and that it was due to a mistake on the part of A; third, that B has omitted to draw the mistake to the notice of A. And I think there must be a fourth element involved, namely that the mistake must be one calculated to benefit B. If these requirements are satisfied, the court may regard it as inequitable to allow B to resist rectification to give effect to A's intention on the ground that the mistake was not, at the time of execution of the document, a common mistake.

Eveleigh LJ [at 1090]: ... Where a party is aware that the instrument does not give effect to the common intention of the parties as communicated each to the other, there may well be an inference of sharp practice or unfair dealing. In my opinion, this will not always be so. I do not think that it is always necessary to show sharp practice. In a case like the present if one party alone knows that the instrument does not give effect to the common intention and changes his mind without telling the other party, then he will be estopped from alleging that the common intention did not continue right up to the moment of the execution of the clause. There is no need to decide whether his conduct amounted to sharp practice. I think he might at that time have had no intention of taking advantage of the mistake of the other party. I do not think that it is necessary to show that the mistake would benefit the party who is aware of it. It is enough that the inaccuracy of the instrument as drafted would be detrimental to the other party, and this may not always mean that it is beneficial to the one who knew of the mistake.

I agree that the lease should be rectified …

Appeal dismissed

INTERNATIONAL PERSPECTIVES

The *United Nations Convention on the Use of Electronic Communications in International Contracts 2005* includes an article dealing with 'input errors' made in electronic communications with automated systems.[53] Where it applies (which will depend on domestic legislation in each jurisdiction) a party who makes an 'input error' in an electronic communication involving the automated message system which does not provide an opportunity to correct the error— such as a confirmation screen—will be able to withdraw that error provided they notify the other party as soon as possible and derive no material benefit from the transaction. Despite being limited in scope, if such a provision was introduced into Australian law it would permit a remedy for unilateral mistake in circumstances not currently permitted by common law or equity.

Under the *Indian Contract Act* unilateral mistake will not make a contract void or voidable.[54] However, such a mistake may result in there being an absence of consent necessary to form a binding contract.[55] Alternatively, if the mistake is caused by the fraud or misrepresentation of the unmistaken party there will be no 'free consent' by the mistaken party and they will have the option of avoiding the contract.

Article 54 of the Chinese *Contract Law* covers cases of unilateral mistake. The law also specifically refers to cases in which a contract is induced by the fraud of one of the parties.

---

53   The Convention has not yet been signed in Australia, following the release of a discussion paper and the receipt of submissions supporting accession to the Convention, the Standing Committee of Attorneys-General announced, in April 2009, that variations would be made to the state and territory uniform Electronic Transactions Acts to enable Australia to accede to the Convention. This was followed by the passage of the *Electronic Transactions Amendment Act 2011* designed to align Australia's electronic transactions regime with the Convention with a view to accession.

54   See *AA Singh v Union of India* AIR 1970 Mani 16 and *Haji Abdul Rehman Allarakhia v Bombay and Persia Steam Navigation Co* (1892) 16 Bom 561.

55   See *Tarsem Singh v Sukhminder Singh* (1998) 3 SCC 471, where each party intended land to be sold in different units of measurement and the agreement was held to be void.

2005 United Nations Convention on the Use of Electronic Communications in International Contracts

Article 14. Error in electronic communications

(1) Where a natural person makes an input error in an electronic communication exchanged with the automated message system of another party and the automated message system does not provide the person with an opportunity to correct the error, that person, or the party on whose behalf that person was acting, has the right to withdraw the portion of the electronic communication in which the input error was made if:
   (a) The person, or the party on whose behalf that person was acting, notifies the other party of the error as soon as possible after having learned of the error and indicates that he or she made an error in the electronic communication; and
   (b) The person, or the party on whose behalf that person was acting, has not used or received any material benefit or value from the goods or services, if any, received from the other party.
(2) Nothing in this article affects the application of any rule of law that may govern the consequences of any error other than as provided for in paragraph 1.

Indian Contract Act, 1872

Section 22

… A contract is not voidable merely because it was caused by one of the parties to it being under a mistake as to a matter of fact.

Section 13

'Consent' defined - Two or more person are said to consent when they agree upon the same thing in the same sense.

Section 14

'Free consent' defined - Consent is said to be free when it is not caused by - …
(3) fraud, … or
(4) misrepresentation, … or
(5) mistake, subject to the provisions of sections 20, 21, and 22.
   Consent is said to be so caused when it would not have been given but for the existence of such … fraud, misrepresentation, or mistake.

Section 17. 'Fraud' defined

'Fraud' means and includes any of the following acts committed by a party to a contract, or with his connivance, or by his agents, with intent to deceive another party thereto his agent, or to induce him to enter into the contract;
…

(2) the active concealment of a fact by one having knowledge or belief of the fact;

...

(4) any other act fitted to deceive;

...

Section 19. Voidability of agreements without free consent

When consent to an agreement is caused by coercion, fraud or misrepresentation, the agreement is a contract voidable at the option of the party whose consent was so caused. A party to contract, whose consent was caused by fraud or misrepresentation, may, if he thinks fit, insist that the contract shall be performed, and that he shall be put in the position in which he would have been if the representations made had been true.

Exception: If such consent was caused by misrepresentation or by silence, fraudulent within the meaning of section 17 (which includes 'the active concealment of a fact by one having knowledge or belief of the fact'), the contract, nevertheless, is not voidable, if the party whose consent was so caused had the means of discovering the truth with ordinary diligence.

Explanation: A fraud or misrepresentation which did not cause the consent to a contract of the party on whom such fraud was practised, or to whom such misrepresentation was made, does not render a contract voidable.

Contract Law of the People's Republic of China, 1999

Article 54

...

If a party induced the other party to enter into a contract against its true intention by fraud ... the aggrieved party is entitled to petition the People's Court or an arbitration institution for amendment or cancellation of the contract.

5 Non est factum

Where a party is mistaken about the very nature of the document they are signing, as opposed to merely being mistaken about its terms, the defence of *'non est factum'*—'it is not my deed'—may be available to relieve them of their obligations. Where successful, a plea of *non est factum* will result in a contract being void.

As a result of the potential this remedy has to impact on innocent third parties and because of the commercial desirability of requiring parties to remain bound to the documents they sign, three preconditions must be satisfied before this defence will be made out:

- the defendant must either belong to a class of persons unable to read due to blindness or illiteracy and dependent on others for advice about what they are signing *or*, through no fault of their own, are unable to understand the meaning or significance of the document they are signing[56]
- the defendant must show that when they signed the document they believed it to be radically different from what it was in fact
- the defendant's failure to read or understand the document must not have been due to their own carelessness.[57]

Petelin v Cullen

(1975) 132 CLR 355, High Court of Australia

[Petelin was a landowner who spoke only limited English and could not read English. Cullen wished to purchase his land for the purpose of development and sought from Petelin an option to purchase. Cullen's agent gave Petelin a document granting a six-month option to purchase Petelin's property for $31,000 and advised him to consult a solicitor. The appellant took the document and later brought it back to Cullen's agent, signed but with certain parts excised. Petelin received a cheque for $50 consideration in return. At the expiry of sixth months Cullen sought an extension of the option and sent Petelin a letter which read, in part:

'Please find enclosed a cheque for $50.00 for a further six months' extension of the option on your property.'

Subsequently Cullen's agent saw Petelin and asked if he had received the $50, showed him a document proposing the six-month extension and asked Petelin to 'Sign it that you received $50.' The appellant signed the document without reading it. Cullen subsequently sought to exercise the option and Petelin refused to sign a contract.

Petelin succeeded at first instance, the Court finding that he had signed the document in the belief that it was merely a receipt for the $50. Cullen succeeded in having this decision reversed by the NSW Court of Appeal. Petelin appealed to the High Court.]

The Court (Barwick CJ, McTiernan, Gibbs, Stephen and Mason JJ) [at 359]: The principle which underlies the extension of the plea [of *non est factum*] to cases in which a defendant has actually signed the instrument on which he is sued has not proved easy of precise formulation. The problem is that the principle must accommodate two policy considerations which pull in opposite directions: first, the injustice of holding a person to a bargain to which he has not brought a consenting mind; and, secondly, the necessity of holding a person who signs a document to that document, more particularly so as to protect innocent persons who rely on that signature when there is no reason to doubt its validity. The [law assigns great]

---

56 *Petelin v Cullen* (1975) 132 CLR 355 at 359–360.
57 Note that the requirement of carelessness is likely to apply only against 'innocent' parties, so that where the mistake as to the nature of the document is due to the conduct of the other party it will not be necessary for the defendant to prove this element: *Petelin v Cullen* (1975) 132 CLR 355.

importance ... to the act of signing and to the protection of innocent persons who rely upon a signature ...

The class of persons who can avail themselves of the defence is limited. It is available to those who are unable to read owing to blindness or illiteracy and who must rely on others for advice as to what they are signing; it is also available to those who through no fault of their own are unable to have any understanding of the <360> purport of a particular document. To make out the defence a defendant must show that he signed the document in the belief that it was radically different from what it was in fact and that, at least as against innocent persons, his failure to read and understand it was not due to carelessness on his part. Finally, it is accepted that there is a heavy onus on a defendant who seeks to establish the defence. ...

It is now settled beyond any shadow of doubt that when we speak of negligence or carelessness in connexion with *non est factum* we are not referring to the tort of negligence but to a mere failure to take reasonable precautions in ascertaining the character of a document before signing it. The insistence that such precautions should be taken as a condition of making out the defence is of fundamental importance when the defence is asserted against an innocent person, whether a third party to the transaction or not, who relies on the document and the signature which it bears and who is unaware of the circumstances in which it came to be executed. It is otherwise when the defence is asserted against the other party to the transaction who is aware of the circumstances in which it came to be executed and who knows (because the document was signed on his representation) or has reason to suspect that it was executed under some misapprehension as to its character. In such a case the law must give effect to the policy which requires that a person should not be held to a bargain to which he has not brought a consenting mind for there is no conflicting or countervailing consideration to be accommodated—no innocent person has placed reliance on the signature without reason to doubt its validity.

On this analysis the element of carelessness has no relevance for the present case. As the learned judge found, the appellant's belief that the document was a receipt was inspired by the agent's representation that the document acknowledged the payment of the sum of $50. It is scarcely to be conceived that the respondent was unaware of what his agent said and did; but even if he was not informed by the agent he must take responsibility for his action. Consequently as against the appellant, the respondent is not to be considered as an innocent person without knowledge or reason to doubt the validity of the appellant's signature. <361>

... The appellant's difficulties in reading and understanding must have been present to Mr Clements' mind when the extension was signed; yet he contented himself with a demand that the document be signed and omitted to give an explanation of its character.

The matters to which we have referred would in any event support the independent conclusion that there was no carelessness on the part of the appellant. He could not read English; it was beyond his capacity to understand what the document provided. He was therefore faced with the choice of relying on what Mr Clements said or of incurring the expense and inconvenience of taking it to a solicitor for advice. Vis-à-vis Mr Clements and the respondent, he was justified in relying on what he was told by Mr Clements. After all, Mr Clements had previously advised him to consult a solicitor when that was necessary; on this occasion no such advice was given; nor did he give any indication that the document granted rights additional to those previously conferred.

The other element in the defence which requires to be mentioned is the necessity that the appellant should show that he believed the document to be radically different from what it was in fact. Once it is accepted that the primary judge could properly find that the appellant believed it to be a receipt, this point of contention disappears from the case. ...

Appeal allowed

[footnotes omitted]

The defence of *non est factum* also arose in the case of *Paul George Pty Ltd v George as Executor for the late Hasbie George*.[58] Mrs George, a widow aged almost 90, entered into a deed, for no personal benefit, which surrendered her rights to her property for the benefit of a company controlled by her son. At the time Mrs George suffered from periods of confusion, needed daily care and had impaired hearing and sight. She received no independent legal advice and could not read or write in English (her native language was Arabic). A few years later Mrs George died and the executor of her estate sought to have the deed set aside on the basis of *non est factum*. Sheppard AJA, with whom Powell and Stein JJA's agreed, noted that this was a case in which no innocent person had placed reliance on the signature of Mrs George and therefore absence of negligence of carelessness was not required to be proven by Mrs George. His Honour concluded (at 56,978):

> What concerns me is whether it can truly be said that the nature and effect of the document was so fundamentally different from what Mrs George was told about it that she was misled as to its legal effect. ... <56,979> ... I think it was. She was told she was to receive two allotments of land. In fact, she received no benefit of all. ... If ... the defence of *non est factum* was not available, little would change. ... the defence of unconscionability was plainly made out.

INTERNATIONAL PERSPECTIVES

Under the *Indian Contract Act*, where one party makes a fraudulent misrepresentation as to the *character* of the document being signed, so that the other party is mistaken about the nature of the promise being made, the transaction will be void under s 13 due to lack of true consent.[59]

Absent fraud, a plea of *non est factum* is available in essentially the same circumstances as under Australian law.

Chinese law does not recognise a plea of *non est factum*, but the same circumstances may enable a party to avoid on the basis of material mistake under Article 54(i) extracted above.

---

58 [2000] ANZ ConvR 4 (Supreme Court of New South Wales).
59 See *Dularia Devi v Janardan Singh* AIR 1990 SC 1173.

6 Summary

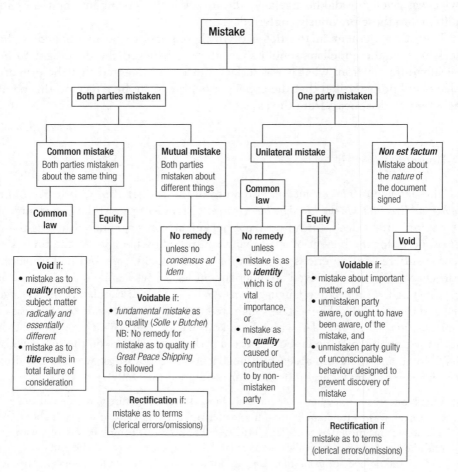

7 Questions

1. Louis is an art lover. On 4 April he walked past a garage sale and recognised an original 'old master' painting by Van Gogh. He couldn't believe his luck and inquired as to the price. Valerie, a 65-year-old retired seamstress, told him the price was $400. Feigning surprise, Louis replied that $400 was a bit out of his price range and seemed a bit much for the 'old and dusty' painting which was contained in a damaged frame. Valerie had always thought the painting to be very beautiful, but had no room to hang it in her small home and had to admit that the frame was a bit battered. As she had no idea of the value of the painting (she had inherited it from her parents) and had never really thought she would get $400 for the painting, she agreed to reduce it to $300 and was very happy when Louis agreed to pay that amount.

Unfortunately for Louis, he had encountered the garage sale by accident and did not have enough cash on him to complete the purchase. However, he asked Valerie to accept $50 as his deposit and to hold the painting for him until he returned later in the day with the remaining $250. Valerie agreed.

A short time later Richard visited the garage sale and saw the painting, which was now marked with a 'sold' sticker. He immediately recognised the painting as an original Van Gogh and asked Valerie if she was aware of the identity and value of the painting. She was very surprised to learn that the painting was worth at least $20m—and probably much more.

Valerie has since refused to hand over the art to Louis, claiming she was mistaken about its value. She has offered to refund Louis' deposit, but he has refused, claiming that he is entitled to the painting and that Valerie has no right to keep it from him. Valerie has come to you for advice about whether or not she must hand the painting over to Louis. Please advise her.

2   Helen and Bernie own a private yacht. One day while sailing they struck rocks and their yacht begin to take on water. Although there was no immediate threat, there was a risk that if it continued to take on water it would capsize. In addition to concerns about personal safety, Helen and Bernie were concerned that if the yacht capsized several valuable antiques which they kept on board would be lost. As a result, they transmitted a request for salvage to vessels in the area. Initially the only response received was from *Save Me Pty Ltd* with the result that Helen and Bernie entered into a contract with that company to perform rescue and salvage operations. At this time both parties believed that *Save Me's* salvage vessel was only a few hours from Helen and Bernie's yacht and that there were no other salvage ships in the vicinity.

However, a few hours later it was discovered that *Save Me's* vessel was further away than both parties first thought and would not reach them for another four to five hours. They also learned that there was another salvage vessel, operated by *Marine Security Pty Ltd*, which was less than an hour away from Helen and Bernie's yacht. This vessel was initially overlooked because heavy weather had interfered with radio signals, with the result that *Marine Security* did not immediately respond to Helen and Bernie's salvage request. Eager to save themselves and their vessel, which they believed would sink before *Save Me's* vessel arrived, Helen and Bernie immediately contracted with *Marine Security* to salvage their vessel and notified *Save Me* that their services were no longer required.

Nick, the managing director of *Save Me Pty Ltd*, has come to you for advice. He claims that *Save Me* had a valid contract with Helen and Bernie which they have breached by hiring someone else to provide the salvage operation. Please advise Nick about whether or not *Save Me* has any contractual remedies against Helen and Bernie.

3   Alex is a karate instructor who runs a local Karate dojo. Fiona has a son, Dillon, who attended classes at Alex's dojo. Dillon showed great promise and Fiona was keen to accelerate his karate training. To this end she offered to pay Alex $200 a week to provide private tuition to Dillon. Alex agreed, but asked Fiona if the agreement would be recorded in writing for tax purposes. Jill quickly typed up the following agreement.

> 'I, Fiona Rider, agree to pay Alex King a sum of $2000 per week for a period of six months in exchange for Alex King agreeing to teach judo to my son, Dillon Rider, for at least two hours each week.'

Fiona quickly scribbled a signature on the document without noticing the reference to '$2000' rather than the $200 she thought she had typed. Alex skimmed the document and signed without noticing the price.

Fiona and Alex have had a falling out and Alex is now demanding that Fiona pay $2,000 per week for the tuition. Fiona has refused, claiming the real agreement was for $200 per week. Please advise Alex about whether she is entitled to claim $2,000 per week as stipulated in their written agreement.

CHAPTER 14

Duress

1	Introduction	403
2	The elements of duress	404
	a Illegitimate pressure	404
	b Inducing the contract	405
3	Types of duress	405
	a Duress of the person	405
	b Duress of goods	409
	c Economic duress	411
	d The effect of duress at common law	416
4	Statutory duress	417
5	Summary	421
6	Questions	421

1 Introduction

Duress has long been recognised by the common law courts as providing grounds upon which a contract may be avoided. Duress is concerned with an inequality of power between parties at the time the contract is entered into as a result of the dominant party (D) exerting illegitimate pressure on the weaker party (W), thereby inducing that party to enter into a contract.

> The crux of the modern law of duress lies in one party making a threat that induces the other party, who has no reasonable alternative, to manifest contractual assent, with the result that the transaction thereby created is voidable at the election of the victim.[1]

It is not necessary that there be an inequality of power between the parties prior to the exertion by D of illegitimate pressure, although this will frequently be the case. Consequently, it was possible for the United States government to argue it was dominated by a steel company which, it alleged, exerted illegitimate pressure

---

1   R Bigwood, 'Coercion in Contract: The Theoretical Constructs of Duress' (1996) 46 *The University of Toronto Law Journal* 201 at 208.

over it by charging unreasonably high prices for ship building when there were ship shortages caused by World War I.[2]

Traditionally the 'illegitimate pressure' required for duress involved actual or threatened physical violence but more recently it has extended to threats relating to property and to economic duress. Where established, a contract formed under duress will be voidable at the option of the weaker party.

2 The elements of duress

A contract will be voidable for duress where it is brought about through the exertion of illegitimate pressure.

a Illegitimate pressure

The onus rests upon the party seeking to avoid the contract (W) to demonstrate that they were subjected to illegitimate pressure from D. Traditionally this required W to establish that the pressure exerted was such that their 'free will' was overborne. This requirement has now been rejected so that it is sufficient if the pressure 'went beyond what the law is prepared to countenance as legitimate'.[3] The range of conduct that may be categorised as illegitimate is not closed. In *Crescendo Management Pty Ltd v Westpac Banking Corp* McHugh JA observed that pressure 'will be illegitimate if it consists of unlawful threats or amounts to unconscionable conduct'.[4] More recently, the New South Wales Court of Appeal has suggested that duress should be limited to 'threatened or actual unlawful conduct' and that lawful, but unconscionable, threats should be dealt with under the doctrine of undue influence or unconscionable conduct.[5] The High Court has yet to restrict the doctrine of duress in this way and therefore it is suggested that, at least outside New South Wales, illegitimate pressure may, in appropriate circumstances, extend to lawful but improper conduct.

---

2   *United States v Bethlehem Steel Corporation et al* 315 US 289 (1942). The United States failed in its claim of duress (mainly because the majority of the Court considered that there were other alternatives—such as commandeering the steel plants—open to the Government), but the case does demonstrate that it is the nature of the pressure rather than the pre-existing position of the parties that is relevant to duress. This is in contrast to both undue influence and unconscionability which will be discussed in the next two chapters.

3   *Crescendo Management Pty Ltd v Westpac Banking Corp* (1988) 19 NSWLR 40 at 45, per McHugh JA. Note that it remains the position in the UK that the will of the victim must be overborne before duress will be established: *Occidental Worldwide Investment Corp v Skibs A/S Avanti (The 'Siboen' and the 'Sibotre')* [1976] 1 Lloyd's Rep 293. The circumstances in which the courts will be prepared to accept that the victim's will has been overborne appear, however, to be expanding so that in practice there is limited difference between the two tests.

4   (1988) 19 NSWLR 40 at 45, per McHugh JA.

5   *Australia and New Zealand Banking Group Limited v Karam* [2005] NSWCA 344.

b   Inducing the contract

If W succeeds in establishing illegitimate pressure the burden shifts to D to prove that this pressure was not a cause of W entering into the contract. The illegitimate pressure need not be the sole cause of W entering into the contract; it is sufficient if it is 'a' reason they entered into the contract.

In assessing whether the pressure induced the contract, W's response to the pressure will be relevant. For example, a protest may help demonstrate the contract was induced by the pressure; conversely, failure to take advantage of other reasonable commercial alternatives or effective legal action[6] will suggest that the pressure was not an inducement. None of these factors will be determinative and the result will depend upon the individual facts of the case. It will, however, only be in rare circumstances that, having established illegitimate pressure was applied, D will be able to discharge the burden of establishing it did not influence W's decision to enter into the contract.[7]

3   Types of duress

The forms of illegitimate pressure recognised by the courts fall within three categories:

- duress of the person
- duress of goods
- economic duress.

a   Duress of the person

Traditionally, duress was limited to circumstances in which W—or a close relative of W—was subjected to actual or threatened violence or deprivation of liberty unless they entered into a contract with D.[8]

Examples

i   D threatens to kill W if he does not sign the contract.[9]
ii D repeatedly punches W and insists the beating will not stop until the contract is signed.
iii D threatens to kill W's children unless W signs.[10]

---

6   For example, breach of contract. However, legal action will not normally be considered a practical alternative given the expense and delay involved.
7   See, for example, *Crescendo Management Pty Ltd v Westpac Banking Corp* (1988) 19 NSWLR 40, which represents an exception to the norm, and *Barton v Armstrong* [1976] AC 104.
8   These cases have rarely come before the courts. It is perhaps not surprising that a party who has made such unlawful threats would not wish to go to court to have the resultant contract enforced. See GB Glover, *The Doctrine of Duress in the Law of Contract and Unjustified Enrichment in South Africa*, PhD Thesis, Rhodes University, October 2003 at 182.
9   *Barton v Armstrong* [1976] AC 104.
10 *Saxon v Saxon* [1976] 4 WWR 300 (Canada) and *Byle v Byle* (1990) 65 DLR (4th) 641 (Canada).

> iv D invites W to his office to negotiate a contract. W will not agree to D's terms. D blocks W's exit from the office and tells him that he will not let him leave unless he signs the contract.
> v D endeavours to get W to sign a contract. W refuses. D replies 'The city is not as safe as it used to be. If you do not sign you will be sorry.'[11]
> vi D threatens to go to the police and accuse W's husband of beating him up unless W agrees to buy his car for $10,000. W's husband has had previous arrests for violent crimes and, although he did not in fact beat up D, W is concerned that the police will believe D and reluctantly agrees to buy D's car.[12]

In all these examples, if W signs the contract it will be voidable for duress. The first of these scenarios was discussed in the following case.

Barton v Armstrong

[1976] AC 104, Privy Council on appeal from the Supreme Court of New South Wales

[This case involved a complex business agreement between Barton and Armstrong involving various companies, including Landmark Corporation Ltd, of which Barton was the managing director. Barton alleged the agreement was the product of duress in the form of a threat by Armstrong to have him killed and other unlawful threats. Barton failed in the Supreme Court of New South Wales and an appeal to the Court of Appeal was dismissed. He then appealed to the Privy Council.]

Lord Cross of Chelsea, Lord Kilbrandon and Sir Garfield Barwick [at 112]: Barton [alleges] that Armstrong ... coerced him into [entering into the agreement] by threatening to have him murdered and by otherwise exerting unlawful pressure on him. ...

[The trial judge found that on many occasions] <113> Armstrong had threatened Barton with death; and that Barton was justified in taking and did take these threats seriously. On the other hand he held that though Barton was ... in real fear for the safety of himself and his family, these threats and the fear engendered by them did not in fact coerce him into entering into the agreement. ... 'It was' to quote another passage, 'what [he] ... regarded as sheer commercial necessity that was the real and quite possibly the sole motivating factor' underlying the agreement ...

The threats alleged were as follows:

(1) Barton said that when ... he ... suggested that [Armstrong] should resign, Armstrong, ... said:

> 'The city is not as safe as you may think between office and home. You will see what I can do against you and you will regret the day when you decided not to work with me'. ....

---

11 *Barton v Armstrong* [1976] AC 104.
12 Note, in certain cases threats such as these will enable a contract to be avoided on the ground of 'equitable coercion' even if the accused party did commit the crime alleged.

(2) Barton … began to receive telephone calls in the middle of the night. … on some occasions a voice would say 'You will be killed'. … on one occasion … he recognised this voice as Armstrong's. …

(3) Barton said that … his house was being watched by a man named Hume. There was some evidence to show that he was Armstrong's 'strong arm' man. … <114> …

(4) … Armstrong said to [Barton]:

> '… I will show you what I can do against you and you had better watch out. You can get killed.' …

(5) … Armstrong came into the board room and shouted at Barton: 'You stink; you stink. I will fix you.' Later he [said] that by virtue of his wealth and his position … he could procure police officers to do his bidding; that organised crime was moving into Sydney and that for 2,000 dollars you could have someone killed. The judge found … that Barton was justifiably seriously perturbed by them. Indeed … he hired a bodyguard to watch over his safety …

(7) … Armstrong said to [Barton] …

> Unless Landmark buys my interest in Paradise Waters (Sales) Pty Ltd for 100,000 dollars and the company repays 400,000 dollars owing to me and you buy my shares for 60 cents each I will have you fixed. …

(8) On January 7 … Vojinovic … told Barton that Hume had hired him to kill him promising him £2,000 for doing so and that Hume was acting on instructions from Armstrong. … Barton … reported the matter …. Vojinovic was promptly arrested and made a statement asserting that he had indeed been hired on Armstrong's behalf to kill Barton. … <115> … The judge … did not consider that the evidence justified him in finding that Vojinovic was in fact employed directly or indirectly by Armstrong. He had, however, no doubt that Barton believed that Armstrong had hired a criminal to kill him and was seriously and justifiably alarmed for his safety. …

(9) Barton said that … Armstrong rang him up at the company's office and said 'You had better sign this agreement—or else' …

[Their Lordships discussed some of the commercial factors that led Barton to enter into the agreement and continued (at 116)]: The [trial] judge … went so far as to hold that Armstrong was, as he put it, a 'reluctant vendor' and that his threats were not intended and were not thought by Barton to be intended to induce him to enter into the agreement but were simply manifestations of blind malevolence. …

[Their Lordships disagreed, holding that (at 117)]: Armstrong was not a 'reluctant vendor' and that such threats as he uttered … were intended by him to induce and were understood by Barton to be intended to induce him to enter into the agreement. … On the facts proved the inference that Armstrong was responsible for Hume's 'watching' of Barton is irresistible. … Armstrong—being the sort of man he was—had every reason to threaten Barton in order to induce him to go through with the agreement and their Lordships have no doubt that such threats as he made during the negotiations were made for this purpose and that Barton was well aware of the fact. ...

[Their Lordships went on to consider the legal result of the factual findings (at 118)]: ... if A threatens B with death if he does not execute some document and B, who takes A's threats seriously, executes the document it can be only in the most unusual circumstances that there can be any doubt whether the threats operated to induce him to execute the document. But this is a most unusual case and the findings of fact made below do undoubtedly raise the question whether it was necessary for Barton in order to obtain relief to establish that he would not have executed the deed in question but for the threats. ... <119> ... Their Lordships think that ... if Armstrong's threats were 'a' reason for Barton's executing the deed he is entitled to relief even though he might well have entered into the contract if Armstrong had uttered no threats to induce him to do so.

It remains to apply the law to the facts. ... it was for Armstrong to establish, if he could, that the threats which he was making and the unlawful pressure which he was exerting for the purpose of inducing Barton to sign the agreement and which Barton knew were being made and exerted for this purpose in fact contributed nothing to Barton's decision to sign. ... <120> ... before the documents were executed Barton was in genuine fear that Armstrong was planning to have him killed if the agreement was not signed. His state of mind was ... one of 'very real mental torment' and he believed that his fears would be at an end when once [sic] the documents were executed. It is true that the judge was not satisfied that Vojinovic had been employed by Armstrong but if one man threatens another with unpleasant consequences if he does not act in a particular way, he must take the risk that the impact of his threats may be accentuated by extraneous circumstances for which he is not in fact responsible. It is true that ... Armstrong's threats may have been unnecessary; but it would be unrealistic to hold that they played no part in making Barton decide to execute the documents. The proper inference to be drawn from the facts found is ... that though it may be that Barton would have executed the documents even if Armstrong had made no threats and exerted no unlawful pressure to induce him to do so the threats and unlawful pressure in fact contributed to his decision to sign the documents and to recommend their execution by Landmark and the other parties to them.

[Lord Wilberforce and Lord Simon of Glaisdale dissented, upholding the trial judge's finding that the threats were not a reason Barton entered into the contract.]

Appeal allowed

The cases have, to date, restricted duress of the person to cases in which it is the victim or a close relative of the victim involved. It has, however, been suggested that there is no reason in principle why violent threats directed to other persons should not also constitute duress.[13]

Lawful threats have also been held to constitute duress in appropriate circumstances. In most cases involving lawful conduct the threats have been in

---

13   See P Vout (ed), *Unconscionable Conduct – The Laws of Australia*, Lawbook Co, Sydney, 2006, 269.

the nature of blackmail. Thus, for example, a threat to reveal information which would embarrass the weaker party unless they agreed to contract may constitute duress. This occurred in *Robertson v Robertson* where a husband's threat to reveal an alleged infidelity in order to induce his wife to agree to transfer land to him was held to constitute duress.[14]

b   Duress of goods

A contract will also be voidable for duress where the stronger party applies illegitimate pressure in relation to the property of the weaker party.

Examples

i   D says to W 'sign this contract or I'll burn your house down'.[15]
ii   D threatens to slash a valuable painting owned by W unless W signs the contract.[16]
iii D steals W's car and refuses to return it until W signs the contract.

In all these cases the contract would be voidable for duress despite no threat to the physical integrity of the weaker party. This situation arose in *Vantage Navigation Corporation v Suhail and Saud Bahwan Building Materials LLC* (*The 'Alev'*). Vantage Navigation chartered a ship to a third party. The ship contained a consignment of steel for delivery to Suhail. The third party went bankrupt during the voyage and was unable to pay Vantage Navigation for the charter. Maritime law nevertheless bound Vantage Navigation to deliver the steel to Suhail. This involved considerable cost and Vantage Navigation threatened to delay delivery or dump the cargo at another port unless Suhail paid them certain expenses. Suhail reluctantly agreed. The threat was held to be illegitimate and duress was established.[17]

A withholding of goods was also held to constitute duress in the following case.

Hawker Pacific Pty Ltd v Helicopter Charter Pty Ltd

(1991) 22 NSWLR 298, New South Wales Court of Appeal

[Helicopter Charter (the respondent) engaged Hawker Pacific (the appellant) to repaint its helicopter for a price of $5,200. The helicopter was repainted but not to the respondent's satisfaction. The helicopter was re-delivered to the appellant

---

14   [1930] QWN 41.
15   *Occidental Worldwide Investment Corp v Skibs A/S Avanti* (*The 'Siboen' and the 'Sibotre'*) [1976] 1 Lloyd's Rep 293 at 335, per Kerr J (Queens Bench).
16   *Occidental Worldwide Investment Corp v Skibs A/S Avanti* (*The 'Siboen' and the 'Sibotre'*) [1976] 1 Lloyd's Rep 293 at 335, per Kerr J (Queens Bench).
17   [1989] 1 Lloyd's Rep 138 (Queens Bench). Note, this was considered both economic duress and duress of goods. See further Glover, above n 8 at 183–4.

for further work. When the respondent's agent, Mr Hough, sought to collect the helicopter, which it needed for a charter that day, he was presented with a document for signing. This obliged the respondent to pay $4,300 for the paint job and release the appellant from liability in relation to it. Mr Hough signed, reasonably believing this to be the only way of obtaining the helicopter at that time, but subsequently did not make payment. The respondent claimed the agreement was void for duress and succeeded at first instance. The appellant appealed.]

Priestley JA [at 302]: [The trial judge] said that the appellant's conduct ... viewed objectively, amounted to a holding out to the respondent that the helicopter would not be released unless the respondent first promised to pay $4,300 to the defendant and signed the document ... this represented a finding of conduct by the appellant analogous to threatened duress by the appellant applied to either or both of the respondent's helicopter or the respondent's right to take its helicopter away from the appellant's premises ...

The respondent was entitled to take away its helicopter from the appellant's premises ... [Despite making no express threat, the] appellant's conduct showed, and [the respondent's agent] believed, that the appellant would not permit it to be taken away unless the respondent did what the appellant wanted. On [the trial judge's] findings, ... <303> ... fully supported by the evidence, the respondent's need for the helicopter for business purposes that day was so urgent that recourse to legal proceedings for its recovery clearly would not have solved the company's practical problem.

[His Honour considered the appellant's argument that, by not claiming duress for a number of weeks after signing the contract—referred to as the 'fobbing-off' period—but merely refusing to make payment under the contract, the respondent had affirmed the contract (at 304)]: ... the relevant rule [has been stated] that because a contract entered into under duress was voidable and not void, a person who had entered into such a contract might either affirm or avoid it after the duress had ceased, and that acting under such a contract with full knowledge of the circumstances after escaping from the duress and taking no steps to set aside the transaction, a person might be found to have affirmed it. ... In my opinion [affirmation] covers situations governed by two particular legal theories, election and estoppel. That is, in my opinion, to make a case of affirmation the appellant here needs to show either that the respondent elected not to avoid the contract or became estopped from asserting its right to avoid the contract.

So far as election is concerned, two considerations appear ... One is that the party which has the election is not bound to elect immediately. The party 'may keep the question open so long as the delay does not cause prejudice to the other side' ... The other consideration is that 'The words or conduct ordinarily required to constitute an election must be unequivocal in the sense that it is consistent only with the exercise of one of the two sets of rights and inconsistent with the exercise of the other' ...

In the present case I doubt whether the fobbing-off period ... caused any significant prejudice to the appellant. [More significantly (at 305)] I do not think the respondent's conduct during the fobbing-off period was unequivocal in the necessary sense. The words being spoken on the respondent's behalf taken by themselves might be regarded as unequivocal in that they recognised the existence of the transaction of release, without protest about it; but, accompanying the ... words was the conduct of non-payment. ...

[Clarke JA and Handley JA both agreed that the appeal should be dismissed.]

Appeal dismissed

[footnotes omitted]

c Economic duress

It is now well established that illegitimate economic pressure can ground a claim of duress. This may take a wide variety of forms, most commonly threatening not to perform a contract or threatening to take legal action in circumstances where the claim is not *bona fide*. The leading case in Australia on economic duress is *Crescendo Management*.

Crescendo Management Pty Ltd v Westpac Banking Corporation

(1988) 19 NSWLR 40, New South Wales Court of Appeal

[Hilbrink was a director of two companies, Upward Production and Upward Publishing. A relocation of company premises necessitated the sale of Hilbrink's family home and the purchase of another. The net proceeds of approximately $31,000 were received by Westpac and Hilbrink requested that 50 per cent of the proceeds be transferred to his wife's account. Instead the bank disbursed approximately $3,500 into paying out two of Hilbrink's accounts and refused to release the balance unless Hilbrink and his wife executed certain documents as security for the debts of Hilbrink's properties, including a mortgage by Crescendo Management Pty Ltd. The documents were duly executed by Crescendo Management, without any expressed reluctance by Mr Hilbrink or anyone else, and the money was released. Crescendo Management alleged that the mortgage was obtained by duress.

The trial judge held that there was no duress and that the bank was entitled to retain the money because of guarantees that Mr Hilbrink had previously provided which were in default. His Honour did not consider it relevant that Mrs Hilbrink was not a guarantor.]

McHugh JA [at 45]: The rationale of the doctrine of economic duress is that the law will not give effect to an apparent consent which was induced by pressure exercised upon one party by another party when the law regards that pressure as illegitimate: *Universe Tankships* ... per Lord Diplock. ... the consequence is that the 'consent is treated in law as revocable unless approbated either expressly or by implication after the illegitimate pressure has ceased to operate on his mind' .... In the same case Lord Scarman declared [that] there are two elements in the realm of duress: (a) pressure amounting to compulsion of the will of the victim and (b) the illegitimacy of the pressure exerted. 'There must be pressure', said Lord Scarman 'the practical effect of which is compulsion or the absence of choice'.

The reference in *Universe Tankships* ... and other cases to compulsion 'of the will' of the victim is unfortunate. ...

In my opinion the overbearing of the will theory of duress should be rejected. A person who is the subject of duress usually knows only too well <46> what he is doing. But he chooses to submit to the demand or pressure rather than take an alternative course of action. The proper approach in my opinion is to ask whether any applied pressure induced the victim to enter into the contract and then ask whether that pressure went beyond what the law is prepared to countenance as legitimate? Pressure will be illegitimate if it consists of unlawful threats or amounts to unconscionable conduct. But the categories are not closed. Even overwhelming pressure, not amounting to unconscionable or unlawful conduct, however, will not necessarily constitute economic duress. ...

It is unnecessary, however, for the victim to prove that the illegitimate pressure was the sole reason for him entering into the contract. It is sufficient that the illegitimate pressure was one of the reasons for the person entering into the agreement. Once the evidence establishes that the pressure exerted on the victim was illegitimate, the onus lies on the person applying the pressure to show that it made no contribution to the victim entering into the agreement ...

In the present case ... Westpac had no right to retain the moneys which represented Mrs Hilbrink's interest in the fund. ... I do not think that Westpac was entitled to deal with the moneys owing to Mr Hilbrink in the way which it did. Westpac was certainly entitled to appropriate part of the moneys to pay out Mr Hilbrink's personal accounts. It was also entitled under its guarantee to appropriate the balance <47> of the moneys owing to Mr Hilbrink from the Oyster Bay sale to reduce the indebtedness of Upward Publishing ... However, Westpac did not purport to appropriate the money for that purpose. It simply refused to hand it over to Mr Hilbrink unless Crescendo executed the mortgage in question.

Although the pressure applied by Westpac to Mr and Mrs Hilbrink was unlawful, I am of the opinion that it played no part in the execution of the mortgage which had occurred before the pressure was applied. ... the directors and their wives were aware of the need to amalgamate the debts of the two companies ... They seem to have been quite happy to give the guarantees and mortgages. Certainly they raised no objection. Indeed they were simply bowing to the inevitable. Refusal to enter into the arrangements would have probably brought immediate problems for the companies ...

[Samuels and Mahoney JJA agreed with McHugh JA in holding that any pressure applied by Westpac was not the cause of the execution of the mortgage documents.]

Appeal dismissed

Threat to break a contract

Frequently economic duress takes the form of threatening not to perform a contract.[18] This occurred in *Austin Instrument Inc v Loral Corp*.[19] In that case Loral (W) had contracted with the navy to produce radar sets. These sets were made up of 40 component parts for which Austin (D) was sub-contracted to provide 23. W subsequently received another navy contract for radar sets. D bid to supply all 40 components. After W indicated it would only award a contract to Austin in respect of components for which it was the lowest bidder, D threatened to stop delivery of the original 23 components unless it received a price increase on the first contract and a sub-contract for all 40 components for the second contract. D subsequently halted delivery of parts due under the first contract. W, unable to obtain the full supply from another subcontractor, reluctantly agreed to D's demands in order to avoid breaching its contract with the navy. The Court held that D's conduct was wrongful in seeking to deny W goods which it needed and which it knew could not be obtained from another source. This constituted economic duress.

Economic duress of this nature was considered in Australia in the following case.

North Ocean Shipping Co Ltd v Hyundai Construction Co Ltd
[1979] 1 QB 705, Queens Bench

[Hyundai Construction entered into a contract to build a tanker, the *Atlantic Baron*, for North Ocean Shipping. Payment was to be made in five instalments and in US dollars. Hyundai agreed to open a letter of credit[20] in the North Ocean Shipping's favour to enable return of payments in case of default. After payment of the first instalment the US dollar was devalued by 10 per cent and Hyundai claimed an increase of 10 per cent on the remaining instalments. North Ocean Shipping refused and paid the second and third instalments without the 10 per cent increase. This was refused by Hyundai who returned the money. North Ocean Shipping, who were negotiating a contract for the charter of the tanker to Shell, agreed to pay the increase 'without prejudice' to their rights. They requested, and

---

18   See further Nathan Tamblyn, 'Causation and Bad Faith in Economic Duress' (2011) 27 *Journal of Contract Law* 140. This paper discusses some of the difficulties with identifying the precise scope of economic duress.
19   (1971) 29 NY 2d 124 (New York Court of Appeals).
20   A letter of credit provides a guarantee of payment to one party on the happening of a particular event. In this case, Hyundai took out a letter of credit with its bank in favour of North Open Shipping in case it defaulted. This constituted a guaranteed promise to pay North Open Shipping upon the happening of a specified event—in this case it's default in providing the ship contracted for. Had it defaulted North Open Shipping could have called in the letter of credit and Hyundai's bank would have been obliged to pay North Open Shipping the money specified in the letter. In this way the letter of credit removes the risk North Open Shipping might otherwise have to take in making payment before being supplied with the goods.

Hyundai provided, a corresponding increase in the value of the letter of credit. The tanker was subsequently delivered and approximately seven months later North Ocean Shipping made a claim for the return of the additional 10 per cent paid, alleging payment was made under economic duress.]

Mocatta J [at 714]: [His Honour first noted that the provision of an extra 10 per cent payment was supported by consideration in the form of the increased value of the letter of credit taken out by Hyundai.]

... I must next consider whether even if that agreement, varying the terms of the original contract ... was made under a threat to break that original contract and the various increased instalments were made consequently under the varied agreement, the increased sums can be recovered as money had and received. Mr Longmore [for North Ocean Shipping] submitted that they could be, provided they were involuntary payments and not made, albeit perhaps with some grumbling, to close the transaction.

Certainly this is the well-established position if payments are made, <715> for example, to avoid the wrongful seizure of goods where there is no prior agreement to make such payments. ... Lord Reading CJ [in *Maskell v Horner* [1915] 3 KB 106] did not say that express words of protest were always necessary, though they might be useful evidence to negative voluntary payments; the circumstances taken as a whole must indicate that the payments were involuntary. ...

Mr Longmore referred me to other cases decided in this country bordering upon what he called economic duress as distinct from duress to goods. ... *Close v Phipps* (1844) 7 Man & G 586, in which the attorney of a mortgagee threatened to sell the mortgaged property unless certain costs, to which he was not entitled, were paid in addition to the mortgage money. The <716> additional costs were paid under protest and were subsequently recovered as money had and received. It was stressed in argument, rightly I think, that this was a case of money paid under duress, the duress being a threatened breach of contract ...

[After reviewing some more case law his Honour continued (at 718)]: It would seem ... that the Australian courts would be prepared to allow the recovery of excess money paid, even under a new contract, as the result of a threat to break an earlier contract, since the threat or compulsion would be applied to the original contractual right of the party subject to the compulsion or economic duress. ...

<719> ... I do not take the view that the recovery of money paid under duress other than to the person is necessarily limited to duress to goods falling within one of the categories hitherto established by the English cases. ... the compulsion may take the form of 'economic duress' if the necessary facts are proved. A threat to break a contract may amount to such 'economic duress.' Thirdly, if there has been such a form of duress leading to a contract for consideration, I think that the contract is a voidable one which can be avoided and the excess money paid under it recovered.

I think the facts found in this case do establish that the agreement to increase the price by 10 per cent reached at the end of June 1973 was caused by what may be called 'economic duress.' [Hyundai was] adamant in insisting on the increased price without having any legal justification for so doing and the owners realised that [Hyundai] would not accept anything other than an unqualified agreement to the increase. ... in view of the position of [North Ocean Shipping] vis-à-vis their relations with Shell it would be unreasonable to hold that [claiming damages in arbitration] is the course they should have taken ... The owners made a very reasonable offer of arbitration coupled with security for any award in [Hyundai's] favour that might be made, but this was refused. They then made their agreement, which can truly I think be said to have been made under compulsion, by the telex of June 28 without prejudice to their rights. I do not consider [Hyundai's] ignorance of the Shell charter material. It may well be that had they known of it they would have been even more exigent.

If I am right in the conclusion reached with some doubt earlier that <720> there was consideration for the 10 per cent increase agreement ... and it be right to regard this as having been reached under a kind of duress in the form of economic pressure ... [that contract] is voidable and not void.

[His Honour then noted that, as a result of the duress, North Ocean Shipping could choose to affirm or avoid the contract after the duress ceased. In this case his Honour noted a delay of approximately seven months before any further protest was made by North Open Shipping regarding the increase in price and held that in the circumstances this constituted an affirmation of the variation of the contract increasing the price.]

Claim denied

Not all threats to break a contract which give rise to a further or amended contract will constitute economic duress. For example, it will normally be necessary to demonstrate that the weaker party had no reasonable choice but to accede to the demand.

Example

W has a contract with D to supply 100 power drills for purposes of re-supply. D subsequently refuses to supply the drills unless W agrees to a 50 per cent increase in price. There are, however, a number of other suppliers of the same drill who would be able to supply W with the drills it needs by the date required. In these circumstances duress would not be established; W should obtain the drills from another source and then recover any damages suffered as a result of D's conduct in an action for breach of contract.[21]

It is also important to distinguish threats to break a contract from requests to renegotiate the terms of a contract.

---

21   See *Austin Instrument Inc v Loral Corp* (1971) 29 NY 2d 124 (New York Court of Appeals).

> **Examples**
>
> i   D has a contract with W to build several houses for a new residential development. As a result of a breach of contract by an electrical subcontractor D has difficulty performing the contract in a timely manner. D explains the problem to W and then asks 'I wonder if you would consider an increase in the electrical component of the contract; that would make it easier for me to find another electrical contractor to perform the job in the time required.' W agrees to vary the contract in this way.
>
> ii   D has a contract with W to build several houses for a new residential development. A week before the contractual date for completion D approaches W and says 'I will stop work on the development now unless you agree to pay me an additional 20 per cent for the job.' W is unable to find another contractor in time and needs the work completed on time due to contractual obligations to third-party purchasers. W reluctantly agrees to the price increase.

It is only the second scenario that might give rise to a successful claim of economic duress.

Threat to institute legal proceedings

A threat to institute legal proceedings that is *bona fide*—that is, the threatening party honestly believes that they have a legal claim against the other party—will not enable the threatened party to avoid any resulting contract on the grounds of duress. However, *mala fide* threats may permit the threatened party to rescind a resulting contract for duress.

> **Example**
>
> W is a building contractor. D is a plumber. After W receives a large contract for a new commercial development D approaches W and says 'I want you to sub-contract me for all the plumbing work on the new development or I'll sue you for payments owed under our last contract.' W agrees. Provided D honestly believes he has a claim for overdue payments this threat will not enable W to avoid the new contract for economic duress.[22]

d   The effect of duress at common law

Where duress is established the contract thereby created will be voidable at the option of the victim. If the victim of the duress wishes to avoid the contract they should do so as soon as the threat—or illegitimate pressure—has been removed; failure to do so may constitute an affirmation of the contract which cannot later be

---

22   See *Westpac Banking Corporation v Cockerill* (1998) 152 ALR 267 (Full Federal Court).

avoided.[23] The party who engaged in the vitiating conduct has no right to avoid the contract on the basis of their duress.

Where the contract is set aside any property or money that has passed between the parties must be returned. Similarly, restitution in the form of a *quantum meruit* may be ordered for services.

Example

D kidnaps W's wife and refuses to release her unless W, a builder, agrees to build a new garage for D for the sum of $100. W agrees and signs a contract to that effect. After expending around $10,000 on materials and 50 man-hours in building the garage D pays W $100 and releases W's wife. W immediately goes to the police and D is arrested. W subsequently takes action to avoid the contract and recover his expenses.

There is clear duress in this case and W has done nothing to affirm or ratify the contract; as soon as the duress had passed—that is, once his wife had been released—he went to the police and indicated an intention to avoid the contract. The court will avoid the contract and order restitution. W could recover the $10,000 in materials and a fair market rate for his labour in building the garage. D would be entitled to recover the $100 paid for the job.

---

4 Statutory duress

The common law doctrine of duress is given statutory force in the *Australian Consumer Law (ACL)*. The *ACL* is derived from the *Competition and Consumer Act 2010* (Cth), Schedule 2.

Australian Consumer Law

Section 50. Harassment and coercion

(1) A person must not use physical force, or undue harassment or coercion, in connection with:
   (a) the supply or possible supply of goods or services; or
   (b) the payment for goods or services; or
   (c) the sale or grant, or the possible sale or grant, of an interest in land; or
   (d) the payment for an interest in land.

Note: A pecuniary penalty may be imposed for a contravention of this subsection.

Until 2011 statutory duress was prohibited by s 60 of the *Trade Practices Act 1974* (Cth) and the various state and territory Fair Trading Acts. With the

---

23 See *Hawker Pacific Pty Ltd v Helicopter Charter Pty Ltd* (1991) 22 NSWLR 298 and *North Ocean Shipping Co Ltd v Hyundai Construction Co Ltd* (1979) 1 QB 705.

exception of Victoria, these prohibitions were restricted to consumer transactions. However, this restriction was not incorporated into s 50 of the *ACL*. As a result, s 50 will capture harassment and coercion in connection with the supply of goods or services, or the sale or grant of interests in land, or the payment for such supply. The reference to 'physical force, or undue harassment or coercion' remains the same as in s 60 of the *Trade Practices Act*, so that case law applying that provision will remain relevant.

'Physical force, or undue harassment or coercion' may constitute duress of the person or duress of goods. For example, in *Australian Competition & Consumer Commission v Davis*,[24] Lee J found the provision had been breached when, in the process of attempting to seize the consumer's vehicle by attaching it to a tow-truck (which they were entitled to do), the respondents pinned the consumer (who had emerged from his house in his underwear to protest the seizure) down on the ground while the car was removed from the premises.

More frequently, however, the harassment or coercion will take the form of economic duress. It is not essential that the 'harassment or coercion' constitute an illegal act.[25] The harassment must, however, be *undue*. The concept of 'undue harassment' was discussed by French J in *Australian Competition and Consumer Commission v McCaskey*:[26]

The word 'harassment' as used in s 60 must serve two broad purposes. It describes a range of conduct, in connection with the supply of goods or services which involve, *inter alia*, applying repeated pressure to a consumer who is under no pre-existing obligation to acquire. It also describes conduct in relation to a consumer who is under an unfulfilled obligation to pay for goods or services. Given the range of cases that it can cover, the question whether or not there is harassment involves evaluative judgment. The word 'undue' adds an extra layer of evaluation which is more relevant to the case of debt recovery than to the sale of goods or services. Repeated unwelcome approaches to a potential acquirer of goods or services could qualify as harassment and, so qualified, require very little additional evidence, if any, to attract the characterisation of 'undue harassment'. On the other hand a consumer who owes money to a supplier can expect repeated unwelcome approaches requesting payment of the debt if he or she does not pay. No doubt such approaches might also qualify as harassment. If legitimate demands are reasonably made, on more than one occasion, for the purpose of reminding the debtor of his or her obligation and drawing the debtor's attention to the likelihood of legal proceedings if payment is not made, then that conduct, if it be harassment, is not undue harassment. If, however, the frequency, nature or content of the approaches and communications associated with them is such that they are calculated to intimidate or demoralise, tire out or exhaust a debtor rather than convey the demand and an associated legitimate threat of proceedings, the harassment will be undue.

---

24   [2003] FCA 1227.
25   *Campbell v Metway Leasing Ltd* (1998) ATPR 41-630.
26   (2000) 104 FCR 8 at [48].

In the same case French J also considered the concept of 'undue coercion':[27]

> The collection of debts may involve coercion in the sense that the debtor is subjected to the pressure of the demand and the legitimate threat of civil process for recovery with the additional cost and damage to credit which that can involve. Such pressure may be thought of as coercion but is entirely legitimate and not 'undue'. Where the demand includes content which does not serve legitimate purposes of reminding the debtor of the obligation and threatening legal proceedings for recovery but is calculated otherwise to intimidate or threaten the debtor, then the coercion may be undue. So if a threat is made of criminal proceedings, or of the immediate seizure and sale of house and property, a remedy not available in the absence of retention of title or some form of security, the coercion is likely to be seen as undue. The threat of criminal proceedings itself may be an offence against state laws. Quite apart from content the manner or circumstances of a demand or communication, including the language used, the time and place at which it is made and the person to whom it is communicated, may go beyond the legitimate purposes of drawing attention to the existence of the obligation and the consequences for non-compliance. Again such a communication may amount to undue coercion. Obvious examples include the use of personally abusive or obscene language, conveying the demand to uninvolved family members, particularly children, or conveying the demand through a third party in order to embarrass the debtor when the debtor could reasonably have been the subject of a direct communication. Each case will turn on its own facts. ... The recovery of unpaid debts can be pursued with firmness, determination and civility. It can do all those things without resorting to bullying, bluff, misrepresentation or stand-over tactics. If it does the first and avoids the second it is unlikely to contravene the law.

Where s 50 of the *ACL* is contravened remedies include injunctions,[28] ancillary orders, which may include rescission or variation of the contract,[29] and damages.[30]

INTERNATIONAL PERSPECTIVES

> Duress is recognised in the contract laws of both India and China. In the case of India, duress to person and property and economic duress involving unlawful threats will prevent a contract arising. In China, duress, which would appear to include economic duress as well as the more traditional concepts of duress, will provide a ground for amendment or cancellation of a contract.
>
> ### India
>
> In order to constitute a contract under the *Indian Contract Act* an agreement must be made by the 'free consent' of the parties (s 10). There will be no free consent where the consent is caused by coercion (s 14).

---

27 Para 51.
28 *ACL* Part 5-2, Division 2.
29 *ACL* s 243.
30 *ACL* s 236.

> ## Indian Contract Act, 1872
>
> Section 15
>
> 'Coercion' is the committing, or threatening to commit, any act forbidden by the Indian Penal Code.
>
> Coercion encompasses what in Australia would be classified as duress against a person or property and extends to all threats to commit unlawful acts. In some important respects it extends beyond Australian law; in particular, the threat inducing the contract may be made by any person—not only the other party to the contract—and the threat may be directed at any person. Consequently, a threat to harm a person unknown to the other party will constitute duress if it was a cause of that party agreeing to the contract.
>
> As is the case in Australia, it is not necessary that the free will of the weaker party be overborne by the coercion.[31]
>
> Economic duress may also be prohibited as a form of undue influence where one party is in a position to dominate another.[32]

China

A contract influenced by duress may be validly formed in China, but will be declared invalid where the duress harms the interest of the state and, in other cases, will enable the influenced party to seek amendment or cancellation of the tainted contract.

> ## Contract Law of the People's Republic of China, 1999
>
> Article 52. Invalidating Circumstances
>
> A contract is invalid in any of the following circumstances:
>
> (i) One party induced conclusion of the contract through fraud or duress, thereby harming the interests of the state; ...
>
> Article 54. Contract Subject to Amendment or Cancellation
>
> ... If a party induced the other party to enter into a contract against its true intention by fraud or duress, or by taking advantage of the other party's hardship, the aggrieved party is entitled to petition the People's Court or an arbitration institution for amendment or cancellation of the contract.
>
> Where a party petitions for amendment of the contract, the People's Court or arbitration institution may not cancel the contract instead.

---

31   *Karuppayee Ammal v Karuppish Pillai* (1987) 1 Mad LJ 138 (Madras High Court).
32   *Shrimati v Sudhakar R Bhatkar AIR* 1998 Bom 122 (Bombay High Court).

5   Summary

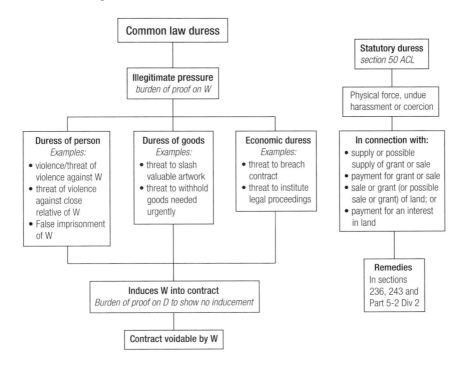

6   Questions

1   Toby is the owner of a small printing service, Pretty Pamphlets Pty Ltd. Suzanne runs a professional seminar program for teachers and regularly uses Pretty Pamphlets for assistance in designing and printing her seminar documents and advertising material. In March, Suzanne ordered 1,000 glossy colour brochures for use in a series of seminars to run in May at a cost of $10 per brochure.

In April, two weeks before the seminars were to commence, Toby contacted Suzanne and told her that, while he had printed 650 brochures at the agreed price of $10, the latest batch of high quality brochure paper had cost him significantly more than anticipated due to fluctuations in the exchange rate and he could not supply the remaining 350 brochures for less than $12 each (an additional $700 in total). Suzanne protested that they had an agreement and that he should honour it, but Toby responded that at $12 a copy he was still operating at a loss and that he simply could not afford to print the brochures at the original rate without laying off staff to offset the increased costs. Although not impressed, Suzanne did not wish to be responsible for anyone losing their job and she knew she would be unable to get equivalent brochures printed in time, so agreed to pay the higher rate for the remaining brochures.

The brochures were printed and delivered in May and were a great hit at the seminars. However, after receiving the invoice for the brochures Suzanne had a change of heart and refused to pay the additional $700 above the original agreed price.

Please advise Toby about whether he can claim the additional $700. Would your advice change if Toby had demanded an additional $10 per brochure and the price change had nothing to do with increased production costs?

2   Stacy runs her own business as a financial planner. She is also a keen horse enthusiast and, unfortunately, as a result of spending too much time with her horses and too little time servicing her customers, she has exposed herself to numerous negligence claims and her business has run into financial difficulties.

One of her clients, Mark, seeking to bypass the court system, followed Stacy to a gymkhana (a horse event) and stole her horse. Mark then confronted Stacy and threatened to cause harm to the horse if she did not immediately sign a contract he had prepared. Pursuant to this, she agreed to pay him $10,000 in exchange for him agreeing not to sue her for negligence over poor advice she had given him. Distraught, Stacy signed the contract. However, as a result of the financial difficulties experienced by her business, Stacy is unable to honour the contract.

She has approached you for advice. Please advise Stacy whether or not she is obliged to pay Mark $10,000.

3   Jack was particularly fond of a piece of movie memorabilia owned by a friend of his, Harry. Jack regularly asked Harry if he would sell the item to him, but on each occasion Harry indicated that he would not sell it at any price. Jack grew increasingly obsessed with obtaining the item and Jack and Harry's friendship became strained as a result.

On one occasion, after a bout of drinking, Jack said to Harry: 'Just sell the damn thing to me or I swear I will beat the crap out of you.' Harry didn't believe Jack and simply walked away. However, the next day Jack approached Harry and said: 'I'm not kidding. I'm sick of asking and if you don't sell it to me I will get you.' Harry told him to grow up and get over the fact he was never going to get the item. Jack then punched Harry in the guts. Jack said 'Sell it to me or there'll be more of that.' Harry was shocked and agreed to sell Jack the item for $1,000 (a fair market price). Jack agreed and told him he'd be over to collect it the next day.

Harry has come to see you. Please advise Harry about whether or not he is required to give the item to Jack as agreed.

CHAPTER 15

Undue Influence

1	Introduction	423
2	Domination or express undue influence	424
3	Antecedent relationships of trust—presumed undue influence	425
	a Relationships deemed to give rise to presumed undue influence	426
	b Other relationships of trust and confidence	427
4	Third parties	432
5	Summary	437
6	Questions	437

1   Introduction

Undue influence, like duress, is concerned with an inequality of power between the parties which leads the weaker party (W) to enter into a contract or other transaction, such as a gift, with the dominant party (D) or a third party (T).

Not all *influence* leading to a contract will provide a remedy. Only *influence* that reaches such a degree that the courts are prepared to classify it as *undue* will provide W with a remedy. In this respect there are two categories of undue influence recognised by the courts:

- **Domination or express undue influence:** this occurs when D's influence is such that it effectively deprives W of their free will. This is sometimes referred to as 'equitable coercion' and overlaps with the common law doctrine of duress.
- **Presumed undue influence:** this occurs where D holds a position of trust or confidence over W such that the law will presume that transactions between them are the result of undue influence unless D can demonstrate that this is not the case.

Where established, undue influence will render a contract voidable at the option of W. W may elect to rescind the contract and recover money paid or property transferred—except that transferred to an innocent third party—under the contract, or they may affirm the contract.

2 Domination or express undue influence

In cases of express undue influence the burden of demonstrating that D exerted undue influence over W in relation to their transaction lies upon W. W must also demonstrate that it was this influence that brought about the contract in question. Express undue influence overlaps with duress and, as it is often brought about by misleading statements, commonly also gives rise to a statutory claim of misleading and deceptive conduct.

This situation arose in *Odorizzi v Bloomfield School District*. The plaintiff, a school teacher, was arrested for homosexual behaviour.[1] After being questioned, booked and released on bail, having not slept for a period of 40 hours, he was visited at his home by the superintendent of the school district and his school principal. They pressured him to sign a resignation in return for the school hushing up his 'crime'. Specifically, they told him that:

> ... he should take their advice and immediately resign his position with the district, that there was no time to consult an attorney, that if he did not resign immediately the district would suspend and dismiss him from his position and publicize the proceedings, his 'aforedescribed arrest' and cause him 'to suffer extreme embarrassment and humiliation'; but that if he resigned at once the incident would not be publicized and would not jeopardize his chances of securing employment as a teacher elsewhere.[2]

The plaintiff signed the resignation. He was later acquitted of the charges and sought to be reinstated. The school refused and he brought an action seeking to rescind his resignation on the ground of undue influence.

In his judgment Fleming J[3] observed that undue influence is normally accompanied by several of the following elements:

> (1) discussion of the transaction at an unusual or inappropriate time, (2) consummation of the transaction in an unusual place, (3) insistent demand that the business be finished at once, (4) extreme emphasis on untoward consequences of delay, (5) the use of multiple persuaders by the dominant side against a single servient party, (6) absence of third-party advisers to the servient party, (7) statements that there is no time to consult financial advisers or attorneys.[4]

In this case a number of these elements were present. His Honour therefore held that excessive pressure had been exerted upon the plaintiff and the cause of action for rescission based on undue influence was made out. His Honour also observed that the difference between legitimate and undue influence often rests in the 'manner in which the parties go about their business'. In this case, for example, he observed that:

---

1 The behaviour involved was illegal in California at the time.
2 246 Cal App 2d 123 (1966) at 127.
3 The leading judgment was delivered by Fleming J with Roth PJ and Herndon J concurring.
4 246 Cal App 2d 123 (1966) at 133.

> ... if a day or two after [the plaintiff's] release on bail the superintendent of the school district had called him into his office during business hours and directed his attention to those provisions of the Education Code compelling his leave of absence and authorizing his suspension on the filing of written charges, had told him that the district contemplated filing written charges against him, had pointed out the alternative of resignation available to him, had informed him he was free to consult counsel or any adviser he wished and to consider the matter overnight and return with his decision the next day, it is extremely unlikely that any complaint about the use of excessive pressure could ever have been made against the school district.[5]

In determining whether or not there has been undue influence, one of the factors the court will look to is the adequacy of consideration provided. This is not a determinative factor; a contract might be voidable for undue influence despite generous consideration being provided.[6] Nevertheless, the more improvident the transaction from the weaker party's perspective the easier it will be to demonstrate the contract was tainted by undue influence. It is important, however, to recognise that there is a difference between legitimate commercial persuasion and *undue influence*. This distinction was highlighted by Fleming J in *Odorizzi v Bloomfield School District* when his Honour said:[7]

> Undue influence cannot be used as a pretext to avoid bad bargains or escape from bargains which refuse to come up to expectations. A woman who buys a dress on impulse, which on critical inspection by her best friend turns out to be less fashionable than she had thought, is not legally entitled to set aside the sale on the ground that the saleswoman used all her wiles to close the sale. A man who buys a tract of desert land in the expectation that it is in the immediate path of the city's growth and will become another Palm Springs, an expectation cultivated in glowing terms by the seller, cannot rescind his bargain when things turn out differently. If we are temporarily persuaded against our better judgment to do something about which we later have second thoughts, we must abide the consequences of the risks inherent in managing our own affairs ...

3 Antecedent relationships of trust—presumed undue influence

If a relationship of trust and confidence exists between the parties prior to a contract being entered into, undue influence will be presumed; the dominant party will then have the burden of rebutting this presumption in order to enforce the contract. The most obvious means of doing this is to demonstrate that W received independent legal advice prior to entering into the transaction,[8] although it is still possible for D to overcome the burden without proof of such advice.

---

5   246 Cal App 2d 123 (1966) at 134–135.
6   Note that this is not the case in the UK where the transaction must be improvident before undue influence will arise: *National Westminster Bank v Morgan* [1985] 1 AC 686.
7   *Odorizzi v Bloomfield School District* (1966) 246 Cal App 2d 123 at 132.
8   *Johnson v Buttress* (1936) 56 CLR 113 at 120, per Latham CJ.

In some situations the parties will be deemed to be in a relationship of trust and confidence; in others, this relationship must be positively demonstrated before the presumption will arise.

a   Relationships deemed to give rise to presumed undue influence

There is no exhaustive list of relationships that will result in undue influence being presumed. There are, however, a number of relationships which are firmly established as giving rise to such a presumption. These include solicitor and client, parent and child, doctor and patient, trustee and beneficiary, and cases where there is a religious influence.[9]

Example

A solicitor, D, is engaged by W to settle his deceased parents' estate. The estate includes a residential property. D is quite taken with the property and decides to purchase it for herself. W agrees to the sale.

The solicitor and client relationship is one in which undue influence will be presumed. Consequently it will be presumed that the sale of the property to D was tainted by undue influence, even if D purchased the property at a fair market value. In order to enforce the contract D must demonstrate that W entered into the contract freely and that D did not breach the fiduciary obligations created through its position of trust and confidence.

The relationship of husband and wife, on the other hand, is not one in which the presumption automatically arises. The reason for this exclusion was described by Dixon J in the High Court in *Yerkey v Jones*:

> ... there is nothing unusual or strange in a wife from motives of affection or even of prudence conferring a large proprietary or pecuniary benefit upon her husband. The Court of Chancery was not blind to the opportunities of obtaining and unfairly using influence over his wife which a husband often possesses. But in the relations comprised within the category to which the presumption of undue influence applies, there is another element besides the mere existence of an opportunity of obtaining ascendancy or confidence and of abusing it. It will be found that in none of those relations is it natural to expect the one party to give property to the other. That is to say, the character of the relation itself is never enough to explain the transaction and to account for it without suspicion of confidence abused.
>
> ... while the relation of a husband to his wife is not one of influence, and no presumption exists of undue influence, it has never been divested completely of what may be called equitable presumptions of an invalidating tendency.[10]

---

9   See *Johnson v Buttress* (1936) 56 CLR 113 at 119, per Latham CJ.
10   (1939) 63 CLR 649 at 675.

While the relationship of husband and wife is not one in which the law will deem that trust and confidence resides, it remains possible for a spouse to prove that such a relationship of trust and confidence does in fact exist or, alternatively, that actual undue influence was exerted.

b   Other relationships of trust and confidence

Where the relationship involved does not fall within one of the recognised categories W may still be able to demonstrate that the relationship was of such a nature that undue influence ought to be presumed. In this respect W must demonstrate there was a relationship of trust and confidence between the parties and that W actually did repose trust and confidence in D. This situation commonly arises where D experiences a conflict of interest. It also frequently arises in respect of relationships of intimacy. Equity's treatment of other relationships of trust and confidence was discussed in the following case.

Johnson v Buttress
(1936) 56 CLR 113, High Court of Australia

[Buttress (the deceased) was 67 years old, illiterate and of less than average intelligence with no capacity for business. He owned land on which a cottage was erected; this was substantially all the property he possessed. Buttress had known Johnson (the defendant) for many years, had been living on land owned by her and planned to continue to do so until his death. The Court found that there was ample reason for the deceased to hold gratitude for her and also that 'a relation of trust and confidence obtained between [him and the defendant] of such a character that he relied upon her for advice on any matter of business'.[11]

During his lifetime the deceased transferred his land to the defendant. The transfer of land was executed at the office of the defendant's solicitor and the deceased did not receive independent advice regarding the transfer. The trial judge found that the defendant did not understand that he was parting with his property permanently. Following his death, the defendant's son and beneficiary under his will brought an action seeking to have the transfer set aside on the grounds of undue influence.]

Latham CJ [at 119]: The jurisdiction of a court of equity to set aside gifts *inter vivos* which have been procured by undue influence is exercised where undue influence is proved as a fact, or where, undue influence being presumed from the relations existing between the parties, the presumption has not been rebutted. Where certain special relations exist undue influence is presumed in the case of such gifts. These relations include those of parent and child, guardian and ward, trustee and *cestui que trust*, solicitor and client, physician and patient and cases of religious influence. The relations mentioned, however, do not constitute

---

[11]   Latham CJ at 122.

an exhaustive list of the cases in which undue influence will be presumed from personal relations. Wherever the relation between donor and donee is such that the latter is in a position to exercise dominion over the former by reason of the trust and confidence reposed in the latter, the presumption of undue influence is raised.

Where such a relation of what may be called, from one point of view, dominion, and from another point of view, dependence, exists, the age and condition of the donor are irrelevant so far as raising the presumption of undue influence is concerned. It must be affirmatively shown by the donee that the gift was ... 'the pure, voluntary, well-understood act of the mind' of the donor.

It may not be necessary in all cases to show that the donor received competent independent advice <120> ... But evidence that such advice has been given is one means, and the most obvious means, of helping to establish that the gift was the result of the free exercise of independent will; and the absence of such advice, even if not sufficient in itself to invalidate the transaction, would plainly be a most important factor in determining whether the gift was in fact the result of a free and genuine exercise of the will of the donor.

In the case of an illiterate or weak-minded person it will be more difficult for the donee to discharge the prescribed onus of proof than in other cases. The burden will be still heavier upon the donee where the donor has given him all or practically all of his property ...

<121> ... It cannot be denied that the absolute transfer to the defendant of the property which was his sole source of income was highly improvident. It is true that the defendant and her daughter gave evidence that it was understood that the defendant would support him for the rest of his life, but the learned judge has found that there was no contract to that effect, and, if the defendant had died the day after the transfer, the deceased would have been left practically without any property and without any enforceable rights to ensure his support.

[The deceased received no independent advice. Due to the relationship of trust and confidence between the deceased and the defendant (at 123)] in order to maintain the transaction, it was necessary for the defendant to show affirmatively that the deceased knew what he was doing when he made the transfer, in the sense that he understood its effect and significance in relation to himself, and further to show that the transfer was the result of his own will. ...

... the findings of the learned judge, ... show that though it has not been affirmatively proved against the defendant that she exercised undue influence, yet she has not displaced the presumption of undue influence which arises in the circumstances of this case. Thus the transaction cannot stand by reason of the general policy of the law directed to preventing the possible abuse of relations of trust and confidence. ...

Dixon J [at 134]: ... parties may antecedently stand in a relation that gives to one an authority or influence over the other from the abuse of which it is proper that he should be protected. When they stand in such a relation, the party in the position of influence cannot maintain his beneficial title to property of substantial value made over to him by the other as a gift, unless he satisfies the court that he took no advantage of the donor, but that the gift was the independent and well-understood act of a man in a position to exercise a free judgment based on information as full as that of the donee. This burden is imposed upon one of the parties to certain well-known relations as soon as it appears that the relation existed and that he has obtained a substantial benefit from the other. A solicitor must thus justify the receipt of such a benefit from his client, a physician from his patient, a parent from his child, ... But while in these and perhaps one or two other relationships their very nature imports influence, the doctrine which throws upon the recipient the burden of justifying the transaction is confined to no fixed category. It rests upon a principle. It applies whenever one party occupies or assumes <135> towards another a position naturally involving an ascendancy or influence over that other, or a dependence or trust on his part. [When one] occupying such a position ... takes from that man a substantial gift of property, it is incumbent upon him to show that it cannot be ascribed to the inequality between them which must arise from his special position. ...

<137> ... in this peculiar case it is the man's illiteracy, his ignorance of affairs, and his strangeness in disposition and manner that provide the foundation for the suggested relation. For many years he had leant upon his wife, and it is evident that, after her death, he was at a loss for guidance and support. He turned first to one and then to another for a prop. ... <138> [the facts] draw a picture of an ignorant labouring man depending in many essential matters upon one whom he regarded as having all the advantages of education and position and in whom he confided ... such matters of business as he had occasion to transact were managed by, or under the supervision of, Mrs Johnson. ... he was constantly in her company and that he relied upon her advice and depended on her kindness.

I think that when the circumstances of the case are considered, with the character and capacity of Buttress they lead to the conclusion that an antecedent relation of influence existed which throws upon Mrs Johnson the burden of justifying the transfer by showing that it was the result of the free exercise of the donor's independent will. This, in my opinion, she has quite failed to do.

[Evatt J agreed with Dixon J; Starke and McTiernan JJ delivered separate judgments in favour of the plaintiff.]

Appeal dismissed

[footnotes omitted]

INTERNATIONAL PERSPECTIVES

Indian Contract Act, 1872

The *Indian Contract Act* recognises the concept of undue influence. There will be no 'free consent' and, therefore, no contract, where consent is caused by undue influence. Similar circumstances to those that give rise to undue influence in

Australia will result in consent being negated in India.[12] In particular, undue influence will be presumed in all cases where a relationship of trust and confidence exists between the parties[13] unless the dominant party can demonstrate they did not use this position to obtain an unfair advantage over the weaker party.[14]

Similarly, where one party is in a position to dominate the other and the resulting contract is apparently unconscionable, or unfair, the law will presume the weaker party's consent was obtained as a result of undue influence. The dominant party will then have the onus of proving they did not in fact overbear the will of the weaker party.[15]

Section 10. What agreements are contracts

All agreements are contracts if they are made by the free consent of parties ...

Section 14. Free consent defined

Consent is said to be free when it is not caused by-

...

(2) Undue influence, as defined in section 16, or

...

Consent is said to be so caused when it would not have been given but for the existence of such ... undue influence, ...

Section 16. Undue influence defined

(1) A contract is said to be induced by undue influence where the relations subsisting between the parties are such that one of the parties is in a position to dominate the will of the other and uses that position to obtain an unfair advantage over the other.

(2) In particular and without prejudice to the generality of the foregoing principle, a person is deemed to be in a position to dominate the will of another-
   (a) Where he holds a real or apparent authority over the other, or where he stands in a fiduciary relation to the other; or
   (b) Where he makes a contract with a person whose mental capacity is temporarily or permanently affected by reason of age, illness, or mental or bodily distress.

---

12 See *Smith v Kay* (1859) 7 HLC 750 at 779; the burden lies upon the plaintiff to prove the other party was in a position to dominate their will and also that this influence was used to obtain the plaintiff's consent.

13 Similar relationships give rise to the presumption in India; for example doctors and patients, lawyers and clients, and spiritual advisors and their inferiors constitute presumed relationships of trust. Indian law will also presume undue influence involving contracts made with a *pardanashin* woman—that is, a woman secluded from all normal social interaction: *Kalibaksh Singh v Ram Gopal Singh* (1913) 41 IA 23. As in Australia, marital relations will not give rise to a presumption of undue influence.

14 See *Chand Singh v Ram Kaur* (1987) 2 Punj LR 70.

15 See *Wajid Khan v Raja Ewaz Ali Khan* (1891) 18 IA 144 which involved an elderly and illiterate woman conferring a pecuniary benefit on her confidential managing agent.

(3) Where a person who is in position to dominate the will of another, enters into a contract with him, and the transaction appears, on the face of it or on the evidence adduced, to be unconscionable, the burden of proving that such contract was not induced by undue influence shall be upon the person in a position to dominate the will of the other.

...

Illustrations
(a) A having advanced money to his son, B, during his minority, upon B's coming of age obtains, by misuse of parental influence, a bond from B for a greater amount than the sum due in respect of the advance. A employs undue influence.
(b) A, a man enfeebled by disease of age, is induced, by influence over him as his medical attendants to agree to pay B an unreasonable sum for his professional services. B employees undue influence.
(c) A, being in debt to B, the money-lender of his village, contracts a fresh loan on terms which appear to be unconscionable. It lies on B to prove that the contract was not induced by undue influence.
(d) A applies to a banker for a loan at a time when there is stringency in the money market. The banker declines to make the loan except at an unusually high rate of interest. A accepts the loan on these terms. This is a transaction in the ordinary course of business, and the contract is not induced by undue influence.

Section 19A. Power to set aside contract induced by undue influence

When consent to an agreement is caused by undue influence, the agreement is a contract voidable at the option of the party whose consent was so caused.

Any such contract may be set aside either absolutely or, if the party who was entitled to avoid it has received any benefits thereunder, upon such terms and conditions as to the Court may seem just.

Illustrations
(a) A's son has forged B's name to a promissory note. B under threat of prosecuting A's son, obtains a bond from A for the amount of the forged note. If B sues on this bond, the Court may set the bond aside.
(b) A, a money-lender, advances Rs 100 to B, an agriculturist, and, by undue influence, induces B to execute a bond for Rs 200 with interest at 6 percent, per month. The Court may set the bond aside, ordering B to repay the Rs 100 with such interest as may seem just.

China

The Chinese Contract law does not recognise undue influence as providing a separate ground for amendment or cancellation of a contract. The law does, however, permit amendment or cancellation of a contract in circumstances where one party was induced to enter into the contract 'against its true intention' by the other party's fraud, duress or the taking advantage of that party's hardship.[16] This is discussed further in chapters 12, 14 and 16.

4 Third parties

As noted above, wives are not in a presumed relationship of undue influence with their husbands. Nevertheless, the courts have indicated that where such a relationship exists a third-party creditor is taken to be on notice that any actual undue influence on the part of the husband will invalidate the transaction. This was made clear by the High Court in *Yerkey v Jones*:

> Although the relation of husband to wife is not one of influence, yet the opportunities it gives are such that if the husband procures his wife to become surety for his debt a creditor who accepts her suretyship obtained through her husband has been treated as taking it subject to any invalidating conduct on the part of her husband even if the creditor be not actually privy to such conduct. ...[17]

This issue arose in the following case which makes clear that even if there is no *actual* undue influence on the part of the husband, where the wife is a *volunteer* to the transaction, the court will not permit a third-party creditor to take the benefit of a transaction if the transaction and its effects have not been sufficiently explained to the wife.

Garcia v National Australia Bank

(1998) 194 CLR 395, High Court of Australia

[Mrs Garcia, a physiotherapist, and her husband, executed a mortgage over their home in favour of the bank. The mortgage secured moneys owing under future guarantees. Mrs Garcia's husband conducted a business, Citizens Gold, of which she was also a director. Guarantees were also given in respect of this business. The husband had assured her there was no danger in the guarantee and she signed the document at the bank. No explanation of the transaction was provided by the bank officer. The trial judge found that Mrs Garcia understood what a guarantee was but did not understand that the guarantee was 'secured by the all moneys mortgage which she had signed in 1979'.[18]

The Garcia's subsequently divorced and Mrs Garcia sought a declaration that the guarantees given by her in respect of Citizens Gold were void. The trial judge found in favour of Mrs Garcia. The Court of Appeal overturned this decision and Mrs Garcia appealed to the High Court.]

---

16 *Contract Law of the People's Republic of China*, Article 54.
17 (1939) 63 CLR 649 at 678, per Dixon J.
18 Gaudron, McHugh, Gummow and Hayne JJ at 401.

Gaudron, McHugh, Gummow and Hayne JJ [at 402]: ... Although the appellant had pleaded a case of actual undue influence by her husband, the trial judge made no positive finding that the appellant's execution of the November 1987 guarantee had been procured by actual undue influence. He did find that 'the husband pressured the wife to sign the document' and that '[s]he appeared to have done so because her husband consistently pointed out what a fool she was in commercial matters whereas he was an expert, and because she was trying to save her marriage'. ... <403> ...

The Court of Appeal held that it was not bound to follow ... the principle in *Yerkey v Jones* [because] 'at its heart ... [it] is based upon general assumptions about the capacity of married women rather than upon evidence of the circumstances of the particular case' ...

... we consider that the principles spoken of by Dixon J in *Yerkey v Jones* are simply particular applications of accepted equitable principles which have as much application today as they did then. ... It was submitted that changes in Australian society since 1939, when *Yerkey v Jones* was decided, require that equitable rules move on to meet these changed circumstances.

That Australian society, and particularly the role of women in that society, has changed in the last six decades is undoubted. But some things are unchanged. There is still a significant number of women in Australia in relationships which are, ... marked by disparities of economic and other power between the <404> parties. However, the rationale of *Yerkey v Jones* is not to be found in notions based on the subservience or inferior economic position of women. Nor is it based on their vulnerability to exploitation because of their emotional involvement, save to the extent that the case was concerned with actual undue influence.

... *Yerkey v Jones* ... is based on trust and confidence, in the ordinary sense of those words, between marriage partners. The marriage relationship is such that one, often the woman, may well leave many, perhaps all, business judgments to the other spouse. In that kind of relationship, business decisions may be made with little consultation between the parties and with only the most abbreviated explanation of their purport or effect. Sometimes, with not the slightest hint of bad faith, the explanation of a particular transaction given by one to the other will be imperfect and incomplete, if not simply wrong. That that is so is not always attributable to intended deception, to any imbalance of power between the parties, or, even, the vulnerability of one to exploitation because of emotional involvement. It is, at its core, often a reflection of no more or less than the trust and confidence each has in the other.

It may be that the principles applied in *Yerkey v Jones* will find application to other relationships, more common now than was the case in 1939, to long term and publicly declared relationships short of marriage between members of the same or of opposite sex. ... It may be that those principles will find application where the husband acts as surety for the wife but ... that is not a problem that falls for decision here. This case concerns a husband and wife ...

In his reasons for decision in *Yerkey v Jones*, Dixon J dealt with at least two kinds of circumstances: the first in which there is actual undue influence by a husband over a wife and the second, ... in which there is no undue influence but there is a failure to explain adequately and accurately the suretyship transaction which the husband seeks to have the wife enter for the immediate economic benefit not of the wife but of the husband, or the <405> circumstances in which her liability may arise. The former kind of case is one concerning what today is seen as an imbalance of power. In point of legal principle, however, it is actual undue influence in that the wife, lacking economic or other power, is overborne by her husband and goes surety for her husband's debts when she does not bring a free mind and will to that decision. The latter case is not so much concerned with imbalances of power as with lack of proper information about the purport and effect of the transaction. The present appeal concerns circumstances of the latter kind rather than the former. ...

<409> ... the analysis of the second kind of case identified in *Yerkey v Jones* is not one which depends upon any presumption of undue influence by the husband over the wife. ... Nor does the analysis depend upon identifying the husband as acting as agent for the creditor in procuring the wife's agreement to the transaction. Rather, it depends upon the surety being a volunteer and mistaken about the purport and effect of the transaction, and the creditor being taken to have appreciated that because of the trust and confidence between surety and debtor the surety may well receive from the debtor no sufficient explanation of the transaction's purport and effect. To enforce the transaction against a mistaken volunteer when the creditor, the party that seeks to take the benefit of the transaction, has not itself explained the transaction, and does not know that a third party has done so, would be unconscionable. ...

<411> ... the only question of notice that arises is whether the creditor knew at the time of the taking of the guarantee that the surety was then married to the creditor. ...

... the creditor may readily avoid the possibility that the surety will later claim not to have understood the purport and effect of the transaction that is proposed. If the creditor itself explains the transaction sufficiently, or knows that the surety has received 'competent, independent and disinterested' advice from a third party, it would not be unconscionable for the creditor to enforce it against the surety even though the surety is a volunteer and it later emerges that the surety claims to have been mistaken.

... The trial judge found that the appellant did not understand the purport or effect of the transaction. She knew it was a guarantee but she thought it was a guarantee of limited overdraft accommodation to be applied only in the purchase of gold. Nor did she understand that her obligations under the guarantee were secured by the mortgage which she had given over her home. It being found that the bank took no step to explain the transaction to her and knew of no independent advice to her about it (there having been no such independent advice) the conclusion that the appellant was entitled to succeed in her claim to set the transaction aside was inevitable if she was a volunteer. ...

<412> ... Although the trial judge found that from time to time some benefit flowed to the family from the companies, he found that they were companies that were in the 'complete control' of the appellant's husband. Taken as a whole, those findings demonstrate that the appellant in fact obtained no real benefit from her entering the transaction; she was a volunteer. ...

Kirby J [at 415]: ... [His Honour noted the claim that Mrs Garcia was a volunteer in the transaction and continued]: The wife was fully aware that she was guaranteeing her husband's transactions and those of Citizens Gold, the company through which he operated. She was herself involved in Citizens Gold, both as a shareholder and director. The wife was not deluded nor coerced by the husband into signing the guarantee. Nor was her will overborne in a technical sense. Had the husband's investments prospered, in ordinary circumstances this would have secured economic advantages for the wife, or at least the children of the marriage. She was therefore not entirely a volunteer, in the sense of having no economic interest in the success of his business ventures. The couple lived together in a jointly owned home. By inference, the reason for her accepting an office of director in Citizens Gold, and for providing the guarantee, was that the husband's economic position was, however indirectly, bound up in the economic position of the whole family. If the financial transactions in which Citizens Gold was involved had proved profitable, and if the personal relationships of the husband and wife had improved, it scarcely seems <416> likely that the wife would have disclaimed the economic benefits as vigorously as she has now sought to escape the economic burdens.

[His Honour considered that Dixon J's reasons in *Yerkey* which provided a special equity for wives based on their stereotypical need for the protection should not be endorsed. Instead his Honour indicated he would adopt a broader principle designed to encompass relationships involving emotional dependency. Applied to the present case his Honour agreed that as the bank knew, or ought to have known, that Mrs Garcia reposed trust and confidence in her husband in relation to financial affairs, and having failed 'to take reasonable steps to satisfy itself that she entered the obligation freely and with knowledge of the relevant facts' they were unable to enforce it against her. His Honour further noted that the fact that she was intelligent and articulate, while relevant, was not determinative.]

[Justice Callinan delivered a separate judgment in which he upheld *Yerkey* and agreed with the orders of the majority.]

Appeal allowed

[footnotes omitted]

The House of Lords has since extended this principle beyond sexual relationships to all non-commercial relationships of trust and confidence, holding that:

> [applying the principle only to sexual relationships] would be an arbitrary boundary ... the reality of life is that relationships in which undue influence can be exercised are infinitely various. They cannot be exhaustively defined. Nor is it possible to

produce a comprehensive list of relationships where there is a substantial risk of the exercise of undue influence, ... Human affairs do not lend themselves to categorisations of this sort.

These considerations point forcibly to the conclusion that there is no rational cut-off point, with certain types of relationship being susceptible ... and others not. Further, if a bank is not to be required to evaluate the extent to which its customer has influence over a proposed guarantor, the only practical way forward is to regard banks as 'put on inquiry' in every case where the relationship between the surety and the debtor is non-commercial. The creditor must always take reasonable steps to bring home to the individual guarantor the risks he is running by standing as surety. As a measure of protection, this is valuable. But, in all conscience, it is a modest burden for banks and other lenders. It is no more than is reasonably to be expected of a creditor who is taking a guarantee from an individual. If the bank or other creditor does not take these steps, it is deemed to have notice of any claim the guarantor may have that the transaction was procured by undue influence or misrepresentation on the part of the debtor.[19]

This broader principle has not yet been endorsed by Australian courts.[20] Thus, in *Kranz v National Australia Bank Ltd* (2003) 8 VR 310, the Victorian Court of Appeal has made clear that while the *Garcia* principle extends beyond intimate personal relationships, it does not yet extend to encompass the principle set out in *Etridge* above.[21]

---

19   *Royal Bank of Scotland v Etridge (No 2)* [2002] AC 773 at 813–814, per Lord Nicholls.
20   See *Watt v State Bank of New South Wales* [2003] ACTCA 7 and for discussion see M Brown, 'Garcia – surely it's *not* just about sex!' (2004) 32 *ABLR* 254.
21   This case involved the provision of a guarantee by the brother-in-law of the beneficiary. Charles JA held that there was no reason to suppose that, as between the brothers-in-law, there was an 'emotional or influential relationship' which might put the bank on notice that the guarantor was in a 'position of special disability in respect of the transaction'. Winneke P and Eames J agreed with Charles JA. Despite developments in the United Kingdom, the High Court considered this case unsuitable for discussion of these issues and refused special leave to appeal: *Kranz & Anor v National Australia Bank Ltd* [2004] HCATrans 211. Gleeson CJ considered the findings of fact made the case an unsuitable vehicle for discussion of issues raised and also that there were 'insufficient prospects of success of an appeal to warrant a grant of special leave'. See also *ANZ Banking Group Ltd v Alirezai; Alirezai v ANZ Banking Group Ltd & Anor* [2004] QCA 6.

5 Summary

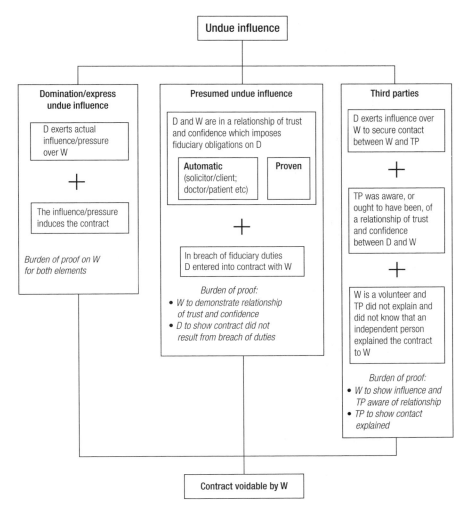

6 Questions

1. Lisa runs her own accounting business. She is highly educated and has worked at a major national accounting firm for many years. Greg owns a farm in rural Victoria, near Horsham, which he inherited from his parents. Greg left school at the age of 16 to start work on the family farm and pursue his love of horses and the outdoors. Although not formally educated in business, he has enjoyed success through managing his farm.

    Several years ago Lisa and Greg met when Greg approached her accounting firm for tax advice. They fell in love and Lisa decided to leave her high-flying job and follow Greg to the farm. Shortly after marrying Greg, Lisa started up a local accounting business, run from a detached office at their home on the farm. She has enjoyed some success in advising local farmers and managing their accounts. Unfortunately, Lisa developed an online gambling addiction. What started with small bets on football games began to spiral out of control. She was soon spending all her business profits—and more—on gambling, without enjoying any great success. As a consequence, her business fell into debt.

Realising her difficulties, Lisa sought counselling for her gambling addiction. She was confident that, with help, she could turn her business around, provided she could overcome her businesses' current cash-flow problems. To this end she visited the Horsham Credit Institute Ltd (HCI) seeking a short-term business loan. Kathy, the loans manager at HCI, told Lisa that HCI would be prepared to lend her up to $100,000, but only if she could provide security. Unfortunately for Lisa, she owned no assets of any value. Kathy told her that she would not be able to obtain the loan unless Greg offered a guarantee, secured by the farm (an asset that was registered in Greg's name alone).

After speaking to Kathy, Lisa rushed home and prepared a candlelit picnic dinner for Greg. That evening, they enjoyed a wonderful and romantic meal under the stars. The next morning, as Greg was recovering from the pleasures of the previous evening, Lisa broached the subject of providing her with a guarantee, secured by the farm, to enable her to obtain a loan she needed for her business. As Greg was under the impression that the business was thriving, he was slightly puzzled by the request. Lisa assured him that a small cash-injection was needed to expand the business. Greg, who relied on Lisa for financial guidance, was satisfied she knew what she was doing and there would be no real risk to the farm.

The following Monday Lisa and Greg both attended a meeting with Kathy at the HCI offices. Kathy spoke to them about mortgaging the farm. Greg was asked to sign a number of documents. Kathy suggested that Greg read the documents thoroughly and seek advice from his solicitor before signing. Greg, while literate, knew he wouldn't understand all the legal and financial aspects of the document so he asked Lisa to read them for him. Lisa read them and assured him the terms were quite standard. Satisfied, Greg signed the documents without bothering to seek other advice. In fact, the documents, while quite standard, provided that the mortgage was to be used as security for any future loans made to Lisa's business as well as securing all existing debt.

Lisa's business did not improve. Six months later, HCI called in the debt. Lisa was unable to make the payments and HCI sought to enforce the mortgage and sell the farm.

Greg is distraught and comes to you for advice. Please advise Greg whether or not HCI can take his home.

2   Bill is Don's solicitor and friend. Following an amicable divorce, Don and his now ex-wife, Carol, approached Bill to assist them in drafting new wills and to assist them in the sale of the matrimonial property. The proceeds of the sale were to be split evenly between Don and Carol. Bill, who always loved Don and Carol's house, told them he would love to purchase the property and, if they wanted a quick sale (and to avoid agent fees), he would be happy to offer to pay a fair market price. He told them he could draft something to confirm the sale right away. Don and Carol were slightly hesitant about making a decision on the spot. Bill assured them that they should feel under no pressure and that he would not be offended if they wanted to put the house on the market. As it was approaching lunchtime he suggested that Don and Carol go out to lunch to talk about his proposal and that they could meet again at 2pm to discuss it further.

Over lunch, Don and Carol decided that it would make their lives easier if they just sold to Bill. They had already had the house valued at $650,000 and agreed that, provided Bill was prepared to pay that sum, they would sell the property to him. When they returned they informed Bill of their decision. Bill instantly agreed to pay the $650,000 and arranged to meet them again the next day to sign the documents. The next day the documents were drawn up and Don and Carol arrived and signed them. Transfer of the property was to take place in three months.

Don and Carol's post-divorce relationship has since deteriorated after Carol discovered Don had been having an affair with work colleague. Carol has also discovered that the person who valued their house was notorious for under-valuation and she has since had the property valued by two other experts. They place its value at closer to $1m. Carol now wishes to get out of the contract of sale with Bill and has come to you for advice.

Please advise Carol whether or not she can halt the sale of the property to Bill.

CHAPTER 16

Unconscionable Conduct

1	Introduction	440
2	The nature and effect of unconscionable conduct	440
3	The equitable doctrine of unconscionable conduct	442
	a Abuse of position	442
	b Harsh and oppressive transaction	448
	c Remedies for unconscionable conduct in equity	448
4	Statutory unconscionability	449
	a The *Australian Consumer Law*	449
	b *Australian Securities and Investments Commission Act 2001* (Cth)	462
	c State and territory legislation	463
5	*Contracts Review Act 1980* (NSW)	464
6	*National Credit Code*	471
7	Summary	475
8	Questions	475

1 Introduction

The prohibition of unconscionable conduct, like duress and undue influence, is aimed at encouraging fairness and good faith in contractual dealings. The equitable doctrine of unconscionability has long provided remedies for contracting parties whose weaker position has been unjustly exploited by a more dominant party. In Australia the equitable doctrine has, in recent years, been embedded in federal, state and territory legislation with the result that a broader range of remedies and dispute resolution procedures are now available to parties who have been subjected to unconscionable practices in the formation of their contracts. More recently this legislation has expanded the scope of unconscionable conduct for which the law will provide a remedy. This chapter will consider the traditional doctrine of unconscionable conduct and the more recent statutory developments.

2 The nature and effect of unconscionable conduct

Unconscionable conduct, like duress and undue influence, is concerned with the abuse of a dominant position by one contracting party over a weaker contracting party. Consequently, there is considerable scope for overlap between these doctrines. This is particularly so in relation to unconscionable conduct and undue influence. Nevertheless, the criteria for each doctrine are distinct, as Mason J made clear in *Amadio*:

> Although unconscionable conduct in this narrow sense bears some resemblance to the doctrine of undue influence, there is a difference between the two. In the latter the will of the innocent party is not independent and voluntary because it is overborne. In the former the will of the innocent party, even if independent and voluntary, is the result of the disadvantageous position in which he is placed and of the other party unconscientiously taking advantage of that position.[1]

It is possible, however, for the same conduct to give rise to an action for undue influence and unconscionability and often both are pleaded.

INTERNATIONAL PERSPECTIVES

> The type of *procedural* unconscionability with which Australian and English law are concerned does not have an equivalent in Indian or Chinese law, though China will allow remedies for unconscionable contracts in limited circumstances.
>
> ### Indian Contract Act, 1872
>
> The *Indian Contract Act* does not provide a general prohibition on unconscionable dealings. Instead, reliance is placed on the specific prohibitions of undue influence and fraud. These were discussed in chapters 14 and 15.
>
> ### Contract Law of the People's Republic of China, 1999
>
> Transactions which are unconscionable, either in substance or by virtue of one party taking advantage of another's hardship, may enable the weaker party to have the contract amended or even cancelled.
>
> Article 54. Contract Subject to Amendment or Cancellation
>
> Either of the parties may petition the People's Court or an arbitration institution for amendment or cancellation of a contract if:
>
> ...
>
> (a)(ii) the contract was grossly unconscionable at the time of its conclusion.
>
> If a party induced the other party to enter into a contract against its true intention by ... taking advantage of the other party's hardship, the aggrieved party is entitled to petition the People's Court or an arbitration institution for amendment or cancellation of the contract.
>
> ...
>
> Where cancelled the contract will have the effect of being void *ab initio*.[2]

---

1   *Commercial Bank of Australia v Amadio* (1983) 151 CLR 447 at 461.
2   Article 56.

3 The equitable doctrine of unconscionable conduct

Equity will intervene where one contracting party has taken advantage of a 'special disability' held by the other party. In most, if not all, cases it will also be necessary to establish that the resultant contract is harsh and oppressive from the perspective of the weaker party.

a Abuse of position

The key requirement of equitable unconscionable conduct is that a stronger party takes advantage of a 'special disability' held by a weaker party. The range of circumstances which may constitute a special disability for this purpose are not capable of exhaustive definition. Most commonly age, illiteracy and lack of education have been held, in appropriate cases, to constitute such a disability. This form of 'disability' arose for consideration in the following case.[3]

Commercial Bank of Australia v Amadio
(1983) 151 CLR 447, High Court of Australia

[Vincenzo Amadio was the managing director of a building company (the company). The bank provided an overdraft account for the company, the limit of which was repeatedly exceeded. The bank agreed to increase the overdraft limit provided the overdraft was secured by a property owned by Vincenzo's parents (the Amadio's).

Vincenzo asked his parents to provide the security, telling them that the mortgage would be limited to $50,000 and a duration of six months. In fact, it was not so limited. The Amadio's were Italian migrants in their seventies with limited understanding of written English. They agreed to execute the mortgage and the bank manager, Mr Virgo, attended the Amadio's home to obtain their signatures on the security deed. During that visit Vincenzo told his parents the security was limited to six months and Mr Virgo corrected him, informing the Amadio's that it was not so limited. Mr Virgo did not, however, make any attempt to explain the document to them. The Amadio's executed the deed without reading it. The Amadio's were mistaken about the extent of liability and would not have executed the deed had they known the truth.

The company subsequently went into liquidation and the bank demanded payment in excess of $200,000 under the guarantee. The Amadio's sought to avoid the guarantee on the grounds of unconscionable conduct. The trial judge found in favour of the bank, holding that Mr Virgo reasonably believed that Vincenzo

---

3   See also *Elkofairi v Permanent Trustee Co Ltd* [2002] NSWCA 413 where the Court held that it was unconscientious for the respondent to lend large sums of money to the appellant, who was illiterate, understood only basic spoken English and had no income, in circumstances where they knew that if repayments were not met it could re-sell her only asset (at para 59).

had sufficiently explained the transaction to his parents. The Supreme Court of South Australia allowed an appeal and ordered the mortgage be set aside. The bank appealed to the High Court.]

Mason J [at 461]: ... relief on the ground of 'unconscionable conduct' is usually taken to refer to the class of case in which a party makes unconscientious use of his superior position or bargaining power to the detriment of a party who suffers from some special disability or is placed in some special situation of disadvantage, ... it is impossible to describe definitively all the situations in which relief will be granted on the ground of unconscionable conduct. ...

... [there is a] general principle which may be invoked whenever one party by reason of some condition of circumstance is placed at a special disadvantage *vis-à-vis* another and unfair or unconscientious advantage is then taken of the opportunity thereby created. I qualify the word 'disadvantage' by the adjective 'special' in order to disavow any suggestion that the principle applies whenever there is some difference in the bargaining power of the parties and in order to emphasize that the disabling condition or circumstance is one which seriously affects the ability of the innocent party to make a judgment as to his own best interests, when the other party knows or ought to know of the existence of that condition or circumstance and of its effect on the innocent party.

... <463> ... The situation of special disadvantage in which the respondents were placed was the outcome of their reliance on and their confidence in their son who, in order to serve his own interests, urged them to provide the mortgage guarantee which the bank required as a condition of increasing the approved overdraft limit of his company, ... and misled them as to the financial position of the company. Their reliance on their son was due in no small degree to their infirmities—they were Italians of advanced years, aged 76 and 71 respectively, having a limited command of written English and no experience of business in the field or at the level in which their son and the company engaged. They believed that the company's business was a flourishing and prosperous enterprise, though temporarily in need of funds. In reality, as the bank well knew, the company was in a perilous financial condition.

In the weeks immediately preceding the execution of the mortgage guarantee the company was unable to pay its debts as they fell due. In this situation the bank had selectively paid cheques drawn by the company in favour of suppliers in order to ensure continuity in the supply of building materials, the company being a building contractor. In this period the bank had regularly and continuously dishonoured other cheques, the payment of which was not essential to the maintenance of the supply of building materials. ...

<465> ... The effect of the respondents' execution of the mortgage guarantee was disastrous for them though advantageous to the bank. ...

No doubt the respondents' age and lack of business experience <466> played a part in their reliance on their son's judgment and in their failure to make any inquiries as to the financial position of the company and their failure to seek advice as to the probable or possible consequences of the transaction into which they entered. Their lack of command of English, especially written English, apart from contributing to their reliance on their son, had an additional importance. ... The primary judge found that if Vincenzo 'had disabused his parents' minds of their confidence in him, his parents would not have helped him'. ...

In deciding whether the bank took unconscientious advantage of the position of disadvantage in which the respondents were placed, we must ask, first, what knowledge did the bank have of the respondents' situation?

Mr Virgo was aware that the respondents were Italians, that they were of advanced years and that they did not have a good command of English. He knew that Vincenzo had procured their agreement to sign the mortgage guarantee. He had no reason to think that they had received advice and guidance from anyone but their son. ... It must have been obvious to Mr Virgo, as to anyone else having knowledge of the facts, that the transaction was improvident from the viewpoint of the respondents. In these circumstances it is inconceivable that the possibility did not occur to Mr Virgo that the respondents' entry into the transaction was due to their inability to make a judgment as <467> to what was in their best interests, owing to their reliance on their son, ...

... if A having actual knowledge that B occupies a situation of special disadvantage in relation to an intended transaction, so that B cannot make a judgment as to what is in his own interests, takes unfair advantage of his (A's) superior bargaining power or position by entering into that transaction, his conduct in so doing is unconscionable. And if, instead of having actual knowledge of that situation, A is aware of the possibility that that situation may exist or is aware of facts that would raise that possibility in the mind of any reasonable person, the result will be the same.

The knowledge of Mr Virgo was the knowledge of the bank.

[His Honour then held that the Amadio's were 'entitled to an order setting aside the mortgage guarantee'.]

Deane J [at 474]: The jurisdiction of courts of equity to relieve against unconscionable dealing ... is long established as extending generally to circumstances in which (i) a party to a transaction was under a special disability in dealing with the other party with the consequence that there was an absence of any reasonable degree of equality between them and (ii) that disability was sufficiently evident to the stronger party to make it *prima facie* unfair or 'unconscientious' that he procure, or accept, the weaker party's assent to the impugned transaction in the circumstances in which he procured or accepted it. Where such circumstances are shown to have existed, an onus is cast upon the stronger party to show that the transaction was fair, just and reasonable: ...

The adverse circumstances which may constitute a special disability for the purposes of the principles relating to relief against unconscionable dealing may take a wide variety of forms and are not susceptible to being comprehensively catalogues [sic]. ... <475>

... In most cases where equity courts have granted relief against unconscionable dealing, there has been an inadequacy of consideration moving from the stronger party. It is not, however, essential that that should be so ... Notwithstanding that adequate consideration may have moved from the stronger party, a transaction may be unfair, unreasonable and unjust from the view point of the party under the disability. An obvious instance of circumstances in which that may be so is the case where the benefit of the consideration does not move to the party under the disability but moves to some third party involved in the transaction. Thus, it is established that the jurisdiction extends, in an appropriate case, to relieve a guarantor of the burden of a guarantee of existing and future indebtedness ...

[His Honour then considered whether Mr and Mrs Amadio were under a relevant disability in dealing with the bank and concluded, for substantially the same reasons as Mason J, that they were.]

[Gibbs CJ, while finding for the Amadio's as a result of Vincenzo's misrepresentation, would not have held the conduct of the bank to be unconscionable.[4] Wilson J agreed with Deane J. Dawson J dissented.]

Appeal dismissed

[footnotes omitted]

It is, however, clear that age alone will not constitute a special disability. In *Davey v Challenger Managed Investments Ltd* elderly parents guaranteed a loan for the benefit of their children's business and mortgaged their homes as security. The business subsequently failed and the security was called upon. The parents had received independent legal advice and no fraud, misrepresentation or actual undue influence was alleged. The Court had little difficulty dismissing the claim for unconscionable conduct, finding the parents were in 'full possession of their faculties', in general good health, were literate and English was their first language. While they had no capacity to repay the debt should the children default, this did not render the transaction unconscionable. Guarantees of this nature may well often prove successful and for the benefit of the community which might be rendered a disservice 'if it treated age and pensioner status as disabling parents from helping their children in this way'.[5]

Other, less permanent disabilities, such as drunkenness, have also been recognised as constituting a special disability. Taking advantage of a person's drunken state arose for consideration by the High Court in *Blomley v Ryan*. In that case the 'weaker' defendant was an elderly man of failing intellect who was prone to bouts of drinking which 'reduced him to a state of stupidity'.[6] He owned a property found to be worth well in excess of £30,000. One afternoon the father and the agent of the plaintiff visited the defendant at his property. The defendant

---

4   See pages 459–460: 'In the present case it is true that the respondents were elderly, did not have a complete mastery <460> of the English language and had had no formal education. However, the bank did not take unfair advantage of any of those disabilities, if disabilities they were. ....'
5   *Davey v Challenger Managed Investments Ltd* [2003] NSWCA 172, per Handley JA at para 24.
6   *Blomley v Ryan* (1956) 99 CLR 362 at 367, per Taylor J [trial judge]. This case was also discussed in the context of contractual capacity in chapter 6.

was drunk at the time and was invited to drink more by the plaintiff's agent who then sought to negotiate the sale of the property. At that time the defendant was in a condition 'such that he was incapable of considering the question of the sale of his property with any real degree of intelligent appreciation of the matters involved'[7] and this was evident to the agent. A 'deal' for the sale of the property at £25,000 was reached. The agent sought to have the defendant sign a sale contract on the spot but he refused. Anxious to proceed quickly with the sale the agent told the defendant he would pick him up the next morning and take him to a solicitor's office to sign the documents. This he did. The defendant was still drunk when the agent picked him up and took him to the solicitor's office where he signed the documents. He received no independent legal advice prior to signing the contract. In the course of setting aside the contract on the grounds of unconscionable conduct Fullagar J, while first observing that '*mere* drunkenness affords no ground for resisting a suit to enforce a contract', continued:

> ... where the court is satisfied that a contract disadvantageous to the party affected has been obtained by 'drawing him in to drink', or that there has been real unfairness in taking advantage of his condition, the contract may be set aside ...
>
> The circumstances adversely affecting a party, which may induce a court of equity either to refuse its aid or to set a transaction aside, are of great variety and can hardly be satisfactorily classified. Among them are poverty or need of any kind, sickness, age, sex, infirmity of body or mind, drunkenness, illiteracy or lack of education, lack of assistance or explanation where assistance or explanation is necessary. The common characteristic seems to be that they have the effect of placing one party at a serious disadvantage vis-à-vis the other. It does not appear to be essential in all cases that the party at a disadvantage should suffer loss or detriment by the bargain. ... But inadequacy of consideration, while never of itself a ground for resisting enforcement, will often be a specially important element in cases of this type. It may be important in either or both of two ways—firstly as supporting the inference that a position of disadvantage existed, and secondly as tending to show that an unfair use was made of the occasion. Where, as here, intoxication is the main element relied upon as creating the position of disadvantage, the question of adequacy or inadequacy of consideration is, I think, likely to be a matter of major, and perhaps decisive, importance. ...[8]

It is also possible for a professional person to be classified as being in a position of special disability in appropriate circumstances. This issue arose for consideration in the following case.

---

7   *Blomley v Ryan* (1956) 99 CLR 362 at 370, per Taylor J [trial judge].
8   *Blomley v Ryan* (1956) 99 CLR 362 at 405. Justice McTiernan delivered a separate judgment in which he found that contract should be set aside due to the conduct of the plaintiff's agents. Justice Kitto dissented, believing the respondent to have been capable of judging his interests and said he did not believe the plaintiff's agents had taken unfair advantage of him.

Louth v Diprose

(1992) 175 CLR 621, High Court of Australia

[Louis Diprose, a solicitor, was infatuated with Carol Louth. They formed a friendship in 1981 and had intercourse on two occasions in the first year of their relationship but after that their sexual relationship ended. Diprose proposed marriage in 1982 and was rejected by Louth. Louth moved to Adelaide in August 1982 after Diprose was unsuccessful in persuading her to stay in Launceston. Diprose subsequently moved to Adelaide. Over the years he composed for Louth many love poems and regularly provided her with gifts as well as occasionally paying her household bills.

In 1983 Louth told Diprose she was depressed and contemplating suicide. Late in 1984 Louth's sister's marriage broke down. Louth was in financial difficulties and was living in a house owned by her sister's husband. Louth told Diprose that the house would have to be sold as part of a property settlement and she would be required to leave and, if forced to leave, she would commit suicide. In fact, Louth was not under pressure from her brother-in-law to vacate the house. Despite limited personal assets Diprose agreed to buy the house for Louth and purchased it in her name after she insisted that having title in her name was essential to her security.

Subsequently, in 1988, the relationship of the parties deteriorated and Diprose sought an order that the property be transferred to him.

Diprose succeeded at trial, the judge finding 'the appellant manufactured an atmosphere of crisis with respect to the house where none really existed so as to influence the respondent to provide the money for the purchase of the house …'.[9] A majority of the Supreme Court of South Australia dismissed an appeal by Louth who then appealed to the High Court.]

Deane J [at 638]: [After discussing the requirements for setting a contract aside for unconscionable dealing his Honour continued]: On the findings of the learned trial judge in the present case, the relationship between the respondent and the appellant at the time of the impugned gift was plainly such that the respondent was under a special disability in dealing with the appellant. That special disability arose not merely from the respondent's infatuation. It extended to the extraordinary vulnerability of the respondent in the false 'atmosphere of crisis' in which he believed that the woman with whom he was 'completely in love' and upon whom he was emotionally dependent was facing eviction from her home and suicide unless he provided the money for the purchase of the house. The appellant was aware of that special disability. Indeed, to a significant extent, she had deliberately created it. She manipulated it to her advantage to influence the respondent to make the gift of the money to purchase the house. When asked for restitution she refused. From the respondent's point of view, the whole transaction was plainly a most improvident one.

---

9   Mason CJ at 624.

In these circumstances, the learned trial judge's conclusion that the appellant had been guilty of unconscionable conduct in procuring and retaining the gift of $59,206.55 was not only open to him. In the context of his Honour's findings of fact, it was inevitable and plainly correct. On those findings, the case was not simply one in which the respondent had, under the influence of his love for, or infatuation with, the appellant, made an imprudent gift in her favour. The case was one in which the appellant deliberately used that love or infatuation and her own deceit to create a situation in which she could unconscientiously manipulate the respondent to part with a large proportion of his property. The intervention of equity is not merely to relieve the plaintiff from the consequences of his own foolishness. It is to prevent his victimization.

[Mason CJ and Brennan J delivered separate judgments agreeing with Deane J on this issue. Dawson, Gaudron and McHugh JJ delivered a separate joint judgment agreeing with Deane J. Toohey J dissented, holding there was no special situation of disadvantage.]

Appeal dismissed

[footnotes omitted]

b Harsh and oppressive transaction

The courts have stopped short of requiring that a contract formed as a result of a dominant party taking advantage of the weaker party's special disability must be harsh and oppressive for the weaker party. In practice, however, the courts have only intervened when the contract has been of this nature. Such a result will, of course, be integral in demonstrating that there has been an abuse, by the stronger party, of the dominant position they held over the weaker party. In this respect Fullagar J in *Blomley v Ryan* observed:

> ... inadequacy of consideration, while never of itself a ground for resisting enforcement, will often be a specially important element. ... It may be important in either or both of two ways—firstly as supporting the inference that a position of disadvantage existed, and secondly as tending to show that an unfair use was made of the occasion. ...[10]

c Remedies for unconscionable conduct in equity

Where unconscionable conduct is established the resulting contract or gift is voidable in equity. Consequently it will continue to operate unless and until it is rescinded by the weaker party, at which point the contractual obligations will be terminated *ab initio*, returning the parties to the position they were in at the time of contracting. Precise restitution is not essential in equity, but it must be possible to substantially place the parties in effectively the same position they were in at the time of contracting.

---

10   (1956) 99 CLR 362 at 405.

4 Statutory unconscionability

In addition to the equitable doctrine and remedies, statute prohibits certain forms of unconscionable conduct. These prohibitions and their associated remedies are now contained in the *Australian Consumer Law*, which applies both at a federal level and, by virtue of enabling legislation, in all the state and territories. In addition to superior remedies, the prohibition of unconscionable conduct in the *Australian Consumer Law* (ACL) enables the Australian Competition and Consumer Commission (ACCC) and state and territory fair trade directors to bring actions in the public interest on the part of aggrieved parties who might otherwise not be able to afford litigation.

a The *Australian Consumer Law*

Nationally consistent prohibitions on unconscionable conduct are now contained in Part 2-2 of the *ACL*. The first of these prohibitions entrenches into statute the equitable doctrine of unconscionable conduct as described above, thereby extending the range of remedies available to parties affected by unconscionable conduct. The second prohibition extends the concept of unconscionability beyond that recognised in equity and can be relied upon by all persons, other than listed corporations, who acquire or supply goods or services in trade or commerce.

Section 20

Section 20 of the *ACL* prohibits unconscionability engaged in by a person[11] 'within the meaning of the unwritten law'.[12] To prevent overlap, s 20 will not apply where s 21 applies.

Australian Consumer Law

Section 20(1)

A person must not, in trade or commerce, engage in conduct that is unconscionable within the meaning of the unwritten law, from time to time.

---

11 For constitutional reasons this prohibition applies only where the conduct is engaged in by a corporation. Note there are extension provisions enabling conduct of a 'person', not being a corporation, to be caught in limited circumstances as provided in s 6 of the Act. Note also that state legislation, discussed below, is not so limited, extending to conduct by all 'persons'.

12 It has been argued this prohibition may be unconstitutional by in effect providing the judiciary with the ability to change legislation by changing the 'unwritten law'. The constitutional validity of the provision was addressed by French J in *ACCC v C G Berbatis Holdings Pty Ltd* (No 2) (2000) 96 FCR 491 and resolved in favour of the provision's validity. In the course of his decision his Honour noted that 'The statutory formula in s 51AA, referring to the unwritten law of the State and Territories from time to time, must be taken to be the common law of Australia' (at para 12) and (at para 28) 'that s 51AA does not purport to adopt the unwritten law relating to unconscionable conduct and give to it the force of statute. In form it uses the unwritten law to the extent that it provides for the characterisation of conduct as unconscionable and then prohibits such conduct'.

Note: A pecuniary penalty may be imposed for a contravention of this sub-section.

This provision is in the same terms as its predecessor, s 51AA of the *Trade Practices Act 1974* (Cth), with the result that case law discussing that provision will remain relevant. The requirements that there be 'engaging in conduct' by 'a' person acting 'in trade or commerce' have been discussed in the context of misleading and deceptive conduct[13] and have the same meaning here. The core requirement in s 20 is that the conduct involved be 'unconscionable within the meaning of the unwritten law'. The courts have resolved this to mean the equitable doctrine relating to unconscionable dealings involving the taking advantage by one party of a special disability held by another.[14] Thus, for example, it will encompass the kind of conduct that occurred in *Blomley v Ryan* and *Amadio*,[15] discussed above.

ACCC v CG Berbatis Holdings Pty Ltd

(2003) 214 CLR 51, High Court of Australia

[Berbatis owned the Farrington Fair shopping centre in which the Roberts leased a fish shop. A group of tenants, including the Roberts, instituted proceedings against Berbatis in 1996 over charges they believed had been wrongly levied against them. The Roberts believed the overpayments amounted to approximately $50,000.

The Roberts' lease was due to expire in February 1997. Due, at least in part, to a desire to provide care for their sick daughter, the Roberts decided to sell their business and, in October 1996, entered into a sale agreement, subject to the requirement that the Roberts obtain a renewal of the lease and permission to assign it to the new purchaser.

In negotiations with Berbatis for the extension and assignment of the lease, a release clause was included requiring, as a condition for the assignment and renewal, that the Roberts release Berbatis from any legal claims. Action was subsequently brought in which it was alleged that the inclusion of the release clause was 'unconscionable' within s 51AA of the *TPA*.]

Gleeson CJ [at 61]: The specific question is whether the lessors of premises in a shopping centre engaged in conduct that was 'unconscionable within the meaning of the unwritten law' in stipulating, as a condition of their consent to a proposed renewal or extension of a lease, in contemplation of its assignment, a requirement that the lessees would abandon certain claims against them. The lessees were in a difficult bargaining position. They had no option to renew their lease. Their prospects of making an advantageous sale of their business depended upon the cooperation of the lessors, which they were not obliged to give. ...

---

13   See chapter 12.
14   Initially it was thought that the concept of unconscionability might extend beyond the general law of unconscionability to undue influence and duress (see French J in *ACCC v CG Berbatis Holdings Pty Ltd* (1999) 95 FCR 292) however it now seems clear it does not extend that far.
15   The explanatory memorandum noted it was intended to capture the type of conduct that occurred in *Blomley v Ryan* and *Amadio*.

<62> ... senior counsel for the appellant argued the case on the basis that the relevant form of unconscionable conduct in question was 'the knowing exploitation by one party of the special disadvantage of another.' He said that, by special disadvantage, he meant 'a disabling circumstance seriously affecting the ability of the innocent party to make a judgment in [that party's] own best interests.' Applied to a case such as the present, that approach is consistent with what the Act calls the unwritten law concerning unconscionable conduct, bearing in mind that the Act also allows for development of the law from time to time. It is also consistent with the legislative history of s 51AA. ...

<63> ... In the present case, [the trial judge] French J said that the lessees suffered from a 'situational' as distinct from a 'constitutional' disadvantage, in that it did not stem from any inherent infirmity or weakness or deficiency. ...

<64> ... A person is not in a position of relevant disadvantage, constitutional, situational, or otherwise, simply because of inequality of bargaining power. Many, perhaps even most, contracts are made between parties of unequal bargaining power, and good conscience does not require parties to contractual negotiations to forfeit their advantages, or neglect their own interests. ...

In the present case, there was neither a special disadvantage on the part of the lessees, nor unconscientious conduct on the part of the lessors. All the people involved in the transaction were business <65> people, concerned to advance or protect their own financial interests. The critical disadvantage from which the lessees suffered was that they had no legal entitlement to a renewal or extension of their lease; and they depended upon the lessors' willingness to grant such an extension or renewal for their capacity to sell the goodwill of their business for a substantial price. They were thus compelled to approach the lessors, seeking their agreement to such an extension or renewal, against a background of current claims and litigation in which they were involved. They were at a distinct disadvantage, but there was nothing 'special' about it. ... They had the benefit of legal advice. They made a rational decision, ... They suffered from no lack of ability to judge or protect their financial interests. What they lacked was the commercial ability to pursue [both the sale and the litigation] at the same time.

... French J spoke of the lessors using '[their] bargaining power to extract a concession [that was] commercially irrelevant to the terms and conditions of any proposed new lease.' ... Parties to commercial negotiations frequently use their bargaining power to 'extract' concessions from other parties. That is the stuff of ordinary commercial dealing. What is relevant to a commercial negotiation is whatever one party to the negotiation chooses to make relevant. ...

In truth, there was no lack of ability on their part to make a judgment about anything. Rather, there was a lack of ability to get their own way. That is a disability that affects people in many circumstances in commerce, and in life. It is not one against which the law ordinarily provides relief. ...

[Gummow, Hayne and Callinan JJ also found that there was no unconscionable conduct on the facts. Justice Kirby dissented. While agreeing that inequality of bargaining power is not sufficient in itself to create a 'special disadvantage', in this case in light of the fact that the shopping centre already had a number of empty shops and that the Roberts' and the proposed assignees were 'objectively acceptable' he considered it clear that apart from the Roberts' immediate need to sell the premises (and the Centre's knowledge and exploitation of this) they would not have been subjected to such a term. His Honour held (at 88) that it was

> ... open to the primary judge to view the insistence on that requirement as an opportunistic attempt to take advantage of the special position in which the Roberts found themselves. ... [93] ... The change of stance of the owners and the belated revival of their insistence upon the clause had all the hallmarks of a well-tuned demand, imposed by those with proportionately greater economic power to take advantage of the vulnerable position that the Roberts found themselves in, given the course of dealings and their commercial, financial and personal circumstances at the time. ... They were taken by surprise and without sufficient opportunity or 'time to act with caution'. This was the way in which the information upon which the Roberts were proceeding was contrived, as was their ultimate assent to the transaction. This is why it can be said that there was no real bargaining over the term and, in the circumstances, the Roberts were unable to assess properly their options and interests.]

Appeal dismissed

[footnotes omitted]

Sections 21 and 22: Unconscionable conduct in connection with goods or services

Section 21[16] prohibits unconscionable conduct in connection with the supply or acquisition of goods or services by or from a person (other than a listed public company). Section 21 expressly provides that it is not intended to be 'limited by the unwritten law relating to unconscionable conduct' and that relevant factors extend beyond 'consideration of the circumstances relating to formation of the contract' (procedural unconscionable conduct) to the terms of the contract themselves (substantive unconscionable conduct). In addition, section 22 sets out a range of factors a court may consider when determining whether conduct is unconscionable.

Australian Consumer Law

21 Unconscionable conduct in connection with goods or services

(1) A person must not, in trade or commerce, in connection with:
    (a) the supply or possible supply of goods or services to a person (other than a listed public company); or

---

16   This was originally inserted in the *Trade Practices Act 1974* (Cth) as s 52A(1) and was re-numbered s 51AA of the *TPA* in 1998. A modified version of the provision became s 21 of the *Australian Consumer Law* on 1 January 2011. This was subsequently repealed and replaced with a new ss 21–22 (which effectively combined the existing consumer and small business unconscionable conduct provisions) following the passage of the *Competition and Consumer Legislation Amendment Act 2011*.

(b) the acquisition or possible acquisition of goods or services from a person (other than a listed public company);

engage in conduct that is, in all the circumstances, unconscionable.

(2) This section does not apply to conduct that is engaged in only because the person engaging in the conduct:
  (a) institutes legal proceedings in relation to the supply or possible supply, or in relation to the acquisition or possible acquisition; or
  (b) refers to arbitration a dispute or claim in relation to the supply or possible supply, or in relation to the acquisition or possible acquisition.
(3) For the purpose of determining whether a person has contravened subsection (1):
  (a) the court must not have regard to any circumstances that were not reasonably foreseeable at the time of the alleged contravention; and
  (b) the court may have regard to conduct engaged in, or circumstances existing, before the commencement of this section.
(4) It is the intention of the Parliament that:
  (a) this section is not limited by the unwritten law relating to unconscionable conduct; and
  (b) this section is capable of applying to a system of conduct or pattern of behaviour, whether or not a particular individual is identified as having been disadvantaged by the conduct or behaviour; and
  (c) in considering whether conduct to which a contract relates is unconscionable, a court's consideration of the contract may include consideration of:
    (i) the terms of the contract; and
    (ii) the manner in which and the extent to which the contract is carried out;
  and is not limited to consideration of the circumstances relating to formation of the contract.

22 Matters the court may have regard to for the purposes of section 21

(1) Without limiting the matters to which the court may have regard for the purpose of determining whether a person (the supplier) has contravened section 21 in connection with the supply or possible supply of goods or services to a person (the customer), the court may have regard to:
  (a) the relative strengths of the bargaining positions of the supplier and the customer; and
  (b) whether, as a result of conduct engaged in by the supplier, the customer was required to comply with conditions that were not reasonably necessary for the protection of the legitimate interests of the supplier; and
  (c) whether the customer was able to understand any documents relating to the supply or possible supply of the goods or services; and
  (d) whether any undue influence or pressure was exerted on, or any unfair tactics were used against, the customer or a person acting on behalf of the customer by the supplier or a person acting on behalf of the supplier in relation to the supply or possible supply of the goods or services; and

(e) the amount for which, and the circumstances under which, the customer could have acquired identical or equivalent goods or services from a person other than the supplier; and

(f) the extent to which the supplier's conduct towards the customer was consistent with the supplier's conduct in similar transactions between the supplier and other like customers; and

(g) the requirements of any applicable industry code; and

(h) the requirements of any other industry code, if the customer acted on the reasonable belief that the supplier would comply with that code; and

(i) the extent to which the supplier unreasonably failed to disclose to the customer:

  (i) any intended conduct of the supplier that might affect the interests of the customer; and

  (ii) any risks to the customer arising from the supplier's intended conduct (being risks that the supplier should have foreseen would not be apparent to the customer); and

(j) if there is a contract between the supplier and the customer for the supply of the goods or services:

  (i) the extent to which the supplier was willing to negotiate the terms and conditions of the contract with the customer; and

  (ii) the terms and conditions of the contract; and

  (iii) the conduct of the supplier and the customer in complying with the terms and conditions of the contract; and

  (iv) any conduct that the supplier or the customer engaged in, in connection with their commercial relationship, after they entered into the contract; and

(k) without limiting paragraph (j), whether the supplier has a contractual right to vary unilaterally a term or condition of a contract between the supplier and the customer for the supply of the goods or services; and

(l) the extent to which the supplier and the customer acted in good faith.

(2) Without limiting the matters to which the court may have regard for the purpose of determining whether a person (the acquirer) has contravened section 21 in connection with the acquisition or possible acquisition of goods or services from a person (the supplier), the court may have regard to:

(a) the relative strengths of the bargaining positions of the acquirer and the supplier; and

(b) whether, as a result of conduct engaged in by the acquirer, the supplier was required to comply with conditions that were not reasonably necessary for the protection of the legitimate interests of the acquirer; and

(c) whether the supplier was able to understand any documents relating to the acquisition or possible acquisition of the goods or services; and

(d) whether any undue influence or pressure was exerted on, or any unfair tactics were used against, the supplier or a person acting on behalf of the supplier by the acquirer or a person acting on behalf of the acquirer

in relation to the acquisition or possible acquisition of the goods or services; and
(e) the amount for which, and the circumstances in which, the supplier could have supplied identical or equivalent goods or services to a person other than the acquirer; and
(f) the extent to which the acquirer's conduct towards the supplier was consistent with the acquirer's conduct in similar transactions between the acquirer and other like suppliers; and
(g) the requirements of any applicable industry code; and
(h) the requirements of any other industry code, if the supplier acted on the reasonable belief that the acquirer would comply with that code; and
(i) the extent to which the acquirer unreasonably failed to disclose to the supplier:
  (i) any intended conduct of the acquirer that might affect the interests of the supplier; and
  (ii) any risks to the supplier arising from the acquirer's intended conduct (being risks that the acquirer should have foreseen would not be apparent to the supplier); and
(j) if there is a contract between the acquirer and the supplier for the acquisition of the goods or services:
  (i) the extent to which the acquirer was willing to negotiate the terms and conditions of the contract with the supplier; and
  (ii) the terms and conditions of the contract; and
  (iii) the conduct of the acquirer and the supplier in complying with the terms and conditions of the contract; and
  (iv) any conduct that the acquirer or the supplier engaged in, in connection with their commercial relationship, after they entered into the contract; and
(k) without limiting paragraph (j), whether the acquirer has a contractual right to vary unilaterally a term or condition of a contract between the acquirer and the supplier for the acquisition of the goods or services; and
(l) the extent to which the acquirer and the supplier acted in good faith.

22A: Presumptions relating to whether representations are misleading

Section 4 applies for the purposes of sections 21 and 22 in the same way as it applies for the purposes of Division 1 of Part 3-1.

Prior to the passage of the *Competition and Consumer Legislation Amendment Act 2011* (*CCLA Act*), the Act contained separate prohibitions for unconscionable conduct in dealings with small business (section 21 of the *ACL* and, prior to that, s 51AC of the *TPA*) and consumers (section 21 of the *ACL* and, prior to that s 51AB of the *TPA*). The *CCLA Act* effectively combined these two prohibitions into a new s 21, but case law dealing with the former s 51AB and 51AC of the *TPA* will remain relevant to the interpretation of ss 21–22.

The application of s 51AB, involving a consumer transaction, was discussed in the following case.

ACCC v Radio Rentals Ltd

[2005] FCA 1133, Federal Court of Australia

[The ACCC brought proceedings on behalf of Mr Ronald Groth arising from dealings he had with Radio Rentals over a six-year period. This included 15 rental, two loan and 19 service agreements with Radio Rentals relating to electrical goods, with payments made exceeding $20,000. Mr Groth has an intellectual disability and a schizophrenic illness and relies on a disability pension as his sole source of income. The ACCC alleged that by entering into these agreements with Mr Roth, Radio Rentals was guilty of unconscionable conduct under ss 51AA and 51AB of the *TPA*. The following extract deals only with the claim under s 51AB.]

Finn J [at 2]: Before outlining Mr Groth's condition, capacities and personal history, it is important that I emphasise that this case is not concerned with Mr Groth's objective circumstances as such. Rather its concern is with how he was, or ought to have been, perceived by the Radio Rentals employees with whom he dealt or who dealt with his affairs. As will become apparent, this difference is of fundamental importance to the proper resolution of this matter. To anticipate my conclusion, notwithstanding the significant disability and incapacities from which he suffers, these were not so made evident to Radio Rentals as to justify the conclusion that Radio Rentals and Walker Stores engaged in unconscionable conduct for the purposes of s 51AA and s 51AB of the TP Act.

...

[38] It cannot seriously be disputed that Mr Groth suffers some level of intellectual retardation and that he has significant incapacities. As I earlier indicated, it is not necessary that I reach a definitive view on the level of his retardation and the extent of his incapacities as such. My concern rather is with what ought to have been apparent to others from how he presented, his conduct and his actions and with what these suggested about his abilities and capacity. ...

[23] Section 51AB(1) provides that a corporation shall not, in trade or commerce, in connection with the supply or possible supply of goods or services to a person, engage in conduct that is, in all the circumstances, unconscionable. The term 'unconscionable' is undefined. However, s 51AB does refer to a non-exhaustive list of matters to which the Court may have regard in determining whether a corporation has contravened s 51AB(1).

[24] Unlike s 51AA, s 51AB does not limit unconscionable conduct to conduct that is unconscionable within the meaning of the unwritten law. As others have pointed out, there is no reason when construing the section to import such a limitation into it: see *ACCC v Simply No-Knead (Franchising) Pty Ltd* (2000) 104 FCR 253 at [30]-[37]; *Australian Competition and Consumer Commission v C G Berbatis Holdings Pty Ltd (No 2)* (2000) 96 FCR 491 at [24]. Indeed the

section on its face in referring to a *'possible* supply' travels beyond the unwritten law as I understand it. There is, in my view, no reason not to give the term its ordinary possible meanings in the context of a supply or possible supply of goods or services. These have been expressed, variously, as 'serious misconduct [or] something clearly unfair or unreasonable': *Cameron v Qantas Airways Ltd* (1994) 55 FCR 147 at 179; 'showing no regard for conscience; irreconcilable with what is right or reasonable': *ACCC v Samton Holdings Pty Ltd* (2002) 117 FCR 301 at [44]; see also *Hurley v McDonald's Australia Pty Ltd* (2000) ATPR 41-741 at [22]; or, simply, conduct that is 'unfair': *Garry Rogers Motors (Aust) Pty Ltd v Subaru (Aust) Pty Ltd* (1999) ATPR 41-703 at [46]; and see generally *ACCC v Keshow* [2005] FCA 558 at [91] ff.

...

[197] This proceeding has highlighted three matters. The first is the peculiar vulnerability of persons like Mr Groth who are unable in fact to conserve their own interests but who do not, as of course, put people with whom they deal on notice of their incapacities. They are, in consequence, attributed innocently with powers they do not possess. This can redound to their distinct disadvantage, as the circumstances of this matter demonstrate.

[198] The second matter highlighted flows from the first. It is that, in the conduct of day-to-day retail transactions and related dealings, too much cannot be expected of ordinary people doing routine jobs by way of critical appraisal of their employers' customers and their affairs. They ought not have attributed to them powers and responsibilities which are foreign to what can reasonably be expected of them in virtue of what they do in its particular setting. It is for this reason that companies can properly be expected in the protection of their own interests (and, derivatively, of the interests of those with whom they deal) to have in place appropriate risk management practices—practices now facilitated by modern technology. I would emphasise in passing that the present case as pleaded was not about the respondents' risk management practices as such.

[199] The third matter relates to the problem of attributing knowledge or a state of mind to a corporation in light of what might be inferred from aggregating information derived from a multiplicity of discrete transactions and dealings involving corporate employees who adventitiously to participate in some of those matters without suspecting in any way that anything is out of the ordinary. To permit such aggregation in circumstances such as the present for the purposes of attributing a particular state of mind to a company as a prelude to a finding of unconscionable conduct can only 'eviscerate' unconscionable conduct of its meaning: cf *Stern v McArthur* (1988) 165 CLR 489 at 503. For the purposes of the unconscionable dealings doctrine it would result in a company being held guilty of exploitation or victimisation of another without any officer or agent of that company having any suspicion, or any reason to suspect, at all that the company was so acting. In the case of s 51AB, the company would be held to have acted unreasonably or clearly unfairly, without having reason to appreciate it was so acting.

[200] It is one thing to proscribe advantage taking by a commercial enterprise of a specially disadvantaged person. It is quite another to make that enterprise in effect that other's insurer. In light of the findings I have made, the ACCC's principal claim must be dismissed.

[201] For the purposes of the s 51AA claim, while Mr Groth could be said to be in a position of special disadvantage, he was not on my findings knowingly taken advantage of by the respondents. He was not victimised or exploited. ... it is not to the point that, with different risk management practices, the respondents may have been able to detect Mr Groth's circumstances and to take steps to assist him. That is not the case before me although it has faint echo in the ACCC's written closing submission where it is said that corporate businesses and their sales agents 'have a responsibility to ensure that they do not take unfair advantage of customers'. This responsibility, it is said 'requires businesses to be alert to the fact that some of their customers may be vulnerable'. All I would say of this is that the positive, neighbourhood-like, obligation implicit in this stands apart from the law of unconscionable dealing as it has been conceptualised to date and it appears to be distinctly tort like in character, conjuring up as it does a negligent failure to discharge this claimed 'responsibility'.

[202] The unfair conduct judgment required to be made by s 51AB is similarly not open in light of my findings. Doubtless, the relative bargaining positions of the respondents and Mr Groth were unequal: cf s 51AB(2)(a). What the evidence does not disclose is unfair use of this by Radio Rentals. There is little doubt that Mr Groth did not understand the detail of the general terms and conditions of his various agreements with the respondents: cf s 51AB(2)(c). Nonetheless I am satisfied that this was not sufficiently evident to those from Radio Rentals with whom he had dealings. There is no evidence to suggest that the terms he was required to accept differed from those required of other customers or that unfair tactics were used against, or unfair pressure was exerted upon, him in relation to his dealings with the respondents.

[203] The course of events in this matter were unfortunate indeed. But the case as pleaded affords no proper reason for passing adverse judgment on the respondents under s 51AB because of their participation in those events. They have not been shown to have acted unfairly.

...

The application of s 51AC, involving small business dealings, was discussed in the following cases.

ACCC v Simply No-Knead (Franchising) Pty Ltd

(2000) 104 FCR 253, Federal Court of Australia

[Simply No-Knead (Franchising) Pty Ltd (SNK) owned a business, 'Simply No-Knead', which supplied training and materials for making bread at home. SNK had a number of franchisees. Over the years it engaged in various forms of conduct in relation to its franchisees which the ACCC alleged constituted unconscionable conduct under s 51AC. This conduct included refusing to deliver certain products, unreasonably refusing requests for discussion of matters in dispute, producing advertising material omitting the names and contact details of the franchisees, selling and advertising products within the franchisees territories and refusing to provide disclosure documents upon request. The ACCC sought a declaration that SNK had engaged in conduct in contravention of s 51AC.]

Sunberg J [at 265] [31]: ... 'unconscionable' in s 51AC is not limited to the cases of equitable or unwritten law unconscionability the subject of s 51AA. The principal pointer to an enlarged notion of unconscionability in s 51AC lies in the factors to which sub-s (3) permits the Court to have regard. Some of them describe conduct that goes beyond what would constitute unconscionability in equity. For example, factor (j) directs attention to the extent to which the supplier was willing to negotiate the terms and conditions of any contract for supply of the goods or services with the business consumer. Factor (g) relates to the requirements of any applicable industry code. Further, it is to be remembered that the list of factors in sub-s (3) is not exhaustive.

[32] In the second reading speech on the Bill that [introduced s 51AC] the responsible Minister said the section 'will extend the common law doctrine of unconscionability expressed in the existing section 51AA'. ...

[His Honour went on to address each of the forms of unconscionable conduct alleged, noting that on most occasions the conduct of SNK constituted an 'exertion of pressure on, and the use of unfair tactics against, the franchisees within factor (d) in s 51AC(3)'[17] and that other conduct was 'unreasonable, unfair, harsh, oppressive and wanting in good faith'[18] within factor (k) and concluded that 'the accumulation of incidents ... discloses an overwhelming case of unreasonable, unfair, bullying and thuggish behaviour in relation to each franchisee that amounts to unconscionable conduct by SNK for the purposes of s 51AC(1). ... SNK devised a plan intended to cause the franchisees to terminate or not renew their franchise agreements. SNK's conduct achieved its aim. ... SNK's plan and its implementation constitute unconscionable conduct for the purposes of s 51AC(1).'[19]]

The Victorian Court of Appeal also recently considered the application of s 51AC in the following case:

Body Bronze International Pty Ltd v Fehcorp Pty Ltd

[2011] VSCA 196, Supreme Court of Victoria, Court of Appeal

[Body Bronze entered into a franchise agreement with Fehcorp. The agreement was subsequently terminated and, at first instance, Fehcorp succeeded in a claim

---

17　At page 268 [41].
18　At page 269 [46].
19　At page 270 [51].

against Body Bronze for breach of contract and for contraventions of s 51AC and s 52 of the (then) *TPA*. Body Bronze appealed the decision in respect of the statutory claims. In the course of upholding the appeal, the Court made several observations about the operation of s 51AC; in particular, the Court made clear that not every intentional breach of contract will constitute unconscionable conduct.]

Macaulay AJA (with whom Harper and Hansen JJA agreed)

[75] [Sub-section 51AC(3)] sets out a non-exhaustive list of matters to which the court may have regard in determining whether a corporation has contravened sub-section (1). [Author's note: these are substantially the same as those now set out in s 22 of the *ACL*]

...

[76] Not only do these factors assist in comprehending the intended scope and meaning of unconscionable conduct prohibited by the section, but they also provide a useful, although non-exhaustive, set of factors by which to test the particular conduct in question.

...

[86] The meaning of unconscionable conduct under s 51AC has been contrasted with the meaning of the same phrase as it appears in s 51AA of the *TPA* where it is accompanied by the qualifying words 'within the meaning of the unwritten law'. Those qualifying words are absent in s 51AC; rather, the proscribed conduct is conduct that is 'in all the circumstances' unconscionable.

...

[88] Section 51AC prescribes a standard rather than a rule wherein the boundaries of its application are normative rather than logical. In performing its task the Court is aided but not controlled by the factors listed in subsection (3).

[89] In my view the relevant principles for the application of s 51AC have been most helpfully and concisely collected by Foster J in *ACCC v Allphones Retail Pty Ltd (No 2)* [2009] FCA 17 in this way:

(a) The scope of s 51AC is wider than that of s 51AA. The meaning of *unconscionable* for the purposes of s 51AC is not limited to the meaning of the word according to established principles of common law and equity: per French J in *Australian Competition and Consumer Commission v C G Berbatis Holdings Pty Ltd (No 2)* [2000] FCA 2; (2000) 96 FCR 491 at [24] and [25] (p 503); per Sundberg J in *Australian Competition and Consumer Commissioner v Simply No-Knead Franchising Pty Limited* [2000] FCA 1365; (2000) 104 FCR 253 at [31] (p 265); per Selway J in *Australian Competition and Consumer Commission v 4WD Systems Pty Limited* (2003) 59 IPR 435 at [183] (p 487) and per Jacobson J in *Pacific National (ACT) Limited v Queensland Rail* (2006) 28 ATPR 46-268 (p 53,515) at [918] (p 53,527).

(b) The ordinary or dictionary meaning of *unconscionable*, which involves notions of serious misconduct or something which is clearly unfair or unreasonable, is picked up by the use of the word in s 51AC. When used in that section, the expression requires that the actions of the alleged contravenor show no regard for conscience, and be irreconcilable with what is right or reasonable.

Inevitably the expression imports a pejorative moral judgment: per Heerey, Drummond and Emmett JJ in *Hurley v McDonald's Australia Limited* (2000) 22 ATPR 41-741 (p 40,578) at [22] (p 40,585). This helpful articulation of the meaning of the word when used in s 51AC was followed by Selway J in *ACCC v 4WD Systems Pty Ltd* (2003) 59 IPR 435 at [183]–[185] (pp 487–488) and by Sundberg J in *ACCC v Simply No-Knead Franchising Pty Limited* [2000] FCA 1365; (2000) 104 FCR 253 at [30] (p 264); and

(c) Normally, some moral fault or moral responsibility would be involved. This would not ordinarily be present if the critical actions are merely negligent. There would ordinarily need to be a deliberate (in the sense of intentional) act or at least a reckless act: per Selway J in *ACCC v 4WD Systems Pty Ltd* (2003) 59 IPR 435 at [185] (p 488).

[90] Picking up on the notions contained in paragraphs (b) and (c) of the extract above, it has also been said that the notion of unconscionable conduct requires 'a high level of moral obloquy'.

[91] In applying these principles to conduct which involves the breach of a contract, it should be recognised that not every breach of contract, even a deliberate breach, necessarily involves the moral obloquy that the authorities suggest needs be present for unconscionable conduct in breach of s 51AC to be made out. Although it may be true that for an act to have that moral character it will usually be conduct that is intentional or at least reckless, it does not follow that any breach that is intentional necessarily has that moral character. As Weinberg J (as he then was) said in *Macdonald v Australian Wool Innovation Ltd* [[2005] FCA 105 at para 208]:

> Any promise that is deliberately broken could easily by characterised as 'unconscionable'. That is not the sense in which the term is used in s 51AC.

[92] A decision may be taken to break a contract because, upon rational commercial considerations, the burden of performance may be greater and more onerous than the liability to be incurred if the conduct amounts to breach. The party committing the breach may know that it will deliver to the opposite party an opportunity to exercise rights both under and outside the contract that flow from the breach, and that the opposite party has the means to exercise and enforce those rights. Those rights may include seeking injunctive relief to restrain the breach, accepting a repudiation of the contract so as to terminate executory obligations and seeking damages, or keeping the contract on foot and merely seeking damages. There may be nothing offensive to conscience in a commercial participant taking such a commercial decision in given circumstances. Whether or not it amounts to unconscionable conduct does not simply flow from it being a deliberate breach; it must be evaluated in 'all the circumstances'.

[93] The real question is what 'more' is required than conscious breach to convert it into unconscionable conduct. The answer to that question must, at least in part, lie in the value judgment of the particular decision maker. It means, of course, that minds can reasonably differ.

[94] However some guidance in the exercise of that judgment is to be found in the list of matters to which s 51AC(3) directs the court to have regard. That judgment is not to be informed merely by a sense of distaste for the impugned conduct. ...

Remedies

Extensive statutory remedies are available for breaches of the unconscionable conduct provisions. The regulator (normally the ACCC) or any person may apply for an injunction under Part 5-2 Division 2 of the *ACL* in 'such terms as the court determines to be appropriate'. This may involve, for example, ordering a corporation not to engage in a particular form of conduct which the court determines is unconscionable. Where a party may become liable to pay money—for example damages—by virtue of their conduct the court may also make an order prohibiting a person or corporation from disposing of assets.[20]

Most importantly, any person who has suffered loss or damage may seek damages under s 236 of the *ACL* to compensate for that loss or damage. In addition, remedial orders may be sought by the ACCC or any other person where the unconscionable conduct prohibitions have been contravened. These orders are broad-ranging, enabling the court to make 'such order or orders as the court thinks appropriate against the person who engaged in the conduct, or a person involved in that conduct' for the purpose of compensating a person who has suffered loss or damage as a result of the contravention or for the purpose of preventing or reducing loss or damage suffered.[21] In addition, the ACCC may now seek the imposition of civil pecuniary penalties[22] and may issue an infringement notice in relation to unconscionable conduct.[23]

Time limits

A claim for damages or other orders arising from a contravention of ss 20–21 must be brought within six years from the date upon which the applicant has suffered or is likely to suffer damage as a result of the unconscionable conduct.[24]

b   Australian Securities and Investments Commission Act 2001 (Cth)

The unconscionable conduct provisions of the *ACL* do not apply to conduct engaged in relating to financial services or financial products.[25] In 1998 consumer protection provisions relating to financial services were transferred to the *Australian Securities and Investments Commission Act 2001* (Cth) (*ASIC Act*) to enable the Australian Securities and Investments Commission (ASIC) to provide all regulation in relation to financial services. The *ASIC Act* provides equivalent unconscionable conduct

---

20 Competition and Consumer Act 2010 (CCA) S 137F. Such an order may only be made on application of the ACCC or the Minister.
21 Section 237 *ACL*.
22 Section 224(1)(a)(i) *ACL*.
23 Section 134A(2)(a) *CCA*.
24 Sections 236(2) and 237(3) *ACL*.
25 Section 131A(1) *CCA*.

provisions in relation to such financial services and ASIC's powers are equivalent to those of the ACCC for purposes of unconscionable conduct. These provisions apply to conduct engaged in by any persons in relation to such services; it is not limited to corporations.[26]

c State and territory legislation

Prior to the introduction of the *ACL*, state and territory legislation provides similar prohibitions against unconscionable conduct, predominantly in relation to consumer transactions. These have now been repealed to facilitate a nationally consistent consumer law.

However, due to the prevalence of unconscionable conduct in retail leasing, most states and territories have enacted a statutory prohibition on unconscionable conduct specifically directed toward retail leases.[27] These have survived the introduction of the *ACL*.

Retail Leases Act 2003 (Vic)

Section 78. Unconscionable Conduct of a Tenant

(1) A tenant under a retail premises lease or a proposed retail premises lease must not, in connection with the lease or proposed lease, engage in conduct that is, in all the circumstances, unconscionable.

(2) Without in any way limiting the matters to which the Tribunal may have regard for the purpose of determining whether a tenant has contravened sub-section (1), the Tribunal may have regard to-
   [factors (a)-(k) are similar to those contained in s 51AC of the *TPA*, with specific reference to landlords and tenants]
   (l) the extent to which the tenant was not reasonably willing to negotiate the rent under the lease; and
   (m) the extent to which the tenant unreasonably used information about the turnover of the tenant's or a previous tenant's business to negotiate the rent; and
   (n) the extent to which the tenant was willing to incur reasonable fit out costs.

(3) In considering whether a tenant has contravened sub-section (1), the Tribunal—
   (a) must not have regard to any circumstances that were not reasonably foreseeable at the time of the alleged contravention; and
   (b) may have regard to circumstances existing before the commencement of this section but not to conduct engaged in before that commencement.

---

26 Sections 12CA and 12CB *ASIC Act*.
27 See *Leases (Commercial & Retail) Act 2001* (ACT) s 22; *Retail Leases Act 1994* (NSW) ss 62A and 62B; *Business Tenancies (Fair Dealings) Act 2003* (NT) Part 10; *Retail Shop Leases Act 1994* (Qld) s 46A; *Fair Trading (Code of Practice for Retail Tenancies) Regulations 1998* (Tas); *Retail Leases Act 2003* (Vic) s 78.

Section 79. Certain conduct is not unconscionable

A person is not to be taken for the purposes of section ... 78 to engage in unconscionable conduct in connection with a retail premises lease merely because-
(a) the person institutes proceedings in relation to the lease or refers a dispute, application or claim relating to the lease to arbitration, conciliation, mediation or some other form of alternative dispute resolution; or
(b) the person fails to renew the lease or enter into a new lease; or
(c) the person does not agree to having an independent valuation of current market rent carried out.

A landlord or tenant suffering loss or damage by virtue of unconscionable conduct may recover that amount by lodging a claim with VCAT within six years of the conduct occurring.[28]

5   *Contracts Review Act 1980* (NSW)

New South Wales was the first Australian jurisdiction to attempt to provide comprehensive statutory relief in respect of 'unjust' contracts. The introduction of the *Contracts Review Act 1980* (NSW) followed the release of the *Peden Report*,[29] which highlighted the inadequacies of existing common and statutory law in relation to harsh and unconscionable transactions.[30] It was recognised that the traditional principles of sanctity and freedom of contract 'bear little relationship to the climate that often prevails over today's contractual transactions'—particularly consumer transactions—and that the 'common law had failed to keep abreast of the needs of a rapidly changing society by developing a general doctrine for dealing with unconscionable contracts'.[31]

The *Contracts Review Act 1980* (NSW) applies almost exclusively to consumer transactions[32] and the vast majority of cases that have invoked the Act have related to consumer mortgage contracts and lending guarantees.[33]

Unfortunately the *Contracts Review Act* has done little to prevent unfair terms in New South Wales with the courts still focusing on unjust procedures in the creation

---

28   Section 80 *Retail Leases Act 2003* (Vic). In Victoria the *Residential Tenancies Act 1997* also allows parties to challenge harsh and unconscionable *terms* in a tenancy agreement: s 28. The focus here is on the terms of the contract itself rather than the conduct of the landlord, although that will also be relevant.
29   John Peden, *Harsh and Unconscionable Contracts*, Report to the Minister for Consumer Affairs and Cooperative Societies and The Attorney-General for New South Wales, 1976.
30   See further TM Carlin, 'The *Contracts Review Act 1980* (NSW)—20 Years On' (2001) 23 *Sydney L Rev* 125.
31   *Finding a balance: Toward fair trading in Australia*, report by the House of Representatives Standing Committee on Industry, Science and technology, May 1997 at 160 quoting the relevant Minister.
32   The original bill was not restricted to consumers but as a result of business reaction to the Contracts Review Bill 1979 (NSW) it was revised to reduce the coverage of the legislation to predominantly consumers: see further A Terry, 'Unconscionable Contracts in New South Wales: The *Contracts Review Act 1980*' (1982) 10 *ABLR* 311.
33   See Carlin, above n 31, 144.

of the contract rather than the substantive unfairness of the terms themselves.[34] In addition, the Act's focus on individual contracts, rather than specific terms, means that the Act has had little, if any, impact on standard form contracts for consumers, despite the expectation that it would.[35]

Contracts Review Act 1980 (NSW)

Section 4. Definitions

(1) ... 'unjust' includes unconscionable, harsh or oppressive, and 'injustice' shall be construed in a corresponding manner.

Section 7. Principal relief

(1) Where the Court finds a contract or a provision of a contract to have been unjust in the circumstances relating to the contract at the time it was made, the Court may, if it considers it just to do so, and for the purpose of avoiding as far as practicable an unjust consequence or result, do any one or more of the following:
   (a) it may decide to refuse to enforce any or all of the provisions of the contract,
   (b) it may make an order declaring the contract void, in whole or in part,
   (c) it may make an order varying, in whole or in part, any provision of the contract,
   (d) it may, in relation to a land instrument, make an order for or with respect to requiring the execution of an instrument that:
      (i) varies, or has the effect of varying, the provisions of the land instrument, or
      (ii) terminates or otherwise affects, or has the effect of terminating or otherwise affecting, the operation or effect of the land instrument.

(2) ... the declaration or variation shall have effect as from the time when the contract was made or ... from some other time or times as specified in the order.

...

Section 9. Matters to be considered by Court

(1) In determining whether a contract or a provision of a contract is unjust in the circumstances relating to the contract at the time it was made, the Court shall have regard to the public interest and to all the circumstances of the case, including such consequences or results as those arising in the event of:
   (a) compliance with any or all of the provisions of the contract, or
   (b) non-compliance with, or contravention of, any or all of the provisions of the contract.

---

34   Standing Committee on Law and Justice (NSW), *Unfair Terms in Consumer Contracts*, Report 32, November 2006, pp 44–46.
35   Carlin, above n 31, 144.

(2) Without in any way affecting the generality of subsection (1), the matters to which the Court shall have regard shall, to the extent that they are relevant to the circumstances, include the following:
  (a) whether or not there was any material inequality in bargaining power between the parties to the contract,
  (b) whether or not prior to or at the time the contract was made its provisions were the subject of negotiation,
  (c) whether or not it was reasonably practicable for the party seeking relief under this Act to negotiate for the alteration of or to reject any of the provisions of the contract,
  (d) whether or not any provisions of the contract impose conditions which are unreasonably difficult to comply with or not reasonably necessary for the protection of the legitimate interests of any party to the contract,
  (e) whether or not:
    (i) any party to the contract (other than a corporation) was not reasonably able to protect his or her interests, or
    (ii) any person who represented any of the parties to the contract was not reasonably able to protect the interests of any party whom he or she represented,
  because of his or her age or the state of his or her physical or mental capacity,
  (f) the relative economic circumstances, educational background and literacy of:
    (i) the parties to the contract (other than a corporation), and
    (ii) any person who represented any of the parties to the contract,
  (g) where the contract is wholly or partly in writing, the physical form of the contract, and the intelligibility of the language in which it is expressed,
  (h) whether or not and when independent legal or other expert advice was obtained by the party seeking relief under this Act,
  (i) the extent (if any) to which the provisions of the contract and their legal and practical effect were accurately explained by any person to the party seeking relief under this Act, and whether or not that party understood the provisions and their effect,
  (j) whether any undue influence, unfair pressure or unfair tactics were exerted on or used against the party seeking relief under this Act:
    (i) by any other party to the contract,
    (ii) by any person acting or appearing or purporting to act for or on behalf of any other party to the contract, or
    (iii) by any person to the knowledge (at the time the contract was made) of any other party to the contract or of any person acting or appearing or purporting to act for or on behalf of any other party to the contract,
  (k) the conduct of the parties to the proceedings in relation to similar contracts or courses of dealing to which any of them has been a party, and
  (l) the commercial or other setting, purpose and effect of the contract.

...

(4) In determining whether a contract or a provision of a contract is unjust, the Court shall not have regard to any injustice arising from circumstances that were not reasonably foreseeable at the time the contract was made.

(5) In determining whether it is just to grant relief in respect of a contract or a provision of a contract that is found to be unjust, the Court may have regard to the conduct of the parties to the proceedings in relation to the performance of the contract since it was made.

The matters to be considered in determining if a contract is unjust focus predominantly on procedural rather than substantive issues. The result has been that the courts have focused on procedural rather than substantive unfairness[36] and it is very rare that substantive unfairness alone will result in a remedy under the Act.[37] The list of factors to consider has also caused some confusion and uncertainty with different courts weighting factors differently.[38] In this respect it has been observed that the term 'unjust' is 'a slippery word of uncertain content'.[39] Nevertheless, while it is clear that the term 'unjust' does not go so far as to encapsulate all 'unfair' conduct, it is clear that it is wider than the common law notion of unconscionability.[40]

The scope of the *Contracts Review Act* was considered in the following case.

West v AGC (Advances) Ltd

(1986) 5 NSWLR 610, New South Wales Court of Appeal

[Mrs West had a loan secured by a mortgage over her home. She had not paid interest on this loan for nearly three years and the mortgagee was threatening to exercise its power of sale. Her husband then raised with her the possibility of using the home as security for a loan of money that would discharge the existing mortgage and finance the expansion of a company that employed him, Quiche, which was experiencing financial difficulties. A meeting subsequently took place between Mr West and two of the directors of Quiche to discuss the proposal. A copy of the proposal was sent to Mrs West's son, Michael, and noted that discharge of the mortgage and the retention of the property would be dependent upon success of Quiche. Michael advised his mother not to go ahead with the proposal unless, in part, she obtained independent legal advice.

---

36 See further Standing Committee on Law and Justice (NSW), *Unfair Terms in Consumer Contracts*, Report 32, November 2006, p 45.
37 Ibid. Ramensky indicates that statistically in 2000 there were 16 identified breaches of the Act with only one of those cases involving substantive unfairness of a term. For an example of a case in which relief was granted almost exclusively on the basis of substantive unfairness see *Westpac Banking Corporation v Sugden* [1988] NSW ConvR ¶55-377 in which it was held that providing a standard form guarantee to 'commercially naïve customers' without explanation, in circumstances where the guarantee did more than what was necessary to protect the legitimate interests of the bank, was unjust: see further P Vout (ed), *Unconscionable Conduct—The Laws of Australia*, Lawbook Co, Sydney, 2006, p 508.
38 Carlin, above n 31.
39 Carlin, above n 31, citing Samuels JA in *Antonovic v Volker* (1986) 7 NSWLR 151 at 157.
40 Carlin, above n 31, 143.

After Mrs West received a further notice from the existing mortgagee, Quiche wrote to AGC seeking a loan of $85,000. AGC approved a loan to Mrs West of $68,000 to be secured by a mortgage over her home. Arrangements for execution of the deed and mortgage were made by AGC's solicitors and one of the directors of Quiche, who then took the deed and memorandum to Mrs West for execution. It was clear to the director, Mr Young, that the amount to be disbursed to Quiche would not even cover its existing debts and AGC had possession of Quiche's balance sheet. The monthly repayments on the loan were greater than the nett monthly salary earned by Mrs West. It was intended by Mrs West that Quiche and its directors would make the monthly repayments.]

McHugh JA [at 620]: Under s 7(1) a contract may be unjust in the circumstances existing when it was made because of the way it operates in relation to the claimant or because of the way in which it was made or both. Thus a contractual provision may be unjust simply because it imposes an unreasonable burden on the claimant when it was not reasonably necessary for the protection of the legitimate interests of the party seeking to enforce the provision: cf s 9(2)(d). In other cases the contract may not be unjust per se but may be unjust because in the circumstances the claimant did not have the capacity or opportunity to make an informed or real choice as to whether he should enter into the contract: cf s 9(2)(a), 9(2)(e), 9(2)(g), 9(2)(i), 9(2)(j). More often, it will be a combination of the operation of the contract and the manner in which it was made that renders the contract or one of its provisions unjust in the circumstances. Thus a contract may be unjust under the Act because its terms, consequences or effects are unjust. This is substantive injustice. Or a contract may be unjust because of the unfairness of the methods used to make it. This is procedural injustice. Most unjust contracts will be the product of both procedural and substantive injustice.

The definition of 'unjust' in s 4 is not exclusive. It is in my opinion a <621> mistake to think that a contract or one of its terms is only unjust when it is unconscionable, harsh or oppressive. ... The *Contracts Review Act* 1980 is revolutionary legislation whose evident purpose is to overcome the common law's failure to provide a comprehensive doctrinal framework to deal with 'unjust' contracts. Moreover, the provisions of s 9(2) do not exhaustively indicate the criteria as to what can be taken into account in determining whether a contract or any of its provisions is unjust. The provisions of s 9(2) of the Act are concerned for the most part with matters of procedural injustice. But the court is entitled to have regard to all the circumstances of the case, subject to s 9(4), and the public interest. In an appropriate case gross disparity between the price of goods or services and their value may render the contract unjust in the circumstances even though none of the provisions of s 9(2) can be invoked by the applicant. Indeed, notions of unfairness and unreasonableness will, I think, generally be present when a contract or any of its provisions is declared unjust. This will particularly be the case where procedural injustice is relied on. If a contract or one of its relevant provisions is neither unfair nor unreasonable so far as the applicant is concerned, it is difficult to see how the existence of inequality in bargaining power or lack of independent advice, for example, can render the contract or a provision of the contract unjust.

It is important to bear in mind that it is the contract or its provisions which must be unjust. ... 'it is not the transaction but the contract which must be initially examined' ... The *Contracts Review Act* regulates contracts not investments. ...

If a defendant has not been engaged in conduct depriving the claimant of a real or informed choice to enter into a contract and the terms of the contract are reasonable as between the parties, I do not see how that contract can be considered unjust simply because it was not in the interest of the claimant to make the contract or because she had no independent advice. ...

<622> ... under this Act, a contract will not be unjust as against a party unless the contract or one of its provisions is the product of unfair conduct on his part either in the terms in which he has imposed or in the means which he has employed to make the contract. In this respect it stands in marked contrast with [legislation which permits a declaration that] certain types of contact or arrangements [are] void on the ground that they are 'unfair'.

[His Honour noted (at 624) that in this case]: it was reasonably foreseeable that Quiche might be wound up and that Mrs West might have to meet the payments out of her own funds. ... Quiche was wound up in April 1982 [just slightly over a year after the loan was executed].

The question is not whether it was unjust that Mrs West should have borrowed money from AGC on the security of her home for the purpose of discharging her mortgage and lending the balance to Quiche. The question in issue is the narrower one whether *the contract* made between AGC and Mrs West or any of its provisions was unjust in the circumstances relating to it when it was made.

... [It was intended that in return for Mrs West's loan to them Quiche would pay the monthly instalments of $1,191.70.] Mrs West worked ... for Safeways at a nett monthly salary of $819. ... <625> ... It was reasonably foreseeable by AGC that Quiche might not be able to meet the payments which were owed by Mrs West to AGC. ... Mrs West had no solicitor acting for her ... She ... agreed to the proposal to borrow money on the security of her home as soon as her husband asked her to ... the wives of the other directors [of Quiche] had refused to allow their homes to be used as security. [However] Mrs West 'was well aware that she was giving a mortgage over her property, and that (AGC) could have recourse to that property in order to recoup its loan in the event of default'.

... The deed of loan was not unjust ... AGC made a loan to her at ordinary commercial rates to be repaid over four years and took a first mortgage over her property to secure their loan ... there is [nothing] in the terms of the ... mortgage or the deed of loan and guarantee which of itself is harsh, oppressive, unconscionable or unjust. Nor is it suggested that AGC in any way sought to induce Mrs West to enter into the deed or mortgage or applied any pressure to her. ...

<631> ... The *Contracts Review Act* 1980 is beneficial legislation. It must be interpreted liberally. But it operates within and not outside the domain of the

law of contract … By executing the deed of loan and memorandum of mortgage, Mrs West agreed to repay the loan which she obtained from AGC. She did so … with a full appreciation of the consequences and against the advice of her son … The deed and mortgage were ordinary commercial documents containing no unfair or unjust terms. AGC was guilty of no unfair conduct towards her. …

[His Honour noted that any pressure by the directors of Quiche did not render the contract between AGC and Mrs West unjust and it was not unjust simply because she did not receive independent legal advice. She understood the legal and practical effect of the mortgage. His Honour concluded (at 628) that] neither the contract nor any provision of the contract was unjust in providing that Mrs West should repay the loan to AGC and that she should provide a first mortgage over her home.

[Hope JA agreed with McHugh JA. Kirby P dissented, placing particular importance on the lack of independent legal advice.]

Appeal dismissed

Despite the comments of McHugh JA that it is the contract and not the transaction that is to be considered when determining if a contract is unjust, the courts have subsequently been prepared to look at the transaction as informing a decision as to whether a contract is unjust:

> It would appear that the trend of authority since *West* is that the *Contracts Review Act* permits a court not only to look at the terms of the contract *per se*, to see its terms are unjust, but to look at the circumstances in which the contract was made and its effect, having regard to those circumstances.[41]

In *Elkofairi v Permanent Trustee Co Ltd*[42] the appellant, who was dominated by her apparently abusive husband, was illiterate and had a very limited understanding of English, entered—with her husband—into a substantial loan with the respondent secured by her only asset, her joint interest in the matrimonial home. She had no income and this was known to the respondent. The fact that the respondent was prepared to issue a substantial loan without any information as to any income of the appellant or her husband, together with the appellant's limited educational background and illiteracy and her difficult domestic circumstances made the 'contract unjust in the circumstances in which it was made'.[43]

Claims relating to the *Contracts Review Act* are made to the Supreme Court of New South Wales and, subject to some limitation, to lower courts and the Consumer, Trader and Tenancy Tribunal.[44] Relief is available where the plaintiff demonstrates that their contract or its terms are unjust and that the unjust consequences may be avoided by the provision of relief.[45]

---

41 *Elkofairi v Permanent Trustee Co Ltd* [2002] NSWCA 413 at para 78, per Beazley JA.
42 [2002] NSWCA 413.
43 *Elkofairi v Permanent Trustee Co Ltd* [2002] NSWCA 413 at para 79, per Beazley JA.
44 *Contracts Review Act 1980* (NSW) s 4(1). See also Vout, above n 48, 502.
45 *Contracts Review Act 1980* (NSW) s 7(1). See also *Anotonovic v Volker* (1986) 7 NSWLR 151 and Vout, above n 48, 511. Ancillary relief is also available under s 8.

Where successful, the courts may avoid the contract *ab initio*, or may tailor the relief to the circumstances of a particular case by, for example, avoiding a guarantee contract only above a certain monetary unit.[46]

Recently it has been suggested that the *Contracts Review Act* now has a diminished role with the introduction of broader concepts of statutory unconscionability for consumers and small business under the *ACL*, discussed above.[47]

6 National Credit Code

Consumer credit contracts are now regulated nationally by the *National Credit Code*[48] which replaced the state-based Uniform Consumer Credit Code (UCCC) in 2010.

National Credit Code

Section 76. Court may reopen unjust transactions
Power to reopen unjust transactions

(1) The court may, if satisfied on the application of a debtor, mortgagor or guarantor that, in the circumstances relating to the relevant credit contract, mortgage or guarantee at the time it was entered into or changed (whether or not by agreement), the contract, mortgage or guarantee or change was unjust, reopen the transaction that gave rise to the contract, mortgage or guarantee or change.

Matters to be considered by court

(2) In determining whether a term of a particular credit contract, mortgage or guarantee is unjust in the circumstances relating to it at the time it was entered into or changed, the court is to have regard to the public interest and to all the circumstances of the case and may have regard to the following:
   (a) the consequences of compliance, or non-compliance, with all or any of the provisions of the contract, mortgage or guarantee;
   (b) the relative bargaining power of the parties;
   (c) whether or not, at the time the contract, mortgage or guarantee was entered into or changed, its provisions were the subject of negotiation;
   (d) whether or not it was reasonably practicable for the applicant to negotiate for the alteration of, or to reject, any of the provisions of the contract, mortgage or guarantee or the change;

---

46 See further Carlin, above n 31.
47 See further Carlin, above n 31, 143.
48 The *National Credit Code* is contained in Schedule 1 to the *National Consumer Credit Protection Act 2009 (Cth)* and is given force in the states and territories by virtue of enabling legislation: *Credit (Commonwealth Powers) Act 2010* (NSW), *Consumer Credit (National Uniform Legislation) Implementation Act 2010* (NT), *Credit (Commonwealth Powers) Act 2010* (Qld), *Credit (Commonwealth Powers) Act 2010* (SA), *Credit (Commonwealth Powers) Act 2009* (Tas), *Credit (Commonwealth Powers) Act 2010* (Vic), *Credit (Commonwealth Powers) Act 2010* (WA).

(e) whether or not any of the provisions of the contract, mortgage or guarantee impose conditions that are unreasonably difficult to comply with, or not reasonably necessary for the protection of the legitimate interests of a party to the contract, mortgage or guarantee;

(f) whether or not the debtor, mortgagor or guarantor, or a person who represented the debtor, mortgagor or guarantor, was reasonably able to protect the interests of the debtor, mortgagor or guarantor because of his or her age or physical or mental condition;

(g) the form of the contract, mortgage or guarantee and the intelligibility of the language in which it is expressed;

(h) whether or not, and if so when, independent legal or other expert advice was obtained by the debtor, mortgagor or guarantor;

(i) the extent to which the provisions of the contract, mortgage or guarantee or change and their legal and practical effect were accurately explained to the debtor, mortgagor or guarantor and whether or not the debtor, mortgagor or guarantor understood those provisions and their effect;

(j) whether the credit provider or any other person exerted or used unfair pressure, undue influence or unfair tactics on the debtor, mortgagor or guarantor and, if so, the nature and extent of that unfair pressure, undue influence or unfair tactics;

(k) whether the credit provider took measures to ensure that the debtor, mortgagor or guarantor understood the nature and implications of the transaction and, if so, the adequacy of those measures;

(l) whether at the time the contract, mortgage or guarantee was entered into or changed, the credit provider knew, or could have ascertained by reasonable inquiry at the time, that the debtor could not pay in accordance with its terms or not without substantial hardship;

(m) whether the terms of the transaction or the conduct of the credit provider is justified in the light of the risks undertaken by the credit provider;

(n) for a mortgage—any relevant purported provision of the mortgage that is void under section 50;

(o) the terms of other comparable transactions involving other credit providers and, if the injustice is alleged to result from excessive interest charges, the annual percentage rate or rates payable in comparable cases;

(p) any other relevant factor.

Representing debtor, mortgagor or guarantor

(3) For the purposes of paragraph (2)(f), a person is taken to have represented a debtor, mortgagor or guarantor if the person represented the debtor, mortgagor or guarantor, or assisted the debtor, mortgagor or guarantor to a significant degree, in the negotiations process prior to, or at, the time the credit contract, mortgage or guarantee was entered into or changed.

Unforeseen circumstances

(4) In determining whether a credit contract, mortgage or guarantee is unjust, the court is not to have regard to any injustice arising from circumstances that were not reasonably foreseeable when the contract, mortgage or guarantee was entered into or changed.

Conduct

(5) In determining whether to grant relief in respect of a credit contract, mortgage or guarantee that it finds to be unjust, the court may have regard to the conduct of the parties to the proceedings in relation to the contract, mortgage or guarantee since it was entered into or changed.

Application

(6) This section does not apply:
   (a) to a matter or thing in relation to which an application may be made under subsection 78(1); or
   (b) to a change to a contract under this Division.
(7) This section does apply in relation to a mortgage, and a mortgagor may make an application under this section, even though all or part of the mortgage is void under subsection 50(3).

Meaning of unjust

(8) In this section:
   unjust includes unconscionable, harsh or oppressive.

77 Orders on reopening of transactions

The court may, if it reopens a transaction under this Division, do any one or more of the following, despite any settlement of accounts or any agreement purporting to close previous dealings and create a new obligation:

(a) reopen an account already taken between the parties to the transaction;
(b) relieve the debtor and any guarantor from payment of any amount in excess of such amount as the court, having regard to the risk involved and all other circumstances, considers to be reasonably payable;
(c) set aside either wholly or in part or revise or alter an agreement made or mortgage given in connection with the transaction;
(d) order that the mortgagee takes such steps as are necessary to discharge the mortgage;
(e) give judgment for or make an order in favour of a party to the transaction of such amount as, having regard to the relief (if any) which the court thinks fit to grant, is justly due to that party under the contract, mortgage or guarantee;
(f) give judgment or make an order against a person for delivery of goods to which the contract, mortgage or guarantee relates and which are in the possession of that person;
(g) make ancillary or consequential orders.

78 Court may review unconscionable interest and other charges

(1) The court may, if satisfied on the application of a debtor or guarantor that:
   (a) a change in the annual percentage rate or rates under a credit contract to which subsection 64(1) or (4) applies; or
   (b) an establishment fee or charge; or
   (c) a fee or charge payable on early termination of a credit contract; or
   (d) a fee or charge for a prepayment of an amount under a credit contract;
   is unconscionable, annul or reduce the change or fee or charge and may make ancillary or consequential orders.

(2) For the purposes of this section, a change to the annual percentage rate or rates is unconscionable if and only if it appears to the court that:
   (a) it changes the annual percentage rate or rates in a manner that is unreasonable, having regard to any advertised rate or other representations made by the credit provider before or at the time the contract was entered into, the period of time since the contract was entered into and any other consideration the court thinks relevant; or
   (b) the change is a measure that discriminates unjustifiably against the debtor when the debtor is compared to other debtors of the credit provider under similar contracts.

(3) In determining whether an establishment fee or charge is unconscionable, the court is to have regard to whether the amount of the fee or charge is equal to the credit provider's reasonable costs of determining an application for credit and the initial administrative costs of providing the credit or is equal to the credit provider's average reasonable costs of those things in respect of that class of contract.

(4) For the purposes of this section, a fee or charge payable on early termination of the contract or a prepayment of an amount under the credit contract is unconscionable if and only if it appears to the court that it exceeds a reasonable estimate of the credit provider's loss arising from the early termination or prepayment, including the credit provider's average reasonable administrative costs in respect of such a termination or prepayment.

80 Time limit

(1) An application (other than an application under section 78) may not be brought under this Division more than 2 years after the relevant credit contract is rescinded or discharged or otherwise comes to an end.

(2) An application under section 78 may not be brought more than 2 years after the relevant change takes effect or fee or charge is charged under the credit contract or the credit contract is rescinded or discharged or otherwise comes to an end.

7 Summary

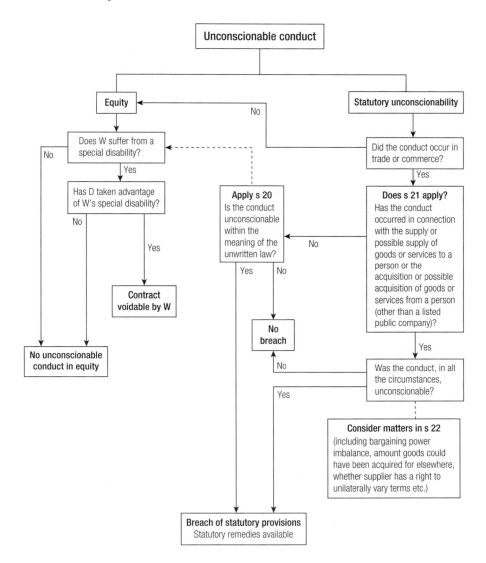

8 Questions

1. Sonia runs her own financial planning business. She is highly educated, having a bachelor degree in accounting and a masters degree in financial planning. Sonia also loves horses and it was in pursuit of her love of horse-riding that she met her husband, Hunter. Hunter owns a farm in rural Victoria, near Horsham (which he inherited from his parents and which

had been in his family for many generations). He left school at the age of 16 to pursue his love of horses and the outdoors and works as a self-employed farrier and general horseman. He earns a modest income.

Sonia and Hunter live on the farm. Sonia also owns a property in Melbourne where she stays when engaged in city business. Sonia's business is primarily conducted through her online financial planning website. She also services the Horsham region of Victoria through a local Horsham office.

Unfortunately, Sonia's business is no longer thriving. As a result of spending too much time with her horses and too little time servicing her online customers, she has exposed herself to numerous negligence claims and her income has dropped below that necessary to maintain rent and insurance payments. As a consequence, her business has fallen into debt.

Despite these financial difficulties, Sonia was confident that she could turn her business around and, to facilitate this, she sought a loan from the Horsham Credit Institute Ltd (HCI) to help revive the business. Greg, the loans manager at HCI, told Sonia that they would be prepared to lend her up to $100,000, but only if she was able to provide security for that amount by means of a mortgage over property. Unfortunately, Sonia's Melbourne home was already subject to two mortgages. As a result, in order to secure the loan she needed to provide a mortgage over the farm, which was registered in Hunter's name alone.

After speaking to Greg, Sonia rushed home and prepared a candlelit picnic dinner for Hunter. That evening, they enjoyed a wonderful and romantic meal under the stars. The next morning Sonia broached the subject of mortgaging the home to secure a loan for her business. As Hunter was under the impression that the business was thriving, he was slightly puzzled by the request. Sonia assured him that a small cash-injection was needed to expand the business and Hunter, who relied on Sonia for financial guidance, was satisfied she knew what she was doing and there would be no real risk to the farm.

The following Monday Sonia and Hunter both attended the HCI and spoke to the manager, Greg, about mortgaging the farm. Hunter was asked to sign a number of documents. Greg suggested that Hunter read the documents thoroughly and seek advice from his solicitor before signing. However, Hunter, while literate, could not understand financial documents and after Sonia assured him the terms were quite standard, signed the documents without bothering to read them or seek other advice. In fact, the documents, while quite standard, provided that the mortgage was to be used as security for any future loans made to Sonia's business as well as securing all existing debt.

Sonia's business did not improve and six months later HCI called in the debt. Sonia was unable to make payment and HCI sought to enforce the mortgage and sell the farm.

Hunter has come to you for advice. He is distressed at the prospect of losing the farm and wishes to know if there is any way he can prevent the bank from taking it from him. Please advise Hunter.

2. Snap Happy Pty Ltd is a small family company that provides a range of photographic goods and services. These range from professional photography services, to the supply of camera equipment and the printing of high quality photographs and other photo products. Snap Happy is owned by Antonio and Francesco Giordano, who recently immigrated to Australia

to be closer to their son (who had married a Melburnian) and, they hoped, their future grandchildren. Although well educated, with bachelor degrees in photography, Antonio and Francesco had no previous experience in running a business, having only worked as employees for a photography company before immigrating to Australia. They agreed that Antonio would complete a postgraduate business course to assist them in the future and both enrolled in English classes to improve their English proficiency. Both could speak and read English at a basic level, but agreed that, until their English improved, they would hire an assistant who would have more direct contact with customers.

Shop Heaven Ltd is a large company that owns several shopping complexes around Australia. Snap Happy entered into a lease of a business premises with Shop Heaven in their Melbourne City complex. The lease was negotiated between Antonio Giordano and the managing director of Shop Heaven's Melbourne complex, Charles Rich.

Charles presented Antonio with a standard form contract, which Antonio quickly perused, but did not really understand. Charles told him that he could 'take it or leave it'. Antonio, who wanted the lease quite desperately, decided to simply accept the terms presented without attempting to read or understand them in any depth. The parties then negotiated a price. Charles described the price in a detailed and complex way, explaining how various pricing components (including power, cleaning, advertising and security) combined to produce the monthly price and he nominated a price well above the market rate for similar premises. Antonio was a bit overwhelmed by the complexity of the pricing and, although the price was above what he wanted to pay, it was within what he considered an acceptable range, so agreed without much further negotiation.

The lease was due for renewal after three years and the Giordano's were keen to extract a better deal from Shop Heaven. The lease provided that the Giordano's would have the option of renewing the lease after three years, but this was subject to any additional terms or conditions Shop Heaven wished to impose.

During the past three years, the Giordano's had acquired better English and business skills, and realised that Antonio had not negotiated a very good deal for the initial lease. In particular, they had discovered that the 'market value' for similar leases was considerably less than they were paying and that some of the more onerous terms in the lease agreement (including those relating to trading hours) had been successfully modified by other tenants in the Melbourne City complex, notwithstanding Charles' claim that the offer was made on a 'take it or leave it' basis.

Unfortunately, when Antonio approached Charles Rich to renegotiate the lease (which contained an option for renewal), Charles refused to negotiate on terms and demanded an even higher price if the Giordano's wanted to continue to lease their premises.

Charles knew that the business was only just beginning to be profitable as a result of the Giordano's investing significant time promoting their business. He also knew that the business depended heavily on a city location and that it would damage business and would impose considerable expense on the Giordano's if they were forced to relocate. Charles had also been informed that the Giordano's were expecting their first grandchild and that they were trying to save money to assist their son with the construction of a home extension to house a nursery. Despite this, Charles was prepared to renew the lease at the existing rate, or even reduce the rate if necessary to keep the Giordano's in the Melbourne City complex, as he thought they were great tenants who added significantly to the quality of the complex. However, he was not going to make any concessions unless he felt it absolutely necessary.

Antonio protested that they were already paying a higher rate than other tenants and could not afford to pay more or give up the lease. Charles would not budge and told Antonio that if he didn't like it, he could walk away. Antonio, knowing he could not afford the damage to his business that would accompany relocation, reluctantly agreed to pay an additional rate to ensure his lease was renewed for a further three years.

Antonio has come to you for advice. His business is struggling to pay the additional monthly rate and he has had to lay off staff and work longer hours to pay the bills. This also means that he and Francesco are unable to visit their new grandson very often, which Antonio knows is causing Francesco considerable distress. He thinks it is unfair that Charles would not renegotiate terms, particularly when it is clear that other retailers in the complex have received much fairer terms and rates. He is worried that in another three years, when it comes time to negotiate a further renewal, Shop Heaven will once again seek to extract higher rents that may cause the business to fail.

Please advise Antonio if there is any way he can return to paying the rent originally agreed to or otherwise renegotiate the terms of his lease.

CHAPTER 17

Unfair Terms

1	Introduction	479
2	*Fair Trading Act 1999* (Vic) Part 2B	480
3	Australian Consumer Law	480
	a Standard form consumer contracts	482
	b Unfair term	483
	c The effect of including an unfair or prescribed unfair term	489
4	Impact of unfair terms legislation	490
5	Unfair terms in contracts for the supply of financial products or services	491
6	Summary	493
7	Questions	494

1 Introduction

In the previous chapters we have dealt predominantly with procedural unfairness or unconscionable conduct in the formation of a contract. This chapter looks at how certain legislation deals with unfairness within the contract itself—substantive unfairness. The law has generally not provided a remedy for substantive unfairness where there has been no associated procedural unfairness.[1] In recent years, however, it has been recognised that there is a need, particularly in relation to consumer contracts, to provide protection in respect of substantive unfairness, even where no procedural irregularities can be demonstrated.[2] Some have argued that to go beyond procedural unconscionability and prohibit unfair terms unduly impinges

---

1   This has been recognised as one of the 'most significant limitations of the current legal framework' dealing with unfair contractual terms: Standing Committee on Law and Justice (NSW), *Unfair Terms in Consumer Contracts*, Report 32, November 2006, p 43. Lynden Griggs has also observed that general 'unfairness or lack of good faith has failed to find a common law foundation for intervention': Ibid p 44.

2   For a discussion of possible theoretical grounds for unfair terms legislation see N Howell, 'Catching up with consumer realities: The need for legislation prohibiting unfair terms in consumer contracts' (2006) 34 *ABLR* 447. The author suggests (at 459) that the current doctrine of freedom of contract be replaced with a 'new framework for consumer contracts that takes an inequality of bargaining power and a lack of negotiation on contract terms as starting points, rather than as exceptions to the norm ...'. See also L Griggs, 'The [ir]rational consumer and why we need national legislation governing unfair contract terms' (2005) 13 *Competition & Consumer Law Journal* 51.

on the doctrine of freedom of contract and party autonomy. Other commentators have rejected this claim, arguing that prohibition of unfair terms

> ... is simply a recognition that the freedom to contract is not a totally unfettered right but exists within a set of social and legal obligations, which the Parliament also has a responsibility to define and protect. Indeed, in commercial life, agreements are valued for the relationships they establish, rather than vice versa. If the relationships they establish are exploitative, they are no longer to be valued. Consequently, far from undermining the institution of contract and economic exchange, any law which insists on standards of fairness in contracts, and commerce more generally, would be protecting the fundamental social and economic purposes of those institutions.[3]

2 Fair Trading Act 1999 (Vic) Part 2B

In 2003 Victoria became the first Australian state to introduce a comprehensive prohibition on *unfair terms* in consumer contracts.[4] This took the form of a new Part 2B of the *Fair Trading Act 1999*, 'Unfair Terms in Consumer Contracts' which came into operation on 9 October 2003.[5] Section 32Y provided that an *unfair term* in a consumer contract was void and that a *prescribed unfair term* in a *standard form* contract was void. In each case, the contract continued 'to bind the parties if ... capable of existing without the unfair term or the prescribed unfair term'.[6]

These provisions were repealed when the first stage of the *Australian Consumer Law (ACL)* was introduced in July 2010.

3 Australian Consumer Law

The *ACL*[7] incorporates a national prohibition on unfair terms in standard form consumer contracts[8] and is modelled, in part, on the Victorian unfair terms legislation.

---

3   *Finding a balance: Toward fair trading in Australia*, report by the House of Representatives Standing Committee on Industry, Science and technology, May 1997 at 167.
4   Note that s 106 *Industrial Relations Act 1996* (NSW) has enabled the Industrial Relations Commission of NSW to void or vary an industry contract which it considers an 'unfair contract'. This, however, is limited to certain employment contracts; see further P Vout (ed), *Unconscionable Conduct—The Laws of Australia*, Lawbook Co, Sydney, 2006 ch 6. Similarly the *Industrial Relations Act 1999* (Qld) permits 'unfair contracts' to be avoided: s 276(1).
5   Part 2B applied to any consumer contract in force on 9 October 2003 and all such contracts entered into since that date.
6   Section 32Y(3).
7   The ACL is contained in Schedule 2 of the *Competition and Consumer Act 2010* (Cth). It applies as a law of the Commonwealth by virtue of Part XI of the CCA and as a law of the states and territories by virtue of state enabling legislation. See, for example, the *Fair Trading Amendment (Unfair Contract Terms) Act 2010* (Vic).
8   The unfair terms provisions were introduced with the first stage of the ACL. They were originally contained in Part 2 of the ACL (ss 2–8), but were renumbered (Part 2-3, ss 23–28) when the second stage of the ACL was implemented on 1 January 2011. For a discussion of the new law see, for example, J Paterson, 'The Australian Unfair Contract Terms Law: The Rise of Substantive Unfairness as a Ground for Review of Standard Form Consumer Contracts' (2009) 33 Melbourne University Law Review 934.

Australian Consumer Law

Part 2-3 Unfair Contract Terms

23 Unfair terms of consumer contracts

(1) A term of a consumer contract is void if:
 (a) the term is unfair; and
 (b) the contract is a standard form contract.
(2) The contract continues to bind the parties if it is capable of operating without the unfair term.
(3) A consumer contract is a contract for:
 (a) a supply of goods or services; or
 (b) a sale or grant of an interest in land;
  to an individual whose acquisition of the goods, services or interest is wholly or predominantly for personal, domestic or household use or consumption.

24 Meaning of *unfair*

(1) A term of a consumer contract is unfair if:
 (a) it would cause a significant imbalance in the parties' rights and obligations arising under the contract; and
 (b) it is not reasonably necessary in order to protect the legitimate interests of the party who would be advantaged by the term; and
 (c) it would cause detriment (whether financial or otherwise) to a party if it were to be applied or relied on.
(2) In determining whether a term of a consumer contract is unfair under subsection (1), a court may take into account such matters as it thinks relevant, but must take into account the following:
 (a) the extent to which the term is transparent;
 (b) the contract as a whole.
(3) A term is transparent if the term is:
 (a) expressed in reasonably plain language; and
 (b) legible; and
 (c) presented clearly; and
 (d) readily available to any party affected by the term.
(4) For the purposes of subsection (1)(b), a term of a consumer contract is presumed not to be reasonably necessary in order to protect the legitimate interests of the party who would be advantaged by the term, unless that party proves otherwise.
 …

28 Contracts to which this Part does not apply

(1) This Part does not apply to:
 (a) a contract of marine salvage or towage; or
 (b) a charterparty of a ship; or
 (c) a contract for the carriage of goods by ship.

…

(3) This Part does not apply to a contract that is the constitution (within the meaning of section 9 of the *Corporations Act 2001*) of a company, managed investment scheme or other kind of body.

a   Standard form consumer contracts

Like the Victorian law, the *ACL* applies only to consumer contracts.[9] However, unlike the Victorian law, the prohibition is limited to 'standard form' contracts.

Consumer contract

A 'consumer contract' is defined, for purposes of the *ACL*, as a contract for a supply of goods or services or sale or grant of an interest in land 'to an individual whose acquisition of the goods, services or interest is wholly or predominantly for personal, domestic or household use or consumption'.[10] The reference to an 'individual' acquiring the goods or services limits the scope of the prohibition to acquisitions by natural persons.[11]

To determine the actual use of the goods or services acquired the courts will look at the purpose of the agreement, rather than the subjective intention of either of the parties.[12] This purpose is to be 'ascertained by reference to the terms of the agreement, which will reflect the intention of all the parties to the agreement'.[13] It is not essential that the goods or services be acquired solely for personal, household or domestic use, provided they are acquired *substantially* for that purpose.[14]

Standard form contract

Standard form contract is not defined in the *ACL*, but a list of factors that the courts may consider when determining whether the contract is a standard form contract is provided. These include whether or not one party was effectively 'required to either accept or reject the terms of the contract … in the form in which they were presented' and 'whether another party was given an effective opportunity to negotiate the terms of the contract'. Where a consumer alleges that a contract is a standard form contract it will be presumed that the contract is a standard form contract unless the other party proves otherwise.

---

9   It was originally proposed that the legislation would apply to all standard form contracts. However, when the Trade Practices (Australian Consumer Law) Bill 2009 (which later became the Trade Practices Amendment (Australian Consumer Law) Bill (No 1) 2010) was introduced it limited the application of the unfair terms laws to terms in standard form consumer contracts.
10   *ACL* s 23(3).
11   *Acts Interpretation Act 1901* (Cth) section 22(1)(aa).
12   *Director of Consumer Affairs Victoria v AAPT Limited (Civil Claims)* [2006] VCAT 1493 at para 30, per Justice Stuart Morris (President). Note, although this case related to the Victorian unfair terms legislation, the relevant requirement was the same under that Act.
13   *Director of Consumer Affairs Victoria v AAPT Limited (Civil Claims)* [2006] VCAT 1493 at para 30, per Justice Stuart Morris (President).
14   *Director of Consumer Affairs Victoria v AAPT Limited (Civil Claims)* [2006] VCAT 1493 at para 27, per Justice Stuart Morris (President): 'a good or service will be supplied for a specific purpose if it is *substantially* supplied for that purpose'.

Australian Consumer Law
Part 2-3 Unfair Contract Terms

27 Standard form contracts

(1) If a party to a proceeding alleges that a contract is a standard form contract, it is presumed to be a standard form contract unless another party to the proceeding proves otherwise.

(2) In determining whether a contract is a standard form contract, a court may take into account such matters as it thinks relevant, but must take into account the following:
   (a) whether one of the parties has all or most of the bargaining power relating to the transaction;
   (b) whether the contract was prepared by one party before any discussion relating to the transaction occurred between the parties;
   (c) whether another party was, in effect, required either to accept or reject the terms of the contract (other than the terms referred to in section 26(1)) in the form in which they were presented;
   (d) whether another party was given an effective opportunity to negotiate the terms of the contract that were not the terms referred to in section 26(1);
   (e) whether the terms of the contract (other than the terms referred to in section 26(1)) take into account the specific characteristics of another party or the particular transaction;
   (f) any other matter prescribed by the regulations.

b Unfair term

A term of a consumer contract is considered an 'unfair term' if it would 'cause significant imbalance in the parties' rights and obligations under the contract' and 'it is not reasonably necessary in order to protect the legitimate interests of the party who would be advantaged by the term' and 'it would cause detriment ... to a party if it were to be applied or relied on'.[15] There is a legal presumption that a term of a consumer contract is not 'reasonably necessary in order to protect the legitimate interests of the party who would be advantaged by the term, unless that party proves otherwise'.[16]

Despite the clear focus on substantive unfairness of terms, procedural factors may continue to influence a decision on whether contractual terms are in fact unfair. Thus, for example, section 24(2) provides that in determining whether a term of a consumer contract is unfair, a court must take into account the extent to which the term is transparent. Assessment of the term must also take into account the contract as a whole.[17] As a consequence, a term which may look unfair in isolation may appear fair when other terms in the contract are also considered.

---

15 ACL s 24.
16 ACL s 24(4).
17 ACL s 24(2)(b).

Some guidance on the concept of 'unfair terms' has been provided by the ACCC in *A Guide to the Unfair Contract Terms Law*.

ACCC, A Guide to the Unfair Contract Terms Law
(2011), pp 11–13

A 'significant imbalance'

The first limb of the test requires the court to consider whether a term of a consumer contract would cause a significant imbalance in the parties' rights and obligations arising under the contract. This would involve a factual assessment of the available evidence.

Under this limb of the test, the claimant is required to prove that, on the balance of probabilities, a term of a consumer contract would cause a significant imbalance in the parties' rights and obligations arising under the contract.

'Not reasonably necessary'

Under the second limb of the test for unfairness, a court must find that the term is not reasonably necessary to protect the legitimate interests of the party that would be advantaged by the term. The meaning of legitimate interest is open to interpretation by the court.

This limb requires that the party advantaged by the term provide evidence to the court to demonstrate why it is necessary for the contract to include the term.

Such evidence might include material relating to the business's costs and business structure, the need for the mitigation of risks or particular industry practices to the extent that such material is relevant.

Detriment

The third limb of the test for unfairness requires the court to find that the term would cause detriment (whether financial or otherwise) to a party if it were to be applied or relied on.

Detriment is not limited to financial detriment. The court will be allowed to consider situations where there may be other forms of detriment such as delay or distress suffered by the consumer as a result of the unfair term.

What will a court consider in determining whether or not a term is unfair?

In determining whether a term of a standard form consumer contract is unfair, a court may take into consideration any matter that it thinks relevant. It must take into consideration:

- the extent to which the term is transparent and
- the contract as a whole.

A transparent term

A lack of transparency regarding a term in a standard form consumer contract may cause a significant imbalance in the parties' rights and obligations.

A term is considered to be transparent if it is:
- expressed in reasonably plain language
- legible
- presented clearly
- readily available to any party affected by the term.

Again, it is important to note that only the court can determine what a transparent term is for the purposes of the unfair contract terms provisions. Examples of terms that may not be considered transparent include terms that are hidden in fine print or schedules, or that are phrased in legalese or in complex or technical language.

Although the court must take into account the transparency requirement, a term that does not meet the transparency requirement will not necessarily be unfair. Further, transparency, on its own account, will not necessarily overcome underlying unfairness in a contract term.

The United Kingdom Unfair Terms in Consumer Contracts Regulation 1999 uses the term 'plain and intelligible language' rather than 'transparent'. Despite the difference in terminology, the finding of Smith J in *Office of Fair Trading v Abbey National plc* [[2009] UKSC 6.] may provide some guidance:

> Regulation 6(2) ... requires not only the actual wording of individual clauses or conditions be comprehensible to consumers, but that the typical consumer can understand how the term affects the rights and obligations that he and the seller or supplier have under the contract

The 'contract as a whole'

The fairness of a particular contractual term cannot be considered in isolation but must be assessed in light of the contract as a whole. Some terms that might seem quite unfair in one context may not be unfair in another.

Conversely, if a particular term was decided by a court in one case to be fair, this does not mean it will always be fair.

An apparently unfair term may be regarded in a better light when seen in the context of other counterbalancing terms. For example, a potentially unfair term may be included in a consumer contract but may be counterbalanced by additional benefits—such as a lower price—being offered to the other party.

However, even if a contract contains terms that favour the consumer, such favourable terms may not counterbalance an unfair term if the consumer is unaware of them. Examples include implied terms, or terms hidden in fine print, in a schedule or in another document, or written in legalese. This may result in an information imbalance in favour of the business. [see *Director of Consumer Affairs Victoria v AAPT Ltd (Civil Claims)* [2006] VCAT 1493.]

[footnotes omitted]

The concept of unfair terms which caused a 'significant imbalance in the parties' rights and obligations under the contract'[18] was considered in the following case, decided pursuant to Victoria's unfair terms legislation.

---

18 This case related to a claim that certain contractual terms were unfair contrary to s 32W *Fair Trading Act 1999* (Vic).

Director of Consumer Affairs Victoria v AAPT Limited (Civil Claims)
[2006] VCAT 1493, Victorian Civil and Administrative Tribunal

[The Director of Consumer Affairs, Victoria, brought an action against AAPT Ltd alleging that a number of terms in their mobile phone contracts were unfair in contravention of Part 2B.]

Justice Morris [at 49]: Are terms in AAPT contracts unfair terms?

... it is clear that many of the terms identified by the Director were unfair terms within the meaning of section 32W of the *FTA* and are void. It is desirable to deal with some of these terms in order to illustrate why they were unfair.

Variations to Agreement

[50] Clause 1.3 of the mobile services standard form of agreement ('mobile SFOA') provided:

> **Variations:** We may vary any term of this Agreement at any time in writing. To the extent required by any applicable laws or determinations made by the Australian Communications Authority (ACA), we will notify you of any such variation.

This term is unfair because it permits AAPT, but not the customer, to change the contract unilaterally. The term has the effect of permitting AAPT, but not the consumer, to avoid or limit the performance of the contract ....

Suspension of service

[51] Clause 3.10 of the mobile SFOA provided:

> **Suspension:** We reserve the right to suspend provision of Services to you, where charges owing to us or any amount owing under this clause remain outstanding after 60 days, unless we have received written notice from you disputing those charges in good faith. If we suspend or terminate the Services for unpaid charges or any other reason, subsequent reconnection may incur a reconnection fee.

[The first sentence of this term is not unfair]. However the second sentence of the term goes too far, as it provides that AAPT may charge a reconnection fee for 'any other reason': and this could embrace a reason which does not involve any breach by the customer of its obligations under the contract.

[52] Clause 9 of the mobile SFOA provided:

> 9.1 We may from time to time and without notice or liability to you suspend any of the Services (and at our discretion disconnect the relevant SIM cards from the Network) in any of the following circumstances:
>
> (a) during any technical failure, modification or maintenance of the Network (but in that event we will procure resumption of the Services as soon as reasonably practicable);
>
> ...
>
> 9.2 Notwithstanding any suspension of the Services under this clause you shall remain liable for all charges due hereunder throughout the period of suspension (including without limitation all monthly access fees, and regardless of whether or not any SIM card has been disconnected from the Network) unless we in our sole discretion determine otherwise.

[The term in clause 9.2] whereby the customer remains liable for all charges throughout the period in which the service is suspended unless AAPT, in its sole discretion, determines otherwise [cannot be justified]. Circumstances could arise where service is suspended for a technical failure and the nature of the failure (and suspension of service) is such that AAPT is not required to pay a fee to the ultimate service supplier. Yet, because clause 9.2 gives AAPT a discretion as to whether or not to charge its customer during the period of suspension, that term is clearly unfair. ....

Immediate termination
[53] Clause 10 of the mobile SFOA provided:

> 10.2 **Immediate termination:** We may terminate this Agreement immediately by notice to you if:
> (a) you have breached this Agreement;
> (b) ...; or
> (c) you change your address or billing contact details without notifying us in accordance with clause 7.4.
> 10.4 You remain liable for all charges payable under the Agreement in respect of Services up to the time of termination.

These provisions potentially have broad application. A customer may have breached the Agreement in a manner which is inconsequential, yet faces the prospect of having the service terminated. Further, if the customer changes his or her address ... this will also provide a ground to AAPT to terminate the Agreement. Because these provisions are so broadly drawn, and are one sided in their operation, they are unfair terms within the meaning of the *FTA*.

Variations to prepaid mobile service
[54] Clause 1.3 of the prepaid mobile service standard form of agreement ('prepaid mobile SFOA') provided:

> 1.3 **Variations:** To the extent permitted by law, AAPT may change a Supplier or its products, or vary our charges from time to time without notice to you. Otherwise, AAPT may vary these terms on 30 days written notice to you.

This term causes a significant imbalance in the parties' rights and obligations arising under the contract, to the detriment of the consumer. For example, it would enable AAPT to reduce the number of calls that a person could make pursuant to a prepaid mobile phone service which the person had entered into in good faith. This term was an unfair term.

...
[footnotes omitted]

To determine whether an identified term is unfair, it is also necessary to refer to ss 25 and 26 of the *ACL*. Section 26 makes clear that the prohibition on unfair terms does not extend to terms to the extent to which they define the main subject of the contract, or set the upfront price payable under the contract or is required or expressly permitted by statute. Consequently, for example, a consumer will not have recourse to the unfair terms provisions to claim that the price paid for a product was 'unfair'. In this respect, the explanatory memorandum to the Trade Practices Amendment (Australian Consumer Law) Bill (No 2) 2010, notes that the 'upfront price', as defined in s 26(2), covers both cash price payable for goods, services or land at the time the contract is made *and* future payment or payments, provided those payments are disclosed at or prior to the conclusion of the contract. It does not include consideration that is contingent.[19] Section 25 sets out a number of examples of the kinds of terms that may be considered unfair.

Australian Consumer Law

Part 2-3 Unfair Contract Terms

25 Examples of unfair terms

(1) Without limiting section 24, the following are examples of the kinds of terms of a consumer contract that may be unfair:
   (a) a term that permits, or has the effect of permitting, one party (but not another party) to avoid or limit performance of the contract;
   (b) a term that permits, or has the effect of permitting, one party (but not another party) to terminate the contract;
   (c) a term that penalises, or has the effect of penalising, one party (but not another party) for a breach or termination of the contract;
   (d) a term that permits, or has the effect of permitting, one party (but not another party) to vary the terms of the contract;
   (e) a term that permits, or has the effect of permitting, one party (but not another party) to renew or not renew the contract;
   (f) a term that permits, or has the effect of permitting, one party to vary the upfront price payable under the contract without the right of another party to terminate the contract;
   (g) a term that permits, or has the effect of permitting, one party unilaterally to vary the characteristics of the goods or services to be supplied, or the interest in land to be sold or granted, under the contract;
   (h) a term that permits, or has the effect of permitting, one party unilaterally to determine whether the contract has been breached or to interpret its meaning;
   (i) a term that limits, or has the effect of limiting, one party's vicarious liability for its agents;
   (j) a term that permits, or has the effect of permitting, one party to assign the contract to the detriment of another party without that other party's consent;
   (k) a term that limits, or has the effect of limiting, one party's right to sue another party;

---

19 See s 26(2) of the *ACL* and the Trade Practices Amendment (Australian Consumer Law) Bill (No 2) 2010 Explanatory Memorandum, paras 5.62–5.70.

(l) a term that limits, or has the effect of limiting, the evidence one party can adduce in proceedings relating to the contract;
(m) a term that imposes, or has the effect of imposing, the evidential burden on one party in proceedings relating to the contract;
(n) a term of a kind, or a term that has an effect of a kind, prescribed by the regulations.
(2) Before the Governor-General makes a regulation for the purposes of subsection (1)(n) prescribing a kind of term, or a kind of effect that a term has, the Minister must take into consideration:
(a) the detriment that a term of that kind would cause to consumers; and
(b) the impact on business generally of prescribing that kind of term or effect; and
(c) the public interest.

26 Terms that define main subject matter of consumer contracts etc. are unaffected

(1) Section 23 does not apply to a term of a consumer contract to the extent, but only to the extent, that the term:
(a) defines the main subject matter of the contract; or
(b) sets the upfront price payable under the contract; or
(c) is a term required, or expressly permitted, by a law of the Commonwealth, a State or a Territory.
(2) The upfront price payable under a consumer contract is the consideration that:
(a) is provided, or is to be provided, for the supply, sale or grant under the contract; and
(b) is disclosed at or before the time the contract is entered into;
but does not include any other consideration that is contingent on the occurrence or non-occurrence of a particular event.

c   The effect of including an unfair or prescribed unfair term

Term void

An unfair term in a standard form consumer contract is void.[20]

If the remainder of the contract is capable of existing without the void term—in other words, if the term is severable—the remainder of the contract will continue to operate. If the term cannot be severed then the whole contract will be declared void.[21]

Other remedies

A party to a consumer contract containing an unfair term may apply to the relevant court or tribunal for:

---

20   *ACL* s 23.
21   *ACL* s 23.

- a declaration that a term of a consumer contract is an unfair term;[22]
- an injunction;[23] and/or
- compensation.[24]

The ACCC or state or territory regulator may apply to the relevant court or tribunal[25] for:

- a declaration that a term of a consumer contract is an unfair term;[26]
- an injunction;[27]
- compensation on behalf of one or more persons injured by the contravention;[28] and/or
- an order to redress loss or damage suffered by non-party consumers.

A limitation period of six years applies to applications for compensation and orders to redress loss or damage suffered by non-party consumers.[29]

4 Impact of unfair terms legislation

The effectiveness of the *ACL* in preventing unfair terms in consumer contracts is yet to be determined. Some reference can, however, be made to its impact in Victoria. Despite the fact that there were only a limited number of cases brought pursuant to the Victorian laws, they had a significant impact on business practice in Victoria. The extent of this impact is difficult to accurately measure, but it is clear that hundreds of standard form contracts were amended to avoid infringing the unfair terms law.[30] Consumer Affairs Victoria (CAV) also investigated particular industries and contract types to ensure they complied with the legislation. In relation to mobile phones, CAV commissioned reviews that demonstrated that, while there were a significant number of unfair terms in the 2004 contracts, 'improvement had been made' by 2006 and it is likely that 'reduction in unfair terms and conditions [had] been brought about as a consequence of [the unfair terms legislation]'.[31] The CAV also investigated gift vouchers and loyalty programs and published some of the changes that were brought about by the legislation:

---

22   *ACL* s 250(1).
23   *ACL* s 232. The injunction can be in 'such terms as the court considers appropriate (s 232(1))' and may include, for example, refunding money, transferring property or honouring a promise (s 232(6)).
24   *ACL* s 237.
25   At the federal level the ACCC would apply to the federal court. At the state or territory level the state or territory regulator would apply to a court or tribunal.
26   *ACL* s 250(1).
27   *ACL* s 232(2)
28   *ACL* s 237(1).
29   *ACL* ss 237(3) and 239(4), respectively.
30   Ibid p 69.
31   E Beal, Communications Law Centre, Submission No 11 to the *Inquiry into Unfair Terms in Consumer Contracts*, submitted 11 October 2006.

Dymocks Bookstores has agreed to revise the terms and conditions of its Booklover Loyalty Program—a program that allows consumers to earn 'reward points' on purchases which can later be exchanged for discounts on future purchases. The main issue was that Dymocks could vary, suspend or terminate the scheme at any time and without obligation to honour accumulated reward points.

Hilton Hotels has agreed to remove several terms in its Hilton Premium Club contracts that allowed the business to not provide what it had promised, change the Club contract, and change the benefits a consumer might receive by joining the Club. They also further amended membership agreements so consumers could obtain a pro-rata refund if Hilton Hotels made changes to which the consumer had not agreed.

Langham Hotels has agreed to review the terms and conditions of its gift vouchers after the agency conciliated an agreement for a consumer who had accidentally thrown away a $150 voucher. The voucher number was tracked by Langhams electronic systems proving the consumer had paid despite the voucher term that stated it would not be replaced if lost or stolen. Consumer Affairs Victoria advised this was unfair and Langhams agreed to re-issue the voucher and alter its practices.[32]

5 Unfair terms in contracts for the supply of financial products or services

The *ACL* unfair contract terms regime does not apply to '... to the supply, or possible supply, of services that are financial services, or of financial products'. Equivalent provisions have, however, been introduced into the *Australian Securities and Investments Commission Act 2001* (Cth).[33]

INTERNATIONAL PERSPECTIVES

There is no unfair terms prohibition under either Indian or Chinese *contract law*. The Chinese *Contract Law* does, however, specify certain levels of fairness and enables contractual avoidance in some cases of substantive unfairness.

India

Indian Contract Act, 1872

Unfair terms will negate free consent, and therefore prevent an agreement constituting a contract, only where they are brought about by coercion, undue influence, fraud or misrepresentation.

The Chinese *Contract Law* provides generally that parties should abide by principles of fairness and good faith in their contractual dealings and prohibits certain terms.

---

32   'Victorian Consumers Protected on Loyalty Contracts', CAV Media Release, 4 October 2006 <http://www.consumer.vic.gov.au>.
33   Sections 12BF–12MB.

China

Contract Law of the People's Republic of China, 1999

Article 5. Fairness

The parties shall abide by the principle of fairness in prescribing their respective rights and obligations.

Article 6. Good Faith

The parties shall abide by the principle of good faith in exercising their rights and performing their obligations.

Similar requirements are imposed on 'standard form contracts' which also require the other party to be informed of certain provisions and invalidate certain other provisions.

Article 39. Standard Terms; Duty to Call Attention

Where a contract is concluded by way of standard terms, the party supplying the standard terms shall abide by the principle of fairness in prescribing the rights and obligations of the parties and shall, in a reasonable manner, call the other party's attention to the provision(s) whereby such party's liabilities are excluded or limited, and shall explain such provision(s) upon request by the other party.

Standard terms are contract provisions which were prepared in advance by a party for repeated use, and which are not negotiated with the other party in the course of concluding the contract.

Article 40. Invalidity of Certain Standard Terms

A standard term is invalid if it falls into any of the circumstances set forth in Article 52 and Article 53 hereof, or if it excludes the liabilities of the party supplying such term, increases the liabilities of the other party, or deprives the other party of any of its material rights.

Article 53. Invalidity of Certain Exculpatory Provisions

The following exculpatory provisions in a contract are invalid:

(i) excluding one party's liability for personal injury caused to the other party;
(ii) excluding one party's liability for property loss caused to the other party by its intentional misconduct or gross negligence.

Contracts which are grossly unconscionable will also be subject to amendment or cancellation. In this context unconscionable focuses on *substantive* rather than procedural unconscionability.

> Article 54. Contract Subject to Amendment or Cancellation
>
> Either of the parties may petition the People's Court or an arbitration institution for amendment or cancellation of a contract if:
>
> (iii) the contract was grossly unconscionable at the time of its conclusion.
>
> ...

6 Summary

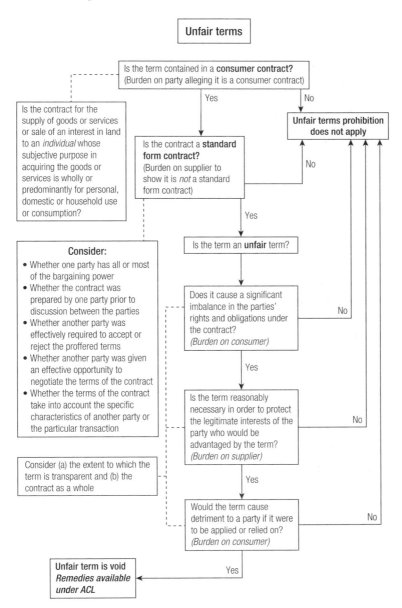

7 Questions

1. Katrina entered into a contract with *Fitness Fast Pty Ltd*, a local gymnasium, with the intention of improving her general health and fitness. When she inquired about joining the gym she was handed a contract containing several pages of terms. The manager of the gymnasium went through the key terms with Katrina, including the following:

   Cl 8:   *Fitness Fast* may relocate its premises by providing you with three weeks notice of the proposed move.

   Cl 9:   *Fitness Fast* may alter its hours of operation at any time.

   Cl 10: *Fitness Fast* may alter, suspend or cancel any of its group fitness classes at any time.

   Cl 76: You may cancel your membership at any time after the expiration of your membership term, provided that you give *Fitness Fast* 30 days written notice by registered post.

   Katrina did not pay much attention to the terms, concerned only with the duration of the contract (12 months) and the cost of $25 per week. Katrina signed the contract on the spot and was handed a membership card.

   Katrina was initially a regular attendee of the *Fitness Fast* gym, but after the first month, as winter approached, her attendance dropped to one group session a week and, occasionally, one weights session. After two months, *Fitness Fast* cancelled the group session she attended. Katrina complained, but was told there was insufficient attendance for them to continue the class. She noticed several other classes had also been cancelled.

   Katrina stopped attending the gym altogether for a while, but five months into her contract she found renewed inspiration and started attending the gym five days a week. This was facilitated in part by her recent purchase of a house within walking distance of the gym.

   Unfortunately, six months into contract, *Fitness Fast* announced it was relocating to bigger premises 10km away and that its opening hours were changing. When Katrina joined the gym the opening hours were 6am–6pm. The new hours were 9am–9pm. This did not suit Katrina, who preferred to use the gym first thing in the morning.

   Despite the inconvenient hours, Katrina tried driving to the new premises. However, she found that the extra hassle of getting into the car after work and hunting for one of the limited number of car parks was too stressful and she stopped attending the gym altogether. Katrina tried to cancel her membership, but was told that she had no grounds to terminate prior to the expiration of the 12-month membership term.

   Eleven months into her 12-month term, Katrina wrote to *Fitness Fast* advising them that she wished to cancel her membership at the expiration of her membership term in 30 days.

   Thirteen months after initially taking out her membership with *Fitness Fast*, Katrina checked her credit card account and noticed that *Fitness Fast* was still debiting her account. She drove to the gym and asked to speak with the manager, Tony. Tony advised her that her account was still being debited because she had not sent her cancellation letter by registered post, as required by the contract. Katrina was furious and told Tony that if he debited her card again she would go straight to her solicitor and sue *Fitness Fast*. Tony replied that he would stop payment 30 days after he received from her a registered letter of cancellation, but not before.

Katrina is furious and has come to you for advice. She wishes to know if she has any claim against *Fitness Fast* for the charges incurred after the expiration of her 12-month term, for the relocation of the gymnasium and changes to opening hours or for the cancellation of her favourite group fitness class. Please advise Katrina.

2   Peter entered into a contract with Advanced Communications Pty Ltd, for the purchase of a mobile phone. He intended to use the phone as both his primary business and home phone. Prior to entering into the contract he discussed the terms with Kevin, the sales manager at Advanced Communications. The contract that Kevin handed Peter contained more than 100 clauses, including the following:

Cl 15:   We may vary any term of this agreement at any time in writing. To the extent required by any applicable laws we will notify you of any such variation.

Cl 17:   We reserve the right to change suppliers at any time.

Cl 18:   We reserve the right to suspend provision of services to you for a period of up to three weeks during the term of the contract. Notwithstanding any suspension of service in accordance with this clause, you will remain liable for all monthly access fees and other charges due.

Cl 20:   If you cancel your service before the contract term expires you must pay *Advanced Communications* an early termination fee of $100 and all the remaining monthly access fees that would have become payable had the service continued for the remainder of the contract term.

In respect of clause 15, Peter asked if *Advanced Communications* would modify the term to require that all variations be notified by Peter, whether or not *Advanced Communications* were required by law to give notice to Peter. Kevin agreed and made the amendment by hand. In respect of clause 18, Peter asked if *Advanced Communications* would alter the reference from three weeks to one week, which he considered more reasonable. Kevin refused, claiming he was not authorised to make that change.

Notwithstanding *Advanced Communications'* refusal to make all requested changes, Peter was still attracted to *their* deal and signed a 12-month contract with them. This included a phone and $100 worth of included calls for a monthly fee of $59.

Unfortunately, after one month, *Advanced Communications* suspended provision of service for two weeks, causing significant disruption to Peter's work. In addition, after three months, *Advanced Communications* changed its supplier, with the result that the satellite signal was very weak whenever Peter ventured out of the city, which he did regularly for work. This caused him to miss several calls and many more others were cut off or distorted as a result of the poor reception.

It is now four months since Peter entered into his contract with *Advanced Communications* and he now wishes to terminate the contract. He has been advised by *Advanced Communications* that early termination will cost him $572 ($100 + 8 x $59).

Peter has come to you for advice. Please advise Peter what, if any, remedies he may have against *Advanced Communications* under the *ACL*.

CHAPTER 18

Illegality and Public Policy

1	Introduction	496
2	Statutory illegality	497
	a Contracts prohibited by statute	497
	b Contracts entered into for an illegal purpose	499
	c Contracts that are performed illegally	501
	d Contracts rendered void by statute	506
3	Common law illegality and contracts contrary to public policy	507
	a Contracts to commit a legal wrong	508
	b Contracts prejudicial to the administration of justice	509
	c Contracts tending to promote corruption in public life	513
	d Contracts prejudicial to public safety or foreign relations	514
	e Contracts to defraud the Revenue	514
	f Contracts that prejudice the status of marriage	514
	g Contracts that promote sexual immorality	519
	h Contracts in restraint of trade	520
4	Effect of illegality	525
	a Exceptions to the general rule that the court will not enforce an illegal contract	525
	b Independent causes of action	529
	c Severance	529
5	Summary	533
6	Questions	534

1 Introduction

Illegality has often been described as a difficult area of the law of contract and concern has been expressed about its scope and the uncertainty it can generate.[1]

---

[1] Justice Kirby in *Fitzgerald v FJ Leonhardt Pty Ltd* (1997) 189 CLR 215 at 231–232 [footnotes omitted] has said 'Illegality, and the associated problems of statutory construction and public policy, have been described as a "shadowy" and "notoriously difficult" area of the law where there are "many pitfalls". Many of the authorities on the point are difficult to reconcile. Commentators claim that some of them are marked by "obscurities, supposed distinctions and questionable techniques of decision". They suggest that this is an area of the law which is "intensely controversial and confused". ...'
See also H Stowe, 'The "Unruly Horse" has bolted: *Tinsley v Milligan*' (1994) *Modern Law Review* 441–449.

In this chapter we will examine the policy behind contractual illegality and the impact illegality may have on the ability of one or both parties to enforce a contract.

As a general principle, the court will not 'lend its aid to a man who founds his cause of action on an immoral or an illegal act'.[2] *Illegality* in the context of the law of contract is not restricted to contracts or conduct which infringes the criminal law, but extends to conduct contrary to civil legislation or the common law and conduct which is immoral or considered so socially undesirable that the court should refuse to enforce it on public policy grounds. In addition to concern about the scope and uncertainty of public policy considerations, in particular, concern has been expressed that in today's increasingly regulated society, minor and unintended transgressions may frequently occur in relation to contractual creation or performance in a way not envisaged when the illegality principles were developed.[3] It is, therefore, essential that we understand the scope and effect that such transgressions may have on the willingness of a court to enforce a contract.

2 Statutory illegality

Statutory illegality is now the most common form of contractual illegality. It occurs whenever legislation or regulations prohibit some aspect of contractual formation or its performance. The key ways in which it might arise are through direct statutory prohibition of the contract itself, where the contract is associated with, or made with, the purpose of frustrating the objects of a statute, or where an otherwise lawful contract is performed in a manner that is prohibited by statute.[4]

a Contracts prohibited by statute

In some cases a statute will prohibit the making of a particular contract. For example, a contract between competitors to form a cartel is prohibited by the *Competition and Consumer Act 2010* (Cth) and, in addition to the remedies and penalties provided within that statute, the courts will refuse to enforce the contract on grounds of illegality.[5]

It is, however, important not to confuse prohibition of contracts themselves with prohibition of certain acts contemplated by a contract. There is, in this respect, an important distinction between contracts which are themselves illegal and contracts which are tainted by illegal performance. The test used to determine

---

2   *Holman v Johnson* [1775–1802] All ER Rep 98; 1 Cowp 341; 98 ER 1120, per Lord Mansfield CJ.
3   See Justice Kirby in *Fitzgerald v FJ Leonhardt Pty Ltd* (1997) 189 CLR 215 at 242: 'The substantial growth of legislative provisions affecting all aspects of the society in which contracts are made presents a legal environment quite different from that in which the doctrine of illegality was originally expressed.'
4   See Gibbs ACJ in *Yango Pastoral Co Pty Ltd v First Chicago Australia Ltd* (1978) 139 CLR 410 at 413.
5   For example, s 45 of the *Competition and Consumer Act* directs attention specifically to contracts by providing (in part) that a corporation must not 'make a contract' if that contract 'has the purpose, or would have or be likely to have the effect, of substantially lessening competition'.

whether or not a contract which prohibits certain acts required or contemplated by a contract is itself an illegal contract is one of statutory intent.[6] It will be necessary, in each case, to ask whether or not the statute intended to penalise the unlawful conduct *only* or whether it also intended to prohibit the contract giving rise to the unlawful performance. This issue arose for consideration in the following case.

St John Shipping Corp v Joseph Rank Ltd

[1957] 1 QB 267, Court of Queens Bench

[Legislation made it an offence to overload a cargo ship so that its 'load line' was submerged. A fine was prescribed for contravention of the legislation which was set at the greater of the increased earning capacity of the ship brought about by the overloading or £100 per inch over the load line.

The master of the ship, *St John*, overloaded his ship by more than 11 inches and was fined the maximum of £1,200. The increased earning capacity due to the overloading was £2,295. The defendants had cargo on the plaintiff's ship and decided to punish the plaintiffs by withholding £2,000 payment (of the almost £19,000 payable) under their contract. The defendants claimed that the plaintiffs could not enforce the contract of carriage against them due to the illegality arising from their contravention of the legislation.]

Devlin J [at 280]: ... Believing, rightly or wrongly, that the plaintiff had deliberately committed a serious infraction of the <281> Act and one which has placed their property in jeopardy, [the defendants] wish to do no more than to take the profit out of his dealing. But the principle which they invoke for this purpose cares not at all for the element of deliberation or for the gravity of the infraction and does not adjust the penalty to the profits unjustifiably earned. The defendants cannot succeed unless they claim the right to retain the whole freight and to keep it whether the offence was accidental or deliberate, serious or trivial. The application of this principle to a case such as this is bound to lead to startling results. ... A shipowner who accidentally overloads by a fraction of an inch will not be able to recover from any of the shippers or consignees a penny of the freight. There are numerous other illegalities which a ship might commit in the course of the voyage which would have the same effect; ...

<282> Of course ... one must not be deterred from enunciating the correct principle of law because it may have starting or even calamitous results. But I confess that I approach the investigation of a legal proposition which has results of this character with a prejudice in favour of the idea that there may be a flaw in the argument somewhere.

Counsel for the defendants ... submits as a general proposition that a person who performs a legal contract in an illegal manner cannot sue on it, ...

---

6   See, for example, Justice Mason in *Yango Pastoral Company Pty Ltd v First Chicago Australia Ltd* (1978) 139 CLR 410 at 425: whether a statute 'prohibits contracts is always a question of construction turning on the particular provisions, the scope and purpose of the statute'. See also *Miller v Miller* [2011] HCA 9 at para 24.

<283> ... There are two general principles. The first is that a contract which is entered into with the object of committing an illegal act is unenforceable. The application of this principle depends on proof of the intent, at the time the contract was made, to break the law; if the intent is mutual the contract is not enforceable at all, and, if unilateral, it is unenforceable at the suit of the party who is proved to have it. This principle is not involved here. ... The second principle is that the court will not enforce a contract which is expressly or impliedly prohibited by statute. If the contract is of this class it does not matter what the intent of the parties is; if the statute prohibits the contract, it is unenforceable whether the parties meant to break the law or not. ...

[In relation to this principle two] <287> questions are involved. The first ... is: does the statute mean to prohibit contracts at all? If this be answered in the affirmative, then one must ask: does this contract belong to the class which the statute intends to prohibit? ...

[In this case the relevant section] provides that the ship '... shall not be so loaded as to submerge...' the appropriate load line. ... an implied prohibition of contracts of loading does not necessarily extend to contracts for the carriage of goods by improperly loaded vessels. Of course if the parties knowingly agree to ship goods by an overloaded vessel, such a contract would be illegal; ... <288> ... The way to test the question whether a particular class of contract is prohibited by the statute is to test it in relation to a contract made in ignorance of its effect.

In my judgment contracts for the carriage of goods are not within the ambit of this statute at all. A court ... ought to be very slow to hold that a statute intends to interfere with the rights and remedies given by the ordinary law of contract. Caution in this respect is, I think, especially necessary in these times when so much of commercial life is governed by regulations of one sort or another which may easily be broken without wicked intent. Persons who deliberately set out to break the law cannot expect to be aided in a court of justice, but it is a different matter when the law is unwittingly broken.

<290> ... a contract for carriage of goods is not to be considered void merely because the ship in which they are carried does not comply with the law. But ... each case must be determined by reference to the relevant statute ...

Judgment for the plaintiff

b   Contracts entered into for an illegal purpose

Contracts not themselves prohibited but which are entered into for an illegal purpose may also be unenforceable. Whether such a contract is unenforceable will depend upon whether, on a case-by-case basis, public policy considerations require that the court should refuse to enforce the contract.[7]

---

7   See French CJ, Gummow, Hayne, Crennan, Kiefel and Bell JJ in *Miller v Miller* [2011] HCA 9 at para 27, observing that where contracts are associated with or in furtherance of an illegal purpose the court must discern 'from the scope and purpose of the statute, ... whether the legislative purpose will be fulfilled without regarding the contract ... as void and unenforceable'.

This issue arose for consideration in the following case:

Nelson v Nelson

(1995) 184 CLR 538, High Court of Australia

[The appellant, Mrs Nelson, provided purchase moneys for a house (the 'Bent St property') that was transferred into the names of her daughter, Elizabeth (the respondent), and her son. The purpose of the appellant putting the house in the names of her children was to enable her to claim the benefit of a subsidised loan under the *Defence Services Homes Act 1918* (Cth) should she subsequently wish to purchase another home. The appellant did later buy a new house and received a subsidy after declaring on her application that she did not own or have an interest in another home.

Soon after the purchase of the second home, the Bent Street property was sold netting proceeds in excess of $230,000. The appellant claimed that, having paid for the house, she was its beneficial owner and therefore entitled to the proceeds of the sale. The respondent claimed that she and her brother were the true owners as a result of the 'presumption of advancement' applicable whenever a parent provides a benefit to a child, and that therefore she was entitled to half the proceeds of the sale. In order to rebut the presumption of advancement (by proving no gift was intended) it was necessary for the appellant to disclose her true purpose in transferring the home into the names of her children; to preserve her entitlement to claim benefits under the Act. As this was an illegal purpose the respondent claimed the appellant could not use evidence of this purpose to rebut the presumption of advancement.

At first instance this argument succeeded and an appeal to the New South Wales Court of Appeal failed. Mrs Nelson appealed to the High Court.]

McHugh J [at 598]: ... the appeal should be allowed. [The presumption that Mrs Nelson intended to transfer property to her daughter (at 599)] is rebuttable. It may be rebutted even where the transfer was made for an illegal purpose unless the circumstances of the transfer are so injurious to the public interest that public policy requires otherwise. Nothing in the Act or its objects nor in the circumstances of this case provided any sound reason in public policy for the Supreme Court refusing to allow Mrs Nelson to rebut the presumption in this case. Consequently, her proven intention to retain the beneficial ownership of the property rebutted the presumption of advancement ...

<603> ... [Counsel for the respondent] contends that ... equity will not permit a person to rebut the presumption ... in respect of property that was transferred to effectuate an illegal <604> purpose. ... In my opinion [this is] erroneous.

... A court that finds that an agreement is unlawful or has an unlawful purpose has merely set the stage for a further inquiry: are the circumstances surrounding the agreement such that the court should deny a relevant remedy to the party seeking the assistance of the court? ...

The argument for Elizabeth naturally relied on the famous dictum of Lord Mansfield that '[n]o Court will lend its aid to a man who founds his cause of action upon an immoral or an illegal act'. The principle contained in this dictum applies in both law and equity. But it is subject to exceptions which allow relief to be granted despite the presence of illegality. ... But [counsel] claims that ... neither the common law courts nor the equity courts will assist a claimant who must rely on his or her unlawful purpose to make out a cause of action. ...

<611> ... The doctrine of illegality ... was formulated in a society that was vastly different from that which exists today. It was a society that was much less regulated. With the rapid expansion of regulation, it is undeniable that the legal environment in which the doctrine of illegality operates has changed. The underlying policy ... is still valid ... the courts must not condone or assist a breach of statute ... However, the ... rule [that] 'No court will lend its aid to a man who founds his cause of action upon an immoral or an illegal act' is too extreme and inflexible to represent sound legal policy in the late twentieth century ...

[In this case, if] a certificate has been issued as a result of a false statement by the applicant ... the Secretary can cancel the subsidy [or (at 616)] require the repayment to the Commonwealth of either the whole of the subsidy already paid, or such amount as the Secretary considers reasonable. ...

The result in this case

In this case, we are concerned with an agreement or transaction that was not, per se, illegal but which was entered into for an illegal purpose. ...

[The Act] contains internal mechanisms for dealing with false declarations ... The Act ... provides for recovery of the subsidy paid .... These provisions lend weight to the submission ... that the policy of the Act will not be defeated if the Court enforces her equitable rights. ...

<617> ...I can see no justification for the courts imposing a further sanction by refusing to enforce the legal or equitable rights of applicants under the Act, particularly when such a refusal may often result, as it does in this case, in a penalty out of all proportion to the seriousness of an applicant's conduct. ...

Appeal allowed

[footnotes omitted]

c   Contracts that are performed illegally

Contracts not prohibited by legislation or entered into for an illegal purpose may nevertheless be tainted by illegal performance. For example, a contract between A and B in which A agrees to transport goods from Melbourne to Geelong for B is lawful and capable of being performed in a lawful manner. However, should A speed when driving or drive while unlicensed or intoxicated then the contract will have been performed in an illegal manner. Incidental illegality of this nature will generally not be sufficient to render the contract itself illegal and unenforceable at common law, at least where the illegal performance was not contemplated at the time of the contract.

In each case it will be necessary to examine the statute or regulations applicable to determine whether the remedies they provide are sufficient to serve the legislative purpose in prohibiting the conduct or whether public policy demands that the courts should also refuse to enforce any associated contract. This issue was discussed in the following cases.

Yango Pastoral Co Pty Ltd v First Chicago Australia Ltd

(1978) 139 CLR 410, High Court of Australia

[The respondent carried on an unauthorised banking business contrary to the requirements of the *Banking Act 1959* (Cth), thereby committing an offence under the Act. In the course of that business it loaned money to the appellant secured by a mortgage and guarantee. The appellant defaulted and the respondent claimed on the mortgage and guarantee. The appellant claimed the mortgage and associated guarantee were void for illegality or, alternatively, that the court should not assist the appellant in giving effect to the transaction. The respondent succeeded in the Supreme Court and an appeal was denied. A further appeal was made to the High Court.]

Gibbs ACJ [at 413]: [The Act] does not render it unlawful to borrow or lend money or to give and take a mortgage, supported by guarantees, to secure its repayment. The contract sued upon was therefore not to do anything which [the Act] forbids. The principal question in the case is whether [the Act] on its proper construction, prohibited the making or performance of the contract. ... if that question is answered in the negative, it will not be possible to say that the contract cannot be enforced on the ground that it was made in order to effect an unlawful purpose or was performed in an unlawful manner.

It is often said that a contract expressly or impliedly prohibited by statute is void and unenforceable. That statement is true as a general rule, ... Where a statute imposes a penalty upon the making or performance of a contract, it is a question of construction whether the statute intends to prohibit the contract in this sense, that is, to render it void and unenforceable, or whether it intends only that the penalty for which it provides shall be inflicted if the contract is made or performed.

The question whether a statute, on its proper construction, intends to vitiate a contract made in breach of its provisions, is one which must be determined in accordance with the ordinary principles that govern the construction of statutes. 'The determining factor is the true effect and meaning of the statute' ... 'One must have regard to the language used and to the scope and <414> purpose of the statute' .... One consideration that has been regarded as important in a great many cases, ... is whether the object of the statute—or one of its objects—is the protection of the public.

[His Honour noted at least one object of the Act was the protection of the public and continued (at 414)]: ... the argument advanced on behalf of the appellants was that the prohibition which it imposes on an unauthorized body corporate from carrying on any banking business extends to all activities which go to make up the business of banking, except such as are merely collateral or peripheral. It was said that a contract to lend money on mortgage supported by guarantee is central to the business of banking and that such a contract, when made by a body corporate unlawfully carrying on the business of banking, and in the course of that business, is prohibited ... However the receipt of money on deposit is equally central to the business of banking, and if the argument put on behalf of the appellants is correct, [the Act] would invalidate not only <415> those contracts by which a body corporate carrying on an unauthorized banking business agreed to lend money, but also all contracts pursuant to which it agreed to receive money from depositors. The result of accepting this argument might be that persons who had deposited money with such a body corporate would be unable to seek the assistance of the courts to recover it. ... In those circumstances 'the avoidance of the contract would cause grave inconvenience and injury to innocent members of the public without furthering the object of the statute' ...

Another relevant consideration is the fact that the penalty which [the Act] imposes is a pecuniary sum for each day during which the contravention continues. ... This is an indication that the Parliament did not intend to prohibit each contract made in the course of the business, but only to penalize the carrying on of the business without authority ...

The language of [the Act] indicates that it is directed, not at the making or performance of particular contracts, but at the carrying on of any banking business. ... <416> ... in making and performing the contract the parties have not done or contracted to do anything which the Act expressly forbids. ... <417>

Having regard to the language of [the Act] and to the matters to which I have referred, I conclude that [the Act], on its proper construction, does not vitiate contracts made by a body corporate in the course of carrying on a banking business in breach of the section. ...

Further it cannot be said that the contract was performed for any illegal purpose. ... Once it is held that neither the making nor the performance of the contract was unlawful, the fact that the contract was made and performed in the course of the conduct of an unlawful business provides no ground for denying relief to the respondent. ...

Mason J [at 426]: Where, as here, a statute imposes a penalty for contravention of an express prohibition against carrying on a business without a licence or an authority and the business is carried on by entry into contracts, the question is whether the statute intends merely to penalize the person who contravenes the prohibition or whether it intends to go further and prohibit contracts the making of which constitute the carrying on of the business. In deciding this question the court will take into account the scope and purpose of the statute and the consequences of the suggested implication with a view to ascertaining whether it would conduce to, or frustrate, the object of the statute. ...

... there is little to be said for the view that the statute intends to prohibit contracts made by unauthorized banks <427> in the course of carrying on banking business. To do so would be to prejudice depositors, not to protect them. The implication of such a prohibition would deny to innocent depositors the right to recover moneys deposited unlawfully ...

It is not rational to suppose that the Parliament intended to inflict such dire consequences on innocent depositors. ... I therefore conclude that the purpose of the Act is adequately served by the imposition of the very heavy penalty which is prescribed for a contravention ... and that it does not prohibit and thereby invalidate contracts and transactions entered into in the course of carrying on banking business in breach of the section. ...

Appeal dismissed

Fitzgerald v FJ Leonhardt Pty Ltd

(1997) 189 CLR 215, High Court of Australia

[The plaintiff (respondent) brought an action to recover money due under a contract with the defendant (appellant). The contract provided that the respondent, a licensed driller, was to dig a minimum of three bores at $1,750 with extra payments dependent on the depth of the bore. Seven bores were dug in order to discover three that would provide the desired water. The *Water Act 1992* (NT) required a permit before a person could 'cause, suffer or permit a bore to be drilled, constructed, altered, plugged, backfilled or sealed off' and prescribed penalties for breach. It was the appellant's obligation to obtain the permits before the drilling started which he failed to do. Following a dispute over payment the plaintiff lodged a claim for almost $25,000 said to be owing under the contract.

The trial judge held that the contract was 'illegal as formed' and unenforceable; but for the illegality the respondent would have succeeded. In the Supreme Court of the Northern Territory Kearney J upheld an appeal on the issue of illegality, finding the contract was not 'illegal as formed' and that nothing in the relevant Act rendered the contract void or unenforceable. On appeal to the Court of Appeal of the Northern Territory the majority agreed with Kearney J. An appeal was made to the High Court.]

Dawson and Toohey JJ [at 219]: ... the Act did not forbid the drilling of a bore. Section 56 forbids an owner, occupier or lessee of land to cause, suffer or permit a bore to be drilled on the land without a permit. ... The obligation to obtain a permit was cast upon the owner, not the driller, ...

Secondly, the drilling contract was not one which the statute expressly or impliedly prohibited. A permit was required if the drilling was not to constitute an offence on the part of the owner, but a contract for the drilling of bores was plainly envisaged by the Act.

Nor was the contract made in order to effect a purpose which the Act rendered unlawful. It was not made for the purpose of causing an offence to be committed ... it was not made for the purpose of causing, suffering or permitting the unauthorised drilling of a bore. ...

Thus, if the contract were to be affected by illegality it could only be because ... although lawful according to its own terms, it might be performed in a manner which the Act prohibited. That category, however, does not stand for the proposition that a contract, which is itself legal, will be unenforceable if something illegal is done in the course of its performance. The cases provide no authority for <220> such a proposition. ...

In this case, the performance of the drilling contract resulted in the commission of an offence by the owner, but the manner of performance by the driller did not turn it into a contract which was forbidden by the Act. ... the Act contemplated drilling by a licensed driller. In other words, s 56 of the Act was intended to penalise conduct—in this case the conduct of the owner in failing to obtain a permit—and not to prohibit contracts.

... It has sometimes been said that a contract is illegal if its performance involves breach of a statute passed for the protection of the public but, stated in that way, the proposition is too broad. The purpose of the statute may be served by the imposition of a penalty, notwithstanding that it is for the protection of the public. ... <221>

[His Honour held that in this case the purpose of the statute was served by the legislative provisions and it was not necessary for the court to refuse performance of the contract in this case.]

McHugh and Gummow JJ [at 227]: ... The question [is] whether, as a matter of public policy, the court should decline to enforce the contract because of its association with the illegal activity of the owner in, if not causing, then at least suffering or permitting the construction and drilling of bores, ... without the grant to the owner of permits .... The refusal of the courts in such a case to regard the contract as enforceable stems not from express or implied legislative prohibition but from the policy of the law, commonly called public policy. Regard is to be had primarily to the scope and purpose of the statute to consider whether the legislative purpose will be fulfilled without regarding the contract as void and unenforceable.

Section 56 prescribes a penalty. ... Here, the imposition of an additional sanction, namely inability of the driller to recover moneys otherwise owing by the owner, would be an inappropriate adjunct to the scheme for which the Act provides. ...

Kirby J [at 249]: It would be absurd if a trivial breach of a statutory provision constituting illegality, connected in some way with a contract or contracting parties, could be held to justify the total withdrawal of the facilities of the courts. It would be doubly absurd if the courts closed their doors to a party seeking to enforce its contractual rights without having regard to the degree of that party's transgression, the deliberateness or otherwise of its breach of the law and its state of mind generally relevant to the illegality. ... It is another to invoke a broad rule of so-called 'public policy' which slams the doors of the court in the face of a person whose illegality may be minor, technical, innocent, lacking in seriousness and wholly incidental or peripheral to a contract which that person is seeking to enforce. ...

Appeal dismissed

[footnotes omitted]

d Contracts rendered void by statute

In addition to statutes that render certain contracts or contractual performance illegal, legislation may declare certain contracts or contractual provisions void. In these cases the legislative intent is clear and the courts will not enforce the affected contracts or contractual provisions. The *Australian Consumer Law (ACL)* provides examples of contractual provisions which will be void and consequently of no effect.

Australian Consumer Law

Section 64(1). Any term of a contact (including a term that is not set out in the contract but is incorporated in the contract by another term of the contract) is void to the extent that the term purports to exclude, restrict or modify, or has the effect of excluding, restricting or modifying:
(a) the application of all or any of the provisions of this Division;
…

INTERNATIONAL PERSPECTIVES

Illegal contracts are not enforceable under either the Indian or Chinese contract laws.

Indian Contract Act, 1872

Illegality arises both as an issue of contractual formation and as a means by which a contract may be declared void. Statutory illegality will generally prevent an agreement being classified as an enforceable contract.

Section 10. What agreements are contracts

All agreements are contracts if they are made by the free consent of parties competent to contract, for a lawful consideration and with a lawful object, and are not hereby expressly declared to be void. Nothing herein contained shall affect any law in force in India, and not hereby expressly repealed, by which any contract is required to be made in writing or in the presence of witnesses, or any law relating to the registration of documents.

Section 23. What consideration and objects are lawful, and what not

The consideration or object of an agreement is lawful, unless -

- it is forbidden by law; or
- is of such nature that, if permitted it would defeat the provisions of any law; or
- is fraudulent; or
- involves or implies, injury to the person or property of another; or
- the Court regards it as immoral, or opposed to public policy.

In each of these cases, the consideration or object of an agreement is said to be unlawful. Every agreement of which the object or consideration is unlawful is void.

In addition, illegality may operate to render an otherwise lawful contract void. This possibility is discussed further at p 525, below.

Contract Law of the People's Republic of China, 1999

In China statutory illegality will render a contract invalid. Where the contract itself contravenes legislation or where the contract has been made for an illegal purpose.

More generally, the *Contract Law of the People's Republic of China* requires parties, when forming or performing their contract, to abide by laws and regulations and consider the public interest. A contract failing to do this may not be protected—or enforced—by the law.

Article 52. Invalidating Circumstances

A contract is invalid in any of the following circumstances:
...
(iii) The parties intended to conceal an illegal purpose under the guise of a legitimate transaction;
...
(v) The contract violates a mandatory provision of any law or administrative regulation.

Article 7. Legality

In concluding or performing a contract, the parties shall abide by the relevant laws and administrative regulations, as well as observe social ethics, and may not disrupt social and economic order or harm the public interests.

Article 8. Binding Effect; Legal Protection

A lawfully formed contract is legally binding on the parties. The parties shall perform their respective obligations in accordance with the contract, and neither party may arbitrarily amend or terminate the contract.

A lawfully formed contract is protected by law.

3 Common law illegality and contracts contrary to public policy

In addition to contracts rendered illegal by statute or regulation, contracts may be illegal or immoral at common law or unenforceable because they are contrary to public policy. This stems from the principle expressed in the maxim *ex turpi causa non oritor actio*; no action arises from a dishonourable cause. The potential scope and uncertainty surrounding public policy in particular has attracted some concern and criticism and prompted Justice Mason to remark:

> ... The difficulties in ascertaining the existence and strength of an identifiable public interest to which the courts should give effect by refusing to enforce a contract are so formidable as to require that they 'should use extreme reserve in holding such a contract to be void as against public policy, and only do so when the contract is incontestably and on any view inimical to the public interest', ...[8]

Contracts that are rendered void as illegal or immoral at common law or which are contrary to public policy have traditionally fallen into the following categories:

- contracts to commit a legal wrong
- contracts prejudicial to the administration of justice
- contracts tending to promote corruption in public life
- contracts prejudicial to public safety or foreign relations
- contracts to defraud the revenue
- contracts that prejudice the status of marriage
- contracts that promote sexual immorality
- contracts in restraint of trade.

a Contracts to commit a legal wrong

A contract between parties to commit a crime or civil wrong will be illegal at common law. For example, a contract in which A engages B to murder her husband, C, will be void for illegality and, should A subsequently refuse to pay B for committing the crime, the courts will not enforce the contract against A. Contracts to commit a crime of this nature (as distinct from the commission of the crime itself) now also constitute statutory illegality in most jurisdictions.[9] This issue arose in the following case.

Holman v Johnson

[1775–1802] All ER Rep 98, (1775) 1 Cowp 341, Court of King's Bench

[The plaintiff sold tea in Dunkirk (France) to the defendant and delivered it at Dunkirk. These goods were prohibited in England and the plaintiff knew that the defendant intended to smuggle them into England for sale. The plaintiff sought to recover money owed under the contract of sale and the defendant claimed that the contract was unenforceable for illegality.]

Lord Mansfield CJ [at 99]: The objection that a contract is immoral or illegal as between plaintiff and defendant ... is founded in general principles of policy ...

---

8   *A v Hayden* (1984) 156 CLR 532 at 559.
9   For example, the *Crimes Act 1958* (Vic) renders illegal any conspiracy to commit an offence: s 321.

The principle of public policy is this: *Ex dolo malo non oritur actio*. No court will lend its aid to a man who founds his cause of action on an immoral or an illegal act. ...

The question, therefore, is whether, in this case, the plaintiff's demand is founded on the ground of any immoral act or contract, or on the ground of his being guilty of anything which is prohibited by a positive law of this country. An immoral contract it certainly is not; ... This is an action brought merely for goods sold and delivered at Dunkirk. Where then, or in what respect, is the plaintiff guilty of any crime? Is there any law of England transgressed by a person making a complete sale of a parcel of goods at Dunkirk and giving credit for them? The contract is complete, and nothing is left to be done. The seller, indeed, knows what the buyer is going to do with the goods, but has no concern in the transaction itself. ... To what a dangerous extent would this go if it were to be held a crime. If contraband clothes are bought in France and brought home hither or if glass bought abroad which ought to pay a great duty is run into England, shall the French tailor or the glass-manufacturer stand to the risk or loss attending their being run into England? Clearly not. Debt follows the person and may be recovered in England, ... Therefore, I am clearly of opinion that the vendors of <100> these goods are not guilty of any offence, nor have they transgressed against the provisions of any Act of Parliament.

... In England, tea, which has not paid duty, is prohibited, and if sold there the contract is null and void. But if sold and delivered at a place where it is not prohibited, as at Dunkirk, and an action is brought for the price of it in England, the buyer shall be condemned to pay the price; because the original contract was good and valid. ... But if the goods sold were to be delivered in England where they are prohibited the contract is void, and the buyer shall not be liable in an action for the price, because it would be an inconvenience and prejudice to the state if such an action could be maintained.

... on the facts of the case, from the first to the last, he clearly has offended against no law of England. ...

[Aston, Willes and Ashurst JJ concurred.]

b   Contracts prejudicial to the administration of justice

Contracts which are prejudicial to the administration of justice are illegal and void at common law. For example, an agreement not to give evidence to police about a civil wrongdoing, such as corporate fraud, would be illegal. A contract might be prejudicial to the administration of justice either because its purpose is to obstruct the administration of justice or because, while no such intent existed at the time of contracting, enforcement of the contract would have the effect of obstructing the administration of justice. The following cases discuss the public policy issues concerning the effective administration of justice and the response of the common law courts.

A v Hayden

(1984) 156 CLR 532, High Court of Australia

[The plaintiffs took part in a training exercise devised by the Australian Secret Intelligence Service (ASIS) which involved the mock rescue of a hostage from a hotel room. It was alleged that they had performed illegal acts in carrying out the exercise and the Victorian Chief Commissioner of Police sought to obtain the identities of the plaintiffs for purposes of criminal investigation. The plaintiffs sought injunctions to prevent this disclosure, claiming, in part, that they each had a contract with the Commonwealth which provided that the Commonwealth would keep their identity confidential. The plaintiffs claimed that they 'had an honest belief that ASIS, before instructing and authorizing them to do any act or thing, would obtain any authority or consent necessary to make such act or thing lawful'.[10] In Justice Mason's words:

> There is an air of unreality about this stated case. It has the appearance of a law school moot based on an episode taken from the adventures of Maxwell Smart. It features the Commonwealth in a new and somewhat unattractive role—recruiting officers to the service of ASIS, its counter-espionage organization, on the footing that their names will be kept secret for reasons of national and personal security, instructing them through superior officers to participate in a bizarre training exercise ... which involved risks of disturbing the peace and of the commission of criminal offences, yet arguing that it is entitled to disclose their names to the Chief Commissioner of Police for Victoria so that he may conduct investigations with a view to enforcing the criminal law against them, the Commonwealth itself being immune from enforcement of the law notwithstanding that through senior officers it initiated the training exercise.[11]]

Gibbs CJ [at 542]: No doubt this absolute contractual obligation [to keep the identities confidential], like any other, would be subject to, and overridden by, the duty of the officers of the Commonwealth to comply with the law of the land ...

<543> [One reason] advanced in support of the argument that the contractual term is unenforceable is that the term has a tendency to obstruct the administration of justice and is therefore contrary to public policy. There is no doubt that a contract which tends to pervert or obstruct the course of justice is against public policy. ... looking at the matter at the time when the contract was made, no criminal act might ever be committed or contemplated by <544> the plaintiffs. The contracts were entered into by the Commonwealth with persons who, we were told, were actuated by high motives and who were joining a service whose functions are important to society and which could not properly operate unless the identity of its agents was kept secret. An agreement to keep the identity of such persons secret is not contrary to public policy, unless, of course, its actual purpose was to shield one of the parties

---

10   Gibbs CJ at 541.
11   Mason J at 550.

from liability for a breach of the law. Where a contract is not unlawful on its face and is capable of performance without any violation of the law, it will be enforceable unless it is proved that one or both of the parties intended to perform it in an illegal manner or to effect an illegal purpose ... The mere possibility that the contract in the present case might, if performed, obstruct the course of justice was not enough to render it invalid. There is no proof that the parties intended the contract to have any effect on the administration of justice. The contractual term was a valid one. ...

The fact that the contractual term is not in itself invalid is not however the end of the matter. The court will refuse to exercise its discretion in favour of granting equitable relief, such as an <545> injunction, to enforce an obligation of confidentiality when the consequence would be to prevent the disclosure of criminality which in all the circumstances it would be in the public interest to reveal. ...

The public interest does not, in every case, require the <546> disclosure of the fact that a criminal offence, however trivial, has been committed. And the administration of justice, although a fundamental public interest, is not an exclusive public interest: ...

It is clear that a person who owes a duty to maintain confidentiality will not be allowed to escape from his obligation simply because he alleges that crimes have been committed and that it is in the public interest that he should disclose information relating to them. He bears the burden of establishing the facts upon which he relies to relieve him of the obligation. ...

The Commonwealth owes an individual obligation of confidentiality to each plaintiff with whom it has contracted. ... The facts stated in the cases do not reveal any ground for belief that any particular plaintiff committed any offence. [His Honour considered that there was insufficient evidence to make a determination on whether the plaintiffs could be reasonably suspected of having committed a breach of the criminal law and so deferred judgment on this issue.]

Mason J [at 553]: ... That there is a powerful public interest in the enforcement of the criminal law as an important element in the administration of justice does not admit of debate. ... <554> ... the perversion of justice may take place in many ways. One example was concealment or procuring the concealment of a felony amounting to the offence of misprision. Another example is an agreement not to prosecute or to stifle a prosecution which at common law is void or unenforceable: .... Yet another example is an agreement between a prosecutor and persons indicted that a witness should not give evidence at a trial for reward. ... The final example is an agreement to compromise legal proceedings for an offence of a public nature which is illegal: ... <555>

... the effective enforcement of the criminal law and the administration of justice, which are central elements in a well ordered democratic society, depend for their efficacy on the unrestricted freedom of each and every citizen to assist and co-operate with the authorities in the investigation and prosecution of criminal offences. There is therefore a powerful public interest in promoting and preserving the citizen's freedom to assist and co-operate with the authorities in the investigation and prosecution of crime. ... <556>

It is obvious that the public interest in the enforcement of the criminal law as an element in the administration of justice would be seriously impaired if the citizen were at liberty to assume in return for a benefit an obligation not to disclose information concerning the commission of a criminal offence. ... <557–559>

... The question which then arises is whether a refusal to disclose the information requested to the Chief Commissioner will have a tendency to interfere with the enforcement of the criminal law. ... Because a principle based on public policy is necessarily a reflection of judicial assessment of public interest, it generally follows that any <560> opposing public interest must be identified and weighed in the balance. ... It may be that the public interest in the administration of justice and the enforcement of the criminal law is so strong that it cannot be outweighed by any countervailing public interest, ... Be this as it may, security presents a particular problem. That there is a public interest in national and international security is beyond question. But in many situations it may be difficult or impossible for a court to satisfy itself that there is a threat or prejudice to security. This is one such case. ...

[In this case] I am unable to hold that there is a countervailing public interest which <561> overcomes or neutralizes the traditional public policy supporting the common law principle.

Deane J [at 595]: ... the defendants' argument based on public policy must prevail. The relevant proposition of law was shortly stated at the commencement of this judgment. It is that the courts of this country will not lend their aid to enforce a promise not to disclose information where the circumstances are such that enforcement or insistence upon observance of the promise would obstruct the due administration of the criminal law of Australia, whether Commonwealth or State. The rationale of that proposition is that, apart from the exceptional case (such as that of a professional legal adviser) where the overall administration of the law itself requires that confidentiality be maintained, it would be contrary to public policy for the courts to enforce a right on the part of one person to insist that another fail or refuse to disclose relevant information to assist those entrusted with the ordinary administration of the criminal law in the proper investigation and prosecution of criminal activity: ... <598>

... In some cases, of course, a balancing process may be involved .... The obvious example is where the promise to maintain confidentiality is that of a professional legal adviser and relates to communications which are properly the subject of legal professional privilege: ...

[Wilson and Dawson JJ delivered a separate judgment holding that the confidentiality agreement could not be enforced for public policy reasons.]

Injunctions refused

Agreements to oust the ordinary jurisdiction of the courts are also considered contrary to public policy; however, agreements to refer matters to arbitration in preference to the courts will generally[12] not be considered contrary to public policy and will be enforceable.[13]

c Contracts tending to promote corruption in public life

Contracts which tend to promote corruption among public figures are illegal at common law and often will also be prohibited by statute. For example, an agreement with a member of parliament to vote a particular way on a proposed bill, or an agreement to pay a sum of money to a police officer in exchange for the officer not issuing a traffic infringement notice would be void and illegal at common law on public policy grounds. This issue arose for consideration in the following case.

Wilkinson v Osborne
(1915) 21 CLR 89, High Court of Australia

[The respondents were members of the NSW State Parliament. The appellant was acting as agent for a land-owner who was negotiating for the sale of land to the Crown. The land-owner was threatening to withdraw his offer which would have denied the appellant his commission. In an attempt to ensure the sale went ahead the appellant engaged the respondents with the promise of a share of his commission, to try to speed through the deal. The completion of the deal was dependent on the approval of the House of which they were members. The respondents brought action against the appellant in respect of his non-payment of the promised commission. They succeeded in the Supreme Court of New South Wales. Wilkinson appealed to the High Court.]

Griffith CJ [at 93]: Put baldly, the contract was one by which the respondents, members of the Legislative Assembly, agreed for a pecuniary consideration to put pressure upon the Government, of which they were supporters, to agree to expend the public funds in the purchase of the land of private persons, the completion of the purchase and earning of the reward being contingent upon the approval of the House of which they were members, so that the completion was or might be dependent on their votes. There cannot be a plainer case of a man attempting to serve two masters. They owed to their employer, the appellant, the duty to press forward the contract regardless of the interests of the public, and as members of the <94> Legislature it was their duty to consider the matter impartially before voting upon it.

It would be deplorable that any doubt should be allowed to exist as to whether such a bargain is tolerated by the civil—I say nothing of the criminal—law.

… The law cannot supervise the conduct of members of Parliament as to the pressure they may bring to bear on Ministers, but if they sell the pressure the bargain is, in my opinion, void as against public policy. …

[Justices Isaacs and Duffy agreed that the appeal should be allowed.]

Appeal allowed

[footnotes omitted]

---

12 There are some statutory restrictions on this right.
13 *Scott v Avery* (1856) 5 HLC 811, per Lord Cranwroth.

d Contracts prejudicial to public safety or foreign relations

Contracts considered prejudicial to public safety or foreign relations will be illegal and unenforceable. For example, an agreement to sell weaponry to the army of an enemy of the state in a time of war will be illegal at common law.

e Contracts to defraud the Revenue

Contracts to defraud the Revenue are contrary to public policy and consequently considered illegal and unenforceable at common law. A contract designed to evade tax obligations will fall into this category in addition to possibly contravening taxation legislation.[14]

f Contracts that prejudice the status of marriage

Contracts prejudicial to the status of marriage have long been considered contrary to public policy and consequently void at common law. These agreements fall into three broad categories:

- contracts to restrain marriage
- contracts to encourage separation
- marriage brokerage contracts.

Contracts to restrain marriage

Any attempt to restrain marriage generally or in particular circumstances will be void. For example, a promise by Peter to pay Joe $1,000 on the condition that Joe promise never to marry his daughter is prejudicial to the status of marriage and unenforceable. This issue arose in the following case.

Lowe v Peers

[1558–1774] All ER 364; (1768) 4 Burr 2225, Court of King's Bench

[After a long courtship the defendant voluntarily entered into a deed with the plaintiff in the following terms:

> I do hereby promise Mrs Catherine Lowe that I will not marry with any person besides herself: if I do, I agree to pay the said Catherine Lowe 1,000 pounds within three months next after I shall marry anybody else.

Several years later the defendant married another woman but did not pay the plaintiff the £1000 agreed. The plaintiff brought an action for the payment.]

Lord Mansfield CJ [at 366]: [It] is objected that this is an engagement in restraint of marriage. ... <367> ... These engagements are liable to many mischiefs, to many dangerous consequences. When persons of different sexes, attached to

---

14 See *Holdcroft v Market Garden Produce Pty Ltd* [2001] 2 Qd R 381.

each other, and thus contracting to marry each other, do not marry immediately, there is always some reason or other against it, as disapprobation of friends and relations, inequality of circumstances, or the like. Both sides ought to continue free. Otherwise such contracts may be greatly abused, as by putting women's virtue in danger by too much confidence in men, or by young men living with women without being married. Therefore, these contracts are not to be extended by implication. Here is not the least ground to say that this man has engaged to marry this woman. ... There is a great difference between promising to marry a particular person and promising not to marry anyone else. ... This is only a restraint upon him against marrying anyone else besides the plaintiff. It is not a reciprocal engagement to marry each other or anything like it. ... this was such a contract as ought not to be carried into execution. ...

Yates J [at 367]: This agreement is in restraint of marriage. It is not a covenant to marry the plaintiff, but is one not to marry anyone else, and yet she was under no obligation to marry him. So that it restrained him from marrying at all if she had chosen not <368> to permit him to marry her. ... This covenant is illegal, and will support no action, and, therefore, the plaintiff ought to recover nothing upon it.

Claim denied

In the past the courts have made a distinction between contracts which restrain a first marriage, as in *Lowe v Peers*, and those that restrain a second marriage; the first was considered immoral and the second was not.[15] It is unlikely this distinction would survive today. It is suggested that were this issue to arise in the courts today there would be no valid moral grounds for distinguishing between first and subsequent marriages.

Contracts to encourage separation

Contracts which encourage separation from a spouse will also be considered immoral and illegal.

Example

John, infatuated with Sally, promises to pay Sally $100,000 if Sally leaves her husband, Bill. Sally subsequently leaves Bill but John refuses to give her the promised money. Sally seeks to enforce the contract against Bill. It is likely the contract will be considered illegal as prejudicial to the status of marriage and the court would not lend aid to its enforcement.

This issue arose in the following case.

---

15   Lord Mansfield CJ and Justice Aston make this observation in *Lowe v Peers* [1558–1774] All ER 364; (1768) 4 Burr 2225.

Andrews v Parker

(1973) Qd R 93, Supreme Court of Queensland

[The plaintiff met the defendant at their workplace. They started meeting for coffee and subsequently the plaintiff became aware that the defendant was married. The defendant claimed to be having marital problems and the pair started to see more of each other until eventually the defendant left her husband and moved into the plaintiff's home.

The pair began living as a de facto couple and the plaintiff, who the judge referred to as 'simple-minded',[16] gave the defendant all his income. Shortly thereafter the defendant began to ask the plaintiff what he was going to do about the house, making clear that she felt that she had no security. The plaintiff offered to leave his house to her in his will but she would not agree, claiming his son would challenge the will and toss her out. He then offered to make her a joint owner of the home which she also refused. Finally the defendant agreed to the plaintiff's offer to transfer the home to her on three conditions, including that if she returned to her husband she would transfer the home back to him.

During this time the defendant had started seeing her husband again and, soon after the transfer took place, she started seeing her husband more frequently and openly. The plaintiff asked her what she planned to do about the house, urging her to do the 'decent' thing and return it to him. To this suggestion the defendant replied: 'I'm not decent. I'm cunning …'

Within three months of the transfer the defendant told the plaintiff that her husband was coming to live at the house and asked him when he would leave. The plaintiff subsequently left the home and the defendant told him that he was not the first man she'd taken for everything and probably would not be the last.

The plaintiff brought this action to recover the home and the defendant claimed that the 'agreement' to transfer back the property was for an immoral consideration and therefore unenforceable.]

Stable J: [After setting out the facts his Honour first observed that there was no arrangement that the defendant could not go back to her husband, just that if she did the plaintiff wanted the house back and continued (at 100)]: The picture which clearly emerges is that of a ruthless, cunning woman who came to realise that in the plaintiff she had found a man who would literally be as clay in the hands of a potter. They were not by any means evenly matched … [after the plaintiff left the defendant] had no hesitation in virtually telling him that he had been the victim of a scheme to which Delilah herself would have given an approving nod. …

… defendant's counsel said that once <101> the plaintiff made it plain that he was not contemplating a brother and sister relationship [with the defendant] the maxim *ex turpi causa non oritur actio*— an action does not arise from a base cause— applied to defeat his claim. He argued that on the plaintiff's evidence he induced

---

16   At p 99.

the woman to remain apart from her husband upon penalty of having to re-transfer the property. Upon the facts as I see them this second argument is not valid. ... the case smells of a scheme to get the plaintiff's home. ... the main argument revolved around the matter of immoral consideration ...

Lord Wright said in *Fender v St John Mildmay* [1938] ...

> 'The law will not enforce an immoral promise, such as a promise between a man and a woman to live together without being married, or to pay a sum of money or give some other consideration in return for immoral association.'

... The original agreement was not one to bring about a state of extramarital cohabitation, for that state existed already. And the agreement provided for the return of his property to the plaintiff when and if the defendant returned to the state of lawful cohabitation. ... The effect of the agreement in the present case was not to bring about an immoral association, but to provide for what was to happen upon its ending. ...

<102> ... are the actions of people today to be judged in the light of the standards of last century? ... what was then by community standards sexual immorality appear to have been decided in the days when for the sake of decency the legs of tables wore drapes, and women (if they simply had to do it) never referred to men's legs as such, but called them their 'understandings'. ... What I am asked literally to apply is the common law which still says that an immoral contract will not be enforced. But I am asked also to apply the standards of the days when the living common law was first laid down. I am not, in my view, to be taken as changing the law if I do not accept that immoral today means precisely what it did in [1866]. I am, I believe, entitled to look at the word under modern social standards. ...

<103> ... in declaring the common law for Australia the court's task is to express what is the law on the subject *as appropriate to current times in Australia* [and] this will not necessarily be identical with the common law of England ... what is obscene like what is in-<104>-decent must be judged according to the current standards of the community. Surely, what is immoral must be judged by the current standards of morality of the community. What was apparently regarded with pious horror when the cases where decided would, I observe, today hardly draw a raised eyebrow or a gentle 'tut-tut'. It is notorious that there are many people living as husband and wife without benefit of clergy [so much so that legislation provides for social service benefits and children born out of wedlock have the same access to family maintenance] ... George Bernard Shaw's Eliza Doolittle (*circa* 1912) thought the suggestion that she have a bath in private with her clothes off was indecent, so she hung a towel over the bathroom mirror. One wonders what she would have thought and said to a suggestion that she wear in public one of today's minuscule and socially accepted bikinis, held miraculously in place apparently with the aid of providence, and, possibly, glue.

The point ... is that notoriously the social judgements of today upon matters of 'immorality' are as different from those of last century as is the bikini from a bustle. So, on this aspect, I hold that if the agreement between the parties was based on an immoral consideration (which I have doubted as a matter of interpretation) then the immorality was not such according to modern standards as to deprive the plaintiff the right to enforce it.

[His Honour went on to note that even were the contract to be considered immoral the parties were not *in pari delicto*—they were not at equal fault. The plaintiff was 'one of those unfortunate people who is over-anxious to please and who hate saying 'No' [who was] caught by a cunning and ruthless woman'.[17] His Honour continued (at 105)]: where the parties to an illegal contract, or one against public policy, are not *in pari delicto*, and public policy is considered as advanced by allowing either, or at least the more excusable of the two to sue for relief against the transaction, relief is given to him. ...

[107] ... ... if the plaintiff's hands are by the standards of today a little soiled the defendant's hands are by comparison filthy. It surely cannot be in accord with the public interest or public policy that she should retain property which she obtained through a deceitful course of conduct designed to get a home for her husband. ...

Claim denied

Legislation in Australia does now permit certain forms of pre-nuptial agreements. Where specifically permitted by statute these agreements will be enforceable at common law.

Marriage brokerage contracts

Marriage brokerage contracts are considered immoral and illegal at common law. This issue arose for consideration in the following case.

Hermann v Charlesworth

[1905] 2 KB 123, English Court of Appeal

[The defendant was a marriage advertising agent. The plaintiff wished to get married and responded to an advertisement placed by the defendant. The defendant agreed to assist the plaintiff in getting married by introducing her to gentlemen in return for the plaintiff agreeing to pay the defendant certain fees, including an advanced 'special client's fee' which was refundable if no engagement or marriage took place within four months. The plaintiff was introduced to various gentlemen but after four months changed her mind and sought her money back.

The plaintiff succeeded in the county court on the basis that this was a 'marriage brokerage contract' and the law would not assist in its enforcement. The defendant successfully appealed to the Divisional Court which held that it was not a marriage brokerage contract but simply a contract to procure introductions with a view to marriage. The plaintiff then appealed to the Court of Appeal.]

---

17   At p 105.

Collins MR [at 129]: I am unable to find any ground for [distinguishing between a contract to 'procure marriage with one particular person' and a contract to make introductions with a view to marriage.] It seems to me that the principle is as much violated in the class of cases to which the present one belongs as in cases where the contract relates to bringing about a marriage with a particular individual. The principle is clearly stated in *Cole v Gibson*, where Lord Hardwicke in his judgment said: 'To be sure, this Court has been extremely jealous of any contract of this kind made with a guardian or servant, especially with a servant, in respect of the marriage of persons over whom they have an influence; (and has been justly so; nothing tending more to introduce improper matches) and by rules established, not regarding whether the match is proper or no, if brought about by a marriage-brocage contract, sets it aside; not for the sake of the particular instance or the person, but of the public, and that marriages may be on a proper foundation: therefore though a proper match, ... yet for the sake of the mischief <130> that would be introduced, and to prevent that influence which servants more especially would gain over young ladies, the Court sets it aside: and if that was the nature of the contract, I do not know, that subsequent confirmations have been permitted to stand in the way of the relief sought.' ... I can see no distinction in this respect between a contract relating to one particular person and a contract that relates to a whole class. Many elements have no doubt entered into the judgments in different cases, but at the root of the question of the illegality of a marriage brokage contract is the introduction of the consideration of a money payment into that which should be free from any such taint. ... <131> ... In my opinion, both on principle and authority, the transaction in this case comes within the rule which invalidates marriage brokage contracts.

[Mathew LJ agreed with Collins MR and Cozens-Handy LJ also agreed that the contract was a marriage brokerage contract and therefore illegal.]

Appeal allowed

Marriage brokerage contracts have not arisen for consideration in recent years and it is uncertain how the courts would treat them today. It is likely that contracts which provide for payment upon the occurrence of marriage will still be held to be immoral and unenforceable. However, contracts with dating agencies will almost certainly be considered acceptable in today's society, at least where no additional payment is contingent upon a marriage or engagement.

g   Contracts that promote sexual immorality

Contracts promoting sexual immorality are generally considered to be immoral and void. The type of conduct that constitutes sexual immorality today is likely to be vastly different from that of a century ago and each case will turn on its peculiar facts as assessed against current community standards.[18] The following case discusses sexual immorality in the context of unlawful prostitution.

---

18   See further *Andrews v Parker* (1973) Qd R 93 at 102–103, extracted above.

Pearce v Brooks

[1861–73] All ER Rep 102; [1866] LR 1 Ex 213, Court of Exchequer (UK)

[The plaintiffs, coach builders, entered into a contract to let one of their coaches to the defendant, a prostitute, with the knowledge that she intended to use the coach for purposes associated with prostitution. The plaintiff sued the defendant for certain payments said to be due under the contract.]

Pollock CB [at 103]: I take the rule to be that any person who contributes to the performance of an illegal act, knowing that the subject-matter is to be so applied, cannot recover the price of such subject-matter, and that the old notion, if any such ever existed, which I do not wish to affirm, that the price must be intended to be paid out of the profits of the illegality, has ceased to be part of the law, if ever it was so. I do not think that for this purpose we should make any distinction between an illegal and an immoral act. The rule now is, *ex turpi causa non oritur actio*, and whether such turpitude be an immorality or an illegality, the effect is the same; no cause of action can arise out of one or the other. ... If, therefore, this article was furnished for the purpose of a display favourable to the defendant's immoral vocation, it seems to me no cause of action can arise. I cannot agree in thinking it necessary that these matters should be proved with an accuracy repugnant to decency. In certain criminal matters there is a necessity for absolute proof, but there is no such necessity for the purposes of civil actions. If there was enough evidence of the defendant's profession and of the plaintiffs' knowledge <104> of its nature from which the jury could infer that the article was to the plaintiffs' knowledge intended to facilitate the exercise of her vocation, that is enough.

[Martin, Pigott and Bramwell, BB agreed with Pollock CB.]

Appeal dismissed

h Contracts in restraint of trade

Contracts that restrict the freedom of a person to pursue their trade or profession are illegal at common law if the restraint imposed is unreasonable. Restraints will generally be considered unreasonable if they do more than is necessary to protect the legitimate interests of the party imposing the restraint or if they are contrary to the public interest. Restrictive contracts, such as these, may also risk contravening the competition law provisions in Part IV of the *Trade Practices Act 1974* (Cth) or the *Restraints of Trade Act 1976* (NSW).

Nordenfelt v The Maxim Nordenfelt Guns and Ammunition Company Ltd

[1894] AC 535, House of Lords

[The appellant was a manufacturer of guns and ammunitions. He transferred his business to the respondents with the covenant that he would not, for a period of twenty-five years, engage in the trade or business of gun and ammunition manufacture or compete in any other way with the respondents.

The appellant subsequently entered into an agreement with other manufacturers of guns and ammunition. The respondents brought an action seeking to enforce the covenant and succeeded in the Court of Appeal. An appeal was brought before the House of Lords, the appellant claiming the agreement was unenforceable on public policy grounds.]

Lord Macnaghten [at 564]: In the age of Queen Elizabeth all restraints of trade, whatever they were, general or partial, were thought to be contrary to public policy, and therefore void ... In time, however, it was found that a rule so rigid and far-reaching must seriously interfere with transactions of every-day occurrence. Traders could hardly venture to let their shops out of their own hands; the purchaser of a business was at the mercy of the seller; every apprentice was a possible rival. So the rule was relaxed. It was relaxed as far as the exigencies of trade for the time being required, gradually and not without difficulty, until it came to be recognised that all partial restraints might be good, though it was thought that general restraints, that is, restraints of general application extending throughout the kingdom, must be bad. Why was the relaxation supposed to be thus limited? Simply because nobody imagined in those days that a general restraint could be reasonable, not because there was any inherent or essential distinction between the two cases. ...

The true view at the present time I think, is this: The public have an interest in every person's carrying on his trade freely: so has the individual. All interference with individual liberty of action in trading, and all restraints of trade of themselves, if there is nothing more, are contrary to public policy, and therefore void. That is the general rule. But there are exceptions: restraints of trade and interference with individual liberty of action may be justified by the special circumstances of a particular case. It is a sufficient justification, and indeed it is the only justification, if the restriction is reasonable—reasonable, that is, in reference to the interests of the parties concerned and reasonable in reference to the interests of the public, so framed and so guarded as to afford adequate protection to the party in whose favour it is imposed, while at the same time it is in no way injurious to the public. ...

When the question is how far interference with the liberty of an individual in a particular trade offends against the interest of the public, there is not much difficulty in measuring the offence and coming to a judgment on the question. The difficulty is much greater when the question of public policy is considered at large and without direct reference to the interests of the individual under restraint. It is a principle of law and of public policy that trading should be encouraged and that trade should be free; but a fetter is placed on trade and trading is discouraged if a man who has built up a valuable business is not to be permitted to dispose of the fruits of his labours to the best advantage. ... <565–572>

... in the present case it was hardly disputed that the restraint was reasonable, having regard to the interests of the parties at the time when the transaction was entered into. It <573> enabled Mr Nordenfelt to obtain the full value of what he had to sell; without it the purchasers could not have been protected in the possession of what they wished to buy. Was it reasonable in the interests of the public? It can hardly be injurious to the public, that is, the British public, to prevent a person from carrying on a trade in weapons of war abroad. But apart from that special feature in the present case, how can the public be injured by the transfer of a business from one hand to another? If a business is profitable there will be no lack of persons ready to carry it on. In this particular case the purchasers brought in fresh capital, and had at least the opportunity of retaining Mr Nordenfelt's services. But then it was said there is another way in which the public may be injured. Mr Nordenfelt has 'committed industrial suicide,' and as he can no longer earn his living at the trade which he has made peculiarly his own, he may be brought to want and become a burden to the public. My Lords, this seems to me to be very far-fetched. Mr Nordenfelt received over £200,000 for what he sold. He may have got rid of the money. I do not know how that is. But even so, I would answer the argument in the words of Tindal CJ: 'If the contract is a reasonable one at the time it is entered into we are not bound to look out for improbable and extravagant contingencies in order to make it void': ….

… I think the only true test in all cases, whether of partial or general restraint, is the test proposed by Tindal CJ: What is a reasonable restraint with reference to the particular case? I think that the restraint in the present case is reasonable in every point of view, and therefore I agree that the appeal should be dismissed.

[Lord Chancellor Herschell, Lord Watson, Lord Morris and Lord Ashbourne all delivered separate judgments in which they agreed that the appeal should be dismissed.]

Appeal dismissed

[footnotes omitted]

INTERNATIONAL PERSPECTIVES

Both the Indian and Chinese contract laws render unenforceable contracts which are illegal or contrary to public policy. The *Indian Contract Act* also makes specific reference to contracts which are immoral.

Indian Contract Act, 1872

Contracts for which the consideration stipulated involves personal injury or property damage or which are otherwise immoral or contrary to public policy are unlawful and void. This would encompass the same sorts of contracts as are considered illegal, immoral or contrary to public policy at common law in Australia.

Section 23. What consideration and objects are lawful, and what not

The consideration or object of an agreement is lawful, unless [it] involves or implies, injury to the person or property of another; or the Court regards it as immoral, or opposed to public policy.

In each of these cases, the consideration or object of an agreement is said to be unlawful. Every agreement of which the object or consideration is unlawful is void.

Contracts that have been held to have an immoral purpose include contracts related to prostitution or infidelity.[19]

As in Australia agreements in restraint of marriage are void. Contracts which relate to proposed adulterous affairs[20] and marriage brokerage contracts will fall within this category.[21]

Section 26. Agreement in restraint of marriage, void

Every agreement in restraint of the marriage of any person, other than a minor, is void.

Agreements in restraint of trade are, subject to a goodwill exception, void.

Section 27. Agreement in restraint of trade, void

Every agreement by which anyone is restrained from exercising a lawful profession, trade or business of any kind, is to that extent void.

Exception 1: Saving of agreement not to carry on business of which good will is sold—One who sells the goodwill of a business may agree with the buyer to refrain from carrying on a similar business, within specified local limits, so long as the buyer, or any person deriving title to the goodwill from him, carries on a like business therein, provided that such limits appear to the court reasonable, regard being had to the nature of the business.

As is the case in Australia, agreements prejudicial to the administration of justice will be considered void under Indian contract law.

Section 28. Agreements in restraint of legal proceedings, void

Every agreement,
(a) by which any party thereto is restricted absolutely from enforcing his rights under or in respect of any contract, by the usual legal proceedings in the ordinary tribunals, or which limits the time within which he may thus enforce his rights; or
(b) which extinguishes the rights of any party thereto, or discharges any party thereto, from any liability, under or in respect of any contract on the expiry of a specified period so as to restrict any party from enforcing his rights, is void to that extent.

---

19 See *Bani Muncharan v Regina* ILR 32 Bom 581 involving the lease of premises for purposes of prostitution; *Rajendra v Abdul* 39 IC 767 in which money was loaned for the purpose of enabling the other party to visit a brothel; and *Upfull v Wright* [1911] 1 KB 506 involving the lease of premises for the purpose of keeping a mistress.
20 See *Kandaswami v Narayanaswami* 45 MLJ 551.
21 See also *Baivijli v Nansa Nagar* (1885) 10 Bom 152 in which a promise by a woman to leave her husband and marry another for financial reward was held to be immoral and void.

Exception 1: Saving of contract to refer to arbitration dispute that may arise. This section shall not render illegal a contract, by which two or more persons agree that any dispute which may arise between them in respect of any subject or class of subjects shall be referred to arbitration, and that only the amount awarded in such arbitration shall be recoverable in respect of the dispute so referred.

Exception 2: Saving of contract to refer question that have already arisen.—Nor shall this section render illegal any contract in writing, by which two or more persons agree to refer to arbitration any question between them which has already arisen, or affect any provision of any law in force for the time being as to reference to arbitration.

Agreements by way of wager are also considered void in India as contrary to public policy.

Section 30. Agreements by way of wager, void

Agreements by way of wager are void; and no suit shall be brought for recovering anything alleged to be won on any wager, or entrusted to any person to abide by the result of any game or other uncertain event on which any wager is made.

Exception on favour of certain prizes for horse-racing; This section shall not be deemed to render unlawful a subscription or contribution, or agreement to subscribe or contribute, made or entered into for or toward any place, prize or sum of money, of the value or amount of five hundred rupees or upwards, to be awarded to the winner or winners of any horse-race. ...

Contract Law of the People's Republic of China, 1999

In China contracts that are contrary to the public interest are invalid. It is not yet clear what sort of conduct would be considered contrary to the public interest in China, but it is likely that it would encompass much of the same conduct prohibited as common law illegality in Australia, including contracts prejudicial to the administration of justice or tending to promote corruption in public life.

Article 52. Invalidating Circumstances

A contract is invalid in any of the following circumstances:
...
(iv) The contract harms public interests;
...

4 Effect of illegality

The general rule is that contracts affected by statutory or common law illegality or which are deemed contrary to public policy will be unenforceable[22] by either party to the contract. As a consequence, while property can pass under the contract, no party can rely on the contract to obtain a court order for property transfer or payment of moneys due under an illegal contract. This general rule might, at times, lead to harsh consequences far exceeding the gravity of the unlawful conduct in which one or both parties have engaged. As a result, a number of exceptions have developed permitting limited remedies in some cases. In this respect Kirby J observed in *Fitzgerald v FJ Leonhardt Pty Ltd* that:

> ... it should not be assumed that the apparently inflexible operation of the law as to illegality always leaves the party affected without other remedies in a proper case.[23]

a Exceptions to the general rule that the court will not enforce an illegal contract

The circumstances in which a court will enforce an illegal contract were discussed in the following case.

Nelson v Nelson
(1995) 184 CLR 538, High Court of Australia

[The facts were set out above at p 500]

McHugh J [at 612]: ...If courts withhold relief because of an illegal transaction, they necessarily impose a sanction on one of the parties to that transaction, a sanction that will deprive one party of his or her property rights and effectively vest them in another person who will almost always be a willing participant in the illegality. ... such a sanction can only be justified if two conditions are met.

First, the sanction imposed should be proportionate to the seriousness of the illegality involved. It is not in accord with contemporaneous notions of justice that the penalty for breaching a <613> law or frustrating its policy should be disproportionate to the seriousness of the breach. The seriousness of the illegality must be judged by reference to the statute whose terms or policy is contravened. It cannot be assessed in a vacuum. The statute must always be the reference point for determining the seriousness of the illegality; otherwise the courts would embark on an assessment of moral turpitude independently of and potentially in conflict with the assessment made by the legislature.

Second, the imposition of the civil sanction must further the purpose of the statute and must not impose a further sanction for the unlawful conduct if

---

22 The courts often refer to illegal contracts as being 'void' or 'void and unenforceable'. In the majority of cases the true effect (despite language used) is that such agreements are merely unenforceable; they are not completely devoid of legal effect and may, for example, pass property.

23 (1997) 189 CLR 215 at 238–239.

Parliament has indicated that the sanctions imposed by the statute are sufficient to deal with conduct that breaches or evades the operation of the statute and its policies. In most cases, the statute will provide some guidance, express or inferred, as to the policy of the legislature in respect of a transaction that contravenes the statute or its purpose. It is this policy that must guide the courts in determining, consistent with their duty not to condone or encourage breaches of the statute, what the consequences of the illegality will be. Thus, the statute may disclose an intention, explicitly or implicitly, that a transaction contrary to its terms or its policy should be unenforceable. On the other hand, the statute may inferentially disclose an intention that the only sanctions for breach of the statute or its policy are to be those specifically provided for in the legislation.

Accordingly ... courts should not refuse to enforce legal or equitable rights simply because they arose out of or were associated with an unlawful purpose unless: (a) the statute discloses an intention that those rights should be unenforceable in all circumstances; or (b) (i) the sanction of refusing to enforce those rights is not disproportionate to the seriousness of the unlawful conduct; (ii) the imposition of the sanction is necessary, having regard to the terms of the statute, to protect its objects or policies; and (iii) the statute does not disclose an intention that the sanctions and remedies contained in the statute are to be the only legal consequences of a breach of the statute or the frustration of its policies.

The ability to enforce an illegal contract will depend on the type of illegality involved, the legislative intent of any applicable statute and the degree of guilty intent that may be attributable to each of the parties.

Subject to limited exceptions, where the contract itself is illegal at common law it will be void and neither party will be able to recover money or property transferred or due under the contract. Where the contract is lawful and the illegality arises from an illegal or immoral purpose or illegal performance then a number of exceptions to the general rule may arise. These exceptions were set out by Justice McHugh in *Nelson v Nelson*:

> First, the courts will not refuse relief where the claimant was ignorant or mistaken as to the factual circumstances which render an agreement or arrangement illegal. Second, the courts will not refuse relief where the statutory scheme rendering a contract or arrangement illegal was enacted for the benefit of a class of which the claimant is a member. Third, the courts will not refuse relief where an illegal agreement was induced by the defendant's fraud, oppression or undue influence. Fourth, the courts will not refuse relief where the illegal purpose has not been carried into effect.[24]

Where the parties are not in pari delicto

Parties may not always be equally implicated in the illegal purpose or conduct. In this respect, the maxim *in pari delicto potior est conditio defendentis* (where the

---

24 (1995) 184 CLR 538 at 604–605.

parties are equally at fault the courts will favour the defendant) provides that the court will not aid a party equally implicated in the illegality. Conversely, however, a court may assist a party who is not equally at fault. In *Andrews v Parker* Justice Stable said:

> ... where the parties to an illegal contract, or one against public policy, are not *in pari delicto*, and public policy is considered as advanced by allowing either, or at least the more excusable of the two to sue for relief against the transaction, relief is given to him. ...[25]

Similarly Devlin J in *St John Shipping Corp v Joseph Rank Ltd* has indicated that where an illegal *intent* is unilateral it will be unenforceable at the suit of the party who has that intent but enforceable by the other party to the contract.[26]

Where the statute is intended to benefit a class of persons which includes the claimant

Where the purpose of the statute rendering the contract illegal is to protect a class of which the claimant is a member, the court will not regard the parties as being *in pari delicto* and will generally allow that party to enforce the contract. The statute must, however, be intended for the protection of an identifiable class and not the public at large. This issue was addressed in the following case.

South Australian Cold Stores Ltd v Electricity Trust of South Australia

(1965) 115 CLR 247, High Court of Australia

[The Electricity Trust (the Trust) was established by legislation. The State Prices Commissioner had the power to make orders fixing the maximum rates the Trust could charge its customers. In 1952 the Prices Commissioner purported to make an order increasing the maximum rate and the Trust increased the rate accordingly. South Australian Cold Stores (the Company) was a customer of the Trust and challenged the validity of the new rates. The new rates were found to be ineffective due to a failure to comply with certain formal requirements in the *Prices Act*. The Company then sought to recover past money paid above the maximum lawful rates at the time. The Company failed in the Supreme Court and then appealed to the High Court.]

Kitto J [at 257]: The appellant's principal contention was that it can recover the amount of its overpayments as money had and received by the respondent to the appellant's use. ... All the payments were voluntarily made, and in order to succeed in recovering them as having been made illegally the appellant would have to make good its contention that it was not *in pari delicto* with the respondent. The

---

25 (1973) Qd R 93 at 105.
26 [1957] 1 QB 267

contention must be upheld or rejected according [to whether] the appellant is or is not a member of a class of persons for whose protection the prohibition <258> in the *Prices Act*, 1948–1951 (SA) is enacted: ... If it is a member of such a class, it is entitled to succeed, ... The *Prices Act* is directed to the regulation of prices generally, and for that reason is to be contrasted with legislation which is directed only to the regulation of amounts payable in respect of a particular kind of transaction. ... a general *Prices Act* [has] on its face the purpose of preventing or curbing a decline in the value of money. It is that value which is the subject of its protection, not purchasers. ... both vendor and purchaser are forbidden to contribute to the upward pressure on prices generally in the community by giving or receiving more than the amounts fixed ... A vendor and a purchaser are therefore to be held *in pari delicto* if the one charges and the other pays more than the amount fixed under the Act. <2563> ...

[His Honour then noted the rule stated by Lord Mansfield in *Browning v Morris* is that]: ... where contracts or transactions are prohibited by positive statutes, for the sake of protecting one set of men from another set of men, the one, from their situation and condition, being liable to be oppressed or imposed upon by the other; there the parties are not *in pari delicto*; and in furtherance of these statutes, the person injured, after the transaction is finished and completed, may bring his action and defeat the contract'. [His Honour rejected the appellant's argument that this case fell within that principle and continued]: The *Prices Act* was passed for the protection of the community as a whole against the mischiefs of inflation and the community is not a 'class' or 'set' of men within the meaning of the rule. ...

Appeal dismissed

[footnotes omitted]

Fraud

When one party was induced into an illegal contract by the fraud of the other party the contract will generally be enforceable by the party so induced who will not be considered equally at fault with the fraudulent party. The party induced into the contract by fraud may also have remedies in tort or under the *Trade Practices Act 1974* (Cth).

Where the illegal purpose has not been carried into effect

If there is some illegal intent associated with a contract and one party pulls out of performing that illegal act the courts may allow that party to enforce the contract. For example, parties may contract for the sale of a stereo with the intention that the seller will steal the stereo in order to fulfil his contractual obligations. If that party has a change of heart and instead lawfully acquires the stereo to fulfil his contractual obligations then the court will enforce the contract despite the illegal purpose at the time of contracting.[27]

---

27   See *Payne v McDonald* (1908) 6 CLR 201 at 212. See further L Willmott, S Christensen and D Butler, *Contract Law*, 2nd edn, Oxford University Press, Melbourne, 2005, 636–637.

Where statute does not require the courts to deny enforcement

In addition to the specific exceptions recognised by the court in *Nelson v Nelson*, the court in *Fitzgerald v FJ Leonhardt* noted the importance, in cases of statutory illegality, of determining whether or not the purpose of the statute required the courts to refuse enforcement or whether the penalties imposed by the statute were sufficient to address any public policy concerns associated with the illegality.

Fitzgerald v FJ Leonhardt Pty Ltd
(1997) 189 CLR 215, High Court of Australia

[The facts were set out above.]

Dawson and Toohey JJ [at 220]: ... even if the performance of the contract by the driller were seen as involving a breach of the Act, that would not necessarily mean that the contract was illegal. It has sometimes been said that a contract is illegal if its performance involves breach of a statute passed for the protection of the public but, stated in that way, the proposition is too broad. The purpose of the statute may be served by the imposition of a penalty, notwithstanding that it is for the protection of the public.

McHugh and Gummow JJ [at 227]: Section 56 prescribes a penalty. In such a case, the role of the common law in determining the legal consequences of commission of the offence may thereby be diminished because the purpose of the statute is sufficiently served by the penalty. Here, the imposition of an additional sanction, namely inability of the driller to recover moneys otherwise owing by the owner, would be an inappropriate adjunct to the scheme for which the Act provides. The contrary decision would cause prejudice to an innocent party without furthering the objects of the legislation. ...

Kirby P [at 244]: ... if the legislation provides in a detailed way for sanctions and remedies for breach of its terms, courts will require good reason to add to those express provisions additional civil penalties, such as the deprivation of contractual rights, which Parliament has not chosen to enact. ...

b   Independent causes of action

Independent causes of action may also be open to one or both parties to an illegal contract. For example, if an illegal contract was induced by misleading or deceptive conduct, the victim of that conduct, while unable to enforce the contract, may be able to bring an action under the *Trade Practices Act 1974* (Cth), s 52.

c   Severance

It may be possible in some cases to sever the otherwise void parts of an illegal or immoral contract so that rights and obligations may still be enforced for the remainder of the contract. Before a court will sever any illegal portions of a contract it must be satisfied that the contract is capable of operating as intended without the severed portion and that it would not be contrary to public policy to enforce the remainder of the contract.

The policy considerations surrounding the issue of severing illegal portions of a contract were discussed in the following cases.

Brooks v Burns Philp Trustee Co Ltd

(1969) 121 CLR 433, High Court of Australia

[A married couple entered into deed prior to petition for dissolution of their marriage which included the following provisions:

- Clause 1 included a covenant by the husband to pay weekly amounts to the wife during her life.
- Clause 2 contained a covenant by the wife to accept the terms of the deed 'in full settlement of all claims against the husband for alimony and maintenance of any description'.

Following the death of the husband his estate (the respondents) sought a determination of the question of whether the estate was required to make the weekly payments to the wife (the appellant) provided for in the deed.

The Supreme Court of New South Wales declared that the husband's estate was not required to make payment and the wife appealed.]

Kitto J [at 437]: [Clause 2] bound the wife not to ask the Court for more than the terms of the deed provided and not to take more by virtue of any order that the Court might see fit to make. Thus its operation, if it was valid, was to nullify as between the parties the Court's discretion as to alimony and maintenance ... <438> ... the Divorce Court would refuse to treat such a covenant as binding, and any other court would refuse on the ground of public policy to enforce it.

Clause 2 was therefore devoid of legal effect, and the question arises whether the covenant in [clause 1 for the weekly payments to the wife] stands ... or is inoperative because of the invalidity of cl 2. ... I do not think it is possible to read the document as a whole without perceiving that the intention was to substitute a limited liability in covenant for every other liability of the husband in respect of alimony or maintenance. This means that the husband's covenants in [clause 1] and the wife's covenant in cl 2 were intended to be the obverse and reverse of the one coin, to operate reciprocally or not at all. Questions of severability are often difficult, ... but in some cases— and I think this is one—the intended reciprocity of obligation between promises is sufficiently clear to necessitate an inference that the legal validity of each promise is a condition of the operation of the other. Accordingly I am of opinion that cl 1 (b) failed to take effect as a source of legally enforceable obligation. ...

Owen J [at 478]: [The trial judge] considered that cl 2 of the deed was void as being a provision which purported to oust the jurisdiction of the Court and that the deceased's covenant in cl 1 (b) to pay to the appellant the weekly sum of £13 7s and the appellant's covenant to accept those payments in full settlement of all claims for alimony and maintenance were so dependent, the one upon the other, that they were incapable of severance so that if the appellant's covenant was void, the deceased's covenant failed with it. <479>

I am of opinion that his Honour's decision on both points was correct. There is no doubt that an agreement which purports to oust the jurisdiction of the courts is void as being against public policy and, applying that general principle, a promise by a wife that, in the event of the dissolution of their marriage, she will accept an amount agreed upon between herself and her husband in full settlement of all claims for alimony or maintenance, is void and unenforceable. [Clause 2 and clause 1 were dependent covenants and therefore] the two clauses are incapable of severance and each is void.

[Taylor J agreed with Kitto J that clause 2 could not be severed. Menzies J did not consider clause 2 to be void and would therefore have allowed the appeal. Windeyer J dissented believing that the offending clause was not capable of separation from the remainder of the contract].

Appeal denied

Thomas Brown & Sons Ltd v Fazal Deen

(1962) 108 CLR 391, High Court of Australia

[Pursuant to a contract of bailment the plaintiff [Fazel Deen] deposited gold, gems and a safe with the defendant for safe keeping. It was kept in a strong room on the premises for many years before it mysteriously disappeared. After discovering the goods were missing the plaintiff sought recovery of the goods or their value and succeeded at first instance. The defendants appealed.

The defendant claimed, in part, that the goods (or their value) could not be recovered because the contract of bailment under which they were kept was illegal. Legislation at the time required that all gold be delivered to the Commonwealth Bank; consequently, storing the gold elsewhere contravened this legislation. The Court agreed that, at least in relation to the gold, the contract was illegal with the result that the gold (or its value) could not be recovered. The Court then went on to consider whether or not the other goods subject of the bailment contract could be recovered.]

Kitto, Windeyer and Owen JJ [at 410]: So far as the gold was concerned, the performance of that agreement would, and in fact it did, contravene the regulations but it does not follow that <411> the bailment of the gems and of the safe was tainted by illegality. If the terms of the bailment relating to the gold were severable from those relating to the gems and the safe the bailment of the latter chattels would be lawful. The test of severability [is] 'If the elimination of the invalid promises changes the extent only but not the kind of contract, the valid promises are severable: ...'. Applying that test, it is clear that the plaintiff's rights of action in respect of the gems and the safe would not be answered by a defence of illegality based upon a breach of the [regulations] since the contractual obligation upon the company as to the return of the plaintiff's property on demand applied to every part of the property deposited whether demanded together with the rest of it or separately. In the case of the gold, however, the plaintiff could not succeed if he was obliged to rely upon the illegal transaction to establish his case. The learned trial judge considered that proof of the bailment was not an essential part of the plaintiff's case. … [Their Honours disagreed, noting (at 412) that the plaintiff] was obliged to prove the contract of bailment and, to support his claim …, to rely upon the failure of the company to comply with the obligation imposed by it to redeliver the goods upon the demand which he made in 1959. It follows from what has been said that the plaintiff's claim to recover the value of the gold cannot be supported …

Appeal upheld in part

[footnotes omitted]

INTERNATIONAL PERSPECTIVES

India

The effect of illegality in India is very similar to that in Australia.

Agreements or contracts that are illegal, immoral or otherwise contrary to public policy are void. Generally, money paid and property transferred pursuant to such a contract cannot be recovered. As is the case in Australia, however, there are exceptions to this rule. Most notably, where parties were unaware of the illegality involved in the contract or where the parties were not *in pari delicto*, the party, or parties, who did not have the illegal purpose will be able to recover money or property paid under the contract.[28]

Despite section 24, below, severance will be possible under the *Indian Contract Act* provided the unlawful portion can be severed without affecting the other lawful portions.[29]

The Courts have also held that where no part of the illegal purpose has been executed any payment or benefits passed under the contract may be recovered.[30]

Indian Contract Act, 1872

Section 24. Agreements void, if consideration are objects unlawful in part

If any part of a single consideration for one or more objects, or any one or any part of any one of several consideration of a single object, is unlawful, the agreement is void.

China

Chinese law makes no specific exceptions for recovering money or benefits that have passed under an illegal contract, simply providing that such contracts are invalid.

---

28 See *Indian Contract Act, 1872*, s 65 and *Ram Singh v Jethamal Wadhumal & Co* AIR 1964 Raj 232.
29 See A Singh, *Law of Contract and Specific Relief*, 9th edn, EBC, Lucknow, 2005 at 252 and *Poonoo Bibi v Fyaz Buksh* (1874) 15 BLR App 5.
30 See *Dharindhar v Kanhji Sahay*, AIR 1949 Pat 250 and Singh, above n 28 at 364.

5 Summary

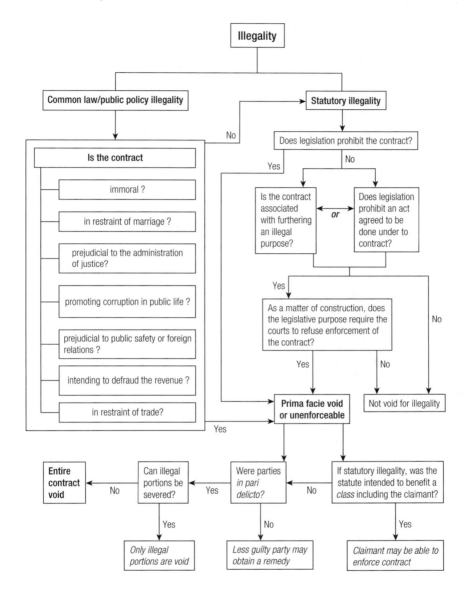

6 Questions

1. Donna is a local Judo champion. She runs a Judo academy and provides both group and private instruction. One of her private clients was Libby Lane. During one session Libby explained to Donna that her ex-boyfriend, Jordan, had been harassing her new boyfriend, Clay, and she was concerned that if it continued Clay may give up and leave her. She asked Donna if there was something she could do to help frighten off Jordan. Donna expressed sympathy, but told Libby she would rather not get involved. Libby broke down and told Donna that she was really desperate to get Jordan to leave her and Clay alone and that she feared for their safety if someone didn't intervene. She begged Donna to help and offered to pay her $1,000 if she would 'send a message' to Jordan that he would regret any continued harassment. She assured Donna that she didn't want her to cause Jordan serious or permanent injury, but a few punches and threats of further violence if he didn't back off should do the trick. Donna was still a bit reluctant, but was struggling to pay her weekly bills and found the $1,000 payment too difficult to resist. She agreed to do as Libby asked. Libby expressed great relief and told Donna she could give her $500 now and the remaining $500 would be paid after Donna had confronted Jordan.

    Two weeks later Donna advised Libby that she had confronted Jordan, given him a black eye he wouldn't soon forget, and received his assurance that he would leave both Libby and Clay alone in the future. In the meantime, however, Libby had discovered that Clay had been cheating on her and had broken off their relationship. As a result, she was no longer concerned if Jordan harassed Clay, and refused to pay the remaining $500 to Donna. Donna protested that they had an agreement and she'd performed her end of the bargain so Libby should pay up. Libby refused.

    Donna has come to you for advice. She wishes to know whether or not she has any claim to the $500 Libby promised her for roughing up Jordan.

2. David is a home-owner in Ballarat. He arrived home from work one day to discover that his television and various other electronic items had been stolen. Fortunately, he had comprehensive contents insurance with Trusty Ltd and immediately called them about making a claim. They sent him a form which required, among other things, that he list the items that had been stolen. He did this accurately until it came to the claim for the television. The stolen television was an old box 24" set that he had been meaning to replace. He reasoned that, had he purchased a new 52" plasma 3D television prior to the robbery, the insurance company would have compensated him for it, so it wouldn't hurt anyone if he just made a 'slight' modification to the insurance claim to reflect his hypothetical purchase. Consequently, while everything else in his claim (which comprised the majority of the claim) was accurate, when it came to indicating the model of television stolen he wrote '52" Plasma 3D'.

    David was, however, justifiably concerned that Trusty Ltd might query his claim. Consequently, he quickly visited a small electronics store a friend had told him about, Dodgy Brothers Televisions Pty Ltd, and asked if they would backdate a receipt for the purchase of a 52" television. He told the manager that he would pay for the television once the insurance claim came through. The manager agreed to backdate the receipt, but only if payment was made upfront. David reluctantly agreed and the manager gave him a receipt indicating payment and delivery of a television valued at $1,500. They agreed that David would collect the television if his insurance came through and that if his claim was unsuccessful Dodgy Brothers Televisions would refund the payment.

Several weeks later David's insurance claim was paid and he returned to Dodgy Brothers Televisions, excited about collecting his new television. He once again spoke to the manager, who had had a change of heart and refused to give David the television. David insisted that they had an agreement and that he was entitled to the television. The manager replied 'tell it to the court' and walked away.

David has come to see you for advice. He admits that he lied on his insurance claim, but insists that he paid $1,500 to Dodgy Brothers Televisions and should be entitled to the new television. Please advise David. You may assume, for purposes of this question, that there is insurance legislation in place which imposes a financial penalty of $1,000 for making false insurance claims.

3. John is a 19-year-old student. He was dating Kate, who was also a student. Paul is Kate's father. One evening, after John dropped Kate home following a romantic dinner, Paul asked to speak with John. John thought Paul wanted to discuss the sale of his old Ford Falcon, which John had previously offered to buy for $5,000. Instead, the conversation focussed on John's relationship with Kate. Paul told John that, while he liked him, he wanted him to stop seeing his daughter. Although he did not say so expressly, it was clear that Paul considered John lacked a certain social 'class' that was important to Paul. Paul offered to pay John $20,000 if he promised to call off his relationship with Kate and agreed never to see her again. He also told John he would sell him his old Ford Falcon for $5,000, if John still wanted it.

John was clearly stunned and Paul told him to think about it overnight and return the next day. John left and considered Paul's offer. Although he thought he loved Kate and they had already discussed marriage, he convinced himself that, because he and Kate were still quite young, they were probably just being naive about their future together and they would both have plenty of time to find somebody else. He also had to admit that the $20,000 would provide him with some desperately needed cash to help him complete his university studies. Consequently, when he returned to Paul's house the next day he reluctantly agreed to Paul's offer.

Paul quickly pulled out a contract he had drafted the previous night. It contained two clauses. The first provided that John would call off his relationship with Kate within a week and would not engage in a romantic relationship with her anytime in the future. It further provided that $20,000 would be paid one month after the signing of the contract. The second clause provided that Paul would sell his old car to John for a sum of $5,000. John signed the contract, wrote Paul a cheque for $5,000 and drove home in his newly acquired Ford Falcon.

The next day John arranged to meet Kate for dinner. He struggled to find a way to break off the relationship and eventually broke down and told her exactly what had transpired between himself and Kate's father. He told her that he loved her and wanted to marry her, but he had no money and her father would make both their lives difficult if they continued their relationship. Kate was furious with her father and insisted that she would not let him stand between them. They agreed that John would tell Paul he was withdrawing from the agreement and they would somehow manage to save the money to get married as soon as possible.

When John confronted Paul, Paul flew into a rage and told him that he could never marry his daughter, that they had a contract and that if he even thought of continuing his relationship with Kate, not only would he never see his $20,000, but Paul would sue him breach of contract and would also seek to recover the car he'd sold him for the bargain price of $5,000.

John and Kate have come to see you for advice. They wish to know whether Paul has any claim for breach of contract in relation to their continuing relationship and whether or not he is able to recover the old Ford Falcon he sold to John. Please advise them.

PART 5

Performance and Termination

Part 5 deals with the related topics of contractual performance and the termination of contractual rights and obligations. 'Performance' concerns what the parties must do before it can be said that they have discharged their obligations under the contract sufficiently to be able to require the other party to perform their side of the contract, or to pay compensation for not doing so. 'Termination' refers to the situations in which a contract may come to an end because of events that occurred since it was entered into. In this regard, termination is to be contrasted with 'Avoidance', the subject of Part 4, which is concerned with the forms of pre-contractual conduct that prevent the proper formation of a contract and which, where applicable, allow a contract to be rescinded *ab initio*; that is, from the beginning.

The situations that will terminate a contract are

- Performance (chapter 19)
- Agreement (chapter 20)

- Breach (chapter 21)
- Frustration (chapter 22)

Although in many respects these situations are quite different from each other, when they operate they do so to terminate the contract only *in futuro*; that is, for the future. As a result, they bring to an end only those contractual rights and obligations that were due to arise sometime after the date of termination; they do not bring to an end those that have already fallen due for performance before that time. This has important consequences for the remedies available to the parties after termination.

CHAPTER 19

Performance

1	Introduction	539
2	The nature of performance	539
	a General rule	539
	b Exceptions to the general rule	540
3	Entire and severable contracts	544
	a Entire contracts	544
	b The doctrine of substantial performance	547
	c Apportionment legislation	548
	d Severable contracts	549
4	Time for performance	550
5	Prevention of performance	560
6	Summary	562
7	Questions	562

1 Introduction

Most contracts come to an end as a result of the parties performing their contractual obligations. In this chapter we assess the requirements for discharging a contract in this manner and, in particular, the impact of defective performance on the rights and obligations of the parties.

2 The nature of performance

a General rule

As a general rule parties must perform their contractual obligations strictly and completely.[1] Determination of whether or not this has occurred involves a comparison between the contractual obligations assumed by the parties[2] and the acts that they have performed. It is only when the assumed obligations precisely

---

1   See *Re Moore & Co and Landauer & Co* [1921] 2 KB 519.
2   The way in which contractual terms are determined was addressed in chapter 10.

match the acts of performance that complete and exact performance will have been achieved and the contractual relationship brought to its intended end.

b Exceptions to the general rule

The general rule relating to performance is, however, subject to modification by the parties either expressly or by implication. The parties may, for example, agree that exact compliance with contractual obligations is not required or, in appropriate circumstances a court may be willing to imply a term to this effect. This issue arose in the following case.

Luna Park (NSW) Ltd v Tramways Advertising Pty Ltd

(1938) 61 CLR 286, High Court of Australia

[The plaintiff (Tramways) entered into a contract with the defendant (Luna Park) by which Tramways agreed to display 53 roof boards advertising Luna Park's amusement park for at least eight hours per day for a minimum of 52 weeks in total over three seasons. The agreement provided, in part:

> We guarantee that these boards will be on the tracks at least eight hours per day throughout your season.

The agreement also provided that Luna Park would make payment at the rate of £20 per week 'from date of the first appearance of complete number of boards 53 in all, payable monthly'.

Tramways brought an action to recover payments it claimed due for displaying the roof boards and Luna Park cross-claimed for damages for breach of contract. An issue arose as to whether Tramways had completely performed its obligations under the contract.

Luna Park succeeded at first instance with the trial judge holding that the contract required the display of boards for eight hours each day and that this had not occurred. Consequently, Tramways' action failed. The majority of the Full Court of the Supreme Court of New South Wales allowed an appeal by Tramways. Luna Park appealed to the High Court.]

Latham CJ [at 296]: After the second season the Luna Park Co objected that the display contracted for was not being provided. The company contended that the provision quoted meant that each of the fifty-three boards would be on the tracks for at least eight hours on every day during three seasons. It is admitted that this service was not given. The advertising company, on the other hand, contended that the obligation imposed by the clause was performed if during each season each board was displayed for an average time of at least eight hours per day. According to this view of the meaning of the provision there would be no breach if no boards at all or only a small number of boards were shown on some days, provided that the display on other days was such as to bring the average for each board over a season to at least eight hours per day. It is admitted that if the provision bears this meaning the advertising company has performed its contract.

[His Honour discussed the plaintiff's contention that the guarantee that the boards would be displayed for 'at least eight hours' per day meant an average of eight hours per day and continued (at 299)]: In my opinion this contention is opposed to the natural meaning of the words. What is called the guarantee is a guarantee as to each and every board. It is an undertaking that each board will be on the tracks for at least eight hours on every day all through each season. ... The effect of the undertaking, ... is that, whatever might be the average time that cars were on the track, the roof boards were to be displayed for at least eight hours on every day. The guarantee contains no reference to averages, and it is apparent that there may be business reasons why the defendant required regular and continuous publicity.

It follows that in my opinion the plaintiff must fail upon the claim because the plaintiff sues upon the special contract and has not <300> performed the contract in accordance with its terms.

In the cross-action, the defendant claimed damages for breach of contract by the plaintiff in not displaying the fifty-three roof boards daily throughout the whole contract period of fifty-two weeks. ...

<301> The essential character of the clause in question appears both from its own terms and from the circumstances in which the contract was made. In the first place the words 'we guarantee' are particularly suited, in a contract drawn by laymen, to emphasize <303> the importance of the clause which they introduce. In the next place, the payment of £20 per week was not to begin until the complete number of roof boards, namely, fifty-three, were all displayed at the same time. The money is made payable 'from date of first appearance of complete number of boards 53 in all.' Thus, if the advertising company displayed even as many as fifty-two boards on every day throughout a whole season, it would never become entitled to recover any payment. This provision in the contract therefore supports the view that the parties regarded the completeness of the display contracted for as an essential element in the contract. <304> Accordingly any breach of the clause would entitle the defendant to determine the contract.

But it is still necessary to consider what default will amount to a breach of the clause. The clause used the words 'at least eight hours,' but, in my opinion, such a phrase should not be interpreted with absolute mathematical exactitude in a commercial contract of this class. In some contracts it may be proper to construe references to time with absolute and precise accuracy down to minutes and seconds, but in a contract dealing with the display of roof boards on trams for at least eight hours per day the words 'eight hours per day' should be understood as meaning substantially eight hours per day. The clause would not, in my opinion, be broken by small occasional deficiencies. ... I take the admission that each board was not exhibited for at least eight hours a day as an admission that it was not the case that each board was exhibited for substantially eight hours each day. I am accordingly of opinion that the defendant was entitled to determine the contract by reason of the past breaches of the plaintiff. ...

[Rich and McTiernan JJ, in separate judgments, held that the contract required the boards to be exhibited for an aggregate of eight hours each and every day and that this had not occurred. Dixon J dissented, taking the view that the term would be satisfied by display of boards for an 'average' of eight hours per day.]

Appeal allowed

[footnotes omitted]

INTERNATIONAL PERSPECTIVES

India

The *Indian Contract Act, 1872* requires the parties to perform (or offer to perform) their contractual obligations in the manner and at the time required by the contract (s 50) unless the need for performance is dispensed with or excused under the Act (s 37). The promisee may allow the promisor to perform at a different time or in a different manner (s 50) and may even dispense with the need for performance altogether (s 63). Death of the promisor does not excuse performance by the promisor's representatives (s 37). Failure to perform permits the promisee to bring the contract to an end (s 39).

Indian Contract Act, 1872

Section 37. Obligations of parties to contracts

The parties to a contract must either perform, or offer to perform, their respective promises, unless such performance is dispensed with or excused under the provisions of this Act, or of any other law.

Section 38. Effect of refusal to accept offer of performance

Where a promisor has made an offer of performance to the promisee, and the offer has not been accepted, the promisor is not responsible for non-performance, nor does he thereby lose his rights under the contract.

Every such offer must fulfil the following conditions—

(1) it must be unconditional;
(2) it must be made at a proper time and place, and under such circumstances that the person to whom it is made may have a reasonable opportunity of ascertaining that the person by whom it is been made is able and willing there and then to do the whole of what he is bound by his promise to do
…

Section 39. Effect of refusal of party to perform promise wholly

When a party to a contract has refused to perform, or disabled himself from performing, his promise in its entirety, the promisee may put an end to the

contract, unless he has signified, by words or conduct, his acquiescence in its continuance.
Illustrations

(a) A, a singer, enters into contract with B, the manager of a theatre, to sing at his theatre two nights in every week during next two months, and B engages to pay her 100 rupees for each night's performance. On the sixth night A wilfully absents herself from the theatre. B is at liberty to put an end to the contract. ...

Section 50. Performance, in manner or at time prescribed or sanctioned by promisee

The performance of any promise may be made in any manner, or at any time which the promisee prescribes or sanctions.

Section 63. Promisee may dispense with or remit performance of promise

Every promisee may dispense with or remit, wholly or in part, the performance of the promise made to him, or may extend the time for such performance, or may accept instead of it any satisfaction which he thinks fit.

China

The *Contract Law of the People's Republic of China* requires performance in accordance with contractual obligations and provides that a contract is discharged upon such performance.

Contract Law of the People's Republic of China, 1999

Article 60. Full Performance; Performance in Good Faith

The parties shall fully perform their respective obligations in accordance with the contract.

The parties shall abide by the principle of good faith, and perform obligations such as notification, assistance, and confidentiality, etc in light of the nature and purpose of the contract and in accordance with the relevant usage.

Article 91. Conditions for Discharge

The rights and obligations under a contract are discharged in any of the following circumstances:

(i) The obligations were performed in accordance with the contract; ...

Chinese law also enables a promisee to reject partial performance of a contract.

Article 72. Right to Reject Partial Performance; Exception

An obligee may reject the obligor's partial performance, except where such partial performance does not harm the obligee's interests.

Any additional expense incurred by the obligee due to the obligor's partial performance shall be borne by the obligor.

3 Entire and severable contracts

a Entire contracts

An entire contract is one in which performance of one party's obligations is dependent on the performance of the other party's obligations. In these cases performance of the first party's obligations is viewed as a condition precedent to the performance of the second party's obligations. Whether a contract is an 'entire' contract or not is determined by reference to the intention of the parties, viewed objectively, at the time of contracting. This issue was discussed in the following cases.

Cutter v Powell

(1795) All ER Rep 159; 6 Term Rep 320, Court of King's Bench

[Cutter was hired by Powell as a sailor for a voyage under a note which stated:

> Ten days after the ship 'Governor Parry,' myself master, arrives at Liverpool, I promise to pay to Mr T Cutter the sum of thirty guineas, provided he proceeds, continues and does his duty as second mate in the said ship from hence to the port of Liverpool, Kingston, ...

Cutter sailed on 2 August and continued to perform his duty as second mate until his death on 20 September, prior to the ship's arrival in the port of Liverpool. The administratrix of Cutter's estate sought to recover from Powell a proportion of the promised wages for work and labour done during the voyage on a *quantum meruit*.]

Lord Kenyon Ch J [at 162]: Here the defendant expressly promised to pay the intestate 30 guineas provided he proceeded, continued and did his duty as second mate in the ship from Jamaica to Liverpool, and the accompanying circumstances disclosed in the case are that the common rate of wages is 4 pounds per month when the party is paid in proportion to the time he serves, and that this voyage is generally performed in two months. Therefore, if there had been no contract between these parties, all that the intestate could have recovered on a *quantum meruit* for the voyage would have been 8 pounds, whereas here the defendant contracted to pay 30 guineas provided the mate continued to do his duty as mate during the whole voyage, in which case the latter would have received nearly four times as much as if he were paid for the number of months he served. He stipulated to receive the larger sum if the whole duty were performed, and nothing unless the whole of that duty were performed. It was a kind of insurance. On this particular contract, my opinion is formed at present. ...

Ashhurst J [at 161]: This is a written contract, and it speaks for itself. As it is entire and, as the defendant's promise depends on a condition precedent to be performed by the other party, the condition must be performed before the other party is entitled to receive anything under it. ... wherever there is an express contract the parties must be guided by it, and one party cannot relinquish or abide by it as it may suit his advantage. ...

Grose J [at 161]: ... in this case the agreement is conclusive. The defendant only engaged to pay the intestate on condition of his continuing to do his duty on board during the whole voyage, and the latter was to be entitled either to 30 guineas or to nothing, for such was the contract between the parties. When we recollect how large a price was to be given in the event of the mate continuing on board during the whole voyage instead of the small sum which is usually given per <162> month, it may fairly be considered that the parties themselves understood that, if the whole duty were performed, the mate was to receive the whole sum and that he was not to receive anything unless he did continue on board during the whole voyage. ...

[Lawrence J agreed.]

Judgment for the defendant

Automatic Fire Sprinklers Proprietary Limited v Watson

(1946) 72 CLR 435, High Court of Australia

[Watson was appointed as the general manager of the appellants' (Automatic Fire Sprinklers) companies. The agreement permitted termination of the employment contract by the companies on one month's notice (or payment of one month's salary in lieu of notice) if the directors were of opinion that Watson had become unfit to act as general manager.

After Watson had acted as general manager for more than six years the directors sent him a letter dated 29 September in which they stated that they considered he was unfit to act as General Manager and, in accordance with the contract, were terminating his employment and paying him one month's salary in lieu of notice. It was determined as a matter of fact that the directors never in fact considered Watson unfit to act as General Manager and that the letter purporting to terminate his employment constituted a breach of contract. Watson refused to accept this termination and continued to attend his office where he was ready and willing to perform the duties of General Manager until the company eventually excluded him from the premises.

[The following extract deals with the issue of whether the company was obliged to pay Watson a salary for the period between his receipt of the ineffective letter of termination and the time at which he was excluded from the premises, almost a year later.]

Dixon J [at 465]: A contract for the establishment of the relation of master and servant falls into the ... general category of agreements to pay in respect of the consideration when and so often as it is executed, and is, therefore, commonly understood as involving no liability for wages or salary unless earned by service, even though the failure to serve is a consequence of the master's wrongful act.

It is, of course, possible for the parties to make a contract for the payment of periodical sums by the master to the servant independently of his service. ... The common understanding of a contract of employment at wages or salary periodically payable is that it is the service that earns the remuneration and even a wrongful discharge from the service means that wages or salary cannot be earned however ready and willing the employee may be to serve and however much he stand by his contract and decline to treat it as discharged by breach. ...

His only remedy is in unliquidated damages for wrongful dismissal. ... <466>.

... wages are incident to the subsisting relationship of master and servant. ... That relationship may be ended by the servant forsaking the master or the master discharging the servant, although the act of the one or of the other amounts to a breach of contract.

In the present case the question for decision is, in substance, whether the general manager of two companies which, without justification, purported to dismiss him from that position can recover wages for a period in which he continued to proffer his service, or must be content with unliquidated damages. ... in my opinion, ... there is nothing in the agreement which makes the <467> payment of salary independent of actual service, or which would operate to give the employee a title to salary, notwithstanding that he had been discharged from the service of the companies, however wrongfully. ...

<469> ... there is nothing in the general law preventing the wrongful dismissal of a servant operating to discharge him from service, notwithstanding that he declines to accept the dismissal as absolving him from further performance but keeps the contract open and remains ready and willing to serve.

There is nothing in the special terms of the contract in this case entitling the employee to salary in respect of a period in which he did not serve and, therefore, [save for legislation which operated in this case] the employee's remedy would from 29th September 1944 be for unliquidated damages.

[In this case legislation entitled the employee to a salary for the period he continued to proffer his services and, as a result, the appeal failed. The other members of the Court agreed that wages could not be recovered at common law following the breach.]

Appeal dismissed

b The doctrine of substantial performance

In response to the harsh consequences that may result from entire contracts, the courts developed the doctrine of 'substantial performance' permitting recovery of the contract price where the plaintiff has substantially performed their obligations under a contract. A defendant, however, will still maintain the right to claim damages for any loss suffered as a result of the plaintiff's failure to strictly adhere to their contractual obligations. This doctrine was applied in the following cases.

Hoenig v Isaacs

[1952] 2 All ER 176, Court of Appeal (England)

[The plaintiff (Isaacs) was an interior decorator and designer of furniture. He entered into a contract with the defendant (Hoenig) to decorate and furnish Hoenig's flat for a sum of £750. The contract provided for the payment of certain sums 'as the work proceeds' with 'balance on completion'.

Hoenig paid £400 by way of three instalments and occupied the flat and used the furniture. However, in response to a claim by Isaacs for the balance of £350 Hoenig refused to pay, alleging Isaacs had failed to perform his contract due to defective workmanship. Isaacs succeeded in his claim for the balance before the Official Referee, despite a finding that some items of furniture needed replacing or alteration. Hoenig appealed.]

Denning LJ [at 180]: This case raises the familiar question: Was entire performance a condition precedent to payment? That depends on the true construction of the contract. ...

In determining this issue the first question is whether, on the true construction of the contract, entire performance was a condition precedent to payment. It was a lump sum contract, but that does not mean that entire performance was a condition precedent to payment. When a contract provides for a specific sum to be paid on completion of specified work, the courts lean against a construction of the contract which would deprive the contractor of any payment at all simply because there are some defects or omissions. The promise to complete the work is, therefore, construed as a term of the contract, but not <181> as a condition. It is not every breach of that term which absolves the employer from his promise to pay the price, but only a breach which goes to the root of the contract, such as an abandonment of the work when it is only half done. Unless the breach does go to the root of the matter, the employer cannot resist payment of the price. He must pay it and bring a cross-claim for the defects and omissions, or, alternatively, set them up in diminution of the price. The measure is the amount which the work is worth less by reason of the defects and omissions, and is usually calculated by the cost of making them good .... It is, of course, always open to the parties by express words to make entire performance a condition precedent. A familiar instance is when the contract provides for progress payments to be made as the work proceeds, but for retention money to be held until completion. Then entire performance is usually a condition precedent to payment of the retention money, but not, of course, to the progress payments. The contractor is entitled to payment pro rata as the work proceeds, less a deduction for retention money. But he is not entitled to the retention money until the work is entirely finished, without defects or omissions. In the present case the contract provided for 'net cash, as the work proceeds; and balance on completion.' If the balance could be regarded as retention money, then it might well be that the contractor ought to have done all the work correctly, without defects or omissions, in order to be entitled to the balance. But I do not think the balance should be regarded as retention money. Retention money is usually only ten per cent, or fifteen per cent, whereas this balance was more than fifty per cent. I think this contract should be regarded as an ordinary lump sum contract. It was substantially performed. The contractor is entitled, therefore, to the contract price, less a deduction for the defects. ...

Romer LJ [at 182]: In certain cases it is right that the rigid rule for which the defendant contends should be applied, for example, if a man tells a contractor to build a ten foot wall for him in his garden and agrees to pay £x for it, it would not be right that he should be held liable for any part of the contract price if the contractor builds the wall to two feet and then renounces further performance of the contract, or builds the wall of a totally different material from that which was ordered, or builds it at the wrong end of the garden. The work contracted for has not been done and the corresponding obligation to pay consequently never arises. But when a man fully performs his contract in the sense that he supplies all that he agreed to supply but what he supplies is subject to defects of so minor a character that he can be said to have substantially performed his promise, it is, in my judgment, far more equitable to apply the [substantial performance] principle than to deprive him wholly of his contractual rights and relegate him to such remedy (if any) as he may have on a *quantum meruit*...

[Somervell LJ agreed the appeal should be dismissed.]

Appeal dismissed

[footnotes omitted]

c Apportionment legislation

As a result of the harsh and unfair consequences which may result from application of the rule in *Cutter v Powell*, apportionment legislation has been developed in all Australian states and territories.[3]

---

[3] (1795) 6 TR 320. See *Civil Law (Property) Act 2006* (ACT) Pt 2.6; *Conveyancing Act 1919* (NSW) ss 142 and 144; *Law of Property Act 2002* (NT) ss 211–213; *Property Law Act 1974* (Qld) Pt 17; *Law of Property Act 1936* (SA) Pt 7; *Apportionment Act 1871* (Tas) ss 2–3; *Supreme Court Act 1986* (Vic) ss 53–56; *Property Law Act 1969* (WA) Pt XV.

Supreme Court Act 1986 (Vic), s 54

All rents, annuities, dividends and other periodical payments in the nature of income (whether reserved or made payable under an instrument in writing or otherwise) are to be considered as accruing from day to day and are apportionable in respect of time accordingly.

The apportionment provisions are, however, limited by the fact that they only apply in relation to periodical payments (not lump sum payments) and may be excluded by express agreement between the parties. Consequently, because in *Cutter v Powell* the payment was in the form of a lump sum, the apportionment provisions would not have assisted the plaintiff.

d Severable contracts

A severable (or 'divisible') contract is one in which the rights and obligations of the parties are not dependent on complete performance of their contractual obligations. These include contracts consisting of a number of smaller 'entire' obligations, for which the obligation to pay arises for each performed obligation and also contracts for which payment is not dependent on the performance of any obligation by the other party.

Examples

i   A and B enter into a contract under which A agrees to supply 1,000 bales of hay by five monthly instalments of 200 bales. The total contract price for the hay is $5,000 to be paid by way of five monthly instalments of $1,000 each. The contract is severable; B's payment falls due upon each instalment, regardless of whether or not A performs its obligations in relation to future instalments.

ii C (a landlord) enters into a lease agreement with D (a tenant) whereby D is required to make regular payments regardless of whether C adheres to its contractual obligations to keep the premises in good repair. In this case the contract is severable and the tenant's obligation to pay rent is independent of the landlord's contractual obligations.

Consequently, in these cases one party may sue the other for breach of contract even if they are also in breach.[4]

INTERNATIONAL PERSPECTIVES

India

The *Indian Contract Act, 1872* provides that where the promisor has failed to perform their obligations in their entirety the promisee may end the contract.[5]

---

4   See *Huntoon Company v Kolynos (Incorporated)* [1930] 1 Ch 528.
5   *Indian Contract Act, 1872* s 39 (extracted above) at p 542.

However, the courts appear to have read this down so that partial failure, which does not go to the root of the contract, would not allow the other party to bring the contract to an end.[6]

Indian Contract Act, 1872

Section 51. Promisor not bound to perform, unless reciprocal promisee ready and willing to perform

When a contract consists of reciprocal promises to be simultaneously performed, no promisor need perform his promise unless the promisee is ready and willing to perform his reciprocal promise.
Illustrations

(a) A and B contract that A shall deliver goods to B to be paid for by B on delivery. A need not deliver the goods, unless B is ready and willing to pay for the goods on delivery.
(b) B need not pay for the goods, unless A is ready and willing to deliver them on payment.

China

The *Contract Law of the People's Republic of China* provides that where one party is required to perform their obligations first, their failure to perform in accordance with the contract will relieve the other party from their obligation to perform.

Contract Law of the People's Republic of China, 1999

Article 67. Consecutive Performance

Where the parties owe performance toward each other and there is an order of performance, prior to performance by the party required to perform first, the party who is to perform subsequently is entitled to reject its requirement for performance. If the party required to perform first rendered non-conforming performance, the party who is to perform subsequently is entitled to reject its corresponding requirement for performance.

4 Time for performance

Contractual obligations must be performed in the time stipulated—whether expressly or by implication—by the contract. Where no time is stipulated, performance must occur within a reasonable time, determined by reference to

---

6   See further A Singh, *Law of Contract and Specific Relief*, 9th edn, EBC, Lucknow, 2005, pp 396–399.

the particular circumstances of the case. At common law, unless otherwise agreed, time stipulations were required to be adhered to strictly. Failure to adhere to this requirement would enable the non-breaching party to rescind the contract. Equity, however, was less severe in its treatment of late performance so that parties could not rescind a contract in cases of late performance unless the lapse of time was substantial. Equity's approach to time stipulations has now been embedded in legislation.[7]

Property Law Act 1958 (Vic)

Section 41

Stipulations in a contract, as to time or otherwise, which according to rules of equity are not deemed to be or to have become of the essence of the contract, shall be construed and have effect at law in accordance with the same rules.

Subject-specific legislation may also assist in determining the relevance of a failure to perform at the time stipulated in a contract. Thus, for example, the Victorian *Goods Act 1958* provides that time stipulations will not be considered of the essence unless a contrary intention appears in the contract.

Goods Act 1958 (Vic)

Section 15

Unless a different intention appears from the terms of the contract, stipulations as to time of payment are not deemed to be of the essence of a contract of sale. Whether any other stipulation as to time is of the essence of the contract or not depends on the terms of the contract.

As a consequence of this legislative intervention, time will only be of the essence if:

- the parties expressly provide that time is of the essence;
- the circumstances indicate parties intended time to be of the essence; or
- subsequent to a party failing to adhere to a time requirement in a contract, the non-defaulting party gives notice requiring performance to be made within a reasonable period of time.

The relevance of timely performance was recently discussed by the High Court in the following case.

---

7   See *Conveyancing Act 1919* (NSW) s 13; *Property Law Act 1974* (Qld) s 62; *Law of Property Act 1936* (SA) s 16; *Supreme Court Civil Procedure Act 1932* (Tas) s 11(7); *Property Law Act 1958* (Vic) s 41; *Property Law Act 1969* (WA) s 21. See also *Goods Act 1988* (Vic) s 14.

Tanwar Enterprises Pty Ltd v Cauchi

(2003) 217 CLR 315, High Court of Australia

[The respondent vendors (Cauchi) entered into contracts for the sale of three adjoining parcels of land to the appellant purchaser (Tanwar) in October 1999. The combined price of the properties was just over $4.5 million. The agreed completion date was 28 February 2000 (later amended by agreement, for which the purchasers paid $80,000 consideration, to August 2000) and time was not stipulated as being of the essence.

The purchaser paid deposit moneys totalling just over $450,000 and, later, additional payments of nearly $400,000 toward the purchase price. On 20 August 2000 the vendors issued notices of termination in respect of the contracts. However, as a result of negotiations these notices were withdrawn and replaced with deeds providing for a new completion date of 25 June 2001 which each provided that time was of the essence. The deeds also stipulated that if the purchaser did not complete the sale all moneys paid pursuant to the contract would be forfeited. The purchasers were unable to access the necessary funds on 25 June 2001 and sought to make payment on 26 June. The vendors issued notices of termination whereupon the purchaser sought an order for specific performance of the contract. The purchaser failed at first instance and on appeal to the New South Wales Court of Appeal. The purchaser appealed to the High Court.]

Kirby J <at 345 [91]>: The nineteenth century English cases: The traditional strictness of the common law's approach to contractual provisions as to time was nowhere more rigorously enforced than in time stipulations for the completion of contracts for the sale of land. ... <346> ... Originally, the distinction between 'essential' and 'non-essential' conditions did not exist at common law in respect of stipulations as to the time for completion of a contract for the sale of land. This was because all such stipulations, where they were found, were regarded as essential.

[92] Courts of equity, however, adopted a distinct approach to stipulations as to time. In the application of that approach, such courts, at least by the early nineteenth century, would intervene to grant equitable remedies, including the remedy of relief against forfeiture and specific performance, against the legal consequence following a party's inability to enforce its interests because of a breach of a contractual stipulation as to time. In early cases, regard was had by equity to such considerations as the length of the defaulting party's delay, the extent of any affirmation of the contract despite the delay, whether the delay was 'not sufficiently apologised for' and whether there was waiver or acquiescence. ...

[94] ... equity drew a distinction between 'essential' and ' non-essential' conditions as to time. It imposed upon the party who set up the provision as to time the onus of establishing the essentiality of the stipulation. ... <347>

[95] Unsurprisingly, the response of common lawyers in retaliation against these developments was to draft contracts that contained express provisions stipulating that time was of the essence of the agreement between the parties. Such stipulations were included in the obvious hope of repelling equitable intervention

by providing a foothold for the argument that it would be unjust, and indeed unconscionable, for equity to intervene to defeat the expressly agreed legal rights and obligations of the parties.

[96] Notwithstanding such express terms, a series of decisions in England ... maintained the opinion that equity could relieve a defaulting purchaser against forfeiture of an interest in land, even when that party had failed to comply with the condition of the contract stipulating that time was of the essence. ... These decisions were sometimes viewed in Australia as having preserved the right of equity to give relief ... notwithstanding the express contractual stipulation as to time. ...

The applicable principles

[106] It is now necessary to state the principles applicable to cases such as the present that I take to emerge from legal authority applicable in Australia:

(1) The basic principle is that, subject to statute, a party of full capacity is bound by legal obligations assumed in a valid agreement with another. Equity, it is said, mends no man's bargain. ... <351> ... Certainty in contractual obligations, freely assumed, is an economically valuable feature of a modern market economy. ... If parties agree to be contractually bound by a provision that stipulates that time is essential to their contractual dealings, *prima facie* they should be held to that agreement. ...

(2) Nevertheless, in Australia, equitable relief may be granted against forfeiture of property in established cases. The mere fact that the agreement between the parties makes time essential does not exclude equity's jurisdiction to afford relief. However, such jurisdiction is reserved to cases in which 'exceptional circumstances' are shown. In judging whether the circumstances are 'exceptional', regard must be had to the entire relationship between the parties, the concern of equity being with substance, not form. The entire circumstances must be judged as exceptional. ....

(3) Whatever may be the precise content of the 'equitable interest' of a purchaser under a contract for the sale of land, it is now accepted that, in a proper case, it is sufficient to sustain equitable jurisdiction to relieve that party against forfeiture of such an interest for time default, even in respect of a time provision agreed to be essential. The equitable interest has developed to relieve from forfeiture a party with a substantial stake in the property in consequence of an exercise of legal rights that is shown to be the result of fraud, mistake, accident or surprise or otherwise unconscionable in all the circumstances.

(4) In deciding whether it would be unconscientious conduct for a party to take advantage of the forfeiture consequent on a breach of an essential time stipulation leading to a termination of the contract, various factual considerations, typical of such cases, have often been taken into account. ... <352> ... factual considerations that may be taken into account in judging the existence or absence of unconscionable conduct for this purpose include (a) the

character of the contract in which the time stipulation appears (ie whether it is of a commercial, domestic or personal kind); (b) the relevant background facts explaining any special significance of the stipulation as to time; (c) whether the parties have access to appropriate independent legal advice; and (d) any degree to which the party in default may be regarded as disadvantaged, vulnerable or in need of equity's protection from the insistence on its rights of a party in a superior economic or other position. Generally speaking, equity is more solicitous for the plight of the vulnerable. ....

(5) In deciding whether relief should be offered, it is proper to expect the moving party, seeking the exceptional intervention of equity, to establish by admissible evidence any fact said to be relevant to that intervention. ... They should not normally be left to inference, speculation or suggested common knowledge. ...

[107] I turn to apply these principles to the present appeal.

Unconscionable conduct is not demonstrated
[108] *Consideration of the parties' dealings*: To the extent that the evidence permitted, the primary judge and the Court of Appeal were correct to take into account the history of the dealings between the parties that led to the execution of the deeds of 5 June 2001. Sometimes, perhaps often, an express stipulation in a contract for the sale of land, to the effect that time is of the essence, will be included as a standard provision in a printed form. But the terms of the deeds of 5 June 2001 applicable in this case deny that character to the special conditions upon which the parties agreed. The opening clause of each deed acknowledged a withdrawal by the vendors of a notice of termination that they had given to the purchaser on 20 August 2000. The vendors were therefore surrendering any rights that they may have had under that notice to bring previous defaults in timely settlement to a head and to be returned to a position where they once again had unrestricted control over the disposition of their property. The language of the deeds is emphatic. It is clear and specific. The circumstance of the negotiation, and rejection, of the four week period for settlement sought by the purchaser adds evidentiary emphasis to the vendors' insistence on adherence to the 'final arrangement' as it was described in ... the deeds. <354>

[110] *Terms of the deeds and exceptional circumstances*: The language of the deeds, reinforced by the evidence as to their origin, sustains the conclusion that this was a time stipulation that both sides consciously entered into to govern their future dealings. Having bound themselves to conform to such a clear stipulation, the vendors had the legal right, in the default that occurred, to exercise the powers conferred on them ... to terminate the sale. That right the vendors exercised. ... Correctly, the purchaser accepted that the vendors had not caused, or contributed to, the default which was wholly its own.

[111] To obtain relief from equity, it was therefore the obligation of the purchaser to show, relevantly, exceptional circumstances and that it would be unconscientious for the vendors to terminate the sale and to take advantage of

the forfeiture. This was not a case where the breach was inadvertent. True, it was unintended. But knowing as it did the strict provisions of the deeds and the earlier refusal of the vendors to agree to a four week interval for settlement, it was extremely perilous for the purchaser to proceed on the footing that strict conformity as to time would be waived if the funds were not available for the settlement on the date 'finally arranged'. In some circumstances, it might conceivably be safe to draw down funds on a second mortgage at the last possible minute. But this was not such a case. At least it was open to the judges below to so conclude. No error is shown in the conclusions that they reached.

[112] *Absence of special vulnerability*: Nor can it be said that the purchaser was specially disadvantaged, vulnerable or in need of the protection of equity from the vendors' misuse of a superior position. The purchaser is a development company with access to good legal advice. ...

[His Honour concluded that the vendors were entitled to terminate the contract in this case.]

[Gleeson CJ, McHugh, Gummow, Hayne and Heydon JJ, in a joint judgment, also held that it was not unconscientious in the circumstances for the vendors to exercise their right to terminate the contract. In a separate judgment Callinan J held that this was not an exceptional case for which the purchaser could obtain relief against forfeiture.]

Appeal dismissed

[footnotes omitted]

Where time is not stipulated to be of the essence and one party does not perform within the stipulated time (or if no time is stipulated, within a reasonable time) that party will be in breach but the other party will not have an automatic right to terminate the contract. However, if the non-breaching party gives notice to the other party requiring performance of their obligations within a reasonable time, that new time stipulation will be considered 'of the essence' and failure to comply will enable the non-breaching party to rescind the contract and recover damages.

Louinder v Leis

(1982) 149 CLR 509, High Court of Australia

[On 1 November 1979 the appellant (Louinder) contracted to sell to the respondent (Leis) a property near Sydney for the amount of $79,500 payable by $7,950 deposit upon signing and the balance on completion. The contract did not stipulate a date for completion but included a provision enabling Louinder to give notice for completion of the contract in specified circumstances. On 8 February 1980 Louinder gave notice to complete the contract within 21 days. Completion did not occur in this time and Louinder gave notice rescinding the contract. Leis received finance to purchase the property on 14 April and sought specific performance of the contract.

Louinder claimed he was entitled to give the notice of completion he did. The trial judge disagreed, holding that notice to complete could not be given unless there was 'great and improper delay' or other misconduct on the part of Louinder. The Court of Appeal agreed. Louinder appealed.]

Mason J [at 519]: The principal issue in the appeal is: in what circumstance is a party to a contract for the sale of land entitled to give notice to complete making time the essence of the contract? ... At the outset we need to keep in mind (a) the difference between a contract which does not fix a time for completion and one which does, though not making time of the essence; and (b) the difference between breach of an obligation to complete the contract on a stipulated date or within a reasonable time, as the case may be, and a breach of some other obligation imposed by the contract, ... The entitlement to give notice having the effect of making time of the essence varies in these situations. ...

<524> ... a mere failure to comply with a non-essential stipulation as to time justifies the giving of a notice having the effect of making time the essence of performance of that stipulation, even though the failure to comply does not involve an unreasonable delay. The non-essential stipulation as to time is a term of the contract enforceable by an action for damages and it is the breach of this term that justifies the giving of the notice. ...

<526> ... delay beyond the stipulated date will give rise to a liability in damages. But because equity treats the time stipulation as non-essential, mere breach of it does not justify rescission by the innocent party and will not bar specific performance at the suit of the party in default. Unreasonable delay in complying with the stipulation in substance amounting to a repudiation is essential to justify rescission. It is to this end that, following breach, the innocent party gives notice fixing a reasonable time for performance of the relevant contractual obligation. The result of non-compliance with the notice is that the party in default is guilty of unreasonable delay in complying with a non-essential time stipulation. The unreasonable delay amounts to a repudiation and this justifies rescission.

<527> ... This solution is not unfair to the party who is guilty of a mere breach of contract. He is entitled to a notice which fixes a reasonable time in all the circumstances and those circumstances will include the fact that he has not been guilty of a serious breach of contract or of unreasonable or gross delay.

<528> ... the general rule that a breach of a non-essential term entitles the innocent party to give a notice having the effect of making time of the essence in respect of that term is qualified so as to permit the giving of a notice having the effect of making time of the essence of the contract in respect of completion when the breach of the particular stipulation amounts to a breach of the obligation to complete or has the practical effect of making it impossible to complete the contract within the time stipulated or contemplated by the contract.

[In this case the notice was not effective because, as the contract did not fix a time for completion, an unreasonable delay was required before there could be said to be a breach which would justify the giving of notice. That was not the case here.]

[Gibbs CJ, Stephen, Wilson and Brennan JJ agreed on this point.]

Appeal dismissed

Where a date for performance is stipulated in a contract the parties have until midnight on that date to perform unless the contract or trade usage provides otherwise.[8]

Afovos Shipping Co SA v Pagnan (The 'Afovos')

[1983] 1 All ER 449, House of Lords

[By a time charter-party, Pagnan, the owners, let a vessel to the charterers, Afovos. Under the terms of the charter-party hire was payable semi-monthly in advance and, in the event of the charterers failing to pay the hire punctually and regularly, the owners were at liberty to withdraw the vessel from hire. This was, however, subject to a proviso in clause 31 that, if the hire was not received when due, the owners were to give the charterers 48 hours notice and would not withdraw the vessel if payment was made within those 48 hours.

Due to a bank error, the charterer's failed to make payment on the due date of 14 June 1979. At 4:40pm on 14 June the owners notified the charterers by telex that they intended to withdraw the charter. Payment was not received within 48 hours of the receipt of the telex and the owners claimed an entitlement to withdraw the vessel.

The charterers claimed that the general rule that payment is not due until midnight on a specified date meant that the telex of 14 June was sent prematurely and the 48 hours could not begin until after midnight. The owners, on the other hand, claimed that where payment was to be made to a bank, the time for performance was not midnight but rather the normal closing time for the bank and that therefore their notice of 14 June was not premature.

The trial judge held that the owners were entitled to give notice at any time on the due date. An appeal to the Court of Appeal succeeded, the Court holding that the charterers were not due to make payment until midnight on 14 June and therefore the notice was premature. The owners appealed.]

Lord Hailsham of St Marylebone LC [at 452]: Both the grammatical meaning of cl 31 and the policy considerations underlying the contract require that the moment of time at which the 48 hours' notice must be given did not arise until after the moment of time at which, apart from the clause, the right of withdrawal would have accrued. ... The argument which appealed to the judge that notice could be given at any time during the last day available for payment of the instalment (ie at any time after midnight on 13–14 June or alternatively at some point of time when it was unlikely that the instalment would be paid timeously) failed to make any impression on me at all. The notice can only be given 'when hire is due and not received', which cannot arise before the time postulated by the answer given to the first question (whatever that answer may be), and the notice can only be given when there is (or apart from cl 31 would be) already in existence, an 'option'

---

8   Patteson J in *Startup v Macdonald* (1843) 134 ER 1029 at 1040.

capable of exercise of 'withdrawing the vessel from the Charter-Party', and that option can only be exercised after the arrival of the same point of time.

... <453> ... In the result, I conclude that the crux of this case depends on the answer given to [the following question]: at what point of time can the charterers be said to have been 'failing the punctual and regular payment of the hire'? [Put simply] what is the latest point of time on 14 June 1979 which would have constituted punctual payment of the instalment? To this question I believe that, in principle, only one answer is possible, namely at midnight on the last day available to them for the due and punctual payment of the hire, ... I take it to be a general principle of law not requiring authority that where a person under an obligation to do a particular act has to do it on or before a particular date he has the whole of that day to perform his duty. No doubt as the hours pass it becomes less and less probable that he will be able to do it. That is the risk he runs. But he is not actually in default until the time arrives. ... <454> ... The question is not when the charterer would cease to be likely to pay in time but when ... 'punctual payment' would have failed. In my opinion this moment must relate to a particular hour, and is not dependent on the modalities of the recipient bank. It is the hour of midnight to which the general rule applies.

[Lord Diplock, Lord Keith of Kinkel, Lord Roskill and Lord Brightman agreed with Lord Hailsham of St Marylebone LC.]

Appeal dismissed

INTERNATIONAL PERSPECTIVES

India

Unlike the position at common law, when performance may be rendered any time before midnight on the date specified, under the *Indian Contract Act, 1872* where a date is stipulated as the day for performance, performance must take place within the ordinary business hours for performance. The Indian Act also provides a guide to remedies where time is, or is not, of the essence.

Indian Contract Act, 1872

Section 46. Time for performance of promise, where no application is to be made and no time is specified

Where, by the contract, a promisor is to perform his promise without application by the promisee, and no time for performance is specified, the engagement must be performed within a reasonable time.

Explanation: The question 'what is a reasonable time' is, in each particular case, a question of fact.

Section 47. Time and place for performance of promise, where time is specified and no application to be made

When a promise is to be performed on a certain day, and the promisor has undertaken to perform it without the application by the promisee, the promisor may perform it at any time during the usual hours of business on such day and at the place at which the promise ought to be performed.

Illustration

A promise to deliver goods at B's warehouse on the first of January. On that day, A brings the goods to B's warehouse, but after the usual hour for closing it, and they are not received. A has not performed his promise.

Section 48. Application for performance on certain day to be at proper time and place

When a promise is to be performed on a certain day, and the promisor has not undertaken to perform it without application by the promisee, it is the duty of the promisee to apply for the performance at a proper place and within the usual hours of business

Explanation: The question 'what is proper time and place' is, in each particular case, a question of fact.

Section 55. Effect of failure to perform at fixed time, in contract in which time is essential

When a party to a contract promises to do a certain thing at or before a specified time, or certain things at or before a specified time and fails to do such thing at or before a specified time, the contract or so much of it as has not been performed, becomes voidable at the option of the promisee, if the intention of the parties was that time should be of essence of the contract.

Effect of such failure when time is not essential: If it was not the intention of the parties that time should be of the essence of the contract, the contract does not become voidable by the failure to do such thing at or before the specified time; but the promisee is entitled to compensation from the promisor for any loss occasioned to him by such failure.

Effect of acceptance of performance at time other than that agreed upon: If, in case of a contract voidable on account of the promisor's failure to perform his promise at the time agreed, the promisee accepts performance of such promise at any time other than that agreed, the promisee cannot claim compensation of any loss occasioned by the non-performance of the promise at the time agreed, unless, at the time of acceptance, he gives notice to the promisor of his intention to do so.

China

The *Contract Law of the People's Republic of China* has no provisions dealing with whether or not time is 'of the essence' and the consequences of this, but does provide guidance as to when performance must take place where the parties have not stipulated a time for performance in their contract.

> #### Contract Law of the People's Republic of China, 1999
>
> Article 62. Gap Filling
>
> Where a relevant term of the contract was not clearly prescribed, and cannot be determined in accordance with [normal usage] one of the following provisions applies:
> (...iv) If the time of performance was not clearly prescribed, the obligor may perform, and the obligee may require performance, at any time, provided that the other party shall be given the time required for preparation; ...

5 Prevention of performance

If the promisee prevents the promisor from performing their obligations under the contract this will excuse the promisor from performance and the promisee cannot thereafter rely on non-performance as a basis for a contractual claim or as a defence to a claim brought by the promisor.

INTERNATIONAL PERSPECTIVES

India

The *Indian Contract Act, 1872* provides that where one party prevents performance of the contract by the other, the latter may avoid the contract and recover compensation for any loss suffered.

> #### Indian Contract Act, 1872
>
> Section 53. Liability of party preventing event on which contract is to take effect
>
> When a contract contains reciprocal promises, and one party to the contract prevents the other from performing his promise, the contract becomes voidable at the option of the party so prevented; and he is entitled to compensation from the other party for any loss which he may sustain in consequence of the non-performance of the contract.

Illustration

A and B contract that B shall execute some work for A for a thousand rupees. B is ready and willing to execute the work accordingly, but A prevents him from doing so. The contract is voidable at the option of B; and, if he elects to rescind it, he is entitled to recover from A compensation for any loss which he has incurred by its non-performance.

Section 54. Effect of default as to the promise which should be performed, in contract consisting of reciprocal promises

When a contract consists of reciprocal promises, such that one of them cannot be performed, or that its performance cannot be claimed till the other has been performed, and the promisor of the promise last mentioned fails to perform it, such promisor cannot claim the performance of the reciprocal promise, and must make compensation to the other party to the contract for any loss which such other party may sustain by the non-performance of the contract.

Section 67. Effect of neglect of promisee to afford promisor reasonable facilities for performance

If any promisee neglects or refuses to afford the promisor reasonable facilities for the performance of his promise, the promisor is excused by such neglect or refusal as to any non-performance caused thereby.
Illustration

(a) A contracts with B to repair B's house.
(b) B neglects or refuses to point out to A the places in which his house requires repair. A is excused for the non-performance of the contract, if it is caused by such neglect or refusal.

China

The *Contract Law of the People's Republic of China* does not directly provide for the prevention by one party of performance by the other. However, the general requirement that performance by the parties occur in good faith is likely to oblige a promisee not to prevent the performance by the promisor of their obligations (Article 60).

6 Summary

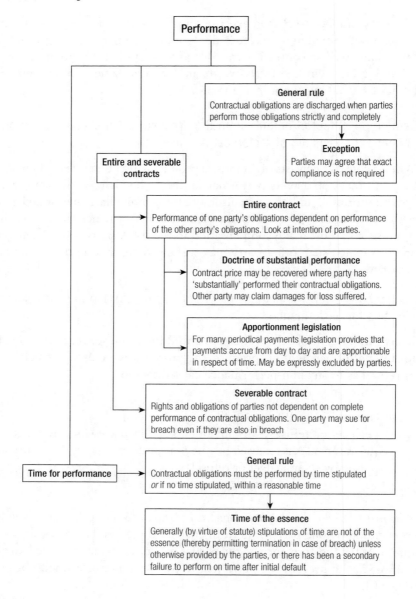

7 Questions

1   Suzanne is a champion netballer. She has been an Australian and Victorian representative player. She has recently retired from professional sport and returned to her home town to live with her husband and two young children. Seizing this opportunity, the local netball club, the Hawthorn Hawks, approached her to play for them. The Hawks had been struggling for years. Suzanne told the club that she was not keen to sign on for the season because of

unpredictable family commitments. The club was, however, quite desperate to get Suzanne on board and told her that if she agreed to play for the season with the Hawks, they would pay her $5,000. Suzanne found the promise of money, combined with the opportunity to play the sport she loved, too good to resist, and agreed to their proposal.

Suzanne began training with the Hawks and, when the season started, she helped them to their first victory in years, playing in the key 'goal attack' position. This arrangement continued for the next few weeks, at which point the Hawks were well on their way to their first finals berth in years.

Just before round 10, with only two games remaining before the finals, Suzanne's eldest son succeeded in making the state football team. Her son's game was scheduled to play at the same time as her netball game. She decided that watching her son play in the state team was much more important than her own sporting commitments. She notified her netball coach that she would not be playing in the round 10 game. Her coach expressed great disappointment and begged her to reconsider, but she refused.

The Hawks lost their round 10 encounter in Suzanne's absence. Suzanne played in the round 11 game, which the team won. However, the Hawks fell just short of making the finals.

At the end of the season Suzanne approached the club seeking the $5,000 they had promised her for her participation. They refused, claiming that she missed a vital game and had therefore not lived up to her part of the bargain.

Suzanne has come to you for advice. Please advise Suzanne whether she can recover all or part of the promised payment.

2. Louis is an art lover and holds an extensive private collection. To make room for some new acquisitions, he decided to sell a few paintings that, while valuable, were not among his favorites. One of these paintings was sold to Tobias for $900,000 on 20 June. Tobias did not have immediate access to $900,000 and it was agreed between the parties that settlement would occur on 20 July, giving Tobias sufficient time to arrange finance.

Tobias did not make payment by the agreed date and Louis reluctantly agreed to an extension of the settlement date until 14 August. On 15 August, when Tobias has still not made payment, Louis notified him by email that he was terminating the contract and that he planned to sue Tobias for any loss suffered as a result of his failure to make payment as agreed. After receiving the email Tobias called Louis and begged him to give him an extra couple of days to finalise the financial arrangements. Louis refused.

Tobias has come to you for advice. He tells you that he had finance approved, but it had taken a bit longer than expected for the financiers to make the funds available to him. He advises that he now has the funds and could have made payment on 16 August if Louis had agreed. He wishes to know if there is any way Louis can be compelled to allow him to make payment and, if not, whether he could be liable to Louis for damages, as Louis had claimed.

CHAPTER 20

Discharge by Agreement

1	Introduction	564
2	Termination by separate agreement	564
3	Termination provisions	567
4	The consequences of discharge by agreement	570
5	Summary	571
6	Questions	571

1 Introduction

The general principle of freedom of contract that facilitates parties entering into a contract also operates to allow parties to end their contract by agreement.

There are two ways a contract can be discharged by agreement. First, a contract can be discharged as a result of a separate and subsequent agreement being reached by the parties. Second, a contract can be discharged pursuant to a term of the existing contract giving the parties the right to terminate the contract upon the occurrence or non-occurrence of a specified event.

2 Termination by separate agreement

After the formation of a contract, but prior to complete performance, parties may wish to bring their contractual rights and obligations to an end. Often this will be due to a change in circumstances of one or both of the parties and may also be used as part of a dispute resolution mechanism between the parties.

In order to effectively terminate an existing contract the new agreement must meet all the criteria of a binding contract. Consequently, unless the contract is made by deed, consideration must be provided by both parties. In the case of a wholly executory contract, in which neither party has fully performed their contractual obligations, this presents no practical difficulties; the consideration of each party will be the promise to release the other from its obligations under the existing contract.[1] On the other hand, where one party has fully performed its contractual

---

[1] See *Creamoata Limited v The Rice Equalization Association Limited* (1953) 89 CLR 286 at 306, per Williams ACJ.

obligations but the other party has not, the performing party's consideration will be releasing the non-performing party from their existing contractual obligations but the non-performing party must provide separate consideration in order for the termination contract to be binding. These agreements are known as 'accord and satisfaction' agreements.[2]

> Accord and satisfaction is the purchase of a release from an obligation arising under contract or tort by means of any valuable consideration, not being the actual performance of the obligation itself. The accord is the agreement by which the obligation is discharged. The satisfaction is the consideration which makes the agreement operative. Formerly it was necessary that the consideration should be executed: 'I release you from your obligation in consideration of 50 pounds now paid by you to me.' Later it was conceded that the consideration might be executory: 'I release you from your obligation in consideration of your promise to pay me 50 pounds, and give me a letter of withdrawal.' The consideration on each side might be an executory promise, the two mutual promises making an agreement enforceable in law, a contract.[3]

In some cases an agreement to terminate may be inferred from inordinate delay by the parties in performing, or requiring performance, of contractual obligations. In such a case the contract will be said to have been 'abandoned'. This issue was discussed in the following case.

Fitzgerald v Masters

(1956) 95 CLR 420, High Court of Australia

[The plaintiff (respondent) made a contract with John Fitzgerald (the deceased) for the transfer of an interest in the deceased's farm. The agreement provided for a partnership arrangement in which the plaintiff would work part of the land and after full payment was made the deceased would transfer to the plaintiff the agreed share in the land. The plaintiff paid a substantial sum under the contract but, at the request of the deceased (for legal reasons relating to certain disclosures made to his bank), did not make further payment. The partnership arrangement broke down and the plaintiff left the farm a few years later. Twenty-six years after making the contract, the plaintiff sought specific performance against the defendants (appellants) as executors of the deceased's estate. The plaintiff succeeded in the Supreme Court of New South Wales and the defendants appealed. The defendants argued that the contract had been abandoned as a result (in part) of a lapse of time.]

Dixon CJ and Fullagar J [at 432]: There can be no doubt that, where what has been called an 'inordinate' length of time has been allowed to elapse, during which neither party has attempted to perform, or called upon the other to perform, a contract made between them, it may be inferred that the contract has been abandoned. ... What is really inferred in [abandonment cases] is that the contract

---

2 See *Butler v Fairclough* (1917) 23 CLR 78.
3 Scrutton LJ in *British Russian Gazette and Trade Outlook Ltd v Associated Newspapers Ltd* [1933] 2 KB 616 at 643–644.

has been discharged by agreement, each party being entitled to assume from a long-continued ignoring of the contract on both sides that ... 'the matter is off altogether'.

It is impossible, in our opinion, to infer a discharge of the contract in the present case. ... The position was simply that each party had promised to do something, and for a long period no act was done in performance of the contract, and no step was taken to require any act to be done in performance of the contract. Here the contract had been partly performed by the respondent. Before he left the property, he had paid more than half of the purchase price, and he had an equitable interest in the land. He had registered his contract. It is impossible to suppose ... that he ever intended simply to allow the deceased to keep both the money and the land, and no suggestion that the money should be repaid to him was ever made. As Taylor J observed during argument, if he had at any time regarded the contract as at an end, the first thing one would have expected him to do <433> was to demand repayment of his money. The truth is, we think, that the equitable interest in the land, which the respondent had acquired, could not be lost or destroyed by mere inaction on his part. It could only be lost or destroyed by release or express agreement on his part, or if the deceased lawfully rescinded the contract. ...

McTiernan, Webb and Taylor JJ [at 440]: After leaving the property the respondent did not return to it nor, indeed, did he see it again until after 1951 when the deceased died. Upon the evidence there can be no suggestion that the respondent intended to abandon his rights under the contract at the time when he left the property for the deceased undertook to work the property during his absence. ... That the respondent had no thought of abandoning his rights under the agreement is borne out by an incident that occurred shortly before he left the property. The difficulties ... had arisen between the respondent and the deceased and some question arose between them concerning the registration of the agreement for sale. ... After receiving advice [the respondent] had the agreement registered with the Department of Lands and this he did after notice to the deceased and in spite of the latter's requests that he should forbear from doing so for the time being.

... Nothing more passed between the parties until 1937 and thereafter there was silence until September 1948. We forbear to discuss the correspondence which passed between the parties at this later stage but it continued sporadically until the death of the deceased in 1951. ...

After discussing the question of the respondent's delay with as much particularity as the meagre evidence permitted the learned trial judge expressed the view that if no other factor remained for consideration the equitable relief sought by the respondent should be refused. With this view we agree. The suit was instituted some twenty-six years after the date when the contract was made and some twenty years after the date when, if the instalments of purchase money had been paid in accordance with the terms of the agreement, the full amount of the purchase money would have been paid. And, notwithstanding the unusual circumstances in which the respondent left the property, the delay was of such a character as to justify <441> entirely the conclusion that equitable relief sought should be refused. Indeed, in our view, it is doubtful whether any other conclusion would fairly have been open. But [Moratorium legislation subsequently came into force which postponed the prescribed dates for payment of further instalments] and ultimately the time for payment was extended until 'prescribed dates' in the year 1952. The result was that except, perhaps, for a very short period in 1930 the respondent was not in default in payments of any instalment during the lifetime of the deceased. Indeed, after December 1930 no further instalments became due and payable until some time in 1952 and before this—in March 1951—the respondent was moving to assert his rights. ... It was, as already appears, only in [1952] that the outstanding instalments began to fall due and it is only too plain that the appellants were not then prepared to recognise the respondent's claim. In these circumstances we fail to see how it can be said that a case of unreasonable delay was made out. The respondent was not entitled to a transfer of an interest in the land until he had paid the balance of the purchase money and he was under no obligation to pay it until 1952. And at that stage the appellants refused and thereafter continued to refuse to perform the agreement on their part. There was not, as was suggested on behalf of the appellants, a delay on the part of the respondent of something like twenty years in seeking to enforce his right to a transfer; on the contrary as long as the balance of purchase money remained outstanding he had no such right and as long as his obligation to pay such balance was postponed by the operation of the Moratorium Acts there was no delay of which the deceased, in his lifetime, or the appellants, thereafter, could take advantage.

<442> ... In any event the evidence makes it clear that at no time did the deceased furnish the respondent with information which would have enabled the latter to discharge his obligations ... and, in these circumstances, it does not lie in the mouth of the appellants to assert that the respondent was guilty of unreasonable delay in making such payments or that his failure to make such payments establishes that he was not a ready and willing purchaser.

Appeal dismissed

3 Termination provisions

Frequently an existing contract will provide a mechanism for termination, either expressly or by implication. Whether this is the case, and how the provision operates, is a matter of construction in each case. A contract may contain a provision expressly giving one or both parties the right to terminate the contract upon the occurrence or non-occurrence of a specified event or it may provide for automatic termination in certain circumstances. This sort of provision is common in commercial contracts such as partnerships and joint venture and also in employment contracts. In these cases the provision acts both as a form of risk management and as a deterrent against non-performance.

In addition to express provisions, termination clauses may, in appropriate cases, be implied into a contract. This will most often arise in the case of open-ended contracts, such as those for the lease of premises or for the provision of on-going personal services. This issue arose in the following case.

Crawford Fitting Co v Sydney Valve and Fitting Pty Ltd

(1988) 14 NSWLR 438, New South Wales Court of Appeal

[Crawford Fitting (manufacturer) appointed Sydney Valve (distributor) to be the exclusive agent for its products for an indefinite period of time. Sydney Valve later breached this agreement by distributing competing products. Crawford Fitting then sought to terminate by serving six months notice on Sydney Valve. One issue that arose was whether or not a term could be implied that the agreement could be terminated on the provision of reasonable notice. The trial judge held that such a term could not be implied and that Crawford Fitting was in breach of contract by purporting to terminate in the way it did. Crawford Fitting appealed.]

McHugh JA [at 443]: When the question arises whether a commercial agreement for an indefinite period may be terminated, the answer depends upon whether the agreement contains an implied term to that effect. ... The existence of the term is a matter of construction. But the question of construction does not depend only upon a textual examination of the words or writings of the parties. It also involves consideration of the subject matter of the agreement, the circumstances in which it was made, and the provisions to which the parties have or have not agreed ...

<444> ... In principle, the better view would seem to be that, although there is a presumption against implying a term that an agreement is terminable, ordinarily the nature of a commercial agreement will lead to the conclusion that the parties must have intended it to be terminable on notice. ...

Whether a contract is terminable on reasonable notice instead of at will also depends upon the existence of an implied term. ... That question is determined by the circumstances existing at the date of the contract ... However, the reasonableness of the period of notice depends upon the circumstances existing when the notice is given. ...

When a contract is terminable on reasonable notice, the period of notice must be sufficiently long to enable the recipient to deploy his labour and equipment in alternative employment, to carry out his commitments, to bring current negotiations to fruition and to wind up the association in a businesslike manner ...

<447> ... The implication of a term that a distributorship or agency should continue for a reasonable period gives effect to the reasonable expectations of the parties. The distributor is frequently obliged to invest his own or borrowed money in the establishment or development of the business, in purchasing stock and plant, and in employing workers. He has no hope of recouping his initial expenditure or effort if the manufacturer can terminate the agreement at will or by a period of notice sufficient only to enable the distributor to deploy his labour and equipment elsewhere. ...

<448> ... The chief purpose of a notice for a reasonable period, therefore, is to enable the parties to bring to an end in an orderly way a relationship which, *ex hypothesi*, has existed for a reasonable period so that they will have a reasonable opportunity to enter into alternative arrangements and to wind up matters which arise out of their relationship. Matters to be wound up will include carrying out existing commitments, bringing current negotiations to fruition, and, where

appropriate, obtaining the fruits of any extraordinary expenditure or effort carried out within the scope of the agreement. The line between ordinary recurrent expenditure and effort and extraordinary expenditure and effort will not always be easy to draw. But in general it will be determined by what the parties would reasonably have contemplated was extraordinary effort or expenditure.

[In this case the Court held that Sydney Valve had failed to discharge their onus of proving that the notice given by Crawford was unreasonable.]

[Priestley JA agreed with McHugh JA. Clarke JA dissented.]

Appeal allowed

INTERNATIONAL PERSPECTIVES

India

The *Indian Contract Act, 1872* permits parties to agree to the termination of their contract and also permits a promisee to unilaterally dispose of the need for performance by the promisor, even where the latter provides no valuable consideration in return. Accord and satisfaction agreements are also effective in terminating a contract based on general contractual principles.[4]

Indian Contract Act, 1872

Section 62. Effect of novation, rescission, and alteration of contract

If the parties to a contract agree to substitute a new contract for it, or to rescind or alter it, the original contract need not be performed.

Section 63. Promisee may dispense with or remit performance of promise

Every promisee may dispense with or remit, wholly or in part, the Performance of the promise made to him, or may extend the time for such performance, or may accept instead of it any satisfaction which he thinks fit.

Illustrations

(a) A promises to paint a picture for B. B afterwards forbids him to do so. A is no longer bound to perform the promise.

(b) A owes B 5,000 rupees. A pays to B, and B accepts, in satisfaction of the whole debt, 2,000 rupees paid at the time and place at which the 5,000 rupees were payable. The whole debt is discharged.

China

The *Contract Law of the People's Republic of China* provides specifically for the amendment and termination of contracts. It also provides for termination clauses

---

4   See A Singh, *Law of Contract and Specific Relief*, 9th edn, EBC, Lucknow, 2005, pp 382–384. See also *Kapur Chand Godha v Mir Nawab Himayatalikhan Azamjah* 1963 AIR 250 (in which the Supreme Court also applied s 63 of the Act).

within contracts. Unlike the position in Australia, no consideration is required for discharge, so that a party that has fully performed their obligations may discharge the other party from performance without the provision of separate consideration.

> ### Contract Law of the People's Republic of China, 1999
>
> Article 91. Conditions for Discharge
>
> The rights and obligations under a contract are discharged in any of the following circumstances ...
>
> (v) The obligee released the obligor from performance;
> (vi) Both the obligee's rights and obligor's obligations were assumed by one party;
> (vii) Any other discharging circumstance provided by law or prescribed by the parties occurred.
>
> Article 92. Post-discharge Obligations
>
> Upon discharge of the rights and obligations under a contract, the parties shall abide by the principle of good faith and perform obligations such as notification, assistance and confidentiality, etc in accordance with the relevant usage.
>
> Article 93. Termination by Agreement; Termination Right
>
> The parties may terminate a contract if they have so agreed.
>
> The parties may prescribe a condition under which one party is entitled to terminate the contract. Upon satisfaction of the condition for termination of the contract, the party with the termination right may terminate the contract.

4 The consequences of discharge by agreement

Discharge by agreement will relieve both parties from their obligations under the contract discharged. This includes obligations that had already accrued as well as future obligations. However, where unconditional rights have accrued for the benefit of the non-breaching party, such as claims for rent in arrears, those rights continue. Consequently, in *Shevill v The Builders Licensing Board*,[5] where a lease contract was terminated pursuant to a termination clause, the High Court held that the non-breaching landlord was not entitled to any damages as compensation for loss it would sustain as a result of the tenant failing to fulfil its term in accordance with the contract, but could recover rent in arrears.

---

5   (1981) 149 CLR 620. This is discussed further in chapter 21.

5 Summary

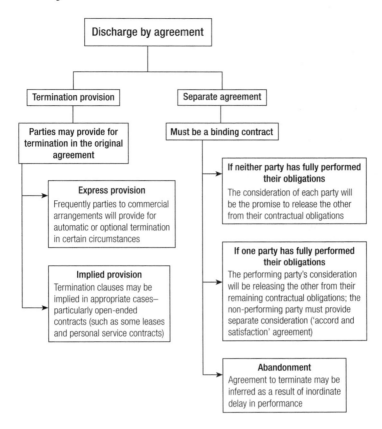

6 Questions

1. Bronwyn is a gardener. She entered into a contract with Gloria to mow her lawns for a period of two years. The contract provided that Bronwyn would mow Gloria's garden every Monday and that Gloria would pay Bronwyn $50 per week for this service. The contract entitled either party to terminate on six week's notice. The contract further provided, in clause 3, that in the event that Bronwyn failed to mow the lawns for two successive weeks without prior agreement, Gloria could terminate the contract immediately by providing notice to Bronwyn.

    Bronwyn mowed Gloria's lawn each week for 12 months. Unfortunately, after 12 months, Bronwyn's son became very ill and required hospitalisation. Bronwyn stayed with her son around the clock as they tried to determine the cause of his sudden illness. After almost a fortnight the doctor's were able to determine the cause of the illness and prescribe a course of medication which improved his health sufficiently to enable him to return home.

    Bronwyn, who had been distraught with worry over her son's health, had not performed any gardening work during this time. When she returned home with her son she found a note from Gloria informing her that Gloria was terminating her mowing contract, effective immediately, and that Gloria would be pursuing legal action against Bronwyn seeking the difference between the agreed price of $50 a week (for the remainder of the term of the contract) and the cost of her new gardener, who was charging $60 per week.

Please advise Bronwyn whether Gloria has a right to terminate the agreement without notice and/or sue her for damages as a result of her failing to mow Gloria's lawns for two weeks.

2   Joe entered into a contract with Ebony pursuant to which Joe agreed to build a carport for Ebony in exchange for $5,000, payable up front. Ebony made this payment and Joe began constructing the carport in accordance with the contract.

After about half of the carport was complete, Ebony discovered she was pregnant. She and her husband agreed that they would need to extend their house to accommodate their new arrival and to do this they would need to dismantle the carport. Ebony discussed this with Joe, who informed her that he did not have the expertise necessary to build a home extension. However, following further discussion he agreed to stop work on the carport and refund Ebony the sum of $1,000 paid for the construction of the carpark.

Unfortunately, Joe has struggled to secure any building contracts since he agreed to stop working for Ebony.

He has now come to you for advice, claiming that he only agreed to the refund of $1,000 because he thought he would quickly find new work. He would now like the money back and would like to know if he has any legal claim to the $1,000. Please advise Joe.

CHAPTER 21

Discharge for Breach

1	Introduction	573
2	Breaches that allow a contract to be discharged	574
	a Contractual provisions	574
	b Repudiatory breach	580
	c Serious breach of contract	587
3	An election to discharge the contract	594
	a Requirement and nature	594
	b Limitations on the right of election	598
4	Consequences of discharge for breach	602
	a The general effect	602
	b The effect on payments made or due	605
	c Relief against forfeiture	611
	d Recovery under a *quantum meruit*	612
5	Summary	614
6	Questions	614

1 Introduction

A breach of contract may bring it to an end; in other words, may 'discharge', or 'terminate', the contract. Not every breach has this effect. As a general rule, what is required is a particular type of breach by one party (who we refer to as the 'guilty party'[1]) followed by an election to end the contract by the other (who we refer to as 'the innocent party').[2] When this combination has occurred, the contract is discharged *in futuro*; that is, for the future. Unlike the effect of vitiating factors such as mistake, duress or undue influence which terminate the contract *ab initio* and

---

1 The terms 'innocent' and 'guilty' are used for ease of reference and refer to only the breach of contract that is in issue in a particular case. Being described as 'innocent' does not imply that a party has not been guilty of some other breach of the contract. More importantly, as we shall see below, one of the complications in this area of law is that these descriptions of the parties may change when an 'innocent' party wrongfully rescinds a contract and that conduct is then treated as a repudiatory breach.

2 See *Heyman v Darwins Ltd* [1942] AC 356. In the words of Viscount Simon in this case at 361, 'It takes two to end [a contract], by repudiation, on the one side, and acceptance of the repudiation on the other.'

require the parties to be returned, at least substantially, to their original position, discharge for breach terminates only their future rights and obligations—those that would have arisen under the contract had it not been discharged.

Three types of breach will allow the innocent party to discharge a contract. The first is a breach which the contract itself provides will allow the innocent party to do this. The second is a repudiatory breach in which the guilty party renounces the contract in some way and the third is an actual breach that is very serious in nature.[3]

Unless the contract provides otherwise, breach of contract will not discharge a contract automatically; no matter how serious it is. Rather, the innocent party will almost always have a choice—to discharge the contract, or to affirm it and continue to require proper performance. Because the innocent party has this choice, discharge for breach both describes a situation in which a contract will come to an end and a remedy available to the innocent party—a remedy that will often be pursued as part of the latter's response to the guilty party's breach of contract. This dual quality makes discharge for breach very important in practice.

The election to discharge a contract for breach is often referred to as 'rescinding' the contract and in the present context the word 'rescission' is frequently used interchangeably with 'discharge' or 'termination'. Some commentators, however, criticise this use of 'rescission', arguing that the term should be employed only in connection with factors, such as misrepresentation, duress, unconscionable conduct or undue influence, that so adversely affect the formation of a contract that it is rendered voidable.[4] Although this argument has been lost, it remains important to remember, as noted above, that the effect of rescission for breach is significantly different from the effect of rescission on the other grounds mentioned.

In this chapter we will examine:

- the types of breach that will allow a contract to be discharged
- the nature and duration of the election open to the innocent party and the restrictions that may exist on that election
- the consequences of a contract being discharged for breach.

2 Breaches that allow a contract to be discharged

a Contractual provisions

A contract may provide that in the event of a particular breach the innocent party can elect to bring it to an end. It is also possible, though uncommon, for a contract to make discharge automatic.[5] What kinds of breach will have this effect is a matter

---

3   The courts have used many different phrases to describe how serious the breach must be including 'a fundamental breach', a breach 'going to the root of the contract' and 'breach of condition'. This issue and the different types of breach that can occur are considered below.
4   For a brief discussion of this issue, see N Seddon and MP Ellinghaus *Cheshire and Fifoot's Law of Contract*, 8th edn, LexisNexis, Sydney, 2002, at 21.8.
5   Ibid at 21.2.

for agreement so that the parties can restrict it to only very serious breaches of contract, or provide that any breach, regardless of how serious it is in substance, will allow the contract to be discharged. Similarly, the parties can provide what the consequences of discharge are to be. In particular, they may provide that should the innocent party discharge the contract this will be the only remedy available, or that the right to discharge will be additional to any other rights the law may give that party. These issues are illustrated by the following extracts.

Holland v Wiltshire

(1954) 90 CLR 409, High Court of Australia

[The Hollands (defendants) contracted with Wiltshire (the plaintiff) to purchase a house property and paid a deposit of £2. This contract contained a forfeiture clause to the effect that if the purchaser did not pay the contract price, the vendor could sell the land, rescind the contract and forfeit any money that had been paid on account of the purchase price as and for liquidated damages. Subsequently, the Hollands repudiated the contract. Wiltshire responded by saying that unless they completed the transaction by a nominated date he would take action for breach of contract. The Hollands did not reply and eventually Wiltshire resold the property for a lower price. He then commenced proceedings, seeking as damages the difference between the contract price and the price for which he had resold the house, less the deposit paid. He was successful at first instance and in the Hollands' appeal to the South Australian Full Court. The Hollands then appealed to the High Court.]

Dixon CJ [at 412]: At the trial the defendants took more than one defence, but in the end the grounds of their appeal from the Local Court's judgment come down to one point. It is that there is a special clause in the contract which governs the matter and that it prescribes the only compensation which the vendor may have, namely the forfeiture of the moneys paid on account of the purchase as liquidated damages, that is to say, the amount of £2 paid as deposit. … <413> …. They say that what the vendor has done is to sell the property and rescind the contract in the exercise of the power it is expressed to confer, and that thereupon the damages became liquidated or ascertained by the clause at £2. It follows, they say, that the vendor, the plaintiff respondent, is entitled under the contract to no more. … <414>

It may be remarked that this contention assumes that when the clause says 'and any moneys paid on account of the purchase shall … be forfeited to the vendor as and for liquidated damages' it means that the forfeiture shall take place independently of the vendor's volition. It is, however, plain that the clause is intended for his benefit only and it would not be an unnatural reading to treat the forfeiture as dependent upon his election. But however that may be, there is no sufficient reason for regarding the vendor <415> as having exercised the power conferred by the clause. On the contrary everything points to his having treated the contract as discharged by breach, and as having sold in the exercise of his right as owner unfettered by the contract. … <416>

In these circumstances, the vendor was entitled to treat the contract as discharged by breach. He himself was ready and willing up to the expiration of the notice. His election to treat the contract as discharged by the purchasers' breach was sufficiently manifested by his proceeding to advertise the property for sale, and by his selling it. By that time, the purchasers were in actual breach and that breach was accompanied by an intention clearly evinced of setting the contract at nought. It is hard to see why this should not enable the vendor to treat the whole contract as discharged by the purchasers' breach or in other words to treat the contract as no longer binding upon him. This means that both parties would be discharged from further performance of the contract. The whole contract was involved, including the clause relating to rescission.

When the plaintiff respondent, the vendor, notified the defendants appellants, the purchasers, that he would take proceedings for breach of contract, he must have been understood as saying that he would seek to recover damages and that necessarily meant that he was putting on one side the restriction of the compensation to which he was entitled to the forfeiture under the clause of the £2 already paid.

The proper conclusion is that the vendor proceeded not under the contractual provision but on the footing that the purchasers had discharged him from the obligation of the contract. It follows that he is entitled to sue for unliquidated damages.

[Kitto and Taylor JJ delivered separate judgments to the same effect.]

Appeal dismissed

Shevill v The Builders Licensing Board

(1982) 149 CLR 620, High Court of Australia

[The Shevills guaranteed Shevill Truck Sales and Service Pty Ltd when it leased land from the Board for a number of years. Clause 3 of the lease provided that the rent was to be paid in advance in monthly instalments and Clause 9(a) provided that if the rent was unpaid for 14 days, or if certain other terms were breached, or if the lessee went into bankruptcy or liquidation then the lessor could re-enter the land 'without prejudice to any action or other remedy the lessee has or might or otherwise could have for arrears of rent or breach of covenants or for damages as a result of any such event'. The lessee was regularly late in paying rent. Eventually, the Board terminated the lease and claimed overdue rent and damages for breach of contract in an amount equal to the rent that would have been paid for the balance of the term of the lease. The Board succeeded at first instance and in the New South Wales Court of Appeal; the Shevills then appealed to the High Court.]

Gibbs CJ [at 625]: It is not … disputed that the appellants are liable under the guarantee for whatever damages are payable by the lessee to the respondent. The question for decision is whether the lessee is in the circumstances liable for damages.

The primary submission made on behalf of the respondent was that since the breaches of contract committed by the lessee entitled the respondent to terminate the contract, it followed that when the respondent exercised its right to do so it became entitled to damages for loss of the benefits which performance of the contract would have conferred upon it. This submission treated the breaches of the covenant to pay rent as a breach of an essential term of the contract. In the alternative it was submitted that the conduct of the lessee revealed such an unwillingness or inability to perform the contract as to amount to a repudiation of it.

This argument proceeded on the basis that the general principles of the law of contract, so far as they are relevant to the questions that arise in this case, are equally applicable to leases. ... I am content to assume that the ordinary principles of contract law are applicable.

As Lord Wright pointed out in *Heyman v Darwins Ltd* repudiation is an ambiguous word and is used in various senses. We are of course concerned only with a case in which it is admitted that there was a valid and binding contract. Such a contract may be repudiated if one party renounces his liabilities under it—if he evinces an intention no longer to be bound by the contract (*Freeth v Burr*) or shows that he intends to fulfil the contract only in a manner substantially inconsistent with his <626> obligations and not in any other way (*Ross T Smyth & Co Ltd v TD Bailey, Son & Co; Carr v JA Berriman Pty Ltd*). In such a case the innocent party is entitled to accept the repudiation, thereby discharging himself from further performance, and sue for damages: *Heyman v Darwins Ltd*. It is convenient to say that the injured party in these circumstances rescinds the contract, although there is, of course, no rescission *ab initio*: *Johnson v Agnew*. The present case was not one of this kind. There is nothing to suggest that the lessee had any intention other than to fulfil the contract, according to its terms, to the best of its ability. However, if one party, although wishing to perform the contract, proves himself unable to do so, his default in performance will give the other party a right to rescind the contract, if the breach goes 'so much to the root of the contract that it makes further commercial performance of the contract impossible': *Hongkong Fir Shipping Co Ltd v Kawasaki Kisen Kaisha Ltd*. ... [I]n either case the innocent party can rescind the contract and recover damages to compensate him for the failure to perform the contractual obligations. Counsel for the respondent, in their alternative argument, sought to bring the case within this principle. A third situation in which a right to rescission arises is where there has been a breach of a fundamental or essential term of the contract. In *Suisse Atlantique Societe d'Armement Maritime SA v NV Rotterdamsche Kolen Centrale*, Lord Upjohn said:

> A fundamental term of a contract is a stipulation which the parties have agreed either expressly or by necessary implication or which the general law regards as a condition which goes to the root of the contract so that any breach of that term may at once and without further reference to the facts and circumstances <627> be regarded by the innocent party as a fundamental breach ...

The primary argument of the respondent is that … the covenant for the payment of the rent, read in conjunction with cl 9(a), was a fundamental or essential term and that any breach of it which resulted in rent being unpaid for fourteen days gave to the respondent the right to terminate the contract and sue for damages for the breach.

It is clear that a covenant to pay rent in advance at specified times would not, without more, be a fundamental or essential term having the effect that any failure, however slight, to make payment at the specified times would entitle the lessor to terminate the lease. However, the parties to a contract may stipulate that a term will be treated as having a fundamental character although in itself it may seem of little importance, and effect must be given to any such agreement: see *Wickman Tools v Schuler AG*. In other words, a right to forfeit a lease might arise 'in the case of any breach of covenant however trifling, if the parties had agreed that a breach of that covenant should create a forfeiture': *Campbell v Payne and Fitzgerald*. In the present case cl 9(a) undoubtedly gave to the respondent a right to re-enter if rent should be unpaid for fourteen days. … However, the respondent's argument is that because cl 9(a) gave a right to re-enter for any breach of cl 3 that resulted in rent being unpaid for fourteen days, the covenant in cl 3 as to payment, together with the provisions of cl 9(a), became an essential term, or at least gave the respondent the same rights as are available under the general law to a party who elects to terminate a contract for repudiation or fundamental breach.

In my opinion it does not follow from the fact that the contract gave the respondent the right to terminate the contract that it conferred on it the further right to recover damages as compensation for the loss it will sustain as a result of the failure of the lessee to pay the rent and observe the covenants for the rest of the term. Clause 9(a) specifies a number of circumstances in which the rights <628> conferred by that clause will arise. The first of those circumstances—where the rent is unpaid for fourteen days—is not described by reference to any breach, although it necessarily involves a default. The second case—that in which the lessee commits or suffers to occur any breach or default in the observance of any of the covenants of the lease—does depend entirely upon the lessee causing or suffering a breach to occur. The other conditions on which re-entry is available do not necessarily involve a breach of any covenant or condition of the lease. In some cases, whether or not there has been a breach, the right of re-entry given by cl 9(a) may become available although the circumstances would not suggest that the position of the lessor under the lease has been substantially affected or threatened. For example, a lessee, who usually makes prompt payment of the rent, may allow a small amount of rent to fall in arrears for fourteen days. He may commit a minor breach of covenant, such as an insignificant failure to paint or repair or keep the premises clean. He may make an arrangement with his creditors the effect of which will nevertheless be that he can continue to pay the rent fully and on time. In all these circumstances the lessor is given the right to re-enter. However it would require very clear words to bring about the result, which in some circumstances would be quite unjust, that whenever a lessor could exercise the right given by the clause to re-enter, he could also recover damages for the loss resulting from the failure of the lessee to carry out all the covenants of the lease—covenants which, in some cases, the lessee might have been both willing and able to perform had it not been for the re-entry.

The words of cl 9(a) afford no support to the respondent's argument. The rights which the lessee is to have if any of the circumstances mentioned in the clause exist are exhaustively defined by the clause. There are preserved to the lessor 'any action or other remedy which the Lessor has or might or otherwise could have for arrears of rent or breach of covenants or for damages as a result of any such event.' In my opinion these words refer, distributively, to the three different sorts of circumstances in which the provisions of cl 9(a) take effect. First there is the case in which the rent has been unpaid for fourteen days; in that case the lessor can recover the arrears of rent. The second case is that in which the lessee commits or suffers to occur any breach or default in the performance of the covenants, and in that case the remedy preserved is for breach of covenants. Thirdly, events may occur (such as liquidation and bankruptcy) which do not amount to breaches of covenants. It would appear that it is to such events, and to no other, that the words 'damages as a result of any such event' refer. It is true that <629> the word 'events', where it first occurs in the clause, refers to the non payment of the rent and to the breaches of covenants as well as to the other events mentioned, but if it had this wide meaning in the phrase 'any such event', the reference to 'breach of covenants', at least, would be redundant. If this view of the clause is correct the only remedy of the respondent in the present case was to recover arrears of rent.

However, if I am wrong, and if the words 'any such event' include the non payment of rent for fourteen days, cl 9(a) does no more than preserve any right to recover damages resulting from such non payment. The clause does not confer a right to recover damages which result from the fact that the lessee will pay no further rent during the remainder of the term. It does not refer to damages for the loss of the benefits conferred by the lease as a whole. Although cl 9(a) deals with the situation in which the lessor may bring the lease to an end, there is nothing in its provisions to indicate any intention to give to a lessor who exercises the right to re-enter the same rights as would have been available to him if he had accepted a repudiation of the contract or had rescinded it on the ground that the lessee had committed a breach of an essential term. It would have been easy, although inequitable, to provide that in any of the circumstances mentioned in cl 9(a) the lessor would be entitled to damages for loss of the benefits which performance of the covenants of the lease would have conferred on him in the future. However, the rights of the lessor are limited to the recovery of arrears of rent and damages for breaches and other events that occurred before re-entry. ... <630> ...

For these reasons in my opinion the respondent was entitled to recover the arrears of rent but was not entitled to the damages which the learned trial judge awarded.

[Murphy and Brennan JJ agreed with Gibbs CJ; in a separate judgment Wilson J also agreed, although placing a different interpretation on one aspect of cl 9(a).]

Appeal allowed

[footnotes omitted]

b Repudiatory breach

The nature of a repudiatory breach

A repudiatory breach is any form of conduct by a party that evinces an intention not to be bound by the contract. Examples include expressly refusing to perform part or all of a contract, or insisting that the other party perform the contract in a manner that it does not require or sanction. It may also take the form of a continued failure to perform the contract. In all of these cases, it is not essential that the guilty party intends to repudiate the contract. Thus, for example, if that party believes that the contract requires the other to perform in a certain manner and insists that they do so, then, should this belief prove to be erroneous, their conduct will constitute a repudiatory breach even though they wanted the contract to be performed.

As the crucial ingredient in all cases of repudiation is the guilty party's evinced intention not to perform the contract, a repudiatory breach can occur even where any actual breach is of a relatively minor nature. Thus, although breach of a relatively unimportant term will not allow the innocent party to discharge the contract on the grounds of actual breach of contract, should such a breach be accompanied by statements, or action, on the part of the guilty party indicating that they do not intend to perform the contract in the future, discharge will be possible on the grounds of repudiatory breach.[6]

The concept of a repudiatory breach also reveals one of the dangers facing the innocent party where the seriousness of the guilty party's breach is contested. If the innocent party purports to discharge the contract on the grounds of the guilty party's breach and it is subsequently determined that the breach was not sufficiently serious to justify such action, then the innocent party's conduct may amount to a repudiatory breach entitling the other party (who will now be characterised as the 'innocent party') to discharge the contract on that ground.

The forms in which repudiatory breach may occur and what is required for a breach to be of this nature are discussed in the following extracts.

Federal Commerce and Navigation Ltd v Molena Alpha Inc

[1979] AC 757, House of Lords

[Federal chartered three ships from Molena to carry grain from the Great Lakes to Europe. Subsequently, a dispute arose between the parties concerning certain deductions made by the charters (Federal) from the hire payments due to Molena. In response, Molena instructed the masters of all three ships to refuse to issue bills of lading freight pre-paid. Federal demanded that this instruction be withdrawn, saying that it placed the company in an impossible position commercially. When Molena refused, Federal treated its conduct as a repudiation of the contract. The validity of this action was referred to arbitration and in connection with those proceedings a special case was stated for the court. Kerr J held that Federal had

---

6   See, for example, *Allphones Retail Pty Ltd v Hoy Mobile Pty Ltd* (2009) ATPR 42-294, esp at 41,135.

not validly terminated the contract. However, Federal successfully appealed to the Court of Appeal; Molena then appealed to the House of Lords.]

Lord Wilberforce [at 778]: [T]his is one of the more perspicuous branches of the law of contract and the modern position is clear. The form of the critical question may differ slightly as it is put in relation to varying situations:

> '... an intimation of an intention to abandon and altogether to refuse performance of the contract [or to] evince an intention no longer to be bound by the contract ....' (*Freeth v Burr* (1874) LR 9 CP 208, 213 *per* Lord Coleridge CJ)
>
> 'I do not say that it is necessary to show that the party alleged to have repudiated should have an actual intention not to fulfil the contract. He may intend in fact to fulfil it, but may be determined to do so only in a manner substantially inconsistent with his obligations, and not in any other way.' (*Ross T Smyth & Co Ltd v* <779> *T D Bailey, Son & Co* [1940] 3 All ER 60, 72 *per* Lord Wright such as to deprive) 'the charters of substantially the whole benefit which it was the intention of the parties ... that the charterers should obtain from the further performance of their own contractual undertakings' (*Hong Kong Fir Shipping Co Ltd v Kawasaki Kisen Kaisha Ltd* [1962] 2 QB 26, 72 *per* Diplock CJ)
>
> 'To constitute repudiation, the threatened breach must be such as to deprive the injured party of a substantial part of the benefit to which he is entitled under the contract ... will the consequences of the breach be such that it would be unfair to the injured party to hold him to the contract and leave him to the remedy in damages ...?' (*Decro-Wall International SA v Practitioners in Marketing Ltd* [1971] 1 WLR 361, 380 *per* Buckley LJ).

The difference in expression between these two last formulations does not, in my opinion, reflect a divergence of principle, but arises from and is related to the particular contract under consideration. They represent, in other words, applications to different contracts of the common principle that to amount to repudiation a breach must go to the root of the contract.

My Lords, I do not think there can be any doubt that the owners' breach or threatened breach in the present case, consisting in their announcement that their masters would refuse to issue bills of lading freight pre-paid and not 'claused' so as to refer to the charters, *prima facie* went to the root of the contract as depriving the charterers of substantially the whole benefit of the contract. ... It was in fact the owners' intention to put irresistible pressure on the charterers ('to compel the charters to pay over all sums deducted from hire by the charters which the owners disputed, irrespective of whether such deductions should ultimately be determined to be valid or invalid' ...) through the action they threatened to take. If the charterers had not given way, the charters would have become useless for the purpose for which they were granted. I do not think that this was disputed by the owners; in any event it was not disputable. What was said was that the action of the owners, in the circumstances in which it was taken, should not be taken to be repudiatory. They had, on 21st September 1977, referred the whole question of deductions to arbitration; in a short time the whole issue would be cleared up one way or another, after which the charters would continue to be operated in accordance with the arbitrators' decision. The owners' action was of an interim character designed to have effect only until the position as to deductions could be clarified. The owners' interest was strongly in the direction of maintaining the charters; their move was simply a tactical one designed to resolve a doubtful situation. The sums which they were forcing the charterers to pay were inconsiderable. The charterers had already offered to pay them in 'escrow'.

My Lords, with genuine respect for the judgment of Kerr J who in substance agreed with this argument, I find myself obliged to reject it. ... <780> ... [T]he owners' action must be regarded as going to the root of the contract. The issue of freight pre-paid bills of lading in respect of each of the three vessels was an urgent, indeed an immediate, requirement. ...

These were pending transactions, and 'the Charterers were likely to incur very substantial liabilities to Continental Grain if the cargoes which were being loaded or which were about to be loaded on 5th October were not completed and if freight pre-paid unclaused bills of lading were not issued promptly'. ... Blacklisting by Continental Grain was likely to follow. Thus the resolution of the deductions issue by arbitration, however soon this might be achieved, would still have left the charterers in a position where they might have lost the whole benefit of the time charters. That a 'without prejudice' agreement was in fact entered into which averted these consequences is of course irrelevant though the fact that it was made does underline the extent of the pressure on the charterers. It is also irrelevant that the steps the charterers were being compelled, under threat of a breach of contract, to take were not very serious for them. A threat to commit a breach, having radical consequences, is nonetheless serious because it is disproportionate to the intended effect. It is thirdly irrelevant that it was in the owners' real interest to continue the charters rather than put an end to them. If a party's conduct is such as to amount to a threatened repudiatory breach, his subjective desire to maintain the contract cannot prevent the other party from drawing the consequences of his actions. ...

For these reasons I agree with the decision of the Court of Appeal that the charterers were entitled to determine the contracts.

[Viscount Dilhorne and Lord Scarman agreed with Lord Wilberforce; Lords Fraser and Russell delivered separate speeches to the same effect.]

Appeal dismissed

Laurinda Pty Ltd v Capalaba Park Shopping Centre Pty Ltd

(1988–1989) 166 CLR 623, High Court of Australia

[On 31 October 1985, Laurinda entered into a deed of agreement with Capalaba whereby the latter agreed to lease its premises within a retail shopping centre that was then under construction. This agreement required Laurinda to execute a lease and deliver it to Capalaba and to pay for the stamping and registration of that lease. Capalaba was required to fill in certain details in the lease when the commencement of its term was known and have it registered. The centre opened on 1 December 1985 and having fulfilled all its obligations in relation to the lease, in

January and March 1986 Laurinda asked Capalaba for a copy. However, Capalaba did not register the lease. On 21 August 1986 Laurinda wrote to Capalaba requiring the latter to register the lease within 14 days and saying that if this did not occur it would reserve its position. The lease was not registered within that time and on 5 September Laurinda advised Capalaba that it no longer regarded itself as bound by the lease. In these proceedings, Laurinda sought a declaration that the lease had been validly discharged. It succeeded at first instanced but an appeal by Capalaba to the Queensland Full Court was successful. Laurinda then appealed to the High Court.]

Brennan J [at 647]: Repudiation is not ascertained by an inquiry into the subjective state of mind of the party in default; it is to be found in the conduct, whether verbal or other, of the party in default which conveys to the other party the defaulting party's inability to perform the contract or promise or his intention not to perform it or to fulfil it only in a manner substantially inconsistent with his obligations and not in any other way. In *Freeth v Burr*, Lord Coleridge CJ spoke of acts or conduct which 'do or do not amount to an intimation of an intention to abandon and altogether <648> to refuse performance of the contract' or of acts and conduct which 'evince an intention no longer to be bound by the contract'. This was followed by the Earl of Selborne LC in *Mersey Steel and Iron Co v Naylor, Benzon & Co*:

> I am content to take the rule as stated by Lord Coleridge in Freeth v Burr, which is in substance, as I understand it, that you must look at the actual circumstances of the case in order to see whether the one party to the contract is relieved from its future performance by the conduct of the other; you must examine what that conduct is, so as to see whether it amounts to a renunciation, to an absolute refusal to perform the contract, such as would amount to a rescission if he had the power to rescind, and whether the other party may accept it as a reason for not performing his part.

And in *Carswell v Collard*, Lord Herschell LC stated the question precisely:

> Of course, the question was not what actually influenced the defender, but what effect the conduct of the pursuer would be reasonably calculated to have upon a reasonable person.

Forslind v Bechely-Crundall is in accord with this view, though Lord Shaw of Dunfermline may be thought to go beyond Lord Herschell's test in emphasizing the effect of the defaulting party's conduct on the mind of the innocent party.

The question whether an inference of repudiation should be drawn merely from continued failure to perform requires an evaluation of the delay from the standpoint of the innocent party. Would a reasonable person in the shoes of the innocent party clearly infer that the other party would not be bound by the contract or would fulfil it only in a manner substantially inconsistent with that party's obligations and in no other way? Different minds may easily arrive at different answers. ... <649> ...

The long and unexplained delay from March to September 1986 ending with a letter stating that the solicitors required further instructions with respect to completing what had been promised over five months earlier is sufficient foundation for the drawing of an inference of repudiation. It is the inference which

Laurinda drew and, although it cannot be said that no other reasonable inference is open, it is a reasonable inference which can be clearly drawn. I have vacillated in arriving at this conclusion but, having arrived at it, I would allow the appeal and restore the judgment of Connolly J.

[Mason CJ, Deane, Dawson and Gaudron JJ delivered separate judgments to the same effect.]

Appeal allowed

[footnotes omitted]

Anticipatory breach

Anticipatory breach occurs when the guilty party repudiates the contract *before* the date on which they were due to perform their obligations and the innocent party elects to discharge the contract as a result. In such a case, the guilty party is not in actual breach of contract, as the date set for performance has not arrived. Nevertheless, the law allows the innocent party to rescind because it will usually be in the interests of both parties that they do so. From the perspective of the innocent party, it reduces the uncertainty they face by allowing them to seek substitute performance and where they are able do this, thereby reduce (and possibly even eliminate) their loss. From the perspective of the guilty party, where the innocent party's loss is reduced, it will concomitantly reduce the damages they will be required to pay for breach of contract.[7]

Anticipatory breach will occur, however, only if the innocent party elects to rescind the contract. If, instead, the contract is affirmed, the innocent party cannot claim damages unless and until the guilty party is in actual breach of contract. Thus, if the guilty party recants and performs the contract, or if a supervening event occurs that justifies their eventual non-performance, damages will not be recoverable.[8]

As well as through repudiation, anticipatory breach can be constituted by the guilty party being unable to perform their contractual obligations before performance is due. However, to justify rescission in such circumstances the innocent party must be able to show that performance would have been impossible. This requirement and other aspects of anticipatory breach are illustrated by the following extracts.

Taylor v Johnston
Sup 123 Cal Rptr 641 (1975), Supreme Court of California

[Johnston contracted to have her stallion service Taylor's mares but subsequently repudiated this contract by selling the stallion to a third party. However, when Taylor insisted upon performance she arranged for the stallion to be available at

---

7   See *Hochster v De La Tour* (1853) 2 E & B 678.
8   See *Avery v Bowden* (1855) 5 E & B 714 and *Peter Turnbull & Co Pty Ltd v Mundus Trading Co (Australasia) Pty Ltd* (1953–1954) 90 CLR 235 esp at 250, per Kitto J.

the premises of the third party and the mares were shipped there. Breeding was not successful and Taylor sued for breach of contract. He was successful at first instance whereupon Johnston appealed to the Supreme Court.]

Sullivan J [at 646]: Anticipatory breach occurs when one of the parties to a bilateral contract repudiates the contract. The repudiation may be express or implied. An express repudiation is a clear, positive, unequivocal refusal to perform ...; an implied repudiation results from conduct where the promisor puts it out of his power to perform so as to make substantial performance of his promise impossible. ...

When a promisor repudiates a contract, the injured party faces an election of remedies: he can treat the repudiation as an anticipatory breach and immediately seek damages for breach of contract, thereby terminating the contractual relationship between the parties, or he can treat the repudiation as an empty threat, wait until the time for performance arrives and exercise his remedies for actual breach if a breach does in fact occur at such time. ... However, if the injured party disregards the repudiation and treats the contract as still in force, and <647> the repudiation is retracted prior to the time of performance, then the repudiation is nullified and the injured is left with his remedies, if any, invocable at the time of his performance. ...

As we have pointed out, the trial court found that the whole course of conduct of defendants and their agents Dr Pessin and Mrs Judy from the time of the sale of Fleet Nasrullah up to and including June 13, 1966, amounted to a repudiation which plaintiff was justified in treating as an anticipatory breach. ... However, when the principles of law governing repudiation just described are applied to the facts constituting this course of conduct as found by the trial court, it is manifest that such conduct cannot be treated as an undifferentiated continuum amounting to a single repudiation but must be divided into two separate repudiations.

First, defendants clearly repudiated the contracts when, after selling Fleet Nasrullah and shipping him to Kentucky, they informed the plaintiff '[y]ou are, therefore, released from your reservations made to the stallion.' However, the trial court additionally found that '[p]laintiff did not wish to be 'released' from his 'reservations' ... insist[ed] on performance of the stud service agreements ... [and] threaten[ed] litigation if the contracts were not honoured by defendants ...' Accordingly defendants arranged for performance of the contracts by making Fleet Nasrullah available for stud service to plaintiff in Kentucky through their agents Dr Pessin and Mrs Judy. Plaintiff elected to treat the contracts as in force and shipped the mares to Kentucky to effect the desired performance. The foregoing facts lead us to conclude that the subsequent arrangements by defendants to make Fleet Nasrullah available to service plaintiff's mares in Kentucky constituted a retraction of the repudiation. Since at the time plaintiff had not elected to treat the repudiation as an anticipatory breach and had in fact shipped the mares to Kentucky in reliance on defendants arrangements, this nullified the repudiation. Thus, plaintiff was then left with this remedies that might arise at the time of performance.

[His Honour found that there was no evidence to substantiate a finding that Johnston had subsequently repudiated or not performed the contract. The other members of the Court concurred and therefore the judgment in favour of Taylor was reversed.]

National Engineering Pty Ltd v Chilco Enterprises Pty Ltd

[2001] NSWCA 291, New South Wales Court of Appeal

[National Engineering (National) contracted to hire a Demag CC4800 crane or equivalent from Chilco to assist with the construction of the Olympic Stadium at Homebush. This was a large crane owned by Van Seumeren. Subsequently, National formed the view that Chilco would not be able to deliver the crane on time. Therefore, it terminated the contract and commenced proceedings seeking a declaration that it had been entitled to do this and to recover the deposit it had paid. At first instance it was held that Chilco had not committed a breach of contract and that National's purported termination amounted to a repudiation of the contract which entitled Chilco to damages. National appealed to the Court of Appeal.]

Ipp AJA [at 49]: Repudiation of a contract may be regarded as an anticipatory breach entitling the innocent party to terminate the contract: *Laurinda Pty Limited v Capalaba Park Shopping Centre Pty Limited* per Brennan J at 641–644; *Sunbird Plaza Pty Limited v Maloney* (1988) 166 CLR 245 per Mason CJ at 262, per Gaudron J at 278–279. In addition, a party may terminate a contract for anticipatory breach where, at the point of termination, 'the other party was wholly and finally disabled from performing its contractual obligations when the time for performance, so far as it is of the essence, should arrive' per Gaudron J (at 280) in *Sunbird Plaza Pty Limited v Maloney* (see also Mason CJ at 262). As her Honour went on to remark: 'That total disability must be proved 'in fact and not in supposition'.—per Devlin J in *Universal Cargo Carriers Corporation v Citati* [1957] 2 QB 401 at 450'.

[50] For the appellant to succeed in establishing an anticipatory breach entitling it to terminate the contract, it therefore had to prove that, as at 25 March 1997 (the termination date), the respondent was wholly and finally disabled from supplying a crane as stipulated by the contract.

[51] Windeyer J held that:

> There was certainly a possibility that at the date of the purported termination [the respondent] would have been able to prevail upon Van Seumeren to provide an equivalent crane. ...

Hence, his Honour found against the appellant on this issue.

[52] His Honour was correct, with respect, in adopting this approach. The onus was on the appellant to prove on a balance of probabilities, in fact and not in supposition, that, as at 25 March 1997, there was no possibility of Van Seumeren providing a crane as stipulated by the contract. It was only in that event that it could be found that the respondent, as at 25 March 1997, was wholly and finally disabled from performing the obligation in question. Once it was found that there was a possibility that Van Seumeren would supply such a crane, the appellant had failed to discharge the onus upon it.

[After considering the evidence his Honour concluded]:

[74] In all the circumstances, in my opinion, the Van Seumeren letter and the other evidence on which the appellant relied does not establish—as a matter of fact and not supposition—that, as at 25 March, the respondent was wholly and finally disabled from obtaining a CC4800 crane or its equivalent. I am not persuaded Windeyer J was incorrect when he found that there was a possibility that at 25 March the respondent would have been able to prevail upon Van Seumeren to provide an equivalent crane.

[Heydon and Hodgson JJA agreed.]

Appeal dismissed

c Serious breach of contract

An actual breach of contract, either in the form of non-performance or defective performance, will entitle the innocent party to discharge the contract where the breach is a serious breach, as distinct from a minor one in respect of which the innocent party can be adequately compensated by an award of damages. The key issues in this area have centred on how to best characterise the breaches of contract that will permit rescission and how to determine, in a particular case, whether the breach involved was of this nature.

Characterisation

Over the years, the courts have adopted various characterisations to describe the kinds of breach that will allow a contract to be discharged for breach. Some of these have focused on the nature of the terms of the contract; for example, on whether they were dependent or independent covenants,[9] or whether the term breached was a condition precedent, or not, to the obligations of the innocent party.[10] By far the most important example of this approach has been the characterisation of terms as promissory[11] conditions or warranties with any breach of the former, but not the latter, allowing the innocent party to rescind a contract. This approach was considered in chapter 10[12] and is illustrated by the following extract from *Luna Park (NSW) Ltd v Tramways Advertising Pty Ltd*, endorsed by the High Court in *Koompahtoo Local Aboriginal Land Council v Sanpine Pty Ltd* (2007) HCA 61.

---

9   If the terms were independent of each other, the innocent party's obligation to perform existed independently of whether the guilty party also performed its obligations and so rescission for breach was not possible. However, if they were dependent, the guilty party's non-performance relieved the innocent party of its obligation to perform; in other words, rescission for breach was possible: see *Kingston v Preston* (1773) 2 Doug 689 and *Newcombe v Newcombe* (1934) 34 SR (NSW) 446.
10 In such a case, breach would entitle the innocent party to rescind: see *Bettini v Gye* (1876) 1 QBD 183.
11 A promissory condition is to be distinguished from a condition upon which rights or obligations are contingent but which is not promised; for example should A promise to pay B $100 if Collingwood wins the premiership, payment is contingent upon Collingwood winning the premiership but A does not promise that it will do so.
12 See, in particular, the extracts from *Associated Newspapers Ltd v Bancks* (1951) 83 CLR 322 and *Cehave NV v Bremer Handelsgesellschaft mbH* [1976] 1 QB 441.

It is not always possible, however, to characterise a particular term as a condition or a warranty and where this is the case it is necessary for the courts to focus instead on the nature of the breach. This approach requires an inquiry into the effect of the breach on the innocent party to determine whether it is so serious that they should be excused from performing their side of the contract. The leading exposition of this approach is the judgment of Diplock LJ in *Hongkong Fir Shipping Co Ltd v Kawasaki Kisen Kaisha Ltd*, extracted below, which the High Court confirmed in *Koomphatoo* reflected Australian law.[13]

Luna Park (NSW) Ltd v Tramways Advertising Pty Ltd

(1938) SR (NSW) 632, New South Wales (Supreme Court)

(1938) 61 CLR 286, High Court of Australia

[Tramways Advertising contracted to display boards advertising Luna Park on a number of Sydney trams. Under this contract Tramways said that it would 'guarantee that these boards will be on the tracks for at least eight hours per day'. This did not occur. Tramways contended that the true construction of the contract required the boards to be displayed only for an average of eight hours per day. Further, it indicated that it was prepared to continue performing the contract only on this basis. When Tramways brought an action claiming money under the contract, Luna Park argued that the contract had been discharged for breach and counter-claimed for damages for breach of contract. Tramways failed at first instance but succeeded on appeal to the New South Wales Full Court. Luna Park then appealed to the High Court. Although, as we will see, Luna Park's appeal to the High Court was successful, the judgment of Jordan CJ in the Full Court was accepted as a correct statement of the law and is seen as a seminal one in the area. For this reason, it has been extracted below in addition to an extract from the reasoning of the High Court. Other aspects of this case were discussed in chapter 19.]

Jordan CJ [at 641]: In considering the legal consequences flowing from a breach of contract, it is necessary to remember that (i) the breach may extend to all or to some only of the promises of the defaulting party, (ii) the promises broken may be important or unimportant, (iii) the breach of any particular promise may be substantial or trivial, (iv) the breach may occur or be discovered (a) when the innocent party has not yet performed any or some of the promises on his part, or after he has performed them all, and (b) when the innocent party has received no performance from the defaulting party, or has received performance in whole or in part; and to remember also that the resultant rights of the innocent party and the nature of the remedies available to him may depend upon some or all of these matters.

The nature of the promise broken is one of the most important of the matters. If it is a condition that is broken, ie, an essential promise, the innocent party, when he becomes aware of the breach, has ordinarily the right at his option either to

---

13   See above at p 291.

treat himself as discharged from the contract and to recover damages for loss of the contract, or else to keep the contract on foot and recover damages for the particular breach. If it is a warranty that is broken, ie, a non-essential promise, only the latter alternative is available to the innocent party: in that case he cannot of course obtain damages for loss of the contract: *AH McDonald & Co Pty Ltd v Wells*.

The question whether a term in a contract is a condition or a warranty, ie, an essential or a non-essential promise, depends upon the intention of the parties as appearing in or from the contract. The test of essentiality is whether it appears from the general nature of the contract considered as a whole, or from some particular term or terms, that the promise is of such importance to the promisee that he would not have entered into the contract unless he had been assured of a strict or a substantial performance of the promise, as the case may be, and that this ought to have been apparent <642> to the promisor: *Flight v Booth; Bettini v Gye; Bentsen v Taylor Sons & Co (No 2); Fullers' Theatres Ltd v Musgrove; Bowes v Chaleyer; Clifton v Coffey*. If the innocent party would not have entered into the contract unless assured of a strict and literal performance of the promise, he may in general treat himself as discharged upon any breach of the promise, however slight. If he contracted in reliance upon a substantial performance of the promise, any substantial breach will ordinarily justify a discharge. In some cases it is expressly provided that a particular promise is essential to the contract, eg, by a stipulation that it is the basis or of the essence of the contract: *Bettini v Gye*; but in the absence of express provision the question is one of construction for the Court, when once the terms of contract have been ascertained: ….

[On appeal to the High Court]

Latham CJ [at 301]: In the Supreme Court a great deal of attention was devoted to the consideration of the question whether the particular clause in question was a condition or a warranty. <302>

I agree with the Full Court that the guarantee clause was a condition and not a warranty in the sense in which those words are used by *Fletcher-Moulton* LJ in *Wallis, Son & Wells v Pratt & Haynes*. It was a term of the contract which went so directly to the substance of the contract or was so 'essential to its very nature that its non-performance may fairly be considered by the other party as a substantial failure to perform the contract at all.' The breach of such a term by one party entitles the other party not only to obtain damages but also to refuse to perform any of the obligations resting upon him.

The essential character of the clause in question appears both from its own terms and from the circumstances in which the contract was made. In the first place the words 'we guarantee' are particularly suited, in a contract drawn by laymen, to emphasize <303> the importance of the clause which they introduce. In the next place, the payment of £20 per week was not to begin until the complete number of roof boards, namely, fifty-three, were all displayed at the same time. The money is made payable 'from date of first appearance of complete number of boards 53 in all.' Thus, if the advertising company displayed even as many as fifty-two boards on every day throughout a whole season, it would never become entitled to recover any payment. This provision in the contract therefore supports the view that the parties regarded the completeness of the display contracted for as an essential element in the contract. Further, the preliminary correspondence shows that the advertising company represented continuity of display as an important feature. In a letter of 27th November 1935 the company emphasized the offer as an offer of 'an exclusive full-powered type of publicity that is *continuous day in day out and gets* 100 *per cent attention all the time.*' Reference was made in the same letter to the advantages of the 'tremendous full-attention coverage available *continuously over the entire week.*' (The words italicized were typed in large print in the letter.) Reference to these statements is permissible because, when the question is whether a promise is a condition or a warranty, 'there is no way of deciding that question except by looking at the contract in the light of the surrounding circumstances, and then making up one's mind whether the intention of the parties, as gathered from the instrument itself, will best be carried out by treating the promise as a warranty sounding only in damages, or as a condition precedent by the failure to perform which the other party is relieved of his liability. In order to decide this question of construction, one of the first things you would look to is, to what extent the accuracy of the statement—the truth of what is promised—would be likely to affect the substance and foundation of the adventure which the contract is intended to carry out' (per *Bowen* LJ in *Bentson v Taylor, Sons & Co (No 2)*); and see *Halsbury's Laws of England*, 2nd ed, vol 7, p 333. A discontinuous and irregular display is a different thing from a guaranteed continuous and regular display. For these reasons, in my opinion, <304> the clause was a condition and not a mere warranty. Accordingly any breach of the clause would entitle the defendant to determine the contract.

[His Honour went on to decide that Tramways was in breach of the clause as it required the boards to be displayed for substantially eight hours every day and this had not occurred. Therefore, Luna Park was justified in rescinding the contract. He also found that Tramways had repudiated the contract by saying that it would perform the contract only on the basis that the boards were displayed for an average of eight hours per day. Rich and McTiernan JJ reached the same conclusion as Latham CJ; Dixon J dissented.]

Appeal allowed

[footnotes omitted]

Determining the effect of a breach in practice

By adopting the nomenclature of conditions and warranties, legislation, such as the State and Territory Sale of Goods Acts, can make it clear that the breach of certain terms will allow the innocent party to rescind the contract, while the breach of others will not do so. Similarly, the parties can do likewise in the contract itself, although in that case merely using the description 'condition' may be insufficient if the term in question is inherently of minor importance.[14] Where neither legislation, nor the parties have made it clear what the consequences of breach are to be then recourse must be had to the seriousness of the particular breach in the circumstances of the particular case to determine whether it will allow the innocent party to rescind.

Hongkong Fir Shipping Co Ltd v Kawasaki Kisen Kaisha Ltd
[1962] 2 QB 26, English Court of Appeal

[Kawasaki chartered a vessel from Hongkong Fir for 24 months. The contract described the vessel as fitted for ordinary cargo service and required the owners to maintain it in an efficient state. However, for substantial periods the vessel was not fit for service and could not be used by Kawasaki. After approximately six months Kawasaki purported to discharge the contract for breach. At this time, however, there were no reasonable grounds for thinking that the owners would be unable to make the vessel seaworthy and in fact shortly thereafter it was seaworthy in all respects. Hongkong Fir treated Kawasaki's action as a wrongful repudiation of the contract and commenced proceedings seeking damages for breach of contract. At first instance, it was decided that the breaches did not justify discharge and Hongkong Fir's claim succeeded. Kawasaki appealed.]

Diplock LJ [at 65]: Every synallagmatic contract contains in it the seeds of the problem: in what event will a party be relieved of his undertaking to do that which he has agreed to do but has not yet done? The contract may itself expressly define some of these events, <66> as in the cancellation clause in a charterparty, but, human prescience being limited, it seldom does so exhaustively and often fails to do so at all. In some classes of contracts, such as sale of goods, marine insurance, contracts of affreightment evidenced by bills of lading and those between parties to bills of exchange, Parliament has defined by statute some of the events not provided for expressly in individual contracts of that class; but, where an event occurs the occurrence of which neither the parties nor Parliament have expressly stated will discharge one of the parties from further performance of his undertakings, it is for the court to determine whether the event has this effect or not.

The test whether an event has this effect or not has been stated in a number of metaphors all of which I think amount to the same thing: does the occurrence of the event deprive the party who has further undertakings still to perform of substantially the whole benefit which it was the intention of the parties as expressed in the contract that he should obtain as the consideration for performing those undertakings?

This test is applicable whether or not the event occurs as a result of the default of one of the parties to the contract, but the consequences of the event are different in the two cases. ...

---

14   See *Schuler AG v Wickman Machine Tool Sales* Ltd [1974] AC 235.

[at 69] Once it is appreciated that it is the event and not the fact that the event is a result of a breach of contract which relieves the party not in default of further performance of his obligations, two consequences follow: (i) The test whether the event relied on has this consequence is the same whether the event is the result of the other party's breach of contract or not, as Devlin J, pointed out in *Universal Cargo Carriers Corporation v Citati*. (ii) The question whether an event which is the result of the other party's breach of contract has this consequence cannot be answered by treating all contractual undertakings as falling into one of two separate categories: 'conditions', the breach of which gives rise to an event which relieves the party not in default of further performance of his obligations, and 'warranties', the breach of which does not give rise to such an event.

Lawyers tend to speak of this classification as if it were comprehensive, partly for the historical reasons which I have already mentioned, and partly because Parliament itself adopted it in the *Sale of Goods Act, 1893*, as respects a number of implied terms in contracts for the sale of goods and has in that Act used the expressions 'condition' and 'warranty' in that meaning. But it is by no means true of contractual undertakings in general at common law.

No doubt there are many simple contractual undertakings, sometimes express, but more often because of their very simplicity ('It goes without saying') to be implied, of which it can be predicated that every breach of such an undertaking must give rise to an event which will deprive the party not in default of substantially the whole benefit which it was intended that he should obtain from the contract. And such a stipulation, unless the parties have agreed that breach of it shall not entitle the non-defaulting party to treat the contract as repudiated, is a <70> 'condition'. So, too, there may be other simple contractual undertakings of which it can be predicated that no breach can give rise to an event which will deprive the party not in default of substantially the whole benefit which it was intended that he should obtain from the contract; and such a stipulation, unless the parties have agreed that breach of it shall entitle the non-defaulting party to treat the contract as repudiated, is a 'warranty'.

There are, however, many contractual undertakings of a more complex character which cannot be categorised as being 'conditions' or 'warranties' if the late nineteenth century meaning adopted in the *Sale of Goods Act, 1893*, and used by Bowen LJ, in *Bentsen v Taylor, Sons & Co*, be given to those terms. Of such undertakings, all that can be predicated is that some breaches will, and others will not, give rise to an event which will deprive the party not in default of substantially the whole benefit which it was intended that he should obtain from the contract; and the legal consequences of a breach of such an undertaking, unless provided for expressly in the contract, depend on the nature of the event to which the breach gives rise and do not follow automatically from a prior classification of the undertaking as a 'condition' or a 'warranty'. ... <71> ...

Consequently, the problem in this case is, in my view, neither solved nor soluble by debating whether the owners' express or implied undertaking to tender a seaworthy ship is a 'condition' or a 'warranty'. It is, like so many other contractual terms, an undertaking one breach of which may give rise to an event which relieves the charterer of further performance of his undertakings if he so elects, and another breach of which may not give rise to such an event but entitle him only to monetary compensation in the form of damages. ... <72> ...

What the learned judge had to do in the present case as in any other case where one party to a contract relies on a breach by the other party as giving him a right to elect to rescind the contract, was to look at the events which had occurred as a result of the breach at the time at which the charterers purported to rescind the charterparty, and to decide whether the occurrence of those events deprived the charterers of substantially the whole benefit which it was the intention of the parties as expressed in the charterparty that the charterers should obtain from the further performance of their own contractual undertakings.

[His Lordship concluded that the trial judge had done this and for that reason, the appeal should be dismissed. In separate judgments, Sellers and Upjohn LJJ reached the same conclusion.]

Appeal dismissed

[footnotes omitted]

It is useful to compare the approach taken in *Hongkong Fir* with the following description of the position in the United States of America, taken from the Second Restatement of the Law of Contracts.

Restatement of the Law, Second, Contracts, S 241

The American Law Institute, 1981

S 241. Circumstances Significant in Determining Whether a Failure Is Material

In determining whether a failure to render or to offer performance is material, the following circumstances are significant:

(a) the extent to which the injured party will be deprived of the benefit which he reasonably expected;
(b) the extent to which the injured party can be adequately compensated for the part of that benefit of which he will be deprived;
(c) the extent to which the party failing to perform or to offer to perform will suffer forfeiture;
(d) the likelihood that the party failing to perform or to offer to perform will cure his failure, taking account of all the circumstances including any reasonable assurances;
(e) the extent to which the behavior of the party failing to perform or to offer to perform comports with standards of good faith and fair dealing.

3 An election to discharge the contract

a Requirement and nature

Unless a contract provides otherwise (and this would be unusual), breach—no matter how serious—will not discharge it automatically. Rather, the innocent party is presented with the choice of rescinding the contract and thereby bringing it to an end, or affirming it and insisting that the guilty party perform as promised. If the innocent party elects to rescind, that decision must be communicated to the guilty party and as a general rule it will not be effective until this has occurred.[15] Once made it is 'final and irrevocable'.[16] On the other hand, if the innocent party elects to affirm the contract both parties will remain bound. Furthermore, as we saw above in *Taylor v Johnston*,[17] the innocent party's election to affirm is final and they cannot subsequently have a change of heart and rescind on the grounds of the original breach; rescission will only be possible after affirmation should the guilty party be again in serious breach.[18]

The nature of the innocent party's right of election and what is required before an election will be regarded as having been made are examined in the following extracts.

Holland v Wiltshire
(1954) 90 CLR 409, High Court of Australia

[The facts of this case are set out above at p 575. The following extract deals only with the issue of whether Wiltshire had affirmed the contract so as to preclude him from discharging it for breach.]

Dixon CJ [at 415]: In the present case … there was more than … a default. There was a renunciation of and refusal to perform the entire contract on the part of the purchaser. True it is that it was not accepted at once either as a breach or as an anticipatory breach. What was done was to place the purchasers on notice that they would be sued for breach if they did not complete before the date named by the notice. This was not an unconditional affirmation of the contract notwithstanding the renunciation. It was a demand for performance coupled with an intimation that refusal or failure to perform would result in proceedings for damages. That is to say it kept the contract open for a limited time and conditionally upon compliance. If time

---

15 This is confirmed by statute in some cases: see *Fair Trading Act 1999* (Vic) s 32PA which applies to the supply of goods, other than where rejection is available under the *ACL*.
16 *Tramways Advertising Pty Ltd v Luna Park (NSW) Ltd* (1938) SR (NSW) 632 at 643, per Jordan CJ. However, if the guilty party seeks to avoid communication, it may be sufficient for the innocent party to merely take reasonable steps to achieve this: see *Car & Universal Finance Co Ltd v Caldwell* [1963] 2 All ER 547.
17 Sup 123 Cal Rptr 641 (1975).
18 Such a breach may be constituted by a new breach that is sufficiently serious, or a failure to remedy the earlier breach where this evinces an intention by the guilty party not to be bound by the contract: see *Ogle v Comboyuro Investments Pty Ltd* (1976) 136 CLR 444.

is an essential condition, to extend it does not waive the effect of the stipulation as a condition: see per Jessel MR Barclay v Messenger and per Talbot J, Bernard v Williams. In the same way to give a party refusing to perform a fixed time to resile from his refusal and to notify him that failing his doing so he will be sued for his breach does not amount to an unconditional waiver of the refusal as a renunciation. Here the inference of fact is plain that the purchasers were maintaining their attitude of refusal to go on with the sale. <416> In these circumstances, the vendor was entitled to treat the contract as discharged by breach. He himself was ready and willing up to the expiration of the notice. His election to treat the contract as discharged by the purchasers' breach was sufficiently manifested by his proceeding to advertise the property for sale, and by his selling it.

[footnotes omitted]

Immer (No 145) Pty Ltd v The Uniting Church in Australia Property Trust (NSW)

(1992–1993) 182 CLR 26, High Court of Australia

[The Trust owned certain air space rights which it could transfer, provided that it first restored to the satisfaction of the Sydney City Council an historic building to which those rights were related. On 14 October 1988, the Trust sold the rights to Immer under a contract which provided that completion was to occur within seven days of notice that the Council's requirements had been met. However, it also provided that if Council approval had not been granted by 1 April 1989, Immer was entitled to rescind. On 26 June 1989, mistakenly thinking that Council approval had been given, Immer's solicitor sent settlement documents to the Trust's solicitors. Shortly afterwards, the Council informed Immer that the Trust had not yet met its requirements and that it was not yet in a position to complete the transfer. On 25 August Immer gave the Trust notice of rescission on the grounds that Council approval had not been given by 1 April. In these proceedings, the Trust sought a declaration that the contract subsisted and an order for specific performance. It failed at first instance but succeeded on appeal to the New South Wales Court of Appeal; Immer then appealed to the High Court.]

Deane, Toohey, Gaudron and McHugh JJ [at 40]: [Immer submitted] that there could have been no election for, on 26 June 1989, it did not have the requisite knowledge of the relevant circumstances. Immer accepted that it could have been held to an election without awareness of the legal situation which would have allowed it to rescind, but said that it could not have been so held unless it was aware of the facts giving rise to the right to avoid the deed. In this regard it pointed to the judgment of Mason, Brennan, Deane and Dawson JJ in *Khoury v Government Insurance Office (NSW)*

> 'It would seem however that, at least where the alternative rights arise under the terms of the one contract, a party may be held to have elected to affirm it notwithstanding that he was unaware of the actual right to avoid it ... Even in such

a case however, the party alleged to have elected to affirm the contract must be at least aware of the facts giving rise to the right to avoid the contract.' <41>

On this basis, Immer argued that on 26 June 1989 it was not aware of the facts giving rise to its right to rescind the agreement because it did not know that the Council was actively asserting that the relevant permission had not been given. The answer to this submission is that the evidence does not support a conclusion that Immer was unaware of the fact giving rise to the right to rescind under cl 7 of the deed, that is to say, the fact that 'approval' had not been 'granted by 1.4.89'. Nonetheless, Immer's mistaken belief that the approval of the City Council had been given at some subsequent time is, as will be seen, relevant to the question whether it lost the right to rescind the deed by reason of an election to affirm it.

The true nature of election is brought out in this sentence from the seminal work of Spencer Bower and Turner, *The Law Relating to Estoppel by Representation*: 'It is of the essence of election that the party electing shall be 'confronted' with two mutually exclusive courses of action between which he must, in fairness to the other party, make his choice.' When Immer's solicitors wrote their letter of 26 June 1989, the date 1 April 1989 in cl 7 of the deed had passed. It was then open to Immer, as purchaser, to rescind the deed, subject to any question that might arise as to whether rescission could be effected peremptorily or only after reasonable notice. Can it be said that Immer was then confronted with two mutually exclusive courses of action between which it must choose? Were its actions consistent only with an intention to keep the agreement on foot and inconsistent with the exercise of the right to rescind?

If a party to a contract, faced with the choice of terminating the contract or keeping it on foot, terminates the contract that party will ordinarily have acted in a way that leaves no doubt as to the choice made. And that choice will be clearly inconsistent with the exercise of the right to keep the contract on foot because the contract no longer exists. But where, as here, the situation is the converse the question is not answered so readily. Immer was proceeding on the footing that the Council had approved the transfer of air space rights and that completion of the transfer was possible. Mr Dixon-Smith wrote the letter of 26 June 1989 in that belief. But it was not the case. Not only was it not the case but Mrs Dale would have been aware at the time she received the letter that it was not the <42> case and that restoration and refurbishment of Pilgrim House was still a condition of that approval being obtained.

As Spencer Bower and Turner point out in the passage quoted earlier, at the heart of election is the idea of confrontation which in turn produces the necessity of making a choice. But in a case such as the present one, the choice is not merely one of affirming the agreement; it involves as well the abandonment of the right to rescind. Abandonment is more readily inferred in some circumstances, for instance where the choice arises once and for all. Here, by reason of cl 7 of the deed, Immer was entitled at any time after 1 April 1989 to rescind the deed. There is of course a danger of circularity here because the Uniting Church says: 'Yes, so long as Immer did not elect not to rescind.' The point is that where the right to rescind is a continuing one, it is not so readily concluded that the party entitled to rescind has abandoned that right completely as opposed to taking no action to exercise the right at the time in question.

There can be no doubt that when Mr Dixon-Smith wrote the letter of 26 June 1989 it was Immer's understanding that the Council had approved a transfer of air space rights and that there was no obstacle to early completion on the transaction. That is manifest from the correspondence. In *Tropical Traders Ltd v Goonan* Kitto J commented:

> Not that election is a matter of intention. It is an effect which the law annexes to conduct which would be justifiable only if an election had been made one way or the other.

On the other hand, in *Sargent v ASL Developments Ltd* Mason J said of the elements essential to the making of a binding election:

> The question is complicated because in some instances election may take place as a matter of conscious choice with knowledge of the existence of the alternative right and in other cases it may occur when the law attributes the character of an election to the conduct of a party.

But, in drawing this distinction, Mason J was focusing on the dichotomy between awareness of the right to rescind and awareness of the facts giving rise to the right. We do not read that passage from his Honour's judgment as implying that a party to a contract who is aware either of the right to rescind or of facts giving rise to a right to rescind will necessarily be held to have elected to affirm a <43> contract if he or she acts on the basis that the contract remains on foot. Such an implication is at odds with the notion of being confronted with the necessity of making a choice. In the present case it cannot truly be said that Immer was confronted with the necessity of making a choice at the time the letter in question was written, even less that it was abandoning for all time its rights under cl 7 of the deed.

[T]he forwarding by Immer's solicitors on 26 June 1989 of documents for settlement, including the draft deed of assignment reciting the approval of the Council, was clearly on the basis that the Council had, by then, approved. In a context where the Council had not, in fact, approved the transfer and where the stage had not been reached where Immer was required to make an election either to rescind the contract or to abandon the right to rescind, the forwarding of the documents for settlement did not constitute an election to affirm the contract regardless of whether the Council had or had not approved. ...

No prejudice was caused to the Uniting Church by Immer's actions; the possibility of rescission was due to the Church's inability to obtain the approval for the Council to the transfer of air space rights, an approval which was not obtained until September 1990.

In our view Immer's actions in and about June 1989 did not constitute an election on its part not to exercise its right of rescission.

[In a separate judgment, Brennan J reached the same conclusion.]

Appeal allowed

[footnotes omitted]

b   Limitations on the right of election

The innocent party's rights may be limited in two ways; first, the particular circumstances may be such that they have no practical choice but to rescind the contract. And second, even when that choice remains, they may be required to exercise it in a particular manner. The principal limitations of this nature are as follows.

Fair conduct

The courts are reluctant to allow the parties to exercise their rights oppressively and to this extent, the innocent party's right of election is never completely unfettered. For example, an innocent party may not be able to affirm the contract without having a legitimate interest in doing so, at least where this would impose a greater burden on the guilty party than would rescission. This issue is discussed in the following extract.[19]

White and Carter (Councils) Ltd v McGregor

[1961] 3 All ER 1178, House of Lords

[The plaintiff council and the defendant entered into a contract which provided that the council would make and display on its litter bins advertisements for the defendant's business. Almost immediately, and before the council had done any work performing the contract, it was repudiated by the defendant. Nevertheless, the council went ahead, made and displayed the advertisements and claimed the amount due under the contract. The defendant argued that the council should have discharged the contract and claimed damages.]

Lord Reid [at 1181]: The general rule cannot be in doubt. It was settled in Scotland at least as early as 1848 and it has been authoritatively stated time and again in both Scotland and England. If one party to a contract repudiates it in the sense of making it clear to the other party that he refuses or will refuse to carry out his part of the contract, the other party, the innocent party, has an option. He may accept that repudiation and sue for damages for breach of contract whether or not the time for performance has come; or he may if he chooses disregard or refuse to accept it and then the contract remains in full effect. ...

---

19   Compare *Finelli v Dee* (1968) 67 DLR 393 in which the opposite result was reached. However, in this case, the 'innocent' party was guilty of trespassing on the defendant's land in order to perform the contract, despite the defendant's repudiation.

I need not refer to the numerous authorities. They are not disputed by the respondent but he points out that in all of them the party who refused to accept the repudiation had no active duties under the contract. The innocent party's option is generally said to be to *wait* until the date of performance and then to claim damages estimated as at that date. There is no case in which it is said that he may, in face of the repudiation, go on and incur useless expense in performing the contract and then claim the contract price. The option, it is argued, is merely as to the date as at which damages are to be assessed. Developing this argument, the respondent points out that in most cases the innocent party cannot complete the contract himself without the other party doing, allowing or accepting something, and that it is purely fortuitous that the appellants can do so in this case. In most cases by refusing co-operation the party in breach can compel the innocent party to restrict his claim to damages. Then it was said that even where the innocent party can complete the contract without such co-operation it is against the public interest that he should be allowed to do so. An example was developed in argument. A company might engage an expert to go abroad and prepare an elaborate report and then repudiate the contract <1182> before anything was done. To allow such an expert then to waste thousands of pounds in preparing the report cannot be right if a much smaller sum of damages would give him full compensation for his loss. It would merely enable the expert to extort a settlement giving him far more than reasonable compensation. [After deciding that the authority relied upon by the respondent was wrongly decided his Lordship concluded at 1183]:

It may well be that, if it can be shown that a person has no legitimate interest, financial or otherwise, in performing the contract rather than claiming damages, he ought not to be allowed to saddle the other party with an additional burden with no benefit to himself. If a party has no interest to enforce a stipulation he cannot in general enforce it: so it might be said that if a party has no interest to insist on a particular remedy he ought not to be allowed to insist on it. And, just as a party is not allowed to enforce a penalty, so he ought not to be allowed to penalise the other party by taking one course when another is equally advantageous to him. If I may revert to the example which I gave of a company engaging an expert to prepare an elaborate report and then repudiating before anything was done, it might be that the company could show that the expert had no substantial or legitimate interest in carrying out the work rather than accepting damages: I would think that the *de minimis* principle would apply in determining whether his interest was substantial and that he might have a legitimate interest other than an immediate financial interest. But if the expert had no such interest then that might be regarded as a proper case for the exercise of the general equitable jurisdiction of the court. But that is not this case. Here the respondent did not set out to prove that the appellants had no legitimate interest in completing the contract and claiming the contract price rather than claiming damages, there is nothing in the findings of fact to support such a case, and it seems improbable that any such case could have been proved. It is, in my judgment, impossible to say that the appellants should be deprived of their right to claim the contract price merely because the benefit to them as against claiming damages and reletting their advertising space might be small in comparison with the loss to the respondent.

[Lord Hodson with whom Lord Tucker agreed, delivered a separate speech to the same effect; Lords Morton and Keith dissented.]

Appeal allowed

Where the guilty party's co-operation is required

Affirmation may not be possible where the participation of the guilty party is required for the innocent party to be able to perform. For example, if the guilty party refuses to allow the innocent party to enter property so that the latter is prevented from carrying out building work as contracted, the innocent party will be absolved from performance.[20] This may relegate them to a claim for damages, rather than the contract price.[21]

Contractual restrictions

An innocent party wishing to take advantage of a contractual termination clause must comply with any procedural or timing requirements that term imposes. Failure to do so may prevent reliance on the clause.

Statutory restrictions

Statutory restrictions are sometimes imposed on the innocent party's right to rescind. This is common where the statute has created the right to rescind in the first place; however, there are other provisions that restrict, or regulate, that party's common law rights in this respect. The following extracts are, respectively, an example of each type of provision.

Fair Trading Act 1999, (Vic)

Section 32P. Discharge or rescission of contract of supply of goods

(1) This section applies if a purchaser—
   (a) discharges a contract of supply of goods by reason of repudiation or breach of condition by the supplier; or
   (b) in accordance with section 32OA(1) rescinds a contract of supply of goods after an innocent misrepresentation is made.
(2) If the goods have been delivered to the purchaser and have not been returned to the supplier, the purchaser must return the goods to the supplier or permit the supplier to take possession of the goods.
(3) The purchaser is liable to the supplier for loss or damage caused to the goods—
   (a) by the purchaser wilfully or by the purchaser's negligence while the goods are in the purchaser's possession during a period of 21 days after discharging or rescinding the contract; and

---

20 See *Tramways Advertising Pty Ltd v Luna Park (NSW) Ltd* (1938) 38 SR (NSW) 632, esp at 645.
21 This may be the explanation for *Finelli v Dee* (1968) 67 DLR 393.

(b) by the purchaser wilfully while the goods are in the purchaser's possession after the expiration of a period of 21 days after discharging or rescinding the contract.
(4) If the property in the goods passed to the purchaser before the discharge or the rescission, the property re-vests in the supplier.
(5) The supplier is liable to the purchaser for money paid and for the value of any other consideration paid or provided under the contract by the purchaser to the supplier.
(6) If—
   (a) the purchaser used the goods before the discharge or rescission; and
   (b) the supplier acted honestly and reasonably in supplying the goods—
   the court may, if it is satisfied that, in all the circumstances, it is just and convenient to do so, allow the supplier to recover from the purchaser an amount equal to the whole or any part of the fair value to the purchaser of the purchaser's use of the goods.

32PA. When does a discharge or rescission have effect?

(1) If a purchaser purports to discharge or rescind a contract of supply of goods, the purported discharge or rescission has effect only if—
   (a) the supplier is aware that the purchaser treats the contract as at an end, whether by reason of the return of the goods to the supplier or by reason of any other information which comes to the knowledge of the supplier; or
   (b) if the purchaser is unable, due to the conduct or omission of the supplier, after taking reasonable steps, to inform the supplier or to cause the supplier to become aware that the purchaser treats the contract as at an end—
      (i) the purchaser treats the contract as at an end; and
      (ii) by the purchaser's conduct, shows unequivocally that the purchaser treats the contract as at an end.
(2) This section does not apply to a rejection under the Australian Consumer Law (Victoria).

Property Law Act 1974, (Qld)

Section 72. Restriction on vendor's right to rescind

(1) An instalment contract shall not be determinable or determined because of default on the part of the purchaser in payment of any instalment or sum of money (other than a deposit or any part of a deposit) due and payable under the contract until the expiration of a period of 30 days after service upon the purchaser of a notice in the approved form.
(2) A purchaser upon whom a notice in the approved form has been served may within the period mentioned in subsection (1) pay or tender to the vendor or the vendor's agent such sum as would have been due and payable under the contract at the date of such payment or tender but for such default (including any sum in respect of which the default was made).

(3) Upon payment or tender under subsection (2) any right or power of the vendor to determine the contract because of the default specified in the notice shall cease and the purchaser shall be deemed not to be in default under the contract.

(4) A notice shall be deemed to be to the like effect of that in the approved form if it is reasonably sufficient fully and fairly to apprise the purchaser of the purchaser's default and of the effect of the purchaser's failure to remedy the default within the time specified in this section.

4 Consequences of discharge for breach

a   The general effect

Discharge for breach terminates the contract *in futuro*; this is, for the future. This means that the parties are relieved of those obligations and lose those rights that would have arisen after the date of termination, had termination not occurred. However, it does not relieve the parties of those obligations, or take away those rights, that had already accrued by that time. Furthermore, the terms of the contract regulating the rights and liabilities of the parties may also survive the contract being discharged. Also, termination does not relieve the guilty party of liability for breach of contract and regard can still be paid to the contract for the purpose of assessing the damages to be awarded to the innocent party. The general effect of discharge for breach and its effect on the rights and obligations of the parties is discussed in the following extracts.

Heyman v Darwins Ltd

[1942] AC 356, House of Lords

[The parties entered into an agency contract which provided that if a dispute arose between them it would be submitted to arbitration. A dispute did arise and Heyman alleged that this discharged the contract. Heyman then commenced proceedings, seeking a declaration that the contract had been discharged and damages for breach. Darwins responded by applying to have the action stayed so that the dispute could go to arbitration. A stay was refused at first instance, but granted by the Court of Appeal; Heyman then appealed to the House of Lords.]

Lord Macmillan [at 373]: Repudiation, ... in the sense of a refusal by one of the parties to a contract to perform his obligations thereunder, does not, of itself, abrogate the contract. The contract is not rescinded. It obviously cannot be rescinded by the action of the one of the parties alone. But, even if the so-called repudiation is acquiesced in or accepted by the other party, that does not end the contract. The wronged party has still his right of action for damages under the contract which has been broken, and the contract provides the measure of these damages. It is inaccurate to speak in such cases of repudiation of the contract.

The contract stands, but one of the parties has declined to fulfil his part of it. There has been what is called a total breach or a breach going to the root of the contract and this relieves the party of any further obligation to perform what he for his part, has undertaken. Now, in this state of matters, why should it be said that the arbitration clause, if the contract contains one, is no longer operative or effective? A partial breach leaves the arbitration clause effective. Why should a total breach abrogate it? The repudiation being not of the contract but of obligations undertaken by one of the parties, why should it imply a repudiation of the arbitration clause so that it can no longer be invoked for the settlement of disputes arising in consequence of the repudiation? I do not think that this is the result of what is termed repudiation. Suppose the injured party prefers to have his claim of damages for the other party's total breach assessed by arbitration, can he not invoke and enforce the arbitration clause for that purpose? Can he be effectually met by a plea on the part of the wrongdoer that the wrongdoer has repudiated the contract and with it the arbitration clause which is consequently no longer operative? I do not think that this result follows even if the injured party acquiesces in the total breach—accepts the repudiation, as it is put—and contents himself with his claim of damages. I think he is entitled to insist on having his damages assessed by arbitration notwithstanding the other party's repudiation.

I venture to think that not enough attention has been directed to the true nature and function of an arbitration clause in a contract. It is quite distinct from the other clauses. The other clauses set out the obligations which the partied undertake towards each other *hinc inde*, but the arbitration clause does not impose on one of the parties an obligation in favour of the other. It embodies the agreement of both <374> parties that, if any dispute arises with regard to the obligations which the one party has undertaken to the other, such dispute shall be settled by a tribunal of their own constitution. …

I am, accordingly, of opinion that what is commonly called repudiation or total breach of a contract, whether acquiesced in by the other party or not, does not abrogate the contract, though it may relieve the injured party of the duty of further fulfilling the obligations which he has by the contract undertaken to the repudiating party. The contract is not put out of existence, though all further performance of the obligations undertaken by each party in favour of the other may cease. It survived for the purpose of measuring the claims arising out of the breach, and the arbitration clause survives for determining the mode of their settlement. The purposes of the contract have failed, but the arbitration clause is not one of the purposes of the contract.

[His Lordship went on to conclude that as the dispute fell within the terms of the arbitration clause the action should be stayed. Viscount Simon LC, and Lords Russell, Wright and Porter delivered speeches to the same effect.]

Appeal dismissed

Moschi v Lep Air Services

[1972] 2 All ER 393, House of Lords

[A company controlled by Moschi became indebted to Lep Air Services (Lep). To secure the release of goods it owned and over which Lep was exercising a lien in respect of the debt, the company entered into an agreement with Lep to repay it by periodic instalments. As part of this arrangement, Moschi guaranteed the payment of these instalments. The company breached the agreement and it was rescinded by Lep. Lep then sought to enforce the guarantee. Lep succeeded at first instance and in Moschi's appeal to the Court of Appeal; Moschi then appealed to the House of Lords. A key issue in the appeal was whether the discharge of the company's contract with Lep meant that Moschi was not liable under the guarantee for payments that would have fallen due after that date.]

Lord Diplock [at 402]: My Lords, it has become usual to speak of the exercise by one party to a contract of his right to treat the contract as rescinded in circumstances such as these, as an 'acceptance' of the wrongful repudiation of the contract by the other party as a rescission of the contract. But it would be quite erroneous to suppose that any fresh agreement between the parties or any variation of the terms of the original contract is involved when the party who is not in default elects to exercise his right to treat the contract as rescinded because of a repudiatory breach of the contract by the other party. He is exercising a right conferred on him by law of which the sole source is the original contract. He is not varying that contract; he is enforcing it.

It is no doubt convenient to speak of a contract as being terminated or coming to an end when the party who is not in default exercises his right to treat it as rescinded. But the law is concerned with the effect of that election on those obligations of the <403> parties of which the contract was the source, and this depends on the nature of the particular obligation and on which party promised to perform it.

Generally speaking, the rescission of the contract puts an end to the primary obligations of the party not in default to perform any of his contractual promises which he has not already performed by the time of the rescission. It deprives him of any right as against the other party to continue to perform them. It does not give rise to any secondary obligation in substitution for a primary obligation which has come to an end. The primary obligations of the party in default to perform any of the promises made by him and remaining unperformed likewise come to an end as does his right to continue to perform them. Bur for his primary obligations there is substituted by operation of law a secondary obligation to pay to the other party a sum of money to compensate him for the loss he has sustained as a result: of the failure to perform the primary obligations. This secondary obligation is just as much an obligation arising from the contract as are the primary obligations that it replaces (see *R V Ward Ltd v Bignall*).

Although this is the general rule as to the effect of rescission of the contract on obligations of which it was the source, there may be exceptional primary obligations which continue to exist notwithstanding that the contract has been rescinded. These are obligations that are ancillary to the main purpose of the contract—which is, of course, that the parties should perform their primary obligations voluntarily. Mutual promises to submit to arbitration disputes arising as to the performance by the parties of their other obligations arising from the contract may be expressed in terms which make it clear that it was the common intention of the parties that their primary obligation to continue to perform these promises should continue notwithstanding that their other primary obligations had come to an end *(Heyman v Darwins Ltd)*.

But this is the exception. Although in the instant appeal the Court of Appeal came to the right decision, I cannot accept entirely that part of their reasoning in support of it in which they suggest that the primary obligation of the debtor to continue to pay the instalments which he had promised under cl (IX) of the contract was not ended by the rescission of the contract but remained in existence although the law no longer permitted him to pay them. A legal obligation to continue to perform is inconsistent with the withdrawal of any legal right to do so. The better explanation is that which I have already given, namely, that on rescission of the contract the primary obligation of the debtor to pay the instalments was converted by operation of law into a secondary obligation either to pay damages for failure to perform it; or, as these were instalments of a debt existing at the date of the contract, it may be a revived obligation to pay the balance of the whole debt immediately. The guarantor's obligation under his contract of guarantee does not, as the Court of Appeal appear to suggest, depend on the debtor's primary obligation continuing to exist after the contract had been rescinded. Nor is it affected by whether the debtor's secondary obligation which was substituted for it by operation of law is classified as an obligation to pay damages or as an obligation to pay the debt. It was the debtor's failure to perform his primary obligation to pay the instalments in circumstances which put an end to it that constituted a failure by the guarantor to perform his own primary obligation to the creditor to see that the instalments were paid by the debtor, and substituted for it a secondary obligation of the guarantor to pay to the creditor a sum of money for the loss he thereby sustained. It is the guarantor's own secondary obligation, not that of the debtor, that the creditor is enforcing in his claim for damages for breach of his contract of guarantee.

[In separate speeches Lords Reid, Gardiner, Simon and Kilbrandon agreed that the appeal should be dismissed.]

Appeal dismissed

[footnotes omitted]

b The effect on payments made or due

Before a contract was discharged for breach money may have been paid by one party to the other, or a payment may have fallen due. For example, a purchaser may have paid to the seller a deposit, or instalments of the purchase price. Similarly, instalments of the purchase price, or other forms of periodic payments, may have fallen due but remained unpaid at the time of discharge; indeed, non-payment of an amount due is one of the more common grounds upon which contracts are discharged for breach. The effect of the contract being discharged on such payments can be summarised as follows:

- Where a contract is discharged for breach, money that has been paid by one party to the other can be recovered from the payee provided there has been a total failure of the consideration that was to be provided for that payment. As a corollary, payments due, but unpaid, at the time of discharge cease to be payable.
- In the case of contracts for the sale of goods, or land, the consideration for the purchaser paying the price will normally be the seller transferring ownership of the land, or goods, to them. In such cases, if the seller discharges the contract because of the purchaser's breach of contract, and hence does not transfer ownership, any instalments of the price paid by the purchaser will be recoverable as there will have been a total failure of consideration. However, if a contract is structured in such a manner that consideration has been provided for payments due before the contract is discharged for breach, those payments will be irrecoverable by the payee.
- The consideration for a deposit paid by a purchaser will normally be the seller entering into the contract of sale. Consequently, it will be irrecoverable by the purchaser if the contract is discharged by the seller because of the purchaser's breach as there will not have been a total failure of consideration. For the same reason, a deposit that was payable by the purchaser, but which had not been paid when the contract was discharged, will be recoverable by the seller. However, relief against such forfeiture is available in equity and under statute.

These situations are discussed in the following extracts.

McDonald v Dennys Lascelles Ltd

(1933) 48 CLR 457, High Court of Australia

[McDonald guaranteed the payment of an instalment due to Dennys Lascelles under a contract for the sale of land. This instalment had not been paid when, for other reasons, the contract of sale was discharged. Dennys Lascelles sought to enforce the guarantee. It succeeded at first instance and McDonald appealed to the High Court.]

Dixon J [at 476]: When a party to a simple contract, upon a breach by the other contracting party of a condition of the contract, elects to treat the contract as no longer binding upon him, the contract is not rescinded as from the beginning. Both parties <477> are discharged from the further performance of the contract, but rights are not divested or discharged which have already been unconditionally acquired. Rights and obligations which arise from the partial execution of the contract and causes of action which have accrued from its breach alike continue unaffected. When a contract is rescinded because of matters which affect its formation, as in the case of fraud, the parties are to be rehabilitated and restored, so far as may be, to the position they occupied before the contract was made. But when a contract, which is not void or voidable at law, or liable to be set aside in equity, is dissolved at the election of one party because the other has not observed an essential condition or has committed a breach going to its root, the contract is determined so far as it is executory only and the party in default is liable for damages for its breach. … It does not, however, necessarily follow from these principles that when, under an executory contract for the sale of property, the price or part of it is paid or payable in advance, the seller may both retain what he has received, or recover overdue instalments, and at the same time treat himself as relieved from the obligation of transferring the property to the buyer. When a contract stipulates for payment of part of the purchase money in advance, the purchaser relying only on the vendor's promise to give him a conveyance, the vendor is entitled to enforce payment before the time has arrived for conveying the land; yet his title to retain the money has been considered not to be absolute but conditional upon the subsequent completion of the contract. 'The very idea of payment falls to the ground when both have treated the bargain as at an end; and from that moment the vendor holds the money advanced to the use of the purchaser' (*Palmer v Temple*). In *Laird v Pim*, Parke B says: 'It is clear he cannot <478> have the land and its value too'; … It is now beyond question that instalments already paid may be recovered by a defaulting purchaser when the vendor elects to discharge the contract (*Mayson v Clouet*). Although the parties might by express agreement give the vendor an absolute right at law to retain the instalments in the event of the contract going off, yet in equity such a contract is considered to involve a forfeiture from which the purchaser is entitled to be relieved (see the judgment of *Long Innes* J in *Pitt v Curotta*). [After discussing various authorities his Honour continued]: [T]hese cases establish the purchaser's right to recover the instalments, other than the deposit, although the contract is not carried into execution. If a vendor under a contract containing an express power to forfeit instalments at first determined the contract and retained the instalments but afterwards resiled from his former election to treat the contract as discharged and insisted that, if the purchaser was unwilling to forfeit his instalments according to the tenor of the agreement, he should at least carry out the sale, perhaps the purchaser as a term of equitable relief against forfeiture would be required to carry out his contract. But, where there is no express agreement excluding the implication made at law, by which the instalments become repayable upon the discharge of the obligation to convey and the purchaser has a legal right to the return of the purchase money already paid which makes it needless to resort to equity and submit to equity as a condition of obtaining relief, the <479> vendor appears to be unable to deduct from the amount of the instalments the amount of his loss occasioned by the purchaser's abandonment of the contract. A vendor may, of course, counterclaim for damages in the action in which the purchaser seeks to recover the instalments.

In the present case, the contract of resale contains no provision for the retention or forfeiture of the instalments. If, therefore, the instalment originally due on 24th January 1930 had been paid by the purchasers to the vendors, they would, in my opinion, have been entitled to recover it from the vendors. The right so to recover it is legal and not equitable. ... It appears to me inevitably to follow from the principles upon which instalments paid are recoverable that an unpaid overdue instalment ceases to be payable by the purchasers when the contract is discharged.

[His Honour went on to conclude that as the liability McDonald had guaranteed had been discharged by the termination of the contract of sale, his liability under the guarantee was likewise discharged. Rich and McTiernan JJ agreed with Dixon J and in separate judgment Starke J reached the same conclusion; Evatt J dissented.]

Appeal allowed

[footnotes omitted]

Hyundai Heavy Industries Co Ltd v Papadopoulos
[1980] 2 All ER 29, House of Lords

[Hyundai contracted to build a ship for a Liberian company. This contract provided that the price (US$14.3m) was to be paid in five instalments; the first and second were each to be 2.5 per cent of the total price, the third 10 per cent, the fourth 17.5 per cent and the fifth 67.5 per cent. The contract provided that if the buyers did not pay the second instalment Hyundai could rescind the contract, retain any money paid and sell the ship. In a related agreement, Papadopoulos guaranteed Hyundai that the buyers would make these payments in accordance with the contract. The buyers paid the first instalment but defaulted in paying the second. As a result, Hyundai rescinded the shipbuilding contract and commenced proceedings against Papadopoulos under the guarantee, claiming the second instalment and interest. Hyundai succeeded at first instance and on Papadopoulos' appeal to the Court of Appeal. Papadopoulos then appealed to the House of Lords.]

Lord Fraser [at 45]: [Counsel for Papadopoulos argued that] once the contract has been cancelled the price must cease to be payable; the purchasers can no longer be liable to pay the price for a vessel which the builders are no longer obliged to sell to them, and which the builders said they have no intention of selling to the purchasers. The argument was supported by reference to a statement by Lord Denman CJ in *Palmer v Temple* (1839) 9 Ad & El 508 at 520–521, 112 ER 1304 at 1309, where he said:

> 'But the very idea of payment falls to the ground when both [parties] have treated the bargain as at an end; and from that moment the vendor holds the money advanced to the use of the purchaser.'

Palmer v Temple was a case where the plaintiff had contracted to purchase landed property and had paid a sum 'by way of deposit, and in part of £5,500', which was the purchase price, and had then failed to pay the balance of the price or to complete the contract. He was held to be entitled to recover his deposit, but the actual decision turned on the terms of the particular contract. In *Dies v British and International Mining Corporation* [1939] 1 KB 724 at 740–742, where a passage from Lord Denman's judgment in *Palmer v Temple* including the statement that

I have quoted was relied on by Stable J, the contract was again purely one of sale, in that case of rifles and ammunition. The vendor was a merchant or middle man who had intended to buy the goods from the manufacturer and to resell them to the purchaser at a profit. Stable J held that the purchaser who had paid a large sum as an advance of the purchase price, and who had then failed to complete payment or to take delivery of the goods, was entitled to recover his advance payment under deduction of an agreed sum of liquidated damages. Counsel for the guarantors in the instant case argued that if the buyer in the *Dies* case was entitled to recover an advance which had already been paid, then a fortiori the buyers in the instant case could not be liable to make an advance that was due but unpaid; if they did make it, said counsel, they would be entitled to immediate repayment of it.

I do not accept that argument. In my opinion the Dies case and Palmer v Temple are both distinguishable from the present case because in both these cases the contracts were simply contracts of sale which did not require the vendor to perform any work or incur any expense on the subjects of sale. But the contract in the instant case is not of that comparatively simple character. The obligations of the buyers were not confined to selling the vessel but included designing and building it and there were special provisions (art 2) that the contract price 'shall include payment for services in the inspection, tests, survey and classification of the vessel' and also 'all costs and expenses for designing and supplying all necessary drawings for the vessel in accordance with the specifications'. Accordingly the builders were obliged to carry out work and to incur expense, starting from the moment that the contract had been signed, including the wages of designers and workmen, fees for inspection and for cost of purchasing materials. It seems very likely that the increasing proportions of the contract price represented by the five instalments bore some relation to the anticipated rate of expenditure, but we have no information on which to make any nice comparison between the amount of expenses that the builders would have to bear from time to time, and the amounts of the instalments payable by the buyers. I do not think that such comparisons are necessary. It is enough that the builders were bound to incur considerable expense in carrying out their part of the contract long before the actual sale could take place. <45>

There was no evidence either way whether the builders had in fact carried out their obligations to start designing and building the vessel, but in my opinion we must assume, in the absence of evidence or even averment to the contrary, that they had carried out their part of the bargain up till the date of cancellation.

Much of the plausibility of the argument on behalf of the guarantors seemed to me to be derived from the assumption that the contract price was simply a purchase price. That is not so, and once that misconception has been removed I think it is clear that the shipbuilding contract has little similarity with a contract of sale and much more similarity, so far as the present issues are concerned, with contracts in which the party entitled to be paid had either performed work or provided services for which payment is due by the date of cancellation. In contracts of the latter class, which of course includes building and construction contracts, accrued rights to payment are not (in the absence of express provisions) destroyed by cancellation of the contract. … <46>

In the instant case the buyers have not actually enjoyed any benefit from the work which the builders have performed, but it has been performed (or at least we must so assume, in the absence of evidence to the contrary) on the faith of the buyers' promise to pay the instalments on the due dates. The builders had acquired a vested right to the debt which was owed by the buyers at the date of cancellation and I see no reason for holding it to be cancelled. ...

For these reasons I am of opinion that the cancellation of the contract did not release the buyers from their liability for the second instalment, the due date for payment of which had passed before cancellation. That remained, and still remains, a debt due by the buyers to the builders.

Appeal dismissed

Bot v Ristevski

[1981] VR 120, Supreme Court of Victoria

[Bot contracted to sell a house and land to Ristevski. The contract required a deposit to be paid upon signing and the balance on a later date. Part of the deposit was paid but before payment of the balance Ristevski repudiated the contract. This was accepted by Bot as discharging the contract; Bot then claimed payment of the balance of the deposit.]

Brooking J [at 120]: Where the vendor discharges a contract for breach, the contract may expressly empower him to forfeit instalments of purchase money payable in advance of conveyance or transfer, so as to make it necessary for the purchaser to invoke equitable relief against forfeiture. If the contract gives no express power of forfeiture, the purchaser may recover by action at law instalments of purchase money paid in advance of conveyance or transfer and will have a good defence at law to an action by the vendor claiming payment of instalments of purchase money which were overdue by the time when the contract was discharged. The vendor's title to retain or recover the purchase money is conditional upon the subsequent completion of the contract by conveyance or transfer; if the contract is not completed, the consideration wholly fails: *McDonald v Dennys Lascelles Ltd supra*, at pp 477–9; *Berry v Mahony*, [1933] VLR 314, at p 320; *Real Estates Securities Ltd v Kew Golf Links Estate Pty Ltd*, [1935] VLR 114, at pp 119–20; *Automatic Fire Sprinklers Pty Ltd v Watson* (1946), 72 CLR 435, at pp 464–5 *Cowan v Stanhill Estates Pty Ltd (No 2)*, [1967] VR 641, at p 650.

The vendor's title to retain or recover a deposit is not conditional in this sense, and accordingly it will not be defeated or divested by the subsequent discharge of the contract: *Ettridge v Vermin Board of the District of Mural Bay*, [1928] SASR 124, at p 128. True it is that a deposit wears two aspects: if the purchase is carried out, it goes against the purchase money, but its primary purpose is that it is a guarantee that the purchaser means business *(Depree v Bedhorough* (1863), 4 Gift 479; 66 ER 795; *Howe v Smith* (1884), 27 ChD 89, at p 101, per Fry LJ; *Soper v Arnold* (1889), 14 AC 429, at p 435, per Lord Macnaghten). There is no failure of consideration if the land is not conveyed or transferred, for the purchaser has had the benefit of the entry into the contract of sale by the vendor.

> Here the purchaser made an unconditional promise to pay a deposit immediately and, although if the contract was completed the moneys would according to ordinary principles be credited towards the purchase price and until then would constitute an earnest for performance, the agreement to pay was not in consideration of conveyance but was in consideration of the contract. It was the price or part of the price of the vendor's promise to sell ... *Farrant v Leburn.* [1970] WAR 179, at p 184. <124>

I ... approach the problem by asking whether an unconditional right to recover and retain the deposit arose before the contract was discharged. If such a right did arise, it will survive the determination of the contract, and if the money has been paid before discharge the purchaser will not get it back, while if the money has not been paid before discharge the purchaser will be compelled to pay it. Whether the vendor obtained an unconditional right to recover <125> and retain the deposit will depend upon whether the discharge of the contract will give rise to a total failure of the consideration for payment of the deposit. If it will, then the consequence of discharge will be that the vendor cannot recover the deposit, if unpaid, or retain it, if paid. Either there was an unconditional right to recover and retain the deposit, or there was not. ...

[After reviewing various authorities his Honour concluded at [129]: Principle and authority have combined to lead me to the conclusion ... that a vendor who discharges the contract in consequence of the purchaser's repudiation of it can recover a deposit that should have been paid before the contract was discharged ...

c Relief against forfeiture

As Dixon J explained in *McDonald v Dennys Lascelles*, equity has the power to grant relief against the forfeiture of payments made by a purchaser as instalments of the purchase price, even where the contract provides that they are to be forfeited should the contract be discharged as a result of that party's breach of contract. However, as we saw in *Bot v Ristevski*, this does not apply to payments made as deposits. One consequence of this difference between the treatment of instalments and deposits is that vendors may be tempted to characterise payments due under a contract of sale as the latter, rather than the former, so that should the contract be discharged because of the purchaser's breach of contract the payment can be retained, or recovered. Fortunately, unconscionable exploitation of this possibility was thwarted by the Privy Council in *Workers Trust and Merchant Bank Ltd v Dojap Investments Ltd*[22] which decided that a payment will be treated as a deposit only if the amount is 'reasonable'; usually, this will require it not to exceed 10 per cent of the purchase price.

In Victoria and New South Wales further relief against the forfeiture of deposits is provided by statute. These provisions empower a court to order the return of a deposit 'if it thinks fit'.[23]

---

22   [1993] AC 573.
23   See *Conveyancing Act 1919* (NSW) s 55(2A) and *Property Law Act 1958* (Vic) s 49(2).

d Recovery under a *quantum meruit*

If a contract is discharged for breach the innocent party, rather than claiming damages for breach of contract, can choose instead to sue on a *quantum meruit* for the value of any benefit conferred on the guilty party or of the work they have carried out.[24] On the other hand, the guilty party cannot similarly recover the value of a benefit conferred on the innocent party, prior to termination, unless a fresh contract to pay for this work can be discerned[25] or the contract is divisible, or the doctrine of substantial performance operates.[26]

INTERNATIONAL PERSPECTIVES

India

The law in India relating to discharge for breach is derived from the English common law with very little statutory modification.[27] As a result, it is essentially the same as it is in England and Australia. In the case of anticipatory breach, s 39 of the *Indian Contract Act, 1872* restates the common law and has been interpreted in line with current English cases; the rule that damages can be claimed after an innocent party has rescinded is restated in s 75.

Indian Contract Act, 1872

Section 39. Effect of refusal of party to perform promise wholly

When a party to a contract has refused to perform, or disabled himself from performing, his promise in its entirety, the promisee may put an end to the contract, unless he has signified, by words or conduct, his acquiescence in its continuance.

Section 75. Party rightfully rescinding contract, entitled to compensation

A person who rightfully rescinds a contract is entitled to compensation for any damage which he has sustained through the non-fulfilment of the contract.

China

The *Contract Law* makes specific provision for anticipatory breach (Article 108) and for a contract to be discharged for other forms of serious breach (Article 94). There are also provisions dealing with the effect of termination (Article 97) and with deposits (Articles 115 and 116) that are similar to the common law.

---

24   See *Segur v Franklin* (1934) 34 SR (NSW) 67.
25   See *Sumpter v Hedges* [1898] 1 QB 673.
26   See p 547, above.
27   See A Singh, *Law of Contract and Specific Relief*, 9th edn, EBC, Lucknow, 2005, ch 9.

Contract Law of the People's Republic of China, 1999

Article 94. Legally Prescribed Conditions Giving Rise to Termination Right

The parties may terminate a contract if:

(i)   force majeure frustrated the purpose of the contract;
(ii) before the time of performance, the other party expressly stated or indicated by its conduct that it will not perform its main obligations;
(iii) the other party delayed performance of its main obligations, and failed to perform within a reasonable time after receiving demand for performance;
(iv) the other party delayed performance or otherwise breached the contract, thereby frustrating the purpose of the contract;
(v)   any other circumstance provided by law occurred.

Article 97. Remedies in Case of Termination

Upon termination of a contract, a performance which has not been rendered is discharged; if a performance has been rendered, a party may, in light of the degree of performance and the nature of the contract, require the other party to restore the subject matter to its original condition or otherwise remedy the situation, and is entitled to claim damages.

Article 108. Anticipatory Breach

Where one party expressly states or indicates by its conduct that it will not perform its obligations under a contract, the other party may hold it liable for breach of contract before the time of performance.

Article 115. Deposit

The parties may prescribe that a party will give a deposit to the other party as assurance for the obligee's right to performance in accordance with the *Security Law of the People's Republic of China*. Upon performance by the obligor, the deposit shall be set off against the price or refunded to the obligor. If the party giving the deposit failed to perform its obligations under the contract, it is not entitled to claim refund of the deposit; where the party receiving the deposit failed to perform its obligations under the contract, it shall return to the other party twice the amount of the deposit.

Article 116. Election Between Deposit or Liquidated Damages Clauses

If the parties prescribed payment of both liquidated damages and a deposit, in case of breach by a party, the other party may elect in alternative to apply the liquidated damages clause or the deposit clause.

5 Summary

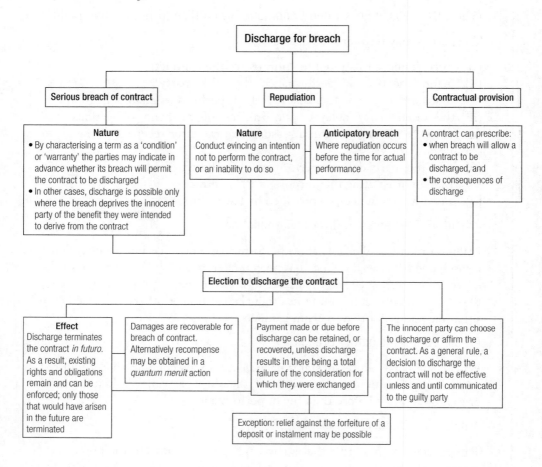

6 Questions

1. On 1 February, Peggy entered into a contract with Great Land Development Ltd (Greater Land) to purchase a house and land package for $290,000. This agreement provided for the immediate payment by Peggy of a deposit of $30,000 and for the payment of the balance in four equal instalments of $65,000 on 1 April, 1 May, 1 June and 1 July. It also provided that the house and the land would be transferred to Peggy upon payment of the final instalment on 1 July.

    Peggy paid the deposit of $30,000. On 2 February, Greater Land commenced building the house on the land chosen by Peggy and by the end of March the foundations and timber frame were completed. However, on 27 March, Peggy was advised that she would be transferred from her job in Melbourne to one located in Perth. Therefore, having no option but to move to Perth, she wrote to Greater Land later that day saying that, regrettably, she could no longer proceed with the contract. She advised Greater Land that, as a result, she would not make the payments due under the contract and asked it to return the deposit she had already paid to the company. On 8 April, Greater Land's solicitors replied saying that the company was treating this letter as a breach of contract and that it intended to keep the deposit paid to it as compensation for the building work it had so far carried out. They also said that Greater Land expected the instalment due on 1 April to be paid. Peggy did not make this payment. Greater Land completed the house on the land Peggy had contracted to purchase and sold to a third party for $280,000, the highest price it could get.

Please advise Greater Land of its rights and liabilities in relation to Peggy arising out of this transaction.

2   In January, Farm Ltd ('Farm') entered into a contract with Tanks Ltd ('Tanks') for the supply and installation of three large water tanks on its horse stud. The total price under the contract was $30,000, being calculated as $10,000 for the supply and installation of each tank. Under this contract, the tanks were to be installed in line with other work being carried out on the property, the first on 1 March, the second on 1 May and the third on 1 July. The total price was to be paid as a lump sum on 4 July after all the tanks had been delivered and installed.

Tank 1 was installed on 1 March. However, Tanks failed to supply and install tank 2 on 1 May. Having tried unsuccessfully for several days to contact the company, on 10 May Farm wrote to Tanks saying that it would engage another company to do the work. Still not having heard from Tanks, on 20 May Farm entered into a contract with Rural Water Ltd ('RW') to supply and install the second and third tanks for a total price of $22,000 (being $11,000 per tank) on 1 August and 1 September, with payment due in full on 4 September. On that day (20 May) Farm wrote to Tanks, advising of the action it had taken.

RW installed tank 2 on 1 August as agreed. However, on 15 August, as part of a water conservation strategy, the state government banned the filling of water tanks installed after that date. As a result, on 20 August, Farm wrote to RW saying that it did not wish to proceed with its acquisition of tank 3 as this would no longer be of any use to its enterprise. To compound Farm's problems, late in August, during the first period of significant rainfall after it was installed, tank 1 ruptured badly and has required extensive repairs costing $5,000.

In November 2003, Tanks wrote to Farm demanding the contract price of $30,000, saying that it had been at all times ready and willing to perform the contract and had merely experienced a minor supply problem in May. In December, RW also wrote to Farm asking for payment of its account of $22,000, saying that it had been willing and able to install tank 3 as contracted.

Please advise Farm about its rights and liabilities in relation to Tanks and RW.

CHAPTER 22

Discharge by Frustration

1	Introduction	616
2	The development of the doctrine of frustration	617
	a Absolute obligations	617
	b The foundation for the modern doctrine of frustration	618
	c The theoretical basis of frustration	620
3	The current position in Australia	622
4	Events that may frustrate a contract	627
	a Destruction of something essential	628
	b Non-occurrence of an essential event	628
	c Impossibility of performance	630
	d Events causing delay or making performance more expensive	631
	e Changes in the law	632
5	Situations preventing frustration	632
	a Where the contract makes provision for the supervening event	632
	b When the frustrating event is caused by one of the parties	635
6	Application of the doctrine to leases	637
7	The consequences of frustration	639
	a Common law	639
	b Statutory modification	642
8	Summary	648
9	Questions	648

1 Introduction

The doctrine of frustration deals with the allocation of risks and losses which occur as a result of an unanticipated change in circumstances occurring after the parties have entered into a contract. Frustration generally arises when a contracting party refuses to perform or has failed to perform its obligations in whole or in part because performance of the contract has become either physically impossible, illegal or is no longer commercially viable. Typically this arises as a result of an unexpected supervening event. Where, in such a case, it would be 'positively unjust to hold the parties bound'¹ under the dramatically changed circumstances, the courts will terminate the contract and discharge both parties from their future obligations under the contract.

Whether changed circumstances will amount to a frustrating event will be a matter of construction in each case. The court will compare the performance the parties had expected at the time of contracting with performance under the changed circumstances to determine whether the requirements for performance of the contract under those changed circumstances would be rendered something radically different from that which was contemplated by the parties at the time of making the contract. If so, the doctrine of frustration will operate.

Where the supervening event is a 'frustrating' event, the contract will be automatically discharged and both parties excused from further performance of the contractual obligations. The rights and obligations accrued up to the point of frustration remain enforceable.²

This chapter will discuss the development of the doctrine of frustration, the circumstances in which frustration will operate and the effect of frustration on the parties.

2 The development of the doctrine of frustration

a Absolute obligations

There was an early reluctance at common law to absolve a party from the consequences of his failure to perform contractual obligations; contractual obligations were regarded as absolute and the parties were taken to have promised to perform them 'come what may'. This strict approach was best demonstrated in *Paradine v Jane*.

Paradine v Jane

[1558–1774] All ER Rep 172; 82 ER 897, Court of King's Bench

[In an action of debt, Paradine (landlord), sued Jane (tenant) for three years rent in arrears. Jane denied liability on the ground that during that three-year period he had been forcibly evicted from the land as a result of the invasion by an army led by Prince Rupert of the Rhine.]

Bacon and Rolle JJ [at 173]: [I]t was resolved that the matter of the plea was insufficient, for although the whole army had been alien enemies, yet the defendant ought to pay the rent. This difference was taken, that where the law

---

1   See Lord Denning in *Ocean Tramp Tankers Corporation v V/O Sovfracht 'The Eugenia'* [1964] 2 QB 226 at 239.
2   See further *National Carriers v Panalpina (Northern) Ltd* [1981] AC 675 and *Codelfa Construction Pty Ltd v State Rail Authority of NSW* (1982) 149 CLR 337.

creates a duty or charge, and the party is disabled from performing it without any default in him, and has no remedy over, there the law will excuse him. ... But when the party by his own contract creates a duty or charge upon himself he is bound to make it good, if he may, notwithstanding any accident by inevitable necessity because he might have provided against it by his contract. Therefore, if the lessee covenants to repair a house, although it is burnt by lightning or thrown down by enemies ... yet he ought to repair it ...

The rent is a duty created by the parties upon the reservation, and had there been a covenant to pay it there would have been no question but the lessee must have made it good, notwithstanding the interruption by enemies, for the law would not protect him beyond his own agreement, no more than in the case of reparations. ... Another reason was added, that as the lessee is to have the advantage of casual profits, so he must run the hazard of casual losses <174> and not lay the whole burden of them upon his lessor.

Judgment for the plaintiff

b The foundation for the modern doctrine of frustration

The harshness of a strict insistence on contractual performance in circumstances where that performance has been rendered fundamentally different from that envisaged at the time of contract resulted in the development of the doctrine of frustration.[3]

The modern doctrine of frustration has its foundation in the decision of the Queen's Bench in the following case. In this case, while the Court did not use the word 'frustration', it was prepared to imply a term that certain supervening events should terminate contractual obligations.

Taylor v Caldwell

[1861–1873] All ER Rep 24; (1863) 3 B & S 826, Court of Queen's Bench

[The defendants (Caldwell) agreed to let the plaintiff (Taylor) use the Surrey Gardens and Music Hall for a period of four days in exchange for payment of 100 pounds per day. The gardens and hall were to be used for concerts and other entertainment and the plaintiffs expended moneys promoting these events. After entering into this agreement, but prior to the date of the first concert, the Music Hall burnt down. As a result the concerts could not take place as planned and the

---

3   Bingham LJ in *J Lauritzen AS v Wijsmuller BV* [1990] 1 Lloyd's Rep 1 at 8 stated that the doctrine of frustration has developed 'to mitigate the rigor of the common law's insistence on literal performance of absolute promises' and that its object is 'to give effect to the demands of justice, to achieve a just and reasonable result, to do what is reasonable and fair, as an expedient to escape from injustice where such would result from enforcement of a contract in its literal term after a significant change in circumstances'.

plaintiffs sued the defendants for their losses incurred in promoting the concerts. The defendants relied on the destruction of the hall as excusing their performance.]

Blackburn J [at 27]: [The destruction of the hall], we must take it on the evidence, was without the fault of either party, and was so complete that in consequence the concerts could not be given as intended. And the question we have to decide is whether, under these circumstances, the loss which the plaintiffs have sustained is to fall upon the defendants. The parties when framing their agreement, evidently had not present to their minds the possibilities of such a disaster, and have made no express stipulation with reference to it, so that the answer to the question must depend upon the general rules of law applicable to such a contract.

There seems no doubt that where there is a positive contract to do a thing, not in itself unlawful, the contractor must perform it or pay damages for not doing it, although in consequence of unforeseen accidents, the performance of his contract has become unexpectedly burthensome or even impossible. ... But this rule is only applicable when the contract is positive and absolute, and not subject to any condition either express or implied: and there are authorities which, as we think, establish the principle that where, from the nature of the contract, it appears that the parties must from the beginning have known that it could not be fulfilled unless when the time for the fulfilment of the contract arrived some particular specified thing continued to exist, so that, when entering into the contract, they must have contemplated such continuing existence as the foundation of what was to be done; there, in the absence of any express or implied warranty that the thing shall exist, the contract is not to be construed as a positive contract, but as subject to an implied condition that the parties shall be excused in case, before breach, performance becomes impossible from the perishing of the thing without default of the contractor.

There seems little doubt that this implication tends to further the great object of making the legal construction such as to fulfil the intention of those who entered into the contract. For in the course of affairs men in making such contracts in general would, if it were brought to their minds, say that there should be such a condition.

... <29> ... The principle seems to us to be that, in contracts in which the performance depends on the continued existence of a given person or thing, a condition is implied that the impossibility of performance arising from the perishing of the person or thing shall excuse the performance. ...

In the present case, looking at the whole contract, we find that the parties contracted on the basis of the continued existence of the Music Hall at the time when the concerts were to be given; that being essential to their performance. We think, therefore, that the Music Hall having ceased to exist, without fault of either party, both parties are excused, the plaintiffs from taking the gardens and paying the money, the defendants from performing their promise to give the use of the Hall and Gardens and other things. Consequently the rule must be absolute to enter the verdict for the defendant.

Judgment for the defendants

c The theoretical basis of frustration

Five theories have been advanced as the jurisprudential foundation on which the doctrine of frustration rests.[4] These theories were set out by Lord Wilberforce in *National Carriers v Panalpina (Northern) Ltd*[5] as including:

- implied term theory[6]
- construction of the contract
- removal of the foundation of the contract
- total failure of consideration and
- justice.

The implied term theory found early favour with the courts but has since been discarded by most as a legitimate basis for the doctrine:

> [T]he theory of an implied term has now been discarded by everyone, or nearly everyone, for the simple reason that it does not represent the truth. The parties would not have said: 'It is all over between us.' They would have differed about what was to happen. Each would have sought to insert reservations or qualifications of one kind or another.[7]

The modern formulation of the doctrine of frustration was expressed by Lord Radcliffe in the following case.

Davis Contractors Ltd v Fareham Urban District Council

[1956] AC 696, House of Lords

[As a result of a successful tender the appellants contracted to build 78 houses for the respondent council within an eight month period. Due to circumstances beyond the control of either party adequate supplies of labour were not available during that period and the building works took more than 22 months to complete.

The appellants claimed the contract had been frustrated and that they were entitled to recover for extra expenses incurred. The appellants succeeded before an arbitrator but lost an appeal to the Court of Appeal which concluded the contract had not been frustrated. An appeal was then made to the House of Lords.]

---

4   Lord Reid in *Davis Contractors Ltd v Fareham Urban District Council* [1956] AC 696 stated that 'So long as each theory produces the same result as the other, as normally it does, it matters little which theory is avowed.' Lord Wilberforce in *National Carriers v Panalpina (Northern) Ltd* [1981] AC 675 described it 'as a device by which the rules as to absolute contracts are reconciled with a special exception which justice demands'.
5   [1981] AC 675.
6   See also *Taylor v Caldwell* [1861–1873] All ER Rep 24, per Blackburn J.
7   Denning LJ in *Ocean Tramp Tankers Corporation v V/O Sovfracht 'The Eugenia'* [1964] 2 QB 226 at 238. See also Lord Hailsham of St Marylebone LC in *National Carriers v Panalpina (Northern) Ltd* [1981] AC 675 at 687: 'In the present case, had the officious bystander pointed out [the event would occur] and asked them what they would do in the event of [the event occurring] I have not the least idea what they would have said, or whether either would have entered into the lease at all.'

Lord Radcliffe: [After analysing the frustration theory of implied terms, his Lordship continued at 729]: [F]rustration occurs whenever the law recognises that, without default of either party, a contractual obligation has become incapable of being performed because the circumstances in which performance is called for would render it a thing radically different from that which was undertaken by the contract. *Non haec in foedera veni.* It was not this that I promised to do.

There is, however, no uncertainty as to the materials upon which the court must proceed. 'The data for decision are, on the one hand, the terms and construction of the contract, read in the light of the surrounding circumstances, and, on the other hand, the events which have occurred' … In the nature of things there is often no room for any elaborate inquiry. The court must act on a general impression of what its rule requires. It is for that reason that special importance is necessarily attached to the occurrence of any unexpected event that, as it were, changes the face of things. But, even so, it is not hardship or inconvenience or material loss itself which calls the principle of frustration into play. There must be as well such a change in the significance of the obligation that the thing undertaken would, if performed, be a different thing from that contracted for.

I am bound to say that, if this is the law, the appellants' case seems to me a long way from a case of frustration. Here is a building contract entered into by a housing authority and a big firm of contractors in all the uncertainties of the post-war world. … <730> …

The contract, it is said, was an eight months' contract, as indeed it was. Through no fault of the parties it turned out that it took 22 months to do the work contracted for. The main reason for this was that, whereas both parties had expected that adequate supplies of labour and material would be available to allow for completion in eight months, the supplies that were, in fact, available were much less than adequate for the purpose. Hence, it is said, the basis or the footing of the contract was removed before the work was completed; or, slightly altering the metaphor, the footing of the contract was so changed by the circumstance that the expected supplies were not available that the contract built on that footing became void. …

<731> … Two things seem to me to prevent the application of the principle of frustration to this case. One is that the cause of the delay was not any new state of things which the parties could not reasonably be thought to have foreseen. On the contrary, the possibility of enough labour and materials not being available was before their eyes and could have been the subject of special contractual stipulation. It was not made so. The other thing is that, though timely completion was, no doubt, important to both sides, it is not right to treat the possibility of delay as having the same significance for each. The owner draws up his conditions in detail, specifies the time within which he requires completion, protects himself both by a penalty clause for time exceeded and by calling for the deposit of a guarantee bond, and offers a certain measure of security to a contractor by his escalator clause with regard to wages and prices. In the light of these conditions the contractor makes his tender, and the tender must necessarily take into account the margin of profit that

he hopes to obtain on his adventure, and in that any appropriate allowance for the obvious risks of delay. To my mind, it is useless to pretend that the contractor is not at risk if delay does occur, even serious delay. And I think it a misuse of legal terms to call in frustration to get him out of his unfortunate predicament. ...

[Viscount Simonds, Lord Morton of Henryton, Lord Reid and Lord Somervell of Harrow all delivered separate judgments in which they agreed that the contract was not frustrated.]

Appeal dismissed

3 The current position in Australia

Australian courts have adopted the modern doctrine as expressed in *Davis Contractors*. The High Court considered the doctrine of frustration in the following cases.[8]

Codelfa Construction Pty Ltd v State Rail Authority of New South Wales

(1982) 149 CLR 337, High Court of Australia

[The facts of this case are set out at page 265 above]

Mason J [at 357]: [I] agree with ... the approach adopted by Lord Reid and Lord Radcliffe in *Davis Contractors*. Lord Reid said that the task of the court is to determine 'on the true construction of the terms which are in the contract read in light of the nature of the contract and of the relevant surrounding circumstances', 'whether the contract which they did make is ... wide enough to apply to the new situation: if it is not, then it is at an end'. Later he described frustration as 'the termination of the contract by operation of law on the emergence of a fundamentally different situation'. ...

[Lord Radcliffe] noting that special importance attaches to an unexpected event, observed 'There must be as well such a change in the significance of the obligation that the thing undertaken would, if performed, be a different thing from that contracted for'.

It is implicit, if not explicit ... in the speeches of Lord Reid and Lord Radcliffe in *Davis Contractors*, that to express a preference for this view of frustration as against the theory of the implied condition and other suggested bases is not to cast doubt on the authority of earlier decisions. This is of critical importance because the earlier cases provide many illustrations of the proposition that a contract will be frustrated when the parties enter into it on the common assumption that some particular thing or state of affairs essential to its performance will continue to exist

---

8   See also *Brisbane City Council v Group Projects Pty Ltd* (1979) 145 CLR 143.

or be available, neither party undertaking responsibility in that regard, and that common assumption proves to be mistaken ... Two objections may be urged to the width of the proposition I have stated.

The first is that the common assumption must be found in the contract itself. The answer to this objection is that, granted that the assumption needs to be contractual, in the case of frustration, as <358> with the implication of a term, it is legitimate to look to extrinsic evidence in the form of relevant surrounding circumstances to assist us in the interpretation of the contract, unless its language is so plain that recourse to surrounding circumstances would amount to no more than an attempt to contradict or vary the terms of the contract. ...

<359> ... The second objection is that the proposition does not sufficiently acknowledge the fact that the event which generally, if not universally, works a frustration, is an event which supervenes after the making of the contract, viz a change in the law which makes it impossible for the parties to execute the contract. It is not surprising that the cases commonly throw up situations of supervening impossibility caused by a change in the law—they are the more common instances of the unforeseen or unexpected occurrence. But in principle there is no reason why a mutual assumption arising from a mistaken view that an activity is immune from injunctive relief should not attract the principle of frustration. No doubt it is more difficult in such a case to show that the grant of injunctive relief was not foreseen or could not reasonably have been foreseen, but if that can be shown then the doctrine of frustration should apply. The injunction is a supervening event though it does not stem from any alteration in the law.

An unusual element in the present case is that the parties appear to have received, accepted and acted on erroneous legal advice that the contract work could not be impeded by the grant of an injunction to restrain noise or other nuisance, ... One might have expected the parties and their advisers to have had reservations about the correctness of the advice and to have given consideration to the possibility that, despite the advice, an injunction might be granted. However, the findings do not reflect the existence of any reservations; indeed, they record Codelfa's acceptance of the representations made by the Authority. ...

<360> The critical issue then is whether the situation resulting from the grant of the injunction is fundamentally different from the situation contemplated by the contract on its true construction in the light of the surrounding circumstances. The contract itself did not require that the work be carried out on a three-shift continuous basis six days a week without restriction as to Sundays. But it required completion of the works within 130 weeks. And Codelfa with its tender had submitted a construction programme which involved a three-shift continuous basis six days a week. By cl S6 of the specifications Codelfa was required to submit a revised programme of work to the Engineer for his determination within thirty calendar days of the issue of a notice to proceed under the contract. This Codelfa did. Again it made provision for the method of operation already mentioned. It was accepted by the Engineer. ...

<361> The submission of the proposed programme of work with the tender, its supersession by the revised programme ... provide a link between the contract and the antecedent discussions so as to enable us ... to say that the contract contemplated that completion would be achieved within the time stipulated by the method of work already mentioned, it being assumed that it could not be disturbed by the grant of an injunction. ...

<362> Once the injunctions were granted the Engineer gave notices reflecting the provisions of the injunctions, restricting the hours of work so as to prohibit work at night and thereby inhibited Codelfa from continuing with its three-shift operation under the contract. ...

I come back then to the question whether the performance of the contract in the new situation was fundamentally different from performance in the situation contemplated by the contract. The answer must, I think, be in the affirmative. ... The finding [of the Arbitrator] proceeds on the footing that the contract work could not be carried out as contemplated by the contract once injunctions were granted, ... <363> .... Performance by means of a two shift operation, necessitated by the grant of the injunctions, was fundamentally different from that contemplated by the contract.

There is, of course, no inconsistency between the conclusion that a term cannot be implied and the conclusion that events have occurred which have brought about a frustration of the contract. I find it impossible to imply a term because I am not satisfied that in the circumstances of this case the term sought to be implied was one which parties in that situation would necessarily have agreed upon as an appropriate provision to cover the eventuality which has arisen. On the other hand I find it much easier to come to the conclusion that the performance of the contract in the events which have occurred is radically different from performance of the contract in the circumstances which it, construed in the light of surrounding circumstances, contemplated. ...

Aickin J [at 375]: The Contractor's argument was that the grant of the injunction had such a drastic effect upon its construction programme, both physically and financially, that it was transformed into an obligation radically different from that which it had undertaken on the common erroneous understanding. ...

<376> The manner in which the doctrine of frustration is generally expressed has undergone some change, though it has not been suggested that its content has changed. When it was first developed it was usual to express it as arising from an implied term: ... The doctrine is now generally expressed as depending on changes in the significance of the obligations undertaken and the surrounding circumstances in which the contract was made. ...

<381> ... both parties proceeded upon the assumption that the works could be lawfully completed within the specified time by continuous work on a three-shift basis for six days a week. The situation became one in which it was impossible to perform the contract in accordance with its terms, impossible because court orders restrained the mode of performance, which was held to constitute a nuisance, but which was critical to the completion of the works within the time allowed.

It is a different situation from that in which one party has been prevented from completing the contract work within the specified time because of shortage of labour or shortage of materials, or both. Those cases are not cases in which the completion of the work in the contract period is rendered impossible because injunctions have prevented the work being done in a manner and at times which, from the outset, both parties knew were essential to completion on time. ...

<383> In my opinion the grant of the injunction produced frustration in the true sense of that term. It had become unlawful to perform the work in a manner which would have complied with the requirement of the contract, a requirement well known to both parties. The fact that both parties to the contract had an understanding of the law which led them to believe that the performance of the contract on the three-shift basis could not be interfered with by any private or public litigant seeking to restrain a nuisance caused by the performance of the work, does not prevent the application of the doctrine of frustration. ...

[Stephen and Wilson JJ agreed with Mason and Aicken JJ on the issue of frustration. Brennan J dissented, noting (at 409) that the 'injunction limiting working hours did no more than enforce judicially a limitation by which Codelfa was already legally bound'.]

Appeal allowed

[footnotes omitted]

Brisbane City Council v Group Projects Proprietary Limited

(1979) 145 CLR 143, High Court of Australia

[The respondent developer, Group Projects, entered into a contract with the appellant Council, by which it agreed to undertake construction works on and around land it owned in exchange for the Council making an application to the minister to have land re-zoned to permit residential development. The agreement expressly contemplated the future subdivision of the land for which the respondent intended to profit through future residential development. Subsequently the parties were notified that the Crown intended to resume some of the land to which the agreement related for the purpose of building a school. Despite this, Group Projects asked the Council to proceed with the re-zoning application. The Council made the application and the land was re-zoned. Group Projects subsequently applied for a declaration that it was not bound by the agreement. Group Projects succeeded at trial and on appeal to the full court of the Supreme Court of Queensland. The Council appealed to the High Court.]

Stephen J [at 156]: [T]he question for me is ... whether Group Projects will be in breach of its obligations under the deed if it fails to perform them or whether it may instead invoke the doctrine of frustration so as to bring the deed ... to an end. ...

In any consideration of the claim that this is a case of frustration, two features of the case should be noted at the outset. The first is that this is not the common case of two contracting parties, both interested in a commercial venture, one of them supplying to the other, in return for a money payment, goods or land or services. The Council is a public body and the principal obligation which the deed imposes upon it is performance of an act, the making of an application for re-zoning, which is of a kind which the statute contemplates that it will from time to time have occasion to perform in carrying out its public functions. The inducement offered to the Council is not in essence monetary gain. Its relevant primary concern is, no doubt, that areas destined for residential development should be provided with proper amenities, with electric light, water, a sewerage system, good roads, parks and the like. To induce it to apply for re-zoning, Group Projects undertakes materially to assist in the provision of these amenities. No doubt the Council has in mind that its own funds should not unnecessarily be expended in providing those amenities; … However, <157> essentially the advantages which the Council seeks are not its own financial or commercial advancement but the attainment in a new subdivisional area of appropriate standards of amenity. This distinguishes the present case from those in which questions of frustration usually arise.

The second feature calling for mention is that *in principle* this is not a case in which performance of contractual obligations has either been rendered impossible or more onerous by the frustrating event. I use the qualifying expression 'in principle' because, as it happens, some of Group Projects' obligations would in fact have involved the carrying out of work on the land itself, which has now become Crown land to which it no longer has access, let alone the right to carry out engineering works on it. But the bulk of the work contracted for, or towards the cost of which it has promised to contribute, was to be done *off* the acquired land, so that its acquisition by the Crown in no way prevents the doing of that work or alters its nature or cost. That this is not so in relation to all the work to be done is in a sense fortuitous and the great bulk of the work can still be performed with no greater difficulty or expense than before. If frustration is to apply its application cannot, in these circumstances, be accommodated very comfortably within any theory of frustration which is said to be based upon such a 'change in the significance of the obligation that the thing undertaken would, if performed, be a different thing from that contracted for' (*Davis Contractors* …).

There is, I suppose, no doubt but that the acquisition of the land by the Crown for use as the site of a school has deprived Group Projects of all desire to now proceed with the work and expenditure which it has contracted for under the deed. To do that work and incur that expenditure would be to provide, at great cost to itself, facilities for land in which it no longer has the remotest interest. … it is clear that, although Group Projects no doubt remains able to perform the bulk of the obligations which it has undertaken, being that part <158> of the work which is not to be undertaken on the acquired land, and although that work will have neither changed in character nor become more onerous, yet the acquisition of the land for a school site has wholly destroyed Group Projects' purpose in undertaking any obligations at all.

Whichever of the competing theories, said to underlie and give conceptual validity to the doctrine of frustration, is to be preferred, and the truth may, indeed, not lie in a choice of one and the rejection of all others, there is no doubt that an examination of the parties' agreement and of the surrounding circumstances provides an appropriate starting point.

I have already spoken of the role of the Council, a public body performing public duties, and of the complete aborting of Group Projects' plans as a result of the acquisition of the land for a school site. The terms of the deed both reflect this role of the Council and also emphasize that it was upon the basis of development of the land as a residential subdivision that the parties entered into it. ... <159> ...

The task is to set this alongside the doctrine of frustration and to see whether the result is that the law will regard the contract as frustrated or will, <160> instead, regard non-performance by Group Projects as actionable at the suit of the Council. ...

[In *Davis Contractors* Lord Reid] rejected the notion of the implied term as the basis of the doctrine. He says that the task for a court, confronted with the parties' contract, is to determine, on the true construction of the terms of the contract, read in the light of the nature of the contract and of the relevant surrounding circumstances when the parties made it, 'whether the contract which they did make is, on its true construction, wide enough to apply to the new situation: if it is not, then it is at an end.' Frustration he describes as 'the termination of the contract by operation of law on the emergence of a fundamentally different situation'. What I understand his Lordship's approach to involve is, then, a comparison between the contemplated situation, as revealed by the terms of the contract on its true construction, and the situation in fact resulting from the frustrating event. If they be 'fundamentally different' the contract is frustrated subject, of course, to the frustrating event not being the fault of the party seeking to rely upon the doctrine. ...

<162> ... There has arisen, as a result of the compulsory acquisition of the land by the Crown for a school site, such a fundamentally different situation from that contemplated when the contract was entered into that it is properly to be regarded as having come to an end at the date of acquisition by the Crown. ...

[Murphy J agreed with Stephen J on this issue. Gibbs, Mason and Wilson JJ dismissed the appeal for different reasons and did not find it necessary to address the issue of frustration.]

Appeal dismissed

[footnotes omitted]

4 Events that may frustrate a contract

There are a number of 'events' that the courts have recognised as rendering a contract 'radically different' from that which was contemplated. Each case will, however, depend on its own peculiar circumstances and these cases can, therefore, only provide a guide to possible future applications of the doctrine of frustration. When determining whether the doctrine of frustration operates in any particular case, consideration should be given to the terms of the contract, the nature of the event that has occurred and the type of contract that is involved; then an assessment may be made of whether or not the operation of the contract following the event is radically different from that originally contemplated.

a Destruction of something essential

If the continuing existence of a thing or a person is assumed by both parties as the foundation of the contract, the destruction of that thing or person may invoke the doctrine of frustration. Thus, the destruction of the Music Hall in *Taylor v Caldwell* excused the parties in that case from further performance.

b Non-occurrence of an essential event

If the occurrence of an essential event is assumed by both parties as the basis of their contract relationship, the non-occurrence of that event may invoke the doctrine of frustration. The most famous examples are the Coronation cases, in which contracts made upon an understanding that coronation processions would take place at a particular time and place were held to have been frustrated when, as a result of the King's serious illness, the processions did not take place.

Krell v Henry

[1903] 2 KB 740, English Court of Appeal

[On 20 June 1902 the defendant entered into a contract with the plaintiff for the lease of the plaintiff's flat in Pall Mall on 26 and 27 June 1902. It had been announced that coronation processions would take place along Pall Mall on those dates. The contract itself made no express reference to the processions. As a result of the King's serious illness the processions did not take place as planned. The plaintiff sought payment of the balance of the agreed price and the defendant counter-claimed for a return of the deposit on the grounds that there had been a total failure of consideration. The trial judge found for the defendant on the basis that there was an implied condition in the contract that the procession would take place.]

Vaughan Williams LJ [at 748]: … the English law applies the principle [of frustration] not only to cases where the performance of the contract becomes impossible by the cessation of existence of the thing which is the subject-matter of the contract, but also to cases where the event which renders the contract incapable of performance is the cessation or non-existence of an express condition or state of things, going to the root of the contract, and essential to its performance. It is said, on the one side, that the specified thing, state of things, or condition the continued existence of which is necessary for the fulfilment of the contract, so that the parties entering into the contract must have contemplated the continued existence of that thing, condition, or state of things as the foundation of what was to be done under the contract, is limited to things which are either the subject-matter of the contract or a condition or state of things, present or anticipated, which is expressly <749> mentioned in the contract. But, on the other side, it is said that the condition or state of things need not be expressly specified, but that it is sufficient if that condition or state of things clearly appears by extrinsic evidence to have been assumed by the parties to be the foundation or basis of the contract, and the event which causes the impossibility is of such a character that it cannot reasonably be supposed to have been in the contemplation of the contracting parties when the contract was made. In such a case the contracting parties will not be held bound by the general words which, though large enough to include, were not used with reference to a possibility of a particular event rendering performance of the contract impossible. I do not think that the principle … is limited to cases in which the event causing the impossibility of performance is the destruction or non-existence of some thing which is the subject-matter of the contract or of some condition or state of things expressly specified as a condition of it. I think that you first have to ascertain, not necessarily from the terms of the contract, but, if required, from necessary inferences, drawn from surrounding circumstances recognised by both contracting parties, what is the substance of the contract, and then to ask the question whether that substantial contract needs for its foundation the assumption of the existence of a particular state of things. If it does, this will limit the operation of the general words, and in such case, if the contract becomes impossible of performance by reason of the non-existence of the state of things assumed by both contracting parties as the foundation of the contract, there will be no breach of the contract thus limited. Now what are the facts of the present case? The contract is contained in two letters …. These letters do not mention the coronation, … But the [evidence shows] that the plaintiff exhibited on his <750> premises, … an announcement to the effect that windows to view the Royal coronation procession were to be let, and that the defendant was induced by that announcement … In my judgment the use of the rooms was let and taken for the purpose of seeing the Royal procession. … It is a licence to use rooms for a particular purpose and none other. And in my judgment the taking place of those processions on the days proclaimed along the proclaimed route, … was regarded by both contracting parties as the foundation of the contract; and I think that it cannot reasonably be supposed to have been in the contemplation of the contracting parties, when the contract was made, that the coronation would not be held on the proclaimed days, or the processions not take place on those days along the proclaimed route; and I think that the words imposing on the defendant the obligation to accept and pay for the use of the rooms for the named days, although general and unconditional, were not used with reference to the possibility of the particular contingency which afterwards occurred. …

<751> … Each case must be judged by its own circumstances. In each case one must ask oneself, first, what, having regard to all the circumstances, was the foundation of the contract? Secondly, was the performance of the contract

prevented? Thirdly, was the event which prevented the performance of the contract of such a character that it cannot reasonably be said to have been in the contemplation of the parties at the date of the contract? If all these questions are answered in the affirmative (as I think they should be in this case), I think both parties are discharged from further performance of the contract. I think that the coronation procession was the foundation of this contract, and that the non-happening of it prevented the performance of the contract; and, secondly, I think that the <752> non-happening of the procession, ... was an event 'of such a character that it cannot reasonably be supposed to have been in the contemplation of the contracting parties when the contract was made, and that they are not to be held bound by general words which, though large enough to include, were not used with reference to the possibility of the particular contingency which afterwards happened.' The test seems to be whether the event which causes the impossibility was or might have been anticipated and guarded against. It seems difficult to say, in a case where both parties anticipate the happening of an event, which anticipation is the foundation of the contract, that either party must be taken to have anticipated, and ought to have guarded against, the event which prevented the performance of the contract. ... <754> ... I myself am clearly of opinion that in this case, where we have to ask ourselves whether the object of the contract was frustrated by the non-happening of the coronation and its procession on the days proclaimed, parol evidence is admissible to shew that the subject of the contract was rooms to view the coronation procession, and was so to the knowledge of both parties. When once this is established, I see no difficulty whatever in the case. It is not essential to the application of the principle of *Taylor v Caldwell* that the direct subject of the contract should perish or fail to be in existence at the date of performance of the contract. It is sufficient if a state of things or condition expressed in the contract and essential to its performance perishes or fails to be in existence at that time. In the present case the condition which fails and prevents the achievement of that which was, in the contemplation of both parties, the foundation of the contract, is not expressly mentioned either as a condition of the contract or the purpose of it; but I think for the reasons which I have given that the principle of *Taylor v Caldwell* ought to be applied.

[Romer and Stirling LJJ agreed with Vaughan Williams.]

Appeal dismissed

[footnotes omitted]

c Impossibility of performance

If, as a result of a supervening event, a contract becomes impossible to perform, either physically or commercially, the doctrine of frustration may operate to discharge the contract. In *Fibrosa Spolka Akcyjna v Fairbairn Lawson Combe Barbour Ltd*[9] the House of Lords held that a contract under which goods were to

---

9   [1943] AC 32.

be delivered to Gydnia was frustrated when, after the date of contract but prior to delivery, Gydnia became enemy-occupied territory such that it became illegal for the sellers to deliver the goods. Performance may also be rendered impossible by the death or incapacity of the promisor, at least where the contract depends on some special skill or knowledge of the promisor.

d Events causing delay or making performance more expensive

Events which merely delay performance or render it more expensive than contemplated will not frustrate a contract. However, where the delay or increased expense is such that the contract becomes one that is radically different from that contemplated by the parties the doctrine of frustration may operate.[10] Consequently, in *Codelfa Constructions* the Court held that delay caused by an injunction not contemplated by the parties frustrated the contract. This issue also arose in the following case.

Wong Lai Ying v Chinachem Investment Co Ltd
(1979) 13 Build LR 81, Privy Council

[The appellant purchasers separately contracted with the respondent developer to buy flats the respondent was building in an area to be known as 'University Heights'. Work commenced in December 1971 and was to be completed in May 1973. Time was stipulated as being of the essence, subject to the possibility of an extension of no more than one year in specified circumstances. The purchase price was payable at the conclusion of the contract. In June 1972 a large landslide, which was accepted as being an unforeseeable natural disaster, destroyed a block of flats and buried the construction site. No building was permitted at the site while a lengthy investigation took place and the respondent was not given permission to recommence construction until November 1975. As a consequence, the earliest day on which it was possible to complete the works was October 1976.

The trial judge and the Hong Kong Court of Appeal held the landslip was a 'frustrating event'. The purchasers appealed seeking a declaration that their contracts were not frustrated and an order for specific performance of the contract.]

Lord Scarman [at 92]: The law is now well settled. A frustrating event is an interruption of the performance of a contract, which is an event of such a character and duration as to make the contract when resumed a different contract from the contract when broken off … <93>.

[If] there was a frustrating event, it was the landslip [which] was an unforeseeable natural disaster. …

<94> … The landslip was a major interruption fundamentally changing the character and the duration of the contract performance. The contract, which was one for the sale of an undivided share in land upon the express condition that the

---

10 See, for example, *Jackson v The Union Marine Insurance Company, Limited* [1873] LR 10 CP 125 and *Horlock v Beal* [1916] 1 AC 486.

vendor would erect and within a stipulated period complete a building on the land to include a flat for the purchaser, was entered into when plans had been approved by the Building Authority but no work begun. The purchaser was required to pay a substantial deposit at once (in Wong Lai Ying's case, the whole purchase price). Not surprisingly, time was made the essence of the contract. Clause 3, which imposed the time limit upon the vendor and spelt out the purchaser's rights in the event of delay, made express provision only for a limited period of delay, and no provision at all for an event arising which made further performance uncertain and the character and duration of any further performance (should any prove possible) radically different from that which the original contract contemplated ...

<95> ... As Lord Denning MR remarked in *The Eugenia* ... frustration is a common law doctrine designed to achieve justice where it would be 'positively unjust to hold the parties bound'. On the facts as found concurrently by the trial judge and Court of Appeal it would be unjust to hold the parties bound. <96> ... The common law, supplemented by legislation, enables the vendor in this case to be relieved of a performance radically different from that which he originally undertook and the purchaser to be repaid his money with interest from the date of payment.

The Lordships will humbly advise Her Majesty that these appeals be dismissed with costs.

Appeal dismissed

[footnotes omitted]

e   Changes in the law

A subsequent change in the law may frustrate a contract, even if it does not render performance of the contract illegal, provided it substantially affects the parties so that the contract becomes different in nature than that contemplated by the parties. The obtaining of an injunction against a party in *Codelfa Constructions*,[11] which substantially affected the ability of the plaintiff to perform the contract in the manner contemplated, was held to frustrate the contract. Similarly, in *Fibrosa*,[12] the outbreak of war which rendered performance of the contract illegal under the *Trading with the Enemy Act 1939* (UK) caused the contract to be frustrated.

5   Situations preventing frustration

a   Where the contract makes provision for the supervening event

Where the parties have contemplated a supervening event and made provision for it in their contract there is no scope for the operation of the doctrine of frustration. This was considered in the following case.[13]

---

11   See case extracted above on p 622.
12   This case is extracted below.
13   See also *Wong Lai Ying and Others v Chinachem Investment Co Ltd* (1979) 13 Build LR 81.

Bank Line, Limited v Arthur Capel and Company

[1919] AC 435, House of Lords

[In February 1915, the defendant owners agreed to let a steamer (the *Quito*) to the plaintiff charterers for a period of 12 months to run from the time the vessel was delivered. The contract provided that if the steamer was not delivered by 30 April 1915 the charterers would have the option of cancelling the contract and they would also have the option of cancelling if the steamer was commandeered by the government during the term of the charter. The steamer was not delivered by the agreed date and was subsequently requisitioned by the government. However, the plaintiffs did not exercise their option of cancelling the contract. In August 1915 the defendants contracted to sell the steamer to a third party, subject to it being released from the government. The government agreed to the release and the sale went ahead. The plaintiffs claimed damages for non-delivery and the defendants responded the contract had been frustrated.

The defendants succeeded at trial but the plaintiffs successfully appealed to the Court of Appeal. A further appeal was made to the House of Lords.]

Lord Sumner [at 450]: From the time when the *Quito* was requisitioned her owners never were in a position to put her at the charterers' disposal for any purpose until after they had sold her. By finding a substitute for her they might possibly have induced the Admiralty to set her free, for such things had been done; but it was uncertain if such an attempt would succeed, and mere importunity proved unavailing. They had not contracted to make this special effort for the benefit of the charterers. It is true that, when they did so for their own benefit, they succeeded, and having got possession of her, they might have been bound to place her at the charterers' disposal under the charter, if that still subsisted, the sale notwithstanding; <451> but the question is whether the charter had previously come to an end by frustration. If it had, they were not bound to give the charterers a first chance of a new contract. ...

<454> ... Rights ought not to be left in suspense or to hang on the chances of subsequent events. The contract binds or it does not bind, and the law ought to be that the parties can gather their fate then and there. What happens afterwards may assist in showing what the probabilities really were, if they had been reasonably forecasted, but when <455> the causes of frustration have operated so long or under such circumstances as to raise a presumption of inordinate delay, the time has arrived at which the fate of the contract falls to be decided. That fate is dissolution or continuance and, if the charter ought to be held to be dissolved, it cannot be revived without a new contract. The parties are free.

... <456> ... In the present case three clauses are relied on as express provisions for the event and consequences of an Admiralty requisition delaying or preventing the placing of the *Quito* at the charterers' disposal, Nos. 14, 26, and 31. When the Admiralty requisitioned her she became subject to a restraint of princes, one of the causes mentioned in clause 14, which says 'throughout this charter losses or damages, whether in respect of goods carried or to be carried or in other respects arising or occasioned by the following causes, shall be absolutely excepted.' In the first place, I think this claim is not for 'loss or damage' within that clause, but in the second the meaning of such an ordinary clause of exception is well settled. It excuses breaches of the contract caused by matters which fall within its terms; it suspends the liability to pay hire without finally determining it; but relief from the liability to pay damages or hire and complete discharge from further obligation to perform the contract are different things. ...

The same may be said of clause 31. It means that, if the Admiralty should requisition the ship, the charter may be forthwith cancelled by the charterers, without waiting to see or having to show that its object is thereby frustrated. ... As to clause 26, the cancelling clause, I am unable to accept the construction of it, which makes it mean that after April 30 and until the <457> ship is delivered for the chartered service, however long the interval may be, the charterers can at any moment spring on the shipowners a cancellation of the contract, and can hold them bound so long as they choose to hold their own tongues. ... After all, it is a stipulation in the charterers' favour, and cannot be given so extreme a meaning, unless that meaning is clearly expressed. The parties never meant that the shipowners should remain indefinitely at the charterers' mercy. ...

<458> Delay even of considerable length and of wholly uncertain duration is an incident of maritime adventure, which is clearly within the contemplation of the parties, such as delay caused by ice or neaping, so much so as to be often the subject of express provision. Delays such as these may very seriously affect the commercial object of the adventure, for the ship's expenses and over-head charges are running on and ... the margin of profit is quickly run off. None the less this <459> is not frustration; the delay is ordinary in character, and in most cases the charterer is getting the use of the chartered ship, even though it is unprofitable to him. ...

<460> ... My Lords, applying these considerations I am of opinion that the requisitioning of the *Quito* destroyed the identity of the chartered service and made the charter as a matter of business a totally different thing. It hung up the performance for a time, which was wholly indefinite and probably long. The return of the ship depended on considerations beyond the ken or control of either party. Both thought its result was to terminate their contractual relation by the middle of June and, as they must have known much more about it than I do, there is no reason why I should not think so too. I should allow the appeal.

[Lord Finlay LC, Lord Shaw of Dunfermline and Lord Wrenbury also held that the contract had been frustrated and, in particular, that the doctrine of frustration was not excluded in these circumstances by the terms of the charterparty. Viscount Haldane agreed that there was nothing in the contract excluding the doctrine of frustration, but did not consider that the requisition of the steamer by the government constituted a frustrating event in this case.]

Appeal allowed

b When the frustrating event is caused by one of the parties

Where the event relied on was caused by one of the parties it will not operate to frustrate the contract.[14] This issue arose in the following cases.

Maritime National Fish Limited v Ocean Trawlers Limited

[1935] AC 524, Privy Council

[Maritime (the appellants) chartered a steam trawler (the *St Cuthbert*) from Ocean Trawlers (the respondents) for a period of one year. The charterparty provided that the trawler was only permitted to be used in the fishing industry. However, Canadian legislation made it an offence to leave a Canadian port with intent to fish using this type of vessel unless a licence was first obtained. The appellants were only able to obtain three licences and applied them to other vessels. They subsequently claimed that as the contract had become impossible to perform the contract had been frustrated.]

Lord Wright (delivering the judgment of the Panel which also comprised Lord Atkin, Lord Tomlin and Lord MacMillan) [at 529]: ... It is clear that the appellants were free to select any three of the five trawlers they were operating and could, had they willed, have selected the *St Cuthbert* as one, in which event <530> a licence would have been granted to her. It is immaterial to speculate why they preferred to put forward for licences the three trawlers which they actually selected. Nor is it material, as between the appellants and the respondents, that the appellants were operating other trawlers to three of which they gave the preference. What matters is that they could have got a licence for the *St Cuthbert* if they had so minded. If the case be figured as one in which the *St Cuthbert* was removed from the category of privileged trawlers, it was by the appellants' hand that she was so removed, because it was their hand that guided the hand of the Minister in placing the licences where he did and thereby excluding the *St Cuthbert*. The essence of 'frustration' is that it should not be due to the act or election of the party. ...

[T]heir Lordships are of <531> opinion that the loss of the *St Cuthbert's* licence can correctly be described, quoad the appellants, as 'a self induced frustration.' ...

On this ground ... their Lordships are of opinion that the appeal should be dismissed with costs. ...

Appeal dismissed

---

14 Latham CJ, in *Scanlan's New Neon Ltd v Tooheys Ltd* (1943) 67 CLR 169 at 186, held that 'a state of facts brought about by the act of a party cannot be used as an excuse for failure to perform a contractual obligation'. See also *Ocean Tramp Tankers Corporation v V/O Sovfracht 'The Eugenia'* [1964] 2 QB 226.

J Lauritzen AS v Wijsmuller BV (the 'Super Servant Two')

[1990] 1 Lloyds Rep 1, English Court of Appeal (Civil Division)

[The defendants (Wijsmuller) entered into a contract with the plaintiff (Lauritzen) to carry the plaintiff's drilling rig (the *Dan King*) from Japan to a specified location in the North Sea. The contract was dated July 1980 and the rig was to be delivered between June and August 1981 using a 'transportation unit', defined as either '*Super Servant One*' or '*Super Servant Two*'. The defendants intended to use *Super Servant Two* to transport the rig but, in January 1981 this transportation unit sank. The defendants had already entered into contracts with other parties requiring the use of the *Super Servant One*. In February 1981 the defendants informed the plaintiffs they could no longer transport the rig as agreed. A subsequent 'without prejudice' agreement was reached pursuant to which the rig was transported using a barge by a tug.

The plaintiffs sought damages for loss and the defendants counter-claimed for increased expenses they had incurred. On the issue of frustration the trial judge held that the sinking of the *Super Servant Two* did not constitute a frustrating event.]

Bingham LJ [at 8]: The argument in this case raises important issues on the English law of frustration. ...

Certain propositions, established by the highest authority, are not open to question:

(1) The doctrine of frustration was evolved to mitigate the rigour of the common law's insistence on literal performance of absolute promises ... The object of the doctrine was to give effect to the demands of justice, to achieve a just and reasonable result, to do what is reasonable and fair, as an expedient to escape from injustice where such would result from enforcement of a contract in its literal terms after a significant change in circumstances ...
(2) Since the effect of frustration is to kill the contract and discharge the parties from further liability under it, the doctrine is not to be lightly invoked, must be kept within very narrow limits and ought not to be extended ...
(3) Frustration brings the contract to an end forthwith, without more and automatically ...
(4) The essence of frustration is that it should not be due to the act or election of the party seeking to rely on it ... A frustrating event must be some outside event or extraneous change of situation ...
(5) A frustrating event must take place without blame or fault on the side of the party seeking to rely on it ...

<9> ... Had the *Dan King* contract provided for carriage by *Super Servant Two* with no alternative, and that vessel had been lost before the time for performance, then assuming no negligence by Wijsmuller (as for purposes of this question we must), I feel sure the contract would have been frustrated. The doctrine must avail a party who contracts to perform a contract of carriage with a vessel which, through

no fault of his, no longer exists. But that is not this case. The *Dan King* contract did provide an alternative. When that contract was made one of the contracts eventually performed by *Super Servant One* during the period of contractual carriage of *Dan King* had been made, the other had not, at any rate finally. Wijsmuller have not alleged that when the *Dan King* contract was made either vessel was earmarked for its performance. That, no doubt, is why an option was contracted for. Had it been foreseen when the *Dan King* contract was made that *Super Servant Two* would be unavailable for performance, whether because she had been deliberately sold or accidentally sunk Lauritzen at least would have thought it no matter since the carriage could be performed with the other. I accordingly accept [the] submission that the present case does not fall within the very limited class of cases in which the law will relieve one party from an absolute promise he has chosen to make. ...

[Dilllon LJ agreed that the appeal should be dismissed.]

Appeal dismissed

6 Application of the doctrine to leases

For many years it was thought that the doctrine of frustration could never be applied to leases because of its dual operation as a contract and a means of conveying an interest in land. In the United Kingdom, however, it has been recognised that should a supervening event take place which deprives the lessee of substantial use of the property as contemplated by the parties, the doctrine of frustration is capable of applying to bring the lease to an end. The cases in which the doctrine will apply to leases are, however rare.

National Carriers v Panalpina (Northern) Ltd

[1981] AC 675, House of Lords

[National Carriers leased a warehouse from Panalpina for a term of 10 years from 1 January 1974. In May 1979 the local authority closed the street which provided the only access to the warehouse. The closure of the street prevented the appellants from using the warehouse for the only purpose contemplated by the lease and from May 1979 they stopped paying rent. In July 1979 Panalpina brought an action against the appellants claiming payment of rent in arrears. National Carriers contended that they were not liable to pay the rent because the lease was frustrated as a result of the closure of the street. On an application for summary judgment by the plaintiffs Master Waldman and Justice Sheen rejected this defence on the ground that they were bound by authority to hold that the doctrine of frustration could not apply to a lease. National Carriers appealed to the House of Lords.]

Lord Wilberforce [at 693]: Because of [the closure of the street] which made the warehouse unusable for the only purpose for which it could be used under the lease, the appellant contended that the lease was frustrated, so that rent ceased to be payable. ...

I can ... give fairly briefly the reasons which have persuaded me, on the whole, that the [argument that the doctrine of frustration can apply to leases] ought to be preferred.

(1) The doctrine of frustration of contracts made its appearance in English law in answer to the proposition ... that an obligation expressed in absolute and unqualified terms, such as an obligation to pay rent, had to be performed and could not be excused by supervening circumstances. ...

(2) ... <694> ... the doctrine can now be stated generally as part of the law of contract; as all judicially evolved doctrines it is, and ought to be, flexible and capable of new applications.

(3) In view of this generality, the onus, in my opinion, lies on those who assert that the doctrine can never apply to leases. ... To place leases of land beyond a firm line of exclusion seems to involve anomalies, to invite fine distinctions, or at least to produce perplexities. ... Refusal ever to apply the doctrine to leases of land must be based upon some firm legal principle which cannot be departed from: ...

(4) Two arguments only by way of principle have been suggested. The first is that a lease is more than a contract: it conveys an estate in land. ...the English law of frustration ... requires, when it applies, not merely adjustment of the contract, but its termination. But this argument, by itself, is incomplete as a justification for denying that frustration is possible. ...

... if the argument is to have any reality, it must be possible to say that frustration of leases cannot occur because in any event the tenant will have that which he bargained for, namely, the leasehold estate. Certainly this may be so in many cases—let us say most cases. ... But there may also be cases where this is not so. ...

<695> ... The second argument of principle is that on a lease the risk passes to the lessee, as on a sale it passes to the purchaser .... But the two situations are not parallel. Whether the risk—or any risk—passes to the lessee depends on the terms of the lease: it is not uncommon, indeed, for some risks—of fire or destruction—to be specifically allocated. So in the case of unspecified risks, which may be thought to have been mutually contemplated, or capable of being contemplated by reasonable men, why should not the court decide on whom the risks are to lie? ... <696> ...

(5) ... it would be wrong to erect a total barrier [against the application of the doctrine of frustration to leases] inscribed 'You shall not pass.' ...

It is said that to admit the possibility of frustration of leases will lead to increased litigation. Be it so, if that is the route to justice. But even <697> if the principle is admitted, hopeless claims can always be stopped at an early stage, if the facts manifestly cannot support a case of frustration. The present may be an example. In my opinion, therefore, though such cases may be rare, the doctrine of frustration is capable of application to leases of land. ...

I now come to the second question which is whether on the facts of the case the appellant should be given leave to defend the action: can it establish that there is a triable issue? .... At first sight, it would appear to my mind that the case might be one for possible frustration. But examination of the facts leads to a negative conclusion.

... the position is that the parties to the lease contemplated, when Kingston Street was first closed, that the closure would probably last for a year or a little longer. In fact it seems likely to have lasted for just over 18 months. Assuming that the street is reopened in January 1981, the lease will have three more years to run.

My Lords, no doubt, even with this limited interruption the appellant's business will have been severely dislocated. It will have had to move goods from the warehouse before the closure and to acquire alternative accommodation. After reopening the reverse process must take place. But this does not approach the gravity of a frustrating event. Out of 10 years it will have lost under two years of use: there will be nearly three years left after the interruption has ceased. This is a case, similar to <698> others, where the likely continuance of the term after the interruption makes it impossible for the lessee to contend that the lease has been brought to an end. The obligation to pay rent under the lease is unconditional, ... I am of opinion therefore that the lessee has no defence to the action for rent, that leave to defend should not be given and that the appeal must be dismissed.

[Lord Hailsham of St Marylebone LC, Lord Simon of Glaisdale and Lord Roskill all agreed the doctrine of frustration *could* apply to leases but did not apply in the present case.]

Appeal dismissed

This case has been followed in Australia.[15] The courts have, however, cautioned that the circumstances in which the doctrine of frustration will apply to leases of land will be extremely rare.[16]

7 The consequences of frustration

a Common law

The effect of frustration at common law is to terminate a contract automatically. Consequently, there is no need for either party to 'elect' to terminate. The contract is terminated *in futuro*,[17] so that accrued rights and obligations remain. In relation to money paid or services rendered under a contract that has been frustrated, the early position of the common law was that the loss lay where it fell. Thus,

---

15   *Progressive Mailing House Pty Ltd v Tabali Pty Ltd* (1985) 157 CLR 17 and *Wilson Parking Australia 1992 Pty Ltd v Leda Holdings Pty Ltd and National Mutual Trustee Ltd* [1996] 982 FCA 1.
16   *Progressive Mailing House Pty Ltd v Tabali Pty Ltd* (1985) 157 CLR 17, per Deane J at 52–53.
17   See *Baltic Shipping Co v Dillon* (1993) 176 CLR 344 at 356, per Mason CJ.

money paid under a frustrated conduct for services to occur in the future could not be recovered, nor could recompense be obtained for services rendered where payment only fell due after the frustrating event. This principle was expressed by Collins MR in *Chandler v Webster*:

> [W]here the doctrine of *Taylor v Caldwell* ... applies, the result is that the law leaves the parties where they were when the further performance of the contract became impossible. It treats the contract as a good and subsisting contract with regard to things done and rights accrued in accordance with it up to that time; but, as the basis of the contract has failed, it excuses the parties from further responsibility under it.[18]

The potential for this principle to produce harsh consequences has resulted in it being overturned. Instead, the law now permits recovery of moneys due and paid prior to a frustrating event in circumstances where there has been a total failure of consideration.

Fibrosa Spolka Akcyjna v Fairbairn Lawson Combe Barbour Ltd
[1943] AC 32, House of Lords

[In July 1939 the respondents (Fairbairn) contracted to sell and install machinery to the appellants (Fibrosa) in Gdynia, Poland. The contract required one-third payment (amounting to £1,600) to be paid at the time of contract. The appellants made payment of £1,000 in July. Following the outbreak of war, in September 1939 Poland became an enemy-occupied territory. The appellants claimed the contract had been frustrated as a result and sought to recover the payment of £1,000.]

Lord Atkin [at 50]: ... I have no doubt that the contract in this case came to an end before the time for complete performance had arrived by reason of the arising of a state of war which caused an indefinite delay not contemplated by the parties, and eventually on account of the legal impossibility of delivering the goods at a port occupied by the enemy. In other words, to use a short phrase of frequent occurrence since the beginning of the last war, the commercial adventure was frustrated. The legal effects of 'frustration' are not in dispute. ... It is well-settled that, when a contract which is still executory on one or both sides is subject to frustration, the law is that, when the event happens, the parties are excused from further performance, but have to give effect to rights under the contract already accrued before the happening of the event. A sells a horse to B for £50, delivery to be made in a month, the price to be paid forthwith, but the property not to pass till delivery, and B to pay A each week an agreed sum for keep of the horse during the month. The horse dies in a fortnight. A is excused from delivery and B, from taking delivery; B is bound to pay the sum due for the fortnight during which the horse was kept; but what is the position as to the £50, the price paid in advance? This is in

---

18 [1904] 1 KB 493 at 500–510.

simple terms the problem in the present case. The answer which I venture to think would occur to most people, whether laymen or lawyers, would be that the buyer ought to get his money back, having had nothing for <51> it, and the lawyer would support the claim by saying that it is money had and received to the use of the buyer, being money paid on a consideration which has wholly failed. That was not the answer given in similar cases in the coronation cases, and it is those decisions that come up for review in the present case. The question arose in the neatest form in *Chandler v Webster*, where the leading judgment was given in the Court of Appeal by Sir Richard Collins MR, [who held] that where the contract has become impossible in the circumstances there stated 'it remains a perfectly good contract up to that point, and everything previously done in pursuance of it must be treated as rightly done, but the parties are both discharged from further performance of it.' So far the statement is unassailable; but he proceeded as follows: 'If the effect were that the contract <52> were wiped out altogether, no doubt the result would be that money paid under it would have to be repaid as on a failure of consideration. But that is not the effect of the doctrine; it only releases the parties from further performance of the contract. Therefore the doctrine of failure of consideration does not apply.' …

My Lords, the difficulty which this decision causes me is to understand how this great lawyer came to the conclusion that the claim for money paid on a consideration which wholly failed could only be made where the contract was wiped out altogether. I have sought for some construction of his words which stopped short of that absolute statement, but I can find none. I know of no authority for the proposition. … <53> … With great respect, therefore, to the judgment in *Chandler v Webster*, I do not agree with that part of it which refused to give effect to the plaintiff's claim for the return of the sum which he had paid on the ground of total failure of consideration. Some discussion arose as to the precise meaning of this term. It was pointed out that the consideration for the part payment by the plaintiffs was the promise by defendants to deliver the goods cif at Gdynia; and the promise was always effective until further performance was excused. I personally agree with that statement of what the consideration was, and I do not think it necessary to use the word 'consideration' in two meanings. I understand by the phrase that the promise to deliver goods totally failed because no goods were or could be delivered, and that, therefore, a cause of action accrued to the plaintiff. I should add that, if it was wrong in *Chandler v Webster* to refuse the plaintiff relief on his claim, it was also wrong to give the defendant judgment on his counterclaim. It is true that the right to receive the balance had accrued before frustration: but, if the money had been paid, it could have been recovered back as the £100 could, …

<54> That the result of the law may cause hardship when a contract is automatically stayed during performance and any further right to performance is denied to each party is incontrovertible. One party may have almost completed

expensive work, yet he can get no compensation. The other <55> party may have paid the whole price, and, if he has received but a slender part of the consideration, he can get no compensation. At present it is plain that, if no money has been paid on the contract, there is no legal principle by which loss can be made good. What is being now decided is that the application of an old-established principle of the common law does enable a man who has paid money and received nothing for it to recover the money so expended. At any rate, it can be said it leaves the man who has received the money and given nothing for it in no worse position than if he had received none. Many commercial contracts provide for various risks. It is always possible to provide for the risk of frustration; …

[Viscount Simon LC, Lord Russell of Killowen, Lord Macmillan, Lord Wright, Lord Roche and Lord Porter all delivered separate judgments agreeing that the appeal should be allowed and that the finding in *Chandler v Webster* did not represent good law.]

Appeal allowed

This case has found support in Australia[19] and would appear to represent the current Australian common law position. This position may, however, still produce harsh results where there has been only partial, not a total, failure of consideration. Thus, for example, where, as a result of frustration, only a small part of consideration has been provided (such as one day of a month-long holiday) in exchange for a large benefit (for example, the full purchase price) that benefit can not be recovered.[20]

Parties may, however, protect against the harshness of this outcome by making provision in their contract for what should happen in the event of frustration.

b Statutory modification

As a result of the hardships that may result from application of common law principles relating to frustration, three Australian states have introduced legislation modifying the rights of the parties following frustration of a contract.[21] Thus, for example, in Victoria provision is made for the return of all or part of moneys paid and for payment for services rendered in a wide range of circumstances. This legislation also permits severance of parts of a frustrated contract in limited circumstances.

---

19 See *Lombok Pty Ltd v Supetina Pty Ltd* (1987) 14 FCR 226.
20 For a discussion of the concept of partial failure of consideration see J Edelman, 'The New Doctrine of Partial Failure of Consideration' (1996) 15 *Australian Bar Review* 229.
21 *Frustrated Contracts Act 1978* (NSW) ss 11–13; *Frustrated Contracts Act 1988* (SA) and *Fair Trading Act 1999* (Vic) Part 2C. Note that the statutory provisions differ significantly between these states, so the Victorian law as extracted should not be considered indicative of the frustration laws in NSW and SA.

Fair Trading Act 1999 (Vic)
Part 2C

S 33ZF Contracts to which this Part applies

(1) This part applies to a contract if the parties to the contract are discharged from the further performance of the contract because—
  (a) performance of the contract becomes impossible; or
  (b) the contract is otherwise frustrated; or
  (c) the contract is avoided by the operation of section 12 of the Goods Act 1958 *[rendering void any agreement for the sale of specific goods where, without fault of the parties, the goods perish before risk passes to the buyer]*.

…

(3) This Part does not apply to [most charter-parties or other contracts for carriage of goods by sea, or any contracts for insurance]

S 33ZG Adjustment of amounts paid or payable to parties to discharged contracts

(1) All amounts paid to any party under a discharged contract before the time of discharge are recoverable
(2) All amounts payable to any party under a discharged contract before the time of discharge cease to be payable.

S 33ZH Court may allow amounts paid or payable to be recovered or paid

Despite section 32ZG, the court may, if it considers it just to do so having regard to all the circumstances of the case, allow a party to a discharged contract—

(a) to whom amounts were paid or are payable under that contract before the time of discharge; and
(b) who has incurred expenses before the time of discharge in or for the purpose of the performance of that contract

to retain or recover (as the case may be) the whole or any part of the amounts paid or payable to that party under the contract in an amount not exceeding the expenses incurred.

S 32ZI Parties to pay an amount for valuable benefits obtained

(1) This section applies if a party to a discharged contract obtained a valuable benefit (other than a payment of money to which section 32ZG or 32ZH applies) before the time of discharge because of anything done by another party in or for the purpose of the performance of the contract.
(2) Despite section 32ZG, the benefited party is liable to pay to that other party any amount (not exceeding the benefit of the amount obtained) that the court considers just having regard to all the circumstances of the case.

(3) For the purpose of subsection (2), the Court may have regard in particular to—
   (a) the amount of any expenses the benefited party incurred before the time of discharge in or for the purpose of the performance of the contract, including any amount paid or payable by the benefited party to any other party under the contract and retained or recoverable by that party under section 32ZG or 32ZH; or
   (b) the effect, in relation to the benefit obtained, of the circumstances giving rise to the frustration or avoidance of the contract.
(4) For the purpose of this section, if a party to the contract has assumed obligations under the contract in consideration of the conferral of a benefit by another party to the contract on any other person (whether or not that person is a party to the contract), the court may, if in all the circumstances of the case it considers it just to do so, treat any benefit conferred on that other person as a benefit obtained by the party who has assumed those obligations.

32ZJ Calculation of expenses incurred

In estimating, for the purposes of this Division, the amount of any expenses incurred by any party to a discharged contract, the court may include an amount that appears reasonable for—

(a) overhead expenses; and
(b) work or services performed personally by the party.

32ZK Circumstances in which amounts payable under contract of insurance excluded

In considering whether any amount is to be retained or recovered by any party to a discharged contract, the court must not take into account any amounts payable to a party under a contract of insurance because of the circumstances giving rise to the frustration or avoidance of the contract unless an obligation to insure is imposed—

(a) by an express provision in the frustrated or avoided contract; or
(b) by or under any enactment.

32ZL Circumstances in which contract provisions continue to have effect despite frustration

If any contract to which this Part applies contains a provision that on the true construction of the contract—

(a) is intended to continue to have effect in circumstances that operate or would, but for that provision, operate to frustrate or avoid the contract; or
(b) is intended to have effect whether or not circumstances that operate or would, but for that provision, operate to frustrate or avoid the contract arise—
   the court must give effect to that provision and must only give effect to Division 2 to the extent that the court is satisfied that it is consistent with the provision of the contract.

32ZM Performed part of contract not frustrated

If it appears to the court that part of a contract to which this Part applies—

(a) is wholly performed before the time of discharge; or
(b) is wholly performed before the time of discharge except for payment in respect of that part of the contract of amounts that are or can be ascertained under the contract—

> the court must treat that part of the contract as if it were a separate contract that had not been frustrated or avoided and Division 2 will only apply to the remainder of that contract.

INTERNATIONAL PERSPECTIVES

India

The *Indian Contract Act, 1872* makes express provision for frustrating events in limited circumstances, providing that where a contract provides for the performance of an act that becomes 'impossible or unlawful' it will become void at that time. The Supreme Court of India has held, however, that impossible does not mean 'physically impossible'[22] and extends to most cases in which frustration will occur at common law.[23] As is the case in Australia, commercial hardship alone will not render the contract void.

Indian Contract Act, 1872

Section 56. Agreement to do impossible act

An agreement to do an act impossible in itself is void.

Contract to do act afterwards becoming impossible or unlawful: A contract to do an act which, after the contract is made, becomes impossible or, by reason of some event which the promisor could not prevent, unlawful, becomes void when the act becomes impossible or unlawful.

Compensation for loss through non-performance of act known to be impossible or unlawful: Where one person has promised to do something which he knew or, with reasonable diligence, might have known, and which the promisee did not know to be impossible or unlawful, such promisor must make compensation to such promisee for any loss which such promisee sustains through the non-performance of the promise.

Illustrations

(a) A agrees with B to discover treasure by magic. The agreement is void.
(b) A and B contract to marry each other. Before the time fixed for the marriage, A goes mad. The contract becomes void.

---

22 *Satyabrata v Mugneeram* (1954) SCR 310 (India).
23 See further A Singh, *Law of Contract and Specific Relief*, 9th edn, EBC, Lucknow, 2005 at 335–360.

(c) A contracts to marry B, being already married to C, and being forbidden by the law to which he is subject to practise polygamy. A must make compensation to B for the loss caused to her by the non-performance of his promise.

(d) A contracts to take in cargo for B at a foreign port. A's Government afterwards declares war against the country in which the port is situated. The contract becomes void when war is declared.

(e) A contracts to act at a theatre for six months in a consideration of a sum paid in advance by B. On several occasions A is too ill to act. The contract to act on those occasions becomes void.

Where a contract is rendered void by virtue of impossibility of performance, the *Indian Contract Act, 1872* provides for restoration of payments or compensation for benefits conferred up until that point.

Section 65. Obligation of person who has received advantage under void agreement, or contract that becomes void

When an agreement is discovered to be void, or when a contract becomes void, any person who has received any advantage under such agreement or contract is bound to restore, it, or to make compensation for it, to the person from whom he received it.

Illustrations

(a) A pays B 1,000 rupees, in consideration of B's promising to marry C, A's daughter. C is dead at the time of promise. The agreement is void, but B must repay A the 1,000 rupees.

(b) A contracts with B to deliver to him 250 maunds of rice before the first of May. A delivers 130 maunds only before that day, and none after. B retains the 130 maunds after the first of May. He is bound to pay A for them.

(c) A, a singer, contracts with B, the manager of a theatre, to sing at his theatre for two nights in every week during the next two months, and B engages to pay her hundred rupees for each night's performance. On the sixth night, A wilfully absents herself from the theatre, and B, in consequence, rescinds the contract. B must pay A for the five nights on which she had sung.

(d) A contracts to sing for B at a concert for 1,000 rupees, which are paid in advance. A is too ill to sing. A is not bound to make compensation to B for the loss of profit which B would have made if A had been able to sing, but must refund to B the 1,000 rupees paid in advance.

China

In China, the doctrine of frustration is addressed under the general provisions for *force majeure*,[24] termination and specific performance provisions of the *Contract Law of People's Republic of China*.

---

24 *Force majeure* literally means 'greater force' and, when included in a contract, relieves parties from obligations as a result of extraordinary events occurring without fault of the parties. A *force majeure* clause will normally capture a greater range of conduct that the common law doctrine of frustration.

Contract Law of the People's Republic of China, 1999

Article 117. Force Majeure

A party who was unable to perform a contract due to force majeure is exempted from liability in part or in whole in light of the impact of the event of force majeure, except as otherwise provided by law. Where an event of force majeure occurred after the party's delay in performance, it is not exempted from liability.

For purposes of this Law, force majeure means any objective circumstance which is unforeseeable, unavoidable and insurmountable.

Article 118. Duty to Notify in Case of Force Majeure

If a party is unable to perform a contract due to force majeure, it shall timely notify the other party so as to mitigate the loss that may be caused to the other party, and shall provide proof of force majeure within a reasonable time.

Article 94. Legally Prescribed Conditions Giving Rise to Termination Right

The parties may terminate a contract if:
(i) force majeure frustrated the purpose of the contract;
…

Article 110. Non-monetary Specific Performance;

Exceptions
Where a party fails to perform, or rendered non-conforming performance of, a non-monetary obligation, the other party may require performance, except where:
(i) performance is impossible in law or in fact;
…

Article 231. Lessee's Remedies in Case of Damage Not Attributable to Itself

Where the lease item was damaged or lost in part or in whole due to any reason not attributable to the lessee, the lessee may require reduction in rent or refuse to pay rent; where the purpose of the contract is frustrated due to damage to or loss of the lease item in part or in whole, the lessee may terminate the contract.

8 Summary

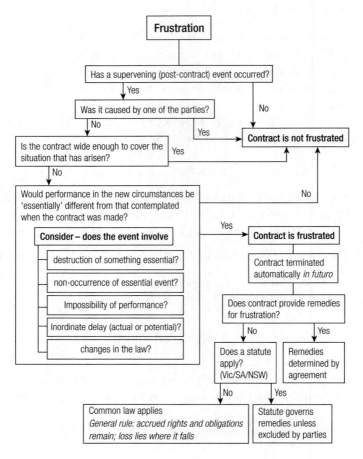

9 Questions

1   Kathy engaged Artistic Desire Pty Ltd to paint a portrait of her father, which was to be a gift for him on his 60th birthday. The contract provided that the portrait would be completed by Lilly Collins, one of the artists employed by Artistic Desire. Kathy had been shown some of Lilly's previous works and was thrilled when Artistic Desire told her that Lilly would be available to paint her father's portrait. Pursuant to the contract, Kathy paid $2,500 up front and agreed to pay a further $2,500 when the portrait was complete.

Lilly held two sittings with Kathy's father, in which she drew some sketches and took a variety of photographs to enable her to complete the work.

Unfortunately, when the portrait was only half-finished, Lilly was killed in a car accident. Artistic Desire informed Kathy that they would have another of their artists complete the painting, but Kathy responded that if Lilly couldn't paint it she didn't want anybody painting it and has demanded her money back.

The managing director of Artistic Desire, Paul, has come to you for advice. He wants to know:

- whether he has to refund Kathy's money and
- whether he can claim any additional money from Kathy, given that Artistic Desire was prepared to have someone else complete the portrait.

Please advise Paul.

2   Katrina purchased a 1969 Ford Mustang Shelby from Classic Imports Pty Ltd for AU$200,000 and paid a deposit of AU$20,000. The contract provided that the car would be delivered within 90 days, with the remaining payment to be made on delivery.

Classic Imports regularly sourced vehicles from all over Europe and North America. It sourced the Mustang from a dealer in Alabama, USA. As a result of an arrangement they had with the dealer, Classic Imports put a hold on the vehicle. They arranged that following the sale to Katrina, they would purchase the car for US$150,000, with payment to be made on delivery.

Unfortunately for Classic Imports, between the time at which they purchased the car and the time it was delivered, the US stock market experienced an unprecedented revival, with the result that the US dollar, which had been trading at an even AU$1, was now trading at AU$1.50. As a result, the cost of the vehicle to Classic Imports was AU$225,000, rather than the AU$150,000 that had been anticipated.

In addition, during the time that the car was being shipped, the Australian government raised import duties on luxury vehicles (including the Ford Mustang) by 100% (from 1%, as it had been when Katrina's order was made, to 100% by the time the car passed through customs). This meant that instead of paying an anticipated AU$1,500 customs duty (1% of $150,000), Classic Imports was required to pay AU$225,000 customs duties.

As a result of its increased costs, Classic Imports has refused to supply the car to Katrina unless she agrees to pay an additional AU$250,000. Classic Imports insists it is not trying to rip Katrina off, but is just trying to break even on the sale. Katrina has refused to pay and is demanding that Classic Imports transfer the car to her immediately.

Please advise the parties of their rights and obligations.

3   In March, Geekville Pty Ltd, a popular retail store specialising in science-fiction memorabilia, engaged Krane Konstructions Pty Ltd to re-develop their retail premises in Essendon. The renovations were to be completed by the end of May. Geekville paid a deposit of $5,000, with a further $45,000 to be paid at completion.

Unfortunately, on 15 April, a severe storm hit Melbourne and surrounding suburbs, including Essendon, causing flash flooding and serious damage to a number of buildings in the vicinity of Geekville's premises. One of the buildings damaged was a high-rise building which neighboured Geekville's premises. Council building inspectors visited the high-rise building after the floods and declared them to be unsafe and in need of demolition. In addition, because of the risk that the building might collapse at any time, Council issued an order prohibiting any retail activity or construction work in buildings neighbouring the high rise until the demolition was complete. The demolition was scheduled for 15 May.

As a result of the Council's order, Krane Konstructions was not able to conduct any work at the premises prior to the demolition. It advised Geekville that it would not be able to complete by the end of May, as they had agreed. Geekville advised that, as a result of the devastation occasioned by the storm, and the harm it had done to retail trading in the area, it had decided to relocate its premises elsewhere and no longer wanted the work done.

Krane Konstructions' managing director, Bob, has come to you for advice. He informs you that the company is ready and willing to complete the work as agreed and will be able to do so as soon as the Council ban order is lifted. He also tells you that they have completed half of the project at an estimated cost of $15,000 in material and $10,000 in labour. Bob wants to know whether he can recover any or all of these costs and whether he can recover any further damages as a result of Geekville's refusal to allow them to complete the construction.

Please advise Bob.

PART 6

Remedies

Where one party has breached their contract by failing to perform their obligations, properly or at all, the principal remedies at common law and in equity are:

- discharge by breach
- damages
- recovery of a debt
- liquidated damages
- restitution of property transferred under the contract
- *quantum meruit* claim for the value of any benefit conferred pursuant to that contract
- specific performance
- injunction.

Discharge of contract for breach was considered in chapter 21, together with *quantum meruit* claims. The remaining remedies are considered in this Part. Chapter 23 considers common law damages, debt and liquidated claims. Chapter 24 examines the equitable remedies of specific performance and injunctions and equitable damages.

The remedies examined in Part 6 should not be confused with remedies available as a result of certain pre-contractual conduct, such as misleading conduct, duress or undue influence, which were considered in Part 4.

CHAPTER 23

Damages and Liquidated Claims

1	Introduction		654
	a	Compensatory damages	654
	b	Restitutionary damages	654
2	Loss		655
	a	The plaintiff must prove loss	655
	b	The plaintiff's loss is recoverable, not the defendant's profit	657
	c	Difficulty of assessment	657
	d	Losses by a third party	657
3	Causation		661
4	Remoteness of damage		663
	a	Damage must not be too remote from the breach	663
	b	The rule in *Hadley v Baxendale*	663
5	Types of loss recognised		667
	a	Mental distress	667
	b	Loss of chance	669
	c	Wasted expenditure—reliance damages	673
	d	The cost of repairs	676
	e	Loss of the use of money	681
	f	The rule in *Bain v Fothergill*	681
6	The assessment of damages		681
	a	The date for assessing damages	681
	b	Mitigation of loss	682
	c	Contributory negligence	685
7	Liquidated (agreed) damages		687
8	Restitutionary damages for breach of contract		690
9	Other common law remedies for breach of contract		694
	a	Debt	694
	b	Termination clauses	694
	c	Retention of deposits paid	694
10	Summary		698
	a	Overview	698
	b	Approach to damages	699
11	Questions		700

1 Introduction

a Compensatory damages

Damages for breach of contract are *compensatory* in nature.[1] This was established by Parke B in *Robinson v Harman* who held that the object of an award of damages is to place the plaintiff in the position they would have been in had the contract been performed and not to punish the defendant for their breach.[2] In this respect, damages function as a substitute for performance of the contract.[3]

The following preconditions must be established before a plaintiff will be awarded substantial damages for breach of contract:

- that the plaintiff suffered loss
- a causal connection between the defendant's breach and the plaintiff's loss
- that the loss suffered is not too remote from the breach of contract
- that the loss suffered is of a kind recognised by the law.

Subject to an express contractual provision to the contrary, a court has no discretion to refuse an award of damages where a breach of contract has been established. However, where loss cannot be proved the plaintiff will only be entitled to recover nominal damages.

b Restitutionary damages

More recently there has been some movement towards permitting restitutionary-type damages for breach of contract in cases where loss is not easily ascertained, or where the compensatory measure of damages would not do adequate justice between the parties. Thus, for example, where the breaching party profits from their breach without causing demonstrable loss to the non-breaching party, the courts have, in limited cases, been prepared to require the breaching party to disgorge their profits in favour of the non-breaching party.

In this chapter we will discuss the prerequisites for obtaining an award of damages including:

- the types of loss commonly recognised by the courts
- the manner in which damages are assessed
- the possibility of obtaining restitutionary damages in exceptional circumstances
- the availability of other common law remedies for breach of contract.

---

1   *Attorney General v Blake (Jonathan Cape Ltd Third Party)* [2001] 1 AC 268.
2   'The rule of the common law is that where a party sustains a loss by reason of a breach of contract, he is, so far as money can do it, to be placed in the same situation, with respect to damages, as if the contract had been performed.': *Robinson v Harman* [1848] All ER Rep 383, per Parke B.
3   Damages are what is necessary to 'put the plaintiff in the same position as if the contract had been performed. It is a substitute for performance. That is why it is necessarily compensatory. …': *Attorney General v Blake (Jonathan Cape Ltd Third Party)* [2001] 1 AC 268.

INTERNATIONAL PERSPECTIVES

India

The remedies for breach of contract in India are designed to be compensatory in nature. Section 73 of the *Indian Contract Act, 1872* uses the term 'compensation' in relation to the entitlement of a party suffering loss as a result of breach. Unlike the position at common law, while the court may award nominal damages if no loss is demonstrated, this is at the discretion of the court.

China

The *Contract Law of the People's Republic of China* does not specify the measure of damages recoverable but refers, in some provisions, to the 'loss' suffered by the non-breaching party, suggesting damages are intended to be compensatory and not punitive in nature.

2 Loss

a The plaintiff must prove loss

In order to recover damages for breach of contract beyond nominal damages it is necessary for the plaintiff to demonstrate that they have suffered loss. Loss need not necessarily be physical or monetary in nature, although this will normally be the case, and it is not necessary that loss be determined with exact precision.[4] The requirement of proving loss was discussed by the High Court in the following case.

Placer (Granny Smith) Pty Ltd v Thiess Contractors Pty Ltd

[2003] HCA 10, High Court of Australia

[Thiess contracted to carry out mining operations for Placer based on Thiess's 'genuine estimates' of the cost of those operations. After relations broke down between the parties Placer claimed that Thiess had inflated its costs estimates in breach of its contractual obligations and that this resulted in Placer overpaying Thiess for the work performed. Placer sought to recover these overpayments.]

Hayne J [at para 14]: [The trial judge found that] in breach of its obligations under the contract, Thiess Contractors submitted rates to Placer which were not a genuine estimate of Thiess Contractors' costs. He assessed damages for this breach in the sum of $4,853,000.

[15] ... The Full Court held, however, that the method adopted by the trial judge for calculation of damages was flawed [and] that the method of calculation advanced by Placer at trial not only had failed but was bound to fail, to provide

---

4 See *Chaplin v Hicks* [1911] 2 KB 786.

an accurate measure of what had been lost. The Full Court, therefore, held that Placer had not proved its damages. [They] ordered that Placer have judgment for the nominal sum of $100. ...

[17] ... Thiess Contractors admitted that the estimates which it provided to Placer ... exceeded its actual *bona fide* estimates of costs to be incurred in performing work under the contract by $2,713,940. ... it follows from the admitted facts that Placer overpaid Thiess Contractors ... The amount admittedly overpaid was $2,713,940 plus 5 per cent, which was the agreed profit margin. ...

[20] Given the admission that was made, it follows that the orders of the Full Court, substituting an award of nominal damages for the judgment entered by the trial judge, must be set aside. On its own pleadings Thiess Contractors admitted that Placer had suffered damage of at least $2,713,940 plus 5 per cent. On this basis alone, the appeal to this Court must be allowed. ...

[37] Placer undoubtedly bore the burden of proving not only that it had suffered damage as a result of Thiess Contractors' breach of contract, but also the amount of the loss it had sustained. It goes without saying that it had to prove these matters on the balance of probabilities and with as much precision as the subject matter reasonably permitted.

[40] Once it was accepted, as the trial judge found, that estimated costs closely approximated actual costs, the profit that should have been earned could be calculated with considerable, and for present purposes, sufficient precision. ...

[41] ... The proof tendered by Placer, and accepted by the trial judge, supported the conclusion that the trial judge reached: that Placer had paid $4.853 million more than it would have paid if Thiess Contractors had not breached its contract. ...

Callinan J [at para 72]: ... in assessing damages a court does the best it can. A judge relies on predictions and probabilities. Precision will rarely be possible with respect to future costs and profits, particularly when deceit by one party obscures the true position. ...

[Gleeson CJ, McHugh and Kirby JJ agreed with Hayne J.]

Appeal allowed

[footnotes omitted]

The Court in *Placer v Thiess* made clear that it is not essential for loss to be demonstrated with exact precision. However, where the extent of a breach itself cannot be demonstrated a calculation of loss will be impossible and the plaintiff will be entitled to receive only nominal damages. This was discussed in the following case.

Luna Park (NSW) Ltd v Tramways Advertising Pty Ltd

(1938) 61 CLR 286, High Court of Australia

[Tramways was an advertising agent and agreed with Luna Park to display roof boards advertising Luna Park on tram-cars in Sydney for an average period of eight hours per day for a total period of 52 weeks over three seasons in exchange for a sum of £20 per month. Tramways failed to display every roof board for the agreed period of time. The Court accepted that there was a breach of contract. The following extract deals only with the Court's discussion of damages.]

Latham CJ [at 300]: [If there is a breach of contract then] as a matter of course, the defendant is entitled to nominal damages. ...

<301> ... there are many authorities which establish that substantial damages can be awarded where a breach of contract is established, even though the calculation of the damages is 'not only difficult but incapable of being carried out with certainty or precision' ... In all these cases, however, the extent of the breach was established. There was a complete failure on one side to perform the contract. In the present case, however, there has not been a complete, but only a partial, failure to perform the contract. The extent of the failure is unascertained. Thus the evidence which the defendant was content to put before the court does not make it possible to reach any estimate of damage suffered. ... If a party chooses to go to trial with incomplete evidence he must abide the consequences. ... Thus the defendant must be content ... with nominal damages.

[McTiernan and Rich JJ agreed on the issue of damages. Dixon J dissented.]

Appeal allowed

b The plaintiff's loss is recoverable, not the defendant's profit

The compensatory nature of damages for breach of contract means that where the defendant obtains a profit as a result of their breach of contract this profit is generally not recoverable by the plaintiff unless a commensurate amount of loss can be proved. However, as indicated earlier, there has been a recent move towards allowing restitutionary damages in exceptional cases which may permit the plaintiff to recover profits gained through the defendant's breach. This form of damages will be discussed later in this chapter.

c Difficulty of assessment

Where breach of contract has caused loss, damages are recoverable even where the extent of that loss is difficult to assess.[5] Thus, for example, loss of chance and damage caused through mental distress are recognised forms of loss capable of being compensated by an award of damages for breach of contract despite the inherent difficulties associated with assessing this loss in financial terms.

d Losses by a third party

A plaintiff can only recover loss suffered by them personally. Consequently, loss suffered by a third party to the contract as a result of the defendant's breach of

---

[5] See *Placer (Granny Smith) Pty Ltd v Thiess Contractors Pty Ltd* [2003] HCA 10, above.

contract with the plaintiff cannot be recovered by the plaintiff.[6] Where, however, the breach exposes the plaintiff to liability to the third party, loss will be demonstrated.

In very limited cases a plaintiff may directly enforce a contract on behalf of third parties who might suffer loss as a result of a breach.

Linden Gardens Trust Ltd v Lenesta Sludge Disposals Ltd
[1994] 1 AC 85, House of Lords

[The plaintiffs were property developers and began a development of shops, offices and flats. They entered into a building contract with the defendants. The plaintiffs subsequently assigned their rights in the property to a third party. Several years later the building work was found to have been defective and remedial works were required at a substantial cost to the third party. The plaintiffs and the third party both sought to recover this loss. The plaintiff did not suffer any direct financial loss as a result of the defendant's breach of contract. The Court held that the third party could not recover directly against the plaintiff. The following extract deals with the Court's discussion of whether the plaintiff could recover damages for the defendant's breach.]

Lord Browne-Wilkinson [at 109]: [The defendant] submits, [the plaintiff] is only entitled to nominal damages. [The plaintiff] has suffered no loss: it had parted with its interest in the property (and therefore with the works when completed) before any breach of the building contract; moreover [the plaintiff] received full value for that interest on its disposal to [the third party]. Therefore, it is said, neither of the plaintiffs has any right to substantial damages: [The third party] has incurred damage (being the cost of rectifying the faulty work) but has no cause of action; [the plaintiff] has a cause of action but has suffered no loss. If this is right, in the words of my noble and learned friend, Lord Keith of Kinkel in *GUS Property Management Ltd v Littlewoods Mail Order Stores Ltd*, 1982 SLT 533, 538, 'the claim to damages would disappear ... into some legal black hole, so that the wrongdoer escaped scot-free.'

The Court of Appeal was able to avoid this result by reason of the continuing liability on [the plaintiff] to indemnify [the third party] against the cost of remedying the defects. ...

<110> Attractive as this argument is, [counsel for the defendant] has satisfied me that it is erroneous because the damage being claimed is too remote. ...

Since, before the date of any breach of contract by [the defendant], [the plaintiff] had disposed of all its interest in the property on which the building works were carried out, [the plaintiff] has suffered no loss. [The plaintiff] received the full value of the property from [the third party]. The measure of damages for defective performance of a building contract is the diminution in value of the plaintiff's property, which diminution is usually properly reflected by the cost of

---

6   See *Linden Gardens Trust Ltd v Lenesta Sludge Disposals Ltd* [1994] 1 AC 85.

carrying out the repairs necessary to effect reinstatement: ... Since at the date of breach [the plaintiff] did not own the property, [the plaintiff] suffered no loss by any diminution in its value nor could [the plaintiff] carry out any works of reinstatement. Therefore, it is said, [the plaintiff] has suffered no loss.

<112> ... the facts of this case bring it within the class of exceptions to the general rule to which Lord Diplock referred in *The Albazero*.

In *The Albazero* Lord Diplock said [1977] AC 774, 846:

> Nevertheless, although it is exceptional at common law that a plaintiff in an action for breach of contract, although he himself has not suffered any loss, should be entitled to recover damages on behalf of some third person who is not a party to the action for a loss which that third person has sustained, the notion that there may be circumstances in which he is entitled to do so was not entirely unfamiliar to the common law ...

<114> ... In my judgment the present case falls within the rationale of the exceptions to the general rule that a plaintiff can only recover damages for his own loss. The contract was for a large development of property which, to the knowledge of both [the plaintiff] and [the defendant], was going to be occupied, and possibly purchased, by third parties and not by [the plaintiff] itself. Therefore it could be foreseen that damage caused by a breach would cause loss to a later owner and not merely to the original contracting party, [the plaintiff]. As in contracts for the carriage of goods by land, there would be no automatic vesting in the occupier or owners of the property for the time being who sustained the loss of any right of suit against [the defendant]. On the contrary, [the defendant] had <115> specifically contracted that the rights of action under the building contract could not without [the defendant's] consent be transferred to third parties who became owners or occupiers and might suffer loss. In such a case, it seems to me proper, as in the case of the carriage of goods by land, to treat the parties as having entered into the contract on the footing that [the plaintiff] would be entitled to enforce contractual rights for the benefit of those who suffered from defective performance but who, under the terms of the contract, could not acquire any right to hold [the defendant] liable for breach. It is truly a case in which the rule provides 'a remedy where no other would be available to a person sustaining loss which under a rational legal system ought to be compensated by the person who has caused it'.

... If the ultimate purchaser is given a direct cause of action against the contractor (as is the consignee or endorsee under a bill of lading) the case falls outside the rationale of the rule. The original building owner will not be entitled to recover damages for loss suffered by others who can themselves sue for such loss. I would therefore hold that [the plaintiff] is entitled to substantial damages for any breach by [the defendant] of the building contract. ...

[Lord Keith of Kinkel, Lord Bridge of Harwick, Lord Griffiths and Lord Ackner agreed with Lord Browne-Wilkinson on this issue.]

Appeal on this issue dismissed

INTERNATIONAL PERSPECTIVES

India

Under the *Indian Contract Act, 1872* compensation is available for loss suffered as a result of a breach of contract. To obtain damages the onus is on the plaintiff to prove loss.[7] In this respect the Privy Council in *AKAS Jamal v Moolla Dawood Sons & Co* held that s 73 of the *Indian Contract Act, 1872* was declaratory of the common law as to damages.[8]

Indian Contract Act, 1872

Section 73. Compensation of loss or damage caused by breach of contract

When a contract has been broken, the party who suffers by such breach is entitled to receive, from the party who has broken the contract, compensation for any loss or damage caused to him thereby, which naturally arose in the usual course of things from such breach, or which the parties knew, when they made the contract, to be likely to result from the breach of it.

China

The *Contract Law of the People's Republic of China* provides a remedy of damages as well as the ability to require the breaching party to rectify goods or property in accordance with contractual obligations. The law does not specify the measure of damages to be applied, although it suggests it would be the equivalent to the loss sustained as a result of the breach.[9]

Contract Law of the People's Republic of China, 1999

Article 97. Remedies in Case of Termination

Upon termination of a contract, a performance which has not been rendered is discharged; if a performance has been rendered, a party may, in light of the degree of performance and the nature of the contract, require the other party to restore the subject matter to its original condition or otherwise remedy the situation, and is entitled to claim damages.

Article 111. Liabilities in Case of Quality Non-compliance

Where a performance does not meet the prescribed quality requirements, the breaching party shall be liable for breach …. Where the liabilities for breach were not prescribed or clearly prescribed [in the contract], and cannot be

---

7   See *Sudesh Prabhakar Volvoikar v Gopal Babu Savolkar* (1996) 5 Bom CR 1.
8   [1916] 1 AC 175, Lord Wrenbury for the Panel (including Viscount Haldane, Sir John Edge and Mr Ameer Ali).
9   See Article 112 which refers to the non-breaching party sustaining 'loss'.

determined in accordance with Article 61 hereof, the aggrieved party may, … require the other party to assume liabilities for breach by way of repair, replacement, remaking, acceptance of returned goods, or reduction in price or remuneration, etc.

Article 112. Liability for Damages Notwithstanding Subsequent Performance or Cure of Non-conforming Performance

Where a party failed to perform or rendered non-conforming performance, if notwithstanding its subsequent performance or cure of non-conforming performance, the other party has sustained other loss, the breaching party shall pay damages.

3 Causation

In addition to proving loss the plaintiff must prove its loss was caused by the defendant's breach of contract. This is normally a simple matter, but difficulties arise where the loss can be attributed to more than one cause. Where this is the case the plaintiff must prove the defendant's breach was at least one of the causes of the loss suffered and also that the defendant could foresee that loss would arise as a result of its breach.[10]

Reg Glass Pty Ltd v Rivers Locking Systems Pty Ltd

(1968) 120 CLR 516, High Court of Australia

[The plaintiff was a menswear retailer. It engaged the defendants to install a 'burglar-proof door' at the back of its shop. The defendant fitted and hung a door and subsequently thieves broke into the shop by forcing the door out of position. The trial judge found as a matter of fact that there was an area of softwood exposed around the 'fitted' door that was apparent to anyone looking at it. The plaintiff succeeded at first instance but lost an appeal to the Court of Appeal of the Supreme Court of New South Wales. The plaintiff appealed to the High Court.]

Barwick CJ, McTiernan and Menzies JJ: [Their Honours first held that there was no breach of any of the express terms of the contract by the defendants in the way that they hung the door and continued (at 521)]: By common law, however, there was a term to be implied in the contract. The business of the defendant was to provide burglar-proof protection and the plaintiff unquestionably relied upon its skill and ability to supply, fit and hang a door which would provide reasonable protection against persons seeking to break in when the locking devices were in operation. … The problem, as we see it therefore, is whether the Supreme Court

---

10   See *National Australia Bank v Nemur Varity Pty Ltd* (2000) 4 VR 252.

was correct in setting aside the finding of the learned trial judge that the manner of the hanging of the door was such that the door did not provide reasonable protection against persons seeking to enter the shop.

In our opinion the learned trial judge's finding was correct. ...

<522> ... The defendant could, in a variety of ways, have fulfilled its obligation to supply, fit and hang a door so that it would constitute reasonably fit protection against thieves, ... the work as it was done did not constitute the door a reasonable deterrent to thieves wanting to break into the shop, and it is not the point that the contract did not provide a particular means of making it such a deterrent. ... Of course the defendant did not undertake to provide a door which would defeat all endeavours of determined thieves to break in and steal, and its implied obligation was, of necessity, qualified. Nevertheless we are not prepared to express that qualification more particularly than by using terms indicating reasonable fitness for the purpose for which the door was being installed; ... Of <523> course the door as fitted would delay progress longer than would the hollow core wooden door which it replaced, but that, we think, is not enough. What the plaintiff contracted for was a door which when locked would be reasonably fit to keep would-be breakers out of the shop and the door as fitted and hung by the defendant was, as the learned trial judge found, not of that character. We think that finding was open; indeed we agree with it. ...

The question of damages has its difficulties. The learned trial judge decided that the entry was due to the breach and that the measure of damages was the value of the goods stolen. This the respondent disputes. ... In our opinion, however, nothing appears to show that his Honour's conclusion about the plaintiff's loss by theft was wrong. The more fundamental question, however, is whether the measure of damages for the breach of contract was the value of the goods stolen. Upon the whole we agree with his Honour, the learned trial judge, that it was. It is true that it cannot be predicated that a door complying with the warranty would have prevented the thieves from breaking into the shop but once breach of warranty is established, and it appears that the actual entry made was due to the breach of warranty, we think that the loss suffered from the entry is *prima facie* the measure of damages for breach of warranty. This involves two steps. First that the loss suffered resulted from the breach, and secondly that the loss suffered was, when the contract was made, reasonably foreseeable as likely to result from such a breach. His Honour's affirmative finding as to both these matters cannot, we think, be disturbed. ...

[Windeyer and Owen JJ dissented, holding there was no breach of contract and, if there was, the loss did not flow from that breach as it was not certain the breaking and entering would not still have taken place.]

Appeal allowed

4 Remoteness of damage

a Damage must not be too remote from the breach

Once the plaintiff has demonstrated both that they have suffered loss and that that loss was caused by the defendant's breach, they must show that the loss suffered was not too remote from the breach. In *Chaplin v Hicks*, Lord Justice Fletcher Moulton provided an example of a loss that, while caused by breach, was too remote to be recovered:

> For example, an innkeeper furnishes a chaise to a son to drive to see his dying father; the chaise breaks down; the son arrives too late to see his father, who has cut him out of his will in his disappointment at his not coming to see him; in such a case it is obvious that the actual damage to the plaintiff has nothing to do with the contract to supply the chaise. ...[11]

b The rule in *Hadley v Baxendale*

The test to be applied in determining whether loss is too remote from the breach is to ask whether the loss would have been in the 'reasonable contemplation' of the parties as a possible consequence of the breach. This is known as the rule in *Hadley v Baxendale*.

Hadley v Baxendale
(1854) 9 Ex 341, Court of Exchequer

Alderson B [at 354]: Where two parties have made a contract which one of them has broken the damages which the other party ought to receive in respect of such breach of contract should be such as may fairly and reasonably be considered as either arising naturally, ie, according to the usual course of things, from such breach of contract itself, or such as may reasonably be supposed to have been in the contemplation of both parties at the time they made the contract as the probable result of the breach of it. If special circumstances under which the contract was actually made were communicated by the plaintiffs to the defendants, and thus known to both parties, the damages resulting from the breach of such a contract which they would reasonably contemplate would be the amount of injury which would ordinarily follow from a breach of contract under the special circumstances so known and communicated. But, on the other hand, if these special circumstances were wholly unknown to the party breaking the contract, he, at the most, could only be supposed to have had in his contemplation the amount of injury which would arise generally, and in the real multitude of cases not affected by any special circumstances, from such a breach of contract. For, had the special circumstances

---

11 [1911] 2 KB 786 at 794.

been known, the parties might have specially provided for the breach of contract by special terms as to the damages in that case; and of this advantage it would be very unjust to deprive them.

This rule was discussed and applied in the following case.

Koufos v C Czarnikow ('The Heron II')
[1969] 1 AC 350, House of Lords

[The respondents [plaintiffs] chartered the appellant's [defendant's] vessel, *Heron II*, to carry a cargo of sugar to Basrah. In breach of contract the vessel made deviations which delayed its arrival in Basrah by nine days. The respondents intended to sell the cargo of sugar promptly on arrival in Basrah. Although the appellant was aware there was a sugar market in Basrah they did not know of the respondents' plans.

Between the time at which the vessel ought to have arrived and the time it did arrive the market price for sugar dropped. The respondent claimed they were entitled to damages amounting to the difference between the price the sugar would have fetched had the vessel arrived on time and the price at the time of arrival.

The appellant succeeded at trial but the respondent successfully appealed to the Court of Appeal which held the loss in price was not too remote to be recovered. The appellant appealed to the House of Lords.]

Lord Reid [at 382]: There is no finding that [the respondents] had in mind any particular date as the likely date of arrival at Basrah or that they had any knowledge or expectation that in late November or December there would be a rising or a falling market. The shipowner was given no information about these matters by the charterers. He did not know what the charterers intended to do with the sugar. But he knew there was a market in sugar at Basrah, and it appears to me that, if he had thought about the matter, he must have realised that at least it was not unlikely that the sugar would be sold in the market at market price on arrival. And he must be held to have known that in any ordinary market prices are apt to fluctuate from day to day: …

So the question for decision is whether a plaintiff can recover as damages for breach of contract a loss of a kind which the <383> defendant, when he made the contract, ought to have realised was not unlikely to result from a breach of contract causing delay in delivery. I use the words 'not unlikely' as denoting a degree of probability considerably less than an even chance but nevertheless not very unusual and easily foreseeable. …

<385> … a type of damage which was plainly foreseeable as a real possibility but which would only occur in a small minority of cases cannot be regarded as arising in the usual course of things or be supposed to have been in the contemplation of the parties: the parties are not supposed to contemplate as grounds for the recovery of damage any type of loss or damage which on the knowledge available to the defendant would appear to him as only likely to occur in a small minority of cases.

In cases like ... the present case it is not enough that in fact the plaintiff's loss was directly caused by the defendant's breach of contract. It clearly was so caused ... The crucial question is whether, on the information available to the defendant when the contract was made, he should, or the reasonable man in his position would, have realised that such loss was sufficiently likely to result from the breach of contract to make it proper to hold that the loss flowed naturally from the breach or that loss of that kind should have been within his contemplation.

The modern rule of tort is quite different and it imposes a much wider liability. The defendant will be liable for any type of damage which is reasonably foreseeable as liable to happen even in the most unusual case, unless the risk is so small that a reasonable man would in the whole circumstances feel justified <386> in neglecting it. And there is good reason for the difference. In contract, if one party wishes to protect himself against a risk which to the other party would appear unusual, he can direct the other party's attention to it before the contract is made ... But in tort there is no opportunity for the injured party to protect himself in that way, and the tortfeasor cannot reasonably complain if he has to pay for some very unusual but nevertheless foreseeable damage which results from his wrongdoing. ...

[His Honour considered that in this case the loss was not too remote to be recovered.]

Lord Morris [at 396]: While the appellant did not know precisely what plans the respondents had made he could be reasonably sure of one thing, namely that they had contracted for the appellant's ship to proceed at all convenient speed to its destination because they wanted to have their cargo delivered at its destination at such time as the ship could be expected to arrive. ... The appellant could and should at the very least have contemplated that if his ship was nine days later in arriving than it could and should have arrived some financial loss to the respondents ... Must the loss of the respondents be such that the appellant could see that it was certain to result? Or would it suffice if the loss was probable or was likely to result or was liable to result? ...

I think that it is clear that the loss need not be such that the contract-breaker could see that it was certain to result. ...

<397> If a party has suffered some special and peculiar loss in reference to some particular arrangements of his which were unknown to the other party and were not communicated to the other party and were not therefore in the contemplation of the parties at the time when they made their contract, then it would be unfair and unreasonable to charge the contract-breaker with such special and peculiar loss. If, however, there are no 'special and extraordinary circumstances beyond the reasonable prevision of the parties' ... then it becomes very largely a question of fact as to whether in any particular case a loss can 'fairly and reasonably' be considered as arising in the normal course of things. ...

<399> ... in order to make a contract-breaker liable under what was called 'either rule' in *Hadley v Baxendale* it is not necessary that he should actually have asked himself what loss is liable to result from a breach but that it suffices that if he had considered the question he would as a reasonable man have concluded

that the loss in question was liable to result. Nor need it be proved, ... that upon a given state of knowledge he could, as a reasonable man, foresee that a breach must necessarily result in that loss. ...

... I entertain no doubt that if at the time of their contract the parties had considered what the consequence would be if the arrival of the ship <400> at Basrah was delayed they would have contemplated that some loss to the respondents was likely or was liable to result. The appellant at the time that he made his contract must have known that if in breach of contract his ship did not arrive at Basrah when it ought to arrive he would be liable to pay damages. He would not know that a loss to the respondents was certain or inevitable but he must, as a reasonable business man, have contemplated that the respondents would very likely suffer loss, and that it would be or would be likely to be a loss referable to market price fluctuations at Basrah. I cannot think that he should escape liability by saying that he would only be aware of a possibility of loss but not of a probability or certainty of it. ...

The carriage of sugar from the Black Sea to Iraqi ports (including Basrah) is a recognised trade. The appellant knew that there was a sugar market at Basrah. When he contracted with the respondents to carry their sugar to Basrah, though he did not know what were the actual plans of the respondent, he had all the information to enable him to appreciate that a delay in arrival might in the ordinary course of things result in their suffering some loss. He must have known that the price in a market may fluctuate. He must have known that if a price goes down someone whose goods are late in arrival may be caused loss.

... where there is delay in arrival, in many cases the actual loss suffered ... can be measured by comparing the market price of the goods at the date when they should have arrived and the market price when they did arrive. That *prima facie* is the measure of the damages. ...

[Lords Hodson, Pearce and Upjohn also dismissed the appeal.]

Appeal dismissed

[footnotes omitted]

INTERNATIONAL PERSPECTIVES

India

Section 73 of the *Indian Contract Act, 1872* imports the notion of remoteness into its assessment of damages.

Indian Contract Act, 1872

Section 73

When a contract has been broken, the party who suffers by such breach is entitled to receive, from the party who has broken the contract, compensation for any loss or damage caused to him thereby, which naturally arose in the usual course of things from such breach, or which the parties knew, when they made the contract, to be likely to result from the breach of it.

Such compensation is not to be given for any remote and indirect loss or damage sustained by reason of the breach.

China

The *Contract Law of the People's Republic of China* also restricts loss recoverable to that which was or should have been foreseen by the breaching party at the time the contract was concluded.

Contract Law of the People's Republic of China, 1999

Article 113. Calculation of Damages; Damages to Consumer

Where a party failed to perform or rendered non-conforming performance, thereby causing loss to the other party, the amount of damages payable shall be equivalent to the other party's loss resulting from the breach, including any benefit that may be accrued from performance of the contract, provided that the amount shall not exceed the likely loss resulting from the breach which was foreseen or should have been foreseen by the breaching party at the time of conclusion of the contract.

5 Types of loss recognised

Most forms of loss arising from breach of contract are recognised as compensable at common law. Some of these forms of loss are discussed below.

a Mental distress

Mental distress alone will not ordinarily be regarded as a compensable form of loss resulting from a breach of contract. However, if the object of the contract is to provide enjoyment then mental distress resulting from a breach of contract may be recoverable.[12]

Baltic Shipping v Dillon

(1993) 176 CLR 344, High Court of Australia

[The respondent was a passenger on the appellant's cruise vessel, the *Mikhail Lermontov*. The cruise commenced on 7 February and was scheduled to return on

---

12 In the United Kingdom the circumstances in which damage for mental distress may be recovered have been expanded following the decision of the House of Lords in *Farley v Skinner* [2002] 2 AC 732. See further J Hartshorne, 'Damages for Contractual Mental Distress after *Farley v Skinner*' (2006) 22 JCL 118.

21 February. On 16 February the vessel struck a shoal and sank. The respondent lost her luggage and suffered injury. An issue arose as to whether the respondent could claim damage as compensation for 'disappointment and distress' relating to the loss of entertainment and enjoyment that had been promised. The trial judge held that she could and awarded the respondent $5,000. The Court of Appeal, by majority, dismissed the appellant's appeal and a further appeal was made to the High Court. This extract deals only with the issue of damages for loss of enjoyment.]

Mason CJ [at 359]: ... for a long time it was considered that, in general, damages for injured feelings of the kind just mentioned could not be awarded in an action for breach of contract.

<361> The general rule that damages for anxiety, disappointment and distress are not recoverable in actions for breach of contract is, ... subject to exceptions. ... The scope of the exceptions has been expanded by judicial decision in recent years, so much so that the authority of the general rule is now somewhat uncertain.

The conceptual and policy foundations of the general rule are by no means clear. It seems to rest on the view that damages for breach of contract are in essence compensatory and that they are confined to the award of that sum of money which will put the injured party in the financial position the party would have been in had the breach of contract not taken place. On that approach, anxiety and injured feelings do not, generally speaking, form part of the plaintiff's compensable loss which flows from a breach of contract. ...

<362> ... This policy is based on an apprehension that the recovery of compensation for injured feelings will lead to inflated awards of damages in commercial contract cases, if not contract cases generally. ...

... anxiety and injured feelings are recognized as heads of compensable damage, at least outside the realm of the law of contract. ... We are then left with a rule which rests on flimsy policy foundations and conceptually is at odds with the fundamental principle governing the recovery of damages, the more so now that the approaches in tort and contract are converging.

It is convenient now to take stock of the exceptions to the general rule. ... it is beyond question that a plaintiff can recover damages for pain and suffering, including mental suffering and anxiety, where the defendant's breach of contract causes physical injury to the plaintiff. ... there are cases in which damages for breach of contract have included compensation for the physical inconvenience suffered by the plaintiff in certain circumstances. They include the physical inconvenience suffered by a plaintiff when the <363> defendant's train did not carry him to the stipulated destination ... courts have included compensation for an element of subjective mental suffering where the plaintiff has sustained physical inconvenience as a result of the defendant's breach of contract and the mental suffering is directly related to that physical inconvenience. Finally, there are other cases in which the plaintiff has recovered damages for distress, vexation and frustration where the very object of the contract has been to provide pleasure, relaxation or freedom from molestation. ... plaintiffs have recovered damages for disappointment and distress caused by the breach of a contract to provide a stipulated holiday, entertainment or enjoyment, the object of the contract being to provide pleasure or relaxation. ...

<365> ... as a matter of ordinary experience, it is evident that, while the innocent party to a contract will generally be disappointed if the defendant does not perform the contract, the innocent party's disappointment and distress are seldom so significant as to attract an award of damages on that score. For that reason, if for no other, it is preferable to adopt the rule that damages for disappointment and distress are not recoverable unless they proceed from physical inconvenience caused by the breach or unless the contract is one the object of which is to provide enjoyment, relaxation or freedom from molestation. In cases falling within the last-mentioned category, the damages flow directly from the breach of contract, the promise being to provide enjoyment, relaxation or freedom from molestation. In these situations the court is not driven to invoke notions such as 'reasonably foreseeable' or 'within the reasonable contemplation of the parties' because the breach results in a failure to provide the promised benefits. ...

<366> In the present case, the contract, which was for what in essence was a 'pleasure cruise', must be characterized as a contract the object of which was to provide for enjoyment and relaxation. It follows that the respondent was entitled to an award of damages for disappointment and distress and physical inconvenience flowing from that breach of contract. Indeed, an award for disappointment and distress consequential upon physical inconvenience was justified on that account alone. ...

[Toohey and Gaudron JJ agreed with Mason CJ on this issue. Brennan, Deane and Dawson JJ agreed that damages for disappointment and distress are available where the contract was one by which the defendant promised pleasure, entertainment or relaxation. McHugh J held that such damages were available where the distress or disappointment arose from breach of a term (express or implied) that the defendant would provide pleasure or enjoyment or if the distress arose as a result of suffering physical injury.]

Appeal allowed

[footnotes omitted]

b Loss of chance

Loss of chance is difficult to quantify with precision. Nevertheless, the courts have recognised that the loss of chance of gaining some benefit under a contract due to the defendant's breach can give rise to substantial damages. Thus, for example, damages might be recoverable if a party, in breach of contract, fails to proceed with the purchase of a house which deprives the vendor of the opportunity to sell to someone else. In determining loss the court will take into consideration the prospect of success of the lost opportunity.[13] Damages for loss of chance were first recognised as recoverable in the following case.

---

13   See *Sellars v Adelaide Petroleum NL* (1994) 179 CLR 332.

Chaplin v Hicks

[1911] 2 KB 786, English Court of Appeal

[The defendant, an actor and theatrical manager, offered young ladies the opportunity of obtaining engagements as actresses by a competition which involved ladies sending in their photographs and an application form. Approximately 6,000 applications were received. Three hundred photographs were published in the newspaper and voted on by readers. From these votes the top 50 candidates were to be given the opportunity to be interviewed by the defendant who would personally select 12 to receive acting engagements.

The plaintiff was voted in the top 50 eligible for selection by the defendant. The defendant sent a letter to the plaintiff asking her to see the defendant on a particular date. However, the letter did not arrive in time for the plaintiff to make her appointment and, despite attempts, she was not given an opportunity to make another appointment. The trial judge found that the defendant was in breach of contract by not giving the plaintiff an opportunity to be interviewed for selection and awarded her damages. The defendant appealed.]

Vaughan Williams LJ [at 790]: It is contended ... that the breach of contract was such that the damages (if any) obtainable in respect of it could only be nominal. The argument for the defendant was based upon two propositions, first, that the damages were remote, and, secondly, that they were unassessable.

As regards remoteness, the test that is generally applied is to see whether the damages sought to be recovered follow so naturally or by express declaration from the terms of the contract that they can be said to be the result of the breach. This generally resolves itself into the question whether the <791> damages flowing from a breach of contract were such as must have been contemplated by the parties as a possible result of the breach. Now, the moment it is admitted that the contract was in effect one which gave the plaintiff a right to present herself and to take her chance of getting a prize, and the moment the jury find that she did not have a reasonable opportunity of presenting herself on the particular day, we have a breach attended by neglect of the defendant to give her a later opportunity; and when we get a breach of that sort and a claim for loss sustained in consequence of the failure to give the plaintiff an opportunity of taking part in the competition, it is impossible to say that such a result and such damages were not within the contemplation of the parties as the possible direct outcome of the breach of contract. I cannot think these damages are too remote.

Then came the [argument] that the damages were of such a nature as to be impossible of assessment. It was said that the plaintiff's chance of winning a prize turned on such a number of contingencies that it was impossible for any one, ... to say that there was any assessable value of that loss. It is said that in a case which involves so many contingencies it is impossible to say what was the plaintiff's pecuniary loss. I am unable to agree with that contention. I agree that the presence of all the contingencies upon which the gaining of the prize might depend makes the calculation not only difficult but incapable of being carried out with certainty or precision. The proposition is that, whenever the contingencies on which the result depends are numerous and difficult to deal with, it is impossible to recover any damages for the loss of the chance or opportunity of winning the prize. In the present case I understand that there were fifty selected competitors, of whom the plaintiff was one, and twelve prizes, so that the average chance of each competitor was about one in four. Then it is said that the questions which might arise in the minds of the judges are so numerous that it is impossible to say that the case is one in which it <792> is possible to apply the doctrine of averages at all. I do not agree with the contention that, if certainty is impossible of attainment, the damages for a breach of contract are unassessable. I agree, however, that damages might be so unassessable that the doctrine of averages would be inapplicable because the necessary figures for working upon would not be forthcoming; ... [I] wish to deny with emphasis that, because precision cannot be arrived at [damages cannot be awarded.]

... [there have been] many cases in which it was difficult to apply definite rules. In the case of a breach of a contract for the delivery of goods the damages are usually supplied by the fact of there being a market in which similar goods can be immediately bought, and the difference between the contract price and the price given for the substituted goods in the open market is the measure of damages; that rule has been always recognized. Sometimes, however, there is no market for the particular class of goods; but no one has ever suggested that, because there is no market, there are no damages. ... But the fact that damages cannot be assessed with certainty does not relieve the wrong-doer of the necessity of paying damages for his breach of contract. ...

<793> ... taking away from the plaintiff of the opportunity of competition, as one of a body of fifty, when twelve prizes were to be distributed, deprived the plaintiff of something which had a monetary value. ...

Fletcher Moulton LJ [at 793]: I have come to the same conclusion. ...

<794> ... there is no other universal principle as to the amount of damages than that it is the aim of the law to ensure that a person whose contract has been broken shall be placed as near as possible in the same position as if it had not. The assessment is sometimes a matter of great difficulty. ...

<795> To my mind the contention that [the damages] are too remote is unsustainable. The very object and scope of the contract were to give the plaintiff the chance of being selected as a prize-winner, and the refusal of that chance is the breach of contract complained of and in respect of which damages are claimed as compensation for the exclusion of the plaintiff from the limited class of competitors. In my judgment nothing more directly flowing from the contract and the intentions of the parties can well be found.

... it is said that the damages cannot be arrived at because it is impossible to estimate the quantum of the reasonable probability of the plaintiff's being a prize-winner. I think that, where it is clear that there has been actual loss resulting from the breach of contract, which it is difficult to estimate in money, it is for the jury to do their best to estimate; it is not necessary that there should be an absolute measure of damages in each case. …

<796> … Where by contract a man has a right to belong to a limited class of competitors, he is possessed of something of value, … The present case is a typical one. From a body of six thousand, who sent in their photographs, a smaller body of fifty was formed, of which the plaintiff was one, and among that smaller body twelve prizes were allotted for distribution; by reason of the defendant's breach of contract she has lost all the advantage of being in the limited competition, and she is entitled to have her loss estimated. [In determining damages consideration must be given to the fact] that the plaintiff's chance is only one out of four and that they cannot tell whether she would have ultimately proved to be the winner. But having considered all this they may well think that <797> it is of considerable pecuniary value to have got into so small a class, and they must assess the damages accordingly.

[Farwell LJ agreed the appeal should be dismissed.]

Appeal dismissed

In Australia this issue was addressed further in the following case.

Howe v Teefy

(1927) 27 SR (NSW) 301, Supreme Court of New South Wales

[The defendant (appellant) leased a racehorse to the plaintiff (respondent), a horse trainer, for a period of three years. After only four months the defendant, without justification, took the horse from the plaintiff. The plaintiff brought an action for damages resulting from lost profits from betting on the horse and loss of stable commissions (supplying information to others for reward). The plaintiff succeeded at trial and the defendant appealed, alleging both that the loss was too remote and that it was too contingent to be recovered as damages.]

Street CJ [at 304]: Assuming that the damages claimed are capable of assessment, I do not think that it can be said that they are too remote … The sole object of the agreement was to give [the plaintiff] a chance of making money by training and racing the horse, and what is complained of is that it was taken from him and that he was deprived of that chance. Nor does the fact that his opportunities of making money depended upon contingencies, including the volition of other people, suffice to render the damages for the defendant's breach of contract incapable of assessment. …

<306> The presence of contingencies … even when the volition of a third person comes into the matter, does not render the damages incapable of assessment though it may make the calculation of the pecuniary loss sustained incapable of being carried out with certainty or precision. The question in every case is has there been any actual loss resulting from the breach of contract complained of. …

<307> In the present case the question is whether the plaintiff, by having the horse wrongfully taken out of his possession sustained any loss which had a monetary value and which he was entitled to have estimated by a jury. I think that it is clear that he was deprived of something which was of value. The injury which he sustained was the deprivation of his right under his agreement to train and race the horse, and make what profit he could out of doing so. ... The calculation which [the jury] had to make was not how much he would probably have made in the shape of profit out of his use of the horse, but how much his chance of making that profit, by having the use of that horse, was worth in money. ...

[Gordon and Campbell JJ concurred.]

Appeal dismissed

c Wasted expenditure—reliance damages

Where the plaintiff has expended money in the expectation of the defendant's performance which is wasted as a result of the defendant's breach, this loss may be recovered in an action for damages for breach of contract, at least where the plaintiff would have recouped the loss had the contract been performed. The issue of recoupment of reliance damages was discussed by the High Court in the following case.[14]

Commonwealth of Australia v Amann Aviation Pty Ltd

(1991) 174 CLR 64, High Court of Australia

[Amman Aviation won a tender to provide aerial surveillance for the Commonwealth of Australia's northern coastline for a period of three years. A six-month preparatory period was contemplated by the parties and, after winning the tender, Amann acquired and fitted out 14 aircraft which it proposed to use for the surveillance.

After the six-month preparatory period Amann commenced surveillance for the Commonwealth but, due to delays associated with fitting out the aircraft, it did not have all its aircraft ready and conforming with contractual specifications. On the same day Amann's surveillance commenced the Commonwealth terminated their contract by notice, specifying Amann's failure to comply with the contract. This notice was held to be ineffective and itself constituted a breach of contract. The only issue on appeal concerned damages available to Amann as a result of the Commonwealth's breach.]

Mason CJ and Dawson J [at 74]: The trial judge assessed damages on the basis of lost profits and arrived at an amount very substantially less than that claimed by Amann. Amann contended that it was entitled to damages on a 'reliance' basis as

---

14   For a discussion of the effect of the court's decision in this case see G Ng, 'The Onus of Proof in a Claim for Reliance Damages for Breach of Contract' (2006) 22 *JCL* 139.

it had incurred heavy expenditure in equipping itself to carry out its contractual obligations, this expenditure having been wasted by virtue of the Commonwealth's repudiation of the contract. By 12 September, apart from incurring pre-operational expenditure of $854,943, Amann had arranged for the acquisition and fitting out of aircraft at a cost of $5,281,521. It was common ground between the parties that the resale value of the aircraft was only $917,329, a difference of $4,364,192. This large discrepancy is to be explained both by the fact that the aircraft had been adapted to a special use for which there was a very limited demand and by the cost of transporting them to an available market.

Amann's prospects of making a substantial profit rested on its prospect of securing a renewal of the contract. The cost and value of the aircraft were such that a period of operation significantly longer than three years was needed in order to generate a substantial profit. The prospect of the contractor securing a renewal was strong …

<77> … The Full Court, unlike the trial judge, concluded <78> that Amann was entitled to have its damages assessed on the basis of its expenditure rendered futile by the Commonwealth's repudiation; in other words, to be compensated for the expenses it had incurred in reliance on the contract and in equipping itself for the contract. Their Honours acknowledged that such a loss could not be claimed where, even if the breach of contract had not occurred, the returns from the contract would not have been sufficient to recoup the expenditure. However, the Full Court was of the view that the onus of establishing such insufficiency was on the defaulting party. …

<80> … The award of damages for breach of contract protects a plaintiff's expectation of receiving the defendant's performance. That expectation arises out of or is created by the contract. Hence, damages for breach of contract are often described as 'expectation damages'. The onus of proving damages sustained lies on a plaintiff and the amount of damages awarded will be commensurate with the plaintiff's expectation, objectively determined, rather than subjectively ascertained. That is to say, a plaintiff must prove, on the balance of probabilities, that his or her expectation of a certain outcome, as a result of performance of the contract, had a likelihood of attainment rather than being mere expectation.

<81> In the ordinary course of commercial dealings, a party supplying goods or rendering services will enter into a contract with a view to securing a profit, … It is for this reason that expectation damages are often described as damages for loss of profits. Damages recoverable as lost profits are constituted by the combination of expenses justifiably incurred by a plaintiff in the discharge of contractual obligations and any amount by which gross receipts would have exceeded those expenses. …

The expression 'damages for loss of profits' should not be understood as carrying with it the implication that no damages are recoverable either in the case of a contract in which no net profit would have been generated or in the case of a contract in which the amount of profit cannot be demonstrated. … If the performance of a contract would have resulted in a plaintiff, while not making a profit, nevertheless recovering costs incurred in the course of performing contractual obligations, then that plaintiff is entitled to recover damages in an amount equal to those costs ... Similarly, where it is not possible for a plaintiff to demonstrate whether or to what extent the performance of a contract would have resulted in a profit for the plaintiff, it will be open to a plaintiff to seek to recoup expenses incurred, damages in such a case being described as reliance damages or damages for wasted expenditure. ...

<84> ... if a plaintiff's expenditure would not have been fully recouped had the contract been performed, then full compensation for the wasted expenditure would not be awarded. A plaintiff is only entitled to damages for an amount equivalent to that which would have been earned had the contract been fully performed. In this way, the award of damages assessed by reference to a plaintiff's expenditure is in complete conformity with the principle that an award of damages for breach of contract should place a plaintiff in the same position as if the contract had been performed. ...

<85> ... Naturally, the categories of case in which a plaintiff is likely to make a claim for the recovery of expenditure incurred are those in which the plaintiff has not suffered a loss of profits and those in which it is impossible to assess what would have been the outcome had the contract been performed or those in which that outcome is otherwise uncertain. ...

An award of damages for expenditure reasonably incurred under a contract in which no net profit would have been realized, while placing the plaintiff in the position he or she would have been in had the contract been fully performed, also restores the plaintiff to <86> the position he or she would have been in had the contract not been entered into. ...

It should be observed that, in a case where it is not possible to predict what position a plaintiff would have been in had the contract been fully performed, ... it is not possible as a matter of strict logic to assess damages in accordance with the principle in *Robinson v Harman*. But the law considers the just result in such a case is to allow a plaintiff to recover such expenditure as is reasonably incurred in reliance on the defendant's promise. In this case, the law *assumes* that a plaintiff would at least have recovered his or her expenditure had the contract been fully performed. It will still be open to a defendant, however, to argue that, notwithstanding the fact that it is impossible to assess what profits, if any, the plaintiff would have made had the contract been fully performed, the expenditure claimed by a plaintiff would nevertheless not have been recovered ...

... there is strong authority to the effect that, where a plaintiff claims damages for expenditure reasonably incurred, it is *prima facie* sufficient for that plaintiff to prove his or her expenditure and that it was reasonably incurred. The onus then shifts to the party in breach of contract to establish that such expenditure would not have been recouped even if the contract had been fully performed. If this onus is not discharged, a plaintiff's entitlement to reliance damages remains intact. ...

<87> ... The placing of the onus of proof on a defendant in the manner described amounts to the erection of a presumption that a party would not enter into a contract in which its costs were not recoverable. ...

[Brennan, Deane, Toohey and Gaudron JJ all agreed that the company was entitled to damages for wasted expenditure. Deane J agreed with Mason CJ and Dawson J that the onus was on the defendant to demonstrate that the wasted expenditure would not have been recouped. Brennan J also placed this onus with the defendant, but only where it was the defendant's breach that made it impossible for the plaintiff to predict loss with certainty. Toohey and Gaudron JJ placed the onus on the plaintiff both to prove the wasted expenditure and that it would have been recovered but for the defendant's breach. McHugh J dissented.]

Appeal dismissed

d The cost of repairs

Loss in the form of the cost of repairs will most commonly arise where the defendant is a tradesman who has defectively performed the work contracted for. In these cases the general rule is that the defendant can recover the amount necessary to put it in the position it would have been in had the work been performed properly and not merely the difference between the value of the work performed and the value of the work contracted for.[15]

Bellgrove v Eldridge
(1954) 90 CLR 613, High Court of Australia

[The appellant builder entered into a contract with the respondent to build a two-storey 'brick house villa' in accordance with plans. The appellant brought an action claiming payment for the building work. The respondent refused payment and cross-claimed for damages resulting from substantial departures the appellant had made from the building plans which had resulted in the 'grave instability' of the building. The respondent succeeded at first instance and an appeal was made to the High Court on the issue of the damages recoverable for the appellant's breach.]

The Court (Dixon CJ, Webb and Taylor JJ) [at 615]: [The trial judge held that] '... In this case the departure from contract is in my opinion so substantial that the only remedy which will place the plaintiff in substantially the position in which she would be if the contract were carried out, is to award her such damages as will enable her to have this building demolished and a new building erected in accordance with the contract and specifications ... <616> ... The only remedy for this, apart from demolishing the building, is either to under-pin the building as suggested by the plaintiff or to remove the existing foundations in

---

15 For a discussion of the difference between the 'difference in value' test, normally applied where goods are defective, and the 'cost or cure' test, normally applied in relation to defective building works, see AFH Loke, 'Cost of Cure or Differences in Market Value? Toward a sound choice in the basis for quantifying expectation damages' (1996) 10 *JCL* 189. See also *Tabcorp Holdings Ltd v Bowen Investments Pty Ltd* (2009) 236 CLR 272.

small sections and replace them by new foundations. It is extremely doubtful if this work could be successfully done or would be a proper remedy for the defects now existing. It would be a hazardous operation at the best. That is why in my opinion the defendant's damages should be assessed on the basis of demolition and reconstruction'. ... <617> ...

In the present case, the respondent was entitled to have a building erected *upon her land* in accordance with the contract and the plans and specifications which formed part of it, and her damage is the loss which she has sustained by the failure of the appellant to perform his obligation to her. This loss cannot be measured by comparing the value of the building which has been erected with the value it would have borne if erected in accordance with the contract; her loss can, *prima facie*, be measured only by ascertaining the amount required to rectify the defects complained of and so give to her the equivalent of a building on her land which is substantially in accordance with the contract. ... Departures from the plans and specifications forming part of a contract for the erection of a building may result in the completion of a building which, whilst differing in some particulars from that contracted for, is no less valuable. For instance, particular rooms in such a building may be finished in one colour instead of quite a different colour as specified. Is the owner in these circumstances without a remedy? In our opinion he is not; he is entitled to the reasonable cost of rectifying the departure or defect so far as that is possible. Subject to a qualification to which we shall refer presently the rule is, we think, correctly stated in Hudson on *Building Contracts*, 7th ed (1946), p 343. 'The measure of the damages recoverable by the building owner for the breach of a building contract is, it is submitted, the difference between the contract price of the work <618> or building contracted for and the cost of making the work or building conform to the contract, with the addition, in most cases, of the amount of profits or earnings lost by the breach'. ... But the work necessary to remedy defects in a building and so produce conformity with the plans and specifications may, and frequently will, require the removal or demolition of some part of the structure. And it is obvious that the necessary remedial work may call for the removal or demolition of a more or less substantial part of the building. Indeed—and such was held to be the position in the present case—there may well be cases where the only practicable method of producing conformity with plans and specifications is by demolishing the whole of the building and erecting another in its place. In none of these cases is anything more done than that work which is required to achieve conformity and the cost of the work, whether it be necessary to replace only a small part, or a substantial part, or, indeed, the whole of the building is, subject to the qualification ... to which we shall refer, together with any appropriate consequential damages, the extent of the building owner's loss.

The qualification, however, to which this rule is subject is that, not only must the work undertaken be necessary to produce conformity, but that also, it must be a reasonable course to adopt. No one would doubt that where pursuant to a building contract calling for the erection of a house with cement rendered external walls of second-hand bricks, the builder has constructed the walls of new bricks of first quality the owner would not be entitled to the cost of demolishing the walls and re-erecting them in second-hand bricks. In such circumstances the work of demolition and re-erection would be quite unreasonable … <619> … Many examples may, of course, be given of remedial work, which though necessary to produce conformity would not constitute a reasonable method of dealing with the situation and in such cases the true measure of the building owner's loss will be the diminution in value, if any, produced by the departure from the plans and specifications or by the defective workmanship or materials.

As to what remedial work is both 'necessary' and 'reasonable' in any particular case is a question of fact. But the question whether demolition and re-erection is a reasonable method of remedying defects does not arise when defective foundations seriously threaten the stability of a house and when the threat can be removed only by such a course. That work, in such circumstances, is obviously reasonable and in our opinion, may be undertaken at the expense of the builder. …

Appeal dismissed

The Court in *Bellgrove* indicated that the general rule in building contracts that a defendant can recover the costs necessary to put them in the position they would have been in had the contract been properly performed was subject to the qualification that that course of action must be reasonable in the circumstances. The issue of reasonableness was discussed in the following case.[16]

Ruxley Electronics and Construction Ltd v Forsyth

[1995] 1 AC 344, House of Lords

[The appellants contracted to build a swimming pool for the respondent. The contract specified the diving area for the pool should be 7 feet 6 inches deep. The diving area in the finished pool was in fact only 6 feet deep. This was still deep enough for diving and the difference in depth did not affect the value of the property. It would have cost £21,560 to rebuild the pool to the contractual specifications.

On the issue of damages for the appellant's breach the trial judge considered that the cost of reinstatement of the pool at the contracted depth was unreasonable in the circumstances and awarded damages of £2,500. A majority of the Court of Appeal allowed the respondent's appeal, holding the loss was that which was necessary to put him in the position he would have been in had the breach not occurred. On appeal to the House of Lords.]

Lord Bridge of Harwich [at 353]: My Lords, damages for breach of contract must reflect, as accurately as the circumstances allow, the loss which the claimant

---

16   See also *Tabcorp Holdings Ltd v Bowen Investments Pty Ltd* (2009) 236 CLR 272 in which it was held to be reasonable for a landlord to recover the cost of restoring the premises to its original state after, without approval, the tenant constructed a new foyer.

has sustained because he did not get what he bargained for. There is no question of punishing the contract breaker. ...

The circumstances giving rise to the present appeal exemplify a situation which one might suppose to be of not infrequent occurrence. A landowner contracts for building works to be executed on his land. When the work is complete it serves the practical purpose for which it was required perfectly satisfactorily. But in some minor respect the finished work falls short of the contract specification. The difference in commercial value between the work as built and the work as specified is nil. But the owner can honestly say: 'This work does not please me as well as would that for which I expressly stipulated. It does not satisfy my personal preference. In terms of amenity, convenience or aesthetic satisfaction I have lost something.' Nevertheless the contractual defect could only be remedied by demolishing the work and starting again from scratch. The cost of doing this would be so great in proportion to any benefit it would confer on the owner that no reasonable owner would think of incurring it. What is the measure of the loss which the owner has sustained in these circumstances? ...

<354> ... to hold in a case such as this that the measure of the building owner's loss is the cost of reinstatement, however unreasonable it would be to incur that cost, seems to me to fly in the face of common sense.

My Lords, since the populist image of the geriatric judge, out of touch with the real world, is now reflected in the statutory presumption of judicial incompetence at the age of 75, this is the last time I shall speak judicially in your Lordships' House. I am happy that the occasion is one when I can agree with your Lordships still in the prime of judicial life who demonstrate so convincingly that common sense and the common law here go hand in hand. ...

Lord Jauncey of Tullichettle [at 357]: Damages are designed to compensate for an established loss and not to provide a gratuitous benefit to the aggrieved party from which it follows that the reasonableness of an award of damages is to be linked directly to the loss sustained. If it is unreasonable in a particular case to award the cost of reinstatement it must be because the loss sustained does not extend to the need to reinstate. ...

<358> ... A man contracts for the building of a house and specifies that one of the lower courses of brick should be blue. The builder uses yellow brick instead. In all other respects the house conforms to the contractual specification. To replace the yellow bricks with blue would involve extensive demolition and reconstruction at a very large cost. It would clearly be unreasonable to award to the owner the cost of reconstructing because his loss was not the necessary cost of reconstruction of his house, which was entirely adequate for its design purpose, but merely the lack of aesthetic pleasure which he might have derived from the sight of blue bricks. Thus in the present appeal the respondent has acquired a perfectly serviceable swimming pool, albeit one lacking the specified depth. His loss is thus not the lack of a useable pool with consequent need to construct a new one. Indeed were he to receive the cost of building a new one and retain the existing one he would

have recovered not compensation for loss but a very substantial gratuitous benefit, something which damages are not intended to provide.

What constitutes the aggrieved party's loss is in every case a question of fact and degree. ... if a building is constructed so defectively that it is of no use for its designed purpose the owner may have little difficulty in establishing that his loss is the necessary cost of reconstructing. Furthermore in taking reasonableness into account in determining the extent of loss it is reasonableness in relation to the particular contract and not at large. Accordingly if I contracted for the erection of a folly in my garden which shortly thereafter suffered a total collapse it would be irrelevant to the determination of my loss to argue that the erection of such a folly which contributed nothing to the value of my house was a crazy thing to do.

However where the contractual objective has been achieved to a substantial extent the position may be very different.

<359> My Lords, the trial judge found that it would be unreasonable to incur the cost of demolishing the existing pool and building a new and deeper one. In so doing he implicitly recognised that the respondent's loss did not extend to the cost of reinstatement. He was, in my view, entirely justified in reaching that conclusion. ...

Lord Lloyd of Bewick [at 366]: In building cases, the pecuniary loss is almost always measured in one of two ways; either the difference in value of the work done or the cost of reinstatement. Where the cost of reinstatement is less than the difference in value, the measure of damages will invariably be the cost of reinstatement. By claiming the difference in value the plaintiff would be failing to take reasonable steps to mitigate his loss. In many ordinary cases, too, where reinstatement presents no special problem, the cost of reinstatement will be the obvious measure of damages, even where there is little or no difference in value, or where the difference in value is hard to assess. This is why it is often said that the cost of reinstatement is the ordinary measure of damages for defective performance under a building contract.

But it is not the only measure of damages. Sometimes it is the other way round. ...

<367> ... the cost of reinstatement is not the appropriate measure of damages if the expenditure would be out of all proportion to the benefit to be obtained, and, secondly, the appropriate measure of damages in such a case is the difference in value, even though it would result in a nominal award. ...

<369> ... If the court takes the view that it would be unreasonable for the plaintiff to insist on reinstatement, as where, for example, the expense of the work involved would be out of all proportion to the benefit to be obtained, then the plaintiff will be confined to the difference in value. ...

[Lord Mustill agreed the appeal should be allowed.]

Appeal allowed

e   Loss of the use of money

Damages for the loss of use of money are recoverable in Australia. Deprivation of the use of money may cause loss in the form of the costs associated with borrowing money from another source or through the loss of interest. Provided such loss is foreseeable then damages for that loss will be recoverable.[17]

f   The rule in *Bain v Fothergill*

In *Bain v Fothergill* the House of Lords held that where a vendor of land fails to complete as a result of a defect in title, the purchaser is restricted to recovering losses associated with investigating the title as well as any deposit paid unless the vendor is guilty of fraud or bad faith.[18] This rule has been abolished in the United Kingdom but still applies in Australia, save for Queensland and New South Wales where it has been abolished by legislation.[19]

6   The assessment of damages

a   The date for assessing damages

Once a recognised loss is demonstrated which was caused by the defendant's breach and which was not too remote to the contract, the plaintiff will be entitled to recover damages for that loss. The date for assessing damages is generally the date the plaintiff's cause of action arose which will normally be the date on which the defendant's breach occurred. However, where assessment on that date would not fairly compensate the plaintiff for the loss caused as a result of the breach another date may be used.

Hoffman v Cali

[1985] Qd R 253, Supreme Court of Queensland (Full Court)

[In March 1981 the plaintiff, Mrs Hoffman, entered into a contract with the defendant developers to purchase, for the price of $89,000, a unit in a multi-storey block of home units they were to erect. As required by the contract, Mrs Hoffman paid $4,500 representing a partial deposit. Time was stipulated to be of the essence but no completion date was fixed. The trial judge held that it was to be implied that the building must be completed within a reasonable time which he estimated at 18 months (September 1982). The defendants did not proceed with the construction

---

17   The normal measure of damages will be the amount of interest lost as a result of not having the money: see *Hungerfords v Walker* (1989) 171 CLR 125.
18   *Bain v Fothergill* (1874) LR 7 HL 158.
19   *Property Law Act 1974* (Qld) s 68; *Conveyancing Act 1919* (NSW) s 54B. To a limited extent it has also been abolished in Western Australia.

and in September 1981 offered to cancel Mrs Hoffman's contract and refund the deposit. Mrs Hoffman requested performance of the contract.

Subsequently Mrs Hoffman commenced action, seeking damages for breach of contract. An issue arose as to the time at which damages should be calculated.]

McPherson J [at 259]: The only question [on appeal] is the proper measure of [damages for the defendants' breach of contract]. It is accepted that one of the components in the calculation is the contract price of $89,000.00, and that the other is the value or market price. ... [The trial judge] held that the relevant date at which the market price was to be taken was between December 1981 and February 1982 [which was when the plaintiff elected to accept the defendants' repudiation of the contract]. ... The market price of the unit during this period was found to be $130,000.00. ...

[The defendants argue that the] appropriate time for determining the market price [is] September 1982 [the date at which construction ought to have been completed] ...

The question of what is the appropriate date for determining the market price, and hence the difference between it and the contract price, <260> [involves] a choice between the date of breach ... and the date for completion ...

... it is the date of breach rather than performance that is relevant ... There is indeed an element of ambiguity about the statement that damages are to be assessed by <261> reference to circumstances prevailing at the date of breach, because in a case such as this there are really two such dates. These are the dates of the repudiation or anticipatory breach and the date of failure to perform the contract. ...

<264> In the present case there are no special features that would displace the general rule laid down in *Frost v Knight* (1872) LR 7 Ex 111, 113, as applicable to cases of anticipatory breach, namely that a plaintiff who accepts such a repudiation is entitled to such damages as would have arisen from non-performance of the contract at the appointed time; nor is there any reason for displacing the principle stated by *McGregor* and adopted in *Ella v Wenham* [1972] QdR 90, namely that damages for breach of a contract for the sale of land are ordinarily to be measured by the difference between market value and contract price at the contractual date for completion.

[In this case] damages should have been assessed at the difference between $89,000.00 and the prevailing market price payable for a similar unit in September 1982. [The market price at that date is estimated at] $104,000.00.

[Andrews SPJ agreed the appeal should be allowed and damages assessed at September 1982.]

Appeal allowed

b Mitigation of loss

The plaintiff must do what is reasonable to reduce ('mitigate') the loss suffered as a result of a defendant's breach. Where the plaintiff has not mitigated their loss any damages awarded will be reduced by the amount the defendant could have reasonably reduced their loss. Any costs associated with mitigating loss—for example, advertising goods for sale—can be recovered as damages. The defendant has the onus of demonstrating the plaintiff could have mitigated their loss in order to receive a reduction in damages.[20]

Burns v MAN Automotive (Aust) Pty Ltd

(1986) 161 CLR 653, High Court of Australia

[The appellant, Burns, and the respondent, MAN Automotive, entered into a contract by which the respondent agreed to sell a prime mover to a hire-purchase company who would hire it to the appellant for use in his one-man haulage business. The respondent warranted that the engine had been fully reconditioned. In fact the engine had not been fully reconditioned and was in a 'deplorable condition' which caused significant problems for the appellant's haulage business.

It would have cost between $7,000 and $8,000 to recondition the engine, which the appellant could not afford. The appellant sought, unsuccessfully, to get the respondent to recondition the engine. The appellant then borrowed money to carry out some repair work sufficient to enable the prime mover to be used for local, but not interstate, haulage. During this time the haulage business operated at a loss. The prime mover eventually broke down and was repossessed by the hire-purchase company.

The appellant brought an action for damage suffered, including loss of profits, for the period of four years after the date of purchase; this was the period in which the engine should have continued to operate had it been in the state promised by the respondent. The following extract deals only with the issue of mitigation of loss.]

Gibbs CJ [at 657]: There can be no doubt that it was within the reasonable contemplation of the parties at the time when the contract was made that if the warranty was broken the appellant might lose the profits which he might otherwise have made in the business of an interstate haulier. ... The appellant had made known to representatives of the respondent the purpose for which he intended to use the vehicle, and if the engine was not in a fully reconditioned state a loss of profits was a serious possibility ...

<658> ... this is a case in which it is necessary to consider whether the appellant did what he could to mitigate the damage caused by the breach of warranty. ... any damage which resulted from a breach of the contract, and was reasonably within the contemplation of the parties when the contract was made, is recoverable even though the appellant's impecuniosity contributed to it: ... However, the appellant was bound to take all reasonable steps to mitigate the loss, and one course open to

---

20   See *Metal Fabrications (Vic) Pty Ltd v Kelcey* [1986] VR 507 and *TCN Channel 9 Pty Ltd v Hayden Enterprises Pty Ltd* (1989) 16 NSWLR 130.

him to mitigate the damage, if he could have afforded to take it, was to have the engine reconditioned or to buy another to replace it. However, his impecuniosity prevented him from taking that course. The question arises whether it should be held that the appellant is <659> debarred from claiming such part of the damages as is attributable to his failure to take the necessary steps in mitigation, when he was unable to take those steps because of his lack of means.

That question must be answered in the negative. …

… a plaintiff's duty to mitigate his damage does not require him to do what is unreasonable and it would seem unjust to prevent a plaintiff from recovering in full damages caused by a breach of contract simply because he lacked the means to avert the consequences of the breach. There are in the present case, the additional features that the financial difficulties of the appellant were largely brought about by the actions of the respondent in supplying him with a defective engine and refusing properly to rectify the defects, although the respondent should have known that the appellant lacked the financial resources that would have enabled him to pay to have the engine reconditioned. …

<660> However, there is another reason why the appellant did not do all that he reasonably could to mitigate his damage. It was not reasonable for him to carry on his business with the defective prime mover, once he knew that he was operating at a loss and should have known that he had no prospect of making a profit. …

Brennan J [at 675]: The limitation placed on the recovery of loss resulting from breach of contract when the loss would have been avoided by the injured party taking reasonable steps to mitigate the loss is not so draconian as to deny recovery to an impecunious victim who, if he were not impecunious, could have avoided the loss but who, being impecunious, has suffered it. …

<676> The possible choices which confronted the appellant when he discovered in July 1978 that the engine which had been warranted reconditioned was in fact in a deplorable state were fourfold: to complain to the respondent and request it to recondition the engine, to deliver the prime mover to Esanda and terminate the hire-purchase agreement, to pay sufficient to repair the engine to a condition where the vehicle could be used for haulage work on a reduced scale, or to pay the full cost of reconditioning. Consider each of those choices. The first was not available. Though the appellant sought redress from the respondent it was refused. … The second option would have left the appellant without any prospect of working his way out of the Esanda debt. In July 1978 his total liability to Esanda stood at $34,622.15. If the prime mover as warranted had been worth $31,000 in July 1977, it is unlikely that its resale with known defects in July 1978 would have brought enough to discharge the debt … However, it was reasonable to try to haul supplies to the central Queensland coal mines in an effort to earn sufficient to pay out the hire-purchase liability. That was the third choice and the one he took: … he obtained the money to pay for the needed repairs and he thus obtained a chance to use the vehicle profitably. The fourth choice would have involved an outlay of $7,000 to $8,000 which he did not have. He was not

bound to take <677> it. I would apply to this case what Megaw LJ said in *Dodd Properties*:

> 'A plaintiff who is under a duty to mitigate is not obliged, in order to reduce the damages, to do that which he cannot afford to do: particularly where, as here, the plaintiffs' "financial stringency," so far as it was relevant at all, arose, as a matter of common sense, if not as a matter of law, solely as a consequence of the defendants' wrongdoing.'

It would be wrong to find that the course taken by the appellant in having some repairs done to the engine in 1978 was an unreasonable step to take in mitigating his loss unless it appeared that he was bound to suffer further losses when he went back on the road. The respondent, on whom the onus lay, did not establish that fact. ...

... the reasonableness of the steps taken to mitigate must be assessed in the light of the appellant's actual financial situation, not by reference to a supposition which puts in his hands the money which he needed but did not have to put an end to the losses inflicted on him. ...

[In their joint judgment Wilson, Deane and Dawson JJ did not consider that this was a case of mitigation of damage, but simply called for a determination of whether the damage alleged was too remote to be recovered.]

Appeal dismissed

c Contributory negligence

Legislation provides that in cases where a contract imposes a duty of care on a party and that duty is breached, but the other contracting party is partly responsible for the loss they suffered, damages for breach of contract may be reduced by the an amount proportional to the extent that the other party was responsible for their own loss.[21]

Wrongs Act 1958 (Vic)

Section 25. Definitions

In this Part unless inconsistent with the context or subject-matter—
'wrong' means an act or omission that—

(a) gives rise to a liability in tort in respect of which a defence of contributory negligence is available at common law; or
(b) amounts to a breach of a contractual duty of care that is concurrent and co-extensive with a duty of care in tort.

---

21 See *Civil Law (Wrongs) Act 2002* (ACT) s 102; *Law Reform (Miscellaneous Provisions) Act 1965* (NSW) Part 3; *Law Reform (Miscellaneous Provisions) Act* (NT) Part V; *Law Reform Act 1995* (Qld); *Law Reform (Contributory Negligence and Apportionment of Liability) Act 2001* (SA); *Law Reform (Contributory Negligence and Tortfeasors' Contribution) Act 1947* (WA); *Wrongs Act 1954* (Tas) s 4.

Section 26. Liability for contributory negligence

(1) If a person (the claimant) suffers damage as the result partly of the claimant's failure to take reasonable care (contributory negligence) and partly of the wrong of any other person or persons—
   (a) … a claim in respect of the damage is not defeated by reason of the contributory negligence of the claimant; and
   (b) the damages recoverable in respect of the wrong must be reduced to such extent as the court thinks just and equitable having regard to the claimant's share in the responsibility for the damage.

(1A) Sub-section (1) does not operate to defeat any defence arising under a contract.

(1B) If any contract or enactment providing for the limitation of liability is applicable to the claim, the amount of damages awarded to the claimant by virtue of sub-section (1) is not to exceed the maximum limit so applicable.

INTERNATIONAL PERSPECTIVES

India

The *Indian Contract Act, 1872* requires a court to take into consideration the extent to which a party has mitigated their loss when assessing damages.

Indian Contract Act, 1872

Section 73. Explanation

In estimating the loss or damage arising from a breach of contract, the means which existed of remedying the inconvenience caused by the non-performance of the contract must be taken into account.

In *AKAS Jamal v Moolla Dawood Sons & Co* the Privy Council, on appeal from the Chief Court of Lower Burma, observed that under the *Indian Contract Act:* 'It is undoubted law that a plaintiff who sues for damages owes the duty of taking all reasonable steps to mitigate the loss consequent upon the breach and cannot claim as damages any sum which is due to his own neglect.'[22]

China

The *Contract Law of the People's Republic of China* also imposes a duty on the non-breaching party to mitigate the loss they suffer as a result of the other party's breach of contract.

---

22 [1916] 1 AC 175.

Contract Law of the People's Republic of China, 1999

Article 119. Non-Breaching Party's Duty to Mitigate Loss in Case of Breach

Where a party breached the contract, the other party shall take the appropriate measures to prevent further loss; where the other party sustained further loss due to its failure to take the appropriate measures, it may not claim damages for such further loss.

Any reasonable expense incurred by the other party in preventing further loss shall be borne by the breaching party.

7 Liquidated (agreed) damages

The parties may include a term in their contract which specifies the amount that will be payable in the event that one of the parties breaches their obligations. Provided the sum stipulated constitutes a genuine estimate of the likely damage that would be caused by the breach it will be enforced by the courts. If, on the other hand, the sum specified is in reality a penalty, it will not be enforced. A court will, however, be slow to find an agreed damages clause is a penalty.[23] The issue of liquidated damages and penalties arose for consideration in the following case.[24]

Dunlop Pneumatic Tyre Company Ltd v New Garage and Motor Company Ltd

[1915] AC 79, House of Lords

[The appellants entered into a contract for the supply of goods with the respondents. The respondents agreed, among other things, that they would not sell at prices less than Dunlop's list price. The contract also provided that the respondents agreed to pay Dunlop the sum of 5*l* per tyre offered or sold in breach of this agreement 'by way of liquidated damages and not as a penalty'. The trial judge held that the agreed sum was in fact for liquidated damages and was not a penalty. The respondents

---

23   See *Ringrow Pty Ltd v BP Australia Pty Ltd* (2005) 224 CLR 656 in which the High Court approved and applied the following statement from the judgments of Mason and Wilson JJ in *AMEV-UDC Finance Ltd v Austin* (1986) 162 CLR 170 at 699: '[T]here is much to be said for the view that the courts should return to ... allowing parties to a contract greater latitude in determining what their rights and liabilities will be, so that an agreed sum is only characterized as a penalty if it is out of all proportion to damage likely to be suffered as a result of breach.'

24   This case represents the law in Australia: *Ringrow Pty Ltd v BP Australia Pty Ltd* (2005) 224 CLR 656. See also E Peden and JW Carter, 'Agreed Damages Clauses—Back to the Future?' (2006) 22 JCL 189 and *AMEV-UDC Finance Ltd v Austin* (1986) 162 CLR 170, JW Carter and E Peden, 'A Good Faith Perspective on Liquidated Damages' ((2007) 23 *Journal of Contract Law* 157 and PD Baron, 'Confused in Words: Unconscionability and the Doctrine of Penalties' (2008) 34 *Monash University Law Review* 286.

appealed and the majority held that the fixed sum was a penalty. A further appeal was made to the House of Lords.]

Lord Dunedin [at 86]: I shall content myself with stating succinctly the various propositions which I think are deducible from the decisions which rank as authoritative:—

(1) Though the parties to a contract who use the words 'penalty' or 'liquidated damages' may *prima facie* be supposed to mean what they say, yet the expression used is not conclusive. ...
(2) The essence of a penalty is a payment of money stipulated as *in terrorem* [a tactic intended to intimidate or frighten the other party] of the offending party; the essence of liquidated damages is a genuine covenanted pre-estimate of damage ...
(3) The question whether a sum stipulated is penalty or liquidated damages is a question of construction to be decided <87> upon the terms and inherent circumstances of each particular contract, judged of as at the time of the making of the contract, not as at the time of the breach ...
(4) To assist this task of construction various tests have been suggested, ...
   (a) It will be held to be penalty if the sum stipulated for is extravagant and unconscionable in amount in comparison with the greatest loss that could conceivably be proved to have followed from the breach. ...
   (b) It will be held to be a penalty if the breach consists only in not paying a sum of money, and the sum stipulated is a sum greater than the sum which ought to have been paid ...
   (c) There is a presumption (but no more) that it is penalty when 'a single lump sum is made payable by way of compensation, on the occurrence of one or more or all of several events, some of which may occasion serious and others but trifling damage'

On the other hand:
   (d) It is no obstacle to the sum stipulated being a genuine pre-estimate of damage, that the consequences of the breach are such <88> as to make precise pre-estimation almost an impossibility. On the contrary, that is just the situation when it is probable that pre-estimated damage was the true bargain between the parties ...

Turning now to the facts of the case, it is evident that the damage apprehended by the appellants owing to the breaking of the agreement was an indirect and not a direct damage. So long as they got their price from the respondents for each article sold, it could not matter to them directly what the respondents did with it. Indirectly it did [because it affected their distribution system.] But though damage as a whole from such a practice would be certain, yet damage from any one sale would be impossible to forecast. It is just, therefore, one of those cases where it seems quite reasonable for parties to contract that they should estimate that damage at a certain figure, and provided that figure is not extravagant there would seem no reason to suspect that it is not truly a bargain to assess damages, but rather a penalty to be held *in terrorem*.

[In this case the sum specified was a sum for liquidated damages and not a penalty.]

Lord Atkinson [at 95]: ... although it may be true ... that a presumption is raised in favour of a penalty <96> where a single lump sum is to be paid by way of compensation in respect of many different events, some occasioning serious, some trifling damage, it seems to me that that presumption is rebutted by the very fact that the damage caused by each and every one of those events, however varying in importance, may be of such an uncertain nature that it cannot be accurately ascertained. The damage has been proved to be of that nature in the present case, and the very fact that it is so renders it all the more probable that the sum of 5*l* was not stipulated for merely *in terrorem*, but was really and genuinely a pre-estimate of the appellants' probable or possible interest in the due performance of the contract. ...

[Lords Parker of Waddington and Parmoor agreed that the appeal should be allowed.]

Appeal allowed

[footnotes omitted]

INTERNATIONAL PERSPECTIVES

India

Under the *Indian Contract Act, 1872* parties may stipulate a sum as liquidated damages. Where the sum is a reasonable pre-estimate of loss likely to be suffered as a result of breach then that pre-estimate may be taken by the court to be the appropriate measure of 'reasonable compensation'.[25] However, where a sum stipulated is a penalty for breach the court must only award such a sum as is reasonable compensation in the circumstances.

Indian Contract Act, 1872

Section 74. Compensation for breach of contract where penalty stipulated for

When a contract has been broken, if a sum is named in the contract as the amount to be paid in case of such breach, or if the contract contains any other stipulation by way of penalty, the party complaining of the breach is entitled, whether or not actual damage or loss is proved to have been caused thereby, to receive from the party who has broken the contract reasonable compensation not exceeding the amount so named or, as the case may be, the penalty stipulated for.

---

25 *Oil & Natural Gas Corpn Ltd v Saw Pipes Ltd* [2003] INSC 236 (Supreme Court of India) per Shah J.

China

The *Contract Law of the People's Republic of China* permits the parties to prescribe a sum of liquidated damages to be paid in the event of breach. This amount may, however, be increased or decreased on petition to bring it to an amount approximating actual loss resulting from the breach.

Contract Law of the People's Republic of China, 1999

Article 114. Liquidated Damages; Adjustment; Continuing Performance Notwithstanding Payment of Liquidated Damages

The parties may prescribe that if one party breaches the contract, it will pay a certain sum of liquidated damages to the other party in light of the degree of breach, or prescribe a method for calculation of damages for the loss resulting from a party's breach.

Where the amount of liquidated damages prescribed is below the loss resulting from the breach, a party may petition the People's Court or an arbitration institution to increase the amount; where the amount of liquidated damages prescribed exceeds the loss resulting from the breach, a party may petition the People's Court or an arbitration institution to decrease the amount as appropriate.

Where the parties prescribed liquidated damages for delayed performance, the breaching party shall, in addition to payment of the liquidated damages, render performance.

8 Restitutionary damages for breach of contract

In *Attorney-General v Blake* the House of Lords held that restitutionary-type damages could be recovered for breach of contract in a limited number of cases where compensatory damages alone would not achieve justice.[26] Lord Nicholls in that case held that while a restitutionary remedy for an account of profits was discretionary in nature and no fixed rules could be prescribed for its provision,[27] they should be available whenever the 'plaintiff had a legitimate interest in preventing the defendant's profit making activity and, hence, in depriving him of his profit'.[28]

---

26 [2001] 1 AC 268. See further R Cunnington, 'Equitable Damages: A Model for Restitutionary Damages' (2001) 17 *Journal of Contract Law* 212 and A Phang and PW Lee, 'Rationalising Restitutionary Damages in Contract Law—An Elusive or Illusory Quest?' (2001) 17 JCL 240. In Australia, some positive treatment for such a remedy has been found in *Town & Country Property Management Services Pty Ltd v Kaltoum* [2002] NSWSC 166.

27 This has been criticised as leading to uncertainty in commercial law: see Cunnington, above n 25 at 212.

28 *Attorney-General v Blake* [2001] 1 AC 268 at 285.

Attorney-General v Blake

[2001] 1 AC 268, House of Lords

[Blake was employed as a member of the United Kingdom security and intelligence services from 1944 to 1961. During this time he became an agent for the Soviet Union, disclosing secret information gained during his employment. He was convicted on charges relating to this disclosure and sentenced to 42 years imprisonment. He escaped from prison and fled to Moscow. While still a fugitive in Moscow he wrote an autobiography, part of which contained information obtained as an intelligence officer. Despite the fact that this information was no longer confidential or damaging to the public interest, Blake's employment contract prohibited him from disclosing this information even after his employment with the security services ceased. The Attorney-General sought to prevent Blake receiving the profits associated with the breach of contract—the substantial royalties for the book.

On the issue of damages recoverable for breach of contract the Court of Appeal expressed the view that restitutionary damages consisting of profits made from breach of contract could be obtained in appropriate circumstances. These circumstances included where the profit was obtained by doing the very thing the defendant was contracted not to do. That, they said, was the case here and consequently the profit could be recovered. The matter then came on appeal to the House of Lords.]

Lord Nicholls of Birkenhead [at 277]: This is a subject on which there is a surprising dearth of judicial decision. By way of contrast, ... there has been no lack of academic writing. ... <278> ... Most writers have favoured the view that in some circumstances the innocent party to a breach of contract should be able to compel the defendant to disgorge the profits he obtained from his breach of contract. However, there is a noticeable absence of any consensus on what are the circumstances in which this remedy should be available. ... The broad proposition that a wrongdoer should not be allowed to profit from his wrong has an obvious attraction. The corollary is that the person wronged may recover the amount of this profit when he has suffered no financially measurable loss. ... the corollary is not so obviously persuasive. ...

<279> ... More difficult is the alignment of this measure of damages within the basic compensatory measure. Recently there has been a move towards applying the label of restitution to awards of this character: ... However that may be, these awards cannot be regarded as conforming to the strictly compensatory measure of damage for the injured person's loss unless loss is given a strained and artificial meaning. The reality is that the injured person's rights were invaded but, in financial terms, he suffered no loss. ...

<282> [For breach of contract the] basic remedy is an award of damages. In the much quoted words of Baron Parke, the rule of the common law is that where a party sustains a loss by reason of a breach of contract, he is, so far as money can do it, to be placed in the same position as if the contract had been

performed: *Robinson v Harman* ... Leaving aside the anomalous exception of punitive damages, damages are compensatory. That is axiomatic. It is equally well established that an award of damages, assessed by reference to financial loss, is not always 'adequate' as a remedy for a breach of contract. The law recognises that a party to a contract may have an interest in performance which is not readily measurable in terms of money. On breach the innocent party suffers a loss. He fails to obtain the benefit promised by the other party to the contract. To him the loss may be as important as financially measurable loss, or more so. An award of damages, assessed by reference to financial loss, will not recompense him properly. ...

The classic example of this type of case, as every law student knows, is a contract for the sale of land. The buyer of a house may be attracted by features which have little or no impact on the value of the house. An award of damages, based on strictly financial criteria, would fail to recompense a disappointed buyer for this head of loss. The primary response of the law to this type of case is to ensure, if possible, that the contract is performed in accordance with its terms. To this end the court has wide powers to grant injunctive relief. The court will, for instance, readily make orders for the specific performance of contracts for the sale of land, ...

All this is trite law. But these remedies are not always available. For instance, confidential information may be published in breach of a non-disclosure agreement before the innocent party has time to apply to the court for urgent relief. Then the breach is irreversible. Further, these specific remedies are discretionary. Contractual obligations vary infinitely. So do the circumstances in which breaches occur, and the circumstances in which remedies are sought. The court may, for instance, decline to grant specific relief on the ground that this would be oppressive. ...

<283> ... in contract as well as tort damages are not always narrowly confined to recoupment of financial loss. In a suitable case damages for breach of contract may be measured by the benefit gained by <284> the wrongdoer from the breach. The defendant must make a reasonable payment in respect of the benefit he has gained. In the present case the Crown seeks to go further. The claim is for all the profits of Blake's book which the publisher has not yet paid him. This raises the question whether an account of profits can ever be given as a remedy for breach of contract. The researches of counsel have been unable to discover any case where the court has made such an order on a claim for breach of contract. ...

My conclusion is that there seems to be no reason, in principle, why the court must in all circumstances rule out an account of profits as a remedy for breach of contract. I prefer to avoid the unhappy expression 'restitutionary damages'. Remedies are the law's response to a wrong (or, more precisely, to a cause of action). When, exceptionally, a just response to a breach of contract so requires, the court should be able to grant the discretionary <285> remedy of requiring a defendant to account to the plaintiff for the benefits he has received from his breach of contract. In the same way as a plaintiff's interest in performance of a contract may render it just and equitable for the court to make an order for specific performance or grant an injunction, so the plaintiff's interest in performance may make it just and equitable that the defendant should retain no benefit from his breach of contract.

... when awarding damages, the law does not adhere slavishly to the concept of compensation for financially measurable loss. When the circumstances require, damages are measured by reference to the benefit obtained by the wrongdoer. This applies to interference with property rights. ... I consider it would be only a modest step for the law to recognise openly that, exceptionally, an account of profits may be the most appropriate remedy for breach of contract. ...

The main argument against the availability of an account of profits as a remedy for breach of contract is that the circumstances where this remedy may be granted will be uncertain. This will have an unsettling effect on commercial contracts where certainty is important. I do not think these fears are well founded. I see no reason why, in practice, the availability of the remedy of an account of profits need disturb settled expectations in the commercial or consumer world. An account of profits will be appropriate only in exceptional circumstances. Normally the remedies of damages, specific performance and injunction, coupled with the characterisation of some contractual obligations as fiduciary, will provide an adequate response to a breach of contract. It will be only in exceptional cases, where those remedies are inadequate, that any question of accounting for profits will arise. No fixed rules can be prescribed. The court will have regard to all the circumstances, including the subject matter of the contract, the purpose of the contractual provision which has been breached, the circumstances in which the breach occurred, the consequences of the breach and the circumstances in which relief is being sought. A useful general guide, although not exhaustive, is whether the plaintiff had a legitimate interest in preventing the defendant's profit-making activity and, hence, in depriving him of his profit. ...

<286> *The present case*
The present case is exceptional. ... Blake deliberately [breached] his express undertaking. ...

<287> ... an account of profits [given] the special circumstances of the intelligence services ... would be a just response to the breach. ...

<288> ... the appropriate form of order on this appeal is a declaration that the Attorney General is entitled to be paid a sum equal to whatever amount is due and owing to Blake ...

Lord Steyn [at 291]: [There are] difficulties inherent in creating a general remedy for the recovery of restitutionary damages for breach of contract. ... [In academic debate] there is no or virtually no support for a general action for disgorgement of profits made by a contract breaker by reason of his breach. ... [this] is a notoriously difficult subject. ...

<292> ... The distinctive feature of this case is ... that Blake gave an undertaking not to divulge any information, confidential or otherwise, obtained by him during his work in the intelligence services. This obligation still applies to Blake. He was, ... in a very similar position to a fiduciary. ... Secondly, I bear in mind that the enduring

strength of the common law is that it has been developed on a case-by-case basis by judges for whom the attainment of practical justice was a major objective of their work. ... These observations are almost banal: the public would be astonished if it was thought that judges did not conceive it as their prime duty to do practical justice whenever possible. ... For my part practical justice strongly militates in favour of granting an order for disgorgement of profits against Blake. ... Our law is also mature enough to provide a remedy in such a case but does so by the route of the exceptional recognition of a claim for disgorgement of profits against the contract breaker. ...

[His Honour also agreed with the reasons of Lord Nicholls of Birkenhead.]

[Lord Goff of Chieveley and Lord Browne-Wilkinson agreed with the reasons of Lord Nicholls of Birkenhead. Lord Hobhouse of Woodborough dissented].

Appeal dismissed

9 Other common law remedies for breach of contract

a Debt

Where the breach of contract takes the form of not paying a sum of money the remedy of the non-breaching party takes the form of an action to recover the sum owed rather than a claim for damages. There is no necessity, in such a case, for the non-breaching party to prove loss. Thus, for example, if P contracts to sell their car to D and transfers ownership to D on the date stipulated but D fails to pay the price, P can maintain an action in debt for the agreed price. Damages may be recoverable in addition to the debt owed where failure to pay on time results in additional loss to the plaintiff.

b Termination clauses

Where a contract is terminated in reliance on a termination clause in the contract damages may not be recoverable by the innocent party. Whether this is the case will be a matter of construction in each case. This was discussed by the High Court in *Shevill v The Builders Licensing Board*[29] which was discussed and extracted in chapter 21.

c Retention of deposits paid

A deposit paid pursuant to a contract may be retained in the event of a breach by the other party.[30] The non-breaching party may also recover from the breaching

---

29 (1982) 149 CLR 620.
30 This is normally provided for expressly in the contract; where this is not the case the court will need to determine the intention of the parties. See further chapter 21 discussing the effect of breach of contract on payments made or due.

party a deposit due at the time of the breach but not yet paid. This is the case even where the non-breaching party has suffered no demonstrable loss as a result of the breach, provided that the deposit is itself reasonable. A deposit of 10 per cent of the purchase price will ordinarily be considered reasonable; conversely, a deposit exceeding this amount will not generally be reasonable and instead will be considered to be a penalty which must be repaid to the breaching party. Where loss beyond the amount of the deposit is suffered the non-breaching party may also maintain an action for damages.

Workers Trust and Merchant Bank Ltd v Dojap Investments Ltd
[1993] AC 573, Privy Council

[The appellant bank sold premises at auction to the respondent. The contract required a deposit of 25 per cent which was duly paid. The remainder of the purchase price was to be paid within 14 days and the contract stipulated that should the purchaser fail to comply with this obligation the deposit shall be forfeited to the vendor. Payment was not made within 14 days and the bank retained the deposit. The respondent sought recovery of the deposit. The Court of Appeal of Jamaica held the respondent was entitled to recover that part of the deposit that exceeded 10 per cent.]

Lord Browne-Wilkinson (for the Board) [at 577]: This case raises the question whether a deposit in excess of 10 per cent paid under a contract for the sale of land can be lawfully forfeited by the vendor in the event of a failure by the purchaser to complete on the due date.

<578> In general, a contractual provision which requires one party in the event of his breach of the contract to pay or forfeit a sum of money to the other party is unlawful as being a penalty, unless such provision can be justified as being a payment of liquidated damages being a genuine pre-estimate of the loss which the innocent party will incur by reason of the breach. One exception to this general rule is the provision for the payment of a deposit by the purchaser on a contract for the sale of land. Ancient law has established that the forfeiture of such a deposit (customarily 10 per cent of the contract price) does not fall within the general rule and can be validly forfeited even though the amount of the deposit bears no reference to the anticipated loss to the vendor flowing from the breach of contract.

This exception is anomalous ... The special treatment afforded to such a deposit derives from the ancient custom of providing an earnest for the performance of a contract in the form of giving either some physical token of earnest (such as a ring) or earnest money. The history of the law of deposits can be traced to the Roman law ... Ever since the decision in *Howe v Smith*, the nature of such a deposit has been settled in English law. Even in the absence of express contractual provision, it is an earnest for the performance of the contract: in the event of completion of the contract the deposit is applicable towards payment of the purchase price; in the event of the purchaser's failure to complete in accordance with the terms <579> of the contract, the deposit is forfeit, equity having no power to relieve against such forfeiture.

However, the special treatment afforded to deposits is plainly capable of being abused if the parties to a contract, by attaching the label 'deposit' to any penalty, could escape the general rule which renders penalties unenforceable. ...

... It is not possible for the parties to attach the incidents of a deposit to the payment of a sum of money unless such sum is reasonable as earnest money. The question therefore is whether or not the deposit of 25 per cent in this case was reasonable as being in line with the traditional concept of earnest money or was in truth a penalty intended to act *in terrorem*.

<580> ... In their Lordships' view the correct approach is to start from the position that, without logic but by long continued usage both in the United Kingdom and formerly in Jamaica, the customary deposit has been 10 per cent. A vendor who seeks to obtain a larger amount by way of forfeitable deposit must show special circumstances which justify such a deposit.

... formerly the normal practice in Jamaica was to require a deposit of 10 per cent. This was changed [as a result of a 7.5 per cent transfer tax imposed by legislation in 1971 so that] in practice ... the contractual deposit is increased to at least 17½ per cent.

<581> The question therefore arises whether the court has jurisdiction to relieve against the express provision of the contract that the deposit of 25 per cent was to be forfeited. ...

<582> In the view of their Lordships, since the 25 per cent deposit was not a true deposit by way of earnest, the provision for its forfeiture was a plain penalty. ...

The Court of Appeal took a middle course by ordering the repayment of 15 per cent. out of the 25 per cent deposit, leaving the bank with its normal 10 per cent deposit which it was entitled to forfeit. Their Lordships are unable to agree that this is the correct order. The bank has contracted for a deposit consisting of one globular sum, being 25 per cent of the purchase price. If a deposit of 25 per cent constitutes an unreasonable sum and is not therefore a true deposit, it must be repaid as a whole. The bank has never stipulated for a reasonable deposit of 10 per cent: therefore it has no right to such a limited payment. If it cannot establish that the whole sum was truly a deposit, it has not contracted for a true deposit at all.

... Finally, it appears that the bank may have suffered some damage as a result of the purchaser's failure to complete. If so, the bank is entitled <583> to deduct the amount of such damages from the 'deposit' of 25 per cent. ...

Appeal dismissed

INTERNATIONAL PERSPECTIVES

India

It has been held that under the *Indian Contract Act, 1872* a deposit which represents 'earnest money' may be retained upon breach even if no loss can be demonstrated.[31]

China

Similarly, the *Contract Law of the People's Republic of China* entitles a non-breaching party to retain a deposit paid by a breaching party. However, where it is the party who has received the deposit who is in breach of contract that party must return an amount equal to twice the deposit to the non-breaching party.

Where parties stipulate both for the payment of a deposit and liquidated damages, a party in breach must elect either to retain the deposit or recover the amount of liquidated damages.

Contract Law of the People's Republic of China, 1999

Article 115. Deposit

The parties may prescribe that a party will give a deposit to the other party as assurance for the obligee's right to performance ... Upon performance by the obligor, the deposit shall be set off against the price or refunded to the obligor. If the party giving the deposit failed to perform its obligations under the contract, it is not entitled to claim refund of the deposit; where the party receiving the deposit failed to perform its obligations under the contract, it shall return to the other party twice the amount of the deposit.

Article 116. Election Between Deposit or Liquidated Damages Clauses

If the parties prescribed payment of both liquidated damages and a deposit, in case of breach by a party, the other party may elect in alternative to apply the liquidated damages clause or the deposit clause.

---

31 *Maula Bux v Union of India* (1969) 2 SCC 554 (Supreme Court of India).

698 • Part 6: Remedies

10 Summary

a Overview

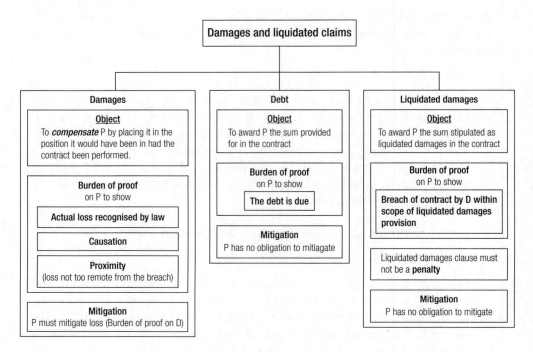

b Approach to damages

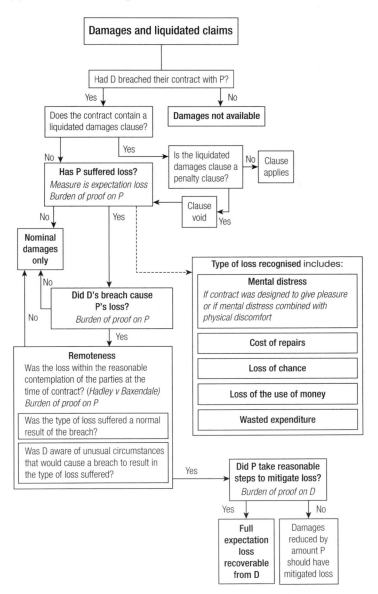

11 Questions

1. On 12 May Sparky Electrics Ltd (Sparky) agreed to carry out electrical work for Victoria Holdings Ltd (Victoria) for the sum of $25,000. In breach of contract, Sparky carried out this work carelessly. As a result, in July the same year, Victoria's premises caught fire causing property damaged estimated at $10m and the loss of all the company's accounts. The loss of these accounts concealed a fraud that was being perpetrated by Brock Jones, Victoria's chief accountant. In January the following year this fraud culminated in Jones withdrawing and absconding with $2m from Victoria's accounts, never to be seen or heard from again.

   As a result of Jones' fraud, Victoria suffered financial difficulties, as it was not insured against this kind of loss. Also, because of the property damage it had suffered, it was unable to proceed with a new project that had been underway when Sparky carried out its electrical work. Estimates suggest that Victoria would have made a profit of $4m from this project in the following financial year. Victoria's financial difficulties have also caused Victoria's CEO, Lorna Lane, great distress. This culminated in her suffering a heart attack on 1 June, causing the company and herself considerable financial loss.

   Please advise Victoria whether or not it has any claim for damages against Sparky for any of the various losses it has suffered and, if so, the extent of those claims.

2. Martin sold 10 crates of apples to Glenda's Groceries Pty Ltd each month at a cost of $50 per crate. This was pursuant to an ongoing contract, which contained a clause permitting either party to terminate on two months notice. In breach of contract, Glenda's Groceries refused to take delivery of the crates supplied by Martin in March. Glenda's Groceries' owner, Alice, informed Martin that she had obtained apples elsewhere at a better rate and no longer needed or wanted his apples.

   Martin was upset at Alice's refusal to take delivery, as it left him with a surplus of apples and deprived him of the profit he had anticipated making on each crate. On his way home he stopped at one of his neighbours, who ran a horse stud farm, and offered to sell him the apples at $5 a crate to feed his horses. His neighbour readily agreed.

   The following week Martin was able to find a retailer willing to purchase his apples in the future, but as a result of a recent increase in competition he was only able to extract a fee of $40 per crate.

   Martin has come to you for advice. He wants to know whether he can recover any damages from Glenda's Groceries resulting from their refusal to take delivery of his apples. Please advise Martin.

3. Paul's Pools (PP) entered into a contract with the Werribee Aquatic Centre (WAC) to construct a 50m Olympic class swimming pool. The WAC advised PP that it intended to use the pool both for community sport, amateur and professional training and, it hoped, for national and international competitive events.

   PP constructed the pool by the requisite contract date. Unfortunately it was later discovered that the pool was 1cm short of 50m, with the result that it could not be used for professional competitive events. WAC demanded that PP pay the cost of repairing the pool. This would involve significant demolition and reconstruction and cost almost as much as the original construction. PP objected, stating that, while they were prepared to pay some compensation for their mistake, WAC's demand that they pay for the repair was unreasonable.

In light of PP's objection, WAC's managing director, Kathy, has approached you for advice. She tells you that WAC has already had to cancel a proposed competitive event because the pool did not meet the requisite standard. Please advise Kathy what, if any, damages she can claim against WAC.

CHAPTER 24

Equitable Remedies

1	Introduction	702
2	The nature of equitable remedies	702
3	Specific performance	703
	a The nature of specific performance	703
	b The approach to claims for specific performance	703
	c Contracts for which the courts routinely award specific performance	710
	d Contracts which will not be specifically enforced	714
4	Injunctions	722
5	Damages in lieu of equitable remedy	730
6	Summary	734
7	Questions	735

1 Introduction

In this chapter we discuss the equitable remedies of specific performance and injunction for breach of contract. An award of specific performance directs the person against whom it is made to perform their contractual obligations and, is, therefore, the most appropriate equitable remedy for a party seeking to enforce a *positive* obligation. Injunctions, on the other hand, are more appropriate where a party wishes to prevent a breach of a *negative* contractual obligation, such as not to disclose confidential information.

2 The nature of equitable remedies

In the previous chapter we saw that damages at common law are designed to *compensate* a party for loss that has been suffered as a result of a breach of contract. Equitable remedies, on the other hand, seek to compel performance of assumed contractual obligations and consequently may, where appropriate, prove a more desirable option for the innocent party. These remedies are not, however, available as a matter of course. Equitable remedies are discretionary in nature and, in each case, the court will be required to decide whether it is appropriate for it to exercise its *discretion* to grant the remedy sought. The courts will generally only exercise their discretion to award equitable remedies where it can be demonstrated that common law remedies, such as damages, would be inadequate to compensate the plaintiff for the defendant's breach, or anticipated breach, of contract.[1]

In *Co-Operative Insurance Society Ltd v Argyll Stores (Holdings) Ltd* Lord Hoffman explained the nature of equitable remedies in the following terms:

> A decree of specific performance is of course a discretionary remedy ... There are well-established principles which govern the exercise of the discretion but these, like all equitable principles, are flexible and adaptable to achieve the ends of equity, which is, as Lord Selborne LC once remarked, to 'do more perfect and complete justice' than would be the result of leaving the parties to their remedies at common law: .... Much therefore depends upon the facts of the particular case ...
>
> Specific performance is traditionally regarded in English law as an exceptional remedy, as opposed to the common law damages to which a successful plaintiff is entitled as of right. ... by the 19th century it was orthodox doctrine that the power to decree specific performance was part of the discretionary jurisdiction of the Court of Chancery to do justice in cases in which the remedies available at common law were inadequate. This is the basis of the general principle that specific performance will not be ordered when damages are an adequate remedy.[2]

Where it can be demonstrated that common law remedies provide inadequate compensation for breach of contract, a court may nevertheless refuse to exercise its discretion if the granting of an equitable remedy would not be appropriate in the circumstances of the particular case.[3]

3 Specific performance

a The nature of specific performance

An order for specific performance directs the party against whom it is made to perform obligations promised under the contract. It is generally used as a method of enforcing *positive* obligations, rather than to prevent parties from engaging in conduct prohibited by a contract, for which an injunction would be the more appropriate remedy.

b The approach to claims for specific performance

Specific performance is not available automatically following a breach, or anticipated breach, of contract. As noted above, it is a matter for the court's discretion in

---

1 See Lord Redesdale in *Harnett v Yielding* (1805) 2 Sch & Lef 549, Dixon J in *Dougan v Ley* (1946) 71 CLR 142 and Lord Hoffmann in *Co-Operative Insurance Society Ltd v Argyll Stores (Holdings) Ltd* [1998] AC 1.
2 [1998] AC 1 at 9–11.
3 The circumstances in which equitable remedies may be refused on other grounds are discussed below. In *Stewart v Kennedy* (1890) 15 AC 75, at 102 Lord Watson observed in this respect: 'Specific performance is not a matter of legal right, but a purely equitable remedy, which the Court can withhold when there are sufficient reasons of conscience or expediency against it.'

each case. When approaching a claim of specific performance a court will generally adopt the following process in deciding whether or not it is appropriate to exercise their discretion.[4]

(1) The plaintiff must be entitled to some remedy in respect of the breach of contract alleged.
(2) Damages must not provide an adequate remedy for the breach or anticipated breach by the defendant.
(3) Specific performance must provide a more adequate remedy than damages for the plaintiff.
(4) If all the other elements are met, the court must then be satisfied that it would be fair to the defendant to order specific performance.

Plaintiff entitled to some remedy

This will normally be easily satisfied. Breach of a valid contract automatically entitles the non-breaching party to at least nominal damages. However, if the contract is invalid or unenforceable for some reason this element may not be satisfied.

Damages do not provide adequate compensation

If damages adequately compensate the plaintiff there is no cause for equity to intervene. Consequently, in each case, the court will only exercise its discretion to grant specific performance where it can be demonstrated that common law damages will provide an inadequate compensation for the plaintiff.[5] Damages may not provide adequate compensation where, for example, the item contracted for is unique, such as is normally the case for contracts for the sale of land. Damages may also be inadequate where contractual remedies are not available at law as a result of a failure to comply with statutory formalities.[6]

Another situation in which damages will be routinely considered inadequate will be where a contract was made principally for the benefit of a third party who is not able to sue directly to enforce that benefit.[7] In the latter case the non-breaching party may have suffered no measurable loss for which substantial damages can be recovered, despite the other party failing to perform all or most of their bargain. This was discussed in the following case.

---

4 This approach was adopted by Lord Buckley in *Price v Strange* [1978] Ch 337, [1977] 3 All ER 371: '… the questions which should be asked by any court which is invited to enforce specific performance of a contractual obligation should be: (1) is the plaintiff entitled to a remedy of some kind in respect of the alleged breach of contract? (2) if so, would damages be an adequate remedy? (3) if not, would specific performance be a more adequate remedy for the plaintiff? (4) if so, would it be fair to the defendant to order him to perform his part of the contract specifically?'

5 This was expressed by Buckley LJ in *Price v Strange* [1978] Ch 337, [1977] 3 All ER 371 (Court of Appeal, UK) as follows: 'For breaches of some kinds of contract, pre-eminently contracts for the sale of land, the common law remedy of damages was inadequate. …'

6 Thus, specific performance may be ordered for part performance of a contract that is unenforceable by virtue of s 126 *Instruments Act* (Vic) (see further chapter 7) even though, if formalities had been complied with damages would have provided an adequate remedy: see further, *JC Williamson Limited V Lukey and Mulholland* (1931) 45 CLR 282.

7 See further chapter 8.

Beswick v Beswick

[1968] AC 58, House of Lords

[The plaintiff agreed to transfer his business to his nephew, the defendant, in consideration for the defendant employing him until his death and then paying a sum to the plaintiff's wife until her death. Following the plaintiff's death, less than two years later, the defendant refused to pay his wife the sum agreed. The plaintiff (through his estate) sued for specific performance of the agreement. The plaintiff was unsuccessful at first instance but succeeded in the Court of Appeal.]

Lord Hodson [at 78]: ... The only question is, 'What is the appropriate remedy?' It would be strange if the only remedy were nominal damages recoverable at common law or a series of actions at law to enforce the performance of a continuing obligation. ...

<81> ... it was argued at one time that the equitable remedy of specific performance of a contract to make a money payment was not available. This [is an] untenable contention. ... Further, it was argued that specific performance would not be granted where the remedy at law was adequate and so should not be ordered. The remedy at law is plainly inadequate, as was pointed out by the Court of Appeal, as (1) only nominal damages can be recovered; (2) in order to enforce a continuing obligation it may be necessary to bring a series of actions whereas specific performance avoids multiplicity of action. ...

<83> In such a case as this, there having been an unconscionable breach of faith, the equitable remedy sought is apt. The appellant has had the full benefit of the contract and the court will be ready to see that he performs his part ...

Lord Pearce [at 88]: It is argued that the estate can only recover nominal damages and that no other remedy is open, either to the estate or to the personal plaintiff. Such a result would be wholly repugnant to justice and commonsense. And if the argument were right it would show a very serious defect in the law.

... this is a case in which, as the Court of Appeal rightly decided, the more appropriate remedy is that of specific performance.

The administratrix is entitled, if she so prefers, to enforce the agreement rather than accept its repudiation, and specific performance is more convenient than an action for arrears of payment followed by separate actions as each sum falls due. Moreover, damages for breach would be a less appropriate remedy since the parties to the agreement were intending an annuity for a widow; and a lump sum of damages does not accord with this. ... <89>

The present case presents all the features which led the equity courts to apply their remedy of specific performance. The contract was for the sale of a business. The defendant could on his part clearly have obtained specific performance of it if Beswick senior or his administratrix had defaulted. Mutuality is a ground in favour of specific performance.

Moreover, the defendant on his side has received the whole benefit of the contract and it is a matter of conscience for the court to see that he now performs his part of it. ...

Lord Upjohn [at 96]: ... surely on a number of grounds this is a case for specific performance. ...

<97> ... when the money payment is not made once and for all but in the nature of an annuity there is an even greater need for equity to come to the assistance of the common law. Equity is to do true justice to enforce the true contract that the parties have made and to prevent the trouble and expense of a multiplicity of actions. This has been well settled for over a century: ...

<98> It is in such common sense and practical ways that equity comes to the aid of the common law and it is sufficiently flexible to meet and satisfy the justice of the case in the many different circumstances that arise from time to time. ...

[Lord Reid and Lord Guest agreed on the issue of specific performance.]

Appeal dismissed

[footnotes omitted]

Specific performance must provide a more adequate remedy

If, despite damages not providing adequate compensation, specific performance would not provide *more* adequate compensation in the circumstances, then it would not be necessary or appropriate for equity to intervene. Thus, for example, if a contract is for the sale of unique goods which have subsequently been lost or destroyed then an order of specific performance requiring a defendant to hand over those goods would not provide a more adequate remedy than damages because the plaintiff would be in no position to comply with that order.[8]

Is it fair to order specific performance?

Once all the other elements are satisfied a court may still refuse to order specific performance if to do so would be unfair in the circumstances. The courts will consider factors such as mutuality of obligations, adequacy of consideration and hardship to the defendant to determine whether or not the discretion should be exercised.

- **Lack of mutuality.** Equity will not order specific performance for the benefit of one contracting party unless it can ensure that any unperformed obligations of the other party can also be the subject of an order for specific performance.[9] This is referred to as the principle of mutuality. The date for determining if there is a mutuality of obligations is the date at which specific performance is sought and not the time at which the parties entered into their contract.[10] This principle was expressed by Buckley LJ in *Price v Strange* as follows:

---

8 See *Johnson v Agnew* [1980] AC 367.
9 See *Price v Strange* [1978] Ch 337, [1977] 3 All ER 371 (Court of Appeal, UK) per Buckley LJ.
10 See *Price v Strange* [1978] Ch 337, [1977] 3 All ER 371 (Court of Appeal, UK) per Buckley LJ. See also Lord Goff in the same case: 'Surely the defence of want of mutuality should be governed by the state of affairs as seen at the hearing, since one is dealing not with a question affecting the initial validity of the contract, but with whether or not the discretionary remedy of specific performance should be granted. ...'

... the court will not compel a defendant to perform his obligations specifically if it cannot at the same time ensure that any unperformed obligations of the plaintiff will be specifically performed, unless, perhaps, damages would be an adequate remedy to the defendant for any default on the plaintiff's part. ....[11]

- **Delay.** If a party delays in seeking an order for specific performance a court will be less inclined to exercise their jurisdiction to make the order in their favour.
- **Hardship to the defendant.** Where an order for specific performance would cause unreasonable hardship to the defendant the courts are unlikely to exercise their discretion to order specific performance. This issue arose for consideration in the following case.

Dowsett v Reid

(1912) 15 CLR 695, High Court of Australia

[This case involved a complex lease agreement. The appellant (defendant) was the lessor. He was illiterate but otherwise a 'shrewd' business man. The respondent's (plaintiff's) husband visited the appellant a week before the contract was signed, asking whether he would sell the property. The appellant indicated he was interested in selling and a preliminary agreement was drawn up. The respondent's husband went back to the appellant a week later with a formal agreement prepared by his solicitor. He claimed to have read it to the appellant and also took the document to the postmaster who read it carefully to the appellant who appeared to be satisfied with the document. The appellant subsequently claimed he was drunk at the time and did not know anything about the transaction. This claim was, however, rejected at trial and the High Court did not disturb this finding. Relevantly, the appellant argued that this was a 'hard and unconscionable bargain' and that, as a consequence, the court should refuse to exercise its discretion to grant specific performance of the lease contract. The Supreme Court of Western Australia granted specific performance. An appeal was made to the High Court.]

Griffith CJ [at 705]: I now come to the third defence, that it was a hard and unconscionable bargain. That is an appeal to the discretion of the Court, and it raises more difficulty. Some recent cases seem to have gone so far as to suggest that in every case where there is a valid contract the Court is bound to grant specific performance; but that is not the old doctrine of the Court, nor do I think it is the present doctrine. In *Fry on Specific Performance*, 3rd ed, p 152, sec 334, it is said: 'Nothing is more established in this Court, said Lord Hardwicke, speaking of contracts which the Court will enforce, than that every agreement of this kind ought to be certain, fair, and just in all its parts. If any of those ingredients are wanting in the case, this Court will not decree a specific performance. I lay it down as a general proposition, said Lord Rosslyn, to which I know no limitation, that all agreements, in order to be executed in this Court, must be certain and defined: secondly, they must be equal and fair; for this Court, unless they are fair, will not

---

11   *Price v Strange* [1978] Ch 337, [1977] 3 All ER 371 (Court of Appeal, UK) per Buckley LJ.

execute them.' At page 194, sec 417, the doctrine is thus stated:—'It is a well established doctrine that the Court will not enforce the specific performance of a contract the result of which would be to impose great hardship on either of the parties to it; and this although the party seeking specific performance may be free from the least impropriety of conduct.' … <706> …

In my judgment the old doctrine is still the doctrine of the Court. The Court is not bound to enforce a bargain which would work great hardship upon either party. …

[His Honour then discussed the details of the contract in this case and, after concluding the bargain would leave the appellant substantially out of pocket and provide a windfall benefit to the respondent, concluded (at 707)]: it appears to me on these facts that the bargain is one which the Court ought not, in its discretion, to enforce upon the lessor; but as the plaintiff cannot get it set aside I think the Court ought to … give him such damages as he can prove that he has sustained. …

[Barton J agreed with Griffith CJ. Higgins J agreed specific performance should not be granted in the circumstances; in particular he noted that the agreement had been drawn up for the respondent by the respondent's solicitors and contained clauses very favourable to the respondent which were not part of the original draft agreement between the parties, that the agreement was long and complicated and that the appellant was illiterate and had no independent advice.]

Appeal allowed in part

[footnotes omitted]

- **Mistake or misrepresentation.** Where the defendant has been the victim of a mistake or misrepresentation the court may choose not to order specific performance against him or her even where the mistake or misrepresentation is not such as to provide a remedy at common law.
- **Inadequacy of consideration.** Inadequacy of consideration does not prevent a contract being formed, but will be a factor considered by the courts in determining whether equitable remedies, such as specific performance, should be awarded against a defendant.[12]
- **Plaintiff also in breach.** Where a plaintiff is also in breach of an essential obligation under a contract or is not ready, willing and able to perform their contractual obligations, the courts will not order specific performance in their favour. This is a manifestation of the general equitable maxim that 'he who comes to equity must come with clean hands'.

Green v Sommerville

(1979) 141 CLR 594, High Court of Australia

[The appellants (Mr and Mrs Green) entered into a contract to sell a parcel of land to the respondent. The respondent paid a deposit but was unable to pay the full

---

12 See *Dowsett v Reid* (1912) 15 CLR 695.

contract price at settlement. Nevertheless, she was keen to purchase the property and anticipated being in a position to pay shortly thereafter. The appellants allowed her to take possession of the property in exchange for a weekly rental. A new settlement date was set and the respondent tendered the sum she thought due under the contract. The appellant believed a higher sum, including an amount for interest resulting from the delayed payment, was due. They rejected the tendered amount and sought to rescind the contract. The respondent made a claim for specific performance. She failed at first instance but succeeded on appeal to the Full Court of the Supreme Court of Western Australia. The vendors appealed to the High Court.]

Barwick CJ [at 597]: [After noting that the purported revocation was ineffective and therefore didn't prevent an order for specific performance his Honour continued (at 600)]: It is a condition precedent to success in a purchaser's action for specific performance that the purchaser should, at the institution of the suit, be ready and willing to perform the contract. ... on the facts as they appeared before the primary judge, it <601> could not be said that the respondent was unwilling to perform the contract according to that construction of it which the Court might put upon it. The adoption by a party of an erroneous construction of the contract is not necessarily fatal to the proposition that, none the less, the party remains ready and willing to perform the contract according to its terms properly construed. ...

Accordingly, I am of opinion that the Full Court was not in error in ordering specific performance ...

Mason J [at 605]: According to Burt CJ [in the Full Court], the respondent was ready, willing and able to pay the balance of the purchase price and by tendering the balance she remedied the breach of contract which occurred on 10th November 1976. ... Her refusal to pay interest as well as rent went to an 'inessential term' and amounted to no more than an assertion of a wrong view of the contract. In the result, the appeal was allowed and an order for specific performance made. ...

<607> ... The respondent remedied the requirement in the earlier notice that the balance of the purchase price due on 10th November 1976 be paid. This she did by tendering an amount in excess of $23,400.00 on 30th May 1977, the date for settlement subsequently agreed upon by the parties. Her failure to complete the contract by making payment of all the interest due on 30th May 1977 was not to the point. ... it did not give rise to an automatic rescission ...

<609> ... the respondent was, in my opinion, in breach of contract by failing to pay on 30th May 1977 the interest which was then due. ...

[The] obligation to pay interest, though not a trivial term, is ... not an essential term.

<610> ... Does the respondent's failure to pay the amount of interest due on settlement, though not a breach of an essential term, disentitle her to specific performance on the ground that she was not ready and willing? In my opinion,

it does not. It is well settled that a plaintiff in a suit for specific performance is not required to show that he has strictly complied with all his obligations under the contract; it is enough that he has performed and is ready and willing to perform the substance of the contract ...

<611> ... the respondent was, on the view which I take of the contract, ready and willing to perform her essential obligation under the contract, that is, by paying the balance of the purchase price. Secondly, it is a general principle of the law of contract that the court will not readily infer from a party's insistence on a wrong construction of a contract that he is unwilling to perform it according to its true construction. This principle applies to the plaintiff's readiness and willingness in a suit for specific performance ... I can see no reason why the principle should not apply to a case in which there is a dispute as to the nature and effect of an oral agreement and the view for which the plaintiff contends is bona fide held by her. The fact is ... that both parties maintained an incorrect view as to the amount of interest payable. ... it was a case in which the respondent 'though asserting a wrong view of a contract because he believes it to be correct, is willing to perform the contract according to its tenor'. It was not a case in which the plaintiff persisted in an untenable view of the contract. Nor was it a case in which it could be said that the respondent came with unclean hands. This is important because the concept of readiness and willingness is an exemplification of the maxim 'He who comes to equity must come with clean hands.'

[Murphy and Aickin JJ agreed that for the reasons expressed by Mason J the appeal should be dismissed. Wilson J also agreed the appeal should be dismissed.]

Appeal dismissed

[footnotes omitted]

c Contracts for which the courts routinely award specific performance

The issue of determining whether specific performance should be ordered is a matter for the court's discretion in each case. However, there are some classes of contract for which the courts have routinely ordered specific performance.

Contracts for rare or unique goods

The general rule in relation to contracts for the sale of goods is that damages will constitute an adequate remedy. This is because the plaintiff can generally recover the difference between the contract price of goods and the market price following the breach, thereby enabling them to either sell or purchase the items contracted for without suffering any net financial loss. However, in relation to goods for which there is no current 'market', damages might not prove adequate. This will most often be the case in relation to rare or unique items or items that, while of limited monetary value, nevertheless have a sentimental value that cannot be measured through an award of damages.[13] This issue arose in the following case.

Dougan v Ley

(1946) 71 CLR 142, High Court of Australia

[The defendant (appellant) owned a registered taxi and licence. He contracted to sell the taxi and the related registration and licence to the plaintiff (respondent). The defendant refused to proceed with the sale and the plaintiff sought specific performance of the contract. At the time, legislation limited the number of taxi licences available in the relevant area. The trial judge gave an order for specific performance and the defendant appealed.]

Dixon J [at 149]: The subject matter, it is said, is the sale of a chattel and, in general, a suit for the specific performance of an agreement to sell and deliver chattels will not be entertained. But, when the substance of the matter is considered, the agreement is not of this simple character. The legislation has resulted in a restriction upon the number of registered and licensed vehicles with which the calling of taxi-driving may be pursued. The contract is in fact for the transfer of a valuable privilege annexed to a chattel. Of the amount of the consideration, somewhat the greater part appears to represent the registration and licence and the lesser part the vehicle itself. The number of taxi-cabs licensed for the city and suburbs of Sydney which had not been already sold once since the commencement of Act No 22 of 1945 was shown to be only 880. Thirty-seven taxis had, according to the <150> evidence, been sold since that date and the prices paid for the licences of the vehicles were said to have averaged £1,318. The subject of the sale is thus shown to be a special right attached to a chattel, transferable only with it, and numerically restricted.

... So it became the received doctrine that the foundation of decrees for specific performance was 'that damages at law would not give the party the compensation to which he was entitled; that is, would not put him in a situation as beneficial to him as if the agreement were specifically performed' ....

'The Court gives specific performance instead of damages, only when it can by that means do more perfect and complete justice' ...

In the case of goods or securities obtainable upon the market, damages at law place the disappointed buyer or seller in as good a position as delivery of the articles or receipt of the price because it enables him to go upon the market. ...

<151> It was not difficult to say that a purchaser of 'articles of unusual beauty rarity and distinction' was entitled to obtain them *in specie* (*Falcke v Gray* ...).

---

13 See *Fells v Read* [1896] All ER Rep 525 involving an ornamental silver tobacco-box, enclosed in two larger silver cases containing various engravings which had been held by a religious society for at least several decades. When the overseer of the society refused to return the cases to the society upon leaving office, an order of specific performance was sought to have the item returned. Lord Loughborough LC noted that 'In all cases where the object of the suit is not liable to a compensation by damages, it would be strange if the law of this country did not afford a remedy' and ordered the box returned.

Though a less obvious case, it was settled that 'a certain number of railway shares of a particular description, which railway shares are limited in number' and are not to be obtained by going on the share market, are a subject in respect of which a contract of sale will be enforced specifically (*Duncuft v Albrecht* ...). ...

In the present case I think that we should have no difficulty in concluding that, because of the limited number of vehicles registered and licensed as taxi-cabs, because of the extent to which the price represents the value of the licence, and because of the essentiality to the purchasers' calling of the chattel and the licence annexed thereto, we should treat the contract as within the scope of the remedy of specific performance.

Williams J [at 153]: It is clear that the Court of Equity will not decree specific performance of a contract where a money payment, or in other words damages, will afford an adequate remedy for the breach, and that this is the position in the case of most forms of personal property, such as goods which can be readily purchased in the market. ... But it is equally clear that the Court of Equity will decree specific performance of contracts for the sale of chattels which are unique or have for some other reason a special or peculiar value. ...

[Rich, Starke and McTiernan JJ all agreed the appeal should be dismissed.]

Appeal dismissed

[footnotes omitted]

Contracts involving land

The courts have generally accepted that contracts relating to interests in land are of such a nature that a breach is not capable of adequate compensation through an award of damages. Consequently, specific performance has been routinely considered a proper remedy for breaches of contracts relating to land.[14]

Pianta v National Finance & Trustees Ltd

(1964) 180 CLR 146, High Court of Australia

[The appellant, Pianta, was the owner of a property of nearly 50 acres on which he lived and conducted a horse stud. The respondent approached the appellant expressing an interest in purchasing the land. The respondent drew up a contract and negotiations continued involving the appellant's solicitors. The appellant subsequently sold the property to a third party. The respondent objected, claiming to have reached a binding agreement for the sale of the property through the appellant's solicitor and sought an order for specific performance. The trial judge determined that there was a binding contract between the appellant and respondent but refused an order for specific performance.]

---

14 See Dixon J in *Dougan v Ley* (1946) 71 CLR 142 at 150. See also *Hillingdon Estate co v Stonefield Estate Ltd* [1952] Ch 627.

Barwick CJ [at 151]: I can discover no reason why a decree for specific performance should not have been made, if there was a binding agreement between the appellants and the respondent. ... There was a faint endeavour made on behalf of the appellants to support the refusal of a decree for specific performance on the ground that, because the respondent was a land developer, damages would be an adequate remedy. But in my opinion this proposition is without foundation in law, even if the respondent had had no other business than that of subdividing and selling land and had made a decision to subdivide and sell the subject land.

[Barwick CJ went on to find that there was no binding contract for the sale of the property between the appellant and respondent and on that ground the appeal succeeded].

[Menzies and Owen JJ did not find it necessary to address the issue of specific performance, having determined there was no binding contract between the parties. Kitto and Windeyer JJ agreed with the judgments of Barwick CJ, Menzies and Owen JJ.]

Appeal allowed

Recently, however, the Supreme Court of Canada has questioned whether land should be so unquestionably considered incapable of adequate compensation through damages. In *Semelhago v Paramedevan*, La Forest J observed:

[para 14] Different considerations apply where the thing which is to be purchased is unique. Although some chattels such as rare paintings fall into this category, the concept of uniqueness has traditionally been peculiarly applicable to agreements for the purchase of real estate. Under the common law every piece of real estate was generally considered to be unique. ... Accordingly, damages were an inadequate remedy and the innocent purchaser was generally entitled to specific performance. ...

[para 20] ... While at one time the common law regarded every piece of real estate to be unique, with the progress of modern real estate development this is no longer the case. Both residential, business and industrial properties are mass produced much in the same way as other consumer products. If a deal falls through for one property, another is frequently, though not always, readily available.

[para 21] It is no longer appropriate, therefore, to maintain a distinction in the approach to specific performance as between realty and personalty. It cannot be assumed that damages for breach of contract for the purchase and sale of real estate will be an inadequate remedy in all cases. The common law recognized that the distinction might not be valid when the land had no peculiar or special value. ...

[para 22] Courts have tended, however, to simply treat all real estate as being unique and to decree specific performance unless there was some other reason for refusing equitable relief: ... Some courts, however, have begun to question the assumption that damages will afford an inadequate remedy for breach of contract for the purchase of land. ...

Specific performance should, therefore, not be granted as a matter of course absent evidence that the property is unique to the extent that its substitute would not be readily available. ...

[footnotes omitted][15]

d   Contracts which will not be specifically enforced

In addition to establishing certain types of contracts in which specific performance will generally be awarded, the authorities establish certain types of contract for which specific performance will not be an appropriate remedy.

Contracts of personal service

Contracts of personal service, such as employment contracts, will not be ordered to be specifically performed.[16] This would require parties to maintain a personal relationship in circumstances in which mutual trust and confidence between the parties has been broken. Compulsion in these circumstances is considered undesirable and is likely to infringe on the civil liberties of employees.

Contracts requiring constant supervision

Contracts requiring the courts to constantly supervise the performance of obligations will not be suitable for an award of specific performance. This issue arose in the following cases.

JC Williamson Ltd v Lukey and Mulholland
(1931) 45 CLR 282, High Court of Australia

[The parties entered into a contract whereby the plaintiffs (Lukey and Mulholland) would take over the lease of a sweets shop adjacent to the Theatre Royal in Melbourne for the expiry of the existing term and an additional five year term and, during that period, would have an exclusive right to sell sweets and confectionery in the Theatre Royal (the defendants held the rights to grant this exclusive licence). The defendants subsequently repudiated the plaintiff's right to sell sweets exclusively in the area promised and granted that right to a third party. The plaintiffs sought both specific performance and an injunction to enforce their contractual rights to sell sweets exclusively. The plaintiffs succeeded in the Supreme Court of Victoria and the defendants appealed.]

Starke J [at 292]: Courts of equity have, no doubt, exercised jurisdiction to enforce contracts specifically and to restrain the breach of contracts which such a

---

15   (1996) 136 DLR (4th) 1.
16   See, for example, *Lucy v Commonwealth* (1923) 33 CLR 229 in which Knox CJ observed that save for 'the purpose of preventing the breach or intended breach of a negative stipulation' an order for specific performance of a contract of service will not be granted (at 238).

Court would specifically enforce and to restrain the breach of negative stipulations in contracts whether in the particular case the Court would or would not specifically enforce the whole contract. ... But over and over again it is asserted in the books that a Court of equity will not compel one party to perform his part of a contract unless justice can be done as regards the other party ... Nor will it as a rule enforce <293> contracts of personal service or any other contract the execution whereof would require continued superintendence by the Court ...

... it is clear, on the principles already referred to, that no Court of equity would have enforced, specifically or by way of injunction, the right of the respondents to sell sweets in the theatre. Nor would any such Court have enforced the right of the appellant to supervise and control the right of selling sweets in the theatre. The enforcement of either right would have required a continued and effective superintendence of acts and services which would be impossible for any Court. So we limit our consideration to the stipulation that the respondents should have the exclusive right to sell sweets in the theatre. This positive stipulation imports the negative that no other person should be allowed the right of selling sweets in the theatre. ...

<294> ... it is contrary to all equitable principles to enforce part of an agreement and leave the parties without any remedy whatever as to all other obligations of that agreement. It would result substantially in very different legal obligations, and great injustice to both parties. In the present case the respondents would have no redress if the appellant refused to allow them to sell sweets in the theatre, and the appellant could not recover the charges payable in respect of the sweet rights or have any redress if the respondents violated its directions as to the dress, deportment and behaviour of their employees. Indeed, I dissent entirely from the notion that this agreement can be divided into two parts, one enforceable and the other wholly unenforceable. Consequently, in my opinion, a Court of equity would, in the case before us, have had no jurisdiction or authority whatever to enforce the stipulation giving the respondents the exclusive right of selling sweets in the theatre by restraining the appellant from permitting or allowing any other person to sell them. ...

Dixon J [at 297]: It must be remembered that, although the remedy of specific performance is commonly applied in aid of a legal right, it extends to cases where, for one reason or another, there is no remedy at law, as well as to cases where the remedy at law is inadequate. ... But it is evident from a mere statement of the nature of the agreement in this case that it falls outside the scope of the remedy of specific performance. The parties meant their oral contract to be a final expression of obligation for the regulation of their future relations. It was not an agreement preliminary to a further transaction which, when carried out, should define their relative positions. ... Specific performance, in the proper sense, is a remedy to compel the execution *in specie* of a contract which requires some definite thing to be done before the transaction is complete and the parties rights are settled and defined in the manner intended. Moreover, the remedy is not available unless complete relief can be given, and the contract carried into full and final execution so that the parties are put in the relation contemplated by their agreement. Specific performance is inapplicable when the [298] continued supervision of the Court is necessary in order to ensure the fulfilment of the contract. It is not a form of relief which can be granted if the contract involves the performance by one party of services to the other or requires their continual co-operation. … In the present case the condition of the contract which entitles the plaintiffs and their servants to admission for the purpose of selling confectionery in the theatre is concurrent with the conditions governing the time, place and manner of supply, the character of the goods supplied, and the appearance, dress and behaviour of their servants. It would be contrary to principle to bind the Company by a decree to perform its obligations leaving it only a remedy sounding in damages in the event of a breach by the plaintiffs of the conditions to be observed by them. It would be equally contrary to principle for the Court to undertake the supervision of the specific fulfilment of these conditions. It, therefore, could not be contended that a decree of specific performance might be made, ….

[Duffy CJ agreed with Dixon J. In separate judgments Evatt and McTiernan JJ agreed the appeal should be allowed.]

Appeal allowed

Co-Operative Insurance Society Ltd v Argyll Stores (Holdings) Ltd

[1998] AC 1, House of Lords

[The plaintiffs granted a lease to the defendants of a unit in its shopping centre for a term of 35 years. The lease imposed an obligation on the defendants to keep the premises (containing a Safeway supermarket) open during the usual hours of business. This was important to the plaintiffs as the supermarket was the largest store in the centre and of commercial benefit to the other tenants. Almost 16 years later the defendants decided to close their Safeway supermarket which was the subject of the lease, and did so despite the plaintiff's protests. The plaintiffs sought, *inter alia*, specific performance of the contract. The trial judge granted damages but refused specific performance. The plaintiffs succeeded on appeal to the Court of Appeal which granted specific performance. The defendants appealed. There was no question that the defendants had breached their lease obligations; the only issue was whether an award of specific performance was appropriate.]

Lord Hoffmann [at 11]: The principles upon which English judges exercise the discretion to grant specific performance are reasonably well settled …

<12> The practice of not ordering a defendant to carry on a business is not entirely dependent upon damages being an adequate remedy. …

The most frequent reason given in the cases for declining to order someone to carry on a business is that it would require constant supervision by the court. …

There has, I think, been some misunderstanding about what is meant by continued superintendence. It may at first sight suggest that the judge (or some other officer of the court) would literally have to supervise the execution of the order. ... It is the possibility of the court having to give an indefinite series of ... rulings in order to ensure the execution of the order which has been regarded as undesirable.

Why should this be so? A principal reason is that ... the only means available to the court to enforce its order is the quasi-criminal procedure of punishment for contempt. This is a powerful weapon; so powerful, in fact, as often to be unsuitable as an instrument for adjudicating upon the disputes which may arise over whether a business is being run in accordance with the terms of the court's order. The heavy-handed nature of the enforcement mechanism is a consideration which may go to the exercise of the court's discretion in other cases as well, but its use to compel the running of a business is perhaps the paradigm case of its disadvantages and it is in this context that I shall discuss them.

<13> The prospect of committal or even a fine, with the damage to commercial reputation which will be caused by a finding of contempt of court, is likely to have at least two undesirable consequences. First, the defendant, who *ex hypothesi* did not think that it was in his economic interest to run the business at all, now has to make decisions under a sword of Damocles which may descend if the way the business is run does not conform to the terms of the order. This is, as one might say, no way to run a business. In this case the Court of Appeal made light of the point because it assumed that, once the defendant had been ordered to run the business, self-interest and compliance with the order would thereafter go hand in hand. But, as I shall explain, this is not necessarily true.

Secondly, the seriousness of a finding of contempt for the defendant means that any application to enforce the order is likely to be a heavy and expensive piece of litigation. The possibility of repeated applications over a period of time means that, in comparison with a once-and-for-all inquiry as to damages, the enforcement of the remedy is likely to be expensive in terms of cost to the parties and the resources of the judicial system. ...

<15> There is a further objection to an order requiring the defendant to carry on a business, ... This is that it may cause injustice by allowing the plaintiff to enrich himself at the defendant's expense. The loss which the defendant may suffer through having to comply with the order (for example, by running a business at a loss for an indefinite period) may be far greater than the plaintiff would suffer from the contract being broken. ...

It is true that the defendant has, by his own breach of contract, put himself in such an unfortunate position. But the purpose of the law of contract is not to punish wrongdoing but to satisfy the expectations of the party entitled to performance. A remedy which enables him to secure, in money terms, more than the performance due to him is unjust. From a wider perspective, it cannot be in the public interest for the courts to require someone to carry on business at a loss if there is any plausible alternative by which the other party can be given compensation. It is not <16> only a waste of resources but yokes the parties together in a continuing hostile relationship. The order for specific performance prolongs the battle. If the defendant is ordered to run a business, its conduct becomes the subject of a flow of complaints, solicitors' letters and affidavits. This is wasteful for both parties and the legal system. An award of damages, on the other hand, brings the litigation to an end. The defendant pays damages, the forensic link between them is severed, they go their separate ways and the wounds of conflict can heal.

The cumulative effect of these various reasons, none of which would necessarily be sufficient on its own, seems to me to show that the settled practice is based upon sound sense. Of course the grant or refusal of specific performance remains a matter for the judge's discretion. There are no binding rules, but this does not mean that there cannot be settled principles, founded upon practical considerations of the kind which I have discussed, which do not have to be re-examined in every case, but which the courts will apply in all but exceptional circumstances. ...

[In this case there was no flaw in the trial judge's reasoning refusing an order of specific performance and that decision should be restored.]

[Lord Browne-Wilkinson, Lord Slynn of Hedley, Lord Hope of Craighead and Lord Clyde all agreed with Lord Hoffman.]

Appeal allowed

[footnotes omitted]

INTERNATIONAL PERSPECTIVES

India

The *Indian Contract Act, 1872* does not make provision for an award of specific performance. However, the *Specific Relief Act 1963* does permit this form of relief and provides, in some detail, the circumstances in which specific performance will or will not be available to a plaintiff. Those circumstances are substantially the same as those under Australian common law. In particular, a key requirement before specific performance will be available is that damages are unable to be calculated or would not provide adequate compensation in the circumstances of the case.[17] Land contracts are presumed not to be capable of adequate compensation through damages.

Specific Relief Act 1963

Section 10. Cases in which specific performance of contract enforceable

Except as otherwise provided in this Chapter, the specific performance of any contract may, in the discretion of the court, be enforced—

(a) when there exists no standard for ascertaining the actual damage caused by the non-performance of the act agreed to be done; or

---

17   See *MS Madhusoodhanan v Kerala Kaumudi P Ltd* (2004) 9 SCC 204.

(b) when the act agreed to be done is such that compensation in money for its non-performance would not afford adequate relief.

Explanation—Unless and until the contrary is proved, the court shall presume—

(i) that the breach of a contract to transfer immovable property cannot be adequately relieved by compensation in money; and
(ii) that the breach of a contract to transfer movable property can be so relieved except in the following cases:—
   (a) where the property is not an ordinary article of commerce, or is of special value or interest to the plaintiff, or consists of goods which are not easily obtainable in the market;
   (b) where the property is held by the defendant as the agent or trustee of the plaintiff.

Section 12. Specific performance of part of contract

(1) Except as otherwise hereinafter provided in this section, the court shall not direct the specific performance of a part of a contract.
(2) Where a party to a contract is unable to perform the whole of his part of it, but the part which must be left unperformed bears only a small proportion to the whole in value and admits of compensation in money, the court may, at the suit of either party, direct the specific performance of so much of the contract as can be performed, and award compensation in money for the deficiency.

The remaining parts of s 12 set out a variety of other circumstances in which specific performance of part of a contract may be available.

As is the case under Australian common law, the *Specific Relief Act 1963* provides for certain circumstances in which specific performance will not be available, including for contracts requiring continued supervision of the courts.

Section 14. Contracts not specifically enforceable

(1) The following contracts cannot be specifically enforced, namely:—
   (a) a contract for the non-performance of which compensation in money is an adequate relief;
   (b) a contract which runs into such minute or numerous details or which is so dependent on the personal qualifications or volition of the parties, or otherwise from its nature is such, that the court cannot enforce specific performance of its material terms;
   (c) a contract which is in its nature determinable;
   (d) a contract the performance of which involves the performance of a continuous duty which the court cannot supervise.

Sub-section 3 sets out a number of cases in which specific performance may, despite the provisions of sub-section 1, still be enforced, including where the claim is for enforcement of a contract for construction of a building or any other work on land, provided terms are sufficiently precise.

Specific performance is available to any party to a contract or representative of a party provided that, where personal skills are involved, the contractual interest in specific performance is not assigned (unless that personal performance has already occurred) (s 15). The Act also sets out special cases in which other persons may have a right to claim specific performance (s 15).

Section 16. Personal bars to relief

Specific performance of a contract cannot be enforced in favour of a person—

(a) who would not be entitled to recover compensation for its breach; or
(b) who has become incapable of performing, or violates any essential term of, the contract that on his part remains to be performed, or acts in fraud of the contract, or wilfully acts at variance with, or in subversion of, the relation intended to be established by the contract; or
(c) who fails to aver and prove that he has performed or has always been ready and willing to perform the essential terms of the contract which are to be performed by him, other than terms the performance of which has been prevented or waived by the defendant.

Section 17. Contract to sell or let property by one who has no title, not specifically enforceable

(1) A contract to sell or let any immovable property cannot be specifically enforced in favour of a vendor or lessor—
   (a) who, knowing himself not to have any title to the property, has contracted to sell or let the property;
   (b) who, though he entered into the contract believing that he had a good title to the property, cannot at the time fixed by the parties or by the court for the completion of the sale or letting, give the purchaser or lessee a title free from reasonable doubt.
(2) The provisions of sub-section (1) shall also apply, as far as may be, to contracts for the sale or hire of movable property.

The *Specific Relief Act 1963* also makes clear that a court's decision to award specific performance is discretionary in nature. Issues of fairness may be considered by the courts.

Section 20. Discretion as to decreeing specific performance

(1) The jurisdiction to decree specific performance is discretionary, and the court is not bound to grant such relief merely because it is lawful to do so; but the discretion of the court is not arbitrary but sound and reasonable, guided by judicial principles and capable of correction by a court of appeal.

(2) The following are cases in which the court may properly exercise discretion not to decree specific performance—
   (a) where the terms of the contract or the conduct of the parties at the time of entering into the contract or the other circumstances under which the contract was entered into are such that the contract, though not voidable, gives the plaintiff an unfair advantage over the defendant; or
   (b) where the performance of the contract would involve some hardship on the defendant which he did not foresee, whereas its non-performance would involve no such hardship on the plaintiff;
   (c) where the defendant entered into the contract under circumstances which though not rendering the contract voidable, makes it inequitable to enforce specific performance.

Explanation

(1) Mere inadequacy of consideration, or the mere fact that the contract is onerous to the defendant or improvident in its nature, shall not be deemed to constitute an unfair advantage within the meaning of clause (a) or hardship within the meaning of clause (b).
(2) The question whether the performance of a contract would involve hardship on the defendant within the meaning of clause (b) shall, except in cases where the hardship has resulted from any act of the plaintiff subsequent to the contract, be determined with reference to the circumstances existing at the time of the contract.
(3) The court may properly exercise discretion to decree specific performance in any case where the plaintiff has done substantial acts or suffered losses in consequence of a contract capable of specific performance.
(4) The court shall not refuse to any party specific performance of a contract merely on the ground that the contract is not enforceable at the instance of the other party.

China

The *Contract Law of the People's Republic of China* provides that specific performance is available at the option of the non-breaching party unless such performance is impossible, or the cost of performing would be excessive or where specific performance has not been requested within a reasonable time. The *Law* also precludes specific performance where 'the obligation does not lend itself to enforcement by specific performance'.[18] While the *Law* does not set out the circumstances in which an obligation will not lend itself to specific enforcement, this is likely to cover similar contracts to those for which specific performance is routinely denied in Australia—such as, for example, contracts requiring the constant supervision of the courts.

---

18 Article 110.

> ### Contract Law of the People's Republic of China, 1999
>
> Article 107. Types of Liabilities for Breach
>
> If a party fails to perform its obligations under a contract, or rendered non-conforming performance, it shall bear the liabilities for breach of contract by specific performance, cure of non-conforming performance or payment of damages, etc.
>
> Article 109. Monetary Specific Performance
>
> If a party fails to pay the price or remuneration, the other party may require payment thereof.
>
> Article 110. Non-monetary Specific Performance; Exceptions
>
> Where a party fails to perform, or rendered non-conforming performance of, a non-monetary obligation, the other party may require performance, except where:
>
> (i) performance is impossible in law or in fact;
> (ii) the subject matter of the obligation does not lend itself to enforcement by specific performance or the cost of performance is excessive;
> (iii) the obligee does not require performance within a reasonable time.

4 Injunctions

An injunction is ordinarily sought where one contracting party wishes to restrain the other from committing a contractual breach (a *prohibitory* injunction) or to reverse a breach that has already occurred (a *mandatory* injunction). Frequently, injunctions are sought to prevent disclosure of confidential information or to enforce a legal restraint of trade clause.

Lumley v Wagner

[1852] All ER Rep 368, Lord Chancellor's Court

[By contract, Wagner (the defendant) agreed to sing at Lumley's (the plaintiff's) theatre for a certain number of nights each week for a period of three months. Wagner was offered another singing engagement for a larger sum which would have required her to abandon the agreement with the Lumley. Lumley sought an injunction to prevent Wagner singing elsewhere during the time of their contract. Lumley succeeded at trial and Wagner appealed.]

Lord St Leonards LC [at 371]: As I understand the points taken by the defendants' counsel in support of this appeal they in effect come to this, namely, that a court of equity ought not to grant an injunction except in cases connected with specific performance, or where the injunction, being to compel a party to forbear from committing an act (and not to perform an act) that injunction will complete the whole of the agreement remaining unexecuted.

... <372> ... At an early stage of the argument I adverted to the familiar cases of attorneys' clerks, and surgeons' and apothecaries' apprentices, and the like, in which this court has constantly interfered, simply to prevent the violation of negative covenants, but it was said that in such cases the court only acted on the principle that the clerk or apprentice had received all the benefit and that the prohibition operated upon a concluded contract, and, therefore, the injunction fell within one of the exceptional cases. I do not, however, apprehend that the jurisdiction of the court depends upon any such principle. ... <373> ...

The present is a mixed case, consisting not of two correlative acts to be done, one by the plaintiff and the other by the defendants, which state of facts may have and in some cases has introduced a very important difference, but of an act to be done by Johanna Wagner alone, to which is superadded a negative stipulation on her part to abstain from the commission of any act which will break in upon her affirmative covenant—the one being ancillary to, and concurrent and operating together with the other. The agreement to sing for the plaintiff during three months at his theatre, and during that time not to sing for anybody else, is not a correlative contract. It is, in effect, one contract, and though beyond all doubt this court could not interfere to enforce the specific performance of the whole of this contract, yet in all sound construction and according to the true spirit of the agreement, the engagement to perform for three months at one theatre must necessarily exclude the right to perform at the same time at another theatre. It was clearly intended that Johanna Wagner was to exert her vocal abilities to the utmost to aid the theatre to which she agreed to attach herself. I am of opinion that if she had attempted, even in the absence of any negative stipulation, to perform at another theatre, she would have broken the spirit and true meaning of the contract as much as she would now do with reference to the contract into which she has actually entered. Wherever this court has not proper jurisdiction to enforce specific performance, it operates to bind men's consciences, as far as they can be bound, to a true and literal performance of their agreements, and it will not suffer them to depart from their contracts at their pleasure, leaving the party with whom they have contracted to the mere chance of any damages which a jury may give. ...

It was objected that the operation of the injunction in the present case was mischievous, excluding the defendant Johanna Wagner from performing at any other theatre while this court had no power to compel her to perform at Her Majesty's Theatre. It is true that I have not the means of compelling her to sing, but she has no cause of complaint if I compel her to abstain from the commission of an act which she has bound herself not to do, and thus possibly cause her to fulfil her engagement. The jurisdiction which I now exercise is wholly within the power of the court, and, being of opinion that it is a proper case for interfering, I shall leave nothing unsatisfied by the judgment I pronounce. ... <374> ... The injunction may also, as I have said, tend to the fulfilment of her engagement, though, in continuing the injunction, I disclaim doing indirectly what I cannot do directly. ...

Motion refused

Warner Bros v Nelson

[1937] 1 KB 209, Court of King's Bench

[The defendant, Nelson (Bette Davis), entered into a contract with the plaintiff, Warner Bros, for a period of one year, pursuant to which she agreed to render her services exclusively to the plaintiffs and would not, during the time of the contract, render her services elsewhere. In breach of this agreement the defendant entered into a contract to make a film with a third party. The plaintiff sought an injunction to restrain the defendant from making the film with the third party.]

Branson J [at 213]: In June of this year the defendant, for no discoverable reason except that she wanted more money, declined to be further bound by the agreement, left the United States and, in September, entered into an agreement in this country with a third person. This was a breach of contract on her part, … <214> it was contended [for the defendant] that no injunction could as a matter of law be granted in the circumstances of the case. …

I turn then to the consideration of the law applicable to this case on the basis that the contract is a valid and enforceable one. It is conceded that our Courts will not enforce a positive covenant of personal service; and specific performance of the positive covenants by the defendant to serve the plaintiffs is not asked in the present case. The practice of the Court of Chancery in relation to the enforcement of negative covenants is stated on the highest authority by Lord Cairns in the House of Lords in *Doherty v Allman*. His Lordship says: 'My Lords, if there had been a negative covenant, I apprehend, according to well settled practice, a <215> Court of Equity would have had no discretion to exercise. If parties, for valuable consideration, with their eyes open, contract that a particular thing shall not be done, all that a Court of Equity has to do is to say, by way of injunction, that which the parties have already said by way of covenant, that the thing shall not be done; and in such case the injunction does nothing more than give the sanction of the process of the Court to that which already is the contract between the parties. It is not then a question of the balance of convenience or inconvenience, or of the amount of damage or of injury—it is the specific performance, by the Court, of that negative bargain which the parties have made, with their eyes open, between themselves.' …

The defendant, having broken her positive undertakings in the contract without any cause or excuse … <216> … contends that she cannot be enjoined from breaking the negative covenants also. The mere fact that a covenant which the Court would not enforce, if expressed in positive form, is expressed in the negative instead, will not induce the Court to enforce it. … The Court will attend to the substance and not to the form of the covenant. Nor will the Court, true to the principle that specific performance of a contract of personal service will never be ordered, grant an injunction in the case of such a contract to enforce negative covenants if the effect of so doing would be to drive the defendant either to starvation or to specific performance of the positive covenants: …

<217> The conclusion to be drawn from the authorities is that, where a contract of personal service contains negative covenants the enforcement of which will not amount either to a decree of specific performance of the positive covenants of the contract or to the giving of a decree under which the defendant must either remain idle or perform those positive covenants, the Court will enforce those negative covenants; but this is subject to a further consideration. An injunction is a discretionary remedy, and the Court in granting it may limit it to what the Court considers reasonable in all the circumstances of the case.

... <219> ... The case before me is ... one in which it would be proper to grant an injunction unless to do so would in the circumstances be tantamount to ordering the defendant to perform her contract or remain idle or unless damages would be the more appropriate remedy.

With regard to the first of these considerations, it would, of course, be impossible to grant an injunction covering all the negative covenants in the contract. That would, indeed, force the defendant to perform her contract or remain idle; but this objection is removed by the restricted form in which the injunction is sought. It is confined to forbidding the defendant, without the consent of the plaintiffs, to render any services for or in any motion picture or stage production for any one other than the plaintiffs.

It was also urged that the difference between what the defendant can earn as a film artiste and what she might expect to earn by any other form of activity is so great that she will in effect be driven to perform her contract. That is not the criterion adopted in any of the decided cases. The defendant is stated to be a person of intelligence, capacity and means, and no evidence was adduced to show that, if enjoined from doing the specified acts otherwise than for the plaintiffs, she will not be able to employ herself both usefully and remuneratively in other spheres of activity, though not as remuneratively as in her special line. She will not be driven, although she may be tempted, to perform the contract, and the fact that she may be so tempted is no objection to the <220> grant of an injunction. ...

With regard to the question whether damages is not the more appropriate remedy, I have the uncontradicted evidence of the plaintiffs as to the difficulty of estimating the damages which they may suffer from the breach by the defendant of her contract. I think it is not inappropriate to refer to the fact that, in the contract between the parties ... there is a formal admission by the defendant that her services, being 'of a special, unique, extraordinary and intellectual character' gives them a particular value 'the loss of which cannot be reasonably or adequately compensated in damages' and that a breach may 'cost the producer great and irreparable injury and damage,' and the artiste expressly agrees that the producer shall be entitled to the remedy of <221> injunction. Of course, parties cannot contract themselves out of the law; but it assists, at all events, on the question of evidence as to the applicability of an injunction in the present case, to find the parties formally recognizing that in cases of this kind injunction is a more appropriate remedy than damages.

I think that ... an injunction should be granted in regard to the specified services.

Then comes the question as to the period for which the injunction should operate. ... the Court should make the period such as to give reasonable protection and no more to the plaintiffs against the ill effects to them of the defendant's breach of contract. ... The main difficulty that the plaintiffs apprehend is that the defendant might appear in other films whilst the films already made by them and not yet shown are in the market for sale or <222> hire and thus depreciate their value. I think that if the injunction is in force during the continuance of the contract or for three years from now, whichever period is the shorter, that will substantially meet the case. ...

Injunction granted

[footnotes omitted]

The same considerations as those that apply in determining whether the court should exercise its discretion to order specific performance apply in determining whether discretion should be exercised to grant an injunction. In particular, a key factor in determining whether an injunction should be ordered will be whether or not damages would provide an adequate remedy.

Dickson Property Management Services Pty Ltd v Centro Property Management (Vic) Pty Ltd

(2000) 180 ALR 485, Federal Court of Australia

[In November 1999, Dickson (the applicant) agreed to provide cleaning services for Box Hill Central Shopping Centre for three years. The contract permitted the owner of the centre (Centro Management), in its discretion, to terminate the contract by giving 90 days notice. In July 2000 Centro Property Management (the respondent), which had taken over ownership of the Centre, gave Dickson notice that it was exercising this right. Dickson sought an interlocutory injunction to restrain Centro Property from terminating the contract, arguing that Centro Management had not acted in good faith in exercising its discretion to terminate the contract.]

Ryan J [at 487[12]]: ... I have come to the clear view that it would not be an appropriate exercise of the court's discretion to grant the interlocutory injunction which the applicant seeks. That reflects principally my conviction that damages will be an adequate remedy if Dickson Property makes out its entitlement to relief either in contract or under s 51AA of the *Trade Practices Act*. The measure of those damages will be the remuneration which Dickson Property would have derived had the cleaning contract run its full term less the costs which it would have incurred in performing the contract over that term.

[13] There is in the evidence nothing to suggest that Centro could not satisfy an award of damages measured in that way. I am not unaware that Dickson Property will be required, if an injunction is refused, to mitigate those damages by making redundant or otherwise redeploying the employees presently engaged at the shopping centre. Nor am I without sympathy for the prospects of unemployment

which will be visited on those employees. I also realise that Dickson Property will be required to relieve itself, as far as it can, of its liability under leases of centre-specific equipment. However, all of those considerations will be matters of mitigation on which Centro will bear the onus at trial. Cash-flow implications for Dickson Property can, I consider, be ameliorated, if it succeeds in the event, by having an early trial ...

[15] A related consideration is that, if the court by injunction keeps the cleaning contract on foot, it can only do so on the basis that it is conditional on Dickson Property's maintaining a satisfactory standard of cleaning. That, I think, has the <488> potential to involve the court, to an unacceptable extent, in supervising the performance of a detailed contract equivalent to a contract for personal services by a party, in whom the other part asserts, not totally unbelievably, that it has lost confidence. ...

Application for interlocutory injunction dismissed

Hill v C A Parsons & Co Ltd

[1971] 3 All ER 1345, [1971] 3 WLR 995, [1972] 1 Ch 305, English Court of Appeal

[The Draughtsmen's and Allied Technicians Association (DATA), a trade union, extracted an agreement from CA Parsons & Co Ltd (the respondents) that it would employ only members of its union. Pursuant to the agreement Hill (and others) were sent notice of a change in employment conditions which required them to become members of DATA. Hill and the others did not join DATA and they subsequently received notice that their employment was being terminated on the basis of a failure to comply with this new condition. Hill was a long serving employee of 35 years who was due to retire in two years. It was important to the value of his pension entitlements that his employment not be terminated. Hill sought an injunction to restrain the respondents from terminating his employment contract. The trial judge refused injunctive relief and Hill appealed.]

Lord Denning MR [at 1349]: ... the company seemed to think that they could change the conditions of Mr Hill's employment without his consent. They had no power to do any such thing. ... In the letter of 30th July 1971 the company purported to terminate Mr Hill's employment by giving one month's notice. They had no power to do any such thing. ...

Then comes the important question: what is the effect of an invalid notice to terminate? ...

... *In the ordinary course of things* [a] servant cannot claim specific performance of the contract of employment. ... He is <1350> left to his remedy in damages against the master for breach of the contract ...

I would emphasise, however, that that is the consequence in the ordinary course of things. The rule is not inflexible. It permits of exceptions. The court can in a proper case grant a declaration that the relationship still subsists and an injunction to stop the master treating it as at an end. ...

<1351> [In this case] it is of the utmost importance to Mr Hill and the other 37 that the notices given to them should not be held to terminate their employment. Damages would not be at all an adequate remedy. If ever there was a case where an injunction should be granted against the employers, this is the case. It is quite plain that the employers have done wrong. I know that the employers have been under pressure from a powerful trade union. That may explain their conduct, but it does not excuse it. ... They cannot be allowed to break the law in this way. It is, to my mind, a clear case for an injunction. ...

[Sachs LJ agreed that the appeal should be allowed and the injunction granted. Stamp LJ dissented.]

Appeal allowed

INTERNATIONAL PERSPECTIVES

India

The *Indian Contract Act, 1872* does not make provision for injunctive relief. However, the *Specific Relief Act 1963* does permit this form of relief at the discretion of the court.

Specific Relief Act 1963

Section 36. Preventive relief how granted

Preventive relief is granted at the discretion of the court by injunction, temporary or perpetual.

Section 37. Temporary and perpetual injunctions

(1) Temporary injunctions are such as are to continue until a specified time, or until the further order of the court, and they may be granted at any stage of a suit, ...
(2) A perpetual injunction can only be granted by the decree made at the hearing and upon the merits of the suit; the defendant is thereby perpetually enjoined from the assertion of a right, or from the commission of an act, which would be contrary to the rights of the plaintiff.

Section 38. Perpetual injunction when granted

(1) Subject to the other provisions ... a perpetual injunction may be granted to the plaintiff to prevent the breach of an obligation existing in his favour, whether expressly or by implication.
(2) When any such obligation arises from contract, the court shall be guided by the rules and provisions contained in Chapter II.
(3) When the defendant invades or threatens to invade the plaintiff's right to, or enjoyment of, property, the court may grant a perpetual injunction in the following cases, namely:—

(a) where the defendant is trustee of the property for the plaintiff;
(b) where there exists no standard for ascertaining the actual damage caused, or likely to be caused, by the invasion;
(c) where the invasion is such that compensation in money would not afford adequate relief;
(d) where the injunction is necessary to prevent a multiplicity of judicial proceedings.

Section 39. Mandatory injunctions

When, to prevent the breach of an obligation, it is necessary to compel the performance of certain acts which the court is capable of enforcing, the court may in its discretion grant an injunction to prevent the breach complained of, and also to compel performance of the requisite acts.

Section 41. Injunction when refused

An injunction cannot be granted—

(a) to restrain any person from prosecuting a judicial proceeding pending at the institution of the suit in which the injunction is sought, unless such restraint is necessary to prevent a multiplicity of proceedings;
(b) to restrain any person from instituting or prosecuting any proceeding in a court not subordinate to that from which the injunction is sought;
(c) to restrain any person from applying to any legislative body;
(d) to restrain any person from instituting or prosecuting any proceeding in a criminal matter;
(e) to prevent the breach of a contract the performance of which would not be specifically enforced;
(f) to prevent, on the ground of nuisance, an act of which it is not reasonably clear that it will be a nuisance;
(g) to prevent a continuing breach in which the plaintiff has acquiesced;
(h) when equally efficacious relief can certainly be obtained by any other usual mode of proceeding except in case of breach of trust;
(i) when the conduct of the plaintiff or his agents has been such as to disentitle him to the assistance of the court;
(j) when the plaintiff has no personal interest in the matter.

Section 42. Injunction to perform negative agreement

Notwithstanding anything contained in clause (e) of section 41, where a contract comprises an affirmative agreement to do a certain act, coupled with a negative agreement, express or implied, not to do a certain act, the circumstance that the court is unable to compel specific performance of the affirmative agreement shall not preclude it from granting an injunction to perform the negative agreement:

Provided that the plaintiff has not failed to perform the contract so far as it is binding on him.

> ### China
>
> The *Contract Law of the People's Republic of China* does not provide directly for injunctive relief. However, Article 110, extracted above, would appear wide enough to allow the court to order specific performance of both positive and negative obligations.

5   Damages in lieu of equitable remedy

Damages may be awarded in lieu of, or in addition to, the equitable remedies of specific performance or an injunction. This may be of particular importance where a party fails to comply with an order for specific performance, where specific performance or an injunction is refused on discretionary grounds, such as lack of mutuality, where additional loss has been suffered by the non-breaching party or where damages are not available at law because, for example, there has been a failure to comply with statutory formalities.[19] The remedy of equitable damages stems from *Lord Cairns' Act 1858* (UK). This Act was passed to enable a party to claim damages from the Court of Chancery rather than having to bring a separate action in the common law courts. This legislation has been repealed, but the principles it established in relation to equitable damages remain. In particular, whenever a court has jurisdiction to entertain an equitable remedy of specific performance or injunction, damages in equity may be awarded in addition to or in substitution for those awards.[20] This is the position in equity and is also re-enforced by legislation in all Australian states except Queensland.[21]

> ### Supreme Court Act 1986 (Vic)
>
> #### Section 38. Damages in addition to or in place of other remedies
>
> If the Court has jurisdiction to entertain an application for an injunction or specific performance, it may award damages in addition to, or in substitution for, an injunction or specific performance.

As with other equitable remedies, the award of equitable damages is discretionary. The measure of damages will normally be the same as an award of damages would have been at common law. However, the courts have suggested that if to follow the common law rules would 'give rise to injustice' the measure of damages may be assessed differently.[22]

---

19   For example, s 126 *Instruments Act 1958* (Vic) requiring, *inter alia*, contracts for the sale of land to be evidenced in writing.
20   For further discussion of the *Lord Cairns' Act* see, for example, R Cunnington, 'Equitable Damages: A Model for Restitutionary Damages' (2001) 17 *Journal of Contract Law* 212 from 217.
21   *Supreme Court Act 1933* (ACT) ss 26–27; *Supreme Court Act 1970* (NSW) s 68; *Supreme Court Act* (NT) ss 62–63; *Supreme Court Act 1935* (SA) s 30; *Supreme Court Civil Procedure Act 1932* (Tas) s 11(13); *Supreme Court Act 1986* (Vic) s 38.
22   *Johnson v Agnew* [1980] AC 367 per Lord Wilberforce.

Johnson v Agnew

[1980] AC 367, House of Lords

[The respondent, Agnew, entered into a contract to sell a property, *Sheepcote Grange*, to the appellant, Johnson. The appellant subsequently refused to complete on the contract date of 6 December 1973. Additional time was granted by the respondent and the appellant still failed to complete. The respondent then obtained an order for specific performance which was entered in November 1974. The appellant still failed to perform. In August 1974 the respondent's mortgagee took possession of the property and sold it in April 1975. Consequently, from this date, specific performance became impossible. The respondent then sought to have the order for specific performance dissolved and damages awarded in its place.]

Lord Wilberforce [at 394]: ... if the order for specific performance is not complied with by the purchaser, the vendor may either apply to the court for enforcement of the order, or may apply to the court to dissolve the order and ask the court to put an end to the contract. ... It follows, indeed, automatically from the facts that the contract remains in force after the order for specific performance and that the purchaser has committed a breach of it of a repudiatory character which he has not remedied, or ... that he is refusing to complete.

... there only remains the question whether, if the vendor takes the latter course, ie of applying to the court to put an end to the contract, he is entitled to recover damages for breach of the contract. On principle one may ask 'Why ever not?' If, as is clear, the vendor is entitled (after and notwithstanding that an order for specific performance has been made) if the purchaser still does not complete the contract, to ask the court to permit him to accept the purchaser's repudiation and to declare the contract to be terminated, why, if the court accedes to this, should there not follow the ordinary consequences, undoubted under the general law of contract, that on such acceptance and termination the vendor may recover damages for breach of contract?

[His Lordship discussed and dismissed the arguments against an award of damages in these circumstances and continued (at 398)]: ... a party, who has chosen to seek specific performance, may quite well thereafter, if specific performance fails to be realised, say, 'Very well, then, the contract should be regarded as terminated.'
....

<399> Once the matter has been placed in the hands of a court of equity, or one exercising equity jurisdiction, the subsequent control of the matter will be exercised according to equitable principles. The court would not make an order dissolving the decree of specific performance and terminating the contract (with recovery of damages) if to do so would be unjust, in the circumstances then existing, to the other party, in this case to the purchaser. ... This is why there was, in the Court of Appeal, rightly, a relevant and substantial argument, repeated in this House, that the non-completion of the contract was due to the default of the vendors; if this had been made good, the court could properly have refused them

the relief sought. But the Court of Appeal came to the conclusion that this non-completion, and the ultimate impossibility of completion, was the fault of the purchaser. I agree with their conclusion. ...

It is now necessary to deal with questions relating to the measure of damages. The Court of Appeal, while denying the vendors' right to <400> damages at common law, granted damages under *Lord Cairns's Act*. Since on the view which I take, damages can be recovered at common law, two relevant questions now arise: (1) whether *Lord Cairns's Act* provides a different measure of damages from the common law? If so, the respondents would be in a position to claim the more favourable basis to them; and (2) if the measure of damages is the same, on what basis they should be calculated?

... it is clear that the jurisdiction to award damages in accordance with s 2 of *Lord Cairns's Act* (accepted by the House as surviving the repeal of the Act) may arise in some cases in which damages could not be recovered at common law; examples of this would be damages in lieu of a *quia timet* injunction and damages for breach of a restrictive covenant to which the defendant was not a party. To this extent the Act created a power to award damages which did not exist before at common law. But apart from these, and similar cases where damages could not be claimed at all at common law, there is sound authority for the proposition that the Act does not provide for the assessment of damages on any new basis. ...

... the purpose of the Act was to enable a court of equity to grant those damages which another court might give; ... I find in the Act no warrant for the court awarding damages differently from common law damages, but the question is left open on what date such damages, however awarded, ought to be assessed.

(2) The general principle for the assessment of damages is compensatory, ie that the innocent party is to be placed, so far as money can do so, in the same position as if the contract had been performed. Where the contract is one of sale, this principle normally leads to assessment of damages as at the date of the breach, ... <401> .... But this is not an absolute rule; if to follow it would give rise to injustice, the court has power to fix such other date as may be appropriate in the circumstances.

In cases where a breach of a contract for sale has occurred, and the innocent party reasonably continues to try to have the contract completed, it would to me appear more logical and just rather than tie him to the date of the original breach, to assess damages as at the date when (otherwise than by his default) the contract is lost. ...

In the present case if it is accepted, as I would accept, that the vendors acted reasonably in pursuing the remedy of specific performance, the date on which that remedy became aborted (not be the vendors' fault) should logically be fixed as the date on which damages should be assessed. Choice of this date would be in accordance both with common law principle, as indicated in the authorities ...

[Lord Salmon, Lord Fraser of Tullybelton, Lord Krith of Kinkel and Lord Scarman all agreed with the reasons of Lord Wilberforce.]

Appeal dismissed subject to variation of date for assessment of damages

INTERNATIONAL PERSPECTIVES

India

The *Specific Relief Act 1963* provides for a form of equitable damages in addition to or in substitution for specific performance or injunctive relief.

Specific Relief Act 1963

Section 21. Power to award compensation in certain cases

(1) In a suit for specific performance of a contract, the plaintiff may also claim compensation for its breach, either in addition to, or in substitution of, such performance.

Section 40. Damages in lieu of, or in addition to, injunction.

(1) The plaintiff in a suit for perpetual injunction under section 38, or mandatory injunction under section 39, may claim damages either in addition to, or in substitution for, such injunction and the court may, if it thinks fit, award such damages.

(2) No relief for damages shall be granted under this section unless the plaintiff has claimed such relief in his plaint:

Provided that where no such damages have been claimed in the plaint, the court shall, at any stage of the proceedings, allow the plaintiff to amend the plaint on such terms as may be just for including such claim.

(3) The dismissal of a suit to prevent the breach of an obligation existing in favour of the plaintiff shall bar his right to sue for damages for such breach.

China

The *Contract Law of the People's Republic of China* does not provide for damages as a substitute for specific performance.

6 Summary

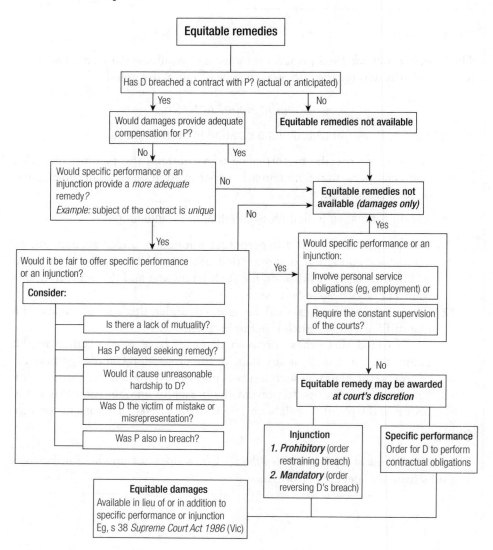

7 Questions

1. Sally entered into a contract with Regina to purchase an autographed first edition of Jane Austen's *Pride and Prejudice*. Sally has been a fan of Austen for as long as she can remember and was always on the lookout for Austen memorabilia. She was thrilled when she saw the book advertised and called Regina immediately to arrange an inspection.

   Satisfied with her inspection, Sally agreed to pay the asking price of $75,000 for the book. It was further agreed that payment and transfer of the book would occur in two weeks, enabling Sally to access the necessary funds for the purchase.

   Two weeks later Sally visited Regina with a bank cheque for $75,000, as agreed. She was surprised and disappointed when Regina refused to accept the cheque and hand over the book. Regina was very apologetic, claiming that she had only agreed to the sale because she was desperate for money. However, since agreeing to the sale, Regina had won Tattslotto and no longer needed to sell the book in order to pay her bills. Sally objected, demanding that Regina hand over the book. Regina refused and Sally had no choice but to leave without the book.

   Sally has now come to you for advice. She tells you that she will not be satisfied with anything short of obtaining the book. Please advise Sally whether Regina can be compelled to hand over the book.

2. Clyde entered into a contract with Rhys, pursuant to which Clyde agreed to train Rhys' racehorse, on a weekly basis, in exchange for a fee. The contract was stipulated to run for one year, with an option for renewal.

   After six months Clyde informed Rhys that he no longer wished to train Rhys' racehorse. He told Rhys that his horse would never be a successful racer and that he'd been offered a more lucrative job training a much more promising horse. Rhys asked him to reconsider, but Clyde would hear nothing of it, telling Clyde that his mind was made up.

   Clyde has come to you for advice. He tells you that Clyde was the best trainer in the state and was the only trainer that had a relationship with his star racehorse. As a result, he claims, his prospects of success in this year's race season without Clyde are greatly diminished. He wants to know if there is any way he can force Clyde to continue training his horse or, at the very least, if Clyde can be stopped from training another horse, which is likely to compete with his own in the forthcoming race season. Please advise Clyde.

Index

acceptance
   communication 59–75
   conduct, by 52–3
   definition 50
   entitlement to accept 52
   international perspectives 28–30, 58–9, 71–5
   intervening correspondence 53–9
   mode specified by offeror 68–9
ad idem, *see* consensus *ad idem*
administration of justice, contracts prejudicial to 509–13
advertisements
   bait 37–40
   offers in 36–7
agency, privity and 235
agreement
   contractual nature 26–8
   Indian law 28
   international perspectives 27–8
   joking 26
   offer and acceptance 28–30
   summary chart 84
   voluntariness 26
   without offer and acceptance 75–8
   see also consensus *ad idem*; intention to create contractual relations relations
agreements
   to agree or negotiate 97–101
   illusory 88–91
   to negotiate in good faith 101
ambiguity, *see* uncertainty
American contract law
anticipatory breach 584–7
auctions 33–6
Australian contract law, *see* contract law
avoidance of contract, *see* capacity; duress; illegality; misleading or deceptive conduct; mistake; public policy, illegal contracts and; unconscionable conduct; undue influence; unfair terms

Bain v Fothergill rule 681
bankruptcy
   breach of covenant, not constituting 579
   capacity and 177
bilateral contracts 78–83
breach of contract
   anticipatory 584–7
   both parties, specific performance and 708
   debt recovery 694
   effect of 573
   miscellaneous common law remedies 694–8
   remoteness of damage 663–7
   repudiatory 580–4
   restitutionary damages for 690–4
   retention of deposits paid deposit, retention for breach 694–6
   serious 587–93
   termination clauses 694

capacity
   bankrupts 177
   Crown 177–8
   international perspectives 170–1, 174
   intoxication and 175–6
   mental incapacity 171–4
   minors 171–85
case law 7–8
causation, of damage 661–2
certainty, summary chart 112
Chinese contract law
   acceptance 58–9
   capacity 170–1
   common mistake 383–4
   communication of acceptance 71–5

• 737

Chinese contract law (cont.)
  consideration   115
  exclusion clauses   312–13
  illegal contracts   506–7, 532
  intention to create legal relations   165
  mutual mistake   385
  nature and duration of offers   47–9
  nature of an agreement   27–8
  nature of contract law   20–1
  non est factum   399
  offer and acceptance   29–30
  performance   543–4
  public policy illegality   522, 524
  unconscionable dealings   441
  undue influence   431–2
  unfair terms   491–3
  unilateral mistake   394–5
claims, forgone, as consideration   141–3
classification of terms
  conditions   286–9
  importance   286–93
  intermediate terms   289
  nature of operation   286
  nature of term   285
  warranties   289
coercion, *see* duress
collateral contracts   246–50
common law
  duress, summary chart   421
  frustration   639–42
  illegality   507–24
  remedies   694–8
  see also damages
companies
  capacity   186–7
  misleading or deceptive conduct   323
  pre-incorporation contracts   186–7
compensation, *see* damages
  equitable remedies, specific
    performance   219–26, 702–22
compensatory damages   654
conditional contracts   104–11
conditions, *see* terms
conduct, *see* duress; illegality;
  unconscionable conduct; misleading
  or deceptive conduct; public
  policy, illegal contracts and;
  undue influence; unfair terms;
  remedies
consensus ad idem
  insufficient by itself   153
  necessary   13, 26, 27, 52, 386–8

consideration
  anything stipulated by promisor   122–4
  claim forgone as   141–3
  contemporaneity   126–8
  contractual duty
    owed to promisor   130–5
    owed to third party   135–6
  debt part-paid as   139–41
  definitions   116, 121, 353
  doctrine of   116–21, 145–6
  enforcement and   176
  existing duty as   130–9
  international perspectives   115–16,
    143–5
  moving from promisee   128–9
  nature of   122–45
  need not pass to promisor   128–9
  privity of contract and   218
  public duty as   137–9
  real, of value   124–6
  rule in *Pinnel's Case*   139, 141
  specific performance and   708
  summary chart   150
construction
  aids to   284–5
  basic rule   276–7
  exclusion clauses   300–10
  parol evidence exceptions   279–84
  parol evidence rule   277–9
consumer contracts   194–5
  definition   482
  formalities   194–5
  regulation   7, 240–1, 271–4, 310–13,
    479–80
  standard form   482–3
  trade or commerce, in   324–5
  unfair terms, in   481–2
contract
  definitions   3–4, 28, 51, 122, 144,
    145, 166
  law of, terminology   9
  summary chart   22
contract law
  China, *see* Chinese contract law
  importance   2–6
  India, *see* Indian contract law
  introduction   1
  judge-made   7–8
  nature of   7–9
  relationship with other branches   9
contract theory   4–18
  bargain theory   14

miscellaneous theories   17–18
promise theory   14–15
reasonable expectations theory   15–16
reliance theory   16–17
will theory   12–13
contracts
   bilateral and unilateral   78–83
   conditional   104–11
   formation, *see* formation of contracts
   void/voidable distinction   316
contracts of employment, beneficial   180
contracts of guarantee   193–4
contracts of personal service   714
contractual efficacy, terms for   265–8
contractual obligations
   nature of   8–9
   see also contract theory
contractual relations, *see* intention to create contractual relations
contributory negligence, damages and   685–6
corporations, *see* companies
correspondence, between offer and acceptance   53–9
corruption in public life, contracts promoting   513
counter-offers
   acceptance as   52
   intervening correspondence   53–9
   offer/acceptance analysis, limitations   76
   rejection by offeree as   45–6
   see also offers
course of dealing, terms in   259–61
Crown, capacity of   177–8
custom, terms implied by   269–71
Cutter v Powell rule   548–9

damage
   causation and   661–2
   remoteness of   663–7
damages
   assessment of   681–6
   compensatory   654
   contributory negligence and   685–6
   cost of repairs   676–80
   date for assessing   681–2
   defendant's profit not recoverable   657
   difficulty of assessment   657
   in lieu of equitable remedy   730–3
   international perspectives   655, 660–1, 666–7
   liquidated (agreed)   687–9
   loss of chance   669–73

loss of use of money   681
loss requirement   655–61
losses by a third party   657–9
mental distress   667–9
misleading or deceptive conduct   344–53
misrepresentation, for   358–9
mitigation of loss   682–5
other common law remedies   694–8
plaintiff's loss recoverable   657
privity and   221–6
restitutionary   654
rule in Hadley v Baxendale   663–6
rule in *Potts v Miller*   352
summary charts   698, 699
types of loss recognised   667–81, 689–90
wasted expenditure (reliance damages)   673–6
damages and liquidated claims, summary chart   698, 699
death
   offeror or offeree   46, 129
   performance rendered impossible by   631
debt
   liquidated, summary chart   698
   part payment, as consideration   139–41
   recovery, after breach   694
   unliquidated   141
deeds, *see* formalities; land
defrauding the revenue   514
diagrams, *see* summary charts
discharge
   agreement to discharge
      consequences of   570
      international perspectives   569–70
      summary chart   571
      termination by separate agreement   564–7
      termination provisions   567–70
   breach, consequent upon
      anticipatory breach   584–7
      consequences of   602–13
      contractual provisions   574–9
      contractual restrictions and   600
      effect of breach in practice, 590–30
      effect on payments made or due   605–11
      election to discharge   594–602
      fair conduct and   598–600
      general effect   602–5
      guilty party's co-operation and   600
      in futuro   573
      international perspectives   612–13

discharge (*cont.*)
    limitations on election right 598–602
    nature of election requirement 594–8
    recovery under quantum meruit 612
    relief against forfeiture 611–12
    repudiatory breach 580–4
    situations permitting 574–93
    statutory restrictions and 600–2
    summary chart 614
    terminology 590–1
  frustration, consequent upon
    absolute obligations 617–18
    changes in law 632
    common law 639–42
    consequences of frustration 639–45
    current position in Australia 622–7
    destruction of something essential 628
    doctrine 617
    events causing delay 631–2
    events increasing expense of performance 631–2
    events that qualify 627–32
    foundation for the modern doctrine 618–19
    frustrating event caused by a party 635–6
    impossibility of performance 630–1
    international perspectives 645–7
    leases and 637–9
    non-occurrence of essential event 628–30
    situations preventing frustration 632–7
    statutory modification 642–5
    summary chart 648
    theoretical basis 620–2
documents, rule in *L'Estrange v Graucob* 250, 254
domestic agreements, *see* intention to create contractual relations
duress
  economic 411–16
  effect at common law duress, statutory 417–19
  enforcement and 132–3
  goods, in connection with 409–11
  illegitimate pressure as 404–5
  inducing the contract 405
  international perspectives 419–20
  of the person 405–9
  threats as 413–17
  types of 405–17
  see also undue influence

electronic communications 69–71
  definition 50
employment contracts 567–9, 714, 727
enforcement of contracts
  consideration and 176
  contracts for the benefit of third parties 219–33
  duress and 132–3
  expenses of, consumer credit 194
  international perspectives 191–2
  public policy and 507–24
  theory and 5, 12, 13, 15, 17, 18
  voluntary promises 149
  see also capacity; equitable remedies
engaging in conduct, defined 325, 328
English contract law, diminishing influence 18–20
equitable remedies
  estoppel 4, 64, 147, 410, 596
  injunctions 722–8
  nature of 702–3
  promissory estoppel 115, 141, 146–50, 236
  rescission 356–8
  specific performance 219–26, 703–22
  summary chart 734
  unconscionable conduct 448
estoppel, *see* equitable remedies
evidence, parol 277–84
ex turpi causa non oritor actio 507–8, 516, 520
exclusion clauses
  aids to construction 303–10
  construction of 300–10
  contra proferentem reading 303–4
  deviation from route 307–8
  four corners rule 306–7
  importance 298
  international perspectives 312–13
  legislative control 310–13
  main purpose rule 304–5
  misrepresentation 359
  nature and operation 297–300
  negligence only rule 305–6
  preconditions to effectiveness 299–300
  summary chart 313
  types 297–8
  use of 298–9
executed contracts, rule in *Seddon's case* 358, 359
express terms, *see* terms

family agreements, *see* intention to create contractual relations
financial services   323, 462–3, 491
foreign relations, contracts prejudicial to   514
formalities
   common law rights independent of contract   199–201
   consequences of non-compliance   198–206
   consumer contracts   194–5
   contracts of guarantee   193–4
   documents used in proceedings   198
   equitable doctrine of part performance and   202–6
   estoppel and   206
   guarantees   193–4
   international perspectives   191–2
   note or memorandum   195–7
   sales of goods   193
   sales of land   192–3
   satisfying   195–8
   signatures   198
   when necessary   192–5
formation of contracts, *see* agreement; capacity; certainty; consideration; formalities; intention to create contractual relations
formula provisions   96
fraud, definitions   360, 361
frustration
   development of the doctrine   617
   summary chart   648
   see also discharge by frustration

good faith, negotiation agreements   101
goods and services
   display not an offer   32–3
   rare or unique   710–12
   sales contracts   193
   sales puff   242, 327
   unconscionability   449–62
governments, agreements with   164–6
guarantees
   formalities   193–4
   see also terms; inducements; sales puff
guilt and innocence, use of terms in contract law   573

Hadley v Baxendale, rule in   663–6
Hague Rules   229, 298
harassment, *see* duress
honour clause   163

illegality
   at common law
      contracts contrary to public policy   507–9
      contracts in restraint of trade   520–2
      contracts prejudicial to public safety or foreign relations   514
      contracts prejudicial to the administration of justice   509–13
      contracts prejudicing status of marriage   514
      contracts promoting corruption   513
      contracts promoting sexual immorality   519–20
      contracts to commit a legal wrong   508–9
      contracts to defraud the revenue   514
      contracts to encourage separation   515–16
      marriage brokerage contracts   518–19
   effect of   525–32
   exceptions to unenforceability   525–32
   independent causes of action   529
   induced by fraud   528
   international perspectives   506–7, 522–4, 532
   parties not *in pari delicto*   526–7
   purpose not carried into effect   528
   severance and   529–32
   statute not requiring denial of enforcement   529
   statutes intended to benefit claimant's class   527
   statutory   497–507
      illegal-purpose contracts   499–501
      illegally performed contracts   501–6
      prohibited contracts   497–9
      severance of illegal parts   529–32
      void contracts   506–7
   summary chart   533
immorality
   contracts promoting   519–20
   ex turpi causa   507–8, 516, 520
implied terms, *see* terms
incompleteness   91–7
Indian contract law
   acceptance   58–9
   capacity   170–1
   common mistake   383–4

Indian contract law (*cont.*)
   communication of acceptance   71–3
   consideration   115–16
   exclusion clauses   312–13
   illegal contracts   506–7, 532
   intention to create legal relations   165
   mutual mistake   385
   nature and duration of offers   47–8
   nature of contract law   20–1
   nature of an agreement   27–8
   non est factum   399
   offer and acceptance   29–30
   performance   542–3
   public policy illegality   522–3
   unconscionable dealings   441
   undue influence   429–31
   unfair terms   491–3
   unilateral mistake   394–5
inducements
   bargain theory   14
   illegality, by fraud   528
   pressure as, *see* duress   404–5
   inducements, sole or partial   347, 356
   test of esentiality   243–6, 288
   see also duress; sales puff; misleading or deceptive conduct
injunctions   219–26
   international perspectives   728–30
   mandatory   722
   prohibitory   722
   see also equitable remedies; specific performance
insurance contracts, privity and   234–5
intention to create contractual relations
   agreements with governments   164–6
   commercial agreements   163–4
   domestic agreements   158–63
   international perspectives   164–5
   proving   158–60
   rebuttable presumptions   158–9, 162
   social agreements   158–63
   summary chart   167
intermediate terms   285, 289–93
   see also terms
intoxication
   capacity and   175–6
invitation to deal
   cf offer   31–40
   displayed goods   32–3

judge-made law   7–8

land
   formalities required for contracts   192–3
   rule in *Bain v Fothergill*   681
   third party interests in   387
leases, doctrine of frustration and   637–9
legal relations, *see* intention to create contractual relations
L'Estrange v Graucob rule   250, 254
liquidated claims, summary chart   698
liquidated damages   687–89
loss
   damages for   655–61
   mitigation of   682–5
   plaintiff must prove   655–7
loss of chance, damages for   669–73
lump sum payments, rule in *Cutter v Powell*   548–9

machinery provisions   96–7
marriage
   brokerage contracts   518–19
   contracts prejudicing status of   514
   contracts to restrain   514–16
mental distress, damages for   667–9
mental incapacity   171–4
   see also capacity
minds, meeting, *see consensus ad idem*
minority, effect   178–81
minors
   beneficial contracts of employment   180
   common law capacity   178–81
   contracts for necessities   178–9
   international perspectives   185–6
   statutory capacity   181–5
misleading or deceptive conduct
   application to contracts   326–43
   causation and   344–5
   common law, *see* misrepresentation   320
   contractual promises   337–9
   by corporation or person   323
   damages   344–54
   definition   325
   engaging in   323
   exclusion clauses   342–3
   expressions of opinion or law   326–7
   failure to exercise care   343
   failure to take care   348–9
   financial services, in   323, 462–3, 491
   liability of persons 'involved'   353–4
   measure of   349–53
   nature and scope   322–3
   other remedies   354–5

preconditions to liability   323–6
prohibitions on   321–2
relaying information   339–42
remedies   343–55
representations of fact   326
remoteness   345–6
sales puffs   327
silence or non-disclosure   327–8
scope of the remedy   344
statements about the future   333–7
summary chart   365
terminology   325–6
trade or commerce, in   324–5
types of loss compensable   348
vicarious liability   343
misrepresentation
   common law conduct   355–64
   damages for   358–9
   definition   355
   exclusion clauses   359
   international perspectives   360–4
   legislative modifications   359–64
   limits on right to rescind   357–8
   pre-contractual   355–6
   remedies   356–9
   rescission for   356–8
   specific performance and   708
mistake
   common law, at   369–78, 386–7
   common mistake   369–84
   contract terms, as to   375
   equity, in   379–84, 387–95
   existence of subject matter, as to   370–2
   international perspectives   383–5, 394–5, 399
   mutual   384–5
   non est factum   396–9
   quality, as to   372–5
   rectification and   381–4, 391–6
   regarding law   378
   rescission and   379–81, 387–91
   specific performance and   708
   summary chart   400
   title, as to   375–8
   unilateral   386–96
   see also consensus ad idem
money, damages for loss of use   681
moral turpitude (*ex turpi causa*)   507–8, 516, 520

negotiations
   precontractual agreements   97–101

non est factum   396–9
non-contractual rights and liabilities   218–19

offers
   advertisements   36–7
   auctions   33–6
   calls for tender   37–40
   death of offeror or offeree   46
   invitations to deal distinguished   31–40
   failure of a condition   47
   international perspectives   28–30, 47–9
   intervening correspondence   53–9
   lapse of time   46
   made to whom   30–1
   nature and duration   30–49
   offer/acceptance analysis, limitations of   76
   rejection   45–6
   requests for information distinguished   40
   revocation   40–4
   specific performance and   219–21
   statements of future terms distinguished   40
   termination   40–9
   see also acceptance; advertisements; counter-offers

parol evidence rule   277–9
   exceptions   279–84
part performance, contract formalities and   202–6
parties, promisees   218
performance
   apportionment legislation   548–9
   doctrine of substantial performance   547–8
   entire contracts   544–6
   general rule   539–40
   general rule exceptions   540–4
   international perspectives   542–3, 549–50, 558–60, 560–1
   nature of   539–44
   prevention of   560–1
   rule in *Seddon's case*   358, 359
   severable contracts   549–50
   summary chart   562
   time for   550–60
   see also part performance, contract formalities and
personal service contracts   714
persons
   affected   219, 235

persons (cont.)
    engaging in conduct   323
    involved   353, 462
Pinnel's Case rule   139, 141
Potts v Miller rule   352
postal acceptance rule   64–8
pre-contractual events
    misrepresentation   355–6
    preconditions   355–6
    statements as terms   241–2
pre-incorporation contracts, companies   186–7
presumptions
    rebuttable, as to intention   158–9, 162
    representations, as to   455
privity of contract
    abolition (WA, Qld, NT)   232–4
    agency and   235
    circumventions   235–7
    consideration and   218
    contracts for the benefit of third parties   219–31, 233
    contracts obligating third parties   231–2
    damages and   221–6
    enforcement by joint promisee   226
    enforcement by promisee   219–26
    enforcement by third party   226–31
    exceptions to doctrine   232–7
    finding contracts between B and C   228–31
    injunction   219–21
    insurance contracts   234–5
    non-contractual rights and liabilities   218–19
    origins and development   213–17
    rights of third parties   235
    scope of doctrine   213–19
    specific exceptions   234–5
    specific performance   219–21
    trusts and   235
    vicarious immunity   227
promisees, parties by definition   218
promissory estoppel, *see* equitable remedies
property, *see* land; title
public policy, illegal contracts and   507–9
public safety, contracts prejudicial to   514
puff, sales   242, 327

quantum meruit, recovery under   612

remedies
    contract formalities and   206
    unfair terms   489–90
    see also damages; discharge (breach, consequent upon); equitable remedies; liquidated claims, summary chart
repairs, damages for cost of   676–80
representations   243
    cf terms, test for   243–6
    see also terms; inducements; sales puff
repudiatory breach   580–4
rescission
    completed contracts, rule in *Seddon's case*   358, 359
    see also equitable remedies
restitutionary damages   654
    for breach   690–4
restraint of trade   520–2

sale contracts
sales of land, contract formalities   192–3
sales puff   242, 327
Seddon's case rule   358, 359
separation, contracts to encourage   515–16
settlement
severability   103–4
    of illegal parts   529–32
    performance and   549–50
sexual immorality, contracts promoting   519–20
signed documents, terms   250–5
silence   62–4
social agreements, *see* intention to create contractual relations
special disability   442
specific performance   219–26
    approach to claims for   703–4
    consideration inadequate   708
    contracts for benefit of thirs parties   219–26
    contracts for rare or unique goods   710–12
    contracts involving land   712–13
    contracts of personal service   714
    contracts requiring constant supervision   714–18
    damages in lieu   730–3
    damages inadequate as compensation   704–6
    fairness of order for   706–10
    injunctions   722–8
    international perspectives   718–22
    misrepresentation and   708

mistake and   708
  plaintiff also in breach   708
  plaintiff entitled to a remedy   704
  proving the remedy more adequate   706
  when not awarded   714–18
  when routinely awarded   710–14
  see also equitable remedies
standard form contracts, definition   482
standard terms, *see* terms
statutory unconscionability
  Australian law   449–63
  state and territory law   463–71
subject to contract   104–6
subject to finance   106–11
summary charts
  agreement   84
  certainty   112
  common law duress   421
  consideration   150
  contract   22
  damages and liquidated claims   698, 699
  discharge for breach   614
  discharge by agreement   571
  equitable remedies   734
  exclusion clauses   313
  frustration   648
  illegality   533
  intention to create contractual
    relations   167
  misleading or deceptive conduct   365
  mistake   400
  performance   562
  unconscionable conduct   475
  undue influence   437
  unfair terms   493
supervening events, *see* discharge by
    frustration
supervision, contracts requiring   714–18

termination, *see* breach; discharge; frustration;
    performance
termination *ab initio*   574
termination clauses   694
terms
  classification   286–93
  collateral contract   243, 246–9
  common law   261–71
  custom, implied by   269–71
  for contractual efficacy   265–8
  course of dealing   259–61
  displayed or delivered   255–9
  express   241–61

  good faith and fair dealing, requiring   269
  implied terms   261–74
  intermediate   285, 289–93
  international, *see* UNIDROIT Principles
      of International Commercial
      Contracts 2004
  international perspectives   272–3
  pre-contractual statements   241–2
  representations   243
  requiring good faith and fair dealing   269
  sales puff   242, 327
  signed documents   250–5
  standard implied terms   268
  statutory   271–4
  term of the contract   242
  test for essentiality   243–, 288
  tripartite collateral contracts   249–50
  unfair, *see* unfair terms
  vague or ambiguous   87
  void/voidable distinction   316
  warranties   289
  for workability   268
third parties
  common mistake and   369
  conferral of rights on   235
  contracts for the benefit of   219–31, 233
  contracts obligating   231–2
  damages and   657–59
  enforcement by   226–31
  finding contracts between B and C
      228–31
  interests in title   387
  losses by   657–9
  non est factum and   396
  notice of undue influence   432–6
  pre-contractual statements by   241–2, 356
  relaying information   339–42
  tripartite collateral contracts   249–50
  undue influence   423, 432–6
  void contracts, effect   316
  voidable contracts, effect   316
  see also privity of contract
threats
  to break contract   413–16
  institute legal proceedings   416–17
title
  third party interests and   387
  land, specific performance and   712–13
  defects, rule in *Bain v Fothergill*   681
trade or commerce
  conduct in   324–5
  see also consumer contracts

tripartite collateral contracts 249–50
trusts, privity and 235

uncertainty
  international perspectives 101–3
  summary chart, certainty 112
  types 86–103
UNCITRAL Model Law on Electronic
    Commerce 69
unconscionability, statutory 449–74
  Australian Consumer Law 449–63,
    471–4
  goods or services, in 449–62
  remedies unconscionability, statutory,
    time limits
  state and territory law 463–71
  unjust transactions 471–4
unconscionable conduct
  abuse of position and 442–8
  equitable doctrine 442–8
  equitable remedies for 448
  harsh and oppressive transactions 448
  international perspectives 441
  nature and effect 440–1
  not limited by definition 456
  summary chart 475
undue influence
  antecedent trust relationships 425–32
  deemed in established
      categories 426–7
  domination or express 423, 424–5
  indefinable 435
  international perspectives 429–32
  presumed 423, 425–32
  proved in other relationships 427–9
  summary chart 437
  third party notice of 432–6
unfair terms
  consumer contracts 482
  contract as a whole 485–8
  definition 483–5
  effect of including 489–90
  examples 488–9
  financial products or services 491

impact of legislation 490–1
international perspectives 492
national consumer law 480–90
standard form contract 482–3
state legislation 480
summary chart 493
void 489
UNIDROIT Principles of International
    Commercial Contracts 2004 114,
    192, 269, 272
unilateral contracts 78–83
United Nations Convention on the Use of
    Electronic Communications in
    International Contracts
    2005 394, 395
unjust contracts, definition 465, 468
unjust transactions 471–4
upfront price 488

vagueness, *see* uncertainty
Vienna Convention 44–47, 58
vitiating factors, *see* capacity; duress;
    illegality; misleading or deceptive
    conduct; mistake; public policy,
    illegal contracts and; unconscionable
    conduct; undue influence;
    unfair terms
void and voidable
  distinction 316
  see also capacity; duress; illegality;
      misleading or deceptive conduct;
      mistake; public policy, illegal
      contracts and; unconscionable
      conduct; undue influence;
      unfair terms

waiver 60–1
warranties, *see* terms; inducements;
    pre-contractual events
wasted expenditure, reliance damages
    for 673–6
wrongs
  contracts to commit 508–9
  definition 685